COMMENTARY ON THE OLD TESTAMENT

C. F. KEIL and F. DELITZSCH

VOLUME 2

JOSHUA, JUDGES, RUTH
1 AND 2 SAMUEL

TWO VOLUMES IN ONE

 HENDRICKSON PUBLISHERS

PEABODY, MASSACHUSETTS 01961 3473

COMMENTARY ON THE OLD TESTAMENT, 10 Volume set

Hendrickson Publishers, Inc. edition

ISBN: 0-943575-24-9

reprinted from the edition originally published by
William B. Eerdmans Publishing Company, Grand Rapids, 1986

First printing — February, 1989

Printed in the United States of America

COMMENTARY ON THE OLD TESTAMENT

C. F. KEIL and F. DELITZSCH

JOSHUA, JUDGES, RUTH

TRANSLATED BY

JAMES MARTIN

TABLE OF CONTENTS

--------◆--------

THE BOOK OF JUDGES.

INTRODUCTION.

EXPOSITION.

THE BOOK OF RUTH.

INTRODUCTION

EXPOSITION.

INTRODUCTION

THE PROPHETICAL HISTORIES OF THE OLD TESTAMENT

THE *thorah*, or five books of Moses, which contains an account of the founding of the Old Testament kingdom of God, and the laws which were given through Moses, is followed in the Hebrew canon by the writings of the "earlier prophets," נביאים ראשונים, *prophetæ priores*. This collective name is given to the four historical books of *Joshua*, *Judges*, *Samuel*, and *Kings*, which trace, in the light of divine revelation, and of the gradual unfolding of the plan of salvation, the historical development of this kingdom of God from the death of Moses, the mediator of the old covenant, or from the entrance of the people of Israel into the land of Canaan promised to their fathers, till the dissolution of the kingdom of Judah, and the Babylonian captivity; the whole embracing a period of nearly nine hundred years. The names given to these books are taken from the men whom the God-king of Israel called and appointed at different times as the leaders and rulers of His people and kingdom, and indicate, very suitably on the whole, the historical periods to which the books refer.

The book of *Joshua* describes the introduction of the people of Israel into the promised land of Canaan, through the conquest effected by Joshua, and the division of the land among the tribes of Israel. As Joshua only completed what Moses had commenced but had not been permitted to carry out, on account of his sin at the water of strife (Num. xx. 12); and as he had not only been called by the Lord, and consecrated by the laying on of the hands of Moses, to accomplish this work, but had also been favoured with direct revelations from God, and with His miraculous help in the execution of it; the book which is named after him, and contains the account of what he did in the power of the Lord, is more closely related to the Pentateuch, both in its form and contents, than any other book of the Old Testament. In this respect, therefore, it might be regarded as an appendix, although it was never actually joined to it so as to form part of the same work, but was from the very first a separate writing, and simply stood in the same dependent relation to the writings of Moses, as that in which Joshua stood to Moses himself, of whom he was both the servant and successor.

The book of *Judges* embraces the period of 350 years, from the death of Joshua to the rise of Samuel as a prophet of the Lord; that is to say, the time appointed to the people of Israel to establish themselves in the complete and sole possession of the land that had been given them for an inheritance, by fighting against the Canaanites who remained in the land and exterminating them, and, when settled in this inheritance as the congregation of the Lord, to set up the covenant concluded with God at Sinai, and to maintain and build up the kingdom of God according to the principles and ordinances, the laws and rights, prescribed by Moses in the law. The Lord had promised His help to the covenant nation in carrying on the conflict with the remaining Canaanites, on condition that they adhered with fidelity to His covenant, and willingly obeyed His commandments. It was but very imperfectly, however, that the tribes of Israel observed these conditions, which had been earnestly impressed upon their hearts, not only by Moses, but also by Joshua before his death. They soon grew weary of the task of fighting against the Canaanites and destroying them, and contented themselves with making them merely tributary; in fact, they even began to form friendships with them, and worship their gods. As a punishment for this, the Lord gave them over to their enemies, so that they were repeatedly oppressed and deeply humiliated by the Canaanites, and the nations that were living round about Canaan. But whenever they repented and turned again in their distress to the Lord their God, He raised up helpers and deliverers for them in the persons of the judges, whom He filled with the power of His Spirit, so that they smote the enemy, and delivered both the people and the land from their oppression. But inasmuch as in every instance the judge was no sooner dead than the people fell into idolatry again, they sank deeper and deeper into bondage to the heathen, the theocratic constitution fell more and more into decay, and the life of the nation as a religious community was rapidly coming to an end. This constant alternation, of apostasy from the Lord to the Canaanitish Baals and Astartes and the consequent punishment by deliverance into the power of their enemies on the one hand, and of temporary return to the Lord and deliverance by the judges out of their bondage on the other, which characterizes the post-Mosaic period of the Israelitish history, is clearly set forth in the book of Judges, and placed distinctly before the eye in separate pictures of the various oppressions and deliverances of Israel, each one being complete in itself, and the whole arranged in chronological order. Whilst the book of Joshua shows how the Lord fulfilled His promise to Israel with a mighty arm, and led His people into the land promised to the fathers, the book of Judges shows how Israel continually broke the covenant of its God in the land which He had given it for an inheritance, and thus fell into bondage to its foes, out of which the judges were not able to secure it a permanent deliverance ; so that the Lord was obliged to create a new thing in Israel, in order to carry out His purpose of salvation, and to found and erect His kingdom in Canaan, through the medium of the children of Israel. This new thing consisted in the institution of prophecy as promised by Moses, or rather in the introduction of it into the political and national life, as a spiritual power by which it was henceforth to be pervaded, guided, and controlled ; as neither the judges, nor the priests as custodiers of the sanctuary, were able to uphold the authority of the law of God in the nation, or turn the idolatrous nation to the Lord. It is true we meet with certain prophets as early as the times of the judges ; but the true founder of the Old Testament prophecy (*prophetenthums*, prophethood) was Samuel, with whom the prophets first began their continuous labours, and the prophetic gift was developed into a power which exerted an influence, as strong as it was salutary, upon the future development of the Israelitish state.

The books of *Samuel* contain the history of Israel from the appearance of Samuel as a prophet to the end of the reign of David, and include the renewal of the theocracy by the labours of Samuel, and the establishment of the earthly monarchy by Saul and David. At the close of the period of the judges, when the ark of the covenant had fallen into the hands of the Philistines, and the removal of this visible symbol and substratum of the presence of God from the tabernacle had caused the central sanctuary of the congregation to lose all its significance as the place where God manifested himself, and when the judgments of God had even fallen upon the members of the high-priesthood itself, in the death of Eli and his worthless sons, when the word of Jehovah was dear, and there was little prophecy to be found (1 Sam. iii. 1),—the Lord raised up Samuel, the son of the pious Hannah, who had been asked for of the Lord and consecrated to His service from his mother's womb, to be His prophet, and appeared to him continually at Shiloh; so that all Israel acknowledged him as the prophet appointed by the Lord, and through his prophetic labours was converted from dead idols to serve the living God. In consequence of this conversion, the Lord gave to the Israelites, in answer to Samuel's prayer, a complete and wondrous victory over the Philistines, by which they were delivered from the heavy oppression they had endured for forty years at the hands of these foes. From that time forward Samuel judged all Israel. But when he had grown old, and his sons, who had been appointed by him as judges, failed to walk in his steps, the people desired a king to judge them, to go before them, and to conduct their wars. In accordance with the command of God, Samuel chose Saul the Benjamite as king, and then laid down his own office as judge. He continued, however, to the very end of his life to labour as a prophet, in and through the schools of the prophets, which he had called into existence for the strengthening and confirmation of Israel in its fidelity to the Lord; and not only announced to King Saul his rejection by God, on account of his frequent resistance to the divine command, as made known to him by the prophet, but anointed David to be his successor as king over Israel. He died at the close of the reign of Saul, and did not live to see the accession and reign of David, with which the second book of Samuel is occupied. The reason why the name of Samuel is given to both these books, which form, both in style and contents, an indivisible whole, is in all probability therefore, that Samuel not only inaugurated the monarchy in Israel by anointing Saul and David, but exerted so decided an influence upon the spirit of the government of both these kings, through his prophetic labours, that even the latter may be regarded in a certain sense as the continuation of that reformation of the Israelitish state which the prophet himself began. It was in David that the true king of the kingdom of God under the Old Testament arose,—a mighty warrior in conflict with the enemies of Israel, and yet at the same time a pious servant of the Lord,—a man of true humility and faithful obedience to the word and commandment of God, who not only raised the state to a lofty height of earthly power and glory, through the strength and justice of his rule, but who also built up the kingdom of God, by reviving and organizing the public worship of God, and by stimulating and fostering the true fear of God, through the cultivation of sacred song. When God had given him rest from all his enemies round about, he wished to build a temple to the Lord. But God did not grant him this desire of his heart : He gave him a promise, however, instead, viz. that He would build him a house, and establish the throne of his kingdom for ever ; and that He would raise up his seed after him, who would build a house to the name of the Lord (2 Sam. vii.). This promise formed not only the culminating point in the life and reign of David, but the indestructible basis for the further development of the Israelitish state and kingdom, and was not only a sure pledge of the continuance of the Davidic monarchy, but a firm anchor of hope for the covenant nation in all time to come.

Lastly, the books of *Kings* carry on the history of the Old Testament kingdom of God through a period of 450 years, viz. from the accession of Solomon to the Babylonian captivity, and furnish the historical proof that the promise given by the Lord to His servant David was stedfastly fulfilled. Notwithstanding the attempt of Adonijah to usurp the throne, He preserved the whole of the kingdom of David to his son Solomon, who had been chosen as his successor, and at the very commencement of his reign renewed His promise to him, so that Solomon was able to carry out the work of building the temple ; and under his wise and peaceful government in Judah and Israel every one could sit in safety under his own vine and fig-tree. But when Solomon allowed himself to be drawn away by his foreign wives to turn from the Lord and worship idols, the Lord chastened him with the rod of men, and with the stripes of the children of men; but His mercy did not depart away from him, as He had promised to David (2 Sam. vii. 14, 15). After Solomon's death, the ten tribes, it is true, revolted from the house of David, and founded a kingdom of their own under Jeroboam ; but one tribe (Judah along with Benjamin) remained with his son Rehoboam, and along with this tribe the capital, Jerusalem, and the temple. During the whole time that this one brother-nation was divided into two distinct kingdoms, which were frequently engaged in hostility with one another, the Lord preserved the throne to the seed of David ; and the kingdom of Judah survived the kingdom of the ten tribes of Israel 134 years, having as firm a political foundation in the unbroken succession of the royal family of David, as it had a strong spiritual foundation in the capital Jerusalem, with the temple which had been sanctified by the Lord as the dwelling-place of His name. In the kingdom of the ten tribes, on the other hand, Jeroboam introduced the germ of what eventually led to its destruction, by establishing as the state religion the unlawful worship of the golden calves. The destruction of his house was at once foretold to him on account of this sin (1 Kings xiv. 7); and this threat was carried out in the person of his son (1 Kings xv. 28 sqq.). As the kings of Israel who followed did not desist from this sin of Jeroboam, but, on the contrary, the dynasty of the house of Omri attempted to make the worship of Baal the leading religion of the kingdom, and the king and people gave no heed to the voice of the prophets, and did not return with sincerity of heart to the Lord, He gave up the sinful kingdom and people to the consequences of their sins, so that one dynasty overthrew another; and after the lapse of 250 years, the kingdom, which was already shattered by the frequently recurring civil wars, fell a prey to the Assyrians, by whom the whole land was conquered, and its inhabitants were led into captivity. The kingdom of Judah was also hard pressed by this powerful empire, and brought to the very verge of destruction; but in answer to the prayer of the pious king Hezekiah, it was delivered and preserved by the Lord for His own and His servant David's sake, until at length the godless king Manasseh filled up the measure of its sins, so that even the good king Josiah could only suspend the destruction for a certain time, but could not ward it off altogether. A short time after his death the judgment fell upon Judah and Jerusalem on account of the sins of Manasseh (2 Kings xxiii. 26, 27, xxiv. 3), when King Nebuchadnezzar came from Babylon, conquered the land, and laid it waste; and having taken Jerusalem, led away Jehoiachim to Babylon, with a considerable portion of the people. And when even Zedekiah, who had been raised by him to the throne, rebelled against him, the Chaldeans returned and put an end to the kingdom of Judah, by destroying Jerusalem and burning the temple, Zechariah himself being deprived of his sight, and led away into captivity with a large number of prisoners. Yet even when Judah and its king were rejected and scattered among the heathen, the Lord did not leave His servant David without any light shining; but after Jehoiachim had been in prison for thirty-seven years, paying the penalty of his own and his father's sins, he was released from his imprisonment by Evil-merodach, the king of

Babylon, and his seat was placed above the seats of the kings who were with him in Babylon (2 Kings xxv. 27–30). This joyful turn in the destinies of Jehoiachim, with which the books of Kings are brought to a close, throws the first gleam into the dark night of the captivity of that better future which was to dawn upon the seed of David, and through it upon the people of Israel when they should be delivered out of Babylon.

These four historical writings have been very justly called *prophetical books of history*: not, however, because they all, but more especially the books of Samuel and the Kings, give very full accounts of the labours of the prophets in Israel; nor merely because, according to the early Jewish tradition, they were written by prophets; but rather because they describe the history of the Old Testament covenant nation and kingdom of God in the light of the divine plan of salvation, setting forth the divine revelation, as it was accomplished in the historical development of Israel, or showing how the Almighty God and Lord of the whole earth continued as King of Israel uninterruptedly to fulfil the covenant of grace which He had concluded with the fathers and had set up at Sinai, and built up His kingdom, by leading the people whom He had chosen as His own possession, notwithstanding all the opposition of their sinful nature, further and further onwards towards the goal of their divine calling, and thus preparing the way for the salvation of the whole world. These books, therefore, do not contain a general history of the natural development of the Israelitish nation from a political point of view, but trace the history of the people of God, or Israel, in its theocratic development as a covenant nation, and as the channel of that salvation which was to be manifested to all nations in the fulness of time. Their authors, therefore, by virtue of prophetic illumination, have simply selected and described such events and circumstances from among the rich and plentiful variety contained in the accounts handed down by tradition, whether relating to families, tribes, or the nation as a whole, as were of importance to the history of the kingdom of God; that is to say, in addition to the divine revelations in word and deed, the wonders wrought by God, and the prophetic declarations of His counsel and will, they have recorded chiefly such points in the life and conduct of the nation and its more prominent members as affected advantageously or otherwise the development of the divine kingdom in Israel. Whatever had no inward connection with this higher aim and peculiar calling of Israel, was, as a rule, passed over altogether, or, at all events, was only touched upon and mentioned so far as it served to exhibit the attitude of the nation generally, or of its rulers and leaders, towards the Lord and His kingdom. This will help to explain not only the apparent inequality in the treatment of the history, or the fact that here and there we have long periods merely referred to in a few general remarks, whereas, on the other hand, the adventures and acts of particular individuals are depicted with biographical minuteness, but also another distinctive peculiarity, viz. that the natural causes of the events which occurred, and the subjective motives which determined the conduct of historical personages, are for the most part left unnoticed, or only briefly and cursorily alluded to, whilst the divine interpositions and influence are constantly brought into prominence, and, so far as they were manifested in an extraordinary manner, are carefully and circumstantially described.

In all these respects the prophetic histories are so intimately connected with the historical narrative in the books of Moses, that they may be regarded as a simple continuation of those books. This not only applies to the book of Joshua, but to the other prophetic histories also. Just as the book of Joshua is linked on to the death of Moses, so the book of Judges is linked on to the death of Joshua; whilst the books of Kings commence with the termination of the reign of David, the point to which the history of David is brought in the books of Samuel. These books, again, are connected just as closely with the book of Judges; for, after giving an account of the high-priesthood of Eli, and the birth and youth of Samuel, which forms the introduction to the labours of Samuel, they describe the continuance and close of the subjugation of Israel by the Philistines, the commencement and prolongation of which are related in the last section of the book of Judges, although in this case the link of connection is somewhat hidden by the appendices to the book of Judges (chap. xvii.–xxi.), and by the introduction to the history of Samuel (1 Sam. i.–iii.). This close connection between all the writings in question, which is still further strengthened by their evident agreement in the selection and treatment of the historical materials, does not arise, as some suppose, from the fact that they received a last finish from the editorial hand of some one man, by whom this harmony and the so-called theocratic pragmatism which is common to them all was stamped upon the history; but it arose from the very nature of the historical facts themselves, *i.e.* from the fact that the history of Israel was not the result of a purely natural development, but was the fruit and result of the divine training of the covenant nation. The prophetic character, by which these works are distinguished from the other sacred histories of the Israelites, consists in the fact that they do not trace the theocratic history from an individual point of view, but according to its actual course, and in harmony with the successive steps in the development of the divine counsels of salvation; and thus furnish their own proof that they were written by prophets, to whom the Spirit of the Lord had given a spiritual insight into the divine law of the kingdom.

With regard to the *origin* of the prophetical books of history, and the *date of their composition*, all that can be determined with certainty is, that they were all composed some time after the last event which they record, but were founded upon written contemporaneous accounts of the different events referred to. Although no sources are mentioned in the books of Joshua, of the Judges, and of Samuel, with the exception of the "book of Jasher" (Josh. x. 13, and 2 Sam. i. 18), from which the poetical extracts contained in the passages have been taken, there can be no doubt that the historical materials even of these books have been obtained, so far as everything essential is concerned, either from public documents or private writings. In the books of Kings we meet for the first time with the original sources regularly cited at the close of each king's reign; and, judging from the titles, "book of the Acts of Solomon" (1 Kings xi. 41), and "book of the Chronicles (or 'daily occurrences,' *i.e.* contemporaneous history) of the Kings of Israel and Judah" (1 Kings xiv. 19, 29, etc.), they were in all probability fuller annals to which reference is made, as containing further accounts of the acts and undertakings of the several kings. We find a similar work cited in the books of the Chronicles under different titles, whilst certain prophetic works are referred to for the history of particular kings, such as words of Samuel the seer, Nathan the prophet, and Gad the seer (1 Chron. xxix. 29); of Shemaiah the prophet, and Iddo the seer (2 Chron. xii. 15), and others; also the prophecies (vision) of Isaiah (2 Chron. xxxii. 32), and words of Jehu the prophet (2 Chron. xx. 34), both of which are expressly said to have been received into the book of the kings of Israel (or of Judah and Israel). It is obvious from these statements, not only that prophetic writings and collections of oracles were incorporated in the more comprehensive annals of the kingdom, but also that the prophets themselves were engaged in various

ways in committing the history of Israel to writing. The foundation for this occupation had no doubt been laid in the companies or
schools of the prophets, which had been called into existence by
Samuel, and in which not only sacred music and sacred song were
cultivated, but sacred literature also, more especially the history of
the theocracy. Consequently, as *Oehler* supposes, in all probability
the foundation was laid even in the *cœnobium* at Ramah (1 Sam.
xix. 19 sqq.) for that great historical work, which was composed by
prophets during the following centuries and is frequently referred
to in the books of Kings, and which certainly lay before the writer
of the Chronicles, though possibly in a revised form. The task of
writing down the history of the theocracy was very closely connected with a prophet's vocation. Called as they were to be watchers
(*zophim* or *mezappim : vid.* Micah vii. 4; Jer. vi. 17; Ezek. iii. 17,
xxxiii. 7) of the theocracy of the Lord, it was their special duty to
test and judge the ways of the nation and its rulers according to
the standard of the law of God, and not only to work in every
possible way for the recognition of the majesty and sole glory of
Jehovah, to bear witness before both high and low against every
instance of apostasy from Him, against every violation of His
ordinances and rights, and to proclaim judgment upon all who
hardened themselves against the word of God and salvation and
deliverance to the penitent and desponding; but also to set forth
the guidance of Israel in the light of the saving purpose of God,
and the inviolable rule of divine retribution,—to pass sentence upon
the past circumstances of the nation, particularly the life and conduct of its kings, according to the standard of the law,—and to
exhibit in their fate the reality of the divine promises and threats;
and through all this to hold up, in the past history of the fathers,
a mirror for the warning and comfort of future generations.
With all these facts before us, we are fully warranted in assuming,
that the prophetic works of history were employed as sources even
in the composition of the books of Samuel. But this is not a probable
supposition so far as the times of the judges are concerned, as we can
find no certain traces of any organized prophetic labours by which
the national life could be at all deeply influenced, notwithstanding
the fact, that beside the prophetess Deborah (Judg. iv. 4), there is
a prophet mentioned in Judg. vi. 7 sqq., and 1 Sam. ii. 27. But
even if the author of our book of Judges could not avail himself
of any prophetic writings, we must not on that account deny that
he may have made use of other written statements and accounts,

handed down by contemporaries of the events. In the book of Joshua it is almost universally admitted, that at all events the geographical portions have been taken from public documents.—For further remarks upon this subject, see the introductions to the different books.

The employment of written sources, from living auditors or eye-witnesses of the events, in all the prophetic books of history, is evident as a general fact from the contents of the books, from the abundance of genuine historical details which they contain although many of them extend over very long periods of time; from the exactness of the geographical *data* connected with the different accounts, and the many genealogical as well as chronological particulars; and, in fact, from the clearness and certainty of the descriptions given of circumstances and occurrences which are often very complicated in their character. But this is still more obvious from the style in which the different books are written, where the gradual development of the language, and the changes which occurred in the course of centuries, are unmistakeably apparent. For whilst the books of Kings, which date from the time of the captivity, contain many words, forms, and phrases that indicate that corruption of the Hebrew through Aramæan idioms, which commenced with the invasions of Israel and Judah by the Assyrians and Chaldeans, there are no certain traces of the decline of the language to be found in the books of Samuel and Judges, but the style throughout is the pure style of the age of David and Solomon; whilst in the book of Joshua, as a whole, we still find the old forms of the Mosaic times, although the actual archaisms of the Pentateuch have already disappeared. This difference in the words employed in the different books cannot be satisfactorily explained from the simple fact, that the sources used, and from which extracts were made, were written in different ages. To quote but one example, since the fuller discussion of this point belongs to the introduction to the separate books, this is perfectly obvious from the use of the word פַּחוֹת, in connection with Solomon's governors, in 1 Kings x. 15; since the author of our books of Kings cannot possibly have taken this word from his original sources for the history of Solomon's reign, as it was not till the time of the Chaldean and Persian dominion that this foreign word was adopted into the Hebrew language.

The peculiarities in the language of the different prophetic books of history do furnish decisive evidence, however, against the hypothesis propounded by *Spinoza,* and lately revived by *Stähelin* and

Bertheau, viz. that "in the historical books, from Gen. i. to 2 Kings xxv., in the form and connection in which we possess them now, we have not several historical works which have been composed independently of one another, but rather a connected treatment of the history from the beginning of the world to the time of the captivity" (*Bertheau*), or "*one* work, which owes its present form to *one* man, or at any rate to *one* age" (*Stähelin*). The arguments adduced in support of this are all very weak. "The close connection in which these writings stand to one another, so that each book in succession is closely connected with the one before it, and presupposes all that the latter contains, and none goes back to an earlier period than that at which the previous book closes" (*Stähelin*), does prove indeed that they have not been written independently of one another; but it by no means proves that they belong to one author, or even to *one* age. Nor can we infer that they have been composed or finally revised by one man, from the fact, "that very often, in some one writing, as it has come down to us, we not only find two different styles, or a totally different mode of description, so that we can with certainty conclude that the work is founded upon two different sources, but these sources run through writings that are separated from one another, and are frequently ascribed to entirely different ages." For the circumstance, that a writing is founded upon two sources, is no proof at all that it is nothing more than a portion of a larger work; and the proof which *Stähelin* adduces of his assertion, that the same source runs through several of the works in question, is much too weak and untenable to be regarded as an established fact, not to mention that, according to the first rules of logic, what applies to *several* cannot therefore be predicated of *all.* The actual root of this hypothesis is to be found in the naturalistic assumption of modern critics, that the theocratic spirit, which is common to all the prophetic histories, was not to be found in the historical facts, but was simply the "theocratic pragmatism" of the historians themselves, which had at the most a certain subjective truth, but no objective reality. From such an assumption, however, it is impossible to come to a correct conclusion with regard to either the contents or the origin of the prophetic histories of the Old Testament.

THE BOOK OF JOSHUA

INTRODUCTION.

CONTENTS, DATE, AND CHARACTER OF THE BOOK.

THE book of Joshua derives its name, יהושע, 'Ιησοῦς Ναυή or υἱὸς Ναυή (LXX.), not from its author, but from its contents, viz. the history of the guidance of Israel into the land of Canaan, the land promised to the fathers, by Joshua the son of Nun. It commences immediately after the death of Moses, with the command addressed by the Lord to Joshua, to lead the children of Israel over the Jordan into Canaan, and not only to take possession of this land, but to divide it among the tribes of Israel (chap. i. 1–9), and closes with the death and burial of Joshua and his contemporary, the high priest Eleazar (chap. xxiv. 29–33). The contents may be divided into two parts of nearly equal length,—the conquest of Canaan (chap. i.–xii.), and the division of it among the tribes of Israel (chap. xii.–xxiv.); chap. i. 1–9 forming the introduction, and chap. xxiv. 29–33 the conclusion. After the introductory notice, that when Moses was dead the Lord commanded Joshua, who had been called to be the leader of Israel in his stead, to carry out the work entrusted to him, and encouraged him by the promise of His omnipotent help in the completion of it (chap. i. 1–9), the history opens in the *first part*, (1) with the preparations made by Joshua for advancing into Canaan; viz. (*a*) the command of Joshua to the people to prepare for crossing the Jordan, the summons to the two tribes and a half to help their brethren to conquer Canaan (chap. i. 10–18), and the despatch of spies to Jericho (chap. ii.); (*b*) the crossing of the river, which had been laid dry by a divine miracle (chap. iii. and iv.); and (*c*) the preparation of Israel for the conquest of the land, by the performance of circumcision and the passover at Gilgal (chap. v. 1–12). Then follow (2) the conquest and subjugation of Canaan; viz. (a) the commencement of it by the miraculous fall of Jericho (chap. v. 13–vi. 27), the attack upon Ai, and capture of that town, after the expiation of the guilt that had been brought upon the congregation through the sin of Achan against the ban (chap. vii.–viii. 29), and the solemn act of setting up the law in the land on Ebal and Gerizim (chap. viii. 30–35), (b) the further conquest of the land through the subjugation of the Gibeonites, who had succeeded surreptitiously in obtaining a treaty from Israel which guaranteed their safety (chap. ix.); the two great victories over the allied kings of Canaan in the south (chap. x.) and north (chap. xi.), with the capture of the fortified towns of the land; and lastly, at the close of the first part, the list of the conquered kings (ch. xii.).—The *second part* commences with the command of God to Joshua to divide the whole land among the nine tribes and a half for a possession, although several parts of it still remained unconquered; as two tribes and a half had already received from Moses their inheritance on the eastern side of the Jordan, the boundaries and towns of which are then described (chap. xiii.). Accordingly Joshua, with the heads of the people appointed for the purpose, proceeded to the distribution of the land, first of all (a) in the camp at Gilgal, where Caleb was the first to receive his inheritance (chap. xiv.), and then, according to the lot, the tribes of Judah (chap. xv.) and Joseph, *i.e.* Ephraim and (half) Manasseh (chap. xvi. and xvii.); and afterwards (b) at Shiloh, where the tabernacle was first of all erected, and a description of the land to be divided written down (chap. xviii. 1–10), and then the rest of the tribes—Benjamin (chap. xviii. 11–28), Simeon, Zebulun, Issachar, Asher, Naphtali, and Dan (chap. xix.) —received their inheritance, after which the cities of refuge were selected (chap. xx.), and forty-eight cities were given up by the twelve tribes for the Levites to occupy (chap. xxi.); and finally, (c) the warriors belonging to the tribes beyond Jordan were sent back by Joshua to their own inheritance (chap. xxii.). To this there is appended, in the next place, an account of what Joshua did towards the end of his life to establish the tribes of Israel securely in their inheritance: viz. (a) an exhortation to the heads of the tribes, who were gathered round him, to carry out their calling with fidelity (chap. xxiii.); and (b) the renewal of the covenant at the diet at Shechem (chap. xxiv. 1–28). This is followed by an account of the close of Joshua's life, and the conclusion of the whole book (chap. xxiv. 29–33). Thus the two parts or halves of the book correspond exactly to one another, both in form and in contents. As the events described in ch. i. 10–v. 12 were preparatory to the conquest of Canaan, so the diets held by Joshua after the distribution of the land by lot (chap. xxiii.–xxiv. 28) had no other object than to establish the covenant people firmly in the inheritance bestowed upon them by God, by exhorting them to be faithful to the Lord. And just as chap. xii. rounds off the first part, as a kind of appendix which completes the history of the conquest of the land, so chap. xxii. is obviously an appendix to the distribution of the land among the tribes. which brings to a close the dismission of the people to the separate portions of their inheritance.

The book of Joshua is not intended merely as a continuation of the history of Israel from the death of Moses to the death of Joshua, still less as a description of the acts of Joshua only. The purpose of the book is rather to show how, after the death of Moses, the faithful covenant God fulfilled to the children of Israel, whom He had adopted as His people of possession through the mediation of His servant, the promise which He had made to the patriarchs ; how the Canaanites were destroyed, and their land given to the tribes of Israel for an hereditary possession through the medium of Joshua, the servant of Moses, whom he had consecrated as leader of the people through the laying on of hands and by putting some of his honour upon him. As the servant of Moses treading in his footsteps, Joshua finished the work which Moses was not allowed to bring to a conclusion on account of his sin at the water of strife, viz. the planting and establishment of Israel in Canaan, the land of its inheritance, which the Lord had selected for His dwelling (Ex. xv. 17) and chosen as the nursery ground of His kingdom. As Joshua simply carried on in this respect, and brought to completion, the work which Moses had begun, arranged, and set on foot, the book of Joshua is naturally connected very closely with the books of Moses, though without forming an integral part, or the last portion of it, and without being written by Joshua himself.

The *origin* of the book of Joshua is involved in obscurity, as we can neither find out its author, nor determine with certainty the date of its composition. Whereas, on the one hand, the historical account bears throughout the mark of having been written by an eye-witness, and even by one who had taken part in the events described, and the description given of the possessions allotted to the different tribes according to their respective boundaries and the cities which they contained is unquestionably founded upon contemporaneous writings, and in one passage the writer actually classes himself with those who crossed over Jordan into Canaan under the guidance of Joshua (chap. v. 1, "until we were passed over"); on the other hand we find a number of historical statements in the book, which point beyond the life of Joshua and are opposed to the idea that it was written by Joshua himself. We do not include in these either the closing accounts of the death of Joshua and Eleazar (chap. xxiv. 29, 33), or the allusion to the "book of the righteous" (chap. x. 13): for these accounts might have been appended to a writing of Joshua's by a later hand, just as in the case of the Pentateuch; and the book of the righteous is not a work that was composed after the time of Joshua, but a collection of odes in praise of the acts of the Lord in Israel, which were composed by pious minstrels during the conquest of the land, and were added one by one to this collection. Even the frequent repetition of the statement that this or the other has continued "to this day," furnishes no certain proof that the book was not written in the closing years of Joshua's life, when we consider the purely relative signification of the formula, which is sometimes used in connection with things that only lasted a few years. Apart from such passages as chap. xxii. 3, 17, and xxiii. 8, 9, in which no one has discovered any allusion to a later time than that of Joshua, we find the formula "to this day" in chap. iv. 9, v. 9, vi. 25, vii. 26, viii. 28, 29, ix. 27, xiii. 13, xiv. 14, xv. 63, and xvi. 10. But if the remark made in chap. vi. 25 with regard to Rahab, "she dwelleth in Israel unto this day," was certainly written during her lifetime, such statements as that the first encampment of Israel in Canaan "is called Gilgal unto this day," on account of the circumcision of the people that took place there, and that the valley in which Achan was stoned is called Achor "unto this day" (chap. v. 9, vii. 26), or that the memorial stones set up in the bed of the Jordan (chap. iv. 9), and the heaps of stones raised upon the bodies of Achan and the king of Ai (chap. vii. 26, viii. 29), remain "unto this day;" that "unto this day" Ai remains an heap (chap. viii. 28), the Gibeonites are hewers of wood and drawers of water to the congregation (chap. ix. 27), and Hebron is the inheritance of Caleb (chap. xiv. 14); that the Geshurites and Maachathites have not been expelled (chap. xiii. 13), nor the inhabitants of Jerusalem and Gezer (chap. xv. 63, xvi. 10), but dwell among and by the side of Israel "unto this day," may be just as easily understood, if they were made ten or fifteen years after the conquest and division of Canaan, as if they were made after an interval of eighty or a hundred years. For even in giving names, the remark that the new name has remained to this day is of greater significance at the end of ten years than after an interval of a century, since its permanence would be fully secured if it made its way to general adoption during the first ten years. The formula " to this day" proves nothing more than that the written record was not quite contemporaneous with the events; but it does not warrant us in concluding that the book itself was written several generations, or even centuries, after the settlement of Israel in Canaan.

It is different with the accounts of the conquest of Hebron by Caleb, Debir by Othniel, and Leshem by the Danites (chap. xv. 13-19 and xix. 47). Considered by themselves, these conquests could no doubt have taken place before the death of Joshua, as he lived for some time after the distribution of the land and the settlement of the different tribes in the possessions allotted to them (compare chap. xix. 50 and xxiii. 1, with chap. xxii. 4 and xxi. 43, 44). But if we compare these accounts with the parallel accounts of the same conquests in Judg. i. 10-16 and xviii., there can be no doubt that it was after Joshua's death that the places mentioned were taken permanently from the Canaanites, and came into the actual and permanent possession of the Israelites. For, according to Judg. i. 1-15, the Israelites inquired of the Lord, after the death of Joshua, who should begin the war with the Canaanites, i.e. with those who had not yet been destroyed, and received this reply, " Judah shall go up: behold, I have delivered the land into his hand;" whereupon Judah and Simeon smote the Canaanites at Bezek, then advanced against Jerusalem, took this city and set it on fire, and " afterward" (ver. 9) proceeded against the Canaanites on the mountains and in the south, and took Hebron and Debir. From this account it is evident at once that even the capture of Jerusalem did not take place till after the death of Joshua, and that even then the Jebusites were not driven out of Jerusalem, but continued to dwell there by the side of the Benjamites (Judg. i. 21), so that the same statement in Joshua xv. 63 also points beyond the death of Joshua. It is equally evident from Judg. xviii. that the Danites of Zorah and Eshtaol did not enter upon the expedition against Leshem or Laish till after Joshua's death. This also applies to the other statements concerning the failure to expel the Canaanites out of different districts and towns, which are common to this book and the book of Judges (compare chap. xiii. 2-5, xvi. 10, and xvii. 11, 12, with Judg. iii. 3, i. 29, and i. 27, 28), so that we might infer from every one of these passages that this book of Joshua was not written till after Joshua's death, and therefore that the closing accounts of his death in chap. xxiv. 29-33 formed a part of the original work.

If we endeavour to determine the date of composition more exactly, we have first of all to bear in mind the fact, that the wars and conquests just referred to cannot have occurred a very long time after Joshua's death ; for, in the first place, it was in the very nature of things, that when the different tribes of Israel proceeded into their different possessions, even if they did not commence the attack upon the remaining Canaanites immediately, they would certainly do so very soon, in order that they might obtain complete and undisputed possession of the land. Moreover, when the division of the land by lot took place, Caleb was eighty-five years old ; and yet he lived to see the capture of Hebron and Debir, and even took part in it, inasmuch as he not only promised but was able to give his daughter to the conqueror of Debir for a wife (chap. xv. 13-19 ; Judg. i. 11 sqq.). It was no doubt shortly after these wars, in which Judah took possession of the mountains, but was unable to destroy the Canaanites who dwelt in the valley, because of their possessing iron chariots (Judg. i. 19), that the Danites felt obliged to go northwards to conquer Leshem, and take it for a possession, on account of the inheritance assigned them by lot between Judah and Ephraim being too small for them, because the Canaanites had not been expelled. And whilst all these occurrences, which are mentioned in the book of Joshua, fell within the period immediately succeeding the death of Joshua, we can find distinct evidence in the book itself that it was not written after, but before, the establishment of the monarchy in Israel. According to chap. xvi. 10, the Canaanites were still dwelling in Gezer ; yet they were destroyed at the close of David's reign, or the commencement of that of Solomon, when Pharaoh, the king of Egypt, conquered the town (1 Kings ix. 16). According to chap. xv. 63, the Jebusites had not yet been driven out of Jerusalem ; but this was accomplished by David at the beginning of his reign over all the tribes of Israel (2 Sam. v. 3, 6-9). According to chap. ix. 27, the place for the temple had not yet been chosen, but this was done in the time of David (2 Sam. xxiv. 18 sqq. ; 1 Chron. xxi. 16 sqq). And the

Gibeonites were still hewers of wood and drawers of water to the congregation for the altar of the Lord, by virtue of the treaty which Joshua and the elders had made with them; whereas this treaty was violated by Saul, who endeavoured to destroy the Gibeonites (2 Sam. xxi. 1 sqq.). If we add to this, that our book shows no traces whatever of later times and circumstances either in its style or contents, but that it is closely connected with the Pentateuch in the language as well as in its peculiar stand-point,—for example, when the only Phœnicians mentioned are the Sidonians, and they are reckoned as belonging to the Canaanites who were to be destroyed (chap. xiii. 4–6), whereas in the time of David we find the circumstances entirely changed (2 Sam. v. 11; 1 Kings v. 15; 1 Chron. xiv. 1); and again when Sidon is referred to as the chief city of Phœnicia, and the epithet " great" is applied to it (chap. xi. 8, xix. 28), whereas Tyre had outstripped Sidon even in the days of David,—the conclusion becomes an extremely probable one, that the book was written not later than twenty or twenty-five years after the death of Joshua, in all probability by one of the elders who crossed the Jordan with Joshua, and had taken part in the conquest of Canaan (*vid.* chap. v. 1, 6), but who survived Joshua a considerable time (chap. xxiv. 31; Judg. ii. 7).

But even if the book of Joshua was not composed till some time after the events recorded (and the authorship cannot be determined with certainty), this does not affect its *historico-prophetic character;* for both the contents and form of the book show it to be an independent and simple work composed with historical fidelity, and a work which is as thoroughly pervaded with the spirit of the Old Testament revelation as the Pentateuch itself. However closely it is connected with the Pentateuch both in language and contents, there is no tenable ground for the hypothesis set up in various forms by modern critics, that it has arisen, just like the Pentateuch, from the fusion of two or three earlier writings, and was composed by the so-called " Deuteronomist." For, even if we leave altogether out of sight the fact that this hypothesis is unfounded and untenable in the case of the Pentateuch, the supposed community of authorship between the book of Joshua and that of Deuteronomy, as well as the rest of the Pentateuch, in the revised form in which it has come down to us, is founded chiefly upon the opinion that the death of Moses, with which the Pentateuch closes, " does not form a fitting conclusion for a work which commenced with the creation, and treated the earlier history in the manner in which this is done

in the Pentateuch;" because " it is hardly conceivable that a
historical work, which was written at any rate some time after the
conquest of the land of Canaan by the Israelites, should describe
all the preparations that were made for the conquest of the land,
and then break off without including either the capture of the
land, or the division of it among the remaining tribes" (*Bleek's
Einleitung, Stähelin,* and others). But, in the first place, it is to be
observed that the Pentateuch was not written " some time after the
conquest of Canaan by the Israelites," and is not to be regarded as
a historical work in the sense intended by these critics. It is the
law book of the Old Testament, to which, as even *Bleek* admits,
the book of Deuteronomy forms an appropriate close. And, in the
second place, although the book of Joshua is closely connected with
the Pentateuch, and carries on the history to the conquest of the
promised land by the Israelites, there is evidence that it is an independent work, in the fact that it repeats the account of the conquest
of the land on the east of Jordan, and its distribution by Moses
among the two tribes and a half, and also of the cities of refuge
which Moses had already appointed in that part of the land, for the
purpose of giving a full and complete account of the fulfilment of
the promise made by God to the patriarchs, that their seed should
receive the land of Canaan for a possession ; and still more in the
peculiarities of language by which it is obviously distinguished from
the books of Moses. In the book of Joshua not only do we find
none of the archaisms which run pretty uniformly through all the
books of the Pentateuch, such as הוּא for הִיא, נַעַר for נַעֲרָה, הָאֵל
for הָאֵלֶּה, and other words which are peculiar to the Pentateuch ;
but we find, on the other hand, words and expressions which never
occur in the Pentateuch, *e.g.* the constant form יְרִיחוֹ (chap. ii. 1–3,
etc., in all twenty-six times) instead of the form יְרֵחוֹ, which is quite
as uniformly adopted in the Pentateuch (Num. xxii. 1, xxvi. 3,
etc., in all eleven times) : also מַמְלְכוּת, for the kingdom of Sihon
and Og (chap. xiii. 12, 21, 27, 30, 31), instead of מַמְלֶכֶת (Num.
xxxii. 33 ; Deut. iii. 4, 10, etc.) ; קַנּוֹא (chap. xxiv. 19) instead of
קַנָּא (Ex. xx. 5, xxxiv. 14 ; Deut. iv. 24, v. 9, etc.) ; שֵׁמַע, *fama*
(chap. vi. 27, ix. 9), for שֵׁמַע (Gen. xxix. 13, etc.) ; יְרֵא (chap. xxii.
25) for יִרְאָה (Deut. iv. 10, v. 26, etc.) ; and lastly, גִּבּוֹרֵי הַחַיִל
(chap. i. 14, vi. 2, viii. 3, x. 7) for בְּנֵי חַיִל (Deut. iii. 18) ; נֹאד, a
bottle (chap. ix. 4, 13), for חֵמֶת (Gen. xxi. 14, 15, 19) ; הִצִּית, to set
on fire or burn (chap. viii. 8, 19) ; צָנַח, to spring down (chap. xv.
18) ; קָצִין, a prince or leader (chap. x. 24) ; שָׁקַט, to rest (chap. xi. 23,

xiv. 15) ; and other words besides, which you seek for in vain in the Pentateuch, whereas they frequently occur in the later books.[1]

Whilst the independence of the book of Joshua is thus placed beyond all doubt, its internal unity, or the singleness of the authorship, is evident in general from the arrangement and connection of the contents, as shown above, and in particular from the fact, that in the different parts of the book we neither meet with material differences or discrepancies, nor are able to detect two different styles. The attempt which was formerly made by *De Wette, Hauff*, and others, to show that there were material discrepancies in the different parts, has been almost entirely given up by *Bleek* and *Stähelin* in their introductions. What *Bleek* still notices in this respect, in chaps. iii. and iv., viii. 1–29 and other passages, will be examined in our exposition of the chapters in question, along with the arguments which *Knobel* employs against the unity of the book. The many traces of different modes of thought which were adduced by *Stähelin* in 1843, have been dropped in his special introduction (1862) : the only one that he insists upon now is the fact, that the way in which Joshua acts in chap. xviii. 1–10 is very different from chap. xiv. sqq. ; and that in the historical sections, as a rule, Joshua is described as acting very differently from what would be expected from Num. xxvii. 21, inasmuch as he acts quite independently, and never asks the high priest to give him an answer through the Urim and Thummim. This remark is so far correct, that throughout the whole book, and not merely in the historical sections, Joshua is never said to have inquired the will of the Lord through the medium of the Urim and Thummim of the high priest, and Eleazar is not mentioned at all in the historical portions. But it does not follow from this that there is any such difference in the mode of thought as would point to a difference of authorship. For,

[1] How completely the hypothesis that the book of Joshua was written by the Deuteronomist is wrecked on these differences in language, is evident even from the attempts which have been made to set them aside. For example, when *Stähelin* observes that the later editor retained the form יְרֵחוֹ in the Pentateuch as he found it in the original work, whereas in the book of Joshua he altered the original work into the form he commonly used, this assumption is just as incredible as the hitherto unheard of assertion that the archaistic use of הוּא as a feminine instead of הִיא· is traceable to a later form. What can have induced the later editor, then, to alter the form מַמְלֶכֶת, which he so commonly uses in Deuteronomy, into מַמְלְכוּת in Joshua ? The "reliable" *Bleek* prefers, therefore, to take no notice of these differences, or at least to express no opinion about them.

on the one hand, Joshua is blamed in chap. ix. 14 for having made a treaty with the Gibeonites, without asking at the mouth of Jehovah, and in this there is evidently a gentle allusion to Num. xxvii. 21; and on the other hand, even Num. xxvii. 21 by no means implies that God would only make known His will to Joshua through the Urim and Thummim : so that when Joshua is there referred to the high priest for instructions, all other communications, such as those which he received directly from the Lord with regard to the conquest and division of Canaan, are thereby precluded. If the Lord made known to him what he was to do in this respect, partly by the direct communication of His will, and partly by His angel (chap. v. 13 sqq.), there was no occasion at all for Eleazar to be mentioned in the historical portion of the book, since the direction of the army to fight battles and conquer towns did not form part of the official functions of the high priest, even if he did accompany Joshua in his campaigns. In the geographical portion, however, Eleazar is only mentioned in connection with the committee of heads of the nation appointed according to the law in Num. xxxiv. 17 sqq. for the distribution of the land (chap. xiv. 1, xix. 51, xxi. 1) ; and even here he does not stand out with any peculiar prominence, as Joshua was still at the head of the whole nation when this was performed (chap. xiii. 1, 7). Consequently, not only did Caleb apply to Joshua with the request for the inheritance promised him by the Lord (chap. xiv. 6 sqq.) ; but even in other cases, where there was no reason for enumerating the different members of the commission for dividing the land, Joshua is mentioned as appointing and superintending the casting of the lots (chap. xviii. 3–10, xx. 1). The proofs adduced of the " double style" of the book are equally weak. The principal ones are the fact, that the word generally used for tribe in the historical sections is *shebet*, whereas *matteh* is the word employed in the geographical sections, and that in the latter the word *machaloketh* is altogether wanting (chap. xi. 23, xii. 7). But the interchange of *shebet* and *matteh* may be fully explained from the difference in the meaning of these two words, *shebet* denoting the tribe as a political corporation, possessing independence and power, and *matteh* having simple regard to its genealogical aspect,— a distinction which is not overthrown by the assurance, that " in chap. vii. 14, 16, 18, and xxii. 1, as compared with chap. xiii. 29, and in chap. iii. 12, as compared with Num. xxxiv. 18, the charge is perfectly arbitrary." But whether it be involuntary or carefully considered, there is no ground for inferring that there have been two writers engaged upon the work, for the simple reason that both words occur in the historical as well as the geographical sections,— sometimes, in fact, in the very same verse, *e.g.* chap. xiii. 29 and Num. xviii. 2, where we cannot possibly imagine a fusion of different documents to have taken place. (For further remarks, see at chap. vii. 1.) The word *machaloketh,* however, is not synonymous with *mishpachah,* as *Stähelin* supposes, but denotes the various subdivisions of the tribes into families, fathers' houses and families; and this also not only occurs in chap. xi. 23 and xii. 7, but in the geographical portion also, in chap. xviii. 10. The other remark, viz. that " in the place of the רָאשֵׁי אָבוֹת, who are the leading actors in the *geographical* sections, we find the elders, judges, heads רָאשִׁים and שֹׁטְרִים in the *historical,* or else simply the *shoterim* (chap. i. 10, iii. 2, viii. 33, xxiii. 2, xxiv. 1), or the elders," is neither quite correct, nor in the least degree conclusive. It is incorrect, inasmuch as even in the geographical portion, namely chap. xvii. 4, the נְשִׂיאִים are mentioned instead of the רָאשֵׁי אָבוֹת, along with Eleazar and Joshua. But the notion upon which this argument is founded is still more erroneous, viz. that " the שֹׁפְטִים זְקֵנִים, רָאשֵׁי אָבוֹת, נְשִׂיאִים, and שֹׁטְרִים are all the same, as we may clearly see from Deut. i. 15 ;" for the identity of the terms elders and heads with the terms judges and officers (*shoterim*) cannot possibly be inferred from this passage, in which the judges and *shoterim* are said to have been chosen from the elders of the nation. Even the " heads of the fathers' houses" (see at Ex. vi. 14) were only a section of the princes and heads of the nation, and those mentioned in the book of Joshua are simply those who were elected as members of the distribution committee, and who are naturally referred to in connection with the division of the land by lot; whereas the judges and *shoterim* had nothing to do with it, and for this very reason are not mentioned at all in the geographical sections.—And if, instead of confining ourselves to the words, we turn our attention to the facts, all the peculiarities that we meet with in the different parts of the book may be explained in this way, and the seeming differences brought into harmony. In a work which embraces two such different subjects as the forcible conquest and the peaceable distribution of the land of Canaan, the same ideas and expression cannot possibly be constantly recurring, if the words are to be at all in conformity with the actual contents. And not the smallest conclusion can be drawn from such differences as these with regard to the composition of the book ; much less can they be adduced as proofs of diversity of authorship. Moreover, the unity of authorship is not to be overthrown by proving, or showing it to be probable, that the author made use of written documents for some of the sections—such, for example, as the official records prepared for the distribution of the land by lot—in his description of the possessions of the different tribes.

Lastly, the historical fidelity of the book of Joshua cannot justly be called in question; and so far as all the narratives and descriptions are concerned, which lie within the sphere of the ordinary laws of nature, this is generally admitted. This applies not only to the description of the possessions of the different tribes according to their boundaries and towns, which are almost universally acknowledged to have been derived from authentic records, but to such historical passages as the words of Caleb (chap. xiv. 6 sqq.), the address of Phinehas, and the reply of the two tribes and a half (chap. xxii.), the complaint of the children of Joseph on account of the smallness of the possessions that had fallen to their lot, and Joshua's answer (chap. xvii. 14 sqq.), which are so thoroughly original, and so perfectly appropriate to the persons and circumstances, that their historical credibility cannot be disputed.[1] It is chiefly at the miraculous occurrences that the opponents of the biblical revelation have taken offence: partly therefore because of the miracles themselves, and partly because the statement that God commanded the destruction of the Canaanites is irreconcilable with correct (?) views of the Godhead, they deny the historical character of the whole book. But the miracles recorded in this book do not stand alone; on the contrary, they are most intimately connected with the great work of divine revelation, and the redemption of the human race; so that it is only through unscriptural assumptions as to the character of God, and His operations in nature and the world of men, that they can be pronounced unreal, or altogether denied. And the objection, that the destruction of the Canaanites, as an act commanded by God, "cannot be reconciled even with only half correct notions of the Deity," as *Eichhorn* maintains, rests upon totally unscriptural and irrational views of God and the divine government, which

---

[1] Even *Eichhorn*, for example, says in his Introduction, "The words of Caleb, in chap. xiv. 1 sqq., in which he asks for the inheritance that had been promised him, bear too strongly the characteristics of an appeal from the mouth of an old man of eighty years of age, and breathe too thoroughly in every word his spirit, and age, and peculiar situation, for it to be possible that it should be merely the composition of a later writer, who placed himself in imagination in his situation, and put the words into his mouth."

deny *a priori* all living influence on the part of the "Deity" upon the earth and its inhabitants. But the true God is not a Deity who can neither help nor injure men (Jer. x. 5); He is the almighty creator, preserver, and governor of the world. This God was Jehovah, who chose Israel for His own people, "a living God, an everlasting King" (Jer. x. 10); who not only fixed for the nations the bounds of their habitations, but their appointed times as well, that they should seek Him, if haply they might feel after Him, and find Him (Deut. xxxii. 8; Acts xvii. 26, 27); who, because He has given to every nation upon earth life and being, property and land, to be rightly used, and to promote their own happiness through the glorification of the name of God, possesses both the power and the right to deprive them of all their possessions, and wipe out every trace of them from the earth, if they dishonour and disgrace the name of God by an obstinate abuse of the blessings and gifts entrusted to them. Thus the only true God, who judges the earth in eternally unchangeable wisdom and righteousness, and manifests His wrath in great judgments, as well as His mercy in innumerable blessings to all the children of men, had promised to Abraham that He would give him the land of Canaan for a possession for his seed the children of Israel, when the iniquity of the Amorites, who possessed it at that time, was full, *i.e.* had reached its full measure (Gen. xii. 7, xv. 13–16). The expulsion of the Canaanites, therefore, from possessions which they had no doubt rightfully held, but to which they had forfeited their right through the misuse they had made of them, is to be regarded quite as decidedly as an act of penal justice on the part of God, as the presentation of this land to Israel was an act of His free grace; and the destruction of the Canaanites by the Israelites, as well as their capture of the possession which the Canaanites had forfeited through their sins (*vid.* Lev. xviii. 24–28; Deut. xii. 29–31), was perfectly justifiable, if, as our book affirms, the Israelites were only acting as instruments in the hands of the Lord. It is true they were not warranted in carrying on a war of extermination against the Canaanites simply because the land had been given them by God, any more than David was warranted in putting Saul to death and wresting the kingdom from him, although he had been rejected by the Lord, simply because Samuel had promised him the kingdom by the command of God, and had even anointed him king over Israel. But the Israelites did not proceed from Egypt to Canaan of their own accord, or by their own power; they were brought out of this land of their bondage by the God of their fathers with a mighty arm, and led by Him through the wilderness into the promised land. Joshua acted, as Moses had done before him, by the immediate command of God; and the fact that this command was real and well-founded, and not a mere fancy, is proved by the miraculous signs through which God accredited the armies of Israel as the servants of His judicial righteousness, who were fighting in His name and by His command, when the Lord of the whole earth divided the waters of Jordan before them, threw down the walls of Jericho, filled the Canaanites with fear and despair, killed them with hailstones at Gibeon, and brought to nought all their plans and endeavours to resist the advance of Israel, so that Joshua smote great and mighty nations, and no one could stand before him. Hence the Psalmist was able to write, "Thou didst drive out the heathen with Thy hand, and plantedst them (the Israelites); Thou hast destroyed nations, and cast them out. For they got not the land in possession by their own sword, neither did their own arm help them; but Thy right hand, and Thine arm, and the light of Thy countenance, because Thou hadst a favour unto them" (Ps. xliv. 2, 3).—And whilst the Israelites were thus proved to be the executors of the penal judgments of God, they acted in perfect accordance with this vocation by the manner in which they carried out the judgment entrusted to them. They submitted cheerfully and obediently to all the appointments of Joshua; they sanctified themselves by the circumcision of all who had remained uncircumcised in the desert and by keeping the passover at Gilgal; they set up the law of the Lord upon Ebal and Gerizim; they executed the ban upon the Canaanites, as the Lord had commanded, and punished Achan and his house for transgressing this ban, that they might expunge the sin from their midst; they vowed, in the most solemn manner, that when they had come into peaceable possession of the promised inheritance, they would renounce all idolatry, would serve Jehovah their God alone, and would hearken to His voice, to renew the covenant with the Lord; and they served the Lord as long as Joshua lived, and the elders after him, who knew all the works of the Lord which He had done for Israel.—(For further remarks upon this subject, see *Hengstenberg's* Dissertations on the Pentateuch, vol. ii. pp. 387–417, Eng. trans., Art. "On the Right of the Israelites to Palestine.")

Thus the contents of the book have their higher unity and their truth in the idea of the justice, holiness, and grace of God, as they were manifested in the most glorious manner in the great historical event which forms the subject of the whole. Whilst justice was revealed in the case of the Canaanites, and grace in that of the Israelites, the holiness of the Almighty God was manifested in both,—in the Canaanites, who were liable to judgment, through their destruction; and in the Israelites, who were chosen to fellowship with the Lord, through the sanctification of their lives to the faithful performance of the duties of their vocation, both to the honour of God and the glory of His name.

The different views that have been expressed as to the time when the book was written are given more fully in *Keil's* Commentary on Joshua (1847, Eng. trans. 1857), where the exegetical aids are also given.

EXPOSITION.

THE PREAMBLE.

CHAP. I. 1–9.

AFTER the death of Moses the Lord summoned Joshua, the servant of Moses, whom He had appointed as the leader of Israel into Canaan, to go with all the people across the Jordan, and take the land which had been promised to the fathers on oath, assuring him at the same time of His powerful aid, on condition that he observed the law of Moses faithfully. This summons and promise of God form the preamble to the whole book, which is linked on to the conclusion of the Pentateuch by the introductory words, "And it came to pass after the death of Moses, the servant of the Lord," though it is not so closely connected as to warrant the conclusion that the two works have been written by the same author.—Ver. 1. The imperfect with *vav consec.*, the standing mode of expressing a continued action or train of thought, "simply attaches itself by the conjunction 'and' to a completed action, which has either been mentioned before, or is supposed to be well known" (*Ewald*, § 231, *b.*). "*After the death of Moses*," *i.e.* after the expiration of the thirty days of general mourning for him (*vid.* Deut. xxxiv. 8). "*Servant of Jehovah*" is a standing epithet applied to Moses as an honourable title, and founded upon Num. xii. 7, 8 (*vid.* Deut. xxxiv. 5; 1 Kings viii. 56; 2 Kings xviii. 12; Ps. cv. 26, etc.).

On "*Joshua, Moses' minister,*" see at Ex. xvii. 9 and Num. xiii. 16. *Minister* (*meshareth*), as in Ex. xxiv. 13, etc. Although Joshua had already been called by the mouth of the Lord to be the successor of Moses in the task of leading the people into Canaan (Num. xxvii. 15 sqq.), and had not only been presented to the people in this capacity, but had been instituted in this office by the Lord, with the promise of His help (Deut. xxxi. 3–7 and 23), the word of the Lord came to him a second time after the death of Moses, with the command to enter upon the office to which he had been called, and with the promise that He would help him to fulfil its duties, as he had already helped His servant Moses. " Because even some of the bravest men, although fully prepared beforehand, either stand still or hesitate when the thing has to be done : this exhortation to Joshua, to gird himself at once for the expedition, was by no means superfluous ; though his call was ratified again not only for his own sake, but in order that the people might not hesitate to follow him with their minds collected and calm, when they saw that he took no step without the guidance of God" (*Calvin*).— Joshua received this word of the Lord by a direct address from God, and not through the intervention of the Urim and Thummim of the high priest ; for this appointed medium for the revelation of the will of God, to which he had been referred on the occasion of his first call (Num. xxvii. 21), whenever difficulties should arise in connection with his office, was not sufficient for the renewal and confirmation of his divine calling, since the thing required here was not merely that the will of God should be made known to him, but that he should be inspired with courage and strength for the fulfilment of it, *i.e.* for discharging the duties of his office, just as he afterwards was when in front of the fortified town of Jericho which he was directed to take, where the angel of the Lord appeared to him and assured him of its fall (chap. v. 13). Moreover, the conquest of Canaan formed part of the work which the Lord entrusted to His servant Moses, and in which therefore Joshua was now Moses' successor. Consequently the Lord would be with him as He had been with Moses (ver. 5) ; and for this reason He revealed His will directly to him, as He had done to Moses, though without talking with him mouth to mouth (Num. xii. 8).—Ver. 2. As Moses had died without having brought the Israelites to Canaan, Joshua was to arise and go with all the nation over *this* Jordan (*i.e.* the river then before him) into the land which the Lord would give them.— Ver. 3. " *Namely, every place that the sole of your foot shall tread upon*," *i.e.* I have given you the whole land, not excepting a single foot's breadth. The perfect, "*I have given*," refers to the counsel of God as having been formed long before, and being now about to be carried into execution. These words, which are connected with Deut. xi. 24, so far as the form is concerned, rest upon the promise of God in Ex. xxiii. 30, 31, to which the words "as I said unto Moses" refer.—Ver. 4. The boundaries of the land are given as in Deut. xi. 24, with the simple difference in form, that the boundary line from the desert (of Arabia) and Lebanon, *i.e.* from the southern and northern extremity, is drawn first of all towards the east to the great river, the Euphrates, and then towards the west to "the great sea, toward the going down of the sun," *i.e.* the Mediterranean ; and then between these two *termini ad quem* the more precise definition is inserted, " all the land of the Hittites ; " whereas in Deuteronomy the southern, northern, and eastern boundaries are placed in antithesis to the western boundary, and the more precise definition of the country to be taken is given by an enumeration of the different tribes that were to be destroyed by the Israelites (ver. 23). On the oratorical character of these descriptions, see at Gen. xv. 18. The demonstrative pronoun "this," in connection with Lebanon, may be explained from the fact that Lebanon, or at all events Antilibanus, was visible from the Israelitish camp. The expression "*the Hittites*" (see at Gen. x. 15) is used here in a broader sense for Canaanites in general, as in 1 Kings x. 29 ; 2 Kings vii. 6 ; Ezek. xvi. 3. The promise in ver. 5*a* is adopted from Deut. xi. 25, where it was made to the whole nation, and specially transferred to Joshua ; and ver. 5*b* is repeated from Deut. xxxi. 8, as compared with ver. 6.—Vers. 6-9. The promise is followed by the condition upon which the Lord would fulfil His word. Joshua was to be firm and strong, *i.e.* well-assured, courageous, not alarmed (*vid.* Deut. xxxi. 6). In the first place (ver. 6), he was to rely firmly upon the Lord and His promise, as Moses and the Lord had already told him (Deut. xxxi. 7 and 23), and as is again repeated here, whilst at the same time the expression, "*thou shalt divide for an inheritance*," recalls to mind Deut. i. 38, iii. 28 ; and in the second place (vers. 7, 8), he was to strive to attain and preserve this firmness by a careful observance of the law. "*Observe to do*," etc., as Moses had already impressed upon the hearts of all the people (Deut. v. 29, cf. xxviii. 14 and ii. 27). The suffix in מִמֶּנּוּ is to be explained on the supposition that the speaker had the book of the law in his mind. The further expansion, in ver. 8, is not only attached to the exhortations, with which Moses urges upon all the people in Deut. vi. 6, 7, and xi. 18, 19, an uninterrupted study and laying to heart of the commandments of God, but even more closely to the directions to the king, to read every day in the law (Deut. xvii. 19). "*Not to depart out of the mouth*," is to be constantly *in* the mouth. The law is in our mouth, not only when we are incessantly preaching it, but when we are reading it intelligently for ourselves, or conversing about it with others. To this there was to be added meditation, or reflection upon it both day and night (*vid.* Ps. i. 2). הָגָה does not mean theoretical speculation about the law, such as the Pharisees indulged in, but a practical study of the law, for the purpose of observing it in thought and action, or carrying it out with the heart, the mouth, and the hand. Such a mode of employing it would be sure to be followed by blessings. "*Then shalt thou make thy way prosperous*," *i.e.* succeed in all thine undertakings (*vid.* Deut. xxviii. 29), "*and act wisely*" (as in Deut. xxix. 8).—Ver. 9. In conclusion, the Lord not only repeats His exhortation to firmness, but the promise that He gave in vers. 5 and 6. "*Have I not*" (*nonne*) is a rhetorical mode of saying, "Behold, I have," the assurance being clothed in the form of an affirmative question. On the words "*be not afraid*," etc., see Deut. xxxi. 6 and 8.

I.—THE CONQUEST OF CANAAN.

Chap. i.–xii.

PREPARATIONS FOR ENTERING CANAAN.—CHAP. I. 10–II. 24.

In consequence of the divine command (chap. i. 2–9), Joshua began without delay to make the necessary preparations for carrying out the work appointed him ; *first* of all by issuing instructions to the people to make ready for crossing the river (i. 10, 11) ; *secondly*, by reminding the tribes of Reuben, Gad, and half Manasseh of their promise to help the other tribes to conquer Canaan, and calling upon them to fulfil it (vers. 12–18) ; and *thirdly*, by sending two spies to Jericho, to explore the land, and discover the feelings of its inhabitants (chap. ii.).

Chap. i. 10–18. PREPARATIONS FOR CROSSING THE JORDAN.

—Vers. 10, 11. For the purpose of carrying out the commands of the Lord, Joshua first of all directed the officers of the people (*shoterim*: see at Ex. v. vi.), whose duty it was, as the keepers of the family registers, to attend not only to the levying of the men who were bound to serve in the army, but also to the circulation of the commands of the general, to issue orders to the people in the camp to provide themselves with food, so that they might cross the Jordan within three days, and take the land that was promised them by God. By *zedah*, provision for a journey (Gen. xlii. 25, etc.), we are not to understand manna, for that had already ceased (see at chap. v. 12), but simply the natural produce of the inhabited country. The expression " *in three days*," *i.e.*, as we may see from comparing Gen. xl. 13, 19, with ver. 20, on the third day from the publication of the command, " *will ye go over the Jordan*," is not to be regarded as a prediction of the time when the crossing actually took place, but to be taken as the latest time that could be allowed to the people to prepare for crossing : viz. in this sense, " Prepare you victuals for crossing over the Jordan within three days," *i.e.* that you may be able to leave Shittim within that time, to cross over the Jordan, and commence the conquest of Canaan. If we understand the words in this way, they are in perfect harmony with chap. ii. and iii. According to chap. ii., Joshua sent out spies from Shittim to Jericho, who were obliged to hide themselves for three days in the mountains after their flight from that city (chap. ii. 22), before they could return to the Israelitish camp ; so that they were absent three or four days at any rate, and came back at the earliest in the evening or night of the fourth day after they had been sent out. It was not till the morning after this that the Israelites left Shittim and proceeded to the Jordan, where they halted again. Then, three days afterwards, they went across the river (chap. iii. 1, 2), so that at least $4 + 1 + 3$, *i.e.* eight whole days must have intervened between the day when the spies were sent out and the day on which the people crossed the river. Joshua no doubt intended to proceed to the Jordan and cross it within three days after despatching the spies ; he therefore sent the spies to Jericho on the same day on which he issued the command to the people to prepare for crossing within three days, so that he might reasonably hope that they would fulfil their commission and return in two or three days. But as they were compelled to hide themselves for three days in the mountains, in consequence of the unexpected discovery of their arrival in Jericho, and the despatch of men in pursuit of them, Joshua could not remove with the people from Shittim and proceed to the Jordan till the day after their return; and even then he could not cross the river at once, but waited three days after reaching the bank of the river before he crossed to the other side (*vid*. chap. iii. 1 sqq.).[1]

Vers. 12–18. Joshua's appeal to the two tribes and a half, to remember the condition on which Moses gave them the land on the east of the Jordan for an inheritance, and to fulfil it, met with a ready response; so that these tribes not only promised to obey his commandments in every respect, but threatened every one with death who should refuse obedience. In recalling this condition to the recollection of the tribes referred to, Joshua follows the expressions in Deut. iii. 18-20, where Moses himself recapitulates his former command, rather than the original passage in Num. xxxii. The expression "*this land*" shows that the speaker was still on the other side of the Jordan. חֲמֻשִׁים, *with the loins girded, i.e.* prepared for war, synonymous with חֲלֻצִים in Deut. iii. 18 and Num. xxxii. 32 (see at Ex. xiii. 18). כָּל־גִּבּוֹרֵי חַיִל, *all the mighty men of valour, i.e.* the brave warriors (as in chap. vi. 2, viii. 3, x. 7, and very frequently in the later books), is not common to this book and Deuteronomy, as *Knobel* maintains, but is altogether strange to the Pentateuch (see p. 9). The word "*all*" (ver. 14, like Num. xxxii. 21, 27) must not be pressed. According to chap. iv. 13, there were only about 40,000 men belonging to the two tribes and a half who crossed the Jordan to take part in the war; whereas, according to Num. xxvi. 7, 18, 34, there were 110,000 men in these tribes who were capable of bearing arms, so that 70,000 must have remained behind for the protection of the women and children and of the flocks and herds, and to defend the land of which they had taken possession. On ver. 15 see Deut. iii. 18; and on the more minute definition of "*on this side* (*lit.* beyond) *Jordan*" by "*toward the sun-rising*,"

---

[1] In this way the different statements in the three chapters harmonize perfectly well. But the majority of commentators have arranged the order of succession differently and in a very arbitrary way, starting with the unwarrantable assumption that the time referred to in this verse, "within three days," is identical with that in chap. iii. 2, "it came to pass after three days." Upon the strength of this groundless assumption, *Knobel* maintains that there is great confusion in the order of succession of the events described in chap. i.–iii., that chap. i. 11 is irreconcilable with chap. iii. 1–6, and that accounts written by three different authors have been mixed up together in these chapters. (For the different attempts to reconcile the accounts, see *Keil's* Commentary on Joshua, pp. 72–75, note, Eng. trans. Clark, 1857.)

compare the remarks on Num. xxxii. 19. The answer of the two tribes and a half, in which they not only most cheerfully promise their help in the conquest of Canaan, but also express the wish that Joshua may have the help of the Lord (ver. 17 compared with ver. 4), and after threatening all who refuse obedience with death, close with the divine admonition, "*only be strong and of a good courage*" (ver. 18, cf. ver. 6), furnishes a proof of the wish that inspired them to help their brethren, that all the tribes might speedily enter into the peaceable possession of the promised inheritance. The expression "*rebel* against the commandment" is used in Deut. i. 26, 43, ix. 23, 1 Sam. xii. 14, to denote resistance to the commandments of the Lord; here it denotes opposition to His representative, the commander chosen by the Lord, which was to be punished with death, according to the law in Deut. xvii. 12.

Chap. ii. TWO SPIES SENT OVER TO JERICHO. — Ver. 1. Although Joshua had received a promise from the Lord of His almighty help in the conquest of Canaan, he still thought it necessary to do what was requisite on his part to secure the success of the work committed to him, as the help of God does not preclude human action, but rather presupposes it. He therefore sent two men out secretly as spies from Shittim the place of encampment at that time (see at Num. xxv. 1), to view, *i.e.* explore, the land, especially Jericho, the strongly fortified frontier town of Canaan (chap. vi. 1). The word "*secretly*" is connected by the accents with "*saying*," giving them their instructions secretly; but this implies that they were also sent out secretly. This was done partly in order that the Canaanites might not hear of it, and partly in order that, if the report should prove unfavourable, the people might not be thrown into despair, as they had been before in the time of Moses. The spies proceeded to Jericho, and towards evening they entered the house of a harlot named Rahab, and lodged there, *lit.* laid themselves down, intended to remain or sleep there. *Jericho* was two hours' journey to the west of the Jordan, situated in a plain that was formerly very fertile, and celebrated for its palm trees and balsam shrubs, but which is now quite desolate and barren. This plain is encircled on the western side by a naked and barren range of mountains, which stretches as far as Beisan towards the north and to the Dead Sea on the south. Every trace of the town has long since passed away, though it evidently stood somewhere near, and probably on the northern side of, the miserable and dirty village of

Rîha, by the Wady Kelt (see *Robinson,* Pal. ii. pp. 279 sqq., 289 sqq. ; *v. Raumer,* Pal. pp. 206 sqq.). *Rahab* is called a *zonah, i.e.* a *harlot,* not an innkeeper, as *Josephus,* the *Chaldee* version, and the *Rabbins* render the word. Their entering the house of such a person would not excite so much suspicion. Moreover, the situation of her house against or upon the town wall was one which facilitated escape. But the Lord so guided the course of the spies, that they found in this sinner the very person who was the most suitable for their purpose, and upon whose heart the tidings of the miracles wrought by the living God on behalf of Israel had made such an impression, that she not only informed the spies of the despondency of the Canaanites, but, with believing trust in the power of the God of Israel, concealed the spies from all the inquiries of her countrymen, though at the greatest risk to herself.

Vers. 2–6. When the king of Jericho was informed of the fact that these strange men had entered the house of Rahab, and suspecting their reason for coming, summoned Rahab to give them up, she hid them (*lit. hid him, i.e.* each one of the spies : for this change from the plural to the singular see *Ewald,* § 219), and said to the king's messengers: כֵּן, *recte,* " It is quite correct, the men came to me, but I do not know where they were from ; and when in the darkness the gate was at the shutting (*i.e.* ought to be shut : for this construction, see Gen. xv. 12), they went out again, I know not whither. Pursue them quickly, you will certainly overtake them." The writer then adds this explanation in ver. 6 : she had hidden them upon the roof of her house among stalks of flax. The expression "*to-night*" (*lit. the* night) in ver. 2 is more precisely defined in ver. 5, viz. as night was coming on, before the town-gate was shut, after which it would have been in vain for them to attempt to leave the town. "*Stalks of flax,*" not "cotton pods" (*Arab., J. D. Mich.*), or "tree-flax, *i.e.* cotton," as *Thenius* explains it, but flax stalks or stalk-flax, as distinguished from carded flax, in which there is no wood left, λινοκαλάμη, *stipula lini* (LXX., *Vulg.*). Flax stalks, which grow to the height of three or four feet in Egypt, and attain the thickness of a reed, and would probably be quite as large in the plain of Jericho, the climate of which resembles that of Egypt, would form a very good hiding-place for the spies if they were piled up upon the roof to dry in the sun. The falsehood by which Rahab sought not only to avert all suspicion from herself of any conspiracy with the Israelitish men who had entered her house, but to prevent any further search for them in her house, and to frustrate the attempt to arrest them, is not to be justified as a lie of necessity told for a good purpose, nor, as *Grotius* maintains, by the unfounded assertion that, " before the preaching of the gospel, a salutary lie was not regarded as a fault even by good men." Nor can it be shown that it was thought " allowable," or even " praise-worthy," simply because the writer mentions the fact without express-ing any subjective opinion, or because, as we learn from what fol-lows (vers. 9 sqq.), Rahab was convinced of the truth of the miracles which God had wrought for His people, and acted in firm faith that the true God would give the land of Canaan to the Israelites, and that all opposition made to them would be vain, and would be, in fact, rebellion against the Almighty God himself. For a lie is always a sin. Therefore even if Rahab was not actuated at all by the desire to save herself and her family from destruction, and the motive from which she acted had its roots in her faith in the living God (Heb. xi. 31), so that what she did for the spies, and thereby for the cause of the Lord, was counted to her for righteousness (" justified by works," James ii. 25), yet the course which she adopted was a sin of weakness, which was forgiven her in mercy because of her faith.[1]

Vers. 7–14. Upon this declaration on the part of the woman, the king's messengers (" the men ") pursued the spies by the road to the Jordan which leads across the fords. Both the circumstances themselves and the usage of the language require that we should interpret the words in this way; for עַל הַמַּעְבְּרוֹת cannot mean " as far as the fords," and it is very improbable that the officers should have gone across the fords. If they did not succeed in overtaking the spies and apprehending them before they reached the fords, they certainly could not hope to do this on the other side of the river in the neighbourhood of the Israelitish camp. By " *the fords*" with the article we are to understand the ford near to Jericho which was generally used at that time (Judg. iii. 22 ; 2 Sam. xix. 16 sqq.) ; but whether this was the one which is commonly used now at the

---

[1] *Calvin's* estimate is also a correct one : " It has often happened, that even when good men have endeavoured to keep a straight course, they have turned aside into circuitous paths. Rahab acted wrongly when she told a lie and said that the spies had gone ; and the action was acceptable to God only because the evil that was mixed with the good was not imputed to her. Yet, although God wished the spies to be delivered, He did not sanction their being protected by a lie." *Augustine* also pronounces the same opinion concerning Rahab as that which he expressed concerning the Hebrew midwives (see the comm. on Ex. i. 21).

mouth of Wady *Shaib*, almost in a straight line to the east of Jericho, or the more southerly one, *el Helu*, above the mouth of Wady Hesban (*Rob.* Pal. ii. p. 254), to the south of the bathing-place of Christian pilgrims, or *el Meshra* (*Lynch*, p. 155), or *el Mocktaa* (*Seetzen*, ii. p. 320), it is impossible to determine. (On these and other fords near Beisan, and as far up as the Sea of Galilee, see *Rob.* ii. p. 259, and *Ritter Erdk.* xv. pp. 549 sqq.) After the king's messengers had left the town, they shut the gate to prevent the spies from escaping, in case they should be still in the town. אַחֲרֵי כַּאֲשֶׁר for אַחֲרֵי אֲשֶׁר is uncommon, but it is analogous to אַחֲרֵי־כֵן אֲשֶׁר in Gen. vi. 4.—Vers. 8 sqq. Notwithstanding these precautions, the men escaped. As soon as the officers had left Rahab's house, she went to the spies, who were concealed upon the roof, before they had lain down to sleep, which they were probably about to do upon the roof, —a thing of frequent occurrence in the East in summer time,—and confessed to them all that she believed and knew, namely, that God had given the land to the Israelites, and that the dread of them had fallen upon the Canaanites (" *us*," in contrast with " *you*," the Israelites, signifies the Canaanites generally, and not merely the inhabitants of Jericho), and despair had seized upon all the inhabitants of the land. The description of the despair of the Canaanites (ver. 9) is connected, so far as the expressions are concerned, with Ex. xv. 15 and 16, to show that what Moses and the Israelites had sung after crossing the Red Sea was now fulfilled, that the Lord had fulfilled His promise (Ex. xxiii. 27 compared with Deut. ii. 25 and xi. 25), and had put fear and dread upon the Canaanites.—Ver. 10. The report of the drying up of the Red Sea (Ex. xiv. 15 sqq.), of the defeat of the mighty kings of the Amorites, and of the conquest of their kingdoms, had produced this effect upon the Canaanites. Even in the last of these occurrences the omnipotence of God had been visibly displayed, so that what the Lord foretold to Moses (Deut. ii. 25) had now taken place; it had filled all the surrounding nations with fear and dread of Israel, and the heart and courage of the Canaanites sank in consequence.—Ver. 11. " *When we heard this*"—Rahab proceeded to tell them, transferring the feelings of her own heart to her countrymen—" *our heart did melt*" (it was thus that the Hebrew depicted utter despair; " the hearts of the people melted, and became as water," chap. vii. 5), " *and there did not remain any more spirit in any one :*" *i.e.* they lost all strength of mind for acting, in consequence of their fear and dread (*vid.* chap. v. 1, though in 1 Kings x. 5 this phrase is used to signify being out of one's-self from mere astonishment). *" For Jehovah your God is God in heaven above, and upon the earth beneath."* To this confession of faith, to which the Israelites were to be brought through the miraculous help of the Lord (Deut. iv. 39), Rahab also attained; although her confession of faith remained so far behind the faith which Moses at that time demanded of Israel, that she only discerned in Jehovah a Deity (*Elohim*) in heaven and upon earth, and therefore had not yet got rid of her polytheism altogether, however close she had come to a true and full confession of the Lord. But these miracles of divine omnipotence which led the heart of this sinner with its susceptibility for religious truth to true faith, and thus became to her a savour of life unto life, produced nothing but hardness in the unbelieving hearts of the rest of the Canaanites, so that they could not escape the judgment of death.—Vers. 12–14. After this confession Rahab entreated the spies to spare her family (father's house), and made them promise her on oath as a sign of their fidelity, that on the capture of Jericho, which is tacitly assumed as self-evident after what had gone before, they would save alive her parents, and brothers and sisters, and all that belonged to them (*i.e.*, according to chap. vi. 23, the children and families of her brothers and sisters), and not put them to death; all of which they promised her on oath. *" A true token,"* *lit.* a sign of truth, *i.e.* a sign by which they guaranteed the truth of the kindness for which she asked. This sign consisted in nothing but the solemn oath with which they were to confirm their assurance, and, according to ver. 14, actually did confirm it. The oath itself was taken in these words, *" our soul shall die for you,"* by which they pledged their life for the life of Rahab and her family in this sense : God shall punish us with death if we are faithless, and do not spare thy life and the lives of thy relations. Though the name of God is not really expressed, it was implied in the fact that the words are described as swearing by Jehovah. But the spies couple their assurance with this condition, *" if ye utter not this our business,"* do not betray us, *sc.* so that we should be pursued, and our life endangered; *" then will we show thee mercy and truth"* (cf. Gen. xxiv. 27).

Vers. 15–24. Rahab then let them down by a rope through the window, namely, into the open country; for her house stood against or upon the town wall, so that she lived upon the wall, and advised them to get to the mountains, that they might not meet the men who had been sent out in pursuit of them, and to hide themselves there for three days, when the pursuers would have returned.—

Vers. 17–20. In conclusion, the spies guarded against any arbitrary interpretation and application of their oath, by imposing three conditions, on the non-fulfilment of which they would be released from their oath. הַזֶּה for הַזֹּאת is to be explained in ver. 17 from the fact that the gender is often disregarded in the use of the pronoun (see *Ewald*, § 183, *a.*), and in ver. 18 from the fact that there the gender is determined by the *nomen rectum* (see *Ewald*, § 317, *d.*). —Ver. 18. The *first* condition was, that when the town was taken Rahab should make her house known to the Israelites, by binding " *the cord of this crimson thread*," *i.e.* this cord made of crimson thread, in the window from which she had let them down. The demonstrative " *this*" leads to the conclusion adopted by *Luther* and others, that " *this cord*" is the rope (חבל) mentioned in ver. 15, as no other cord had been mentioned to which they could refer ; and the fact that nothing has been said about the sign in question being either given or received, precludes the idea that the spies gave the cord to Rahab for a sign. The crimson or scarlet colour of the cord (תּוֹלַעַת שָׁנִי = שָׁנִי ; see at Ex. xxv. 4), as the colour of vigorous life, made this cord an expressive sign of the preservation of Rahab's life and the lives of her relations. The *second* condition was, that when the town was taken, Rahab should collect together her parents, and her brothers and her sisters, into her own house.—Ver. 19. Whoever went outside the door, his blood should be upon his own head ; *i.e.* if he was slain outside by the Israelitish soldiers, he should bear his death as his own fault. But every one who was with her in the house, his blood should fall upon their (the spies') head, if any hand was against them, *i.e.* touched them or did them harm (*vid.* Ex. ix. 3). The formula, " *his blood be upon his head*," is synonymous with the legal formula, " his blood be upon him" (Lev. xx. 9). The *third* condition (ver. 20) is simply a repetition of the principal condition laid down at the very outset (ver. 14).— Ver. 21. When Rahab had accepted all these conditions, she let the men go, and bound the red cord in the window. It is not to be supposed that she did this at once, but merely as soon as it was necessary. It is mentioned here for the purpose of bringing the subject to a close.—Ver. 22. The spies remained three days in the mountains, till the officers returned to the town, after searching for them the whole way in vain. The mountains referred to are probably the range on the northern side of Jericho, which afterwards received the name of *Quarantana* (Arab. *Kuruntul*), a wall of rock rising almost precipitously from the plain to the height of 1200 or

1500 feet, and full of grottoes and caves on the eastern side. These mountains were well adapted for a place of concealment; moreover, they were the nearest to Jericho, as the western range recedes considerably to the south of Wady Kelt (*vid. Rob.* ii. p. 289).— Vers. 23, 24. After this they returned to the camp across the Jordan, and informed Joshua of all that had befallen them, and all that they had heard. On ver. 24, see ver. 9.

PASSAGE THROUGH THE JORDAN.—CHAP. III. AND IV.

The following morning, after the return of the spies into the camp, Joshua proceeded with the people from Shittim to the bank of the Jordan, to complete the necessary preparations there, and then cross the river and enter Canaan (chap. iii. 1). The crossing of this boundary river of Canaan, or rather the passage through the bed of the river, which had been dried up by a miracle of divine omnipotence at the place of crossing, is narrated in these two chapters in the following manner: first (chap. iii. 1*b*–6), the final preparations for crossing; and then the passage through the bed of the river, and the erection of stones as a permanent memorial of this miracle. This is arranged in three parts: viz. vers. 7–17, the commencement of the crossing; chap. iv. 1–14, its further progress; and chap. iv. 15–24, its close. The account is also arranged upon the following plan: in every one of these three sections the command of God to Joshua is mentioned first (cf. chap. iii. 7, 8, iv. 2, 3, iv. 15, 16); then the communication of this command to the people by Joshua; and finally its execution (chap. iii. 9–17, iv. 4–13, iv. 17–20). This arrangement was adopted by the author for the purpose of bringing distinctly out to view, not only the miracle itself, but also the means with which God associated the performance of the miracle, and also of impressing deeply upon the memory of the people both the divine act and the end secured. In doing this, however, some repetitions were inevitable, in consequence of the endeavour, so peculiar to the Hebrew mode of writing history, to mark and round off the several points in the occurrences described, by such comprehensive statements as anticipate the actual course of events. It is to this arrangement and dovetailing of the different points that we must attribute the distribution of the revelation and commands which Joshua received from God, over the several portions of the history; and consequently we are not to suppose, that at each separate point during the passage God revealed to Joshua what he was to do, but must rather assume that He actually revealed and commanded whatever was requisite all at once, on the day before the miraculous passage.[1]

Chap. iii. 1–6. *Arrangements for the Passage through the Jordan.* —When they reached the Jordan, the Israelites rested till they passed over. לִין, *to pass the night;* then in a wider sense to tarry, Prov. xv. 31 ; here it means to rest. According to ver. 2, they stayed there three days. "*At the end* (after the expiration) *of three days*" cannot refer to the three days mentioned in chap. i. 11, if only because of the omission of the article, apart from the reasons given in the note upon chap. i. 11, which preclude the supposition that the two are identical. The reasons why the Israelites stayed three days by the side of the Jordan, after leaving Shittim, are not given, but they are not difficult to guess; for, in the first place, before it could be possible to pass into an enemy's country, not only with an army, but with all the people, including wives, children, and all their possessions, and especially when the river had first of all to be crossed, it must have been necessary to make many preparations, which would easily occupy two or three days. Besides this, the Jordan at that time was so high as to overflow its banks, so that it was impossible to cross the fords, and they were obliged to wait till this obstruction was removed. But as soon as Joshua was assured that the Lord would make a way for His people, he issued the following instructions through the proper officers to all the people in the camp: "*When ye see the ark of the covenant of the Lord your God, and* (see) *the Levitical priests bear it, then ye shall remove from your place, and go after it : yet there shall be a space between you and it, about two thousand cubits by measure : come not near unto it; that ye may know the way by which ye must go : for ye have not passed this way yesterday and the day before.*" On the expression "the Levitical priests," see at Deut. xxxi. 25, as compared with ver. 9 and xvii. 9. בֵּינְו, both here and in chap. viii. 11, should probably be pointed בֵּינוֹ (*vid. Ewald,* § 266, *a.*). This command referred simply to the march from the last resting-place by the Jordan into the river itself, and not to the passage through the

---

[1] The assertion made by *Paulus, Eichhorn, Bleek, Knobel,* and others, that the account is compounded from two different documents, is founded upon nothing else than a total oversight of the arrangement explained above and doctrinal objections to its miraculous contents. The supposed contradictions, which are cited as proofs, have been introduced into the text, as even *Hauff* acknowledges (*Offenbarungsgl.* pp. 209, 210).

river, during which the priests remained standing with the ark in the bed of the river until the people had all passed through (vers. 8 and 17).[1] The people were to keep about 2000 cubits away from the ark. This was not done, however, to prevent their going wrong in the unknown way, and so missing the ford, for that was impossible under the circumstances; but the ark was carried in front of the people, not so much to show the road as to make a road by dividing the waters of the Jordan, and the people were to keep at a distance from it, that they might not lose sight of the ark, but keep their eyes fixed upon it, and know the road by looking at the ark of the covenant by which the road had been made, *i.e.* might know and observe how the Lord, through the medium of the ark, was leading them to Canaan by a way which they had never traversed before, *i.e.* by a miraculous way.—Vers. 5, 6. Joshua then issued instructions (*a*) to the people to sanctify themselves, because on the morrow the Lord would do wonders among them; and (*b*) to the priests, to carry the ark of the covenant in front of the people. The issuing of these commands with the prediction of the miracle presupposes that the Lord had already made known His will to Joshua, and serves to confirm our conclusions as to the arrangement of the materials. The sanctification of the people did not consist in the washing of their clothes, which is mentioned in Ex. xix. 10, 14, in connection with the act of sanctification, for there was no time for this; nor did it consist in merely changing their clothes, which might be a substitute for washing, according to Gen. xxxv. 2, or in abstinence from connubial intercourse (Ex. xix. 15), for this was only the outward side of sanctification. It consisted in spiritual purification also, *i.e.* in turning the heart to God, in faith and trust in His promise, and in willing obedience to His commandments, that they should lay to heart in a proper way the miracle of grace which the Lord was about to work in the midst of them and on their behalf on the following day. " *Wonders :*" those miraculous displays of the omnipotence of God for the realization of His covenant of grace, which He had already promised in connection

---

[1] *Knobel* maintains that this statement, according to which the Israelites were more than 2000 cubits from the place of crossing, is not in harmony with ver. 1, where they are said to have been by the Jordan already; but he can only show this supposed discrepancy in the text by so pressing the expression, they " came to Jordan," as to make it mean that the whole nation was encamped so close to the edge of the river, that at the very first step the people took their feet would touch the water.

with the conquest of Canaan (Ex. xxxiv. 10). In ver. 6, where the command to the priests is given, the fulfilment of the command is also mentioned, and the course of events anticipated in consequence.

Vers. 7–17. *Commencement of the Crossing.*—First of all (in vers. 7 and 8), the revelation made by God to Joshua, that He would begin this day to make him great, *i.e.* to glorify him before the Israelites, and the command to the priests who bore the ark of the covenant to stand still in the river, when they came to the water of the Jordan; then (vers. 9–13) the publication of this promise and command to the people; and lastly (vers. 14–17), the carrying out of the command. אָחֵל, I will *begin* to make thee great. The miraculous guidance of the people through the Jordan was only the beginning of the whole series of miracles by which the Lord put His people in possession of the promised land, and glorified Joshua in the sight of Israel in the fulfilment of his office, as He had glorified Moses before. Just as Moses was accredited in the sight of the people, as the servant of the Lord in whom they could trust, by the miraculous division of the Red Sea (Ex. xiv. 31), so Joshua was accredited as the leader of Israel, whom the Almighty God acknowledged as He had His servant Moses, by the similar miracle, the division of the waters of Jordan. Only the most important points in the command of God to the priests are given in ver. 8. The command itself is communicated more fully afterwards in the address to the people, in ver. 13. When they came with the ark to the end of the waters of Jordan,—*i.e.* not to the opposite side, but to the nearest bank; that is to say, as soon as they reached the water in the bed of the river,—they were to stand still (*vid.* ver. 15, and chap. iv. 11), in order, as we see from what follows, to form a dam as it were against the force of the water, which was miraculously arrested in its course, and piled up in a heap. Moses divided the waters of the Red Sea with his *rod;* Joshua was to do the same to the Jordan with the *ark of the covenant,* the appointed symbol and vehicle of the presence of the Almighty God since the conclusion of the covenant. Wherever the ordinary means of grace are at hand, God attaches the operations of His grace to them ; for He is a God of order, who does not act in an arbitrary manner in the selection of His means.—Vers. 9, 10. The summons to the children of Israel, *i.e.* to the whole nation in the persons of its representatives, to draw near (גֹּשׁוּ for גִּשׁוּ, as in 1 Sam. xiv. 38; Ruth ii. 14) to hear the words of the Lord its God, points to the importance of the following announcement, by which Israel was to learn that there was a living God in the midst of it, who had the power to fulfil His word. Jehovah is called a "living God," in contrast with the dead gods of the heathen, as a God who proved himself to be living, with special reference to those "divine operations by which God had shown that He was living and watchful on behalf of His people; just as His *being in the midst* of the people did not denote a naked presence, but a striking degree of presence on the part of God in relation to the performance of extraordinary operations, or the manifestation of peculiar care" (*Seb. Schmidt*). The God of Israel would now manifest himself as a living God by the extermination of the Canaanites, seven tribes of whom are enumerated, as in Deut. vii. 1 (see the remarks on this passage). Joshua mentions the destruction of these nations as the purpose which God had in view in the miraculous guidance of Israel through the Jordan, to fill the Israelites with confidence for their entrance into the promised land.[1]—Vers. 11–13. After this inspiring promise, Joshua informed the people what the Lord intended to do first: "*Behold, the ark of the covenant of the Lord of the whole earth will go before you into Jordan.*" אֲדוֹן כָּל־הָאָרֶץ is a genitive dependent upon אֲרוֹן הַבְּרִית, the strict subordination of the construct state being loosened in this case by the article before the *nomen regens*. The punctuators have therefore separated it from the latter by *sakeph-katon*, without thereby explaining it as in opposition or giving any support to the mistaken exposition of *Buxtorff* and *Drusius*, that "the ark of the covenant is called the ruler of the whole earth." The description of Jehovah as "Lord of the whole earth," which is repeated in ver. 13, is very appropriately chosen for the purpose of strengthening confidence in the omnipotence of the Lord. This epithet "exalted the government of God over all the elements of the world, that the Israelites might have no doubt that as seas and rivers are under His control, the waters, although liquid by nature, would become stable at His nod" (*Calvin*). The expression, "*passeth over before you into Jordan*," is more precisely explained in the course of the narrative:

[1] " He extends the force of the miracle beyond their entrance into the land, and properly so, since the mere opening of a way into a hostile country, from which there would be no retreat, would be nothing but exposure to death. For they would either easily fall, through being entangled in difficulties and in an unknown region, or they would perish through want. Joshua therefore foretold, that when God drove back the river it would be as if He had stretched out His hand to strike all the inhabitants of the land, and that the proof which He gave of His power in their crossing the Jordan would be a certain presage of victory, to be gained over all the tribes."

the ark of the covenant went (was carried) before the people into the river, and then stood still, as the bulwark of the people, till the passage was completed; so that the word "before" indicates the protection which it would afford.—Ver. 12. "*And take to you (i.e. appoint) twelve men out of the tribes of Israel, one for each tribe.*" For what purpose is not stated here, but is apparent from what follows (chap. iv. 2 sqq.). The choice or appointment of these men was necessarily commanded before the crossing commenced, as they were to stand by the side of Joshua, or near the bearers of the ark of the covenant, so as to be at hand to perform the duty to be entrusted to them (chap. iv. 3 sqq.). Joshua then concludes by foretelling the miracle itself: "*It will come to pass, that when the soles of the feet of the priests who bear the ark of the Lord shall settle down in the water of the Jordan, the waters of the Jordan shall be cut off; namely, the waters flowing down from above, and shall stand still as one heap.*" "*Shall be cut off,*" so as to disappear; namely, at the place where the priests stand with the ark of the covenant. This took place through the waters standing still as a heap, or being heaped up, at some distance above the standing-place. נֵד אֶחָד is an accusative of more precise definition. The expression is taken from the song of Moses (Ex. xv. 8).

The event corresponded to the announcement.—Vers. 14–16. When the people left their tents to go over the Jordan, and the priests, going before with the ark of the covenant, dipped their feet in the water ("the brim of the water," ver. 15, as in ver. 8), although the Jordan was filled over all its banks throughout the whole time of harvest, the waters stood still: the waters flowing down from above stood as a heap at a very great distance off, by the town of Adam, on the side of Zarthan; and the waters flowing down to the salt sea were entirely cut off, so that the people went through the dried bed of the river opposite to Jericho. Vers. 14–16 form one large period, consisting of three protases (vers. 14, 15), the first and third of which are each of them more precisely defined by a circumstantial clause, and also of three apodoses (ver. 16). In the protases the construction passes from the infinitive (בִּנְסֹעַ and כְּבוֹא) into the finite verb (נִטְבְּלוּ),—a thing of frequent occurrence (see *Ewald*, § 350). The circumstantial clause (ver. 15*b*), "*and the Jordan was filled over all its banks all the days of harvest,*" brings out in all its fulness the miracle of the stoppage of the water by the omnipotence of God. Every attempt to explain the miracle as a natural occurrence is thereby prevented; so that *Eichhorn* pronounces the clause a gloss, and endeavours in this manner to get rid of it altogether. עַל־כָּל־גְּדוֹתָיו might mean full against all its banks, flowing with its banks full, or "full to the brim" (*Robinson*, Pal. ii. p. 262, according to the LXX. and *Vulg.*); but if we compare chap. iv. 18, "the waters of Jordan returned to their place, and went over all its banks as before," with the parallel passage in Isa. viii. 7, "the river comes up over all its channels and goes over all its banks," there can be no doubt that the words refer to an overflowing of the banks, and not merely to their being filled to the brim, so that the words must be rendered "go over the banks." But we must not therefore understand them as meaning that the whole of the Ghor was flooded. The Jordan flows through the Ghor, which is two hours' journey broad at Beisan, and even broader to the south of that (see at Deut. i. 1), in a valley about a quarter of an hour in breadth which lies forty or fifty feet lower, and, being covered with trees and reeds, presents a striking contrast to the sandy slopes which bound it on both sides. In many places this strip of vegetation occupies a still deeper portion of the lower valley, which is enclosed by shallow banks not more than two or three feet high, so that, strictly speaking, we might distinguish three different banks at the places referred to : namely, the upper or outer banks, which form the first slope of the great valley; the lower or middle banks, embracing that strip of land which is covered with vegetation; and then the true banks of the river's bed (see *Burckhardt*, Syr. pp. 593 sqq., and *Robinson*, Pal. ii. pp. 254 sqq., and Bibl. Researches, pp. 333 sqq.). The flood never reaches beyond the lower line of the Ghor, which is covered with vegetation, but even in modern times this line has sometimes been overflowed. For example, *Robinson* (Pal. ii. p. 255, compared with p. 263) found the river so swollen when he visited it in 1838, that it filled its bed to the very brim, and in some places flowed over and covered the ground where the bushes grew. This rise of the water still takes place at the time of harvest in April and at the beginning of May (see at Lev. xxiii. 9 sqq.), and therefore really at the close of the rainy season, and after the snow has been long melted upon Hermon, as it is then that the lake of Tiberias reaches its greatest height, in consequence of the rainy season and the melting of the snow, so that it is only then that the Jordan flows with its full stream into the Dead Sea (*Robinson*, ii. p. 263). At this time of the year the river cannot of course be waded through even at its shallowest fords, whereas this is possible in the summer season, when the water is low. It is only by swimming that it can possibly be crossed, and even that cannot be accomplished without great danger, as it is ten or twelve feet deep in the neighbourhood of Jericho, and the current is very strong (*vid. Seetzen*, R. ii. pp. 301, 320–1; *Rob.* ii. p. 256). Crossing at this season was regarded as a very extraordinary feat in ancient times, so that it is mentioned in 1 Chron. xii. 15 as a heroic act on the part of the brave Gadites. It may possibly have been in this way that the spies crossed and recrossed the river a few days before. But that was altogether impossible for the people of Israel with their wives and children. It was necessary, therefore, that the Lord of the whole earth should make a road by a miracle of His omnipotence, which arrested the descending waters in their course, so that they stood still as a heap "*very far*," sc. from the place of crossing, "*by the town of Adam*" (בְּאָדָם must not be altered into מֵאָדָם, from Adam, according to the *Keri*), "*which is by the side of Zarthan.*" The city of *Adam*, which is not mentioned anywhere else (and which *Luther* has erroneously understood as an appellative, according to the Arabic, "people of the city"), is not to be confounded with *Adamah*, in the tribe of Naphtali (chap. xix. 36). The town of *Zarthan*, by the side of which Adam is situated, has also vanished. *Van de Velde* and *Knobel* imagine that the name *Zarthan* has been preserved in the modern *Kurn* (Horn) *Sartabeh*, a long towering rocky ridge on the south-west of the ford of *Damieh*, upon which there are said to be the ruins of a castle. This conjecture is not favoured by any similarity in the names so much as by its situation. For, on the one hand, the mountain slopes off from the end of this rocky ridge, or from the loftiest part of the horn, into a broad shoulder, from which a lower rocky ridge reaches to the Jordan, and seems to join the mountains on the east, so that the Jordan valley is contracted to its narrowest dimensions at this point, and divided into the upper and lower Ghor by the hills of Kurn Sartabeh; and consequently this was apparently the most suitable point for the damming up of the waters of the Jordan (see *Robinson*, Bibl. Researches, pp. 293–4). On the other hand, this site tallies very well with all the notices in the Bible respecting the situation of the town of Zarthan, or Zeredetha (1 Kings vii. 46, compared with 2 Chron. iv. 17): viz. at 1 Kings iv. 12, where Zarthan is said to have been by the side of the territory of Beth-shean; also at 1 Kings vii. 46, where Zarthan and Succoth are opposed to one another; and at Judg. vii. 22, where the reading should be צְרֵדָתָה, according to the Arabic and Syriac versions.

Hence *Knobel* supposes that *Adam* was situated in the neighbour-hood of the present ford *Damieh,* near to which the remains of a bridge belonging to the Roman era are still to be found (*Lynch,* Expedition). The distance of Kurn Sartabeh from Jericho is a little more than fifteen miles, which tallies very well with the expression "very far." Through this heaping up of the waters coming down from above, those which flowed away into the Dead Sea (the sea of the plain, see Deut. iv. 49) were completely cut off (תַּמּוּ נִכְרָתוּ are to be taken together, so that תַּמּוּ merely expresses the adverbial idea wholly, completely), and the people went over, probably in a straight line from Wady Hesbân to Jericho.—Ver. 17. But the priests stood with the ark of the covenant "*in the midst of Jordan,*" *i.e.* in the bed of the river, not merely by the river, "*upon dry ground,* הָכֵן," lit. *firmando, i.e. with a firm foot,* whilst all Israel went over upon dry ground, "*till all the people were passed over.*" This could easily have been accomplished in half a day, if the people formed a procession of a mile or upwards in breadth.

Chap. iv. 1–14. *Crossing the River.*—In the account of the crossing, the main point is their taking twelve stones with them from the bed of the river to the opposite side to serve as a memorial. To set forth the importance of this fact as a divine appointment, the command of God to Joshua is mentioned first of all (vers. 2, 3); then the repetition of this command by Joshua to the men appointed for the work (vers. 4–7); and lastly, the carrying out of the in-structions (ver. 8). This makes it appear as though God did not give the command to Joshua till after the people had all crossed over, whereas the twelve men had already been chosen for the purpose (chap. iii. 12). But this appearance, and the discrepancy that seems to arise, vanish as soon as we take the different clauses, —which are joined together here by *vav consec.,* according to the simple form of historical composition adopted by the Hebrews, "*and Jehovah spake, saying,*" etc. (vers. 2, 3); "*and Joshua called the twelve men,*" etc. (ver. 4),—and arrange them in logical order, and with their proper subordination to one another, according to our own modes of thought and conversation, as follows : "Then Joshua called the twelve men,—as Jehovah had commanded him, saying, 'Take you twelve men out of the people,' etc.,—and said to them,"[1]

---

[1] So far as the meaning is concerned, *Kimchi, Calvin,* and many others, were perfectly correct in taking vers. 1b–3 as a parenthesis, and rendering וַיֹּאמֶר as a pluperfect, though, grammatically considered, and from a Hebrew point of view, the historical sense with *vav consec.* does not correspond to our pluperfect, but

etc.—Vers. 1 sqq. When all the people had crossed over Jordan,[1] Joshua issued to the twelve men who had been appointed by the twelve tribes the command given to him by God : " *Go before the ark of Jehovah into the midst of Jordan, and take every man a stone upon his shoulder, according to the number of the tribes of the Israelites*," or, as it is expressed in the fuller explanation in the divine command in ver. 3, " *from the standing-place of the priests, the setting up of twelve stones* (הָכִין is an infinitive used as a substantive, or else it should be pointed as a substantive), *and carry them over with you, and lay them down in the place of encampment where ye shall pass the night.*"—Vers. 6, 7. This (viz. their taking the twelve stones with them and setting them up) was to be a sign in Israel ; the stones were to serve as a memorial of the miraculous crossing of the Jordan to all succeeding generations. For the expression " *if your children ask to-morrow* (in future)," etc., see Ex. xiii. 14, xii. 26, 27, and Deut. vi. 20, 21.—Ver. 8. The children of Israel carried out these instructions. The execution is ascribed to the " children of Israel," *i.e.* to the whole nation, because the men selected from the twelve tribes acted in the name of the whole nation, and the memorial was a matter of equal importance to all. יַנִּחוּם does not signify that they set up the stones as a memorial, but simply that they laid them down in their place of encampment. The setting up at Gilgal is mentioned for the first time in ver. 20. In addition to this, Joshua set up twelve stones for a memorial, on the spot where the feet of the priests had stood as they bore the ark of the covenant, which stones were there " *to this day*," *i.e.* the time when the account was written. There is nothing to warrant our calling this statement in question, or setting it aside as a probable gloss, either in the circumstance that nothing is said about any divine command to set up these stones, or in the opinion that such

always expresses the succession either of time or thought. This early Hebrew form of thought and narrative is completely overlooked by *Knobel*, when he pronounces vers. 1*b*–3 an interpolation from a second document, and finds the apodosis to ver. 1*a* in ver. 4. The supposed discrepancy—namely, that the setting up of the memorial is not described in vers. 5 sqq. as a divine command, as in vers. 8, 10—by which *Knobel* endeavours to establish his hypothesis, is merely a deduction from the fact that Joshua did not expressly issue his command to the twelve men as a command of Jehovah, and therefore is nothing more than an unmeaning *argumentum e silentio*.

[1] The *piska* in the middle of ver. 1 is an old pre-Masoretic mark, which the Masorites have left, indicating a space in the midst of the verse, and showing that it was the commencement of a *parashah*.

a memorial would have failed of its object, as it could not possibly have remained, but would very speedily have been washed away by the stream. The omission of any reference to a command from God proves nothing, simply because divine commands are frequently hinted at but briefly, so that the substance of them has to be gathered from the account of their execution (compare chap. iii. 7, 8, with iii. 9–13, and iv. 2, 3, with iv. 4–7); and consequently we may assume without hesitation that such a command was given, as the earlier commentators have done. Moreover, the monument did not fail of its object, even if it only existed for a short time. The account of its erection, which was handed down by tradition, would necessarily help to preserve the remembrance of the miraculous occurrence. But it cannot be so absolutely affirmed that these stones would be carried away at once by the stream, so that they could never be seen any more. As the priests did not stand in the middle or deepest part of the river, but just in the bed of the river, and close to its eastern bank, and it was upon this spot that the stones were set up, and as we neither know their size nor the firmness with which they stood, we cannot pronounce any positive opinion as to the possibility of their remaining. It is not likely that they remained there for centuries; but they were intended rather as a memorial for the existing generation and their children, than for a later age, which would be perpetually reminded of the miraculous help of God by the monument erected in Gilgal.—Vers. 10, 11. Whilst Joshua was carrying out all that Jehovah had commanded him to say to the people, according to the command of Moses,—that is to say, whilst the people were passing through the Jordan before the ark, and the twelve men were carrying over the stones out of the river to the resting-place on the other side, and Joshua himself was setting up twelve stones in Jordan for a memorial,—during all this time, the priests stood with the ark in the bed of the river; but after all the people, including the twelve men who took the stones out of the Jordan, had finished crossing, the ark of the Lord passed over, with the priests, before the people: that is to say, it stationed itself again, along with the priests, at the head of the people. The words " *according to all that Moses had commanded Joshua* " do not refer to any special instructions which Moses had given to Joshua with reference to the crossing, for no such instructions are to be found in the Pentateuch, nor can they be inferred from Num. xxvii. 23, Deut. iii. 28, or xxxi. 23 ; they simply affirm that Joshua carried out all the commands which the Lord had

given him, in accordance with the charge which he received from
Moses at the time when he was first called.   Moses had called him
and instructed him to lead the people into the promised land, in
consequence of a divine command; and had given him the promise,
at the same time, that Jehovah would be with him as He had
been with Moses. This contained *implicite* an admonition to Joshua
to do only what the Lord should command him.   And if this was
how Joshua acted, the execution of the commands of God was also
an observance of the command of Moses.   The remark in ver. 10*b*,
"*and the people hastened and passed over,*" i.e. passed hastily through
the bed of the river, is introduced as an explanation of the fact that
the priests stood still in the bed of the river the whole time that the
crossing continued.   As the priests stood in one spot whilst all the
people were passing over, it was necessary that the people should
hasten over, lest the strength of the priests should be exhausted.
This reason for hastening, however, does not preclude the other,—
namely, that the crossing had to be finished in one day, before night
came on.   The statement in ver. 11, that when all the people had
passed over, the ark of the Lord also passed over with the priests,
is so far anticipatory of the actual course of the events, that up to
this time nothing has been said about the fighting men belonging
to the two tribes and a half having passed over (vers. 12, 13); nor
has the command of God for the ark to pass over been mentioned
(vers. 15 sqq.), though both of these must have preceded the crossing
of the ark in order of time.   It is to be observed, that, in the words
"*the ark of the Lord passed over, and the priests,*" the priests are
subordinate to the ark, because it was through the medium of the
ark of the Lord that the miracle of drying up the river had been
effected: it was not by the priests, but by Jehovah the Almighty
God, who was enthroned upon the ark, that the waters were commanded to stand still.   "*Before the people*" (*Eng. Ver.* "in the
presence of the people") has the same signification in ver. 11 as in
chap. iii. 6, 14.—Vers. 12, 13. The account of the fighting men of
the tribes on the east of the Jordan passing over along with them,
in number about 40,000, is added as a supplement, because there
was no place in which it could be appropriately inserted before, and
yet it was necessary that it should be expressly mentioned that these
tribes performed the promise they had given (chap. i. 16, 17), and
in what manner they did so.   The words וַיַּעַבְרוּ וגו׳ do not imply
that these 40,000 men crossed over behind the priests with the ark,
which would not only be at variance with the fact so expressly

stated, that the ark of the covenant was the medium of the miraculous division of the water, but also with the distinct statement in ver. 18, that when the priests, with the ark, set their feet upon the dry land, the waters filled the river again as they had done before. The imperfect with *vav consec.* here expresses simply the order of thought, and not of time. *"Arboth Jericho,"* the steppes of Jericho, were that portion of the Arabah or Ghor which formed the environs of Jericho, and which widens here into a low-lying plain of about three and a half or four hours' journey in breadth, on account of the western mountains receding considerably to the south of the opening of the Wady Kelt (*Rob.* Pal. ii. pp. 263 sqq.).—In ver. 14 the writer mentions still further the fact that the Lord fulfilled His promise (in chap. iii. 7), and by means of this miracle so effectually confirmed the authority of Joshua in the eyes of Israel, that the people feared him all the days of his life as they had feared Moses. " This was not the chief end of the miracle, that Joshua increased in power and authority; but since it was a matter of great importance, so far as the public interests were concerned, that the government of Joshua should be established, it is very properly mentioned, as an addition to the benefits that were otherwise conferred, that he was invested as it were with sacred insignia, which produced such a feeling of veneration among the people, that no one dared to treat him with disrespect" (*Calvin*).

Vers. 15-24. *Termination of the miraculous Passage through the Jordan.*—As soon as the priests left their standing-place in the river with the ark of the covenant, according to the command of God made known to them by Joshua; and the soles of their feet " *tore themselves loose upon the dry ground*" (נִתְּקוּ אֶל הֶחָרָבָה, *constructio prægnans*, for they tore themselves loose from the soft soil of the river, and trode upon the dry or firm ground), the waters of the Jordan returned again to their place, and went over all its banks as before (*vid.* chap. iii. 15). This affirms as clearly as possible that it was the ark which kept back the stream.—Ver. 19. The crossing took place on the tenth day of the first month, that is to say, on the same day on which, forty years before, Israel had begun to prepare for going out of Egypt by setting apart the paschal lamb (Ex. xii. 3). After crossing the river, the people encamped at Gilgal, on the eastern border of the territory of Jericho. The place of encampment is called *Gilgal* proleptically in vers. 19 and 20 (see at chap. v. 9).—Vers. 20 sqq. There Joshua set up the twelve stones, which they had taken over with them out of the Jordan, and explained to the people at the same time the importance of this memorial to their descendants (vers. 21, 22), and the design of the miracle which had been wrought by God (ver. 24). On vers. 21, 22, see vers. 6, 7.   אֲשֶׁר (ver. 23), *quod*, as (see Deut. ii. 22).   The miracle itself, like the similar one at the Dead Sea, had a double intention, viz. to reveal to the Canaanites the omnipotence of the God of Israel, the strong hand of the Lord (compare Ex. xiv. 4, 18, with chap. vi. 6 ; and for the expression " the hand of the Lord is mighty," see Ex. iii. 19, vi. 1, etc.), and to serve as an impulse to the Israelites to fear the Lord their God always (see at Ex. xiv. 31).

CIRCUMCISION OF THE PEOPLE, AND CELEBRATION OF THE PASSOVER AT GILGAL.—CHAP. V. 1—12.

When the Israelites had trodden the soil of Canaan, Joshua began immediately to make arrangements for conquering the land, and destroying its inhabitants. As the Lord had only promised him His assistance on condition that the law given by Moses was faithfully observed (chap. i. 7 sqq.), it was necessary that he should proceed first of all to impose it as an inviolable obligation, not only upon himself, but also upon all the people entrusted to his charge, to fulfil all the precepts of the law, many of which could not be carried out during the journey through the wilderness, whilst many others had only been given with special reference to the time when the people should be dwelling in Canaan. The first duty which devolved upon him in this respect, was to perform the rite of circumcision upon the generation that had been born in the wilderness, and had grown up without circumcision, so that the whole congregation might be included in the covenant of the Lord, and be able to keep the passover, which was to be celebrated in a few days in the manner prescribed by the law.

Vers. 1–9. CIRCUMCISION OF THE PEOPLE.—Ver. 1. Whilst, on the one hand, the approach of the passover rendered it desirable that the circumcision of those who had remained uncircumcised should be carried out without delay, on the other hand the existing circumstances were most favourable for the performance of this covenant duty, inasmuch as the miracle wrought in connection with the passage through the Jordan had thrown the Canaanites into such alarm that there was no fear of their attacking the Israelitish camp. To indicate this, the impression produced by this miracle is described, namely, that all the kings of Canaan had been thrown into despair in consequence. All the tribes of Canaan are grouped together here under the names of Amorites and Canaanites, the tribes in possession of the mountains being all called Amorites, and those who lived by the sea, *i.e.* by the shore of the Mediterranean, Canaanites (*vid.* chap. i. 4) : for the Amorites upon the mountains were the strongest of all the Canaanitish tribes at that time (see at Gen. x. 16); whilst the name Canaanite, *i.e.* the bent one (see at Gen. ix. 25), was peculiarly appropriate to the inhabitants of the lowlands, who relied upon trade more than upon warfare, and were probably dependent upon the strong and mighty Amorites. The application of the expression " *beyond Jordan*" (*Eng. Ver.* " on the side of ") to the country on this side, may be explained on the ground that the historian was still writing from the stand-point of the crossing. But in order to prevent any misunderstanding, he adds " *towards the west*," as he had previously added " towards the sunrise," in chap. i. 15, when speaking of the land on the eastern side. That we have the report of an eye-witness here is evident from the words, " until *we* were passed over :" the reading of the *Keri*, עָבְרָם (till *they* were passed over), is nothing but an arbitrary and needless conjecture, and ought not to have been preferred by *Bleek* and others, notwithstanding the fact that the ancient versions and some MSS. also adopt it.—Vers. 2-8. At that time (*sc.* the time of their encampment at Gilgal, and when the Canaanites were in despair) Joshua had the people " *circumcised again, the second time.*" The word שֵׁנִית (a second time) is only added to give emphasis to שׁוּב, or as an explanation of it, and is not to be pressed, either here or in Isa. xi. 11, as though it denoted the repetition of the same act in every respect, *i.e.* of an act of circumcision which had once before been performed upon the whole nation. It merely expresses this meaning, " circumcise the people again, or the second time, as it was formerly circumcised" (*i.e.* a circumcised people, not in the same manner in which it once before had circumcision performed upon it). When the people came out of Egypt they were none of them uncircumcised, as distinctly affirmed in ver. 5 ; but during their journey through the wilderness circumcision had been neglected, so that now the nation was no longer circumcised, and therefore it was necessary that circumcision should be performed upon the nation as a whole, by circumcising all who were uncircumcised. The opinion of *Masius* and *O. v. Gerlach*, that the expression "the second time" refers to the introduction of circumcision, when Abraham was circumcised with all his house, is very far-fetched. חַרְבוֹת צֻרִים are not "sharp knives," but "*stone knives*," which were used according to ancient custom (see at Ex. iv. 25), literally knives of rocks (the plural *zurim* is occasioned by *charboth*, as in Num. xiii. 32, etc.; the singular might have been used: see *Ewald*, § 270, *c*.).—Ver. 3. Joshua had the circumcision performed "*at the hill of the foreskins*," as the place was afterwards called from the fact that the foreskins were buried there.—Vers. 4–7. The reason for the circumcision of the whole nation was the following: all the fighting men who came out of Egypt had died in the wilderness by the way; for all the people that came out were circumcised; but all that were born in the wilderness during the journey had not been circumcised (בְּצֵאתָם מִמִּצְרַיִם, on their coming out of Egypt, which only came to an end on their arrival in Canaan). They walked forty years in the wilderness; till all the people—that is to say, all the fighting men—who came out of Egypt were consumed, because they had not hearkened to the voice of the Lord, and had been sentenced by the Lord to die in the wilderness (ver. 6; cf. Num. xiv. 26 sqq., xxvi. 64, 65, and Deut. ii. 14–16). But He (Jehovah) set up their sons in their place, *i.e.* He caused them to take their place; and these Joshua circumcised (*i.e.* had them circumcised), for they were uncircumcised, because they had not been circumcised by the way. This explains the necessity for a general circumcision of all the people, but does not state the reason why those who were born in the wilderness had not been circumcised. All that is affirmed in vers. 5 and 7 is, that this had not taken place "by the way." The true reason may be gathered from ver. 6, if we compare the statement made in this verse, "for the children of Israel walked forty years in the wilderness, till all the men that were capable of bearing arms were consumed . . . unto whom the Lord sware that He would not show them the land promised to the fathers," with the sentence pronounced by God to which these words refer, viz. Num. xiv. 29–34. The Lord is then said to have sworn that all the men of twenty years old and upwards, who had murmured against Him, should perish in the wilderness; and though their sons should enter the promised land, they too should pasture, *i.e.* lead a nomad life, for forty years in the wilderness, and bear the apostasy of their fathers, till their bodies had fallen in the desert. This clearly means, that not only was the generation that came out of Egypt sentenced to die in the wilderness because of its rebellion against the Lord, and therefore rejected by God, but the sons of this generation had to bear the whoredom, *i.e.* the apostasy of their fathers from the Lord, for the period of forty years, until the latter had been utterly consumed; that is to say, during all this time they were to endure the punishment of rejection along with their fathers : with this difference alone, that the sons were not to die in the wilderness, but were to be brought into the promised land after their fathers were dead. The sentence upon the fathers, that their bodies should fall in the desert, was unquestionably a rejection of them on the part of God, an abrogation of the covenant with them. This punishment was also to be borne by their sons ; and hence the reason why those who were born in the desert by the way were not circumcised. As the covenant of the Lord with the fathers was abrogated, the sons of the rejected generation were not to receive the covenant sign of circumcision. Nevertheless this abrogation of the covenant with the generation that had been condemned, was not a complete dissolution of the covenant relation, so far as the nation as a whole was concerned, since the whole nation had not been rejected, but only the generation of men that were capable of bearing arms when they came out of Egypt, whilst the younger generation which had grown up in the desert was to be delivered from the ban, which rested upon it as well, and brought into the land of Canaan when the time of punishment had expired. For this reason the Lord did not withdraw from the nation every sign of His grace ; but in order that the consciousness might still be sustained in the young and rising generation, that the covenant would be set up again with them when the time of punishment had expired, He left them not only the presence of the pillar of cloud and fire, but also the manna and other tokens of His grace, the continuance of which therefore cannot be adduced as an argument against our view of the time of punishment as a temporary suspension of the covenant. But if this was the reason for the omission of circumcision,[1] it did

---

[1] This reason was admitted even by *Calvin*, and has been well supported by *Hengstenberg* (Diss. ii. pp. 13 sqq.). The arguments adduced by *Kurtz* in opposition to this view are altogether unfounded. We have already observed that the reason for the suspension is not given in ver. 7 ; and the further remark, that in ver. 5 ("all the people that were born in the wilderness by the way as they came forth out of Egypt, them they had not circumcised") the book of Joshua dates the suspension not from the sentence of rejection, but expressly and undoubtedly (?) from the departure from Egypt, has no force whatever, unless we so press the word *all* ("all the people that were born in the desert ")

not commence till the second year of their journey, viz. at the time
when the murmuring nation was rejected at Kadesh (Num. xiv.);
so that by "all the people that were born in the wilderness" we are
to understand those who were born after that time, and during the
last thirty-eight years of their wanderings, just as "all the people
that came out of Egypt" are to be understood as signifying only
those men who were twenty years old and upwards when they came
out. Consequently circumcision was suspended as long as the nation
was under the ban of the divine sentence pronounced upon it at
Kadesh. This sentence was exhausted when they crossed the brook
Zared and entered the country of the Amorites (compare Deut. ii.
14 with Num. xxi. 12, 13). Why, then, was not the circumcision
performed during the encampment in the steppes of Moab either

as not to allow of the slightest exception. But this is decidedly precluded by
the fact, that we cannot imagine it possible for God to have established His
covenant with the people at a time when they had neglected the fundamental
law of the covenant, the transgression of which was threatened with destruction
(Gen. xvii. 14), by neglecting to circumcise all the children who had been born
between the departure from Egypt and the conclusion of the covenant at Sinai.
We are also prevented from pressing the little word "all" in this manner by
the evident meaning of the words before us. In vers. 4 and 5 the Israelites are
divided into two classes: (1) All the people that came out of Egypt and were
circumcised; and (2) All the people that were born in the desert and were
uncircumcised. The first of these died in the wilderness, the second came to
Canaan and were circumcised by Joshua at Gilgal. But if we should press the
word "all" in these clauses, it would follow that all the male children who
were under twenty years of age at the time of the exodus, either died in the
desert or were circumcised a second time at Gilgal. Lastly, it does not follow
from ver. 6 that the circumcision was suspended for exactly forty years; for
the forty years during which Israel journeyed in the desert until the murmuring generation was consumed, are to be interpreted by Num. xiv. 33, 34,
and amounted, chronologically considered, to no more than thirty-eight years
and a few months (see the commentary on Num. xxiv. 28 sqq.). On the other
hand, the other very general view which *Kurtz* adopts—namely, that the circumcision was omitted during the journey through the desert on account of the
hardships connected with travelling, and because it was impossible to have regard
to particular families who might wish for longer rest on account of their children who had just been circumcised, and were suffering from the wound, just
at the time when they had to decamp and journey onward, and they could not
well be left behind—throws but little light upon the subject, as the assumption
that the people were constantly wandering about for forty years is altogether
an unfounded one. The Israelites were not always wandering about: not only
did they stay at Sinai for eleven whole months, but even after that they halted
for weeks and months at the different places of encampment, when they might
have circumcised their children without the slightest danger of their suffering
from the wound.

before or after the numbering, since all those who had been sentenced to die in the wilderness were already dead (Num. xxvi. 65)? The different answers which have been given to this question are some of them wrong, and others incomplete. For example, the opinion held by some, that the actual reason was that the forty years had not yet expired, is incorrect (see Deut. ii. 14). And the uncertainty how long they would remain in the steppes of Moab cannot be adduced as an explanation, as there were no circumstances existing that were likely to occasion a sudden and unexpected departure from Shittim. The reason why Moses did not renew the circumcision before the end of his own life, is to be sought for in the simple fact that he would not undertake an act of such importance without an express command from the Lord, especially as he was himself under sentence to die without entering the promised land. But the Lord did not enjoin the renewal of the covenant sign before Israel had been conducted into the promised land, because He saw fit first of all to incline the hearts of the people to carry out His commandment through this magnificent proof of His grace. It is the rule of divine grace first to give and then to ask. As the Lord did not enjoin circumcision as a covenant duty upon Abraham himself till He had given him a practical proof of His grace by leading him to Canaan, and by repeated promises of a numerous posterity, and of the eventual possession of the land ; and just as He did not give the law to the children of Israel at Sinai till He had redeemed them with a mighty arm from the bondage of Egypt, and borne them on eagles' wings, and brought them to Himself, and had thereby made them willing to promise gladly to fulfil all that He should say to them as His covenant nation ; so now He did not require the renewal of circumcision, which involved as the covenant sign the observance of the whole law, till He had given His people practical proofs, through the help afforded in the defeat of Sihon and Og, the kings of the Amorites, and in the miraculous division of the waters of Jordan, that He was able to remove all the obstacles that might lie in the way of the fulfilment of His promises, and give them the promised land for their inheritance, as He had sworn to their fathers.

Ver. 8. When the rite of circumcision had been performed upon them all, the people remained quietly in the camp till those who were circumcised had recovered. *" They abode in their places,"* i.e. sat still as they were, without attempting anything. חָיָה, to revive (Gen. xlv. 27 ; Job xiv. 14), or recover (2 Kings i. 2, viii. 8, etc.). The circumcision of the people could not be performed earlier than the day after the crossing of the Jordan, *i.e.*, according to chap. iv. 19, not earlier than the 11th day of the first month. Now, as the passover was to be kept, and actually was kept, on the 14th (ver. 10), the two accounts are said to be irreconcilable, and the account of the circumcision has been set down as a later and unhistorical legend. But the objections made to the historical credibility of this account—viz. that the suffering consequent upon circumcision made a person ill for several days, and according to Gen. xxxiv. 25 was worst on the third day, so that the people could not have kept the passover on that day, and also that the people could not possibly have been all circumcised on one day—are founded upon false assumptions. In the latter, for example, the number of persons to be circumcised is estimated, most absurdly, at a million ; whereas, according to the general laws of population, the whole of the male population of Israel, which contained only 601,730 of twenty years of age and upwards, besides 23,000 Levites of a month old and upwards, when the census was taken a short time before in the steppes of Moab, could not amount to more than a million in all, and of these between 280,000 and 330,000 were thirty-eight years old, and therefore, having been born before the sentence was pronounced upon the nation at Kadesh, and for the most part before the exodus from Egypt, had been already circumcised, so that there were only 670,000, or at the most 720,000, to be circumcised now. Consequently the proportion between the circumcised and uncircumcised was one to three or three and a half ; and the operation could therefore be completed without any difficulty in the course of a single day. As regards the consequences of this operation, Gen. xxxiv. 25 by no means proves that the pain was most acute on the third day ; and even if this really were the case, it would not prevent the keeping of the passover, as the lambs could have been killed and prepared by the 280,000 or 330,000 circumcised men ; and even those who were still unwell could join in the meal, since it was only Levitical uncleanness, and not disease or pain, which formed a legal impediment to this (Num. ix. 10 sqq.).[1] But if there were about 300,000 men of the age of forty and upwards who could not only perform the rite of circumcision upon their sons or younger brothers, but, if necessary, were able at any moment to draw the sword, there was no reason what-

---

[1] For the basis upon which this computation rests, see *Keil's* Commentary on Joshua, p 139 (Eng. trans. 1857).

ever for their being afraid of an attack on the part of the Canaanites, even if the latter had not been paralyzed by the miraculous crossing of the Jordan.—Ver. 9. When the circumcision was completed, the Lord said to Joshua, " *This day have I rolled away the reproach of Egypt from off you.*" " The reproach of Egypt" is the reproach proceeding from Egypt, as " the reproach of Moab," in Zeph. ii. 8, is the reproach heaped upon Israel by Moab (cf. Isa. li. 7; Ezek. xvi. 57). We are not to understand by this the Egyptian bondage, or the misery which still cleaved to the Israelites from Egypt, and the still further misery which they had suffered during their journey, on account of the displeasure of Jehovah (*Knobel*), but the reproach involved in the thoughts and sayings of the Egyptians, that Jehovah had brought the Israelites out of Egypt to destroy them in the desert (Ex. xxxii. 12 ; Num. xiv. 13–16 ; Deut. ix. 28), which rested upon Israel as long as it was condemned to wander restlessly about and to die in the wilderness. This reproach was rolled away from Israel with the circumcision of the people at Gilgal, inasmuch as this act was a practical declaration of the perfect restoration of the covenant, and a pledge that the Lord would now give them the land of Canaan for their inheritance. From this occurrence the place where the Israelites were encamped received the name of *Gilgal*, viz. " rolling away," from בָּלַל, to roll. This explanation and derivation of the name is not to be pronounced incorrect and unhistorical, simply because it merely preserves the subordinate idea of rolling, instead of the fuller idea of the rolling away of reproach. For the intention was not to form a word which should comprehend the whole affair with exhaustive minuteness, but simply to invent a striking name which should recall the occurrence, like the name *Tomi*, of which Ovid gives the following explanation : *Inde Tomos dictus locus est quia fertur in illo membra soror fratris consecuisse sui* (*Trist.* iii. 9, 33). *Knobel* is wrong in maintaining that the name should be explained in a different way, and that this *Gilgal* is the same as *Geliloth* (circles) in chap. xviii. 17 (see the explanation given at chap. xv. 7). The word *gilgal*, formed from בָּלַל, to roll, signifies primarily rolling, then a wheel (Isa. xxviii. 28) ; and if by possibility it signifies *orbis* also, like בְּלִיל, this is neither the original nor the only meaning of the word. According to *Josephus* (Ant. v. 1, 4), Israel encamped fifty stadia, *i.e.* two hours and a half, from the Jordan, and ten stadia, or half an hour, from Jericho,—that is to say, in the plain or steppe between Jericho and the Jordan, in an uninhabited and unculti-

vated spot, which received the name of *Gilgal* for the first time, as
the place where the Israelites were encamped. No town or village
ever existed there, either at the period in question or at any later
time. The only other places in which this Gilgal can be shown to
be evidently referred to, are Micah vi. 5 and 2 Sam. xix. 16, 41 ; and
the statement made by *Eusebius* in the *Onom. s. v. Galgala*, δείκνυται
ὁ τόπος ἔρημος ὡς ἱερὸς θρησκευόμενος, which *Jerome* paraphrases
thus, " Even to the present day a deserted place is pointed out at
the second mile from Jericho, which is held in amazing reverence
by the inhabitants of that region," by no means proves the existence of a town or village there in the time of the Israelites. Consequently it is not to be wondered at, that in spite of repeated
search, *Robinson* has not been able to discover any remains of
Gilgal to the east of Jericho, or to meet with any Arab who could
tell him of such a name in this locality (see *Rob.* Pal. ii. pp. 287–8
and 278). On the situation of the Gilgal mentioned in chap. ix. 6,
x. 6, etc., see at chap. viii. 35.

Vers. 10–14. THE PASSOVER AT GILGAL.—When the whole
nation had been received again into covenant with the Lord by
circumcision, they kept the passover, which had no doubt been
suspended from the time that they left Sinai (Num. ix. 1 sqq.), on
the 14th of the month (Nisan), in the evening (according to the
law in Ex. xii. 6, 18, Lev. xxiii. 5, Num. xxviii. 16, Deut. xvi. 6).
The next day, *i.e.* on the 16th, or the day after the first feast-day,
they ate unleavened loaves and parched corn (" roasted grains," see
at Lev. ii. 14) of the produce of the land (עָבוּר,[1] which only oċcurs
in vers. 11 and 12, is synonymous with תְּבוּאָה[2] in ver. 12), *i.e.* corn
that had grown in the land of Canaan, as the manna entirely
ceased from this day forwards. " *The morrow after the passover*"
is used in Num. xxxiii. 3 for the 15th Nisan ; but here it must be
understood as signifying the 16th, as the produce of the land, of
which they ate not only on that day, but, according to ver. 12,
throughout that year, cannot mean the corn of the previous year,
but the produce of this same year, *i.e.* the new corn, and they were
not allowed to eat any of that till it had been sanctified to the
Lord by the presentation of the wave sheaf on the second day of
the passover (Lev. xxiii. 11). According to Lev. xxiii. 11, the
presentation was to take place on the day after the Sabbath, *i.e.* the

---

[1] Rendered " old corn" in the Eng. version.
[2] Rendered *fruit* in our version.

first day of the feast of Mazzoth, which was kept as a Sabbath, or the 16th of Nisan, as the seven days' feast of Mazzoth commenced on the 15th (Lev. xxiii. 6; Num. xxviii. 17). " On the morrow after the passover" is the same as " on the morrow after the Sabbath" in Lev. xxiii. 11, the term passover being used here not in its original and more restricted sense, in which it applies exclusively to the observance of the paschal meal, which took place on the evening of the 14th, and is expressly distinguished from the seven days' feast of *Mazzoth* (Ex. xii. 23, 27; Lev. xxiii. 5; Num. xxviii. 16), but in the broader sense, which we have already met with in Deut. xvi. 2, in which the name was gradually extended to the whole of the seven days' feast. The writer assumed that the facts themselves were already well known from the Mosaic law, and therefore did not think it necessary to give any fuller explanation. Moreover, the words, " they did eat of the fruit of the land," etc., are not to be understood as signifying that they began to eat un- leavened bread for the first time on the 16th Nisan (they had already eaten it as an accompaniment to the paschal lamb); but unleavened bread of the produce of the land, the green corn of that year, was what they ate for the first time on that day. Especial prominence is given to this by the words, " in the self- same day," because not only did the eating of the new corn com- mence on that day, but from that day forward " *the children of Israel had manna no more.*" This statement is evidently related to Ex. xvi. 35, and must be understood, according to that passage, as merely signifying, that on that day the gift of the manna entirely ceased (see Pentateuch, vol. ii. pp. 70 sqq.).

APPEARANCE OF THE ANGEL OF THE LORD, AND CONQUEST OF JERICHO.—CHAP. V. 13–VI. 27.

Having been confirmed and fortified in the covenant with the Lord through the observance of the passover, Joshua determined to proceed at once to the work entrusted to him, viz. the conquest of the land of Canaan. But the town of Jericho, which was sur- rounded with strong walls, as the border defence of Canaan against any foe approaching from the east, had its gates shut before the children of Israel. And whilst Joshua was deep in meditation concerning its capture, the angel of the Lord appeared to him to announce that the Lord had given Jericho and its king into his power, and would miraculously throw down its walls.

Chap. v. 13–vi. 5. APPEARANCE AND MESSAGE OF THE ANGEL
OF THE LORD.—Vers. 13–15. When Joshua was by Jericho, בִּירִיחוֹ,
lit. in Jericho (בְּ expressing immediate proximity, the entrance as
it were into some other object, vid. Ewald, § 217),—that is to say,
inside it in thought, meditating upon the conquest of it,—he saw, on
lifting up his eyes, a man standing before him with a drawn sword
in his hand ; and on going up to him, and asking, " Dost thou belong
to us or to our enemies ?" he received this reply : " Nay (לֹא is not
to be altered into לוֹ, which is the reading adopted in the Sept.,
Syr., and a few MSS.), but I am the prince of the army of Jehovah ;
now I am come." The person who had appeared neither belonged
to the Israelites nor to their enemies, but was the prince of the
army of Jehovah, i.e. of the angels. " The Lord's host" does not
mean "the people of Israel, who were just at the commencement
of their warlike enterprise," as v. Hofmann supposes ; for although
the host of Israel who came out of Egypt are called " the hosts of
the Lord" in Ex. xii. 41, the Israelites are never called the host or
army of Jehovah (in the singular). " The host of Jehovah" is
synonymous with " the host of heaven" (1 Kings xxii. 19), and
signifies the angels, as in Ps. cxlviii. 2 and ciii. 21. With the
words " now I am come," the prince of the angels is about to enter
upon an explanation of the object of his coming; but he is interrupted
in his address by Joshua, who falls down before him, and says,
" What saith my lord to his servant?" so that now he first of all commands Joshua to take off his shoes, as the place on which he stands
is holy. It by no means follows that because Joshua fell down
upon the ground and יִשְׁתָּחוּ (Eng. Ver. " did worship"), he must
have recognised him at once as the angel of the Lord who was
equal with God ; for the word הִשְׁתַּחֲוָה, which is connected with the
falling down, does not always mean divine worship, but very frequently means nothing more than the deep Oriental reverence paid
by a dependant to his superior or king (e.g. 2 Sam. ix. 6, xiv. 33),
and Joshua did not address the person who appeared to him by the
name of God, אֲדֹנָי, but simply as אֲדֹנִי, " My lord." In any case,
however, Joshua regarded him at once as a superior being, i.e. an
angel. And he must have recognised him as something more than
a created angel of superior rank, that is to say, as the angel of
Jehovah who is essentially equal with God, the visible revealer of
the invisible God, as soon as he gave him the command to take
off his shoes, etc.,—a command which would remind him of the
appearance of God to Moses in the burning bush, and which im-

plied that the person who now appeared was the very person who had revealed himself to Moses as the God of Abraham, Isaac, and Jacob. (On the meaning of the command to take off the shoes, see the exposition of Ex. iii. 5.) The object of the divine appearance was indicated by the drawn sword in the hand (cf. Num. xxii. 31), by which he manifested himself as a heavenly warrior, or, as he describes himself to Joshua, as prince of the army of Jehovah. The drawn sword contained in itself this practical explanation: "I am now come with my heavenly army, to make war upon the Canaanites, and to assist thee and thy people" (*Seb. Schmidt*). It was not in a vision that this appearance took place, but it was an actual occurrence belonging to the external world; for Joshua saw the man with the drawn sword at a certain distance from himself, and went up to him to address him,—a fact which would be perfectly incompatible with an inward vision.

Chap. vi. 1–5. When Joshua had taken off his shoes, the prince of the army of God made known to him the object of his coming (vers. 2–5). But before relating the message, the historian first of all inserts a remark concerning the town of Jericho, in the form of an explanatory clause, for the purpose of showing the precise meaning of the declaration which follows.[1] This meaning is to be found not merely in the fact that the Lord was about to give Jericho into the hands of the Israelites, but chiefly in the fact that the town which He was about to give into their hands was so strongly fortified.—Ver. 1. "*Jericho was shutting its gates* (vid. Judg. ix. 51), *and closely shut.*" The participles express the permanence of the situation, and the combination of the active and passive in the emphatic form מְסֻגֶּרֶת (LXX. συγκεκλεισμένη καὶ ὠχυρωμένη; *Vulg. clausa erat atque munita*) serves to strengthen the idea, to which still further emphasis is given by the clause, "*no one was*

---

[1] If there is any place in which the division of chapters is unsuitable, it is so here; for the appearance of the prince of the angels does not terminate with chap. v. 15, but what he had come to communicate follows in chap. vi. 2–5, and chap. vi. 1 merely contains an explanatory clause inserted before his message, which serves to throw light upon the situation (*vid. Ewald*, § 341). If we regard the account of the appearance of the angel as terminating with chap. v. 15, as *Knobel* and other commentators have done, we must of necessity assume either that the account has come down to us in a mutilated form, or that the appearance ceased without any commission being given. The one is as incredible as the other. The latter especially is without analogy; for the appearance in Acts x. 9 sqq., which *O. v. Gerlach* cites as similar, contains a very distinct explanation in vers. 13–16.

going out and in," *i.e.* so firmly shut that no one *could* go out or in.
—Ver. 2. "*And the Lord said to Joshua:*" this is the sequel to
chap. v. 15, as ver. 1 is merely a parenthesis and Jehovah is the
prince of the army of Jehovah (chap. v. 14), or the angel of
Jehovah, who is frequently identified with Jehovah (see Pentateuch, vol. i. pp. 184 sqq.). "*See, I have given into thy hand
Jericho and its king, the mighty men of valour.*" ("Have given,"
referring to the purpose of God, which was already resolved upon,
though the fulfilment was still in the future.) "*The mighty men
of valour*" (brave warriors) is in apposition to Jericho, regarded as
a community, and its king. In vers. 3–5 there follows an explanation of the way in which the Lord would give Jericho into the
hand of Joshua. All the Israelitish men of war were to go round
the town once a day for six days. הַקֵּיף ... פַּעַם אֶחָת, "*going round
about the city once,*" serves as a fuller explanation of סַבּוֹתֶם ("*ye
shall compass*"). As they marched in this manner round the city,
seven priests were to carry seven jubilee trumpets before the ark,
which implies that the ark itself was to be carried round the city in
solemn procession. But on the seventh day they were to march
round the town seven times, and the priests to blow the trumpets;
and when there was a blast with the jubilee horn, and the people
on hearing the sound of the trumpet raised a great cry, the wall of
the town should fall down "*under itself.*" The "jubilee trumpets"
(*Eng. Ver.* "trumpets of rams' horns") are the same as the "jubilee
horn" (*Eng. Ver.* "rams' horn") in ver. 5, for which the abbreviated
form *shophar* (trumpet, ver. 5; cf. Ex. xix. 16) or *jobel* (jubilee:
Ex. xix. 13) is used. They were not the silver trumpets of the
priests (Num. x. 1 sqq.), but large horns, or instruments in the
shape of a horn, which gave a loud far-sounding tone (see at Lev.
xxiii. 24, xxv. 11). For תְּקַע בש׳, blow the trumpet (*lit.* strike the
trumpet), in ver. 4, מָשַׁךְ בְּקֶרֶן, draw with the horn, *i.e.* blow the horn
with long-drawn notes, is used in ver. 5 (see at Ex. xix. 13). The
people were then to go up, *i.e.* press into the town over the fallen
wall; "*every one straight before him,*" *i.e.* every one was to go
straight into the town without looking round at his neighbour either
on the right hand or on the left (*vid.* ver. 20).

Vers. 6–27. TAKING OF JERICHO.—In the account of this we
have first of all a brief statement of the announcement of the
divine message by Joshua to the priests and the people (vers. 6, 7);
then the execution of the divine command (vers. 8–20); and lastly

the burning of Jericho and deliverance of Rahab (vers. 21-27).—
Vers. 6, 7. In communicating the divine command with reference
to the arrangements for taking Jericho, Joshua mentions in the
first place merely the principal thing to be observed. The plural
וַיֹּאמְרוּ (" they said"), in ver. 7, must not be altered, but is to be
explained on the ground that Joshua did not make the proclamation to the people himself, but through the medium of the *shoterim*,
who were appointed to issue his commands (see chap. i. 10, 11, iii.
2, 3). In this proclamation the more minute instructions concerning
the order of march, which had been omitted in vers. 3-5, are given;
namely, that הֶחָלוּץ was to march in front of the ark. By הֶחָלוּץ,
" *the equipped* (or armed) *man*," we are not to understand all the
fighting men, as *Knobel* supposes; for in the description of the
march which follows, the whole of the fighting men (" all the men
of war," ver. 3) are divided into הֶחָלוּץ and הַמְאַסֵּף (*Eng. Ver.* " the
armed men" and "the rereward," vers. 9 and 13), so that the former
can only have formed one division of the army. It is very natural
therefore to suppose, as *Kimchi* and *Rashi* do, that the former were
the fighting men of the tribes of Reuben, Gad, and half Manasseh
(חֲלוּצֵי הַצָּבָא, chap. iv. 13), and the latter the fighting men of the rest
of the tribes. On the meaning of מְאַסֵּף, see at Num. x. 25. If
we turn to the account of the facts themselves, we shall see at once,
that in the report of the angel's message, in vers. 3-5, several
other points have been passed over for the purpose of avoiding too
many repetitions, and have therefore to be gathered from the
description of what actually occurred. First of all, in vers. 8-10,
we have the appointment of the order of marching, namely, that
the ark, with the priests in front carrying the trumpets of jubilee,
was to form the centre of the procession, and that one portion of
the fighting men was to go in front of it, and the rest to follow
after; that the priests were to blow the trumpets every time they
marched round during the seven days (vers. 8, 9, 13); and lastly,
that it was not till the seventh time of going round, on the seventh
day, that the people were to raise the war-cry at the command of
Joshua, and then the walls of the town were to fall (vers. 10, 16).
There can be no doubt that we are right in assuming that Joshua
had received from the angel the command which he issued to the
people in vers. 17 sqq., that the whole town, with all its inhabitants
and everything in it, was to be given up as a ban to the Lord, at the
time when the first announcement concerning the fall of the town
was made.

Vers. 8–20. *Execution of the divine Command.*—Vers. 8–11.
The march round on the first day; and the instructions as to the
war-cry to be raised by the people, which are appended as a supplement in ver. 10. "*Before Jehovah*," instead of "before the ark of
Jehovah," as the signification of the ark was derived entirely from
the fact, that it was the medium through which Jehovah communi
cated His gracious presence to the people. In ver. 9, תָּקְעוּ is in the
perfect tense, and we must supply the relative אֲשֶׁר, which is sometimes omitted, not only in poetry, but also in prose, after a definite
noun in the accusative (*e.g.* Ex. xviii. 20; see *Ewald*, § 332, *a.*).
There is not sufficient ground for altering the form of the word
into תִּקְעֵי, according to the *Keri*, as תָּקַע is construed in other cases
with the accusative הַשּׁוֹפָר, instead of with בְּ, and that not only in
poetry, but also in prose (*e.g.* Judg. vii. 22, as compared with vers.
18–20). הָלוֹךְ וְתָקוֹעַ, "*trumpeting continually*" (*Eng. Ver.* "going
on and blowing"). הָלוֹךְ is used adverbially, as in Gen. viii. 3, etc.
—Ver. 11. "*So the ark of the Lord compassed the city*," not "Joshua
caused the ark to compass the city." The *Hiphil* has only an
active, not a causative, meaning here, as in 2 Sam. v. 23, etc.—Vers.
12–14. The march on each of the next five days resembled that on
the first. "*So they did six days.*" In ver. 13, וְתָקְעוּ does not stand
for וְתָקֹעַ, but corresponds to וְתָקְעוּ in ver. 8; and the participle הוֹלֵךְ
is used interchangeably with the *inf. abs.* הָלוֹךְ, as in Gen. xxvi. 13,
Judg. iv. 24, etc., so that the *Keri* הָלוֹךְ is an unnecessary emendation.—Vers. 15–19. On the seventh day the marching round the town
commenced very early, at the dawning of the day, that they might
go round seven times. כַּמִּשְׁפָּט, in the manner prescribed and
carried out on the previous days, which had become a *right* through
precept and practice. On the seventh circuit, when the priests had
blown the trumpet, Joshua commanded the fighting men to raise a
war-cry, announcing to them at the same time that the town, with
all that was in it, was to be a ban to the Lord, with the exception
of Rahab and the persons in her house, and warning them not to
take of that which was laid under the ban, that they might not
bring a ban upon the camp of Israel. The construction in ver. 16,
"*it came to pass at the seventh time the priests had blown the trumpets,
then Joshua said, . . .*" is more spirited than if the conjunction כַּאֲשֶׁר
had been used before תָּקְעוּ, or בִּתְקוֹעַ had been used. Because the
Lord had given Jericho into the hands of the Israelites, they were
to consecrate it to Him as a ban (*cherem*), *i.e.* as a holy thing belonging to Jehovah, which was not to be touched by man, as being

the first-fruits of the land of Canaan. (On *cherem*, see the remarks at Lev. xxvii. 28, 29.) Rahab alone was excepted from this ban, along with all that belonged to her, because she had hidden the spies. The inhabitants of an idolatrous town laid under the ban were to be put to death, together with their cattle, and all the property in the town to be burned, as Moses himself had enjoined on the basis of the law in Lev. xxvii. 29. The only exceptions were metals, gold, silver, and the vessels of brass and iron ; these were to be brought into the treasury of the Lord, *i.e.* the treasury of the tabernacle, as being holy to the Lord (ver. 19 ; *vid.* Num. xxxi. 54). Whoever took to himself anything that had been laid under the ban, exposed himself to the ban, not only because he had brought an abomination into his house, as Moses observes in Deut. vii. 25, in relation to the gold and silver of idols, but because he had wickedly invaded the rights of the Lord, by appropriating that which had been laid under the ban, and had wantonly violated the ban itself. The words, " *beware of the ban, that ye do not ban and take of the ban*" (ver. 18), point to this. As *Lud. de Dieu* observes, " the two things were altogether incompatible, to devote everything to God, and yet to apply a portion to their own private use ; either the thing should not have been devoted, or having been devoted, it was their duty to abstain from it." Any such appropriation of what had been laid under the ban would make the camp of Israel itself a ban, and trouble it, *i.e.* bring it into trouble (*conturbare*, cf. Gen. xxxiv. 30). In consequence of the trumpet-blast and the war-cry raised by the people, the walls of the town fell together, and the Israelites rushed into the town and took it, as had been foretold in ver. 5. The position of וַיָּרַע הָעָם is not to be understood as signifying that the people had raised the war-cry before the trumpet-blast, but may be explained on the ground, that in his instructions in ver. 16 Joshua had only mentioned the shouting. But any misinterpretation is prevented by the fact, that it is expressly stated immediately afterwards, that the people did not raise the great shout till they heard the trumpet-blast.

As far as the event itself is concerned, the different attempts which have been made to explain the miraculous overthrow of the walls of Jericho as a natural occurrence, whether by an earthquake, or by mining, or by sudden storming, for which the inhabitants, who had been thrown into a false security by the marvellous procession repeated day after day for several days, were quite unprepared (as *Ewald* has tried to explain the miracle away), really deserve no serious refutation, being all of them arbitrarily forced upon the text. It is only from the naturalistic stand-point that the miracle could ever be denied; for it not only follows most appropriately upon the miraculous guidance of Israel through the Jordan, but is in perfect harmony with the purpose and spirit of the divine plan of salvation. " It is impossible," says *Hess*, " to imagine a more striking way, in which it could have been shown to the Israelites that Jehovah had given them the town. Now the river must retire to give them an entrance into the land, and now again the wall of the town must fall to make an opening into a fortified place. Two such decisive proofs of the co-operation of Jehovah so shortly after Moses' death, must have furnished a pledge, even to the most sensual, that the same God was with them who had led their fathers so mightily and so miraculously through the Red Sea." That this was *in part* the intention of the miracle, we learn from the close of the narrative (ver. 27). But this does not explain the *true object* of the miracle, or the reason why God gave up this town to the Israelites without any fighting on their part, through the miraculous overthrow of their walls. The reason for this we have to look for in the fact that Jericho was not only the first, but the strongest town of Canaan, and as such was the key to the conquest of the whole land, the possession of which would open the way to the whole, and give the whole, as it were, into their hands. The Lord would give His people the first and strongest town of Canaan, as the first-fruits of the land, without any effort on their part, as a sign that He was about to give them the whole land for a possession, according to His promise; in order that they might not regard the conquest of it as their own work, or the fruit of their own exertions, and look upon the land as a well-merited possession which they could do as they pleased with, but that they might ever use it as a gracious gift from the Lord, which he had merely conferred upon them as a trust, and which He could take away again, whenever they might fall from Him, and render themselves unworthy of His grace. This design on the part of God would of necessity become very obvious in the case of so strongly fortified a town as Jericho, whose walls would appear impregnable to a people that had grown up in the desert and was so utterly without experience in the art of besieging or storming fortified places, and in fact would necessarily remain impregnable, at all events for a long time, without the interposition of God. But if this was the reason why the Lord gave up Jericho to the Israelites by a miracle, it does not explain either the connection between the blast of trumpets or the war-cry of the people and the falling of the walls, or tne reason for the divine instructions that the town was to be marched round every day for seven days, and seven times on the seventh day. Yet as this was an appointment of divine wisdom, it must have had some meaning.

The significance of this repeated marching round the town culminates unquestionably in the ark of the covenant and the trumpet-blast of the priests who went before the ark. In the account before us the ark is constantly called the ark of the Lord, to show that the Lord, who was enthroned upon the cherubim of the ark, was going round the hostile town in the midst of His people; whilst in ver. 8 Jehovah himself is mentioned in the place of the ark of Jehovah. Seven priests went before the ark, bearing jubilee trumpets and blowing during the march. The first time that we read of a trumpet-blast is at Sinai, where the Lord announced His descent upon the mount to the people assembled at the foot to receive Him, not only by other fearful phenomena, but also by a loud and long-continued trumpet-blast (Ex. xix. 16, 19, xx. 14 (18)). After this we find the blowing of trumpets prescribed as part of the Israelitish worship in connection with the observance of the seventh new moon's day (Lev. xxiii. 24), and at the proclamation of the great year of jubilee (Lev. xxv. 9). Just as the trumpet-blast heard by the people when the covenant was made at Sinai was as it were a herald's call, announcing to the tribes of Israel the arrival of the Lord their God to complete His covenant and establish His kingdom upon earth; so the blowing of trumpets in connection with the round of feasts was intended partly to bring the people into remembrance before the Lord year by year at the commencement of the sabbatical month, that He might come to them and grant them the Sabbath rest of His kingdom, and partly at the end of every seven times seven years to announce on the great day of atonement the coming of the great year of grace and freedom, which was to bring to the people of God deliverance from bondage, return to their own possessions, and deliverance from the bitter labours of this earth, and to give them a foretaste of the blessed and glorious liberty to which the children of God would attain at the return of the Lord to perfect His kingdom (*vid.* Pentateuch, vol. ii. pp. 466–7). But when the Lord comes to found, to build up, and to perfect His kingdom upon earth, He also comes to overthrow and destroy the worldly power which opposes His kingdom. The revelation of the grace and mercy of God to His children, goes ever side by side with the revelation of justice and judgment towards the ungodly who are His foes. If therefore the blast of trumpets was the signal to the congregation of Israel of the gracious arrival of the Lord its God to enter into fellowship with it, no less did it proclaim the advent of judgment to an ungodly world. This shows clearly enough the meaning of the trumpet-blast at Jericho. The priests, who went before the ark of the covenant (the visible throne of the invisible God who dwelt among His people) and in the midst of the hosts of Israel, were to announce through the blast of trumpets both to the Israelites and Canaanites the appearance of the Lord of the whole earth for judgment upon Jericho, the strong bulwark of the Canaanitish power and rule, and to foretel to them through the falling of the walls of this fortification, which followed the blast of trumpets and the war-cry of the soldiers of God, the overthrow of all the strong bulwarks of an ungodly world through the omnipotence of the Lord of heaven and earth. Thus the fall of Jericho became the symbol and type of the overthrow of every worldly power before the Lord, when He should come to lead His people into Canaan and establish His kingdom upon earth. On the ground of this event, the blowing of trumpets is frequently introduced in the writings of the prophets, as the signal and symbolical omen of the manifestations of the Lord in great judgments, through which He destroys one worldly power after another, and thus maintains and extends His kingdom upon earth, and leads it on towards that completion to which it will eventually attain when He descends from heaven in His glory at the time of the last trump, with a great shout, with the voice of the archangel and the trump of God, to raise the dead and change the living, to judge the world, cast the devil, death, and hell into the lake of fire, create a new heaven and new earth, and in the new Jerusalem erect the tabernacle of God among men for all eternity (1 Cor. xv. 51 sqq.; 1 Thess. iv. 16, 17; Rev. xx. and xxi.).

The appointment of the march round Jericho, which was to be continued for seven days, and to be repeated seven times on the seventh day, was equally significant. The number seven is a symbol in the Scriptures of the work of God and of the perfection already produced or to be eventually secured by Him; a symbol founded upon the creation of the world in six days, and the completion of the works of creation by the resting of God upon the seventh day. Through this arrangement, that the walls of Jericho were not to fall till after they had been marched round for seven days, and not till after this had been repeated seven times on the seventh day, and then amidst the blast of the jubilee trumpets and the war-cry of the soldiers of the people of God, the destruction of this town, the key to Canaan, was intended by God to become a type of the final destruction at the last day of the power of this world, which exalts itself against the kingdom of God. In this way He not only showed to His congregation that it would not be all at once, but only after long-continued conflict, and at the end of the world, that the worldly power by which it was opposed would be overthrown, but also proved to the enemies of His kingdom, that however long their power might sustain itself in opposition to the kingdom of God, it would at last be destroyed in a moment.

Vers. 21 27. After the taking of Jericho, man and beast were banned, *i.e.* put to death without quarter (ver. 21; cf. ver. 17); Rahab and her relations being the only exceptions. Joshua had directed the two spies to fetch them out of her house, and in the first instance had them taken to a place of safety outside the camp of Israel (vers. 22, 23). "*Her brethren,*" *i.e.* her brothers and sisters, as in chap. ii. 13, not her brothers only. "*All that she had*" does not mean all her possessions, but all the persons belonging to her house; and "*all her kindred*" are all her relations by birth or marriage, with their dependants (cf. chap. ii. 13). *Clericus* is correct in observing, that as Rahab's house was built against the town-wall, and rested partly upon it (chap. ii. 15), when the wall fell down, that portion against or upon which the house stood cannot have fallen along with the rest, "otherwise when the wall fell no one would have dared to remain in the house." But we must not draw the further inference, that when the town was burned Rahab's house was spared.[1] וַיַּנִּיחוּם מִחוּץ וגו' (ver. 23; cf. Gen. xix. 16), "*they let them rest,*" *i.e.* placed them in safety, "*outside the camp of Israel,*" *sc.* till they had done all that was requisite for a formal reception into the congregation of the Lord, viz. by giving up idolatry and heathen superstition, and turning to the God of Israel as the only true God (to which circumcision had to be added in the case of the men), and by whatever lustrations and purifications were customary at the time in connection with reception into the covenant with Jehovah, of which we have no further information.—Vers. 24, 25. After man and beast had been put to death,

---

[1] The statements made by travellers in the middle ages, to the effect that they had seen Rahab's house (*Rob.* Pal. ii. pp. 295-6), belong to the delusions of pious superstition.

and Rahab and her relatives had been placed in security, the
Israelites set the town on fire with everything in it, excepting the
metals, which were taken to the treasury of the tabernacle, as had
been commanded in ver. 19. On the conquest of the other towns
of Canaan the inhabitants only were put to death, whilst the cattle
and the rest of the booty fell to the conquerors, just as in the case of
the conquest of the land and towns of Sihon and Og (compare chap.
viii. 26, 27, x. 28, with Deut. ii. 34, 35, and iii. 6, 7), as it was only
the inhabitants of Canaan that the Lord had commanded to be put
under the ban (Deut. vii. 2, xx. 16, 17). In the case of Jericho,
on the contrary, men, cattle, and booty were all put under the ban,
and the town itself was to be laid in ashes. This was because
Jericho was the first town of Canaan which the Lord had given up
to His people. Israel was therefore to sacrifice it to the Lord as
the first-fruits of the land, and to sanctify it to Him as a thing
placed under the ban, for a sign that they had received the whole
land as a fief from his hand, and had no wish to grasp as a prey
that which belonged to the Lord.—Ver. 25. But Rahab and all
that belonged to her Joshua suffered to live, so that she dwelt in
Israel "*unto this day.*" It is very evident from this remark, that
the account was written not very long after the event.[1]

Vers. 26, 27. But in order to complete the ban pronounced
upon Jericho in perfect accordance with the command of God in
Deut. xiii. 17, and to make the destruction of it a memorial to posterity of the justice of God sanctifying itself upon the ungodly,
Joshua completed the ban with an oath : "*Cursed be the man before
the Lord that riseth up and buildeth this city Jericho ; he shall lay
the foundation thereof at the price of his first-born, and set up its
gates at the price of his youngest son*" (בְּ denoting the price of a

---

[1] Rahab is no doubt the same person as the Rachab mentioned in the
genealogy of Jesus Christ, who married Salmon the tribe prince of Judah, to
whom she bore Boaz, an ancestor of David (Matt. i. 5). The doubts which
Theophylact expressed as to the identity of the two, and which *J. Outhov* has
since sought to confirm, rest for the most part upon the same doctrinal scruples
as those which induced the author of the Chaldee version to make Rahab
an innkeeper, namely, the offence taken at her dishonourable calling. *Jerome's*
view, on the other hand, is a very satisfactory one. "In the genealogy of the
Saviour," he says, "none of the holy women are included, but only those
whom the Scriptures blame, that He who came on behalf of sinners, being
himself born of sinners, might destroy the sins of all." The different ways in
which the name is written, viz. ἡ Ῥαχάβ in Matthew, and Ῥααβ in the Sept.
version of Joshua, and in Heb. xi. 31 and James ii. 25, is not enough to throw

thing). The rhythmical parallelism is unmistakeable in this curse. The two last clauses express the thought that the builder of the town would pay for its restoration by the loss of all his sons, from the first-born to the very youngest. The word " buildeth," however, does not refer to the erection of houses upon the site of the town that had been burnt to ashes, but to the restoration of the town as a fortification, the word בָּנָה being frequently used to denote the fortification of a town (e.g. 1 Kings xv. 17; 2 Chron. xi. 6, xiv. 5, 6). This is evident in general from the fact that a town is not founded by the erection of a number of houses upon one spot, but by the joining of these houses together into an enclosed whole by means of a surrounding wall, but more particularly from the last words of the verse, in which בָּנָה is explained as יְיַסְּדֶנָּה (lay the foundation thereof) and יַצִּיב דְּלָתֶיהָ (set up the gates of it). Setting up the gates of a town is not setting up doors to the houses, but erecting town-gates, which can only be done when a town-wall has been built. But if setting up the gates would be a sign of the completion of the wall, and therefore of the restoration of the town as a fortification, the " founding" (laying the foundation) mentioned in the parallel clause can only be understood as referring to the foundation of the town-wall. This view of the curse, which is well supported both by the language and the facts, is also confirmed by the subsequent history. Joshua himself allotted Jericho to the Benjamites along with certain other towns (chap. xviii. 21), which proves that he intended them to inhabit it; and accordingly we find the city of palms, i.e. Jericho, mentioned afterwards as an inhabited place (Judg. iii. 13; 2 Sam. x. 5), and yet it was not till the time of Ahab that Joshua's curse was fulfilled, when Hiel the Bethelite undertook to make it into a fortified town (1 Kings xvi.

any doubt upon the identity of the two, as *Josephus* always calls the harlot Rahab ἡ Ῥαχάβη. The chronological difficulty, that Salmon and Rahab lived much too soon to have been the parents of Boaz, which is adduced by *Knobel* as an argument against the identity of the mother of Boaz and the harlot Rahab, has no force unless it can be proved that *every* link is given in the genealogy of David (in Ruth iv. 21, 22; 1 Chron. ii. 11; Matt. i. 5), and that Boaz was really the great-grandfather of David; whereas the very opposite, viz. the omission from the genealogies of persons of no celebrity, is placed beyond all doubt by many cases that might be cited. Nothing more is known of Rahab. The accounts of the later Rabbins, such as that she was married to Joshua, or that she was the mother of eight prophets, and others of the same kind, are fables without the slightest historical foundation (see *Lightfoot, hor. hebr. et talm.* in Matt. i. 5).

34).[1]—Ver. 27. Thus the Lord was with Joshua, fulfilling His promise to him (chap. i. 5 sqq.), so that his fame spread through all the land.

ACHAN'S THEFT AND PUNISHMENT.—CHAP. VII.

Ver. 1. At Jericho the Lord had made known to the Canaanites His great and holy name; but before Ai the Israelites were to learn that He would also sanctify Himself on them if they transgressed His covenant, and that the congregation of the Lord could only conquer the power of the world so long as it was faithful to His covenant. But notwithstanding the command which Joshua had enforced upon the people (chap. vi. 18), Achan, a member of the tribe of Judah, laid hands upon the property in Jericho which had been banned, and thus brought the ban upon the children of Israel, the whole nation. His breach of trust is described as unfaithfulness (a trespass) on the part of the children of Israel in the ban, in consequence of which the anger of the Lord was kindled against the whole nation. מָעַל מַעַל, to commit a breach of trust (see at Lev. v. 15), generally against Jehovah, by purloining or withholding what was sanctified to Him, here in the matter of the ban, by appropriating what had been banned to the Lord. This crime was imputed to the whole people, not as *imputatio moralis, i.e.* as though the whole nation had shared in Achan's disposition, and cherished in their hearts the same sinful desire which Achan had carried out in action in the theft he had committed; but as *imputatio civilis,* according to which Achan, a member of the nation, had robbed the whole nation of the purity and holiness which it ought to possess before God, through the sin that he had committed, just as the whole body is affected by the sin of a single member.[2] Instead of

---

[1] *Knobel's* opinion, that the Jericho mentioned between the times of Joshua and Ahab in all probability did not stand upon the old site which Hiel was the first to build upon again, is at variance with 1 Kings xvi. 34, as it is not stated there that he rebuilt the old site of Jericho, but that he began to build the town of Jericho, which existed, according to 2 Sam. x. 5 and Judg. iii. 13, in the time of David, and even of the judges, *i.e.* to restore it as a fortified town; and it is not raised into a truth by any appeal to the statements of *Strabo, Appian,* and others, to the effect that Greeks and Romans did not choose places for building upon which any curse rested.

[2] In support of this I cannot do better than quote the most important of the remarks which I made in my former commentary (*Keil* on Joshua, pp. 177-8, Eng. trans.): "However truly the whole Scriptures speak of each man as indi-

Achan (the reading here and in chap. xxii. 20) we find *Achar* in 1 Chron. ii. 7, the liquids *n* and *r* being interchanged to allow of a play upon the verb עָכַר in ver. 25. Hence in *Josephus* the name is spelt *Acharos*, and in the *Cod. Vat.* of the LXX. *Achar*, whereas the *Cod. Al.* has *Achan*. Instead of *Zabdi*, we find *Zimri* in 1 Chron. ii. 6, evidently a copyist's error. *Zerah* was the twin-brother of Pharez (Gen. xxxviii. 29, 30). *Matteh*, from נָטָה, to spread out, is used to denote the tribe according to its genealogical ramifications; whilst *shebet* (from an Arabic root signifying " uniform, not curled, but drawn out straight and long without any curvature at all ") was applied to the sceptre or straight staff of a magistrate or ruler (never to the stick upon which a person rested), and differed from *matteh* not only in its primary and literal meaning, but also in the derivative meaning *tribe*, in which it was used to designate the division of the nation referred to, not according to its genealogical ramifications and development, but as a corporate body possessing authority and power. This difference in the ideas expressed by the two words will explain the variations in their use: for example, *matteh* is used here (in vers. 1 and 18), and in chap. xxii. 1–14, and in fact is the term usually employed in the geographical sections; whereas *shebet* is used in vers. 14, 16, in chap. iii. 12, iv. 2, and on many other occasions, in those portions of the historical narratives in which the tribes of Israel are introduced as military powers.

Vers. 2–5. The anger of God, which Achan had brought upon Israel, was manifested to the congregation in connection with their attempt to take *Ai.* This town was situated near Bethaven, on the east of Bethel. *Bethel* was originally called *Luz* (see at Gen. xxviii. 19), a place on the border of Ephraim and Benjamin (chap.

---

vidually an object of divine mercy and justice, they teach just as truly that a nation is one organic whole, in which the individuals are merely members of the same body, and are not atoms isolated from one another and the whole, since the state as a divine institution is founded upon family relationship, and intended to promote the love of all to one another and to the invisible Head of all. As all then are combined in a fellowship established by God, the good or evil deeds of an individual affect injuriously or beneficially the welfare of the whole society. And, therefore, when we regard the state as a divine organization and not merely as a civil institution, a compact into which men have entered by treaty, we fail to discover caprice and injustice in consequences which necessarily follow from the moral unity of the whole state; namely, that the good or evil deeds of one member are laid to the charge of the entire body. Caprice and injustice we shall always find if we leave out of sight this fundamental unity, and merely look at the fact that the many share the consequences of the sin of one."

xvi. 2, xviii. 13). It is frequently mentioned, was well known at a later time as the city in which Jeroboam established the worship of the calves, and was inhabited again even after the captivity (see *v. Raumer, Pal.* pp. 178, 179). It has been preserved, in all probability, in the very extensive ruins called *Beitin* (see *Robinson, Pal.* ii. pp. 126 sqq.), about four hours' journey on horseback to the north of Jerusalem, and on the east of the road which leads from Jerusalem to Sichem (Nablus).[1] No traces have ever been discovered of Bethaven. According to chap. xviii. 12, 13, the northern boundary of the tribe of Benjamin, which ran up from Jericho to the mountains on the west, passed on to the desert of Bethaven, and so onwards to Luz (Bethel). If we compare with this the statement in 1 Sam. xiii. 5, that the Philistines who came against Israel encamped at Michmash before (in front of) Bethaven, according to which Bethaven was on the east or north-east of Michmash (Mukhmas), the desert of Bethaven may very possibly have been nothing more than the table-land which lies between the Wady Mutyah on the north and the Wadys Fuwar and Suweinit (in *Robinson's* map), or Wady Tuwâr (on *Van de Velde's* map), and stretches in a westerly direction from the rocky mountain Kuruntel to Abu Sebah (Subbah). Bethaven would then lie to the south or south-east of Abu Sebah. In that case, however, Ai (*Sept. Gai* or *Aggai*, Gen. xii. 8) would neither be found in the inconsiderable ruins to the south of the village of Deir Diwan, as *Robinson* supposes (Pal. ii. pp. 312 sqq.), nor on the site of the present Tell el Hajar, *i.e.* stone hill, three-quarters of an hour to the s.e. of Beitin, on the southern side of the deep and precipitous Wady Mutyah, as *Van de Velde* imagines; but in the ruins of *Medinet Chai* or *Gai*, which *Krafft*[2] and *Strauss*[3] discovered on the flat surface of a mountain that slopes off towards the east, about forty minutes on the eastern side of Geba (Jeba), where " there are considerable ruins surrounded by a circular wall, whilst the place is defended on the south by the valley of Farah, and on the north by the valley of Es Suweinit, with steep shelving walls of rock" (*Strauss : vid. C. Ritter Erdk.* xvi. pp. 526-7). On the advice of the men who were sent out to explore the land, and who

---

[1] The statements of the *Onomasticon* of *Eusebius s. v.* 'Αγγαί agree with this : Κεῖται Βαιθὴλ ἀπιόντων εἰς Αἰλίαν ἀπὸ Νέας πόλεως ἐν λαιοῖς τῆς ὁδοῦ ἀμφὶ τὸ δωδέκατον ἀπ' Αἰλίας σημεῖον. Also *s. v.* Βαιθήλ : καὶ νῦν ἐστὶ κώμη, Αἰλίας ἄποθεν σημείοις ιβ' (twelve Roman miles are four or five hours' journey).

[2] Topograph. v. Jerusalem, p. ix.   [3] Sinai u. Golgoth. pp. 326-7.

described the population on their return as small ("*they are but few*"), Joshua did not send the whole of the fighting men against *Ai*, but only about 3000 men. As there were not more than 12,000 inhabitants (chap. viii. 25), there could hardly have been 3000 fighting men, who might easily have been beaten by 3000 Israelitish warriors. But when the Israelites attacked the town they fled before its inhabitants, who slew about thirty-six men, and pursued them before the gate, *i.e.* outside the town, to the stone quarries, and smote them on the sloping ground. The *Shebarim*, from *sheber*, a breach or fracture, were probably stone quarries near the slope on the east of the town. Nothing more can be decided, as the country has not been thoroughly explored by travellers. On account of this repulse the people lost all their courage. "*The hearts of the people melted*" (see chap. ii. 15): this expression is strengthened still further by the additional clause, "*and became as water.*"

Vers. 6–9. Joshua and the elders of the people were also deeply affected, not so much at the loss of thirty-six men, as because Israel, which was invincible with the help of the Lord, had been beaten, and therefore the Lord must have withdrawn His help. In the deepest grief, with their clothes rent (see at Lev. x. 6) and ashes upon their heads, they fell down before the ark of the Lord (*vid.* Num. xx. 6) until the evening, to pour out their grief before the Lord. Joshua's prayer contains a complaint (ver. 7) and a question addressed to God (vers. 8, 9). The complaint, "*Alas, O Lord Jehovah, wherefore hast Thou brought this people over Jordan, to deliver us into the hand of the Amorites, to destroy us?*" almost amounts to murmuring, and sounds very much like the complaint which the murmuring people brought against Moses and Aaron in the desert (Num. xiv. 2, 3); but it is very different from the murmuring of the people on that occasion against the guidance of God; for it by no means arose from unbelief, but was simply the bold language of faith wrestling with God in prayer,—faith which could not comprehend the ways of the Lord,—and involved the most urgent appeal to the Lord to carry out His work in the same glorious manner in which it had been begun, with the firm conviction that God could neither relinquish nor alter His purposes of grace. The words which follow, "*Would to God that we had been content* (see at Deut. i. 5) *to remain on the other side of the Jordan,*" assume on the one hand, that previous to the crossing of the river Israel had cherished a longing for the possession of Canaan, and on the other hand, that this longing might possibly have been the cause of the calamity which had fallen upon the people now, and therefore express the wish that Israel had never cherished any such desire, or that the Lord had never gratified it. (On the unusual form הֶעֱבַרְתְּ for הֶעֱבַרְתָּ, see Ges. § 63, anm. 4, and Ewald, § 41, b.) The inf. abs. הַעֲבִיר (with the unusual i in the final syllable) is placed for the sake of emphasis after the finite verb, as in Gen. xlvi. 4, etc. The Amorites are the inhabitants of the mountains, as in Gen. xlvi. 4, etc.—Vers. 8, 9. The question which Joshua addresses to God he introduces in this way : " Pray (בִּי contracted from בְּעִי), Lord, what shall I say?" to modify the boldness of the question which follows. It was not because he did not know what to say, for he proceeded at once to pour out the thoughts of his heart, but because he felt that the thought which he was about to utter might involve a reproach, as if, when God permitted that disaster, He had not thought of His own honour ; and as he could not possibly think this, he introduced his words with a supplicatory inquiry. What he proceeds to say in vers. 8, 9, does not contain two co-ordinate clauses, but one simple thought : how would God uphold His great name before the world, when the report that Israel had turned their back before them should reach the Canaanites, and they should come and surround the Israelites, and destroy them without a single trace from off the face of the earth.[1] In the words, "the Canaanites and all the inhabitants of the land," there is involved the thought that there were other people living in Canaan beside the Canaanites, e.g. the Philistines. The question, " What wilt Thou do with regard to Thy great name?" signifies, according to the parallel passages, Ex. xxxii. 11, 12, Num. xiv. 13 sqq., Deut. ix. 28, " How wilt Thou preserve Thy great name, which Thou hast acquired thus far in the sight of all nations through the miraculous guidance of Israel, from being misunderstood and blasphemed among the heathen?" (" what wilt Thou do?" as in Gen. xxvi. 29).

Vers. 10-15. The answer of the Lord, which was addressed to Joshua directly and not through the high priest, breathed anger against the sin of Israel. The question, " Wherefore liest thou upon

---

[1] Calovius has therefore given the correct interpretation: " When they have destroyed our name, after Thou hast chosen us to be Thy people, and brought us hither with such great wonders, what will become of Thy name? Our name is of little moment, but wilt Thou consult the honour of Thine own name, if Thou destroyest us? For Thou didst promise us this land ; and what people is there that will honour Thy name if ours should be destroyed?"

thy face?" ("fallest," as in Deut. xxi. 1) involved the reproof that Joshua had no reason to doubt the fidelity of the Lord. Instead of seeking for the cause of the calamity in God, he ought to seek it in the sin of the people.—Ver. 11. Israel had sinned, and that very grievously. This is affirmed in the clauses which follow, and which are rendered emphatic by the repetition of גַם as an expression of displeasure. The sin of one man was resting as a burden upon the whole nation in the manner explained above (on ver. 1). This sin was a breach of the covenant, being a transgression of the obligation into which the people had entered in their covenant with the Lord, to keep His commandments (Ex. xix. 8, xxiv. 7); yea, it was a grasping at the ban, and a theft, and a concealment, and an appropriation of that which was stolen to their own use. The first three clauses describe the sin in its relation to God, as a grievous offence; the three following according to its true character, as a great, obstinate, and reckless crime. "*They have put it among their own stuff*" (house furniture), viz. to use and appropriate it as their own property. As all that had been stolen was a property consecrated to the Lord, the appropriation of it to private use was the height of wickedness.—Ver. 12. On account of this sin the Israelites could not stand before their foes, because they had fallen under the ban (cf. chap. vi. 18). And until this ban had been removed from their midst, the Lord would not help them any further.—Vers. 13–15. Joshua was to take away this ban from the nation. To discover who had laid hands upon the ban, he was to direct the people to sanctify themselves for the following day (see at chap. iii. 5), and then to cause them to come before God according to their tribes, families, households, and men, that the guilty men might be discovered by lot; and to burn whoever was found guilty, with all that he possessed. נִקְרַב, "*to come near,*" sc. to Jehovah, *i.e.* to come before His sanctuary. The tribes, families, households, and men, formed the four classes into which the people were organized. As the tribes were divided into families, so these again were subdivided into houses, commonly called fathers' houses, and the fathers' houses again into men, *i.e.* fathers of families (see the remarks on Ex. xviii. 25, 26, and my Bibl. Archæology, § 140). Each of these was represented by its natural head, so that we must picture the affair as conducted in the following manner: in order to discover the tribe, the twelve tribe princes came before the Lord; and in order to discover the family, the heads of families of the tribe that had been taken and so on to the end, each one in turn being

subjected to the lot.   For although it is not distinctly stated that
the lot was resorted to in order to discover who was guilty, and
that the discovery was actually made in this way, this is very evident from the expression אֲשֶׁר־יִלְכְּדֶנָּה (which the Lord taketh), as this
was the technical term employed, according to 1 Sam. xiv. 42, to
denote the falling of the lot upon a person (see also 1 Sam. x. 20).
Moreover, the lot was frequently resorted to in cases where a crime
could not be brought home to a person by the testimony of eye-
witnesses (see 1 Sam. xiv. 41, 42; Jonah i. 7; Prov. xviii. 18), as
it was firmly believed that the lot was directed by the Lord (Prov.
xvi. 33).   In what manner the lot was cast we do not know.   In
all probability little tablets or potsherds were used, with the names
written upon them, and these were drawn out of an urn.   This
may be inferred from a comparison of chap. xviii. 11 and xix. 1,
with xviii. 6, 10, according to which the casting of the lot took
place in such a manner that the lot came up (עָלָה, chap. xviii. 11,
xix. 10; Lev. xvi. 9), or came out (יָצָא, chap. xix. 1, xvii. 24;
Num. xxxiii. 54).   הַנִּלְכָּד בַּחֵרֶם, the person taken in (with) the ban,
i.e. taken by the lot as affected with the ban, was to be burned with
fire, of course not alive, but after he had been stoned (ver. 25).
The burning of the body of a criminal was regarded as heightening
the punishment of death (vid. Lev. xx. 14).   This punishment was
to be inflicted upon him, in the first place, because he had broken
the covenant of Jehovah; and in the second place, because he had
wrought folly in Israel, that is to say, had offended grievously
against the covenant God, and also against the covenant nation.
" Wrought folly :" an expression used here, as in Gen. xxxiv. 7, to
denote such a crime as was irreconcilable with the honour of Israel
as the people of God.

Vers. 16-26. Execution of the Command.—Vers. 16–18. Dis
covery of the guilty man through the lot.   In ver. 17 we should
expect "the tribe" (shebet) or " the families" (mishpachoth) of
Judah, instead of " the family."   The plural mishpachoth is adopted
in the LXX. and Vulgate, and also to be met with in seven MSS.;
but this is conjecture rather than the original reading.   Mishpachah
is either used generally, or employed in a collective sense to denote
all the families of Judah.   There is no ground for altering לִגְבָרִים (man
by man) into לְבָתִּים (house by house) in ver. 17, according to some
of the MSS.; the expression "man by man" is used simply because
it was the representative men who came for the lot to be cast, not
only in the case of the fathers' houses, but in that of the families also.

—Ver. 19. When Achan had been discovered to be the criminal, Joshua charged him to give honour and praise to the Lord, and to confess without reserve what he had done. It is not ironically, or with dissimulation, that Joshua addresses him as "my son," but with "sincere paternal regard."[1] "*Give glory to the Lord:*" this is a solemn formula of adjuration, by which a person was summoned to confess the truth before the face of God (cf. John ix. 24). "*And give Him praise:*" the meaning is not, "make confession," but give praise, as Ezra x. 11 clearly shows. Through a confession of the truth Achan was to render to God, as the Omniscient, the praise and honour that were due.—Vers. 20, 21. Achan then acknowledged his sin, and confessed that he had appropriated to himself from among the booty a beautiful Babylonish cloak, 200 shekels of silver, and a tongue of gold of 50 shekels weight. The form וָאֶרְאֶה is not to be abbreviated into וָאֵרֶא, according to the *Keri*, as the form is by no means rare in verbs ל"ה. "*A Babylonish cloak*" (*lit.* a cloak of Shinar, or Babylon) is a costly cloak, artistically worked, such as were manufactured in Babylon, and distributed far and wide through the medium of commerce.[2] Two hundred shekels of silver was about £25. "*A tongue of gold*" (according to *Luther*, "ornaments made in the shape of tongues") was certainly a golden ornament in the form of a tongue, the use of which is unknown; it was of considerable size, as it weighed 50 shekels, *i.e.* 13,700 grains. It is not necessary to suppose that it was a golden dagger, as many do, simply because the ancient Romans gave the name *lingula* to an oblong dagger formed in the shape of a tongue. Achan had hidden these things in the ground in the midst of his tent, and the silver "*under it,*" *i.e.* under these things (the suffix is neuter, and must be understood as referring to all the things with the exception of the silver). The Babylonish cloak and the tongue of gold were probably placed in

---

[1] To these remarks *Calvin* also adds : " This example serves as a lesson to judges, that when punishing crimes they should moderate their rigour, and not lose all the feelings of humanity ; and, on the other hand, that whilst merciful they should not be careless or remiss."

[2] *Plinius h. n.* viii. 48 : *Colores diversos picturæ vestium intexere Babylon maxime celebravit et nomen imposuit.* (See *Heeren Ideen.* i. 2, pp. 205 sqq., and *Movers Phönizier*, ii. 3, pp. 258 sqq.) The *Sept.* rendering is ψιλὴ ποικίλη, *i.e.* a Babylonian cloak ornamented with pictures. It is called ψιλή because it was cut smooth, and ποικίλη because it was covered with coloured figures, either of men or animals, sometimes woven, at other times worked with the needle (*Fischer de vers. græc. libr.* V. T. pp. 87–8).

a chest; at any rate they would be carefully packed up, and the silver was placed underneath. The article in הָאַהֳלִי, which occurs twice, as it also does in chap. viii. 33, Lev. xxvii. 33, Micah ii. 12, is probably to be explained in the manner suggested by *Hengstenberg*, viz. that the article and noun became so fused into one, that the former lost its proper force.—Vers. 22, 23. Joshua sent two messengers directly to Achan's tent to fetch the things, and when they were brought he had them laid down before Jehovah, *i.e.* before the tabernacle, where the whole affair had taken place. הִצִּיק, here and in 2 Sam. xv. 24, signifies to lay down (synonymous with הִצִּיג), whilst the *Hiphil* form is used for pouring out.—Vers. 24, 25. Then Joshua and all Israel, *i.e.* the whole nation in the person of its heads or representatives, took Achan, together with the things which he had purloined, and his sons and daughters, his cattle, and his tent with all its furniture, and brought them into the valley of Achor, where they stoned them to death and then burned them, after Joshua had once more pronounced this sentence upon him in the place of judgment : " *How hast thou troubled us* " (עָכַר, as in chap. vi. 18, to bring into trouble) ! " *The Lord will trouble thee this day.* " It by no means follows from the expression " stoned him " in ver. 25, that Achan only was stoned. The singular pronoun is used to designate Achan alone, as being the principal person concerned. But it is obvious enough that his children and cattle were stoned, from what follows in the very same verse : " *They burned them* (the persons stoned to death, and their things) *with fire, and heaped up stones upon them.* " It is true that in Deut. xxiv. 16 the Mosaic law expressly forbids the putting to death of children for their fathers' sins; and many have imagined, therefore, that Achan's sons and daughters were simply taken into the valley to be spectators of the punishment inflicted upon the father, that it might be a warning to them. But for what reason, then, were Achan's cattle (oxen, sheep, and asses) taken out along with him? Certainly for no other purpose than to be stoned at the same time as he. The law in question only referred to the punishment of ordinary criminals, and therefore was not applicable at all to the present case, in which the punishment was commanded by the Lord himself. Achan had fallen under the ban by laying hands upon what had been banned, and consequently was exposed to the same punishment as a town that had fallen away to idolatry (Deut. xiii. 16, 17). The law of the ban was founded upon the assumption, that the conduct to be punished was not a crime of which the individual only was guilty, out one in which the whole family of the leading sinner, in fact everything connected with him, participated. Thus, in the case before us, the things themselves had been abstracted from the booty by Achan alone; but he had hidden them in his tent, buried them in the earth, which could hardly have been done so secretly that his sons and daughters knew nothing of it. By so doing he had made his family participators in his theft; they therefore fell under the ban along with him, together with their tent, their cattle, and the rest of their property, which were all involved in the consequences of His crime. The clause וַיִּסְקְלוּ אֹתָם בָּאֲבָנִים does not refer to the stoning as a capital punishment, but to the casting of stones upon the bodies after they were dead and had been burned, for the purpose of erecting a heap of stones upon them as a memorial of the disgrace (vid. chap. viii. 29; 2 Sam. xviii. 17).—In ver. 26, the account of the whole affair closes with these two remarks: (1) That after the punishment of the malefactor the Lord turned from the fierceness of His anger; and (2) That the valley in which Achan suffered his punishment received the name of Achor (troubling) with special reference to the fact that Joshua had described his punishment as well as Achan's sin as עָכַר (troubling: see ver. 25), and that it retained this name down to the writer's own time. With regard to the situation of this valley, it is evident from the word וַיַּעֲלוּ in ver. 24 that it was on higher ground than Gilgal and Jericho, probably in one of the ranges of hills that intersect the plain of Jericho, and from chap. xv. 7, where the northern border of the possessions of Judah is said to have passed through this valley, that it is to be looked for to the south of Jericho. The only other places in which there is any allusion to this event are Hos. ii. 17 and Isa. lxv. 10.

CONQUEST OF AI. BLESSINGS AND CURSES UPON GERIZIM AND EBAL.—CHAP. VIII.

Vers. 1-29. CONQUEST AND BURNING OF AI.—Vers. 1, 2. After the ban which rested upon the people had been wiped away, the Lord encouraged Joshua to make war upon Ai, promising him that the city should be taken, and giving him instructions what to do to ensure the success of his undertaking. With evident allusion to Joshua's despair after the failure of the first attack, the Lord commences with these words, " Fear not, neither be thou dismayed" (as in Deut. i. 21, xxxi. 8), and then commands him to go against

Ai with all the people of war. By "all the people of war" we are hardly to understand all the men out of the whole nation who were capable of bearing arms; but as only a third of these were contributed by the two tribes and a half to cross over into Canaan and take part in the war (see p. 32), the other tribes also are not likely to have levied more than a third, say about 160,000, which would form altogether an army of about 200,000 men. But even such an army as this seems out of all proportion to the size of Ai, with its 12,000 inhabitants (ver. 25). On the other hand, however, we must bear in mind that the expression "*all* the people of war" simply denotes the whole army, in contrast with the advice of the spies that only a portion of the army should be sent (chap. vii. 3), so that we are not warranted in pressing the word "all" too absolutely;[1] and also that this command of God was not given with reference to the conquest of Ai alone, but applied at the same time to the conquest of the whole land, which Joshua was not to attempt by sending out detachments only, but was to carry out with the whole of the force at his command. עָלָה, to go up, is applied to the advance of an army against a hostile town, independently of the question whether the town was situated upon an eminence or not, as every town that had to be taken was looked upon as a height to be scaled, though as a fact in this instance the army had really to ascend from Jericho to Ai, which was situated up in the mountains. (On ver. 1*b*, see chap. vi. 2.) "*His land*" is the country round, which belonged to the town and was under its king. —Ver. 2. Joshua was to do the same to Ai and her king as he had already done to Jericho and her king, except that in this case the conquerors were to be allowed to appropriate the booty and the cattle to themselves. In order to conquer the town, he was to lay an ambush behind it.[2] אֹרֵב, a collective noun, signifying the persons concealed in ambush; מַאֲרָב (ver. 9), the place of ambush. "*Behind it*," *i.e.* on the west of the town.

Vers. 3–13. Accordingly Joshua set out with all the people of war against Ai, and selected 30,000 brave men, and sent them out in the night, with instructions to station themselves as an ambuscade

---

[1] " As we have just before seen how their hearts melted, God *consulted their weakness*, by putting no heavier burden upon them than they were able to bear, until they had recovered from their alarm, and hearkened readily to His commands."—*Calvin.*

[2] The much agitated question, whether it could be worthy of God to employ stratagem in war, to which different replies have been given, has been answered

behind the town, and at no great distance from it. As the distance from Gilgal to Ai was about fifteen miles, and the road runs pretty straight in a north-westerly direction from Jericho through the Wady Faran, the detachment sent forward might easily accomplish the distance in a night, so as to arrive on the western side of Ai before the break of day. They were then to hold themselves in readiness to fight. He (Joshua) himself would approach the town with the people of war that remained with him; and if the inhabitants of Ai should come out against him as they did before, they would flee before them till they had drawn them quite away from their town (ver. 5). This was to be expected; "*for they will say, They flee before us, as at the first: and we will flee before them.*" (ver. 6). When this was done, the warriors were to come forth from their ambush, fall upon the town, and set it on fire (vers. 7, 8). Having been sent away with these instructions, the 30,000 men went into ambush, and posted themselves "*between Bethel and Ai, on the west side of Ai*" (ver. 9), *i.e.*, according to *Strauss*, in the Wady es Suweinit, to the north-west of Ai, where it forms almost a perpendicular wall, near to which the ruins of *Chai* are to be found, though "not near enough to the rocky wady for it to be possible to look down its almost perpendicular wall" (*Ritter*, Erdk. xvi. p. 528). Joshua remained for the night in the midst of the people, *i.e.* in the camp of that portion of the army that had gone with him towards Ai; not in Gilgal, as *Knobel* supposes.—Ver. 10. The next morning he mustered the people as early as possible, and then went, with the elders of Israel, "before the people of Ai." The elders of Israel are not "military tribunes, who were called *elders* because of their superiority in military affairs," as *Masius* supposes, but, as in every other case, the heads of the people, who accompanied Joshua as counsellors.—Ver. 11. The whole of the people of war also advanced with him to the front of the town, and encamped on the north of Ai, so that the valley was between it (בינו, as in chap. iii. 4) and Ai. This was probably a side valley branching off towards the south from the eastern continuation of the Wady es Suweinit.—In vers. 12, 13, the account of the prepara-

quite correctly by *Calvin*. "Surely," he says, "wars are not carried on by striking alone; but they are considered the best generals who succeed through art and counsel more than by force. . . . Therefore, if war is lawful at all, it is beyond all controversy that the way is perfectly clear for the use of the customary arts of warfare, provided there is no breach of faith in the violation of treaty or truce, or in any other way."

tions for the attack is rounded off by a repetition of the notice as to the forces engaged, and in some respects a more exact description of their disposition. Joshua, it is stated in ver. 12, took about 5000 men and placed them in ambush between Bethel and Ai, on the west of the town. As the place where this ambuscade was posted is described in precisely the same terms as that which was occupied, according to ver. 9, by the 30,000 men who were sent out to form an ambuscade in the night before the advance of the main army against Ai (for the substitution of "*the city*" for Ai cannot possibly indicate a difference in the locality), the view held by the majority of commentators, that ver. 12 refers to a second ambuscade, which Joshua sent out in addition to the 30,000, and posted by the side of them, is even more than questionable, and is by no means raised into a probability by the expression אֶת־עֲקֵבוֹ (*Eng.* "their liers in wait") in ver. 13. The description of the place, "on the west of the city," leaves no doubt whatever that "their liers in wait" are simply the ambuscade (אֹרֵב) mentioned in ver. 12, which was sent out from the whole army, *i.e.* the ambuscade that was posted on the west of the town. עָקֵב signifies literally the lier in wait (Ps. xlix. 5), from עָקַב, *insidiari*, and is synonymous with אֹרֵב. The meaning which *Gesenius* and others attach to the word, viz. the rear or hinder part of the army, cannot be sustained from Gen. xlix. 19. If we add to this the fact that ver. 13*a* is obviously nothing more than a repetition of the description already given in ver. 11 of the place where the main army was posted, and therefore bears the character of a closing remark introduced to wind up the previous account, we cannot regard ver. 12 as anything more than a repetition of the statements in vers. 3, 9, and can only explain the discrepancy with regard to the number of men who were placed in ambush, by supposing that, through a copyist's error, the number which was expressed at first in simple letters has in one instance been given wrongly. The mistake, however, is not to be found in the 5000 (ver. 12), but in the 30,000 in ver. 3, where ה has been confounded with ל. For a detachment of 5000 men would be quite sufficient for an ambuscade that had only to enter the town after the soldiers had left it in pursuit of the Israelites, and to set it on fire, whereas it hardly seems possible that 30,000 men should have been posted in ambush so near to the town.[1]—In ver. 13*a*, הָעָם

[1] We need have no hesitation in coming to the conclusion that there is a mistake in the number given in ver. 3, as the occurrence of such mistakes in the historical books is fully established by a comparison of the numbers given

(the people) is to be taken as the subject of the sentence : " *The people had set all the host, that was on the north of the city, and its ambuscade on the west of the city.*" In the night, namely the night before the army arrived at the north of the town, Joshua went through the midst of the valley, which separated the Israelites from the town, so that in the morning he stood with all the army close before the town.

Vers. 14–23. When the king of Ai saw the Israelites, he hurried out in the morning against them to battle at the (previously) appointed place (לַמּוֹעֵד, *in locum condictum,* as in 1 Sam. xx. 35) before the steppe (*Arabah,* not the valley of the Jordan, but the steppe or desert of Bethaven ; see at chap. vii. 2), as he knew nothing of the ambuscade behind the town.—Ver. 15. But the Israelites let them beat them, and fled along the desert (of Bethaven).—Vers. 16, 17. And all the people in the town were called together to pursue the Israelites, and were drawn away from the town, so that not a man, *i.e.* not a single soldier who could take part in the pursuit, remained either in Ai or the neighbouring town of Bethel, and the town stood open behind them. It is evident from ver. 17 that the inhabitants of Bethel, which was about three hours' journey from Ai, took part in the battle, probably in consequence of a treaty which the king of Ai had made with them in the expectation of a renewed and still stronger attack on the part of the Israelites. Nothing further is known upon this point ; nor can anything be inferred from the fact that the king of Bethel is included in the list of the kings slain by Joshua (chap. xii. 16). Consequently, we cannot decide whether the Bethelites came to the help of the Aites

in the books of Samuel and Kings with those in the books of Chronicles, and is admitted by every commentator. In my earlier commentary on Joshua, I attempted to solve the difficulty by the twofold assumption : *first,* that ver. 12 contains a supplementary statement, in which the number of the men posted in ambush is given for the first time ; and *secondly,* that the historian forgot to notice that out of the 30,000 men whom Joshua chose to make war upon Ai, 5000 were set apart to lie in ambush. But, on further examination of the text, I have come to the conclusion that the second assumption is irreconcilable with the distinct words of ver. 3, and feel obliged to give it up. On the other hand, I still adhere to the conviction that there is not sufficient ground either for the assumption that vers. 12, 13, contain an old marginal gloss that has crept into the text, or for the hypothesis of *Ewald* and *Knobel,* that these verses were introduced by the last editor of the book out of some other document. The last hypothesis amounts to a charge of thoughtlessness against the latest editor, which is hardly reconcilable with the endeavour, for which he is praised in other places, to reconcile the discrepancies in the different documents.

for the first time on the day of the battle itself, or, what is more
probable, had already sent men to Ai, to help to repulse the expected attack of the Israelites upon that town.—Vers. 18, 19. At
the command of God Joshua now stretched out the javelin in his
hand towards the town. At this sign the ambuscade rose hastily
from its concealment, rushed into the town, and set it on fire.
נָטָה בַּכִּידוֹן signifies to stretch out the hand with the spear. The
object יָד, which is missing (cf. vers. 19, 26), may easily be supplied
from the apposition אֲשֶׁר בְּיָדֶךָ. The raising of the javelin would
probably be visible at a considerable distance, even if it was not
provided with a small flag, as both earlier and later commentators
assume, since Joshua would hardly be in the midst of the flying
Israelites, but would take his station as commander upon some
eminence on one side. And the men in ambush would have
scouts posted to watch for the signal, which had certainly been
arranged beforehand, and convey the information to the others.—
Vers. 20, 21. The men of Ai then turned round behind them, being
evidently led to do so by the Israelites, who may have continued
looking round to the town of Ai when the signal had been given
by Joshua, to see whether the men in ambush had taken it and set
it on fire, and as soon as they saw that this had been done began to
offer still further resistance to their pursuers, and to defend themselves vigorously against them. On looking back to their town
the Aites saw the smoke of the town ascending towards heaven:
" *and there were not hands in them to flee hither and thither,*" *i.e.* they
were utterly unable to flee. " *Hands,*" as the organs of enterprise
and labour, in the sense of " strength," not " room," for which we
should expect to find לָהֶם instead of בָּהֶם. There is an analogous
passage in Ps. lxxvi. 6, " None of the men of might have found
their hands." For the people that fled to the wilderness (the
Israelitish army) turned against the pursuers (the warriors of Ai),
or, as is added by way of explanation in ver. 21, when Joshua and
all Israel saw the town in the hands of the ambuscade, and the
smoke ascending, they turned round and smote the people of Ai;
and (ver. 22) these (*i.e.* the Israelites who had formed the ambuscade) came out of the town to meet them. " *These*" (*Eng.* the
other), as contrasted with " the people that fled" in ver. 20, refers
back to " the ambush" in ver. 19. In this way the Aites were in
the midst of the people of Israel, who came from this side and that
side, and smote them to the last man. " *So that they let none of
them remain :*" as in Num. xxi. 35 and Deut. iii. 3, except that in

this case it is strengthened still further by וּפָלִיט, "*or escape.*"—Ver. 23. The king of Ai was taken alive and brought to Joshua.

Vers. 24–29. When all the men of Ai, who had come out to pursue the Israelites, had been slain upon the field (namely) in the desert, all Israel returned to Ai and smote it (the town, *i.e.* the inhabitants), so that on that day there fell of men and women 12,000, all the people of Ai : for Joshua did not draw back his hand, which had been stretched out with the javelin, till all the inhabitants of Ai were smitten with the ban, *i.e.* put to death ; according to the common custom of war, that the general did not lower the war-signal till the conflict was to cease (see *Suidas* in Σημεῖα, and *Lipsius de militia, Rom.* iv. *dial.* 12).—Ver. 27. Only the cattle and the rest of the booty the conquerors retained for themselves, according to the word of the Lord (ver. 2).—Ver. 28. Joshua had the town burnt down and made into a heap of rubbish for ever.—Ver. 29. He had the king of Ai hanged upon a tree, *i.e.* put to death, and then suspended upon a stake (see Num. xxv. 4) until the evening; but at sunset he had him taken down (in accordance with Deut. xxi. 22, 23), and thrown at the entrance of the town-gate, and a heap of stones piled upon him (as in the case of Achan, chap. vii. 26).

Vers. 30–35. BLESSINGS AND CURSES UPON GERIZIM AND EBAL.—After the capture of Ai, Israel had gained so firm a footing in Canaan that Joshua was able to carry out the instructions of Moses in Deut. xxvii., that, after crossing the Jordan, he was to build an altar upon Mount Ebal for the setting up of the covenant. The fulfilment of these instructions, according to the meaning of this solemn act, as a symbolical setting up of the law of the Lord to be the invariable rule of life to the people of Israel in the land of Canaan (see at Deut. xxvii.), was not only a practical expression of thanksgiving on the part of the covenant nation for its entrance into this land through the almighty assistance of its God, but also a practical acknowledgment, that in the overthrow of the Canaanites thus far it had received a strong pledge of the conquest of the foes that still remained and the capture of the whole of the promised land, provided only it persevered in covenant faithfulness towards the Lord its God. The account of this transaction is attached, it is true, to the conquest of Ai by the introduction, "*Then Joshua built,*" etc. (ver. 30); but simply as an occurrence which had no logical connection with the conquest of Canaan and the defeat of its kings. The particle אָז (*sequ. imperf.*) is used, for example, in cases where the historian either wishes to introduce contemporaneous facts, that do not carry forward the main course of the history, or loses sight for the time of the strictly historical sequence and simply takes note of the occurrence of some particular event (*vid. Ewald*, § 136, *b.*). The assertion of modern critics, which *Knobel* repeats, that this account is out of place in the series of events as contained in chap. vi.–xii., is so far correct, that the promulgation of the law and the renewal of the covenant upon Ebal form no integral part of the account of the conquest of Canaan; but it by no means proves that this section has been interpolated by the Jehovist from his first document, or by the last editor of this book from some other source, and that what is related here did not take place at the time referred to. The circumstance that, according to chap. vi.–viii. 29, Joshua had only effected the conquest of Jericho in the south of the land from Gilgal as a base, and that even in chap. ix. and x. he was still engaged in the south, by no means involves the impossibility or even the improbability of a march to *Shechem*, which was situated further north, where he had not yet beaten the Canaanites, and had not effected any conquests. The distance from Ai to Shechem between Gerizim and Ebal is about thirty miles in a straight line. *Robinson* made the journey from Bireh (Beeroth) to Sichem on mules in eleven and a half hours, and that not by the most direct route (Pal. iii. pp. 81–2), and Ai was not more than an hour to the south of Beeroth; so that Joshua could have gone with the people from Ai to Gerizim and Ebal in two days without any excessive exertion. Now, even if the conquests of the Israelites had not extended further north than Ai at that time, there was no reason why Joshua should be deterred from advancing further into the land by any fear of attack from the Canaanites, as the people of war who went with him would be able to repulse any hostile attack; and after the news had spread of the fate of Ai and Jericho, no Canaanitish king would be likely to venture upon a conflict with the Israelites alone. Moreover, Shechem had no king, as we may gather from the list of the thirty-one kings who were defeated by Joshua. To the further remark of *Knobel*, that "there was no reason for their hurrying with this ceremony, and it might have been carried out at a later period in undisturbed security," we simply reply, that obedience to the command of God was not a matter of such indifference to the servant of the Lord as *Knobel* imagines. There was no valid reason after the capture of

Ai for postponing any longer the solemn ceremony of setting up
the law of Jehovah which had been enjoined by Moses; and if we
consider the reason for this solemnity, to which we have already
referred, there can be no doubt that Joshua would proceed without
the least delay to set up the law of the Lord in Canaan as early as
possible, even before the subjugation of the whole land, that he might
thereby secure the help of God for further conflicts and enterprises.

The account of this religious solemnity is given very briefly. It
presupposes an acquaintance with the Mosaic instructions in Deut.
xxvii., and merely gives the leading points, to show that those
instructions were carefully carried out by Joshua. Of the three
distinct acts of which the ceremony consisted, in the book of Deuteronomy the setting up of the stones with the law written upon
them is mentioned first (Deut. xxvii. 2-4), and then (vers. 5-7)
the building of the altar and the offering of sacrifice. Here, on
the contrary, the building of the altar and offering of sacrifice are
mentioned first (vers. 30, 31), and then (ver. 32) the writing of
the law upon the stones; which was probably the order actually
observed.—In ver. 30 Jehovah is called "*the God of Israel*," to
show that henceforth no other god was to be worshipped in Canaan
than the God of Israel. On Mount *Ebal*, see at Deut. xi. 29 and
xxvii. 4.—Ver. 31. "*As Moses commanded:*" namely, Deut. xxvii.
5. "*As it is written in the book of the law of Moses:*" viz. in Ex.
xx. 22 (25). On the presentation of burnt-offerings and slain-
offerings, see at Deut. xxvii. 6, 7.—In ver. 32 nothing is mentioned
but the writing of the law upon the stones; all the rest is presupposed from Deut. xxvii. 2 sqq., to which the expression "*the*
stones" refers. "*Copy of the law:*" as in Deut. xvii. 18; see the
explanation at Deut. xxvii. 3. In connection with the third part
of the ceremony, the promulgation of the law with the blessing
and cursing, the account of the Mosaic instructions given in Deut.
xxvii. 11 sqq. is completed in ver. 33 by the statement that "*all
Israel, and their elders* (*i.e.* with their elders), *and shoterim, and
judges,*" stood on both sides of the ark before the Levitical priests,
the stranger as well as the native, *i.e.* without any exception, one
half (*i.e.* six tribes) towards Mount Ebal, and the other half towards
Mount Gerizim. For further remarks, see at Deut. xxvii. 11 sqq.
"*As Moses commanded to bless the people before:*" *i.e.* as he had
previously commanded. The fact that the thought itself does not
suit the context is quite sufficient to show that the explanation given
by many commentators, viz. that they were to commence with the

blessings, is incorrect. But if, on the other hand, we connect the word "before" with the principal verb of the sentence, "commanded," the meaning will be that Moses did not give the command to proclaim the blessings and cursings to the people for the first time in connection with these instructions (Deut. xxvii.), but had done so before, at the very outset, namely, as early as Deut. xi. 29. —Ver. 34. "*And afterwards* (after the people had taken the place assigned them) *he read to them all the words of the law*," *i.e.* he had the law proclaimed aloud by the persons entrusted with the proclamation of the law, viz. the Levitical priests. קָרָא, *lit.* to call out or proclaim, then in a derivative sense to read, inasmuch as reading aloud is proclaiming (as, for example, in Ex. xxiv. 7). The words "*the blessing and the curse*" are in apposition to "*all the words of the law*," which they serve to define, and are not to be understood as relating to the blessings in Deut. xxviii. 1–14, and the curses in Deut. xxvii. 15–26 and xxviii. 15–68. The whole law is called "the blessing and the curse" with special reference to its contents, inasmuch as the fulfilment of it brings *eo ipso* a blessing, and the transgression of it *eo ipso* a curse. In the same manner, in Deut. xi. 26, Moses describes the exposition of the whole law in the steppes of Moab as setting before them blessing and cursing. In ver. 35 it is most distinctly stated that Joshua had the whole law read to the people; whilst the expression "all Israel," in ver. 33, is more fully explained as signifying not merely the congregation in its representatives, or even the men of the nation, but "all the congregation of Israel, with the women, and the little ones, and the strangers that were in the midst of it."

Nothing is said about the march of Joshua and all Israel to Gerizim and Ebal. All that we know is, that he not only took with him the people of war and the elders or heads of tribes, but all the people. It follows from this, however, that the whole of the people must have left and completely vacated the camp at Gilgal in the valley of the Jordan. For if all Israel went to the mountains of Gerizim and Ebal, which were situated in the midst of the land, taking even the women and children with them, it is not likely that they left their cattle and other possessions behind them in Gilgal, exposed to the danger of being plundered in the meantime by the Canaanites of the southern mountains. So again we are not informed in what follows (chap. ix. sqq.) in which direction Joshua and the people went after these solemnities at Ebal and Gerizim were over. It is certainly not stated that he went back to Gilgal

in the Jordan valley, and pitched his tent again on the old site.
No doubt we find Gilgal still mentioned as the encampment of
Israel, not only in chap. ix. 6, x. 6, 9, 15, 43, but even after the
defeat and subjugation of the Canaanites in the south and north,
when a commencement was made to distribute the land (chap. xiv.
6). But when it is asked whether this Gilgal was the place of
encampment on the east of Jericho, which received its name from
the circumcision of the whole nation which took place there, or the
town of Gilgal by the side of the terebinths of Moreh, which is
mentioned in Deut. xi. 30, and by which Moses defines the situation
of Gerizim and Ebal, this question cannot be answered unhesitat-
ingly according to the traditional view, viz. in favour of the encampment in the Jordan valley. For when not only the army, but
all the people with their wives and children, had once proceeded
from the Jordan valley to the mountains of Gerizim and Ebal, we
cannot imagine any reason why Joshua should go back again to the
plain of Jericho, that is to say, to the extreme corner of Canaan on
the east, for the purpose of making that the base of his operations
for the conquest and extermination of the Canaanites. And there
is just as much improbability in the assumption, that after Joshua
had not only defeated the kings of southern Canaan, who had
allied themselves with Adonizedek of Jerusalem in the battle
fought at Gibeon (chap. x.), but had also overthrown the kings
of northern Canaan, who were allied with Jabin of Hazor at the
waters of Merom above the Sea of Galilee (chap. xi.), he should
return again to Gilgal in the Jordan valley, and there quietly
encamp with all the people, and commence the distribution of the
land. The only thing that could bring us to assent to such
extremely improbable assumptions, would be the fact that there was
no other Gilgal in all Canaan than the encampment to the east of
Jericho, which received the name of Gilgal for the first time from
the Israelites themselves. But as the other Gilgal by the side of
the terebinths of Moreh—i.e. the present *Jiljilia*, which stands upon
an eminence on the south-west of Shiloh at about the same distance
from Jerusalem as from Sichem—was a well-known place even
in Moses' days (Deut. xi. 30), and from its situation on a lofty
ridge, from which you can see the great lowlands and the sea
towards the west, the mountains of Gilead towards the east, and
far away in the north-east even Hermon itself (*Rob.* Pal. iii. p.
81), was peculiarly well adapted for a place of encampment, from
which Joshua could carry on the conquest of the land toward both

the north and south, we can come to no other conclusion than
that this Gilgal or Jiljilia was the Gilgal mentioned in chap. ix. 6,
x. 6, 9, 15, 43, and xiv. 6, as the place where the Israelites were
encamped. We therefore assume, that after the setting up of
the law on Gerizim and Ebal, Joshua did not conduct the people
with their wives and children back again to the camp which they
had left in the Jordan valley on the other side of Jericho, but
chose the Gilgal which was situated upon the mountains, and only
seven hours' journey to the south of Sichem, as the future place of
encampment, and made this the central point of all his further
military operations; and that this was the place to which he returned
after his last campaign in the north, to commence the division
of the conquered land among the tribes of Israel (chap. xiv. 6),
and where he remained till the tabernacle was permanently erected
at Shiloh, when the further distribution was carried on there (chap.
xviii. 1 sqq.).   This view, which even *Van de Velde* (Memoir, p.
316) has adopted as probable, is favoured still further by the fact
that this Gilgal or Jiljilia, which is still a large village, is frequently
mentioned in the subsequent history of Israel, not only in 2 Kings
ii. 1 and iv. 38, as the seat of a school of the prophets in the time
of Elijah and Elisha, and in Hos. iv. 15, ix. 15, xii. 12, Amos iv. 4,
v. 5, as a place which was much frequented for the purpose of
idolatrous worship; but even at an earlier date still, namely, as one
of the places where Samuel judged the people (1 Sam. vii. 16), and
as the place where he offered sacrifice (1 Sam. x. 8 ; cf. xiii. 7–9),
and where he gathered the people together to confirm the monarchy
of Saul (1 Sam. xi. 14, 15), at a time when the tabernacle at Shiloh
had ceased to be the only national sanctuary of Israel, on account
of the ark having been taken away.   Gilgal had no doubt acquired
this significance along with Bethel, which had been regarded as a
holy place ever since the time of Jacob, from the fact that it was
there that Joshua had established the camp of Israel with the ark
of the covenant, until the land was divided, and Shiloh was appointed as the site for the national sanctuary.

STRATAGEM OF THE GIBEONITES, AND THEIR CONSEQUENT PRESERVATION.—CHAP. IX.

The victorious advance of the Israelites in the land induced
the kings of Canaan to form a common league for the purpose of
resisting them.   But, as frequently happens, the many kings and

lords of the towns and provinces of Canaan were not all united, so
as to make a common and vigorous attack. Before the league had
been entered into, the inhabitants of Gibeon, one of the largest
towns in the central part of Canaan, together with the smaller
neighbouring towns that were dependent upon it, attempted to
anticipate the danger which threatened them by means of a stratagem, and to enter into a friendly alliance with the Israelites. And
they succeeded, inasmuch as Joshua and the elders of the congregation of Israel fell into the snare that was laid for them by the
ambassadors of the Gibeonites, who came to the camp at Gilgal,
and made the desired treaty with them, without inquiring of the
Lord. "This account," as *O. v. Gerlach* says, "is a warning to the
Church of God of all ages against the cunning and dissimulation
of the world, which often seeks for a peaceable recognition on the
part of the kingdom of God, and even for a reception into it,
whenever it may be its advantage to do so."

Vers. 1, 2, form the introduction to chaps. ix.–xi., and correspond to the introduction in chap. v. 1. The news of the miraculous passage of the Israelites through the Jordan had thrown all
the kings of Canaan into such despair, that they did not venture
to make any attack upon Israel. But they gradually recovered
from their first panic, partly, no doubt, in consequence of the
failure of the first attack of the Israelites upon Ai, and resolved to
join together in making war upon the foreign invaders. The kings
of Canaan did this when they heard, *sc.* what Israel had hitherto
undertaken and accomplished, not merely "what Joshua had done
to Jericho and Ai" (*Knobel*) : that is to say, all the kings across
the Jordan, *i.e.* in the country to the west of the Jordan (עֵבֶר הַיַּרְדֵּן,
as in chap. v. 1), viz. "*upon the mountains*" (not only the mountains of Judah, as in chap. x. 40, xi. 16, etc., but all the mountains
which run throughout the whole length of Canaan, as in Deut. i. 7
and Num. xiii. 17 : see the explanation of the latter passage) ; "*in
the lowlands*" (*shephelah*, the low-lying country between the mountains and the sea-coast, which is simply intersected by small ranges
of hills ; see at Deut. i. 7) ; "*and on all the coast of the Great Sea
towards Lebanon,*" *i.e.* the narrow coast of the Mediterranean Sea
from Joppa up to the Ladder of Tyre (see at Deut. i. 7). The
different tribes of the Canaanites are also mentioned by name, as
in chap. iii. 10, except that the Girgashites are omitted. These
gathered themselves together to fight with Joshua and Israel with
one mouth, or with one accord (1 Kings xxii. 13).

Vers. 3–5. But the inhabitants of a republic, which included not only Gibeon the capital, but the towns of Chephirah, Beeroth, and Kirjath-jearim also, acted differently from the rest. *Gibeon* (Γαβάων, *Gabaon*, LXX. *Vulg.*) was larger than Ai, being one of the royal cities (chap. x. 2), and was inhabited by Hivites, who were a brave people (chap. x. 7, xi. 19). It was afterwards allotted to the tribe of Benjamin, and set apart as a Levitical town (chap. xviii. 25, xxi. 17). After the destruction of Nob by Saul, the tabernacle was removed thither, and there it remained till the building of Solomon's temple (1 Chron. xvi. 39, xxi. 29 ; 1 Kings iii. 4, 5 ; 2 Chron. i. 3 sqq.). According to *Josephus*, it was forty or fifty stadia from Jerusalem, and judging from its name was built upon a hill. It is to be found in the modern *Jib*, two good hours' journey to the north-west of Jerusalem, a village of moderate size, on a long chalk hill which overlooks a very fertile, well cultivated plain, or rather a basin, consisting of broad valleys and plains, and rises like a vineyard, in the form of separate terraces (*Strauss*, Sinai, p. 332). The remains of large massive buildings of great antiquity are still to be seen there, also some fountains, and two large subterraneous reservoirs (*vid. Rob.* Pal. ii. p. 136). When the Gibeonites heard of the fate of Jericho and Ai, they also did (something) with stratagem. In the expression נַם הֵמָּה ("*they also*") there is a reference implied to what Joshua had done at Jericho and Ai ; not, however, to the stratagem resorted to in the case of Ai, as such an allusion would not apply to Jericho. *They set out as ambassadors :* יִצְטַיָּרוּ, from צִיר, which occurs in every other instance in the form of a noun, signifying a messenger (Prov. xiii. 17, etc.). In the *Hithpael* it means to make themselves ambassadors, to travel as ambassadors. The translators of the ancient versions, however, adopted the reading יִצְטַיָּדוּ, they provided themselves with food ; but this was nothing more than a conjecture founded upon ver. 12, and without the slightest critical value. They also took " *old sacks upon their asses, and old mended wineskins.*" מְצֹרָרִים, from צָרַר, *lit.* bound together, is very characteristic. There are two modes adopted in the East of repairing skins when torn, viz. inserting a patch, or tying up the piece that is torn in the form of a bag. Here the reference is to the latter, which was most in harmony with their statement, that the skins had got injured upon their long journey. Also " *old mended sandals upon their feet, and old clothes upon them* (upon their bodies) ; *and all the bread of their provisions had become dry and quite mouldy.*" נִקֻּדִים, *lit.*

furnished with points; נָקֹד, pointed, speckled (Gen. xxx. 32 sqq.).
Hence the rendering of the LXX., εὐρωτιῶν; *Theod.*, βεβρωμένοι;
Luther schimmlicht, mouldy; whereas the rendering adopted by
Aquila is ἐψαθυρωμένος; by *Symmachus,* κάπορος, *i.e. adustus,
torridus;* and by the *Vulgate, in frusta comminuti, i.e.* crumbled.

Vers. 6–15. Having made these preparations, they went to the
Israelitish camp at Gilgal (Jiljilia), introduced themselves to the
men of Israel (אִישׁ, in a collective sense, the plural being but little
used, and only occurring in Prov. viii. 4, Isa. liii. 3, and Ps. cxli. 4)
as having come from a distant land, and asked them to make a
league with them. But the Israelites hesitated, and said to the
Hivites, *i.e.* the Gibeonites who were Hivites, that they might perhaps be living in the midst of them (the Israelites), *i.e.* in the land of
Canaan, which the Israelites already looked upon as their own; and
if so, how could they make a league with them? This hesitation
on their part was founded upon the express command of God, that
they were not to make any league with the tribes of Canaan (Ex.
xxiii. 32, xxxiv. 12; Num. xxxiii. 55; Deut. vii. 2, etc.). In reply
to this the Gibeonites simply said, " *We are thy servants*" (ver. 8),
i.e. we are at thy service, which, according to the obsequious language common in the East, was nothing more than a phrase intended to secure the favour of Joshua, and by no means implied a
readiness on their part to submit to the Israelites and pay them
tribute, as *Rosenmüller, Knobel,* and others suppose; for, as *Grotius*
correctly observes, what they wished for was " a friendly alliance,
by which both their territory and also full liberty would be secured
to themselves." Tho *Keri* וַיֹּאמֶר (ver. 7) is nothing more than a
critical conjecture, occasioned not so much by the singular אִישׁ,
which is frequently construed in the historical writings as a collective noun with a plural verb, as by the singular suffix attached to
בְּקִרְבִּי, which is to be explained on the ground that only one of the
Israelites (viz. Joshua) was speaking as the mouthpiece of all the
rest. The plural וַיֹּאמְרוּ is used, because Joshua spoke in the name
of the people.—Ver. 8. To the further question put by Joshua,
where they had come from, the Gibeonites replied, " *From a very
distant land have thy servants come, because of the name of Jehovah
thy God,*" or as they themselves proceed at once to explain: " *for
we have heard the fame (fama) of Him, and all that He did in Egypt,
and to Sihon and Og, the two kings of the Amorites.*" They very
wisely say nothing about the miracles connected with the crossing
of the Jordan and the taking of Jericho, since, " as the inhabit-

ants of a very far distant region, they could not have heard anything about things that had occurred so lately, even by report"
(*Masius*).—Vers. 11 sqq. When these tidings reached them, they
were sent off by the elders (the leaders of the republic) and the
inhabitants of the land to meet the Israelites, that they might offer
them their service, and form an alliance with them. In confirmation of this, they point to their dried provisions, and their torn and
mended skins and clothes.—Vers. 14, 15. The Israelites suffered
themselves to be taken in by this pretence. " *The men* (the elders
of Israel) *took of their provisions; but they did not ask the mouth
of the Lord.*" Instead of inquiring the will of the Lord in this
matter through the Urim and Thummim of the high priest (Num.
xxvii. 21), they contented themselves with taking some of the bread
that was shown them, and tasting it; as if the dry mouldy bread
furnished a safe guarantee of the truth of the words of these
foreign ambassadors. Some commentators regard their taking of
their provisions as a sign of mutual friendship, or of the league
which they made; but in that case their eating with them would
at any rate have been mentioned. Among the Arabs, simply eating
bread and salt with a guest is considered a sign of peace and friendship.—Ver. 15. So Joshua made (granted) them peace (*vid.* Isa.
xxvii. 5), and concluded a covenant with them (לָהֶם, in their
favour), to let them live; and the princes of the congregation sware
unto them. Letting them live is the only article of the league that
is mentioned, both because this was the main point, and also with
special reference to the fact that the Gibeonites, being Canaanites,
ought properly to have been destroyed. It is true that Joshua and
the princes of the congregation had not violated any express command of God by doing this; for the only thing prohibited in the
law was making treaties with the *Canaanites*, which they did not
suppose the Gibeonites to be, whilst in Deut. xx. 11, where wars
with foreign nations (not Canaanites) are referred to, permission is
given to make peace with them, so that all treaties with foreign
nations are not forbidden. But they had failed in this respect, that,
trusting to the crafty words of the Gibeonites, and to outward
appearances only, they had forgotten their attitude to the Lord
their God, who had promised to His congregation, in all important
matters, a direct revelation of His own will.

Vers. 16–27. Three days after the treaty had been concluded,
the Israelites discovered that they had been deceived, and that
their allies dwelt among them (see ver. 7). They set out therefore

to deal with the deceivers, and reached their towns Gibeon, Chephirah, Beeroth, and Kirjath-jearim on the third day. *Chephirah*,
which was afterwards allotted to the tribe of Benjamin along with
Gibeon and Beeroth, and was still inhabited after the captivity
(chap. xviii. 25, 26; Ezra ii. 25; Neh. vii. 29), is to be seen in the
ruins of *Kefir*, an hour's journey to the east of Yalo, in the mountains, and three hours to the west of Gibeon (see *Rob.* Bibl. Res.
p. 146, and *Van de Velde*, Memoir, pp. 303–4). *Beeroth*, Βηρώθ,
according to *Eusebius* (*Onom. s. v.*) a hamlet near Jerusalem, and
seven miles on the road to *Nicopolis* (it should read *Neapolis*), was
in the tribe of Benjamin (2 Sam. iv. 2), and still exists in the
large village of *Bireh*, which is situated upon a mountain nine
Roman miles to the north of Jerusalem in a stony and barren
district, and has still several springs and a good well, besides
the remains of a fine old church of the time of the Crusades (see
Rob. Pal. ii. pp. 130 sqq.; *Seetzen*, R. ii. pp. 195–6). *Kirjath-
jearim*, also called *Kirjath-baal* (chap. xv. 60), *Baalah* (chap. xv.
9), and *Baal-Jehuda* (2 Sam. vi. 2), was allotted to the tribe of
Judah. It stood upon the boundary between Judah and Benjamin
(chap. xv. 60, xviii. 15); and the ark remained there, after it had
been sent back by the Philistines, until the time of David (1 Sam.
vii. 2; 2 Sam. vi. 2; 1 Chron. xiii. 5, 6). According to the
Onom., s. v. Καριαθιαρείμ and Βαάλ, it was nine or ten Roman
miles from Jerusalem, on the road to Diospolis (Lydda), and is
probably to be seen in the present *Kuryet el Enab*, a considerable
village with a large number of olive trees, figs, pomegranates, and
vineyards, from the last of which the old "town of the forests" has
received the more modern name of "town of the vine" (see *Rob.*
Pal. ii. p. 335, and Bibl. Res. pp. 156–7; and *Seetzen*, ii. p. 65).
These towns, which formed one republic with Gibeon, and were
governed by elders, were at so short a distance from Gilgal (Jiljilia),
that the Israelites could reach it in one or two days. The expression
"*on the third day*" is not at variance with this; for it is not stated
that Israel took three days to march there, but simply that they
arrived there on the third day after receiving the intelligence of the
arrival of the ambassadors.—Ver. 18. "*The Israelites smote them
not,*" *sc.* with the edge of the sword, "*because the princes of the
congregation had sworn to them,*" *sc.* to let them live (ver. 15); but,
notwithstanding the murmuring of the congregation, they declared
that they might not touch them because of their oath. "*This* (*sc.*
what we have sworn) *we will do to them, and let them live* (הַחֲיֵה, *inf.*

abs. with special emphasis instead of the finite verb), *lest wrath come upon us because of the oath."* *Wrath* (*sc.* of God), a judgment such as fell upon Israel in the time of David, because Saul disregarded this oath and sought to destroy the Gibeonites (2 Sam. xxi. 1 sqq.).

But how could the elders of Israel consider themselves bound by their oath to grant to the Gibeonites the preservation of life which had been secured to them by the treaty they had made, when the very supposition upon which the treaty was made, viz. that the Gibeonites did not belong to the tribes of Canaan, was proved to be false, and the Gibeonites had studiously deceived them by pretending that they had come from a very distant land? As they had been absolutely forbidden to make any treaties with the Canaanites, it might be supposed that, after the discovery of the deception which had been practised upon them, the Israelitish rulers would be under no obligation to observe the treaty which they had made with the Gibeonites in full faith in the truth of their word. And no doubt from the stand-point of strict justice this view appears to be a right one. But the princes of Israel shrank back from breaking the oath which, as is emphatically stated in ver. 19, they had sworn by Jehovah the God of Israel, not because they assumed, as *Hauff* supposes, "that an oath simply regarded as an outward and holy transaction had an absolutely binding force," but because they were afraid of bringing the name of the God of Israel into contempt among the Canaanites, which they would have done if they had broken the oath which they had sworn by this God, and had destroyed the Gibeonites. They were bound to observe the oath which they had once sworn, if only to prevent the sincerity of the God by whom they had sworn from being rendered doubtful in the eyes of the Gibeonites; but they were not justified in taking the oath. They had done this without asking the mouth of Jehovah (ver. 14), and thus had sinned against the Lord their God. But they could not repair this fault by breaking the oath which they had thus imprudently taken, *i.e.* by committing a fresh sin; for the violation of an oath is always sin, even when the oath has been taken inconsiderately, and it is afterwards discovered that what was sworn to was not in accordance with the will of God, and that an observance of the oath will certainly be hurtful (*vid.* Ps. xv. 4).[1] By taking an oath to the ambassadors that they

---

[1] "The binding power of an oath ought to be held so sacred among us, that we should not swerve from our bond under any pretence of error, even though we had been deceived: since the sacred name of God is of greater worth than all the riches of the world. Even though a person should have sworn therefore

would let the Gibeonites live, the princes of Israel had acted unconsciously in violation of the command of God that they were to destroy the Canaanites. As soon therefore as they discovered their error or their oversight, they were bound to do all in their power to ward off from the congregation the danger which might arise of their being drawn away to idolatry—the very thing which the Lord had intended to avert by giving that command. If this could by any possibility be done without violating their oath, they were bound to do it for the sake of the name of the Lord by which they swore ; that is to say, while letting the Gibeonites live, it was their duty to put them in such a position, that they could not possibly seduce the Israelites to idolatry. And this the princes of Israel proposed to do, by granting to the Gibeonites on the one hand the preservation of their lives according to the oath they had taken, and on the other hand by making them slaves of the sanctuary. That they acted rightly in this respect, is evident from the fact that their conduct is never blamed either by the historian or by the history, inasmuch as it is not stated anywhere that the Gibeonites, after being made into temple slaves, held out any inducement to the Israelites to join in idolatrous worship, and still more from the fact, that at a future period God himself reckoned the attempt of Saul to destroy the Gibeonites, in his false zeal for the children of Israel, as an act of blood-guiltiness on the part of the nation of Israel for which expiation must be made (2 Sam. xxi. 1 sqq.), and conse- quently approved of the observance of the oath which had been sworn to them, though without thereby sanctioning the treaty itself.

Ver. 21. The princes declared again most emphatically, " *They shall live*." Thus the Gibeonites became hewers of wood and drawers of water to the congregation, as the princes had said to them, *i.e.* had resolved concerning them. This resolution they communicated to the congregation at the time, using the expression יִחְיוּ (*let them live*) ; but the historian has passed this over at ver. 21*a*, and instead of mentioning the resolution proceeds at once to describe its execu- tion.—Vers. 22, 23. Joshua then summoned the Gibeonites, charged them with their deceit, and pronounced upon them the curse of

without sufficient consideration, no injury or loss will release him from his oath." This is the opinion expressed by *Calvin* with reference to Ps. xv. 4 ; yet for all that he regards the observance of their oath on the part of the princes of Israel as a sin, because he limits this golden rule in the most arbitrary manner to private affairs alone, and therefore concludes that the Israelites were not bound to observe this " wily treaty."

eternal servitude : " *There shall not be cut off from you a servant,*" *i.e.*
ye shall never cease to be servants, ye shall remain servants for over
(*vid.* 2 Sam. iii. 29 ; 1 Kings ii. 4), " *and that as hewers of wood
and drawers of waters for our God's house.*" This is a fuller definition of the expression " for all the congregation" in ver. 21. The
Gibeonites were to perform for the congregation the slaves' labour
of hewing wood and drawing water for the worship of the sanctuary,
—a duty which was performed, according to Deut. xxix. 10, by the
lowest classes of the people. In this way the curse of Noah upon
Canaan (Gen. ix. 25) was literally fulfilled upon the Hivites of the
Gibeonitish republic.—Vers. 24, 25. The Gibeonites offered this
excuse for their conduct, that having heard of the command of God
which had been issued through Moses, that all the Canaanites were
to be destroyed (Deut. vii. 1, xx. 16, 17), they had feared greatly
for their lives, and readily submitted to the resolution which
Joshua made known to them.—Vers. 26, 27. " *And so did he
unto them, and delivered them out of the hand of the children of
Israel, that they slew them not. He made them hewers of wood and
drawers of water for the congregation, and indeed for the altar of the
Lord,*" (assigning them) " *to the place which God would choose,*"
viz. for the altar. אֶל־הַמָּקוֹם (to the place) is grammatically dependent upon וַיִּתְּנֵם (he " gave them "). It by no means follows,
however, that Joshua sent them there at that very time, but simply
that he sentenced them to service at the altar in the place which
would be chosen for the sanctuary. From the words " *unto this
day,*" it no doubt follows, on the one hand, that the account was
written after the fact had taken place ; but, on the other hand, it
also follows from the future יִבְחַר (should, or shall choose), that it
was written before the place was definitely fixed, and therefore
before the building of Solomon's temple.

VICTORY AT GIBEON, AND CONQUEST OF SOUTHERN CANAAN.— CHAP. X.

Vers. 1–5. The report that Joshua had taken Ai, and put it,
like Jericho, under the ban, and that the Gibeonites had concluded
a treaty with Israel, filled Adonizedek the king of Jerusalem with
alarm, as Gibeon was a large town, like one of the king's towns,
even larger than Ai, and its inhabitants were brave men. He
therefore joined with the kings of Hebron, Jarmuth, Lachish, and
Eglon, to make a common attack upon Gibeon, and punish it for

its alliance with the Israelites, and at the same time to put a check upon the further conquests of Israel. *Adonizedek, i.e.* lord of righteousness, is synonymous with *Melchizedek* (king of righteousness), and was a title of the Jebusite kings, as Pharaoh was of the Egyptian. *Jerusalem, i.e.* the founding or possession of peace, called *Salem* in the time of Abraham (Gen. xiv. 18), was the proper name of the town, which was also frequently called by the name of its Canaanitish inhabitants *Jebus* (Judg. xix. 10, 11; 1 Chron. xi. 4), or "city of the Jebusites" (*Ir-Jebusi*, Judg. xix. 11), sometimes also in a contracted form, *Jebusi* (הַיְבוּסִי, chap. xviii. 16, 28, xv. 8; 2 Sam. v. 8).[1] On the division of the land it was allotted to the tribe of Benjamin (chap. xviii. 28); but being situated upon the border of Judah (chap. xv. 8), it was conquered, and burned by the sons of Judah after the death of Joshua (Judg. i. 8). It was very soon taken again and rebuilt by the Jebusites, whom the sons of Judah were unable to destroy (Judg. xv. 63, xix. 12), so that both Benjaminites and Judahites lived there along with the Jebusites (Judg. i. 21, xv. 63); and the upper town especially, upon the summit of Mount Zion, remained as a fortification in the possession of the Jebusites, until David conquered it (2 Sam. v. 6 sqq.), made it the capital of his kingdom, and called it by his own name, "the city of David," after which the old name of Jebus fell into disuse. *Hebron*, the town of *Arba* the Anakite (chap. xiv. 15, etc.; see at Gen. xxiii. 2), was twenty-two Roman miles south of Jerusalem, in a deep and narrow valley upon the mountains of Judah, a town of the greatest antiquity (Num. xiii. 22), now called *el Khalil, i.e.* the friend (of God), with reference to Abraham's sojourn there. The ruins of an ancient heathen temple are still to be seen there, as well as the Haram, built of colossal blocks, which contains, according to Mohammedan tradition, the burial-place of the patriarchs (see at Gen. xxiii. 17). *Jarmuth*, in the lowlands of Judah (chap. xv. 35; Neh. xi. 29), according to the *Onom.* (*s. v. Jermus*) a hamlet, *Jermucha* (Ἱερμοχῶς), ten Roman miles from Eleutheropolis, on the road to Jerusalem, is the modern *Jarmuk*, a village on a lofty hill, with the remains of walls and cisterns of a very ancient date, the name of which, according to *Van de Velde* (Mem. pp. 115–6), is pronounced *Tell 'Armuth* by the Arabs (see *Rob.* Pal. ii. p. 344). *Lachish*, in the lowlands of Judah (chap. xv. 39), was fortified

---

[1] In our English version, we have the Hebrew word itself simply transposed in Joshua xviii. 16, 28; whilst it is rendered "the Jebusite" in chap. xv. 8, and "the Jebusites" in 2 Sam. v. 8.—Tr.

by Rehoboam (2 Chron. xi. 9), and besieged by Sennacherib and Nebuchadnezzar (2 Kings xviii. 14, xix. 8; Jer. xxxiv. 7), and was still inhabited by Jews after the return from the captivity (Neh xi. 30). It is probably to be found in *Um Lakis,* an old place upon a low round hill, covered with heaps of small round stones thrown together in great confusion, containing relics of marble columns; it is about an hour and a quarter to the west of Ajlun, and seven hours to the west of Eleutheropolis.[1] *Eglon :* also in the lowlands of Judah (chap. xv. 39). The present name is *Ajlân,* a heap of ruins, about three-quarters of an hour to the east of Um Lakis (see *Rob.* Pal. ii. p. 392, and *Van de Velde,* Mem. p. 308). In the *Onom.* (*s. v. Eglon*) it is erroneously identified with *Odollam ;* whereas the situation of *Agla,* " at the tenth stone, as you go from Eleutheropolis to Gaza" (*Onom. s. v.* Βηθαλαίμ, *Bethagla*), suits *Eglon* exactly.—Ver. 5. These five kings marched against Gibeon and besieged the town. The king of Jerusalem headed the expedition, as his town was so near to Gibeon that he was the first to fear an attack from the Israelites.

Vers. 6–11. The Gibeonites then sent to Joshua to the camp at Gilgal, and entreated him to come to his help as speedily as possible. " *Slack not thy hand from thy servants,*" *i.e.* withhold not thy help from us. The definition appended to "the kings of the Amorites" ("*that dwelt in the mountains*") is to be understood *a potiori,* and does not warrant us in drawing the conclusion, that all the towns mentioned in ver. 3 were in the mountains of Judah. The Amorites who dwelt in the mountains were the strongest of all the Canaanites.—Ver. 7. In accordance with this petition Joshua advanced from Gilgal (יעל, not went up) with all the people of war, even (*vav. expl.*) all the men of valour.—Ver. 8. The Lord then renewed the assurance of His help in this particular war, in which Joshua was about to fight for the first time with several allied kings of Canaan (cf. chap. ii. 24, vi. 2, viii. 1, 18).—Ver. 9. Joshua came

---

[1] It is true that *Robinson* disputes the identity of *Um Lakis* with the ancient *Lachish* (Pal. ii. p. 388), but " not on any reasonable ground " (*Van de Velde,* Mem. p. 320). The statement in the *Onom.* (*s. v. Lochis*), that it was seven Roman miles to the south of Eleutheropolis, cannot prove much, as it may easily contain an error in the number, and *Robinson* does not admit its authority even in the case of Eglon (Pal. ii. p. 392). Still less can *Knobel's* conjecture be correct, that it is to be found in the old place called *Sukkarijeh,* two hours and a half to the south-west of Beit Jibrin (Eleutheropolis), as *Sukkarijeh* is on the east of Ajlun, whereas, according to vers. 31–36, Lachish is to be sought for on the west of Eglon.

suddenly upon them (the enemy), as he had marched the whole night from Gilgal, *i.e.* had accomplished the entire distance in a night. Jiljilia is fully fifteen miles from el-Jib.—Ver. 10. " *Jehovah threw them into confusion,*" as He had promised in Ex. xxiii. 27, and in all probability, judging from ver. 11, by dreadful thunder and lightning (*vid.* 1 Sam. vii. 10; Ps. xviii. 15, cxliv. 6: it is different in Ex. xiv. 24). " *Israel smote them in a great slaughter at Gibeon, and pursued them by the way of the ascent of Bethhoron,*" *i.e.* Upper Bethhoron (*Beit Ur, el-Foka*), which was nearest to Gibeon, only four hours distant on the north-west, on a lofty promontory between two valleys, one on the north, the other on the south, and was separated from Lower Bethhoron, which lies further west, by a long steep pass, from which the ascent to Upper Bethhoron is very steep and rocky, though the rock has been cut away in many places now, and a path made by means of steps (see *Rob.* Pal. iii. p. 59). This pass between the two places leads downwards from Gibeon towards the western plain, and was called sometimes the ascent, or going up to Bethhoron, and sometimes the descent, or going down from it (ver. 11), ἀνάβασις καὶ κατάβασις Βαιθωρῶν (1 Macc. iii. 16, 24). Israel smote the enemy still further, " *to Azekah and Makkedah:*" so far were they pursued and beaten after the battle (cf. vers. 16, 21). If we compare ver. 11, according to which the enemy was smitten, from Bethhoron to Azekah, by a violent fall of hail, it is very evident that the two places were on the west of Beth-horon. And it is in perfect harmony with this that we find both places described as being in the lowland; Azekah in the hill-country between the mountains and the plain (chap. xv. 35), Makkedah in the plain itself (chap. xv. 41). *Azekah,* which was fortified by Rehoboam (2 Chron. xi. 9), besieged by Nebuchadnezzar (Jer. xxxiv. 7), and still inhabited after the captivity (Neh. xi. 30), was not far from Socoh, according to chap. xv. 35; whilst sideways between the two was *Ephes-dammim* (1 Sam. xvii. 1). *Van de Velde* has discovered the latter in the ruins of *Damûm,* about an hour's journey east by south from Beit Nettif (Mem. p. 290), and consequently imagines that *Azekah* is to be found in the village of *Ahbek,* which stands upon a lofty mountain-top a mile and a half to the north of Damûm, and about four or five miles N.N.E. of Shuweikeh, supposing this to be *Aphek.* The statement in the *Onom.* (*s. v.* Ἀζηκά), ἀνάμεσον Ἐλευθεροπόλεως καὶ Αἰλίας, agrees with this. *Makkedah* is described in the *Onom.* as being eight Roman miles to the east of Eleutheropolis, and hence *Knobel* supposes it to have been near *Terkumieh*, or *Morak*; but he is wrong in his supposition, as in that case it would have been in the hill-country or upon the mountains, whereas it was one of the towns in the plain (chap. xv. 41). *Van de Velde's* conjecture (p. 332) is a much more probable one, viz. that it is to be found in *Summeil*, a considerable village on an eminence in the plain, with a large public well 110 feet deep and 11 feet in diameter, with strongly built walls of hewn stones, where there is also part of an old wall, which to all appearance must formerly have belonged to a large square castle built of unce-mented stones, resembling in some respects the oldest foundation wall of Beit Jibrin (*Rob.* Pal. ii. p. 368). It is two hours and a half to the north-west of Beit Jibrin, and there *Van de Velde* dis-covered the large cave (see at ver. 16), which *Robinson* has not observed (see his Journey through Syria and Palestine).—Ver. 11. The large stones which the Lord threw upon the flying foe at the slope of Bethhoron were hail-stones (see Isa. xxx. 30), not stone-hail, or a shower of stones, but a terrible hail-storm, in which hail fell upon the foe in pieces as large as stones (see Wisd. xlvi. 6), and slew a greater number of them than the swords of the Israel-ites. This phenomenon, which resembled the terrible hail in Egypt (Ex. ix. 24), was manifestly a miraculous occurrence produced by the omnipotent power of God, inasmuch as the hail-stones slew the enemy without injuring the Israelites, who were pursuing them. By this the Israelites were to be made to see that it was not their own power, but the supernatural help of their God, which had given them the victory; whilst the enemy discovered that it was not only the people of Israel, but the God of Israel, that had devoted them to destruction.

Vers. 12-15. In firm reliance upon the promise of God (ver. 8), Joshua offered a prayer to the Lord during the battle, that He would not let the sun go down till Israel had taken vengeance upon their foes; and the Lord hearkened to the prayer of His servant, and the sun hastened not to go down till the defeat of the Amorites was accomplished. This miraculous victory was celebrated by the Israelites in a war-song, which was preserved in the " *book of the Righteous.*" The author of the book of Joshua has introduced the passage out of this book which celebrates the mighty act of the Lord for the glorification of His name upon Israel, and their foes the Amorites. It is generally admitted, that vers. 12-15 contain a quotation from the " book of Jasher," mentioned in ver. 13. This quotation, and the reference to the work itself, are analogous to the notice of " the book of the wars of the Lord," in Num. xxi. 14, and to the strophes of a song which are there interwoven with the historical narrative ; the object being, not to confirm the historical account by referring to an earlier source, but simply to set forth before other generations the powerful impression which was made upon the congregation by these mighty acts of the Lord. The " *book of Jasher,*" *i.e.* book of the upright, or righteous man, that is to say, of the true members of the theocracy, or godly men. יָשָׁר (*Jasher,* the righteous) is used to denote the genuine Israelite, in the same sense as in Num. xxiii. 10, where Balaam calls the Israelites " the righteous," inasmuch as Jehovah, the righteous and upright one (Deut. xxxii. 4), had called them to be His people, and to walk in His righteousness. In addition to this passage, the " book of the righteous (*Jasher*)" is also mentioned in 2 Sam. i. 18, as a work in which was to be found David's elegy upon Saul and Jonathan. From this fact it has been justly inferred, that the book was a collection of odes in praise of certain heroes of the theocracy, with historical notices of their achievements interwoven, and that the collection was formed by degrees ; so that the reference to this work is neither a proof that the passage has been interpolated by a *later* hand, nor that the work was composed at a very late period. That the passage quoted from this work is extracted from a song, is evident enough, both from the poetical form of the composition, and also from the parallelism of the sentences. The quotation, however, does not begin with וַיֹּאמֶר (*and he said*) in ver. 12*b*, but with בְּיוֹם תֵּת (*in the day when the Lord delivered*) in ver. 12*a*, and vers. 13 and 14 also form part of it ; so that the title of the book from which the quotation is taken is inserted in the middle of the quotation itself. In other cases, unquestionably, such formulas of quotation are placed either at the beginning (as in Num. xxi. 14, 27 ; 2 Sam. i. 18), or else at the close of the account, which is frequently the case in the books of Kings and Chronicles ; but it by no means follows that there were no exceptions to this rule, especially as the reason for mentioning the original sources is a totally different one in the books of Kings, where the works cited are not the simple vouchers for the facts related, but works containing fuller and more elaborate accounts of events which have only been cursorily described. The poetical form of the passage in ver. 13 also leaves no doubt whatever that vers. 13 and 14 contain the words of the old poet, and are not a prose comment made by the historian upon the poetical passage quoted. The only purely his-

torical statement is ver. 15 ; and this is repeated in ver. 43, at the
close of the account of the wars and the victory. But this literal
repetition of ver. 15 in ver. 43, and the fact that the statement, that
Joshua returned with all the people to the camp at Gilgal, anticipates the historical course of the events in a very remarkable
manner, render it highly probable, if not absolutely certain, that
ver. 15 was also taken from the book of the righteous.

In the day when Jehovah delivered up the Amorites to the
children of Israel (" before," as in Deut. ii. 31, 33, etc.), Joshua
said before the eyes (*i.e.* in the presence) of Israel, so that the
Israelites were witnesses of his words (*vid.* Deut. xxxi. 7) : " *Sun,
stand still* (wait) *at Gibeon ; and, Moon, in the valley of Ajalon.*"
דָּמַם, to be silent, to keep one's self quiet or still, to wait (1 Sam. xiv.
9). The address to the sun and moon implies that they both of them
stood, or were visible in the heavens at the time ; and inasmuch as
it was spoken to the Lord, involves a prayer that the Lord and
Creator of the world would not suffer the sun and moon to set till
Israel had taken vengeance upon its foes. This explanation of the
prayer is only to be found, it is true, in the statement that the
sun and moon stood still at Joshua's word ; but we must imagine it
as included in the prayer itself. גּוֹי without an article, when used
to denote the people of Israel, is to be regarded as a poetical
expression. In the sequel (ver. 13*b*) the sun only is spoken of :
" *and the sun stood still in the midst of heaven, and hasted not to go
down about a whole day.*" The poetical word אוּץ, to press or hurry,
is founded upon the idea that the sun runs its course like a strong
man, with vigour, and without weariness or cessation (Ps. xix. 6, 7).
It follows from this, that Joshua merely prayed for the day to be
lengthened, *i.e.* for the setting of the sun to be delayed ; and that
he included the moon (ver. 12), simply because it was visible at the
time. But even if this is the case, we are not therefore to conclude,
as *C. v. Lapide, Clericus,* and others have done, that Joshua spoke
these words in the afternoon, when the sun was beginning to set,
and the moon had already risen. The expression בַּחֲצִי הַשָּׁמַיִם, " *in
the half,*" *i.e.* the midst, " *of the sky,*" is opposed to this view, and
still more the relative position of the two in the sky, the sun at
Gibeon and the moon in the valley of Ajalon, *i.e.* in the fine broad
basin on the north side of *Yalo* (see at chap. xix. 42), the present
Merj Ibn Omeir (*Rob.* iii. pp. 63, 64), which is four hours' journey
to the west of Gibeon. As Joshua smote the enemy at Gibeon,
and they fled to the south-west, he was no doubt on the west of

Gibeon when he commanded the sun and moon to stand still ; and therefore from his point of view the sun would be in the east when it stood over Gibeon, and the moon in the far west when it stood over the valley of Ajalon. But that could only be the case before noon, a few hours after sunrise, when the moon had not yet set in the western sky. In all probability the battle took place quite early in the morning, as Joshua had marched from Gilgal the night before, and fell quite suddenly upon the enemy (ver. 9). But after the conflict had lasted for some hours, and Joshua began to be anxious lest he should be unable to overcome the enemy before night came on, he addressed the prayer to the Lord to lengthen out the day, and in a short time saw his prayer so far fulfilled, that the sun still stood high up in the sky when the enemy was put to flight. We take for granted that these words were spoken by Joshua before the terrible hail-storm which fell upon the enemy in their flight, when they were near Bethhoron, which is about two hours from Gibeon, and smote them to Azekah. There is nothing to prevent our assuming this. The fact, that in the historical account the hail is mentioned before the desire expressed by Joshua and the fulfilment of that desire, may be explained on the simple ground, that the historian, following the order of importance, relates the principal incident in connection with the battle first, before proceeding to the special point to be cited from the book of the righteous. כְּיוֹם תָּמִים, " towards (about, or as it were) a whole day," neither signifies " when the day was ended" (Clericus), nor "as it usually does when the day is perfected or absolutely finished" (Rosenmüller); but the sun did not hasten or press to go down, delayed its setting, almost a whole day (" day" being the time between sunrise and sunset).

What conception are we to form of this miraculous event ? It is not stated that the sun actually stood still in one spot in the heavens,—say, for instance, in the zenith. And if the expression, " the sun stood still in the midst of heaven," which is added as an explanation of וַיִּדֹּם, is so pressed as to mean that the sun was miraculously stopped in its course, this is hardly reconcilable with לֹא אָץ לָבוֹא, "it hasted not to go down," as these words, if taken literally, merely denote a slower motion on the part of the sun, as many of the Rabbins have observed. All that is clearly affirmed in vers. 12 and 13 is, that at Joshua's word the sun remained standing in the sky for almost a whole day longer. To this there is added, in ver. 14, "*There was no day like that before it, or after it, that*

Jehovah hearkened to the voice of a man ; for Jehovah fought for Israel." This expression must not be pressed too far, as the analogous passages (" there was none like him," etc.) in 2 Kings xviii. 5 and xxiii. 25 clearly show. They merely express this thought: no other day like this, which God so miraculously lengthened, ever occurred either before or afterwards. So much, therefore, is obvious enough from the words, that the writer of the old song, and also the author of the book of Joshua, who inserted the passage in his narrative, were convinced that the day was miraculously prolonged. At the same time, it must be borne in mind that it is not stated that God lengthened that day at the request of Joshua almost an entire day, or that He made the sun stand still almost a whole day, but simply that God hearkened to the voice of Joshua, *i.e.* did not permit the sun to go down till Israel had avenged itself upon its enemies. This distinction is not without importance : for a miraculous prolongation of the day would take place not only if the sun's course or sun's setting was delayed for several hours by the omnipotent power of God, and the day extended from twelve to eighteen or twenty hours, but also if the day seemed to Joshua and all Israel to be miraculously prolonged ; because the work accomplished on that day was so great, that it would have required almost two days to accomplish it without supernatural aid. It is not easy to decide between these two opposite views ; in fact, it is quite impossible if we go to the root of the matter. When we are not in circumstances to measure the length of the day by the clock, it is very easy to mistake its actual length, especially in the midst of the pressure of business or work. The Israelites at that time had neither sun-clocks nor any other kind of clock; and during the confusion of the battle it is hardly likely that Joshua, or any one else who was engaged in the conflict, would watch the shadow of the sun and its changes, either by a tree or any other object, so as to discover that the sun had actually stood still, from the fact that for hours the shadow had neither moved nor altered in length. Under such circumstances, therefore, it was quite impossible for the Israelites to decide whether it was in reality, or only in their own imagination, that the day was longer than others. To this there must be added the poetical character of the verses before us. When David celebrates the miraculous deliverance which he had received from the Lord, in these words, " In my distress I called upon the Lord. . . . He heard my voice out of His temple. . . . He bowed the heavens also, and came down. . . . He sent from above, He took me, He drew me out of many waters" (Ps. xviii. 7-17), who would ever think of interpreting the words literally, and supposing them to mean that God actually came down from the sky, and stretched out His hand to draw David out of the water? Or who would understand the words of Deborah, "They fought from heaven, the stars in their courses fought against Sisera" (Judg. v. 20), in their literal sense? The truthfulness of such utterances is to be sought for in the subjective sphere of religious intuition, and not in a literal interpretation of the words. And it may be just the same with these verses, without their actual contents being affected, if the day was merely *subjectively* lengthened,—that is to say, in the religious conviction of the Israelites. But even if the words really affirmed that a miraculous and objective lengthening of the day did actually take place, we should have no reason whatever for questioning the credibility of the statement. All the objections that have been raised with reference to the reality or possibility of such a miracle, prove to have no force when we examine the subject more closely. Thus, for example, the objection that the annals of the other nations of the earth contain no account of any such miracle, which must have extended over the whole world, loses all its significance from the simple fact that there are no annals in existence belonging to other nations and reaching back to that time, and that it is altogether doubtful whether the miracle would extend far beyond the limits of Palestine. Again, an appeal to the unchangeableness of the motions of the stars according to eternal and unchangeable laws, is not adapted to prove the impossibility of such a miracle. The eternal laws of nature are nothing more than phenomena, or forms of manifestation, of those divine creative powers, the true character of which no mortal has ever fathomed. And does not the almighty Creator and Upholder of nature and all its forces possess the power so to direct and govern the working of these forces, as to make them subservient to the realization of His purposes of salvation? And lastly, the objection that a sudden stoppage of the revolution of the earth upon its axis would have dashed to pieces all the works of human hands that were to be found upon its surface, and hurled the earth itself, with its satellite the moon, out of their orbits, cannot prove anything, because it leaves out of sight the fact that the omnipotent hand of God, which not only created the stars, but gave them the power to revolve with such regularity in their orbits as long as this universe endures, and which upholds and governs all things in heaven and on earth, is not too short to guard against any such disastrous consequences as these. But to this we may add, that even the strictest and most literal interpretation of the words does not require us to assume, as the fathers and earlier theologians did, that the sun itself was miraculously made to stand still, but simply supposes an optical stopping of the sun in its course,—that is to say, a miraculous suspension of the revolution of the earth upon its axis, which would make it appear to the eye of an observer as if the sun itself were standing still. *Knobel* is by no means warranted in pronouncing this view of the matter an assumption at variance with the text. For the Scriptures speak of the things of the visible world as they appear ; just as we speak of the sun as rising and setting, although we have no doubt whatever about the revolution of the earth. Moreover, the omnipotence of God might produce such an optical stoppage of the sun, or rather a continuance of the visibility of the sun above the horizon, by celestial phenomena which are altogether unknown to us or to naturalists in general, without interfering with the general laws affecting the revolution of the heavenly bodies. Only we must not attempt, as some have done, to reduce the whole miracle of divine omnipotence to an unusual refraction of the light, or to the continuance of lightning throughout the whole night.

Vers. 16–27. The five kings fled and hid themselves in the cave that was at Makkedah. When they were discovered there, Joshua ordered large stones to be rolled before the entrance to the cave, and men to be placed there to watch, whilst the others pursued the enemy without ceasing, and smote their rear (*vid.* Deut. xxv. 18), and prevented their entering into their cities. He himself remained at Makkedah (ver. 21).—Vers. 20, 21. When the great battle and the pursuit of the enemy were ended, and such as remained had reached their fortified towns, the people returned to the camp to Joshua at Makkedah in peace, *i.e.* without being attacked by anybody. " *There pointed not* (a dog) *its tongue against the sons of Israel, against any one*" (see at Ex. xi. 7). לְאִישׁ is in apposition to לִבְנֵי יִשְׂרָאֵל, and serves to define it more precisely. It is possible, however, to regard the לְ as a copyist's error, as *Houbigant* and *Maurer* do, in which case אִישׁ would be the nominative to the verb. —Vers. 22–27. Joshua then commanded the five kings to be fetched out of the cave, and directed the leaders of the army to set their feet upon the necks of the kings ; and when this had been done, he ordered the kings to be put to death, and to be hanged upon trees until the evening, when their bodies were to be thrown into the cave in which they had concealed themselves. Of course this did not take place till the day after the battle, as the army could not return from their pursuit of the foe to the camp at Makkedah till the night after the battle; possibly it did not take place till the second day, if the pursuit had lasted any longer. In ver. 24, *" all the men of Israel"* are all the warriors in the camp. הֶהָלְכוֹא, with הֶ artic., instead of the relative pronoun (see *Ges.* §109; *Ew.* § 331, *b.*); and the ending וא for וּ or ן, as in Isa. xxviii. 12 (see *Ew.* § 190, *b.*). The fact that the military leaders set their feet at Joshua's command upon the necks of the conquered kings, was not a sign of barbarity, which it is necessary to excuse by comparing it with still greater barbarities on the part of the Canaanites, as in Judg. i. 7, but was a symbolical act, a sign of complete subjugation, which was customary in this sense even in the Eastern empire (see *Bynæus de calceis*, p. 318, and *Constant. Porphyrogen de cerimon. aulæ Byzant.* ii. 19). It was also intended in this instance to stimulate the Israelites to further conflict with the Canaanites. This is stated in the words of Joshua (ver. 25): *" Fear not, nor be dismayed (vid.* chap. i. 9, viii. 1); *for thus shall the Lord do to all your enemies."* On the putting to death and then hanging, see chap. viii. 29 and Deut. xxi. 22, 23. The words וַיְשִׂימוּ וגו׳ (ver. 27*b*) are generally understood as signifying, that after the bodies of the kings had been cast into the cave, the Israelites placed large stones before the entrance, just as in other cases heaps of stones were piled upon the graves of criminals that had been executed (*vid.* chap. vii. 25), and that these stones remained there till the account before us was written. But this leaves the words עַד עֶצֶם unexplained, as עֶצֶם never occurs in any other case where the formula " until this day " is used with the simple meaning that a thing had continued to the writer's own time. עֶצֶם הַיּוֹם הַזֶּה expresses the thought that the day referred to was the very same day about which the author was writing, and no other (see chap. v. 11; Gen. vii. 13, xvii. 23; Ex. xii. 17, etc.). If, therefore, it has any meaning at all in the present instance, we must connect the whole clause with the one preceding, and even construe it as a relative clause: *" where they* (the kings) *had hidden themselves, and they* (the Israelites) *had placed large stones at the mouth of the cave until that very day"* (on which the kings were fetched out and executed).

Vers. 28–39. Further prosecution of the victory, by the conquest of the fortified towns of the south, into which those who

escaped the sword of the Israelites had thrown themselves.—Ver. 28.
On the same day on which the five kings were impaled, Joshua
took Makkedah (see at ver. 10), and smote the town and its king
with the edge of the sword, banning the town and all the persons
in it, *i.e.* putting all the inhabitants to death (many MSS. and some
editions adopt the reading אתה for אתם, as in ver. 37), taking the
cattle and the property in the town as booty, as in the case of Ai
(chap. viii. 27, 28), and treating its king like the king of Jericho,
who was suspended upon a stake, to judge from chap. viii. 2, 29,
although this is not stated in chap. vi.—Vers. 29, 30. From Makkedah he went with all Israel, *i.e.* all the men of war, against *Libnah*,
and after effecting the conquest of it, did just the same as he had
done to Makkedah.   *Libnah* was one of the towns of the plain or
of the hill-country of Judah (chap. xv. 42) ; it was allotted to the
priests (chap. xxi. 13), revolted from Judah in the reign of Joram
(2 Kings viii. 22), and was besieged by Sennacherib (Isa. xxxvii. 8).
It is to be sought on the north-west of Lachish, not on the south
as *Knobel* erroneously infers from Isa. xxxvii. 8.   According to the
Onom. (*s. v. Lebna*), it was at that time *villa in regione Eleuthero-*
politana, quæ appellatur Lobna.   It has not been discovered yet ;
but according to the very probable conjecture of *V. de Velde* (Mem.
p. 330), the ruins of it may perhaps be seen upon the hill called
Arâk el Menshiyeh, about two hours to the west of Beit Jibrin.[1]—
Vers. 31, 32.   *Lachish, i.e. Um Lakis* (see at ver. 3), shared the same
fate.—Ver. 33.   Joshua also smote the king of *Gezer*, who had come
with his people to the help of Lachish, and left no one remaining.
Nothing is said about the capture of the town of Gezer.   According
to chap. xvi. 10 and Judg. i. 29, it was still in the possession of the
Canaanites when the land was divided, though this alone is not
sufficient to prove that Joshua did not conquer it, as so many of the
conquered towns were occupied by the Canaanites again after the
Israelites had withdrawn.   But its situation makes it very probable
that Joshua did not conquer it at that time, as it was too much out
of his road, and too far from Lachish.   *Gezer* (LXX. Γάζερ, in
1 Chron. xiv. 16 Γαζηρά, in 1 Macc. Γαζήρα or Γάζαρα plur., in

---

[1] *Knobel* is decidedly wrong in his supposition, that *Libnah* is to be seen in
the considerable ruins called *Hora*, which lie in the plain (*Seetzen* and *V. de
Velde*) and are called *Hawara* by *Robinson*.   He founds his conjecture upon
the fact that the name signifies *white*, and is the Arabic translation of the
Hebrew name.   But *Hora* is only two hours and a half to the north of Beersheba,
and is not in the plain at all, but in the Negeb.

Josephus Γάζαρα, Ant. vii. 4, 1, viii. 6, 1, and also Γάδαρα, v. 1, 22, xii. 7, 4) was on the southern boundary of Ephraim (chap. xvi. 3), and was given up by that tribe to the Levites (chap. xvi. 9, 10, xxi. 20, 21. It is very frequently mentioned. David pursued the Philistines to Gezer (Gazer), after they had been defeated at Gibeon or Geba (2 Sam. v. 25 ; 1 Chron. xiv. 16). At a later period it was conquered by Pharaoh, and presented to his daughter, who was married to Solomon ; and Solomon built, *i.e.* fortified it (1 Kings ix. 16, 17). It was an important fortress in the wars of the Maccabees (1 Macc. ix. 52 ; 2 Macc. x. 32 ; cf. 1 Macc. iv. 15, vii. 45, xiii. 53, xiv. 34, xv. 28, 35). According to the *Onom.* (*s. v. Gazer*), it was four Roman miles to the north of Nicopolis, *i.e.* Anwas, and was called Γαζάρα. This is not only in harmony with chap. xvi. 3, according to which the southern border of Ephraim ran from Lower Bethhoron to Gezer, and then on to the sea, but also with all the other passages in which Gezer is mentioned,[1] and answers very well to the situation of *el Kubab*, a village of considerable size on a steep hill at the extreme north of the mountain

[1] The statement in 1 Macc. vii. 45, that Judas Maccabæus pursued the army of Nicanor, which had been beaten at Adasa, for a day's journey, as far as Gazera (" a day's journey from Adasa into Gazera"), is perfectly reconcilable with the situation of *el Kubab;* for, according to *Josephus* (Ant. xii. 10, 5), Adasa was thirty stadia from Bethhoron, and Bethhoron is ten miles to the west of Kubab (measuring in a straight line upon the map); so that Judas pursued the enemy fifteen miles —a distance which might very well be called " a day's journey," if we consider that the enemy, when flying, would not always take the straightest road, and might even make a stand at intervals, and so delay their pursuers. Still less do the statement in 1 Macc. xiv. 34, that Simon fortified Joppa on the sea, and Gazara on the border of Ashdod, the combination of Joppa, Gazara, and the tower that is in Jerusalem (1 Macc. xv. 28, 35), and the fact that the country of Gadaris, with the town of Gadara, occurs between Joppa and Jamnia in *Strabo* xvi. 759, warrant us in making a distinction between Gazara (Gezer) and the place mentioned in the *Onom.*, as *Grimm* does (on 1 Macc. iv. 15), and identifying it with the village of *Jazûr*, an hour and a half from Jaffa, although *Arvieux* calls this village *Gesser*. The objections of *Van de Velde* against the identity of Kubab and Gazer are without any force. It does not necessarily follow from the expression " went up," that Lachish stood on higher ground than Gezer, as going up often signifies nothing more than making a hostile attack upon a fortification. And no importance can be attached to the conjecture, that with the great distance of Kubab from Um Lakis, the king of Gezer would have come to the help of the kings of Makkedah and Libnah, who were much nearer and were attacked first, as the circumstances which determined his conduct are too thoroughly unknown to us, for it to be possible to pronounce an opinion upon the subject with any certainty.

chain which runs to the north-west of Zorea, and slopes off towards
the north into the broad plain of Merj el Omeir, almost in the
middle of the road from Ramleh to Yalo. For this village, with
which *Van Semden* identifies Gezer (*Van de Velde*, Mem. p. 315),
was exactly four Roman miles north by west of Anwas, according
to *Robinson's* map, and not quite four hours from Akir (Ekron),
the most northerly city of the Philistines; so that *Josephus* (Ant.
vii. 4, 1) could very properly describe Gazara as the frontier of the
territory of the Philistines. *Robinson* discovered no signs of antiquity, it is true, on his journey through Kubab, but in all probability he did not look for them, as he did not regard the village
as a place of any importance in connection with ancient history
(Bibl. Res. pp. 143-4).

Vers. 34, 35. From Lachish Joshua proceeded eastwards against
Eglon (Ajlan, see ver. 3), took the town, and did to it as he had
done to Lachish.—Vers. 36, 37. From Eglon he went up from the
lowland to the mountains, attacked Hebron and took it, and did to
this town and its king, and the towns belonging to it, as he had
already done to the others. The king of Hebron cannot of course
be the one who was taken in the cave of Makkedah and put to
death there, but his successor, who had entered upon the government while Joshua was occupied with the conquest of the towns
mentioned in vers. 28-35, which may possibly have taken more
than a year. "*All the cities thereof*" are the towns dependent upon
Hebron as the capital of the kingdom.—Vers. 38, 39. Joshua then
turned southwards with all Israel (*i.e.* all the army), attacked *Debir*
and took it, and the towns dependent upon it, in the same manner
as those mentioned before. *Debir*, formerly called *Kirjath-sepher*,
i.e. book town, πόλις γραμμάτων (LXX. chap. xv. 15; Judg. i. 11),
and *Kirjath-sanna*, *i.e.* in all probability the city of palm branches
(chap. xv. 49), was given up by Judah to the priests (chap. xxi. 15).
It stood upon the mountains of Judah (chap. xv. 49), to the south
of Hebron, but has not yet been certainly discovered, though *V. de
Velde* is probably correct in his supposition that it is to be seen in
the ruins of *Dilbeh*, on the peak of a hill to the north of Wady
Dilbeh, and on the road from Dhoberiyeh to Hebron, about two
hours to the south-west of the latter. For, according to *Dr Stewart*,
there is a spring at *Dilbeh*, the water of which is conducted by an
aqueduct into the Birket el Dilbeh, at the foot of the said hill,
which would answer very well to the upper and lower springs at
Debir, if only Debir might be placed, according to chap. xv. 49, so

far towards the north.[1] Moreover, not very long afterwards, probably during the time when the Israelites were occupied with the subjugation of northern Canaan, Hebron and Debir were taken again by the Canaanites, particularly the Anakites, as Joshua had not entirely destroyed them, although he had thoroughly cleared the mountains of Judah of them, but had left them still in the towns of the Philistines (chap. xi. 21, 22). Consequently, when the land was divided, there were Anakites living in both Hebron and Debir; so that Caleb, to whom these towns were given as his inheritance, had first of all to conquer them again, and to exterminate the Anakites (chap. xiv. 12, xv. 13–17: cf. Judg. i. 10–13).[2]

Vers. 40–43. *Summary of the Conquest of the whole of Southern Canaan.*—In the further prosecution of his victory over the five allied kings, Joshua smote the whole land, *i.e.* the whole of the south of Canaan from Gibeon onwards, in all its districts, namely

---

[1] *Knobel* imagines that Debir is to be found in the modern village of *Dhoberiyeh* (*Dhabarije*), five hours to the south-west of Hebron, on the south-west border of the mountains of Judah, upon the top of a mountain, because, in addition to the situation of this village, which is perfectly reconcilable with chap. xv. 49, there are remains of a square tower there (according to *Krafft*, a Roman tower), which point to an ancient fortification (*vid.* Rob. Pal. i. pp. 308 sqq.; *Ritter*, Erdk. xvi. pp. 202 sqq.), and because the name, which signifies "placed behind the back," agrees with *Debir*, the hinder part or back (?), and *Kirjath-sepher*, if interpreted by the Arabic words, which signify "*extremitas, margo, ora.*" But both reasons prove very little. The meanings assigned to *Debir* and *Kirjath-sepher* are improbable and arbitrary. Moreover, it has not been shown that there are any springs near Dhoberiyeh, such as there were in the neighbourhood of Debir (chap. xv. 19 sqq.). The view held by *Rosenmüller*, and adopted by *Bunsen*, with regard to the situation of *Debir*,—namely, that it was the same as the modern *Idwirbân* or *Dewirbân*, an hour and a quarter to the west of Hebron, because there is a large spring there with an abundant supply of excellent water, which goes by the name of *Ain Nunkûr*,—is also quite untenable; for it is entirely at variance with chap. xv. 49, according to which Debir was not on the west of Hebron, but upon the mountains to the south, and rests entirely upon the erroneous assumption that, according to ver. 38 (וַיָּשׇׁב, he turned round), as Joshua came from Eglon, he conquered Hebron first, and after the conquest of this town turned *back* to Debir, to take it also. But שׁוּב does not mean only to turn round or turn back: it signifies turning generally; and it is very evident that this is the sense in which it is used in ver. 38, since, according to chap. xv. 49, Debir was on the south of Hebron.

[2] By this simple assumption we get rid of the pretended contradictions, which neological critics have discovered between chap. x. 36–39 on the one hand, and chap. xi. 21, 22, and xiv. 12, xv. 13–17 on the other, and on account of which *Knobel* would assign the passages last named to a different document. On the first conquest of the land by Joshua, *Masius* observes that "in

the mountains (chap. xv. 48), the Negeb (the south land, chap. xv. 21), the lowlands (chap. xv. 33), and the slopes, *i.e.* the hill region (chap. xii. 8, and comm. on Num. xxi. 15), and all the kings of these different districts, banning every living thing (כָּל־נֶפֶשׁ = כָּל־נְשָׁמָה, vers. 28, 30, *i.e.* all the men ; *vid.* Deut. xx. 16), as Jehovah had commanded, viz. Num. xxxiii. 51 sqq. ; Deut. vii. 1, 2, xx. 16. He smote them from Kadesh-barnea, on the southern boundary of Canaan (chap. xv. 3 ; see at Num. xii. 16), to Gaza (see at Gen. x. 9), and all the country of *Goshen*, a different place from the Goshen of Egypt, deriving its name in all probability from the town of *Goshen* on the southern portion of the mountains (chap. xv. 51). As the line *"from Kadesh-barnea to Gaza"* defines the extent of the conquered country from south to north on the western side, so the parallel clause, *"all the country of Goshen, even unto Gibeon,"* defines the extent from south to north on the eastern side. There is no tenable ground for the view expressed by *Knobel*, which rests upon very uncertain etymological combinations, that the land of Goshen signifies the hill country between the mountains and the plain, and is equivalent to אֲשֵׁדוֹת.—Ver. 42. All these kings and their country Joshua took *"once,"* *i.e.* in one campaign, which lasted, however, a considerable time (cf. chap. xi. 18). He was able to accomplish this, because Jehovah the God of Israel fought for Israel (see ver. 14). After this he returned with the army to the camp at Gilgal (Jiljilia, see p. 93 ; cf. ver. 15).

DEFEAT OF THE KINGS OF NORTHERN CANAAN. SUBJUGATION OF THE WHOLE LAND.—CHAP. XI.

Vers. 1–15. THE WAR IN NORTHERN CANAAN.—Vers. 1–3. On receiving intelligence of what had occurred in the south, the king of Hazor formed an alliance with the kings of Madon, Shimron, and Achshaph, and other kings of the north, to make a common attack upon the Israelites. This league originated with Jabin the king of Hazor, because Hazor was formerly the head of

this expedition Joshua ran through the southern region with an armed band, in too hurried a manner to depopulate it entirely. All that he needed was to strike such terror into the hearts of all through his victories, that no one should henceforth offer any resistance to himself and to the people of God. Those whom he pursued, therefore, he destroyed according to the commands of God, not sparing a single one, but he did not search out every possible hiding-place in which any could be concealed. This was left as a gleaning to the valour of each particular tribe, when it should take possession of its own inheritance."

all the kingdoms of northern Canaan (ver. 10). *Hazor*, which Joshua conquered and burned to the ground (vers. 10, 11), was afterwards restored, and became a capital again (Judg. iv. 2 ; 1 Sam. xii. 9) ; it was fortified by Solomon (1 Kings ix. 15), and taken by Tiglath-Pileser (2 Kings xv. 29). It belonged to the tribe of Naphtali (chap. xix. 36), but has not yet been discovered. According to *Josephus* (Ant. v. 5, 1), it was above the Lake of Samochonitis, the present Bahr el Huleh. *Robinson* conjectures that it is to be found in the ruins upon Tell *Khuraibeh*, opposite to the north-west corner of the lake of Huleh, the situation of which would suit Hazor quite well, as it is placed between Ramah and Kedesh in chap. xix. 35, 36 (see Bibl. Res. p. 364). On the other hand, the present ruins of *Huzzur* or *Hazireh*, where there are the remains of large buildings of a very remote antiquity (see *Rob.* Bibl. Res. p. 62), with which *Knobel* identifies Hazor, cannot be thought of for a moment, as these ruins, which are about an hour and a quarter to the south-west of Yathir, are so close to the Ramah of Asher (chap. xix. 29) that Hazor must also have belonged to Asher, and could not possibly have been included in the territory of Naphtali. There would be more reason for thinking of Tell *Hazûr* or *Khirbet Hazûr*, on the south-west of Szafed (see *Rob.* Bibl. Res. p. 81) ; but these ruins are not very ancient, and only belong to an ordinary village, and not to a town at all. *Madon* is only mentioned again in chap. xii. 19, and its situation is quite unknown. *Shimron*, called Shimron-meron in chap. xii. 20, was allotted to the tribe of Zebulun (chap. xix. 15), and is also unknown. For *Meron* cannot be connected, as *Knobel* supposes, with the village and ruins of *Marôn*, not far from Kedesh, on the south-west (see *Rob.* Pal. iii. p. 371), or *Shimron* with the ruins of *Khuraibeh*, an hour to the south of Kedesh ; as the territory of Zebulun, to which Shimron belonged, did not reach so far north, and there is not the slightest ground for assuming that there were two Shimrons, or for making a distinction between the royal seat mentioned here and the Shimron of Zebulun. There is also no probability in *Knobel's* conjecture, that the *Shimron* last named is the same as the small village of *Semunieh*, probably the *Simonias* of *Josephus* (Vita, § 24), on the west of Nazareth (see *Rob.* Pal. iii. p. 201). *Achshaph*, a border town of Asher (chap. xix. 25), is also unknown, and is neither to be sought, as *Robinson* supposes (Bibl. Res. p. 55), in the ruins of *Kesâf*, which lie even farther north than *Abel* (*Abil*), in the tribe of Naphtali, and therefore much too far to the north to have formed the boundary of Asher; nor to be identified with *Acco* (*Ptolemais*), as *Knobel* imagines, since *Acco* has nothing in common with *Achshaph* except the letter *caph* (see also at chap. xix. 25).—Ver. 2. Jabin also allied himself with the kings of the north "*upon the mountains*," *i.e.* the mountains of Naphtali (chap. xx. 7), and "*in the Arabah to the south of Chinnereth*" (chap. xix. 35), *i.e.* in the Ghor to the south of the sea of Galilee, and "*in the lowland*," *i.e.* the northern portion of it, as far down as Joppa, and "*upon the heights of Dor.*" The town of *Dor*, which was built by Phœnicians, who settled there on account of the abundance of the purple mussels (*Steph. Byz. s. v. Δῶρος*), was allotted to the Manassites in the territory of Asher (chap. xvii. 11; cf. xix. 26), and taken possession of by the children of Joseph (1 Chron. vii. 29). It was situated on the Mediterranean Sea, below the promontory of Carmel, nine Roman miles north of Cæsarea, and is at the present time a hamlet called *Tantura* or *Tortura*, with very considerable ruins (*Wilson*, The Holy Land, ii. 249, and *V. de Velde*, Journey, i. p. 251). The old town was a little more than a mile to the north, on a small range of hills, which is covered with ruins (*Ritter*, Erdk. xvi. pp. 608–9; *V. de Velde*, Mem. p. 307), and on the north of which there are rocky ranges, with many grottos, and houses cut in the rock itself (*Buckingham*, Syria, i. pp. 101–2). These are "the heights of Dor," or "the high range of Dor" (chap. xii. 23; 1 Kings iv. 11).—Ver. 3. "*Namely, with the Canaanites on the east and west, the Amorites*" and other tribes dwelling upon the mountains (*vid.* chap. iii. 10), and "*the Hivites under the Hermon in the land of Mizpah*," *i.e.* the country below *Hasbeya*, between *Nahr Hasbany* on the east, and *Merj Ayûn* on the west, with the village of *Mutulleh* or *Mtelleh*, at present inhabited by Druses, which stands upon a hill more than 200 feet high, and from which there is a splendid prospect over the Huleh basin. It is from this that it has derived its name, which signifies prospect, *specula*, answering to the Hebrew *Mizpah* (see *Robinson*, Bibl. Res. p. 372).

Vers. 4–9. These came out with their armies, a people as numerous as the sand by the sea-shore (*vid.* Gen. xxii. 17, etc.), and very many horses and chariots. All these kings agreed together, *sc.* concerning the war and the place of battle, and encamped at *Merom* to fight against Israel. The name *Merom* (*Meirûm* in the Arabic version) answers to *Meirôm*, a village whose name is also pronounced *Meirûm*, a celebrated place of pilgrimage among the

Jews, because Hillel, Shammai, Simeon ben Jochai, and other noted Rabbins are said to be buried there (see *Robinson*, Pal. iii. p. 333), about two hours' journey north-west of Szafed, upon a rocky mountain, at the foot of which there is a spring that forms a small brook and flows away through the valley below Szafed (*Seetzen*, R. ii. pp. 127–8; *Robinson*, Bibl. Res. pp. 73 sqq.). This stream, which is said to reach the Lake of Tiberias, in the neighbourhood of Bethsaida, is in all probability to be regarded as the "waters of of Merom," as, according to Josephus (Ant. v. 1, 18), "these kings encamped at Berothe (de. Bell. Jud. xx. 6, and Vit. 37, '*Meroth*'), a city of Upper Galilee, not far from Kedese."[1]

Vers. 6 sqq. On account of this enormous number, and the might of the enemy, who were all the more to be dreaded because of their horses and chariots, the Lord encouraged Joshua again,[2] as in chap. viii. 1, by promising him that on the morrow He would deliver them all up slain before Israel; only Joshua was to lame their horses (Gen. xlix. 6) and burn their chariots. אָנֹכִי before נֹחֵן gives emphasis to the sentence : "I will provide for this; by my power, which is immeasurable, as I have shown thee so many times, and by my nod, by which heaven and earth are shaken, shall these things be done" (*Masius*).—Vers. 7, 8. With this to inspirit them, the Israelites fell upon the enemy and smote them, chasing them towards the north-west to Sidon, and westwards as far as Misrephothmaim, and into the plain of Mizpah on the east. *Sidon* is called the great (as in chap. xix. 28), because at that time it was the metropolis of Phœnicia; whereas even by the time of David it had lost its ancient splendour, and was outstripped by its daughter city Tyre. It is still to be seen in the town of *Saida*, a town of five or six thousand inhabitants, with many large and well-built

---

[1] The traditional opinion that "waters of Merom" is the Old Testament name for the Lake of Samochonitis, or Huleh, is not founded upon any historical evidence, but is simply an inference of *Hadr. Reland* (Pal. Ill. p. 262), (1) from the statement made by *Josephus* (Ant. v. 5, 1), that Hazor was above the Lake of Samochonitis, it being taken for granted without further reason that the battle occurred at Hazor, and (2) from the supposed similarity in the meaning of the names, viz. that *Samochonitis* is derived from an Arabic word signifying to be high, and therefore means the same as *Merom* (height), though here again the *zere* is disregarded, and *Merom* is arbitrarily identified with *Marom*.

[2] "As there was so much more difficulty connected with the destruction of so populous and well-disciplined an army, it was all the more necessary that he should be inspired with fresh confidence. For this reason God appeared to Joshua, and promised him the same success as He had given him so many times before."—*Calvin*.

houses (see *Rob.* Pal. iii. p. 415, and *Movers*, Phönizier, ii. 1, pp. 86
sqq.). *Misrephothmaim* (mentioned also at chap. xiii. 6), which the
Greek translators have taken as a proper name, though the Rabbins
and some Christian commentators render it in different ways, such
as salt-pits, smelting-huts, or glass-huts (see *Ges.* Thes. p. 1341), is
a collection of springs, called *Ain Mesherfi*, at the foot of the promontory to which with its steep pass the name of *Ras el Nakhûra*
is given, the *scala Tyriorum* or *Passepoulain* of the Crusaders (see
V. de Velde, Mem. p. 335, and *Ritter*, Erdk. xvi. p. 807). בִּקְעַת מִצְפֶּה
(*Eng. Ver.* "the valley of Mizpeh") is probably the basin of the
Huleh lake and of Nahr *Hasbany*, on the western side of which lay
the land of *Mizpah* (ver. 3).—Ver. 9. Joshua carried out the command of the Lord with regard to the chariots and horses.

Vers. 10–15. After destroying the foe, and returning from the
pursuit, Joshua took Hazor, smote its king and all the inhabitants
with the edge of the sword, and burned the town, the former leader
of all those kingdoms. He did just the same to the other towns,
except that he did not burn them, but left them standing upon
their hills. הָעֹמְדוֹת עַל־תִּלָּם (ver. 13) neither contains an allusion to
any special fortification of the towns, nor implies a contrast to the
towns built in the valleys and plains, but simply expresses the
thought that these towns were still standing upon their hill, *i.e.*
upon the old site (cf. Jer. xxx. 18 : the participle does not express
the preterite, but the present). At the same time, the expression
certainly implies that the towns were generally built upon hills.
The pointing in תִּלָּם is not to be altered, as *Knobel* suggests. The
singular "*upon their hill*" is to be taken as distributive : standing,
now as then, each upon its hill.—With ver. 15, "*as Jehovah commanded His servant Moses*" (cf. Num. xxxiii. 52 sqq. ; Deut. vii. 1
sqq., xx. 16), the account of the wars of Joshua is brought to a
close, and the way opened for proceeding to the concluding remarks
with reference to the conquest of the whole land (vers. 16–23).
לֹא הֵסִיר דָּבָר, he put not away a word, *i.e.* left nothing undone.

Vers. 16–23. RETROSPECTIVE VIEW OF THE CONQUEST OF
THE WHOLE LAND.—Vers. 16, 17. Joshua took all this land,
namely, those portions of Southern Canaan that have already been
mentioned in chap. x. 40, 41 ; also the Arabah, and the mountains
of Israel and its lowlands (see ver. 2), *i.e.* the northern part of the
land (in the campaign described in vers. 1–15), that is to say,
Canaan in all its extent, "*from the bald mountain which goeth up to*

Seir" in the south, *" to Baal-gad, in the valley of Lebanon under Hermon."* The *"bald mountain"* (*Halak*), which is mentioned here and in chap. xii. 7 as the southern boundary of Canaan, is hardly the row of white cliffs which stretches obliquely across the Arabah eight miles below the Dead Sea and forms the dividing line that separates this valley into *el-Ghor* and *el-Araba* (*Rob. Pal.* ii. pp. 489, 492), or the present *Madara*, a strange-looking chalk-hill to the south-west of the pass of Sufah (*Rob.* ii. p. 589), a steep bare mountain in a barren plain, the sides of which consist of stone and earth of a leaden ashy hue (*Seetzen*, R. iii. pp. 14, 15); but in all probability the northern edge of the Azazimeh mountain with its white and glistening masses of chalk. *Baal-gad, i.e.* the place or town of Baal, who was there worshipped as Gad (see Isa. lxv. 11), also called *Baal-hermon* in Judg. iii. 3 and 1 Chron. v. 23, is not Baalbek, but the *Paneas* or *Cæsarea Philippi* of a later time, the present *Banjas* (see at Num. xxxiv. 8, 9). This is the opinion of *v. Raumer* and *Robinson*, though *Van de Velde* is more disposed to look for Baal-gad in the ruins of *Kalath* (the castle of) *Bostra*, or of *Kalath Aisafa*, the former an hour and a half, the latter three hours to the north of Banjas, the situation of which would accord with the biblical statements respecting Baal-gad exceedingly well. The *"valley of Lebanon"* is not *Cœle-Syria*, the modern *Bekâa*, between Lebanon and Antilibanus, but the valley at the foot of the southern slope of Jebel Sheik (Hermon).—Vers. 18 sqq. Joshua made war with the kings of Canaan a long time; judging from chap. xiv. 7, 10, as much as seven years, though Josephus (*Ant.* v. 1, 19) speaks of five (see at chap. xiv. 10). No town submitted peaceably to the Israelites, with the exception of Gibeon: they took the whole in war. *" For it was of the Lord"* (ver. 20), *i.e.* God ordered it so that they (the Canaanites) hardened their heart to make war upon Israel, that they might fall under the ban, and be destroyed without mercy. On the hardening of the heart as a work of God, see the remarks upon the hardening of Pharaoh (Ex. iv. 21). It cannot be inferred from this, that if the Canaanites had received the Israelites amicably, God would have withdrawn His command to destroy them, and allowed the Israelites to make peace with them; for when they made peace with the Gibeonites, they did not inquire what was the will of the Lord, but acted in opposition to it (see at chap. ix. 14). The remark is made with special reference to this, and has been correctly explained by *Augustine* (qu. 8 in Jos.) as follows: *"* Because the Israelites had

shown mercy to some of them of their own accord, though in oppo
sition to the command of God, therefore it is stated that they (the
Canaanites) made war upon them so that none of them were spared,
and the Israelites were not induced to show mercy to the neglect of
the commandment of God."

In vers. 21, 22, the destruction of the Anakites upon the mountains of Judah and Israel is introduced in a supplementary form,
which completes the history of the subjugation and extermination
of the Canaanites in the south of the land (chap. x.). This supplement is not to be regarded either as a fragment interpolated by
a different hand, or as a passage borrowed from another source.
On the contrary, the author himself thought it necessary, having
special regard to Num. xiii. 28, 31 sqq., to mention expressly that
Joshua also rooted out from their settlements the sons of Anak,
whom the spies in the time of Moses had described as terrible
giants, and drove them into the Philistine cities of Gaza, Gath,
and Ashdod. *"At that time"* points back to the "long time,"
mentioned in ver. 18, during which Joshua was making war upon
the Canaanites. The words "cut off," etc., are explained correctly
by *Clericus:* "Those who fell into his hands he slew, the rest he
put to flight, though, as we learn from chap. xv. 14, they afterwards
returned." (On the *Anakim*, see at Num. xiii. 22.) They had
their principal settlement upon the mountains in Hebron (*el Khulil*,
see chap. x. 3), Debir (see at chap. x. 38), and Anab. The last
place (*Anab*), upon the mountains of Judah (chap. xv. 50), has been
preserved along with the old name in the village of *Anâb*, four or
five hours to the south of Hebron, on the eastern side of the great
Wady *el Khulil*, which runs from Hebron down to Beersheba
(*Rob.* Pal. ii. p. 193). *"And from all* (the rest of) *the mountains
of Judah, and all the mountains of Israel:"* the latter are called the
mountains of Ephraim in chap. xvii. 15. The two together form
the real basis of the land of Canaan, and are separated from one
another by the large Wady *Beit Hanina* (see *Rob.* Pal. ii. p. 333).
They received their respective names from the fact that the southern
portion of the mountain land of Canaan fell to the tribe of Judah
as its inheritance, and the northern part to the tribe of Ephraim
and other tribes of Israel.[1] *Gaza, Gath,* and *Ashdod* were towns

---

[1] The distinction here made may be explained without difficulty even from
the circumstances of Joshua's own time. Judah and the double tribe of Joseph
(Ephraim and Manasseh) received their inheritance by lot before any of the
others. But whilst the tribe of Judah proceeded into the territory allotted to

of the Philistines; of these Gaza and Ashdod were allotted to the tribe of Judah (chap. xv. 47), but were never taken possession of by the Israelites, although the Philistines were sometimes subject to the Israelites (see at chap. xiii. 3).—With ver. 23*a*, " *thus Joshua took the whole land*" etc., the history of the conquest of Canaan by Joshua is brought to a close; and ver. 23*b*, " *and Joshua gave it for an inheritance unto Israel*," forms a kind of introduction to the second part of the book. The list of the conquered kings in chap. xii. is simply an appendix to the first part.

The taking of the *whole* land does not imply that all the towns and villages to the very last had been conquered, or that all the Canaanites were rooted out from every corner of the land, but simply that the conquest was of such a character that the power of the Canaanites was broken, their dominion overthrown, and their whole land so thoroughly given into the hands of the Israelites, that those who still remained here and there were crushed into powerless fugitives, who could neither offer any further opposition to the Israelites, nor dispute the possession of the land with them, if they would only strive to fulfil the commandments of their God and persevere in the gradual extermination of the scattered remnants. Moreover, Israel had received the strongest pledge, in the powerful help which it had received from the Lord in the conquests thus far obtained, that the faithful covenant God would continue His help in the conflicts which still remained, and secure for it a complete victory and the full possession of the promised land. Looking,

them in the south, all the other tribes still remained in Gilgal; and even at a later period, when Ephraim and Manasseh were in their possessions, all Israel, with the exception of Judah, were still encamped at Shiloh. Moreover, the two parts of the nation were now separated by the territory which was afterwards assigned to the tribe of Benjamin, but had no owner at this time; and in addition to this, the altar, tabernacle, and ark of the covenant were in the midst of Joseph and the other tribes that were still assembled at Shiloh. Under such circumstances, then, would not the idea of a distinction between Judah, on the one hand, and the rest of Israel, in which the double tribe of Joseph and then the single tribe of Ephraim acquired such peculiar prominence, on the other, shape itself more and more in the mind, and what already existed in the germ begin to attain maturity even here? And what could be more natural than that the mountains in which the " children of Judah" had their settlements should be called the mountains of *Judah*; and the mountains where all the rest of Israel was encamped, where the " children of Israel" were gathered together, be called the mountains of *Israel*, and, as that particular district really belonged to the tribe of Ephraim, the mountains of *Ephraim* also? (chap. xix. 50, xx. 7; also xxiv. 30.)

therefore, at the existing state of things from this point of view, Joshua had taken possession of the whole land, and could now proceed to finish the work entrusted to him by the Lord, by dividing the land among the tribes of Israel. Joshua had really done all that the Lord had said to Moses. For the Lord had not only promised to Moses the complete extermination of the Canaanites, but had also told him that He would not drive out the Canaanites at once, or "in one year," but only little by little, until Israel multiplied and took the land (Ex. xxiii. 28–30; cf. Deut. vii. 22). Looking at this promise, therefore, the author of the book could say with perfect justice, that "*Joshua took the whole land according to all that* (precisely in the manner in which) *the Lord had said to Moses.*" But this did not preclude the fact, that a great deal still remained to be done before all the Canaanites could be utterly exterminated from every part of the land. Consequently, the enumeration of towns and districts that were not yet conquered, and of Canaanites who still remained, which we find in chap. xiii. 1–6, xvii. 14 sqq., xviii. 3, xxiii. 5, 12, forms no discrepancy with the statements in the verses before us, so as to warrant us in adopting any critical hypotheses or conclusions as to the composition of the book by different authors. The Israelites could easily have taken such portions of the land as were still unconquered, and could have exterminated all the Canaanites who remained, without any severe or wearisome conflicts; if they had but persevered in fidelity to their God and in the fulfilment of His commandments. If, therefore, the complete conquest of the whole land was not secured in the next few years, but, on the contrary, the Canaanites repeatedly gained the upper hand over the Israelites; we must seek for the explanation, not in the fact that Joshua had not completely taken and conquered the land, but simply in the fact that the Lord had withdrawn His help from His people because of their apostasy from Him, and had given them up to the power of their enemies to chastise them for their sins.—The distribution of the land for an inheritance to the Israelites took place "*according to their divisions by their tribes.*" מַחְלְקוֹת denote the division of the twelve tribes of Israel into families, fathers' houses, and households; and is so used not only here, but in chap. xii. 7 and xviii. 10. Compare with this 1 Chron. xxiii. 6, xxiv. 1, etc., where it is applied to the different orders of priests and Levites. "*And the land rested from war:*" *i.e.* the war was ended, so that the peaceable task of distributing the land by lot could now be proceeded with (*vid.* chap. xiv. 15; Judg. iii. 11, 30, v. 31).

LIST OF THE KINGS SLAUGHTERED BY THE ISRAELITES.— CHAP. XII.

In the historical account of the wars of Joshua in the south and north of Canaan, the only kings mentioned by name as having been conquered and slain by the Israelites, were those who had formed a league to make war upon them; whereas it is stated at the close, that Joshua had smitten all the kings in the south and north, and taken possession of their towns (chap. x. 40, xi. 17). To complete the account of these conquests, therefore, a detailed list is given in the present chapter of all the kings that were slain, and not merely of those who were defeated by Joshua in the country on this side of the Jordan, but the two kings of the Amorites who had been conquered by Moses are also included, so as to give a complete picture of all the victories which Israel had gained under the omnipotent help of its God.

Vers. 1-6. List of the *kings* whom the Israelites smote, and whose land they took, *on the other side of the Jordan,*—namely, the land by the brook Arnon (Mojeb; see Num. xxi. 13) to Hermon (Jebel es Sheikh, Deut. iii. 8), and the whole of the eastern Arabah (the valley of the Jordan on the eastern side of the river).—Vers. 2, 3. On Sihon and his kingdom, see Num. xxi. 24; Deut. ii. 36, iii. 16, 17. "*Aroër on the Arnon:*" the present ruins of *Araayr*, on the northern bank of the Mojeb (see Num. xxxii. 34). וְתוֹךְ הַנַּחַל, "*and* (from) *the middle of the valley onwards:*" *i.e.*, according to the parallel passages in chap. xiii. 9, 16, and Deut. ii. 36, from the town in the Arnon valley, the city of Moab mentioned in Num. xxii. 36, viz. *Ar* or *Areopolis* (see at Num. xxi. 15) in the neighbourhood of Aroër, which is mentioned as the exclusive *terminus a quo* of the land taken by the Israelites along with the inclusive terminus Aroër. "*Half-Gilead,*" *i.e.* the mountainous district on the south side of the Jabbok (see at Deut. iii. 10), "*to the river Jabbok,*" *i.e.* the upper Jabbok, the present Nahr Ammân (see at Num. xxi. 24).—Ver. 3. "*And* (over) *the Arabah, etc., Sihon reigned,*" *i.e.* over the eastern side of the Ghor, between the Sea of Galilee and the Dead Sea (see at Deut. iii. 17). "*By the way to Bethjeshimoth, and towards the south below the slopes of Pisgah*" (see at Num. xxi. 15 and xxvii. 12), *i.e.* to the north-eastern border of the desert by the Dead Sea (see at Num. xxii. 1). —Vers. 4, 5. *"And the territory of Og,"* sc. they took possession of (ver. 1). On Og, *vid.* Deut. iii. 11; and on his residences, *Ash-taroth* (probably to be seen in Tell *Ashtereh*) and *Edrei* (now *Draa* or *Dêra*), see at Gen. xiv. 5 and Num. xxi. 33. On his territory, see Deut. iii. 10, 13, 14.—Ver. 6. These two kings were smitten by Moses, etc.: *vid.* Num. xxi. 21 sqq., and xxxii. 33 sqq.

Vers. 7–24. List of the *thirty-one kings of Canaan* whom Joshua smote on the western side of the Jordan, *"from Baal-gad, in the valley of Lebanon, to the bald mountain that goeth up towards Seir"* (see chap. xi. 17). This land Joshua gave to the other tribes of Israel. (On the different parts of the land, see at chap. ix. 1, x. 40, and xi. 2.)—Vers. 9 sqq. The different kings are given in the order in which they were defeated: Jericho (chap. vi. 1); Ai (chap. vii. 2); Jerusalem, Hebron, Jarmuth, Lachish, and Eglon (chap. x. 3); Gezer (chap. x. 33); and Debir (chap. x. 38). Those given in vers. 13b and 14 are not mentioned by name in chap. x. *Geder*, possibly the same as *Gedor* upon the mountains of Judah (chap. xv. 58), which has been preserved under the old name of *Jedur* (*Rob.* Pal. ii. p. 186, and Bibl. Res. p. 282). *Hormah* (*i.e.* banning) was in the south of Judah (chap. xv. 30), and was allotted to the Simeonites (chap. xix. 4). It was called *Zephath* by the Canaanites (Judg. i. 17; see at Num. xxi. 3), was on the southern slope of the mountains of the Amalekites or Amorites, the present ruins of *Sepâta*, on the western slope of the table-land of *Rakhma*, two hours and a half to the south-west of Khalasa (Elusa: see *Ritter*, Erdk. xiv. p. 1085). *Arad*, also in the Negeb, has been preserved in Tell *Arad* (see at Num. xxi. 1). *Libnah* (see at chap. x. 29). *Adullam*, which is mentioned in chap. xv. 35 among the towns of the plain between Jarmuth and Socoh, was in the neighbourhood of a large cave in which David took refuge when flying from Saul (1 Sam. xxii. 1; 2 Sam. xxiii. 13). It was fortified by Rehoboam (2 Chron. xi. 7), and is mentioned in 2 Macc. xii. 38 as the city of Odollam. The *Onomast.* describes it as being ten Roman miles to the east of Eleutheropolis; but this is a mistake, though it has not yet been discovered. So far as the situation is concerned, *Deir Dubbán* would suit very well, a place about two hours to the north of Beit Jibrin, near to a large number of caves in the white limestone, which form a kind of labyrinth, as well as some vaulted grottos (see *Rob.* Pal. ii. p. 353, and *Van de Velde*, Reise. pp. 162–3). *Makkedah*: possibly *Summeil* (see at chap. x. 10).   *Bethel, i.e. Beitin* (see chap. viii. 17).   The situation of the towns which follow in vers. 17 and 18 cannot be determined with certainty, as the names *Tappuach, Aphek,* and *Hefer* are met with again in different parts of Canaan, and *Lassaron* does not occur again.   But if we observe, that just as from ver. 10 onwards those kings'-towns are first of all enumerated, the capture of which has already been described in chap. x., and then in vers. 15 and 16 certain other towns are added which had been taken in the war with the Canaanites of the south, so likewise in vers. 19 and 20 the capitals of the allied kings of northern Canaan are given first, and after that the other towns that were taken in the northern war, but had not been mentioned by name in chap. xi. : there can be no doubt whatever that the four towns in vers. 17 and 18 are to be classed among the kings'-towns taken in the war with the king of Jerusalem and his allies, and therefore are to be sought for in the south of Canaan and not in the north. Consequently we cannot agree with *Van de Velde* and *Knobel* in identifying *Tappuach* with *En-Tappuach* (chap. xvii. 7), and looking for it in *Atûf,* a place to the north-east of Nablus and near the valley of the Jordan ; we connect it rather with *Tappuach* in the lowlands of Judah (chap. xv. 34), though the place itself has not yet been discovered.   *Hefer* again is neither to be identified with Gath-hepher in the tribe of Zebulun (chap. xix. 13), nor with *Chafaraim* in the tribe of Issachar (chap. xix. 19), but is most probably the capital of the land of *Hefer* (1 Kings iv. 10), and to be sought for in the neighbourhood of Socoh in the plain of Judah. *Aphek* is probably the town of that name not far from Ebenezer (1 Sam. iv. 1), where the ark was taken by the Philistines, and is most likely to be sought for in the plain of Judah, though not in the village of *Ahbek* (*Rob.* Pal. ii. p. 343) ; but it has not yet been traced.   *Knobel* imagines that it was Aphek near to Jezreel (1 Sam. xxix. 1), which was situated, according to the *Onom.,* in the neighbourhood of Endor (1 Sam. xxix. 1; 1 Kings xx. 26, 30) ; but this Aphek is too far north.   *Lassaron* only occurs here, and hitherto it has been impossible to trace it.   *Knobel* supposes it to be the place called *Saruneh,* to the west of the lake of Tiberias, and conjectures that the name has been contracted from Lassaron by aphæresis of the liquid.   This is quite possible, if only we could look for Lassaron so far to the north.   *Bachienne* and *Rosenmüller* imagine it to be the village of *Sharon* in the celebrated plain of that name, between Lydda and Arsuf.—Vers. 19, 20. *Madon, Hezor,*

Shimron-meron, and *Achshaph* (see at chap. xi. 1).—Ver. 21. *Taa-nach,* which was allotted to the Manassites in the territory of Issachar, and given up to the Levites (chap. xvii. 11, xxi. 25), but was not entirely wrested from the Canaanites (Judg. i. 27), is the present Tell *Taënak,* an hour and a quarter to the south-east of Lejun, a flat hill sown with corn; whilst the old name has been preserved in the small village of *Taânak,* at the south-eastern foot of the Tell (see *Van de Velde,* i. p. 269, and *Rob.* Pal. iii. p. 156).—*Megiddo,* which was also allotted to the Manassites in the territory of Issachar, though without the Canaanites having been entirely expelled (chap. xvii. 11; Judg. i. 27), was fortified by Solomon (1 Kings ix. 15), and is also well known as the place were Ahaziah died (2 Kings ix. 27), and where Josiah was beaten and slain by Pharaoh Necho (2 Kings xxiii. 29, 30; 2 Chron. xxxv. 20 sqq.). *Robinson* has shown that it was preserved in the *Legio* of a later time, the present *Lejun* (Pal. iii. pp. 177 sqq.; see also Bibl. Res. p. 116).—Ver. 22. *Kedesh,* a Levi-tical city and city of refuge upon the mountains of Naphtali (chap. xix. 37, xx. 7, xxi. 32), the home of Barak (Judg. iv. 6), was con-quered and depopulated by Tiglath-Pileser (2 Kings xv. 29), and was also a well-known place after the captivity (1 Macc. xi. 61 sqq.). It is now an insignificant village, still bearing the ancient name, to the north-west of the lake of Huleh, or, according to *Van de Velde* (Reise. ii. p. 355), nothing but a miserable farmstead upon a Tell at the south-west extremity of a well-cultivated table-land, with a large quantity of antiquities about, viz. hewn stones, relics of columns, sarcophagi, and two ruins of large buildings, with an open and extensive prospect on every side (see also *Rob.* Bibl. Res. pp. 367 sqq.). *Jokneam,* near *Carmel,* was a Levitical town in the territory of Zebulun (chap. xix. 11, xxi. 34). *Van de Velde* and *Robinson* (Bibl. Res. p. 114) suppose that they have found it in Tell *Kaimôn,* on the eastern side of the Wady *el Milh,* at the north-west end of a chain of hills running towards the south-east; this Tell being 200 feet high, and occupying a very commanding situation, so that it governed the main pass on the western side of Esdraelon towards the southern plain. *Kaimôn* is the Arabic form of the ancient Καμμωνά, *Cimana,* which *Eusebius* and *Jerome* describe in the *Onom.* as being six Roman miles to the north of *Legio,* on the road to Ptolemais.—Ver. 23. *Dor:* see chap. xi. 2. *Gilgal :* the seat of the king of the *Goyim* (a proper name, as in Gen. xiv. 1), in all probability the same place as the *villa nomine Galgulis* mentioned in the *Onom. (s. v. Gelgel)* as being six Roman miles to the north of Antipatris, which still exists in the Moslem village of *Jiljule* (now almost a ruin ; see *Rob.* Bibl. Res. p. 136), although this village is only two miles E.S.E. of Kefr Sâba, the ancient Antipatris (see *Ritter*, Erdk. xvi. pp. 568–9). *Thirza*, the capital of the kings of Israel down to the time of Omri (1 Kings xiv. 17, xv. 21, 33, xvi. 6 sqq.), is probably the present Talluza, an elevated and beautifully situated place, of a considerable size, surrounded by large olive groves, two hours to the north of Shechem (see *Rob.* Bibl. Res. p. 302, and *Van de Velde*, ii. p. 294).

II. DIVISION OF THE LAND OF CANAAN AMONG THE TRIBES OF ISRAEL.

CHAP. XIII.–XXIV.

The distribution of the conquered land among the Israelites is introduced by the command of the Lord to Joshua to enter upon this work, now that he was old, although different portions of land were still unconquered (chap. xiii. 1–7) ; and to this there is appended a description of the land on the east of the Jordan which had already been conquered and divided among the two tribes and a half (chap. xiii. 8–33). The distribution of the land on this side among the nine tribes and a half is related in its historical order ; so that not only are the territories assigned by lot to the different tribes described according to their respective boundaries and towns, but the historical circumstances connected with the division and allotting of the land are also introduced into the description. These historical accounts are so closely connected with the *geographical* descriptions of the territory belonging to the different tribes, that the latter alone will explain the course pursued in the distribution of the land, and the various ways in which the different territories are described (see the remarks on chap. xiv. 1). For example, in the account of the inheritance which fell to the lot of the tribes of Judah and Benjamin, not only are the boundaries most carefully traced, but the towns are also enumerated one by one (chap. xv. and xviii. 11–28) ; whereas in the tribe of Joseph (Ephraim and half Manasseh) the list of the towns is altogether wanting (chap. xvi. and xvii.) ; and in the possessions of the other tribes, either towns alone are mentioned, as in the case of Simeon and Dan (chap. xix. 1–9, 40–48), or the boundaries and towns are mixed up together, but both of them given incompletely, as in the case of Zebulun, Issachar, Asher, and Naphtali (chap. xix. 10–16, 17–23, 24–31, 32–39). This incompleteness, particularly in the territories of the tribes mentioned last, may be explained from the fact, that in northern Canaan there were still very many tracts of land in the hands of the Canaanites, and the Israelites had not acquired a sufficiently exact or complete knowledge of the country, either through Joshua's campaign in the north, or through the men who were sent out to survey the northern land before it was divided (chap. xviii. 4–9), to enable them to prepare a complete account of the boundaries and towns at the very outset. In the same way, too, we may explain the absence of the list of towns in the case of the tribes of Ephraim and half Manasseh,—namely, from the fact that a large portion of the territory assigned to the tribe of Joseph was still in the possession of the Canaanites (vid. chap. xvii. 14–18); whilst the omission of any account of the boundaries in the case of Simeon and Dan is attributable to the circumstance that the former received its inheritance within the tribe of Judah, and the latter between Judah and Ephraim, whilst the space left for the Danites was so small, that Ephraim and Judah had to give up to them some of the towns in their own territory. Thus the very inequality and incompleteness of the geographical accounts of the possessions of the different tribes decidedly favour the conclusion, that they are the very lists which were drawn up at the time when Joshua divided the land. There is nothing to preclude this supposition in the fact that several towns occur with different names, e.g. Beth-shemesh and Ir-shemesh (chap. xv. 10, xix. 41, xxi. 16), Madmannah and Beth-marcaboth, Sansanna and Hazar-susa (chap. xv. 31, xix. 5), Shilchim and Sharuchen (chap. xv. 32, xix. 6), Remeth and Jarmuth (chap. xix. 21, xxi. 29), or in other smaller differences. For variations of this kind may be sufficiently explained from the fact that such places were known by two different names, which could be used promiscuously; whilst in other cases the difference in the name amounts to nothing more than a different mode of writing or pronouncing it: e.g. Kattah and Kartah (chap. xix. 15, xxi. 34), Eshtemoh and Eshtemoa (chap. xv. 50, xxi. 14), Baalah and Balah (chap. xv. 29, xix. 3); or simply in the contraction of a composite name, such as Ramoth in Gilead for Ramoth-mizpeh (chap. xxi. 36, xiii. 26); Bealoth and Baalath-beer (chap. xv. 24, xix. 8), Lebaoth and Beth-lebaoth (chap. xv. 32, xix. 6), Hammath and *Hammoth-dor* (chap. xix. 35, xxi. 32). If the author, on the other hand, had drawn from later sources, or had simply given the results of later surveys, as *Knobel* supposes, there can be no doubt that much greater uniformity would be found in the different lists.[1]

COMMAND OF GOD TO DIVIDE THE LAND OF CANAAN. DESCRIPTION OF THE TERRITORY OF THE TWO TRIBES AND A HALF. —CHAP. XIII.

Vers. 1–14. INTRODUCTION TO THE DIVISION OF THE LAND. —Vers. 1–7. Command of the Lord to Joshua to distribute the land of Canaan by lot among the nine tribes and a half. Ver. 1 contains only the commencement of the divine command; the conclusion follows in ver. 7. Vers. 2–6 form a parenthesis of several clauses, defining the last clause of ver. 1 more fully. When Joshua had grown old, the Lord commanded him, as he was advanced in years, and there was still much land to be taken, to divide "*this land,*" *i.e.* the whole of the land of Canaan, for an inheritance to

---

[1] The arguments employed by *Knobel* in support of his assertion, consist on the one hand of inconclusive and incorrect assertions, and are founded on the other hand upon arbitrary assumptions. In the first place, for example, he asserts that " a large number of towns are omitted from the lists, which were within the boundaries mentioned and were in existence in the very earliest times, viz. *in the south*, Tamar (Gen. xiv. 7), Arad (Num. xxi. 1), Atbach, Rachal, Aroer, and Siphamoth (1 Sam. xxx. 28 sqq.), Gerar (Gen. xx. 26); *in the Shephelah*, Gaza, Askalon, Gath, Ashdod, Jabne, and Joppa (see chap. xv. 45 sqq.); in *Benjamin*, Michmash and Nob (1 Sam. xiii. 2 sqq., xxii. 19); in the *north*, Aphek, Lassaron, Madon, Shimron-meron, and Merom (chap. xi. 5, xii. 18–20), as well as Meroz and Ajjalon (Judg. v. 23, xii. 12); and these with other places would assuredly not be wanting here, if Joshua and his associates had distributed the towns as well as the land, and furnished our author with the lists." But it would be difficult to bring forward the proofs of this, since *Knobel* himself acknowledges that there are gaps in the lists which have come down to us, some of which can be proved to be the fault of the copyists,—such, for example, as the want of a whole section after chap. xv. 19 and xxi. 35. Moreover, the Philistine towns of Ashdod and Gaza are really mentioned in chap. xv. 46, and the others at all events hinted at; whereas *Knobel* first of all arbitrarily rejects chap. xv. 45–47 from the text, in order that he may afterwards be able to speak of it as omitted. Again, with many of the places mentioned as omissions, such as Atbach, Rachal, Siphamoth, etc., it is very questionable whether they were towns at all in Joshua's time, or, at all events, such towns as we should expect to find mentioned. And lastly, not only are no catalogues of towns given at all in the case of Ephraim and Manasseh, but we have only imperfect catalogues in the case of Zebulun, Asher, and Naphtali; and, as we

the nine tribes and a half, and promised him at the same time that
He would drive out the Canaanites from those portions of the land
that were not yet conquered (ver. 6). The words "*grown old and
come into years*" (*vid.* Gen. xxiv. 1, xviii. 11, etc.) denote advanced
age in its different stages up to the near approach of death (as,
for example, in chap. xxiii. 1). Joshua might be ninety or a hundred years old at this time. The allusion to Joshua's great age
serves simply to explain the reason for the command of God. As
he was already old, and there still remained much land to be taken,
he was to proceed to the division of Canaan, that he might accomplish this work to which he was also called before his death; whereas
he might very possibly suppose that, under existing circumstances,
the time for allotting the land had not yet arrived.—In vers. 2–6
the districts that were not yet conquered are enumerated separately.
—Vers. 2, 3. All the *circles of the Philistines* (*geliloth*, circles of
well-defined districts lying round the chief city). The reference
is to the five towns of the Philistines, whose princes are mentioned
in ver. 3. "*And all Geshuri:*" not the district of Geshur in Peræa

have already observed, this incompleteness and these gaps can be satisfactorily
explained from the historical circumstances under which the allotment of the
land took place. *Secondly, Knobel* also maintains, that " Joshua's conquests
did not extend to the Lebanon (chap. xiii. 4, 5), and yet the author mentions
towns of the Asherites there (chap. xix. 28, 30): Bethel was not taken till after
the time of Joshua (Judg. i. 22 sqq.), and this was also the case with Jerusalem
(Judg. i. 8), and in the earliest times of the judges they had no Hebrew inhabitants (Judg. xix. 12), yet the author speaks of both places as towns of the
Benjamites (chap. xviii. 22, 28); Jericho and Ai were lying in ruins in Joshua's
time (chap. vi. 24, viii. 28), yet they are spoken of here as towns of Benjamin
that had been rebuilt (chap. xviii. 21, 23); it is just the same with Hazor in
Naphtali (chap. xi. 13, xix. 36); and according to Judg. i. 1, 10 sqq., Hebron
and Debir also were not conquered till after Joshua's time." But all this rests
(1) upon the false assumption, that the only towns which Joshua distributed by
lot among the tribes of Israel were those which he permanently conquered,
whereas, according to the command of God, he divided the whole land among
the Israelites, whether it was conquered or not; (2) upon the erroneous opinion,
that the towns which had been destroyed, such as Jericho, Ai, and Hazor, were
allotted to the Israelites as " rebuilt," whereas there is not a word about this
in the text. It is just the same with the arguments used by *Knobel* in proof
of the composition of chap. xiii.–xxi. from three different documents. The
material discrepancies have been forced upon the text, as we shall see when we
come to an explanation of the passages in question; and the verbal differences
prove nothing more than that the geographical account of the boundaries and
towns contains no allusion to the priesthood, to sacrifice, or to certain other
things which no one would think of looking for here.

(vers. 11, 13, xii. 5 ; Deut. iii. 14), but the territory of the Geshurites, a small tribe in the south of Philistia, on the edge of the north-western portion of the Arabian desert which borders on Egypt; it is only mentioned again in 1 Sam. xxvii. 8. The land of the Philis-tines and Geshurites extended from the Sichor of Egypt (on the south) to the territory of Ekron (on the north). *Sichor (Sihor), lit.* the black river, is not the Nile, because this is always called הַיְאֹר (the river) in simple prose (Gen. xli. 1, 3 ; Ex. i. 22), and was not " before Egypt," *i.e.* to the east of it, but flowed through the middle of the land. The " *Sichor before Egypt* " was the brook (*nachal*) of Egypt, the ʿΡινοκορούρα, the modern Wady *el Arish*, which is mentioned in chap. xv. 4, 47, etc., as the southern border of Canaan towards Egypt (see at Num. xxxiv. 5). *Ekron* (Ἀρρα-κών, LXX.), the most northerly of the five chief cities of the Philistines, was first of all allotted to the tribe of Judah (chap. xv. 11, 45), then on the further distribution it was given to Dan (chap. xix. 43); after Joshua's death it was conquered by Judah (Judg. i. 18), though it was not permanently occupied. It is the present Akîr, a considerable village in the plain, two hours to the south-west of Ramlah, and on the east of Jamnia, without ruins of any antiquity, with the exception of two old wells walled round, which probably belong to the times of the Crusaders (see *Rob.* Pal. iii. p. 23). " *To the Canaanites is reckoned* (the territory of the) *five lords of the Philistines*," *i.e.* it was reckoned as belonging to the land of Canaan, and allotted to the Israelites like all the rest. This remark was necessary, because the Philistines were not descendants of Canaan (see at Gen. x. 14), but yet were to be driven out like the Canaanites themselves as being invaders of Canaanitish terri-tory (cf. Deut. ii. 23). סַרְנֵי, from סֶרֶן, the standing title of the princes of the Philistines (*vid.* Judg. iii. 3, xvi. 5 sqq.; 1 Sam. v. 8), does not mean kings, but princes, and is interchangeable with שָׂרִים (cf. 1 Sam. xxix. 6 with vers. 4, 9). At any rate, it was the native or Philistian title of the Philistine princes, though it is not derived from the same root as *Sar*, but is connected with *seren, axis rotæ*, in the tropical sense of *princeps*, for which the Arabic fur-nishes several analogies (see *Ges.* Thes. p. 972). The capitals of these five princes were the following. *Azzah* (*Gaza, i.e.* the strong): this was allotted to the tribe of Judah and taken by the Judæans (chap. xv. 47; Judg. i. 18), but was not held long. It is at the present time a considerable town of about 15,000 inhabitants, with the old name of *Ghazzeh,* about an hour from the sea, and with a

seaport called *Majuma;* it is the farthest town of Palestine towards
the south-west (see *Rob.* Pal. ii. pp. 374 sqq. ; *Ritter,* Erdk. xvi.
pp. 35 sqq.; *Stark,* Gaza, etc., pp. 45 sqq.). *Ashdod* (*Aζωτος,
Azotus*) : this was also allotted to the tribe of Judah (chap. xv.
46, 47), the seat of Dagon-worship, to which the Philistines carried
the ark (1 Sam. v. 1 sqq.). It was conquered by Uzziah (2 Chron
xxvi. 6), was afterwards taken by Tartan, the general of Sargon
(Isa. xx. 1), and was besieged by Psammetichus for twenty-nine
years (Herod. ii. 157). It is the present *Esdud,* a Mahometan
village with about a hundred or a hundred and fifty miserable huts,
upon a low, round, wooded height on the road from Jamnia to
Gaza, two miles to the south of Jamnia, about half an hour from
the sea (*vid. Rob.* i. p. 368). *Ashkalon :* this was conquered by
the Judæans after the death of Joshua (Judg. i. 8, 9) ; but shortly
afterwards recovered its independence (*vid.* Judg. xiv. 19; 1 Sam.
vi. 17). It is the present *Askulân* on the sea-shore between Gaza
and Ashdod, five hours to the north of Gaza, with considerable and
widespread ruins (see *v. Raum.* pp. 173–4; *Ritter,* xvi. pp. 69 sqq.).
Gath (*Γέθ*) : this was for a long time the seat of the Rephaites,
and was the home of Goliath (chap. xi. 22; 1 Sam. xvii. 4, 23;
2 Sam. xxi. 19 sqq.; 1 Chron. xx. 5 sqq.) ; it was thither that the
Philistines of Ashdod removed the ark, which was taken thence
to Ekron (1 Sam. v. 7–10). David was the first to wrest it from
the Philistines (1 Chron. xviii. 1). In the time of Solomon it was
a royal city of the Philistines, though no doubt under Israelitish
supremacy (1 Kings ii. 39, v. 1). It was fortified by Rehoboam
(2 Chron. xi. 8), was taken by the Syrians in the time of Joash
(2 Kings xii. 18), and was conquered again by Uzziah (2 Chron.
xxvi. 6; Amos vi. 2); but no further mention is made of it, and
no traces have yet been discovered[1] (see *Rob.* ii. p. 420, and *v.*

---

[1] According to the *Onom.* (*s. v. Geth*), it was a place five Roman miles from
Eleutheropolis towards Diospolis, whereas Jerome (on Micah i.) says: " *Gath*
was near the border of Judæa, and on the road from Eleutheropolis to Gaza; it
is still a very large village;" whilst in the commentary on Jer. xxv. he says:
" *Gath* was near to and conterminous with Azotus," from which it is obvious
enough that the situation of the Philistine city of Gath was altogether unknown
to the Fathers. *Hitzig* and *Knobel* suppose the Βαιτογάβρα of *Ptolemy* (v. 16,
6), *Betogabri* in *Tab. Peuting.* ix. *e.* (the Eleutheropolis of the Fathers, and the
present *Beit Jibrin*, a very considerable ruin), to be the ancient Gath, but this
opinion is only founded upon very questionable etymological combinations;
whereas *Thenius* looks for it on the site of the present *Deir Dubban,* though
without any tenable ground.

Raumer, Pal. pp. 191–2). *" And the Avvites* (Avvæans) *towards the south."* Judging from Deut. ii. 23, the *Avvim* appear to have belonged to those tribes of the land who were already found there by the Canaanites, and whom the Philistines subdued and destroyed when they entered the country. They are not mentioned in Gen. x. 15–19 among the Canaanitish tribes. At the same time, there is not sufficient ground for identifying them with the Geshurites as *Ewald* does, or with the Anakites, as *Bertheau* has done. More-over, it cannot be decided whether they were descendants of Ham or Shem (see *Stark.* Gaza, pp. 32 sqq.). מִתֵּימָן (*from,* or on, *the south*) at the commencement of ver. 4 should be attached to ver. 3, as it is in the Septuagint, Syriac, and Vulgate, and joined to הָעַוִּים (the Avvites). The Avvæans dwelt to the south of the Philistines, on the south-west of Gaza. It gives no sense to connect it with what follows, so as to read *" towards the south all the land of the Canaanites;"* for whatever land to the south of Gaza, or of the territory of the Philistines, was still inhabited by Canaanites, could not possibly be called " all the land of the Canaanites." If, how-ever, we were disposed to adopt the opinion held by *Masius* and *Rosenmüller,* and understand these words as relating to the southern boundaries of Canaan, " the possessions of the king of Arad and the neighbouring petty kings who ruled in the southern extremity of Judæa down to the desert of Paran, Zin, Kadesh," etc., the fact that Arad and the adjoining districts are always reckoned as belonging to the Negeb would at once be decisive against it (com-pare chap. xv. 21 sqq. with chap. x. 40, xi. 16, also Num. xxi. 1). Moreover, according to chap. x. 40, 41, and xi. 16, 17, Joshua had smitten the whole of the south of Canaan from Kadesh-barnea to Gaza and taken it; so that nothing remained unconquered there, which could possibly have been mentioned in this passage as not yet taken by the Israelites. For the fact that the districts, which Joshua traversed so victoriously and took possession of, were not all permanently held by the Israelites, does not come into considera-tion here at all. If the author had thought of enumerating all these places, he would have had to include many other districts as well.

Beside the territory of the Philistines on the south-west, there still remained to be taken (vers. 4, 5) in the north, " *all the land of the Canaanites,"* i.e. of the Phœnicians dwelling on the coast, and " *the caves which belonged to the Sidonians unto Aphek."* *Mearah* (the cave) is the present *Mugr Jezzin, i.e.* cave of Jezzin, on the east of

Sidon, in a steep rocky wall of Lebanon, a hiding-place of the
Druses at the present time (see at Num. xxxiv. 8 ; also *F. v. Richter*,
Wallfahrten in Morgenland, p. 133). *Aphek*, or *Aphik*, was allotted
to the tribe of Asher (chap. xix. 30 ; Judg. i. 31) ; it was called
᾽Αφακα by the Greeks ; there was a temple of Venus there, which
Constantine ordered to be destroyed, on account of the licentious
nature of the worship (*Euseb.* Vita Const. iii. 55). It is the present
Afka, a small village, but a place of rare beauty, upon a terrace of
Lebanon, near the chief source of the river *Adonis* (*Nahr Ibrahim*),
with ruins of an ancient temple in the neighbourhood, surrounded
by groves of the most splendid walnut trees on the north-east of
Beirut (see *O. F. v. Richter*, pp. 106–7 ; *Rob.* Bibl. Res. p. 663 ;
and *V. de Velde*, Reise. ii. p. 398). " *To the territory of the Amorites :*" this is obscure. We cannot imagine the reference to be to
the territory of Og of Bashan, which was formerly inhabited by
Amorites, as that did not extend so far north ; and the explanation
given by *Knobel*, that farther north there were not Canaanites, but
Amorites, who were of Semitic origin, rests upon hypotheses which
cannot be historically sustained.—Ver. 5. There still remained to
be taken (2) " *the land of the Giblites*," *i.e.* the territory of the
population of *Gebal* (1 Kings v. 32 ; Ezek. xxvii. 9), the *Byblos*
of the classics, on the Mediterranean Sea, to the north of Beirut,
called *Jebail* by the Arabs, and according to *Edrisi* (ed. *Jaubert*,
i. p. 356), " a pretty town on the sea-shore, enclosed in good walls,
and surrounded by vineyards and extensive grounds planted with
fruit trees" (see also *Abulfed.* Tab. Syr. p. 94). It is still a town
with an old wall, some portions of which apparently belong to the
time of the Crusades (see *Burckhardt*, Syr. p. 296, and *Ritter*,
Erdk. xvii. pp. 60 sqq.).[1] " *And all Lebanon toward the sunrising :*"
i.e. not Antilibanus (*Knobel*), but the Lebanon which is to the east
of the territory of Gebal, " *from Baal-gad under Mount Hermon*,"
i.e. Paneas Banjas at the foot of Hermon (see at chap. xi. 17),
" *unto the entering in to Hamath*," *i.e.* as far up as the territory of
the kingdom of Hamath, with the capital of the same name on the
Orontes (see at Num. xxxiv. 8). Lastly, there still remained (3)
" *all the inhabitants of the mountains, from Lebanon to Misrephothmaim*," *i.e.* the promontory of *Nakura* (see at chap. xi. 8), namely
" *all the Sidonians*," *i.e.* all the Phœnicians who dwelt from Lebanon
southwards, from the boundary of the territory of Hamath down

---

[1] The evidence adduced by *Movers* (Phönizier, ii. 1, p. 103), that the Giblites
did not belong to the Canaanites, has more plausibility than truth.

to the promontory of Nakura. According to ancient usage, the Sidonians stand for the Phœnicians generally, as in Homer, on account of Sidon being the oldest capital of Phœnicia (see *Ges.* on Is. i. pp. 724 sqq.). All these the Lord would root out before Israel, and therefore Joshua was to divide the whole of northern Canaan, which was inhabited by Phœnicians, among the Israelites. "*Only divide thou it by lot for an inheritance,*" etc. רַק, only, *i.e.* although thou hast not yet taken it. הַפִּיל, to cause it to fall, here used with reference to the lot, *i.e.* to divide by lot. "Fulfil thy duty in the distribution of the land, not even excepting what is still in the firm grasp of the enemy; for I will take care to perform what I have promised. From this we may learn to rely so perfectly upon the word of God, when undertaking any duty, as not to be deterred by doubts or fears" (*Calvin*).

Vers. 8–14. To the command of God to divide the land on this side the Jordan among the nine tribes and a half (ver. 7), the historian appends the remark, that the other two tribes and a half had already received their inheritance from Moses on the other side (ver. 8). This he proceeds to describe in its full extent (vers. 9–13), and then observes that the tribe of Levi alone received no landed inheritance, according to the word of the Lord (ver. 14). After this he gives a description in vers. 15–33 of the land assigned by Moses to each of the two tribes and a half.[1] The remark in ver. 8 is so closely connected with what precedes by the expression "with whom" (*lit. with it*), that this expression must be taken as somewhat indefinite: "with whom," viz. with half Manasseh, really signifying with the *other* half of Manasseh, with which the Reubenites and Gadites had received their inheritance (see Num. xxxii. and Deut. iii. 8–17). The last words of ver. 8, "*as Moses the servant of Jehovah gave them,*" are not a tautological repetition of the clause "which Moses gave them," but simply affirm that these tribes received the land given them by Moses, in the manner commanded by Moses, without any alteration in his arrangements. The boundaries of the land given in vers. 9–13 really agree with those given in chap. xii. 2–5 and Deut. iii. 8, although the expression

---

[1] *Knobel's* remark, that vers. 8–14 anticipate the following section (vers. 15–33) in an unsuitable manner, rests upon a thorough misunderstanding of the whole; for the account of the division of the land to the east of the Jordan among the two tribes and a half (vers. 15–33) could not be introduced in a more appropriate manner than by a description of the circumference of the land and of its principal parts (vers. 9–13).

varies in some respects. The words of ver. 9, " *the city that is in the midst of the river*," *i.e.* the city in the valley, viz. *Ar*, are more distinct than those of chap. xii. 2, " and from the middle of the river." " *All the plain*" is the Amoritish table-land, a tract of land for the most part destitute of trees, stretching from the Arnon to Heshbon, and towards the north-east to Rabbath-Ammân (see at Deut. iii. 10), which is called in Num. xxi. 20 the field of Moab *Medeba*, now called *Medaba* (see at Num. xxi. 30). *Dibon*, now a ruin called *Dibân*, to the north of Arnon (see at Num. xxi. 20).—Ver. 10, as in chap. xii. 2.—Ver. 11. *Gilead* is the whole country of that name on both sides of the Jabbok (see at chap. xii. 2 and Deut. iii. 10), the present Belka and Jebel Ajlun, for the description of which see the remarks at Num. xxxii. 1. " *The territory of the Geshurites and Maachathites*" is referred to in chap. xii. 5 as the boundary of the kingdom of Og, and in Deut. iii. 14 as the boundary of the land which was taken by Jair the Manassite ; here it is included in the inheritance of the tribes on the other side of the Jordan, but it was never really taken possession of by the Israelites, and (according to ver. 13) it had probably never been really subject to king Og. The other notices in vers. 11 and 12 are the same as in chap. xii. 4, 5.—Ver. 14. The tribe of Levi was to receive no land, but the firings of Jehovah, *i.e.* the offerings, including the tithes and first-fruits (Lev. xxvii. 30–32, compared with Num. xviii. 21–32), were to be its inheritance ; so that the God of Israel himself is called the inheritance of Levi in ver. 33 as in Num. xviii. 20, to which the words " as He said unto them" refer (see the commentary on Num. xviii. 20).

Vers. 15–33. THE POSSESSIONS OF THE TWO TRIBES AND A HALF.—Vers. 15–23. The tribe of *Reuben* received its inheritance in the south—namely, the territory from Aroër in the Arnon valley, and from Ar in that valley, onwards, and the plain (table-land) by Medeba (see ver. 9), with Heshbon the capital and her towns, *i.e.* the towns dependent upon it, in the plain. *Heshbon*, almost in the centre between the Arnon and the Jabbok, was situated upon the border of the inheritance of the Reubenites, and was ceded to the Gadites, who gave it up to the Levites (chap. xxi. 39 ; 1 Chron. vi 66 : see at Num. xxxii. 37). *Dibon*, called Dibon of Gad in Num. xxxiii. 45, because the Gadites had built, *i.e.* fortified it, was on the south of Heshbon, only an hour from Aroër, on the Arnon (ver. 9). *Bamoth-baal*, also called Bamoth simply (Num. xxi. 20 ; Isa. xv. 2),

is to be sought for on the Jebel Attarus (see at Num. xxi. 20).
It was thence that Balaam saw the end of the Israelitish camp
(Num. xxii. 41). *Bethbaal-meon*, the present ruin of *Myun*, three-
quarters of an hour s.e. of Heshbon (see at Num. xxxii. 38). *Jahza*,
where Sihon was defeated, was to the east of Medeba, according to
the *Onom.*; and Dibon was on the border of the desert (see at Num.
xxi. 23). *Kedemoth*, on the border of the desert, to the north-west
of Kalaat Balua, is to be sought on the northern bank of the
Balua, or upper Arnon (see at Num. xxi. 13). *Mephaath*, where
there was a garrison stationed (according to the *Onom.*) as a defence
against the inhabitants of the desert, is to be sought for in the
neighbourhood of Jahza, with which it is always associated (Jer.
xlviii. 21). Kedemoth and Mephaath were given up to the Levites
(chap. xxi. 37 ; 1 Chron. vi. 64).—Vers. 19, 20. *Kirjathaim*, where
Chedorlaomer defeated the Emim, is probably to be found in the
ruins of *et-Teym*, half an hour to the west of Mcdaba (see at Gen.
xiv. 5). *Sibmah* (Num. xxxii. 38), according to *Jerome* (on Isa.
xvi. 8), only 500 paces from Heshbon, appears to have hopelessly
disappeared. *Zereth-hashachar, i.e. splendor auroræ*, which is only
mentioned here, was situated " *upon a mountain of the valley.*"
According to ver. 27, the valley was the Jordan valley, or rather
(according to Gen. xiv. 3, 8) the vale of Siddim, a valley running
down on the eastern side of the Dead Sea. *Seetzen* conjectures
that the town referred to is the present ruin of *Sará*, on the south
of Zerka Maein.—*Beth-peor*, opposite to Jericho, six Roman miles
higher than (to the east of) *Libias :* see at Num. xxiii. 28. The
" *slopes of Pisgah*" (chap. xii. 3; Deut. iii. 17) : to the south of the
former, on the north-eastern shore of the Dead Sea (see at Num.
xxvii. 12). *Beth-jeshimoth* (chap. xii. 3), in the Ghor el Seisabân,
on the north-east side of the Dead Sea (see at Num. xxii. 1). In
ver. 21*a*, the places which Reuben received in addition to those
mentioned by name are all summed up in the words, " *and all the*
(other) *towns of the plain, and all the kingdom of Sihon,*" *sc.* so far
as it extended over the plain. These limitations of the words are
implied in the context : the first in the fact that towns in the plain
are mentioned in ver. 17 ; the second in the fact that, according to
ver. 27, " the rest of the kingdom of Sihon," *i.e.* the northern
portion of it, was given to the Gadites. The allusion to Sihon
induced the author to mention his defeat again ; see at Num. xxxi.,
where the five Midianitish vassals who were slain with Sihon are
noticed in ver. 8, and the death of Balaam is also mentioned.

" *Dukes of Sihon,*" properly vassals of Sihon ; נְסִיכִים does not signify anointed, however, but means literally poured out, *i.e.* cast, moulded, enfeoffed. The word points to the " creation of a prince by the communication or pouring in of power" (*Gusset. s. v.*).—Ver. 23. " *And* (this) *was the boundary of the sons of Reuben, the Jordan and its territory,*" *i.e.* the Jordan, or rather land adjoining it. The meaning is, that the territory of Reuben, viz. with the places mentioned last (ver. 20), reached to the territory of the Jordan ; for so far as the principal part was concerned, it was on the east of the Dead Sea, as it only reached from the Arnon to Heshbon, *i.e.* up to the latitude of the northern extremity of the Dead Sea. " *The towns and their villages.*" חָצֵר, farm premises, used, as in Lev. xxv. 31, to denote places not enclosed by a wall.

Vers. 24-28. Inheritance of the tribe of *Gad.*—This tribe received *Jaëzer* (probably *es Szyr :* see at Num. xxi. 32) and " *all the towns of Gilead,*" *i.e.* of the southern half of Gilead, which belonged to the kingdom of Sihon ; for the northern half, which belonged to the kingdom of Og, was given to the Manassites (ver. 31), " *and the half of the land of the sons of Ammon, to Aroër before Rabbah,*" *i.e.* that portion of the land of the Ammonites between the Arnon and the Jabbok, which the Amorites under Sihon had taken from the Ammonites, namely, the land on the east of Gilead, on the western side of the upper Jabbok (Nahr Ammân : Deut. ii. 37, iii. 16 ; cf. Judg. xi. 13) ; for the land of the Ammonites, *i.e.* the land which they still held in the time of Moses, on the eastern side of Nahr Ammân, the Israelites were not allowed to attack (Deut. ii. 19). *Aroër* before Rabbah, *i.e.* Ammân (see Deut. iii. 11), is Aroër of Gad, and must be distinguished from Aroër of Reuben on the Arnon (ver. 16). It is only mentioned again in Judg. xi. 33 and 2 Sam. xxiv. 5, and was situated, according to 2 Sam., in the valley of Gad, that is to say, in a wady or valley through which *Gesenius* supposes an arm of the Jabbok to have flowed, and *Thenius* the Jabbok itself, though neither of them has sufficient ground for his conjecture. It is also not to be identified with the ruin of *Ayra* to the south-west of Szalt, as this is not in a wady at all ; but in all probability it is to be sought for to the north-east of Rabbah, in the Wady Nahr Ammân, on the side of the Kalat *Zerka Gadda*, the situation of which suits this verse and 2 Sam. xxiv. 5 very well, and may easily be reconciled with Judg. xi. 33.—In ver. 26 the extent of the territory of Gad is first of all described from north to south : viz. from Heshbon (see ver. 17) to *Ramath-mizpeh*, or *Ramoth* in Gilead (chap. xx. 8), probably on the site of the present *Szalt* (see at Deut. iv. 43), " *and Betonim*," probably the ruin of *Batneh*, on the mountains which bound the Ghor towards the east between the Wady Shaib and Wady Ajlun, in the same latitude as Szalt (*V. de Velde*, Mem. p. 298) ; and then, *secondly*, the northern boundary is described from west to east, " *from Mahanaim to the territory of Lidbir*." *Mahanaim* (double-camp ꞉ Gen. xxxii. 2), which was given up by Gad to the Levites (chap. xxi. 30), in which Ishbosheth was proclaimed king (2 Sam. ii. 8, 9), and to which David fled from Absalom (2 Sam. xvii. 24, 27 ; 1 Kings ii. 8), is not to be sought for, as *Knobel* supposes, in the ruins of *Meysera*, to the south of Jabbok, four hours and a half from Szalt, but was on the north of the Jabbok, since Jacob did not cross the ford of the Jabbok till after the angel had appeared to him at Mahanaim (Gen. xxxii. 3, 23). It was in or by the valley of the Jordan (according to 2 Sam. xviii. 23, 24), and has probably been preserved in the ruins of *Mahneh*, the situation of which, however, has not yet been determined (see at Gen. xxxii. 3). *Lidbir* is quite unknown ; the *lamed*, however, is not to be taken as a prefix, but forms part of the word. *J. D. Michaelis* and *Knobel* suppose it to be the same as *Lo-debar* in 2 Sam. ix. 4, 5, xvii. 27, a place from which provisions were brought to David at Mahanaim on his flight from Absalom, and which is to be sought for on the east of Mahanaim.—Ver. 27. On the north, the territory of Gad seems to have extended to the Jabbok, and only to have stretched beyond the Jabbok at Mahanaim, which formed the boundary of half-Manasseh, according to ver. 30. In the valley of the Jordan, on the other hand, the boundary reached to the Sea of Galilee. " *The valley* " is the valley of the Jordan, or the Arabah from Wady Hesbân above the Dead Sea up to the Sea of Galilee, along the east side of the Jordan, which belonged to the kingdom of Sihon (chap. xii. 3 ; Deut. iii. 17). The northern boundary of the tribe of Reuben must have touched the Jordan in the neighbourhood of the Wady Hesbân. In the Jordan valley were *Beth-haram*, the future *Libias*, and present *er Rameh* (see at Num. xxxii. 36) ; *Beth-nimra*, according to the *Onom.* five Roman miles to the north, the present ruin of *Nimrein* (see at Num. xxxii. 36) ; *Succoth*, according to the *Onom. trans Jordanem in parte Scythopoleos* (see at Gen. xxxiii. 17) ; *Zaphon* (*i.e.* north), probably not far from the southern extremity of the Sea of Galilee. " *The rest of the kingdom of Sihon*," the other part having been given to the Reubenites (ver. 21).

Vers. 29–31. The territory of the *half tribe of Manasseh* extended from Mahanaim onwards, and embraced all Bashan, with the sixty Jair towns and the (northern) half of Gilead (see the comm. on Deut. iii. 13–15).—Ver. 32 is the concluding formula. (For the fact itself, see Num. xxxiv. 14, 15.)—Ver. 33 is a repetition of ver. 14.

COMMENCEMENT OF THE DIVISION OF THE LAND OF CANAAN. INHERITANCE OF CALEB.—CHAP. XIV.

Vers. 1–5 form the heading and introduction to the account of the division of the land among the nine tribes and a half, which reaches to chap. xix., and is brought to a close by the concluding formula in chap. xix. 51. The division of the land of Canaan according to the boundaries laid down in Num. xxxiv. 2–12 was carried out, in accordance with the instructions in Num. xxxiv. 16–29, by the high priest Eleazar, Joshua, and ten heads of fathers' houses of the nine tribes and a half, whose names are given in Num. xxxiv. 18–28. "*By the lot of their inheritance*," *i.e.* by casting lots for it : this is dependent upon the previous clause, "*which they distributed for inheritance to them.*" "*As the Lord commanded through Moses*" (Num. xxvi. 52–56, xxxiii. 54, and xxxiv. 13), "*to the nine tribes and a half*" (this is also dependent upon the clause "which they distributed for inheritance").—Vers. 3, 4. So many tribes were to receive their inheritance, for the two tribes and a half had already received theirs from Moses on the other side of the Jordan, and the tribe of Levi was not to receive any land for an inheritance. According to this, there seem to be only eight tribes and a half to be provided for ($2\frac{1}{2} + 1 + 8\frac{1}{2} = 12$); but there were really nine and a half, for the sons of Joseph formed two tribes in consequence of the adoption of Ephraim and Manasseh by the patriarch Jacob (Gen. xlviii. 5). But although the Levites were to have no share in the land, they were to receive towns to dwell in, with pasture adjoining for their cattle ; these the other tribes were to give up to them out of their inheritance, according to the instructions in Num. xxxv. 1–8 (see the notes upon this passage).

So far as the division of the land itself was concerned, it was to be distributed by lot, according to Num. xxvi. 52 sqq. ; but, at the same time, the distribution was carried out with such special regard to the relative sizes of the different tribes, that the more numerous tribe received a larger share of the land than one that was not so numerous. This could only be accomplished, however, by their restricting the lot to the discrimination of the relative situation of the different tribes, and then deciding the extent and boundaries of their respective possessions according to the number of families of which they were composed.[1] The casting of the lots was probably effected, as the Rabbins assumed, by means of two urns, one filled with slips having the names of the tribes upon them; the other, with an equal number, representing separate divisions of the land: so that when one slip, with a name upon it, was taken out of one urn, another slip, with a division of the land upon it, was taken from the other. The result of the lot was accepted as the direct decree of God; "for the lot was not controlled in any way by the opinion, or decision, or authority of men" (Calvin). See the fuller remarks at Num. xxvi. 56. In the account of the casting of the lots, the first fact which strikes us is, that after the tribes of Judah and Joseph had received their inheritance, an interruption took place, and the camp was moved from Gilgal to Shiloh, and the tabernacle erected there (chap. xviii. 1–9); after which the other tribes manifested so little desire to receive their inheritance, that Joshua reproved them for their indolence (chap. xviii. 3), and directed them to nominate a committee of twenty-one from their own number, whom he sent out to survey the land and divide it into seven parts; and it was not till after this had been done that the casting of the lots was proceeded with, and each of these seven tribes received its inheritance. The reason for this interruption is not given; and the commentators have differed in their opinions as to the cause (see Keil's former Comm. on Joshua, pp. 347 sqq.). The following appears to be the most probable supposition. When Joshua received the command from the Lord to divide the land among the tribes, they made an approximative division of the land into nine or ten parts, according to the general idea of its extent and principal features, which they had obtained in connection with the conquest

---

[1] "This was the force of the lot: there were ten lots cast in such a manner as to decide that some were to be next to the Egyptians, some to have the seacoasts, some to occupy the higher ground, and some to settle in the valleys. When this was done, it remained for the heads of the nation to determine the boundaries of their different territories according to some equitable standard. It was their place, therefore, to ascertain how many thousand heads there were in each tribe, and then to adjudicate a larger or smaller space according to the size of the tribe" (Calvin). Or, as Clericus observes (Num. xxvi. 52), "the lot seems to have had respect to the situation alone, and not to the extent of territory at all."

of the country, and then commenced distributing it without any
more minute survey or more accurate measurement, simply fixing
the boundaries of those districts which came out first according
to the size of the tribes upon whom the lots fell. As soon as that
was done, these tribes began to move off into the territory allotted
to them, and to take possession of it. The exact delineation of the
boundaries, however, could not be effected at once, but required a
longer time, and was probably not finally settled till the tribe had
taken possession of its land. In this manner the tribes of Judah,
Ephraim, and half Manasseh had received their inheritance one
after another. And whilst they were engaged in taking possession,
Shiloh was chosen, no doubt in accordance with divine instructions,
as the place where the tabernacle was to be permanently erected;
and there the sanctuary was set up, the whole camp, of course,
removing thither at the same time. But when the casting of the
lots was about to be continued for the remainder of the tribes, they
showed no great desire for fixed abodes, as they had become so
accustomed to a nomad life, through having been brought up in the
desert, that they were much more disposed to continue it, than to
take possession of a circumscribed inheritance,—a task which would
require more courage and exertion, on account of the remaining
Canaanites, than a life in tents, in which they might wander up and
down in the land by the side of the Canaanites, and supply their
wants from its productions, as Abraham, Isaac, and Jacob had formerly done, since the Canaanites who were left were so weakened by
the war that the Israelites had no occasion for a moment's anxiety
about them, provided they did not attempt to expel or to exterminate them. But Joshua could not rest contented with this, if he
would remain faithful to the charge which he had received from
the Lord. He therefore reproved these tribes for their tardiness,
and commanded them to take steps for continuing the casting of
lots for the land. But as the tribe of Joseph had expressed its
dissatisfaction with the smallness of the inheritance allotted to it,
and by so doing had manifested its cowardice, which prevented it
from attacking the Canaanites who were still left in the territory
that had fallen to their lot, Joshua may possibly have had his eyes
opened in consequence to the fact that, if the casting of lots was
continued in the manner begun, and with nothing more than an
approximative definition of the different portions of the land, there
was a possibility of still greater dissatisfaction arising among the
other tribes, since some of them at any rate would be sure to receive

portions of the land in which the Canaanites were more numerous and still stronger than in the possessions of Ephraim. He therefore gave orders, that before the casting of lots was proceeded with any further, the rest of the land should be carefully surveyed and divided into seven districts, and that a statement of the result should be laid before him, that these seven districts might be divided by lot among the seven tribes. This survey of the land no doubt very clearly showed that what remained, after deducting the possessions of Judah and Joseph, was too small for the remaining seven tribes, in proportion to what had been already divided. Moreover, it had also been discovered that Judah's share was larger than this tribe required (chap. xix. 9). Consequently it was necessary that certain partial alterations should be made in the arrangements connected with the first division. The lot itself could not be pronounced invalid when it had once been cast, as its falling was regarded as the decision of God himself, and therefore it was impossible to make a fresh division of the *whole* land among all the tribes. The only thing that could be done was to leave the two tribes in those districts which had fallen to them by lot (chap. xviii. 5), but to take certain parts of their territory for the other tribes, which would leave the lot in all its integrity, as the lot itself had not determined either the size or the boundaries. This will serve to explain both the interruption to the casting of the lots, which had been commenced at Gilgal, and also the peculiar manner in which it was continued at Shiloh.

Vers. 6–15. CALEB'S INHERITANCE.—Vers. 6 sqq. Before the casting of the lots commenced, Caleb came to Joshua along with the sons of Judah, and asked for the mountains of Hebron for his possession, appealing at the same time to the fact, that forty-five years before Moses had promised it to him on oath, because he had not discouraged the people and stirred them up to rebellion, as the other spies that were sent from Kadesh to Canaan had done, but had faithfully followed the Lord.[1] This occurred at Gilgal, where

[1] The grounds upon which *Knobel* follows *Maurer* and others in affirming that this account does not belong to the so-called Elohist, but is merely a fragment taken from the first document of the Jehovist, are formed partly from misinterpretations of particular verses and partly from baseless assumptions. To the former belongs the assertion, that, according to vers. 8, 12, Joshua was not one of the spies (see the remarks on ver. 8) ; to the latter the assertion, that the Elohist does not represent Joshua as dividing the land, or Caleb as receiving so large a territory (see on the contrary, however, the

the casting of the lots was to take place. *Caleb* was not "the head of the Judahites," as *Knobel* maintains, but simply the head of a father's house of Judah, and, as we may infer from his surname, "the Kenizzite" or descendant of Kenaz ("*the Kenizzite*" here and Num. xxxii. 12 is equivalent to "son of Kenaz," ch. xv. 17, and Judg. i. 13), head of the father's house which sprang from *Kenaz, i.e.* of a subdivision of the Judahite family of Hezron; for Caleb, the brother of Jerahmeel and father of Achzah, according to 1 Chron. ii. 42 (cf. 1 Chron. ii. 49), was the same person as Caleb the descendant of Hezron mentioned in 1 Chron. ii. 18. From the surname "the Kenizzite" we are of course not to understand that Caleb or his father Jephunneh is described as a descendant of the Canaanitish tribe of Kenizzites (Gen. xv. 19); but *Kenaz* was a descendant of Hezron, the son of Perez and grandson of Judah (1 Chron. ii. 5, 18, 25), of whom nothing further is known Consequently it was not the name of a tribe, but of a person, and, as we may see from 1 Chron. iv. 15, where one of the sons of Caleb is called Kenaz, the name was repeated in the family. The sons of Judah who came to Joshua along with Caleb were not the Judahites generally, therefore, or representatives of all the families of Judah, but simply members or representatives of the father's house of Judah which took its name from Kenaz, and of which Caleb was the head at that time. Caleb reminded Joshua of the word which the Lord had spoken concerning them in Kadesh-barnea, *i.e.* of the promise of God that they should both of them enter the land of Canaan (Num. xiv. 24, 30), and then proceeded to observe (ver. 7): "*When I was forty years old, and was sent by Moses as a spy to Canaan, I brought back an answer as it was in my mind,*" *i.e.* according to the best of my convictions, without fear of man or regard to the favour of the people.—Ver. 8. Whereas the other spies discouraged the people by exaggerated reports concerning the inhabitants of Canaan, he had followed the Lord with perfect fidelity (Num. xiii. 31–33). He had not been made to waver in his faithfulness to the Lord and His promises either by the evil reports which the other spies had brought of the land, or by the murmuring and threats of the excited crowd (see Num. xiv. 6–10). "*My brethren*" (ver. 8) are the rest of the spies, of course with the exception of Joshua, to whom Caleb was speaking.[1] הִמְסִיו,

exposition of ver. 13), as well as the enumeration of all kinds of words which are said to be foreign to the Elohistic document.

[1] That Joshua was not included was evident from this circumstance alone.

for הִמְסוּ (see *Ges.* § 75, anm. 17, and *Ewald*, § 142, *a.*), from מָסַס = מָסָה (see chap. ii. 11).—Ver. 9. Jehovah swore at that time, that the land upon which his (Caleb's) foot had trodden should be an inheritance for him and his sons for ever. This oath is not mentioned in Num. xiv. 20 sqq., nor yet in Deut. i. 35, 36, where Moses repeats the account of the whole occurrence to the people. For the oath of Jehovah mentioned in Num. xiv. 21, 24, viz. that none of the murmuring people should see the land of Canaan, but that Caleb alone should come thither and his seed should possess it, cannot be the one referred to, as the promise given to Caleb in this oath does not relate to the possession of Hebron in particular, but to the land of Canaan generally, *" the land which Jehovah had sworn to their fathers."* We must assume, therefore, that in addition to what is mentioned in Num. xiv. 24, God gave a special promise to Caleb, which is passed over there, with reference to the possession of Hebron itself, and that Joshua, who heard it at the time, is here reminded of that promise by Caleb. This particular promise from God was closely related to the words with which Caleb endeavoured to calm the minds of the people when they rose up against Moses (Num. xiii. 30), viz. by saying to them, " We are well able to overcome it," notwithstanding the Anakites who dwelt in Hebron and had filled the other spies with such great alarm on account of their gigantic size. With reference to this the Lord had promised that very land to Caleb for his inheritance. Upon this promise Caleb founded his request (vers. 10–12) that Joshua would give him these mountains, of which Joshua had heard at that time that there were Anakites and large fortified cities there, inasmuch as, although forty-five years had elapsed since God had spoken these words, and he was now eighty-five years old, he was quite as strong as he had been then. From the words, "The Lord hath kept me alive these forty-five years," *Theodoret* justly infers, that the conquest of Canaan by Joshua was completed in seven years, since God spake these words towards the end of the second year after the exodus from Egypt, and therefore thirty-eight years before the entrance into Canaan. The clause אֲשֶׁר הָלַךְ וגו' (ver. 10)

and consequently it is a complete perversion on the part of *Knobel* to argue, that because the expression is a general one, *i.e.* because Joshua is not expressly excepted by name, therefore he cannot have been one of the spies, not to mention the fact that the words " concerning me *and thee*," in ver. 6, are sufficient to show to any one acquainted with the account in Num. xiii., xiv., that Joshua was really one of them.

is also dependent upon זֶה אַרְבָּעִים וגו׳ : viz. *"these forty-five years
that Israel has wandered in the desert"* (on this use of אֲשֶׁר, see
Ewald, § 331, c.). The expression is a general one, and the years
occupied in the conquest of Canaan, during which Israel had not
yet entered into peaceful possession of the promised land, are
reckoned as forming part of the years of wandering in the desert.
As another reason for his request, Caleb adds in ver. 11 : *"I am
still as strong to-day as at that time ; as my strength was then, so is
it now for war, and to go out and in"* (see Num. xxvii. 17).—Ver.
12. *"The mountain,"* according to the context, is the mountainous
region of Hebron, where the spies had seen the Anakites (Num.
xiii. 22, 28). The two clauses, in ver. 12, beginning with כִּי are
not to be construed as subordinate to one another, but are co-
ordinate clauses, and contain two distinct motives in support of his
petition : viz. *"for thou heardest in that day,"* sc. what Jehovah said
to me then, and also *"for* (because) *the Anakites are there ;"* . . .
"perhaps Jehovah is with me (אֹתִי for אִתִּי, see *Ges.* § 103, 1, anm.
1, and *Ewald*, § 264, b.), *and I root them out"* (*vid.* chap. xv. 14).
The word "perhaps" does not express a doubt, but a hope or
desire, or else, as *Masius* says, "hope mixed with difficulty ; and
whilst the difficulty detracts from the value, the hope stimulates
the desire for the gift."—Ver. 13. Then Joshua blessed Caleb, *i.e.*
implored the blessing of God upon his undertaking, and gave him
Hebron for an inheritance. Hebron is mentioned as the chief
city, to which the surrounding country belonged ; for Caleb had
asked for the mountains (ver. 9), *i.e.* the mountainous country with
and around Hebron, which included, for example, the fortified
town of Debir also (chap. xv. 15).—Ver. 14. This inheritance, the
historian adds, was awarded to Caleb because he had followed the
God of Israel with such fidelity.—In ver. 15 there follows another
notice of the earlier name of Hebron (see at Gen. xxiii. 2). The
expression לְפָנִים (before), like the words "to this day," applies to
the time when the book was composed, at which time the name
Kirjath-arba had long since fallen into disuse ; so that it by no
means follows that the name Hebron was not so old as the name
Kirjath-arba, which was given to Hebron for the first time when
it was taken by Arba, "the great man among the Anakites," *i.e.*
the strongest and most renowned of the Anakites (*vid.* chap. xv.
13). The remark, *"and the land had rest from war,"* is repeated
again at the close of this account from chap. xi. 23, to show that
although there were Anakites still dwelling in Hebron whom Caleb

hoped to exterminate, the work of distributing the land by lot was not delayed in consequence, but was carried out in perfect peace

INHERITANCE OF THE TRIBE OF JUDAH.—CHAP. XV

Under the superintending providence of God, the inheritance which fell to the tribe of Judah by lot was in the southern part of Canaan, where Caleb had already received his inheritance, so that he was not separated from his tribe. The inheritance of Judah is first of all described according to its boundaries (vers. 1–12); then for the sake of completeness it is stated once more with regard to Caleb, that he received Kirjath-arba for his inheritance, and took possession of it by expelling the Anakites and conquering Debir (vers. 13–20); and after this a list is given of the towns in the different parts (vers. 21–63).

Vers. 1–12 —*Boundaries of the inheritance of the tribe of Judah.* —Ver. 1. Its situation in the land. "*And there was* (*i.e.* fell, or came out; cf. chap. xvi. 1, xix. 1) *the lot to the tribe of Judah according to its families to the frontier of Edom* (see at Num. xxxiv. 3), *to the desert of Zin southward, against the extreme south*" (*lit.* from the end or extremity of the south), *i.e.* its inheritance fell to it, so that it reached to the territory of Edom and the desert of Zin, in which Kadesh was situated (see at Num. xiii. 21), on the extreme south of Canaan.—Vers. 2–4. *The southern boundary.* This was also the southern boundary of the land of Israel generally, and coincided with the southern boundary of Canaan as described in Num. xxxiv. 3–5. It went out "*from the end of the salt sea, namely, from the tongue which turneth to the south,*" *i.e.* from the southern point of the Dead Sea, which is now a salt marsh.—Vers. 3, 4. Thence it proceeded "*to the southern boundary of the ascent of Akrabbim,*" *i.e.* the row of lofty whitish cliffs which intersects the Arabah about eight miles below the Dead Sea (see at Num. xxxiv. 4), "*and passed across to Zin,*" *i.e.* the Wady *Murreh* (see at Num. xiii. 21), "*and went up to the south of Kadesh-barnea,*" *i.e.* by *Ain Kudes* (see at Num. xx. 16), "*and passed over to Hezron, and went up to Adar, and turned to Karkaa, and went over to Azmon, and went out into the brook of Egypt,*" *i.e.* the Wady *el Arish.* On the probable situation of *Hezron, Adar, Karkaa,* and *Azmon,* see at Num. xxxiv. 4, 5. "*And the outgoings of the boundary were to the sea*" (the Mediterranean). The Wady el Arish, a marked boundary, takes first of all a northerly and then a north-

westerly course, and opens into the Mediterranean Sea (see Pent.
vol. ii. p. 58). הָיָה in the singular before the subject in the plural
must not be interfered with (see *Ewald,* § 316, *a.*).—The words
" this shall be your south coast" point back to the southern boundary of Canaan as laid down in Num. xxxiv. 2 sqq., and show that
the southern boundary of the tribe-territory of Judah was also the
southern boundary of the land to be taken by Israel.—Ver. 5*a.*
" The eastern boundary was the salt sea to the end of the Jordan,"
i.e. the Dead Sea, in all its length up to the point where the Jordan
entered it.

In vers. 5*b*–11 we have a description of the *northern* boundary,
which is repeated in chap. xviii. 15–19 as the southern boundary
of Benjamin, though in the opposite direction, namely, from west
to east. It started *" from the tongue of the* (salt) *sea, the end* (*i.e.*
the mouth) *of the Jordan, and went up to Beth-hagla,"*—a border
town between Judah and Benjamin, which was afterwards allotted
to the latter (chap. xviii. 19, 21), the present *Ain Hajla,* an hour
and a quarter to the south-east of *Riha* (Jericho), and three-quarters of an hour from the Jordan (see at Gen. l. 11, note),—*" and
went over to the north side of Beth-arabah,"* a town in the desert of
Judah (ver. 61), afterwards assigned to Benjamin (chap. xviii. 22),
and called *Ha-arabah* in chap. xviii. 18, about twenty or thirty
minutes to the south-west of *Ain Hajla,* in a " level and barren
steppe" (*Seetzen,* R. ii. p. 302), with which the name very well
agrees (see also *Rob.* Pal. ii. pp. 268 sqq.). *" And the border went
up to the stone of Bohan, the son of Reuben."* The expression
"went up" shows that the stone of *Bohan* must have been on
higher ground, *i.e.* near the western mountains, though the opposite
expression " went down" in chap. xviii. 17 shows that it must have
been by the side of the mountain, and not upon the top. According
to chap. xviii. 18, 19, the border went over from the stone of
Bohan in an easterly direction *" to the shoulder over against* (Beth)
Arabah northwards, and went down to (Beth) *Arabah, and then
went over to the shoulder of Beth-hagla northwards,"* *i.e.* on the
north side of the mountain ridge of Beth-arabah and Beth-hagla.
This ridge is "the chain of hills or downs which runs from *Kasr
Hajla* towards the south to the north side of the Dead Sea, and is
called *Katar Hhadije, i.e.* a row of camels harnessed together."—
Ver. 7. The boundary ascended still farther to *Debir* from the
valley of *Achor.* *Debir* is no doubt to be sought for by the Wady
Daber, which runs down from the mountains to the Dead Sea

to the south of *Kasr Hajla*, possibly not far from the rocky grotto called *Choret ed Daber*, between the Wady *es Sidr* and the Khan *Chadrur* on the road from Jerusalem to Jericho, about half-way between the two. On the valley of *Achor* see at chap. vii. 24. Then "*it turned northwards to Gilgal, opposite to the ascent of Adummim south of the brook.*" *Gilgal*, which must not be confounded, as it is by *Knobel*, with the first encampment of the Israelites in Canaan, viz. the *Gilgal* between Jericho and the Jordan, is called *Geliloth* in chap. xviii. 17. The situation of this place, which is only mentioned again in Judg. iii. 19, and was certainly not a town, probably only a village or farm, is defined more precisely by the clause "*opposite to the ascent of Adummim.*" *Maaleh Adummim*, which is correctly explained in the *Onom.* (*s. v. Adommim*) as ἀνάβασις πύρρων, *ascensus rufforum*, "was formerly a small villa, but is now a heap of ruins, which is called even to the present day *Maledomim*—on the road from Ælia to Jericho" (*Tobler*). It is mentioned by ancient travellers as an inn called *a terra ruffa, i.e.* "the red earth;" *terra russo*, or "the red house." By later travellers it is described as a small place named *Adomim*, being still called "the red field, because this is the colour of the ground; with a large square building like a monastery still standing there, which was in fact at one time a fortified monastery, though it is deserted now" (*Arvieux*, Merk. Nachr. ii. p. 154). It is the present ruin of *Kalaat el Dem*, to the north of the road from Jerusalem to Jericho, or *Kalaat ed Domm*, near the Khan *Chadrur*. *Gilgal*, or *Geliloth* (circle), was probably the "small round valley" or "field of *Adommim*," of which *Pococke* speaks as being at the foot of the hill on which the deserted inn was standing (viz. *ed Domm;* see *Pococke*, Reise ins Morgenland, ii. p. 46). The valley (*nachal*, rendered *river*) to the south of which Gilgal or the ascent of Adummim lay, and which was therefore to the north of these places, may possibly be the Wady *Kelt*, or the brook of Jericho in the upper part of its course, as we have only to go a quarter or half an hour to the east of Khan Chadrur, when a wide and splendid prospect opens towards the south across the Wady Kelt as far as Taiyibeh; and according to *Van de Velde's* map, a brook-valley runs in a northerly direction to the Wady Kelt on the north-east of Kalaat *ed Dem*. It is probable, however, that the reference is to some other valley, of which there are a great many in the neighbourhood. The boundary then passed over to the water of *En Shemesh* (sun-fountain), *i.e.* the present Apostle's Well, *Ain el Hodh* or *Bir el Khôt*, below Bethany, and on the road to Jericho (*Tobler*, Topogr. v. Jerus. ii. pp. 398, 400; *Van de Velde*, Mem. p. 310), and then ran out at the fountain of *Rogel* (the spies), the present deep and copious *fountain of Job* or *Nehemiah* at the south-east corner of Jerusalem, below the junction of the valley of *Hinnom* and the valley of *Jehoshaphat* or *Kedron* valley (see *Rob.* Pal. i. p. 491, and *Tobler*, Topogr. v. Jerus. ii. pp. 50 sqq.).—Ver. 8. It then went up into the more elevated valley of *Ben-hinnom*, on the south side of the Jebusite town, *i.e.* Jerusalem (see at chap. x. 1), and still farther up to the top of the mountain which rises on the west of the valley of *Ben-hinnom*, and at the farthest extremity of the plain of *Rephaim* towards the north. The valley of *Ben-hinnom*, or *Bne-hinnom* (the son or sons of Hinnom), on the south side of Mount Zion, a place which was notorious from the time of Ahaz as the seat of the worship of Moloch (2 Kings xxiii. 10; 2 Chron. xxviii. 3, xxxiii. 6; Jer. vii. 31, etc.), is supposed to have derived its name from a man who had possessions there, but of whom nothing further is known (see *Robinson*, Pal. i. pp. 402 sqq.). The plain of *Rephaim* (LXX. γῆ ʽΡαφαείν, in 2 Sam. v. 18, 22, xxiii. 13 κοιλὰς τῶν Τιτάνων), probably named after the gigantic race of *Rephaim*, and mentioned several times in 2 Sam. as a battle-field, is on the west of Jerusalem, and is separated from the edge of the valley of *Ben-hinnom* by a small ridge of rock. It runs southwards to *Mar Elias*, is an hour long, half an hour broad, and was very fertile (Isa. xvii. 5); in fact, even to the present day it is carefully cultivated (see *Rob.* Pal. i. p. 323; *Tobler*, Topogr. v. Jerus. ii pp. 401 sqq.). It is bounded on the north by the mountain ridge already mentioned, which curves westwards on the left side of the road to *Jaffa*. This mountain ridge, or one of the peaks, is " the mountain on the west of the valley of Hinnom," at the northern end of the plain referred to.—Ver. 9. From this mountain height the boundary turned to the fountain of the waters of *Nephtoah*, *i.e.*, according to *Van de Velde's* Mem. p. 336, the present village of *Liftah* (*nun* and *lamed* being interchanged, according to a well-known law), an hour to the north-west of Jerusalem, where there is a copious spring, called by the name of Samuel, which not only supplies large basons, but waters a succession of blooming gardens (*Tobler*, Topogr. v. Jerus. ii. pp. 758 sqq.; *Dieterici*, Reisebilder, ii. pp. 221-2). It then "*went out to the towns of Mount Ephraim*," which is not mentioned again, but was probably the steep and lofty mountain ridge on the west side of the Wady *Beit Hanina* (Terebinth valley), upon which *Kulonia*, a place which the road to Joppa passes, *Kastal* on a lofty peak of the mountain, the fortress of *Milane, Soba*, and other places stand (*Seetzen*, R. ii. pp. 64, 65; *Rob.* Bibl. Res. p. 158). The boundary then ran to *Baala, i.e. Kirjath-jearim*, the modern *Kureyet el Enab*, three hours to the north-west of Jerusalem (see at chap. ix. 17).—Ver. 10. From this point *"the boundary* (which had hitherto gone in a north-westerly direction) *turned westwards to Mount Seir, and went out to the shoulder northwards* (*i.e.* to the northern side) *of Har-jearim, that is Chesalon, and went down to Beth-shemesh, and passed over to Timnah.*" Mount *Seir* is the ridge of rock to the south-west of *Kureyet el Enab*, a lofty ridge composed of rugged peaks, with a wild and desolate appearance, upon which *Saris* and *Mishir* are situated (*Rob.* Bibl. Res. p. 155). *Chesalon* is the present *Kesla* on the summit of a mountain, an elevated point of the lofty ridge between Wady *Ghurâb* and *Ismail*, south-west of Kureyet el Enab (*Rob.* Bibl. Res. p. 154). *Beth-shemesh* (*i.e.* sun-house), a priests' city in the territory of Judah (chap. xxi. 16; 1 Chron. vi. 44), is the same as *Ir-shemesh* (chap. xix. 41), a place on the border of Dan, where the ark was deposited by the Philistines (1 Sam. vi. 9 sqq.), and where Amaziah was slain by Joash (2 Kings xiv. 11, 12; 2 Chron. xxv. 21). It was conquered by the Philistines in the time of Ahaz (2 Chron. xxviii. 18). According to the *Onom.* it was ten Roman miles, *i.e.* four hours, from Eleutheropolis towards Nicopolis. It is the present *Ain Shems*, upon a plateau in a splendid situation, two hours and a half to the south-west of Kesla (*Rob.* Pal. iii. p. 17; Bibl. Res. p. 153). *Timnah*, or *Timnatah*, belonged to Dan (chap. xix. 43); and it was thence that Samson fetched his wife (Judg. xiv. 1 sqq.). It is the present *Tibneh*, three-quarters of an hour to the west of Ain Shems (*Rob.* Pal. i. p. 344).—Ver. 11. Thence *"the border went out towards the north-west to the shoulder of Ekron* (*Akir:* see at chap. xiii. 3), *then bent to Shichron, passed over to Mount Baalah, and went out to Jabneel.*" *Shichron* is possibly *Sugheir*, an hour to the south-west of Jebna (*Knobel*). But if this is correct, the mountain of *Baalah* cannot be the short range of hills to the west of Akir which runs almost parallel with the coast (*Rob.* Pal. iii. p. 21), as *Knobel* supposes; but must be a mountain on the south side of the Wady Surar, since the boundary had already crossed this wady between Ekron and Shichron. *Jabneel* is the Philistine town of *Jabneh*, the walls of which were demolished by Uzziah (2 Chron. xxvi. 6), a place frequently mentioned in the books of Maccabees as well as by *Josephus* under the name of *Jamnia*. It still exists as a good-sized village, under the name of *Jebnah*, upon a small eminence on the western side of Nahr Rubin, four hours to the south of Joppa, and an hour and a half from the sea (*Rob.* Pal. iii. p. 22). From Jabneh the boundary went out to the (Mediterranean) Sea, probably along the course of the great valley, *i.e.* the *Nahr Rubin*, as *Robinson* supposes (Pal. ii. p. 343). The *western boundary* was the Great Sea, *i.e.* the Mediterranean.

Vers. 13–19. The account of the conquest of the inheritance, which Caleb asked for and received before the lots were cast for the land (chap. xiv. 6–15), by the extermination of the Anakites from Hebron, and the capture of the fortified town of Debir, is repeated with very slight differences in Judg. i. 10–15, in the enumeration of the different conflicts in which the separate tribes engaged after the death of Joshua, in order to secure actual possession of the inheritance which had fallen to them by lot, and is neither copied from our book by the author of the book of Judges, nor taken from Judges by the author of Joshua; but both of them have drawn it from one common source, upon which the accounts of the conquest of Canaan contained in the book of Joshua are generally founded.—Ver. 13. As an introduction to the account of the conquest of Hebron and Debir, the fact that they gave Caleb his portion among the sons of Judah, namely Hebron, is first of all repeated from chap. xiv. 13. נָתַן impers., they gave, *i.e.* Joshua (chap. xiv. 13). The words " *according to the command of Jehovah to Joshua* " are to be explained from chap. xiv. 9–12, according to which Jehovah had promised, in the hearing of Joshua, to give Caleb possession of the mountains of Hebron, even when they were at Kadesh (chap. xiv. 12). The " father of Anak" is the tribe father of the family of Anakites in Hebron, from whom this town received the name of *Kirjath-arba;* see at Num. xiii. 22 and Gen. xxiii. 2.—Ver. 14. Thence, *i.e.* out of Hebron, Caleb drove (וַיֹּרֶשׁ, *i.e.* rooted out: cf. יֹבוּ, Judg. i. 10) the three sons of Anak, *i.e.* families of the Anakites, whom the spies that were sent out from Kadesh had already found there (Num. xiii. 22). Instead of Caleb, we find the sons of Judah (Judæans) generally mentioned in Judg. i. 10 as the persons who drove out the Anakites, according to the plan of the history in that book, to describe the conflicts in which the several tribes engaged with the Canaanites. But the one does not preclude the other. Caleb did not take Hebron as an individual, but as the head of a family of Judæans, and with their assistance. Nor is there any discrepancy between this account and the fact stated in chap. xi. 21, 22, that Joshua had already conquered Hebron, Debir, and all the towns of that neighbourhood, and had driven out the Anakites from the mountains of Judah, and forced them back into the towns of the Philistines, as *Knobel* fancies. For that expulsion did not preclude the possibility of the Anakites and Canaanites returning to their former abodes, and taking possession of the towns again, when the Israelitish army had withdrawn and was engaged in the war with the Canaanites of the north; so that when the different tribes were about to settle in the towns and districts allotted to them, they were obliged to proceed once more to drive out or exterminate the Anakites and Canaanites who had forced their way in again (see the remarks on chap. x. 38, 39, p. 117, note).—Vers. 15, 16. From Hebron Caleb went against the inhabitants of *Debir*, to the south of Hebron. This town, which has not yet been discovered (see at chap. x. 38), must have been very strong and hard to conquer; for Caleb offered a prize to the conqueror, promising to give his daughter Achzah for a wife to any one that should take it, just as Saul afterwards promised to give his daughter to the conqueror of Goliath (1 Sam. xvii. 25, xviii. 17).—Ver. 17. Othniel took the town and received the promised prize. *Othniel*, according to Judg. iii. 9 the first judge of the Israelites after Joshua's death, is called בֶּן קְנַז אֲחִי כָלֵב, *i.e.* either "the son of Kenaz (and) brother of Caleb," or "the son of Kenaz the brother of Caleb." The second rendering is quite admissible (comp. 2 Sam. xiii. 3, 32, with 1 Chron. ii. 13), but the former is the more usual; and for this the Masorites have decided, since they have separated *achi Caleb* from *ben-Kenaz* by a *tiphchah*. And this is the correct one, as "the son of Kenaz" is equivalent to "the Kenizzite" (chap. xiv. 6). According to Judg. i. 13 and iii. 9, Othniel was Caleb's younger brother. Caleb gave him his daughter for a wife, as marriage with a brother's daughter was not forbidden in the law (see my Bibl. Archäol. ii. § 107, note 14).—Vers. 18, 19. When Achzah had become his wife (" *as she came,*" *i.e.* on her coming to Othniel, to live with him as wife), she urged him to ask her father for a field. " *A field:*" in Judg. i. 14 we find " the field," as the writer had the particular field in his mind. This was not " the field belonging to the town of Debir" (*Knobel*), for Othniel had no need to ask for this, as it naturally went with the town, but a piece of land that could be cultivated, or, as is shown in what follows, one that was not deficient in springs of water. What Othniel did is not stated, but only what Achzah did to attain her end, possibly because her husband could not make up his mind to present the request to her father. She sprang from the ass upon which she had ridden when her father brought her to Othniel. צָנַח, which only occurs again in Judg. iv. 21, and in the parallel passage, Judg. i. 14, is hardly connected with צָנַע, to be lowly or humble (*Ges.*); the primary meaning is rather that suggested by *Fürst*, to force one's self, to press away, or further; and hence in this case the meaning is, to spring down quickly from the animal she had ridden, like נָפַל in Gen. xxiv. 64. Alighting from an animal was a special sign of reverence, from which Caleb inferred that his daughter had some particular request to make of him, and there-fore asked her what she wanted : " *What is to thee ?*" or, " *What wilt thou ?*" She then asked him for a blessing (as in 2 Kings v. 15); " *for*," she added, " *thou hast given me into barren land.*" אֶרֶץ הַנֶּגֶב (rendered a south land) is *accus. loci;* so that *negeb* is not to be taken as a *proper name*, signifying the southernmost district of Canaan (as in ver. 21, etc.), but as an appellative, " the dry or arid land," as in Ps. cxxvi. 4. " *Give me springs of water,*" *i.e.* a piece of land with springs of water in it. Caleb then gave her the " *upper springs and lower springs :*" this was the name given to a tract of land in which there were springs on both the higher and lower ground. It must have been somewhere in the neighbourhood of Debir, though, like the town itself, it has not yet been found.— Ver. 20 contains the closing formula to vers. 1–19, *i.e.* to the de-scription of the territory of Judah by its boundaries (*vid.* chap. xviii. 20).

In vers. 21–63 there follows a *list of the towns* of the tribe of Judah, arranged in the four districts into which the land was divided, according to the nature of the soil, viz. the south-land (*negeb*), the lowland (*shephelah*) on the Mediterranean Sea, the mountains, and the desert of Judah.

Vers. 21–32. The towns in the *south land.*—*Negeb* (south-land) was the name given to the southernmost district of Canaan in its full extent, from the Arabah, at the southern end of the Dead Sea, right across to the coast of the Mediterranean, and from the southern border of Canaan, as described in vers. 2–4, as far north as Wady *Sheriah*, below Gaza, on the western side, and up to the mountains and desert of Judah on the east, stretching across the wadys of *es Seba, Milh,* and *Ehdeib,* above which that part of

Palestine commences where rain is more abundant, and to which, as we have already observed at Num. xiii. 17, the *Negeb* formed a kind of intermediate link between the fertile land and the desert. It was a line of steppe-land, with certain patches here and there that admitted of cultivation, but in which tracts of heath prevailed, for the most part covered with grass and bushes, where only grazing could be carried on with any success. The term which *Eusebius* and *Jerome* employ for *Negeb* in the *Onom.* is *Daroma*, but they carry it farther northwards than the *Negeb* of the Old Testament (see *Reland*, Pal. Ill. pp. 185 sqq.). The numerous towns mentioned in vers. 21–32 as standing in the *Negeb*, may none of them have been large or of any importance. In the list before us we find that, as a rule, several names are closely connected together by the copula *vav*, and in this way the whole may be divided into four separate groups of towns.

Vers. 21–23. *First* group of nine places.—Ver. 21. The towns " *from*," *i.e.* at " *the end of the tribe-territory of Judah, towards the territory of Edom.*" *Kabzeel*: the home of the hero Benaiah (2 Sam. xxiii. 20), probably identical with *Jekabzeel*, which is mentioned in Neh. xi. 25 in connection with *Dibon*, but has not been discovered. This also applies to *Eder* and *Jagur.*—Ver. 22. *Kinah*: also unknown. *Knobel* connects it with the town of the *Kenites*, who settled in the domain of Arad, but this is hardly correct; for with the exception of Judg. i. 16, where the Kenites are said to have settled in the south of Arad, though not till after the division of the land, the Kenites are always found in the western portion of the Negeb (1 Sam. xv. 6, xxvii. 10, xxx. 29), whereas *Kinah* is unquestionably to be looked for in the east. *Dimonah*, probably the same as *Dibon* (Neh. xi. 25); possibly the ruins of *el Dheib*, on the south side of the wady of the same name, to the north-east of Arad (*V. de Velde*, Mem. p. 252), although *Robinson* (Pal. ii. p. 473) writes the name *Ehdeib*. *Adadah* is quite unknown.—Ver. 23. *Kedesh*, possibly *Kadesh-barnea* (ver. 3). *Hazor* might then be Hezron, in the neighbourhood of Kadesh-barnea (ver. 3). *Ithnan* is unknown.

Vers. 24, 25. *Second* group of five or six places.—Of these, *Ziph* and *Telem* are not met with again, unless *Telem* is the same as *Telaim*, where Saul mustered his army to go against the Amalekites (1 Sam. xv. 4). Their situation is unknown. There was another *Ziph* upon the mountains (see ver. 55). *Knobel* supposes the one mentioned here to be the ruins of *Kuseifeh*, to the south-west of Arad (*Rob.* Pal. ii. p. 620). *Ziph* would then be contracted from Ceziph ; but the contraction of *Achzib* (chap. xix. 29) into Zib does not present a corresponding analogy, as in that case the abbreviated form is the later one, whereas in the case of Ziph a lengthening of the name must have taken place by the addition of a K. *Bealoth,* probably the same as the Simeonitish *Baaloth-beer* (chap. xix. 8), which is called *Baal* simply in 1 Chron. iv. 33, and which was also called *Ramath-negeb* (chap. xix. 8) and *Ramoth-negeb* (1 Sam. xxx. 27). It is not to be identified with *Baalath,* however (chap. xix. 45 ; 1 Kings ix. 18), as *V. de Velde* supposes (Reise, ii. pp. 151–2). *Knobel* fancies it may be the ridge and place called *Kubbet el Baul,* between Milh and Kurnub (*Rob.* ii. p. 617) ; but *Baul* and *Baal* are very different. *Hazor Hadatta* (*Chazor Chadathah*), *i.e.* new Hazor, might be the ruins of *el Hudhaira* on the south of Jebel Khulil (*Rob.* Appendix). *Kenoth* was supposed by *Robinson* (Pal. ii. p. 472, and Appendix) to be the ruins of *el Kuryetein,* on the north-east of Arad and at the foot of the mountains, and with this *V. de Velde* agrees. *Reland* (Pal. p. 708) connects the following word *Hezron* with *Kenoth,* so as to read *Kenoth-hezron, i.e.* Hezron's towns, also called *Hazor.* This is favoured by the *Sept.* and *Syriac,* in which the two words are linked together to form one name, and probably by the Chaldee as well, also by the absence of the copula *vav* (*and*) before Hezron, which is not omitted anywhere else throughout this section, except at the beginning of the different groups of towns, as, for example, before Ziph in ver. 24, and *Amam* in ver. 26, and therefore ought to stand before Hezron if it is an independent town. The Masoretic pointing cannot be regarded as a decisive proof of the contrary.

Vers. 26–28. *Third* group of nine towns.—Ver. 26. *Amam* is not mentioned again, and is quite unknown. *Shema,* which is called *Sheba* in chap. xix. 2, and is mentioned among the towns of the Simeonites between Beersheba and Moladah, is supposed by *Knobel* to be the ruins of *Saâwe* (*Sâweh*) between Milh and Beersheba (see *V. de Velde,* ii. p. 148). *Molada,* which was given to the Simeonites (chap. xix. 2 ; 1 Chron. iv. 28) and was still inhabited by Jews after the captivity (Neh. xi. 26), was the later Μάλαδα, an Idumæan fortress (*Josephus,* Ant. xviii. 6, 2), which *Eusebius* and *Jerome* describe as being twenty Roman miles, *i.e.* eight hours, to the south of Hebron on the road to Aila (Elath). It has been identified by *Robinson* (Pal. ii. p. 621) in the ruins of *el Milh,* by the Wady *Malath* or *Malahh.*—Ver. 27. *Hazar-gaddah, Heshmon,* and *Beth-palet* have not yet been identified. The last of the three is mentioned again in Neh. xi. 26, by the side of Molada, as still inhabited by Judæans.—Ver. 28. *Hazar-shual, i.e.* fox-court, which was assigned to the Simeonites (chap. xix. 3) and still inhabited after the captivity (Neh. xi. 27), answers, so far as the name is concerned, to the ruins of *Thály* (*Rob.* Pal. iii. App.). *Beersheba,* which was a well-known place in connection with the history of the patriarchs (Gen. xxi. 14 sqq., xxii. 19, etc.), and is frequently mentioned afterwards as the southern boundary of the land of Israel (Judg. xx. 1; 2 Sam. xvii. 11, etc.), was also given up to the Simeonites (chap. xix. 2), and still inhabited after the captivity (Neh. xi. 27). It is the present *Bir es Seba* on the Wady *es Seba* (see at Gen. xxi. 31). *Bizjothjah* is unknown.

Vers. 29–32. The *four groups* of thirteen towns in the western portion of the Negeb.—Ver. 29. *Baalah,* which was assigned to the Simeonites, is called *Balah* in chap. xix. 3, and *Bilhah* in 1 Chron. iv. 29. *Knobel* identifies it with the present *Deir Belah,* some hours to the south-west of Gaza (*Rob.* iii. App.; *Ritter,* Erdk. xvi. pp. 41, 42); but it cannot have been so far to the west, or so near the coast as this. *Iim* (or Ivvim, according to the Aνείμ of the LXX.) is probably the ruins of *Beit-auwa* (*Rob.* iii. App.). *Azem,* which was also given up to the Simeonites (chap. xix. 3; 1 Chron. iv. 29), is supposed by *Knobel* to be *Eboda,* the present *Abdeh,* eight hours to the south of *Elusa,* a considerable mass of ruins on a ridge of rock (*Rob.* i. p. 287), because the name signifies firmness or strength, which is also the meaning of the Arabic name —a very precarious reason.—Ver. 30. *Eltolad,* which was given to the Simeonites (chap. xix. 4), and is called *Tolad* (without the Arabic article) in 1 Chron. iv. 29, has not been discovered. *Chesil,* for which the LXX. have Βαιθήλ, is probably, as *Reland* supposes, simply another name, or as *Knobel* suggests a corrupt reading, for *Bethul* or *Bethuel,* which is mentioned in chap. xix. 4 and 1 Chron. iv. 30, between *Eltolad* and *Hormah,* as a town of the Simeonites, and the same place as *Beth-el* in 1 Sam. xxx. 27. As this name points to the seat of some ancient sanctuary, and there was an idol called *Khalasa* worshipped by the Arabs before the time of Mahomet, and also because *Jerome* observes (*vita Hilar.* c. 25) that there was a temple of Venus at *Elusa,* in which the Saracens worshipped Lucifer (see *Tuch,* Deutsch. Morgenl. Ztschr. iii. pp. 194 sqq.), *Knobel* supposes *Bethul* (*Chesil*) to be Elusa, a considerable collection of ruins five hours and a half to the south of Beersheba (see *Rob.* i. p. 296): assuming first of all that the name *el Khulasa*, as the Arabs called this place, was derived from the Mahometan idol already referred to; and secondly, that the Saracen Lucifer mentioned by *Jerome* was the very same idol whose image and temple *Janhari* and *Kamus* call *el Khalasa.* *Hormah:* *i.e. Zephoth*, the present *Sepata* (see at chap. xii. 14). *Ziklag*, which was assigned to the Simeonites (chap. xix. 5; 1 Chron. iv. 30), burnt down by the Amalekites (1 Sam. xxx. 1 sqq.), and still inhabited after the captivity (Neh. xi. 28), is supposed by *Rowland* to be the ancient place called *Asluj* or *Kasluj*, a few hours to the east of Zepata, with which *Knobel*, however, in a most remarkable manner, identifies the *Asluj* to the south-west of Milh on the road to Abdeh, which is more than thirty-five miles distant (see *Rob.* Pal. ii. p. 621). Both places are too far to the south and east to suit Ziklag, which is to be sought for much farther west. So far as the situation is concerned, the ruins of Tell *Sheriah* or Tell *Mellala*, one of which is supposed by *V. de Velde* to contain the relics of Ziklag, would suit much better; or even, as *Ritter* supposes (Erdk. xvi. pp. 132–3), Tell *el Hasy*, which is half an hour to the south-west of Ajlan, and in which *Felix Fabri* found the ruins of a castle and of an ancient town, in fact of the ancient Ziklag, though *Robinson* (i. pp. 389 sqq.) could discover nothing that indicated in any way the existence of a town or building of any kind. *Madmannah* and *Sansannah* cannot be traced with any certainty. *Madmannah*, which is confounded in the *Onom.* (*s. v. Medemena*) with *Madmena*, a place to the north of Jerusalem mentioned in Isa. x. 31, though elsewhere it is correctly described as *Menois oppidum juxta civitatem Gazam*, has probably been preserved in the present *Miniay* or *Minieh*, to the south of Gaza. *Sansannah, Knobel* compares with the Wady *Suni*, mentioned by *Robinson* (i. p. 299), to the south of Gaza, which possibly received its name from some town in the neighbourhood. But in the place of them we find *Beth-marcaboth* (*i.e.* carriage-house) and *Hazar-susa* (*i.e.* horse-court) mentioned in chap. xix. 5 and 1 Chron. iv. 31 among the towns of the Simeon-ites, which *Reland* very properly regards as the same as Mad-mannah and Sansannah, since it is very evident from the meaning of the former names that they were simply secondary names, which were given to them as stations for carriages and horses.—Ver. 32. *Lebaoth*, one of the Simeonite towns, called Beth-lebaoth (*i.e.* lion-house) in chap. xix. 6, and *Beth-birei* in 1 Chron. iv. 31, has not been discovered yet. *Shilchim*, called *Sharuchen* in chap. xix. 6, and *Shaaraim* in 1 Chron. iv. 31, may possibly have been preserved in Tell *Sheriah*, almost half-way between Gaza and Beersheba (*V. de Velde*, ii. p. 154). *Ain* and *Rimmon* are given as Simeonite towns, and being written without the copula, are treated as one name in chap. xix. 7 and 1 Chron. iv. 32, although they are reckoned as two separate towns in chap. xix. 7. But as they were also called *En Rimmon* after the captivity, and are given as one single place in Neh. xi. 29, they were probably so close together that in the course of time they grew into one. *Rimmon*, which is mentioned in Zech. xiv. 10 as the southern boundary of Judah, probably the *Eremmon* of the *Onom.* (" a very large village of the Judæans, sixteen miles to the south of Eleuthcropolis in Daroma"), was probably the present ruin called *Um er Rummanim*, four hours to the north of Beersheba (*Rob.* iii. p. 8). Not more than thirty or thirty-five minutes distant from this, between Tell *Khuweilifeh* (*Rob.* iii. p. 8) or *Chewelfeh* (*V. de Velde*) and Tell *Hhora*, you find a large old but half-destroyed well, the large stones of which seem to belong to a very early period of the Israelitish history (*V. de Velde*, ii. p. 153). This was mentioned as a very important drinking-place even in the lifetime of Saladin, whilst to the present day the Tiyâlah Arabs water their flocks there (see *Rob.* iii. p. 8). To all appearance this was *Ain* (see *V. de Velde*, Mem. p. 344). "*All the cities were twenty and nine, and their villages.*" This does not agree with the number of towns mentioned by name, which is not twenty-nine, but thirty-six ; so that the number twenty-nine is probably an error of the text of old standing, which has arisen from a copyist confounding together different numeral letters that resembled one another.[1]

[1] Some commentators and critics explain this difference on the supposition that originally the list contained a smaller number of names (only twenty-nine), but that it was afterwards enlarged by the addition of several other places by a different hand, whilst the number of the whole was left just as it was before. But such a conjecture presupposes greater thoughtlessness on the part of the editor than we have any right to attribute to the author of our book. If the author himself made these additions to his original sources, as *Hävernick* supposes, or the Jehovist completed the author's list from his second document, as *Knobel* imagines, either the one or the other would certainly have altered the sum of the whole, as he has not proceeded in so thoughtless a manner in any other case. The only way in which this conjecture could be defended, would be by supposing, as *J. D. Michaelis* and others have done, that the names added were originally placed in the margin, and that these marginal glosses were afterwards interpolated by some thoughtless copyist into the

Vers. 33–47. Towns in the *lowland* or *shephelah*.—The lowland (*shephelah*), which is generally rendered ἡ πεδινή in the *Sept.*, rarely τὸ πεδίον (Deut. i. 7), but which is transferred as a proper name ἡ Σεφηλά in Obad. 19, Jer. xxxii. 44, xxxiii. 13, as well as in 1 Macc. xii. 38, where even *Luther* has *Sephela*, is the name given to the land between the mountains of Judah and the Mediterranean Sea,—a broad plain of undulating appearance, intersected by heights and low ranges of hills, with fertile soil, in which corn fields alternate with meadows, gardens, and extensive olive groves. It is still tolerably well cultivated, and is covered with villages, which are situated for the most part upon the different hills. Towards the south, the *shephelah* was bounded by the Negeb (ver. 21) ; on the north, it reached to Ramleh and Lydda, or Diospolis, where the plain of Sharon began,—a plain which extended as far as Carmel, and was renowned for the beauty of its flowers. Towards the east the hills multiply and shape themselves into a hilly landscape, which forms the intermediate link between the mountains and the plain, and which is distinguished from the *shephelah* itself, in chap. x. 40 and xii. 8, under the name of *Ashedoth*, or *slopes*, whereas here it is reckoned as forming part of the *shephelah*. This hilly tract is more thickly studded with villages than even the actual plain. (See *Rob. Pal.* ii. p. 363, and iii. p. 29.) The towns in the *shephelah* are divided into four groups.

Vers. 33–36. The *first* group contains the towns in the northern part of the hilly region or slopes, which are reckoned as forming part of the lowland : in all, fourteen towns. The most northerly part of this district was given up to the tribe of Dan on the second division (chap. xix. 41 sqq.). *Eshtaol* and *Zoreah*, which were assigned to the tribe of Dan (chap. xix. 41), and were partly in-

text. But this conjecture is also rendered improbable by the circumstance that, in the lists of towns contained in our book, not only do other differences of the same kind occur, as in ver. 36, where we find only fourteen instead of fifteen, and in chap. xix. 6, where only thirteen are given instead of fourteen, but also differences of the very opposite kind,—namely, where the gross sum given is larger than the number of names, as, for example, in chap. xix. 15, where only five names are given instead of twelve, and in chap. xix. 38, where only sixteen are given instead of nineteen, and where it can be shown that there are gaps in the text, as towns are omitted which the tribes actually received and ceded to the Levites. If we add to this the fact that there are two large gaps in our Masoretic text in chap. xv. 59, 60, and xxi. 35, which proceed from copyists, and also that many errors occur in the numbers given in other historical books of the Old Testament, we are not warranted in tracing the differences in question to any other cause than errors in the text.

habited by Danites (Judg. xiii. 25, xviii. 2, 8, 11) and partly by families of Judah, who had gone out from Kirjath-jearim (1 Chron. ii. 53, iv. 2), probably after the removal of the 600 Danites to Laish-Dan (chap. xix. 47 ; Judg. xviii.), were situated, according to the *Onom.* (*s. v. Esthaul* and *Saara*), ten Roman miles to the north of Eleutheropolis, on the road to Nicopolis. *Zoreah*, the home of Samson, who was buried between Zoreah and Eshtaol (Judg. xiii. 2, xvi. 31), was fortified by Rehoboam, and still inhabited by Judæans after the captivity (2 Chron. xi. 10 ; Neh. xi. 29) ; it has been preserved in the ruins of *Surá*, at the south-western end of the mountain range which bounds the Wady es Surar on the north (*Rob.* ii. p. 341, and Bibl. Res. p. 153). *Eshtaol* has probably been preserved in *Um Eshteiyeh*, to the south-west (*Rob.* ii. p. 342). *Ashnah* is possibly to be read *Ashvah*, according to the LXX., Cod. Vat. (*Ἀσσα*). In that case it might resemble a town on the east of Zorea (*Tobler*, p. 180), as *Knobel* supposes.—Ver. 34. *Zanoah* was still inhabited by Judæans after the captivity (Neh. xi. 30, iii. 13), and is the present *Zanua*, not far from Zorcah, towards the east (see *Rob.* ii. p. 343). *Engannim* and *Tappuah* are still unknown. *Enam*, the same as *Enaim* (Gen. xxxviii. 14 : rendered " an open place "), on the road from Adullam to Timnah on the mountains (ver. 57), has not yet been discovered.—Ver. 35. *Jarmuth, i.e. Jarmûk;* see chap. x. 3. *Adullam* has not yet been discovered with certainty (see at chap. xii. 15). *Socoh*, which was fortified by Rehoboam, and taken by the Philistines in the reign of Ahaz (2 Chron. xi. 7, xxviii. 18), is the present *Shuweikeh* by the Wady Sumt, half an hour to the south-west of *Jarmûk*, three hours and a half to the south-west of Jerusalem (see *Rob.* ii. pp. 343, 349). The *Onom.* (*s. v. Socoh*) mentions two *viculi* named *Sochoth*, one upon the mountain, the other in the plain, nine Roman miles from Eleutheropolis on the road to Jerusalem. On *Azekah*, see at chap. x. 10.—Ver. 36. *Sharaim*, which was on the west of Socoh and Azekah, according to 1 Sam. xvii. 52, and is called *Σακαρίμ* or *Σαργαρείμ* in the *Sept.*, is probably to be sought for in the present Tell *Zakariya* and the village of *Kefr Zakariya* opposite, between which there is the broad deep valley called Wady Sumt, which is only twenty minutes in breadth (*Rob.* ii. p. 350). This is the more probable as the Hebrew name is a dual. *Adithaim* is unknown. *Gederah* is possibly the same as the *Gederoth* which was taken by the Philistines in the time of Ahaz (2 Chron. xxviii. 18), and the *Gedrus* of the *Onom.* (*s. v. Gœdur*, or *Gahedur*), ten Roman miles to the south of Diospolis, on the road to Eleutheropclis, as the *Gederoth* in ver. 41 was in the actual plain, and therefore did not stand between Diospolis and Eleutheropolis. *Gederothaim* is supposed by *Winer, Knobel,* and others, to be an ancient gloss. This is possible no doubt, but it is not certain, as neither the omission of the name from the *Sept.,* nor the circumstance that the full number of towns is given as fourteen, and that this is not the number obtained if we reckon Gederothaim, can be adduced as a decisive proof, since this difference may have arisen in the same manner as the similar discrepancy in ver. 32.

Vers. 37–41. The *second* group, containing the towns of the actual plain in its full extent from north to south, between the hilly region and the line of coast held by the Philistines : *sixteen* towns in all.—Ver. 37. *Zenan,* probably the same as *Zaanan* (Micah i. 11), is supposed by *Knobel* to be the ruins of *Chirbet-es-Senat,* a short distance to the north of Beit-jibrin (*Tobler,* Dritte Wand. p. 124). *Hadashah,* according to the *Mishnah Erub.* v. vi. the smallest place in Judah, containing only fifty houses, is unknown, and a different place from the *Adasa* of 1 Macc. vii. 40, 45, and *Joseph. Ant.* xii. 10, 5, as this was to the north of Jerusalem (*Onom.*).—*Migdal-gad* is unknown. *Knobel* supposes it to be the small hill called *Jedeideh,* with ruins upon it, towards the north of Beit-jibrin (*V. de Velde,* R. ii. pp. 162, 188).—Ver. 38. *Dilean* is unknown ; for *Bet Dula,* three full hours to the east of Beit-jibrin, with some relics of antiquity (*Tobler,* pp. 150–1), with which *Knobel* identifies it, is upon the mountains and not in the plain. *Mizpeh, i.e. specula,* a different place from the *Mizpeh* of Benjamin (chap. xviii. 26), was on the north of Eleutheropolis, according to the *Onom.* (*s. v. Maspha*), and therefore may possibly be the castle *Alba Specula,* or *Alba Custodia* of the middle ages, the present Tell *es Saphieh,* in the middle of the plain and upon the top of a lofty hill, from which there is an extensive prospect in all directions (see *Rob.* ii. p. 363). *Joktheel* has possibly been preserved in the ruins of *Keitulaneh* (*Rob.* Pal. iii. App.), which are said to lie in that neighbourhood.— Ver. 39. *Lachish, i.e. Um Lakis* (see at chap. x. 3). *Bozkath* is unknown : according to *Knobel,* it may possibly be the ruins of *Tubakah,* on the south of Um Lakis and Ajlan (*Rob.* ii. pp. 388, 648). *Eglon, i.e. Ajlan;* see at chap. x. 3.—Ver. 40. *Cabbon,* probably the heap of ruins called *Kubeibeh* or *Kebeibeh,* "which must at some time or other have been a strong fortification, and have formed the key to the central mountains of Judah" (*V. de*

Velde, R. ii. p. 156), and which lie to the south of Beit-jibrin, and two hours and a half to the east of Ajlan (*Rob*. Pal. ii. p. 394). *Lachmas :* according to *Knobel* a corruption of Lachmam, which is the reading given in many MSS. and editions, whilst the *Vulgate* has *Leheman*, and *Luther* (and the *Eng. Ver.*) *Lahmam*. *Knobel* connects it with the ruins of *el Lahem* to the south of Beit-jibrin (*Tobler*). *Kithlish* (*Chitlis*) is unknown, unless it is to be found in Tell *Chilchis*, to the S.S.E. of Beit-jibrin (*V. de Velde*, R. ii. p. 157).—Ver. 41. *Gederoth, Beth-dagon*, and *Naamah* have not yet been traced. The village mentioned in the *Onom.* (*s. v. Beth-dagon*) as *grandis vicus Capher-dagon*, and said to lie between Diospolis and *Jamnia*, the present *Beit-dejan* (*Rob*. iii. p. 30), was far beyond the northern boundary of the tribe of Judah. *Makkedah :* see at chap. x. 10.

Vers. 42–44. The *third* group, consisting of the towns in the southern half of the hilly region : nine towns.—Ver. 42. *Libnah :* see at chap. x. 29. *Ether* and *Ashan*, which were afterwards given to the Simeonites (chap. xix. 7), and are probably to be sought for on the border of the Negeb, have not yet been discovered. The conjecture that *Ether* is connected with the ruins of *Attârah* (*Rob*. iii. App.) in the province of Gaza, is a very uncertain one. *Ashan*, probably the same as *Kor-ashan* (1 Sam. xxx. 30), became a priests' city afterwards (1 Chron. vi. 44 ; see at chap. xxi. 16).—Ver. 43. *Jiphtah, Ashnah*, and *Nezib* have not yet been traced. *Beit-nesib*, to the east of Beit-jibrin on the Wady Sur (*Rob*. ii. p. 344, and iii. p. 13), the Neesib of the *Onom.*, seven Roman miles to the east of Eleutheropolis, does not suit this group so far as its situation is concerned, as it lies within the limits of the first group.—Ver. 44. *Keilah*, which is mentioned in the history of David (1 Sam. xxiii.), and then again after the captivity (Neh. iii. 17), is neither the Κεειλά, *Ceila* of the *Onom.*, on the east of Eleutheropolis, the present *Kila* (*Tobler*, Dritte Wand. p. 151), which lies upon the mountains of Judah ; nor is it to be found, as *Knobel* supposes, in the ruins of *Jugaleh* (*Rob*. iii. App.), as they lie to the south of the mountains of Hebron, whereas *Keilah* is to be sought for in the *shephelah*, or at all events to the west or south-west of the mountains of Hebron. *Achzib* (Micah i. 14), the same as Chesib (Gen. xxxviii. 5), has been preserved in the ruins at *Kussâbeh*, a place with a fountain (*Rob*. ii. p. 391), *i.e.* the fountain of Kesâba, about five hours south by west from Beit-jibrin. *Mareshah*, which was fortified by Rehoboam (2 Chron. xi. 8 ; cf. Micah i. 15), and was the place where

Asa defeated Zerah the Ethiopian (2 Chron. xiv. 9), the home of Eliezer (2 Chron. xx. 37), and afterwards the important town of *Marissa* (see v. *Raumer,* Pal. pp. 211–12), was between Hebron and Ashdod, since Judas Maccabæus is represented in 1 Macc. v. 65–68 (where the reading should be Μαρίσσαν instead of Σαμάρειαν, according to *Joseph.* Ant. xii. 8, 6) as going from Hebron through *Marissa* into the land of the Philistines, and turning to *Ashdod.* According to the *Onom.* (*s. v. Mareshah*), it was lying in ruins in the time of *Eusebius,* and was about two Roman miles from Eleutheropolis,—a description which applies exactly to the ruins of *Maresh,* twenty-four minutes to the south of Beit-jibrin, which *Robinson* supposes for this reason to be Maresa (*Rob.* ii. p. 422), whereas *Knobel* finds it in *Beit-mirsim,* a place four hours to the south of Beit-jibrin.[1]

Vers. 45–47. The *fourth* group, consisting of the towns of the Philistine line of coast, the northern part of which was afterwards given up to the tribe of Dan (chap. xix. 43), but which remained almost entirely in the hands of the Philistines (see at chap. xiii. 3). —Ver. 45. *Ekron, i.e. Akir* (see chap. xiii. 3). " *Her daughters* are the other towns of the principality of Ekron that were dependent upon the capital, and חֲצֵרִים the villages and farms.—Ver. 46. Judah was also to receive " *from Ekron westwards all that lay on the side of Ashdod and their* (*i.e.* Ekron's and Ashdod's) *villages.*" The different places in this district are not given, because Judah never actually obtained possession of them.—Ver. 47. *Ashdod,* now *Esdûd,* and *Gaza,* now *Ghuzzeh:* see at chap. xiii. 3. Also " *the daughter towns*

---

[1] *Knobel* founds his opinion partly upon 2 Chron. xiv. 9, according to which Mareshah was in the valley of Zephatah, which is the bason-like plain at *Mirsim,* and partly upon the fact that the *Onom.* also places *Moraste* on the east (southeast) of Eleutheropolis ; and *Jerome* (ad Mich. i. 1) describes *Morasthi* as *haud grandem viculum juxta Eleutheropolin,* and as *sepulcrum quondam Micheæ prophetæ nunc ecclesiam* (ep. 108 *ad Eustoch.* § 14) ; and this *ecclesia* is in all probability the ruins of a church called *Santa Hanneh,* twenty minutes to the south-east of Beit-jibrin, and only ten minutes to the east of *Marash,* which makes the assumption a very natural one, that the *Maresa* and *Morasthi* of the fathers are only different parts of the same place, viz. of *Moreseth-gath,* the home of Micah (Micah i. 1, 14 ; Jer. xxvi. 18). But neither of these is decisive. The valley of *Zephatah* might be the large open plain which *Robinson* mentions (ii. p. 355) near Beit-jibrin ; and the conjecture that *Morasthi,* which *Euseb.* and *Jer.* place πρὸς ἀνατολὰς, *contra orientem Eleutheropoleos,* is preserved in the ruins which lie in a straight line towards the south from Beit-jibrin, and are called *Marash,* has not much probability in it.

[2] There is no force in the reasons adduced by *Ewald, Bertheau,* and *Knobel,*

and villages, unto the brook of Egypt (Wady *el Arish :* see ver. 4),
and the great sea with its territory," *i.e.* the tract of land lying
between Gaza and the coast of the Mediterranean.   Gath and
Askalon are not mentioned, because they are both of them included
in the boundaries named.   Askalon was between Ashdod and Gaza,
by the sea-coast (see at chap. xiii. 3), and Gath on the east of Ekron
and Ashdod (see chap. xiii. 3), so that, as a matter of course, it was
assigned to Judah.

Vers. 48–60. The towns on the *mountains* are divided into five,
or more correctly, into six groups.   The mountains of Judah, which
rise precipitously from the Negeb, between the hilly district on the
west, which is reckoned as part of the *shephelah,* and the desert of
Judah, extending to the Dead Sea on the east (ver. 61), attain the
height of 3000 feet above the level of the sea, in the neighbourhood
of Hebron, and run northwards to the broad wady of Beit-hanina,
above Jerusalem.   They are a large rugged range of limestone mountains, with many barren and naked peaks, whilst the sides are for
the most part covered with grass, shrubs, bushes, and trees, and the
whole range is intersected by many very fruitful valleys.   *Josephus*
describes it as abounding in corn, fruit, and wine ; and to the
present day it contains many orchards, olive grounds, and vineyards, rising in terraces up the sides of the mountains, whilst the
valleys and lower grounds yield plentiful harvests of wheat, millet,
and other kinds of corn.   In ancient times, therefore, the whole of
this district was thickly covered with towns (see *Rob.* ii. pp. 185,
191–2, and *C. v. Raumer,* Pal. pp. 45 sqq.).

for regarding these verses as spurious, or as a later interpolation from a different
source.   For the statement, that the " Elohist" merely mentions those towns
of which the Hebrews had taken possession, and which they held either partially or wholly in his own day, and also that his list of the places belonging to
Judah in the *shephelah* never goes near the sea, are assertions without the least
foundation, which are proved to be erroneous by the simple fact, that according
to the express statement in ver. 12, the Mediterranean Sea formed the western
boundary of the tribe of Judah ; and according to chap. xiii. 6, Joshua was to
distribute by lot even those parts of Canaan which had not yet been conquered.
The difference, however, which actually exists between the verses before us and
the other groups of towns, namely, that in this case the " towns" (or daughters)
are mentioned as well as the villages, and that the towns are not summed up at
the end, may be sufficiently explained from the facts themselves, namely, from
the circumstance that the Philistine cities mentioned were capitals of small
principalities, which embraced not only villages, but also small towns, and for
that very reason did not form connected groups, like the towns of the other
districts.

Vers. 48–51. The first *group* consists of eleven towns on the south-west of the mountains.—Ver. 48. *Shamir* has probably been preserved in the ruins of *Um Shaumerah*, mentioned by *Robinson* (iii. App.), though the situation of these ruins has not yet been precisely determined. *Jattir*, which was given up to the priests (chap. xxi. 14), and is mentioned again in 1 Sam. xxx. 27, is described in the *Onom.* (*s. v. Jether*) as a large place inhabited by Christians, twenty miles from Eleutheropolis, *in interiori Daroma juxta Malathan*,—a description which suits the ruins of *Attir*, in the southern portion of the mountains (see *Rob.* ii. p. 194; called *Ater* by *Seetzen*, R. iii. p. 6). *Socoh*, two hours N.W. of this, the present *Shuweikeh* (*Rob.* ii. p. 194), called *Suêche* by *Seetzen* (R. iii. p. 29), a village about four hours from Hebron.—Ver. 49. *Dannah* (*Sept., Syr., Renna*) is unknown. *Knobel* imagines that *Dannah* should be *Danah*, for *Deanah*, *plur. Deanoth*, which would then be suggestive of *Zanute*, the last inhabited place upon the mountains, five hours from Hebron, between Shuweikeh and Attir (see *Rob.* ii. p. 626; *Seetzen*, iii. pp. 27, 29). *Kirjath-sannah*, or *Debir*, has not been traced (see at chap. x. 38).—Ver. 50. *Anab*, on the north-east of Socoh (see at chap. xi. 21). *Eshtemoh*, or *Eshtemoa*, which was ceded to the priests (chap. xxi. 14; 1 Chron. vi. 42), and is mentioned again in 1 Sam. xxx. 28, 1 Chron. iv. 17, 19, is the present *Semua*, an inhabited village, with remains of walls, and a castle of ancient date, on the east of Socoh (*Rob.* ii. pp. 194, 626; *Seetzen*, iii. 28; and *v. Schubert*, R. ii. p. 458). *Anim*, contracted, according to the probable conjecture of *Wilson*, from *Ayanim* (fountains), a place still preserved in the ruins of the village of *el Ghuwein*, on the south of *Semua*, though *Robinson* erroneously connects it with *Ain* (ver. 32: see *Rob.* Pal. ii. p. 626).—Ver. 51. *Goshen, Holon,* and *Giloh*, are still unknown. On *Goshen*, see at chap. x. 41. *Holon* was given up to the priests (chap. xxi. 15; 1 Chron. vi. 43); and *Giloh* is mentioned in 2 Sam. xv. 12 as the birth-place of Ahithophel.

Vers. 52–54. The *second* group of nine towns, to the north of the former, in the country round Hebron.—Ver. 52. *Arab* is still unknown; for we cannot connect it, as *Knobel* does, with the ruins of *Husn el Ghurab* in the neighbourhood of Semua (*Rob.* i. p. 312), as these ruins lie within the former group of towns. *Duma*, according to *Eusebius* the largest place in the Daromas in his time, and seventeen miles from Eleutheropolis, is probably the ruined village of *Daumeh*, by the Wady Dilbeh (*Rob.* i. p. 314), which is fourteen miles in a straight line to the south-east of Eleutheropolis according to the map. *Es'an* (Eshean) can hardly be identified with Asar, (1 Chron. iv. 32), as *Van de Velde* supposes, but is more likely *Korasan* (1 Sam. xxx. 30). In that case we might connect it with the ruins of *Khursah*, on the north-west of Daumeh, two hours and a half to the south-west of Hebron (*Rob.* iii. p. 5). As the Septuagint reading is *Σομά*, *Knobel* conjectures that Eshean is a corrupt reading for *Shema* (1 Chron. ii. 43), and connects it with the ruins of *Simia*, on the south of Daumeh (*Seetzen*, iii. 28, and *Rob.* iii. App.). —Ver. 53. *Janum* is still unknown. *Beth-tappuah* has been preserved in the village of *Teffuh*, about two hours to the west of Hebron (*Rob.* ii. p. 428). *Apheka* has not been discovered.—Ver. 54. *Humtah* is also unknown. *Kirjath-arba*, or *Hebron* : see at chap. x. 3. *Zior* has also not been traced ; though, " so far as the name is concerned, it might have been preserved in the heights of *Tugra*, near to Hebron" (*Knobel*).

Vers. 55–57. The *third* group of ten towns, to the east of both the former groups, towards the desert.—Ver. 55. *Maon*, the home of Nabal (1 Sam. xxv. 2), on the border of the desert of Judah, which is here called the desert of Maon (1 Sam. xxiii. 25), has been preserved in Tell *Maîn*, on a conical mountain commanding an extensive prospect, east by north of Semua, three hours and three-quarters to the s.s.e. of Hebron (*Rob.* ii. p. 193). *Carmel*, a town and mountain mentioned in the history of David, and again in the time of Uzziah (1 Sam. xv. 12, xxv. 2 sqq. ; 2 Chron. xxvi. 10). In the time of the Romans it was a large place, with a Roman garrison (*Onom.*), and is the present *Kurmul*, on the north-west of Maon, where there are considerable ruins of a very ancient date (*Rob.* ii. pp. 196 sqq.). *Ziph*, in the desert of that name, to which David fled from Saul (1 Sam. xxiii. 14 sqq., xxvi. 2, 3), was fortified by Rehoboam (2 Chron. xi. 8), and has been preserved in the ruins upon the hill *Ziph*, an hour and three-quarters to the south-east of Hebron (*Rob.* ii. p. 191). *Juttah*, which was assigned to the priests (chap. xxi. 16), and was a *vicus prægrandis Judæorum* in the time of the fathers (*Onom. s. v. Jethan*), was eighteen Roman miles to the south (south-east) of Eleutheropolis, and is the present *Jutta* or *Jitta*, a large Mahometan place with ruins, an hour and three-quarters to the south of Hebron (*Seetzen*, iii. p. 8 ; *Rob.* ii. pp. 191, υ28).—Ver. 56. *Jezreel*, the home of Ahinoam (1 Sam. xxv. 43, xxvii. 3, etc.), a different place from the Jezreel in the plain of Esdraelon, has not yet been discovered. This also applies to *Jokdeam* and *Zanoah*, which are only met with here.—Ver. 57. *Cain*

(*Hakkain*) is possibly the same as *Jukin*, on the south-east of Hebron (*Rob.* ii. p. 449). *Gibeah* cannot be the *Gabatha* near Bethlehem, mentioned in the *Onom.* (*s. v. Gabathon*), or the *Gibea* mentioned by *Robinson* (ii. p. 327), *i.e.* the village of *Jeba*, on a hill in the Wady el Musurr, as this does not come within the limits of the present group ; it must rather be one of the two places (*Gebaa* and *Gebatha*) described as *viculi contra orientalem plagam Daromœ*, though their situation has not yet been discovered. *Timnah*, probably the place already mentioned in Gen. xxxviii. 12 sqq., has not been discovered.

Vers. 58, 59. The *fourth* group of six towns, on the north of Hebron or of the last two groups.—*Halhul*, according to the *Onom.* (*s. v. Elul*) a place near Hebron named *Alula*, has been preserved in the ruins of *Halhûl*, an hour and a half to the north of Hebron (*Rob.* i. p. 319, ii. p. 186, and Bibl. Res. p. 281). *Beth-zur*, which was fortified by Rehoboam (2 Chron. xi. 7), and is frequently mentioned in the time of the Maccabees as a border defence against the Idumæans (1 Macc. iv. 29, 61, etc.), was twenty (? fifteen) Roman miles from Jerusalem, according to the *Onom.* (*s. v. Beth-zur*), on the road to Hebron. It is the present heap of ruins called *Beit-zur* on the north-west of Halhûl (*Rob.* Bibl. Res. pp. 276–7 ; *Ritter*, Erdk. xvi. pp. 236, 267–8). *Gedor*, the ruins of *Jedûr*, an hour and a half to the north-west (*Rob.* ii. p. 338 ; Bibl. Res. pp. 282–3).—Ver. 59. *Maarath* and *Eltekon* have not yet been discovered. *Beth-anoth* (probably a contraction of *Beth-ayanoth*) has been discovered by *Wolcott* in the ruins of *Beit-anum*, on the east of Halhûl (*Rob.* Bibl. Res. p. 279 ; cf. Pal. ii. p. 186).

Between vers. 59 and 60, the *fifth* group of towns given in the Septuagint is wanting in the Masoretic text. This group lay to the north of the fourth, and reached as far as Jerusalem. It comprised a district in which even now there are at least fifteen places and ruins, so that we have not an arbitrary interpolation made by the LXX., as *Jerome* assumed, but rather a gap in the Hebrew text, arising from the fact that an ancient copyist passed by mistake from the word וְחַצְרֵיהֶן in ver. 59 to the same word at the close of the missing section. In the Alexandrian version the section reads as follows in *Cod. Al. and Vat.*: Θεκὼ καὶ ᾽Εφραθά, αὕτη ἐστὶ Βαιθλεεμ, καὶ Φαγὼρ καὶ Αἰτὰν καὶ Κουλὸν καὶ Τατὰμ καὶ Θωβὴς (*Cod. Al.* Σωρὴς) καὶ Καρὲμ καὶ Γαλὲμ καὶ Θεθὴρ (*Cod. Al.* Βαιθὴρ) καὶ Μανοχώ, πόλεις ἕνδεκα καὶ αἱ κῶμαι αὐτῶν.—*Theko*, the well-known Tekoah, the home of the wise woman and of the

prophet Amos (2 Sam. xiv. 2 ; Amos i. 1), was fortified by Rehoboam, and still inhabited after the captivity (2 Chron. xi. 6 ; Neh.
iii. 5, 27). It is the present *Tekua*, on the top of a mountain covered
with ancient ruins, two hours to the south of Bethlehem (*Rob.* ii.
pp. 181–184; *Tobler*, Denkbl. aus Jerus. pp. 682 sqq.). *Ephratah*,
i.e. Bethlehem, the family seat of the house of David (Ruth i. 1,
iv. 11 ; 1 Sam. xvi. 4, xvii. 12 sqq.; Micah v. 2), was fortified by
Rehoboam (2 Chron. xi. 6), and is a place frequently mentioned.
It was the birth-place of Christ (Matt. ii. 1 sqq.; Luke ii. 4), and
still exists under the ancient name of *Beit-lahm*, two hours to the
south of Jerusalem (*Seetzen*, ii. pp. 37 sqq.; *Rob.* ii. pp. 159 sqq. ;
Tobler, Topogr. v. Jerus. ii. pp. 464 sqq.). *Bethlehem* did not receive
the name of *Ephratah* for the first time from the Calebite family
of Ephrathites (1 Chron. ii. 19, 50, iv. 4), but was known by that
name even in Jacob's time (Gen. xxxv. 19, xlviii. 7). *Phagor*,
which was near to Bethlehem according to the *Onom.* (*s. v. Fogor*),
and is also called *Phaora*, is the present *Faghur*, a heap of ruins to
the south-west of Bethlehem (*Rob.* Bibl. Res. p. 275). *Aetan* was
fortified by Rehoboam (2 Chron. xi. 6), and has been preserved in
the *Wady* and *Ain Attan* between Bethlehem and Faghur (*Tobler*,
dritte Wand. pp. 88, 89). *Kulon*, the present village of *Kulomeh*,
an hour and a half west by north from Jerusalem on the road to
Ramleh (see *Rob.* ii. p. 146; Bibl. Res. p. 158 : it is called *Kolony*
by *Seetzen*, ii. p. 64). *Tatam* cannot be traced. *Sores* (for *Thobes*
appears to be only a copyist's error) is probably *Saris*, a small
village four hours to the east of Jerusalem, upon a ridge on the
south of Wady Aly (*Rob.* Bibl. Res. pp. 154–5). *Karem*, now *Ain
Karim*, a large flourishing village two hours to the west of Jerusalem, with a Franciscan convent dedicated to John the Baptist in
the middle, and a fountain (*Rob.* ii. p. 141; Bibl. Res. p. 271).
Galem, a different place from the *Gallim* on the north of Jerusalem (Isa. x. 30), has not yet been discovered. *Baither*, now a
small dirty village called *Bettir* or *Bittir*, with a beautiful spring,
and with gardens arranged in terraces on the western slope of the
Wady Bittir, to the south-west of Jerusalem (*Rob.* Bibl. Res. p.
266). *Manocho*, possibly the same place as *Manachat* (1 Chron.
viii. 6), has not been found.

Ver. 60. The *sixth* group of only two towns, to the west of
Jerusalem, on the northern border of the tribe of Judah.—*Kirjath-
baal*, or *Kirjath-jearim*, the present *Kureyet el Enab ;* see at ver. 9,
and chap. ix. 17. *Rabbah* (*Ha-rabbah*, the great) is quite unknown.

Vers. 61, 62. The *towns in the desert of Judah*, which ran along the Dead Sea from the northern border of Judah (vers. 6, 7) to Wady Fikreh on the south, and reached to the districts of Maon, Ziph, Tekoah, and Bethlehem towards the west. This tract of land is for the most part a terrible desert, with a soil composed of chalk, marl, and limestone, and with bald mountains covered with flint and hornstone, and without the slightest trace of vegetation on the side bordering on the Dead Sea (see *v. Schubert*, Reise, iii. pp. 94, 96; *Rob.* ii. pp. 202, 475, 477). Yet wherever there are springs even this desert is covered with a luxuriant vegetation, as far as the influence of the water extends (*Seetzen*, ii. pp. 249, 258); and even in those parts which are now completely desolate, there are traces of the work of man of a very ancient date in all directions (*Rob.* ii. p. 187). Six towns are mentioned in the verses before us. *Beth-arabah*: see at ver. 6. *Middin* and *Secaca* are unknown. According to *Knobel*, *Middin* is probably the ruins of *Mird* or *Mardeh*, to the west of the northern end of the Dead Sea (*Rob.* ii. p. 270).—Ver. 62. *Nibsan*, also unknown. The city of salt (salt town), in which the Edomites sustained repeated defeats (2 Sam. viii. 13; Ps. lx. 2; 2 Kings xiv. 7; 1 Chron. xviii. 12; 2 Chron. xxv. 11), was no doubt at the southern end of the Dead Sea, in the Salt Valley (*Rob.* ii. p. 483). *Engedi*, on the Dead Sea (Ezek. xlvii. 10), to which David also fled to escape from Saul (1 Sam. xxiv. 1 sqq.), according to the *Onom.* (*s. v. Engaddi*) a *vicus præ-grandis*, the present *Ain-Jidi*, a spring upon a shelf of the high rocky coast on the west of the Dead Sea, with ruins of different ancient buildings (see *Seetzen*, ii. pp. 227–8; *Rob.* ii. pp. 214 sqq.; *Lynch*, pp. 178–9, 199, 200).—In ver. 63 there follows a notice to the effect that the Judæans were unable to expel the Jebusites from Jerusalem, which points back to the time immediately after Joshua, when the Judæans had taken Jerusalem and burned it (Judg. i. 8), but were still unable to maintain possession. This notice is not at variance with either chap. xviii. 28 or Judg. i. 21, since it neither affirms that Jerusalem belonged to the tribe of Judah, nor that Judah alone laid claim to the possession of the town to the exclusion of the Benjamites (see the explanation of Judg. i. 8).

INHERITANCE OF THE TRIBE OF JOSEPH.—CHAP. XVI. XVII

The descendants of Joseph drew one lot, that the inheritance of the half tribe of Manasseh might not be separated from that of the tribe of Ephraim. But the territory was immediately divided between the two separate tribes of the children of Joseph, Ephraim receiving the southern portion of the land that had fallen to it by lot, and half Manasseh the northern. Accordingly we find the southern boundary of the whole territory described first of all in chap. xvi. 1–4, both the boundary which separated it from the tribe of Benjamin (chap. xviii. 11 sqq.), and that which divided it from Dan (chap. xix. 40 sqq.); then the territory of Ephraim is given, with a minute description of the northern boundary (chap. xvi. 5–10); and finally the territory assigned to the families of Manasseh (chap. xvii. 1–13), without any precise delineation of its northern boundaries, all that is stated being that the Manassites touched Asher and Issachar towards the north, and also received some scattered towns with their villages in the territory of both those tribes (chap. xvii. 10, 11). To this there is appended in vers. 14–18 the complaint of the children of Joseph concerning the inheritance that had fallen to them.

Chap. xvi. 1–4. *Territory of the Tribe of Joseph.*—Ver. 1. " *And there came out the lot of the children of Joseph from Jordan by Jericho.*" "The lot came out," viz. from the urn (cf. chap. xix. 1, 17, 24). The expression " came up" is used in the same sense in chap. xviii. 11. The connection of these two words with the rest of the sentence, " *from Jordan by Jericho,*" may be explained on the supposition that the lot which came out of the urn determined the inheritance that fell to the tribe, so that we might paraphrase the verse in this manner : " There came out the lot to the children of Joseph, namely, the inheritance, which goes out from, or whose boundary commences at, the Jordan by Jericho," *i.e.* from that part of the Jordan which is opposite to Jericho, and which is still more precisely defined by the additional clause, " by the water of Jericho eastward." The water of Jericho is the present fountain of *es Sultan,* half an hour to the north-west of *Riha,* the only large fountain in the neighbourhood of Jericho, whose waters spread over the plain, and form a small brook, which no doubt flows in the rainy season through the Wady Kelt into the Jordan (see *Rob.* ii. pp. 283–4; *Tobler,* Topogr. v. Jerus. ii. pp. 558–9). " *The wilderness*" is in opposition to " the lot," so that the sense is, " *namely, the desert going up from Jericho to the mountains to Bethel.*" According to chap. xviii. 12, the reference is to the desert of Beth-aven, which was on the east of Bethel, between the Wady *Suwar* (*Tuwar*) and Mutyah (see at chap. vii. 2). Towards the east this desert terminates with the Jebel Kuruntul (Quarantana) on the north-west of Jericho, where it descends precipitously into the valley of the Jordan, or *v. v.*, where it rises out of the Jordan valley. According to chap. xviii. 12, the same boundary went up by the shoulder of Jericho towards the north, *i.e.* along the northern range of mountains by Jericho, which cannot be any other than the " conspicuous double height, or rather group of heights," in front of the mountain of Quarantana, at the eastern foot of which lies the fountain of Ain es Sultan (*Rob.* ii. p. 284). In all probability, therefore, the boundary ran up towards the north-west, from the Sultan fountain to Ain Duk, and thence in a westerly direction across to Abu Seba (along which road *Robinson* had a frightful desert on his right hand: Pal. ii. p. 310), and then again towards the north-west to Beitin (Bethel), according to chap. xviii. 13, along the southern shoulder (or side) of Luz, *i.e.* Bethel.—Ver. 2. " *And it went out from Bethel to Luz.*" Bethel is distinguished from Luz in this passage, because the reference is not to the town of Bethel, which was called Luz by the Canaanites (*vid.* Gen. xxviii. 19), but to the southern range of mountains belonging to Bethel, from which the boundary ran out to the town of Luz, so that this town, which stood upon the border, was allotted to the tribe of Benjamin (chap. xviii. 22). From this point the boundary went over " *to the territory of the Arkite to Ataroth.*" We know nothing further about the Arkite than that David's friend Hushai belonged to that family (2 Sam. xv. 32, xvi. 16; 1 Chron. xxvii. 33). *Ataroth*, called *Ataroth-Adar* in chap. xviii. 13, was not the present village of Atâra, an hour and a half to the south of Jiljilia (*Rob.* iii. p. 80), as I once supposed, but the ruins of *Atâra*, three-quarters of an hour to the south of Bireh (Beeroth, *Rob.* ii. p. 314), with which the expression " *descended*" in chap. xviii. 13 perfectly harmonizes. Consequently the boundary was first of all drawn in a south-westerly direction from Beitin to Bireh (chap. xviii. 25), and then southwards to Atârah. —Ver. 3. From this point " *it went down westward to the territory of the Japhletites to the territory of lower Beth-horon,*" or, according to chap. xviii. 13, " to the mountain (or range) which is on the south by lower Beth-horon." The *Japhletite* is altogether unknown, as the Asherite of this name cannot possibly be thought of (1 Chron.

vii. 32, 33). *Lower Beth-horon* is the present *Beit-Ur Tachta*, a village upon a low ridge. It is separated from Upper Beth-horon, which lies farther east, by a deep wady (see at chap. x. 10, and *Rob.* iii. p. 59). " *And to Gezer,*" which was probably situated near the village of *el Kubab* (see at chap. x. 33). " *And the goings out thereof are at the sea*" (the Mediterranean), probably running towards the north-west, and following the Wady Muzeireh to the north of Japho, which was assigned to the Danites, according to chap. xix. 46.—Ver. 4. The territory commencing at the boundary lines mentioned was allotted to Ephraim and Manasseh as theiɪ inheritance.

Vers. 5–10. *Territory of the tribe of Ephraim,* according to its families.—Ver. 5. " *The border of their inheritance was from the east Atroth-addar and* (along the line) *to Upper Beth-horon,*"—a brief description of the southern boundary, which is more minutely described in vers. 1–3. Upper Beth-horon is mentioned here instead of Lower Beth-horon (ver. 3). This makes no difference, however, as the two places stood quite close to one another (see at chap. x. 10). In vers. 6–8 the northern boundary of Ephraim is given, namely, from the middle, or from " a central point near the watershed" (*Knobel*), first towards the east (vers. 6 and 7), and then towards the west (ver. 8). The eastern half of the northern boundary went יָמָּה, *i.e.* when regarded from the west, or looked at towards the west, to the north side of *Michmethah.* According to chap. xvii. 7, this place was before Shechem, and therefore in any case it was not far from it, though it has not been discovered yet. *Knobel* supposes it to have been on the site of the present *Kabate* (*Seetzen,* ii. p. 166), *Kubatiyeh,* an hour and a half to the south of *Jenin* (*Rob.* iii. 154), assuming that *Michmethah* might also have been pronounced *Chemathah,* and that *b* may have been substituted for *m.* But *Kabate* is six hours to the north of Shechem, and therefore was certainly not " *before Shechem*" (chap. xvii. 7). It then turned " *eastward to Taanath-shiloh*" (Τηνὰθ Σηλώ, LXX.), according to the *Onom.* (*s. v. Thenath*) ten Roman miles from Neapolis (Sichem), on the way to the Jordan, most probably the *Thena* of *Ptol.* (v. 16, 5), the present *Tana, Ain Tana,* a heap of ruins on the south-east of Nabulus, where there are large cisterns to be found (see *Rob.* Bibl. Res. p. 295; *Ritter,* Erdk. xv. p. 471). And " *then went by on the east to Janoah*" (*i.e. Jano in Acrabittena regione,* twelve Roman miles from Neapolis: *Onom.*), the present ruins of *Janûn,* a miser-able village, with extensive ruins of great antiquity, about three

hours to the south-east of Nabulus, three-quarters of an hour to the
north-east of Akrabeh (*Rob.* Bibl. Res. p. 297 ; *Van de Velde*, R. ii.
p. 268).—Ver. 7. From Janoah the boundary went down " *to
Ataroth and Naarath.*" *Ataroth*, a different place from the Ataroth
or Atroth-addar mentioned in vers. 3 and 5, is apparently to be
sought for on the eastern slope of the mountains by the side of the
Ghor, judging from the expression " went down ;" but it has not
yet been discovered. *Naarath*, probably the same as *Naaran*, in
eastern Ephraim (1 Chron. vii. 28), is described in the *Onom.*
(*s. v. Naaratha*) as *viculus Judæorum Naorath*, five Roman miles (*i.e.*
two hours) from Jericho, probably on the north-east. The boundary line then touched Jericho, *i.e.* the district of Jericho, namely
on the north side of the district, as Jericho was allotted to the tribe
of Benjamin (chap. xviii. 21). At this point it also coincided with
the southern boundary of the tribe of Joseph (ver. 1) and the
northern boundary of Benjamin (chap. xviii. 12).—Ver. 8. The
western half of the northern boundary went from *Tappuah* westwards to the Cane-brook, and terminated at the sea. *Tappuah*, called
En-tappuah in chap. xvii. 7, as the southern boundary of Manasseh, which is there described, and which ran from Michmethah to
En-tappuah, coincides with the northern boundary of Ephraim,
must not be identified with the royal town of that name mentioned
in chap. xii. 17, and therefore was not *Kefr Kud* (*Capercota*), on
the west of Jenin (Ginäa). This place was so far to the north,
viz. seven hours to the north of Nabulus, that the boundary from
Michmethah, in the neighbourhood of Shechem (Nabulus) onwards,
would have run from south to north instead of in a westerly direction. Still less can *En-tappuah* be found, as *Van de Velde* supposes, in the old well of the deserted village of *Atüf*, five hours to
the east of Nabulus. It must have been to the west of Shechem ;
but it has not yet been discovered, as the country to the west of
Nabulus and Sebastieh has "not been examined" (*Van de Velde*).
The *Cane-brook* is no doubt the brook of that name mentioned
by *Bohad.* (*vita Salad.* pp. 191, 193) ; only it is not quite clear
" whether the *Abu Zabura* is intended, or a brook somewhat farther south, where there is still a *Nahr el Kassab.*"—Ver. 9. The
tribe of Ephraim also received some scattered towns in the territory
of the tribe of Manasseh, in fact all those towns to which Tappuah
belonged, according to chap. xvii. 8, with the dependent villages.[1]—

---

[1] The reason why the Ephraimites received scattered towns and villages in
the tribe-territory of Manasseh, is supposed by *Calvin, Masius*, and others, to

Ver. 10. From Gezer, however (see ver. 3), they could not drive out the Canaanites, so that they still dwelt among the Ephraimites, but were reduced to a state of serfdom. This notice resembles the one in chap. xv. 63, and is to be interpreted in the same way.

Chap. xvii. 1–13. *The inheritance of Manasseh on this side of the Jordan* was on the north of Ephraim.—Vers. 1*b*-6. Before proceeding to the more detailed description of the inheritance, the historian thinks it necessary to observe that the Manassites received a double inheritance. This remark is introduced with the words "*for he was the first-born of Joseph.*" On this account, in addition to the territory already given to him in Gilead and Bashan, he received a second allotment of territory in Canaan proper. With the word לְמָכִיר (for Machir) the more minute account of the division of the Manassites commences. לְמָכִיר וגו׳ is first of all written absolutely at the beginning of the sentence, and then resumed in וַיְהִי לוֹ : "*to Machir, the first-born of Manasseh . . . to him were Gilead and Bashan assigned, because he was a man of war,*" *i.e.* a warlike man, and had earned for himself a claim to the inheritance of Gilead and Bashan through the peculiar bravery which he had displayed in the conquest of those lands. By *Machir*, however, we are not to understand the actual son of Manasseh, but his family ; and אֲבִי הַגִּלְעָד does not mean "father of Gilead," but *lord* (possessor) *of Gilead*, for Machir's son Gilead is always called גִּלְעָד without the article (*vid.* chap. xvii. 3; Num. xxvi. 29, 30, xxvii. 1, xxxvi. 1; 1 Chron. vii. 17), whereas the country of that name is just as constantly called הַגִּלְעָד (see ver. 1, the last clause, ver. 5, chap. xiii. 11, 31 ; Num. xxxii. 40 ; Deut. iii. 10 sqq.). "*And there came, i.e.* the lot fell (the lot is to be repeated from ver. 1), *to the other descendants of Manasseh according to their families,*" which are then enumerated as in Num. xxvi. 30-32. "*These are the male descendants of Manasseh.*" הַזְּכָרִים must not be altered, notwithstanding the fact that it is preceded and followed by הַנּוֹתָרִים ; it is evidently used deliberately as an antithesis to the female descendants of Manasseh mentioned in ver. 3.—Vers. 3 sqq. Among the six families of Manasseh (ver. 2), *Zelophehad*, a descendant of *Hepher*, left no son ; but he had five daughters, whose names are given in ver. 3

---

have been, that after the boundaries had been arranged, on comparing the territory allotted to each with the relative numbers of the two tribes, it was found that Ephraim had received too small a possession. This is quite possible; at the same time there may have been other reasons which we cannot discover now, as precisely the same thing occurs in the case of Manasseh (chap. xvii. 11).

(as in Num. xxvi. 33, xxvii. 1, xxxvi. 10). These daughters had
petitioned Moses for a separate portion in the promised land, and
their request had been granted (Num. xxvii. 2 sqq., compared with
chap. xxxvi.). They therefore came before the committee appointed
for dividing the land and repeated this promise, which was at once
fulfilled. Consequently there were ten families of Manasseh who
had received portions by the side of Ephraim, five male and five
female. " *And* (ver. 5) *there fell the measurements of Manasseh*
(as) *ten*," *i.e.* ten portions were assigned to the Manassites (on the
west of the Jordan), beside the land of Gilead, because (as is again
observed in ver. 6) the daughters of Manasseh, *i.e.* of Zelophehad
the Manassite, received an inheritance among his sons (*i.e.* the rest
of the Manassites).

Vers. 7-13. *Boundaries and extent of the inheritance of the ten
families of Manasseh.*—Vers. 7-10a, the southern boundary, which
coincides with the northern boundary of Ephraim described in
chap. xvi. 6-8, and is merely given here with greater precision
in certain points. It went " *from Asher to Michmethah, before
Shechem.*" *Asher* is not the territory of the tribe of Asher, but a
distinct locality ; according to the *Onom.* (*s. v. Asher*) a place on
the high road from Neapolis to Scythopolis, fifteen Roman miles
from the former. It is not to be found, however, in the ruins of
Tell *Um el Aschera* (*V. de Velde*) or Tell *Um Ajra* (*Rob.* Bibl.
Res. pp. 310, 327), an hour to the south of Beisan, as *Knobel*
supposes, but in the village of *Yasir*, where there are magnificent
ruins, about five hours and ten minutes from Nabulus on the road
to Beisan (*V. de Velde*, Mem. pp. 237, 289 ; R. ii. p. 295). *Michmethah*, before *Shechem*, is still unknown (see chap. xvi. 6). *Shechem*
was founded by the Hivite prince Shechem (Gen. xxxiii. 18), and
is frequently mentioned in the book of Genesis. It stood between
Ebal and Gerizim, was given up by Ephraim to the Levites, and
declared a free city (city of refuge : chap. xxi. 21, xx. 7). It
was there that the ten tribes effected their separation from Judah
(1 Kings xii. 1 sqq.), and Jeroboam resided there (1 Kings xii. 25).
In later times it was the chief city of the country of Samaria, and
the capital of the Samaritans (John iv. 5) ; and the name of
Neapolis, or *Flavia Neapolis*, from which the present *Nabulus* or
Nablus has come, was given to it in honour of Vespasian (see *v.
Raumer*, Pal. pp. 161 sqq.). From this point the boundary went
אֶל־הַיָּמִין (*i.e.* either " *to the right side*," the south side, or *to Yamin*),
" *to the inhabitants of En-tappuah.*" Whether *Yamin* is an appella-

tive or a proper name is doubtful. But even if it be the name of a place, it is quite certain that it cannot be the village of *Yamôn*, an hour to the south-east of *Taanuk* (*Rob.* iii. pp. 161, 167, etc.), as this is much too far north, and, judging from ver. 11, belonged to the territory of Asher. In the case of *En-tappuah*, the inhabitants are mentioned instead of the district, because the district belonged to Manasseh, whilst the town on the border of Manasseh was given to the Ephraimites. The situation of the town has not yet been discovered: see at chap. xvi. 8. From this point the boundary ran down to the Cane-brook (see chap. xvi. 8), namely to the south side of the brook. "*These towns were assigned to Ephraim in the midst of the towns of Manasseh, and* (but) *the territory of Manasseh was on the north of the brook.*" The only possible meaning of these words is the following: From Tappuah, the boundary went down to the Cane-brook and crossed it, so that the south side of the brook really belonged to the territory of Manasseh; nevertheless the towns on this south side were allotted to Ephraim, whilst only the territory to the north of the brook fell to the lot of the Manassites. This is expressed more plainly in ver. 10*a*: "*To the south* (of the brook the land came) *to Ephraim, and to the north to Manasseh.*" In ver. 10*b* the northern and eastern boundaries are only briefly indicated: "*And they* (the Manassites) *touched Asher towards the north, and Issachar towards the east.*" The reason why this boundary was not described more minutely, was probably because it had not yet been fixed. For (ver. 11) Manasseh also received towns and districts in (within the territory of) Issachar and Asher, viz. Beth-shean, etc. *Beth-shean*, to the wall of which Saul's body was fastened (1 Sam. xxxi. 10 sqq.; 2 Sam. xxi. 12), was afterwards called *Scythopolis*. It was in the valley of the Jordan, where the plain of Jezreel slopes off into the valley; its present name is *Beisan*, a place where there are considerable ruins of great antiquity, about two hours from the Jordan (*vid. Seetzen*, ii. pp. 162 sqq.; *Rob.* iii. p. 174; Bibl. Res. p. 325; *v. Raumer*, Pal. pp. 150–1). This city, with its daughter towns, was in the territory of Issachar, which was on the east of Manasseh, and may have extended a considerable distance towards the south along the valley of the Jordan, as the territory of Manasseh and Ephraim did not run into the valley of the Jordan; but Asher (Yasir) is mentioned in ver. 7 as the most easterly place in Manasseh, and, according to chap. xvi. 6, 7, the eastern boundary of Ephraim ran down along the eastern edge of the mountains as far as Jericho, without including the Jordan valley. At the same

time, the Ghor on the western side of the Jordan below Beisan, as
far as the plain of Jericho, was of no great value to any tribe, as
this district, according to *Josephus* (de Bell. Jud. iv. 8, 2, and iii.
10, 7), was uninhabited because of its barrenness. The other
towns, *Ibleam*, etc., with the exception of Endor perhaps, were in
the territory of Asher, and almost all on the south-west border of
the plain of Esdraelon. *Ibleam*, called *Bileam* in 1 Chron. vi. 55
(70), a Levitical town (see at chap. xxi. 25), was not very far from
Megiddo (2 Kings ix. 27), and has probably been preserved in the
ruins of *Khirbet-Belameh*, half an hour to the south of Jenin;
according to *Schultz*, it is the same place as *Belamon, Belmen,* or
Belthem (Judith iv. 4, vii. 3, viii. 3). With וְאֶת־יֹשְׁבֵי דֹאר the construction changes, so that there is an anacolouthon, which can be
explained, however, on the ground that הָיָה לְ may not only mean
to be assigned to, but also to receive or to have. In this last sense
וְאֶת is attached. The inhabitants are mentioned instead of the
towns, because the historian had already the thought present in his
mind, that the Manassites were unable to exterminate the Canaanites
from the towns allotted to them. *Dor* is the present *Tortura* (see
at chap. xi. 2). *Endor*, the home of the witch (1 Sam. xxviii. 7),
four Roman miles to the south of Tabor (*Onom.*), at present a
village called *Endôr*, on the northern shoulder of the Duhy or
Little Hermon (see *Rob.* iii. p. 225; Bibl. Res. p. 340). *Taanach*
and *Megiddo*, the present *Taanuk* and *Lejun* (see at chap. xii. 21).
The three last towns, with the places dependent upon them, are
connected more closely together by שְׁלֹשֶׁת הַנָּפֶת, the three-hill-
country, probably because they formed a common league.—Vers.
12, 13. The Manassites were unable to exterminate the Canaanites
from these six towns, and the districts round; but when they grew
stronger, they made them tributary slaves (cf. chap. xvi. 10).

Vers. 14–18. *Complaint of the Descendants of Joseph respecting
the inheritance allotted to them.*—Ver. 14. As the descendants of
Joseph formed two tribes (Ephraim and Manasseh), they gave
utterance to their dissatisfaction that Joshua had given them
("*me,*" the house of Joseph, ver. 17) but one lot, but one portion
(חֶבֶל, a measure, then the land measured off), for an inheritance,
although they were a strong and numerous people. "*So far hath
Jehovah blessed me hitherto.*" עַד־אֲשֶׁר, to this (*sc.* numerous people),
is to be understood *de gradu;* עַד־כֹּה, hitherto, *de tempore.* There
was no real ground for this complaint. As Ephraim numbered
only 32,500 and Manasseh 52,700 at the second census in the time

of Moses (Num. xxvi.), and therefore Ephraim and half Manasseh together did not amount to more than 58,000 or 59,000, this tribe and a half were not so strong as Judah with its 76,500, and were even weaker than Dan with its 64,400, or Issachar with its 64,300 men, and therefore could not justly lay claim to more than the territory of a single tribe. Moreover, the land allotted to them was in one of the most fertile parts of Palestine. For although as a whole the mountains of Ephraim have much the same character as those of Judah, yet the separate mountains are neither so rugged nor so lofty, there being only a few of them that reach the height of 2500 feet above the level of the sea (see *Ritter*, Erdk. xv. pp. 475 sqq.; *V. de Velde*, Mem. pp. 177 sqq.); moreover, they are intersected by many broad valleys and fertile plateaux, which are covered with fruitful fields and splendid plantations of olives, vines, and fig trees (see *Rob.* iii. p. 78, Bibl. Res. pp. 290 sqq.; *Seetzen*, ii. pp. 165 sqq., 190 sqq.). On the west the mountains slope off into the hill country, which joins the plain of Sharon, with its invariable fertility. "The soil here is a black clay soil of unfathomable depth, which is nearly all ploughed, and is of such unusual fertility that a cultivated plain here might furnish an almost unparalleled granary for the whole land. Interminable fields full of wheat and barley with their waving ears, which were very nearly ripe, with here and there a field of millet, that was already being diligently reaped by the peasants, presented a glorious sight" (*Ritter*, Erdk. xvi. pp. 567–8).—Ver. 15. Joshua therefore sent them back with their petition, and said, "*If thou art a strong people, go up into the wood and cut it away,*" *i.e.* make room for houses, fields, and meadows, by clearing the forests, "*in the land of the Perizzites and Rephaim, if the mountain of Ephraim is too narrow for thee.*" The name "mountain of Ephraim" is used here in a certain sense proleptically, to signify the mountain which received its name from the tribe of Ephraim, to which it had only just been allotted. This mountain, which is also called the mountain of Israel (chap. xi. 16, 21), was a limestone range running from Kirjath-jearim, where the mountains of Judah terminate (see at chap. xi. 21), to the plain of Jezreel, and therefore embracing the greater part of the tribe-territory of Benjamin. The wood, which is distinguished from the mountain of Ephraim, and is also described in ver. 18 as a mountainous land, is either the mountainous region extending to the north of Yasir as far as the mountains of Gilboa, and lying to the west of Beisan, a region which has not yet been thoroughly explored, or else, as *Knobel* supposes, "the broad range of woody heights or low woody hills, by which the mountains of Samaria are connected with Carmel on the north-west (*Rob.* iii. p. 189), between Taanath and Megiddo on the east, and Cæsarea and Dor on the west." Possibly both may be intended, as the children of Joseph were afraid of the Canaanites in Beisan and in the plain of Jezreel (ver. 16). The Rephaim were dwelling there, a tribe of gigantic stature (see at Gen. xiv. 5), also the Perizzites (see at Gen. xiii. 7).—Ver. 16. The children of Joseph replied that the mountain (allotted to them) would not be enough for them (מָצָא, as in Num. xi. 22 ; Zech. x. 10) ; and that all the Canaanites who dwelt in the land of the plain had iron chariots, both those in Beth-shean and its daughter towns, and those in the valley of Jezreel. אֶרֶץ־הָעֵמֶק, the land of the plain or valley land, includes both the valley of the Jordan near Beisan, and also the plain of Jezreel, which opens into the Jordan valley in the neigh-bourhood of Beisan (*Rob.* iii. p. 173). The *plain* of *Jezreel*, so called after the town of that name, is called the "great field of Esdrelom" in Judith i. 4, and τὸ μέγα πεδίον by *Josephus*. It is the present *Merj* (*i.e.* pasture-land) *Ibn Aamer*, which runs in a south-westerly direction from the Mediterranean Sea above Carmel, and reaches almost to the Jordan. It is bounded on the south by the mountains of Carmel, the mountain-land of Ephraim and the range of hills connecting the two, on the north by the mountains of Galilee, on the west by the southern spurs of the Galilean high-land, and on the east by the mountains of Gilboa and the Little Hermon (Jebel Duhy). Within these boundaries it is eight hours in length from east to west, and five hours broad ; it is fertile throughout, though very desolate now (see *v. Raumer*, Pal. iii. pp. 39 sqq.). "*Iron chariots*" are not scythe chariots, for these were introduced by Cyrus, and were unknown to the Medes, Persians, and Arabians, *i.e.* to the early Asiatics before his time (*Xen. Cyr.* vi. 1, 27, 30), as well as to the ancient Egyptians (see *Wilkinson,* Manners and Customs, i. p. 350) ; they were simply chariots tipped with iron, just as the Egyptian war-chariots were made of wood and strengthened with metal nails and tips (*Wilkinson*, pp. 342, 348).—Vers. 17, 18. As the answer of the children of Joseph indicated cowardice and want of confidence in the help of God, Joshua contented himself with repeating his first reply, though more fully and with the reasons assigned. "*Thou art a strong people, and hast great power; there will not be one lot to thee:*" *i.e.*

because thou art a numerous people and endowed with strength, there shall not remain one lot to thee, thou canst and wilt extend thine inheritance. *" For the mountain will be thine, for it is forest, and thou wilt hew it out, and its goings out will become thine."* By the mountain we are not to understand the mountains of Ephraim which were assigned to the Ephraimites by the lot, but the wooded mountains mentioned in ver. 15, which the children of Joseph were to hew out, so as to make outlets for themselves. *" The outgoings of it "* are the fields and plains bordering upon the forest. For the Canaanites who dwelt there (ver. 15) would be driven out by the house of Joseph, just because they had iron chariots and were strong, and therefore only a strong tribe like Joseph was equal to the task.. "Not one of the tribes of Israel is able to fight against them (the Canaanites) because they are strong, but you have strength enough to be able to expel them (*Rashi*).

THE TABERNACLE SET UP AT SHILOH.   SURVEY OF THE LAND
   THAT HAD STILL TO BE DIVIDED.   INHERITANCE OF THE
   TRIBE OF BENJAMIN.—CHAP. XVIII.

Ver. 1. THE TABERNACLE SET UP AT SHILOH.—As soon as the tribe of Ephraim had received its inheritance, Joshua commanded the whole congregation to assemble in Shiloh, and there set up the tabernacle, in order that, as the land was conquered, the worship of Jehovah might henceforth be regularly observed in accordance with the law. The selection of Shiloh as the site for the sanctuary was hardly occasioned by the fitness of the place for this purpose, on account of its being situated upon a mountain in the centre of the land, for there were many other places that would have been quite as suitable in this respect; the reason is rather to be found in the name of the place, viz. *Shiloh, i.e.* rest, which called to mind the promised Shiloh (Gen. xlix. 10), and therefore appeared to be pre-eminently suitable to be the resting-place of the sanctuary of the Lord, where His name was to dwell in Israel, until He should come who was to give true rest to His people as the Prince of Peace. In any case, however, Joshua did not follow his own judgment in selecting Shiloh for this purpose, but acted in simple accordance with the instructions of God, as the Lord had expressly reserved to himself the choice of the place where His name should dwell (Deut. xii. 11). *Shiloh*, according to the *Onom.*,

was twelve Roman miles or five hours to the south of Neapolis
(Nablus), and about eight hours to the north of Jerusalem ; at
present it is a heap of ruins, bearing the name of *Seilun* (see *Rob.*
iii. p. 85). The tabernacle continued standing at Shiloh during
the time of the judges, until the ark of the covenant fell into the
hands of the Philistines, in the lifetime of Eli, when the holy tent
was robbed of its soul, and reduced to the mere shadow of a sanctuary. After this it was removed to Nob (1 Sam. xxi. 2) ; but in
consequence of the massacre inflicted by Saul upon the inhabitants
of this place (1 Sam. xxii. 19), it was taken to Gibeon (1 Kings iii.
4 : see *Keil,* Bibl. Arch. i. § 22). From this time forward Shiloh
continued to decline, because the Lord had rejected it (Ps. lxxviii.
60; Jer. vii. 12, xxvi. 6). That it was destroyed by the Assyrians,
as *Knobel* affirms, is not stated in the history.

Vers. 2–10. Survey of the Land that had yet to be
Divided.—Ver. 2. After the tabernacle had been set up, the
casting of the lots and division of the land among the other seven
tribes were to be continued ; namely at Shiloh, to which the congregation had removed with the sanctuary.—Vers. 3, 4. But, for the
reasons explained in chap. xiv. 1, these tribes showed themselves
" *slack to go to possess the land which the Lord had given them,*" *i.e.*
not merely to conquer it, but to have it divided by lot, and to enter
in and take possession. Joshua charged them with this, and directed
them to appoint three men for each of the seven tribes, that they
might be sent out to go through the land, and describe it according
to the measure of their inheritance. "*According to their inheritance,*"
i.e. with special reference to the fact that seven tribes were to receive
it for their inheritance. The description was not a formal measurement, although the art of surveying was well known in Egypt in
ancient times, and was regularly carried out after the annual inun-
dations of the Nile (*Herod.* ii. 109 ; *Strabo,* xvii. 787 ; *Diod. Sic.* i.
69) ; so that the Israelites might have learned it there. But כָּתַב
does not mean to measure ; and it was not a formal measurement
that was required, for the purpose of dividing the land that yet
remained into seven districts, since the tribes differed in numerical
strength, and therefore the boundaries of the territory assigned them
could not be settled till after the lots had been cast. The meaning
of the word is to describe ; and according to ver. 9, it was chiefly to
the towns that reference was made : so that the description required
by Joshua in all probability consisted simply in the preparation of

lists of the towns in the different parts of the land, with an account
of their size and character; also with " notices of the quality and
condition of the soil; what lands were fertile, and what they produced; where the country was mountainous, and where it was level;
which lands were well watered, and which were dry; and any other
things that would indicate the character of the soil, and facilitate a
comparison between the different parts of the land" (*Rosenmüller*).
The reasons which induced Joshua to take steps for the first time
now for securing a survey of the land, are given in chap. xiv. 1.
The men chosen for the purpose were able to carry out their task
without receiving any hindrance from the Canaanites. For whilst
the latter were crushed, if not exterminated, by the victories which
the Israelites had gained, it was not necessary for the twenty-one
Israelitish men to penetrate into every corner of the land, and every
town that was still inhabited by the Canaanites, in order to accomplish their end.—Vers. 5, 6. " *And divide it into seven parts,*" viz.
for the purpose of casting lots. Judah, however, was still to remain
in its land to the south, and Ephraim in its territory to the north.
The seven portions thus obtained they were to bring to Joshua, that
he might then cast the lot for the seven tribes " before the Lord,"
i.e. before the tabernacle (chap. xix. 51).—Ver. 7. There were only
seven tribes that had still to receive their portions; for the tribe of
Levi was to receive no portion in the land (*vid.* chap. xiii. xiv.), and
Gad, Reuben, and half Manasseh had received their inheritance
already on the other side of the Jordan.—Vers. 8, 9. Execution of
this command.—Ver. 10. Joshua finishes the casting of the lots at
Shiloh.

Vers. 11-28. INHERITANCE OF THE TRIBE OF BENJAMIN.—
Vers. 11-20. *Boundaries* of the inheritance.—Ver. 11. The territory of their lot (*i.e.* the territory assigned to the Benjaminites by
lot) came out (through the falling out of the lot) between the sons
of Judah and the sons of Joseph.—Vers. 12, 13. The *northern
boundary* (" the boundary towards the north side") therefore coincided with the southern boundary of Ephraim as far as Lower
Beth-horon, and has already been commented upon in the exposition
of chap. xvi. 1-3. The *western boundary* follows in ver. 14. At
Beth-horon the boundary curved round and turned southwards on
the western side, namely from the mountain before (in front of)
Beth-horon southwards; and " *the goings out thereof were at Kirjath-
baal, which is Kirjath-jearim,*" the town of the Judæans mentioned

in chap. xv. 60, the present *Kureyet el Enab* (see at chap. ıx. 17).—
Vers. 15–19. "*As for the southern boundary from the end of Kirjath-
jearim onwards, the* (southern) *boundary went out on the west* (*i.e.* it
started from the west), *and went out* (terminated) *at the fountain of
the water of Nephtoah.*" Consequently it coincided with the northern
boundary of Judah, as described in chap. xv. 5–9, except that it is
given there from east to west, and here from west to east (see at
chap. xv. 5–9). In the construction תּוֹצְאוֹתָיו הַגְּבוּל, the noun הַגְּבוּל is
in apposition to the suffix : the outgoings of it, namely of the border
(see *Ewald,* § 291, *b.*).—Ver. 20. The *eastern boundary* was the
Jordan.

Vers. 21–28. The *towns* of Benjamin are divided into two
groups. The *first* group (vers. 21–24) contains twelve towns in the
eastern portion of the territory. *Jericho :* the present *Riha* (see at
chap. ii. 1). *Beth-hoglah,* now *Ain Hajla* (see chap. xv. 6). *Emek-
Keziz :* the name has been preserved in the Wady *el Kaziz,* on the
road from Jerusalem to Jericho, on the south-east of the Apostle's
Well (see *Van de Velde,* Mem. p. 328).—Ver. 22. *Beth-arabah :* see
at chap. xv. 6. *Zemaraim,* probably the ruins of *es Sumrah,* on the
road from Jerusalem to Jericho, to the east of Khan Hadhur, on
Van de Velde's map. *Bethel:* now *Beitin* (see chap. vii. 2).—Ver. 23.
Avvim (*i.e.* ruins) is unknown. *Phara* has been preserved in the
ruins of *Fara,* on Wady Fara, three hours to the north-east of
Jerusalem, and the same distance to the west of Jericho. *Ophrah*
is mentioned again in 1 Sam. xiii. 17, but it is a different place from
the *Ophrah* of Gideon in Manasseh (Judg. vi. 11, 24, viii. 27).
According to the *Onom.* (*s. v. Aphra*), it was a κώμη 'Αφρήλ in the
time of *Eusebius* (*Jer. vicus Effrem*), five Roman miles to the east of
Bethel ; and according to *Van de Velde, v. Raumer,* and others, it is
probably the same place as *Ephron* or *Ephrain,* which Abijah took
from Jeroboam along with *Jeshanah* and *Bethel* (2 Chron. xiii. 19),
also the same as *Ephraim,* the city to which Christ went when He
withdrew into the desert (John xi. 54), as the *Onom.* (*s. v. Ephron*)
speaks of a *villa prægrandis Ephræa nomine* ('Εφραΐμ in *Euseb.*),
although the distance given there, viz. twenty Roman miles to the
north of Jerusalem, reaches far beyond the limits of Benjamin.—
Ver. 24. *Chephar-haammonai* and *Ophni* are only mentioned here,
and are still unknown. *Gaba,* or *Geba* of Benjamin (1 Sam. xiii. 16 ;
1 Kings xv. 22), which was given up to the Levites (chap. xxi. 17 ;
1 Chron. vi. 45), was in the neighbourhood of Ramah (1 Kings xv.
22, 2 Chron. xvi. 6). It is mentioned in 2 Kings xxiii. 8, Zech.

xiv. 10, as the northern boundary of the kingdom of Judah, and was still inhabited after the captivity (Neh. vii. 30). It is a different place from *Gibea*, and is not to be found, as I formerly supposed, in the Moslem village of *Jibia*, by the Wady el Jib, between Beitin and Sinjil (*Rob.* iii. p. 80), but in the small village of *Jeba*, which is lying half in ruins, and where there are relics of antiquity, three-quarters of an hour to the north-east of er-Râm (Ramah), and about three hours to the north of Jerusalem, upon a height from which there is an extensive prospect (*vid. Rob.* ii. pp. 113 sqq.). This eastern group also included the two other towns *Anathoth* and *Almon* (chap. xxi. 18), which were given up by Benjamin to the Levites. *Anathoth*, the home of the prophet Jeremiah (*Jer.* i. 1, xi. 21 sqq.), which was still inhabited by Benjaminites after the captivity (Neh. xi. 32), is the present village of Anâta, where there are ruins of great antiquity, an hour and a quarter to the north of Jerusalem (*Rob.* ii. pp. 109 sqq.). *Almon*, called *Allemeth* in 1 Chron. vi. 45, has been preserved in the ruins of Almît (*Rob.* Bibl. Res. pp. 287 sqq.), or *el-Mid* (*Tobler*, Denkbl. p. 631), on the south-east of Anâta.—Vers. 25–28. The *second* group of fourteen towns in the western portion of Benjamin.—Ver. 25. *Gibeon*, the present *Jib :* see at chap. ix. 3. *Ramah*, in the neighbourhood of Gibeah and Geba (Judg. xix. 13; Isa. x. 29; 1 Kings xv. 17; Ezra ii. 26), most probably the *Ramah* of Samuel (1 Sam. i. 19, ii. 11, xxv. 1, xxviii. 3), is the present village of *er-Râm*, upon a mountain with ruins between Gibeon and Geba, half an hour to the west of the latter, two hours to the north of Jerusalem (see *Rob.* ii. p. 315). *Beeroth*, the present *Bireh :* see at chap. ix. 17.—Ver. 26. *Mizpeh*, commonly called *Mizpah*, where the war with Benjamin was decided upon (Judg. xx. xxi.), and where Samuel judged the people, and chose Saul as king (1 Sam. vii. 5 sqq., x. 17), was afterwards the seat of the Babylonian governor Gedaliah (2 Kings xxv. 23; Jer. xl. 6 sqq.). According to the *Onom.* (*s. v. Massepha*), it was near Kirjath-jearim, and *Robinson* (ii. p. 139) is no doubt correct in supposing it to be the present *Neby Samvil* (*i.e.* prophet Samuel), an hour and a quarter to the east of Kureyet Enab (Kirjath-jearim), two hours to the north-west of Jerusalem, half an hour to the south of Gibeon, a place which stands like a watch-tower upon the highest point in the whole region, and with a mosque, once a Latin church, which is believed alike by Jews, Christians, and Mahometans to cover the tomb of the prophet Samuel (see *Rob.* ii. pp. 135 sqq.). *Chephirah, i.e. Kefir :* see

at chap. ix. 17. *Mozah* is only mentioned here, and is still unknowr.
Ver. 27. This also applies to *Rekem, Irpeel*, and *Taralah.*—Ver. 28
Zelah, the burial-place of Saul and his family (2 Sam. xxi. 14), is
otherwise unknown. *Gibeath* or *Gibeah, i.e.* Gibeah of Benjamin,
which was destroyed by the other tribes of Israel in the time of the
judges, on account of the flagrant crime which had been committed
there (Judg. xix. xx.), is also called *Gibeah of Saul*, as being the
home and capital of Saul (1 Sam. x. 26, xi. 4, etc.), and was situated,
according to Judg. xix. 13 and Isa. x. 29, between Jerusalem and
Ramah, according to *Josephus* (Bell. Jud. v. 2, 1, 8) about twenty
or thirty stadia from Jerusalem. These statements point to the *Tell*
or *Tuleil el Phul, i.e.* bean-mountain, a conical peak about an hour
from Jerusalem, on the road to er-Râm, with a large heap of stones
upon the top, probably the ruins of a town that was built of unhewn
stones, from which there is a very extensive prospect in all directions (*Rob.* ii. p. 317). Consequently modern writers have very
naturally agreed in the conclusion, that the ancient Gibeah of Benjamin or Saul was situated either by the side of or upon this Tell (see
Rob. Bibl. Res. p. 286; *Strauss*, Sinai, etc., p. 331, ed. 6; *v. Raumer*,
Pal. p. 196). *Kirjath* has not yet been discovered, and must not
be confounded with Kirjath-jearim, which belonged to the tribe of
Judah (ver. 14; cf. chap. xv. 60).

INHERITANCE OF THE TRIBES OF SIMEON, ZEBULUN, ISSACHAR, ASHER, NAPHTALI, AND DAN.—CHAP. XIX.

Vers. 1–9. The INHERITANCE OF SIMEON fell within the
inheritance of the children of Judah, because the land allotted to
them at Gilgal was larger than they required (ver. 9). Thus the
curse pronounced upon Simeon by Jacob of dispersion in Israel
(Gen. xlix. 7) was fulfilled upon this tribe in a very peculiar
manner, and in a different manner from that pronounced upon
Levi. The towns allotted to the tribe of Simeon are divided into
two groups, the first (vers. 2–6) consisting of thirteen or fourteen
towns, all situated in the Negeb (or south country); the second
(ver. 7) of four towns, two of which were in the *Negeb* and two in
the *shephelah*. All these eighteen towns have already been enumerated among the towns of Judah (chap. xv. 26–32, 42), and are
mentioned again in 1 Chron. iv. 28–32, in just the same order,
and with only slight differences in the spelling of some of the
names. If the classification of the names in two groups might

seem to indicate that Simeon received a connected portion of land in Judah, this idea is overthrown at once by the circumstance that two of the four towns in the second group were in the south land and two in the lowland, and, judging from chap. xv. 32, 42, at a great distance from one another. At the same time, we cannot decide this point with any certainty, as the situation of several of the towns is still unknown.—Ver. 2. *Beersheba:* see at chap. xv. 28. *Sheba* is wanting in the Chronicles, but has no doubt been omitted through a copyist's error, as *Shema* answers to it in chap. xv. 26, where it stands before *Moladah* just as Sheba does here. —On the names in vers. 3–6*a*, see the exposition of chap. xv. 28–32.—The sum total given in ver. 6*b*, viz. thirteen towns, does not tally, as there are fourteen names. On these differences, see the remarks on chap. xv. 32 (p. 163, the note).—Ver. 7. *Ain* and *Rimmon* were in the south land (chap. xv. 32), *Ether* and *Ashan* in the lowlands (chap. xv. 42).—Vers. 8, 9. In addition to the towns mentioned, the Simeonites received all the villages round about the towns to *Baalath-beer*, the *Ramah* of *the south.* This place, up to which the territory of the Simeonites extended, though without its being actually assigned to the Simeonites, is simply called Baal in 1 Chron. iv. 33, and is probably the same as *Bealoth* in chap. xv. 24, though its situation has not yet been determined (see at chap. xv. 24). It cannot be identified, however, with *Ramet el Khulil*, an hour to the north of Hebron, which *Roediger* supposes to be the Ramah of the south, since the territory of Simeon, which was situated in the Negeb, and had only two towns in the *shephelah*, cannot possibly have extended into the mountains to a point on the north of Hebron. So far as the situation is concerned, *V. de Velde* would be more likely to be correct, when he identifies *Rama of the south* with Tell *Lekiyeh* on the north of Beersheba, if this conjecture only rested upon a better foundation than the untenable assumption, that Baalath-beer is the same as the Baalath of Dan in ver. 44.

Vers. 10–16. The INHERITANCE OF ZEBULUN fell above the plain of Jezreel, between this plain and the mountains of Naphtali, so that it was bounded by Asher on the west and north-west (ver. 27), by Naphtali on the north and north-east (ver. 34), and by Issachar on the south-east and south, and touched neither the Mediterranean Sea nor the Jordan. It embraced a very fertile country, however, with the fine broad plain of *el Buttauf*, the μέγα πεδίον above Nazareth called *Asochis* in *Joseph. vita*, § 41, 45 (see *Rob.* iii. p. 189, Bibl. Res. pp. 105 sqq.; *Ritter*, Erdk. xvi. pp. 742, 758-9).—Ver. 10. "*And the boundary* (the territory) *of their inheritance was* (went) *to Sarid.*" This is no doubt the centre of the southern boundary, from which it is traced in a westerly direction in ver. 11, and in an easterly direction in ver. 12, in the same manner as in chap. xvi. 6. Unfortunately, *Sarid* cannot be determined with certainty. *Knobel's* opinion is, that the name, which signifies "hole" or "incision," after the analogy of שָׂרַד, *perforavit*, and שָׂרַט, *incidit*, does not refer to a town, but to some other locality, probably the southern opening of the deep and narrow wady which comes down from the basin of Nazareth, and is about an hour to the south-east of Nazareth, between two steep mountains (*Seetzen*, ii. pp. 151-2; *Rob.* iii. p. 183). This locality appears suitable enough. But it is also possible that *Sarid* may be found in one of the two heaps of ruins on the south side of the *Mons præcipitii* upon *V. de Velde's* map (so called from Luke iv. 29).— Ver. 11. From this point "*the border went up westwards, namely to Mar'ala, and touched Dabbasheth, and still farther to the brook of Jokneam.*" If *Jokneam* of Carmel has been preserved in the Tell *Kaimûn* (see at chap. xii. 22), the brook before Jokneam is probably the Wady *el Milh*, on the eastern side of which, near the point where it opens into the plain, stands *Kaimûn*, and through which the road runs from Acca to Ramleh, as this wady separates Carmel from the small round hills which run to the south-east (see *Rob.* Bibl. Res. p. 114, and *V. de Velde*, i. p. 249). Here the boundaries of Zebulun and Asher met (ver. 27). *Mar'ala* and *Dabbasheth* are to be sought for between Kaimûn and Sarid. The *Cod. Vat.* has Μαγελδά instead of Μαριλά. Now, however little importance we can attach to the readings of the LXX. on account of the senseless way in which its renderings are made,—as, for example, in this very passage, where עַד־שָׂרִיד : וְעָלָה is rendered Ἐσεδεκγώλα,—the name *Magelda* might suggest a Hebrew reading *Magedlah* or *Mageldah*, and thus lead one to connect the place with the village of *Mejeidil* (*Rob.* Bibl. Res. p. 114), or *Mshedil* (*Seetzen*, ii. p. 143), on the west of *Mons præcipitii*, though neither of these travellers visited the place, or has given us any minute description of it. Its situation upon a mountain would suit *Mar'ala*, to which the boundary went *up* from Sarid. In the case of *Dabbasheth*, the name, which signifies "lump" (see Isa. xxx. 6), points to a mountain. Upon this *Knobel* has founded the conjecture that *Gibeah* or *Gibeath* took the place of this uncommon word, and that this is connected with the *Gabathon* of the *Onom.* (*juxta campum Legionis*), the present *Jebâta* between Mejeidil and Kaimûn, upon an isolated height on the edge of the mountains which skirt the plain of Jezreel, where there are signs of a remote antiquity (*Rob.* iii. p. 201, and Bibl. Res. p. 113; *Ritter,* Erdk. xvi. p. 700); although Tell *Thureh* (*i.e.* mountain) might be intended, a village upon a low and isolated hill a little farther south (see *Rob.* Bibl. Res. p. 116, and *Ritter, ut sup.*).—Ver. 12. "*And from Sarid the boundary turned eastwards toward the sun-rising to the territory of Chisloth-tabor, and went out to Dabrath, and went up to Japhia.*" *Chisloth-tabor, i.e.* according to *Kimchi's* explanation *lumbi Taboris* (French, *les flancs*), was at any rate a place on the side of Tabor, possibly the same as *Kesulloth* in ver. 18, as *Masius* and others suppose, and probably the same place as the *Xaloth* of *Josephus* (Bell. Jud. iii. 3, 1), which was situated in the "great plain," and the *vicus Chasalus* of the *Onom.* (*juxta montem Thabor in campestribus*), *i.e.* the present village of *Iksâl* or *Ksâl,* upon a rocky height on the west of Thabor, with many tombs in the rocks (*Rob.* iii. p. 182). *Dabrath,* a place in the tribe of Issachar that was given up to the Levites (chap. xxi. 28; 1 Chron. vi. 57), called *Dabaritta* in *Josephus* (Bell. Jud. ii. 21, 3) and *Dabira* in the *Onom.* (*villula in monte Thabor*), the present *Deburieh,* an insignificant village which stands in a very picturesque manner upon a stratum of rock at the western foot of Tabor (*Rob.* iii. p. 210; *V. de Velde,* R. ii. p. 324). *Japhia* certainly cannot be the present *Hepha* or *Haifa* (*Khaifa*) on the Mediterranean, and near to Carmel (*Rel.* Pal. p. 826, and *Ges.* Thes. *s. v.*); but it is just as certain that it cannot be the present *Jafa,* a place half an hour to the south-west of Nazareth, as *Robinson* (Pal. iii. p. 200) and *Knobel* suppose, since the boundary was running eastwards, and cannot possibly have turned back again towards the west, and run from Deburieh beyond Sarid. If the positions assigned to Chisloth-tabor and Dabrath are correct, Japhia must be sought for on the east of Deburieh.—Ver. 13. "*From thence it went over towards the east to the sun-rising to Gath-hepher, to Eth-kazin, and went out to Rimmon, which is marked off to Neah.*" *Gath-hepher,* the home of the prophet Jonah (2 Kings xiv. 25), was "*haud grandis viculus Geth*" in the time of Jerome (see *prol. ad Jon.*). It was about two miles from Sephoris on the road to Tiberias, and the tomb of the prophet was shown there. It is the present village of *Meshed,* a place about an hour and a quarter to the north of Nazareth (*Rob.* iii. p. 209; *V. de Velde*, Mem. p. 312). *Eth-kazin* is unknown. *Rimmon*, a Levitical town (chap. xxi. 35; 1 Chron. vi. 62), has probably been preserved in the village of *Rummaneh*, about two hours and a half to the north of Nazareth (*Rob.* iii. p. 195). *Ham-methoar* is not a proper name, but the participle of תֹּאַר, with the article in the place of the relative pronoun, " bounded off," or pricked off. *Neah* is unknown; it is possibly the same place as *Neiel* in the tribe of Asher (ver. 27), as *Knobel* supposes.—Ver. 14. "*And the boundary turned round it* (round Rimmon), *on the north to Channathon, and the outgoings thereof were the valley of Jiphtah-el.*" Judging from the words נָסַב and מִצָּפוֹן, this verse apparently gives the north-west boundary, since the last definition in ver. 13, " to Gath-hepher," etc., points to the eastern boundary. *Jiphtah-el* answers no doubt to the present *Jefât*, two hours and a half to the north of Sefurieh, and is the *Jotapata* which was obstinately defended by *Josephus* (Bell. Jud. iii. 7, 9 : see *Rob.* Bibl. Res. pp 104 sqq.). Consequently the valley of *Jiphtah-el*, at which Zebulun touched Asher (ver. 27), is probably " no other than the large Wady Abilîn, which takes its rise in the hills in the neighbourhood of Jefât" (*Rob.* Bibl. Res. p. 107). And if this be correct, *Channathon* (LXX. Ἐνναθώθ) is probably *Cana* of Galilee, the home of Nathanael (John ii. 1, 11, iv. 46, xxi. 2), the present *Kana el Jelil*, between Rummaneh and Yefât, on the northern edge of the plain of Buttauf, upon a Tell, from which you overlook the plain, fully two hours and a half in a straight line from Nazareth, and directly north of that place, where there are many ruins found (see *Rob.* iii. p. 204; Bibl. Res. p. 108).—Ver. 15. The towns of *Zebulun* were the following. *Kattath*, probably the same as *Kitron*, which is mentioned in Judg. i. 30 in connection with Nahalol, but which is still unknown. *Nehalal*, or *Nahalol* (Judg. i. 30), is supposed by *V. de Velde* (Mem. p. 335), who follows Rabbi *Schwartz*, to be the present village of *Maalul*, a place with ruins on the south-west of Nazareth (see *Seetzen*, ii. p. 143; *Rob.* iii. App.; and *Ritter*, Erdk. xvi. p. 700). *Simron* is supposed by *Knobel* to be the village of *Semunieh* (see at chap. xi. 1). But neither of these is very probable. *Idalah* is supposed by *V. de Velde* to be the village of *Jeda* or *Jeida*, on the west of Semunieh, where are a few relics of antiquity, though *Robinson* (Bibl. Res. p. 113) states the very opposite. *Bethlehem* (of Zebulun), which many regard as the home of the judge Ibzan (Judg. xii. 8), has been preserved under the old name in a miser-

able village on the north of Jeida and Semunieh (see *Seetzen*, ii. p.
139; *Rob.* Bibl. Res. p. 113). The number of the towns is given
as *twelve*, though only five are mentioned by name. It is true that
some commentators have found the missing names in the border
places mentioned in vers. 11–14, as, after deducting Chisloth-tabor
and Dabrath, which belonged to Issachar, the names Sarid, Mara-
lah, Dabbasheth, Japhia, Gittah-hepher, Eth-kazin, and Channathon
give just seven towns. Nevertheless there is very little probability
in this conjecture. For, in the first place, not only would it be a
surprising thing to find the places mentioned as boundaries included
among the towns of the territory belonging to the tribe, especially
as some of the places so mentioned did not belong to Zebulun at
all ; but the copula *vav*, with which the enumeration of the towns
commences, is equally surprising, since this is introduced in other
cases with וְהָיוּ הֶעָרִים (וַיְהִי), *e.g.* chap. xviii. 21, xv. 21. And, in
the second place, it is not a probable thing in itself, that, with the
exception of the five towns mentioned in ver. 15, the other towns of
Zebulun should all be situated upon the border. And lastly, the
towns of *Kartah* and *Dimnah*, which Zebulun gave up to the Levites
(chap. xxi. 34), are actually wanting. Under these circumstances,
it is a natural conclusion that there is a gap in the text here, just
as in chap. xv. 59 and xxi. 36.

Vers. 17–23. THE INHERITANCE OF ISSACHAR.—In this instance only towns are given, and the boundaries are not delineated,
with the exception of the eastern portion of the northern boundary
and the boundary line; at the same time, they may easily be traced
from the boundaries of the surrounding tribes. Issachar received
for the most part the large and very fertile plain of Jezreel (see at
chap. xvii. 16, and *Ritter*, Erdk. xvi. pp. 689 sqq.), and was bounded
on the south by Manasseh, on the west by Manasseh and Asher, on
the north by Zebulun, and farther east by Naphtali also, and on
the east by the Jordan.—Ver. 18. " *And their boundary was towards
Jezreel*," *i.e.* their territory extended beyond Jezreel. *Jezreel*, the
summer residence of Ahab and his house (1 Kings xviii. 45, 46,
etc.), was situated upon a mountain, with an extensive and splendid
prospect over the large plain that was called by its name. It was
afterwards called *Esdraela*, a place described in the *Onom.* (*s. v.
Jezreel*) as standing between Scythopolis and Legio; it is the present Zerîn, on the north-west of the mountains of Gilboa (see
Seetzen, ii. pp. 155-6; *Rob.* iii. pp. 161 sqq.; *Van de Velde*, R. ii.

pp. 320 sqq.). *Chesulloth*, possibly the same as *Chisloth-tabor* (see at ver. 12). *Sunem*, the home of Abishag (1 Kings i. 3–15, etc.), also mentioned in 1 Sam. xxviii. 4 and 2 Kings iv. 8, was situated, according to the *Onom.*, five Roman miles (two hours) to the south of Tabor; it is the present *Solam* or *Sulem*, at the south-western foot of the Duhy or Little Hermon, an hour and a half to the north of Jezreel (see *Rob.* iii. pp. 170 sqq.; *Van de Velde*, R. ii. p. 323).— Ver. 19. *Haphraim*, according to the *Onom.* (*s. v. Aphraim*) *villa Affarœa*, six Roman miles to the north of Legio, is identified by *Knobel* with the village of *Afuleh*, on the west of Sulem, and more than two hours to the north-east of Lejun (*Rob.* iii. pp. 163, 181). *Sion*, according to the *Onom. villa juxta montem Thabor*, has not yet been discovered. *Anaharath* is supposed by *Knobel* to be *Na'urah*, on the eastern side of the Little Hermon (Bibl. Res. p. 337); but he regards the text as corrupt, and following the *Cod. Al.* of the LXX., which has 'Ρενάθ and 'Αῤῥανέθ, maintains that the reading should be *Archanath*, to which *Arâneh* on the north of Jenin in the plain corresponds (*Seetzen*, ii. p. 156; *Rob.* iii. p. 157). But the circumstance that the *Cod. Al.* has two names instead of one makes its reading very suspicious.—Ver. 20. *Harabbit* is supposed by *Knobel* to be *Araboneh*, on the north-east of Arâneh, at the southern foot of Gilboa (*Rob.* iii. p. 157). *Kishion*, which was given up to the Levites (chap. xxi. 28) and is erroneously written *Kedesh* in 1 Chron. vi. 57, is unknown. This also applies to *Abez* or *Ebez*, which is never mentioned again.—Ver. 21. *Remeth*, for which *Jarmuth* stands in the list of Levitical towns in chap. xxi. 29, and *Ramoth* in 1 Chron. vi. 58, is also unknown.[1] *En-gannim*, which was also allotted to the Levites (chap. xxi. 29; also 1 Chron. v. 58, where it is called *Anem*), has been associated by *Robinson* (iii. p. 155) with the Γιναία of *Josephus*, the present *Jenin*. The name *En-gannim* signifies fountain of gardens, and Jenin stands at the southern side of the plain of Jezreel in the midst of gardens

---

[1] *Knobel* imagines *Remeth*, whose name signifies height, to be the village of *Wezar*, on one of the western peaks of Gilboa (*Seetzen*, ii. p. 156; *Rob.* iii. p. 166, and Bibl. Res. p. 339), as the name also signifies " a lofty, inaccessible mountain, or a castle situated upon a mountain." This is certainly not impossible, but it is improbable. For this Mahometan village evidently derived its name from the fact that it has the appearance of a fortification when seen from a distance (see *Ritter*, Erdk. xv. p. 422). The name has nothing in common therefore with the Hebrew *Remeth*, and the travellers quoted by him say nothing at all about the ruins which he mentions in connection with *Wezar* (Wusar).

and orchards, which are watered by a copious spring (see *Seetzen*, ii. pp. 156 sqq.); "unless perhaps the place referred to is the heap of ruins called *Um el Ghanim*, on the south-east of Tabor, mentioned by *Berggren*, ii. p. 240, and *Van de Velde*, Mem. p. 142" (*Knobel*). *En-chadda* and *Beth-pazzez* are only mentioned here, and have not yet been discovered. According to *Knobel*, the former of the two may possibly be either the place by Gilboa called *Judeideh*, with a fountain named *Ain Judeideh* (*Rob.* Bibl. Res. p. 337), or else *Beit-kad* or *Kadd* near Gilboa, mentioned by *Seetzen* (ii. p. 159) and *Robinson* (iii. p. 157).—Ver. 22. "*And the boundary touched Tabor, Sahazim, and Beth-shemesh.*" *Tabor* is not the mountain of that name, but a town upon the mountain, which was given to the Levites, though not by Issachar but by Zebulun (1 Chron. vi. 62), and was fortified afresh in the Jewish wars (*Josephus*, Bell. Jud. iv. 1, 8). In this passage, however, it appears to be reckoned as belonging to Issachar, since otherwise there are not sixteen cities named. At the same time, as there are several discrepancies between the numbers given and the names actually mentioned, it is quite possible that in this instance also the number sixteen is incorrect. In any case, Tabor was upon the border of Zebulun (ver. 12), so that it might have been allotted to this tribe. There are still the remains of old walls and ruins of arches, houses, and other buildings to be seen upon Mount *Tabor;* and round the summit there are the foundations of a thick wall built of large and to a great extent fluted stones (see *Rob.* iii. pp. 453 sqq.; *Seetzen*, ii. p. 148; *Buckingham*, Syr. i. pp. 83 sqq.). The places which follow are to be sought for on the east of Tabor towards the Jordan, as the boundary terminated at the Jordan. *Sachazim* (Shahazimah) *Knobel* connects with *el Hazetheh*, as the name, which signifies heights, points to a town situated upon hills; and *el Hazetheh* stands upon the range of hills, bounding the low-lying land of Ard el Hamma, which belonged to Naphtali. The reason is a weak one, though the situation would suit. There is more probability in the conjecture that *Beth-shemesh*, which remained in the hands of the Canaanites (Judg. i. 33), has been preserved in the ruined village of *Bessum* (*Rob.* iii. p. 237), and that this new name is only a corruption of the old one, like *Beth-shean* and *Beisan*. It is probable that the eastern portion of the northern boundary of Issachar, towards Naphtali, ran in a north-easterly direction from Tabor through the plain to Kefr Sabt, and thence to the Jordan along the Wady Bessum. It is not stated how far the territory of Issachar ran down the valley of the Jordan (see the remarks on chap. xvii. 11, p. 182).

Vers. 24–31. THE INHERITANCE OF ASHER.—Asher received its territory along the Mediterranean Sea from Carmel to the northern boundary of Canaan itself. The description commences with the central portion, viz. the neighbourhood of *Acco* (ver. 25), going first of all towards the south (vers. 26, 27), and then to the north (vers. 28, 30).—Ver. 25. The territory of the Asherites was as follows. *Helkath*, which was given up to the Levites (chap. xxi. 31, and 1 Chron. vi. 75, where *Hukok* is an old copyist's error), is the present *Jelka*, three hours to the east of Acco (Akka: *Scholz*, Reise, p. 257), or *Jerka*, a Druse village situated upon an emi-nence, and judging from the remains, an ancient place (*Van de Velde*, R. i. p. 214; *Rob*. iii. App.). *Hali*, according to *Knobel* possibly *Julis*, between Jerka and Akka, in which case the present name arose from the form *Halit*, and *t* was changed into *s*. *Beten*, according to the *Onom*. (*s. v.* Βατναί: *Bathne*) a *vicus Bethbeten*, eight Roman miles to the east of Ptolemais, has not yet been found. *Achshaph* is also unknown (see at chap. xi. 1). The *Onom*. (*s. v. Achsaph*) says nothing more about its situation than that it was *in tribu Aser*, whilst the statement made *s. v. Acsaph* (᾿Ακσάφ), that it was *villula Chasalus* (κώμη ᾿Εξάδους), eight Roman miles from Diocæsarea *ad radicem montis Thabor*, leads into the territory of Zebulun.—Ver. 26. *Alammalech* has been preserved, so far as the name is concerned, in the Wady *Malek* or *Malik* (*Rob*. Bibl. Res. p. 110), which runs into the Kishon, since in all probability the wady was named after a place either near it or within it. *Amad* is supposed by *Knobel* to be the present *Haifa*, about three hours to the south of Acre, on the sea, and this he identifies with the syca-more city mentioned by *Strabo* (xvi. 758), *Ptolemy* (v. 15, 5), and *Pliny* (*h. n.* v. 17), which was called *Epha* in the time of the Fathers (see *Ritter*, Erdk. xvi. pp. 722 sqq.). In support of this he adduces the fact that the Hebrew name resembles the Arabic noun for sycamore,—an argument the weakness of which does not need to be pointed out. *Misheal* was assigned to the Levites (chap. xxi. 30, and 1 Chron. vi. 74, where it is called *Mashal*). Accord-ing to the *Onom*. (*s. v. Masan*) it was on the sea-coast near to Carmel, which is in harmony with the next clause, " *and reacheth to Carmel westwards, and to Shihor-libnath*." *Carmel* (*i.e.* fruit-field), which has acquired celebrity from the history of Elijah (1 Kings

xviii. 17 sqq.), is a wooded mountain ridge which stretcnes in a north-westerly direction on the southern side of the Kishon, and projects as a promontory into the sea. Its name, "fruit-field," is well chosen; for whilst the lower part is covered with laurels and olive trees, the upper abounds in figs and oaks, and the whole mountain is full of the most beautiful flowers. There are also many caves about it (*vid. v. Raumer*, Pal. pp. 43 sqq.; and *Ritter*, Erdk. xvi. pp. 705-6). The *Shihor-libnath* is not the *Belus*, or glass-river, in the neighbourhood of Acre, but is to be sought for on the south of Carmel, where Asher was bounded by Manasseh (chap. xvii. 10), *i.e.* to the south of Dor, which the Manassites received in the territory of Asher (chap. xvii. 11); it is therefore in all probability the *Nahr Zerka*, possibly the crocodile river of *Pliny* (*Reland*, Pal. p. 730), which is three hours to the south of Dor, and whose name (*blue*) might answer both to *shihor* (black) and *libnath* (white).—Ver. 27. From this point the boundary "*turned towards the east*," probably following the river Libnath for a short distance upwards, "*to Beth-dagon*," which has not yet been discovered, and must not be identified with Beit Dejan between Yafa and Ludd (Diospolis), "*and touched Zebulun and the valley of Jiphtah-el on the north of Beth-emek, and Nehiël, and went out on the left to Cabul*," *i.e.* on the northern side of it. The north-west boundary went from Zebulun into the valley of *Jiphtah-el*, *i.e.* the upper part of the Wady *Abilin* (ver. 14). Here therefore the eastern boundary of Asher, which ran northwards from Wady Zerka past the western side of Issachar and Zebulun, touched the north-west corner of Zebulun. The two places, *Beth-emek* and *Nehiël* (the latter possibly the same as *Neah* in ver. 13), which were situated at the south of the valley of Jiphtah-el, have not been discovered; they may, however, have been upon the border of Zebulun and yet have belonged to Asher. *Cabul*, the κώμη Χαβωλώ of *Josephus* (Vit. § 43), in the district of Ptolemais, has been preserved in the village of *Kabul*, four hours to the south-east of Acre (*Rob.* Bibl. Res. p. 88, and *Van de Velde*, R. i. p. 218).

In vers. 28-30 the towns and boundaries in the northern part of the territory of Asher, on the Phœnician frontier, are given, and the Phœnician cities Sidon, Tyre, and Achzib are mentioned as marking the boundary. First of all we have four towns in ver. 28, reaching as far as Sidon, no doubt in the northern district of Asher. *Ebron* has not yet been traced. As *Abdon* occurs among the towns which Asher gave up to the Levites (chap. xxi. 30; 1 Chron. vi. 59), and in this verse also twenty MSS. have the reading Abdon, many writers, like *Reland* (Pal. p. 514), regard *Ebron* as a copyist's error for *Abdon*. This is possible enough, but it is by no means certain. As the towns of Asher are not all given in this list, since Acco, Achlab, and Helba (Judg. i. 31) are wanting, Abdon may also have been omitted. But we cannot attach any importance to the reading of the twenty MSS., as it may easily have arisen from chap. xxi. 30; and in addition to the Masoretic text, it has against it the authority of all the ancient versions, in which the reading *Ebron* is adopted. But even *Abdon* cannot be traced with certainty. On the supposition that *Abdon* is to be read for *Ebron*, Knobel connects it with the present *Abbadiyeh*, on the east of Beirut (*Rob.* iii. App.; *Ritter*, Erdk. xvii. pp. 477 and 710), or with *Abidat*, on the east (not the north) of Jobail (Byblus), mentioned by *Burckhardt* (Syr. p. 296) and *Robinson* (iii. App.); though he cannot adduce any other argument in support of the identity of Abdon with these two places, which are only known by name at present, except the resemblance in their names. On the supposition, however, that *Abdon* is not the same as *Ebron*, *Van de Velde's* conjecture is a much more natural one; namely, that it is to be found in the ruins of *Abdeh*, on the Wady Kurn, to the north of Acca. *Rehob* cannot be traced. The name occurs again in ver. 30, from which it is evident that there were two towns of this name in the territory of Asher (see at ver. 30). *Schultz* and *Van de Velde* connect it with the village of *Hamûl* by the wady of that name, between Ras el Abyad and Ras en Nakura; but this is too far south to be included in the district which reached to great Sidon. *Knobel's* suggestion would be a more probable one, namely, that it is connected with the village of *Hammana*, on the east of Beirut, in the district of *el Metn*, on the heights of Lebanon, where there is now a Maronite monastery (*vid.* Seetzen, i. p. 260; *Rob.* iii. App.; and *Ritter*, xvii. pp. 676 and 710), if it could only be shown that the territory of Asher reached as far to the east as this. *Kanah* cannot be the village of *Kâna*, not far from Tyre (*Rob.* iii. p. 384), but must have been farther north, and near to Sidon, though it has not yet been discovered. For the supposition that it is connected with the existing place called *Ain Kanieh* (*Rob.* iii. App.; *Ritter*, xvii. pp. 94 and 703), on the north of Jezzin, is overthrown by the fact that that place is too far to the east to be thought of in this connection; and neither *Robinson* nor *Ritter* makes any allusion to " Ain *Kana*, in the neighbourhood of

Jurjera, six hours to the south-east of Sidon," which *Knobel* mentions without quoting his authority, so that the existence of such a place is very questionable. On *Sidon*, now *Saida*, see at chap. xi. 8.—Ver. 29. "*And the boundary turned* (probably from the territory of Sidon) *to Ramah, to the fortified town of Zor.*" *Robinson* supposes that *Rama* is to be found in the village of *Rameh*, on the south-east of Tyre, where several ancient sarcophagi are to be seen (Bibl. Res. p. 63). "The fortified town of *Zor*," *i.e.* Tyre, is not the insular Tyre, but the town of Tyre, which was on the mainland, the present *Sur*, which is situated by the sea-coast, in a beautiful and fertile plain (see *Ritter*, Erdk. xvii. p. 320, and *Movers*, Phönizier, ii. 1, pp. 118 sqq.). "*And the boundary turned to Hosah, and the outgoings thereof were at the sea, by the side of the district of Achzib.*" *Hosah* is unknown, as the situation of *Kausah*, near to the Rameh already mentioned (*Rob.* Bibl. Res. p. 61), does not suit in this connection. מֵחֶבֶל, *lit.* from the district, *i.e.* by the side of it. *Achzib*, where the Asherites dwelt with the Canaanites (Judg. i. 31, 32), is the *Ekdippa* of the Greeks and Romans, according to the *Onom.* (*s. v. Achziph*) nine Roman miles, or according to the *Itiner. Hieros.* p. 584, twelve miles to the north of Acco by the sea, the present *Zib*, a very large village, three good hours to the north of Acre,—a place on the sea-coast, with considerable ruins of antiquity (see *Ges.* Thes. p. 674; *Seetzen*, ii. p. 109; *Ritter*, xvi. pp. 811–12). —In ver. 30 three separate towns are mentioned, which were probably situated in the eastern part of the northern district of Asher, whereas the border towns mentioned in vers. 28 and 29 describe this district in its western half. *Ummah* (LXX. 'Αμμά) may perhaps have been preserved in *Kefr Ammeih*, upon the Lebanon, to the south of Hammana, in the district of Jurd (*Rob.* iii. App.; *Ritter*, xvii. p. 710). *Aphek* is the present *Afka* (see at chap. xiii. 4) *Rehob* cannot be traced with certainty. If it is *Hub*, as *Knobel* supposes, and the name *Hub*, which is borne by a Maronite monastery upon Lebanon, in the diocese of el-Jebail (to the north-east of Jebail), is a corruption of *Rehob*, this would be the northernmost town of Asher (see *Seetzen*, i. pp. 187 sqq., and *Ritter*, xvii. p. 791). The number "*twenty-two towns and their villages*" does not tally, as there are twenty-three towns mentioned in vers. 26–30, if we include Sidon, Tyre, and Achzib, according to Judg. i. 31, 32. The only way in which the numbers can be made to agree is to reckon *Nehiel* (ver. 27) as identical with Neah (ver. 13). But this point cannot be determined with certainty, as the Asherites received

other towns, such as Acco and Aclaph, which are wanting in this
list, and may possibly have simply fallen out.

Vers. 32–39. The Inheritance of Naphtali.—This fell
between Asher and the upper Jordan.   It reached northwards to the
northern boundary of Canaan, and touched Zebulun and Issachar
on the south.   In vers. 33 and 34 the boundary lines are given : viz.
in ver. 33 the western boundary towards Asher, with the northern
and eastern boundaries : in ver. 34 the southern boundary ; but
with the uncertainty which exists as to several of the places
named, it cannot be traced with certainty.—Ver. 33. " *Its boundary was* (its territory reached) *from Heleph, from the oak-forest
at Zaanannim, and Adami Nekeb and Jabneel to Lakkum; and
its outgoings were the Jordan*."   *Heleph* is unknown, though in
all probability it was to the south of Zaanannim, and not very
far distant.   According to Judg. iv. 11, the *oak-forest* (*allon:* see
the remarks on Gen. xii. 6) at *Zaanannim* was near *Kedesh*, on
the north-west of Lake Huleh.   There are still many oaks in that
neighbourhood (*Rob.* Bibl. Res. p. 386) ; and on the south of Bint
Jebail *Robinson* crossed a low mountain-range which was covered
with small oak trees (Pal. iii. p. 372).   *Adami hannekeb, i.e.*
Adami of the pass (*Nekeb*, judging from the analogy of the Arabic,
signifying *foramen, via inter montes*), is supposed by *Knobel* to be
Deir-el-ahmar, i.e. red cloister, a place which is still inhabited,
three hours to the north-west of Baalbek, on the pass from the
cedars to Baalbek (*Seetzen*, i. pp. 181, 185 ; *Burckhardt*, Syr. p. 60 ;
and *Ritter*, Erdk. xvii. p. 150), so called from the reddish colour of
the soil in the neighbourhood, which would explain the name *Adami*.
Knobel also connects *Jabneel* with the lake *Jemun, Jemuni*, or *Jam-
mune*, some hours to the north-west of Baalbek, on the eastern side
of the western Lebanon range (*Rob.* Bibl. Res. p. 548 ; *Ritter*, xvii.
pp. 304 sqq.), where there are still considerable ruins of a very early
date to be found, especially the ruins of an ancient temple and a
celebrated place of pilgrimage, with which the name " God's building" agrees.   And lastly, he associates *Lakkum* with the mountains
of *Lokham*, as the northern part of Lebanon on the Syrian mountains, from the latitude of Laodicea to that of Antioch on the
western side of the Orontes, is called by the Arabian geographers
Isztachri, Abulfeda, and others.   So far as the names are concerned,
these combinations seem appropriate enough, but they are hardly
tenable.   The resemblance between the names *Lakkum* and *Lokham*

is only in appearance, as the Hebrew name is written with ק and the Arabic with כ. Moreover, the mountains of Lokham are much too far north for the name to be adduced as an explanation of Lakkum. The interpretation of *Adami Nekeb* and *Jabneel* is also irreconcilable with the circumstance that the lake *Jamun* was two hours to the west of the red convent, so that the boundary, which starts from the west, and is drawn first of all towards the north, and then to the north-east and east, must have run last of all from the red convent, and not from the Jamun lake to the Jordan. As *Jabneel* is mentioned after *Adami Nekeb*, it must be sought for to the east of Adami Nekeb, whereas the Jamun lake lies in the very opposite direction, namely, directly to the west of the red convent. The three places mentioned, therefore, cannot be precisely determined at present. The Jordan, where the boundary of Asher terminated, was no doubt the upper Jordan, or rather the *Nahr Hasbany*, one of the sources of the Jordan, which formed, together with the Huleh lake and the Jordan itself, between Lake Huleh and the Sea of Tiberias, and down to the point where it issues from the latter, the eastern boundary of Asher.—Ver. 34. From the Jordan below the Lake of Tiberias, or speaking more exactly, from the point at which the Wady *Bessum* enters the Jordan, " *the boundary* (of Asher) *turned westwards to Asnoth-tabor, and went thence out to Hukkok*." This boundary, *i.e.* the southern boundary of Asher, probably followed the course of the Wady *Bessum* from the Jordan, which wady was the boundary of Issachar on the north-east, and then ran most likely from *Kefr Sabt* (see at ver. 22) to *Asnoth-tabor*, *i.e.*, according to the *Onom.* (*s. v. Azanoth*), a *vicus ad regionem Diocæsareæ pertinens in campestribus*, probably on the south-east of *Diocæsarea*, *i.e. Sepphoris*, not far from Tabor, to which the boundary of Issachar extended (ver. 22). *Hukkok* has not yet been traced. *Robinson* (Bibl. Res. p. 82) and *Van de Velde* (Mem. p. 322) are inclined to follow *Rabbi Parchi* of the fourteenth century, and identify this place with the village of *Yakûk*, on the north-west of the Lake of Gennesareth ; but this village is too far to the north-east to have formed the terminal point of the southern boundary of Naphtali, as it ran westwards from the Jordan. After this Naphtali touched " *Zebulun on the south, Asher on the west, and Judah by the Jordan toward the sun-rising or east*." " The Jordan" is in apposition to " Judah," in the sense of " Judah of the Jordan," like " Jordan of Jericho" in Num. xxii. 1, xxvi. 3, etc. The Masoretic pointing, which separates these two words, was founded upon some

false notion respecting this definition of the boundary, and caused
the commentators great perplexity, until *C. v. Raumer* succeeded in
removing the difficulty, by showing that the district of the sixty
towns of Jair, which was upon the eastern side of the Jordan, is
called Judah here, or reckoned as belonging to Judah, because Jair,
the possessor of these towns, was a descendant of Judah on the
father's side through Hezron (1 Chron. ii. 5, 21, 22); whereas in
chap. xiii. 30, and Num. xxxii. 41, he is reckoned *contra morem*,
i.e. against the rule laid down in Num. xxxvi. 7, as a descendant
of Manasseh, on account of his descent from Machir the Manassite,
on his mother's side.[1]

Vers. 35 sqq. The fortified towns of Naphtali were the following.
Ziddim : unknown, though *Knobel* suggests that " it may possibly
be preserved in *Chirbet es Saudeh,* to the west of the southern
extremity of the Lake of Tiberias (*Rob.* iii. App.) ;" but this place is
to the west of the Wady Bessum, *i.e.* in the territory of Issachar.
Zer is also unknown. As the LXX. and Syriac give the name as
Zor, Knobel connects it with *Kerak,* which signifies fortress as well
as *Zor* (= מָצוֹר), a heap of ruins at the southern end of the lake
(*Rob.* iii. p. 263), the place which *Josephus* calls *Taricheæ* (see
Reland, p. 1026),—a very doubtful combination ! *Hammath* (*i.e.*
thermæ), a Levitical town called *Hammoth-dor* in chap. xxi. 32,
and *Hammon* in 1 Chron. vi. 61, was situated, according to statements in the Talmud, somewhere near the later city of Tiberias, on
the western shore of the Lake of Gennesareth, and was no doubt
identical with the κώμη 'Aμμαoύς in the neighbourhood of Tiberias,
a place with warm baths (*Jos.* Ant. xviii. 2, 3 ; Bell. Jud. iv. 1, 3).
There are warm springs still to be found half an hour to the south
of Tabaria, which are used as baths (*Burckhardt,* Syr. pp. 573–4 ;
Rob. iii. pp. 258 sqq.). *Rakkath* (according to the *Talm.* and *Rabb.*
ripa littus) was situated, according to rabbinical accounts, in the
immediate neighbourhood of Hammath, and was the same place as
Tiberias ; but the account given by *Josephus* (Ant. xviii. 2, 3 ; cf.
Bell. Jud. ii. 9, 1) respecting the founding of *Tiberias* by Herod the
tetrarch is at variance with this ; so that the rabbinical statements
appear to have no other foundation than the etymology of the name

---

[1] See *C. v. Raumer's* article on " Judæa on the east of Jordan," in *Tholuck's
litt. Anz.* 1834, Nos. 1 and 2, and his Palästina, pp. 233 sqq. ed. 4 ; and for the
arbitrary attempts that had been made to explain the passage by alterations of
the text and in other ways, see *Rosenmüller's Bibl. Alterthk.* ii. 1, pp. 301–2 ; and
Keil's Comm. on Joshua, pp. 438–9.

Rakkath. *Chinnereth* is given in the Targums as נְגוֹסַר, נִינוֹסַר, גְנֵיסַר, *i.e.* Γεννησάρ. According to *Josephus* (Bell. Jud. iii. 10, 8), this name was given to a strip of land on the shore of the Sea of Galilee, which was distinguished foi its natural beauty, its climate, and its fertility, namely the long plain, about twenty minutes broad and an hour long, which stretches along the western shore of this lake, from el-Mejdel on the south to Khan Minyeh on the north (*Burckhardt,* Syr. pp. 558–9; *Rob.* iii. pp. 279, 290). It must have been in this plain that the town of *Chinnereth* stood, from which the plain and lake together derived the name of *Chinnereth* (Deut. iii. 17) or *Chinneroth* (chap. xi. 2), and the lake alone the name of " Sea of Chinnereth," or " Sea of Chinneroth" (chap. xii. 3, xiii. 27; Num. xxxiv. 11).—Ver. 36. *Adamah* is unknown. *Knobel* is of opinion, that as *Adamah* signifies red, the place referred to may possibly be *Ras el Ahmar, i.e. red-head,* on the north of Safed (*Rob.* iii. p. 370; Bibl. Res. p. 69). *Ramah* is the present *Rameh (Ramea),* a large well-built village, inhabited by Christians and Druses, surrounded by extensive olive plantations, and provided with an excellent well. It stands upon the slope of a mountain, in a beautiful plain on the south-west of Safed, but without any relics of antiquity (see *Seetzen,* ii. p. 129; *Rob.* Bibl. Res. pp. 78–9). *Hazor* has not yet been traced with certainty (see at chap. xi. 1).—Ver. 37. *Kedesh* (see at chap. xii. 2). *Edrei,* a different place from the town of the same name in Bashan (chap. i. 2, 4), is still unknown. *En-hazor* is probably to be sought for in *Tell Hazur* and *Ain Hazur,* which is not very far distant, on the south-west of Rameh, though the ruins upon *Tell Hazur* are merely the ruins of an ordinary village, with one single cistern that has fallen to pieces (*Rob.* Bibl. Res. pp. 80, 81).— Ver. 38. *Jireon (Iron)* is probably the present village of *Jarûn,* an hour to the south-east of Bint-Jebeil, with the ruins of an ancient Christian church (*Seetzen,* ii. pp. 123–4; *Van de Velde,* R. i. p. 133). *Migdal-el,* so far as the name is concerned, might be *Magdala* (Matt. xv. 39), on the western shore of the Lake of Gennesareth, between Capernaum and Tiberias (*Rob.* iii. pp. 279 sqq.); the only difficulty is, that the towns upon this lake have already been mentioned in ver. 35. *Knobel* connects *Migdal-el* with *Chorem,* so as to form one name, and finds *Migdal el Chorem* in the present *Mejdel Kerum,* on the west of Rameh (*Seetzen,* ii. p. 130; *Van de Velde,* i. p. 215), a common Mahometan village. But there is nothing to favour this combination, except the similarity in sound between the two names; whereas it has against it not only the situation of the village, which

was so far to the west, being not more than three hours from Acca,
that the territory of Naphtali can hardly have reached so far, but
also the very small resemblance between *Chorem* and *Kerum*, not to
mention the fact that the accents separate *Chorem* from *Migdal-el*,
whilst the omission of the copula (*vav*) before *Chorem* cannot have
any weight, as the copula is also wanting before *Zer* and *Rakkath*.
Chorem and *Beth-anath* have not yet been discovered. From the
latter place Naphtali was unable to expel the Canaanites (Judg. i.
33). *Beth-shemesh*, a different place from the town of the same
name in Issachar (ver. 22), is also still unknown. The total number
of towns is given as nineteen, whereas only sixteen are mentioned
by name. It is hardly correct to seek for the missing places among
the border towns mentioned in vers. 33 and 34, as the enumeration
of the towns themselves is introduced by עָרֵי מִבְצָר in ver. 35, and
in this way the list of towns is separated from the description of the
boundaries. To this we may add, that the town of Karthan or
Kirjathaim, which Naphtali gave up to the Levites (chap. xxi. 32 ;
1 Chron. vi. 61), does not occur either among the border towns or
in the list of towns, from which we may see that the list of towns
is an imperfect one.

Vers. 40-48. The Inheritance of the Tribe of Dan.—
This fell to the west of Benjamin, between Judah and Ephraim,
and was formed by Judah giving up some of its northern towns,
and Ephraim some of its southern towns, to the Danites, so as to
furnish them with a territory proportionate to their number. It
was situated for the most part in the lowland (*shephelah*), including, however, the hill country between the Mediterranean and the
mountains, and extended over a portion of the plain of Sharon, so
that it belonged to one of the most fruitful portions of Palestine.
The boundaries are not given, because they could be traced from
those of the adjoining territories.—Ver. 41. From Judah the
families of Dan received *Zorea* and *Eshtaol* (see at chap. xv. 33),
and *Ir-shemesh*, also called *Beth-shemesh* (1 Kings iv. 9), on the
border of Judah (see chap. xv. 10) ; but of these the Danites did
not take possession, as they were given up by Judah to the Levites
(chap. xxi. 16 : see at chap. xv. 10). *Saalabbin*, or *Saalbim*, which
remained in the hands of the Canaanites (Judg. i. 35), is frequently
mentioned in the history of David and Solomon (2 Sam. xxiii. 32 ;
1 Chron. xi. 33 ; 1 Kings iv. 9). It may possibly be the present
Selbit (*Rob.* iii. App. ; Bibl. Res. p. 144), some distance to the north

of the three places mentioned (*Knobel*). *Ajalon*, which was also
not taken from the Canaanites (Judg. i. 35), was assigned to the
Levites (chap. xxi. 24; 1 Chron. vi. 54). It is mentioned in the
wars with the Philistines (1 Sam. xiv. 31; 1 Chron. viii. 13), was
fortified by Rehoboam (2 Chron. xi. 10), and was taken by the
Philistines from King Ahaz (2 Chron. xxviii. 18). It has been
preserved in the village of *Yalo* (see at chap. x. 12). *Jethlah* is
only mentioned here, and has not yet been discovered. So far as
the name is concerned, it may possibly be preserved in the Wady
Atallah, on the west of *Yalo* (Bibl. Res. pp. 143-4).—Ver. 43. *Elon*,
which is mentioned again in 1 Kings iv. 9, with the addition of
Beth-hanan, has not yet been traced; according to *Knobel*, it " may
possibly be *Ellin*, near Timnath and Beth-shemesh, mentioned by
Robinson in his Pal. vol. iii. App." *Thimna* (*Thimnathah*) and
Ekron, on the boundary of Judah (see at chap. xv. 10, 11).—Ver.
44. *Eltekeh* and *Gibbethon*, which were allotted to the Levites (chap.
xxi. 23), have not yet been discovered. Under the earliest kings
of Israel, *Gibbethon* was in the hands of the Philistines (1 Kings xv.
27, xvi. 15, 17). *Baalath* was fortified by Solomon (1 Kings ix. 18).
According to *Josephus* (Ant. viii. 6, 1), it was " *Baleth in the
neighbourhood of Geser;*" probably the same place as *Baalah*, on the
border of Judah (chap. xv. 11).—Ver. 45. *Jehud* has probably been
preserved in the village of *Jehudieh* (*Hudieh*), two hours to the
north of Ludd (Diospolis), in a splendidly cultivated plain (*Berggren*, R. iii. p. 162; *Rob.* iii. p. 45, and App.). *Bene-berak*, the
present *Ibn Abrak*, an hour from Jehud (*Scholz*, R. p. 256). *Gath-
rimmon*, which was given to the Levites (chap. xxi. 24; 1 Chron.
vi. 54), is described in the *Onom.* (*s. v.*) as *villa prægrandis in duo-
decimo milliario Diospoleos pergentibus Eleutheropolin*,—a statement
which points to the neighbourhood of Thimnah, though it has not
yet been discovered.—Ver. 46. *Me-jarkon, i.e. aquæ flavedinis*, and
Rakkon, are unknown; but from the clause which follows, " *with
the territory before Japho*," it must have been in the neighbourhood
of Joppa (Jaffa). " *The territory before Japho*" includes the places
in the environs of Joppa. Consequently *Joppa* itself does not
appear to have belonged to the territory of Dan, although, according to Judg. v. 17, the Danites must have had possession of this
town. *Japho*, the well-known port of Palestine (2 Chron. ii. 15;
Ezra iii. 7; Jonah i. 3), which the Greeks called Ἰόππη (Joppa),
the present *Jaffa* (see v. *Raumer*, Pal. pp. 204-5, and *Ritter*, Erdk.
xvi. pp. 574 sqq.).—Ver. 47. Besides this inheritance, the Danites

of Zorea and Eshtaol went, after Joshua's death, and conquered the town of *Leshem* or *Laish*, on the northern boundary of Canaan, and gave it the name of *Dan*, as the territory which was allotted to them under Joshua was too small for them, on account of their inability to drive out the Amorites from several of their towns (Judg. i. 34, 35, xvii. 2). For further particulars concerning this conquest, see Judg. xviii. *Leshem* or *Laish* (Judg. xviii. 7, 27), *i.e.* *Dan*, which the *Onom.* describes as *viculus quarto a Pӕneade miliario euntibus Tyrum*, was the present *Tell el Kadi*, or *el Leddan*, the central source of the Jordan, to the west of Banjas, a place with ancient ruins (see *Rob.* iii. p. 351; Bibl. Res. pp. 390, 393). It was there that Jeroboam set up the golden calves (1 Kings xii. 29, 30, etc.); and it is frequently mentioned as the northernmost city of the Israelites, in contrast with Beersheba, which was in the extreme south of the land (Judg. xx. 1; 1 Sam. iii. 20; 2 Sam. iii. 10: see also *Ritter*, Erdk. xv. pp. 207 sqq.).

Vers. 49–51. *Conclusion of the Distribution of the Land.*—Vers. 49, 50. When the land was distributed among the tribes according to its territories, the Israelites gave Joshua an inheritance in the midst of them, according to the command of Jehovah, namely the town of *Timnath-serah*, upon the mountains of Ephraim, for which he asked, and which he finished building; and there he dwelt until the time of his death (chap. xxiv. 30; Judg. ii. 9). "*According to the word of the Lord*" (*lit.* "at the mouth of Jehovah") does not refer to a divine oracle communicated through the high priest, but to a promise which Joshua had probably received from God at the same time as Caleb, viz. in Kadesh, but which, like the promise given to Caleb, is not mentioned in the Pentateuch (see at chap. xv. 13, xiv. 9). *Timnath-serah*, called *Timnath-heres* in Judg. ii. 9, must not be confounded with *Timnah* in the tribe of Dan (ver. 43, chap. xv. 10), as is the case in the *Onom.* It has been preserved in the present ruins and foundation walls of a place called *Tibneh*, which was once a large town, about seven hours to the north of Jerusalem, and two hours to the west of Jiljilia, standing upon two mountains, with many caverns that have been used as graves (see *Eli Smith* in *Ritter*, Erdk. xvi. pp. 562 sqq., and *Rob.* Bibl. Res. p. 141).—Ver. 51. Closing formula to the account of the distribution of the land, which refers primarily to chap. xviii. 1 sqq., as the expression "*in Shiloh*" shows, but which also includes chap. xiv.–xvii.

SELECTION OF CITIES OF REFUGE, OR FREE CITIES.—CHAP. XX.

After the distribution of the land by lot among the tribes of Israel, six towns were set apart, in accordance with the Mosaic instructions in Num. xxxv., as places of refuge for unintentional manslayers. Before describing the appointment and setting apart of these towns, the writer repeats in vers. 1–6 the main points of the Mosaic law contained in Num. xxxv. 9–29 and Deut. xix. 1–13, with reference to the reception of the manslayers into these towns. תְּנוּ לָכֶם, " give to you," i.e. appoint for yourselves, " cities of refuge," etc. In ver. 6, the two regulations, " until he stand before the congregation for judgment," and " until the death of the high priest," are to be understood, in accordance with the clear explanation given in Num. xxxv. 24, 25, as meaning that the manslayer was to live in the town till the congregation had pronounced judgment upon the matter, and either given him up to the avenger of blood as a wilful murderer, or taken him back to the city of refuge as an unintentional manslayer, in which case he was to remain there till the death of the existing high priest. For further particulars, see at Num. xxxv.—Vers. 7–9. List of the cities: Levitical cities were chosen, for the reasons explained in the Commentary on the Pentateuch, iii. p. 262.—Ver. 7. In the land on this side (viz. Canaan) they sanctified the following cities. In the north, Kedesh (see at chap. xii. 22), in Galil, on the mountains of Naphtali. Galil (a circle) was a district in the northern part of the subsequent province of Galilee; it is called גְּלִיל הַגּוֹיִם, circle of the heathen, in Isa. viii. 23, because an unusually large number of heathen or Gentiles were living there. In the centre of the land, Shechem, upon the mountains of Ephraim (see at chap. xvii. 7). And in the south, Kirjatharba, i.e. Hebron, upon the mountains of Judah (see at chap. x. 3). —Ver. 8. The cities in the land on the other side had already been appointed by Moses (Deut. iv. 41–43). For the sake of completeness, they are mentioned here again : viz. Bezer, Ramoth in Gilead, and Golan (see at Deut. iv. 43). The subject is brought to a close in ver. 9. עָרֵי הַמּוּעָדָה signifies neither urbes congregationis (Kimchi) nor urbes asyli (Gesenius), but cities of appointment,—those which received the appointment already given and repeated again in what follows.

APPOINTMENT OF TOWNS FOR THE PRIESTS AND LEVITES.—
CHAP. XXI.

Vers. 1–3. After the cities of refuge had been set apart, the towns were also selected, which the different tribes were to give up for the priests and Levites to dwell in according to the Mosaic instructions in Num. xxxv. 1–8, together with the necessary fields as pasturage for their cattle. The setting apart of the cities of refuge took place before the appointment of the Levitical towns, because the Lord had given commandment through Moses in Num. xxxv. 6, that they were to give to the Levites the six cities of refuge, and forty-two cities besides, *i.e.* forty-eight cities in all. From the introductory statement in vers. 1, 2, that the heads of the fathers (see Ex. vi. 14, 25) of the Levitical families reminded the distribution committee at Shiloh of the command of God that had been issued through Moses, that towns were to be given them to dwell in, we cannot infer, as *Calvin* has done, that the Levites had been forgotten, till they came and asserted their claims. All that is stated in these words is, " that when the business had reached that point, they approached the dividers of the land in the common name of the members of their tribe, to receive by lot the cities appointed for them. They simply expressed the commands of God, and said in so many words, that they had been deputed by the Levites generally to draw lots for those forty-eight cities with their suburbs, which had been appointed for that tribe" (*Masius*). The clause appended to *Shiloh*, " *in the land of Canaan*," points to the instructions in Num. xxxiv. 29 and xxxv. 10, to give the children of Israel their inheritance *in the land of Canaan*.

Vers. 4–8. *Number of the cities* which the different families of Levi received from each tribe. The tribe of Levi was divided into three branches,—the Gershonites, the Kohathites, and the Merarites (see Num. iii. and Ex. vi. 16–19). The Kohathites again were divided into the four families of Amram, Izhar, Hebron, and Uzziel (Ex. vi. 18) ; and the family of Amram into two lines, consisting of the descendants of Moses and Aaron (Ex. vi. 20). The priesthood was committed to the line of Aaron (Num. xviii. 1–7) ; but the other descendants of Amram, *i.e.* the descendants of Moses, were placed on a par with the other descendants of Levi, and numbered among the simple Levites (Num. iii. ; 1 Chron. v. 27– vi. 34). The towns in which the different families of Levi were to dwell were determined by lot ; but in all probability the towns which each tribe was to give up to them were selected first of all, so that the lot merely decided to which branch of the Levites each particular town was to belong.—Ver. 4. The first lot came out for the families of Kohath, and among these again for the sons of Aaron, *i.e.* the priests. They received thirteen towns from the tribes of Judah, Simeon, and Benjamin. " This did not happen by chance ; but God, according to His wonderful counsel, placed them just in that situation which He had determined to select for His own temple" (*Calvin*).—Ver. 5. The rest of the Kohathites, *i.e.* the descendants of Moses, Izhar, Hebron, and Uzziel, received ten towns from Ephraim, Dan, and half Manasseh.—Ver. 6. The Gershonites received thirteen towns from Issachar, Asher, Naphtali, and half Manasseh in Bashan.—Ver. 7. The Merarites received twelve towns from Reuben, Gad, and Zebulun.

The number of towns thus assigned to the Levites will not appear too large, if we consider, (1) that judging from the number of towns in so small a land, the greater part of them cannot have been very large ; (2) that the Levites were not the sole possessors of these towns, but simply received the number of dwelling-houses which they actually required, with meadow land for their cattle in the suburbs of the towns, whilst the rest of the space still belonged to the different tribes ; and (3) that if the 23,000 males, the number of the Levites at the second census which was taken in the steppes of Moab, were distributed among the thirty-five towns, it would give 657 males, or 1300 male and female Levites for every town. On the other hand, offence has been taken at the statement, that thirteen towns were given up to the priests ; and under the idea that Aaron could hardly have had descendants enough in Joshua's time from his two sons who remained alive to fill even two towns, to say nothing of thirteen, the list has been set down as a document which was drawn up at a much later date (*Maurer*, etc.). But any one who takes this ground not only attributes to the distribution commission the enormous shortsightedness of setting apart towns for the priests merely to meet their existing wants, and without any regard to the subsequent increase which would take place in their numbers, but he also forms too large an estimate of the size of the towns, and too small an estimate of the number of the priests. Moreover, it was never intended that the towns should be filled with priests' families ; and the number of priests alive at that time is not mentioned anywhere. But if we bear in mind that Aaron died in the fortieth year of the journeys of the Israelites, at the age of 123 years (Num. xxxiii. 38), and therefore was eighty-three years old at the time of the exodus from Egypt, his descendants might have entered upon the fourth generation seven years after his death. Now his two sons had twenty-four male descendants, who were the founders of the twenty-four classes instituted by David (1 Chron. xxiv.). And if we only reckon six males to each of the next generations, there would be 144 in the third generation, who would be between the ages of twenty-five and thirty-five when the distribution of the land took place, and who might therefore have had 864 male children living at that time; so that the total number of males in the families of the priests might have amounted to more than 1000, that is to say, might have consisted of at least 200 families.

Vers. 9–42. *Names of the Levitical Towns*.[1]—Vers. 9–19. *The priests' towns :* (*a*) in Judah and Simeon (vers. 9–16); (*b*) in Benjamin (vers. 17–19).—Vers. 9 sqq. In the tribe of Judah the priests received *Kirjath-arba*, or *Hebron*, with the necessary pasturage round about the town (see Num. xxxv. 2), whilst the field of the town with the villages belonging to it remained in the hands of Caleb and his family as their possession (chap. xiv. 12 sqq.).— Ver. 13 contains a repetition of ver. 11, occasioned by the parenthetical remark in ver. 12. They also received *Libnah* in the lowland (see chap. xv. 42, x. 29); *Jattir* (chap. xv. 48), *Eshtemoah*

---

[1] There is a similar list in 1 Chron. vi. 54-81, though in some respects differently arranged, and with many variations in the names, and corruptions of different kinds in the text, which show that the author of the Chronicles has inserted an ancient document that was altogether independent of the book before us. Thus in the Chronicles there are only forty-two towns mentioned by name instead of forty-eight, although it is stated in vers. 45 sqq. that 13 + 10 + 13 + 12, *i.e.* forty-eight towns in all, were given up to the Levites. The names omitted are (1) Jutta in Judah; (2) Gibeon in Benjamin; (3 and 4) Ethekeh and Gibbethon in Dan; (5 and 6) and Jokneam and Nahalal in Zebulun (compare vers. 16, 17, 23, 34, and 35, with 1 Chron. vi. 59, 60, 68, 77. In some cases also the author of the Chronicles gives different names, though some of them indeed are only different forms of the same name, *e.g.* Hilen for Holon, Alemeth for Almon, Ashtaroth for Beeshterah, Mashal for Misheal, Hammon for Hammoth-dor, Kirjathaim for Kartan (compare 1 Chron. vi. 58, 60, 71, 74, 76, with Josh. xxi. 15, 18, 27, 30, 32); or in some cases possibly different names of the same town, *e.g.* Jokmeam for Kibzaim, and Ramoth for Jarmuth, and Anem for En-gannim (1 Chron. vi. 68, 83, and Josh. xxi. 22, 29); whilst some evidently give the true reading, viz. Ashan for Ain, and Bileam for Gath-rimmon (1 Chron. vi. 59, 70; Josh. xxi. 16, 25). The majority, however, are faulty readings, viz. Aner for Tanach, Kedesh for Kishon, Hukok for Helkath, Rimmon and Tabor (compare 1 Chron. vi. 70, 72, 75, 77, with Josh. xxi 25, 28, 31, 34, 35)

(chap. xv. 50), *Holon* (chap. xv. 51), and *Debir* (chap. xv. 15, 49, x. 38) on the mountains of Judah; *Ain*, for which we should read *Ashan* (1 Chron. vi. 44; cf. chap. xv. 42), in the tribe of Simeon (chap. xix. 7); *Juttah* on the mountains (chap. xv. 55); and *Beth-shemesh* in the lowland (chap. xv. 10).—Vers. 17 sqq. In the tribe of Benjamin they received *Gibeon* (see chap. ix. 3), *Geba* (chap. xviii. 24), also *Anathoth* and *Almon*, which are missing in the list of the towns of Benjamin (see at chap. xviii. 24). -Vers. 20–42. *Towns of the Levites.*—Vers. 20–26. The other *Kohathites* received four towns from the tribe of Ephraim (vers. 21, 22), four from Dan (vers. 23, 24), and two from the half tribe of Manasseh on this side of the Jordan (ver. 25). From Ephraim they received *Shechem* (see chap. xvii. 7), *Gezer* (chap. x. 33), *Kibzaim*—for which we find *Jockmeam* in 1 Chron. vi. 68, possibly a different name for the same place, which has not yet been discovered—and *Beth-horon*, whether Upper or Lower is not stated (see chap. x. 10). From Dan they received *Eltheheh* and *Gibbethon* (chap. xix. 44), *Ajalon* and *Gath-rimmon* (chap. xix. 42, 45). From half Manasseh they received *Taanach* (chap. xvii. 11, xii. 21) and *Gath-rimmon*— this is evidently a copyist's error, occasioned by the wandering of the eye to the previous verse, for *Bileam* (1 Chron. vi. 70), *i.e. Jibleam* (chap. xvii. 11).—Ver. 26. Thus they received ten towns in all.— Vers. 27–33. The *Gershonites* received two towns from eastern Manasseh: *Golan* (chap. xx. 8; Deut. iv. 43), and Beeshterah. *Beeshterah* (contracted from *Beth-eshterah*, the house of Astarte), called *Ashtaroth* in 1 Chron. vi. 56, may possibly have been the capital of king Og (*Ashtaroth-karnaim*, Gen. xiv. 5), if not one of the two villages named *Astaroth*, which are mentioned by *Eusebius* in the *Onom. (s. v. Astharoth-karnaim)*, and are described by Jerome as *duo castella in Batanæa, novem inter se millibus separata inter Adaram et Abilam civitates*, though Adara and Abila are too indefinite to determine the situation with any exactness. At any rate, the present *Busra* on the east of the Hauran cannot be thought of for a moment; for this was called $Bό\sigma\sigma o\rho a$ or $Bo\sigma o\rho\rho\acute{a}$, *i.e.* בָּצְרָה, in ancient times, as it is at the present day (see 1 Macc. v. 26, and *Joseph.* Ant. xii. 8, 3), and was corrupted into *Bostra* by the Greeks and Romans. Nor can it be the present *Kul'at Bustra* on the north of Banyas upon a shoulder of the Hermon, where there are the ruins of a magnificent building, probably a temple of ancient date (*Burckhardt*, Syr. pp. 93, 94; *Rob.* Bibl. Res. pp. 414–15), as *Knobel* supposes, since the territory of the Israelites did not reach so far north,

the land conquered by Joshua merely extending to Baal-gad, *i.e.*
Banyas, at the foot of the Hermon (see chap. xi. 17), and the land
to the east of the Jordan, or Bashan, only to the Hermon itself, or
more correctly, merely to the districts of Geshuri and Maacah at the
south-eastern border of the Hermon (see at Deut. iii. 8, 14).—Vers.
28, 29. From Issachar they received four towns : *Kishon* (chap. xix.
20), *Dabrath* (chap. xix. 12), *Jarmuth = Remeth* (see chap. xix. 21),
and *En-gannim* (chap. xix. 21, or *Anem*, 1 Chron. vi. 73).—Vers.
30, 31. From Asher they received four towns : *Mishal* or *Masal*
(chap. xix. 26; cf. 1 Chron. vi. 74), *Abdon* (chap. xix. 28), *Helkath* (chap. xix. 25, called *Hukok* in 1 Chron. vi. 75, probably
a copyist's error), and *Rehob* (chap. xix. 28).—Ver. 32. From
Naphtali they received three towns : *Kedesh* (chap. xix. 37 and
xii. 22), *Hammoth-dor* (called *Hammath* in chap. xix. 35, and
Hammon in 1 Chron. vi. 76), and *Kartan* (contracted from *Kartain*
for *Kirjathaim*, 1 Chron. vi. 76; like *Dothan* in 2 Kings vi. 13,
from *Dothain* in Gen. xxxvii. 17). *Kartan* is not mentioned among
the towns of Naphtali in chap. xix. 33 sqq.; according to *Knobel*
it may possibly be *Katanah*, a place with ruins to the north-east
of Safed (*Van de Velde*, Mem. p. 147).—Ver. 33. They received
thirteen towns in all.—Vers. 34-40. The *Merarites* received twelve
towns. From the tribe of Zebulun they received four : *Jokneam*
(chap. xix. 11 : see at chap. xii. 22), *Kartah* and *Dimnah*,[1] which
are not mentioned among the towns of Zebulun in chap. xix. 11 sqq.,
and are unknown, and *Nahalal* (chap. xix. 15).—Vers. 36, 37. From
Reuben they received four : *Bezer* (chap. xx. 8 : see Deut. iv. 43),
Jahza, Kedemoth, and *Mephaath* (chap. xiii. 18).[2]—Vers. 38, 39.
From Gad they received four towns : *Ramoth* in Gilead, and
Mahanaim (see at chap. xiii. 26), *Heshbon* (chap. xiii. 17) and *Jaezer*
(chap. xiii. 25 : see at Num. xxi. 32).—Ver. 40. They received

---

[1] Many commentators identify *Dimnah* with *Rimmono* in 1 Chron. vi. 77,
but without sufficient reason ; for the text of the Chronicles is no doubt corrupt
in this passage, as it has only two names, *Rimmono* and *Tabor*, instead of four.

[2] *R. Jacob ben Chajim* has omitted vers. 36 and 37 from his Rabbinical Bible
of the year 1525 as spurious, upon the authority of *Kimchi* and the larger
Masora ; but upon insufficient grounds, as these verses are to be found in many
good mss. and old editions of an earlier date than 1525, as well as in all the
ancient versions, and could not possibly have been wanting from the very first,
since the Merarites received twelve towns, which included the four that belonged
to Reuben. In those mss. in which they are wanting, the omission was, no
doubt, a copyist's error, occasioned by the ὁμοιοτελευτόν (see *de Rossi variæ
lectt. ad h. l.*, and *J. H. Michaelis'* Note to his Hebrew Bible).

twelve towns in all.—In vers. 41 and 42 the list of the Levitical towns is closed with a statement of their total number, and also with the repetition of the remark that "these cities were every one with their suburbs round about them." עִיר עִיר וּמ׳, city city, i.e. every city, with its pasture round about it.

Vers. 43–45 form the conclusion to the account of the division of the land in chap. xiii.-xxi., which not only points back to chap. xi. 23, but also to chap. i. 2–6, and connects the two halves of our book together. By the division of Canaan among the tribes of Israel, the promise which Joshua had received from God after the death of Moses was fulfilled (chap. i. 2 sqq.). The Lord had given Israel the whole land which He had sworn to the fathers (Gen. xii. 7, xv. 18, compared with Josh. i. 3, 4); and they had now taken possession of it to dwell therein.—Ver. 44. He had also procured them rest round about, as He had sworn to their fathers, inasmuch as not a man of all their enemies stood against them. The expression " gave them rest," etc., points back to Deut. xii. 9, 10, and refers to all the divine promises of the Pentateuch which assured the Israelites of the peaceable possession of Canaan, such as Ex. xxxiii. 14, Deut. iii. 20, etc. No enemy had been able to withstand them, as the Lord had promised Joshua (chap. i. 5). " The Lord delivered all their enemies into their hand." It is true the Canaanites were not all exterminated; but those who were left had become so powerless, that they could neither accomplish nor attempt anything against Israel, so long as the Israelites adhered faithfully to their God, or so long as Joshua and the elders who were his contemporaries were alive (Judg. ii. 6 sqq.), because the Lord had overwhelmed them with fear and terror before the Israelites.[1]— Ver. 45. Of all the good words which the Lord had spoken to the house of Israel not one had fallen, i.e. remained unfulfilled (Num. vi. 12); all had come to pass (vid. chap. xxiii. 14). כָּל־הַדָּבָר הַטּוֹב relates to the gracious promises of God with regard to the peaceful possession of Canaan, which formed the basis of all the salvation promised to Israel, and the pledge of the fulfilment of all the further

---

[1] " If any one should raise a question as to their actual peace, the solution is easy enough. The tribes of Canaan were so alarmed and broken down with their fear, that in their opinion nothing could serve their purpose better than to purchase peace from the children of Israel by the most obsequious servility. Clearly, therefore, the land was subdued and their home at peace, since no one disturbed them, or attempted anything against them ; there were no threats, no snares, no violence, and no conspiracy."—Calvin.

promises of God. Notwithstanding the fact that many a tract of country still remained in the hands of the Canaanites, the promise that the land of Canaan should be given to the house of Israel for a possession had been fulfilled ; for God had not promised the immediate and total destruction of the Canaanites, but only their gradual extermination (Ex. xxiii. 29, 30 ; Deut. vii. 22). And even though the Israelites never came into undisputed possession of the whole of the promised land, to the full extent of the boundaries laid down in Num. xxxiv. 1-12, never conquering Tyre and Sidon for example, the promises of God were no more broken on that account than they were through the circumstance, that after the death of Joshua and the elders his contemporaries, Israel was sometimes hard pressed by the Canaanites ; since the complete fulfilment of this promise was inseparably connected with the fidelity of Israel to the Lord.[1]

RETURN OF THE TWO TRIBES AND A HALF TO THEIR OWN INHERITANCE.—CHAP. XXII.

Vers. 1-8. After the conquest and division of the land, Joshua sent the auxiliaries of the tribes of Reuben, Gad, and half Manasseh back to their homes, with a laudatory acknowledgment of the help they had given to their brethren, and a paternal admonition to adhere faithfully to the Lord and His law, and with a parting blessing (vers. 1-6). By the expression " *then Joshua called,*" etc., the occurrence described in this chapter is placed in a general manner after the conquest and subjugation of Canaan, though not of necessity at the close of the distribution of the land. As the summons to these tribes to go with their brethren into Canaan, to assist them in the war, formed the commencement of Joshua's plans

---

[1] With reference to this apparent discrepancy between the promises of God and the actual results, *Calvin* observes, that " in order to remove every appearance of discrepancy, it is right to distinguish well between the clear, unwavering, and certain fidelity of God in the fulfilment of His promises, and the weakness and indolence of the people, which caused the blessings of God to slip from their hands. Whatever war the people undertook, in whatever direction they carried their standards, there was victory ready to their hand ; nor was there anything to retard or prevent the extermination of all their enemies except their own slothfulness. Consequently, although they did not destroy them all, so as to empty the land for their own possession, the truth of God stood out as distinctly as if they had ; for there would have been no difficulty in their accomplishment of all that remained to be done, if they had only been disposed to grasp the victories that were ready to their hand. '

for the conquest of Canaan (chap. i. 12 sqq.), their dismission to their home very properly forms the conclusion to the history of the conquest of this land by the Israelites. We might therefore assume, without in any way contradicting the words of the text, that these auxiliaries had been dismissed immediately after the war was ended. Even in that case, the account of their dismission would stand in its proper place, " since it was only right that the history itself, which relates to the conquest and possession of the land, should be fully completed before any other narratives, or any casual occurrences which took place, were introduced to break the thread" (*Lightfoot*, App. i. p. 42). On the other hand, however, the circumstance that the two tribes and a half were dismissed from Shiloh, where the tribes assembled for the first time during the casting of the lots, favours the conclusion that the dismission did not take place till after the lots had been cast; that is to say, contemporaneously with the advance of the other tribes into their possessions.—Vers. 2, 3. Joshua acknowledged that they had done all that they were under any obligation to do towards Moses and himself (Num. xxxii. 20 sqq.; Josh. i. 16, 17). " *Kept the charge of the commandment*," *i.e.* observed what had to be observed in relation to the commandment of the Lord (see at Lev. viii. 35 and Gen. xxvi. 5).—Ver. 4 points back to chap. i. 15. " *Unto your tents*," for to your homes,—an antiquated form of expression, as in Deut. xvi. 7, Judg. vii. 8, etc.—Ver. 5. Remembering, however, the changeableness of the human heart, Joshua appends to the acknowledgment of their fidelity in the performance of their duty the pressing admonition, to continue still to observe the law of Moses faithfully, to walk in the ways of the Lord and serve Him with the whole heart, which was simply a repetition of what Moses had impressed in a fatherly way upon the hearts of the people (see Deut. iv. 4, 29, vi. 5, x. 12, xi. 13, etc.).—Ver. 6. Thus Joshua dismissed them with blessings.—In ver. 7, the writer, for the sake of clearness, refers again to the fact that only half of Manasseh had received its inheritance from Moses in Bashan, whereas the other had received its inheritance through Joshua on the west of the Jordan (cf. chap. xiv. 3, and xviii. 7). To us such repetitions appear superfluous; but they are closely connected with the copious breadth of the early historical style of the Hebrews, which abounded in repetitions. The verb נָתַן (gave) wants its object, אֲחֻזָּתוֹ or נַחֲלָתוֹ, which may easily be supplied from the context. This interpolation involved a further repetition of the fact, that Joshua also dismissed them (the Manassites of the other side) with a blessing, in order that the words might be appended with which Joshua dismissed the two tribes and a half to their homes, namely, the admonition to share the rich booty which they had accumulated with their brethren at home, in accordance with the instructions which Moses had given them with reference to the war with the Midianites (Num. xxxi. 25 sqq.).

Vers. 9–12. On the way home, when the two tribes and a half had reached the border of Canaan, they built a large conspicuous altar in the district of the Jordan, in the land of Canaan, *i.e.* on this side of the Jordan : "*a great altar to see to,*" *i.e.* one which caught the eye on account of its size, since it was to serve for a memorial (vers. 24 sqq.). The definition appended to Shiloh, "*in the land of Canaan*" (ver. 9), serves to bring out the antithesis "*into the land of Gilead,*" by which we are to understand the whole of the country to the east of the Jordan, as in Num. xxxii. 29, Deut. xxxiv. 1, Judg. v. 17, etc. נאחז, both in the form and meaning the same as in Num. xxxii. 30, *made possessors, i.e.* settled down. גְּלִילוֹת הַיַּרְדֵּן, *the circles of the Jordan,* is synonymous with כִּכַּר הַיַּרְדֵּן in Gen. xiii. 10, and signifies that portion of the Ghor which was upon the western side of the Jordan.—Vers. 11, 12. The Israelites (on this side) heard that the tribes in question had built the altar "*opposite to the land of Canaan*" (*lit.* in the face or in front of the land of Canaan), אֶל־עֵבֶר, "*at the opposite region of the children of Israel*" (two descriptions which may be explained on the supposition that the name of Canaan is used in a restricted sense, the valley of the Jordan being expressly excepted, and Canaan considered as only extending to the valley of the Jordan). When they heard this, the whole congregation (in its heads and representatives) assembled at Shiloh, to go up, *i.e.* with the intention of going, to make war against them. The congregation supposed that the altar had been built as a place for sacrifice, and therefore regarded it as a wicked violation of the commandment of God with regard to the unity of the sacrificial altar (Lev. xvii. 8, 9 ; Deut. xii. 4 sqq.), which they ought to punish according to the law in Deut. xiii. 13 sqq. This zeal was perfectly justifiable, and even praiseworthy, as the altar, even if not erected as a place for sacrifice, might easily be abused to that purpose, and thus become an occasion of sin to the whole nation. In any case, the two tribes and a half ought not to have erected such a building without the consent of Joshua or of the high priest.[1]

---

[1] " We know how sternly the law prohibited the use of two altars : because it was the will of God that His worship should be restricted to one place. When,

Vers. 13-20. The congregation therefore sent Phinehas, the son of the high priest and his presumptive successor in this office, with ten princes, one from each tribe (not the tribe-princes, but a head of the fathers' houses of the families of Israel), to Gilead, to the two tribes and a half, to call them to account for building the altar. —Ver. 16. Assuming at the outset that the altar was intended for a second place of sacrifice in opposition to the command of God, the delegates, with Phinehas no doubt as their speaker, began by reproaching them for falling away from the Lord. *" What faith-lessness is this* (מַעַל : see at Lev. v. 15) *that ye have committed against the God of Israel, to turn away this day from Jehovah, in that ye have builded you an altar, that ye might rebel this day against Jehovah?"* מָרַד (to rebel) is stronger than מָעַל.—Vers. 17 sqq. To show the greatness of the sin through apostasy from the Lord, the speaker reminds them of two previous acts of sin on the part of the nation, which had brought severe judgments upon the congregation. *" Is there too little for us in the iniquity of Peor* (*i.e.* with Peor, or through the worship of Peor, Num. xxv. 3), *from which we have not cleansed ourselves till this day, and there came the plague upon the congregation of Jehovah?"* אֶת־עֲוֹן is an accusative: see *Ges.* § 117, 2; *Ewald,* § 277, *d.* That plague, of which 24,000 Israelites died, was stayed through the zeal of Phinehas for the honour of the Lord (Num. xxv. 4-9, 11). The guilt connected with the worship of Peor had thereby been avenged upon the congregation, and the congregation itself had been saved from any further punishment in consequence of the sin. When Phinehas, therefore, affirmed that the congregation had not yet been cleansed from the crime, he did not mean that they were still bearing or suffering from the punish-ment of that crime, but that they were not yet cleansed from that sin, inasmuch as many of them were still attached to idolatry in their hearts, even if they had hitherto desisted from it outwardly from fear of the infliction of fresh judgments.—Ver. 18. *"And*

therefore, from the very appearance it could not fail to occur to the mind of any one that they were establishing a second altar, who would not have condemned them as guilty of sacrilege, for introducing rites and ceremonies at variance with the law of God? And since it might so naturally be regarded as a wicked deed, they ought certainly to have consulted their brethren in so grave and important a matter; and it was especially wrong to pass by the high priest, when the will of God might have been learned from his lips. They were deserving of blame, therefore, because they acted as if they had been alone in the world, and did not consider what offence might easily arise from the novelty of their proceedings."— *Calvin.*

to-day ye turn away from the Lord again," and are about to bring His wrath upon the whole congregation again through a fresh rebellion.—Ver. 19. "*And truly,*" the speaker continued, "*if the land of your possession should be unclean,*" *sc.* so that you think it necessary to have an altar in the neighbourhood to expiate your sins and wipe away your uncleannesses, "*pass over into the land of Jehovah's possession, where His dwelling-place stands, and settle in the midst of us* ('settle,' as in Gen. xxxiv. 10); *but do not rebel against Jehovah nor against us, by building an altar beside the* (one) *altar of Jehovah our God.*" מָרַד is construed first of all with בְּ, and then with the accusative; the only other place in which the latter occurs is Job xxiv. 13.—Ver. 20. He finally reminded them of the sin of Achan, how that had brought the wrath of God upon the whole congregation (chap. vii.); and, moreover, Achan was not the only man who had perished on account of the sin, but thirty-six men had fallen on account of it at the first attack upon Ai (chap. vii. 5). The allusion to this fact is to be understood as an argument *a minori ad majus,* as *Masius* has shown. "If Achan did not perish alone when he committed sacrilege, but God was angry with the whole congregation, what think ye will be the consequence if ye, so great a number, commit so grievous a sin against God?"

Vers. 21–29. In utter amazement at the suspicion expressed by the delegates of the congregation, the two tribes and a half affirm with a solemn oath, that it never entered into their minds to build an altar as a place of sacrifice, to fall away from Jehovah. The combination of the three names of God—EL, the strong one; ELOHIM, the Supreme Being to be feared; and JEHOVAH, the truly existing One, the covenant God (ver. 22)—serves to strengthen the invocation of God, as in Ps. l. 1; and this is strengthened still further by the repetition of these three names. God knows, and let Israel also know, *sc.* what they intended, and what they have done. The אִם which follows is the usual particle used in an oath. "*Verily* (it was) *not in rebellion, nor in apostasy from Jehovah,*" *sc.* that this was done, or that we built the altar. "*Mayst Thou not help us to-day,*" *sc.* if we did it in rebellion against God. An appeal addressed immediately to God in the heat of the statement, and introduced in the midst of the asseveration, which was meant to remove all doubt as to the truth of their declaration. The words which follow in ver. 23, "*that we have built,*" etc., continue the oath : *If we have done this, to build us an altar, to turn away from the Lord, or to offer thereon burnt-offering, meat-offering, or peace-offering, may Jehovah himself require it* (דָּרַשׁ, as in Deut. xviii. 19; cf. 1 Sam. xx. 16). Another earnest parenthetical adjuration, as the substance of the oath, is continued in ver. 24. "*But truly* (וְאִם לֹא, with an affirmative signification) *from anxiety, for a reason* (*lit.* on account of a thing) *have we done this, thinking* (לֵאמֹר, since we thought) *in time to come your sons might say to our sons, What have ye to do with Jehovah, the God of Israel?*" *i.e.* He does not concern you; He is our God. "*Jehovah has made the Jordan a boundary between us and your sons; ye have no part in Jehovah. Thus your sons might make our sons cease to fear Jehovah,*" *i.e.* might make them desist from the worship of Jehovah (for the infinitive form יְרֹא instead of the abbreviated form לֹא used in 1 Sam. xviii. 29, there are analogies in יִצֹק in Ezek. xxiv. 3, and לִישׁוֹן, Eccl. v. 11, whereas יִרְאָה is the only form used in the Pentateuch). There was some reason for this anxiety. For, inasmuch as in all the promises and laws Canaan alone (the land on this side of the Jordan, Num. xxxiv. 1–12) is always mentioned as the land which Jehovah would give to His people for their inheritance, it was quite a possible thing that at some future time the false conclusion might be drawn from this, that only the tribes who dwelt in Canaan proper were the true people of Jehovah.—Vers. 26 sqq. "*So we thought, we will make ourselves to build an altar* (an expression derived from the language of ordinary life, for ' we will build ourselves an altar'), *not for burnt-offerings and slain-offerings; but it shall be a witness between us and you, and between our generations after us, that we may perform the service of Jehovah before His face* (*i.e.* before the tabernacle in which Jehovah was enthroned), *with our burnt-offerings, slain-offerings, and peace-offerings,*"—in order, as they repeat in ver. 27b from vers. 24, 25, that they might not be denied a part in Jehovah in time to come. For if it should so happen in time to come, that this should be said to them and to their descendants, they would say (or reply), "*Behold the copy of the altar of Jehovah, which our fathers made, not for burnt-offerings,*" etc. (ver. 28b, as in vers. 26b, 27a). For this reason they had built the altar according to the pattern of the altar before the tabernacle, and that not in their own land, but on the western side of the Jordan, where the dwelling-place of Jehovah was standing, as a witness that they worshipped one and the same God with the tribes on this side.— Ver. 29. The speakers conclude with an expression of horror at the thought of rebelling against Jehovah. חָלִילָה לָּנוּ מִמֶּנּוּ, "*far be it*

from us away from Him (מֵהוָה=מִמֶּנּוּ, 1 Sam. xxiv. 7, xxvi. 11 ,
1 Kings xxi. 3), *to rebel against Jehovah*," etc.

Vers. 30–34. This explanation pleased the delegates of the congregation, so that Phinehas bore this testimony to the tribes on the
east of the Jordan : " *Now* (to-day) *we perceive that Jehovah is in
the midst of us ; because* (אֲשֶׁר, *quod*, as in Gen. xxxi. 49, etc.) *ye
have not committed this unfaithfulness towards Jehovah, since* (אָז,
then, if ye had only this intention) *ye have saved the children of
Israel out of the hand of Jehovah*," *i.e.* preserved them from His
judgments.—Vers. 32, 33. They then returned to Canaan and
informed the congregation. And the thing pleased them, so that
they praised the Lord, *sc.* for having kept their brethren on the
other side from rebellion, and they thought no more of going to
war against them, or laying waste the land of the tribes on the
east of the Jordan.—Ver. 34. The Reubenites and Gadites (half
Manasseh is omitted in vers. 33, 34, for the sake of brevity) called
the altar " *witness is it between us that Jehovah is God*" (כִּי introduces the words). This is at once a name and an explanation,
namely in this sense : they gave the altar the name of " *witness
between us*," because it was to be a witness that they also acknowledged and worshipped Jehovah as the true God.

JOSHUA'S FAREWELL AND DEATH.—CHAP. XXIII. XXIV.

After the division of the land among the tribes, Joshua had
withdrawn to *Timnath-serah*, on the mountains of Ephraim (chap.
xix. 50), to spend the last days of his life there in the quiet enjoyment of his own inheritance. But when the time of his departure
from the earth was drawing near, remembering the call which he
had received from the Lord (chap. i. 6–8), he felt constrained
to gather the people together once more in the persons of their
representatives, to warn them most earnestly of the dangers of
apostasy from the Lord, and point out the evils that would follow
(chap. xxiii.) ; and then after that, in a solemn assembly of the
nation at Shechem, to review the abundant mercies which the
Lord had conferred upon Israel from the calling of Abraham to
that day, that he might call upon them to remain stedfast and
faithful in the worship of their God, and then solemnly renew the
covenant with the Lord.[1]

---

[1] "The pious solicitude of Joshua furnishes an example worthy of imitation
by all who have the charge of others. For just as a father would not be

Chap. xxiii. EXHORTATION TO THE TRIBES OF ISRAEL TO REMAIN FAITHFUL TO THEIR CALLING.—Vers. 1, 2. The introduction to the discourse which follows is attached in its first part to chap. xxii. 3, 4, and thus also to chap. xxi. 43, 44, whilst in the second part it points back to chap. xiii. 1. The Lord had given the people rest from all their enemies round about, after the land had been subdued and divided by lot (chap. xxi. 43, 44). Joshua was already an old man at the termination of the war (chap. xiii. 1); but since then he had advanced still further in age, so that he may have noticed the signs of the near approach of death. He therefore called together the representatives of the people, either to Timnath-serah where he dwelt (chap. xix. 50), or to Shiloh to the tabernacle, the central sanctuary of the whole nation, as the most suitable place for his purpose. "*All Israel*" is still further defined by the apposition, "*its elders, and its heads, and its judges, and its officers.*" This is not to be understood, however, as referring to four different classes of rulers; but the term *elders* is the general term used to denote all the representatives of the people, who were divided into heads, judges, and officers. And the *heads*, again, were those who stood at the head of the tribes, families, and fathers' houses, and out of whose number the most suitable persons were chosen as judges and officers (Deut. i. 15; see my Bibl. Arch. ii. § 143). Joshua's address to the elders of all Israel consists of two parts, which run parallel to one another so far as the contents are concerned, vers. 2*b*-13 and vers. 14–16. In both parts Joshua commences with a reference to his age and his approaching death, in consequence of which he felt constrained to remind the people once more of all the great things that the Lord had done for them, and to warn them against falling away from their gracious covenant God. Just as Joshua, in this the last act of his life, was merely treading in the footsteps of Moses, who had concluded his life with the fullest exhortations to the people to be faithful to the Lord (Deut. i. 30), so his address consists entirely of reminiscences from the Pentateuch, more especially from Deuteronomy, as he had

regarded as sufficiently careful if he merely thought of the interests of his children up to the time of his own death, and did not extend his thoughtfulness on their behalf still further, and as far as was in his power endeavour to provide for their welfare when he himself should be dead; so good rulers ought to look forward that they may not only leave behind them a well-organized state, but may also strengthen and secure its existence for a long time to come." —*Calvin* (with special reference to 2 Pet. i. 13-15).

nothing fresh to announce to the people, but could only impress the old truth upon their minds once more.

Vers. 2b-13. Joshua commenced his address by reminding them of the greatest manifestations of grace which they had received from the Lord, namely, by referring to what the Lord had done to all these nations (the Canaanites) before them, when He fought for Israel, as Moses had promised them (Deut. i. 30 and iii. 22).—Ver. 3. "*Before you*," *sc.* smiting and driving them away. —Ver. 4. He (Joshua) had now divided by lot among the tribes of Israel as their inheritance these still remaining (Canaanitish) nations, as the Lord had commanded (chap. xiii. 6, 7), "*from Jordan and further all the nations, which I have exterminated* (*i.e.* which Joshua had destroyed when Canaan was taken), *and the great sea* (for 'to the great sea') *in the west*." The breadth of the land of Canaan is here given in a peculiar manner, the *terminus a quo* being mentioned in the first clause, and the *terminus ad quem* (though without the preposition עַד) in the second; and through the parallelism which exists between the clauses, each clause is left to be completed from the other. So that the whole sentence would read thus: "*All these nations which remain . . . from Jordan to the great sea, also all the nations which I have cut off from Jordan, and to the great sea westward*."—Ver. 5. For the Lord would drive all these still remaining nations before the Israelites, and cut them off, and give the Israelites their land for a possession, as He had promised (chap. xiii. 6; cf. Ex. xxiii. 23 sqq.). הָדַף, as in Deut. vi. 19, ix. 4; and the form יְהָדְפֵם, with *Chateph-kametz*, on account of the weakness of the ה, as in Num. xxxv. 20. יְרִשְׁתֶּם, as in chap. i. 15.—Vers. 6 sqq. Only let them be strong, *i.e.* be brave, to keep the law of Moses without fail (cf. chap. i. 7), to enter into no fellowship with these remaining nations (בּוֹא, to enter into close intimacy with a person; see ver. 12), and not to pay reverence to their gods in any way, but to adhere stedfastly to the Lord their God as they had hitherto done. To make mention of the names of the idols (Ex. xxiii. 13), to swear by them, to serve them (by sacrifices), and to bow down to them (to invoke them in prayer), are the four outward forms of divine worship (see Deut. vi. 13, x. 20). The concluding words, "*as ye have done unto this day*," which express a reason for persevering in the attachment they had hitherto shown to Jehovah, "do not affirm that the Israelites had hitherto done all these things fully and perfectly; for who does not know how few mortals there are who devote themselves to God with all the piety and love which He justly demands? But because the nation as a whole had kept the laws delivered to them by Moses, during the time that the government had been in the hands of Joshua, the sins of individual men were left out of sight on this occasion" (*Masius*).—Vers. 9, 10. For this reason the Lord had driven out great and strong nations before the Israelites, so that no one was able to stand before them. The first hemistich points to the fulfilment of Deut. iv. 38, vii. 1, ix. 1, xi. 23; the second to that of Deut. vii. 24, xi. 25. וְאַתֶּם is placed at the beginning absolutely.—In ver. 10*a*, the blessing of fidelity to the law which Israel had hitherto experienced, is described, as in Deut. xxxii. 30, upon the basis of the promise in Lev. xxvi. 7, 8, and Deut. xxviii. 7, and in ver. 10*b* the thought of ver. 3*b* is repeated. To this there is attached, in vers. 11–13, the admonition to take heed for the sake of their souls (cf. Deut. iv. 15), to love the Lord their God (on the love of God as the sum of the fulfilment of the law, see Deut. vi. 5, x. 12, xi. 13). For if they turned, *i.e.* gave up the faithfulness they had hitherto displayed towards Jehovah, and attached themselves to the remnant of these nations, made marriages with them, and entered into fellowship with them, which the Lord had expressly forbidden (Ex. xxxiv. 12–16; Deut. vii. 3), let them know that the Lord their God would not cut off these nations before them any more, but that they would be a snare and destruction to them. This threat is founded upon such passages of the law as Ex. xxiii. 33, Deut. vii. 16, and more especially Num. xxxiii. 55. The figure of a trap, which is employed here (see Ex. x. 7), is still further strengthened by פַּח, *a snare* (cf. Isa. viii. 14, 15). *Shotet*, a *whip or scourge*, an emphatic form of the word derived from the *poel* of שׁוּט, only occurs here. " *Scourges in your sides, and thorns in your eyes*" (see Num. xxxiii. 55). Joshua crowds his figures together to depict the misery and oppression which would be sure to result from fellowship with the Canaanites, because, from his knowledge of the fickleness of the people, and the wickedness of the human heart in its natural state, he could foresee that the apostasy of the nation from the Lord, which Moses had foretold, would take place but too quickly; as it actually did, according to Judg. ii. 3 sqq., in the very next generation. The words "*until ye perish,*" etc., resume the threat held out by Moses in Deut. xi. 17 (cf. chap. xxviii. 21 sqq.).

Vers. 14–16. In the second part of his address, Joshua sums up briefly and concisely the leading thoughts of the first part,

giving greater prominence, however, to the curse which would
follow apostasy from the Lord.—Ver. 14. Now that Joshua was
going the way of all the earth (all the inhabitants of the earth),
i.e. going to die (1 Kings ii. 2), the Israelites knew with all the
heart and all the soul, *i.e.* were fully convinced, that of all the good
words (gracious promises) of God not one had failed, but all had
come to pass (*vid.* chap. xxi. 45). But it was just as certain that
the Lord would bring upon them every evil word that He spake
through Moses (Lev. xxvi. 14–33; Deut. xxviii. 15–68, and xxix.
14–28), if they transgressed His covenant. *" The evil word"* is
the curse of rejection (Deut. xxx. 1, 15). *" Until He have destroyed :"* see Deut. vii. 24, and xxviii. 48. The other words as
in ver. 13*b*. If they went after other gods and served them, the
wrath of the Lord would burn against them, and they would be
quickly destroyed from the good land which He had given them
(*vid.* Deut. xi. 17).

Chap. xxiv. 1–28. RENEWAL OF THE COVENANT AT THE NA-
TIONAL ASSEMBLY IN SHECHEM.—Ver. 1. Joshua brought his
public ministry to a close, as Moses had done before him, with a
solemn renewal of the covenant with the Lord. For this solemn
act he did not choose Shiloh, the site of the national sanctuary, as
some MSS. of the LXX. read, but Shechem, a place which was
sanctified as no other was for such a purpose as this by the most
sacred reminiscences from the times of the patriarchs. He therefore summoned all the tribes of Israel, in their representatives (their
elders, etc., as in chap. xxiii. 2), to Shechem, not merely because it
was at Shechem, *i.e.* on Gerizim and Ebal, that the solemn establishment of the law in the land of Canaan, to which the renewal of
the covenant, as a repetition of the essential kernel of that solemn
ceremony, was now to be appended, had first taken place, but still
more because it was here that Abraham received the first promise
from God after his migration into Canaan, and built an altar at the
time (Gen. xii. 6, 7) ; and most of all, as *Hengstenberg* has pointed
out (Diss. ii. p. 12), because Jacob settled here on his return from
Mesopotamia, and it was here that he purified his house from the
strange gods, burying all their idols under the oak (Gen. xxxiii. 19,
xxxv. 2, 4). As Jacob selected Shechem for the sanctification of
his house, because this place was already consecrated by Abraham
as a sanctuary of God, so Joshua chose the same place for the
renewal of the covenant, because this act involved a practical

renunciation on the part of Israel of all idolatry. Joshua expressly states this in ver. 23, and reference is also made to it in the account in ver. 26. " The exhortation to be faithful to the Lord, and to purify themselves from all idolatry, could not fail to make a deep impression, in the place where the honoured patriarch had done the very same things to which his descendants were exhorted here. The example preached more loudly in this spot than in any other" (*Hengstenberg*). " *And they placed themselves before God.*" From the expression " before God," it by no means follows that the ark had been brought to Shechem, or, as *Knobel* supposes, that an altar was erected there, any more than from the statement in ver. 26 that it was " *by the sanctuary of the Lord.*" For, in the first place, " before God" (*Elohim*) is not to be identified with " before Jehovah," which is used in chap. xviii. 6 and xix. 51 to denote the presence of the Lord above the ark of the covenant; and secondly, even " before Jehovah" does not always presuppose the presence of the ark of the covenant, as *Hengstenberg* has clearly shown. " Before God" simply denotes in a general sense the religious character of an act, or shows that the act was undertaken with a distinct refer-ence to the omnipresent God; and in the case before us it may be attributed to the fact that Joshua delivered his exhortation to the people in the name of Jehovah, and commenced his address with the words, " Thus saith Jehovah."[1]

Vers. 2–15. Joshua's address contains an expansion of two thoughts. He first of all recalls to the recollection of the whole nation, whom he is addressing in the persons of its representatives, all the proofs of His mercy which the Lord had given, from the calling of Abraham to that day (vers. 2–13) ; and then because of these divine acts he calls upon the people to renounce all idolatry, and to serve God the Lord alone (vers. 14, 15). Jehovah is de-scribed as the " God of Israel" both at the commencement (ver. 2) and also at the close of the whole transaction, in perfect accordance with the substance and object of the address, which is occupied throughout with the goodness conferred by God upon the race of

---

[1] " It is stated that they all stood before God, in order that the sanctity and religious character of the assembly may be the more distinctly shown. And there can be no doubt that the name of God was solemnly invoked by Joshua, and that he addressed the people as in the sight of God, so that each one might feel for himself that God was presiding over all that was transacted there, and that they were not engaged in any merely private affair, but were entering into a sacred and inviolable compact with God himself."—*Calvin*.

Israel. The first practical proof of the grace of God towards Israel, was the calling of Abraham from his idolatrous associations, and his introduction to the land of Canaan, where the Lord so multiplied his seed, that Esau received the mountains of Seir for his family, whilst Jacob went into Egypt with his sons.[1] The ancestors of Israel dwelt "*from eternity,*" *i.e.* from time immemorial, on the other side of the stream (the Euphrates), viz. in Ur of the Chaldees, and then at Haran in Mesopotamia (Gen. xi. 28, 31), namely Terah, the father of Abraham and Nahor. Of Terah's three sons (Gen. xi. 27), Nahor is mentioned as well as Abraham, because Rebekah, and her nieces Leah and Rachel, the tribe-mothers of Israel, were descended from him (Gen. xxii. 23, xxix. 10, 16 sqq.). And they (your fathers, Terah and his family) served other gods than Jehovah, who revealed himself to Abraham, and brought him from his father's house to Canaan. Nothing definite can be gathered from the expression " other gods," with reference to the gods worshipped by Terah and his family; nor is there anything further to be found respecting them throughout the whole of the Old Testament. We simply learn from Gen. xxxi. 19, 34, that Laban had *teraphim, i.e. penates,* or household and oracular gods.[2] The question also, whether Abraham was an idolater before his call, which has been answered in different ways, cannot be determined with certainty. We may conjecture, however, that he was not deeply sunk in idolatry, though he had not remained entirely free from it in his father's house; and therefore that his call is not to be regarded as a reward for his righteousness before God, but as an act of free unmerited grace.—Vers. 3, 4. After his

[1] " He commences with their gratuitous training, by which God had precluded them from the possibility of boasting of any pre-eminence or merit. For God had bound them to himself by a closer bond, because when they were on an equality with others, He drew them to himself to be His own peculiar people, for no other reason than His own good pleasure. Moreover, in order that it may be clearly seen that they have nothing whereof to glory, he leads them back to their earliest origin, and relates how their fathers had dwelt in Chaldæa, worshipping idols in common with the rest, and with nothing to distinguish them from the crowd."—*Calvin.*

[2] According to one tradition, Abraham was brought up in Sabæism in his father's house (see *Hottinger,* Histor. Orient. p. 246, and *Philo,* in several passages of his works); and according to another, in the *Targum Jonathan* on Gen. xi. 23, and in the later Rabbins, Abraham had to suffer persecution on account of his dislike to idolatry, and was obliged to leave his native land in consequence. But these traditions are both of them nothing more than conjectures by the later Rabbins.

call, God conducted Abraham through all the land of Canaan (see Gen. xii.), protecting and shielding him, and multiplied his seed, giving him Isaac, and giving to Isaac Jacob and Esau, the ancestors of two nations. To the latter He gave the mountains of Seir for a possession (Gen. xxxvi. 6 sqq.), that Jacob might receive Canaan for his descendants as a sole possession. But instead of mentioning this, Joshua took for granted that his hearers were well acquainted with the history of the patriarchs, and satisfied himself with mentioning the migration of Jacob and his sons to Egypt, that he might pass at once to the second great practical proof of the mercy of God in the guidance of Israel, the miraculous deliverance of Israel out of the bondage and oppression of Egypt.—Vers. 5–7. Of this also he merely mentions the leading points, viz. first of all, the sending of Moses and Aaron (Ex. iii. 10 sqq., iv. 14 sqq.), and then the plagues inflicted upon Egypt. " *I smote Egypt,*" *i.e.* both land and people. נגף is used in Ex. vii. 27 and xii. 23, 27, in connection with the plague of frogs and the slaying of the first-born in Egypt. The words which follow, " *according to that which I did among them, and afterward I brought you out,*" point back to Ex. iii. 20, and show that the Lord had fulfilled the promise given to Moses at his call. He then refers (vers. 6, 7) to the miraculous deliverance of the Israelites, as they came out of Egypt, from Pharaoh who pursued them with his army, giving especial prominence to the crying of the Israelites to the Lord in their distress (Ex. xiv. 10), and the relief of that distress by the angel of the Lord (Ex. xiv. 19, 20). And lastly, he notices their dwelling in the wilderness " *many days,*" *i.e.* forty years (Num. xiv. 33).—Vers. 8–10. The third great act of God for Israel was his giving up the Amorites into the hands of the Israelites, so that they were able to conquer their land (Num. xxi. 21–35), and the frustration of the attack made by Balak king of the Moabites, through the instrumentality of Balaam, when the Lord did not allow him to curse Israel, but compelled him to bless (Num. xxii.–xxiv.). Balak " *warred against Israel,*" not with the sword, but with the weapons of the curse, or *animo et voluntate (Vatabl.).* " *I would not hearken unto Balaam,*" *i.e.* would not comply with his wish, but compelled him to submit to my will, and to bless you ; " *and delivered you out of his* (Balak's) *hand,*" when he sought to destroy Israel through the medium of Balaam (Num. xxii. 6, 11).—Vers. 11–13. The last and greatest benefit which the Lord conferred upon the Israelites, was His leading them by miracles of His omnipotence across the Jordan into Canaan, delivering the " *lords* (or possessors) *of Jericho*," not " the rulers, *i.e.* the king and his heroes," as *Knobel* maintains (see 2 Sam. xxi. 12 ; 1 Sam. xxiii. 11, 12 ; and the commentary on Judg. ix. 6), " *and all the tribes of Canaan into their hand*," and sending *hornets before them*, so that they were able to drive out the Canaanites, particularly the two kings of the Amorites, Sihon and Og, though " *not with their sword and their bow*" (*vid.* Ps. xliv. 4) ; *i.e.* it was not with the weapons at their command that they were able to take the lands of these two kings. On the sending of hornets, as a figure used to represent peculiarly effective terrors, see at Ex. xxiii. 28, Deut. vii. 20. In this way the Lord gave the land to the Israelites, with its towns and its rich productions (vineyards and olive trees), without any trouble on their part of wearisome cultivation or planting, as Moses himself had promised them (Deut. vi. 10, 11).—Vers. 14, 15. These overwhelming manifestations of grace on the part of the Lord laid Israel under obligations to serve the Lord with gratitude and sincerity. " *Now therefore fear the Lord* (יְראוּ for יִרְאוּ, pointed like a verb לְ״ה, as in 1 Sam. xii. 24, Ps. xxxiv. 10), *and serve Him in sincerity and in truth*," *i.e.* without hypocrisy, or the show of piety, in simplicity and truth of heart (*vid.* Judg. ix. 16, 19). " *Put away the gods* (*Elohim* = the strange gods in ver. 23) *which your fathers served on the other side of the Euphrates and in Egypt.*" This appeal does not presuppose any gross idolatry on the part of the existing generation, which would have been at variance with the rest of the book, in which Israel is represented as only serving Jehovah during the lifetime of Joshua. If the people had been in possession of idols, they would have given them up to Joshua to be destroyed, as they promised to comply with his demand (vers. 16 sqq.). But even if the Israelites were not addicted to gross idolatry in the worship of idols, they were not altogether free from idolatry either in Egypt or in the desert. As their fathers were possessed of *teraphim* in Mesopotamia (see at ver. 2), so the Israelites had not kept themselves entirely free from heathen and idolatrous ways, more especially the demon-worship of Egypt (comp. Lev. xvii. 7 with Ezek. xx. 7 sqq., xxiii. 3, 8, and Amos v. 26) ; and even in the time of Joshua their worship of Jehovah may have been corrupted by idolatrous elements. This admixture of the pure and genuine worship of Jehovah with idolatrous or heathen elements, which is condemned in Lev. xvii. 7 as the worship of *Seirim*, and by Ezekiel (*l. c.*) as the idolatrous worship of the people in Egypt, had its roots in the corruption of the natural heart, through which it is at all times led to make to itself idols of mammon, worldly lusts, and other impure thoughts and desires, to which it cleaves, without being able to tear itself entirely away from them. This more refined idolatry might degenerate in the case of many persons into the grosser worship of idols, so that Joshua had ample ground for admonishing the people to put away the strange gods, and serve the Lord.—Ver. 15. But as the true worship of the living God must have its roots in the heart, and spring from the heart, and therefore cannot be forced by prohibitions and commands, Joshua concluded by calling upon the representatives of the nation, in case they were not inclined (" if it seem evil unto you") to serve Jehovah, to choose now this day the gods whom they would serve, whether the gods of their fathers in Mesopotamia, or the gods of the Amorites in whose land they were now dwelling, though he and his house would serve the Lord. There is no necessity to adduce any special proofs that this appeal was not intended to release them from the obligation to serve Jehovah, but rather contained the strongest admonition to remain faithful to the Lord.

Vers. 16–25. The people responded to this appeal by declaring, with an expression of horror at idolatry, their hearty resolution to serve the Lord, who was their God, and had shown them such great mercies. The words, " *that brought us up and our fathers out of the land of Egypt, out of the house of bondage,*" call to mind the words appended to the first commandment (Ex. xx. 2; Deut. v. 6), which they hereby promise to observe. With the clause which follows, " *who did those great signs in our sight,*" etc., they declare their assent to all that Joshua had called to their mind in vers. 3–13. " *We also*" (ver. 18), as well as thou and thy house (ver. 15).— Vers. 19–21. But in order to place most vividly before the minds of the people to what it was that they bound themselves by this declaration, that they might not inconsiderately vow what they would not afterwards observe, Joshua adds, " *Ye cannot serve Jehovah,*" sc. in the state of mind in which ye are at present, or " by your own resolution only, and without the assistance of divine grace, without solid and serious conversion from all idols, and without true repentance and faith" (*J. H. Michaelis*). For Jehovah is " *a holy God,*" etc. *Elohim,* used to denote the Supreme Being (see at Gen. ii. 4), is construed with the predicate in the plural. On the holiness of God, see the exposition of Ex. xix. 6. On the expression " *a jealous God,*" see Ex. xx. 5; and on נִשָּׂא לְפִשְׁעַ, Ex. xxiii. 21. The only other place in which the form קָנוֹא is used for קַנָּא is Nah. i. 2. "*If ye forsake the Lord and serve strange gods, He will turn* (*i.e.* assume a different attitude towards you) *and do you hurt, after He has done you good*," *i.e.* He will not spare you, in spite of the blessings which He has conferred upon you. הֵרַע is used to denote the judgments threatened in the law against transgressors.—Ver. 21. The people adhered to their resolution. לֹא, *minime*, as in chap. v. 14, *i.e.* we will not serve other gods, but Jehovah.—Vers. 22, 23. Upon this repeated declaration Joshua says to them, "*ye are witnesses against yourselves*," *i.e.* ye will condemn yourselves by this your own testimony if ye should now forsake the Lord, "for ye yourselves have chosen you Jehovah to serve Him;" whereupon they answer עֵדִים, "*witnesses are we against ourselves*," signifying thereby, "we profess and ratify once more all that we have said" (*Rosenmüller*). Joshua then repeated his demand that they should put away the strange gods from within them, and incline their hearts (entirely) to Jehovah the God of Israel. אֱלֹהֵי הַנֵּכָר אֲשֶׁר בְּקִרְבְּכֶם might mean the foreign gods which are in the midst of you, *i.e.* among you, and imply the existence of idols, and the grosser forms of idolatrous worship in the nation ; but בְּקֶרֶב also signifies "within," or "in the heart," in which case the words refer to idols of the heart. That the latter is the sense in which the words are to be understood is evident from the fact, that although the people expressed their willingness to renounce all idolatry, they did not bring any idols to Joshua to be destroyed, as was done in other similar cases, viz. Gen. xxxv. 4, and 1 Sam. vii. 4. Even if the people had carried idols about with them in the desert, as the prophet Amos stated to his contemporaries (Amos v. 26; cf. Acts vii. 43), the grosser forms of idolatry had disappeared from Israel with the dying out of the generation that was condemned at Kadesh. The new generation, which had been received afresh into covenant with the Lord by the circumcision at Gilgal, and had set up this covenant at Ebal, and was now assembled around Joshua, the dying servant of God, to renew the covenant once more, had no idols of wood, stone, or metal, but only the "figments of false gods," as *Calvin* calls them, the idols of the heart, which it was to put away, that it might give its heart entirely to the Lord, who is not content with divided affections, but requires the whole heart (Deut. vi. 5, 6). —Vers. 24, 25. On the repeated and decided declaration of the people, "*the Lord our God will we serve, and to His voice will we hearken*," Joshua completed the covenant with them that day. This conclusion of a covenant was really a solemn renewal of the covenant made at Sinai, like that which took place under Moses in the steppes of Moab (Deut. xxviii. 69). " *And set them a statute and right at Shechem,*" sc. through the renewal of the covenant. These words recall Ex. xv. 25, where the guidance of Israel to bitter water, and the sweetening of that water by the means which the Lord pointed out to Moses, are described as setting a *statute and right* for Israel, and then explained by the promise, that if they would hearken to the voice of Jehovah, He would keep them from all the diseases of Egypt. And in accordance with this, by the renewal of the covenant at Shechem, there were set for Israel a חֹק, *i.e.* a *statute*, which bound the people to a renewed and conscientious maintenance of the covenant, and a מִשְׁפָּט, or *right*, by virtue of which they might expect on this condition the fulfilment of all the covenant mercies of the Lord.

Vers. 26–28. All these things (הַדְּבָרִים הָאֵלֶּה are not merely the words spoken on both sides, but the whole ceremony of renewing the covenant) Joshua wrote in the law-book of God, *i.e.* he wrote them in a document which he placed in the law-book of Moses, and then set up a large stone, as a permanent memorial of what had taken place, on the spot where the meeting had been held, " *under the oak that was in the sanctuary of Jehovah.*" As בְּמִקְדָּשׁ neither means " at the sanctuary," nor near the sanctuary, nor " in the place where the sanctuary was set up;" the " sanctuary of Jehovah" cannot signify " the ark of the covenant, which had been brought from the tabernacle to Shechem, for the ceremony of renewing the covenant." Still less can we understand it as signifying the tabernacle itself, since this was not removed from place to place for particular sacred ceremonies ; nor can it mean an altar, in which an oak could not possibly be said to stand ; nor some other illegal sanctuary of Jehovah, since there were none in Israel at that time. The sanctuary of Jehovah under the oak at Shechem was nothing else than the holy place under the oak, where Abraham had formerly built an altar and worshipped the Lord, and where Jacob had purified his house from the strange gods, which he buried under this oak, or rather terebinth tree (Gen. xii. 6, 7, xxxv. 2, 4). This is the explanation adopted by *Masius, J. D. Michaelis,* and *Hengstenberg* (Diss. ii. p. 12). In ver. 27 Joshua explains to the people the meaning of the stone which he had set up. The stone would be a witness against the people if they should deny their God. As a memorial of what had taken place, the stone had heard all the words which the Lord had addressed to Israel, and could bear witness against the people, that they might not deny their God. "*Deny your God,*" viz. in feeling, word, or deed.—Ver. 28. Joshua then dismissed the people, each one to his inheritance. He had done all that was in his power to establish the people in fidelity to the Lord.

Vers. 29–33. DEATH AND BURIAL OF JOSHUA AND ELEAZAR. —With the renewal of the covenant Joshua had ended his vocation. He did not formally lay down his office, because there was no immediate successor who had been appointed by God. The ordinary rulers of the congregation were enough, when once they were settled in Canaan, viz. the elders as heads and judges of the nation, together with the high priest, who represented the nation in its relation to God, and could obtain for it the revelation of the will of God through the right of the Urim and Thummim. In order therefore to bring the history of Joshua and his times to a close, nothing further remained than to give an account of his death, with a short reference to the fruit of his labours, and to add certain other notices for which no suitable place had hitherto presented itself.— Vers. 29, 30. Soon after these events (vers. 1–28) Joshua died, at the age of 110, like his ancestor Joseph (Gen. l. 26), and was buried in his hereditary possessions at Timnath-serah, upon the mountains of Ephraim, to the north of Mount Gaash. *Timnath-serah* is still in existence (see at chap. xix. 50). *Mount Gaash,* however, has not been discovered.—Ver. 31. Joshua's labours had not remained without effect. During his own lifetime, and that of the elders who outlived him, and who had seen all that the Lord did for Israel, all Israel served the Lord. "The elders" are the rulers and leaders of the nation. The account of the burial of Joseph's bones, which the Israelites had brought with them from Egypt to Canaan (Ex. xiii. 19), is placed after the account of Joshua's death, because it could not have been introduced before without interrupting the connected account of the labours of Joshua; and it would not do to pass it over without notice altogether, not only because the fact of their bringing the bones with them had been mentioned in the book of Exodus, but also because the Israelites thereby fulfilled the promise given by their fathers to Joseph when he died. The burial of Joseph in the piece of field which Jacob had purchased at Shechem (*vid.* Gen. xxxiii. 19) had no doubt taken place immediately after the division of the land, when Joseph's descendants received Shechem and the field there for an inheritance. This piece of field, however, they chose for a burial-place for Joseph's bones, not only because Jacob had purchased it, but in all probability chiefly because Jacob had sanctified it for his descendants by building an altar there (Gen. xxxiii. 20). The death and burial of Eleazar, who stood by Joshua's side in the guidance of the nation, are mentioned last of all (ver. 33). When Eleazar died, whether shortly before or shortly after Joshua, cannot be determined. He was buried at Gibeah of Phinehas, the place which was given to him upon the mountains of Ephraim, *i.e.* as his inheritance. *Gibeath Phinehas, i.e.* hill of Phinehas, is apparently a proper name, like Gibeah of Saul (1 Sam. xv. 34, etc.). The situation, however, is uncertain. According to *Eusebius (Onom. s. v. Γαβαάς)*, it was upon the mountains of Ephraim, in the tribe of Benjamin, and was at that time a place named *Gabatha*, the name also given to it by *Josephus* (Ant. v. 1, 29), about twelve Roman miles from Eleutheropolis. This statement is certainly founded upon an error, at least so far as the number twelve is concerned. It is a much more probable supposition, that it is the Levitical town *Geba* of Benjamin, on the north-east of Ramah (chap. xviii. 24), and the name *Gibeah* of Phinehas might be explained on the ground that this place had become the hereditary property of Phinehas, which would be perfectly reconcilable with its selection as one of the priests' cities. As the priests, for example, were not the sole possessors of the towns ceded to them in the possessions of the different tribes, the Israelites might have presented Phinehas with that portion of the city which was not occupied by the priests, and also with the field, as a reward for the services he had rendered to the congregation (Num. xxv. 7 sqq.), just as Caleb and Joshua had been specially considered; in which case Phinehas might dwell in his own hereditary possessions in a priests' city. The situation, "upon the mountains of Ephraim," is not at variance with this view, as these mountains extended, according to Judg. iv. 5, etc., far into the territory of Benjamin (see at chap. xi. 21). The majority of commentators, down to *Knobel*, have thought the place intended to be a *Gibeah* in the tribe of Ephraim, namely the present *Jeeb* or *Jibia*, by the Wady Jib, on the north of Guphna, towards Neapolis (Sichem: see *Rob.* Pal. iii. p. 80), though there is nothing whatever to favour this except the name.

With the death of Eleazar the high priest, the contemporary of Joshua, the times of Joshua came to a close, so that the account of

Eleazar's death formed a very fitting termination to the book. In some MSS. and editions of the Septuagint, there is an additional clause relating to the high priest Phinehas and the apostasy of the Israelites after Joshua's death; but this is merely taken from Judg. ii. 6, 11 sqq. and iii. 7, 12 sqq., and arbitrarily appended to the book of Joshua.

THE BOOK OF JUDGES

INTRODUCTION.

CONTENTS AND CHARACTER, ORIGIN AND SOURCES, OF THE BOOK OF JUDGES.

THE book of Judges, headed *Shophetim* in the Hebrew Bibles, and Κριταί in the Alexandrian version, and called *liber Judicum* in the Vulgate, contains the history of the Israelitish theocracy for a period of about 350 years, from the death of Joshua to the death of Samson, or to the time of the prophet Samuel. It may be divided according to its contents into three parts: (1) an introduction (chap. i.–iii. 6); (2) the history of the several judges (chap. iii. 7–xvi. 31); and (3) a twofold appendix (chap. xvii.–xxi.). In the *Introduction* the prophetic author of the book first of all takes a general survey of those facts which exhibited most clearly the behaviour of the Israelites to the Canaanites who were left in the land after the death of Joshua, and closes his survey with the reproof of their behaviour by the angel of the Lord (chap. i. 1–ii. 5). He then describes in a general manner the attitude of Israel to the Lord its God and that of the Lord to His people during the time of the judges, and represents this period as a constant alternation of humiliation through hostile oppression, when the nation fell away from its God, and deliverance out of the power of its enemies by judges whom God raised up and endowed with the power of His Spirit, whenever the people returned to the Lord (chap. ii. 6–iii. 6). This is followed in the *body of the work* (chap. iii. 7–xvi. 31) by the history of the several oppressions of Israel on the part of foreign nations, with the deliverance effected by the judges who were raised up by God, and whose deeds are for the most part elaborately described in chronological order, and introduced by the standing formula, " And the children of Israel did evil in the sight of the Lord," etc.; or, "And the children of Israel again did evil (added to do evil)," etc. They are arranged in six historical groups: (1) the oppression by the Mesopotamian king, Chushan-rishathaim, with the deliverance from this oppression through *Othniel* the judge (chap. iii. 7–11); (2) the oppression by the Moabitish king Eglon, with the deliverance effected through *Ehud* the judge (chap. iii. 12-30), and the victory achieved by *Shamgar* over the Philistines (chap. iii. 31); (3) the subjugation of Israel by the Canaanitish king Jabin, and the deliverance effected through the prophetess *Deborah* and *Barak* the judge (chap. iv.), with Deborah's song of victory (chap. v.); (4) the oppression by the Midianites, and the deliverance from these enemies through the judge *Gideon*, who was called to be the deliverer of Israel through an appearance of the angel of the Lord (chap. vi.–viii.), with the history of the three years' reign of his son Abimelech (chap. ix.), and brief notices of the two judges *Tola* and *Jair* (chap. x. 1–5); (5) the giving up of the Israelites into the power of the Ammonites and Philistines, and their deliverance from the Ammonitish oppression by *Jephthah* (chap. x. 6–xii. 7), with brief notices of the three judges *Ibzan*, *Elon*, and *Abdon* (chap. xii. 8–15); (6) the oppression by the Philistines, with the account of the life and deeds of *Samson* the judge, who began to deliver Israel out of the power of these foes (chap. xiii.–xvi.). To this there are added two *appendices* in chap. xvii.–xxi.: viz. (1) the account of the worship of images by the Ephraimite Micah, and the transportation of that worship by the Danites to Laish-Dan (chap. xvii. xviii.); and (2) the infamous conduct of the inhabitants of Gibeah, and the war of revenge which was waged by the congregation of Israel against the tribe of Benjamin as a punishment for the crime (chap. xix.–xxi.). Both these events occurred in the earliest part of the period of the judges, as we may gather, in the case of the first, from a comparison of chap. xviii. 1 with chap. i. 34, and in that of the second from a comparison of chap. xx. 28 with Josh. xxii. 13 and xxiv. 33; and they are merely placed at the end of the book in the form of appendices, because they could not well be introduced into the six complete historical *tableaux*; although, so far as the facts themselves are concerned, they are intimately connected with the contents and aim of the book of Judges, inasmuch as they depict the religious and moral circumstances of the times in the most striking manner in two pictures drawn from life. The relation in which the three parts stand to one another, therefore, is this: the introduction depicts the basis on which the deeds of the judges were founded, and the appendices furnish confirmatory evidence of the spirit of the age as manifested in those deeds. The whole book, however, is pervaded and ruled by the idea distinctly expressed in the introduction (chap. ii. 1-3, 11-22), that the Lord left those Canaanites who had not been exterminated by Joshua still in the land, to prove to Israel through them whether it would obey His commandments, and that He chastised and punished His people through them for their disobedience and idolatry; but that as soon as they recognised His chastening hand in the punishment, and returned to Him with penitence and implored His help, He had compassion upon them again in His gracious love, and helped them to victory over their foes, so that, notwithstanding the repeated acts of faithlessness on the part of His people, the Lord remained ever faithful in His deeds, and stedfastly maintained His covenant.

We must not look to the book of Judges, therefore, for a complete history of the period of the judges, or one which throws light upon the development of the Israelites on every side. The character of the book, as shown in its contents and the arrangement of the materials, corresponds entirely to the character of the times over which it extends. The time of the judges did not form a new stage in the development of the nation of God. It was not till the time of Samuel and David, when this period was ended, that a new stage began. It was rather a transition period, the time of free, unfettered development, in which the nation was to take root in the land presented to it by God as its inheritance, to familiarize itself with the theocratic constitution given to it by the Mosaic law, and by means of the peculiar powers and gifts conferred upon it by God to acquire for itself that independence and firm footing in Canaan, within the limits of the laws, ordinances, and rights of the covenant, which Jehovah had promised, and the way to which He had prepared through the revelations He had made to them. This task could be accomplished without any ruler directly appointed by the Lord. The first thing which the tribes had to do was to root out such Canaanites as remained in the land, that they might not only establish themselves in the unrestricted and undisputed possession and enjoyment of the land and its productions, but also avert the danger which threatened them on the part of these tribes of being led away to idolatry and immorality. The Lord had promised them His help in this conflict, if they would only walk in His commandments. The maintenance of civil order and the administration of justice were in the hands of the heads of tribes, families, and households; and for the relation in which the congregation stood to the Lord its God, it possessed the necessary organs and media in the hereditary priesthood of the tribe of Levi, whose head could inquire the will of God in all cases of difficulty through the right of the Urim, and make it known to the nation. Now as long as the generation, which had seen the wonderful works of the Lord in the time of Joshua, was still living, so long did the nation continue faithful to the covenant of its God, and the tribes maintain a successful conflict with the still remaining Canaanites (chap. i. 1–20, 22–25). But the very next generation, to which those mighty acts of the Lord were unknown, began to forget its God, to grow weary and lax in its conflicts with the Canaanites, to make peace with them, and to mix up the worship of Jehovah, the jealous and holy God, with the worship of Baal and Astarte, the Canaanitish deities of nature, and even to substitute the latter in its place. With the loss of love and fidelity to the Lord, the bond of unity which formed the tribes into *one* congregation of Jehovah was also broken. The different tribes began to follow their own separate interests (*vid.* chap. v. 15–17, 23, viii. 5–8), and eventually even to oppose and make war upon one another; whilst Ephraim was bent upon securing to itself the headship of all the tribes, though without making any vigorous efforts to carry on the war with the oppressors of Israel (*vid.* chap. viii. 1 sqq., xii. 1–6). Consequently Israel suffered more and more from the oppression of heathen nations, to which God gave it up as a chastisement for its idolatry; and it would have become altogether a prey to its foes, had not the faithful covenant God taken compassion upon it in its distress as often as it cried to Him, and sent deliverers (מוֹשִׁיעִים, chap. iii. 9, 15; cf. Neh. ix. 27) in those judges, after whom both the age in question and the book before us are called. There are twelve of these judges mentioned, or rather thirteen, as Deborah the prophetess also judged Israel (chap. iv. 4); but there are only eight (Othniel, Ehud, Shamgar, Deborah and Barak, Gideon, Jephthah, and Samson), who are described as performing acts by which Israel obtained deliverance from its oppressors. Of the other five (Tolah, Jair, Ibzan, Elon, and Abdon) we are merely told that they judged Israel so many years. The reason for this we are not to seek in the fact that the report of the heroic deeds of these judges had not been handed down to the time when our book was written. It is to be found simply in the fact that these judges waged no wars and smote no foes.

The judges (*shophetim*) were men who procured justice or right for the people of Israel, not only by delivering them out of the power of their foes, but also by administering the laws and rights of the Lord (chap. ii. 16–19). *Judging* in this sense was different from the administration of civil jurisprudence, and included the idea of government such as would be expected from a king. Thus in 1 Sam. viii. 5, 6, the people are said to have asked Samuel to give them a king " to judge us," to procure us right, *i.e.* to govern us; and in 2 Kings xv. 5 Jotham is said to have *judged*, *i.e.* governed the nation during the illness of his father. The name given to these men (*shophetim*, judges) was evidently founded upon Deut. xvii. 9 and xix. 17, where it is assumed that in after-times there would be a *shophet*, who would stand by the side of the high priest as the supreme judge or leader of the state in Israel. The judges themselves corresponded to the δικασταί of the Tyrians (*Josephus*, c. Ap. i. 21) and the *Suffetes* of the Carthaginians (*qui summus Pœnis est magistratus*, *Liv.* Hist. xxvii. 37, and xxx. 7), with this difference, however, that as a rule the judges of Israel were called directly by the Lord, and endowed with miraculous power for the conquest of the enemies of Israel; and if, after delivering the people from their oppressors, they continued to the time of their death to preside over the public affairs of the whole nation, or merely of several of its tribes, yet they did not follow one another in a continuous line and unbroken succession, because the ordinary administration of justice and government of the commonwealth still remained in the hands of the heads of the tribes and the elders of the people, whilst occasionally there were also prophets and high priests, such as Deborah, Eli, and Samuel (chap. iv. 4; 1 Sam. iv. 18, vii. 15), in whom the government was vested. Thus " Othniel delivered the children of Israel," and " judged Israel," by going out to war, smiting Chushan-rishathaim, the Aramæan king, and giving the land rest for forty years (chap. iii. 9–11); and the same with Ehud and several others. On the other hand, Shamgar (chap. iii. 31) and Samson (chap. xiii.–xvi.) are apparently called judges of Israel, simply as opponents and conquerors of the Philistines, without their having taken any part in the administration of justice. Others, again, neither engaged in war nor gained victories. No warlike deeds are recorded of Tola; and yet it is stated in chap. x. 1, that " he rose up after Abimelech to deliver Israel (לְהוֹשִׁיעַ אֶת־יִשְׂרָאֵל), and judged Israel twenty-three years;" whilst of his successor Jair nothing more is said, than that " he judged Israel twenty-two years." Both of these had delivered and judged Israel, not by victories gained over enemies, but by placing themselves at the head of the tribes over whom Gideon had been judge, at the termination of the ephemeral reign of Abimelech, and by preventing the recurrence of hostile oppression, through the influence they exerted, as well as by what they did for the establishment of the nation in its fidelity to the Lord. This also applies to Ibzan, Elon, and Abdon, who followed Jephthah in direct succession (chap. xii. 8–15). Of these five judges also, it is not stated that Jehovah raised them up or called them. In all probability they merely undertook the government at the wish of the tribes whose judges they were; whilst at the same time it is to be observed, that such cases as these did not occur until the desire for a king had begun to manifest itself throughout the nation (chap. viii. 22, 23).

But if all the judges did not fight against outward enemies of Israel, it might appear strange that the book of Judges should close with the death of Samson, without mentioning Eli and Samuel, as both of them judged Israel, the one forty years, the other for the whole of his life (1 Sam. iv. 18, vii. 15). But Eli was really high priest, and what he did as judge was merely the natural result of his office of high priest; and Samuel was called to be the prophet of the Lord, and as such he delivered Israel from the oppression of the Philistines, not with the sword and by the might of his arm, like the judges before him, but by the power of the word, with which he converted Israel to the Lord, and by the might of his prayer, with which he sought and obtained the victory from the Lord (1 Sam. vii. 3–10); so that his judicial activity not only sprang out of his prophetic office, but was continually sustained thereby. The line of actual judges terminated with Samson; and with his death the office of judge was carried to the grave. Samson was followed immediately by Samuel, whose prophetic labours formed the link between the period of the judges and the introduction of royalty into Israel. The forty years of oppression on the part of the Philistines, from which Samson began to deliver Israel (chap. xiii. 1, 5), were brought to a close by the victory which the Israelites gained through Samuel's prayer (1 Sam. vii.), as will be readily seen when we have determined the chronology of the period of the judges, in the introductory remarks to the exposition of the body of the book. This victory was not gained by the Israelites till twenty years after Eli's death (comp. 1 Sam. vii. 2 with vi. 1 and iv. 18). Consequently of the forty years during which Eli judged Israel as high priest, only the last twenty fell within the time of the Philistine oppression, the first twenty before it. But both Samuel and Samson were born during the pontificate of Eli; for when Samson's birth was foretold, the Philistines were already ruling over Israel (Judg. xiii. 5). The deeds of Samson fell for the most part within the last twenty years of the Philistine supremacy, *i.e.* not only in the interval between the capture of the ark and death of Eli and the victory which the Israelites achieved through Samuel over these foes, which victory, however, Samson did not live to see, but also in the time when Samuel had been accredited as a prophet of Jehovah, and Jehovah had manifested himself repeatedly to him by word at Shiloh (1 Sam. iii. 20, 21). Consequently Samuel completed the deliverance of Israel out of the power of the Philistines, which Samson had commenced.

The book of Judges, therefore, embraces the whole of the judicial epoch, and gives a faithful picture of the political development of the Israelitish theocracy during that time. The author writes throughout from a prophet's point of view. He applies the standard of the law to the spirit of the age by which the nation was influenced as a whole, and pronounces a stern and severe sentence upon all deviations from the path of rectitude set before it in the law. The unfaithfulness of Israel, which went a whoring again and again after Baal, and was punished for its apostasy from the Lord with oppression from foreign nations, and the faithfulness of the Lord, who sent help to the people whenever it returned to Him in its oppression, by raising up judges who conquered its enemies, are the two historical factors of those times, and the hinges upon which the history turns. In the case of all the judges, it is stated that they judged " Israel," or the " children of Israel ;" although it is very obvious, from the accounts of the different deliverances effected, that most of the judges only delivered and judged those tribes who happened to be oppressed and subjugated by their enemies at a particular time. The other tribes, who were spared by this or the other hostile invasion, did not come into consideration in reference to the special design of the historical account, namely, to describe the acts of the Lord in the government of His people, any more than the development of the religious and social life of individual members of the congregation in harmony with the law ; inasmuch as the congregation, whether in whole or in part, was merely fulfilling its divinely appointed vocation, so long as it observed the law, and about this there was nothing special to be related (see the description given of the book of Judges in *Hengsten-berg*, Diss. on the Pentateuch, vol. ii. pp. 16 sqq.).

Lastly, if we take a survey of the gradual development of Israel during the times of the judges, we may distinguish three stages in the attitude of the Lord to His constantly rebelling people, and also in the form assumed by the external and internal circumstances of the nation: viz. (1) the period from the commencement of the apostasy of the nation till its deliverance from the rule of the Canaanitish king Jabin, or the time of the judges Othniel, Ehud, and Shamgar, Deborah and Barak (chap. iii.–v.); (2) the time of the Midianitish oppression, with the deliverance effected by Gideon, and the government which followed, viz. of Abimelech and the judges Tola and Jair (chap. vi.–x. 5); (3) the time of the Ammonitish and Philistine supremacy over Israel, with the judges Jephthah, Ibzan, Elon, and Abdon on the one hand, and that of Samson on the other (chap. x. 6–xvi. 31). Three times, for example, the Lord threatens His people with oppression and subjugation by foreign nations, as a punishment for their disobedience and apostasy from Him: viz. (1) at Bochim (chap. ii. 1–4) through the angel of the Lord; (2) on the invasion of the Midianites (chap. vi. 7–10, through the medium of a prophet; and (3) at the commencement of the Ammonitish and Philistine oppression (chap. x. 10–14). The first time He threatens, " the Canaanites shall be as thorns in your sides, and their gods shall be a snare to you" (chap. ii. 3); the second time, "I delivered you out of the hand of the Egyptians, and out of the hand of all that oppressed you; I said unto you, I am Jehovah, your God; fear not the gods of the Amorites: but ye have not hearkened to my voice" (chap. vi. 9, 10); the third time, "Ye have forsaken me and served other gods: wherefore I will deliver you no more; go and cry unto the gods which ye have chosen; let them deliver you in the time of your tribulation" (chap. x. 13, 14). These threats were fulfilled upon the disobedient nation, not only in the fact that they fell deeper and deeper under the oppression of their foes, but by their also becoming disjointed and separated more and more internally. In the first stage, the oppressions from without lasted a tolerably long time: that of Chushan-rishathaim eight years; that of Eglon the Moabite, eighteen; and that of the Canaanitish king Jabin, as much as twenty years (chap. iii. 8, 14, iv. 3). But, on the other hand, after the first, the Israelites had forty years of peace; after the second, eighty; and after the third, again forty years (chap. iii. 11, 30, v.

31). Under Othniel and Ehud all Israel appears to have risen against its oppressors; but under Barak, Reuben and Gilead, Dan and Asher took no part in the conflict of the other tribes (chap. v. 15–17). In the second stage, the Midianitish oppression lasted, it is true, only seven years (chap. vi. 1), and was followed by forty years of rest under Gideon (chap. viii. 28); whilst the three years' government of Abimelech was followed by forty-five years of peace under Tola and Jair (chap. x. 2, 3); but even under Gideon the jealousy of Ephraim was raised to such a pitch against the tribes who had joined in smiting the foe, that it almost led to a civil war (chap. viii. 1–3), and the inhabitants of Succoth and Penuel refused all assistance to the victorious army, and that in so insolent a manner that they were severely punished by Gideon in consequence (chap. viii. 4–9, 14–17); whilst in the election of Abimelech as king of Shechem, the internal decay of the congregation of Israel was brought still more clearly to light (chap. ix.). Lastly, in the third stage, no doubt, Israel was delivered by Jephthah from the eighteen years' bondage on the part of the Ammonites (chap. xi. 8 sqq.), and the tribes to the east of the Jordan, as well as the northern tribes of the land on this side, enjoyed rest under the judges Jephthah, Ibzan, Elon, and Abdon for thirty-one years (chap. xii. 7, 9, 11, 14); but the Philistine oppression lasted till after Samson's death (chap. xiii. 5, xv. 20), and the internal decay increased so much under this hostile pressure, that whilst the Ephraimites, on the one hand, commenced a war against Jephthah, and sustained a terrible defeat at the hands of the tribes on the east of the Jordan (chap. xii. 1–6), on the other hand, the tribes who were enslaved by the Philistines had so little appreciation of the deliverance which God had sent them through Samson, that the men of Judah endeavoured to give up their deliverer to the Philistines (chap. xv. 9–14). Nevertheless the Lord not only helped the nation again, both in its distress and out of its distress, but came nearer and nearer to it with His aid, that it might learn that its help was to be found in God alone. The first deliverers and judges He stirred up by His Spirit, which came upon Othniel and Ehud, and filled them with courage and strength for the conquest of their foes. Barak was summoned to the war by the prophetess Deborah, and inspired by her with the courage to undertake it. Gideon was called to be the deliverer of Israel out of the severe oppression of the Midianites by the appearance of the angel of the Lord, and the victory over the innumerable army of the foe was given by the

Lord, not to the whole of the army which Gideon summoned to the battle, but only to a small company of 300 men, that Israel might not "vaunt themselves against the Lord," and magnify their own power. Lastly, Jephthah and Samson were raised up as deliverers out of the power of the Ammonites and Philistines; and whilst Jephthah was called by the elders of Gilead to be the leader in the war with the Midianites, and sought through a vow to ensure the assistance of God in gaining a victory over them, Samson was set apart from his mother's womb, through the appearance of the angel of the Lord, as the Nazarite who was to begin to deliver Israel out of the power of the Philistines. At the same time there was given to the nation in the person of Samuel, the son for whom the pious Hannah prayed to the Lord, a Nazarite and prophet, who was not only to complete the deliverance from the power of the Philistines which Samson had begun, but to ensure the full conversion of Israel to the Lord its God.

With regard to the *origin* of the book of Judges, it is evident from the repeated remark, "In those days there was no king in Israel, every man did that which was right in his own eyes" (chap. xvii. 6, xxi. 25; cf. chap. xviii. 1, xix. 1), that it was composed at a time when Israel was already rejoicing in the benefits connected with the kingdom. It is true this remark is only to be found in the appendices, and would have no force so far as the date of composition is concerned, if the view held by different critics were well-founded, viz. that these appendices were added by a later hand. But the arguments adduced against the unity of authorship in all three parts, the introduction, the body of the work, and the appendices, will not bear examination. Without the introduction (chap. i. 1–iii. 6) the historical narrative contained in the book would want a foundation, which is absolutely necessary to make it intelligible; and the two appendices supply two supplements of the greatest importance in relation to the development of the tribes of Israel in the time of the judges, and most intimately connected with the design and plan of the rest of the book. It is true that in chap. i., as well as in the two appendices, the prophetic view of the history which prevails in the rest of the book, from chap. ii. 11 to chap. xvi. 31, is not distinctly apparent; but this difference may be fully explained from the contents of the two portions, which neither furnish the occasion nor supply the materials for any such view,—like the account of the royal supremacy of Abimelech in chap. ix., in which the so-called "theocratical pragmatism" is also wanting. But, on

the other hand, all these portions are just as rich in allusions to the
Mosaic law and the legal worship as the other parts of the book, so
that both in their contents and their form they would be unintelligible apart from the supremacy of the law in Israel. The discrepancies which some fancy they have discovered between chap.
i. 8 and chap. i. 21, and also between chap. i. 19 and chap. iii. 3,
vanish completely on a correct interpretation of the passages themselves. And no such differences can be pointed out in language
or style as would overthrow the unity of authorship, or even render
it questionable. Even *Stähelin* observes (*spez. Einl.* p. 77): " I
cannot find in chap. xvii.–xxi. the (special) author of chap. i.–ii. 5 ;
and the arguments adduced by *Bertheau* in favour of this, from
modes of expression to be found in the two sections, appear to me
to be anything but conclusive, simply because the very same modes
of expression occur elsewhere · יוֹאֶל לָשֶׁבֶת in Ex. ii. 21 ; חֹתֵן in Num.
x. 29 ; נָתַן בְּיַד, Josh. x. 30, xi. 8, Judg. vi. 1, xi. 21 ; נָתַן לְאִשָּׁה,
Gen. xxix. 28, xxx. 4, 9, xxxiv. 8, etc. ; הִכָּה לְפִי חֶרֶב, Num. xxi. 24,
Deut. xiii. 16, Josh. viii. 24, x. 28, 30, 32, etc. Undoubtedly
שָׁאַל בַּי only occurs in Judg. i. 1 and the appendix, and never earlier ;
but there is a similar expression in Num. xxvii. 21 and Josh. ix. 14,
and the first passage shows how the mode of expression could be
so abbreviated. I find no preterites with ו, used in the place of the
future with ו in Judg. i.; for it is evident from the construction
that the preterite must be used in vers. 8, 16, 25, etc.; and thus the
only thing left that could strike us at all is the idiom שִׁלַּח בָּאֵשׁ,
which is common to both sections, but which is too isolated, and
occurs again moreover in 2 Kings viii. 12 and Ps. lxxiv. 7." But
even the "peculiar phrases belonging to a later age," which *Stähelin*
and *Bertheau* discover in chap. xvii.–xxi. do not furnish any tenable
proof of this assertion. The phrase " from Dan to Beersheba," in
chap. xx. 1, was formed after the settlement of the Danites in
Laish-Dan, which took place at the commencement of the time of
the judges. נָשָׂא נָשִׁים, in chap. xxi. 23, is also to be found in Ruth
i. 4; and the others either occur again in the books of Samuel, or
have been wrongly interpreted.

We have a firm *datum* for determining more minutely the time
when the book of Judges was written, in the statement in chap. i.
21, that the Jebusites in Jerusalem had not been rooted out by the
Israelites, but dwelt there with the children of Benjamin "*unto
this day.*" The Jebusites remained in possession of Jerusalem, or
of the citadel Zion, or the upper town of Jerusalem, until the time

when David went against Jerusalem after the twelve tribes had acknowledged him as king, took the fortress of Zion, and made it the capital of his kingdom under the name of the city of David (2 Sam. v. 6–9; 1 Chron. xi. 4–9). Consequently the book was written before this event, either during the first seven years of the reign of David at Hebron, or during the reign of Saul, under whom the Israelites already enjoyed the benefits of a monarchical government, since Saul not only fought with bravery against all the enemies of Israel, and "delivered Israel out of the hands of them that spoiled them" (1 Sam. xiv. 47, 48), but exerted himself to restore the authority of the law of God in his kingdom, as is evident from the fact that he banished the wizards and necromancers out of the land (1 Sam. xxviii. 9). The talmudical statement therefore in *Bava-bathra* (f. 14*b* and 15*a*), to the effect that Samuel was the author of the book, may be so far correct, that if it was not written by Samuel himself towards the close of his life, it was written at his instigation by a younger prophet of his school. More than this it is impossible to decide. So much, however, is at all events certain, that the book does not contain traces of a later age either in its contents or its language, and that chap. xviii. 30 does not refer to the time of the captivity (see the commentary on this passage).

With regard to the *sources* of which the author made use, unless we are prepared to accept untenable hypotheses as having all the validity of historical facts, it is impossible to establish anything more than that he drew his materials not only from oral tradition, but also from written documents. This is obvious from the exactness of the historical and chronological accounts, and still more so from the abundance of characteristic and original traits and expressions that meet the reader in the historical pictures, some of which are very elaborate. The historical fidelity, exactness, and vividness of description apparent in every part of the book are only to be explained in a work which embraces a period of 350 years, on the supposition that the author made use of trustworthy records, or the testimony of persons who were living when the events occurred. This stands out so clearly in every part of the book, that it is admitted even by critics who are compelled by their own dogmatical assumptions to deny the actual truth or reality of the miraculous parts of the history. With regard to the nature of these sources, however, we can only conjecture that chap. i. and xvii.-xxi. were founded upon written accounts, with which the author of the book of Joshua was also acquainted: and that the accounts of Deborah and Barak, of Gideon, and of the life of Samson, were taken from different writings, inasmuch as these sections are distinguished from one another by many peculiarities. (Further remarks on this subject will be found in the exposition itself.)

EXPOSITION.

I.—ATTITUDE OF ISRAEL TOWARDS THE CANAANITES, AND TOWARDS JEHOVAH ITS GOD.

CHAP. I.–III. 6.

HOSTILITIES BETWEEN ISRAEL AND THE CANAANITES AFTER JOSHUA'S DEATH.—CHAP. I. 1–II. 5.

AFTER the death of Joshua the tribes of Israel resolved to continue the war with the Canaanites, that they might exterminate them altogether from the land that had been given them for an inheritance. In accordance with the divine command, Judah commenced the strife in association with Simeon, smote the king of Bezek, conquered Jerusalem, Hebron and Debir upon the mountains, Zephath in the south land, and three of the chief cities of the Philistines, and took possession of the mountains; but was unable to exterminate the inhabitants of the plain, just as the Benjaminites were unable to drive the Jebusites out of Jerusalem (vers. 1–21). The tribe of Joseph also conquered the city of Bethel (vers. 22–26); but from the remaining towns of the land neither the Manassites, nor the Ephraimites, nor the tribes of Zebulun, Asher, and Naphtali expelled the Canaanites: all that they did was to make them tributary (vers. 27–33). The Danites were actually forced back by the Amorites out of the plain into the mountains, because the latter maintained their hold of the towns of the plain, although the house of Joseph conquered them and made them tributary (vers. 34–36). The angel of the Lord therefore appeared at Bochim, and declared to the Israelites, that because they had not obeyed the command of the Lord, to make no covenant with the Canaanites, the Lord would no more drive out these nations, but would cause them and their gods to become a snare to them (chap. ii. 1–5).

From this divine revelation it is evident, on the one hand, that the failure to exterminate the Canaanites had its roots in the negligence of the tribes of Israel; and on the other hand, that the accounts of the wars of the different tribes, and the enumeration of the towns in the different possessions out of which the Canaanites were not expelled, were designed to show clearly the attitude of the Israelites to the Canaanites in the age immediately following the death of Joshua, or to depict the historical basis on which the development of Israel rested in the era of the judges.

Vers. 1–7. With the words " *Now, after the death of Joshua, it came to pass,*" the book of Judges takes up the thread of the history where the book of Joshua had dropped it, to relate the further development of the covenant nation. A short time before his death, Joshua had gathered the elders and heads of the people around him, and set before them the entire destruction of the Canaanites through the omnipotent help of the Lord, if they would only adhere with fidelity to the Lord; whilst, at the same time, he also pointed out to them the dangers of apostasy from the Lord (Josh. xxiii.). Remembering this admonition and warning, the Israelites inquired, after Joshua's death, who should begin the war against the Canaanites who still remained to be destroyed; and the Lord answered, " *Judah shall go up: behold, I have delivered the land into his hand*" (vers. 1, 2). שָׁאַל בַּיהוָֹה, to ask with Jehovah for the purpose of obtaining a declaration of the divine will, is substantially the same as שָׁאַל בְּמִשְׁפַּט הָאוּרִים (Num. xxvii. 21), to inquire the will of the Lord through the Urim and Thummim of the high priest. From this time forward inquiring of the Lord occurs with greater frequency (*vid.* chap. xx. 23, 27; 1 Sam. x. 22, xxii. 10, xxiii. 2, etc.), as well as the synonymous expression " ask of *Elohim*" in chap. xviii. 5, xx. 18; 1 Sam. xiv. 37, xxii. 13; 1 Chron. xiv. 10; whereas Moses and Joshua received direct revelations from God. The phrase יַעֲלֶה אֶל־הַכְּנַעֲנִי, " *go up to the Canaanites,*" is defined more precisely by the following words, " *to fight against them;*" so that עָלָה is used here also to denote the campaign against a nation (see at Josh. viii. 1), without there being any necessity, however, for us to take אֶל in the sense of עַל. עָלָה בַּתְּחִלָּה signifies " *to go up in the beginning,*" *i.e.* to open or commence the war; not to hold the commandership in the war, as the *Sept.*, *Vulgate*, and others render it (see chap. x. 18, where יָחֵל לְהִלָּחֵם is expressly distinguished from being the chief or leader). Moreover, מִי does not mean who? *i.e.* what person, but, as the answer clearly shows, what tribe? Now a tribe could open the war, and take the lead at the head of the other tribes, but could not be the commander-in-chief. In the present instance, however, Judah did not even enter upon the war at the head of all the tribes, but simply joined with the tribe of Simeon to make a common attack upon the Canaanites in their inheritance. The promise in ver. 2*b* is the same as that in Josh. vi. 2, viii. 1, etc. " *The land*" is not merely the land allotted to the tribe of Judah, or Judah's inheritance, as *Bertheau* supposes, for Judah conquered Jerusalem (ver. 8), which had been allotted to the tribe of Benjamin (Josh. xviii. 28), but the land of Canaan generally, so far as it was still in the possession of the Canaanites and was to be conquered by Judah. The reason why Judah was to commence the hostilities is not to be sought for in the fact that Judah was the most numerous of all the tribes (*Rosenmüller*), but rather in the fact that Judah had already been appointed by the blessing of Jacob (Gen. xlix. 8 sqq.) to be the champion of his brethren.—Ver. 3. Judah invited Simeon his brother, *i.e.* their brother tribe, to take part in the contest. This epithet is applied to Simeon, not because Simeon and Judah, the sons of Jacob, were the children of the same mother, Leah (Gen. xxix. 33, 35), but because Simeon's inheritance was within the territory of Judah (Josh. xix. 1 sqq.), so that Simeon was more closely connected with Judah than any of the other tribes. " *Come up with me into my lot* (into the inheritance that has fallen to me by lot), *that we may fight against the Canaanites, and I likewise will go with thee into thy lot. So Simeon went with him,*" *i.e.* joined with Judah in making war upon the Canaanites. This request shows that Judah's principal intention was to make war upon and exterminate the Canaanites who remained in his own and Simeon's inheritance. The different expressions employed, *come up* and *go*, are to be explained from the simple fact that the whole of Simeon's territory was in the *shephelah* and *Negeb*, whereas Judah had received the heart of his possessions upon the mountains.

Ver. 4. " *And Judah went up,*" *sc.* against the Canaanites, to make war upon them. The completion of the sentence is supplied by the context, more especially by ver. 2. So far as the sense is concerned, *Rosenmüller* has given the correct explanation of יַעַל, "Judah entered upon the expedition along with Simeon." " *And they smote the Canaanites and the Perizzites in Bezek,* 10,000 *men.*" The result of the war is summed up briefly in these words ; and then in vers. 5–7 the capture and punishment of the hostile king *Adoni-bezek* is specially mentioned as being the most important event in the war. The foe is described as consisting of Canaanites and Perizzites, two tribes which have been already named in Gen. xiii. 7 and xxxiv. 30 as representing the entire population of Canaan, " *the Canaanites* " comprising principally those in the lowlands by the Jordan and the Mediterranean (*vid.* Num. xiii. 29 ; Josh. xi. 3), and " *the Perizzites* " the tribes who dwelt in the mountains (Josh. xvii. 15). On the *Perizzites,* see Gen. xiii. 7. The place mentioned, *Bezek,* is only mentioned once more, namely in 1 Sam. xi. 8, where it is described as being situated between Gibeah of Saul (see at Josh. xviii. 28) and Jabesh in Gilead. According to the *Onom.* (*s. v. Bezek*), there were at that time two places very near together both named *Bezek,* seventeen Roman miles from Neapolis on the road to *Scythopolis, i.e.* about seven hours to the north of Nabulus on the road to Beisan. This description is perfectly reconcilable with 1 Sam. xi. 8. On the other hand, *Clericus (ad h. l.), Rosenmüller,* and *v. Raumer* suppose the Bezek mentioned here to have been situated in the territory of Judah ; though this cannot be proved, since it is merely based upon an inference drawn from ver. 3, viz. that Judah and Simeon simply attacked the Canaanites in their own allotted territories,—an assumption which is very uncertain. There is no necessity, however, to adopt the opposite and erroneous opinion of *Bertheau,* that the tribes of Judah and Simeon commenced their expedition to the south from the gathering-place of the united tribes at Shechem, and fought the battle with the Canaanitish forces in that region upon this expedition ; since Shechem is not described in Josh. xxiv. as the gathering-place of the united tribes, *i.e.* of the whole of the military force of Israel, and the battle fought with Adoni-bezek did not take place at the time when the tribes prepared to leave Shiloh and march to their own possessions after the casting of the lots was over. The simplest explanation is, that when the tribes of Judah and Simeon prepared to make war upon the Canaanites in the possessions allotted to them, they were threatened or attacked by the forces of the Canaanites collected together by Adoni-bezek, so that they had first of all to turn their arms against this king before they could attack the Canaanites in their own tribe-land. As the precise circumstances connected with the occasion and course of this war have not been recorded, there is nothing to hinder the supposition that Adoni-bezek may have marched from the north against the possessions of Benjamin and Judah, possibly with the intention of joining the Canaanites in Jebus, and the Anakim in Hebron and upon the mountains in the south, and then making a combined attack upon the Israelites. This might induce or even compel Judah and Simeon to attack this enemy first of all, and even to pursue him till they overtook him at his capital Bezek, and smote him with all his army. *Adoni-bezek*, *i.e.* lord of Bezek, is the official title of this king, whose proper name is unknown.

In the principal engagement, in which 10,000 Canaanites fell, Adoni-bezek escaped; but he was overtaken in his flight (vers. 6, 7), and so mutilated, by the cutting off of his thumbs and great toes, that he could neither carry arms nor flee. With this cruel treatment, which the Athenians are said to have practised upon the captured Ægynetes (*Ælian, var. hist.* ii. 9), the Israelites simply executed the just judgment of retribution, as Adoni-bezek was compelled to acknowledge, for the cruelties which he had inflicted upon captives taken by himself. "*Seventy kings*," he says in ver. 7, "*with the thumbs of their hands and feet cut off, were gathering under my table. As I have done, so God hath requited me.*" מְקֻצָּצִים . . . בְּהֹנוֹת, *lit.* "cut in the thumbs of their hands and feet" (see *Ewald*, Lehrb. § 284, *c.*). The object to מְלַקְּטִים, "gathering up" (viz. crumbs), is easily supplied from the idea of the verb itself. Gathering up crumbs under the table, like the dogs in Matt. xv. 27, is a figurative representation of the most shameful treatment and humiliation. "Seventy" is a round number, and is certainly an exaggerated hyperbole here. For even if every town of importance in Canaan had its own king, the fact that, when Joshua conquered the land, he only smote thirty-one kings, is sufficient evidence that there can hardly have been seventy kings to be found in all Canaan. It appears strange, too, that the king of Bezek is not mentioned in connection with the conquest of Canaan under Joshua. Bezek was probably situated more on the side towards the valley of the Jordan, where the Israelites under Joshua did not go. Possibly, too, the culminating point of Adoni-bezek's power, when he conquered so many kings, was before the arrival of the Israelites in Canaan, and it may at that time have begun to decline; so that he did not venture to undertake anything against the combined forces of Israel under Joshua, and it was not till the Israelitish tribes separated to go to their own possessions, that he once more tried the fortunes of war and was defeated. The children of Judah took him with them to Jerusalem, where he died.

Vers. 8–15. After his defeat, Judah and Simeon went against Jerusalem, and conquered this city and smote it, *i.e.* its inhabitants, with the edge of the sword, or without quarter (see Gen. xxxiv. 26), and set the city on fire. שִׁלַּח בָּאֵשׁ, to set on fire, to give up to the flames, only occurs again in chap. xx. 48, 2 Kings viii. 12, and Ps. lxxiv. 7. Joshua had already slain the king of Jerusalem and his four allies after the battle at Gibeon (Josh. x. 3, 18–26), but had not conquered Jerusalem, his capital. This was not done till after Joshua's death, when it was taken by the tribes of Judah and Simeon. But even after this capture, and notwithstanding the fact that it had been set on fire, it did not come into the sole and permanent possession of the Israelites. After the conquerors had advanced still farther, to make war upon the Canaanites in the mountains, in the *Negeb*, and in the *shephelah* (vers. 9 sqq.), the Jebusites took it again and rebuilt it, so that in the following age it was regarded by the Israelites as a foreign city (chap. xix. 11, 12). The Benjaminites, to whom Jerusalem had fallen by lot, were no more able to drive out the Jebusites than the Judæans had been. Consequently they continued to live by the side of the Benjaminites (chap. i. 21) and the Judæans (Josh xv. 63), who settled, as time rolled on, in this the border city of their possessions; and in the upper town especially, upon the top of Mount Zion, they established themselves so firmly, that they could not be dislodged until David succeeded in wresting this fortress from them, and made the city of Zion the capital of his kingdom (2 Sam. v. 6 sqq.).[1]—Vers. 9 sqq. After the conquest of Jerusalem, the children of Judah (together with the Simeonites, ver. 3) went down into their own possessions, to make war upon the Canaanites in the mountains, the *Negeb*, and the *shephelah* (see at Josh. xv. 48, xxi. 33), and to exterminate them. They first of all conquered Hebron and Debir upon the mountains (vers. 10–15), as has already been related in Josh. xv.

---

[1] In this way we may reconcile in a very simple manner the different accounts concerning Jerusalem in Josh. xv. 63, Judg. i. 8, 21, xix. 11 sqq., 1 Sam. xvii. 54, and 2 Sam. v. vi., without there being the slightest necessity to restrict the conquest mentioned in this verse to the city that was built round Mount Zion, as *Josephus* does, to the exclusion of the citadel upon Zion itself; or to follow *Bertheau*, and refer the account of the Jebusites dwelling by the children of Judah in Jerusalem (Josh. xv. 63) to a time subsequent to the conquest of the citadel of Zion by David,—an interpretation which is neither favoured by the circumstance that the Jebusite Araunah still held some property there in the time of David (2 Sam. xxiv. 21 sqq.), nor by the passage in 1 Kings ix. 20 sqq., according to which the descendants of the Amorites, Hittites, Perizzites, Hivites, and Jebusites who still remained in the land were made into tributary bondmen by Solomon, and set to work upon the buildings that he had in hand.

14–19 (see the commentary on this passage). The forms עֲלִית and תַּחְתִּית (ver. 15), instead of עֲלִּוֹת and תַּחְתִּיּוֹת (Josh. xv. 19), are in the singular, and are construed with the plural form of the feminine גֻּלֹּת, because this is used in the sense of the singular, "a spring" (see *Ewald*, § 318, *a*.).

Ver. 16. The notice respecting the Kenites, that they went up out of the palm-city with the children of Judah into the wilderness of Judah in the south of Arad, and dwelt there with the Judæans, is introduced here into the account of the wars of the tribe of Judah, because this migration of the Kenites belonged to the time between the conquest of Debir (vers. 12 sqq.) and Zephath (ver. 17); and the notice itself was of importance, as forming the intermediate link between Num. x. 29 sqq., and the later allusions to the Kenites in Judg. iv. 11, v. 24, 1 Sam. xv. 6, xxvii. 10, xxx. 29. *" The children of the Kenite,"* *i.e.* the descendants of Hobab, the brother-in-law of Moses (compare chap. iv. 11, where the name is given, but קֵין occurs instead of קֵינִי, with Num. x. 29), were probably a branch of the Kenites mentioned in Gen. xv. 19 along with the other tribes of Canaan, which had separated from the other members of its own tribe before the time of Moses and removed to the land of Midian, where Moses met with a hospitable reception from their chief Reguel on his flight from Egypt. These Kenites had accompanied the Israelites to Canaan at the request of Moses (Num. x. 29 sqq.); and when the Israelites advanced into Canaan itself, they had probably remained as nomads in the neighbourhood of the Jordan near to Jericho, without taking any part in the wars of Joshua. But when the tribe of Judah had exterminated the Canaanites out of Hebron, Debir, and the neighbourhood, after the death of Joshua, they went into the desert of Judah with the Judæans as they moved farther towards the south; and going to the south-western edge of this desert, to the district on the south of Arad (Tell Arad, see at Num. xxi. 1), they settled there on the border of the steppes of the Negeb (Num. xxxiii. 40). *" The palm-city"* was a name given to the city of Jericho, according to chap. iii. 13, Deut. xxxiv. 3, 2 Chron. xxviii. 15. There is no ground whatever for thinking of some other town of this name in the desert of Arabia, near the palm-forest, φοινικών, of *Diod. Sic.* (iii. 42) and *Strabo* (p. 776), as *Clericus* and *Bertheau* suppose, even if it could be proved that there was any such town in the neighbourhood. וַיֵּלֶךְ, *" then he went* (the branch of the Kenites just referred to) *and dwelt with the people"* (of the children of Judah), that is to

say, with the people of Israel in the desert of Judah.   The subject
to וַיֵּלֶךְ is קֵינִי, the Kenite, as a tribe.

Vers. 17-21. *Remaining Conquests of the combined Tribes of
Judah and Simeon.*—Ver. 17. *Zephath* was in the territory of
Simeon.   This is evident not only from the fact that Hormah
(Zephath) had been allotted to the tribe of Simeon (compare Josh.
xix. 4 with chap. xv. 30), but also from the words, "Judah went
with Simeon his brother," which point back to ver. 3, and express
the thought that Judah went with Simeon into his territory to
drive out the Canaanites who were still to be found there.   Going
southwards from Debir, Judah and Simeon smote the Canaanites
at Zephath on the southern boundary of Canaan, and executed the
ban upon this town, from which it received the name of *Hormah*,
i.e. banning.   The town has been preserved in the ruins of *Sepâta*,
on the south of Khalasa or Elusa (see at Josh. xii. 14).   In the
passage mentioned, the king of Hormah or Zephath is named
among the kings who were slain by Joshua.   It does not follow
from this, however, that Joshua must necessarily have conquered
his capital Zephath; the king of Jerusalem was also smitten by
Joshua and slain, without Jerusalem itself being taken at that time.
But even if Zephath were taken by the Israelites, as soon as the
Israelitish army had withdrawn, the Canaanites there might have
taken possession of the town again; so that, like many other Canaanitish towns, it had to be conquered again after Joshua's death (see
the commentary on Num. xxi. 2, 3).   There is not much probability in this conjecture, however, for the simple reason that the
ban pronounced by Moses upon the country of the king of Arad
(Num. xxi. 2) was carried out now for the first time by Judah and
Simeon upon the town of Zephath, which formed a part of it.   If
Joshua had conquered it, he would certainly have executed the ban
upon it.   The name *Hormah*, which was already given to Zephath
in Josh. xv. 30 and xix. 4, is no proof to the contrary, since it may
be used proleptically there.   In any case, the infliction of the ban
upon this town can only be explained from the fact that Moses had
pronounced the ban upon all the towns of the king of Arad.—Ver.
18. From the *Negeb* Judah turned into the *shephelah*, and took the
three principal cities of the Philistines along the line of coast, viz.
Gaza, Askelon, and Ekron, with their territory.   The order in
which the names of the captured cities occur is a proof that the
conquest took place from the south.   First of all Gaza, the southernmost of all the towns of the Philistines, the present *Guzzeh;* then

Askelon (*Askulán*), which is five hours to the north of Gaza; and lastly Ekron, the most northerly of the five towns of the Philistines, the present *Akîr* (see at Josh. xiii. 3). The other two, Ashdod and Gath, do not appear to have been conquered at that time. And even those that were conquered, the Judæans were unable to hold long. In the time of Samson they were all of them in the hands of the Philistines again (see chap. xiv. 19, xvi. 1 sqq.; 1 Sam. v. 10, etc.). In ver. 19 we have a brief summary of the results of the contests for the possession of the land. "*Jehovah was with Judah;*" and with His help they took possession of the mountains. And they did nothing more; "*for the inhabitants of the plain they were unable to exterminate, because they had iron chariots.*" הוֹרִישׁ has two different meanings in the two clauses: first (וַיֹּרֶשׁ), to seize upon a possession which has been vacated by the expulsion or destruction of its former inhabitants; and secondly (לְהוֹרִישׁ, with the accusative, of the inhabitants), to drive or exterminate them out of their possessions,—a meaning which is derived from the earlier signification of making it an emptied possession (see Ex. xxxiv. 24; Num. xxxii. 21, etc.). "*The mountain*" here includes the south-land (the *Negeb*), as the only distinction is between mountains and plain. "*The valley*" is the *shephelah* (ver. 9). לֹא לְהוֹרִישׁ, he was not (able) to drive out. The construction may be explained from the fact that לֹא is to be taken independently here as in Amos vi. 10, in the same sense in which אֵין before the infinitive is used in later writings (2 Chron. v. 11; Esther iv. 2, viii. 8; Eccl. iii. 14: see *Ges.* § 132–3, anm. 1; *Ewald*, § 237, *e.*). On the iron chariots, *i.e.* the chariots tipped with iron, see at Josh. xvii. 16.—To this there is appended, in ver. 20, the statement that "*they gave Hebron unto Caleb,*" etc., which already occurred in Josh. xv. 13, 14, and was there explained; and also in ver. 21 the remark, that the Benjaminites did not drive out the Jebusites who dwelt in Jerusalem, which is so far in place here, that it shows, on the one hand, that the children of Judah did not bring Jerusalem into the undisputed possession of the Israelites through this conquest, and, on the other hand, that it was not their intention to diminish the inheritance of Benjamin by the conquest of Jerusalem, and they had not taken the city for themselves. For further remarks, see at ver. 8.

The hostile attacks of the other tribes upon the Canaanites who remained in the land are briefly summed up in vers. 22–36. Of these the taking of Bethel is more fully described in vers. 22–26.

Besides this, nothing more is given than the list of the towns in the territories of western Manasseh (vers. 27, 28), Ephraim (ver. 29), Zebulun (ver. 30), Asher (vers. 31, 32), Naphtali (ver. 33), and Dan (vers. 34, 35), out of which the Canaanites were not exterminated by these tribes. Issachar is omitted; hardly, however, because that tribe made no attempt to disturb the Canaanites, as *Bertheau* supposes, but rather because none of its towns remained in the hands of the Canaanites.

Vers. 22–26. Like Judah, so also ("they also," referring back to vers. 2, 3) did the house of Joseph (Ephraim and western Manasseh) renew the hostilities with the Canaanites who were left in their territory after the death of Joshua. The children of Joseph went up against Bethel, and Jehovah was with them, so that they were able to conquer the city. *Bethel* had indeed been assigned to the tribe of Benjamin (Josh. xviii. 22), but it was situated on the southern boundary of the tribe-land of Ephraim (Josh. xvi. 2, xviii. 13); so that the tribe of Joseph could not tolerate the Canaanites in this border town, if it would defend its own territory against them, and purge it entirely of them. This is a sufficient explanation of the fact that this one conquest is mentioned, and this only, without there being any necessity to seek for the reason, as *Bertheau* does, in the circumstance that the town of Bethel came into such significant prominence in the later history of Israel, and attained the same importance in many respects in relation to the northern tribes, as that which Jerusalem attained in relation to the southern. For the fact that nothing more is said about the other conquests of the children of Joseph, may be explained simply enough on the supposition that they did not succeed in rooting out the Canaanites from the other fortified towns in their possessions; and therefore there was nothing to record about any further conquests, as the result of their hostilities was merely this, that they did not drive the Canaanites out of the towns named in vers. 27, 29, but simply made them tributary. יָתִירוּ, they had it explored, or spied out. תוּר is construed with בְּ here, because the spying laid hold, as it were, of its object. *Bethel*, formerly Luz, now *Beitin:* see at Gen. xxviii. 19 and Josh. vii. 2.—Ver. 24. And *the watchmen* (*i.e.* the spies sent out to explore Bethel) saw a man coming out of the town, and got him to show them the entrance into it, under a promise that they would show him favour, *i.e.* would spare the lives of himself and his family (see Josh. ii. 12, 13); whereupon they took the town and smote it without quarter, according to the law in Deut. xx. 16, 17, letting none but the man and his family go. By " *the entrance into the city* " we are not to understand the gate of the town, but the way or mode by which they could get into the town, which was no doubt fortified. —Ver. 26. The man whom they had permitted to go free, went with his family into the land of the Hittites, and there built a town, to which he gave the name of his earlier abode, viz. *Luz.* The situation of this *Luz* is altogether unknown. Even the situation of the land of the Hittites cannot be more precisely determined ; for we find Hittites at Hebron in the times of Abraham and Moses (Gen. xxiii.), and also upon the mountains of Palestine (Num. xiii. 29), and at a later period in the north-east of Canaan on the borders of Syria (1 Kings x. 29). That the Hittites were one of the most numerous and widespread of the tribes of the Canaanites, is evident from the fact that, in Josh. i. 4, the Canaanites generally are described as Hittites.

Vers. 27, 28. Manasseh did not root out the Canaanites from the towns which had been allotted to it in the territory of Asher and Issachar (Josh. xvii. 11), but simply made them tributary. לֹא הוֹרִישׁ אֶת־בֵּית־שְׁאָן וּגוֹ׳, considered by itself, might be rendered : " *Manasseh did not take possession of Bethshean,*" etc. But as we find, in the further enumeration, the inhabitants of the towns mentioned instead of the towns themselves, we must take הוֹרִישׁ in the sense of rooting out, driving out of their possessions, which is the only rendering applicable in ver. 28 ; and thus, according to a very frequent metonymy, must understand by the towns the inhabitants of the towns. " *Manasseh did not exterminate Bethshean,*" *i.e.* the inhabitants of Bethshean, etc. All the towns mentioned here have already been mentioned in Josh. xvii. 11, the only difference being, that they are not placed in exactly the same order, and that *Endor* is mentioned there after *Dor ;* whereas here it has no doubt fallen out through a copyist's error, as the Manassites, according to Josh. xvii. 12, 13, did not exterminate the Canaanites from all the towns mentioned there. The change in the order in which the towns occur—Taanach being placed next to Bethshean, whereas in Joshua Bethshean is followed by Ibleam, which is placed last but one in the present list—may be explained on the supposition, that in Josh. xvii. 11, Endor, Taanach, and Megiddo are placed together, as forming a triple league, of which the author of our book has taken no notice. Nearly all these towns were in the plain of Jezreel, or in the immediate neighbourhood of the great commercial roads which ran from the coast of the Mediterranean to Damascus and central Asia. The Canaanites no doubt brought all their strength to bear upon the defence of these roads; and in this their war-chariots, against which Israel could do nothing in the plain of Jezreel, were of the greatest service (see ver. 19; Josh. xvii. 16). For further particulars respecting the situation of the different towns, see at Josh. xvii. 11. *Dor* only was on the coast of the Mediterranean (see at Josh. xi. 2), and being a commercial emporium of the Phœnicians, would certainly be strongly fortified, and very difficult to conquer.—Ver. 28. As the Israelites grew strong, they made serfs of the Canaanites (see at Gen. xlix. 15). When this took place is not stated; but at all events, it was only done gradually in the course of the epoch of the judges, and not for the first time during the reign of Solomon, as *Bertheau* supposes on the ground of 1 Kings ix. 20–22 and iv. 12, without considering that even in the time of David the Israelites had already attained the highest power they ever possessed, and that there is nothing at variance with this in 1 Kings iv. 12 and ix. 20–22. For it by no means follows, from the appointment of a prefect by Solomon over the districts of Taanach, Megiddo, and Bethshean (1 Kings iv. 12), that these districts had only been conquered by Solomon a short time before, when we bear in mind that Solomon appointed twelve such prefects over all Israel, to remit in regular order the national payments that were required for the maintenance of the regal court. Nor does it follow, that because Solomon employed the descendants of the Canaanites who were left in the land as tributary labourers in the erection of his great buildings, therefore he was the first who succeeded in compelling those Canaanites who were not exterminated when the land was conquered by Joshua, to pay tribute to the different tribes of Israel.

Vers. 29–35. Ephraim did not root out the Canaanites in *Gezer* (ver. 29), as has already been stated in Josh. xvi. 10.—Ver. 30. Zebulun did not root out the Canaanites in *Kitron* and *Nahalol*. Neither of these places has been discovered (see at Josh. xix. 15). —Ver. 31. Asher did not root out those in *Acco*, etc. *Acco*: a seaport town to the north of Carmel, on the bay which is called by its name; it is called *Ake* by *Josephus, Diod. Sic.*, and *Pliny*, and was afterwards named *Ptolemais* from one of the Ptolemys (1 Macc. v. 15, 21, x. 1, etc.; Acts xxi. 7). The Arabs called it *Akka*, and this was corrupted by the crusaders into *Acker* or *Acre*. During the crusades it was a very flourishing maritime and commercial town; but it subsequently fell into decay, and at the present time has a population of about 5000, composed of Mussulmans, Druses, and Christians (see *C. v. Raumer*, Pal. p. 119; *Rob.* Bibl. Res.; and *Ritter*, Erdk. xvi. pp. 725 sqq.). *Sidon*, now *Saida:* see at Josh. xi. 8. *Achlab* is only mentioned here, and is not known. *Achzib, i.e. Ecdippa:* see at Josh. xix. 29. *Helbah* is unknown. *Aphek* is the present *Afkah:* see Josh. xiii. 4, xix. 30. *Rehob* is unknown : see at Josh. xix. 28, 30. As seven out of the twenty-two towns of Asher (Josh. xix. 30) remained in the hands of the Canaanites, including such important places as Acco and Sidon, it is not stated in ver. 32, as in vers. 29, 30, that " the Canaanites dwelt among them," but that " *the Asherites dwelt among the Canaanites*," to show that the Canaanites held the upper hand. And for this reason the expression " they became tributaries" (vers. 30, 35, etc.) is also omitted.—Ver. 33. Naphtali did not root out the inhabitants of *Beth-shemesh* and *Beth-anath*, two fortified towns, the situation of which is still unknown (see at Josh. xix. 38); so that this tribe also dwelt among the Canaanites, but did not make them tributary.—Vers. 34, 35. Still less were the Danites able to drive the Canaanites out of their inheritance. On the contrary, the Amorites forced Dan up into the mountains, and would not suffer them to come down into the plain. But the territory allotted to the Danites was almost all in the plain (see at Josh. xix. 40). If, therefore, they were forced out of that, they were almost entirely excluded from their inheritance. The Amorites emboldened themselves (see at Deut. i. 5) to dwell in *Har-cheres, Ajalon,* and *Shaalbim.* On the last two places see Josh. xix. 42, where *Ir-shemesh* is also mentioned. This combination, and still more the meaning of the names *Har-cheres, i.e.* sun-mountain, and *Ir-shemesh, i.e.* sun-town, make the conjecture a very probable one, that *Har-cheres* is only another name for *Ir-shemesh, i.e.* the present *Ain Shems* (see at Josh. xv. 10, and *Rob.* Pal. iii. pp. 17, 18). This pressure on the part of the Amorites induced a portion of the Danites to emigrate, and seek for an inheritance in the north of Palestine (see chap. xviii.). On the other hand, the Amorites were gradually made tributary by the powerful tribes of Ephraim and Manasseh, who bounded Dan on the north. " *The hand of the house of Joseph lay heavy,*" *sc.* upon the Amorites in the towns already named on the borders of Ephraim. For the expression itself, comp. 1 Sam. v. 6; Ps. xxxii. 4

Ver. 36. In order to explain the supremacy of the Amorites in the territory of Dan, a short notice is added concerning their extension in the south of Palestine. " *The territory of the Amorites was,*" *i.e.* extended (viz. at the time of the conquest of Canaan by the Israelites), " *from the ascent of Akrabbim, from the rock onwards and farther up.*" *Maaleh-Akrabbim* (*ascensus scorpiorum*) was the sharply projecting line of cliffs which intersected the Ghor below the Dead Sea, and formed the southern boundary of the promised land (see at Num. xxxiv. 4 and Josh. xv. 2, 3). מֵהַסֶּלַע, from the rock, is no doubt given as a second point upon the boundary of the Amoritish territory, as the repetition of the מִן clearly shows, notwithstanding the omission of the copula וְ. הַסֶּלַע, the rock, is supposed by the majority of commentators to refer to the city of *Petra*, the ruins of which are still to be seen in the *Wady Musa* (see *Burckhardt*, Syr. pp. 703 sqq.; *Rob.* Pal. ii. pp. 573 sqq., iii. 653), and which is distinctly mentioned in 2 Kings xiv. 7 under the name of הַסֶּלַע, and in Isa. xvi. 1 is called simply סֶלַע. Petra is to the southeast of the Scorpion heights. Consequently, with this rendering the following word וָמַעְלָה (and upward) would have to be taken in the sense of *ulterius* (and beyond), and *Rosenmüller's* explanation would be the correct one : " The Amorites not only extended as far as the town of Petra, or inhabited it, but they even carried their dwellings beyond this towards the tops of those southern mountains." But a description of the territory of the Amorites in its southern extension into Arabia Petræa does not suit the context of the verse, the object of which is to explain how it was that the Amorites were in a condition to force back the Danites out of the plain into the mountains, to say nothing of the fact that it is questionable whether the Amorites ever really spread so far, for which we have neither scriptural testimony nor evidence of any other kind. On this ground even *Bertheau* has taken וָמַעְלָה as denoting the direction upwards, *i.e.* towards the north, which unquestionably suits the usage of מַעְלָה as well as the context of the passage. But it is by no means in harmony with this to understand הַסֶּלַע as referring to *Petra ;* for in that case we should have two boundary points mentioned, the second of which was farther south than the first. Now a historian who had any acquaintance with the topography, would never have described the extent of the Amoritish territory from south to north in such a way as this, commencing with the Scorpion heights on the north, then passing to Petra, which was farther south, and stating that from this point the territory extended farther towards the north. If וָמַעְלָה therefore refers to the extension of the territory of the Amorites in a northerly direction, the expression " from the rock" cannot be understood as relating to the city of Petra, but must denote some other locality well known to the Israelites by that name. Such a locality there undoubtedly was in the rock in the desert of Zin, which had become celebrated through the events that took place at the water of strife (Num. xx. 8, 10), and to which in all probability this expression refers. The rock in question was at the south-west corner of Canaan, on the southern edge of the *Rakhma* plateau, to which the mountains of the Amorites extended on the south-west (comp. Num. xiv. 25, 44, 45, with Deut. i. 44). And this would be very appropriately mentioned here as the south-western boundary of the Amorites, in connection with the Scorpion heights as their south-eastern boundary, for the purpose of giving the southern boundary of the Amorites in its full extent from east to west.

Chap. ii. 1—5. *The Angel of the Lord at Bochim.*—To the cursory survey of the attitude which the tribes of Israel assumed towards the Canaanites who still remained in their inheritances, there is appended an account of the appearance of the angel of the Lord, who announced to the people the punishment of God for their breach of the covenant, of which they had been guilty through their failure to exterminate the Canaanites. This theophany is most intimately connected with the facts grouped together in chap. i., since the design and significance of the historical survey given there are only to be learned from the reproof of the angel; and since both of them have the same aphoristic character, being restricted to the essential facts without entering minutely into any of the attendant details, very much is left in obscurity. This applies more particularly to the statement in ver. 1*a*, " *Then the angel of Jehovah came up from Gilgal to Bochim.*" The " angel of Jehovah" is not a prophet, or some other earthly messenger of Jehovah, either Phinehas or Joshua, as the *Targums*, the *Rabbins*, *Bertheau*, and others assume, but the angel of the Lord who is of one essence with God. In the simple historical narrative a prophet is never called *Maleach Jehovah*. The prophets are always called either נָבִיא or אִישׁ נָבִיא, as in chap. vi. 8, or else "man of God," as in 1 Kings xii. 22, xiii. 1, etc.; and Hag. i. 13 and Mal. iii. 1 cannot be adduced as proofs to the contrary, because in both these passages the purely appellative meaning of the word *Maleach* is established beyond all question by the context itself. Moreover, no prophet ever identifies himself so entirely with God as the angel of Jehovah does here. The prophets always distinguish between themselves and Jehovah, by introducing their words with the declaration "thus saith Jehovah," as the prophet mentioned in chap. vi. 8 is said to have done. On the other hand, it is affirmed that no angel mentioned in the historical books is ever said to have addressed the whole nation, or to have passed from one place to another. But even if it had been a prophet who was speaking, we could not possibly understand his speaking to the whole nation, or "to all the children of Israel," as signifying that he spoke directly to the 600,000 men of Israel, but simply as an address delivered to the whole nation in the persons of its heads or representatives. Thus Joshua spoke to "all the people" (Josh. xxiv. 2), though only the elders of Israel and its heads were assembled round him (Josh. xxiv. 1). And so an angel, or "the angel of the Lord," might also speak to the heads of the nation, when his message had reference to all the people. And there was nothing in the fact of his coming up from Gilgal to Bochim that was at all at variance with the nature of the angel. When the angel of the Lord appeared to Gideon, it is stated in chap. vi. 11 that he came and sat under the terebinth at Ophra; and in the same way the appearance of the angel of the Lord at Bochim might just as naturally be described as coming up to Bochim. The only thing that strikes us as peculiar is his coming up "from Gilgal." This statement must be intimately connected with the mission of the angel, and therefore must contain something more than a simply literal notice concerning his travelling from one place to another. We are not to conclude, however, that the angel of the Lord came from Gilgal, because this town was the gathering-place of the congregation in Joshua's time. Apart altogether from the question discussed in pp. 92 sqq. as to the situation of Gilgal in the different passages of the book of Joshua, such a view as this is overthrown by the circumstance that after the erection of the tabernacle at Shiloh, and during the division of the land, it was not Gilgal but Shiloh which formed the gathering-place of the congregation when the casting of the lots was finished (Josh. xviii. 1, 10). We cannot agree with *H. Witsius*, therefore, who says in his *Miscell. ss.* (i. p. 170, ed. 1736) that "he came from that place, where he had remained for a long time to guard the camp, and where he was thought to be tarrying still;" but must rather assume that his coming up from Gilgal is closely connected with the appearance of the angel-prince, as described in Josh. v. 13, to announce to Joshua the fall of Jericho after the circumcision of the people at Gilgal. Just as on that occasion, when Israel had just entered into the true covenant relation to the Lord by circumcision, and was preparing for the conquest of Canaan, the angel of the Lord appeared to Joshua as the prince of the army of Jehovah, to ensure him of the taking of Jericho; so here after the entrance of the tribes of Israel into their inheritances, when they were beginning to make peace with the remaining Canaanites, and instead of rooting them out were content to make them tributary, the angel of the Lord appeared to the people, to make known to all the children of Israel that by such intercourse with the Canaanites they had broken the covenant of the Lord, and to foretell the punishment which would follow this transgression of the covenant. By the fact, therefore, that he came up from Gilgal, it is distinctly shown that the same angel who gave the whole of Canaan into the hands of the Israelites when Jericho fell, had appeared to them again at Bochim, to make known to them the purposes of God in consequence of their disobedience to the commands of the Lord. How very far it was from being the author's intention to give simply a geographical notice, is also evident from the fact that he merely describes the place where this appearance occurred by the name which was given to it in consequence of the event, viz. *Bochim, i.e.* weepers. The situation of this place is altogether unknown. The rendering of the LXX., ἐπὶ τὸν Κλαυθμῶνα καὶ ἐπὶ Βαιθὴλ καὶ ἐπὶ τὸν οἶκον Ἰσραήλ, gives no clue whatever; for τὸν Κλαυθμῶνα merely arises from a confusion of בְּכִים with בְּכָאִים in 2 Sam. v. 23, which the LXX. have also rendered Κλαυθμών, and ἐπὶ τὸν Βαιθὴλ κ.τ.λ. is an arbitrary interpolation of the translators themselves, who supposed *Bochim* to be in the neighbourhood of Bethel, "in all probability merely because they thought of *Allon-bachuth,* the oak of weeping, at Bethel, which is mentioned in Gen. xxxv. 8" (*Bertheau*). With regard to the *piska* in the middle of the verse, see the remarks on Josh. iv. 1. In his address the angel of the Lord identifies himself with Jehovah (as in Josh. v. 14 compared with vi. 2), by describing himself as having made them to go up out of Egypt and brought them into the land which He sware unto their fathers. There is something very striking in the use of the imperfect אַעֲלֶה in the place of the perfect (cf. chap. vi. 8), as the substance of the address and the continuation of it in the historical tense וָאָבִיא and וָאֹמַר require the preterite. The imperfect is only to be explained on the supposition that it is occasioned by the *imperf. consec.* which follows immediately afterwards and reacts through its proximity. "*I will*

not break my covenant for ever," *i.e.* will keep what I promised when
making the covenant, viz. that I would endow Israel with blessings
and salvation, if they for their part would observe the covenant
duties into which they had entered (see Ex. xix. 5 sqq.), and obey
the commandments of the Lord. Among these was the commandment to enter into no alliance with the inhabitants of that land, viz.
the Canaanites (see Ex. xxiii. 32, 33, xxxiv. 12, 13, 15, 16; Deut.
vii. 2 sqq.; Josh. xxiii. 12). *"Destroy their altars:"* taken verbatim
from Ex. xxxiv. 13, Deut. vii. 5. The words *"and ye have not
hearkened to my voice"* recall to mind Ex. xix. 5. *" What have ye
done"* (מַה־זֹּאת, literally *"* what is this that ye have done") *sc.* in
sparing the Canaanites and tolerating their altars?—Ver. 3. *"And
I also have said to you:"* these words point to the threat already
expressed in Num. xxxiii. 55, Josh. xxiii. 13, in the event of their
not fulfilling the command of God, which threat the Lord would
now fulfil. From the passages mentioned, we may also explain the
expression וְהָיוּ לָכֶם לְצִדִּים, they shall be in your sides, *i.e.* thorns in
your sides. לְצִדִּים is an abbreviated expression for לְצִנִינִים בְּצִדֵּיכֶם in
Num. xxxiii. 55, so that there is no necessity for the conjecture
that it stands for לְצָרִים. The last clause of ver. 3 is formed after
Ex. xxiii. 33.—Vers. 4, 5. The people broke out into loud weeping
on account of this reproof. And since the weeping, from which
the place received the name of *Bochim,* was a sign of their grief on
account of their sin, this grief led on to such repentance that *" they
sacrificed there unto the Lord,"* no doubt presenting sin-offerings
and burnt-offerings, that they might obtain mercy and the forgiveness of their sins. It does not follow from this sacrifice, however,
that the tabernacle or the ark of the covenant was to be found at
Bochim. In any place where the Lord appeared to His people,
sacrifices might be offered to Him (see chap. vi. 20, 26, 28, xiii. 16
sqq.; 2 Sam. xxiv. 25, and the commentary on Deut. xii. 5). On
the other hand, it does follow from the sacrifice at Bochim, where
there was no sanctuary of Jehovah, that the person who appeared
to the people was not a prophet, nor even an ordinary angel, but
the angel of the Lord, who is essentially one with Jehovah.

CONDUCT OF ISRAEL TOWARDS THE LORD, AND TREATMENT OF
ISRAEL BY THE LORD, IN THE TIME OF THE JUDGES.—CHAP.
II. 6—III. 6.

The attitude which the Israelites assumed towards the Canaanites who were left in their possessions, contained the germ of the
peculiar direction given to the development of the nation of God in
the times of the judges. To exhibit the course of this development
in its most general principles, the age which commenced after
Joshua's death is characterized as a period of constant alternation
between idolatry and consequent subjugation by foreign nations
as a punishment from God for the transgression of His covenant
on the one hand, and return to God after receiving chastisement
and consequent deliverance by judges expressly raised up by God
for that purpose on the other. In this way the righteousness of
the holy God is displayed so clearly in the punishment of the
rebellious, and the mercy of the faithful covenant God in His
forgiveness of the penitent, that the history of Israel at that time
exhibits to us an example of the divine holiness and righteousness
on the one hand, and of His grace and mercy on the other, as
displayed in the church of God of all times, as a warning for the
ungodly and for the consolation of the righteous.

Vers. 6–10. The account of this development of the covenant
nation, which commenced after the death of Joshua and his contemporaries, is attached to the book of Joshua by a simple repetition of the closing verses of that book (Josh. xxiv. 28–31) in vers.
6–10, with a few unimportant differences, not only to form a link
between Josh. xxiv. and Judg. ii. 11, and to resume the thread
of the history which was broken off by the summary just given
of the results of the wars between the Israelites and Canaanites
(*Bertheau*), but rather to bring out sharply and clearly the contrast
between the age that was past and the period of the Israelitish
history that was just about to commence. The *vav consec.* attached
to וַיְשַׁלַּח expresses the order of thought and not of time. The
apostasy of the new generation from the Lord (vers. 10 sqq.) was
a necessary consequence of the attitude of Israel to the Canaanites
who were left in the land, as described in chap. i. 1–ii. 5. This
thought is indicated by the *vav consec.* in וַיְשַׁלַּח; so that the meaning
of vers. 6 sqq. as expressed in our ordinary phraseology would be
as follows: Now when Joshua had dismissed the people, and the
children of Israel had gone every one to his own inheritance to take

possession of the land, the people served the Lord as long as Joshua and the elders who survived him were alive; but when Joshua was dead, and that generation (which was contemporaneous with him) had been gathered to its fathers, there rose up another generation after them which knew not the Lord, and also (knew not) the work which He had done to Israel. On the death and burial of Joshua, see at Josh. xxiv. 29, 30. " *Gathered unto their fathers*" corresponds to "gathered to his people" in the Pentateuch (Gen. xxv. 8, 17, xxxv. 29, xlix. 29, 33, etc.: see at Gen. xxv. 8). They " *knew not the Lord,*" *sc.* from seeing or experiencing His wonderful deeds, which the contemporaries of Joshua and Moses had seen and experienced.

In the general survey of the times of the judges, commencing at ver. 11, the falling away of the Israelites from the Lord is mentioned first of all, and at the same time it is distinctly shown how neither the chastisements inflicted upon them by God at the hands of hostile nations, nor the sending of judges to set them free from the hostile oppression, availed to turn them from their idolatry (vers. 11–19). This is followed by the determination of God to tempt and chastise the sinful nation by not driving away the remaining Canaanites (vers. 20–23); and lastly, the account concludes with an enumeration of the tribes that still remained, and the attitude of Israel towards them (chap. iii. 1–6).

Vers. 11–19. *Repeated falling away of the People from the Lord.* —Vers. 11–13. The Israelites did what was evil in the eyes of the Lord (what was displeasing to the Lord); they served *Baalim.* The plural *Baalim* is a general term employed to denote all false deities, and is synonymous with the expression "other gods" in the clause "other gods of the gods of the nations round about them" (the Israelites). This use of the term *Baalim* arose from the fact that Baal was the chief male deity of the Canaanites and all the nations of Hither Asia, and was simply worshipped by the different nations with peculiar modifications, and therefore designated by various distinctive epithets. In ver. 12 this apostasy is more minutely described as forsaking Jehovah the God of their fathers, to whom they were indebted for the greatest blessing, viz. their deliverance out of Egypt, and following other gods of the heathen nations that were round about them (taken *verbatim* from Deut. vi 14, and xiii. 7, 8), and worshipping them. In this way they provoked the Lord to anger (cf. Deut. iv. 25, ix. 18, etc.).—Ver. 13. Thus they forsook Jehovah, and served Baal and the Asthartes. In this case the singular *Baal* is connected with the plural *Ashtaroth*, because the male deities of all the Canaanitish nations, and those that bordered upon Canaan, were in their nature one and the same deity, viz. *Baal*, a sun-god, and as such the vehicle and source of physical life, and of the generative and reproductive power of nature, which was regarded as an effluence from its own being (see *Movers*, Relig. der Phönizier, pp. 184 sqq., and *J. G. Müller* in Herzog's Cyclopædia). *Ashtaroth*, from the singular *Ashtoroth*, which only occurs again in 1 Kings xi. 5, 33, and 2 Kings xxiii. 13, in connection with the Sidonian Astarte, was the general name used to denote the leading female deity of the Canaanitish tribes, a moon-goddess, who was worshipped as the feminine principle of nature embodied in the pure moon-light, and its influence upon terrestrial life. It corresponded to the Greek *Aphrodite*, whose celebrated temple at Askalon is described in *Herod.* i. 105. In chap. iii. 7, *Asheroth* is used as equivalent to *Ashtaroth*, which is used here, chap. x. 6; 1 Sam. vii. 4, xii. 10. The name *Asheroth*[1] was transferred to the deity itself from the idols of this goddess, which generally consisted of wooden columns, and are called *Asherim* in Ex. xxxiv. 13, Deut. vii. 5, xii. 3, xvi. 21. On the other hand, the word *Ashtoreth* is without any traceable etymology in the Semitic dialects, and was probably derived from Upper Asia, being connected with a Persian word signifying a star, and synonymous with 'Ἀστροάρχη, the star-queen of Sabæism (see *Ges.* Thes. pp. 1083–4; *Movers*, p. 606; and *Müller, ut sup.*).

With regard to the nature of the Baal and Astarte worship, into which the Israelites fell not long after the death of Joshua, and in which they continued henceforth to sink deeper and deeper, it is evident from the more precise allusions contained in the history of Gideon, that it did not consist of direct opposition to the worship of Jehovah, or involve any formal rejection of Jehovah, but that it was simply an admixture of the worship of Jehovah with the heathen or Canaanitish nature-worship. Not only was the ephod which Gideon caused to be made in his native town of Ophrah, and after which all Israel went a whoring (chap. viii. 27), an imitation of the high priest's ephod in the worship of Jehovah; but the worship of Baal-berith at Shechem, after which the Israelites went a whoring again when Gideon was dead (chap. viii. 33), was simply a corruption of the worship of Jehovah, in which Baal was put in the place of Jehovah and worshipped in a similar way,

[1] Rendered *groves* in the English version.—Tr.

as we may clearly see from chap. ix. 27. The worship of Jehovah could even be outwardly continued in connection with this idolatrous worship. Just as in the case of these nations in the midst of which the Israelites lived, the mutual recognition of their different deities and religions was manifested in the fact that they all called their supreme deity by the same name, *Baal,* and simply adopted some other epithet by which to define the distinctive peculiarities of each; so the Israelites also imagined that they could worship the Baals of the powerful nations round about them along with Jehovah their covenant God, especially if they worshipped them in the same manner as their covenant God. This will serve to explain the rapid and constantly repeated falling away of the Israelites from Jehovah into Baal-worship, at the very time when the worship of Jehovah was stedfastly continued at the tabernacle in accordance with the commands of the law. The Israelites simply followed the lead and example of their heathen neighbours. Just as the heathen were tolerant with regard to the recognition of the deities of other nations, and did not refuse to extend this recognition even to Jehovah the God of Israel, so the Israelites were also tolerant towards the Baals of the neighbouring nations, whose sensuous nature-worship was more grateful to the corrupt heart of man than the spiritual Jehovah-religion, with its solemn demands for sanctification of life. But this syncretism, which was not only reconcilable with polytheism, but actually rooted in its very nature, was altogether irreconcilable with the nature of true religion. For if Jehovah is the only true God, and there are no other gods besides or beside Him, then the purity and holiness of His nature is not only disturbed, but altogether distorted, by any admixture of His worship with the worship of idols or of the objects of nature, the true God being turned into an idol, and Jehovah degraded into Baal. Looking closely into the matter, therefore, the mixture of the Canaanitish worship of Baal with the worship of Jehovah was actually forsaking Jehovah and serving other gods, as the prophetic author of this book pronounces it. It was just the same with the worship of Baal in the kingdom of the ten tribes, which was condemned by the prophets Hosea and Amos (see *Hengstenberg,* Christology, i. pp. 168 sqq., Eng. trans.).—Vers. 14, 15. On account of this idolatrous worship, the anger of the Lord burned against Israel, so that He gave them up into the hands of spoilers that spoiled them, and sold them into the hands of their enemies. שֹׁסִים from שָׁסָה, alternated with שָׁסַם in יִשְׁפֹּו, to plunder. This word is not met with in the Pentateuch, whereas מָכַר, to sell, occurs in Deut. xxxii. 30, in the sense of giving helplessly up to the foe. *" They could no longer stand before their enemies,"* as they had done under Joshua, and in fact as long as Israel continued faithful to the Lord; so that now, instead of the promise contained in Lev. xxvi. 7, 8, being fulfilled, the threat contained in Lev. xxvi. 17 was carried into execution. *" Whithersoever they went out,"* i.e. in every expedition, every attack that they made upon their enemies, *" the hand of Jehovah was against them for evil, as He had said"* (Lev. xxvi. 17, 36; Deut. xxviii. 25), and *"had sworn unto them."* There is no express oath mentioned either in Lev. xxvi. or Deut. xxviii.; it is implied therefore in the nature of the case, or *in virtute verborum*, as *Seb. Schmidt* affirms, inasmuch as the threats themselves were words of the true and holy God. וַיֵּצֶר לָהֶם מְאֹד, *" and it became to them very narrow,"* i.e. they came into great straits.—— Vers. 16, 17. But the Lord did not rest content with this. He did still more. *" He raised up judges who delivered them out of the hand of their plunderers,"* to excite them to love in return by this manifestation of His love and mercy, and to induce them to repent. But *" they did not hearken even to their judges,"* namely, so as not to fall back again into idolatry, which the judge had endeavoured to suppress. This limitation of the words is supported by the context, viz. by a comparison of vers. 18, 19.—*" But* (כִּי after a negative clause) *they went a whoring after other gods* (for the application of this expression to the spiritual adultery of idolatrous worship, see Ex. xxxiv. 15), *and turned quickly away* (vid. Ex. xxxii. 8) *from the way which their fathers walked in, to hearken to the commandments of the Lord,"* i.e. from the way of obedience to the divine commands. *" They did not so"* (or what was right) *sc.* as their fathers under Joshua had done (cf. ver. 7).—Vers. 18, 19. *" And when the Lord raised them up judges, and was with the judge, and delivered them out of the hand of their enemies all the days of the judge* (i.e. as long as the judge was living), *because the Lord had compassion upon their sighing, by reason of them that oppressed them, and vexed them* (דָּחַק only occurs again as a verb in Joel ii. 8): *it came to pass when the judge was dead, that they returned and acted more corruptly than their fathers,"* i.e. they turned again to idolatry even more grievously than their fathers had done under the previous judges. *" They did not let fall from their deeds,"* i.e. they did not cease from their evil deeds, and *" from their stiffnecked way."* קָשָׁה, hard, is to be understood as in Ex. xxxii. 9 and xxxiii. 3, where Israel is called a hard-necked people which did not bend under obedience to the commandments of God.

Vers. 20–23. *Chastisement of the rebellious Nation.*—Vers. 20, 21. On account of this idolatry, which was not only constantly repeated, but continued to grow worse and worse, the anger of the Lord burned so fiercely against Israel, that He determined to destroy no more of the nations which Joshua had left when he died, before the people that had broken His covenant. In order to set forth this divine purpose most distinctly, it is thrown into the form of a sentence uttered by God through the expression וגו׳ וַיֹּאמֶר. The Lord said, "Because this people has transgressed my covenant, . . . I also will no longer keep my covenant promise (Ex. xxiii. 23, 27 sqq., xxxiv. 10 sqq.), and will no more drive out any of the remaining Canaanites before them" (see Josh. xxiii. 13).—Ver. 22. The purpose of God in this resolution was " *to prove Israel through them* (the tribes that were not exterminated), *whether they* (the Israelites) *would keep the way of the Lord to walk therein* (cf. Deut. viii. 2), *as their fathers did keep it, or not.*" נַסּוֹת לְמַעַן is not dependent upon the verb עָזַב, as *Studer* supposes, which yields no fitting sense; nor can the clause be separated from the preceding one, as *Bertheau* suggests, and connected as a protasis with ver. 23 (this would be a thoroughly unnatural construction, for which Isa. xlv. 4 does not furnish any true parallel); but the clause is attached in the simplest possible manner to the main thought in vers. 20, 21, that is to say, to the words "*and He said*" in ver. 20: Jehovah said, *i.e.* resolved, that He would not exterminate the remaining nations any further, to tempt Israel through them. The plural בָּם, in the place of the singular בָּהּ, which the foregoing דֶּרֶךְ requires, is to be regarded as a *constructio ad sensum, i.e.* to be attributed to the fact, that keeping the way of God really consists in observing the commandments of God, and that this was the thought which floated before the writer's mind. The thought expressed in this verse, that Jehovah would not exterminate the Canaanites before Israel any more, to try them whether they would keep His commandments, just as He had previously caused the people whom He brought out of Egypt to wander in the wilderness for forty years with the very same intention (Deut. viii. 2), is not at variance with the design of God, expressed in Ex. xxiii. 29, 30, and Deut. vii. 22, not to exterminate the Canaanites all at once, lest the land should become waste, and the wild beasts multiply therein, nor yet with the motive assigned in chap. iii. 1, 2. For the determination not to exterminate the Canaanites in one single year, was a different thing from the purpose of God to suspend their gradual extermination altogether. The former purpose had immediate regard to the well-being of Israel; the latter, on the contrary, was primarily intended as a chastisement for its transgression of the covenant; although even this chastisement was intended to lead the rebellious nation to repentance, and promote its prosperity by a true conversion to the Lord. And the motive assigned in chap. ii. 2 is in perfect harmony with this intention, as our explanation of this passage will clearly show.—Ver. 23. In consequence of this resolution, the Lord let these tribes (those mentioned in chap. iii. 3) remain at rest, i.e. quietly, in the land, without exterminating them rapidly. The expression מָהֵר, hastily, quickly, i.e. according to the distinct words of the following clause, through and under Joshua, appears strange after what has gone before. For what is threatened in ver. 21 is not the suspension of rapid extermination, but of any further extermination. This threat, therefore, is so far limited by the word "hastily," as to signify that the Lord would not exterminate any more of these nations so long as Israel persisted in its idolatry. But as soon as and whenever Israel returned to the Lord its God in true repentance, to keep His covenant, the Lord would recall His threat, and let the promised extermination of the Canaanites go forward again. Had Israel not forsaken the Lord its God so soon after Joshua's death, the Lord would have exterminated the Canaanites who were left in the land much sooner than He did, or have carried out their gradual extermination in a much shorter time than was actually the case, in consequence of the continual idolatry of the people.

Chap. iii. 1–6. *Nations which the Lord left in Canaan:* with a repetition of the reason why this was done.—Ver. 1. The reason, which has already been stated in chap. ii. 22, viz. " to prove Israel by them," is still further elucidated here. In the first place (ver. 1), אֶת־יִשְׂרָאֵל is more precisely defined as signifying " *all those who had not known all the wars of Canaan,*" sc. from their own observation and experience, that is to say, the generation of the Israelites which rose up after the death of Joshua. For " *the wars of Canaan*" were the wars which were carried on by Joshua with the almighty help of the Lord for the conquest of Canaan. The whole thought is then still further expanded in ver. 2 as follows: " *only* (for no other purpose than) *that the succeeding generations* (the generations which followed Joshua and his contemporaries) *of the children of Israel,*

that He (Jehovah) *might teach them war, only those who had not
known them* (the wars of Canaan)." The suffix attached to יְדָעוּם
refers to " the wars of Canaan," although this is a feminine noun,
the suffix in the masculine plural being frequently used in connection with a feminine noun.   At first sight it would appear as though
the reason given here for the non-extermination of the Canaanites
was not in harmony with the reason assigned in chap. ii. 22, which
is repeated in ver. 4 of the present chapter.   But the differences
are perfectly reconcilable, if we only give a correct explanation of
the two expressions, " learning war," and the " wars of Canaan."
Learning war in the context before us is equivalent to learning to
make war upon the nations of Canaan.   Joshua and the Israelites
of his time had not overcome these nations by their own human
power or by earthly weapons, but by the miraculous help of their
God, who had smitten and destroyed the Canaanites before the
Israelites.   The omnipotent help of the Lord, however, was only
granted to Joshua and the whole nation, on condition that they
adhered firmly to the law of God (Josh. i. 7), and faithfully
observed the covenant of the Lord; whilst the transgression of that
covenant, even by Achan, caused the defeat of Israel before the
Canaanites (Josh. vii.).   In the wars of Canaan under Joshua,
therefore, Israel had experienced and learned, that the power to
conquer its foes did not consist in the multitude and bravery of its
own fighting men, but solely in the might of its God, which it could
only possess so long as it continued faithful to the Lord.   This
lesson the generations that followed Joshua had forgotten, and consequently they did not understand how to make war.   To impress
this truth upon them,—the great truth, upon which the very existence as well as the prosperity of Israel, and its attainment of the
object of its divine calling, depended; in other words, to teach it by
experience, that the people of Jehovah could only fight and conquer
in the power of its God,—the Lord had left the Canaanites in the
land.   Necessity teaches a man to pray.   The distress into which
the Israelites were brought by the remaining Canaanites was a
chastisement from God, through which the Lord desired to lead
back the rebellious to himself, to keep them obedient to His commandments, and to train them to the fulfilment of their covenant
duties.   In this respect, learning war, *i.e.* learning how the congregation of the Lord was to fight against the enemies of God and of
His kingdom, was one of the means appointed by God to tempt
Israel, or prove whether it would listen to tne commandments of

God (ver. 4), or would walk in the ways of the Lord. If Israel should so learn to war, it would learn at the same time to keep the commandments of God. But both of these were necessary for the people of God. For just as the realization of the blessings promised to the nation in the covenant depended upon its hearkening to the voice of the Lord, so the conflicts appointed for it were also necessary, just as much for the purification of the sinful nation, as for the perpetuation and growth of the kingdom of God upon the earth.—Ver. 3. The enumeration of the different nations rests upon Josh. xiii. 2-6, and, with its conciseness and brevity, is only fully intelligible through the light thrown upon it by that passage. The five princes of the Philistines are mentioned singly there. According to Josh. xiii. 4 sqq., " *all the Canaanites and the Sidonians and the Hivites*," are the Canaanitish tribes dwelling in northern Canaan, by the Phœnician coast and upon Mount Lebanon. " *The Canaanites :*" viz. those who dwelt along the sea-coast to the south of Sidon. *The Hivites :* those who were settled more in the heart of the country, " from the mountains of Baal-hermon up to the territory of Hamath." *Baal-hermon* is only another name for *Baal-gad,* the present *Banjas,* under the Hermon (cf. Josh. xiii. 5). When it is stated still further in ver. 4, that " they were left in existence (*i.e.* were not exterminated by Joshua) to prove Israel by them," we are struck with the fact, that besides the Philistines, only these northern Canaanites are mentioned ; whereas, according to chap. i., many towns in the centre of the land were also left in the hands of the Canaanites, and therefore here also the Canaanites were not yet exterminated, and became likewise a snare to the Israelites, not only according to the word of the angel of the Lord (chap. ii. 3), but also because the Israelites who dwelt among these Canaanitish tribes contracted marriages with them, and served their gods. This striking circumstance cannot be set aside, as *Bertheau* supposes, by the simple remark, that " the two lists (that of the countries which the tribes of Israel did not conquer after Joshua's death in chap. i., and the one given here of the nations which Joshua had not subjugated) must correspond on the whole," since the correspondence referred to really does not exist. It can only be explained on the ground that the Canaanites who were left in the different towns in the midst of the land, acquired all their power to maintain their stand against Israel from the simple fact that the Philistines on the south-west, and several whole tribes of Canaanites in the north, had been left by Joshua neither exterminated nor even conquered, inasmuch as they so crippled the power of the Israelites by wars and invasions of the Israelitish territory, that they were unable to exterminate those who remained in the different fortresses of their own possessions. Because, therefore, the power to resist the Israelites and oppress them for a time resided not so much in the Canaanites who were dwelling in the midst of Israel, as in the Philistines and the Canaanites upon the mountains of Lebanon who had been left unconquered by Joshua, these are the only tribes mentioned in this brief survey as the nations through which the Lord would prove His people.—Vers. 5, 6. But the Israelites did not stand the test. Dwelling in the midst of the Canaanites, of whom six tribes are enumerated, as in Ex. iii. 8, 17, etc. (see at Deut. vii. 1), they contracted marriages with them, and served their gods, contrary to the express prohibition of the Lord in Ex. xxxiv. 16, xxiii. 24, and Deut. vii. 3, 4.

II.—HISTORY OF THE PEOPLE OF ISRAEL UNDER THE JUDGES.

CHAP. III. 7–XVI. 31.

In order that we may be able to take a distinct survey of the development of the Israelites in the three different stages of their history during the times of the judges, the first thing of importance to be done is to determine *the chronology of the period of the judges,* inasmuch as not only have greatly divergent opinions prevailed upon this point, but hypotheses have been set up, which endanger and to some extent directly overthrow the historical character of the accounts which the book of Judges contains.[1] If we take a superficial glance at the chronological data contained in

---

[1] *Rud. Chr. v. Bennigsen,* for example, reckons up fifty different calculations, and the list might be still further increased by the addition of both older and more recent attempts (see *Winer,* Bibl. Real-Wörterb. ii. pp. 327–8). *Lepsius* (Chronol. der Æg. i. 315–6, 365 sqq. and 377–8) and *Bunsen* (Ægypten, i. pp. 209 sqq. iv. 318 sqq., and Bibelwerk, i. pp. ccxxxvii. sqq.), starting from the position maintained by *Ewald* and *Bertheau,* that the chronological data of the book of Judges are for the most part to be regarded as round numbers, have sought for light to explain the chronology of the Bible in the darkness of the history of ancient Egypt, and with their usual confidence pronounce it an indisputable truth that the whole of the period of the Judges did not last longer than from 169 to 187 years.

the book, it appears a very simple matter to make the calculation required, inasmuch as the duration of the different hostile oppressions, and also the length of time that most of the judges held their office, or at all events the duration of the peace which they secured for the nation, are distinctly given. The following are the numbers that we find:—

1. Oppression by Chushan-rishathaim . .	(chap. iii. 8), .	8 years.
Deliverance by Othniel, and rest . .	(chap. iii. 11), .	40 ,,
2. Oppression by the Moabites . . .	(chap. iii. 14), .	18 ,,
Deliverance by Ehud, and rest . .	(chap. iii. 30), .	80 ,,
3. Oppression by the Canaanitish king Jabin .	(chap. iv. 3), .	20 ,,
Deliverance by Deborah and Barak, and rest	(chap. v. 31), .	40 ,,
4. Oppression by the Midianites . . .	(chap. vi. 1), .	7 ,,
Deliverance by Gideon, and rest . .	(chap. viii. 28), .	40 ,,
Abimelech's reign	(chap. ix. 22), .	3 ,,
Tola, judge	(chap. x. 2), .	23 ,,
Jair, judge	(chap. x. 3), .	22 ,,
	Total, .	301 years.
5. Oppression by the Ammonites . . .	(chap. x. 8), .	18 ,,
Deliverance by Jephthah, who judged Israel	(chap. xii. 7), .	6 ,,
Ibzan, judge	(chap. xii. 9), .	7 ,,
Elon, judge	(chap. xii. 11), .	10 ,,
Abdon, judge	(chap. xii. 14), .	8 ,,
6. Oppression by the Philistines . . .	(chap. xiii. 1), .	40 ,,

At this time Samson judged Israel for 20 years (chap. xv. 20; xvi. 31).

	Total, .	390 years.

For if to this we add (a) the time of Joshua, which is not distinctly mentioned, and . . . . 20 ,,

(b.) The time during which Eli was judge (1 Sam. iv. 18), . . 40 ,,

We obtain . 450 years.[1]

And if we add still further—

(c.) The times of Samuel and Saul combined, . . . 40 ,,

(d.) The reign of David (2 Sam. v. 4; 1 Kings ii. 11), . . 40 ,,

(e.) The reign of Solomon to the building of the temple (1 Kings vi. 1), 3 ,,

The whole time from the entrance of Israel into Canaan to the building of the temple amounted to . . . . . 533 years.

---

[1] The earlier chronologists discovered a confirmation of this as the length of time that the period of the judges actually lasted in Acts xiii. 20, where Paul in his speech at Antioch in Pisidia says, according to the *textus receptus*, " After that He gave unto them judges about the space of four hundred and fifty years

Or if we add the forty years spent in the wilderness, the time that elapsed between the exodus from Egypt and the building of the temple was 573 years. But the interval was not so long as this; for, according to 1 Kings vi. 1, Solomon built the house of the Lord in the 480th year after the children of Israel came out of Egypt, and in the fourth year of his reign. And no well-founded objections can be raised as to the correctness and historical credibility of this statement. It is true that the LXX. have "the 440th year" instead of the 480th; but this reading is proved to be erroneous by *Aquila* and *Symmachus*, who adopt the number 480 in common with all the rest of the ancient versions, and it is now almost unanimously rejected (see *Ewald*, Gesch. ii. p. 479). In all probability it owed its origin to an arbitrary mode of computing the period referred to by reckoning eleven generations of forty years each (see *Ed. Preuss;* die Zeitrechnung der LXX. pp. 78 sqq.). On the other hand, the number 480 of the Hebrew text cannot rest upon a mere reckoning of generations, since the year and month of Solomon's reign are given in 1 Kings vi. 1; and if we deduct this date from the 480, there remain 477 or 476 years, which do not form a cyclical number at all.[1] Again, the exodus of Israel from Egypt

---

until Samuel the prophet." The discrepancy between this verse and the statement in 1 Kings vi. 1, that Solomon built the temple in the four hundred and eightieth year after the children of Israel were come out of Egypt, many have endeavoured to remove by a remark, which is correct in itself, viz. that the apostle merely adopted the traditional opinion of the Jewish schools, which had been arrived at by adding together the chronological data of the book of Judges, without entering into the question of its correctness, as it was not his intention to instruct his hearers in chronology. But this passage cannot prove anything at all; for the reading given in the *lect. rec.* is merely founded upon *Cod. Cant.* and *Laud.*, and the text of *Matthæi;* whilst the oldest reading not only according to the *Codd. Al., Vat., Ephr. S. rescr.*, but according to the *Cod. Sinait. ed. Tischendorf* and several *minuscula*, as well as the *Copt. Sahid. Arm. Vers.* and *Vulg.*, is, καὶ καθελὼν ἔθνη ἑπτὰ ἐν γῇ Χαναὰν κατεκληρονόμησεν αὐτοῖς τὴν γῆν αὐτῶν ὡς ἔτεσιν τετρακοσίοις καὶ πεντήκοντα, καὶ μετὰ ταῦτα ἔδωκεν κριτὰς ἕως Σαμουὴλ τ. πρ. This text is rendered thus in the *Vulgate: et destruens gentes septem in terra Chanaan sorte distribuit eis terram eorum quasi post quadringentos et quinquaginta annos: et post hæc dedit judices usque ad Samuel prophetam,* and can hardly be understood in any other sense than this, that Paul reckoned 450 as the time that elapsed between the call of Abraham (or the birth of Isaac) and the division of the land, namely 215 + 215 (according to the Alex. reading of Ex. xii. 40 : see the comm. on this passage) + 40 = 470, or about 450.

[1] *Bertheau* has quite overlooked this when he endeavours to make the 480 years from the exodus to the building of the temple into a cyclical number, and

was an "epoch-making" event, which was fixed in the recollection of the people as no other ever was, so that allusions to it run through the whole of the Old Testament. Moreover, the very fact that it does not tally with the sum total of the numbers in the book of Judges is an argument in favour of its correctness; whereas all the chronological calculations that differ from this bring us back to these numbers, such, for example, as the different statements of Josephus, who reckons the period in question at 592 years in Ant. viii. 3, 1, and on the other hand, at 612 years in Ant. xx. 10 and c. Ap. ii. 2.[1] Lastly, it may easily be shown that there are several things assumed in this chronological survey which have no foundation in the text. This applies both to the assumed succession of the Ammonitish and Philistine oppressions, and also to the introduction of the forty years of Eli's life as judge after or in addition to the forty years that the Philistines ruled over Israel.

The current view, that the forty years of oppression on the part of the Philistines did not commence till after the death of Jephthah or Abdon, is apparently favoured, no doubt, by the circumstance, that this oppression is not described till after the death of Abdon (chap. xii. 15), and is introduced with the usual formula, "And the

appeals in support of this to 1 Chron. vi. 35 sqq. (cf. v. 29 sqq.), where twelve generations are reckoned from Aaron to Ahimaaz, the contemporary of David. But it is perfectly arbitrary on his part to include Ahimaaz, who was a boy in the time of David (2 Sam. xv. 27, 36, xviii. 19, 22, 27 sqq.), as the representative of a generation that was contemporaneous with David; whereas it was not Ahimaaz, but his father Zadok, *i.e.* the eleventh high priest from Aaron, who anointed Solomon as king (1 Kings i. 39, ii, 35), and therefore there had been only eleven high priests from the exodus to the building of the temple. If therefore this period was to be divided into generations of forty years each on the ground of the genealogies in the Chronicles, there could only be eleven generations counted, and this is just what the LXX. have done.

[1] *Josephus* adds together the numbers which occur in the book of Judges. Reckoning from the invasion of Chushan-rishathaim to the forty years' oppression of the Philistines (inclusive), these amount to 390 years, if we regard Samson's twenty years as forming part of the Philistine oppression, or to 410 years if they are reckoned separately. Let us add to this the forty years of the journey through the wilderness, the twenty-five years which Josephus assigns to Joshua (Ant. v. 1, 29), the forty years of Eli, the twelve years which he allots to Samuel before the election of Saul as king (vi. 13, 5), and the forty years which he reckons to Samuel and Saul together, and lastly, the forty and a half years of David's reign and the four years of Solomon's up to the time when the temple was built, and we obtain $40 + 25 + 40 + 12 + 40 + 40\frac{1}{2} + 4 = 201\frac{1}{2}$ years; and these added to 390 make $591\frac{1}{2}$, or added to 410 they amount to 611 years.

children of Israel did evil again in the sight of the Lord," etc. (chap. xiii. 1). But this formula, taken by itself, does not furnish any certain proof that the oppression which it introduces did not take place till after what has been already described, especially in the absence of any more definite statement, such as the clause introduced into chap. iv. 1, "when Ehud was dead," or the still more definite remark, that the land had rest so many years (chap. iii. 11, 30, v. 31; cf. chap. viii. 32). Now in the case before us, instead of any such statement as to time, we find the general remark in chap. x. 6 sqq., that when the Israelites sank into idolatry again, Jehovah sold them into the hands of the Philistines, and into the hands of the children of Ammon; and after this there simply follows an account of the oppression on the part of the Ammonites, and the eventual deliverance effected by Jephthah (chap. x. 8– xii. 7), together with an enumeration of three judges who succeeded Jephthah (chap. xii. 8–15); but we learn nothing further about the oppression on the part of the Philistines which is mentioned in chap. x. 7. When, therefore, it is still further related, in chap. xiii. 1, that the Lord delivered the Israelites into the hand of the Philistines forty years, this cannot possibly refer to another oppression on the part of the Philistines subsequent to the one noticed in chap. x. 7; but the true explanation must be, that the historian proceeds here for the first time to describe the oppression noticed in chap. x. 7, and introduces his description with the formula he generally adopted: "And the children of Israel did evil again in the sight of the Lord," etc. The oppression itself, therefore, commenced at the same time as that of the Ammonites, and continued side by side with it; but it lasted much longer, and did not come to an end till a short time before the death of Elon the judge. This is confirmed beyond all doubt by the fact, that although the Ammonites crossed the Jordan to fight against Judah, Benjamin, and Ephraim, it was chiefly the tribes of Israel who dwelt on the other side of the Jordan that were oppressed by them (chap. x. 8, 9), and that it was only by these tribes that Jephthah was summoned to make war upon them, and was elected as their head and prince (chap. xi. 5–11), and also that it was only the Ammonites in the country to the east of the Jordan whom he subdued then before the Israelites (chap. xi. 32, 33). From this it is very evident that Jephthah, and his successors Ibzan, Elon, and Abdon, were not judges over all Israel, and neither fought against the Philistines nor delivered Israel from the oppression of those enemies who invaded the land from the south-west; so that the omission of the expression, "the land had rest," etc., from chap. xi. and xii., is very significant.[1]

But if the Ammonitish and Philistine oppressions occurred at the same time, of course only one of them must be taken into account in our chronological calculations as to the duration of the period of the judges; and the one selected must be the one to the close of which the chronological data of the next period are immediately appended. But this is not the case with the account of the Ammonitish oppression, of the deliverance effected by Jephthah, and of the judges who succeeded him (Ibzan, Elon, and Abdon), because the chronological thread of this series of events is broken off with the death of Abdon, and is never resumed again. It is so, however, with the Philistine oppression, which is said to have lasted forty years, though the termination of it is not given in the book of Judges. Samson merely began to deliver Israel out of the power of the Philistines (chap. xiii. 5), but did not accomplish their complete deliverance. He judged Israel for twenty years in the days

[1] Even *Hitzig*, who denies that the oppression of the Philistines was contemporaneous with that of the Ammonites, is obliged to acknowledge that " it is true, the author first of all disposed very properly of the Ammonitish war before entering into the details of the war with the Philistines, with which it had no connection, and which was not brought to a close so soon." When therefore, notwithstanding this, he adduces as evidence that they were not contemporaneous, the fact that " according to the context, and to all analogy (cf. chap. iv. 1, iii. 11, 12), the author intends to write, in chap. xiii. 1, that after the death of Abdon, when there was no judge in Israel, the nation fell back into its former lawlessness, and as a punishment was given up to the Philistines," a more careful study of the passages cited (chap. iv. 1, iii. 11, 12) will soon show that the supposed analogy does not exist at all, since the expression, " the land had rest," etc., really occurs in both instances (see chap. iii. 11 and 31), whereas it is omitted before chap. xiii. 1. The still further assertion, however, that the account of the Philistine war ought to have followed immediately upon that of the war with the Ammonites, if the intention was to describe this with equal fulness, has no force whatever. If neither Jephthah nor the three judges who followed him had anything to do with the Philistines, if they merely judged the tribes that were oppressed and threatened by the Ammonites, it was natural that everything relating to them should be attached to the account of the defeat of the Ammonites, in order that there might be no unnecessary separation of what was so intimately connected together. And whilst these objections are thus proved to have no force, the objection raised to the contemporaneous occurrence of the two oppressions is wrecked completely upon the distinct statement in chap. x. 7, that Jehovah sold the Israelites into the hands of the Philistines and Ammonites, which Hitzig can only get over by declaring, without the slightest foundation, that the words " into the hands of the Philistines" are spurious, simply because they stand in the way of his own assumption.

of the Philistines, *i.e.* during the oppression of the Philistines (chap. xv. 20); consequently the twenty years of his labours must not be taken into account in the chronology of the period of the judges, inasmuch as they are all included in the forty years of the Philistines' rule. At the death of Samson, with which the book of Judges closes, the power of the Philistines was not yet broken; and in chap. iv. of the first book of Samuel we find the Philistines still fighting against the Israelites, and that with such success that the Israelites were defeated by them, and even lost the ark of the covenant. This war must certainly be a continuation of the Philistine oppression, to which the acts of Samson belonged, since the termination of that oppression is not mentioned in the book of Judges; and on the other hand, the commencement of the oppression referred to in 1 Sam. iv. 9 sqq. is not given in the book of Samuel. Consequently even *Hitzig* supports the view which I have expressed, that the forty years' supremacy of the Philistines, noticed in Judg. xiii. 1, is carried on into the book of Samuel, and extends to 1 Sam. vii. 3, 7, and that it was through Samuel that it was eventually brought to a termination (1 Sam. vii. 10 sqq.). But if this is established, then the forty years during which Eli was judge cannot have followed the Philistine oppression and the deeds performed by Samson, and therefore must not be reckoned separately. For since Eli died in consequence of the account of the capture of the ark by the Philistines (1 Sam. iv. 18), and seven months (1 Sam. vi. 1) and twenty years elapsed after this catastrophe before the Philistines were defeated and humiliated by Samuel (1 Sam. vii. 2), only the last half of the forty years of Eli's judicial life falls within the forty years of the Philistine rule over Israel, whilst the first half coincides with the time of the judge Jair. Eli himself was not a judge in the strict sense of the word. He was neither commander of the army, nor secular governor of the nation, but simply the high priest; and in this capacity he administered the civil law in the supreme court, altogether independently of the question whether there was a secular governor at the time or not. After the death of Eli, Israel continued for more than twenty years utterly prostrate under the yoke of the Philistines. It was during this period that Samson made the Philistines feel the power of the God of Israel, though he could not deliver the Israelites entirely from their oppression. Samuel laboured at the same time, as the prophet of the Lord, to promote the inward and spiritual strength of Israel, and that with such success, that the people came to Mizpeh at his summons, and there put away the strange gods that they had hitherto worshipped, and worshipped the Lord alone; after which the Lord hearkened to Samuel's prayer, and gave them a complete victory over the Philistines (1 Sam. vii. 2–11). After this victory, which was gained not very long after the death of Samson, Samuel undertook the supreme government of Israel as judge, and eventually at their own desire, and with the consent of God, gave them a king in the person of Saul the Benjaminite. This was not till Samuel himself was old, and had appointed as his successors in the office of judge his own sons, who did not walk in their father's ways (1 Sam. viii.–x.). Even under Saul, however, Samuel continued to the very end of his life to labour as the prophet of the Lord for the well-being of Israel, although he laid down his office of judge as soon as Saul had been elected king. He announced to Saul how he had been rejected by God on account of his disobedience; he anointed David as king; and his death did not occur till after Saul had begun to be troubled by the evil spirit, and to plot for David's life (1 Sam. xxv. 1), as we may learn from the fact that David fled to Samuel at Ramah when Saul resolved to slay him (1 Sam. xix. 18).

How long Samuel judged Israel between the victory gained at Ebenezer (1 Sam. vii.) and the election of Saul as king of Israel, is not stated in the Old Testament, nor even the length of Saul's reign, as the text of 1 Sam. xiii. 1 is corrupt. But we shall not be very far from the truth, if we set down about forty years as the time covered by the official life of Samuel as judge after that event and the reign of Saul, and reckon from seventeen to nineteen years as the duration of Samuel's judgeship, and from twenty to twenty-two as the length of Saul's reign. For it is evident from the accounts that we possess of the lives and labours of Samuel and Saul, that Saul did not reign forty years (the time given by Paul in Acts xiii. 21, according to the traditional opinion current in the Jewish schools), but at the most from twenty to twenty-two; and this is now pretty generally admitted (see at 1 Sam. xiii. 1). When David was chosen king of Judah at Hebron after the death of Saul, he was thirty years old (2 Sam. v. 1–4), and can hardly have been anointed king by Samuel at Bethlehem before the age of twenty. For though his father Jesse was still living, and he himself was the youngest of Jesse's eight sons, and was feeding the flock (1 Sam. xvi. 6–12), and even after this is still described as נַעַר (1 Sam. xvii. 42, 55), Jesse was זָקֵן (an old man) at the time (1 Sam. xvii. 12), at any rate sixty years old or more, so that his eldest son might be forty years old, and David, the youngest, as much as twenty. For נַעַר was not only applied to a mere boy, but to a young man approaching twenty; and the keeping of sheep was not merely a task performed by shepherd boys, but also by the grown-up sons of a family, among whom we must certainly reckon David, since he had already contended with lions and bears in the steppe, and slain these beasts of prey (1 Sam. xvii. 34–36), and shortly afterwards was not only recommended to king Saul by his courtiers, as " a mighty valiant man, and a man of war, and wise in speech," to cheer up the melancholy king by his playing upon the harp (1 Sam. xvi. 18), but also undertook to fight with the giant Goliath (1 Sam. xvii.), and was placed in consequence over the men of war, and was afterwards made captain of a thousand, and betrothed to his daughter Michal (1 Sam. xviii. 5, 13, 17 sqq.). But if David was anointed by Samuel at the age of about twenty years, Saul could not have reigned more than ten years after that time, as David was made king at the age of thirty. And he cannot have reigned much longer before that time. For, apart from the fact that everything which is related of his former wars and deeds could easily have occurred within the space of ten years, the circumstance that Samuel lived till the last years of Saul's reign, and died but a few years before Saul's death (1 Sam. xxv. 1), precludes the assumption that he reigned any longer than that. For Samuel was already so old that he had appointed his sons as judges, whereupon the people desired a king, and assigned as the reason, that Samuel's sons did not walk in his ways (1 Sam. viii. 1–4), from which it is very evident that they had already filled the office of judge for some considerable time. If we add to this the fact that Samuel was called to be a prophet before the death of Eli, and therefore was no doubt twenty-five or thirty years old when Eli died, and that twenty years and seven months elapsed between the death of Eli and the defeat of the Philistines, so that Samuel may have been about fifty years old at that time, and that he judged the people from this time forward till he had become an old man, and then gave the nation a king in the person of Saul, we cannot assign more than forty years as the interval between the defeat of the Philistines and the death of Saul, without attributing to Samuel an age of more than ninety years, and therefore we cannot reckon more than forty or thirty-nine years as the time that intervened between the installation of Samuel in his office as judge and the commencement of the reign of Saul.

According to this, the chronology of the times of the judges may be arranged as follows :—

a. From the oppression of Chushan-rishathaim to the death of Jair
the judge (*vid.* p. 277), ... 301 years.
b. Duration of the Philistine oppression, ... 40 „
c. Judgeship of Samuel and reign of Saul, . . . 39 „
d. David's reign (7½ and 33 years), ... 40 „
e. Solomon's reign to the building of the temple, . , . 3 „

423 years.

a. The wandering in the desert, ... 40 „
b. The time between the entrance into Canaan and the division of
the land, ... 7 „
c. From the division of Canaan to the invasion of Chushan-rishathaim, ... 10 „

480 years.

These numbers are as thoroughly in harmony with 1 Kings vi. 1, and also with the statement made by Jephthah in his negotiations with the king of the Ammonites, that Israel dwelt in Heshbon and the cities along the bank of the Arnon for three hundred years (Judg. xi. 26), as we could possibly expect so general a statement in round numbers to be. For instance, as the chronological data of the book of Judges give 301 years as the interval between the invasion of Chushan-rishathaim and the commencement of the Ammonitish oppression, and as only about ten years elapsed between the division of Canaan, after which the tribes on the east of the Jordan first established themselves firmly in Gilead, and the invasion of Chushan, the Israelites had dwelt 310 years in the land on the other side of the Jordan at the time of Jephthah's negotiations with the Ammonites, or at the most 328, admitting that these negotiations may possibly not have taken place till towards the end of the eighteen years' oppression on the part of the Ammonites, so that Jephthah could appeal with perfect justice to the fact that they had been in possession of the land for 300 years.

This statement of Jephthah, however, furnishes at the same time an important proof that the several chronological data contained in our book are to be regarded as historical, and also that the events are to be reckoned as occurring successively; so that we have no right to include the years of oppression in the years of rest, as is frequently done, or to shorten the whole period from Othniel to Jephthah by arbitrary assumptions of synchronisms, in direct opposition to the text. This testimony removes all foundation from the hypothesis that the number forty which so frequently occurs is a so-called round number, that is to say, is nothing more than a number derived from a general estimate of the different periods according to generations, or cyclical periods. For if the sum total of the different chronological notices tallies on the whole with the actual duration of the period in question as confirmed by this testimony, the several notices must be regarded as historically true, and that all the more because the greater part of these data consist of such numbers as 6, 8, 18, 20, 22, 23, which can neither be called round nor cyclical. Moreover, the purely cyclical significance of the number forty among the Israelites must first of all be proved. Even *Ewald* (Gesch. ii. pp. 480, 481) most justly observes, that " it is very easy to say that the number forty was a round number in the case of different nations ; but this round number must first of all have had its origin in life, and therefore must have had its limited application." If, however, we look more closely at the different occasions on which the space of forty years is mentioned, between the exodus from Egypt and the building of the temple, we shall find that at any rate the first and last passages contain very definite notices of time, and cannot possibly be regarded as containing merely round or cyclical numbers. In the case of the forty years' wandering in the wilderness, this is placed beyond the reach of doubt by the fact that even the months are given of both the second and fortieth years (Num. x. 11, xx. 1 ; Deut. i. 3), and the intervening space is distinctly stated to have been thirty-eight years (Deut. ii. 14). And the forty years that David is said to have reigned also give the precise number, since he reigned seven and a half years at Hebron, and thirty-three at Jerusalem (2 Sam. v. 4, 5 ; 1 Kings ii. 11). Between these two extreme points we certainly meet with the number forty five times : viz. forty years of rest under Othniel (Judg. iii. 11), the same under Barak and Deborah (chap. v. 31), and the same again under Gideon (chap. viii. 28) ; also forty years of oppression by the Philistines (chap. xiii. 1), and the forty years that Eli was judge (1 Sam. iv. 18) ; and in addition to these, we find eighty years of rest after Ehud's victory (Judg. iii. 30). But there are also twelve or thirteen passages in which we find either odd numbers, or at all events numbers that cannot be called cyclical or round (viz. Judg. iii. 8, 14, iv. 3, vi. 1, ix. 22, x. 2, 3, xii. 7, 9, 11, 14, xv. 20, xvi. 31). What is there then to justify our calling the number forty cyclical or round ? Is it the impossibility or improbability that in the course of 253 years Israel should have had rest from hostile oppression on three occasions for forty years, and on one for eighty? Is there anything impossible in this? Certainly not. Is there even an improbability? If there be, surely improbabilities have very often been perfectly true. And in the case before us, the appearance itself loses all significance, when we consider that although if we take entire years the number forty is repeated, yet it cannot be taken so literally as that we are to understand that entire years are intended every time. If David's reign is reckoned as forty years in 2 Sam. v. 4, although, according to ver. 5, he reigned seven years and six months in Hebron and thirty-three years in Jerusalem, it may also be the case that, although forty years is the number given in the book of Judges, the period referred to may actually have been only thirty-nine years and a half, or may have been forty and a half. To this must be added the fact that the time during which the war with the enemy lasted is also included in the years of rest; and this must always have occupied several months, and may sometimes have lasted even more than a year. Now, if we give all these circumstances their due weight, every objection that can be raised as to the correctness and historical credibility of the chronological data of the book of Judges vanishes away, whilst all the attempts that have been made to turn these data into round or cyclical numbers are so arbitrary as to need no special refutation whatever.[1]

[1] The principal representatives of this hypothesis are *Ewald* and his pupil *Bertheau.* According to *Ewald* (Gesch. ii. pp. 473 sqq.), the twelve judges from Othniel to Samson form the historical groundwork of the book, although there are distinct traces that there were many more such rulers, because it was only of these that any reminiscences had been preserved. When, therefore, after the expiration of the whole of this period, the desire arose to bring out into distinct prominence the most important points connected with it, the first thing that was done was to group together these twelve judges, with such brief remarks as we find in the case of five of them (Tola, Jair, Ibzan, Elon, and Abdon) in chap. x. 1–5 and xii. 8–15. In their case, too, the precise time was given, so far as it could be still remembered. But, independently of this, the attempt was also made to connect the order of the many alternations of war and peace during these 480 years which occurred, according to 1 Kings vi. 1, between the exodus from Egypt and the building of Solomon's temple, to certain grand and easily remembered divisions; and for this the number forty at once presented itself. For since, according to the oldest traditions, Israel spent forty years in the wilderness, and since David also reigned forty years, it might easily be regarded as a suitable thing to divide the whole into twelve equal parts, and to assign to each forty years a great hero and some striking event: *e.g.* (1) Moses and the wilderness; (2) Joshua and the prosperous rule of the elders; (3) the war with Chushan-rishathaim, and Othniel; (4) the Moabites and

The historical character of the chronological data of the book of Judges being thus established, we obtain a continuous chronology for the history of the Israelitish nation, as we may see from the following survey, to which we append a calculation of the years before Christ :—

Ehud; (5) the Aramæans and Jair; (6) the Canaanites under Jabin, and Deborah; (7) the Midianites and Gideon; (8) Tola, with whose opponents we are not acquainted; (9) the Ammonites and Philistines, or Jephthah and Samson; (10) the Philistines and Eli; (11) Samuel and Saul; (12) David. "Finally, then, these twelve judges from Othniel to Samson were necessarily connected with this different mode of reckoning, so that the several numbers, as well as the order in which the judges occur, which show so evidently (?) that the last editor but one compiled the section extending from chap. iii. to xvi. out of a great variety of sources, *must* have been the resultant of many changes." But *Ewald* looks in vain for any reason for this "must." And the question starts up at once, how could the idea ever have entered any one's mind of dividing these 480 years, from the exodus to the building of the temple, among the twelve judges in this particular manner; that to all the judges, concerning whom it was not known how long their period of labour lasted, forty years each were assigned, when it was known that Israel had wandered forty years in the wilderness, that Joshua had governed forty years with the elders, and Samuel and Saul together had ruled for the same time, and David also, so that there only remained for the judges from Othniel to Samson $480 - 4 \times 40$, *i.e.* only 320 years, or, deducting the first three or four years of Solomon's reign, only 317 or 316 years? These years, if divided among twelve judges, would give only twenty-six or twenty-seven years for each. Or how did they come to allot eighty years to Ehud, and only twenty-two to Jair and twenty-three to Tola, if the two latter had also conquered the hostile oppressors of Israel? And lastly, why was Shamgar left without any, when he delivered Israel from the Philistines? To these and many other questions the author of this hypothesis is unable to give any answer at all; and the arbitrary nature of his mode of manufacturing history is so obvious, that it is unnecessary to waste words in proving it. It is no better with *Bertheau's* hypothesis (Judg. pp. xvi. sqq.). According to this hypothesis, out of the twelve generations from Moses to David which he derives from 1 Chron. vi. 35 sqq., only six (or 240 years) belong to the judges from Othniel to Samson. These have been variously reckoned. One calculation takes them as six generations of forty years each; another reckons them more minutely, adopting smaller numbers which were assigned to the twelve judges and the son of Gideon. But six generations and twelve judges could not be combined in any other way than by assigning twenty years to each judge. Now there was not a single judge who judged Israel for twenty years, with the exception of Samson. And the total number of the years that they judged is not 240, but 296 years ($40 + 80 + 40 + 40 + 23 + 22 + 6 + 7 + 10 + 8 + 20 + x$). Consequently we do not find any trace throughout the book, that the period of the judges was reckoned as consisting of six generations of forty years each. (Compare with this a more elaborate refutation by *Bachmann*, pp. 3 sqq.).

CHRONOLOGICAL SURVEY OF THE PRINCIPAL EVENTS FROM THE EXODUS

TO THE BUILDING OF SOLOMON'S TEMPLE.

The Principal Events.	Dura-tion.	Years before the Birth of Christ.
Exodus of Israel from Egypt, ...	—	1492
The law given at Sinai, ...	—	1492—1491
Death of Aaron and Moses in the fortieth year of the wandering in the desert, ...	40	1453
Conquest of Canaan by Joshua, ...	7	1452—1445
From the division of the land to the invasion of Chushan-rishathaim, ...	10	1445—1435
Death of Joshua, ...	—	c. 1442
Wars of the tribes of Israel with the Canaanites, . .	—	1442 onwards
War of the congregation with Benjamin, . .	—	c. 1436
Oppression by Chushan-rishathaim, ...	8	1435—1427
Deliverance by Othniel, and rest, ...	40	1427—1387
Oppression by the Moabites, ...	18	1387—1369
Deliverance by Ehud, and rest, ...	80	1369—1289
Victory of Shamgar over the Philistines, . .	—	
Oppression by Jabin, ...	20	1289—1269
Deliverance by Deborah and Barak, and rest, . .	40	1269—1229
Oppression by the Midianites, ...	7	1229—1222
Deliverance by Gideon, and rest, ...	40	1222—1182
Rule of Abimelech, ...	3	1182—1179
Tola, judge, ...	23	1179—1156
Jair, judge, ...	22	1156—1134
Eli, high priest and judge forty years, . . .	—	1154—1114

After repeated apostasy, oppression

(a) In the East.	(b) In the West.		
By the Ammonites 18 years,	By the Philistines, . .	40	1134—1094
from 1134 to 1116 B.C.	Loss of the ark, . .	—	c. 1114
Jephthah judge 6 years,	Samson's deeds, . .	—	1116—1096
from 1116 to 1110 B.C.	Samuel's prophetic labours,	—	1114 onwards
Ibzan judge 7 years,	Defeat of the Philistines,	—	1094
from 1110 to 1103 B.C.	Samuel, judge, . .	19	1094—1075
Elon judge 10 years,	Saul, king, . . .	20	1075—1055
from 1103 to 1093 B.C.	David king at Hebron, .	7	1055—1048
Abdon judge 8 years,	„ „ at Jerusalem,	33	1048—1015
from 1093 to 1085 B.C.	Solomon's reign to the building of the temple,	3	1015—1012
	Total,	480	years.

All that is required to establish our calculation as to the period of the judges, is to justify our estimate of ten years as the time that intervened between the division of the land and the invasion by Chushan-rishathaim, since the general opinion, founded upon the statement of *Josephus* (Ant. v. 1, 29), that Joshua was στρατηγός of the nation for twenty-five years after the death of Moses, and (vi. 5, 4) that his death was followed by a state of anarchy for eighteen years, is that it was at least thirty-five years. But Josephus at all events ought not to be appealed to, as he had no other sources of information with regard to the earlier portion of the Israelitish history than the Old Testament itself; and he so frequently contradicts himself in his chronological statements, that no reliance can be placed upon them even in cases where their incorrectness cannot be clearly proved. And if we consider, on the other hand, that Joshua was an old man when the two great campaigns in the south and north of Canaan were over, and in fact was so advanced in years, that God commanded him to divide the land, although many districts were still unconquered (Josh. xiii. 1 sqq.), in order that he might finish this part of his calling before his death, there is very little probability that he lived for twenty-five years after that time. The same words are used to describe the last days of his life in chap. xxiii. 1, that had previously been employed to describe his great age (chap. xiii. 1 sqq.). No doubt the statement in chap. xxiii. 1, to the effect that " many days after that the Lord had given rest unto Israel from all their foes;" Joshua called together the representatives of the nation, to renew the covenant of the nation with the Lord before his death, when taken in connection with the statement in chap. xix. 50, that he built the city of Timnathserah, which the tribes had given him for an inheritance after the distribution of the land by lot was over, and dwelt therein, proving very clearly that there were certainly " many days" (*Eng. Ver.* " a long time") between the division of the land and the death of Joshua. But this is so comparative a term, that it hardly embraces more than two or three years. And Joshua might build, *i.e.* fortify Timnath-serah, and dwell therein, even if he only lived for two or three years after the division of the land. On the other hand, there appears to have been a longer interval than the seven or eight years allowed in our reckoning between the death of Joshua and the invasion of Chushan; since it not only includes the defeat of Adoni-bezek, the capture of Jerusalem, Hebron, and other towns, by the tribes of Judah and Simeon (chap. i. 1–14), and the conquest of Bethel by the tribe of Joseph (chap. i. 22 sqq.), but also the war of the congregation with the tribe of Benjamin (chap. xix.–xxi.). But it is only in appearance that the interval allowed is too short. All these events together would not require many years, but might very well have occurred within the space of about five years. And it is quite possible that the civil war of the Israelites might have been regarded by king Chushan-rishathaim as a favourable opportunity for carrying out his design of making Israel tributary to himself, and that he took advantage of it accordingly. The very fact that Othniel delivered Israel from this oppression, after it had continued for eight years, precludes us from postponing the invasion itself to a longer period after the death of Joshua. For Othniel was not Caleb's nephew, as many suppose, but his younger brother (see at Josh. xv. 17). Now Caleb was eighty-five years old when the distribution of the land commenced (Josh. xiv. 10); so that even if his brother Othniel was thirty, or even forty years younger, he would still be fifty-five, or at any rate forty-five years old, when the division of the land commenced. If the statements of Josephus were correct, therefore, Othniel would have been ninety-one years old, or at any rate eighty-one, when he defeated the Aramæan king Chushan-rishathaim; whereas, according to our calculation, he would only have been fifty or sixty years old when Debir was taken, and sixty-three or seventy-three when Chushan was defeated. Now, even if we take the lower number as the correct one, this would be a sufficiently great age for such a warlike undertaking, especially when we consider that Othniel lived for some time afterwards, as is evident from the words of chap. iii. 11, " And the land had rest forty years : and Othniel the son of Kenaz died," though they may not distinctly affirm that he did not die till the termination of the forty years' rest.

The fact that Caleb's younger brother Othniel was the first judge of Israel, also upsets the hypothesis which *Bertheau* has founded upon a mistaken interpretation of chap. ii. 11–iii. 6, that a whole generation of forty years is to be reckoned between the death of Joshua and the invasion of Chushan, and also the misinterpretation of chap. ii. 7, 10 (cf. Josh. xxiv. 31), according to which the sinful generation did not grow up until after Joshua and all the elders who lived a *long time* after him were dead,—an interpretation which has no support in chap. ii. 7, since הֶאֱרִיךְ יָמִים אַחֲרֵי does not mean " to live *long* after a person," but simply " to survive him." The " other generation which knew not the Lord," etc., that arose after the death of Joshua and the elders who outlived him, was not a different generation from the succeeding generations, which were given up to the power of their foes on account of their apostasy from the Lord, but the younger generation generally, which took the place of the older men who had seen the works of the Lord under Joshua; in other words, this is only a comprehensive expression for all the succeeding generations who forgot Jehovah their God and served Baalim. So much may be said in vindication of our calculations as to the period of the judges.

I. TIMES OF THE JUDGES: OTHNIEL; EHUD AND SHAMGAR, DEBORAH AND BARAK.—CHAP. III. 7–V.

In this first stage of the times of the judges, which embraces a period of 206 years, the Israelites were oppressed by hostile nations on three separate occasions: first of all by the Mesopotamian king Chushan-rishathaim, whom they were obliged to serve for eighteen years, until Othniel brought them deliverance, and secured them rest for forty years (chap. iii. 7–11); secondly by the Moabitish king Eglon for eighteen years, until Ehud slew this king and smote the Moabites, and so humiliated them, that the land had rest for eighty years (chap. iii. 12–30), whilst Shamgar also smote a host of Philistines during the same period (chap. iii. 31); and lastly by the Canaanitish king Jabin of Hazor, who oppressed them heavily for twenty years, until Barak gathered an army together at the summons of Deborah the prophetess and with her assistance, and completely defeated the foe (chap. iv.). After this victory, which Deborah celebrated in a triumphal song, the land had rest again for forty years (chap. v.).

Oppression of Israel by Chushan-rishathaim, and Deliverance by Othniel.—Chap. iii. 7–11.

Vers. 7, 8. The first chastisement which the Israelites suffered for their apostasy from the Lord, is introduced with the same formula which had been used before to describe the times of the judges generally (chap. ii. 11, 12), except that instead of וַיַּעַזְבוּ אֶת־יי׳ (" they forsook the Lord") we have here וַיִּשְׁכְּחוּ אֶת־יי׳ (" *they forgot the Lord their God*") from Deut. xxxii. 18 (cf. 1 Sam. xii. 9), and *Asheroth* (rendered " groves") instead of *Ashtaroth* (see at chap. ii. 13). As a punishment for this apostasy, the Lord sold them (chap. ii. 14) into the hand of *Chushan-rishathaim*, the king of Mesopotamia, whom they were obliged to serve for eight years. All that we know about this king of Mesopotamia is what is recorded here. His name, Chushan-rishathaim, is probably only a title which was given to him by the Israelites themselves. *Rishathaim* signifies " *double wickedness*," and the word was rendered as an appellative with this signification in the Targums and the Syriac and Arabic versions. *Chushan* is also formed as an adjective from *Cush*, and may denote the Cushites. According to *M. v. Niebuhr* (Gesch. Assurs u. Babels, p. 272), the rulers of Babylon at that time (1518–1273) were Arabs. " Arabs, however, may have included not only Shemites of the tribe of Joktan or Ishmael, but Cushites also." The invasion of Canaan by this Mesopotamian or Baby lonian king has a historical analogy in the campaign of the five allied kings of Shinar in the time of Abraham (Gen. xiv.).

Vers. 9–11. In this oppression the Israelites cried to the Lord for help, and He raised them up מוֹשִׁיעַ, a deliverer, helper, namely the Kenizzite *Othniel*, the younger brother and son-in-law of Caleb (see at Josh. xv. 17). " *The Spirit of Jehovah came upon him.*" The Spirit of God is the spiritual principle of life in the world of nature and man; and in man it is the principle both of the natural life which we receive through birth, and also of the spiritual life which we receive through regeneration (*vid. Auberlen*, Geist des Menschen, in *Herzog's* Cycl. iv. p. 731). In this sense the expressions " Spirit of God" (*Elohim*) and " Spirit of the Lord" (Jehovah) are interchanged even in Gen. i. 2, compared with Gen. vi. 3, and so throughout all the books of the Old Testament; tho former denoting the Divine Spirit generally in its supernatural causality and power, the latter the same Spirit in its operations upon human life and history in the working out of the plan of salvation. In its peculiar operations the Spirit of Jehovah manifests itself as a spirit of wisdom and understanding, of counsel and might, of knowledge and of the fear of the Lord (Isa. xi. 2). The communication of this Spirit under the Old Testament was generally made in the form of extraordinary and supernatural influence upon the human spirit. The expression employed to denote this is usually וַתְּהִי עָלָיו רוּחַ יי׳ (" the Spirit of Jehovah came upon him :" thus here, chap. xi. 29; 1 Sam. xix. 20, 23; 2 Chron. xx. 14; Num. xxiv. 2). This is varied, however, with the expressions (צָלְחָה) וַתִּצְלַח עָלָיו רוּחַ יי׳ (chap. xiv. 6, 19, xv. 14; 1 Sam. x. 10, xi. 6, xvi. 13) and רוּחַ יי׳ לָבְשָׁה אֶת־פ׳, " the Spirit of Jehovah clothed the man" (chap. vi. 34; 1 Chron. xii. 18; 2 Chron. xxiv. 20). Of these the former denotes the operations of the Divine Spirit in overcoming the resistance of the natural will of man, whilst the latter represents the Spirit of God as a power which envelopes or covers a man. The recipients and bearers of this Spirit were thereby endowed with the power to perform miraculous deeds, in which the Spirit of God that came upon them manifested itself generally in the ability to prophesy (vid. 1 Sam. x. 10, xix. 20, 23 ; 1 Chron xii. 18 ; 2 Chron. xx. 14, xxiv. 20), but also in the power to work miracles or to accomplish deeds which surpassed the courage and strength of the natural man. The latter was more especially the case with the judges ; hence the *Chaldee* paraphrases " the Spirit of Jehovah" in chap. vi. 34 as the " spirit of might from the Lord ;" though in the passage before us it gives the erroneous interpretation רוּחַ נְבוּאָה, " the spirit of prophecy." *Kimchi* also understands it as signifying " the spirit of bravery, under the instigation of which he was able fearlessly to enter upon the war with Chushan." But we are hardly at liberty to split up the different powers of the Spirit of God in this manner, and to restrict its operations upon the judges to the spirit of strength and bravery alone. The judges not only attacked the enemy courageously and with success, but they also judged the nation, for which the spirit of wisdom and understanding was indispensably necessary, and put down idolatry (chap. ii. 18, 19), which they could not have done without the spirit of knowledge and of the fear of the Lord. *" And he judged Israel and went out to war."* The position of וַיִּשְׁפֹּט before וַיֵּצֵא לַמִּלְחָמָה does not warrant us in explaining וַיִּשְׁפֹּט as signifying " he began to discharge the functions of a judge," as *Rosenmüller* has done : for שָׁפַט must not be limited to a settlement of the civil disputes of the people, but means to restore *right* in Israel, whether towards its heathen oppressors, or with regard to the attitude of the nation towards the Lord. *" And the Lord gave Chushan-rishathaim into his hand* (cf. chap. i. 2, iii. 28, etc.), *and his hand became strong over him ;"* i.e. he overcame him (cf. chap. vi. 2), or smote him, so that he was obliged to vacate the land. In consequence of this victory, the land had rest from war (cf. Josh. xi. 23) forty years. *" And then Othniel died :"* the expression וַיָּמָת with וconsec. does not necessarily imply that Othniel did not die for forty years, but simply that he died after rest had been restored to the land.

Oppression of Israel by Eglon, and Deliverance by Ehud;
Shamgar's heroic Deeds.—Chap. iii. 12–31.

In vers. 12–30 the subjugation of the Israelites by *Eglon*, the
king of the Moabites, and their deliverance from this bondage, are
circumstantially described. First of all, in vers. 12–14, *the sub-*
jugation. When the Israelites forsook the Lord again (in the
place of 'וגו אֶת־הָרַע . . . וַיַעֲשׂוּ, ver. 7, we have here the appropriate
expression לַעֲשׂות הָרַע . . . וַיֹּסִפוּ, they added to do, *i.e.* did again, evil,
etc., as in chap. iv. 1, x. 6, xiii. 1), the Lord made Eglon the
king of the Moabites strong over Israel. חִזֵּק עַל, to give a person
strength to overcome or oppress another. עַל כִּי, as in Deut. xxxi.
17, instead of the more usual עַל אֲשֶׁר (cf. Jer. iv. 28; Mal. ii. 14;
Ps. cxxxix. 14). Eglon allied himself with the Ammonites and
Amalekites, those arch-foes of Israel, invaded the land, took the
palm-city, *i.e.* Jericho (see at chap. i. 16), and made the Israelites
tributary for eighteen years. Sixty years had passed since Jerichc
had been burnt by Joshua. During that time the Israelites had
rebuilt the ruined city, but they had not fortified it, on account of
the curse pronounced by Joshua upon any one who should restore
it as a fortress; so that the Moabites could easily conquer it, and
using it as a base, reduce the Israelites to servitude.—Ver. 15. But
when the Israelites cried to the Lord for help, He set them free
through the Benjaminite *Ehud*, whom He raised up as their
deliverer. *Ehud* was "the son of Gera." This probably means
that he was a descendant of Gera, since Gera himself, according to
1 Chron. viii. 3, was a son of Bela the son of Benjamin, and therefore was a grandson of Benjamin; and Shimei the contemporary
of David, a man belonging to the tribe of Benjamin, is also called
a son of Gera in 2 Sam. xvi. 5, xix. 17. At the same time, it is
possible that the name *Gera* does not refer to the same person in
these different passages, but that the name was repeated again and
again in the same family. "*A man shut with regard to his right*
hand," *i.e.* hindered in the use of his right hand, not necessarily
crippled, but in all probability disabled through want of use from
his youth upwards. That the expression does not mean crippled, is
confirmed by the fact that it is used again in connection with the
700 brave slingers in the army of the Benjaminites in chap. xx. 16,
and it certainly cannot be supposed that they were all actual
cripples. So much is certain, however, that it does not mean
ἀμφοτεροδέξιος, *qui utraque manu pro dextera utebatur* (LXX.,

Vulg.), since אָטַר signifies *clausit* (shut) in Ps. lxix. 16. It is merely with reference to what follows that this peculiarity is so distinctly mentioned.—The Israelites sent a present by him to king Eglon. בְּיָדוֹ does not mean *in*, but *through*, his hand, *i.e.* through his intervention, for others were actually employed to carry the present (ver. 18), so that Ehud merely superintended the matter. *Minchah*, a gift or present, is no doubt a euphemism for tribute, as in 2 Sam. viii. 2, 6, 1 Kings v. 1.—Ver. 16. Ehud availed himself of the opportunity to approach the king of the Moabites and put him to death, and thus to shake off the yoke of the Moabites from his nation. To this end he provided himself with a sword, which had two edges (פֵּיוֹת from פֶּה, like שִׂיו, Deut. xxii. 1, from שָׂה), a cubit long (גֹּמֶד, ἀπ. λεγ., signified primarily a staff, here a cubit, according to the Syriac and Arabic; not "a span," σπιθαμή, LXX.), and "*did gird it under his raiment upon his right thigh.*" —Ver. 17. Provided with this weapon, he brought the present to king Eglon, who—as is also mentioned as a preparation for what follows—was a very fat man.—Vers. 18, 19. After presenting the gift, Ehud dismissed the people who had carried the present to their own homes; namely, as we learn from ver. 19, after they had gone some distance from Jericho. But he himself returned from the stone-quarries at Gilgal, *sc.* to Jericho to king Eglon. מִן הַפְּסִילִים refers to some place by Gilgal. In Deut. vii. 25, Isa. xxi. 9, Jer. viii. 19, *pesilim* signifies idols. And if we would retain this meaning here, as the LXX., *Vulg.*, and others have done, we must assume that in the neighbourhood of Gilgal there were stone idols set up in the open air,—a thing which is very improbable. The rendering "stone quarries," from פָּסַל, to hew out stones (Ex. xxxiv. 1, etc.), which is the one adopted in the *Chaldee*, and by *Rashi* and others, is more likely to be the correct one. *Gilgal* cannot be the Gilgal between Jericho and the Jordan, which was the first encampment of the Israelites in Canaan, as is commonly supposed, since Ehud passed the *Pesilim* on his flight from the king's dwelling-place to the mountains of Ephraim (vers. 26, 27); and we can neither assume, as *Bertheau* does, that Eglon did not reside in the conquered palm-city (Jericho), but in some uncultivated place in the neighbourhood of the Jordan, nor suppose that after the murder of Eglon Ehud could possibly have gone from Jericho to the Gilgal which was half an hour's journey towards the east, for the purpose of escaping by a circuitous route of this kind to Seirah in the mountains of Ephraim, which was on the north-west of

Jericho. *Gilgal* is more likely to be *Geliloth*, which was on the west of Jericho opposite to the ascent of Adummim (*Kaalat ed Dom*), on the border of Judah and Benjamin (Josh. xviii. 17), and which was also called *Gilgal* (Josh. xv. 7). Having returned to the king's palace, Ehud sent in a message to him : "*I have a secret word to thee, O king.*" The context requires that we should understand "*he said*" in the sense of "he had him told" (or bade say to him), since Ehud himself did not go in to the king, who was sitting in his room, till afterwards (ver. 20). In consequence of this message the king said : הָס, *lit.* be silent (the imperative of הָסָה) ; here it is a proclamation, Let there be quiet. Thereupon all who were standing round (viz. his attendants) left the room, and Ehud went in (ver. 20). The king was sitting " in his upper room of cooling alone." The "room of cooling" (*Luther, Sommerlaube,* summer-arbour) was a room placed upon the flat roof of a house, which was open to the currents of air, and so afforded a cool retreat, such as are still met with in the East (*vid. Shaw,* pp. 188–9). Then Ehud said, " *A word of God I have to thee ;*" whereupon the king rose from his seat, from reverence towards the word of God which Ehud pretended that he had to deliver to him, not to defend himself, as *Bertheau* supposes, of which there is not the slightest intimation in the text.—Vers. 21, 22. But when the king stood up, Ehud drew his sword from under his garment, and plunged it so deeply into his abdomen that even the hilt followed the blade, and the fat closed upon the blade (so that there was nothing to be seen of it in front, because he did not draw the sword again out of his body), and the blade came out between the legs. The last words have been rendered in various ways. *Luther* follows the Chaldee and *Vulgate,* and renders it " so that the dirt passed from him," taking the ἀπ. λεγ. פַּרְשְׁדֹנָה as a composite noun from פֶּרֶשׁ, *stercus,* and שָׁדָה, *jecit.* But this is hardly correct, as the form of the word פַּרְשְׁדֹנָה, and its connection with יָצָא, rather points to a noun, פַּרְשְׁדֹן, with ה local. The explanation given by *Gesenius* in his *Thes.* and *Heb. lex.* has much more in its favour, viz. *interstitium pedum,* the place between the legs, from an Arabic word signifying *pedes dissitos habuit,* used as a euphemism for *anus, podex.* The subject to the verb is the blade.[1]—Ver. 23. As soon as the deed was

---

[1] At any rate the rendering suggested by *Ewald,* "Ehud went into the open air, or into the enclosure, the space in front of the *Alija,*" is untenable, for the simple reason that it is perfectly irreconcilable with the next clause, " Ehud went forth," etc. (consequently *Fr. Böttcher* proposes to erase this

accomplished, Ehud went out into the porch or front hall, shut the door of the room behind him (בַּעֲדוֹ, not behind himself, but literally round him, *i.e.* Eglon; cf. Gen. vii. 16, 2 Kings iv. 4) and bolted it (this is only added as a more precise explanation of the previous verb).—Vers. 24, 25. When the servants of Eglon came (to enter in to their lord) after Ehud's departure and saw the door of the upper room bolted, they thought "surely (אַךְ, *lit.* only, nothing but) he covers his feet" (a euphemism for performing the necessities of nature; cf. 1 Sam. xxiv. 3), and waited to shaming (cf. 2 Kings ii. 17, viii. 11), *i.e.* till they were ashamed of their long waiting (see at chap. v. 28). At length they opened the door with the key, and found their lord lying dead upon the floor.

Ehud's conduct must be judged according to the spirit of those times, when it was thought allowable to adopt any means of destroying the enemy of one's nation. The treacherous assassination of a hostile king is not to be regarded as an act of the Spirit of God, and therefore is not set before us as an example to be imitated. Although Jehovah raised up Ehud as a deliverer to His people when oppressed by Eglon, it is not stated (and this ought particularly to be observed) that the Spirit of Jehovah came upon Ehud, and still less that Ehud assassinated the hostile king under the impulse of that Spirit. Ehud proved himself to have been raised up by the Lord as the deliverer of Israel, simply by the fact that he actually delivered his people from the bondage of the Moabites, and it by no means follows that the means which he selected were either commanded or approved by Jehovah.—Vers. 26 sqq. Ehud had escaped whilst the servants of Eglon were waiting, and had passed the stone quarries and reached Seirah. *Seirah* is a place that is never mentioned again; and, judging from the etymology (the hairy), it was a wooded region, respecting the situation of which all that can be decided is, that it is not to be sought for in the neighbourhood of Jericho, but "upon the mountains of Ephraim" (ver. 27). For when Ehud had come to Seirah, he blew the trumpet "*upon the mountains of Ephraim,*" to announce to the people the victory that was placed within their reach by the death of Eglon, and to summon them to war with the Moabites, and then went down from the mountain into the plain near Jericho; "*and he was before them,*" *i.e.* went in front as their leader, saying to the people,

clause from the text, without any critical authority whatever). For if Ehud were the subject to the verb, the subject would necessarily have been mentioned, as it really is in the next clause, ver. 23*a*.

"*Follow me ; for Jehovah has given your enemies the Moabites into your hand.*" Then they went down and took (*i.e.* took possession of) the fords near Jericho (see at Josh. ii. 7), לְמוֹאָב, either "*from the Moabites*" or "*towards Moab,*" and let no one (of the Moabites) cross over, *i.e.* escape to their own land.—Ver. 29. Thus they smote at that time about 10,000 Moabites, all fat and powerful men, *i.e.* the whole army of the enemy in Jericho and on this side of the Jordan, not letting a man escape. The expression "at that time" seems to imply that they did not destroy this number in one single engagement, but during the whole course of the war.—Ver. 30. Thus Moab was subdued under the hand of Israel, and the land had rest for eighty years.

Ver. 31. After him (Ehud) was, *i.e.* there rose up, *Shamgar* the son of Anath. He smote the Philistines, who had probably invaded the land of the Israelites, six hundred men, with an ox-goad, so that he also (like Othniel and Ehud, vers. 9 and 15) delivered Israel. מַלְמַד הַבָּקָר, *ἀπ. λεγ.*, signifies, according to the Rabbins and the ancient versions, an instrument with which they trained and drove oxen ; and with this the etymology agrees, as לָמַד is used in Hos. x. 11 and Jer. xxxi. 18 to denote the training of the young ox. According to *Rashi*, מַלְמַד בָּקָר is the same as דָּרְבָן, βούκεντρον, in 1 Sam. xiii. 21. According to *Maundrell* in *Paulus' Samml. der merkw. Reisen nach d. Or.* i. p. 139, the country people in Palestine and Syria use when ploughing goads about eight feet long and six inches in circumference at the thick end. At the thin end they have a sharp point to drive the oxen, and at the other end a small hoe, to scrape off any dirt that may stick to the plough. Shamgar may have smitten the Philistines with some such instrument as this, just as the Edonian prince Lycurgus is described by Homer (Il. vi. 135) as putting Dionysius and the Bacchantines to flight with a βουπλήξ. Nothing is recorded about the descent of Shamgar, either here or in the Song of Deborah, in chap. v. 6. The heroic deed recorded of him must be regarded, as *O. v. Gerlach* affirms, as "merely the result of a holy inspiration that suddenly burst forth within him, in which he seized upon the first weapon that came to his hand, and put to flight the enemy when scared by a terror for God, just as Samson did on a later occasion." For he does not seem to have secured for the Israelites any permanent victory over the Philistines. Moreover, he is not called judge, nor is the period of his labours taken into account, but in chap. iv. 1 the renewed apostasy of Israel from the Lord is dated from the death of Ehud.

Oppression of Israel by Jabin, and Deliverance by Deborah and Barak.—Chap. iv. and v.

This fresh oppression of the Israelites, and the glorious victory which they obtained over Sisera, Jabin's general, through the judge Deborah and the heroic warrior Barak, are so fully described in Deborah's triumphal song in chap. v., that this song may be regarded as a poetical commentary upon that event. It by no means follows from this fact, however, that the historical account in chap. iv. was first of all founded upon the ode, and was merely intended to furnish an explanation of the song itself. Any such assumption is overthrown by the fact that the prose account in chap. iv. contains, as even *Bertheau* acknowledges, some historical details which we look for in vain in the song, and which are of great assistance in the interpretation of it. All that we can infer with any probability from the internal connection between the historical narrative and the Song of Deborah is, that the author of our book took both of them from one common source; though the few expressions and words which they contain, such as שְׂמִיכָה in ver. 18, תִּצְנַח in ver. 21, מָשַׁכְתָּ in ver. 6, and וַיָּהָם in ver. 15, do not throw any light upon the source from which they were derived. For, with the exception of the first, which is not met with again, the whole of them occur in other passages,—the second in chap. i. 14 and Josh. xv. 18, the third in the same sense in chap. xx. 37, and the fourth in Ex. xiv. 24 and Josh. x. 10. And it by no means follows, that because in the passages referred to, " יָהֹם is found in close association with songs or poetical passages" (*Bertheau*), the word itself must be borrowed from the same source as the songs, viz. from the book of Jasher (Josh. x. 13). For הָמַם is found in the same signification in 1 Sam. vii. 10, Ex. xxiii. 27, and Deut. ii. 15, where we look in vain for any songs; whilst it always occurs in connection with the account of a miraculous overthrow of the foe by the omnipotent power of God.

Chap. iv. *The Victory over Jabin and his General Sisera.*—Vers. 1–3. As the Israelites fell away from the Lord again when Ehud was dead, the Lord gave them into the hand of the Canaanitish king *Jabin*, who oppressed them severely for twenty years with a powerful army under *Sisera* his general. The circumstantial clause, " when Ehud was dead," places the falling away of the Israelites from God in direct causal connection with the death of Ehud on the one hand, and the deliverance of Israel into the power of Jabin on the other, and clearly indicates that as long as Ehud lived he kept the people from idolatry (cf. chap. ii. 18, 19), and defended Israel from hostile oppressions. Joshua had already conquered one king, *Jabin* of *Hazor*, and taken his capital (Josh. xi. 1, 10). The king referred to here, who lived more than a century later, bore the same name. The name *Jabin*, "the discerning," may possibly have been a standing name or title of the Canaanitish kings of Hazor, as Abimelech was of the kings of the Philistines (see at Gen. xxvi. 8). He is called "king of Canaan," in distinction from the kings of other nations and lands, such as Moab, Mesopotamia, etc. (chap. iii. 8, 12), into whose power the Lord had given up His sinful people. *Hazor*, once the capital of the kingdoms of northern Canaan, was situated over (above or to the north of) Lake Huleh, in the tribe of Naphtali, but has not yet been discovered (see at Josh. xi. 1). Sisera, the general of Jabin, dwelt in *Harosheth* of the *Goyim*, and oppressed the Israelites most tyrannically (*mightily*: cf. chap. viii. 1, 1 Sam. ii. 16) for twenty years with a force consisting of 900 chariots of iron (see at Josh. xvii. 16). The situation of *Harosheth*, which only occurs here (vers. 2, 13, 16), is unknown; but it is certainly to be sought for in one of the larger plains of Galilee, possibly the plain of *Buttauf*, where Sisera was able to develop his forces, whose strength consisted chiefly in war-chariots, and to tyrannize over the land of Israel.

Vers. 4–11. At that time the Israelites were judged by *Deborah*, a prophetess, the wife of Lapidoth, who dwelt under the Deborah-palm between Ramah (er Râm: see at Josh. xviii. 25) and Bethel (Beitin: see at Josh. vii. 2) in the tribe of Benjamin, upon the mountains of Ephraim. Deborah is called אִשָּׁה נְבִיאָה on account of her prophetic gift, like Miriam in Ex. xv. 20, and Hulda the wife of Shallum in 2 Kings xxii. 14. This gift qualified her to judge the nation (the participle שֹׁפְטָה expresses the permanence of the act of judging), *i.e.* first of all to settle such disputes among the people themselves as the lower courts were unable to decide, and which ought therefore, according to Deut. xvii. 8, to be referred to the supreme judge of the whole nation. The palm where she sat in judgment (cf. Ps. ix. 5) was called after her the *Deborah*-palm. The Israelites went up to her there to obtain justice. The expression "*came up*" is applied here, as in Deut. xvii. 8, to the place of justice, as a spiritual height, independently of the fact that the place referred to here really stood upon an eminence.—Vers. 6 sqq. But in order to secure the rights of her people against their outward foes also, she summoned *Barak* the son of Abinoam from Kedesh,

in the tribe of Naphtali, on the west of the Huleh lake (see at Josh.
xii. 22), and made known to him the commands of the Lord: " *Up
and draw to Mount Tabor, and take with thee* 10,000 *men of the
children of Naphtali and Zebulun; and I will draw to thee into the
brook-valley of Kishon, Sisera the captain of Jabin's army, and his
chariots, and his multitude* (his men of war), *and give him into thy
hand.*" מָשַׁכְתָּ has been explained in different ways. *Seb. Schmidt,
Clericus,* and others supply הַקֶּרֶן or הַשּׁוֹפָר, draw with the trumpet
(cf. Ex. xix. 13, Josh. vi. 5), *i.e.* blow the trumpet in long-drawn
tones, upon Mount Tabor, and regard this as the signal for convening the people; whilst *Hengstenberg* (Diss. ii. pp. 76, 77) refers to
Num. x. 9, and understands the blowing of the horn as the signal
by which the congregation of the Lord made known its need to
Him, and appealed to Him to come to its help. It cannot indeed
be proved that the blowing of the trumpet was merely the means
adopted for convening the people together; in fact, the use of the
following מָשַׁכְתִּי, in the sense of draw, is to be explained on the
supposition that מָשַׁכְתָּ is used in a double sense. " The long-drawn
notes were to draw the Lord to them, and then the Lord would
draw to them Sisera, the captain of Jabin's army. Barak first calls
the helper from heaven, and then the Lord calls the enemy upon
earth." Nevertheless we cannot subscribe to this explanation, *first* of
all because the supposed ellipsis cannot be sustained in this connection, when nothing is said about the blowing of a trumpet either in
what precedes or in what follows; and *secondly,* because Num. x. 9
cannot be appealed to in explanation, for the simple reason that it
treats of the blowing of the *silver trumpets* on the part of the priests,
and they must not be confounded with the *shopharoth.* And the use
made of the trumpets at Jericho cannot be transferred to the passage
before us without some further ground. We are disposed therefore
to take the word מָשַׁךְ in the sense of *draw* (intransitive), *i.e.* proceed
one after another in a long-drawn train (as in chap. xx. 37 and Ex.
xii. 21), referring to the captain and the warriors drawing after
him; whilst in ver. 7 it is to be translated in the same way, though
with a transitive signification. Mount Tabor, called 'Ιταβύριον by
the Greeks (see LXX. Hos. v. 1), the mountain of Christ's transfiguration according to an early tradition of the church, the present
Jebel et Tur, is a large truncated cone of limestone, which is almost
perfectly insulated, and rises to the height of about a thousand feet,
on the north-eastern border of the plain of Jezreel. The sides of
the mountain are covered with a forest of oaks and wild pistachios,

and upon its flat summit, which is about half an hour in circumference, there are the remains of ancient fortifications (see *Robinson*, Pal. iii. pp. 211 sqq., and *v. Raumer*, Pal. pp. 37, 38). The words "and take with thee 10,000 men" are not to be understood as signifying that Barak was to summon the people together upon the top of Mount Tabor, but the assembling of the people is presupposed; and all that is commanded is, that he was to proceed to Mount Tabor with the assembled army, and make his attack upon the enemy, who were encamped in the valley of Kishon, *from that point.* According to ver. 10, the army was collected at Kedesh in Naphtali. *Nachal Kishon* is not only the brook *Kishon*, which is formed by streams that take their rise from springs upon Tabor and the mountains of Gilboa, flows in a north-westerly direction through the plain of Jezreel to the Mediterranean, and empties itself into the bay of Acca, and which is called *Mukatta* by the natives (see *Rob.* iii. pp. 472 sqq., and *v. Raumer*, pp. 39, 50), but the valley on both sides of the brook, *i.e.* the plain of Jezreel (see at Josh. xvii. 16), where the greatest battles have been fought for the possession of Palestine from time immemorial down to the most recent times (see *v. Raumer*, pp. 40 sqq.).—Vers. 8 sqq. Barak replied that he would not go unless she would go with him— certainly not for the reason suggested by *Bertheau*, viz. that he distrusted the divine promise given to him by Deborah, but because his mistrust of his own strength was such that he felt too weak to carry out the command of God. He wanted divine enthusiasm for the conflict, and this the presence of the prophetess was to infuse into both Barak and the army that was to be gathered round him. Deborah promised to accompany him, but announced to him as the punishment for this want of confidence in the success of his undertaking, that the prize of victory—namely, the defeat of the hostile general—should be taken out of his hand; for Jehovah would sell (*i.e.* deliver up) Sisera into the hand of a woman, viz., according to vers. 17 sqq., into the hand of Jael. She then went with him to Kedesh, where Barak summoned together Zebulun and Naphtali, *i.e.* the fighting men of those tribes, and went up with 10,000 men in his train ("at his feet," *i.e.* after him, ver. 14; cf. Ex. xi. 8 and Deut. xi. 6) to Tabor ("went up:" the expression is used here to denote the advance of an army against a place). Kedesh, where the army assembled, was higher than Tabor. זָעַק, *Hiphil* with acc., to call together (cf. 2 Sam. xx. 4, 5). Before the engagement with the foe is described, there follows in ver. 11 a statement that

Heber the Kenite had separated himself from his tribe, the children of Hobab, who led a nomad life in the desert of Judah (chap. i. 16), and had pitched his tents as far as the oak forest at Zaanannim (see at Josh. xix. 33) near Kedesh. This is introduced because of its importance in relation to the issue of the conflict which ensued (vers. 17 sqq.). נִפְרָד with *Kametz* is a participle, which is used in the place of the perfect, to indicate that the separation was a permanent one.

Vers. 12–16. As soon as Sisera received tidings of the march of Barak to Mount Tabor, he brought together all his chariots and all his men of war from Harosheth of the Goyim into the brook-valley of the Kishon. Then Deborah said to Barak, " *Up; for this is the day in which Jehovah hath given Sisera into thy hand. Yea* (הֲלֹא, *nonne*, as an expression indicating lively assurance), *the Lord goeth out before thee*," *sc.* to the battle, to smite the foe; whereupon Barak went down from Tabor with his 10,000 men to attack the enemy, according to chap. v. 19, at Taanach by the water of Megiddo. —Ver. 15. " *And the Lord discomfited Sisera, and all his chariots, and all his army, with the edge of the sword before Barak.*" וַיָּהָם, as in Ex. xiv. 24 and Josh. x. 10, denotes the confounding of the hostile army by a miracle of God, mostly by some miraculous phenomenon of nature: see, besides Ex. xiv. 24, 2 Sam. xxii. 15, Ps. xviii. 15, and cxliv. 6. The expression וַיָּהָם places the defeat of Sisera and his army in the same category as the miraculous destruction of Pharaoh and of the Canaanites at Gibeon; and the combination of this verb with the expression " with the edge of the sword" is to be taken as *constructio prægnans*, in this sense : Jehovah threw Sisera and his army into confusion, and, like a terrible champion fighting in front of Israel, smote him without quarter. Sisera sprang from his chariot to save himself, and fled on foot; but Barak pursued the routed foe to Harosheth, and completely destroyed them. " *All Sisera's army fell by the edge of the sword; there remained not even to one,*" *i.e.* not a single man.

Vers. 17–22. Sisera took refuge in the tent of Jael, the wife of Heber the Kenite, to escape the sword of the Israelites, as king Jabin lived at peace with the house of Heber, *i.e.* with this branch of the Kenites.—Ver. 18. Jael received the fugitive into her tent in the usual form of oriental hospitality (סוּר, as in Gen. xix. 2, 3, to turn aside from the road and approach a person), and covered him with a covering (שְׂמִיכָה, ἅπ λεγ., covering, or rug), that he might be able to sleep, as he was thoroughly exhausted with his

flight.—Ver. 19. On his asking for water to drink, as he was thirsty
(צָמֵתִי, defective form for צָמֵאתִי), she handed him milk from her
bottle, and covered him up again. She gave him milk instead of
water, as Deborah emphatically mentions in her song in chap. v.
25, no doubt merely for the purpose of giving to her guest a friendly
and hospitable reception. When *Josephus* affirms, in his account of
this event (Ant. v. 5, 4), that she gave him milk that was already
spoiled (διεφθορὸς ἤδη), *i.e.* had turned sour, and *R. Tunchum* supposes that such milk intoxicated the weary man, these are merely
later decorations of the simple fact, and have no historical worth
whatever.—Ver. 20. In order to be quite sure, Sisera entreated his
hostess to stand before the door and turn any one away who might
come to her to seek for one of the fugitives. עֲמֹד is the imperative
for עִמְדִי, as the syntax proves that the word cannot be an infinitive.
The anomaly apparent in the use of the gender may be accounted
for on the ground that the masculine was the more general form,
and might therefore be used for the more definite feminine. There
are not sufficient grounds for altering it into עָמוֹר, the *inf. abs.*
Whether Jael complied with this wish is not stated; but in the
place of anything further, the chief fact alone is given in ver. 21,
namely, that Jael took a tent-plug, and went with a hammer in her
hand to Sisera, who had fallen through exhaustion into a deep sleep,
and drove the plug into his temples, so that it penetrated into the
earth, or the floor. The words וְהוּא־נִרְדָּם וַיָּעַף are introduced as
explanatory of the course of the events: "*but he was fallen into
a deep sleep, and exhausted,*" *i.e.* had fallen fast asleep through
exhaustion. "*And so he died.*" וַיָּמֹת is attached as a consequence
to וַתִּצְנַח וגו'.... וַתִּתְקַע, whereas וַיָּעַף belongs to the parenthetical clause
וְהוּא נִרְדָּם. This is the explanation adopted by *Rosenmüller*, and
also in the remark of *Kimchi*: "the words נִרְדָּם וַיָּעַף indicate the
reason why Sisera neither heard Jael approach him, nor was conscious of the blow inflicted upon him." For the combination of
וַיָּעַף with וַיָּמֹת, "then he became exhausted and died," which *Stud.*
and *Bertheau* support, does not give any intelligible thought at all.
A man who has a tent-peg driven with a hammer into his temples,
so that the peg passes through his head into the ground, does not
become exhausted before he dies, but dies instantaneously. And
וַיָּעַף, from עוּף, equivalent to עָיֵף (Jer. iv. 31), or יָעֵף, and written
with *Patach* in the last syllable, to distinguish it from עוּף, *volare,*
has no other meaning than to be exhausted, in any of the passages
in which it occurs (see 1 Sam. xiv. 28, 31; 2 Sam. xxi. 15). The

rendering adopted by the LXX., ἐσκοτώθη, cannot be grammatically sustained.—Ver. 22. When Barak, who was in pursuit of
Sisera, arrived at Jael's tent, she went to meet him, to show him
the deed which she had performed. Thus was Deborah's prediction
to Barak (ver. 9) fulfilled. The Lord had sold Sisera into the hand
of a woman, and deprived Barak of the glory of the victory.
Nevertheless the act itself was not morally justified, either by this
prophetic announcement, or by the fact that it is commemorated in
the song of Deborah in chap. v. 24 sqq. Even though there can
be no doubt that Jael acted under the influence of religious enthusiasm for the cause of Israel and its God, and that she was prompted
by religious motives to regard the connection of her tribe with
Israel, the people of the Lord, as higher and more sacred, not only
than the bond of peace, in which her tribe was living with Jabin
the Canaanitish king, but even than the duties of hospitality, which
are so universally sacred to an oriental mind, her heroic deed cannot
be acquitted of the sins of lying, treachery, and assassination, which
were associated with it, by assuming, as *Calovius, Buddeus,* and others
have done, that when Jael invited Sisera into her tent, and promised
him safety, and quenched his thirst with milk, she was acting with
perfect sincerity, and without any thought of killing him, and that
it was not till after he was fast asleep that she was instigated and
impelled *instinctu Dei arcano* to perform the deed. For Jehovah,
the God of Israel, not only abhors lying lips (Prov. xii. 22), but
hates wickedness and deception of every kind. It is true, He
punishes the ungodly at the hand of sinners; but the sinners whom
He employs as the instruments of His penal justice in carrying out
the plans of His kingdom, are not instigated to the performance of
wicked deeds by an inward and secret impulse from Him. God
had no doubt so ordered it, that Sisera should meet with his death
in Jael's tent, where he had taken refuge; but this divine purpose
did not justify Jael in giving to the enemy of Israel a hospitable
reception into her tent, making him feel secure both by word
and deed, and then murdering him secretly while he was asleep.
Such conduct as that was not the operation of the Spirit of
God, but the fruit of a heroism inspired by flesh and blood; and
even in Deborah's song (chap. v. 24 sqq.) it is not lauded as a
divine act.

Vers. 23, 24. " *So God subdued at that time Jabin the king of
Canaan before the children of Israel; and the hand of the Israelites
became heavier and heavier in its pressure upon him, until they had*

destroyed him." הָלוֹךְ וְקָשָׁה . . . וַתֵּלֶךְ יַד, " the hand . . . increased
more and more, becoming heavy." הָלַךְ, used to denote the progress
or continual increase of an affair, as in Gen. viii. 3, etc., is connected with the infinitive absolute, and with the participle of the
action concerned. קָשָׁה is the feminine participle of קָשֶׁה, like גָּדֵל in
Gen. xxvi. 13 (see *Ges.* § 131, 3, Anm. 3). The overthrow of Jabin
and his rule did not involve the extermination of the Canaanites
generally.

Deborah's Song of Victory.—Chap. v.

This highly poetical song is so direct and lively an utterance of
the mighty force of the enthusiasm awakened by the exaltation of
Israel, and its victory over Sisera, that its genuineness is generally
admitted now. After a general summons to praise the Lord for
the courage with which the people rose up to fight against their
foes (ver. 2), Deborah the singer dilates in the first section (vers.
3–11) upon the significance of the victory, picturing in lively colours
(1) the glorious time when Israel was exalted to be the nation of
the Lord (vers. 3–5); (2) the disgraceful decline of the nation in
the more recent times (vers. 6–8); and (3) the joyful turn of
affairs which followed her appearance (vers. 9–11). After a fresh
summons to rejoice in their victory (ver. 12), there follows in the
second section (vers. 13–21) a lively picture of the conflict and
victory, in which there is a vivid description (*a*) of the mighty
gathering of the brave to battle (vers. 13–15*a*); (*b*) of the cowardice
of those who stayed away from the battle, and of the bravery with
which the braver warriors risked their lives in the battle (vers.
15*b*–18); and (*c*) of the successful result of the conflict (vers.
19–21). To this there is appended in the *third* section (vers.
22–31) an account of the glorious issue of the battle and the victory : first of all, a brief notice of the flight and pursuit of the foe
(vers. 22–24); secondly, a commemoration of the slaying of Sisera
by Jael (vers. 24–27); and thirdly, a scornful description of the
disappointment of Sisera's mother, who was counting upon a large
arrival of booty (vers. 28–30). The song then closes with the hope,
founded upon this victory, that all the enemies of the Lord might
perish, and Israel increase in strength (ver. 31*a*). The whole song,
therefore, is divided into three leading sections, each of which again
is arranged in three somewhat unequal strophes, the first and second
sections being introduced by a summons to the praise of God (vers.
2, 12), whilst the third closes with an expression of hope, drawn

from the contents of the whole, with regard to the future prospects of the kingdom of God (ver. 31*a*).

Ver. 1. The historical introduction (" *Then sang Deborah and Barak the son of Abinoam on that day, saying*") takes the place of a heading, and does not mean that the song of Deborah and Barak which follows was composed by them jointly, but simply that it was sung by them together, in commemoration of the victory. The poetess or writer of the song, according to vers. 3, 7, and 12, was Deborah. The song itself opens with a summons to praise the Lord for the willing and joyful rising up of His people.

Ver. 2. *That the strong in Israel showed themselves strong,*
That the people willingly offered themselves,
Praise ye the Lord!

The meaning of פָּרַע and פְּרָעוֹת is a subject of dispute. According to the Septuagint rendering, and that of *Theodot.*, ἐν τῷ ἄρξασθαι ἀρχηγοὺς ἐν Ἰσραήλ, many give it the meaning to begin or to lead, and endeavour to establish this meaning from an Arabic word signifying to find one's self at the head of an affair. But this meaning cannot be established in Hebrew. פָּרַע has no other meaning than to let loose from something, to let a person loose or free (see at Lev. x. 6); and in the only other passage where פְּרָעוֹת occurs (Deut. xxxii. 42), it does not refer to a leader, but to the luxuriant growth of the hair as the sign of great strength. Hence in this passage also פְּרָעוֹת literally means *comati*, the hairy ones, *i.e.* those who possessed strength; and פָּרַע, to manifest or put forth strength. The persons referred to are the champions in the fight, who went before the nation with strength and bravery. The preposition בְּ before פָּרַע indicates the reason for praising God, or rather the object with which the praise of the Lord was connected. בִּפְרֹעַ וגו׳, literally "in the showing themselves strong." The meaning is, "for the fact that the strong in Israel put forth strength." הִתְנַדֵּב, to prove one's self willing, here to go into the battle of their own free will, without any outward and authoritative command. This introduction transports us in the most striking manner into the time of the judges, when Israel had no king who could summon the nation to war, but everything depended upon the voluntary rising of the strong and the will of the nation at large. The manifestation of this strength and willingness Deborah praises as a gracious gift of the Lord. After this summons to praise the Lord, the first part of the song opens with an appeal to the kings and princes of the earth to hear what Deborah has to proclaim to the praise of God.

Ver. 3. Hear, ye kings ; give ear, ye princes !
  I, to the Lord will I sing,
  Will sing praise to the Lord, the God of Israel.
  4. Lord, when Thou wentest out from Seir,
  When Thou marchedst out of the fields of Edom,
  The earth trembled, and the heavens also dropped ;
  The clouds also dropped water.
  5. The mountains shook before the Lord,
  Sinai there before the Lord, the God of Israel.

The "kings and princes" are not the rulers in Israel, for Israel had no kings at that time, but the kings and princes of the heathen nations, as in Ps. ii. 2. These were to discern the mighty acts of Jehovah in Israel, and learn to fear Jehovah as the almighty God. For the song to be sung applies to Him, the God of Israel. זַמֵּר, ψάλλειν, is the technical expression for singing with an instrumental accompaniment (see at Ex. xv. 2).—Vers. 4, 5. To give the Lord the glory for the victory which had been gained through His omnipotent help over the powerful army of Sisera, and to fill the heathen with fear of Jehovah, and the Israelites with love and confidence towards Him, the singer reverts to the terribly glorious manifestation of Jehovah in the olden time, when Israel was accepted as the nation of God (Ex. xix.). Just as Moses in his blessing (Deut. xxxiii. 2) referred the tribes of Israel to this mighty act, as the source of all salvation and blessing for Israel, so the prophetess Deborah makes the praise of this glorious manifestation of God the starting-point of her praise of the great grace, which Jehovah as the faithful covenant God had displayed to His people in her own days. The tacit allusion to Moses' blessing is very unmistakeable. But whereas Moses describes the descent of the Lord upon Sinai (Ex. xix.), according to its gracious significance in relation to the tribes of Israel, as an objective fact (Jehovah came from Sinai, Deut. xxxiii. 2), Deborah clothes the remembrance of it in the form of an address to God, to bring out the thought that the help which Israel had just experienced was a renewal of the coming of the Lord to His people. Jehovah's going out of Seir, and marching out of the fields of Edom, is to be interpreted in the same sense as His rising up from Seir (Deut. xxxiii. 2). As the descent of the Lord upon Sinai is depicted there as a rising of the sun from the east, so the same descent in a black cloud amidst thunder, lightning, fire, and vapour of smoke (Ex. xix. 16, 18), is represented here with direct allusion to these phenomena as a storm rising up from Seir in the east, in which the Lord advanced to meet His people as they came from the west to Sinai. Before the Lord, who came down upon Sinai in the storm and darkness of the cloud, the earth shook and the heaven dropped, or, as it is afterwards more definitely explained, the clouds dropped with water, emptied themselves of their abundance of water as they do in the case of a storm. The mountains shook (נָזְלוּ, *Niphal* of זָלַל, dropping the reduplication of the ל = נִזֹּלוּ, Isa. lxiii. 19, lxiv. 2), even the strong rocky mountain of Sinai, which stood out so distinctly before the eyes of the singer, that she speaks of it as " this Sinai," pointing to it as though it were locally near. David's description of the miraculous guidance of Israel through the desert in Ps. lxviii. 8, 9, is evidently founded upon this passage, though it by no means follows from this that the passage before us also treats of the journey through the desert, as *Clericus* supposes, or even of the presence of the Lord in the battle with Sisera, and the victory which it secured. But greatly as Israel had been exalted at Sinai by the Lord its God, it had fallen just as deeply into bondage to its oppressors through its own sins, until Deborah arose to help it (vers. 6–8).

> Ver. 6. In the days of Shamgar, the son of Anath,
> In the days of Jael, the paths kept holiday,
> And the wanderers of the paths went crooked ways.
> 7. The towns in Israel kept holiday, they kept holiday,
> Until that I, Deborah, arose,
> That I arose a mother in Israel.
> 8. They chose new gods;
> Then was war at the gates:
> Was there a shield seen and a spear
> Among forty thousand in Israel?

The deep degradation and disgrace into which Israel had sunk before the appearance of Deborah, through its falling away from the Lord into idolatry, forms the dark reverse of that glorification at Sinai. Although, after Ehud, Shamgar had also brought help to the people against their enemies by a victory over the Philistines (chap. iii. 31), and although Jael, who proved herself a heroine by slaying the fugitive Sisera, was then alive, things had got to such a pitch with Israel, that no one would venture upon the public high roads. There are no good grounds for the conjecture that Jael was a different person from the Jael mentioned in chap. iv. 17 sqq., whether a judge who is not further known, as *Ewald* supposes, or a female judge who stood at the head of the nation in these unhappy times (*Bertheau*). חָדְלוּ אֳרָחוֹת, lit. " the paths ceased," sc.

to be paths, or to be trodden by men. הֹלְכֵי נְתִיבוֹת, "*those who went upon paths*," or beaten ways, *i.e.* those who were obliged to undertake journeys for the purpose of friendly intercourse or trade, notwithstanding the burden of foreign rule which pressed upon the land; such persons went by "*twisted paths*," *i.e.* by roads and circuitous routes which turned away from the high roads. And the פְּרָזוֹן, *i.e.* the *cultivated land*, with its open towns and villages, and with their inhabitants, was as forsaken and desolate as the public highways. The word *peruzon* has been rendered judge or guidance by modern expositors, after the example of *Teller* and *Gesenius*; and in ver. 11 decision or guidance. But this meaning, which has been adopted into all the more recent lexicons, has nothing really to support it, and does not even suit our verse, into which it would introduce the strange contradiction, that at the time when Shamgar and Jael were judges, there were no judges in Israel. In addition to the Septuagint version, which renders the word δυνατοὶ in this verse (*i.e.* according to the *Cod. Vat.*, for the *Cod. Al.* has φράζων), and then in the most unmeaning way adopts the rendering αὔξησον in ver. 11, from which we may clearly see that the translators did not know the meaning of the word, it is common to adduce an Arabic word which signifies *segregavit, discrevit rem ab aliis*, though it is impossible to prove that the Arabic word ever had the meaning to judge or to lead. All the old translators, as well as the Rabbins, have based their rendering of the word upon פְּרָזִי, inhabitant of the flat country (Deut. iii. 5, and 1 Sam. vi. 18), and פְּרָזוֹת, the open flat country, as distinguished from the towns surrounded by walls (Ezek. xxxviii. 11; Zech. ii. 8), according to which פְּרָזוֹן, as the place of meeting, would denote both the cultivated land with its unenclosed towns and villages, and also the population that was settled in the open country in unfortified places,—a meaning which also lies at the foundation of the word in Hab. iii. 14. Accordingly, *Luther* has rendered the word *Bauern* (peasants). עַד אֶשֶׁר שַׁקַּמְתִּי for עַד קַמְתִּי. The contraction of אֲשֶׁר into שׁ, with *Dagesh* following, and generally pointed with *Seghol*, but here with *Patach* on account of the ק, which is closely related to the gutturals, belongs to the popular character of the song, and is therefore also found in the Song of Solomon (chap. i. 12, ii. 7, 17, iv. 6). It is also met with here and there in simple prose (Judg. vi. 17, vii. 12, viii. 26); but it was only in the literature of the time of the captivity and a still later date, that it found its way more and more from the language of ordinary conversation into that of the Scriptures. Deborah describes herself as " a mother in Israel," on account of her having watched over her people with maternal care, just as Job calls himself a father to the poor who had been supported by him (Job xxix. 16; cf. Isa. xxii. 21).—Ver. 8 describes the cause of the misery into which Israel had fallen. אֱלֹהִים חֲדָשִׁים is the object to יִבְחַר, and the subject is to be found in the previous term *Israel*. Israel forsook its God and Creator, and chose new gods, *i.e.* gods not worshipped by its fathers (*vid.* Deut. xxxii. 17). Then there was war (לָחֶם, the construct state of לָחֶם, a verbal noun formed from the *Piel*, and signifying conflict or war) at the gates; *i.e.* the enemy pressed up to the very gates of the Israelitish towns, and besieged them, and there was not seen a shield or spear among forty thousand in Israel, *i.e.* there were no warriors found in Israel who ventured to defend the land against the foe. אִם indicates a question with a negative reply assumed, as in 1 Kings i. 27, etc. Shield and spear (or lance) are mentioned particularly as arms of offence and defence, to signify arms of all kinds. The words are not to be explained from 1 Sam. xiii. 22, as signifying that there were no longer any weapons to be found among the Israelites, because the enemy had taken them away (" not seen" is not equivalent to " not found" in 1 Sam. xiii. 22); they simply affirm that there were no longer any weapons to be seen, because not one of the 40,000 men in Israel took a weapon in his hand. The number 40,000 is not the number of the men who offered themselves willingly for battle, according to ver. 2 (*Bertheau*); for apart from the fact that they did not go unarmed into the battle, it is at variance with the statement in chap. iv. 6, 10, that Barak went into the war and smote the enemy with only 10,000 men. It is a round number, *i.e.* an approximative statement of the number of the warriors who might have smitten the enemy and delivered Israel from bondage, and was probably chosen with a reference to the 40,000 fighting men of the tribes on the east of the Jordan, who went with Joshua to Canaan and helped their brethren to conquer the land (Josh. iv. 13). Most of the more recent expositors have given a different rendering of ver. 8. Many of them render the first clause according to the *Peshito* and *Vulgate*, " *God chose something new*," taking *Elohim* as the subject, and *chadashim* (new) as the object. But to this it has very properly been objected, that, according to the terms of the song, it was not *Elohim* but *Jehovah* who effected the deliverance of Israel, and that the Hebrew for new things is not חֲדָשִׁים, but חֲדָשׁוֹת (Isa. xlii.

9, xlviii. 6), or חֲדָשָׁה (Isa. xliii. 19; Jer. xxxi. 22). On these grounds *Ewald* and *Bertheau* render *Elohim* "judges" (they chose new judges), and appeal to Ex. xxi. 6, xxii. 7, 8, where the authorities who administered justice in the name of God are called *Elohim.* But these passages are not sufficient by themselves to establish the meaning "judges," and still less to establish the rendering "new judges" for *Elohim chadashim.* Moreover, according to both these explanations, the next clause must be understood as relating to the specially courageous conflict which the Israelites in their enthusiasm carried on with Sisera; whereas the further statement, that among 40,000 warriors who offered themselves willingly for battle there was not a shield or a lance to be seen, is irreconcilably at variance with this. For the explanation suggested, namely, that these warriors did not possess the ordinary weapons for a well-conducted engagement, but had nothing but bows and swords, or instead of weapons of any kind had only the staffs and tools of shepherds and husbandmen, is proved to be untenable by the simple fact that there is nothing at all to indicate any contrast between ordinary and extraordinary weapons, and that such a contrast is altogether foreign to the context. Moreover, the fact appealed to, that אָז points to a victorious conflict in vers. 13, 19, 22, as well as in ver. 11, is not strong enough to support the view in question, as אָז is employed in ver. 19 in connection with the battle of the kings of Canaan, which was not a successful one, but terminated in a defeat.

The singer now turns from the contemplation of the deep degradation of Israel to the glorious change which took place as soon as she appeared :—

Ver. 9. My heart inclines to the leaders of Israel;
  To those who offered themselves willingly in the nation. Praise ye the Lord!

10. Ye that ride upon white asses;
  Ye that sit upon coverings,
  And that walk in the way, reflect!

11. With the voice of the archers among drawers (of water),
  There praise ye the righteous acts of the Lord,
  The righteous acts in His villages in Israel.
  Then the people of the Lord went down to the gates!

We must supply the *subst. verb* in connection with לְבִּי לְ, "*My heart is* (sc. inclined) *towards the leaders of Israel,*" *i.e.* feels itself drawn towards them. חֹקֵק for מְחוֹקֵק (ver. 14), the determining one, *i.e.* the commander or leader in war: as in Deut. xxxiii. 21. The leaders and willing ones are first of all to praise the Lord for having crowned their willingness with victory.—Ver. 10. And all classes of the people, both high and low, have reason to join in the praise. Those who ride upon white, *i.e.* white-spotted asses, are the upper classes generally, and not merely the leaders (cf. chap. x. 4, xii. 14). צָחֹר, *lit.* dazzling white; but since there are no asses that are perfectly white, and white was a colour that was highly valued both by Hebrews and Arabs, they applied the term white to those that were only spotted with white. Those who sit upon coverings (מִדִּין from מַד, a covering or carpet, with the plural termination ין, which is to be regarded as a poetical Chaldaism) are the rich and prosperous; and those who walk on the way, *i.e.* travellers on foot, represent the middle and lower classes, who have to go about and attend to their affairs. Considered logically, this triple division of the nation is not a very exact one, as the first two do not form a true antithesis. But the want of exactness does not warrant our fusing together the middle term and the first, and understanding by *middin* either saddles or saddle-cloths, as *Ewald* and *Bertheau* have done; for saddle-cloths are still further from forming an antithesis to asses, so that those who ride upon white asses could be distinguished, as the upper classes and leaders, from those who sit upon saddles, or are "somewhat richer." Moreover, there is no reason for regarding these three classes as referring simply to the long line of warriors hastening from the victory to the triumphal fête. On the contrary, all classes of the people are addressed, as enjoying the fruits of the victory that had been obtained: the upper classes, who ride upon their costly animals; the rich resting at home upon their splendid carpets; and the poor travellers, who can now go quietly along the high-road again without fear of interruption from the foe (ver. 6). שִׂיחוּ is rendered "*sing*" by many; but this rendering cannot be sustained from Ps. cv. 2 and cxlv. 5, and it is not necessary in the verse before us, since the well-established meaning of the word "ponder," reflect, *sc.* upon the acts of the Lord, is a perfectly suitable one.— Ver. 11. The whole nation had good reason to make this reflection, as the warriors, having returned home, were now relating the mighty acts of the Lord among the women who were watering their flocks, and the people had returned to their towns once more. This is in all probability the idea of the obscure verse before us, which has been interpreted in such very different ways. The first clause, which has no verb, and cannot constitute a sentence by itself, must be connected with the following clause, and taken as an *anakolouthon*,

as שָׁם יְתַנּוּ does not form a direct continuation of the clause commencing with מִקּוֹל. After the words "*from the voice of the archers*,"
we should expect the continuation "*there is heard*," or "there
sounds forth the praise of the acts of the Lord." Instead of that,
the construction that was commenced is relinquished at שָׁם וְתַנּוּ,
and a different turn is given to the thought. This not only seems
to offer the simplest explanation, but the only possible solution of
the difficulty. For the explanation that מִן is to be taken as signifying "away from," as in Num. xv. 24, etc., in the sense of "far
from the voice of the archers, among the watering women," does not
suit the following word שָׁם, "there," at all. It would be necessary
to attribute to מִן the meaning "no more disquieted by," a meaning
which the preposition could not possibly have in this clause. מְחַצְצִים
are not sharers in the booty, for חָצַץ simply means to cut, to cut in
pieces, to divide, and is never applied to the sharing of booty, for which
חִלֵּק is the word used (*vid.* ver. 30; Ps. lxviii. 13; Isa. ix. 2). מְחַצֵּץ
is to be regarded, as the Rabbins maintain, as a *denom.* from חֵץ, to
hold an arrow, signifying therefore the shooter of an arrow. It was
probably a natural thing for Deborah, who dwelt in Benjamin, to
mention the archers as representatives of warriors generally, since
this was the principal weapon employed by the Benjaminites (see
1 Chron. viii. 40, xii. 2; 2 Chron. xiv. 7, xvii. 17). The tarrying
of the warriors among the drawers of water, where the flocks and
herds were being watered, points to the time of peace, when the
warriors were again occupied with their civil and domestic affairs.
יְתַנּוּ is a simple aorist. תָּנָה, *lit.* to repeat, then to relate, or praise.
"*The righteousness of Jehovah*," *i.e.* the marvellous acts of the Lord
in and upon Israel for the accomplishing of His purposes of salvation, in which the righteousness of His work upon earth was
manifested (cf. 1 Sam. xii. 7, Micah vi. 5). צִדְקוֹת פִּרְזוֹנוֹ has been
rendered by modern expositors, either "the righteous acts of His
guidance or of His decision" (*Ewald* and *Bertheau*), or "the
righteous acts of His commanders," or "the benefits towards His
princes (leaders) in Israel" (*Ros.* and others). But neither of these
can be sustained. We must take פִּרְזוֹן here in just the same sense
as in ver. 7; the country covered with open towns and villages,
together with their inhabitants, whom Jehovah had delivered from
the hostile oppression that had rested upon them, by means of the
victory obtained over Sisera. After that victory the people of the
Lord went down again to their gates, from the mountains and hiding-
places in which they had taken refuge from their foes (vers. 6, 7),

returning again to the plains of the land, and the towns that were now delivered from the foe.

Ver. 12 forms the introduction to the second part, viz. the description of the conflict and the victory. Throwing herself into the great event which she is about to commemorate, Deborah calls upon herself to strike up a song, and upon Barak to lead off his prisoners :

> Ver. 12. Awake, awake, Deborah !
> Awake, awake, utter a song !
> Rise up, Barak, and lead captive thy captives, O son of Abinoam !

עוּרִי has the tone upon the last syllable on the first two occasions, to answer to the rapid summoning burst of the Lord in the opening address (*Bertheau*). שְׁבֵה שֶׁבְיֶ, to lead away captives, as the fruit of the victory; not merely to lead in triumph. On the form וּשֲׁבֵה with *Chateph-patach*, see *Ewald*, § 90, *b*. In the next three strophes of this part (vers. 13–21) the progress of the conflict is described; and in the first two the part taken in the battle by the different tribes (vers. 13–15*a*, and 15*b*–18).

> Ver. 13. Then came down a remnant of nobles of the nation ;
> Jehovah came down to me among the heroes.
> 14. Of Ephraim, whose root in Amalek ;
> Behind thee Benjamin among thy peoples.
> From Machir came down leaders,
> And from Zebulun marchers with the staff of the conductor.
> 15*a*. And princes in Issachar with Deborah,
> And Issachar as well as Barak,
> Driven into the valley through his feet.

Looking back to the commencement of the battle, the poetess describes the streaming of the brave men of the nation down from the mountains, to fight the enemy with Barak and Deborah in the valley of Jezreel ; though the whole nation did not rise as one man against its oppressors, but only a remnant of the noble and brave in the nation, with whom Jehovah went into the battle. In ver. 13 the Masoretic pointing of יְרַד is connected with the rabbinical idea of the word as the *fut. apoc.* of רָדָה : " *then* (now) *will the remnant rule over the glorious*," *i.e.* the remnant left in Israel over the stately foe ; " Jehovah rules for me (or through me) over the heroes in Sisera's army," which *Luther* has also adopted. But, as *Schnurr*. has maintained, this view is decidedly erroneous, inasmuch as it is altogether irreconcilable with the description which follows of the marching of the tribes of Israel into the battle. ירד is to be understood in the same sense as יָרְדוּ in ver. 14, and to be pointed as a perfect יָרַד.[1] "*There came down,*" *sc.* from the mountains of the land into the plain of Jezreel, a remnant of nobles. לְאַדִּירִים is used instead of a closer subordination through the construct state, to bring out the idea of שָׂרִיד into greater prominence (see *Ewald,* § 292). עָם is in apposition to לְאַדִּירִים, and not to be connected with the following word יְהֹוָה, as it is by some, in opposition to the accents. The thought is rather this: with the nobles or among the brave Johovah himself went against the foe. לִ is a *dat. commodi,* equivalent to "for my joy."—Ver. 14. "*From* (מִנִּי, poetical for מִן) *Ephraim,*" *sc.* there came fighting men; not the whole tribe, but only nobles or brave men, and indeed those whose roots were in Amalek, *i.e.* those who were rooted or had taken root, *i.e.* had settled and spread themselves out upon the tribe-territory of Ephraim, which had formerly been inhabited by Amalekites, the mount of the Amalekites, mentioned in chap. xii. 15 (for the figure itself, see Isa. xxvii. 6, Ps. lxxx. 10, and Job v. 3). "*Behind thee,*" *i.e.* behind Ephraim, there followed Benjamin among thy (Ephraim's) people (עֲמָמִים, a poetical form for עַמִּים, in the sense of hosts). Benjamin lived farther south than Ephraim, and therefore, when looked at from the stand-point of the plain of Jezreel, behind Ephraim; "but he came upon the scene of battle, either in subordination to the more powerful Ephraimites, or rushing on with the Ephraimitish hosts" (*Bertheau*). "*From Machir,*" *i.e.* from western Manasseh, there came down leaders (see at ver. 9), *sc.* with warriors in their train. *Machir* cannot refer to the Manassite family of Machir, to which Moses gave the northern part of Gilead, and Bashan, for an inheritance (comp. Josh. xvii. 1 with xiii. 29–31), but it stands poetically for Manasseh generally, as Machir was the only son of Manasseh, from whom all the Manassites were descended (Gen. l. 23; Num. xxvi. 29 sqq., xxvii. 1). The reference here, however, is simply to that portion of the tribe of Manasseh which had received its inheritance by the side of Ephraim, in the land to the west of the Jordan. This explanation of the word is required, not only by the fact that Machir is mentioned after Ephraim and Benjamin, and

---

[1] The *Cod. Al.* of the LXX. contains the correct rendering, τότε κατέβη κατάλειμμα. In the Targum also ירד is correctly translated נְחַת, *descendit,* although the germs of the rabbinical interpretation are contained in the paraphrase of the whole verse: *tunc descendit unus ex exercitu Israel et fregit fortitudinem fortium gentium. Ecce non ex fortitudine manus eorum fuit hoc; sed Dominus fregit ante populum suum fortitudinem virorum osorum eorum.*

before Zebulun and Issachar, but still more decidedly by the introduction of Gilead beyond Jordan in connection with Reuben, in ver.
17, which can only signify Gad and eastern Manasseh. Hence the
two names *Machir* and *Gilead*, the names of Manasseh's son and
grandson, are poetically employed to denote the two halves of the
tribe of Manasseh; Machir signifying the western Manassites, and
Gilead the eastern. " *From Zebulun marchers* (מָשַׁךְ, to approach in
long processions, as in chap. iv. 6) *with the staff of the conductor.*"
סֹפֵר, writer or numberer, was the technical name given to the
musterer-general, whose duty it was to levy and muster the troops
(2 Kings xxv. 19; cf. 2 Chron. xxvi. 11); here it denotes the
military leader generally.—Ver. 15a. שָׂרַי, " *my princes*," does not
furnish any appropriate meaning, as neither Deborah nor Barak
was of the tribe of Issachar, and it is not stated anywhere that the
Issacharites gathered round Deborah as their leader. The reading
שָׂרֵי (*stat. constr.*), adopted by the old versions, must be taken as the
correct one, and the introduction of the preposition בְּ does not preclude this (compare הָרֵי בַגִּלְבֹּעַ, 2 Sam. i. 21, and *Ewald*, § 289, *b.*).
עִם, which is used to denote an outward equality, as in 1 Sam.
xvii. 42, and is substantially the same as the כְּ which follows (" *just
as*"), is construed without בְּ in the first clause, as in Ps. xlviii. 6.
בָּעֵמֶק : into the valley of Jezreel, the plain of Kishon. שֻׁלַּח בְּרַגְלָיו, as
in Job xviii. 8, to be sent off, *i.e.* incessantly impelled, through his
feet ; here it is applied to an irresistible force of enthusiasm for the
battle. The nominative to שֻׁלַּח is Issachar and Barak.

Ver. 15*b*. At the brooks of Reuben were great resolutions of heart.
   16. Why remainest thou between the hurdles,
      To hear the piping of the flocks?
      At the brooks of Reuben were great projects of heart.
   17. Gilead rests on the other side of the Jordan;
      And Dan . . . why tarries he by ships?
      Asher sits on the shore of the sea,
      And by his bays he reposes.
   18. Zebulun, a people that despises its soul even to death,
      And Naphtali upon the heights of the field.

In this strophe Deborah first of all mentions the tribes which
took no part in the conflict (vers. 15*b*–17), and then returns in ver.
18 to the Zebulunites, who staked their life along with Naphtali for
the deliverance of Israel from the yoke of the enemy. The enumeration of the tribes who remained at a distance from the conflict
commences with Reuben (vers. 15*b* and 16). In this tribe there
did arise a lively sympathy with the national elevation. They held

meetings, passed great resolutions, but it led to no practical result; and at length they preferred to remain quietly at home in their own comfortable pastoral life. The meaning brooks for פְּלַגּוֹת is well established by Job xx. 17, and there is no reason whatever for explaining the word as equivalent to פְּלַגּוֹת, מִפְלַגּוֹת, divisions (2 Chron. xxxv. 5, 12; Ezra vi. 18). The territory of Reuben, which was celebrated for its splendid pastures, must have abounded in brooks. The question, Why satest thou, or remainedst thou sitting between the hurdles? *i.e.* in the comfortable repose of a shepherd's life, is an utterance of amazement; and the irony is very apparent in the next clause, to hear the bleating of the flocks, *i.e.* the piping of the shepherds, instead of the blast of the war-trumpets.—Ver. 17. Gilead, Dan, and Asher took no part at all. By *Gilead*, the tribes of Gad and half Manasseh are intended. The use of the term הַגִּלְעָד to denote the whole of the territory of the Israelites on the east of the Jordan probably gave occasion to this, although גִּלְעָד (without the article) does not refer to the land even here, but refers primarily to the grandson of Manasseh, as the representative of his family which dwelt in Gilead. (For further remarks, see at ver. 14.) Dan also did not let the national movement disturb it in its earthly trade and commerce. גּוּר, to keep one's self in a place, is construed here with the accusative of the place, as in Ps. cxx. 5. The territory of Dan included the port of Joppa (see at Josh. xix. 46), where the Danites probably carried on a trade with the Phœnicians. Asher also in his land upon the coast did not allow himself to be disturbed from his rest, to join in the common war of its nation. חוֹף יַמִּים is used, as in Gen. xlix. 13, for the shore of the Mediterranean Sea. מִפְרָצִים, *ἀπ. λεγ.*, literally a rent, and hence applied to a bay, as an incision made in the sea-shore.—Ver. 18. Zebulun and Naphtali acted quite differently. Zebulun showed itself as a people that despised its life even to death, *i.e.* that sacrificed its life for the deliverance of its fatherland. Naphtali did the same in its mountain home. The two tribes had raised 10,000 fighting men at Barak's call (chap. iv. 10), who constituted at any rate the kernel of the Israelitish army.

If we run over the tribes enumerated, it seems strange that the tribes of Judah and Simeon are not mentioned either among those who joined in the battle, or among those who stayed away. The only way in which this can be explained is on the supposition that these two tribes were never summoned by Barak, either because they were so involved in conflict with the Philistines, that they were unable to render any assistance to the northern tribes against their Canaanitish oppressors, as we might infer from chap. iii. 31, or because of some inward disagreement between these tribes and the rest. But even apart from Judah and Simeon, the want of sympathy on the part of the tribes that are reproved is a sufficient proof that the enthusiasm for the cause of the Lord had greatly diminished in the nation, and that the internal unity of the congregation was considerably loosened.

In the next strophe the battle and the victory are described:—

> Ver. 19. Kings came, . . . they fought;
> The kings of Canaan fought
> At Taanach, at the waters of Megiddo.
> A piece of silver they did not take.
> 20. From heaven they fought,
> The stars from their courses fought against Sisera.
> 21. The brook of Kishon swept them away,
> The brook of the olden time, the brook Kishon.
> Go on, my soul, in strength!

The advance of the foe is described in few words. Kings came on and fought. They were the kings of Canaan, since Jabin, like his ancestor (Josh. xi. 1 sqq.), had formed an alliance with other kings of northern Canaan, who went to the battle under the command of Sisera. The battle took place at Taanach (see at Josh. xii. 21), by the water of Megiddo, the present Lejun (see at Josh. xii. 21), i.e. by the brook Kishon (cf. chap. iv. 7). Taanach and Megiddo were not quite five miles apart, and beside and between them there were several brooks which ran into the southern arm of the Kishon, that flowed through the plain to the north of both these towns. The hostile kings went into the battle with the hope of slaying the Israelites and making a rich capture of booty. But their hopes were disappointed. They could not take with them a piece of silver as booty. בֶּצַע, which generally signifies booty or gain, is probably to be taken here in its primary sense of *frustum*, from בָּצַע, to cut off or cut in pieces, a " piece of silver," equivalent to a single piece of valuable booty.—Ver. 20. For not only did the Israelites fight against them, but the powers of heaven also. " *From heaven* " is more minutely defined by " *the stars from their courses.*" These words explain the statement in chap. iv. 15, " the Lord discomfited Sisera;" though in our opinion not so clearly as to enable us to define more precisely the natural phenomenon by which God threw the enemy into confusion. In all probability we have to think of a terrible storm, with thunder and lightning and hail, or the sudden bursting of a cloud, which is poetically described as though the stars of heaven had left their courses to fight for the Lord and His kingdom upon earth.—Ver. 21. The kings of Canaan could do nothing against these powers. They were smitten; the brook Kishon washed them (*i.e.* their corpses) away. The meaning " to wash away" is well established by the dialects and the context, though the verb itself only occurs here. As the battle was fought between Taanach and Megiddo, *i.e.* to the south of the brook Kishon, and the smitten foe fled towards the north, many of them met with their death in the waves of the brook, which was flowing over its banks at the time. The brook is called נַחַל קְדוּמִים, *i.e.* the brook of the old world or the olden time (according to the LXX. *Cod. Vat.* χειμάρρους ἀρχαίων), as the stream that had been flowing from time immemorial, and not, as the Chaldee interprets it, the stream that had been celebrated from olden time on account of the mighty acts that had been performed there. The meaning suggested by *Ewald* and others, " brook of attacks, or slaughters," is not well sustained, although קֶדֶם is sometimes used to denote a hostile encounter. The last clause interrupts the description of the slaughter and the victory. Borne away by the might of the acts to be commemorated, Deborah stimulates her soul, *i.e.* herself, to a vigorous continuation of her song. תִּדְרְכִי is jussive, and עֹז an accusative governed by the verb, in strength, vigorously; for she had still to celebrate the glorious results of the victory. This is done in the third part of the song (vers. 22–31), the first strophe of which (vers. 22–24) describes in brief drastic traits the flight of the foe, and the treatment of the fugitives by the people of the land.

> Ver. 22. Then did the hoofs of the horses stamp
> With the hunting, the hunting of his strong ones.
>
> 23. Curse ye Meroz, saith the angel of the Lord;
> Curse ye, curse ye the inhabitants thereof!
> Because they came not to the help of Jehovah,
> To the help of Jehovah among the mighty.
>
> 24. Blessed before women be Jael,
> The wife of Heber the Kenite,
> Blessed before women in the tent!

The war-chariots of the enemy hunted away in the wildest flight (ver. 22). The horses stamped the ground with the continuous hunting or galloping away of the warriors. דַּהֲרָה, the hunting (cf. דָּהַר, Nah. iii. 2). The repetition of the word expresses the continuance or incessant duration of the same thing (see *Ewald,* § 313, *a.*). אַבִּירִים, strong ones, are not the horses, but the warriors

in the war-chariots. The suffix refers to סוּם, which is used collectively. The mighty ones on horses are not, however, merely the
Canaanitish princes, such as Sisera, as *Ewald* maintains, but the
warriors generally who hunted away upon their war-chariots.—
Ver. 23. The enemy, or at all events Sisera, might have been
destroyed in his flight by the inhabitants of Meroz; but they did
not come to the help of the Israelites, and brought down the curse
of God upon themselves in consequence. That this is the thought
of ver. 23 is evident from the context, and more especially from the
blessing pronounced upon Jael in ver. 24. The situation of Meroz,
which is not mentioned again, cannot be determined with certainty
Wilson and *v. Raumer* imagine that it may be *Kefr Musr* on the
south of Tabor, the situation of which at all events is more suitable than *Marussus*, which was an hour and a half to the north of
Beisan, and which *Rabbi Schwarz* supposed to be Meroz (see *V. de
Velde*, Mem. p. 334). The curse upon the inhabitants of this
place is described as a word or command of the angel of the Lord,
inasmuch as it was the angel of the Lord who fought for Israel
at Megiddo, as the revealer of the invisible God, and smote the
Canaanites. Deborah heard from him the words of the curse
upon the inhabitants of Meroz, because they did not come to help
Jehovah when He was fighting with and for the Israelites. " *Among
the heroes*," or mighty men, *i.e.* associating with the warriors of
Israel.—Ver. 24. Jael behaved altogether differently, although she
was not an Israelite, but a woman of the tribe of the Kenites,
which was only allied with Israel (see chap. iv. 11, 17 sqq.). For
her heroic deed she was to be blessed before women (מִן as in Gen.
iii. 14, literally removed away from women). The " *women in the
tent*" are dwellers in tents, or shepherdesses. This heroic act is
poetically commemorated in the strophe which follows in vers.
25–27.

> Ver. 25. He asked water, she gave him milk ;
> She handed him cream in the dish of nobles.
> 26. She stretched out her hand to the plug,
> And her right hand to the workmen's hammer,
> And hammered Sisera, broke his head,
> And dashed in pieces and pierced his temples.
> 27. Between her feet he bowed, he fell, he lay down :
> Between her feet he bowed, he fell :
> Where he bowed, there he fell down dead.

Assuming that the fact itself is well known, Deborah does not
think it necessary to mention Sisera's name in ver. 25. חֶמְאָה,

which generally signifies thick curdled milk, is used here as synonymous with חָלָב, in the sense of good superior milk. סֵפֶל is only used
here and in chap. vi. 38, and signifies a bowl or vessel for holding
liquids (see *Arab.*, *Chald.*, and *Talm.*; also *Bochart,* Hieroz. i. pp. 625
sqq., ed. *Ros.*). The dish of nobles is a fine costly bowl, such as they
are accustomed to hand to noble guests. The whole verse is simply
intended to express the thought, that Jael had given to her guest
Sisera a friendly reception, and treated him honourably and hospi
tably, simply in order to make him feel secure.—Ver. 26. " *Her*
hand," *i.e.* the left hand, as is shown by the antithesis, " her right
hand," which follows. On the form תִּשְׁלַחְנָה, the third pers. fem.
sing. with נָה attached, to distinguish it the more clearly from the
second pers., see the remarks on Ex. i. 10. הַלְמוּת עֲמֵלִים, *hammer*
or *mallet of the hard workers*, is a large heavy hammer. For the
purpose of depicting the boldness and greatness of the deed, the
words are crowded together in the second hemistich : הָלַם, to hammer,
or smite with the hammer ; מָחַק, ἀπ. λεγ., to smite in pieces, smite
through ; מָחַץ, to smite or dash in pieces ; חָלַף, to pierce or bore
through. The heaping up of the words in ver. 27 answers the
same purpose. They do not " express the delight of a satisfied
thirst for revenge," but simply bring out the thought that Sisera,
who was for years the terror of Israel, was now struck dead with a
single blow. בַּאֲשֶׁר כָּרַע, at the place where he bowed, there he fell
שָׁדוּד, overpowered and destroyed. In conclusion, the singer refers
once more in the last strophe (vers. 28–30) to the mother of Sisera,
as she waited impatiently for the return of her son, and foreboded
his death, whilst the prudent princesses who surrounded her sought
to cheer her with the prospect of a rich arrival of booty.

Ver. 28. Through the window there looks out and cries aloud
  The mother of Sisera, through the lattice work,
  Why does his chariot delay its coming ?
  Why tarry the steps of his team ?
 29. The wise of her princesses reply :
  —But she repeats her words to herself—
 30. Surely they are finding and sharing booty :
  A maiden, two maidens to the head of a man,
  Booty of variegated cloths for Sisera :
  Booty of variegated cloths, garments worked in divers colours,
  A variegated cloth, two garments worked in divers colours for his neck
   as booty.

Sisera's mother looks out with impatience for the return of her
son, and cries aloud out of the window, Why is he never coming?—

foreboding the disastrous result of the war. תְּיַבֵּב, ἁπ. λεγ., signifies to cry; in Aramæan it is used for הֵרִיעַ and רַגֵּן, to denote a loud joyful cry; here it evidently signifies a loud cry of anxiety. For the repeated question, Why does his chariot delay its coming? is evidently expressive of anxiety and alarm. The form אֶחֱרוּ, *perf.* *Piel for* אִחֲרוּ, may be attributed to the influence of the aleph, which favours the seghol sound, like יֵחַמוּ in Gen. xxx. 39. The combination of פַּעֲמֵי מַרְכְּבוֹתָיו, " steps of his chariots," cannot be explained, as it is by *Bertheau*, on the ground that the word פַעֲמֵי, as a general expression for intermittent movement, might also be applied to the jerking of the wheels in rolling, but simply on the supposition that מַרְכָּבוֹת, as a synonym for רֶכֶב, is used for the horses yoked to the chariot in the sense of team, like רֶכֶב in 2 Sam. viii. 4, x. 18, etc.—Ver. 29. The princesses in attendance upon Sisera's mother sought to console her with the remark, that Sisera would have to gather together rich booty, and that his return was delayed in consequence. In the expression " the wisest of her princesses" (see *Ges.* § 119, 2), the irony is very obvious, as the reality put all their wise conjectures to shame. תַּעֲנֶנָּה, third pers. plur. fem. for תַּעֲנֶינָה. The second hemistich of ver. 29 contains a clause inserted as a parenthesis. אַף־הִיא is adversative : " *but she ;*" אַף is only an emphatic copula; the antithesis lies in the emphatic change of subject indicated by הִיא. הָשִׁיב אֲמָרֶיהָ, *lit.* to bring back her words, *i.e.* to repeat. לָהּ is used in a reflective sense, " to herself." The meaning is : But Sisera's mother did not allow herself to be quieted by the words of her wise princesses ; on the contrary, she kept repeating the anxious question, Why does Sisera delay his coming? In ver. 30 there follows the answer of the wise princesses. They imagine that Sisera has been detained by the large amount of booty which has to be divided. הֲלֹא, *nonne,* is he not, in the sense of lively certainty. They will certainly discover rich booty, and divide it. רַחַם, *uterus,* for *puella.* " *A girl* (or indeed probably) *two girls to the head of the man,*" *i.e.* for each man. צְבָעִים, *coloured things,* cloths or clothes. רִקְמָה, *worked stuff,* or garments worked in divers colours (see the remarks on Ex. xxvi. 36), is attached without the *vav cop.* to צְבָעִים, and is also dependent upon שָׁלָל. The closing words, לְצַוְּארֵי שָׁלָל, " *for the necks,*" or (as the plural is also frequently used to signify a single neck, *e.g.* Gen. xxvii. 16, xlv. 14) " *for the neck of the booty,*" do not give any appropriate sense, as שָׁלָל neither signifies animals taken as booty nor the taker of booty. The idea, however, that שָׁלָל is used for אִישׁ שָׁלָל, like הֶלֶךְ in 2 Sam. xii. 4

for אִישׁ הֶלֶךְ, *viator*, and חֶתֶף in Prov. xxiii. 28 for אִישׁ חֶתֶף, seems inadmissible, since שָׁלָל has just before been used three times in its literal sense. There is just the same objection to the application of שָׁלָל to animals taken as booty, not to mention the fact that they would hardly have thought of having valuable cloths upon the necks of animals taken as booty. Consequently the only explanation that remains, is either to alter לְצַוְּארֵי into לְצַוָּארוֹ or לְצַוָּארָיו, or else to change שָׁלָל into שֵׁגַל, the royal spouse. In the former case, שָׁלָל would have to be taken as in apposition to צֶבַע רִקְמָתִים: a variegated cloth, two worked in divers colours for his (Sisera's) neck as booty, as the LXX. have rendered it (τῷ τραχήλῳ αὐτοῦ σκῦλα). *Ewald* and *Bertheau* decide in favour of the second alteration, and defend it on the ground that שָׁלָל might easily find its way into the text as a copyist's error for שֵׁגַל, on account of שָׁלָל having been already written three times before, and that we cannot dispense with some such word as שֵׁגַל here, since the repetition of שָׁלָל three times, and the threefold use of לְ, evidently show that there were three different kinds of people among whom the booty was to be distributed; and also that it was only a fitting thing that Sisera should set apart one portion of the booty to adorn the neck of his wife, and that the wisest of the noble ladies, when mentioning the booty, should not forget themselves.

Ver. 31a. So shall all Thine enemies perish, O Jehovah!
> But let those who love Him be like the rising of the sun in its strength.

This forms the conclusion of the song. כֵּן, *so*, refers to the whole of the song: just in the same manner as Sisera and his warriors. The rising of the sun in its strength is a striking image of the exaltation of Israel to a more and more glorious unfolding of its destiny, which Deborah anticipated as the result of this victory. With the last clause, "*And the land had rest forty years*" (cf. chap. iii. 11, 30, viii. 28), the account of this event is brought to a close.

II. THE TIMES OF GIDEON AND HIS FAMILY, AND OF THE JUDGES TOLA AND JAIR.—CHAP. VI.–X. 5.

In this second stage of the period of the judges, which did not extend over an entire century (only ninety-five years), Israel was only punished for its apostasy from the Lord, it is true, with a seven years' oppression by the Midianites; but the misery which these enemies, who allied themselves with Amalekites and other Arabian hordes, brought upon both land and people, so far surpassed the pressure of the previous chastisements, that the Israelites were obliged to take refuge from the foe in ravines, caves, and strongholds of the mountains. But the more heavily the Lord punished His rebellious nation, the more gloriously did He set forth His nearness to help, and also the way which would lead to a lasting peace, and to true deliverance out of every trouble, in the manner in which He called and fitted Gideon to be its deliverer, and gave him the victory over the innumerable army of the hostile hordes, with only 300 chosen warriors. But the tendency to idolatry and to the worship of Baal had already become so strong in Israel, that even Gideon, that distinguished hero of God, who had been so marvellously called, and who refused the title of king when offered to him from genuine fidelity to the Lord, yielded to the temptation to establish for himself an unlawful worship, in a high-priestly ephod which had been prepared for his use, and thus gave the people an occasion for idolatry. For this reason his house was visited with severe judgments, which burst upon it after his death, under the three years' reign of his son Abimelech; although, notwithstanding the deep religious and moral depravity which was manifested in the doings of Abimelech, the Lord gave His people rest for forty-five years longer after the death of Abimelech under two judges, before He punished their apostasy with fresh hostile oppressions.

The history of Gideon and his family is related very fully, because the working of the grace and righteousness of the faithful covenant God was so obviously displayed therein, that it contained a rich treasure of instruction and warning for the church of the Lord in all ages. The account contains such an abundance of special notices of separate events and persons, as can only be explained on the supposition that the author made use of copious records which had been made by contemporaries and eye-witnesses of the events. At the same time, the separate details do not contain any such characteristic marks as will enable us to discover clearly, or determine with any certainty, the nature of the source or sources which the author employed. The only things peculiar to this narrative are the use of the prefix שֶׁ for אֲשֶׁר, not only in reports of the sayings of the persons engaged (chap. vi. 17), but also in the direct narrative of facts (chap. vii. 12, viii. 26), and the formula רוּחַ יְהוָה לָבְשָׁה (chap. vi. 34), which only occurs again in 1 Chron. xii. 18, 2 Chron. xxiv. 20. On the other hand, neither the interchange of *ha-Elohim* (chap. vi. 36, 39, vii. 14) and *Elohim* (chap. vi. 40, viii. 3, ix. 7, 9, 13, 23, 56, 57) with *Jehovah*, nor the use of the name *Jerubbaal* for *Gideon* (chap. vi. 32, vii. 1, viii. 29, ix. 1, 2, 5, 16, 19, 24, 28), nor lastly the absence of the "theocratical pragmatism" in chap. ix., contains any proof of the nature of the source employed, or even of the employment of two different sources, as these peculiarities are founded upon the contents and materials of the narrative itself.[1]

Oppression of Israel by the Midianites, and call of Gideon to be their Deliverer.—Chap. vi. 1–32.

Vers. 1–10. *Renewed Apostasy of the Nation, and its Punishment.*—Ver. 1. As the Israelites forsook Jehovah their God again, the Lord delivered them up for seven years into the hands of the Midianites. The *Midianites*, who were descendants of Abraham and Keturah (Gen. xxv. 2), and had penetrated into the grassy steppes on the eastern side of the country of the Moabites and

---

[1] Even *Bertheau*, who infers from these data that two different sources were employed, admits that *ha-Elohim* in the mouth of the Midianites (chap. vii. 14) and *Elohim* in Jotham's fable, where it is put into the mouth of the trees, prove nothing at all, because here, from the different meanings of the divine names, the author could not have used anything but *Elohim*. But the same difference is quite as unmistakeable in chap. viii. 3, ix. 7, 23, 56, 57, since in these passages, either the antithesis of man and God, or the idea of supernatural causality, made it most natural for the author to use the general name of God even if it did not render it absolutely necessary. There remain, therefore, only chap. vi. 20, 36, 39, 40, where the use of *ha-Elohim* and *Elohim* instead of Jehovah may possibly have originated with the source made use of by the author. On the other hand, the name *Jerubbaal*, which Gideon received in consequence of the destruction of the altar of Baal (chap. vi. 32), is employed with conscious reference to its origin and meaning, not only in chap. vii. 1, viii. 29, 35, but also throughout chap. ix., as we may see more especially in chap. ix. 16, 19, 28. And lastly, even the peculiarities of chap. ix.—namely, that the names *Jehovah* and *Gideon* do not occur there at all, and that many historical circumstances are related apparently without any link of connection, and torn away from some wider context, which might have rendered them intelligible, and without which very much remains obscure—do not prove that the author drew these incidents from a different source from the rest of the history of Gideon,—such, for example, as a more complete history of the town of Shechem and its rulers in the time of the judges, as *Bertheau* imagines. For these peculiarities may be explained satisfactorily enough from the intention so clearly expressed in chap. viii. 34, 35, and ix. 57, of showing how the ingratitude of the Israelites towards Gideon, especially the wickedness of the Shechemites, who helped to murder Gideon's sons to gratify Abimelech, was punished by God. And no other peculiarities can be discovered that could possibly establish a diversity of sources.

Ammonites (see at Num. xxii. 4), had shown hostility to Israel even in the time of Moses, and had been defeated in a war of retaliation on the part of the Israelites (Num. xxxi.). But they had afterwards recovered their strength, so that now, after an interval of 200 years, the Lord used them as a rod of chastisement for His rebellious people. In vers. 1, 2, 6, they alone are mentioned as oppressors of Israel; but in vers. 3, 33, and chap. vii. 12, the Amalekites and children of the east are mentioned in connection with them, from which we may see that the Midianites were the principal enemies, but had allied themselves with other predatory Bedouin tribes, to make war upon the Israelites and devastate their land. On the *Amalekites*, those leading enemies of the people of God who had sprung from Esau, see the notes on Gen. xxxvi. 12 and Ex. xvii. 8. "*Children of the east*" (see Job i. 3) is the general name for the tribes that lived in the desert on the east of Palestine, "like the name of *Arabs* in the time of *Josephus* (in Ant. v. 6, 1, he calls the children of the east mentioned here by the name of Arabs), or in later times the names of the Nabatæans and Kedarenes" (*Bertheau*). Hence we find in chap. viii. 10, that all the enemies who oppressed the Israelites are called "children of the east."—Vers. 2–5. *The oppression of Israel by Midian and its allies.* Their power pressed so severely upon the Israelites, that before (or because of) them the latter "*made them the ravines which are in the mountains, and the caves, and the strongholds,*" sc. which were to be met with all over the land in after times (viz. at the time when our book was written), and were safe places of refuge in time of war. This is implied in the definite article before מִנְהָרוֹת and the following substantives. The words "*they made them*" are not at variance with the fact that there are many natural caves to be found in the limestone mountains of Palestine. For, on the one hand, they do not affirm that all the caves to be found in the land were made by the Israelites at that time; and, on the other hand, עָשָׂה does not preclude the use of natural caves as places of refuge, since it not only denotes the digging and making of caves, but also the adaptation of natural caves to the purpose referred to, *i.e.* the enlargement of them, or whatever was required to make them habitable. The ἅπ. λεγ. מִנְהָרוֹת does not mean "light holes" (*Bertheau*), or "holes with openings to the light," from נָהַר, in the sense of to stream, to enlighten (*Rashi, Kimchi*, etc.), but is to be taken in the sense of "*mountain ravines*," hollowed out by torrents (from נָהַר, to pour), which the Israelites made into hiding-places. מְצָדוֹת, *fortresses*, mountain strongholds. These ravines, caves, and fortresses were not merely to serve as hiding-places for the Israelitish fugitives, but much more as places of concealment for their possessions and necessary supplies. For the Midianites, like genuine Bedouins, thought far more of robbing and plundering and laying waste the land of the Israelites, than of exterminating the people themselves. *Herodotus* (i. 17) says just the same respecting the war of the Lydian king Alyattes with the Milesians.

Vers. 3, 4. When the Israelites had sown, the Midianites and their allies came upon them, encamped against them, and destroyed the produce of the land (the fruits of the field and soil) as far as Gaza, in the extreme south-west of the land ("till thou come," as in Gen. x. 19, etc.). As the enemy invaded the land with their camels and flocks, and on repeated occasions encamped in the valley of Jezreel (ver. 33), they must have entered the land on the west of the Jordan by the main road which connects the countries on the east with Palestine on the west, crossing the Jordan near Beisan, and passing through the plain of Jezreel; and from this point they spread over Palestine to the sea-coast of Gaza. "*They left no sustenance* (in the shape of produce of the field and soil) *in Israel, and neither sheep, nor oxen, nor asses. For they came on with their flocks, and their tents came like grasshoppers in multitude.*" The *Chethibh* יָבֹאוּ is not to be altered into וּבָאוּ, according to the *Keri* and certain *Codd.* If we connect וְאָהֳלֵיהֶם with the previous words, according to the Masoretic pointing, we have a simple asyndeton. It is more probable, however, that ואהליהם belongs to what follows: "*And their tents came in such numbers as grasshoppers.*" כְּדֵי, *lit.* like a multitude of grasshoppers, in such abundance. "*Thus they came into the land to devastate it.*"—Ver. 6. The Israelites were greatly weakened in consequence (יִדַּל, the *imperf. Niphal* of דָּלַל), so that in their distress they cried to the Lord for help.—Vers. 7–10. But before helping them, the Lord sent a prophet to reprove the people for not hearkening to the voice of their God, in order that they might reflect, and might recognise in the oppression which crushed them the chastisement of God for their apostasy, and so be brought to sincere repentance and conversion by their remembrance of the former miraculous displays of the grace of God. The Lord God, said the prophet to the people, brought you out of Egypt, the house of bondage, and delivered you out of the hand of Egypt (Ex. xviii. 9), and out of the hand of all your oppressors (see chap. ii. 18, iv. 3, x. 12), whom He drove before you (the reference is to the Amorites and Canaanites who were conquered by Moses and Joshua); but ye have not followed His commandment, that ye should not worship the gods of the Amorites. The Amorites stand here for the Canaanites, as in Gen. xv. 16 and Josh. xxiv. 15

Vers. 11–32. *Call of Gideon to be the Deliverer of Israel.*—As the reproof of the prophet was intended to turn the hearts of the people once more to the Lord their God and deliverer, so the manner in which God called Gideon to be their deliverer, and rescued Israel from its oppressors through his instrumentality, was intended to furnish the most evident proof that the help and salvation of Israel were not to be found in man, but solely in their God. God had also sent their former judges. The Spirit of Jehovah had come upon Othniel, so that he smote the enemy in the power of God (chap. iii. 10). Ehud had put to death the hostile king by stratagem, and then destroyed his army; and Barak had received the command of the Lord, through the prophetess Deborah, to deliver His people from the dominion of their foes, and had carried out the command with her assistance. But Gideon was called to be the deliverer of Israel through an appearance of the angel of the Lord, to show to him and to all Israel, that Jehovah, the God of the fathers, was still near at hand to His people, and could work miracles as in the days of old, if Israel would only adhere to Him and keep His covenant. The call of Gideon took place in two revelations from God. First of all the Lord appeared to him in the visible form of an angel, in which He had already made himself known to the patriarchs, and summoned him in the strength of God to deliver Israel out of the hand of the Midianites (vers. 11–24). He then commanded him, in a dream of the night, to throw down his father's altar of Baal, and to offer a burnt-offering to Jehovah his God upon an altar erected for the purpose (vers. 25–32). In the first revelation the Lord acknowledged Gideon; in the second He summoned Gideon to acknowledge Him as his God.

Vers. 11–24. *Appearance of the Angel of the Lord.*—Ver. 11. The angel of the Lord, *i.e.* Jehovah, in a visible self-revelation in human form (see vol. i. pp. 185 sqq.), appeared this time in the form of a traveller with a staff in his hand (ver. 21), and sat down " *under the terebinth which* (was) *in Ophrah, that* (belonged) *to Joash the Abi-ezrite.*" It was not the oak, but Ophrah, that belonged to Joash, as we may see from ver. 24, where the expression " Ophrah of the Abi-ezrite" occurs. According to Josh. xvii. 2 and

1 Chron. vii. 18, *Abiezer* was a family in the tribe of Manasseh, and according to ver. 15 it was a small family of that tribe. *Joash* was probably the head of the family at that time, and as such was the lord or owner of *Ophrah*, a town (chap. viii. 27; cf. ix. 5) which was called "Ophrah of the Abi-ezrite," to distinguish it from Ophrah in the tribe of Benjamin (Josh. xviii. 23). The situation of the town has not yet been determined with certainty. *Josephus* (Ant. v. 6, 5) calls it *Ephran*. *Van de Velde* conjectures that it is to be found in the ruins of *Erfai*, opposite to Akrabeh, towards the S.E., near the Mohammedan Wely of Abu Kharib, on the S.W. of Janun (Mem. pp. 337–8), close to the northern boundary of the tribe-territory of Ephraim, if not actually within it. By this terebinth tree was Gideon the son of Joash "*knocking out wheat in the wine-press.*" חָבַט does not mean to thresh, but to knock with a stick. The wheat was threshed upon open floors, or in places in the open field that were rolled hard for the purpose, with threshing carriages or threshing shoes, or else with oxen, which they drove about over the scattered sheaves to tread out the grains with their hoofs. Only poor people knocked out the little corn that they had gleaned with a stick (Ruth ii. 17), and Gideon did it in the existing times of distress, namely in the pressing-tub, which, like all wine-presses, was sunk in the ground, in a hole that had been dug out or hewn in the rock (for a description of cisterns of this kind, see *Rob.* Bibl. Res. pp. 135–6), "*to make the wheat fly*" (*i.e.* to make it safe) "*from the Midianites*" (הָנִים as in Ex. ix. 20).—Ver. 12. While he was thus engaged the angel of the Lord appeared to him, and addressed him in these words: "*Jehovah* (is) *with thee, thou brave hero.*" This address contained the promise that the Lord would be with Gideon, and that he would prove himself a mighty hero through the strength of the Lord. This promise was to be a guarantee to him of strength and victory in his conflict with the Midianites.—Ver. 13. But Gideon, who did not recognise the angel of the Lord in the man who was sitting before him, replied doubtingly, "*Pray, sir, if Jehovah is with us, why has all this befallen us?*"—words which naturally recall to mind the words of Deut. xxxi. 17, "Are not these evils come upon us because our God is not among us?" "*And where,*" continued Gideon, "*are all His miracles, of which our fathers have told us? . . . But now Jehovah hath forsaken us, and delivered us into the hands of the Midianites.*" Gideon may have been reflecting, while knocking the wheat, upon the misery of his people, and the best means of delivering them from the

oppression of the enemy, but without being able to think of any possibility of rescuing them. For this reason he could not understand the address of the unknown traveller, and met his promise with the actual state of things with which it was so directly at variance, namely, the crushing oppression of his people by their enemies, from which he concluded that the Lord had forsaken them and given them up to their foes.—Ver. 14. " *Then Jehovah turned to him and said, Go in this thy strength, and deliver Israel from the hand of Midian. Have not I sent thee?*" The writer very appropriately uses the name Jehovah here, instead of the angel of Jehovah; for by his reply the angel distinctly manifested himself as Jehovah, more especially in the closing words, " *Have not I sent thee?*" (הֲלֹא, in the sense of lively assurance), which are so suggestive of the call of Moses to be the deliverer of Israel (Ex. iii. 12). " *In this thy strength,*" *i.e.* the strength which thou now hast, since Jehovah is with thee—Jehovah, who can still perform miracles as in the days of the fathers. The demonstrative "*this*" points to the strength which had just been given to him through the promise of God.—Ver. 15. Gideon perceived from these words that it was not a mere man who was speaking to him. He therefore said in reply, not "pray sir" (אֲדֹנִי), but "*pray, Lord*" (אֲדֹנָי, *i.e.* Lord God), and no longer speaks of deliverance as impossible, but simply inquires, with a consciousness of his own personal weakness and the weakness of his family, " *Whereby* (with what) *shall I save Israel? Behold, my family* (lit. ' *thousand,*' equivalent to *mishpachah*: see at Num. i. 16) *is the humblest in Manasseh, and I am the least in my father's house* (my family)."— Ver. 16. To this difficulty the Lord replies, " *I will be with thee* (see Ex. iii. 12, Josh. i. 5), *and thou wilt smite the Midianites as one man,*" *i.e.* at one blow, as they slay a single man (see Num. xiv. 15).—Vers. 17 sqq. As Gideon could no longer have any doubt after this promise that the person who had appeared to him was speaking in the name of God, he entreated him to assure him by a *sign* (אוֹת, a miraculous sign) of the certainty of his appearance. " *Do a sign that thou art speaking with me,*" *i.e.* that thou art really God, as thou affirmest. שָׁאַתָּה, for אֲשֶׁר אַתָּה, is taken from the language of ordinary life. At the same time he presents this request: " *Depart not hence till I* (go and) *come to thee, and bring out my offering and set it before thee;*" and the angel at once assents. *Minchah* does not mean a sacrifice in the strict sense (θυσία, *sacrificium*), nor merely a " gift of food," but a sacrificial gift in the sense of a gift presented to God, on the acceptance of which he hoped to receive the sign, which would show whether the person who had appeared to him was really God. This sacrificial gift consisted of such food as they were accustomed to set before a guest whom they wished especially to honour. Gideon prepared a kid of the goats (עָשָׂה is used to denote the preparation of food, as in Gen. xviii. 7, 8, etc.), and unleavened cakes of an ephah (about 22½ lbs.) of meal, and brought the flesh in a basket and the broth in a pot out to the terebinth tree, and placed it before him.—Vers. 20, 21. The angel of the Lord then commanded him to lay the flesh and the cakes upon a rock close by, and to pour the broth upon it; that is to say, to make use of the rock as an altar for the offering to be presented to the Lord. When he had done this, the angel touched the food with the end of his staff, and fire came out of the rock and consumed the food, and the angel of the Lord vanished out of Gideon's sight. "*This* rock," *i.e.* a rocky stone that was lying near. The departure of the angel from his eyes is to be regarded as a sudden disappearance; but the expression does not warrant the assumption that the angel ascended to heaven in this instance, as in chap. xiii. 19, 20, in the flame of the sacrifice.— Ver. 22. In this miracle Gideon received the desired sign, that the person who had appeared to him was God. But the miracle filled his soul with fear, so that he exclaimed, "*Alas, Lord Jehovah! for to this end have I seen the angel of the Lord face to face.*" אֲהָהּ אֲדֹנָי יהוה is an exclamation, sometimes of grief on account of a calamity that has occurred (Josh vii. 7), and sometimes of alarm caused by the foreboding of some anticipated calamity (Jer. i. 6, iv. 10, xxxii. 17; Ezek. iv. 14, etc.). Here it is an expression of alarm, viz. fear of the death which might be the necessary consequence of his seeing God (see Ex. xx. 16 (19), and the remarks on Gen. xvi. 13). The expression which follows, "*for to this end*," serves to account for the exclamation, without there being any necessity to assume an ellipsis, and supply "that I may die." כִּי־עַל־כֵּן is always used in this sense (see Gen. xviii. 5, xix. 8, xxxiii. 10, etc.).—Vers. 23, 24. But the Lord comforted him with the words, "*Peace to thee; fear not: thou wilt not die.*" These words were not spoken by the angel as he vanished away, but were addressed by God to Gideon, after the disappearance of the angel, by an inward voice. In gratitude for this comforting assurance, Gideon built an altar to the Lord, which he called *Jehovah-shalom,* "the Lord is peace." The intention of this altar, which was preserved "unto this day," *i.e.* till the

time when the book of Judges was composed, is indicated in the
name that was given to it. It was not to serve as a place of sacrifice, but to be a memorial and a witness of the revelation of God
which had been made to Gideon, and of the proof which he had
received that Jehovah was peace, *i.e.* would not destroy Israel in
wrath, but cherished thoughts of peace. For the assurance of peace
which He had given to Gideon, was also a confirmation of His
announcement that Gideon would conquer the Midianites in the
strength of God, and deliver Israel from its oppressors.

The theophany here described resembles so far the appearance
of the angel of the Lord to Abram in the grove of Mamre (Gen.
xviii.), that he appears in perfect human form, comes as a traveller,
and allows food to be set before him; but there is this essential
difference between the two, that whereas the three men who came
to Abraham took the food that was set before them and ate thereof,
—that is to say, allowed themselves to be hospitably entertained by
Abraham,—the angel of the Lord in the case before us did indeed
accept the *minchah* that had been made ready for him, but only as
a sacrifice of Jehovah which he caused to ascend in fire. The
reason for this essential difference is to be found in the different
purpose of the two theophanies. To Abraham the Lord came to
seal that fellowship of grace into which He had entered with him
through the covenant that He had made; but in the case of Gideon
His purpose was simply to confirm the truth of His promise, that
Jehovah would be with him and would send deliverance through
him to His people, or to show that the person who had appeared to
him was the God of the fathers, who could still deliver His people
out of the power of their enemies by working such miracles as the
fathers had seen. But the acceptance of the *minchah* prepared for
Him, as a sacrifice which the Lord himself caused to be miraculously consumed by fire, showed that the Lord would still graciously
accept the prayers and sacrifices of Israel, if they would but forsake the worship of the dead idols of the heathen, and return to
Him in sincerity. (Compare with this the similar theophany in
chap. xiii.)

Vers. 25–32. *Gideon set apart as the Deliverer of his People.*—In
order to be able to carry out the work entrusted to him of setting
Israel free, it was necessary that Gideon should first of all purify
his father's house from idolatry, and sanctify his own life and
labour to Jehovah by sacrificing a burnt-offering.—Ver. 25. " *In
that night*," *i.e.* the night following the day on which the Lord

appeared to him, God commanded him to destroy his father's Baal's altar, with the *asherah-idol* upon it, and to build an altar to Jehovah, and offer a bullock of his father's upon the altar. "*Take the ox-bullock which belongs to thy father, and indeed the second bullock of seven years, and destroy the altar of Baal, which belongs to thy father, and throw down the asherah upon it.*" According to the general explanation of the first clauses, there are two oxen referred to : viz. *first*, his father's young bullock ; and *secondly*, an ox of seven years old, the latter of which Gideon was to sacrifice (according to ver. 26) upon the altar to be built to Jehovah, and actually did sacrifice, according to vers. 27, 28. But in what follows there is no further allusion to the young bullock, or the first ox of his father; so that there is a difficulty in comprehending for what purpose Gideon was to take it, or what use he was to make of it. Most commentators suppose that Gideon sacrificed both of the oxen,—the young bullock as an expiatory offering for himself, his father, and all his family, and the second ox of seven years old for the deliverance of the whole nation (see *Seb. Schmidt*). *Bertheau* supposes, on the other hand, that Gideon was to make use of both oxen, or of the strength they possessed for throwing down or destroying the altar, and (according to ver. 26) for removing the מַעֲרָכָה and the עֲצֵי הָאֲשֵׁרָה to the place of the new altar that was to be built, but that he was only to offer the second in sacrifice to Jehovah, because the first was probably dedicated to Baal, and therefore could not be offered to Jehovah. But these assumptions are both of them equally arbitrary, and have no support whatever from the text. If God had commanded Gideon to take two oxen, He would certainly have told him what he was to do with them both. But as there is only one bullock mentioned in vers. 26–28, we must follow *Tremell.* and others, who understand ver. 25 as meaning that Gideon was to take only one bullock, namely the young bullock of his father, and therefore regard וּפַר הַשֵּׁנִי שׁ' שׁ' as a more precise definition of that one bullock (*vav* being used in an explanatory sense, " and indeed," as in Josh. ix. 27, x. 7, etc.). This bullock is called " the second bullock," as being the second in age among the bullocks of Joash. The reason for choosing this second of the bullocks of Joash for a burnt-offering is to be found no doubt in its age (seven years), which is mentioned here simply on account of its significance as a number, as there was no particular age pre-scribed in the law for a burnt-offering, that is to say, because the seven years which constituted the age of the bullock contained an

inward allusion to the seven years of the Midianitish oppression.
For *seven* years had God given Israel into the hands of the Midianites on account of their apostasy; and now, to wipe away this sin,
Gideon was to take his father's bullock of *seven* years old, and
offer it as a burnt-offering to the Lord. To this end Gideon was
first of all to destroy the altar of Baal and of the *asherah* which his
father possessed, and which, to judge from vers. 28, 29, was the
common altar of the whole family of Abiezer in Ophrah. This
altar was dedicated to Baal, but there was also upon it an *asherah*,
an idol representing the goddess of nature, which the Canaanites
worshipped; not indeed a *statue* of the goddess, but, as we may
learn from the word כָּרַת, to *hew down*, simply a wooden pillar (see
at Deut. xvi. 21). The altar therefore served for the two principal
deities of the Canaanites (see *Movers*, Phönizier, i. pp. 566 sqq.).
Jehovah could not be worshipped along with Baal. Whoever
would serve the Lord must abolish the worship of Baal. The altar
of Baal must be destroyed before the altar of Jehovah could be
built. Gideon was to build this altar "*upon the top of this stronghold*," possibly upon the top of the mountain, upon which the fortress
belonging to Ophrah was situated. בַּמַּעֲרָכָה, "*with the preparation;*"
the meaning of this word is a subject of dispute. As בָּנָה occurs
in 1 Kings xv. 22 with בְּ, to denote the materials out of which (*i.e.*
with which) a thing is built, *Stud.* and *Berth.* suppose that *maaracah*
refers to the materials of the altar of Baal that had been destroyed,
with which Gideon was to build the altar of Jehovah. *Stud.* refers
it to the stone foundation of the altar of Baal; *Bertheau* to the
materials that were lying ready upon the altar of Baal for the
presentation of sacrifices, more especially the pieces of wood. But
this is certainly incorrect, because *maaracah* does not signify either
building materials or pieces of wood, and the definite article attached
to the word does not refer to the altar of Baal at all. The verb עָרַךְ is
not only very frequently used to denote the preparation of the wood
upon the altar (Gen. xxii. 9; Lev. i. 7, etc.), but is also used for
the preparation of an altar for the presentation of sacrifice (Num.
xxiii. 4). Consequently *maaracah* can hardly be understood in any
other way than as signifying the preparation of the altar to be
built for the sacrificial act, in the sense of build the altar with the
preparation required for the sacrifice. This preparation was to
consist, according to what follows, in taking the wood of the
asherah, that had been hewn down, as the wood for the burnt-
offering to be offered to the Lord by Gideon. עֲצֵי הָאֲשֵׁרָה are **not**

trees, but pieces of wood from the *asherah* (that was hewn down).—
Ver. 27. Gideon executed this command of God with ten men of
his servants during the night, no doubt the following night, because
he was afraid to do it by day, on account of his family (his father's
house), and the people of the town.—Vers. 28, 29. But on the
following morning, when the people of the town found the altar of
Baal destroyed and the *asherah* upon it hewn down, and the bullock
sacrificed upon the (newly) erected altar (the bullock would not be
entirely consumed), they asked who had done it, and soon learned
that Gideon had done it all. The accusative אֵת הַפָּר הַשֵּׁנִי is governed
by the *Hophal* הֹעֲלָה (for הָעֳלָה, see *Ges.* s. 63, Anm. 4), according to
a construction that was by no means rare, especially in the earlier
Hebrew, viz. of the passive with אֵת (see at Gen. iv. 18). "*They
asked and sought*," *sc.* for the person who had done it; "*and they
said*," either those who were making the inquiry, according to a
tolerably safe conjecture, or the persons who were asked, and
who were aware of what Gideon had done.—Vers. 30, 31. But
when they demanded of Joash, "*Bring out* (give out) *thy son,
that he may die*," he said to all who stood round, "*Will ye, ye,
fight for Baal, or will ye save him?* ('ye' is repeated with special
emphasis). *Whoever shall fight for him* (Baal), *shall be put to
death till the morning.*" עַד־הַבֹּקֶר, till the (next) morning, is not
to be joined to יוּמַת, in the sense of "very speedily, before the
dawning day shall break" (*Bertheau*),—a sense which is not to be
found in the words : it rather belongs to the subject of the
clause, or to the whole clause in the sense of, Whoever shall
fight for Baal, and seek to avenge the destruction of his altar by
putting the author of it to death, shall be put to death himself;
let us wait till to-morrow, and give Baal time to avenge the insult
which he has received. "*If he be God, let him fight for himself ;
for they have destroyed his altar*," and have thereby challenged his
revenge. Gideon's daring act of faith had inspired his father Joash
with believing courage, so that he took the part of his son, and left
the whole matter to the deity to decide. If Baal were really God,
he might be expected to avenge the crime that had been committed
against this altar.—Ver. 32. From this fact Gideon received the
name of *Jerubbaal*, i.e. "*let Baal fight* (or decide)," since they said,
"*Let Baal fight against him, for he has destroyed his altar.*" יְרֻבַּעַל is
formed from יָרֶב = יְרִיב or יְרִיב and בַּעַל. This surname very soon
became an honourable title for Gideon. When, for example, it
became apparent to the people that Baal could not do him any

harm, *Jerubbaal* became a Baal-fighter, one who had fought against Baal. In 2 Sam. xi. 21, instead of *Jerubbaal* we find the name *Jerubbesheth*, in which *Besheth = Bosheth* is a nickname of Baal, which also occurs in other Israelitish names, *e.g.* in *Ishbosheth* (2 Sam. ii. 8 sqq.) for *Eshbaal* (1 Chron. viii. 33, ix. 39). The name *Jerubbaal* is written ʿΙεροβάαλ by the LXX., from which in all probability *Philo* of Byblus, in his revision of Sanchuniathon, has formed his ʿΙερόμβαλος, a priest of the god ʾΙευώ.

Gideon's Victory over the Midianites.—Chap. vi. 33–viii. 3.

Chap. vi. 33–40. EQUIPMENT OF GIDEON FOR THE BATTLE. —When the Midianites and their allies once more invaded the land of Israel, Gideon was seized by the Spirit of God, so that he gathered together an army from the northern tribes of Israel (vers. 33–35), and entreated God to assure him by a sign of gaining the victory over the enemy (vers. 36–40).—Vers. 33 sqq. The enemy gathered together again, went over (viz. across) the Jordan in the neighbourhood of Beisan (see at chap. vii. 24 and viii. 4), and encamped in the valley of Jezreel (see at Josh. xvii. 16). "*And the Spirit of Jehovah came upon Gideon*" (לָבְשָׁה, clothed, *i.e.* descended upon him, and laid itself around him as it were like a coat of mail, or a strong equipment, so that he became invulnerable and invincible in its might: see 1 Chron. xii. 18, 2 Chron. xxiv. 20, and Luke xxiv. 49). Gideon then blew the trumpet, to call Israel to battle against the foe (see chap. iii. 27); "*and Abiezer let itself be summoned after him.*" His own family, which had recognised the deliverer of Israel in the fighter of Baal, who was safe from Baal's revenge, was the first to gather round him. Their example was followed by all Manasseh, *i.e.* the Manassites on the west of the Jordan (for the tribes on the east of the Jordan took no part in the war), and the neighbouring tribes of Zebulun and Naphtali on the north, which had been summoned by heralds to the battle. "*They advanced to meet them:*" *i.e.* to meet the Manassites, who were coming from the south to the battle, to make war upon the enemy in concert with them and under the guidance of Gideon. עָלָה is used to denote their advance against the enemy (see at Josh. viii. 2), and not in the sense of going up, since the Asherites and Naphtalites would not go up from their mountains into the plain of Jezreel, but could only go down.—Vers. 36 sqq. But before Gideon went into the battle with the assembled army, he asked for a sign from God of the success of his undertaking. "*If Thou*," he said to God, "*art saving Israel through my hand, as Thou hast said, behold, I lay this fleece of wool upon the floor; if there shall be dew upon the fleece only, and dryness upon all the earth* (round about), *I know* (by this) *that Thou wilt save*," etc. גִּזַּת הַצֶּמֶר, *the shorn of the wool; i.e.* the fleece, the wool that had been shorn off a sheep, and still adhered together as one whole fleece. The sign which Gideon asked for, therefore, was that God would cause the dew to fall only upon a shorn fleece, which he would spread the previous night upon the floor, that is to say, upon some open ground, and that the ground all round might not be moistened by the dew.—Ver. 38. God granted the sign. "*And so it came to pass; the next morning, Gideon pressed the fleece together* (יָזַר from זוּר), *and squeezed* (יִמֶץ from מָצָה) *dew out of the fleece a vessel full of water*" (מְלוֹא as in Num. xxii. 18, and סֵפֶל as in chap. v. 25). So copiously had the dew fallen in the night upon the fleece that was exposed; whereas, as we may supply from the context, the earth all round had remained dry.—Vers. 39, 40. But as this sign was not quite a certain one, since wool generally attracts the dew, even when other objects remain dry, Gideon ventured to solicit the grace of God to grant him another sign with the fleece, —namely, that the fleece might remain dry, and the ground all round be wet with dew. And God granted him this request also. Gideon's prayer for a sign did not arise from want of faith in the divine assurance of a victory, but sprang from the weakness of the flesh, which crippled the strength of the spirit's faith, and often made the servants of God so anxious and despondent, that God had to come to the relief of their weakness by the manifestation of His miraculous power. Gideon knew himself and his own strength, and was well aware that his human strength was not sufficient for the conquest of the foe. But as the Lord had promised him His aid, he wished to make sure of that aid through the desired sign.[1] And "the simple fact that such a man could obtain the most daring victory was to be a special glorification of God" (*O. v. Gerlach*). The sign itself was to manifest the strength of the divine assistance to his weakness of faith. Dew in the Scriptures is a symbol of the

[1] "From all these things, the fact that he had seen and heard the angel of Jehovah, and that he had been taught by fire out of the rock, by the disappearance of the angel, by the vision of the night, and by the words addressed to him there, Gideon did indeed believe that GOD both could and would deliver Israel through his instrumentality; but this faith was not placed above or away from the conflict of the flesh by which it was tested. And it is not strange that

beneficent power of God, which quickens, revives, and invigorates the objects of nature, when they have been parched by the burning heat of the sun's rays. The first sign was to be a pledge to him of the visible and tangible blessing of the Lord upon His people, the proof that He would grant them power over their mighty foes by whom Israel was then oppressed. The woollen fleece represented the nation of Israel in its condition at that time, when God had given power to the foe that was devastating its land, and had withdrawn His blessing from Israel. The moistening of the fleece with the dew of heaven whilst the land all round continued dry, was a sign that the Lord God would once more give strength to His people from on high, and withdraw it from the nations of the earth. Hence the second sign acquires the more general signification, "that the Lord manifested himself even in the weakness and forsaken condition of His people, while the nations were flourishing all around" (*O. v. Gerl.*); and when so explained, it served to confirm and strengthen the first, inasmuch as it contained the comforting assurance for all times, that the Lord has not forsaken His church, even when it cannot discern and trace His beneficent influence, but rules over it and over the nations with His almighty power.

Chap. vii. 1–8. MUSTERING OF THE ARMY THAT GIDEON HAD COLLECTED.—Ver. 1. When Gideon had been assured of the help of God by this double sign, he went to the battle early the next morning with the people that he had gathered around him. The Israelites encamped above the fountain of *Harod, i.e.* upon a height at the foot of which this fountain sprang; but the camp of Midian was to him (Gideon) to the north of the hill *Moreh* in the valley (of Jezreel: see chap. vi. 33). The geographical situation of these two places cannot be determined with certainty. The fountain of *Harod* is never mentioned again, though there is a place of that name referred to in 2 Sam. xxiii. 25 as the home of two of David's heroes; and it was from this, no doubt, that the fountain was named. The hill *Moreh* is also unknown. As it was by the valley (of Jezreel), we cannot possibly think of the grove of *Moreh* at Shechem

it rose to its greatest height when the work of deliverance was about to be performed. Wherefore Gideon with his faith sought for a sign from God against the more vehement struggle of the flesh, in order that his faith might be the more confirmed, and might resist the opposing flesh with the greater force. And this petition for a sign was combined with prayers for the strengthening of his faith."—*Seb. Schmidt.*

(Gen. xii. 6; Deut. xi. 30).[1]—Vers. 2, 3. The army of the Israelites amounted to 32,000 men (ver. 4), but that of the Midianites and their allies was about 135,000 (chap. viii. 10), so that they were greatly superior to the Israelites in numbers. Nevertheless the Lord said to Gideon, " *The people that are with thee are too many for me to give Midian into their hands, lest Israel vaunt themselves against me, saying, My hand hath helped me.*" רַב followed by מִן is to be understood as a comparative. Gideon was therefore to have a proclamation made before all the people : " *Whosoever is fearful and despondent, let him turn and go back from Mount Gilead.*" The ἀπ. λεγ. צָפַר, judging from the Arabic, which signifies to plait, viz. hair, ropes, etc., and the noun צְפִירָה, a circle or circuitous orbit, probably signifies to twist one's self round ; hence in this instance to return in windings, to slink away in bypaths. The expression " *from Mount Gilead,*" however, is very obscure. The mountain (or the mountains) of Gilead was on the eastern side of the Jordan ; but the Israelitish army was encamped in or near the plain of Jezreel, in the country to the west of the Jordan, and had been gathered from the western tribes alone ; so that even the inadmissible rendering, Let him turn and go home to the mountains of Gilead, would not give any appropriate sense. The only course left therefore is either to pronounce it an error of the text, as *Clericus* and *Bertheau* have done, and to regard " Gilead" as a mistake for " Gilboa," or to conclude that there was also a mountain or mountain range named *Gilead* by the plain of Jezreel in western Palestine, just as, according to Josh. xv. 10, there was a mountain, or range of mountains, called *Seir,* in the territory of Judah, of which nothing further is known. The appeal which Gideon is here directed to make to the army was prescribed in the law (Deut. xx. 8) for every war

---

[1] *Bertheau* endeavours to settle the position of the place from our knowledge of the country, which is for the most part definite enough. Starting with the assumption that the fountain of *Harod* cannot be any other than the "fountain in Jezreel" mentioned in 1 Sam. xxix. 1, where Saul and the Israelites encamped at Gilboa (1 Sam. xxviii. 4) to fight against the Philistines who were posted at *Shunem,* a place on the western slope of the so-called Little Hermon, he concludes that the fountain of *Harod* must be the present *Ain Jalud,* and the hill of *Moreh* the Little *Hermon* itself. These combinations are certainly possible, for we have nothing definite to oppose to them ; still they are very uncertain, as they simply rest upon the very doubtful assumption that the only fountain in the plain of Jezreel was the celebrated fountain called *Ain Jalud,* and are hardly reconcilable with the account given of the route which was taken by the defeated Midianites (vers. 25 sqq. and chap. viii 4).

in which the Israelites should be engaged, and its general object was to fortify the spirit of the army by removing the cowardly and desponding. But in the case before us the intention of the Lord was to deprive His people of all ground for self-glorification. Hence the result of the appeal was one which Gideon himself certainly did not expect,—namely, that more than two-thirds of the soldiers gathered round him—22,000 men of the people—turned back, and only 10,000 remained.—Ver. 4. But even this number was regarded by the Lord as still too great, so that He gave to Gideon the still further command, " *Bring them* (the 10,000 men) *down to the water*," *i.e.* the waters formed from the fountain of Harod, " *and I will purify them for thee there* (צָרַף, separate those appointed for the battle from the rest of the army ; the singular suffix refers to הָעָם), *and say to thee, This shall go with thee, and that*," *i.e.* show thee each individual who is to go with thee to the battle, and who not.—Vers. 5, 6. Gideon was to divide the people by putting all those who should lick the water with their tongue as a dog licketh into one class, and all those who knelt down to drink into another, and so separating the latter from the former. The number of those who licked the water into their mouth with their hand amounted to 300, and all the rest knelt down to drink. " *To lick with their hand to their mouth*," *i.e.* to take the water from the brook with the hollow of their hand, and lap it into the mouth with their tongue as a dog does, is only a more distinct expression for " licking with the tongue." The 300 men who quenched their thirst in this manner were certainly not the cowardly or indolent who did not kneel down to drink in the ordinary way, either from indolence or fear, as *Josephus, Theodoret*, and others supposed, but rather the bravest,—namely those who, when they reached a brook before the battle, did not allow themselves time to kneel down and satisfy their thirst in the most convenient manner, but simply took up some water with their hands as they stood in their military accoutrements, to strengthen themselves for the battle, and then proceeded without delay against the foe. By such a sign as this, *Bertheau* supposes that even an ordinary general might have been able to recognise the bravest of his army. No doubt: but if this account had not been handed down, it is certain that it would never have occurred to an ordinary or even a distinguished general to adopt such a method of putting the bravery of his troops to the test; and even Gideon, the hero of God, would never have thought of diminishing still further through such a trial an army which had already become so small, or of attempting to defeat an army of more than 100,000 men by a few hundred of the bravest men, if the Lord himself had not commanded it.

Whilst the Lord was willing to strengthen the feeble faith of Gideon by the sign with the fleece of wool, and thus to raise him up to full confidence in the divine omnipotence, He also required of him, when thus strengthened, an attestation of his faith, by the purification of his army, that he might give the whole glory to Him, and accept the victory over that great multitude from His hand alone.—Ver. 7. After his fighting men had been divided into a small handful of 300 men on the one hand, and the large host of 9700 on the other, by the fulfilment of the command of God, the Lord required of him that he should send away the latter, " every man to his place," *i.e.* to his own home, promising that He would save Israel by the 300 men, and deliver the Midianites into their hand. The promise preceded the command, to render it easier to Gideon to obey it. "*All the people,*" after taking out the 300 men, that is to say, the 9700 that remained.—Ver. 8. " *So they* (the 300 picked men) *took the provision of the people in their hand, and their* (the people's) *trumpets* (the suffix points back to הָעָם, the people); *and all the men of Israel* (the 9700) *he had sent away every one to his tents, i.e.* to his home (see at Deut. xvi. 7), *and the three hundred men he had kept by himself; but the camp of the Midianites was below to him in the valley.*" These words bring the preparations for the battle to a close, and the last clause introduces the ensuing conflict and victory. In the first clause הָעָם (the people) cannot be the subject, partly because of the actual sense, since the 300 warriors, who are no doubt the persons intended (cf. ver. 16), cannot be called " the people," in distinction from " all the men of Israel," and partly also because of the expression אֶת־צֵדָה, which would be construed in that case without any article in violation of the ordinary rule. We must rather read אֶת־צֵדַת הָעָם, as the LXX. and the Chaldee have done. The 300 men took the provision of the people, *i.e.* provision for the war, from the people who had been sent away, and the war-trumpets; so that every one of the 300 had a trumpet now, and as the provision of the people was also probably kept in vessels or pitchers (*caddim :* ver. 16), a jug as well. The subject to יָקְחוּ is to be taken from the first clause of the seventh verse. The sentences which follow from וְאֵת כָּל־אִישׁ are circumstantial clauses, introduced to bring out distinctly the situation in which Gideon was now placed. הֶחֱזִיק בְּ, the opposite of שִׁלַּח, to send away, signifies to hold fast, to keep back or by himself, as in Ex. ix. 2. לוֹ, to him, Gideon, who was standing by the fountain of Harod with his 300 men, the situation of Midian was underneath in the valley (see ver. 1, and chap. vi. 33).

Vers. 9–22. GIDEON'S BATTLE AND VICTORY.—Vers. 9–11a. The following night the Lord commanded Gideon to go down to the camp of the enemy, as He had given it into his hand (the perfect is used to denote the purpose of God which had already been formed, as in chap. iv. 14). But in order to fill him with confidence for such an enterprise, which to all human appearance was a very rash one, God added, " *If thou art afraid to go down, go thou with thine attendant Purah down to the camp, and thou wilt hear what they say, and thy hands will thereby become strong.*" The meaning of the protasis is not, If thou art afraid to go down into the camp of the enemy alone, or to visit the enemy unarmed, take Purah thine armour-bearer with thee, to make sure that thou hast weapons to use (*Bertheau*) ; for, apart from the fact that the addition " unarmed" is perfectly arbitrary, the apodosis " thou wilt see," etc., by no means agrees with this explanation. The meaning is rather this : Go with thy 300 men into (בְּ) the hostile camp to smite it, for I have given it into thy hand ; but if thou art afraid to do this, go down with thine attendant to (אֶל) the camp, to ascertain the state and feeling of the foe, and thou wilt hear what they say, *i.e.*, as we gather from what follows, how they are discouraged, have lost all hope of defeating you, and from that thou wilt gather courage and strength for the battle. On the expression " *thine hands shall be strengthened,*" see 2 Sam. ii. 7. The expression which follows, וְיָרַדְתָּ בַּמַּחֲנֶה, is not a mere repetition of the command to go down with his attendant to the hostile camp, but describes the result of the stimulus given to his courage : And then thou wilt go fearlessly into the hostile camp to attack the foe. יָרֵד בַּמַּחֲנֶה (vers. 9, 11) is to be distinguished from יָרֵד אֶל־הַמַּחֲנֶה in ver. 10. The former signifies to go down into the camp to smite the foe ; the latter, to go down to the camp to reconnoitre it, and is equivalent to the following clause : " he went to the outside of the camp."—Vers. 11b–14. But when Gideon came with his attendant to the end of the armed men (*chamushim*, as in Josh. i. 14, Ex. xiii. 18) in the hostile camp, and the enemy were lying spread out with their camels in the valley, an innumerable multitude, he heard one (of the fighting men) relate to his fellow (*i.e.* to another) a dream which he had had : " *Behold a cake of barley bread was rolling into the camp of Midian, and it came to the tent and smote it, so that it fell and turned upwards, and the tent lay along.*" Then the other replied, " *This is nothing else than the sword of Gideon the son of Joash the Israelite : God hath given Midian and all the camp into his hand.*" " The end of fighting men" signifies the outermost or foremost of the outposts in the enemy's camp, which contained not only fighting men, but the whole of the baggage of the enemy, who had invaded the land as nomads, with their wives, their children, and their flocks. In ver. 12, the innumerable multitude of the enemy is described once more in the form of a circumstantial clause, as in chap. vi. 5, not so much to distinguish the fighting men from the camp generally, as to bring out more vividly the contents and meaning of the following dream. The comparison of the enemy to the sand by the sea-side recalls Josh. xi. 4, and is frequently met with (see Gen. xxii. 17, xxxii. 13 ; 1 Sam. xiii. 5). With the word וַיָּבֹא in ver. 13, the thread of the narrative, which was broken off by the circumstantial clause in ver. 12, is resumed and carried further. The ἁπ. λεγ. צְלִיל (*Keri*, צְלִיל) is rendered *cake, placenta*, by the early translators : see *Ges. Thes.* p. 1170. The derivation of the word has been disputed, and is by no means certain, as צָלַל does not give any suitable meaning, either in the sense of to ring or to be overshadowed, and the meaning to roll (*Ges. l. c.*) cannot be philologically sustained; whilst צָלָה, to roast, can hardly be thought of, since this is merely used to denote the roasting of flesh, and קָלָה was the word commonly applied to the roasting of grains, and even " the roasted of barley bread" would hardly be equivalent to *subcinericeus panis ex hordeo* (*Vulgate*). " *The tent*," with the definite article, is probably the principal tent in the camp, *i.e.* the tent of the general. לְמַעְלָה, upwards, so that the bottom came to the top. " *The tent lay along*," or the tent fell, lay in ruins, is added to give emphasis to the words. " *This is nothing if not*," *i.e.* nothing but. The cake of bread which had rolled into the Midianitish camp and overturned the tent, signifies nothing else than the sword of Gideon, *i.e.* Gideon, who is bursting into the camp with his sword, and utterly destroying it.

This interpretation of the dream was certainly a natural one under the circumstances. Gideon is especially mentioned simply as the leader of the Israelites ; whilst the loaf of barley bread, which was the food of the poorer classes, is to be regarded as strictly speaking the symbol of Israel, which was so despised among the nations. The rising of the Israelites under Gideon had not remained a secret to the Midianites, and no doubt filled them with fear; so that in a dream this fear might easily assume the form of the defeat or desolation and destruction of their camp by Gideon. And the peculiar form of the dream is also psychologically conceivable. As the tent is everything to a nomad, he might very naturally picture the cultivator of the soil as a man whose life is all spent in cultivating and baking bread. In this way bread would become almost involuntarily a symbol of the cultivator of the soil, whilst in his own tent he would see a symbol not only of his mode of life, but of his freedom, greatness, and power. If we add to this, that the free pastoral tribes, particularly the Bedouins of Arabia, look down with pride not only upon the poor tillers of the soil, but even upon the inhabitants of towns, and that in Palestine, the land of wheat, none but the poorer classes feed upon barley bread, we have here all the elements out of which the dream of the Midianitish warrior was formed. The Israelites had really been crushed by the Midianites into a poor nation of slaves. But whilst the dream itself admits of being explained in this manner in a perfectly natural way, it acquires the higher supernatural character of a divine inspiration, from the fact that God not only foreknew it, but really caused the Midianite to dream, and to relate the dream to his comrade, just at the time when Gideon had secretly entered the camp, so that he should hear it, and discover therefrom, as God had foretold him, the despondency of the foe. Under these circumstances, Gideon could not fail to regard the dream as a divine inspiration, and to draw the assurance from it, that God had certainly given the Midianites into his hands.—Vers. 15.-18. When therefore he had heard the dream related and interpreted, he worshipped, praising the Lord with joy, and returned to the camp to attack the enemy without delay. He then divided the 300 men into three companies, *i.e.* three attacking columns, and gave them all trumpets and empty pitchers, with torches in the pitchers in their hands. The pitchers were taken that they might hide the burning torches in them during their advance to surround the enemy's camp, and then increase the noise at the time of the attack, by dashing the pitchers to pieces (ver. 20), and thus through the noise, as well as the sudden lighting up of the burning torches, deceive the enemy as to the strength of the army. At the same time he commanded them, " *See from me, and do likewise,*"—a short expression for, As ye see me do, so do ye also (כֵּן, without the previous כְּ, or כַּאֲשֶׁר, as in chap. v. 15; see *Ewald*, § 260, *a.*),—" *I blow the trumpet, I and all who are with me; ye also blow the trumpets round about the entire camp,"* which the 300 men divided into three companies were to surround, *" and say, To the Lord and Gideon."* According to ver. 20, this war-cry ran fully thus : *" Sword to* (for) *the Lord and Gideon."* This addition in ver. 20, however, does not warrant us in inserting *" chereb"* (sword) in the text here, as some of the early translators and MSS. have done.[1]—Ver. 19. Gideon then proceeded with the 100 who were with him, *i.e.* the company which was led by himself personally, to the end of the hostile camp, at the beginning of the middle watch, *i.e.* at midnight. רֹאשׁ is an accusative defining the time: see *Ges.* § 118, 2, and *Ewald,* § 204, *a.* The only other watch that is mentioned in the Old Testament beside the middle night-watch, is the morning night-watch (Ex. xiv. 24 ; 1 Sam. xi. 11), from which it has been correctly inferred, that the Israelites divided the night into three night-watches. The division into four watches (Matt. xiv. 25 ; Mark vi. 48) was first adopted by the Jews from the Romans. *" They* (the Midianites) *had only* (just) *posted the watchmen* (of the middle watch),"—a circumstantial clause, introduced to give greater distinctness to the situation. When the first sentries were relieved, and the second posted, so that they thought they might make quite sure of their night's rest once more, Gideon and his host arrived at the end of the camp, and, as we must supply from the context, the other two hosts at two other ends of the camp, who all blew their trumpets, breaking the pitchers in their hands at the same time. The *inf. abs.* נָפוֹץ, as a continuation of the finite verb יִתְקְעוּ, indicates that the fact was contemporaneous with the previous one (see *Ewald,* § 351, *c.*).—Ver. 20. According to the command which they had received (ver. 17), the other two tribes followed his example. *" Then the three companies*

---

[1] Similar stratagems to the one adopted by Gideon here are recorded by *Polyænus* (Strateg. ii. c. 37) of Dicetas, at the taking of Heræa, and by *Plutarch (Fabius Max.* c. 6) of Hannibal, when he was surrounded and completely shut in by Fabius Maximus. An example from modern history is given by *Niebuhr* (Beschr. von Arabien, p. 304). About the middle of the eighteenth century two Arabian chiefs were fighting for the Imamate of Oman. One of them, Bel-Arab, besieged the other, Achmed ben Said, with four or five thousand men, in a small castle on the mountain. But the latter slipped out of the castle, collected together several hundred men, gave every soldier a sign upon his head, that they might be able to distinguish friends from foes, and sent small companies to all the passes. Every one had a trumpet to blow at a given signal, and thus create a noise at the same time on every side. The whole of the opposing army was thrown in this way into disorder, since they found all the passes occupied, and imagined the hostile army to be as great as the noise.

blew the trumpets, broke the pitchers, and held the torches in their left hands, and the trumpets in their right to blow, and cried, Sword to the Lord and Gideon! And they stood every one in his place round about the camp," sc. without moving, so that the Midianites neces-sarily thought that there must be a numerous army advancing behind the torch-bearers. וַיָּרִיץ וגו', *" and the whole army ran,"* i.e. there began a running hither and thither in the camp of the enemy, who had been frightened out of their night's rest by the unexpected blast of the trumpets, the noise, and the war-cry of the Israelitish warriors; *" and they* (the enemy) *lifted up a cry* (of anguish and alarm), *and caused to fly"* (carried off), sc. their tents (*i.e.* their families) and their herds, or all their possessions (cf. chap. vi. 11, Ex. ix. 20). The *Chethibh* יָנִיסוּ is the original reading, and the *Keri* יָנוּסוּ a bad emendation.—Ver. 22. Whilst the 300 men blew their trumpets, *" Jehovah set the sword of one against the other, and against the whole camp,"* i.e. caused one to turn his sword against the other and against all the camp, that is to say, not merely man against man, but against every one in the camp, so that there arose a terrible slaughter throughout the whole camp. The first clause, *" and the three hundred blew the trumpets,"* simply resumes the statement in ver. 20, *" the three companies blew the trumpets,"* for the purpose of appending to it the further progress of the attack, and the result of the battle. *Bertheau* inserts in a very arbitrary manner the words, *" the second time."* His explanation of the next clause (" then the 300 fighting men of Gideon drew the sword at Jehovah's command, every man against his man") is still more erroneous, since it does violence to the constant usage of the ex-pression אִישׁ בְּרֵעֵהוּ (see 1 Sam xiv. 20, 2 Chron. xx. 23, Isa. iii. 5, Zech. viii. 10). *" And all the camp of the Midianites fled to Beth-shittah to Zeredah, to the shore of Abel-meholah, over Tabbath."* The situation of these places, which are only mentioned here, with the exception of Abel-meholah, the home of Elisha (1 Kings xix. 16, iv. 12), has not yet been determined. According to the Syriac, the Arabic, and some of the MSS., we should read *Zeredathah* instead of *Zererathah*, and *Zeredathah* is only another form for *Zarthan* (comp. 1 Kings vii. 46 with 2 Chron. iv. 17). This is favoured by the situation of *Zarthan* in the valley of the Jordan, probably near the modern *Kurn Sartabeh* (see p. 46), inasmuch as in all probability Beth-shittah and Abel-meholah are to be sought for in the valley of the Jordan ; and according to ver. 24, the enemy fled to the Jordan. *Beth-shittah, i.e.* acacia-house, is not the same place as the village of *Shutta* mentioned by *Robinson* (iii. p. 219), since this village, according to *Van de Velde's* map, was to the north of Gilboa. For although *Shutta* is favoured by the circumstance, that from a very ancient time there was a road running from Jezreel along the valley, between the so-called Little Hermon (Duhy) and the mountains of Gilboa, and past Beisan to the Jordan; and the valley of Jalud, on the northern side of which Shutta was situated, may be regarded as the opening of the plain of Jezreel into the valley of the Jordan (see *v. Raumer*, Pal. p. 41, and *Rob.* iii. p. 176); and *v. Raumer* conjectures from this, that " the flight of the Midianites was apparently directed to Bethsean, on account of the nature of the ground,"—this assumption is rendered very questionable by the fact that the flying foe did not cross the Jordan in the neighbourhood of Beisan, but much farther to the south, viz., according to chap. viii. 4, in the neighbourhood of *Succoth*, which was on the south side of the Nahr Zerka (Jabbok). From this we are led to conjecture, that they were not encamped in the north-eastern part of the plain of Jezreel, in the neighbourhood of Jezreel (Zerin) and Shunem (Solam), but in the south-eastern part of this plain, and that after they had been beaten there they fled southwards from Gilboa, say from the district of Ginæa (Jenin) to the Jordan. In this case we have to seek for Abel-shittah on the south-east of the mountains of Gilboa, to the north of Zeredathah (Zarthan). From this point they fled on still farther to the " *shore of Abel-meholah.*" שְׂפָה does not mean boundary, but brink; here the bank of the Jordan, like שְׂפַת הַיַּרְדֵּן in 2 Kings ii. 13. The bank or strand of *Abel-meholah* is that portion of the western bank of the Jordan or of the Ghor, above which Abel-meholah was situated. According to the *Onom.* (*s. v.* ᾿Αβελμαελαί, *Abelmaula*), this place was in the *Aulon* (or Ghor), ten Roman miles to the south of Scythopolis (Beisan), and was called at that time Βηθμαιελά or *Bethaula*. According to this statement, *Abel-meholah* would have to be sought for near *Churbet es Shuk*, in the neighbourhood of the Wady *Maleh* (see *V. de Velde*, Mem. p. 280). And lastly, *Tabbath* must have been situated somewhere to the south of Abel-meholah.

Ver. 23–chap. viii. 3. *Pursuit of the Enemy as far as the Jordan.* —Ver. 23. As soon as the Midianites had been put to flight, the Israelitish men of Naphtali, Asher, and Manasseh, let themselves be convened for the purpose of pursuing them: *i.e.* the men of these tribes, whom Gideon had sent away before the battle, and who were on their way home, could be summoned back again in a very short time to join in the pursuit of the flying foe. The omission of Zebulun (chap. vi. 35) is, in all probability, simply to be attributed to the brevity of the account.—Vers. 24, 25. In order to cut off the retreat of the enemy who was flying to the Jordan, Gideon sent messengers into the whole of the mountains of Ephraim with this appeal to the Ephraimites, " *Come down* (from your mountains into the lowlands of the Jordan) *to meet Midian, and take the waters from them to Bethbarah and the Jordan,*" *sc.* by taking possession of this district (see chap. iii. 28). " *The waters,*" mentioned before the Jordan and distinguished from it, must have been streams across which the flying foe would have to cross to reach the Jordan, namely, the different brooks and rivers, such as Wady *Maleh, Fyadh, Jamel, Tubâs,* etc., which flowed down from the eastern side of the mountains of Ephraim into the Jordan, and ran through the Ghor to Bethbarah. The situation of *Bethbarah* is unknown. Even *Eusebius* could say nothing definite concerning the place; and the conjecture that it is the same as Bethabara, which has been regarded ever since the time of Origen as the place mentioned in John i. 28 where John baptized, throws no light upon the subject, as the situation of Bethabara is also unknown, to say nothing of the fact that the identity of the two names is very questionable. The Ephraimites responded to this appeal and took possession of the waters mentioned, before the Midianites, who could only move slowly with their flocks and herds, were able to reach the Jordan. They then captured two of the princes of the Midianites and put them to death: one of them, *Oreb, i.e.* the raven, at the rock *Oreb;* the other, *Zeeb, i.e.* the wolf, at the wine-press of *Zeeb.* Nothing further is known about these two places. The rock of *Oreb* is only mentioned again in Isa. x. 26, when the prophet alludes to this celebrated victory. So much, however, is evident from the verse before us, viz. that the Midianites were beaten by the Ephraimites at both places, and that the two princes fell there, and the places received their names from that circumstance. They were not situated in the land to the east of the Jordan, as *Gesenius* (on Isa. x. 26), *Rosenmüller,* and others infer from the fact that the Ephraimites brought the heads of Oreb and Zeeb to Gideon מֵעֵבֶר לַיַּרְדֵּן (ver. 25), but on the western side of the Jordan, where the Ephraimites had taken possession of the waters and the Jordan in front of the Midianites. מֵעֵבֶר לַיַּרְדֵּן does not mean "from the other side of the Jordan," but simply " *on the other side of* (beyond) *the Jordan,*" as in Josh. xiii. 32, xviii. 7, 1

Kings xiv. 15; and the statement here is not that the Ephraimites brought the heads from the other side to Gideon on the west of the river, but that they brought them to Gideon when he was in the land to the east of the Jordan. This explanation of the words is required by the context, as well as by the foregoing remark, " they pursued Midian," according to which the Ephraimites continued the pursuit of the Midianites after slaying these princes, and also by the complaint brought against Gideon by the Ephraimites, which is not mentioned till afterwards (chap. viii. 1 sqq.), that he had not summoned them to the war. It is true, this is given before the account of Gideon's crossing over the Jordan (chap. viii. 4), but in order of time it did not take place till afterwards, and, as *Bertheau* has correctly shown, the historical sequence is somewhat anticipated.

Chap. viii. 1–3. When the Ephraimites met with Gideon, after they had smitten the Midianites at Oreb and Zeeb, and were pursuing them farther, they said to him, " *What is the thing that thou hast done to us* (*i.e.* what is the reason for your having done this to us), *not to call us when thou wentest forth to make war upon Midian? And they did chide with him sharply*," less from any dissatisfied longing for booty, than from injured pride or jealousy, because Gideon had made war upon the enemy and defeated them without the co-operation of this tribe, which was striving for the leadership. Gideon's reply especially suggests the idea of injured ambition: " *What have I now done like you?*" *i.e.* as if I had done as great things as you. " *Is not the gleaning of Ephraim better than the vintage of Abiezer?*" The gleaning of Ephraim is the victory gained over the flying Midianites. Gideon declares this to be better than the vintage of Abiezer, *i.e.* the victory obtained by him the Abiezrite with his 300 men, because the Ephraimites had slain two Midianitish princes. The victory gained by the Ephraimites must indeed have been a very important one, as it is mentioned by Isaiah (x. 26) as a great blow of the Lord upon Midian. " *And what could I do like you?*" *i.e.* could I accomplish such great deeds as you? " *Then their anger turned away from him.*" רוּחַ, the breathing of the nose, snorting, hence " *anger*," as in Isa. xxv. 4, etc.

Pursuit of the Midianites. Other Acts of Gideon; his Appointment as Judge.—Chap. viii. 4–35.

Vers. 4–12. Pursuit and complete Overthrow of the Midianites.—That the Midianites whom God had delivered into

his hand might be utterly destroyed, Gideon pursued those who
had escaped across the Jordan, till he overtook them on the eastern
boundary of Gilead and smote them there.—Vers. 4, 5. When
he came to the Jordan with his three hundred men, who were
exhausted with the pursuit, he asked the inhabitants of Succoth
for loaves of bread for the people in his train. So far as the
construction is concerned, the words from עָבֵר to וְרֹדְפִים form a
circumstantial clause inserted as a parenthesis into the principal
sentence, and subordinate to it : " *When Gideon came to the Jordan,*
passing over he and the three hundred men . . . then he said to the
men of Succoth." "*Exhausted and pursuing,*" *i.e.* exhausted with
pursuing. The *vav* is explanatory, *lit.* " and indeed pursuing," for
" because he pursued." The rendering πεινῶντες adopted by the
LXX. in the *Cod. Alex.* is merely an arbitrary rendering of the
word רֹדְפִים, and without any critical worth. Gideon had crossed
the Jordan, therefore, somewhere in the neighbourhood of Succoth.
Succoth was upon the eastern side of the valley of the Jordan
(Josh. xiii. 27), not opposite to Bethshean, but, according to Gen.
xxxiii. 17, on the south side of the Jabbok (Zerka).—Ver. 6. The
princes of Succoth, however, showed so little sympathy and nation-
ality of feeling, that instead of taking part in the attack upon the
enemies of Israel, they even refused to supply bread to refresh
their brethren of the western tribes who were exhausted with the
pursuit of the foe. They said (the sing. וַיֹּאמֶר may be explained
on the ground that one spoke in the name of all : see *Ewald,* §
319, *a.*), "*Is the fist of Zebah and Zalmunna already in thy hand*
(power), *that we should give thine army bread?*" In these words
there is not only an expression of cowardice, or fear of the vengeance which the Midianites might take when they returned upon
those who had supported Gideon and his host, but contempt of the
small force which Gideon had, as if it were impossible for him to
accomplish anything at all against the foe; and in this contempt
they manifested their utter want of confidence in God.—Ver. 7.
Gideon threatened them, therefore, with severe chastisement in
the event of a victorious return. "*If Jehovah give Zebah and*
Zalmunna into my hand, I will thresh your flesh (your body) *with*
desert thorns and thistles." The verb דּוּשׁ, constructed with a double
accusative (see *Ewald,* § 283, *a.*), is used in a figurative sense : "to
thresh," in other words, to punish severely. "Thorns of the desert"
are strong thorns, as the desert is the natural soil for thorn-bushes.
The ἅπ. λεγ. בַּרְקָנִים also signifies prickly plants, according to the

early versions and the Rabbins, probably "such as grow upon stony ground" (*Bertheau*). The explanation "threshing machines with stones or flints underneath them," which was suggested by *J. D. Michaelis* and *Celsius*, and adopted by *Gesenius*, cannot be sustained.—Vers. 8, 9. The inhabitants of Pnuel on the north bank of the Jabbok (see at Gen. xxxii. 24 sqq.) behaved in the same churlish manner to Gideon, and for this he also threatened them : "*If I return in peace*," *i.e.* unhurt, "*I will destroy this tower*" (probably the castle of Pnuel).—Vers. 10–12. The Midianitish kings were at *Karkor* with all the remnant of their army, about fifteen thousand men, a hundred and twenty thousand having already fallen. Gideon followed them thither by the road of the dwellers in tents on the east of *Nobah* and *Jogbeha;* and falling upon them unawares, smote the whole camp, which thought itself quite secure, and took the two kings prisoners, after discomfiting all the camp. The situation of *Karkor*, which is only mentioned here, cannot be determined with certainty. The statement of *Eusebius* and *Jerome* (*Onom. s. v.* Καρκά, *Carcar*), that it was the castle of *Carcaria*, a day's journey from *Petra*, is decidedly wrong, since this castle is much too far to the south, as *Gesenius* (Thes. p. 1210) has shown. *Karkor* cannot have been very far from *Nobah* and Jogbeha. These two places are probably preserved in the ruins of *Nowakis* and *Jebeiha*, on the north-west of *Ammân* (*Rabbath-ammon;* see at Num. xxi. 31). Now, as *Burckhardt* (Syr. p. 612) also mentions a ruin in the neighbourhood, called *Karkagheisch,* on the left of the road from Szalt to Ammân, and at the most an hour and a half to the north-west of Ammân, *Knobel* (on Num. xxxii. 42) is inclined to regard this ruin as *Karkor*. If this supposition could be proved to be correct, Gideon would have fallen upon the camp of the enemy from the north-east. For "*the way of the dwellers in tents on the east of Nobah and Jogbeha*" cannot well be any other than the way which ran to the east of Nobah and Jogbeha, past the most easterly frontier city of the Gadites, to the nomads who dwelt in the desert. הַשְּׁכוּנֵי בָּאֳהָלִים has the article attached to the governing noun, which may easily be explained in this instance from the intervening preposition. The passive participle שָׁכֵן has an intransitive force (see *Ewald*, § 149, *a.*). The verb הֶחֱרִיד in the circumstantial clause acquires the force of the pluperfect from the context. When he had startled the camp out of its security, having alarmed it by his unexpected attack, he succeeded in taking the two kings prisoners.

Vers. 13–21. Punishment of the Towns of Succoth and
Pnuel, and Execution of the Captured Kings of Midian.
—Vers. 13, 14. Gideon returned victorious from the war, מִלְמַעֲלֵה
הֶחָרֶס, "*from by the ascent* (or *mountain road*) *of Hecheres*," a place
in front of the town of Succoth, with which we are not acquainted.
This is the rendering adopted by the LXX., the Peshito, and the
Arabic; but the rest of the early translators have merely guessed at
the meaning. The *Chaldee*, which has been followed by the *Rabbins*
and *Luther*, has rendered it "before sunset," in utter opposition to
the rules of the language; for although *cheres* is a word used
poetically to denote the sun, מַעֲלֵה cannot mean the setting of the
sun. *Aquila* and *Symmachus*, on the other hand, confound חֶרֶס
with הָרִים.—Gideon laid hold of a young man of the people of
Succoth, and got him to write down for him the princes and elders
(magistrates and rulers) of the city,—in all seventy-seven men.
וַיִּשְׁאָלֵהוּ וַיִּכְתֹּב is a short expression for "he asked him the names of
the princes and elders of the city, and the boy wrote them down."
אֵלָיו, *lit.* to him, *i.e.* for him.—Vers. 15, 16. Gideon then reproached
the elders with the insult they had offered him (ver. 6), and had
them punished with desert thorns and thistles. "*Men of Succoth*"
(vers. 15*a* and 16*b*) is a general expression for "elders of Succoth"
(ver. 16*a*); and elders a general term applied to all the representatives of the city, including the princes. אֲשֶׁר חֵרַפְתֶּם אֹתִי, with
regard to whom ye have despised me. אֲשֶׁר is the accusative of the
more distant or second object, not the subject, as *Stud.* supposes.
"*And he taught the men of Succoth* (*i.e.* caused them to know, made
them feel, punished them) with them (the thorns)." There is no
good ground for doubting the correctness of the reading וַיֹּדַע. The
free renderings of the LXX., *Vulg.*, etc., are destitute of critical
worth; and *Bertheau's* assertion, that if it were the *Hiphil* it would
be written יוֹדַע, is proved to be unfounded by the defective writing
in Num. xvi. 5, Job xxxii. 7.—Ver. 17. Gideon also inflicted upon
Pnuel the punishment threatened in ver. 9. The punishment
inflicted by Gideon upon both the cities was well deserved in all
respects, and was righteously executed. The inhabitants of these
cities had not only acted treacherously to Israel as far as they could,
from the most selfish interests, in a holy conflict for the glory of the
Lord and the freedom of His people, but in their contemptuous
treatment of Gideon and his host they had poured contempt upon
the Lord, who had shown them to be His own soldiers before the
eyes of the whole nation by the victory which He had given them

over the innumerable army of the foe. Having been called by the Lord to be the deliverer and judge of Israel, it was Gideon's duty to punish the faithless cities.—Vers. 18–21. After punishing these cities, Gideon repaid the two kings of Midian, who had been taken prisoners, according to their doings. From the judicial proceedings instituted with regard to them (vers. 18, 19), we learn that these kings had put the brothers of Gideon to death, and apparently not in open fight; but they had murdered them in an unrighteous and cruel manner. And Gideon made them atone for this with their own lives, according to the strict *jus talionis*. אֵיפֹה, in ver. 18, does not mean *where?* but " *in what condition, of what form, were the men whom ye slew at Tabor?*" *i.e.* either in the city of Tabor or at Mount Tabor (see chap. iv. 6, and Josh. xix. 22). The kings replied: " *As thou so they*" (those men), *i.e.* they were all as stately as thou art, " *every one like the form of kings' sons.*" אֶחָד, one, for every one, like אִישׁ אֶחָד in 2 Kings xv. 20, or more frequently אִישׁ alone. As the men who had been slain were Gideon's own brothers, he swore to those who had done the deed, *i.e.* to the two kings, " *As truly as Jehovah liveth, if ye had let them live I should not have put you to death;*" and then commanded his first-born son Jether to slay them, for the purpose of adding the disgrace of falling by the hand of a boy. " *But the boy drew not his sword from fear, because he was yet a boy.*" And the kings then said to Gideon, " *Rise thou and stab us, for as the man so is his strength,*" *i.e.* such strength does not belong to a boy, but to a man. Thereupon Gideon slew them, and took the little moons upon the necks of their camels as booty. " *The little moons*" were crescent-shaped ornaments of silver or gold, such as men and women wore upon their necks (see ver. 26, and Isa. iii. 18), and which they also hung upon the necks of camels,— a custom still prevalent in Arabia (see *Schröder, de vestitu mul. hebr.* pp. 39, 40, and *Wellsted, Reisen in Arab.* i. p. 209).

Vers. 22–32. GIDEON'S REMAINING ACTS, AND DEATH.—Vers. 22, 23. As Gideon had so gloriously delivered Israel from the severe and long oppression on the part of the Midianites, the Israelites offered him an hereditary crown. " *The men of Israel*" were hardly all the twelve tribes, but probably only the northern tribes of the western part of the land already mentioned in chap. vi. 35, who had suffered the most severely from the Midianitish oppression, and had been the first to gather round Gideon to make an attack upon the foe. The temptation to accept the government of Israel was resisted

by this warrior of God. *" Neither I nor my son shall rule over you;*
Jehovah shall rule over you," was his reply to this offer, containing
an evident allusion to the destination and constitution of the tribes
of Israel as a nation which Jehovah had chosen to be His own
possession, and to which He had just made himself known in so
conspicuous a manner as their omnipotent Ruler and King. This
refusal of the regal dignity on the part of Gideon is not at variance
with the fact, that Moses had already foreseen the possibility that
at some future time the desire for a king would arise in the nation,
and had given them a law for the king expressly designed for such
circumstances as these (Deut. xvii. 14 sqq.). For Gideon did not
decline the honour because Jehovah was King in Israel, *i.e.* because
he regarded an earthly monarchy in Israel as irreconcilable with
the heavenly monarchy of Jehovah, but simply because he thought
the government of Jehovah in Israel amply sufficient, and did
not consider either himself or his sons called to found an earthly
monarchy.—Vers. 24 sqq. Gideon resisted the temptation to put an
earthly crown upon his head, from true fidelity to Jehovah; but he
yielded to another temptation, which this appeal on the part of the
people really involved, namely, the temptation to secure to himself
for the future the position to which the Lord had called and exalted
him. The Lord had called him to be the deliverer of Israel by
visibly appearing in His angel, and had not only accepted the gift
which he offered Him, as a well-pleasing sacrifice, but had also
commanded him to build an altar, and by offering an atoning burnt-
sacrifice to re-establish the worship of Jehovah in his family and
tribe, and to restore the favour of God to His people once more.
Lastly, the Lord had made His will known to him again and again;
whilst by the glorious victory which He had given to him and to
his small band over the powerful army of the foe, He had confirmed
him as His chosen servant to be the deliverer and judge of Israel.
The relation which Gideon thus sustained to the Lord he imagined
that he ought to preserve; and therefore, after declining the royal
dignity, he said to the people, *" I will request of you one request,*
that ye give me every one the ring that he has received as booty."
This request the historian explains by adding the remark: *" for*
they (the enemy) *had golden rings, for they were Ishmaelites,"* from
whom therefore the Israelites were able to get an abundance of
rings as booty. *Ishmaelites* is the general name for the nomad
tribes of Arabia, to whom the Midianites also belonged (as in Gen.
xxxvii. 25).—Vers. 25, 26. This request of Gideon's was cheer-

fully fulfilled: "*They spread out the cloth* (brought for collecting the rings), *and threw into it every one the ring that he had received as booty.*" *Simlah*, the upper garment, was for the most part only a large square piece of cloth. The weight of these golden rings amounted to 1700 shekels, *i.e.* about 50 lbs., (לְבַד מִן) separate from, *i.e.* beside, the remaining booty, for which Gideon had not asked, and which the Israelites kept for themselves, viz. the little moons, the ear-pendants (*netiphoth, lit.* little drops, probably pearl-shaped ear-drops: see Isa. iii. 19), and the purple clothes which were worn by the kings of Midian (*i.e.* which they had on), and also apart from the neck-bands upon the necks of their camels. Instead of the *anakoth* or necklaces (ver. 26), the *saharonim*, or little moons upon the necks of the camels, are mentioned in ver. 21 as the more valuable portion of these necklaces. Even at the present day the Arabs are accustomed to ornament the necks of these animals " with a band of cloth or leather, upon which small shells called cowries are strung or sewed in the form of a crescent. The sheiks add silver ornaments to these, which make a rich booty in time of war" (*Wellsted*, Reise, i. p. 209). The Midianitish kings had their camels ornamented with golden crescents. This abundance of golden ornaments will not surprise us, when we consider that the Arabs still carry their luxurious tastes for such things to a very great excess. *Wellsted* (i. p. 224) states that "the women in Omân spend considerable amounts in the purchase of silver ornaments, and their children are literally laden with them. I have sometimes counted fifteen ear-rings upon each side; and the head, breast, arms, and ankles are adorned with the same profusion." As the Midianitish army consisted of 130,000 men, of whom 15,000 only remained at the commencement of the last engagement, the Israelites may easily have collected 5000 golden rings, or even more, which might weigh 1700 shekels.—Ver. 27. "*And Gideon made it into an ephod*," *i.e.* used the gold of the rings obtained from the booty for making an ephod. There is no necessity, however, to understand this as signifying that 1700 shekels or 50 lbs. of gold had been used for the ephod itself, but simply that the making of the ephod was accomplished with this gold. The word *ephod* does not signify an image of Jehovah, or an idol, as *Gesenius* and others maintain, but the shoulder-dress of the high priest, no doubt including the *choshen* belonging to it, with the Urim and Thummim, as in 1 Sam. xiv. 3, xxi. 10, xxiii. 6, 9, etc. The material for this was worked throughout with gold threads; and in addition to that there were

precious stones set in gold braid upon the shoulder-pieces of the
ephod and upon the choshen, and chains made of gold twist for
fastening the choshen upon the ephod (see Ex. xxviii. 6–30). Now,
if 50 lbs. of gold could not be used for these things, there were also
fourteen precious stones to be procured, and the work itself to be
paid for, so that 50 lbs. of gold might easily be devoted to the preparation of this state dress. The large quantity of gold, therefore,
does not warrant us in introducing arbitrarily into the text the
establishment of a formal sanctuary, and the preparation of a golden
image of Jehovah in the form of a bull, as *Bertheau* has done, since
there is no reference to פֶּסֶל or מַסֵּכָה, as in chap. xvii. xviii.; and
even the other words of the text do not point to the founding of a
sanctuary and the setting up of an image of Jehovah.[1] The expression which follows, וַיַּצֵּג אֹתוֹ, does not affirm that " he set it up,"
but may also mean, " *he kept it in his city of Ophrah*." הִצִּיג is never
used to denote the setting up of an image or statue, and signifies
not only to put up, but also to lay down (*e.g.* chap. vi. 37), and to
let a thing stand, or leave behind (Gen. xxxiii. 15). The further
remark of the historian, " *and all Israel went thither a whoring after
it, and it became a snare to Gideon and his house*," does not presuppose the founding of a sanctuary or temple in Ophrah, and the
setting up of a golden calf there. In what the whoring of Israel
after the ephod, *i.e.* the idolatry of the Israelites with Gideon's
ephod which was kept in Ophrah, consisted, cannot be gathered or
determined from the use of the ephod in the worship of Jehovah
under the Mosaic law. " The breastplate upon the coat, and the
holy lot, were no doubt used in connection with idolatry" (*Oehler*),
and Gideon had an ephod made in his town of Ophrah, that he might
thereby obtain revelations from the Lord. We certainly are not
for a moment to think of an exposure of the holy coat for the people
to worship. It is far more probable that Gideon put on the ephod
and wore it as a priest, when he wished to inquire and learn the
will of the Lord. It is possible that he also sacrificed to the Lord
upon the altar that was built at Ophrah (chap. vi. 24). The motive
by which he was led to do this was certainly not merely ambition,

---

[1] *Oehler* has correctly observed in *Herzog's* Cyclopædia, that *Bertheau* acts
very arbitrarily when he represents Gideon as setting up the image of a bull,
as Jeroboam did afterwards, since there is nothing to sustain it in the account
itself. Why cannot Gideon have worshipped without any image of Jehovah,
with the help of the altar mentioned in chap. vi. 24, which was a symbol of
Jehovah's presence, and remained standing till the historian's own time?

as *Bertheau* supposes, impelling the man who, along with his followers, had maintained an independent attitude towards the tribe of Ephraim in the war itself (chap. viii. 1 sqq.), to act independently of the common sanctuary of the congregation which was within the territory of Ephraim, and also of the office of the high priest in the time of peace as well. For there is not the slightest trace to be found of such ambition as this in anything that he did during the conflict with the Midianites. The germs of Gideon's error, which became a snare to him and to his house, lie unquestionably deeper than this, namely, in the fact that the high-priesthood had probably lost its worth in the eyes of the people on account of the worthlessness of its representatives, so that they no longer regarded the high priest as the sole or principal medium of divine revelation ; and therefore Gideon, to whom the Lord had manifested himself directly, as He had not to any judge or leader of the people since the time of Joshua, might suppose that he was not acting in violation of the law, when he had an ephod made, and thus provided himself with a substratum or vehicle for inquiring the will of the Lord. His sin therefore consisted chiefly in his invading the prerogative of the *Aaronic* priesthood, drawing away the people from the one legitimate sanctuary, and thereby not only undermining the theocratic unity of Israel, but also giving an impetus to the relapse of the nation into the worship of Baal after his death. This sin became a snare to him and to his house.

The history of Gideon is concluded in vers. 28–32.—Ver. 28. The Midianites had been so humiliated that they lifted up their head no more, and the land of Israel had rest forty years "*in the days of Gideon*," *i.e.* as long as Gideon lived.—Vers. 29 sqq. Before the account of his death, a few other notices respecting his family are introduced for the purpose of preparing the way for the following history of the doings of his sons, in which the sin of Gideon came to a head, and the judgment burst upon his house. "*And Jerubbaal, the son of Joash, went and dwelt in his house.*" Both the word וַיֵּלֶךְ, which simply serves to bring out the fact more vividly (see the remarks on Ex. ii. 1), and also the choice of the name *Jerubbaal*, merely serve to give greater prominence to the change, from the heat of the war against the Midianites to the quiet retirement of domestic life. Instead of accepting the crown that was offered him and remaining at the head of the nation, the celebrated Baal-fighter retired into private life again. In addition to the seventy sons of his many wives, there was a son born to him by a concubine, who lived at Shechem and is called his maid-servant in chap. ix. 18, and to this son he gave the name of *Abimelech, i.e.* king's father. יַּשֶּׂם אֶת־שְׁמוֹ is not the same as קָרָא אֶת־שְׁמוֹ, to give a person a name, but signifies to add a name, or give a surname (see Neh. ix. 7, and Dan. v. 12 in the Chaldee). It follows from this, that Abimelech received this name from Gideon as a cognomen answering to his character, and therefore not at the time of his birth, but when he grew up and manifested such qualities as led to the expectation that he would be a king's father.—Ver. 32. Gideon died at a good old age (see Gen. xv. 15, xxv. 8), and therefore also died a peaceful death (not so his sons; see chap. ix.), and was buried in his father's grave at Ophrah (chap. vi. 11).

Vers. 33–35 form the introduction to the history of Gideon's sons.—Ver. 33. After Gideon's death the Israelites fell once more into the Baal-worship which Gideon had rooted out of his father's city (chap. vi. 25 sqq.), and worshipped *Baal-berith* as their God. *Baal-berith*, the covenant Baal (equivalent to *El-berith*, the covenant god, chap. ix. 46), is not Baal as the god of covenants, but, according to Gen. xiv. 13, Baal as a god in covenant, *i.e.* Baal with whom they had made a covenant, just as the Israelites had their faithful covenant God in Jehovah (see *Movers*, Phöniz. i. p. 171). The worship of Baal-berith, as performed at Shechem according to chap. ix. 46, was an imitation of the worship of Jehovah, an adulteration of that worship, in which Baal was put in the place of Jehovah (see *Hengstenberg*, Dissertations on the Pentateuch, vol. ii. p. 81).—Vers. 34, 35. In this relapse into the worship of Baal they not only forgot Jehovah, their Deliverer from all their foes, but also the benefits which they owed to Gideon, and showed no kindness to his house in return for all the good which he had shown to Israel. The expression *Jerubbaal-Gideon* is chosen by the historian here, not for the purely outward purpose of laying express emphasis upon the identity of Gideon and Jerubbaal (*Bertheau*), but to point to what Gideon, the Baal-fighter, had justly deserved from the people of Israel.

Judgment upon the House of Gideon, or Abimelech's Sins and End.
—Chap. ix.

After the death of Gideon, Abimelech, his bastard son, opened a way for himself to reign as king over Israel, by murdering his brethren with the help of the Shechemites (vers. 1–6). For this grievous wrong Jotham, the only one of Gideon's seventy sons who

escaped the massacre, reproached the citizens of Shechem in a
parable, in which he threatened them with punishment from God
(vers. 7–21), which first of all fell upon Shechem within a very
short time (vers. 22–49), and eventually reached Abimelech himself
(vers. 50–57).

Vers. 1–6. Having gone to Shechem, the home of his mother
(chap. viii. 31), Abimelech applied to his mother's brothers and the
whole family (all the relations) of the father's house of his mother,
and addressed them thus: " *Speak, I pray you, in the ears of all
the lords of Shechem,*" *i.e.* speak to them publicly and solemnly.
שְׁכֶם בַּעֲלֵי, the lords, *i.e.* the possessors or citizens of Shechem
(compare ver. 46 with ver. 49, where מִגְדָּל בַּעֲלֵי is interchangeable
with מִגְדָּל אַנְשֵׁי; also chap. xx. 5, and Josh. xxiv. 11): they are not
merely Canaanitish citizens, of whom there were some still living
in Shechem according to ver. 28, but all the citizens of the town ;
therefore chiefly Israelites. " *What is better for you, that seventy
men rule over you, all the sons of Jerubbaal, or* (only) *one man* (*i.e.*
Abimelech)? *and remember that I am your flesh and bone*" (blood
relation, Gen. xxix. 14). The name " sons of Jerubbaal," *i.e.* of
the man who had destroyed the altar of Baal, was just as little
adapted to commend the sons of Gideon to the Shechemites, who
were devoted to the worship of Baal, as the remark that seventy
men were to rule over them. No such rule ever existed, or was
even aspired to by the seventy sons of Gideon. But Abimelech
assumed that his brothers possessed the same thirst for ruling as he
did himself ; and the citizens of Shechem might be all the more
ready to put faith in his assertions, since the distinction which
Gideon had enjoyed was thoroughly adapted to secure a prominent
place in the nation for his sons.—Ver. 3. When his mother's
brethren spake to the citizens of Shechem concerning him, *i.e.*
respecting him and his proposal, their heart turned to Abimelech.
—Ver. 4. They gave him seventy shekels of silver from the house
of Baal-berith, *i.e.* from the treasury of the temple that was dedicated to the covenant Baal at Shechem, as temple treasures were
frequently applied to political purposes (see 1 Kings xv. 18). With
this money Abimelech easily hired light and desperate men, who
followed him (attached themselves to him) ; and with their help he
murdered his brethren at Ophrah, seventy men, with the exception
of Jotham the youngest, who had hidden himself. The number
seventy, the total number of his brethren, is reduced by the exception mentioned immediately afterwards to sixty-nine who were

really put to death. רֵיק, *empty*, *i.e.* without moral restraint. פֹּחֵז,
lit. gurgling up, boiling over ; figuratively, *hot, desperate men.*
" *Upon* (against) *one stone,*" that is to say, by a formal execution :
a bloody omen of the kingdom of the ten tribes, which was afterwards founded at Shechem by the Ephraimite Jeroboam, in which
one dynasty overthrew another, and generally sought to establish
its power by exterminating the whole family of the dynasty that
had been overthrown (see 1 Kings xv. 27 sqq., 2 Kings x. 1 sqq.).
Even in Judah, Athaliah the worshipper of Baal sought to usurp
the government by exterminating the whole of the descendants of
her son (2 Kings xi.). Such fratricides have also occurred in quite
recent times in the Mohammedan countries of the East.—Ver. 6.
" *Then all the citizens of Shechem assembled together, and all the
house of Millo, and made Abimelech king at the memorial terebinth
at Shechem.*" *Millo* is unquestionably the name of the castle or
citadel of the town of Shechem, which is called the tower of
Shechem in vers. 46–49. The word *Millo* (Chaldee מִלִּיתָא) signifies
primarily a rampart, inasmuch as it consisted of two walls, with the
space between them filled with rubbish. There was also a *Millo*
at Jerusalem (2 Sam. v. 9 ; 1 Kings ix. 15). " *All the house of
Millo*" are all the inhabitants of the castle, the same persons who
are described in ver. 46 as " all the men (*baale*) of the tower."
The meaning of אֵלוֹן מֻצָּב is doubtful. מֻצָּב, the thing set up, is a
military post in Isa. xxix. 3 ; but it may also mean a monument or
memorial, and here it probably denotes the large stone set up as a
memorial at Shechem under the oak or terebinth (see Gen. xxxv.
4). The inhabitants of Shechem, the worshippers of Baal-berith,
carried out the election of Abimelech as king in the very same
place in which Joshua had held the last national assembly, and had
renewed the covenant of Israel with Jehovah the true covenant
God (Josh. xxiv. 1, 25, 26). It was there in all probability that
the temple of Baal-berith was to be found, namely, according to
ver. 46, near the tower of Shechem or the citadel of Millo.

Vers. 7–21. When Jotham, who had escaped after the murder,
was told of the election which had taken place, he went to the top
of Mount Gerizim, which rises as a steep wall of rock to the height
of about 800 feet above the valley of Shechem on the south side of
the city (*Rob.* iii. p. 96), and cried with a loud voice, " *Hearken to
me, ye lords of Shechem, and God will also hearken to you.*" After
this appeal, which calls to mind the language of the prophets, he
uttered aloud a fable of the trees which wanted to anoint a king

over them,—a fable of true prophetic significance, and the earliest
with which we are acquainted (vers. 8–15).   To the appeal which
is made to them in succession to become king over the trees, the
olive tree, the fig tree, and the vine all reply : Shall we give up our
calling, to bear valuable fruits for the good and enjoyment of God
and men, and soar above the other trees ?   The briar, however, to
which the trees turn last of all, is delighted at the unexpected
honour that is offered it, and says, " *Will ye in truth anoint me
king over you?   Then come and trust in my shadow ; but if not, let
fire go out of the briar and consume the cedars of Lebanon.*"   The
rare form מְלוֹכָה (*Chethib*, vers. 8, 12) also occurs in 1 Sam. xxviii.
8, Isa. xxxii. 11, Ps. xxvi. 2 : see *Ewald*, § 228, *b.*).   מָלְכִי (ver.
10) is also rare (see *Ewald*, § 226, *b.*).   The form הֶחֳדַלְתִּי (vers. 9,
11, 13), which is quite unique, is not "*Hophal* or *Hiphil*, compounded of 'הֶהְחַד or 'הֶהְחַר" (*Ewald*, § 51, *c.*), for neither the
Hophal nor the *Hiphil* of חָדַל occurs anywhere else; but it is a
simple *Kal*, and the obscure *o* sound is chosen instead of the *a* sound
for the sake of euphony, *i.e.* to assist the pronunciation of the gut-
tural syllables which follow one after another. The meaning of the
fable is very easy to understand.   The olive tree, fig tree, and vine
do not represent different historical persons, such as the judges
Othniel, Deborah, and Gideon, as the Rabbins affirm, but in a
perfectly general way the nobler families or persons who bring
forth fruit and blessing in the calling appointed them by God, and
promote the prosperity of the people and kingdom in a manner that
is well-pleasing to God and men. Oil, figs, and wine were the
most valuable productions of the land of Canaan, whereas the briar
was good for nothing but to burn. The noble fruit-trees would
not tear themselves from the soil in which they had been planted
and had borne fruit, to soar (נוּעַ, float about) above the trees, *i.e.*
not merely to rule over the trees, but *obire et circumagi in rebus
eorum curandis.*   נוּעַ includes the idea of restlessness and insecurity
of existence.   The explanation given in the *Berleb.* Bible, " We
have here what it is to be a king, to reign or be lord over many
others, namely, very frequently to do nothing else than float about
in such restlessness and distraction of thoughts, feelings, and desires, that very little good or sweet fruit ever falls to the ground,"
if not a truth without exception so far as royalty is concerned, is
at all events perfectly true in relation to what Abimelech aimed
at and attained, to be a king by the will of the people and not
by the grace of God.   Wherever the Lord does not found the

monarchy, or the king himself does not lay the foundations of his
government in God and the grace of God, he is never anything
but a tree, moving about above other trees without a firm root in a
fruitful soil, utterly unable to bear fruit to the glory of God and
the good of men. The expression " *all the trees*" is to be carefully
noticed in ver. 14. " *All* the trees" say to the briar, Be king over
us, whereas in the previous verse only " *the* trees" are mentioned.
This implies that of all the trees not one was willing to be king
himself, but that they were unanimous in transferring the honour
to the briar. The briar, which has nothing but thorns upon it,
and does not even cast sufficient shadow for any one to lie down in
its shadow and protect himself from the burning heat of the sun, is
an admirable simile for a worthless man, who can do nothing but
harm. The words of the briar, " *Trust in my shadow*," seek refuge
there, contain a deep irony, the truth of which the Shechemites
were very soon to discover. " *And if not*," *i.e.* if ye do not find
the protection you expect, fire will go out of the briar and consume
the cedars of Lebanon, the largest and noblest trees. Thorns
easily catch fire (see Ex. xxii. 5). The most insignificant and most
worthless man can be the cause of harm to the mightiest and most
distinguished.

In vers. 16–20 Jotham gives the application of his fable, for
there was no necessity for any special explanation of it, since it was
perfectly clear and intelligible in itself. These verses form a long
period, the first half of which is so extended by the insertion of
parentheses introduced as explanations (vers. 17, 18), that the
commencement of it (ver. 16) is taken up again in ver. 19*a* for the
purpose of attaching the apodosis. " *If ye have acted in truth and
sincerity, and (i.e.* when ye) *made Abimelech king ; if ye have done
well to Jerubbaal and his house, and if ye have done to him according
to the doing of his hands . . . as my father fought for you . . . but ye
have risen up to-day against my father's house, and have slain . . . if*
(I say) *ye have acted in truth and sincerity to Jerubbaal and his
house this day : then rejoice in Abimelech. . . .*" הִשְׁלִיךְ נַפְשׁוֹ, to throw
away his life, *i.e.* expose to death. מִנֶּגֶד, " *from before him*," serves
to strengthen the הִשְׁלִיךְ. Jotham imputes the slaying of his brothers
to the citizens of Shechem, as a crime which they themselves had
committed (ver. 18), because they had given Abimelech money out
of their temple of Baal to carry out his designs against the sons of
Jerubbaal (ver. 4). In this reproach he had, strictly speaking,
already pronounced sentence upon their doings When, therefore,

he proceeds still further in ver. 19, "If ye have acted in truth towards Jerubbaal . . . then rejoice," etc., this turn contains the bitterest scorn at the faithlessness manifested towards Jerubbaal. In that case nothing could follow but the fulfilment of the threat and the bursting forth of the fire. In carrying out this point the application goes beyond the actual meaning of the parable itself. Not only will fire go forth from Abimelech and consume the lords of Shechem and the inhabitants of Millo, but fire will also go forth from them and devour Abimelech himself. The fulfilment of this threat was not long delayed, as the following history shows (vers. 23 sqq.).—Ver. 21. But Jotham fled to *Beer*, after charging the Shechemites with their iniquity, and dwelt there before his brother Abimelech ("before," *i.e.* "for fear of."— *Jerome*). *Beer* in all probability is not the same place as *Beeroth* in the tribe of Benjamin (Josh. ix. 17), but, according to the *Onom.* (*s. v.* Βηρά), a place eight Roman miles to the north of Eleutheropolis, situated in the plain; at present a desolate village called *el Bireh*, near the mouth of the Wady es Surâr, not far from the former Beth-shemesh (*Rob.* Pal. ii. p. 132).

Vers. 22–24. Abimelech's reign lasted three years. וַיָּשַׂר, from שׂוּר, to govern, is used intentionally, as it appears, in the place of וַיִּמְלֹךְ, because Abimelech's government was not a monarchical reign, but simply a tyrannical despotism. "*Over Israel*," that is to say, not over the whole of the twelve tribes of Israel, but only over a portion of the nation, possibly the tribes of Ephraim and half Manasseh, which acknowledged his sway.—Vers. 23, 24. Then God sent an evil spirit between Abimelech and the citizens of Shechem, so that they became treacherous towards him. "*An evil spirit*" is not merely "an evil disposition," but an evil demon, which produced discord and strife, just as an evil spirit came upon Saul (1 Sam. xvi. 14, 15, xviii. 10); not Satan himself, but a supernatural spiritual power which was under his influence. This evil spirit God sent to punish the wickedness of Abimelech and the Shechemites. *Elohim*, not *Jehovah*, because the working of the divine justice is referred to here. "*That the wickedness to the seventy sons of Jerubbaal might come, and their blood* (the blood of these sons that had been shed), *to lay it upon Abimelech.*" "*And their blood*" is only a more precise definition of "the wickedness to the seventy sons;" and "*to lay it*" is an explanation of the expression "might come." The introduction of לָשׂוּם, however, brings an *anakolouthon* into the construction, since the transitive שׂוּם presupposes *Elohim* as the subject and דָּמָם as the object, whereas the parallel חֲמָס is the subject to the intransitive לָבוֹא : that the wickedness might come, and that God might lay the blood not only upon Abimelech, the author of the crime, but also upon the lords of Shechem, who had strengthened his hands to slay his brethren ; had supported him by money, that he might be able to hire worthless fellows to execute his crime (vers. 4, 5).

Vers. 25–29. The faithlessness of the Shechemites towards Abimelech commenced by their placing liers in wait for him (לוֹ, *dat. incomm.*, to his disadvantage) upon the tops of the mountains (Ebal and Gerizim, between which Shechem was situated), who plundered every one who passed by them on the road. In what way they did harm to Abimelech by sending out liers in wait to plunder the passers-by, is not very clear from the brevity of the narrative. The general effect may have been, that they brought his government into discredit with the people by organizing a system of robbery and plunder, and thus aroused a spirit of discontent and rebellion. Possibly, however, these highway robbers were to watch for Abimelech himself, if he should come to Shechem, not only to plunder him, but, if possible, to despatch him altogether. This was made known to Abimelech. But before he had put down the brigandage, the treachery broke out into open rebellion.—Ver. 26. Gaal, the son of Ebed, came to Shechem with his brethren. עָבַר with בְּ, to pass over into a place. Who Gaal was, and whence he came, we are not informed. Many of the MSS. and early editions, *e.g.* the Syriac and Arabic, read "son of Eber," instead of "son of Ebed." Judging from his appearance in Shechem, he was a knight-errant, who went about the country with his brethren, *i.e.* as captain of a company of freebooters, and was welcomed in Shechem, because the Shechemites, who were dissatisfied with the rule of Abimelech, hoped to find in him a man who would be able to render them good service in their revolt from Abimelech. This may be gathered from the words " *and the lords of Shechem trusted in him.*"—Ver. 27. At the vintage they prepared הִלּוּלִים, " praise-offerings," with the grapes which they had gathered and pressed, eating and drinking in the house of their god, *i.e.* the temple of Baal-berith, and cursing Abimelech at these sacrificial meals, probably when they were excited with wine. הִלּוּלִים signifies, according to Lev. xix. 24, praise-offerings of the fruits which newly-planted orchards or vineyards bore in the fourth year. The presentation of these fruits, by which the vineyard or orchard was sanctified to the Lord, was associated, as we may learn from the passage before us, with sacrificial meals. The Shechemites held a similar festival in the temple of their covenant Baal, and in his honour, to that which the law prescribes for the Israelites in Lev. xix. 23-25.— Vers. 28, 29. At this feast Gaal called upon the Shechemites to revolt from Abimelech. " *Who is Abimelech,*" he exclaimed, "*and who Shechem, that we serve him? Is he not the son of Jerubbaal, and Zebul his officer? Serve the men of Hamor, the father of Shechem! and why should we, we serve him* (Abimelech)?" The meaning of these words, which have been misinterpreted in several different ways, is very easily seen, if we bear in mind (1) that מִי (who is?) in this double question cannot possibly be used in two different and altogether opposite senses, such as " how insignificant or contemptible is Abimelech," and " how great and mighty is Shechem," but that in both instances it must be expressive of disparagement and contempt, as in 1 Sam. xxv. 10; and (2) that Gaal answers his own questions. Abimelech was regarded by him as contemptible, not because he was the son of a maid-servant or of very low birth, nor because he was ambitious and cruel, a parricide and the murderer of his brethren (*Rosenmüller*), but because he was a son of Jerubbaal, a son of the man who destroyed the altar of Baal at Shechem and restored the worship of Jehovah, for which the Shechemites themselves had endeavoured to slay him (chap. vi. 27 sqq.). So also the meaning of the question, Who is Shechem? may be gathered from the answer, " and Zebul his officer." The use of the personal מִי (who) in relation to Shechem may be explained on the ground that Gaal is speaking not so much of the city as of its inhabitants. The might and greatness of Shechem did not consist in the might and authority of its prefect, Zebul, who had been appointed by Abimelech, and whom the Shechemites had no need to serve. Accordingly there is no necessity either for the arbitrary paraphrase of Shechem, given in the *Sept.*, viz. υἱὸς Συχέμ (son of Shechem); or for the perfectly arbitrary assumption of *Bertheau*, that Shechem is only a second name for Abimelech, who was a descendant of Shechem; or even for the solution proposed by *Rosenmüller*, that Zebul was " a man of low birth and obscure origin," which is quite incapable of proof. To Zebul, that one man whom Abimelech had appointed prefect of the city, Gaal opposes " *the men of Hamor, the father of Shechem,*" as those whom the Shechemites should serve (*i.e.* whose followers they should be). *Hamor* was the name of the Hivite prince who had founded the city of

Shechem (Gen. xxxiii. 19, xxxiv. 2 ; compare Josh. xxiv. 32). The
" men of Hamor" were the patricians of the city, who " derived
their origin from the noblest and most ancient stock of Hamor"
(*Rosenmüller*). Gaal opposes them to Abimelech and his representative Zebul.[1] In the last clause, "*why should we serve him*"
(Abimelech or his officer Zebul)? Gaal identifies himself with the
inhabitants of Shechem, that he may gain them fully over to his
plans.—Ver. 29. " *O that this people,*" continued Gaal, "*were in
my hand,*" *i.e.* could I but rule over the inhabitants of Shechem,
"*then would I remove* (drive away) *Abimelech.*" He then exclaimed
with regard to Abimelech (לְ אָמַר, as in ver. 54*b*, Gen. xx. 13, etc.),
"*Increase thine army and come out!*" Heated as he was with wine,
Gaal was so certain of victory that he challenged Abimelech boldly
to make war upon Shechem. רְבֶּה, imper. *Piel* with *Seghol.* צְאָה,
imperative, with ־ה of motion or emphasis.

Vers. 30–45. This rebellious speech of Gaal was reported to
Abimelech by the town-prefect Zebul, who sent messengers to him
בְּתָרְמָה, either with deceit (תָּרְמָה from רְמָה), *i.e.* employing deceit,
inasmuch as he had listened to the speech quietly and with apparent assent, or "*in Tormah,*" the name of a place, תָּרְמָה being a
misspelling for ארמה = אֲרוּמָה (ver. 41). The *Sept.* and *Chaldee* take
the word as an appellative = ἐν κρυφῇ, secretly ; so also do *Rashi*
and most of the earlier commentators, whilst *R. Kimchi* the elder
has decided in favour of the second rendering as a proper name.
As the word only occurs here, it is impossible to decide with certainty in favour of either view. הִנָּם צָרִים, behold they stir up the
city against thee (צָרִים from צוּר in the sense of צָרַר).—Ver. 32. At
the same time he called upon Abimelech to draw near, with the
people that he had with him, during the night, and to lie in wait in
the field (אָרַב, to place one's self in ambush), and the next morning to
spread out with his army against the town ; and when Gaal went
out with his followers, he was to do to him " as his hand should
find," *i.e.* to deal with him as he best could and would under the
circumstances. (On this formula, see at 1 Sam. x. 7, xxv. 8.)—

---

[1] *Bertheau* maintains, though quite erroneously, that serving the men of
Hamor is synonymous with serving Abimelech. But the very opposite of this
is so clearly implied in the words, that there cannot be any doubt on the
question. All that can be gathered from the words is that there were remnants
of the Hivite (or Canaanitish) population still living in Shechem, and therefore
that the Canaanites had not been entirely exterminated,—a fact which would
sufficiently explain the revival of the worship of Baal there.

Ver. 34. On receiving this intelligence, Abimelech rose up during the night with the people that were with him, *i.e.* with such troops as he had, and placed four companies ("heads" as in chap. vii. 16) in ambush against Shechem.—Vers. 35, 36. When Gaal went out in the morning with his retinue upon some enterprise, which is not more clearly defined, and stood before the city gate, Abimelech rose up with his army out of the ambush. On seeing this people, Gaal said to Zebul (who must therefore have come out of the city with him): "*Behold, people come down from the tops of the mountains.*" Zebul replied, for the purpose of deceiving him and making him feel quite secure, "*Thou lookest upon the shadow of the mountains as men.*"—Ver. 37. But Gaal said again, "*Behold, people come down from the navel of the land,*" *i.e.* from the highest point of the surrounding country, "*and a crowd comes by the way of the wizard's terebinths,*"—a place in the neighbourhood of Shechem that is not mentioned anywhere else, and therefore is not more precisely known.—Ver. 38. Then Zebul declared openly against Gaal, and reproached him with his foolhardy speech, whilst Abimelech was drawing nearer with his troops: "*Where is thy mouth now with which thou saidst, Who is Abimelech? Is not this the people that thou hast despised? Go out now and fight with him!*"—Vers. 39 sqq. Then Gaal went out "before the citizens of Shechem;" *i.e.* not at their head as their leader, which is the meaning of לִפְנֵי in Gen. xxxiii. 3, Ex. xiii. 21, Num. x. 35, etc.,—for, according to vers. 33–35, Gaal had only gone out of the town with his own retinue, and, according to vers. 42, 43, the people of Shechem did not go out till the next day,—but "in the sight of the lords of Shechem," so that they looked upon the battle. But the battle ended unfortunately for him. Abimelech put him to flight (רָדַף as in Lev. xxvi. 36), and there fell many slain up to the gate of the city, into which Gaal had fled with his followers.—Ver. 41. Abimelech did not force his way into the city, but remained (יֵשֶׁב, *lit.* sat down) with his army in *Arumah*, a place not mentioned again, which was situated, according to ver. 42, somewhere in the neighbourhood of Shechem. It cannot possibly have been the place called Ῥουμὰ ἡ καὶ Ἀριμα in the *Onom.* of *Eusebius*, which was named Ῥέμφις in his day, and was situated in the neighbourhood of Diospolis (or Lydda). Zebul, however, drove Gaal and his brethren (*i.e.* his retinue) out of Shechem.—Vers. 42–45. The next day the people of Shechem went into the field, apparently not to make war upon Abimelech, but to work in the field, possibly to continue the vintage. But when Abimelech was informed of it, he divided the people, *i.e.* his own men, into three companies, which he placed in ambush in the field, and then fell upon the Shechemites when they had come out of the city, and slew them.—Ver. 44. That is to say, Abimelech and the companies with him spread themselves out and took their station by the city gate to cut off the retreat of the Shechemites into the city, whilst the other two companies fell upon all who were in the field, and slew them.—Ver. 45. Thus Abimelech fought all that day against the city and took it; and having slain all the people therein, he destroyed the city and strewed salt upon it. Strewing the ruined city with salt, which only occurs here, was a symbolical act, signifying that the city was to be turned for ever into a barren salt desert. Salt ground is a barren desert (see Job xxxix. 6, Ps. cvii. 34).

Vers. 46–49. When the inhabitants of the castle of Shechem ("lords of the tower of Shechem" = "all the house of Millo," ver. 6) heard of the fate of the town of Shechem, they betook themselves to the hold of the house (temple) of the covenant god (Baal-berith), evidently not for the purpose of defending themselves there, but to seek safety at the sanctuary of their god from fear of the vengeance of Abimelech, towards whom they also had probably acted treacherously. The meaning of the word צְרִיחַ, which answers to an Arabic word signifying *arx, palatium, omnis structura elatior*, cannot be exactly determined, as it only occurs again in 1 Sam. xiii. 6 in connection with caves and clefts of the rock. According to ver. 49, it had a roof which could be set on fire. The meaning "tower" is only a conjecture founded upon the context, and does not suit, as צְרִיחַ is distinguished from מִגְדָּל.— Ver. 47. As soon as this was announced to Abimelech, he went with all his men to Mount Zalmon, took hatchets in his hand, cut down branches from the trees, and laid them upon his shoulders, and commanded his people to do the same. These branches they laid upon the hold, and set the hold on fire over them (the inhabitants of the tower who had taken refuge there), so that all the people of the tower of Shechem (about one thousand persons) perished, both men and women. Mount *Zalmon*, which is mentioned again in Ps. lxviii. 15, was a dark, thickly-wooded mountain near Shechem,— a kind of "Black Forest," as *Luther* has rendered the name. The plural *kardumoth*, "axes," may be explained on the ground that Abimelech took axes not only for himself but for his people also. מָר in a relative sense, as in Num. xxiii. 3 (see *Ewald*, § 331, *b.*).

Vers. 50–57. At length the fate predicted by Jotham (ver. 20) overtook Abimelech.—Vers. 50, 51. He went from Shechem to Thebez, besieged the town, and took it. *Thebez*, according to the *Onom.* thirteen miles from Neapolis (Shechem) on the road to Scythopolis (Beisan), has been preserved in the large village of *Tubâs* on the north of Shechem (see *Rob.* Pal. iii. p. 156, and Bibl. Res. p. 305). This town possessed a strong tower, in which men and women and all the inhabitants of the town took refuge and shut themselves in. But when Abimelech advanced to the tower and drew near to the door to set it on fire, a woman threw a mill-stone down upon him from the roof of the tower and smashed his skull, whereupon he called hastily to the attendant who carried his weapons to give him his death-blow with his sword, that men might not say of him "a woman slew him." פֶּלַח רֶכֶב, the upper millstone which was turned round, *lapis vector* (see Deut. xxiv. 6). תָּרִיץ: from רָצַץ, with a toneless *i*, possibly to distinguish it from וַתָּרֶץ (from רוץ). גֻּלְגַּלְתּוֹ, an unusual form for גֻּלְגָּלְתּוֹ, which is found in the edition of *Norzi* (Mantua, 1742).—Ver. 55. After the death of Abimelech his army was dissolved. אִישׁ יִשְׂרָאֵל are the Israelites who formed Abimelech's army. In vers. 56, 57, the historian closes this account with the remark, that in this manner God recompensed Abimelech and the citizens of Shechem, who had supported him in the murder of his brothers (ver. 2), according to their doings. After the word "*rendered*" in ver. 56 we must supply "upon his head," as in ver. 57. Thus Jotham's curse was fulfilled upon Abimelech and upon the Shechemites, who had made him king.

The Judges Tola and Jair.—Chap. x. 1–5.

Of these two judges no particular deeds are mentioned, no doubt because they performed none.—Vers. 1, 2. *Tola* arose after Abimelech's death to deliver Israel, and judged Israel twenty-three years until his death, though certainly not all the Israelites of the twelve tribes, but only the northern and possibly also the eastern tribes, to the exclusion of Judah, Simeon, and Benjamin, as these southern tribes neither took part in Gideon's war of freedom nor stood under Abimelech's rule. To explain the clause "*there arose to defend* (or save) *Israel*," when nothing had been said about any fresh oppression on the part of the foe, we need not assume, as *Rosenmüller* does, "that the Israelites had been constantly harassed by their neighbours, who continued to suppress the liberty of the

Israelites, and from whose stratagems or power the Israelites were
delivered by the acts of Tola;" but Tola rose up as the deliverer
of Israel, even supposing that he simply regulated the affairs of
the tribes who acknowledged him as their supreme judge, and succeeded by his efforts in preventing the nation from falling back
into idolatry, and thus guarded Israel from any fresh oppression on
the part of hostile nations. *Tola* was the son of *Puah*, the son of
Dodo, of the tribe of Issachar. The names *Tola* and *Puah* are
already met with among the descendants of Issachar, as founders
of families of the tribe of Issachar (see Gen. xlvi. 13, Num. xxvi.
23, where the latter name is written פֻּוָּה), and they were afterwards
repeated in the different households of these families. *Dodo* is not
an appellative, as the *Sept.* translators supposed (υἱὸς πατραδέλφου
αὐτοῦ), but a proper name, as in 2 Sam. xxiii. 9 (*Keri*), 24, and
1 Chron. xi. 12. The town of *Shamir*, upon the mountains of
Ephraim, where Tola judged Israel, and was afterwards buried,
was a different place from the *Shamir* upon the mountains of Judah,
mentioned in Josh xv. 48, and its situation (probably in the territory of Issachar) is still unknown.—Vers. 3 sqq. After him *Jair*
the Gileadite (born in Gilead) judged Israel for twenty-two years.
Nothing further is related of him than that he had thirty sons who
rode upon thirty asses, which was a sign of distinguished rank in
those times when the Israelites had no horses. They had thirty
cities (the second עֲיָרִים in ver. 4 is another form for עָרִים, from a
singular עָיִר = עִיר, a city, and is chosen because of its similarity in
sound to עֲיָרִים, asses). These cities they were accustomed to call
Havvoth-jair unto this day (the time when our book was written), in
the land of Gilead. The לָהֶם before יִקְרְאוּ is placed first for the sake
of emphasis, " *even these they call*," etc. This statement is not at
variance with the fact, that in the time of Moses the Manassite
Jair gave the name of *Havvoth-jair* to the towns of Bashan which
had been conquered by him (Num. xxxii. 41; Deut. iii. 14); for
it is not affirmed here, that the thirty cities which belonged to the
sons of Jair received this name for the first time from the judge
Jair, but simply that this name was brought into use again by the
sons of Jair, and was applied to these cities in a peculiar sense.
(For further remarks on the *Havvoth-jair*, see at Deut. iii. 14.) The
situation of *Camon*, where Jair was buried, is altogether uncertain.
Josephus (Ant. v. 6, 6) calls it a city of Gilead, though probably
only on account of the assumption, that it would not be likely that
Jair the Gileadite, who possessed so many cities in Gilead, should

be buried outside Gilead. But this assumption is a very question-able one. As Jair judged Israel after Tola the Issacharite, the assumption is a more natural one, that he lived in Canaan proper Yet *Reland* (Pal. ill. p. 679) supports the opinion that it was in Gilead, and adduces the fact that *Polybius* (Hist. v. 70, 12) men-tions a town called Καμοῦν, by the side of Pella and Gefrun, as having been taken by Antiochus. On the other hand, *Eusebius* and *Jerome* (in the *Onom.*) regard our *Camon* as being the same as the κώμη Καμμωνὰ ἐν τῷ μεγάλῳ πεδίῳ, six Roman miles to the north of *Legio* (*Lejun*), on the way to Ptolemais, which would be in the plain of Jezreel or Esdraelon. This is no doubt applicable to the Κναμών of Judith vii. 3; but whether it also applies to our *Camon* cannot be decided, as the town is not mentioned again.

III. PERIOD OF OPPRESSION BY THE AMMONITES AND PHILISTINES. —CHAP. X. 6–XVI.

The third stage in the period of the judges, which extended from the death of Jair to the rise of Samuel as a prophet, was a time of deep humiliation for Israel, since the Lord gave up His people into the hands of two hostile nations at the same time, on account of their repeated return to idolatry; so that the Ammonites invaded the land from the east, and oppressed the Israelites severely for eighteen years, especially the tribes to the east of the Jordan; whilst the Philistines came from the west, and extended their dominion over the tribes on this side, and brought them more and more firmly under their yoke. It is true that Jephthah delivered his people from the oppression of the Ammonites, in the power of the Spirit of Jehovah, having first of all secured the help of God through a vow, and not only smote the Ammonites, but completely subdued them before the Israelites. But the Philistine oppression lasted forty years; for although Samson inflicted heavy blows upon the Philistines again and again, and made them feel the superior power of the God of Israel, he was nevertheless not in a condition to destroy their power and rule over Israel. This was left for Samuel to accomplish, after he had converted the people to the Lord their God.

Israel's renewed Apostasy and consequent Punishment.-- Chap. x. 6–18.

As the Israelites forsook the Lord their God again, and served the gods of the surrounding nations, the Lord gave them up to the power of the Philistines and Ammonites, and left them to groan for eighteen years under the severe oppression of the Ammonites, till they cried to Him in their distress, and He sent them deliverance through Jephthah, though not till He had first of all charged them with their sins, and they had put away the strange gods. This section forms the introduction, not only to the history of Jephthah (chap. xi. 1–xii. 7) and the judges who followed him, viz. Ibzan, Elon, and Abdon (chap. xii. 8–15), but also to the history of Samson, who began to deliver Israel out of the power of the Philistines (chap. xiii.–xvi.). After the fact has been mentioned in the introduction (in ver. 7), that Israel was given up into the hands of the Philistines and the Ammonites at the same time, the Ammonitish oppression, which lasted eighteen years, is more particularly described in vers. 8, 9. This is followed by the reproof of the idolatrous Israelites on the part of God (vers. 10–16); and lastly, the history of Jephthah is introduced in vers. 17, 18, the fuller account being given in chap. xi. Jephthah, who judged Israel for six years after the conquest and humiliation of the Ammonites (chap. xii. 7), was followed by the judges Ibzan, Elon, and Abdon, who judged Israel for seven, ten, and eight years respectively, that is to say, for twenty-five years in all; so that Abdon died forty-nine years (18+6+25) after the commencement of the Ammonitish oppression, *i.e.* nine years after the termination of the forty years' rule of the Philistines over Israel, which is described more particularly in chap. xiii. 1, for the purpose of introducing the history of Samson, who judged Israel twenty years under that rule (chap. xv. 20, xvi. 31), without bringing it to a close, or even surviving it. It was only terminated by the victory which Israel achieved under Samuel at Ebenezer, as described in 1 Sam. vii.

Vers. 6–16. In the account of the renewed apostasy of the Israelites from the Lord contained in ver. 6, seven heathen deities are mentioned as being served by the Israelites: viz., in addition to the *Canaanitish Baals* and *Astartes* (see at chap. ii. 11, 13), the gods of *Aram*, *i.e.* Syria, who are never mentioned by name; of *Sidon*, *i.e.*, according to 1 Kings xi. 5, principally the Sidonian or Phœnician Astarte; of the *Moabites*, *i.e.* Chemosh (1 Kings xi. 33), the principal deity of that people, which was related to Moloch (see at Num. xxi. 29); of the *Ammonites, i.e.* Milcom (1 Kings xi. 5, 33) or Moloch (see at Lev. xviii. 21); and of the *Philistines, i.e.* Dagon (see at chap. xvi. 23). If we compare the list of these seven deities with vers. 11 and 12, where we find seven nations mentioned out of whose hands Jehovah had delivered Israel, the correspondence between the number seven in these two cases and the significant use of the number are unmistakeable. Israel had balanced the number of divine deliverances by a similar number of idols which it served, so that the measure of the nation's iniquity was filled up in the same proportion as the measure of the delivering grace of God. The number *seven* is employed in the Scriptures as the stamp of the works of God, or of the perfection created, or to be created, by God on the one hand, and of the actions of men in their relation to God on the other. The foundation for this was the creation of the world in seven days.—On ver. 7, see chap. ii. 13, 14. The Ammonites are mentioned after the Philistines, not because they did not oppress the Israelites till afterwards, but for purely formal reasons, viz. because the historian was about to describe the oppression of the Ammonites first. In ver. 8 the subject is the "children of Ammon," as we may see very clearly from ver. 9. "*They* (the Ammonites) *ground and crushed the Israelites in the same year*," *i.e.* the year in which God sold the Israelites into their hands, or in which they invaded the land of Israel. רָעַץ and רָצַץ are synonymous, and are simply joined together for the sake of emphasis, whilst the latter calls to mind Deut. xxviii. 33. The duration of this oppression is then added: "*Eighteen years* (they crushed) *all the Israelites, who dwelt on the other side of the Jordan in the land of the Amorites*," *i.e.* of the two Amoritish kings Sihon and Og, who (dwelt) in Gilead. *Gilead*, being a more precise epithet for the land of the Amorites, is used here in a wider sense to denote the whole of the country on the east of the Jordan, so far as it had been taken from the Amorites and occupied by the Israelites (as in Num. xxxii. 29, Deut. xxxiv. 1: see at Josh. xxii. 9).—Ver. 9. They also crossed the Jordan, and made war even upon Judah, Benjamin, and the house of Ephraim (the families of the tribe of Ephraim), by which Israel was brought into great distress. וַתֵּצֶר, as in chap. ii. 15.— Vers. 10–14. When the Israelites cried in their distress to the Lord, "*We have sinned against Thee, namely, that we have forsaken our God and served the Baals*," the Lord first of all reminded them of the manifestations of His grace (vers. 11, 12), and then pointed out to them their faithless apostasy and the worthlessness of their idols (vers. 13, 14). וְכִי, "*and indeed that*," describes the sin more minutely, and there is no necessity to remove it from the text,—an act which is neither warranted by its absence from several MSS. nor by its omission from the Sept., the Syriac, and the Vulgate. *Baalim*

is a general term used to denote all the false gods, as in chap. ii.
11. This answer on the part of God to the prayer of the Israelites
for help is not to be regarded as having been given through an
extraordinary manifestation (theophany), or through the medium
of a prophet, for that would certainly have been recorded; but it
was evidently given in front of the tabernacle, where the people
had called upon the Lord, and either came through the high priest,
or else through an inward voice in which God spoke to the hearts
of the people, *i.e.* through the voice of their own consciences, by
which God recalled to their memories and impressed upon their
hearts first of all His own gracious acts, and then their faithless
apostasy. There is an *anakolouthon* in the words of God. The construction which is commenced with מִמִּצְרַיִם is dropped at וְצִידוֹנִים וגו'
in ver. 12; and the verb הוֹשַׁעְתִּי, which answers to the beginning of
the clause, is brought up afterwards in the form of an apodosis
with וָאוֹשִׁיעָה אֶתְכֶם. " *Did I not deliver you* (1) *from the Egyptians*
(cf. Ex. i.–xiv.); (2) *from the Amorites* (cf. Num. xxi. 3); (3) *from
the Ammonites* (who oppressed Israel along with the Moabites in
the time of Ehud, chap. iii. 12 sqq.); (4) *from the Philistines*
(through Shamgar: see 1 Sam. xii. 9, where the Philistines are
mentioned between Sisera and Moab); (5) *from the Sidonians*
(among whom probably the northern Canaanites under Jabin are
included, as Sidon, according to chap. xviii. 7, 28, appears to have
exercised a kind of principality or protectorate over the northern
tribes of Canaan); (6) *from the Amalekites* (who attacked the
Israelites even at Horeb, Ex. xvii. 8 sqq., and afterwards invaded
the land of Israel both with the Moabites, chap. iii. 13, and also
with the Midianites, chap. vi. 3); *and* (7) *from the Midianites?*"
(see chap. vi. vii.). The last is the reading of the LXX. in *Cod
Al.* and *Vat.*, viz. Μαδίαμ; whereas *Ald.* and *Compl.* read Χαναάν,
also the *Vulgate*. In the Masoretic text, on the other hand, we
have *Maon*. Were this the original and true reading, we might
perhaps think of the *Mehunim*, who are mentioned in 2 Chron. xxvi.
7 along with Philistines and Arabians (cf. 1 Chron. iv. 41), and
are supposed to have been inhabitants of the city of *Maan* on the
Syrian pilgrim road to the east of Petra (*Burckhardt*, Syr. pp. 734
and 1035: see *Ewald*, Gesch. i. pp. 321, 322). But there is very
little probability in this supposition, as we cannot possibly see how
so small a people could have oppressed Israel so grievously at that
time, that the deliverance from their oppression could be mentioned
here; whilst it would be very strange that nothing should be said

about the terrible oppression of the Midianites and the wonderful deliverance from that oppression effected by Gideon. Consequently the Septuagint ($Μαδιάμ$) appears to have preserved the original text.—Ver. 13. Instead of thanking the Lord, however, for these deliverances by manifesting true devotedness to Him, Israel had forsaken Him and served other gods (see chap. ii. 13).—Vers. 14 sqq. Therefore the Lord would not save them any more. They might get help from the gods whom they had chosen for themselves. The Israelites should now experience what Moses had foretold in his song (Deut. xxxii. 37, 38). This divine threat had its proper effect. The Israelites confessed their sins, submitted thoroughly to the chastisement of God, and simply prayed for salvation; nor did they content themselves with merely promising, they put away the strange gods and served Jehovah, *i.e.* they devoted themselves again with sincerity to His service, and so were seriously converted to the living God. "*Then was His* (Jehovah's) *soul impatient* (תִּקְצַר, as in Num. xxi. 4) *because of the troubles of Israel;*" *i.e.* Jehovah could no longer look down upon the misery of Israel; He was obliged to help. The change in the purpose of God does not imply any changeableness in the divine nature; it simply concerns the attitude of God towards His people, or the manifestation of the divine love to man. In order to bend the sinner at all, the love of God must withdraw its helping hand and make men feel the consequences of their sin and rebelliousness, that they may forsake their evil ways and turn to the Lord their God. When this end has been attained, the same divine love manifests itself as pitying and helping grace. Punishments and benefits flow from the love of God, and have for their object the happiness and well-being of men.

Vers. 17, 18. These verses form the introduction to the account of the help and deliverance sent by God, and describe the preparation made by Israel to fight against its oppressors. The Ammonites "*let themselves be called together,*" *i.e.* assembled together (הִצָּעֵק, as in chap. vii. 23), and encamped in Gilead, *i.e.* in that portion of Gilead of which they had taken possession. For the Israelites, *i.e.* the tribes to the east of the Jordan (according to ver. 18 and chap. xi. 29), also assembled together in Gilead and encamped at *Mizpeh*, *i.e.* Ramath-mizpeh or Ramoth in Gilead (Josh. xiii. 26, xx. 8), probably on the site of the present *Szalt* (see at Deut. iv. 43, and the remarks in the Commentary on the Pent. vol. i. p. 300), and resolved to look round for a man who could begin the war, and to make him the head over all the inhabitants of Gilead (the tribes of

Israel dwelling in Perea). The "*princes of Gilead*" are in apposition to "*the people*." "The people, namely, the princes of Gilead," *i.e.* the heads of tribes and families of the Israelites to the east of the Jordan. "*Head*" is still further defined in chap. xi. 6, 11, as "*captain*," or "*head and captain*."

Jephthah elected as Prince; Negotiations with the Ammonites; Victory, Vow, and Office of Judge.[1]—Chap. xi.–xii. 7.

Vers. 1–11. ELECTION OF JEPHTHAH AS PRINCE AND JUDGE OF ISRAEL.—Vers. 1–3. The account begins with his descent and early mode of life. "*Jephthah* (LXX. 'Ιεφθά) the Gileadite was a brave hero" (see chap. vi. 12, Josh. i. 14, etc.); but he was the son of a harlot, and was begotten by Gilead, in addition to other sons who were born of his wife. *Gilead* is not the name of the country, as *Bertheau* supposes, so that the land is mythically personified as the forefather of Jephthah. Nor is it the name of the son of Machir and grandson of Manasseh (Num. xxvi. 29), so that the celebrated ancestor of the Gileadites is mentioned here instead of the unknown father of Jephthah. It is really the proper name of the father himself; and just as in the case of Tola and Puah, in chap. x. 1, the name of the renowned ancestor was repeated in his descendant. We are forced to this conclusion by the fact that the wife of Gilead, and his other sons by that wife, are mentioned in ver. 2. These sons drove their half-brother Jephthah out

---

[1] On the nature of the sources from which the author drew this tolerably elaborate history of Jephthah, all that can be determined with certainty is, that they sprang from some contemporary of this judge, since they furnish so clear and striking a picture of his life and doings. *Bertheau's* hypothesis, that the section extending from chap. xi. 12 to ver. 28 is founded upon some historical work, which is also employed in Num. xxi., Deut. ii. iii., and here and there in the book of Joshua, has really no other foundation than the unproved assumption that the Pentateuch and the book of Joshua were written towards the close of the period of the kings. For the marked agreement between Jephthah's negotiations with the king of the Ammonites concerning the possession of the land to the east of the Jordan, and the account given in the Pentateuch, especially in Num. xx. xxi., may be explained very simply and very perfectly, on the supposition that the author possessed the Pentateuch itself. And the account which is wanting in the Pentateuch, namely, that Israel petitioned the king of Moab also for permission to go through his land (ver. 17), may have been added from oral tradition, as those glorious victories gained by Israel under Moses were celebrated in verse by contemporaneous poets (see Num. xxi. 14, 17, 27); and this certainly contributed not a little to keep alive the memory of those events in the nation for centuries long.

of the house because of his inferior birth, that he might not share
with them in the paternal inheritance; just as Ishmael and the sons
of Keturah were sent away by Abraham, that they might not inherit
along with Isaac (Gen. xxi. 10 sqq., xxv. 6).—Ver. 3. Jephthah
departed from his brothers into the land of *Tob*, *i.e.*, according to
2 Sam. x. 6, 8, a district in the north-east of Perea, on the border
of Syria, or between Syria and Ammonitis, called Τώβιον in 1 Macc.
v. 13, or more correctly Τουβίν, according to 2 Macc. xii. 17, where
loose men gathered round him (cf. chap. ix. 4), and " went out with
him," viz. upon warlike and predatory expeditions like the Bedouins.
—Vers. 4–6. But when the Ammonites made war upon Israel
some time afterwards, the elders of Gilead (= " the princes of
Gilead," chap. x. 18) went to fetch Jephthah out of the land of
Tob, to make this brave warrior their leader. In ver. 4 the account
of the war between the Ammonites and Israel, which is mentioned
in chap. x. 17, is resumed, and its progress under Jephthah is then
more fully described. " *In process of time*" (מִיָּמִים, *a diebus*, *i.e.*
after the lapse of a long period, which cannot be more precisely
defined), *sc.* after the expulsion of Jephthah from his home (see
chap. xiv. 8, xv. 1, Josh. xxiii. 1). קָצִין signifies a leader in war
(Josh. x. 24), and is therefore distinguished in ver. 11 from רֹאשׁ, a
chief in peace and war.—Ver. 7. Jephthah expressed to the elders
his astonishment that they had formerly hated and expelled him,
and now came to him in their distress, *sc.* to make him their leader
in time of war. Thus he lays his expulsion upon the shoulders of
the elders of Gilead, although it was only by his brethren that he
had been driven away from his father's house, inasmuch as they
had either approved of it, or at all events had not interfered as
magistrates to prevent it. We cannot indeed infer from this
reproach, that the expulsion and disinheriting of Jephthah was a
legal wrong; but so much at all events is implied, namely, that
Jephthah looked upon the thing as a wrong that had been done to
him, and found the reason in the hatred of his brethren. The
Mosaic law contained no regulation upon this matter, since the rule
laid down in Deut. xxi. 15–17 simply applied to the sons of different wives, and not to a son by a harlot.—Ver. 8. The elders replied,
" *Therefore* (לָכֵן, because we have formerly done thee wrong) *we have
now come to thee again to make thee our head, if thou comest with us
and fightest against the Ammonites.*" The clauses וְהָלַכְתָּ, וְנִלְחַמְתָּ, and
וְהָיִיתָ, which are formally co-ordinate, are logically to be subordinated
to one another, the first two expressing the condition, the third the

consequence, in this sense, "*If thou go with us and fight, . . . thou shalt be head to us, namely, to all the inhabitants of Gilead,*" *i.e.* to the two tribes and a half on the east of the Jordan.—Ver. 9. Jephthah assented to this : "*If ye will take me back to make war upon the Ammonites, and Jehovah shall give them up to me* (*lit.* 'before me,' as in Josh. x. 12, Deut. ii. 31, etc.), *I will be your head.*" "*I*" is emphatic as distinguished from *ye;* and there is no necessity to regard the sentence as a question, with which the expression in ver. 10, "according to thy words," which presuppose an affirmative statement on the part of Jephthah, and not a question, would be altogether irreconcilable.—Ver. 10. The elders promised this on oath. "*Jehovah be hearing between us,*" *i.e.* be hearer and judge of the things concerning which we are negotiating; "*truly according to thy word so will we do*" (אִם לֹא, a particle used in connection with an oath).—Ver. 11. Then Jephthah went with the elders of Gilead, "*and the people* (*i.e.* the inhabitants of Gilead) *made him head and captain, and Jephthah spoke all his words before Jehovah at Mizpeh :*" *i.e.* he repeated in a solemn assembly of the people, before God at Mizpeh, the conditions and obligations under which he would accept the honour conferred upon him. "*Before Jehovah*" does not necessarily presuppose the presence of the ark at Mizpeh ; nor can we possibly assume this, since the war was resolved upon primarily by the eastern tribes alone, and they had no ark at all. It merely affirms that Jephthah performed this act, looking up to God, the omnipresent head of Israel. Still less do the words warrant the assumption that there was an altar in Mizpeh, and that sacrifices were offered to confirm the treaty, of which there is not the slightest indication in the text. "'Before Jehovah' implies nothing more than that Jephthah confirmed all his words by an oath" (*Hengstenberg*, Diss. ii. pp. 35, 36).

Vers. 12–28. JEPHTHAH'S NEGOTIATIONS WITH THE KING OF THE AMMONITES.—Ver. 12. Before Jephthah took the sword, he sent messengers to the king of the Ammonites, to make complaints to him of his invasion of the land of the Israelites. "*What have we to do with one another* ('what to me and thee?' see Josh. xxii. 24, 2 Sam. xvi. 10), *that thou hast come to me to fight against my land?*" Jephthah's ambassadors speak in the name of the nation ; hence the singulars "*me*" and "*my land.*"—Ver. 13. The king of the Ammonites replied, that when Israel came up out of Egypt, they had taken away his land from the Arnon to the Jabbok (on the north), and to the Jordan (on the west), and demanded that they should now restore these lands in peace. The plural אֶתְהֶן (them) refers *ad sensum* to the cities and places in the land in question. The claim raised by the king of the Ammonites has one feature in it, which appears to have a certain colour of justice. The Israelites, it is true, had only made war upon the two kings of the Amorites, Sihon and Og, and defeated them, and taken possession of their kingdoms and occupied them, without attacking the Ammonites and Moabites and Edomites, because God had forbidden their attacking these nations (Deut. ii. 5, 9, 19); but one portion of the territory of Sihon had formerly been Moabitish and Ammonitish property, and had been conquered by the Amorites and occupied by them. According to Num. xxi. 26, Sihon had made war upon the previous king of Moab, and taken away all his land as far as the Arnon (see the comm. on this passage). And although it is not expressly stated in the Pentateuch that Sihon had extended his conquests beyond Moabitis into the land of the Ammonites, which was situated to the east of Moab, and had taken a portion of it from them, this is pretty clearly indicated in Josh. xiii. 25, since, according to that passage, the tribe of Gad received in addition to Jaezer and all the towns of Gilead, half the land of the children of Ammon, namely, the land to the east of Gilead, on the western side of the upper Jabbok (Nahr Ammân: see at Josh. xiii. 26).[1]—Vers. 14, 15. Jephthah then sent ambassadors again to explain to him the true state of the case, namely, that Israel had neither taken away the land of Moab nor the land of the Ammonites. As a proof of this, Jephthah adduced the leading facts connected with the journey of the Israelites through the desert of Arabia to Canaan, by

---

[1] The explanation which *Masius* gives of this passage (*Eatenus moao sursum in Galaaditidem exporrectam jacuisse Gaditarum hæreditatem, quatenus dimidia Ammonitarum ditio Galaaditidem ab oriente ambiebat*) is not sufficiently in keeping with the words, and too unnatural, to be regarded as correct, as it is by *Reland* (Pal. ill. p. 105) and *Hengstenberg* (Dissertations on the Pentateuch, ii. p. 29); and the reasons assigned by Masius, viz. " that the Israelites were prohibited from occupying the land of the Ammonites," and " the Ammonites are not mentioned in Num. xxi. 26," are too weak to establish anything. The latter is an *argumentum e silentio*, which loses all significance when we bear in mind, that even the allusion to the land of the Moabites in Num. xxi. 26 is only occasioned by the prominence given to Heshbon, and the poetical saying founded upon its fall. But the prohibition against taking the land of the Ammonites from them had just as much force in relation to the land of the Moabites, and simply referred to such land as these tribes still possessed in the time of Moses, and not to that which the Amorites had taken from them.

which this assertion was confirmed, in exact agreement with the accounts of the Pentateuch respecting the matter in dispute.—· Vers. 16, 17. On leaving Egypt, Israel passed through the desert to the Red Sea, and came to Kadesh (Num. xx. 1). They then sent messengers to the king of Edom, to obtain permission to pass through his land ; and this the king of Edom refused (Num. xx. 14–21). They also sent to the king of Moab, who sent back a similar refusal. The embassy to the king of Moab is not mentioned in the Pentateuch, as it had no direct bearing upon the further course of the Israelites (see Pentateuch, vol. iii. p. 132, note 2). "*And Israel abode in Kadesh*" (word for word, as in Num. xx. 1*b*), and "*then passed through the desert*," namely to Mount Hor, then down the Arabah to the Red Sea, and still farther past Oboth to Ijje-abarim in the desert (Num. xx. 22–xxi. 11). In this way they went round the land of Edom and the land of Moab (יְסֹב, like סָבַב in Num. xxi. 4) ; and came from the east to the land of Moab (*i.e.* along the eastern boundary, for Ijje-abarim was situated there, according to Num. xxi. 11) ; and encamped on the other side of the Arnon (Num. xxi. 13), *i.e.* on the upper course of the Arnon where it still flows through the desert (see Pent. iii. p. 144). On this march, therefore, they did not enter the territory of Moab, as the Arnon formed the boundary of Moab, *i.e.* the boundary between Moab and the territory of the Amorites (Num. xxi. 13).—Vers. 19–22 are almost *verbatim* the same as Num. xxi. 21–25. Israel then sent messengers to Sihon the king of the Amorites at Heshbon, to ask permission to pass through his land. "*Into my place*," *i.e.* into the land of Canaan, that Jehovah has appointed for me. But Sihon "*trusted not Israel to pass through his land*," *i.e.* he did not trust to the assurance of Israel that they only wanted to pass peaceably through his land, but supposed the petition to cover an intention to take forcible possession of it. (In Num. xxi. 23 we have לֹא נָתַן instead of לֹא הֶאֱמִין.) He did not confine himself, there-fore, to a refusal of the permission they asked for, but collected his men of war, and marched against the Israelites to the desert as far as Jahza, on the east of Medeba and Dibon (see at Num. xxi. 23), and fought with them. But he was defeated, and lost all his land, from the Arnon (Mojeb) on the south to the Jabbok (Zerka) on the north, and from the desert on the east to the Jordan on the west, of which the Israelites took possession.—Vers. 23, 24. From these facts Jephthah drew this simple but indisputable conclusion : "*Jehovah the God of Israel has rooted out the Amorites before His* *people Israel, and thou wilt take possession of it* (viz. the land of the Amorites)." The suffix to תִּירָשֶׁנּוּ refers to הָאֱמֹרִי, the Amorites, *i.e.* their land. The construction of יָרַשׁ with the accusative of the people (as in Deut. ii. 12, 21, 22, ix. 1) may be explained on the simple ground, that in order to take possession of a country, it is necessary first of all to get the holders of it into your power. Jephthah then proved still further how unwarrantable the claim of the king of the Ammonites was, and said to him (ver. 24), " *Is it not the fact* (הֲלֹא, *nonne*), *that what thy god Chemosh gives thee for a possession, of that thou takest possession; and all that Jehovah makes ownerless before us, of that we take possession?*"—an appeal the validity of which could not be disputed. For *Chemosh*, see at Num. xxi. 29. The verb הוֹרִישׁ combines the three meanings: to drive out of a possession, to deprive of a possessor, and to give for a possession; inasmuch as it is impossible to give a land for a possession without driving away or exterminating its former possessor. —Ver. 25. But not contenting himself with this conclusive deduction, Jephthah endeavoured to remove the lost appearance of right from the king's claim by a second and equally conclusive argument. " *And now art thou better than Balak son of Zippor, the king of Moab? Did he strive* (רוֹב, *inf. abs.* of רִיב or רוֹב) *with Israel, or did he fight against them?*" By the repetition of וְעַתָּה (ver. 25, cf. ver. 23), the new argument is attached to the previous one, as a second deduction from the facts already described. Balak, the king of the Moabites, had indeed bribed Balaam to destroy Israel by his curses; but he did so not so much with the intention of depriving them of the territory of the Amorites which they had conquered, as from the fear that the powerful Israelites might also conquer his still remaining kingdom. Balak had neither made war upon Israel on account of the territory which they had conquered from the Amorites, nor had he put forward any claim to it as his own property, which he certainly might have done with some appearance of justice, as a large portion of it had formerly belonged to the Moabites (see Num. xxi. 26 and the comm. on this passage). If therefore Balak the king of the Moabites never thought of looking upon this land as being still his property, or of asking it back from the Israelites, the king of the Ammonites had no right whatever to lay claim to the land of Gilead as belonging to him, or to take it away from the Israelites by force, especially after the lapse of 300 years. " *As Israel dwells in Heshbon, . . . and in all the cities by the side of the Arnon for three hundred years, why have ye not taken away* (these towns and lands) *within that time"* (*i.e.* during these 300 years)? If the Ammonites had had any right to it, they ought to have asserted their claim in Moses' time. It was much too late now, after the expiration of 300 years. For " if no pre-scriptive right is to be admitted on account of length of time, and if long possession gives no title, nothing would ever be held in safety by any people, and there would be no end to wars and dis-sension" (*Clericus*). On Heshbon and its daughters, see at Num. xxi. 25. Aroër (עֲרֹעוֹר, another form for עֲרֹעֵר, or possibly only a copyist's error) is Aroër of Gad, before *Rabbah* (Josh. xiii. 25), and is to be sought for in the Wady Nahr Ammân, on the north-east of Ammân (see at Josh. *l. c.*), not Aroër of Reuben, on the border of the valley of Arnon (Num. xxxii. 34; Deut. ii. 36, iv. 48; Josh. xii. 2, xiii. 9). This is evident from the fact, that it is distinguished from " all the cities on the side (עַל יְדֵי, see at Num. xxxiv. 3) of the Arnon," which included Aroër of Reuben. *Aroër* of Gad, with its daughter towns, was probably Ammonitish territory before the time of Sihon. On the 300 years, a round number that comes very near the reality, see the *Chronol.* p. 285.—Ver. 27. After Jephthah had adduced all that could be said, to prove that the Israelites were the rightful possessors of the land of Gilead,[1] he closed with these words : " *I* (*i.e.* Israel, whose cause Jephthah was pleading) *have not sinned against thee, but thou doest me wrong in that thou makest war against me. Let Jehovah the Judge be judge this day* (now) *between the children of Israel and the children of Ammon.*" God should decide between the two nations, by giving the victory in war to the side whose cause was the just one.—Ver. 28. But the king of the Ammonites did not hearken to the words of Jephthah " which he had sent to him," *i.e.* had instructed his messengers to address to him ; so that it was necessary that Jehovah should decide for Israel in battle.

Vers. 29-33. JEPHTHAH'S VICTORY OVER THE AMMONITES. —As the negotiations with the king of the Ammonites were fruit-less, Jephthah had no other course left than to appeal to the sword. —Ver. 29. In the power of the Spirit of Jehovah which came upon him (see chap. iii. 10), he passed through Gilead (the land of the tribes of Reuben and Gad between the Arnon and the Jabbok)

---

[1] " Jephthah urged everything that could be pleaded in support of their pre-scriptive right : possession, length of time, the right of conquest, and undisputed occupation."—*Rosenmüller.*

and Manasseh (northern Gilead and Bashan, which the half tribe of Manasseh had received for a possession), to gather together an army to battle, and then went with the assembled army to Mizpeh-Gilead, *i.e.* Ramoth-mizpeh, where the Israelites had already encamped before his call (chap. x. 17), that he might thence attack the Ammonites. עָבַר (to pass over) with an accusative signifies to come over a person in a hostile sense.—Vers. 30, 31. Before commencing the war, however, he vowed a vow to the Lord: "*If Thou givest the Ammonites into my hand, he who cometh to meet me out of the doors of my house, when I return safely* (in peace, *shalom*) *from the Ammonites, shall belong to the Lord, and I will offer him for a burnt-offering.*" By the words הַיּוֹצֵא אֲשֶׁר, "he that goeth out," even if Jephthah did not think "only of a man, or even more definitely still of some one of his household," he certainly could not think in any case of a head of cattle, or one of his flock. "Going out of the doors of his house to meet him" is an expression that does not apply to a herd or flock driven out of the stall just at the moment of his return, or to any animal that might possibly run out to meet him. For the phrase יָצָא לִקְרַאת is only applied to men in the other passages in which it occurs.[1] Moreover, Jephthah no doubt intended to impose a very difficult vow upon himself. And that would not have been the case if he had merely been thinking of a sacrificial animal. Even without any vow, he would have offered, not one, but many sacrifices after obtaining a victory.[2] If therefore he had had an animal sacrifice in his mind, he would certainly have vowed the best of his flocks. From all this there can be no doubt that Jephthah must have been thinking of some human being as at all events included in his vow; so that when he declared that he would dedicate that which came out of his house to meet him, the meaning of the vow cannot

---

[1] *Augustine* observes in his *Quæst.* xlix. in *l. Jud.:* "He did not vow in these words that he would offer some *sheep*, which he might present as a holocaust, according to the law. For it is not, and was not, a customary thing for sheep to come out to meet a victorious general returning from the war. Nor did he say, I will offer as a holocaust *what*ever shall come out of the doors of my house to meet me ; but he says, ' *Who*ever comes out, I will offer *him ;*' so that there can be no doubt whatever that he had then a human being in his mind."

[2] "What kind of vow would it be if some great prince or general should say, ' O God, if Thou wilt give me this victory, the first calf that meets me shall be Thine !' *Parturiunt montes, nascetur ridiculus mus !*"—*Pfeiffer, dubia vex.* p. 356.

have been any other than that he would leave the choice of the sacrifice to God himself. "In his eagerness to smite the foe, and to thank God for it, Jephthah could not think of any particular object to name, which he could regard as great enough to dedicate to God; he therefore left it to accident, *i.e.* to the guidance of God, to determine the sacrifice. He shrank from measuring what was dearest to God, and left this to God himself" (*P. Cassel* in *Herzog's* Real-encycl.). Whomsoever God should bring to meet him, he would dedicate to Jehovah, and indeed, as is added afterwards by way of defining it more precisely, he would offer him to the Lord as a burnt-offering. The וְ before הַעֲלִיתִיהוּ is to be taken as explanatory, and not as disjunctive in the sense of " *or*," which וְ never has. But whether Jephthah really thought of his daughter at the time, cannot be determined either in the affirmative or negative. If he did, he no doubt hoped that the Lord would not demand this hardest of all sacrifices.—Vers. 32, 33. After seeking to ensure the help of the Lord by this vow, he went against the Ammonites to fight against them ; and the Lord delivered them into his hand, so that Jephthah smote them in a very great slaughter " from *Aroër* (or Nahr Ammân ; see ver. 26) to the neighbourhood of ('till thou come to;' see at Gen. x. 19) *Minnith*, (conquering and taking) twenty cities, and to *Abel Keramim* (of the vineyards)." *Minnith*, according to the *Onom.* (*s. v. Mennith*), was a place called *Manith* in the time of *Eusebius*, four Roman miles from Heshbon on the road to Philadelphia, with which the account given by *Buckingham* of the ruins of a large city a little to the east of Heshbon may be compared (see *v. Raum.* Pal. p. 265). The situation of *Abel Keramim* (plain of the vineyards: *Luther* and *Eng. Ver.*) cannot be determined with the same certainty. *Eusebius* and *Jerome* mention two places of this name (*Onom. s. v. Abel vinearum*), a *villa Abela vinetis consita* (κώμη ἀμπελοφόρος Ἄβελ) seven Roman miles from Philadelphia, and a *civitas nomine Abela vini fertilis* twelve Roman miles to the east of Gadara, and therefore in the neighbourhood of the Mandhur. Which of the two is referred to here remains uncertain, as we have no precise details concerning the battle. If the northern *Abela* should be meant, Jephthah would have pursued the foe first of all towards the south to the neighbourhood of Heshbon, and then to the north to the border of Bashan. Through this victory the Ammonites were completely subdued before the Israelites.

Vers. 34–40. JEPHTHAH'S VOW.—Vers. 34, 35. When the victorious hero returned to Mizpeh, his daughter came out to meet him "*with timbrels and in dances*," *i.e.* at the head of a company of women, who received the conqueror with joyous music and dances (see at Ex. xv. 20): "*and she was the only one; he had neither son nor daughter beside her.*" מִמֶּנּוּ cannot mean *ex se*, no other child of his own, though he may have had children that his wives had brought him by other husbands; but it stands, as the greater Masora has pointed it, for מִמֶּנָּה, "besides her," the daughter just mentioned,—the masculine being used for the feminine as the nearest and more general gender, simply because the idea of "*child*" was floating before the author's mind. At such a meeting Jephthah was violently agitated. Tearing his clothes (as a sign of his intense agony; see at Lev. x. 6), he exclaimed, "*O my daughter! thou hast brought me very low; it is thou who troublest me*" (*lit.* thou art among those who trouble me, thou belongest to their class, and indeed in the fullest sense of the word; this is the meaning of the so-called בּ *essentiæ* : see *Ges.* Lehrgeb. p. 838, and such passages as 2 Sam. xv. 31, Ps. liv. 6, lv. 19, etc.) : "*I have opened my mouth to the Lord* (*i.e.* have uttered a vow to Him: compare Ps. lxvi. 14 with Num. xxx. 3 sqq., Deut. xxiii. 23, 24), *and cannot turn it*," *i.e.* revoke it.—Ver. 36. The daughter, observing that the vow had reference to her (as her father in fact had, no doubt, distinctly told her, though the writer has passed this over because he had already given the vow itself in ver. 31), replied, "*Do to me as has gone out of thy mouth* (*i.e.* do to me what thou hast vowed), *since Jehovah has procured the vengeance upon thine enemies the Ammonites.*" She then added (ver. 37), "*Let this thing be done for me* (equivalent to, Let this only be granted me); *let me alone two months and I will go*," *i.e.* only give me two months to go, "*that I may go down to the mountains* (*i.e.* from Mizpeh, which stood upon an eminence, to the surrounding mountains and their valleys) *and bewail my virginity, I and my friends.*" בְּתוּלִים does not mean "youth" (נְעוּרִים), but the condition of virginity (see Lev. xxi. 13). The *Kethibh* רֵעְיָתִי is a less common form of רֵעוֹתַי (*Keri*). —Ver. 38. The father granted this request.—Ver. 39. At the end of two months she returned to her father again, "*and he did to her the vow that he had vowed, and she knew no man.*" In consequence of this act of Jephthah and his daughter, "*it became an ordinance* (a standing custom) *in Israel: from year to year* (see Ex. xiii. 10) *the daughters of Israel go to praise the daughter of Jephthah the*

Gileadite four days in the year." תנה does not mean θρηνεῖν, to lament or bewail (LXX., Chald., etc.), but to praise, as *R. Tanchum* and others maintain.

With regard to *Jephthah's vow*, the view expressed so distinctly by *Josephus* and the Chaldee was the one which generally prevailed in the earlier times among both Rabbins and fathers of the church, viz. that Jephthah put his daughter to death and burned her upon the altar as a bleeding sacrifice to Jehovah. It was not till the middle ages that *Mos.* and *Dav. Kimchi* and certain other Rabbins endeavoured to establish the view, that Jephthah merely dedicated his daughter to the service of the sanctuary of Jehovah in a lifelong virginity. And lastly, *Ludov. Cappellus*, in his *Diatriba de voto Jephtœ*, Salm. 1683 (which has been reprinted in his *Notœ critic.* in Jud. xi., and the *Critici Sacri*, tom. i.), has expressed the opinion that Jephthah put his daughter to death in honour of the Lord according to the law of the ban, because human beings were not allowed to be offered up as burnt-sacrifices. Of these different opinions the third has no foundation in the text of the Bible. For supposing that Jephthah had simply vowed that on his return he would offer to the Lord whatever came to meet him out of his house, with such restrictions only as were involved in the very nature of the case,—viz. offering it as a burnt-offering if it were adapted for this according to the law; and if it were not, then proceeding with it according to the law of the ban,—the account of the fulfilment of this vow would certainly have defined with greater precision the manner in which he fulfilled the vow upon his daughter. The words "he did to her his vow which he had vowed," cannot be understood in any other way than that he offered her as עוֹלָה, *i.e.* as a *burnt-offering*, to the Lord. Moreover, the law concerning the ban and a vow of the ban could not possibly give any individual Israelite the right to ban either his own child or one of his household to the Lord, without opening a very wide door to the crime of murder. The infliction of the ban upon any man presupposed notorious wickedness, so that burnt-offering and ban were diametrically opposed the one to the other. Consequently the other two views are the only ones which can be entertained, and it is not easy to decide between them. Although the words "and I offer him as a burnt-offering" appear to favour the actual sacrifice so strongly, that *Luther's* marginal note, "some affirm that he did not sacrifice her, but the text is clear enough," is perpetually repeated with peculiar emphasis; yet, on looking more closely into the matter, we find insuperable difficulties in the way of the literal interpretation of the words. Since הַיּוֹצֵא אֲשֶׁר יֵצֵא cannot be taken impersonally, and therefore when Jephthah uttered his vow, he must at any rate have had the possibility of some human being coming to meet him in his mind; and since the two clauses " *he shall be the Lord's*," and " *I will offer him up for a burnt-offering*," cannot be taken disjunctively in such a sense as this, it shall *either* be dedicated to the Lord, *or*, if it should be a sacrificial animal, I will offer it up as a burnt-offering, but the second clause simply contains a more precise definition of the first,—Jephthah must at the very outset have contemplated the possibility of a human sacrifice. Yet not only were human sacrifices prohibited in the law under pain of death as an abomination in the sight of Jehovah (Lev. xviii. 21, xx. 2–5; Deut. xii. 31, xviii. 10), but they were never heard of among the Israelites in the early times, and were only transplanted to Jerusalem by the godless kings Ahaz and Manasseh.[1] If Jephthah therefore vowed that he would offer a human sacrifice to Jehovah, he must either have uttered his vow without any reflection, or else have been thoroughly depraved in a moral and religious sense. But what we know of this brave hero by no means warrants any such assumptions. His acts do not show the slightest trace of impetuosity and rashness. He does not take to the sword at once, but waits till his negotiations with the king of the Ammonites have been without effect. Nor does he utter his vow in the midst of the confusion of battle, so that we might fancy he had made a vow in the heat of the conflict without fully weighing his words, but he uttered it before he set out against the Ammonites (see vers. 30 and 32). So far as the religious training of Jephthah was concerned, it is true that he had led the life of a freebooter during his exile from his country and home, and before his election as the leader of the Israelites; but the analogous circumstances connected with David's life preclude us from in-

---

[1] "Human sacrifices do not even belong to heathenism generally, but to the darkest night of heathenism. They only occur among those nations which are the most thoroughly depraved in a moral and religious sense." This remark of *Hengstenberg* (Diss. iii. p. 118) cannot be set aside by a reference to *Euseb. præp. ev.* iv. 16; *Baur*, Symb. ii. 2, pp. 293 sqq.; *Lasaulx*, Sühnopfer der Griechen und Römer, 1841, pp. 8–12; *Ghillany*, die Menschenopfer der alten Hebräer, 1842, pp. 107 sqq., as *Kurtz* supposes, since the uncritical character of the proofs collected together in these writings is very obvious on a closer inspection, and *Eusebius* has simply taken his examples from Porphyry, and other writings of a very recent date.

ferring either moral depravity or religious barbarism from this. When David was obliged to fly from his country to escape from Saul, he also led a life of the same kind, so that all sorts of people came to him, not pious and virtuous people, but all who were in distress and had creditors, or were embittered in spirit (1 Sam. xxii. 2); and yet, even under these circumstances, David lived in the law of the Lord. Moreover, Jephthah was not destitute of the fear of God. This is proved first of all by the fact, that when he had been recalled from his exile he looked to Jehovah to give him the victory over the Ammonites, and made a treaty with the elders of Gilead " before Jehovah " (vers. 9 and 10); and also by the fact, that he sought to ensure the help of God in war through the medium of a vow. And again, we have no right to attribute to him any ignorance of the law. Even if *Kurtz* is correct in his opinion, that the negotiations with the king of the Ammonites, which show the most accurate acquaintance with the Pentateuch, were not carried on independently and from his own knowledge of the law, and that the sending of messengers to the hostile king was resolved upon in the national assembly at Mizpeh, with the priests, Levites, and elders present, so that the Levites, who knew the law, may have supplied any defects in his own knowledge of the law and of the early history of his people; a private Israelite did not need to study the whole of the law of the Pentateuch, and to make himself master of the whole, in order to gain the knowledge and conviction that a human sacrifice was irreconcilable with the substance and spirit of the worship of Jehovah, and that Jehovah the God of Israel was not a Moloch. And again, even if we do not know to what extent the men and fathers of families in Israel were acquainted and familiar with the contents of the Mosaic law, the opinion is certainly an erroneous one, that the Israelites derived their knowledge of the law exclusively from the public reading of the law at the feast of tabernacles in the sabbatical year, as enjoined in Deut. xxxi. 10 sqq.; so that if this public reading, which was to take place only once in seven years, had been neglected, the whole nation would have been left without any instruction whatever in the law. The reason for this Mosaic precept was a totally different one from that of making the people acquainted with the contents of the law (see the commentary on this passage). And again, though we certainly do not find the law of the Lord so thoroughly pervading the religious consciousness of the people, received as it were *in succum et sanguinem*, in the time of the judges, that they were able to resist the bewitching power of nature-worship, but, on the contrary, we find them repeatedly falling away into the worship of Baal; yet we discover no trace whatever of human sacrifices even in the case of those who went a whoring after Baalim. And although the theocratical knowledge of the law seems to have been somewhat corrupted even in the case of such men as Gideon, so that this judge had an unlawful ephod made for himself at Ophrah; the opinion that the Baal-worship, into which the Israelites repeatedly fell, was associated with human sacrifices, is one of the many erroneous ideas that have been entertained as to the development of the religious life not only among the Israelites, but among the Canaanites, and which cannot be supported by historical testimonies or facts. That the Canaanitish worship of Baal and Astarte, to which the Israelites were addicted, required no human sacrifices, is indisputably evident from the fact, that even in the time of Ahab and his idolatrous wife Jezebel, the daughter of the Sidonian king Ethbaal, who raised the worship of Baal into the national religion in the kingdom of the ten tribes, persecuting the prophets of Jehovah and putting them to death, there is not the slightest allusion to human sacrifices. Even at that time human sacrifices were regarded by the Israelites as so revolting an abomination, that the two kings of Israel who besieged the king of the Moabites—not only the godly Jehoshaphat, but Jehoram the son of Ahab and Jezebel—withdrew at once and relinquished the continuance of the war, when the king of the Moabites, in the extremity of his distress, sacrificed his son as a burnt-offering upon the wall (2 Kings iii. 26, 27). With such an attitude as this on the part of the Israelites towards human sacrifices before the time of Ahaz and Manasseh, who introduced the worship of Moloch into Jerusalem, we cannot, without further evidence, impute to Jephthah the offering of a bloody human sacrifice, the more especially as it is inconceivable, with the diametrical opposition between the worship of Jehovah and the worship of Moloch, that God should have chosen a worshipper of Moloch to carry out His work, or a man who was capable of vowing and offering a human-being sacrifice. The men whom God chose as the recipients of His revelation of mercy and the executors of His will, and whom He endowed with His Spirit as judges and leaders of His people, were no doubt affected with infirmities, faults, and sins of many kinds, so that they could fall to a very great depth; but nowhere is it stated that the Spirit of

God came upon a worshipper of Moloch and endowed him with His own power, that he might be the helper and saviour of Israel.

We cannot therefore regard Jephthah as a servant of Moloch, especially when we consider that, in addition to what has already been said, the account of the actual fulfilment of his vow is apparently irreconcilable with the literal interpretation of the words וְהַעֲלִיתִיהוּ עוֹלָה, as signifying a bleeding burnt-offering. We cannot infer anything with certainty as to the mode of the sacrifice, from the grief which Jephthah felt and expressed when his only daughter came to meet him. For this is quite as intelligible, as even the supporters of the literal view of these words admit, on the supposition that Jephthah was compelled by his vow to dedicate his daughter to Jehovah in a lifelong virginity, as it would be if he had been obliged to put her to death and burn her upon the altar as a burnt-offering. But the entreaty of the daughter, that he would grant her two months' time, in order that she might lament her virginity upon the mountains with her friends, would have been marvellously out of keeping with the account that she was to be put to death as a sacrifice. To mourn one's virginity does not mean to mourn because one has to die a virgin, but because one has to live and remain a virgin. But even if we were to assume that mourning her virginity was equivalent to mourning on account of her youth (which is quite untenable, as בְּתוּלִים is not synonymous with נְעוּרִים), "it would be impossible to understand why this should take place *upon the mountains.* It would be altogether opposed to human nature, that a child who had so soon to die should make use of a temporary respite to forsake her father altogether. It would no doubt be a reasonable thing that she should ask permission to enjoy life for two months longer before she was put to death; but that she should only think of bewailing her virginity, when a sacrificial death was in prospect, which would rob her father of his only child, would be contrary to all the ordinary feelings of the human heart. Yet, inasmuch as the history lays special emphasis upon her bewailing her virginity, this must have stood in some peculiar relation to the nature of the vow. When a maiden *bewails* her virginity, the reason for this can only be that she will have to remain a bud that has not been allowed to unfold itself, prevented, too, not by death, but by life" (*P. Cassel,* p. 473). And this is confirmed by the expression, to bewail her virginity " *upon the mountains.*" " If life had been in question, the same tears might have been shed at home. But her lamentations were devoted to her virginity, and such lamentations could not be uttered in the town, and in the presence of men. Modesty required the solitude of the mountains for these. The virtuous heart of the maiden does not open itself in the ears of all; but only in sacred silence does it pour out its lamentations of love" (*P. Cassel*, p. 476). And so, again, the still further clause in the account of the fulfilment of the vow, "and she knew no man," is not in harmony with the assumption of a sacrificial death. This clause would add nothing to the description in that case, since it was already known that she was a virgin. The words only gain their proper sense if we connect them with the previous clause, he "did with her according to the vow which he had vowed," and understand them as describing what the daughter did in fulfilment of the vow. The father fulfilled his vow upon her, and she knew no man; *i.e.* he fulfilled the vow through the fact that she knew no man, but dedicated her life to the Lord, as a spiritual burnt-offering, in a lifelong chastity. It was this willingness of the daughter to sacrifice herself which the daughters of Israel went every year to celebrate,—namely, upon the mountains whither her friends had gone with her to lament her virginity, and which they commemorated there four days in the year. And the idea of a spiritual sacrifice is supported not only by the words, but also most decisively by the fact that the historian describes the fulfilment of the vow in the words " he did to her according to his vow," in such a manner as to lead to the conclusion that he regarded the act itself as laudable and good. But a prophetic historian could never have approved of a human sacrifice; and it is evident that the author of the book of Judges does not conceal what was blameable even in the judges themselves, from his remarks concerning the conduct of Gideon (chap. viii. 27), which was only a very small offence in comparison with the abomination of a human sacrifice. To this we have to add the difficulties connected with such an act. The words " he did to her according to his vow" presuppose undoubtedly that Jephthah offered his daughter as עוֹלָה to Jehovah. But burnt-offerings, that is to say bleeding burnt-offerings, in which the victim was slaughtered and burnt upon the altar, could only be offered upon the lawful altar at the tabernacle, or before the ark, through the medium of the Levitical priests, unless the sacrifice itself had been occasioned by some extraordinary manifestation of God; and that we cannot for a moment think of here. But is it credible that a priest or the priesthood should have consented to offer a sacrifice upon the altar of Jehovah which was denounced in the law as the greatest abomination of the heathen ? This difficulty cannot be set aside by assuming that Jephthah put his daughter to death, and burned her upon some secret altar, without the assistance and mediation of a priest; for such an act would not have been described by the prophetic historian as a fulfilment of the vow that he would offer a burnt-offering to the Lord, simply because it would not have been a sacrifice offered to Jehovah at all, but a sacrifice slaughtered to Moloch.[1]

All these circumstances, when rightly considered, almost compel us to adopt the spiritual interpretation of the words " offer as a burnt-offering." It is true that no exactly corresponding parallel-isms can be adduced from the Old Testament in support of the spiritual view; but the germs of this view, as met with in the Psalms and the writings of the prophets, are contained in the demand of God addressed to Abraham to offer Him his only son Isaac as a burnt-offering, when compared with the issue of Abra-ham's temptation,—namely, that God accepted his willingness to offer up his son as a completed sacrifice, and then supplied him with a ram to offer up as a bleeding sacrifice in the place of his son. As this fact teaches that what God demands is not a corporeal but a spiritual sacrifice, so the rules laid down in the law respecting the redemption of the first-born belonging to the Lord, and of persons vowed to Him (Ex. xiii. 1, 13; Num. xviii. 15, 16; Lev. xxvii. 1 sqq.), show clearly how the Israelites could dedicate themselves and those who belonged to them to the Lord, without burning upon the altar the persons who were vowed to Him. And lastly, it is evident, from the perfectly casual reference to the women who

---

[1] *Auberlen's* remarks upon this subject are very good. " The history of Jephthah's daughter," he says, " would hardly have been thought worth pre-serving in the Scriptures if the maiden had been really offered in sacrifice ; for, in that case, the event would have been reduced, at the best, into a mere family history, without any theocratic significance, though in truth it would rather have been an anti-theocratic *abomination*, according to Deut. xii. 31 (cf. chap. xviii. 9, Lev. xviii. 21, xx. 1–5). Jephthah's action would in that case have stood upon the same platform as the incest of Lot (Gen. xix. 30 sqq.), and would owe its adoption into the canon simply to genealogical considerations, or others of a similar kind. But the very opposite is the case here ; and if, from the conclusion of the whole narrative in chap. xi. 39, 40, the object of it is supposed to be simply to explain the origin of the feast that was held in honour of Jephthah's daughter, even this would tell against the ordinary view. In the eye of the law the whole thing would still remain an abomination, and the canonical Scriptures would not stoop to relate and beautify an institution so directly opposed to the law."

ministered at the tabernacle (Ex. xxxviii. 8 ; 1 Sam. ii. 22), that
there were persons in Israel who dedicated their lives to the Lord
at the sanctuary, by altogether renouncing the world. And there
can be no doubt that Jephthah had such a dedication as this in his
mind when he uttered his vow ; at all events in case the Lord, to
whom he left the appointment of the sacrifice, should demand the
offering up of a human being. The word עֹלָה does not involve the
idea of burning, like our word burnt-offering, but simply that of
going up upon the altar, or of complete surrender to the Lord.
עֹלָה is a whole offering, as distinguished from the other sacrifices,
of which only a part was given up to the Lord. When a virgin,
therefore, was set apart as a spiritual עֹלָה, it followed, as a matter
of course, that henceforth she belonged entirely to the Lord : that
is to say, was to remain a virgin for the remainder of her days.
The fact that Nazarites contracted marriages, even such as were
dedicated by a vow to be Nazarites all their lives, by no means
warrants the conclusion that virgins dedicated to the Lord by a
vow were also free to marry if they chose. It is true that we learn
nothing definite from the Old Testament with regard to this spiritual sacrificial service ; but the absence of any distinct statements
upon the subject by no means warrants our denying the fact.
Even with regard to the spiritual service of the women at the
tabernacle we have no precise information ; and we should not have
known anything about this institution, if the women themselves
had not offered their mirrors in the time of Moses to make the holy
laver, or if we had not the account of the violation of such women
by the sons of Eli. In this respect, therefore, the remarks of
Clericus, though too frequently disregarded, are very true : " It
was not to be expected, as I have often observed, that so small a
volume as the Old Testament should contain all the customs of the
Hebrews, and a full account of all the things that were done among
them. There are necessarily many things alluded to, therefore,
which we do not fully understand, simply because they are not
mentioned elsewhere."

Chap. xii. 1–7. JEPHTHAH'S WAR WITH THE EPHRAIMITES,
AND OFFICE OF JUDGE.—Ver. 1. The jealousy of the tribe of
Ephraim, which was striving after the leadership, had already
shown itself in the time of Gideon in such a way that nothing
but the moderation of that judge averted open hostilities. And
now that the tribes on the east of the Jordan had conquered the

Ammonites under the command of Jephthah without the co-operation of the Ephraimites, Ephraim thought it necessary to assert its
claim to take the lead in Israel in a very forcible manner. The
Ephraimites gathered themselves together, and went over צָפוֹנָה.
This is generally regarded as an appellative noun (*northward*) ;
but in all probability it is a proper name, " to *Zaphon*," the city
of the Gadites in the Jordan valley, which is mentioned in Josh.
xiii. 27 along with Succoth, that is to say, according to a statement
of the *Gemara*, though of a very uncertain character no doubt,
'Αμαθοῦς (*Joseph*. Ant. xiii. 13, 5, xiv. 5, 4 ; Bell. Jud. i. 4, 2,
Reland, Pal. pp. 308 and 559–60), the modern ruins of *Amata* on
the Wady *Rajib* or *Ajlun*, the situation of which would suit this
passage very well.   They then threatened Jephthah, because he
had made war upon the Ammonites without them, and said, " *We
will burn thy house over thee with fire*."   This arrogance and threat
Jephthah opposed most energetically.   He replied (vers. 2, 3), " *A
man of strife have I been, I and my people on the one hand, and the
children of Ammon on the other, very greatly*," *i.e.* I and my people
had a severe conflict with the Ammonites. " *Then I called you,
but ye did not deliver me out of their hand; and when I saw that
thou* (Ephraim) *didst not help me, I put my life in my hand*" (*i.e.* I
risked my own life : see 1 Sam. xix. 5, xxviii. 21, Job xiii. 14.
The *Kethibh* אֶשִׂמָה comes from שִׂים : cf. Gen. xxiv. 33), " *and I
went against the Ammonites, and Jehovah gave them into my hand*."
Jephthah's appeal to the Ephraimites to fight against the Ammonites is not mentioned in chap. xi., probably for no other reason than
because it was without effect. The Ephraimites, however, had very
likely refused their co-operation simply because the Gileadites had
appointed Jephthah as commander without consulting them. Consequently the Ephraimites had no ground whatever for rising up
against Jephthah and the Gileadites in this haughty and hostile
manner; and Jephthah had a perfect right not only to ask them,
" *Wherefore are ye come up against me now* (lit. ' this day '), *to fight
against me ?* " but to resist such conduct with the sword.—Ver. 4.
He therefore gathered together all the men (men of war) of Gilead
and smote the Ephraimites, because they had said, " *Ye Gileadites
are fugitives of Ephraim in the midst of Ephraim and Manasseh*."
The meaning of these obscure words is probably the following:
Ye Gileadites are a mob gathered together from Ephraimites that
have run away ; " ye are an obscure set of men, men of no name,
dwelling in the midst of two most noble and illustrious tribes "

(*Rosenmüller*). This contemptuous speech did not apply to the tribes of Reuben and Gad as such, but simply to the warriors whom Jephthah had gathered together out of Gilead. For the words are not to be rendered *erepti Ephraim*, " the rescued of Ephraim," as they are by *Seb. Schmidt* and *Stud.*, or to be understood as referring to the fact that the Gileadites had found refuge with the Ephraimites during the eighteen years of oppression on the part of the Ammonites, since such an explanation is at variance with the use of the word פָּלִיט, which simply denotes a fugitive who has escaped from danger, and not one who has sought and found protection with another. The Ephraimites had to pay for this insult offered to their brethren by a terrible defeat.—Ver. 5. When the Gileadites had beaten the Ephraimites, they took the fords of the Jordan before the Ephraimites (or towards Ephraim : see chap. iii. 28, vii. 24), to cut off their retreat and prevent their return to their homes. And "*when fugitives of Ephraim wanted to cross, the men of Gilead asked them, Art thou Ephrathi*," *i.e.* an Ephraimite? *And if he said no*, they made him pronounce the word *Shibboleth* (a stream or flood, as in Ps. lxix. 3, 16 ; not an ear of corn, which is quite unsuitable here) ; "*and if he said, Sibboleth, not taking care to pronounce it correctly, they laid hold of him and put him to death at the fords of the Jordan.*" In this manner there fell at that time, *i.e.* during the whole war, 42,000 Ephraimites. The "*fugitives of Ephraim*" were the Ephraimites who had escaped from the battle and wished to return home. The expression is used here in its ordinary sense, and not with the contemptuous sense in which the Ephraimites had used it in ver. 4. From this history we learn quite casually that the Ephraimites generally pronounced *sh* (shin) like *s* (samech). הֵכִין is used elliptically for הֵכִין לֵב, to direct his heart to anything, pay heed (compare 1 Sam. xxiii. 22, 1 Chron. xxviii. 2, with 2 Chron. xii. 14, xxx. 19).—Ver. 7. Jephthah judged Israel six years, though most probably only the tribes on the east of the Jordan. When he died, he was buried in one of the towns of Gilead. The plural בְּעָרֵי גִלְעָד is used quite indefinitely, as in Gen. xiii. 12, Neh. vi. 2, etc. (see *Ges.* Lehrgeb. p. 665), simply because the historian did not know the exact town.

The Judges Ibzan, Elon, and Abdon.—Chap. xii. 8–15.

Of these three judges no particular deeds are related, just as in the case of Tola and Jair (see the remarks on chap. x. 1). But it certainly follows from the expression וַיִּשְׁפֹּט אַחֲרָיו (vers 8, 11, 13)

that they were one after another successors of Jephthah, and therefore that their office of judge also extended simply over the tribes
on the east of the Jordan, and perhaps the northern tribes on this
side.—Vers. 8, 9. *Ibzan* sprang from *Bethlehem*,—hardly, however,
the town of that name in the tribe of Judah, as *Josephus* affirms
(Ant. v. 7, 13), for that is generally distinguished either as Bethlehem "of Judah" (chap. xvii. 7, 9; Ruth i. 2; 1 Sam. xvii. 12),
or Bethlehem *Ephratah* (Micah v. 1), but probably Bethlehem in
the tribe of Zebulun (Josh. ix. 15). He had thirty sons and thirty
daughters, the latter of whom he sent away הַחוּצָה (out of his house),
i.e. gave them in marriage, and brought home thirty women in their
places from abroad as wives for his sons. He judged Israel seven
years, and was buried in Bethlehem.—Vers. 11, 12. His successor
was *Elon* the Zebulunite, who died after filling the office of judge
for ten years, and was buried at *Aijalon*, in the land of Zebulun.
This *Aijalon* has probably been preserved in the ruins of *Jalûn*,
about four hours' journey to the east of Akka, and half an hour
to the s.s.w. of Mejdel Kerun (see *V. de Velde*, Mem. p. 283).—
Vers. 13–15. He was followed by the judge *Abdon*, the son of Hillel
of *Pirathon*. This place, where Abdon died and was buried after
holding the office of judge for eight years, was in the land of
Ephraim, on the mountains of the Amalekites (ver. 15). It is mentioned in 2 Sam. xxiii. 30 and 1 Chron. xi. 31 as the home of Benaiah
the hero; it is the same as Φαραθώ (read Φαραθών) in 1 Macc. ix.
50, and *Joseph*. Ant. xiii. 1, 3, and has been preserved in the village
of *Feráta*, about two hours and a half to the s.s.w. of Nabulus (see
Rob. Bibl. Res. p. 134, and *V. de Velde*, Mem. p. 340). On the
riding of his sons and daughters upon asses, see at chap. x. 4.

Samson's Life, and Conflicts with the Philistines.—Chap. xiii.-xvi.

Whilst Jephthah, in the power of God, was delivering the tribes
on the east of the Jordan from the oppression of the Ammonites,
the oppression on the part of the Philistines continued uninterruptedly for forty years in the land to the west of the Jordan
(chap. xiii. 1), and probably increased more and more after the
disastrous war during the closing years of the high-priesthood of
Eli, in which the Israelites suffered a sad defeat, and even lost the
ark of the covenant, which was taken by the Philistines (1 Sam. iv.).
But even during this period, Jehovah the God of Israel did not
leave himself without witness, either in the case of His enemies
the Philistines, or in that of His people Israel. The triumphant

delight of the Philistines at the capture of the ark was soon changed into great and mortal terror, when Dagon their idol had fallen down from its place before the ark of God and was lying upon the threshold of its temple with broken head and arms; and the inhabitants of Ashdod, Gath, and Ekron, to which the ark was taken, were so severely smitten with boils by the hand of Jehovah, that the princes of the Philistines felt constrained to send the ark, which brought nothing but harm to their people, back into the land of the Israelites, and with it a trespass-offering (1 Sam. v. vi.). At this time the Lord had also raised up a hero for His people in the person of *Samson*, whose deeds were to prove to the Israelites and Philistines that the God of Israel still possessed the power to help His people and smite His foes.

The life and acts of *Samson*, who was to begin to deliver Israel out of the hands of the Philistines, and who judged Israel for twenty years under the rule of the Philistines (chap. xiii. 5 and xv. 20), are described in chap. xiii.–xvi. with an elaborate fulness which seems quite out of proportion to the help and deliverance which he brought to his people. His birth was foretold to his parents by an appearance of the angel of the Lord, and the boy was set apart as a Nazarite from his mother's womb. When he had grown up, the Spirit of Jehovah began to drive him to seek occasions for showing the Philistines his marvellous strength, and to inflict severe blows upon them in a series of wonderful feats, until at length he was seduced by the bewitching Delilah to make known to her the secret of his supernatural strength, and was betrayed by her into the power of the Philistines, who deprived him of the sight of his eyes, and compelled him to perform the hardest and most degraded kinds of slave-labour. From this he was only able to escape by bringing about his own death, which he did in such a manner that his enemies were unable to triumph over him, since he killed more of them at his death than he had killed during the whole of his life before. And whilst the small results that followed from the acts of this hero of God do not answer the expectations that might naturally be formed from the miraculous announcement of his birth, the nature of the acts which he performed appears still less to be such as we should expect from a hero impelled by the Spirit of God. His actions not only bear the stamp of adventure, foolhardiness, and wilfulness, when looked at outwardly, but they are almost all associated with love affairs; so that it looks as if Samson had dishonoured and fooled away the gift entrusted to him, by making it subservient to his sensual lusts, and thus had prepared the way for his own ruin, without bringing any essential help to his people. " The man who carried the gates of Gaza up to the top of the mountain was the slave of a woman, to whom he frivolously betrayed the strength of his Nazarite locks. These locks grew once more, and his strength returned, but only to bring death at the same time to himself and his foes" (*Ziegler*). Are we to discern in such a character as this a warrior of the Lord? Can Samson, the promised son of a barren woman, a Nazarite from his birth, be the head and flower of the judges? We do not pretend to answer these questions in the affirmative; and to justify this view we start from the fact, which *Ewald* and *Diestel* both admit to be historical, that the deep earnest background of Samson's nature is to be sought for in his Nazarite condition, or rather that it is in this that the distinctive significance of his character and of his life and deeds as judge all culminates. The Nazarite was not indeed what *Bertheau* supposes him to have been, " a man separated from human pursuits and turmoil;" but the significance of the Nazarite condition was to be found in a consecration of the life to God, which had its roots in living faith, and its outward manifestations negatively, in abstinence from everything unclean, from drinking wine, and even from fruit of the vine of every description, and positively, in wearing the hair uncut. In the case of Samson this consecration of the life to God was not an act of his own free will, or a vow voluntarily taken; but it was imposed upon him by divine command from his conception and birth. As a Nazarite, *i.e.* as a person vowed to the Lord, he was to begin to deliver Israel out of the hand of the Philistines; and the bodily sign of his Nazarite condition—namely, the hair of his head that had never been touched by the scissors—was the vehicle of his supernatural strength with which he smote the Philistines. In Samson the Nazarite, however, not only did the Lord design to set before His people a man towering above the fallen generation in heroic strength, through his firm faith in and confident reliance upon the gift of God committed to him, opening up before it the prospect of a renewal of its own strength, that by this type he might arouse such strength and ability as were still slumbering in the nation; but Samson was to exhibit to his age generally a picture on the one hand of the strength which the people of God might acquire to overcome their strongest foes through faithful submission to the Lord their God, and on the other hand of the weakness into which they had sunk through unfaithfulness to the covenant and intercourse with the heathen. And it is in this typical character of Samson and his deeds that we find the head and flower of the institution of judge in Israel.

The judges whom Jehovah raised up in the interval between Joshua and Samuel were neither military commanders nor governors of the nation ; nor were they authorities instituted by God and invested with the government of the state. They were not even chosen from the heads of the nation, but were called by the Lord out of the midst of their brethren to be the deliverers of the nation, either through His Spirit which came upon them, or through prophets and extraordinary manifestations of God ; and the influence which they exerted, after the conquest and humiliation of the foe and up to the time of their death, upon the government of the nation and its affairs in general, was not the result of any official rank, but simply the fruit and consequence of their personal ability, and therefore extended for the most part only to those tribes to whom they had brought deliverance from the oppression of their foes. The tribes of Israel did not want any common secular ruler to fulfil the task that devolved upon the nation at that time (see p. 240). God therefore raised up even the judges only in times of distress and trouble. For their appearance and work were simply intended to manifest the power which the Lord could confer upon His people through His Spirit, and were designed, on the one hand, to encourage Israel to turn seriously to its God, and by holding fast to His covenant to obtain the power to conquer all its foes ; and, on the other hand, to alarm their enemies, that they might not attribute to their idols the power which they possessed to subjugate the Israelites, but might learn to fear the omnipotence of the true God. This divine power which was displayed by the judges culminated in Samson. When the Spirit of God came upon him, he performed such mighty deeds as made the haughty Philistines feel the omnipotence of Jehovah. And this power he possessed by virtue of his condition as a Nazarite, because he had been vowed or dedicated to the Lord from his mother's womb, so long as he remained faithful to the vow that had been imposed upon him.

But just as his strength depended upon the faithful observance of his vow, so his weakness became apparent in his natural character, particularly in his intrigues with the daughters of the Philistines ; and in this weakness there was reflected the natural character of the nation generally, and of its constant disposition to fraternize with the heathen. Love to a Philistine woman in

Timnath not only supplied Samson with the first occasion to exhibit his heroic strength to the Philistines, but involved him in a series of conflicts in which he inflicted severe blows upon the uncircumcised. This impulse to fight against the Philistines came from Jehovah (chap. xiv. 4), and in these conflicts Jehovah assisted him with the power of His Spirit, and even opened up a fountain of water for him at Lehi in the midst of his severe fight, for the purpose of reviving his exhausted strength (chap. xv. 19). On the other hand, in his intercourse with the harlot at Gaza, and his love affair with Delilah, he trod ways of the flesh which led to his ruin. In his destruction, which was brought about by his forfeiture of the pledge of the divine gift entrusted to him, the insufficiency of the judgeship in itself to procure for the people of God supremacy over their foes became fully manifest; so that the weakness of the judgeship culminated in Samson as well as its strength. The power of the Spirit of God, bestowed upon the judges for the deliverance of their people, was overpowered by the might of the flesh lusting against the spirit.

This special call received from God will explain the peculiarities observable in the acts which he performed,—not only the smallness of the outward results of his heroic acts, but the character of adventurous boldness by which they were distinguished. Although he had been set apart as a Nazarite from his mother's womb, he was not to complete the deliverance of his people from the hands of the Philistines, but simply to commence it, i.e. to show to the people, by the manifestation of supernatural heroic power, the possibility of deliverance, or to exhibit the strength with which a man could slay a thousand foes. To answer this purpose, it was necessary that the acts of Samson should differ from those of the judges who fought at the head of military forces, and should exhibit the stamp of confidence and boldness in the full consciousness of possessing divine and invincible power.

But whilst the spirit which prevailed in Israel during the time of the judges culminated in the nature and deeds of Samson both in its weakness and strength, the miraculous character of his deeds, regarded simply in themselves, affords no ground for pronouncing the account a mere legend which has transformed historical acts into miracles, except from a naturalistic point of view, which rejects all miracles, and therefore denies a priori the supernatural working of the living God in the midst of His people. The formal character of the whole of the history of Samson, which the oppo nents of the biblical revelation adduce for the further support of this view, does not yield any tenable evidence of its correctness. The external rounding off of the account proves nothing more than that Samson's life and acts formed in themselves a compact and well-rounded whole. But the assertion, that " well-rounded circumstances form a suitable framework for the separate accounts, and that precisely twelve acts are related of Samson, which are united into beautiful pictures and narrated in artistic order" (*Bertheau*), is at variance with the actual character of the biblical account. In order to get exactly twelve heroic acts, *Bertheau* has to fix the stamp of a heroic act performed by Samson himself upon the miraculous help which he received from God through the opening up of a spring of water (chap. xv. 18, 19), and also to split up a closely connected event, such as his breaking the bonds three times, into three different actions.[1] If we simply confine ourselves to the biblical account, the acts of Samson may be divided into two parts. The *first* (chap. xiv. and xv.) contains those in which Samson smote the Philistines with gradually increasing severity; the *second* (chap. xvi.) those by which he brought about his own fall and ruin. These are separated from one another by the account of the time that his judgeship lasted (chap. xv. 20), and this account is briefly repeated at the close of the whole account (chap. xvi. 31). The *first* part includes six distinct acts which are grouped together in twos: viz. (1 and 2) the killing of the lion on the way to Timnath, and the slaughter of the thirty Philistines for the purpose of paying for the solution of his riddle with the clothes that he took off them (chap. xiv.); (3 and 4) his revenge upon the Philistines by burning their crops, because his wife had been given to a Philistine, and also by the great slaughter with which he punished them for having

---

[1] On these grounds, *L. Diestel*, in the article *Samson* in *Herzog's* Cycl., has rejected *Bertheau's* enumeration as unsatisfactory ; and also the division proposed by *Ewald* into five acts with three turns in each, because, in order to arrive at this grouping, *Ewald* is not only obliged to refer the general statement in chap. xiii. 25, " the Spirit of God began to drive Samson," to some heroic deed which is not described, but has also to assume that in the case of one act (the carrying away of the gates of Gaza) the last two steps of the legend are omitted from the present account, although in all the rest *Diestel* follows *Ewald's* view almost without exception. The views advanced by *Ewald* and *Bertheau* form the foundation of *Roskoff's* Monograph, " the legend of Samson in its origin, form, and signification, and the legend of Hercules," in which the legend of Samson is regarded as an Israelitish form of that of Hercules.

burned his father-in-law and wife (chap. xv. 1–8); (5 and 6) the
bursting of the cords with which his countrymen had bound him
for the purpose of delivering him up to the Philistines, and the
slaying of 1000 Philistines with the jaw-bone of an ass (chap. xv.
9–19). The *second* part of his life comprises only three acts : viz.
(1) taking off the town gates of Gaza, and carrying them away
(chap. xvi. 1–3) ; (2) breaking the bonds with which Delilah
bound him three separate times (chap. xvi. 4–14); and (3) his
heroic death through pulling down the temple of Dagon, after he
had been delivered into the power of the Philistines through the
treachery of Delilah, and had been blinded by them (chap. xvi.
15–31). In this arrangement there is no such artistic shaping or
rounding off of the historical materials apparent, as could indicate
any mythological decoration. And lastly, the popular language of
Samson in proverbs, rhymes, and a play upon words, does not
warrant us in maintaining that the popular legend invented this
mode of expressing his thoughts, and put the words into his mouth.
All this leads to the conclusion, that there is no good ground for
calling in question the historical character of the whole account of
Samson's life and deeds.[1]

Chap. xiii. Birth of Samson.—Ver. 1. The oppression of the
Israelites by the Philistines, which is briefly hinted at in chap. x. 7,
is noticed again here with the standing formula, " *And the children
of Israel did evil again in the sight of the Lord*," etc. (cf. chap. x. 6,
iv. 1, iii. 12), as an introduction to the account of the life and acts
of Samson, who began to deliver Israel from the hands of these
enemies. Not only the birth of Samson, but the prediction of his
birth, also fell, according to ver. 5, within the period of the rule of
the Philistines over Israel. Now, as their oppression lasted forty
years, and Samson judged Israel for twenty years during that

---

[1] No safe or even probable conjecture can be drawn from the character of
the history before us, with reference to the first written record of the life of
Samson, or the sources which the author of our book of Judges made use of for
this portion of his work. The recurrence of such expressions as יָחֶל followed
by an infinitive (chap. xiii. 5, 25, xvi. 19, 22), פֶּתִי (chap. xiv. 15, xvi. 5),
הֵצִיק (chap. xiv. 17, xvi. 16, etc.), upon which *Bertheau* lays such stress, arises
from the actual contents of the narrative itself. The same expressions also
occur in other places where the thought requires them, and therefore they form
no such peculiarities of style as to warrant the conclusion that the life of
Samson was the subject of a separate work (*Ewald*), or that it was a fragment
taken from a larger history of the wars of the Philistines (*Bertheau*).

oppression (chap. xv. 20, xvi. 31), he must have commenced his judgeship at an early age, probably before the completion of his twentieth year; and with this the statement in chap. xiv., that his marriage with a Philistine woman furnished the occasion for his conflicts with these enemies of his people, fully agrees. The end of the forty years of the supremacy of the Philistines is not given in this book, which closes with the death of Samson. It did not terminate till the great victory which the Israelites gained over their enemies under the command of Samuel (1 Sam. vii.). Twenty years before this victory the Philistines had sent back the ark which they had taken from the Israelites, after keeping it for seven months in their own land (1 Sam. vii. 2, and vi. 1). It was within these twenty years that most of the acts of Samson occurred. His first affair with the Philistines, however, namely on the occasion of his marriage, took place a year or two before this defeat of the Israelites, in which the sons of Eli were slain, the ark fell into the hands of the Philistines, and the high priest Eli fell from his seat and broke his neck on receiving the terrible news (1 Sam. iv. 18). Consequently Eli died a short time after the first appearance of Samson (see p. 282).

Vers. 2–7. Whilst the Israelites were given into the hands of the Philistines on account of their sins, and were also severely oppressed in Gilead on the part of the Ammonites, the angel of the Lord appeared to the wife of Manoah, a Danite from *Zorea, i.e.* *Sur'a,* on the western slope of the mountains of Judah (see at Josh. xv. 33). *Mishpachath Dani* (the family of the Danites) is used interchangeably with *shebet Dani* (the tribe of the Danites: see chap. xviii. 2, 11, and xviii. 1, 30), which may be explained on this ground, that according to Num. xxvi. 42, 43, all the Danites formed but one family, viz. the family of the Shuhamites. The angel of the Lord announced to this woman, who was barren, " *Thou wilt conceive and bear a son. And now beware, drink no wine or strong drink, and eat nothing unclean: for, behold, thou wilt conceive and bear a son, and no razor shall come upon his head; for a vowed man of God (Nazir) will the boy be from his mother's womb,*" *i.e.* his whole life long, " *to the day of his death,*" as the angel expressly affirmed, according to ver. 7. The three prohibitions which the angel of the Lord imposed upon the woman were the three things which distinguished the condition of a Nazarite (see at Num. vi. 1–8, and the explanation given there of the Nazarite vow). The only other thing mentioned in the Mosaic law is the warning against defilement from contact with the dead, which does not seem to have been enforced in the case of Samson.   When the angel added still further, " *And he* (the Nazarite) *will begin to deliver Israel out of the hand of the Philistines*," he no doubt intended to show that his power to effect this deliverance would be closely connected with his condition as a Nazarite.   The promised son was to be a Nazarite all his life long, because he was to begin to deliver Israel out of the power of his foes.   And in order that he might be so, his mother was to share in the renunciations of the Nazarite vow during the time of her pregnancy.   Whilst the appearance of the angel of the Lord contained the practical pledge that the Lord still acknowledged His people, though He had given them into the hands of their enemies ; the message of the angel contained this lesson and warning for Israel, that it could only obtain deliverance from its foes by seeking after a life of consecration to the Lord, such as the Nazarites pursued, so as to realize the idea of the priestly character to which Israel had been called as the people of Jehovah, by abstinence from the *deliciæ carnis,* and everything that was unclean, as being emanations of sin, and also by a complete self-surrender to the Lord (see Pentateuch, vol. iii. p. 38).—Vers. 6, 7. The woman told her husband of this appearance : " *A man of God,*" she said (*lit. the* man of God, viz. the one just referred to), " *came to me, and his appearance was like the appearance of the angel of God, very terrible ; and I asked him not whence he was, neither told he me his name,*" etc.   " *Man of God*" was the expression used to denote a prophet, or a man who stood in immediate intercourse with God, such as Moses and others (see at Deut. xxxiii. 1).   " *Angel of God*" is equivalent to " angel of the Lord" (chap. ii. 1, vi. 11), the angel in whom the invisible God reveals himself to men.   The woman therefore imagined the person who appeared to her to have been a prophet, whose majestic appearance, however, had produced the impression that he was a superior being; consequently she had not ventured to ask him either his name or where he came from.

Vers. 8–20. Being firmly convinced of the truth of this announcement, and at the same time reflecting upon the obligation which it imposed upon the parents, Manoah prayed to the Lord that He would let the man of God whom He had sent come to them again, to teach them what they were to do to the boy that should be born, *i.e.* how they should treat him.   הַיֶּלֶד, according to the *Keri* הִיְלָד, is a participle *Pual* with the מ dropped (see *Ewald,* § 169, *b.*).   This prayer was heard. The angel of God appeared once more to the woman when she was sitting alone in the field without her husband.—Vers. 10, 11. Then she hastened to fetch her husband, who first of all inquired of the person who had appeared, "*Art thou the man who said to the woman*" (*sc.* what has been related in vers. 3-5)? And when this was answered in the affirmative, he said still further (ver. 12), "*Should thy word then come to pass, what will be the manner of the boy, and his doing?*" The plural דְּבָרֶיךָ is construed *ad sensum* with a singular verb, because the words form one promise, so that the expression is not to be taken distributively, as *Rosenmüller* supposes. This also applies to ver. 17. *Mishpat*, the right belonging to the boy, *i.e.* the proper treatment of him.—Vers. 13, 14. The angel of the Lord then repeated the instructions which he had already given to the woman in ver. 4, simply adding to the prohibition of wine and strong drink the caution not to eat of anything that came from the vine, in accordance with Num. vi. 3.—Ver. 15. As Manoah had not yet recognised in the man the angel of the Lord, as is observed by way of explanation in ver. 16, he wished, like Gideon (chap. vi. 18), to give a hospitable entertainment to the man who had brought him such joyful tidings, and therefore said to him, "*Let us detain thee, and prepare a kid for thee.*" The construction נַעֲשֶׂה לְפָנֶיךָ is a pregnant one: "prepare and set before thee." On the fact itself, see chap. vi. 19.—Ver. 16. The angel of the Lord replied, "*If thou wilt detain me* (*sc.* that I may eat), *I will not eat of thy food* (אָכַל with בְּ, to eat thereat, *i.e.* thereof, as in Ex. xii. 43, Lev. xxii. 11); *but if thou wilt prepare a burnt-offering for Jehovah, then offer it.*"—Ver. 17. Manoah then asked his name: מִי שְׁמֶךָ, *lit.* "*Who is thy name?*" מִי inquires after the person; מָה, the nature or quality (see *Ewald*, § 325, *a.*). "*For if thy word come to pass, we will do thee honour.*" This was the reason why he asked after his name. כִּבֵּד, to honour by presents, so as to show one's self grateful (see Num. xxii. 17, 37, xxiv. 11).—Ver. 18. The angel replied, "*Why askest thou then after my name? truly it is wonderful.*" The *Kethibh* פֶלִאי is the adjectival form פִלְאִי from פֶּלֶא, for which the *Keri* has פֶּלִי, the pausal form of פֶּלִי (from the radical פָּלָה = פָּלָא). The word therefore is not the proper name of the angel of the Lord, but expresses the character of his name; and as the name simply denotes the nature, it expresses the peculiarity of his nature also. It is to be understood in an absolute sense—"absolutely and supremely wonderful" (*Seb. Schmidt*)— as a predicate belonging to God alone (compare the term "Wonderful" in Isa. ix. 6), and not to be toned down as it is by *Bertheau*, who explains it as signifying "neither easy to utter nor easy to comprehend."—Vers. 19, 20. Manoah then took the kid and the *minchah, i.e.,* according to Num. xv. 4 sqq., the meat-offering belonging to the burnt-offering, and offered it upon the rock, which is called an altar in ver. 20, because the angel of the Lord, who is of one nature with God, had sanctified it as an altar through the miraculous acceptance of the sacrifice. מַפְלִא לַעֲשׂוֹת, "*and wonderfully* (miraculously) *did he act*" (הִפְלִיא followed by the infinitive with לְ as in 2 Chron. xxvi. 15). These words form a circumstantial clause, which is not to be attached, however, to the subject of the principal clause, but to לַיהוָֹה: "Manoah offered the sacrifice to the Lord, whereupon He acted to do wonderfully, *i.e.* He performed a wonder or miracle, and Manoah and his wife saw it" (see *Ewald,* Lehrb. § 341, *b.,* p. 724, note). In what the miracle consisted is explained in ver. 20, in the words, "*when the flame went up toward heaven from off the altar;*" that is to say, in the fact that a flame issued from the rock, as in the case of Gideon's sacrifice (chap. vi. 21), and consumed the sacrifice. And the angel of the Lord ascended in this flame. When Manoah and his wife saw this, they fell upon their faces to the earth (*sc.* in worship), because they discovered from the miracle that it was the angel of the Lord who had appeared to them.

Vers. 21–25. From that time forward the Lord did not appear to them again. But Manoah was afraid that he and his wife should die, because they had seen God (on this belief, see the remarks on Gen. xvi. 13 and Ex. xxxiii. 20). His wife quieted his fears, however, and said, "*Jehovah cannot intend to kill us, as He has accepted our sacrifice, and has shown us all this*" (the twofold miracle). "*And at this time He has not let us see such things as these.*" כָּעֵת, at the time in which we live, even if such things may possibly have taken place in the hoary antiquity.—Ver. 24. The promise of God was fulfilled. The boy whom the woman bare received the name of *Samson.* שִׁמְשׁוֹן (LXX., Σαμψών) does not mean sun-like, hero of the sun, from שֶׁמֶשׁ (the sun), but, as *Josephus* explains it (Ant. v. 8, 4), ἰσχυρός, the strong or daring one, from שִׁמְשׁוֹם, from the intensive form שִׁמְשֵׁם, from שָׁמֵם, in its original sense to be strong or daring, not "to devastate." שָׁדַד is an analogous word : *lit.* to be powerful, then to act powerfully, to devastate. The boy grew under the blessing of God (see 1 Sam. ii. 21).—Ver. 25. When he had grown up, the Spirit of Jehovah began to thrust him in the camp of Dan. פָּעַם, to thrust, denoting the operation of the Spirit of God within him, which took possession of him suddenly, and impelled him to put forth supernatural powers. *Mahaneh-Dan*, the camp of Dan, was the name given to the district in which the Danites who emigrated, according to chap. xviii. 12, from the inheritance of their tribe, had pitched their encampment *behind*, *i.e.* to the west of, *Kirjath-jearim*, or according to this verse, between Zorea and Eshtaol. The situation cannot be determined precisely, as the situation of Eshtaol itself has not been discovered yet (see at Josh. xv. 33). It was there that Samson lived with his parents, judging from chap. xvi. 31. The meaning of this verse, which forms the introduction to the following account of the acts of Samson, is simply that Samson was there seized by the Spirit of Jehovah, and impelled to commence the conflict with the Philistines.

Chap. xiv. SAMSON'S FIRST TRANSACTIONS WITH THE PHILISTINES.—Vers. 1–9. At Tibnath, the present *Tibne*, an hour's journey to the south-west of Sur'a (see at Josh. xv. 10), to which Samson had gone down from Zorea or Mahaneh-Dan, he saw a daughter of the Philistines who pleased him ; and on his return he asked his parents to take her for him as a wife (לָקַח, to take, as in Ex. xxi. 9).—Vers. 3, 4. His parents expressed their astonishment at the choice, and asked him whether there was not a woman among the daughters of his brethren (*i.e.* the members of his own tribe), or among all his people, that he should want to fetch one from the Philistines, the uncircumcised. But Samson repeated his request, because the daughter of the Philistines pleased him. The aversion of his parents to the marriage was well founded, as such a marriage was not in accordance with the law. It is true that the only marriages expressly prohibited in Ex. xxxiv. 16 and Deut. vii. 3, 4, are marriages with Canaanitish women; but the reason assigned for this prohibition was equally applicable to marriages with daughters of the Philistines. In fact, the Philistines are reckoned among the Canaanites in Josh. xiii. 3 upon the very same ground. But Samson was acting under a higher impulse, whereas his parents did not know that it was from Jehovah, *i.e.* that Jehovah had so planned it ; " *for Samson was seeking an opportunity on account of the Philistines*," *i.e.* an occasion to quarrel with them, because, as is afterwards added in the form of an explanatory circumstantia clause, the Philistines had dominion over Israel at that time. תֹּאֲנָה, ἅπ. λεγ., an opportunity (cf. הִתְאַנֶּה, 2 Kings v. 7).—Vers. 5, 6.

When Samson went down with his parents to Timnath, a young
lion came roaring towards him at the vineyards of that town. Then
the Spirit of Jehovah came upon him, so that he tore the lion in
pieces as a kid is torn (*lit.* " like the tearing in pieces of the kid"),
although he had nothing, *i.e.* no weapon, in his hand. David, when
a shepherd, and the hero Benaiah, also slew lions (1 Sam. xvii. 34,
35; 2 Sam. xxiii. 20); and even at the present day Arabs sometimes kill lions with a staff (see *Winer*, Bibl. R. W. Art. Löwe).
Samson's supernatural strength, the effect of the Spirit of Jehovah,
which came upon him, was simply manifested in the fact that he
tore the lion in pieces without any weapon whatever in his hand.
But he said nothing about it to his parents, who were not eye-
witnesses of the deed. This remark is introduced in connection
with what follows.—Ver. 7. When he came to Timnath he talked
with the girl, and she pleased him. He had only *seen* her before
(ver. 1); but now that his parents had asked for her, he talked
with her, and found the first impression that he had received of her
fully confirmed.—Ver. 8. When some time had elapsed after the
betrothal, he came again to fetch her (take her home, marry her),
accompanied, as we learn from ver. 9, by his parents. On the way
" *he turned aside* (from the road) *to see the carcase of the lion; and
behold a swarm of bees was in the body of the lion, also honey.*" The
word מַפֶּלֶת, which only occurs here, is derived from נָפַל, like πτῶμα
from πίπτω, and is synonymous with נְבֵלָה, *cadaver,* and signifies not
the mere skeleton, as bees would not form their hive in such a place,
but the carcase of the lion, which had been thoroughly dried up
by the heat of the sun, without passing into a state of putrefaction.
" In the desert of Arabia the heat of a sultry season will often
dry up all the moisture of men or camels that have fallen dead,
within twenty-four hours of their decease, without their passing into
a state of decomposition and putrefaction, so that they remain for
a long time like mummies, without change and without stench"
(*Rosenmüller*, Bibl. Althk. iv. 2, p. 424). In a carcase dried up in
this way, a swarm of bees might form their hive, just as well as in
the hollow trunks of trees, or clefts in the rock, or where wild bees
are accustomed to form them, notwithstanding the fact that bees
avoid both dead bodies and carrion (see *Bochart, Hieroz. ed. Ros.* iii.
p. 355).—Ver. 9. Samson took it (the honey) in his hands, ate some
of it as he went, and also gave some to his father and mother to eat,
but did not tell them that he had got the honey out of the dead body
of the lion; for in that case they would not only have refused to

eat it as being unclean, but would have been aware of the fact, which Samson afterwards took as the subject of the riddle that he proposed to the Philistines. רָדָה, to tread, to tread down; hence to get forcible possession of, not to break or to take out, neither of which meanings can be established. The combination of רָדָה and אֶל־כַּפָּיו is a pregnant construction, signifying to obtain possession of and take into the hands.

Vers. 10–20. *Samson's Wedding and Riddle.*—Ver. 10. When his father had come down to the girl (*sc.* to keep the wedding, not merely to make the necessary preparations for his marriage), Samson prepared for a feast there (in Timnath), according to the usual custom (for so used the young men to do).—Ver. 11. " *And when they saw him, they fetched thirty friends, and they were with him.*" The parents or relations of the bride are the subject of the first clause. They invited thirty of their friends in Timnath to the marriage feast, as " children of the bride-chamber" (Matt. ix. 15), since Samson had not brought any with him. The reading כִּרְאוֹתָם from רָאָה needs no alteration, though *Bertheau* would read כִּרְאֹתָם from יָרֵא, in accordance with the rendering of the LXX. (*Cod. Al.*) and of *Josephus*, ἐν τῷ φοβεῖσθαι αὐτούς. Fear of Samson would neither be in harmony with the facts themselves, nor with the words וַיִּהְיוּ אִתּוֹ, " *they were with him,*" which it is felt to be necessary to paraphrase in the most arbitrary manner " they watched him."—Ver. 12. At the wedding feast Samson said to the guests, " *I will give you a riddle. If you show it to me during the seven days of the meal* (the wedding festival), *and guess it, I will give you thirty sedinim* (σινδόνες, *tunicæ, i.e.* clothes worn next to the skin) *and thirty changes of garments* (costly dresses, that were frequently changed: see at Gen. xlv. 22); *but if ye cannot show it to me, ye shall give me the same number of garments.*" The custom of proposing riddles at banquets by way of entertainment is also to be met with among the ancient Grecians. (For proofs from *Athenæus, Pollux, Gellius,* see *Bochart,* Hieroz. P. ii. l. ii. c. 12; and *K. O. Müller,* Dorier, ii. p. 392). As the guests consented to this proposal, Samson gave them the following riddle (ver. 14): " *Out of the eater came forth meat, and out of the strong came forth sweetness.*" This riddle they could not show, *i.e.* solve, for three days. That is to say, they occupied themselves for three days in trying to find the solution; after that they let the matter rest until the appointed term was drawing near.—Ver. 15. On the seventh day they said to Samson's wife, " *Persuade thy husband to show us the riddle,"* sc. through thee, without his noticing it, *" lest we burn thee and thy father's house with fire. Have ye invited us to make us poor; is it not so?"* In this threat the barbarism and covetousness of the Philistines came openly to light. הַלְיָרְשֵׁנוּ without *Metheg* in the יָ is the *inf. Kal* of יָרַשׁ, to make poor,—a meaning derived from inheriting, not the *Piel* of יָרַשׁ = רוּשׁ, to be poor. הֲלֹא, *nonne,* strengthens the interrogative clause, and has not the signification *" here"* = הֲלֹם. Samson's wife, however, wept over him, *i.e.* urged him with tears in her eyes, and said, *" Thou dost but hate me, and lovest me not; thou hast put forth a riddle unto the children of my people* (my countrymen), *and hast not shown it to me."* חַרְתָּה is from חוּד. Samson replied, that he had not even shown it to his father and mother, *" and shall I show it to thee?"*—Ver. 17. *" Thus his wife wept before him the seven days of the banquet."* This state-ment is not at variance with that in ver. 15, to the effect that it was only on the seventh day that the Philistine young men urged her with threats to entice Samson to tell the riddle, but may be explained very simply in the following manner. The woman had already come to Samson every day with her entreaties from simple curiosity; but Samson resisted them until the seventh day, when she became more urgent than ever, in consequence of this threat on the part of the Philistines. And *" Samson showed it to her, because she lay sore upon him;"* whereupon she immediately be-trayed it to her countrymen.—Ver. 18. Thus on the seventh day, before the sun went down (חַרְסָה = חֶרֶס, chap. viii. 13; Job. ix. 7, with a toneless *ah*, a softening down of the feminine termination: see *Ewald,* § 173, *h.*), the men of the city (*i.e.* the thirty young men who had been invited) said to Samson, *" What is sweeter than honey, and what stronger than a lion?"* But Samson saw through the whole thing, and replied, *" If ye had not ploughed with my heifer, ye had not hit upon* (guessed) *my riddle,"*—a pro-verbial saying, the meaning of which is perfectly clear.—Ver. 19. Nevertheless he was obliged to keep his promise (ver. 12). Then the Spirit of Jehovah came upon him. He went down to Ash-kelon, slew thirty men of them, *i.e.* of the Ashkelonites, took their clothes (חֲלִיצוֹת, *exuviæ:* see 2 Sam. ii. 21), and gave the changes of garments to those who had shown the riddle. This act is described as the operation of the Spirit of Jehovah which came upon Samson, because it showed to the Philistines the superior power of the servants of Jehovah. It was not carnal revenge that had impelled Samson to the deed. It was not till the deed itself was done that his anger was kindled ; and even then it was not against the Philistines, to whom he had been obliged to pay or give the thirty garments, but against his wife, who had betrayed his secret to her countrymen, so that he returned to his father's house, viz. without his wife.— Ver. 20. " *And Samson's wife was given to his friend, whom he had chosen as a friend.*" מֵרֵעַ is no doubt to be understood here in the sense of " the friend of the bridegroom" (John iii. 29), ὁ νυμφαγωγός (LXX.), the conductor of the bride,—namely, one of the thirty companions (ver. 10), whom Samson had entrusted with this office at the marriage festival. The faithlessness of the Philistines towards the Israelites was no doubt apparent here ; for even if Samson went home enraged at the treacherous behaviour of his wife, without taking her with him, he did not intend to break the marriage tie, as chap. xv. 1, 2 clearly shows. So that instead of looking at the wrong by which Samson felt himself aggrieved, and trying to mitigate his wrath, the parents of the woman made the breach irreparable by giving their daughter as a wife to his companion.

Chap. xv. FURTHER ACTS OF SAMSON.—Vers. 1–8. *His revenge upon the Philistines.*—Ver. 1. Some time after, Samson visited his wife in the time of the wheat harvest with a kid,—a customary present at that time (Gen. xxxviii. 17),—and wished to go into the chamber (the women's apartment) to her ; but her father would not allow him, and said, " *I thought thou hatedst her, and therefore gave her to thy friend* (chap. xiv. 20) : *behold her younger sister is fairer than she ; let her be thine in her stead.*"—Ver. 3. Enraged at this answer, Samson said to them (*i.e.* to her father and those around him), " *Now am I blameless before the Philistines, if I do evil to them.*" נִקָּה with מִן, to be innocent away from a person, *i.e.* before him (see Num. xxxii. 22). Samson regarded the treatment which he had received from his father-in-law as but one effect of the disposition of the Philistines generally towards the Israelites, and therefore resolved to avenge the wrong which he had received from one member of the Philistines upon the whole nation, or at all events upon the whole of the city of Timnath.—Vers. 4, 5. He therefore went and caught three hundred *shualim, i.e.* jackals, animals which resemble foxes and are therefore frequently classed among the foxes even by the common Arabs of the present day (see *Niebuhr*, Beschr. v. Arab. p. 166). Their European name is derived from the Persian *schaghal.* These animals, which are still found in great quantities at Joppa, Gaza, and in Galilee, herd

together, and may easily be caught (see *Rosenmüller*, Bibl. Althk.
iv. 2, pp. 155 sqq.). He then took torches, turned tail to tail, *i.e.*
coupled the jackals together by their tails, putting a torch between
the two tails, set the torches on fire, and made the animals run into
the fields of standing corn belonging to the Philistines. Then he
burned "*from the shocks of wheat to the standing grain and to the
olive gardens,*" *i.e.* the shocks of wheat as well as the standing corn
and the olive plantations. כֶּרֶם זַיִת are joined together in the construct state.—Ver. 6. The Philistines found out at once, that Samson
had done them this injury because his father-in-law, the Timnite,
had taken away his wife and given her to his companion. They
therefore avenged themselves by burning her and her father,—
probably by burning his house down to the ground, with its occu-
pants within it, — an act of barbarity and cruelty which fully
justified Samson's war upon them.—Ver. 7. Samson therefore
declared to them, "*If ye do such things, truly* (כִּי) *when I have
avenged myself upon you, then will I cease,*" *i.e.* I will not cease till
I have taken vengeance upon you.—Ver. 8. "*Then he smote them
hip and thigh* (*lit.* 'thigh upon hip;' עַל as in Gen. xxxii. 12), *a
great slaughter.*" שׁוֹק, thigh, strengthened by עַל־יָרֵךְ, is a second
accusative governed by the verb, and added to define the word
אוֹתָם more minutely, in the sense of "on hip and thigh;" whilst
the expression which follows, מַכָּה גְדוֹלָה, is added as an adverbial
accusative to strengthen the verb וַיַּךְ. Smiting hip and thigh is
a proverbial expression for a cruel, unsparing slaughter, like the
German "cutting arm and leg in two," or the Arabic "war in
thigh fashion" (see *Bertheau in loc.*). After smiting the Philistines,
Samson went down and dwelt in the cleft of the rock *Etam*. There
is a town of *Etam* mentioned in 2 Chron. xi. 6, between Bethlehem
and Tekoah, which was fortified by Rehoboam, and stood in all
probability to the south of Jerusalem, upon the mountains of Judah.
But this *Etam*, which *Robinson* (Pal. ii. 168) supposes to be the
village of *Urtas*, a place still inhabited, though lying in ruins, is
not to be thought of here, as the Philistines did not go up to the
mountains of Judah (ver. 9), as *Bertheau* imagines, but simply
came forward and encamped in Judah. The *Etam* of this verse is
mentioned in 1 Chron. iv. 32, along with Ain Rimmon and other
Simeonitish towns, and is to be sought for on the border of the
Negeb and of the mountains of Judah, in the neighbourhood of
Khuweilifeh (see *V. de Velde*, Mem. p. 311). The expression " he
went down " suits this place very well, but not the Etam on the

mountains of Judah, to which he would have had to go up, and not down, from Timnath.

Vers. 9–17. *Samson is delivered up to the Philistines, and smites them with the jaw-bone of an Ass.*—Ver. 9. The Philistines came ("went up," denoting the advance of an army : see at Josh. viii. 1) to avenge themselves for the defeat they had sustained from Samson ; and having encamped in Judah, spread themselves out in *Lechi* (*Lehi*). *Lechi* (לְחִי, in pause לֶחִי, *i.e.* a jaw), which is probably mentioned again in 2 Sam. xxiii. 11, and, according to ver. 17, received the name of *Ramath-lechi* from Samson himself, cannot be traced with any certainty, as the early church tradition respecting the place is utterly worthless. *Van de Velde* imagines that it is to be found in the flattened rocky hill *el Lechieh,* or *Lekieh,* upon which an ancient fortification has been discovered, in the middle of the road from *Tell Khewelfeh* to *Beersheba,* at the south-western approach of the mountains of Judah.—Vers. 10 sqq. When the Judæans learned what was the object of this invasion on the part of the Philistines, three thousand of them went down to the cleft in the rock Etam, to bind Samson and deliver him up to the Philistines. Instead of recognising in Samson a deliverer whom the Lord had raised up for them, and crowding round him that they might smite their oppressors with his help and drive them out of the land, the men of Judah were so degraded, that they cast this reproach at Samson : " *Knowest thou not that the Philistines rule over us ? Wherefore hast thou done this* (the deed described in ver. 8) *? We have come down to bind thee, and deliver thee into the hand of the Philistines.*" Samson replied, " *Swear to me that ye will not fall upon me yourselves.*" פָּגַע with בְּ, to thrust at a person, fall upon him, including in this case, according to ver. 13, the intention of killing.—Ver. 13. When they promised him this, he let them bind him with two new cords and lead him up (into the camp of the Philistines) out of the rock (*i.e.* the cleft of the rock).—Ver. 14. But when he came to Lechi, and the Philistines shouted with joy as they came to meet him, the Spirit of Jehovah came upon him, " *and the cords on his arms became like tow that had been burnt with fire, and his fetters melted from his hands.*" The description rises up to a poetical parallelism, to depict the triumph which Samson celebrated over the Philistines in the power of the Spirit of Jehovah. —Ver. 15. As soon as he was relieved of his bands, he seized upon a fresh jaw-bone of an ass, which he found there, and smote therewith a thousand men. He himself commemorated this victory in a

short poetical strain (ver. 16) : " *With the ass's jaw-bone a heap,
two heaps ; with the ass's jaw-bone I smote a thousand men.*" The
form of the word חֲמוֹר=הֹמֶר is chosen on account of the resemblance to חֲמוֹר, and is found again at 1 Sam. xvi. 20. How Samson
achieved this victory is not minutely described. But the words " a
heap, two heaps," point to the conclusion that it did not take place
in one encounter, but in several. The supernatural strength with
which Samson rent asunder the fetters bound upon him, when the
Philistines thought they had him safely in their power, filled them
with fear and awe as before a superior being, so that they fled, and
he pursued them, smiting one heap after another, as he overtook
them, with an ass's jaw-bone which he found in the way. The
number given, viz. a thousand, is of course a round number signifying a very great multitude, and has been adopted from the song
into the historical account.—Ver. 17. When he had given utterance
to his saying, he threw the jaw-bone away, and called the place
Ramath-lechi, i.e. the jaw-bone height. This seems to indicate that
the name *Lechi* in ver. 9 is used proleptically, and that the place
first received its name from this deed of Samson.

Vers. 18–20. The pursuit of the Philistines, however, and the
conflict with them, had exhausted Samson, so that he was very
thirsty, and feared that he might die from exhaustion ; for it was
about the time of the wheat-harvest (ver. 1), and therefore hot
summer weather. Then he called to the Lord, " *Thou hast through*
(בְּיַד) *Thy servant given this great deliverance; and now I shall die
for thirst, and fall into the hand of the uncircumcised !*" From this
prayer we may see that Samson was fully conscious that he was
fighting for the cause of the Lord. And the Lord helped him out
of this trouble. God split the hollow place at Lechi, so that water
came out of it, as at Horeb and Kadesh (Ex. xvii. 6, and Num. xx.
8, 11). The word מַכְתֵּשׁ, which is used in Prov. xxvii. 22 to signify
a mortar, is explained by rabbinical expositors as denoting the
socket of the teeth, or the hollow place in which the teeth are fixed,
like the Greek ὀλμίσκος, *mortariolum,* according to *Pollux,* Onom.
ii. c. 4, § 21. Accordingly many have understood the statement
made here, as meaning that God caused a fountain to flow miraculously out of the socket of a tooth in the jaw-bone which Samson
had thrown away, and thus provided for his thirst. This view is
the one upon which Luther's rendering, " God split a tooth in
the jaw, so that water came out," is founded, and it has been
voluminously defended by *Bochart* (Hieroz. l. ii. c. 15). But the

expression אֲשֶׁר בַּלֶּחִי, " the *maktesh* which is at *Lechi*," is opposed to
this view, since the tooth-socket in the jaw-bone of the ass would
be simply called מַכְתֵּשׁ הַלֶּחִי or מַכְתֵּשׁ בַּלֶּחִי; and so is also the remark
that this fountain was still in existence in the historian's own time.
And the article proves nothing to the contrary, as many proper
names are written with it (see *Ewald*, § 277, *c.*). Consequently we
must follow *Josephus* (Ant. v. 8), who takes הַמַּכְתֵּשׁ as the name
given to the opening of the rock, which was cleft by God to let
water flow out. "If a rocky precipice bore the name of jaw-bone
(*lechi*) on account of its shape, it was a natural consequence of this
figurative epithet, that the name *tooth-hollow* should be given to a
hole or gap in the rock" (*Studer*). Moreover, the same name,
Maktesh, occurs again in Zeph. i. 11, where it is applied to a locality
in or near Jerusalem. The hollow place was split by *Elohim*,
although it was to *Jehovah* that Samson had prayed, to indicate
that the miracle was wrought by God as the Creator and Lord of
nature. Samson drank, and his spirit returned, so that he revived
again. Hence the fountain received the name of *En-hakkore*, "the
crier's well which is at Lechi," unto this day. According to the
accents, the last clause does not belong to בַּלֶּחִי (in Lechi), but to
קָרָא וגו' (he called, etc.). It received the name given to it unto this
day. This *implies*, of course, that the spring itself was in existence
when our book was composed.—In ver. 20 the account of the
judicial labours of Samson are brought to a close, with the remark
that Samson judged Israel in the days of the Philistines, *i.e.* during
their rule, for twenty years. What more is recorded of him in
chap. xvi. relates to his fall and ruin; and although even in this
he avenged himself upon the Philistines, he procured no further
deliverance for Israel. It is impossible to draw any critical conclusions from the position in which this remark occurs, as to a
plurality of sources for the history of Samson.

Chap. xvi. SAMSON'S FALL AND DEATH.—Samson's judicial
labours reached their highest point when he achieved his great
victory over the Philistines at Lechi. Just as his love to the
daughter of a Philistine had furnished him with the occasion
designed by God for the manifestation of his superiority to the
uncircumcised enemies of Israel, so the degradation of that love
into sensual lust supplied the occasion for his fall which is related
in this chapter. "Samson, when strong and brave, strangled a
lion; but he could not strangle his own love. He burst the fetters

of his foes, but not the cords of his own lusts. He burned up the crops of others, and lost the fruit of his own virtue when burning with the flame enkindled by a single woman." (*Ambros.* Apol. ii., *David.* c. iii.)

Vers. 1–3. *His heroic deed at Gaza.*—Samson went to Gaza in the full consciousness of his superiority in strength to the Philistines, and there went in unto a harlot whom he saw. For Gaza, see Josh. xiii. 3. אֶל בּוֹא is used in the same sense as in Gen. vi. 4 and xxxviii. 16. It is not stated in this instance, as in chap. xiv. 4, that it was of the Lord.—Ver. 2. When this was told to the Gazites, they surrounded him (the object to the verb is to be supplied from the following word לוֹ) and laid wait for him all night at the city gate, but they kept themselves quiet during the night, saying, "*Till the dawning* (אוֹר, *infin.*) *of the morning*," sc. we can wait, "*then will we kill him*." For this construction, see 1 Sam. i. 22. The verb וַיֻּגַּד, "it was told" (according to the LXX. and *Chald.*: cf. Gen. xxii. 20), or וַיֹּאמְרוּ, "they said," is wanting before לְעַזָּתִים, and must have fallen out through a copyist's error. The verb הִתְחָרֵשׁ has evidently the subordinate idea of giving themselves up to careless repose; for if the watchmen who were posted at the city gate had but watched in a regular manner, Samson could not have lifted out the closed gates and carried them away. But as they supposed that he would not leave the harlot before daybreak, they relied upon the fact that the gate was shut, and probably fell asleep.—Ver. 3. But at midnight Samson got up, and "laying hold of the folding wings of the city gate, as well as the two posts, tore them out of the ground with his herculean strength, together with the bar that fastened them, and carried them up to the top of the mountain which stands opposite to Hebron." עַל־פְּנֵי merely means in the direction towards, as in Gen. xviii. 16, and does not signify that the mountain was in the front of Hebron or in the immediate neighbourhood (see Deut. xxxii. 49, where Mount Nebo, which was on the other side of the Jordan, and at least four geographical miles from Jericho, is said to have been over against it, and the same expression is employed). The distance from Gaza to Hebron was about nine geographical miles. To the east of Gaza there is a range of hills which runs from north to south. The highest of them all is one which stands somewhat isolated, about half an hour to the south-east of the town, and is called *el Montar* from a wely which is found upon the top of it. From this hill there is a splendid prospect over the whole of the surrounding country. Hebron itself is not visible from this hill, but the mountains of Hebron are. According to an ancient tradition, it was to the summit of this hill that Samson carried the city gates; and both *Robinson* (Pal. ii. 377) and *V. de Velde* regard this tradition as by no means improbable, although the people of Gaza are not acquainted with it. "The city gate of the Gaza of that time was probably not less than three-quarters of an hour from the hill *el Montar;* and to climb this peak with the heavy gates and their posts and bar upon his shoulders through the deep sand upon the road, was a feat which only a Samson could perform" (*V. de Velde*).

Vers. 4–21. *Samson and Delilah.*—Ver. 4. After this successful act, Samson gave himself up once more to his sensual lusts. He fell in love with a woman in the valley of *Sorek,* named *Delilah* (*i.e.* the weak or pining one), to whose snares he eventually succumbed. With reference to the valley of *Sorek, Eusebius* affirms in the *Onom.* (*s. v. Σωρήχ*), that there was a village called *Βαρήχ* (*l. Καφὰρ σωρήχ* according to *Jerome*) near Zorea, and *ἐν ὁρίοις* (*l. βορείοις* according to *Jerome,* who has *ad septentrionalem plagam*); and also (*s. v. Σωρήκ*) that this place was near to Eshtaol. Consequently the *Sorek* valley would have to be sought for somewhere in the neighbourhood of Samson's birthplace (chap. xiii. 1), and the dwelling-place of his family (ver. 31).—Ver. 5. The princes of the Philistines offered Delilah a considerable sum (they would give her one thousand and one hundred shekels of silver each, *i.e.* a thousand shekels or more: cf. chap. xvii. 2) if she would persuade Samson, and bring out from him "whereby his strength was great," and whereby they could overpower and bind him, לְעַנּוֹתוֹ, to bend him, *i.e.* to oppress him. The Philistine princes thought that Samson's supernatural strength arose from something external, which he wore or carried about with him as an amulet. There was a certain truth at the foundation of this heathen superstition, inasmuch as this gift of divine grace was really bound up with the possession of a corporeal pledge, the loss of which was followed by the immediate loss of the gift of God (see at ver. 17).—Ver. 6. Allured by the reward in prospect, Delilah now sought to get from him the secret of his strength. But he deceived her three times by false statements. He first of all said to her (ver. 7), "*If they bound me with strings that have not been dried, I should be weak and like one of the men*" (*i.e.* like any other man). יֶתֶר signifies a sinew or string, *e.g.* a bow-string, Ps. xi. 2, and in the different dialects either a bow-string or the string of a harp or guitar. As a distinction is made here between the יְתָרִים and the עֲבֹתִים in ver. 11, the strings intended here are those of catgut or animal sinew. The number *seven* is that of a divine act, answering to the divine power which Samson possessed.—Vers. 8, 9. When Delilah told this to the princes of the Philistines, they brought the seven strings required, and Delilah bound Samson with them. " *And the spy sat in the room* (לָהּ, dat. com., lit. 'to her,' *i.e.*) *to help her*," namely, without Samson knowing it, as Delilah had certainly not told him that she should betray the secret of his strength to the Philistines. He was there, no doubt, that he might be at hand and overpower the fettered giant as soon as it becamē apparent that his strength was gone. She then cried out to him, " *Philistines upon thee, Samson !*" And he snapped the strings as one would snap a cord of tow "when it smells fire," *i.e.* is held to the fire.—Vers. 10–12. The second deception : Samson had himself bound with new cords, which had not yet been used for any purpose, and these also he burst from his arms like a thread.—Vers. 13 and 14. The third deception : " *If thou weavest together the seven locks of my hair with the warp. And she drove it in with the plug.*" These words are difficult to explain, partly because several technical terms are used which have more than one meaning, and partly because the account itself is contracted, both Samson's advice and her fulfilment of it being only given in a partial form, so that the one has to be completed from the other. In ver. 19, the only other passage in which מַחְלְפוֹת occurs, it no doubt means the plaits into which Samson's long flowing hair was plaited. הַמַּסֶּכֶת only occurs here (vers. 13 and 14), and probably means the woven cloth, or rather what was still upon the loom, the warp of the cloth, δίασμα (LXX.). Accordingly the meaning of the verse would be this : If thou weavest the seven plaits of my hair along with the warp upon the loom. The commentators are all agreed that, according to these words, there must be something wanting in the account, though they are not of one opinion as to whether the binding of Samson is fully given here, and all that has to be supplied is the clause " *Then shall I be weak,*" etc. (as in vers. 7 and 11), or whether the words וַתִּתְקַע בַּיָּתֵד add another fact which was necessary to the completeness of the binding, and if so, how these words are to be understood. In *Bertheau's* opinion, the words " *and she thrust with the plug*" probably mean nothing more than that she made a noise to wake the sleeping Samson, because it is neither stated here

that she forced the plug into the wall or into the earth to fasten
the plaits with (LXX., *Jerome*), nor that her thrusting with the
plug contributed in any way to the further fastening of the hair.
These arguments are sound no doubt, but they do not prove what
is intended.   When it is stated in ver. 14*b*, that "he tore out the
weaver's plug and the cloth," it is certainly evident that the plug
served to fasten the hair to the cloth or to the loom.   Moreover,
not only would any knocking with the plug to waken Samson
with the noise have been altogether superfluous, as the loud cry,
"Philistines upon thee, Samson," would be amply sufficient for
this; but it is extremely improbable that a fact with so little
bearing upon the main facts would be introduced here at all.
We come therefore to the same conclusion as the majority of
commentators, viz. that the words in question are to be understood
as referring to something that was done to fasten Samson still
more securely.   הַיָּתֵד = הַיְתַד הָאָרֶג (ver. 14) does not mean the
roller or weaver's beam, to which the threads of the warp were
fastened, and round which the cloth was rolled when finished, as
Bertheau supposes, for this is called מְנוֹר אֹרְגִים in 1 Sam. xvii. 7;
nor the σπάθη of the Greeks, a flat piece of wood like a knife,
which was used in the upright loom for the same purpose as our
comb or press, viz. to press the weft together, and so increase the
substance of the cloth (*Braun, de vestitu Sacerd.* p. 253); but the
comb or press itself which was fastened to the loom, so that it
could only be torn out by force.   To complete the account, therefore, we must supply between vers. 13 and 14, "And if thou
fastenest it (the woven cloth) with the plug (the weaver's comb), I
shall be weak like one of the other men; and she wove the seven
plaits of his hair into the warp of the loom."   Then follows in ver.
14, "*and fastened the cloth with the weaver's comb*."   There is no
need, however, to assume that what has to be supplied fell out in
copying.   We have simply an ellipsis, such as we often meet
with.   When Samson was wakened out of his sleep by the cry of
"Philistines upon thee," he tore out the weaver's comb and the
warp (*sc.*) from the loom, with his plaits of hair that had been
woven in.   The reference to his sleeping warrants the assumption
that Delilah had also performed the other acts of binding while he
was asleep.   We must not understand the account, however, as
implying that the three acts of binding followed close upon one
another on the very same day.   Several days may very probably
have elapsed between them.   In this third deception Samson had

already gone so far in his presumptuous trifling with the divine gift entrusted to him, as to suffer the hair of his head to be meddled with, though it was sanctified to the Lord. " It would seem as though this act of sin ought to have brought him to reflection. But as that was not the case, there remained but one short step more to bring him to thorough treachery towards the Lord" (*O. v. Gerlach*).

This last step was very speedily to follow.—Ver. 15. After this triple deception, Delilah said to him, " *How canst thou say, I love thee, as thine heart is not with me*" (*i.e.* not devoted to me) ?—Ver. 16. With such words as these she plagued him every day, so that his soul became impatient even to death (see chap. x. 16). The ἁπ. λεγ. אָלַץ signifies in Aramæan, to press or plague. The form is *Piel*, though without the reduplication of the ל and *Chateph-patach* under ו (see *Ewald*, § 90, *b.*).—Ver. 17. "*And he showed her all his heart*," *i.e.* he opened his mind thoroughly to her, and told her that no razor had come upon his head, because he was a Nazarite from his mother's womb (cf. chap. xiii. 5, 7). "*If I should be shaven, my strength would depart from me, and I should be weak like all other men.*"—Ver. 18. When Delilah saw (*i.e.* perceived, namely from his words and his whole behaviour while making this communication) that he had betrayed the secret of his strength, she had the princes of the Philistines called : "*Come up this time, . . . for he had revealed to her all his heart.*" This last clause is not to be understood as having been spoken by Delilah to the princes themselves, as it is by the Masorites and most of the commentators, in which case לָהּ would have to be altered into לִי; but it contains a remark of the writer, introduced as an explanation of the circumstance that Delilah sent for the princes of the Philistines now that she was sure of her purpose. This view is confirmed by the word וְעָלוּ (came up) which follows, since the use of the perfect instead of the imperfect with *vav consec.* can only be explained on the supposition that the previous clause is a parenthetical one, which interrupts the course of the narrative, and to which the account of the further progress of the affair could not be attached by the historical tense (וַיַּעֲלוּ).[1] The princes of the Philistines came up to Delilah on the receipt of this

---

[1] The *Keri* reading לִי arose simply from a misunderstanding, although it is found in many MSS. and early editions, and is without any critical worth. The Masorites overlooked the fact that the main point is all that is related of the message of Delilah to the princes of the Philistines, namely that they were to

communication, bringing the money, the promised reward of her treachery (ver. 5), in their hands.—Ver. 19. *"Then she made him sleep upon her knees, and called to the man,"* possibly the man lying in wait (vers. 9 and 12), that she might not be alone with Samson when cutting off his hair; and she cut off the seven plaits of his hair, and began to afflict him, as his strength departed from him now.—Ver. 20. She then cried out, *"Philistines upon thee, Samson!"* And he awaked out of his sleep, and thought (*" said," i.e.* to himself), *" I will go away as time upon time* (this as at other times), *and shake myself loose,"* sc. from the fetters or from the hands of the Philistines; *" but he knew not that Jehovah had departed from him."* These last words are very important to observe in order to form a correct idea of the affair. Samson had said to Delilah, "If my hair were cut off, *my strength* would depart from me" (ver. 17). The historian observes, on the other hand, that *" Jehovah* had departed from him." The superhuman strength of Samson did not reside in his hair as hair, but in the fact that Jehovah was with or near him. But Jehovah was with him so long as he maintained his condition as a Nazarite. As soon as he broke away from this by sacrificing the hair which he wore in honour of the Lord, Jehovah departed from him, and with Jehovah went his strength.[1] —Ver. 21. The Philistines then seized him, put out his eyes, and led him to Gaza fettered with double brass chains. The chains are probably called *nechushtaim* (double brass) because both hands or both feet were fettered with them. King Zedekiah, when taken prisoner by the Chaldeans, was treated in the same manner (2 Kings xxv. 7). There Samson was obliged to turn the mill in the prison, and grind corn (the participle טֹחֵן expresses the continuance of the action). Grinding a handmill was the hardest and lowest

come this time, and that the rest can easily be supplied from the context. *Studer* admits how little וְעָלָה suits that view of the clause which the *Keri* reading לֹי requires, and calls it " syntactically impossible." He proposes, however, to read וַיַּעַל, without reflecting that this reading is also nothing more than a change which is rendered necessary by the alteration of לָהּ into לֹי, and has no critical value.

[1] " Samson was strong because he was dedicated to God, as long as he preserved the signs of his dedication. But as soon as he lost those signs, he fell into the utmost weakness in consequence. The whole of Samson's misfortune came upon him, therefore, because he attributed to himself some portion of what God did through him. God permitted him to lose his strength, that he might learn by experience how utterly powerless he was without the help of God. We have no better teachers than our own infirmities."—*Berleb. Bible.*

kind of slave labour (compare Ex. xi. 5 with xii. 29); and both Greeks and Romans sentenced their slaves to this as a punishment (see *Od.* xx. 105 sqq., vii. 103–4; *Terent.* Phorm. ii. 1, 19, Andr. i. 2, 29), and it is still performed by female slaves in the East (see *Chardin* in *Harmar's* Beob. üb. d. Orient. iii. 64)

Vers. 22–31. *Samson's Misery, and his Triumph in Death.*— Ver. 22. The hair of his head began to grow, as he was shaven. In the word כַּאֲשֶׁר, *as* (from the time when he was shaven), there is an indication that Samson only remained in his ignominious captivity till his hair began to grow again, *i.e.* visibly to grow. What follows agrees with this.—Vers. 23, 24. The captivity of this dreaded hero was regarded by the Philistines as a great victory, which their princes resolved to celebrate with a great and joyous sacrificial festival in honour of their god *Dagon*, to whom they ascribed this victory. "*A great sacrifice*," consisting in the offering up of a large number of slain sacrifices. "*And for joy*," viz. to give expression to their joy, *i.e.* for a joyous festival. *Dagon*, one of the principal deities of the Philistines, was worshipped at Gaza and Ashdod (1 Sam. v. 2 sqq., and 1 Macc. x. 83), and, according to Jerome on Isa. xlvi. 1, in the rest of the Philistine towns as well. It was a fish-deity (דָּגֹן, from דָּג, a fish), and in shape resembled the body of a fish with the head and hands of a man (1 Sam. v. 4). It was a male deity, the corresponding female deity being *Atargatis* (2 Macc. xii. 26) or *Derceto*, and was a symbol of water, and of all the vivifying forces of nature which produce their effects through the medium of water, like the Babylonian 'Ωδάκων, one of the four *Oannes*, and the Indian *Vishnu* (see *Movers*, Phöniz. i. pp. 143 sqq., 590 sqq., and *J. G. Müller* in *Herzog's* Cycl.).—Ver. 24. All the people took part in this festival, and sang songs of praise to the god who had given the enemy, who had laid waste their fields and slain many of their countrymen, into their hands.— Vers. 25 sqq. When their hearts were merry (יְטוֹב, *inf.* of יָטַב), they had Samson fetched out of the prison, that he might make sport before them, and "put him between the pillars" òf the house or temple in which the triumphal feast was held. Then he said to the attendant who held his hand, "*Let me loose, and let me touch the pillars upon which the house is built, that I may lean upon it.*" הֲימִישֵׁנִי is the imperative *Hiphil* of the radical verb יָמֵשׁ, which only occurs here; and the *Keri* substitutes the ordinary form הֲמִישׁ from מוּשׁ. "*But the house*," adds the historian by way of preparation for what follows, "*was filled with men and women: all the princes of the Philistines also were there; and upon the roof were about three thousand men and women, who feasted their eyes with Samson's sports"* (רָאָה with בְ, used to denote the gratification of looking).— Ver. 28. Then Samson prayed to Jehovah, *"Lord Jehovah, remember me, and only this time make me strong, O God, that I may avenge myself* (with) *the revenge of one of my two eyes upon the Philistines,"* *i.e.* may take vengeance upon them for the loss of only one of my two eyes (מִשְּׁתֵי, without *Dagesh lene* in the תִ; see *Ewald,* § 267, *b.*),—a sentence which shows how painfully he felt the loss of his two eyes, " a loss the severity of which even the terrible vengeance which he was meditating could never outweigh" (*Bertheau*).—Vers. 29, 30. After he had prayed to the Lord for strength for this last great deed, he embraced the two middle pillars upon which the building was erected, leant upon them, one with his right hand, the other with the left (viz. embracing them with his hands, as these words also belong to יִלְפֹּת), and said, *" Let my soul die with the Philistines."* He then bent (the two pillars) with force, and the house fell upon the princes and all the people who were within. So far as the fact itself is concerned, there is no ground for questioning the possibility of Samson's bringing down the whole building with so many men inside by pulling down two middle columns, as we have no accurate acquaintance with the style of its architecture. In all probability we have to picture this temple of Dagon as resembling the modern Turkish kiosks, namely as consisting of a " spacious hall, the roof of which rested in front upon four columns, two of them standing at the ends, and two close together in the centre. Under this hall the leading men of the Philistines celebrated a sacrificial meal, whilst the people were assembled above upon the top of the roof, which was surrounded by a balustrade" (*Faber,* Archäol. der Hebr. p. 444, cf. pp. 436-7; and *Shaw,* Reisen, p. 190). The ancients enter very fully into the discussion of the question whether Samson committed suicide or not, though without arriving at any satisfactory conclusion. *O. v. Gerlach,* however, has given the true answer. " Samson's deed," he says, " was not suicide, but the act of a hero, who sees that it is necessary for him to plunge into the midst of his enemies with the inevitable certainty of death, in order to effect the deliverance of his people and decide the victory which he has still to achieve. Samson would be all the more certain that this was the will of the Lord, when he considered that even if he should deliver himself in any other way out of the hands of the Philistines, he would always carry

about with him the mark of his shame in the blindness of his eyes,—
a mark of his unfaithfulness as the servant of God quite as much as
of the double triumph of his foes, who had gained a spiritual as well
as a corporeal victory over him." Such a triumph as this the God
of Israel could not permit His enemies and their idols to gain. The
Lord must prove to them, even through Samson's death, that the
shame of his sin was taken from him, and that the Philistines had
no cause to triumph over him. Thus Samson gained the greatest
victory over his foes in the moment of his own death. The terror
of the Philistines when living, he became a destroyer of the temple
of their idol when he died. Through this last act of his he vindi-
cated the honour of Jehovah the God of Israel, against Dagon the
idol of the Philistines. "*The dead which he slew at his death were
more than they which he slew in his life.*"—Ver. 31. This terrible
blow necessarily made a powerful impression upon the Philistines,
not only plunging them into deep mourning at the death of their
princes and so many of their countrymen, and the destruction of
the temple of Dagon, but filling them with fear and terror at the
omnipotence of the God of the Israelites. Under these circumstances it is conceivable enough that the brethren and relatives of
Samson were able to come to Gaza, and fetch away the body of the
fallen hero, to bury it in his father's grave between Zorea and
Eshtaol (see chap. xiii. 25).—In conclusion, it is once more very
appropriately observed that Samson had judged Israel twenty years
(cf. chap. xv. 20).

III.—IMAGE-WORSHIP OF MICAH AND THE DANITES; INFAMOUS
CONDUCT OF THE INHABITANTS OF GIBEAH; VENGEANCE
TAKEN UPON THE TRIBE OF BENJAMIN.

CHAP. XVII.–XXI.

The death of Samson closes the body of the book of Judges,
which sets forth the history of the people of Israel under the judges
in a continuous and connected form. The two accounts, which
follow in chap. xvii.–xxi., of the facts mentioned in the heading are
attached to the book of Judges in the form of *appendices*, as the
facts in question not only belonged to the times of the judges, and
in fact to the very commencement of those times (see p. 238), but
furnished valuable materials for forming a correct idea of the actual

character of this portion of the Israelitish history. The *first* appendix (chap. xvii. xviii.)—viz. the account of the introduction of image-worship, or of the worship of Jehovah under the form of a molten image, by the Ephraimite Micah, and of the seizure of this image by the Danites, who emigrated from their own territory when upon their march northwards, and the removal of it to the city of *Laish-Dan*, which was conquered by them—shows us how shortly after the death of Joshua the inclination to an idolatrous worship of Jehovah manifested itself in the nation, and how this worship, which continued for a long time in the north of the land, was mixed up from the very beginning with sin and unrighteousness. The *second* (chap. xix.–xxi.)—viz. the account of the infamous act which the inhabitants of Gibeah attempted to commit upon the Levite who stayed there for the night, and which they actually did perform upon his concubine, together with its consequences, viz. the war of vengeance upon the tribe of Benjamin, which protected the criminals—proves, on the one hand, what deep roots the moral corruptions of the Canaanites had struck among the Israelites at a very early period, and, on the other hand, how even at that time the congregation of Israel as a whole had kept itself free and pure, and, mindful of its calling to be the holy nation of God, had endeavoured with all its power to root out the corruption that had already forced its way into the midst of it.

These two occurrences have no actual connection with one another, but they are both of them narrated in a very elaborate and circumstantial manner; and in both of them we not only find Israel still without a king (chap. xvii. 6, xviii. 1, and xix. 1, xxi. 25), and the will of God sought by a priest or by the high priest himself (chap. xviii. 5, 6, xx. 18, 23, 27), but the same style of narrative is adopted as a whole, particularly the custom of throwing light upon the historical course of events by the introduction of circumstantial clauses, from which we may draw the conclusion that they were written by the same author. On the other hand, they do not contain any such characteristic marks as could furnish a certain basis for well-founded conjectures concerning the author, or raise *Bertheau's* conjecture, that he was the same person as the author of chap. i. 1–ii. 5, into a probability. For the frequent use of the perfect with ן (compare chap. xx. 17, 33, 37, 38, 40, 41, 48, xxi. 1, 15, with chap. i. 8, 16, 21, 25, etc.) can be fully explained from the contents themselves; and the notion that the perfect is used here more frequently for the historical

imperfect with *vav consec.* rests upon a misunderstanding and misinterpretation of the passages in question.   The other and not very
numerous expressions, which are common to chap. xvii.–xxi. and
chap. i., are not sufficiently characteristic to supply the proof required,
as they are also met with elsewhere: see, for example, שָׁלַח בָּאֵשׁ
(chap. i. 8, xx. 48), which not only occurs again in 2 Kings viii.
12 and Ps. lxxiv. 7, but does not even occur in both the appendices, שָׂרַף בָּאֵשׁ being used instead in chap. xviii. 27.   So much,
however, may unquestionably be gathered from the exactness and
circumstantiality of the history, viz. that the first recorder of these
events, whose account was the source employed by the author of
our book, cannot have lived at a time very remote from the occurrences themselves.   On the other hand, there are not sufficient
grounds for the conjecture that these appendices were not attached
to the book of the Judges till a later age.   For it can neither be
maintained that the object of the first appendix was to show how
the image-worship which Jeroboam set up in his kingdom at Bethel
and Dan had a most pernicious origin, and sprang from the image-
worship of the Ephraimite Micah, which the Danites had established at Laish, nor that the object of the second appendix was to
prove that the origin of the pre-Davidic kingdom (of Saul) was
sinful and untheocratic, *i.e.* opposed to the spirit and nature of
the kingdom of God, as *Auberlen* affirms (Theol. Stud. u. Kr.
1860).   The identity of the golden calf set up by Jeroboam at Dan
with the image of Jehovah that was stolen by the Danites from
Micah the Ephraimite and set up in Laish-Dan, is precluded by
the statement in chap. xviii. 31 respecting the length of time that
this image-worship continued in Dan (see the commentary on the
passage itself).   At the most, therefore, we can only maintain,
with *O. v. Gerlach*, that " both (appendices) set forth, according to
the intention of the author, the misery which arose during the wild
unsettled period of the judges from the want of a governing, regal
authority."   This is hinted at in the remark, which occurs in both
appendices, that at that time there was no king in Israel, and every
one did what was right in his own eyes (chap. xvii. 6, xxi. 25).
This remark, on the other hand, altogether excludes the time of the
falling away of the ten tribes, and the decline of the later kingdom,
and is irreconcilable with the assumption that these appendices
were not added to the book of the Judges till after the division of
the kingdom, or not till the time of the Assyrian or Babylonian
captivity.

IMAGE-WORSHIP OF MICAH THE EPHRAIMITE, AND ITS REMOVAL
TO LAISH-DAN.—CHAP. XVII. XVIII.

Chap. xvii. MICAH'S IMAGE-WORSHIP.—The account of the
image-worship which Micah established in his house upon the
mountains of Ephraim is given in a very brief and condensed
form, because it was simply intended as an introduction to the
account of the establishment of this image-worship in Laish Dan
in northern Palestine. Consequently only such points are for the
most part given, as exhibit in the clearest light the sinful origin
and unlawful character of this worship.

Vers. 1-10. A man of the mountains of Ephraim named Micah
(מִיכָיְהוּ, vers. 1, 4, then contracted into מִיכָה, vers. 5, 8, etc.), who
set up this worship for himself, and "respecting whom the Scriptures do not think it worth while to add the name of his father, or
to mention the family from which he sprang" (*Berleb. Bible*), had
stolen 1100 shekels of silver (about £135) from his mother. This is
very apparent from the words which he spoke to his mother (ver. 2) :
" *The thousand and hundred shekels of silver which were taken from
thee* (the singular לֻקַּח refers to the silver), *about which thou cursedst
and spakest of also in mine ears* (*i.e.* didst so utter the curse that
among others I also heard it), *behold, this silver is with me; I have
taken it.*" אָלָה, to swear, used to denote a malediction or curse (cf.
קוֹל אָלָה, Lev. v. 1). He seems to have been impelled to make this
confession by the fear of his mother's curse. But his mother
praised him for it,—" *Blessed be my son of Jehovah,*"—partly because
she saw in it a proof that there still existed a germ of the fear of
God, but in all probability chiefly because she was about to dedicate
the silver to Jehovah; for, when her son had given it back to her,
she said (ver. 3), " *I have sanctified the silver to the Lord from my
hand for my son, to make an image and molten work.*" The perfect
הִקְדַּשְׁתִּי is not to be taken in the sense of the pluperfect, " I had
sanctified it," but is expressive of an act just performed: I have
sanctified it, I declare herewith that I do sanctify it. " *And now I
give it back to thee,*" namely, to appropriate to thy house of God.—
Ver. 4. Hereupon—namely, when her son had given her back the
silver (" he restored the silver unto his mother" is only a repetition
of ver. 3*a*, introduced as a link with which to connect the appropriation of the silver)—the mother took 200 shekels and gave them
to the goldsmith, who made an image and molten work of them,
which were henceforth in Micah's house. The 200 shekels were

not quite the fifth part of the whole. What she did with the rest is not stated; but from the fact that she dedicated the silver generally, *i.e.* the whole amount, to Jehovah, according to ver. 3, we may infer that she applied the remainder to the maintenance of the image-worship.[1] *Pesel* and *massecah* (image and molten work) are joined together, as in Deut. xxvii. 15. The difference between the two words in this instance is very difficult to determine. *Pesel* signifies an idolatrous image, whether made of wood or metal. *Massecah*, on the other hand, signifies a cast, something poured; and when used in the singular, is almost exclusively restricted to the calf cast by Aaron or Jeroboam. It is generally connected with עֵגֶל, but it is used in the same sense without this definition (*e.g.* Deut. ix. 12). This makes the conjecture a very natural one, that the two words together might simply denote a likeness of Jehovah, and, judging from the occurrence at Sinai, a representation of Jehovah in the form of a molten calf. But there is one obstacle in the way of such a conjecture, namely, that in chap. xviii. 17, 18, *massecah* is separated from *pesel*, so as necessarily to suggest the idea of two distinct objects. But as we can hardly suppose that Micah's mother had two images of Jehovah made, and that Micah had both of them set up in his house of God, no other explanation seems possible than that the *massecah* was something belonging to the *pesel*, or image of Jehovah, but yet distinct from it,—in other words, that it was the pedestal upon which it stood. The *pesel* was at any rate the principal thing, as we may clearly infer from the fact that it is placed in the front rank among the four objects of Micah's sanctuary, which the Danites took with them (chap. xviii. 17, 18), and that in chap. xviii. 30, 31, the *pesel* alone is mentioned in connection with the setting up of the image-worship in Dan. Moreover, there can hardly be any doubt that *pesel*, as a representation of Jehovah, was an image of a bull, like the golden calf which Aaron had made at Sinai (Ex. xxxii. 4), and the golden calves which Jeroboam set up in the kingdom of Israel, and one of which was set up in Dan (1 Kings xii. 29).—Ver. 5. His mother did this, because

---

[1] There is no foundation for *Bertheau's* opinion, that the 200 shekels were no part of the 1100, but the trespass-money paid by the son when he gave his mother back the money that he had purloined, since, according to Lev. v. 24, when a thief restored to the owner any stolen property, he was to add the fifth of its value. There is no ground for applying this law to the case before us, simply because the taking of the money by the son is not even described as a theft, whilst the mother really praises her son for his open confession.

her son Micah had a house of God, and had had an ephod and teraphim made for himself, and one of his sons consecrated to officiate there as a priest. הָאִישׁ מִיכָה (the man Micah) is therefore placed at the head absolutely, and is connected with what follows by לוֹ: "*As for the man Micah, there was to him* (he had) *a house of God.*" The whole verse is a circumstantial clause explanatory of what precedes, and the following verbs וַיַּעַשׂ, וַיְמַלֵּא, and וַיְהִי, are simply a continuation of the first clause, and therefore to be rendered as pluperfects. Micah's *beth Elohim* (house of God) was a domestic temple belonging to Micah's house, according to chap. xviii. 15–18. מִלֵּא אֶת־יָד, to fill the hand, *i.e.* to invest with the priesthood, to institute as priest (see at Lev. vii. 37). The *ephod* was an imitation of the high priest's shoulder-dress (see at chap. viii. 27). The *teraphim* were images of household gods, penates, who were worshipped as the givers of earthly prosperity, and as oracles (see at Gen. xxxi. 19).—In ver. 6 it is observed, in explanation of this unlawful conduct, that at that time there was no king in Israel, and every one did what was right in his own eyes.

Vers. 7–13. *Appointment of a Levite as Priest.*—Vers. 7 sqq. In the absence of a Levitical priest, Micah had first of all appointed one of his sons as priest at his sanctuary. He afterwards found a Levite for this service. A young man from Bethlehem in Judah, of the family of Judah, who, being a Levite, stayed (גָּר) there (in Bethlehem) as a stranger, left this town to sojourn "*at the place which he should find,*" *sc.* as a place that would afford him shelter and support, and came up to the mountains of Ephraim to Micah's house, "making his journey," *i.e.* upon his journey. (On the use of the *inf. constr.* with לְ in the sense of the Latin gerund in *do*, see *Ewald*, § 280, *d.*) Bethlehem was not a Levitical town. The young Levite from Bethlehem was neither born there nor made a citizen of the place, but simply "sojourned there," *i.e.* dwelt there temporarily as a stranger. The further statement as to his descent (*mishpachath Judah*) is not to be understood as signifying that he was a descendant of some family in the tribe of Judah, but simply that he belonged to the Levites who dwelt in the tribe of Judah, and were reckoned in all civil matters as belonging to that tribe. On the division of the land, it is true that it was only to the priests that dwelling-places were allotted in the inheritance of this tribe (Josh. xxi. 9–19), whilst the rest of the Levites, even the non-priestly members of the family of Kohath, received their dwelling-places among the other tribes (Josh. xxi. 20 sqq.). At the same time, as many of the towns which were allotted to the different tribes remained for a long time in the possession of the Canaanites, and the Israelites did not enter at once into the full and undisputed possession of their inheritance, it might easily so happen that different towns which were allotted to the Levites remained in possession of the Canaanites, and consequently that the Levites were compelled to seek a settlement in other places. It might also happen that individuals among the Levites themselves, who were disinclined to perform the service assigned them by the law, would remove from the Levitical towns and seek some other occupation elsewhere (see also at chap. xviii. 30).[1]—Ver. 10. Micah made this proposal to the Levite : " *Dwell with me, and become my father and priest; I will give thee ten shekels of silver yearly, and fitting out with clothes and maintenance.*" אָב, *father*, is an honourable title given to a priest as a paternal friend and spiritual adviser, and is also used with reference to prophets in 2 Kings vi. 21 and xiii. 14, and applied to Joseph in Gen. xlv. 8. לַיָּמִים, *for the days*, sc. for which a person was engaged, *i.e.* for the year (cf. 1 Sam. xxvii. 7, and Lev. xxv. 29). " *And the Levite went*," *i.e.* went to Micah's house. This meaning is evident from the context. The repetition of the subject, " the Levite," precludes our connecting it with the following verb וַיּוֹאֶל.—In vers. 11–13 the result is summed up. The Levite resolved (see at Deut. i. 5) to dwell with Micah, who treated him as one of his sons, and entrusted him with the priesthood at his house of God. And Micah rejoiced that he had got a Levite as priest, and said, " *Now I know that Jehovah will prosper me.*" This belief, or, to speak more correctly, superstition, for which Micah was very speedily to atone, proves that at that time the tribe of Levi held the position assigned it in the law of Moses; that is to say, that it was regarded as the tribe elected by God for the performance of divine worship.

Chap. xviii. THE IMAGE-WORSHIP REMOVED TO LAISH-DAN.

---

[1] There is no reason, therefore, for pronouncing the words מִמִּשְׁפַּחַת יְהוּדָה (of the family of Judah) a gloss, and erasing them from the text, as *Houbigant* proposes. The omission of them from the *Cod. Vat.* of the LXX., and from the Syriac, is not enough to warrant this, as they occur in the *Cod. Al.* of the LXX., and their absence from the authorities mentioned may easily be accounted for from the difficulty which was felt in explaining their meaning. On the other hand, it is impossible to imagine any reason for the interpolation of such a gloss into the text.

—Vers. 1–10. *Spies sent out by the tribe of Dan,* to seek for a place suitable for a settlement, and their success.—Ver. 1. This took place at a time when Israel had no king, and the tribe of the Danites sought an inheritance for themselves to dwell in, because until that day no such portion had fallen to them among the tribes as an inheritance. To the expression לֹא נָפְלָה (had not fallen) we must supply נַחֲלָה as the subject from the previous clause; and בְּנַחֲלָה signifies in the character of a *nachalah, i.e.* of a possession that could be transmitted as hereditary property from father to son. נָפַל, to fall, is used with reference to the falling of the lot (*vid.* Num. xxxiv. 2, Josh. xiii. 6, etc.). The general statement, that as yet no inheritance had fallen to the tribe of Dan by lot, has its limitation in the context. As the Danites, according to ver. 2, sent out five men from Zorea and Eshtaol, and, according to ver. 11, six hundred men equipped for fight went out to Laish, which the spies had discovered to be a place well fitted for a settlement, and had settled there, it is very evident from this that the Danites were not absolutely without an inheritance, but that hitherto they had not received one sufficient for their wants. The emigrants themselves were already settled in Zorea and Eshtaol, two of the towns that had fallen to the tribe of Dan by lot (Josh. xix. 41). Moreover, the six hundred equipped Danites, who went out of these towns, were only a very small part of the tribe of Danites, which numbered 64,400 males of twenty years old and upwards at the last census (Num. xxvi. 43). For a tribe of this size the land assigned by Joshua to the tribe of Dan, with all the towns that it contained, was amply sufficient. But from chap. i. 34 we learn that the Amorites forced the Danites into the mountains, and would not allow them to come down into the plain. Consequently they were confined to a few towns situated upon the sides or tops of the mountains, which did not supply all the room they required. Feeling themselves too weak to force back the Canaanites and exterminate them, one portion of the Danites preferred to seek an inheritance for themselves somewhere else in the land. This enterprise and emigration are described in vers. 2 sqq. The time cannot be determined with perfect certainty, as all that can be clearly inferred from ver. 12, as compared with chap. xiii. 25, is, that it took place some time before the days of Samson. Many expositors have therefore assigned it to the period immediately following the defeat of Jabin by Barak (chap. iv. 24), because it was not till after the overthrow of this powerful king of the Canaanites that conquests were possible in the north of Canaan, and the tribe of Dan at that time still remained in ships (chap. v. 17), so that it had not yet left the territory assigned it by the sea-shore (Josh. xix.). But these arguments have neither of them any force; for there is nothing surprising in the fact that Danites should still be found by the sea-shore in the time of Deborah, even if Danite families from Zorea and Eshtaol had settled in Laish long before, seeing that these emigrants formed but a small fraction of the whole tribe, and the rest remained in the possessions assigned them by Joshua. Moreover, the strengthening of the force of the Canaanites, and the extension of their dominion in the north, did not take place till 150 years after Joshua, in the days of Jabin; so that long before Jabin the town of Laish may have been conquered by the Danites, and taken possession of by them. In all probability this took place shortly after the death of Joshua, as we may infer from ver. 30 (see the exposition of this verse).—Ver. 2. To spy out and explore the land for the object mentioned, the Danites sent out five brave men "*out of their* (the Danites') *ends*," *i.e.* from their whole body (*vid.* 1 Kings xii. 31, xiii. 33, and the commentary on Gen. xix. 4). They came up to the mountains of Ephraim, and as far as Micah's house, where they passed the night.—Vers. 3–6. When they were at Micah's house and recognised the voice of the young Levite, *i.e.* heard his voice, and perceived from his dialect that he was not a native of these mountains, they turned aside there, *sc.* from the road into the house, near to which they rested, and asked him, "*Who brought thee hither, and what doest thou at this place? what hast thou to do here?*" When he told them his history ("thus and thus," *lit.* according to this and that; cf. 2 Sam. xi. 25, 1 Kings xiv. 5), they said to him, "*Ask God, we pray thee, that we may learn whether our way will be prosperous.*" שָׁאַל בֵּאלֹהִים, used for asking the will of God, as in chap. i. 1, except that here the inquiry was made through the medium of the imitation of the ephod and the worship of an image. And he said to them, *sc.* after making inquiry of the divine oracle, "*Go in peace; straight before Jehovah is your way,*" *i.e.* it is known and well-pleasing to Him (*vid.* Prov. v. 21, Jer. xvii. 16).— Ver. 7. Thus the five men proceeded to *Laish*, which is called *Leshem* in Josh. xix. 47, and was named *Dan* after the conquest by the Danites,—a place on the central source of the Jordan, the present *Tell el Kadi* (see at Josh. xix. 47),—and saw the people of the town dwelling securely after the manner of the Sidonians, who lived by trade and commerce, and did not go out to war. יֹשֶׁבֶת is the predicate to אֶת־הָעָם, and the feminine is to be explained from the fact that the writer had the population before his mind (see *Ewald,* § 174, *b.*); and the use of the masculine in the following words, שֹׁקֵט וּבֹטֵחַ, which are in apposition, is not at variance with this. The connection of יֹשֶׁבֶת with בְּקִרְבָּהּ, which *Bertheau* revives from the earlier commentators, is opposed to the genius of the Hebrew language. שֹׁקֵט וּבֹטֵחַ, " *living quietly and safely there.*" וְאֵין־מַכְלִים וגו׳, " *and no one who seized the government to himself did any harm to them in the land.*" הַכְלִים, to shame, then to do an injury (1 Sam. xxv. 7). מַכְלִים דָּבָר, shaming with regard to a thing, *i.e.* doing any kind of injury. עֶצֶר, dominion, namely tyrannical rule, from עָצַר, *imperio coercere.* The rendering " riches" (θησαυρός, LXX.), which some give to this word, is founded simply upon a confounding of עֶצֶר with אוֹצָר. יָרַשׁ does not mean " to possess," but " to take possession of," and that by force (as in 1 Kings xxi. 18). " *And they were far from the Sidonians,*" so that in the event of a hostile invasion they could not obtain any assistance from this powerful city. *Grotius* draws the very probable conclusion from these words, that Laish may have been a colony of the Sidonians. " *And they had nothing to do with* (other) *men,*" *i.e.* they did not live in any close association with the inhabitants of other towns, so as to be able to obtain assistance from any other quarter.—Vers. 8, 9. On their return, the spies said to their fellow-citizens, in reply to the question מָה אַתֶּם, " *What have you accomplished?*" " *Up, let us go up against them* (the inhabitants of Laish), *for the land is very good, and ye are silent,*" *i.e.* standing inactive (1 Kings xxii. 3; 2 Kings vii. 9). " *Be not slothful to go* (to proceed thither), *to come and take possession of the land !*"—Ver. 10. " *When ye arrive, ye will come to a secure people* (*i.e.* a people living in careless security, and therefore very easy to overcome) ; *and the land is broad on both sides* (*i.e.* furnishes space to dwell in, and also to extend : *vid.* Gen. xxxiv. 21, 1 Chron. iv. 40); *for God has given it into your hand.*" They infer this from the oracular reply they had received from the Levite (ver. 6). " *A place where there is no want of anything that is in the land* (of Canaan)."

Vers. 11–29. *Removal of Six Hundred Danites to Laish— Robbery of Micah's Images—Conquest of Laish, and Settlement there.* —Vers. 11, 12. In consequence of the favourable account of the spies who returned, certain Danites departed from Zorea and Eshtaol, to the number of 600 men, accoutred with weapons of war, with their families and their possessions in cattle and goods (see ver. 21), and encamped by the way at Kirjath-jearim (*i.e.* **Kuriyet Enab** ; see Josh. ix. 17), in the tribe territory of Judah, at a place which received the permanent name of *Mahaneh Dan* (camp of Dan) from that circumstance, and was situated behind, *i.e.* to the west of, Kirjath-jearim (see at chap. xiii. 25). The fact that this locality received a standing name from the circumstance described, compels us to assume that the Danites had encamped there for a considerable time, for reasons which we cannot determine from our want of other information. The emigrants may possibly have first of all assembled here, and prepared and equipped themselves for their further march.—Ver. 13. From this point they went across to the mountains of Ephraim, and came to Micah's house, *i.e.* to a place near it.—Ver. 14. Then the five men who had explored the land, viz. Laish (*Laish* is in apposition to הָאָרֶץ, the land), said to their brethren (tribe-mates), " *Know ye that in these houses* (the village or place where Micah dwelt) *there are an ephod and tera-phim, and image and molten work* (see at chap. xvii. 4, 5) ? *and now know what ye will do.*" The meaning of these last words is very easily explained : do not lose this opportunity of obtaining a worship of our own for our new settlement.—Ver. 15. Then they turned from the road thither, and went to the house of the young Levite, the house of Micah, and asked him (the Levite) concerning his health, *i.e.* saluted him in a friendly manner (see Gen. xliii. 27, Ex. xviii. 7, etc.).—Ver. 16. The 600 men, however, placed them-selves before the door.—Ver. 17. Then the five spies went up, *sc.* into Micah's house of God, which must therefore have been in an upper room of the building (see 2 Kings xxiii. 12, Jer. xix. 13), and took the image, ephod, etc., whilst the priest stood before the door with the 600 armed men. With the words בָּאוּ וגו׳ the narra-tive passes from the aorist or historical tense וַיַּעֲלוּ into the perfect. " The perfects do not denote the coming and taking on the part of the five men as a continuation of the previous account, but place the coming and taking in the same sphere of time as that to which the following clause, ' and the priest stood,' etc., belongs" (*Bertheau*). But in order to explain what appears very surprising, viz. that the priest should have stood before the gate whilst his house of God was being robbed, the course which the affair took is explained more clearly afterwards in vers. 18, 19, in the form of a circumstantial clause. Consequently the verbs in these verses ought to be ren-dered as pluperfects, and the different clauses comprised in one period, ver. 18 forming the protasis, and ver. 19 the apodosis.

" *Namely, when those* (five) *men had come into Micah's house, and had taken the image of the ephod, etc., and the priest had said to them,* What *are ye doing? they had said to him, Be silent, lay thy hand upon thy mouth and go with us, and become a father and priest to us* (see chap. xvii. 10). *Is it better to be a priest to the house of a single man, or to a tribe and family in Israel?*" The combination פֶּסֶל הָאֵפוֹד (the ephod-pesel), *i.e.* the image belonging to the ephod, may be explained on the ground, that the use of the ephod as a means of ascertaining the will of God presupposes the existence of an image of Jehovah, and does not prove that the ephod served as a covering for the *pesel*. The priest put on the ephod when he was about to inquire of God. The אוֹ in the second question is different from אִם, and signifies " or rather" (see Gen. xxiv. 55), indicating an improvement upon the first question (see *Ewald,* § 352, *a*.). Consequently it is not a sign of a later usage of speech, as *Bertheau* supposes. The word וּלְמִשְׁפָּחָה (unto a family) serves as a more minute definition or limitation of לְשֵׁבֶט (to a tribe). —Ver. 20. Then was the priest's heart glad (merry; cf. chap. xix. 6, 9, Ruth iii. 7), and he took the ephod, etc., and came amongst the people (the Danites). The first clause of this verse is attached to the supplementary statement in vers. 18, 19, for the purpose of linking on the further progress of the affair, which is given in the second clause; for, according to ver. 17, the priest could only receive the ephod, etc., into his charge from the hands of the Danites, since they had taken them out of Micah's God's house.— Ver. 21. The 600 Danites then set out upon their road again and went away; and they put the children, the cattle, and the valuable possessions in front, because they were afraid of being attacked by Micah and his people from behind. הַטַּף, " the little ones," includes both women and children, as the members of the family who were in need of protection (see at Ex. xii. 37). כְּבוּדָה is literally an adjective, signifying splendid; but here it is a neuter substantive: the valuables, not the heavy baggage. The 600 men had emigrated with their families and possessions.—Vers. 22, 23. The two clauses of ver. 22 are circumstantial clauses : " *When they* (the 600) *had got to some distance from Micah's house, and the men who were in the houses by Micah's house were called together, and had overtaken the Danites, they* (*i.e.* Micah and his people, whom he had called together from the neighbourhood to pursue the emigrants) *called to the Danites; and they turned their faces, and said to Micah, What is to thee* (what is the matter), *that thou hast gathered together?*"—

Vers. 24, 25. And when he replied, " *Ye have taken away my gods which I made, and the priest, and have departed; what is there still to me* (what have I left)? *and how can ye say to me, What is to thee?*" they ordered him to be silent, lest he should forfeit his life : "*Let not thy voice be heard among us, lest men of savage disposition* (מָרֵי נֶפֶשׁ as in 2 Sam. xvii. 8) *should fall upon thee* (*vid.* chap. xv. 12, viii. 21, etc.), *and thou shouldst not save thy life and that of thy household,*" *i.e.* shouldst bring death upon thyself and thy family. וְאָסַפְתָּה is also dependent upon פֶּן.—Ver. 26. Then the Danites went their way; but Micah, seeing that they were stronger than he, turned back and returned home.—Vers. 27, 28. And they (the Danites) had taken what Micah had made, *i.e.* his idols and his priest, and they fell upon Laish (בּוֹא עַל, to come over a person, to fall upon him, as in Gen. xxxiv. 25), a people living quietly and free from care (*vid.* ver. 7), smote them with the edge of the sword (see at Gen. xxxiv. 26), and burned down the city (cf. Josh. vi. 24), as it had no deliverer in its isolated condition (ver. 28a; cf. ver. 7). It was situated "*in the valley which stretches to Beth-rehob.*" This valley is the upper part of the *Huleh* lowland, through which the central source of the Jordan (*Leddan*) flows, and by which *Laish-Dan*, the present *Tell el Kadi*, stood (see at Josh. xix. 47). *Beth-rehob* is most probably the same place as the *Rehob* mentioned in Num. xiii. 21, and the *Beth-rehob* of 2 Sam. x. 6, which is there used to designate a part of Syria, and for which *Rehob* only is also used in ver. 8. *Robinson* (Bibl. Res. pp. 371 sqq.) supposes it to be the castle of *Hunin* or *Honin*, on the south-west of *Tell el Kadi;* but this is hardly correct (see the remarks on Num. xiii. 21, Pent. vol. iii. p. 88). The city, which lay in ashes, was afterwards re-built by the Danites, and called *Dan*, from the name of the founder of their tribe; and the ruins are still to be seen, as already affirmed, on the southern slope of the *Tell el Kadi* (see *Rob.* Bibl. Res. pp. 391–2, and the comm. on Josh. xix. 47).

Vers. 30, 31. *Establishment of the Image-worship in Dan.*— After the rebuilding of Laish under the name of Dan, the Danites set up the *pesel* or image of Jehovah, which they had taken with them out of Micah's house of God. "*And Jehonathan, the son of Gershom, the son of Moses, he and his sons were priests to the tribe of the Danites till the day of the captivity of the land.*" As the Danites had taken the Levite whom Micah had engaged for his private worship with them to Dan, and had promised him the priesthood (vers. 19 and 27), *Jehonathan* can hardly be any other than this Levite. He was a son of Gershom, the son of Moses (Ex. ıı. 22, xviii. 3 ; 1 Chron. xxiii. 14, 15). Instead of בֶּן־מֹשֶׁה, our Masoretic text has בֶּן־מְנַשֶּׁה with a hanging נ. With regard to this reading, the *Talmud* (Baba bathr. f. 109*b*) observes : "Was he a son of Gershom, or was he not rather a son of Moses? as it is written, the sons of Moses were Gershom and Eliezer (1 Chron. xxiii. 14), but because he did the deeds of Manasseh (the idolatrous son of Hezekiah, 2 Kings xxi.) the Scripture assigns him to the family of Manasseh." On this *Rabbabar bar Channa* observes, that "the prophet (*i.e.* the author of our book) studiously avoided calling Gershom *the son of Moses*, because it would have been ignominious to Moses to have had an ungodly son ; but he calls him *the son of Manasseh*, raising the נ, however, above the line, to show that it might either be inserted or omitted, and that he was the son of either מְנַשֶּׁה (Manasseh) or מֹשֶׁה (Moses),—of Manasseh through imitating his impiety, of Moses by descent" (cf. *Buxtorfi Tiber.* p. 171). Later Rabbins say just the same. *R. Tanchum* calls the writing *Menasseh*, with a hanging *nun*, a תִּקּוּן סוֹפְרִים, and speaks of *ben Mosheh* as *Kethibh*, and *ben Menasseh* as *Keri*. *Ben Mosheh* is therefore unquestionably the original reading, although the other reading *ben Menasseh* is also very old, as it is to be found in the *Targums* and the *Syriac* and *Sept.* versions, although some *Codd.* of the LXX. have the reading υἱοῦ Μωϋσῆ (*vid. Kennic. dissert. gener. in V. T.* § 21).[1] *Jerome* also has *filii Moysi.* At the same time, it does not follow with certainty from the reading *ben Gershom* that Jehonathan was actually a son of Gershom, as *ben* frequently denotes a grandson in such genealogical accounts, unknown fathers being passed over in the genealogies. There is very little probability of his having been a son, for the simple reason, that if Jehonathan was the same person as Micah's high priest—and there is no ground for doubting this—he is described as נַעַר in chap. xvii. 7, xviii. 3, 15, and therefore was at any rate a young man, whereas the son of Gershom and grandson of Moses would certainly have passed the age of youth by a few years after the death of Joshua. This Jehonathan and his sons performed the duties of the priesthood at Dan עַד־יוֹם גְּלוֹת הָאָרֶץ. This statement is obscure. גְּלוֹת הָאָרֶץ can hardly mean anything else than the carrying away of the people of the land into exile, that is to say, of

---

[1] These two readings of the LXX. seem to be fused together in the text given by *Theodoret* (*quæst.* xxvi.): Ἰωνάθαν γάρ φησιν υἱὸς Μανασσῆ, υἱοῦ Γερσώμ υἱοῦ Μωσῆ

the inhabitants of Dan and the neighbourhood at least, since גָּלָה is
the standing expression for this. Most of the commentators suppose
the allusion to be to the Assyrian captivity, or primarily to the
carrying away by Tiglath-Pileser of the northern tribes of Israel,
viz. the population of Gilead, Galilee, and the tribe of Naphtali, in
the midst of which Laish-Dan was situated (2 Kings xv. 29). But
the statement in ver. 31, "*And they set them up Micah's graven
image, which he made, all the time that the house of God was in
Shiloh,*" is by no means reconcilable with such a conclusion. We
find the house of God, *i.e.* the Mosaic tabernacle, which the congregation had erected at Shiloh in the days of Joshua (Josh. xviii.
1), still standing there in the time of Eli and Samuel (1 Sam. i. 3
sqq., iii. 21, iv. 3); but in the time of Saul it was at Nob (1 Sam.
xxi.), and during the reign of David at Gibeon (1 Chron. xvi. 39,
xxi. 29). Consequently "the house of God" only stood in Shiloh till
the reign of Saul, and was never taken there again. If therefore
Micah's image, which the Danites set up in Dan, remained there
as long as the house of God was at Shiloh, Jonathan's sons can
only have been there till Saul's time at the longest, and certainly
cannot have been priests at this sanctuary in Dan till the time of
the Assyrian captivity.[1] There are also other historical facts to be
considered, which render the continuance of this Danite image-
worship until the Assyrian captivity extremely improbable, or
rather preclude it altogether. Even if we should not lay any stress
upon the fact that the Israelites under Samuel put away the
Baalim and Astartes in consequence of his appeal to them to turn
to the Lord (1 Sam. vii. 4), it is hardly credible that in the time
of David the image-worship should have continued at Dan by the
side of the lawful worship of Jehovah which he restored and
organized, and should not have been observed and suppressed by
this king, who carried on repeated wars in the northern part of his
kingdom. Still more incredible would the continuance of this
image-worship appear after the erection of Solomon's temple, when
all the men of Israel, and all the elders and heads of tribes, came to
Jerusalem, at the summons of Solomon, to celebrate the consecration of this splendid national sanctuary (1 Kings v.–vii.). Lastly,
the supposition that the image-worship established by the Danites

---

[1] The impossibility of reconciling the statement as to time in ver. 31 with
the idea that "the captivity of the land" refers to the Assyrian captivity, is
admitted even by *Bleek* (Einl. p. 349), who adopts *Houbigant's* conjecture, viz.
גְּלוֹת הָאָרֹן, "the carrying away of the ark."

at Dan still continued to exist, is thoroughly irreconcilable with the fact, that when Jeroboam established the kingdom of the ten tribes he had two golden calves made as images of Jehovah for the subjects of his kingdom, and set up one of them at Dan, and appointed priests out of the whole nation who were not of the sons of Levi. If an image-worship of Jehovah had been still in existence in Dan, and conducted by Levitical priests, Jeroboam would certainly not have established a second worship of the same kind under priests who were not Levitical. All these difficulties preclude our explaining the expression, "the day of the captivity of the land," as referring to either the Assyrian or Babylonian captivity. It can only refer to some event which took place in the last years of Samuel, or the first part of the reign of Saul. *David Kimchi* and many others have interpreted the expression as relating to the carrying away of the ark by the Philistines, for which the words גָּלָה כְבוֹד מִיִשְׂרָאֵל are used in 1 Sam. iv. 21, 22 (*e.g. Hengstenberg*, Beitr. vol. ii. pp. 153 sqq.; *Hävernick*, Einl. ii. 1, p. 109 ; *O. v. Gerlach*, and others). With the carrying away of the ark of the covenant, the tabernacle lost its significance as a sanctuary of Jehovah. We learn from Ps. lxxviii. 59–64 how the godly in Israel regarded that event. They not only looked upon it as a casting away of the dwelling-place of God at Shiloh; but in the fact that Jehovah gave up His might and glory (*i.e.* the ark) into captivity, they discerned a surrender of the nation into the full power of its foes which resembled a carrying away into captivity. For, apart altogether from the description in Ps. lxxviii. 62–64, we may infer with certainty from the account of the tyranny which these foes still exercised over the Israelites in the time of Saul (1 Sam. xiii. 19–23), that, after this victory, the Philistines may have completely subjugated the Israelites, and treated them as their prisoners. We may therefore affirm with *Hengstenberg*, that "the author looked upon the whole land as carried away into captivity in its sanctuary, which formed as it were its kernel and essence." If, however, this figurative explanation of גְּלוֹת הָאָרֶץ should not be accepted, there is no valid objection to our concluding that the words refer to some event with which we have no further acquaintance, in which the city of Dan was conquered by the neighbouring Syrians, and the inhabitants carried away into captivity. For it is evident enough from the fact of the kings of *Zoba* being mentioned, in 1 Sam. xiv. 47, among the different enemies of Israel against whom Saul carried on war, that the Syrians also invaded Israel in the time of the Philistine supremacy, and carried Israelites away out of the conquered towns and districts. The Danite image-worship, however, was probably suppressed and abolished when Samuel purified the land and people from idolatry, after the ark had been brought back by the Philistines (1 Sam. ii. sqq.).

WAR OF THE CONGREGATION WITH THE TRIBE OF BENJAMIN ON ACCOUNT OF THE CRIME AT GIBEAH.—CHAP. XIX. XX.

This account belongs to the times immediately following the death of Joshua, as we may see from the fact that Phinehas, the son of Eleazar, the contemporary of Joshua, was high priest at that time (chap. xx. 28). In chap. xix. we have an account of the infamous crime committed by the inhabitants of Gibeah, which occasioned the war; in chap. xx. the war itself; and in chap. xxi. an account of what was afterwards done by the congregation to preserve the tribe of Benjamin, which was almost annihilated by the war.

Chap. xix. INFAMOUS CRIME OF THE INHABITANTS OF GIBEAH.—Vers. 1–14. At the time when there was no king in Israel, a Levite, who sojourned (*i.e.* lived outside a Levitical town) in the more remote parts of the mountains of Ephraim, took to himself a concubine out of Bethlehem in Judah, who proved unfaithful to him, and then returned to her father's house. יַרְכְּתֵי הַר־אֶפְרַיִם, the hinder or outermost parts of the mountains of Ephraim, are the northern extremity of these mountains; according to ver. 18, probably the neighbourhood of Shiloh. תִּזְנֶה עָלָיו, " *she played the harlot out beyond him,*" *i.e.* was unfaithful to her husband, " *and then went away from him,*" back to her father's house.—Vers. 3, 4. Some time afterwards, namely at the end of four months (אַרְבָּעָה חֳדָשִׁים is in apposition to יָמִים, and defines more precisely the יָמִים, or days), her husband went after her, " *to speak to her to the heart,*" *i.e.* to talk to her in a friendly manner (see Gen. xxxiv. 3), and to reconcile her to himself again, so that she might return; taking with him his attendant and a couple of asses, for himself and his wife to ride upon. The suffix attached to לְהָשִׁיבוֹ refers to לִבָּהּ, " to bring back her heart," to turn her to himself again. The *Keri* הֲשִׁיבָהּ is a needless conjecture. " *And she brought him into her father's house, and her father received his son-in-law with joy, and constrained him* (יֶחֱזַק־בּוֹ, *lit.* held him fast) *to remain there three days."* It is evident from this that the Levite had succeeded in reconciling his wife.—Vers. 5 sqq. Also on the fourth day, when he was about to depart in the morning, the Levite yielded to the persuasion of his father-in-law, that he would first of all strengthen his heart again with a bit of bread (סְעָד לֵב as in Gen. xviii. 5 ; the imperative form with ŏ is unusual) ; and then afterwards, whilst they were eating and drinking, he consented to stay another night. —Ver. 7. When he rose up to go, his father-in-law pressed him ; then he turned back (וַיָּשָׁב is quite in place, and is not to be altered into וַיֵּשֶׁב, according to the LXX. and one Heb. Cod.), and remained there for the night.—Ver. 8. And even in the morning of the fifth day he suffered himself to be induced to remain till the afternoon. הִתְמַהְמְהוּ is an imperative, "Tarry till the day turns," *i.e.* till mid-day is past.—Vers. 9, 10. When at length he rose up, with his concubine and his attendant, to go away, the father entreated his daughter once more : *" Behold the day has slackened to become evening, spend the night here ! Behold the declining of the day, spend the night here,"* etc. חֲנוֹת inf. of חָנָה, to bend, incline. The interchange of the plural and singular may be explained from the simple fact that the Levite was about to depart with his wife and attendant, but that their remaining or departing depended upon the decision of the man alone. But the Levite did not consent to remain any longer, but set out upon the road, and came with his companions to before Jebus, *i.e.* Jerusalem, which is only two hours from Bethlehem (compare *Rob.* Pal. ii. 375 with 379). עַד־נֹכַח, to *before* Jebus, for the road from Bethlehem to Shiloh went past Jerusalem. —Vers. 11 sqq. But as the day had gone far down when they were by Jebus (רַד, third *pers. perf.*, either of יָרַד with ' dropped like תַּתָּה in 2 Sam. xxii. 41 for נָתַתָּה, or from רָדַד in the sense of יָרַד), the attendant said to his master, *" Come, let us turn aside into this Jebusite city, and pass the night in it."* But his master was unwilling to enter a city of the foreigners (נָכְרִי is a genitive), where there were none of the sons of Israel, and would pass over to Gibeah. *" Come* (לְךָ = לְכָה, Num. xxiii. 13), *we will draw near to one of the places* (which he immediately names), *and pass the night in Gibeah or Ramah."* These two towns, the present *Jeba* and *er Râm,* were not a full hour's journey apart, and stood opposite to one another, only about two and a half or three hours from Jerusalem (see at Josh. xviii. 25, 28).—Ver. 14. Then they went forward, and the sun went down upon them as they were near (at) Gibeah of Benjamin.

Vers. 15–30. And they turned aside thither to pass the night in Gibeah; and he (the Levite) remained in the market-place of the town, as no one received them into his house to pass the night. —Vers. 16 sqq. Behold, there came an old man from the field, who was of the mountains of Ephraim, and dwelt as a stranger in Gibeah, the inhabitants of which were Benjaminites (as is observed here, as a preliminary introduction to the account which follows). When he saw the traveller in the market-place of the town, he asked him whither he was going and whence he came; and when he had heard the particulars concerning his descent and his journey, he received him into his house. וְאֶת־בֵּית י' אֲנִי הֹלֵךְ (ver. 18), " *and I walk at the house of Jehovah, and no one receives me into his house*" (*Seb. Schm.*, etc.); not " I am going to the house of Jehovah" (*Ros., Berth.*, etc.), for הָלַךְ אֵת does not signify to go to a place, for which the simple accusative is used either with or without ה local. It either means " to go through a place" (Deut. i. 19, etc.), or " to go with a person," or, when applied to things, " to go about with anything" (see Job xxxi. 5, and *Ges.* Thes. p. 378). Moreover, in this instance the Levite was not going to the house of Jehovah (*i.e.* the tabernacle), but, as he expressly told the old man, from Bethlehem to the outermost sides of the mountains of Ephraim. The words in question explain the reason why he was staying in the market-place. Because he served at the house of Jehovah, no one in Gibeah would receive him into his house,[1] although, as he adds in ver. 19, he had everything with him that was requisite for his wants. " *We have both straw and fodder for our asses, and bread and wine for me and thy maid, and for the young man with thy servants. No want of anything at all,*" so as to cause him to be burdensome to his host. By the words " thy maid" and " thy servants" he means himself and his concubine, describing himself and his wife, according to the obsequious style of the East in olden times, as servants of the man from whom he was expecting a welcome.— Ver. 20. The old man replied, " Peace to thee," assuring him of a welcome by this style of greeting; " *only all thy wants upon me,*" *i.e.* let me provide for them. Thus the friendly host declined the offer made by his guest to provide for himself. " *Only do not pass the night in the market-place.*"—Ver. 21. He then took him into

---

[1] As *Seb. Schmidt* correctly observes, " the argument is taken from the indignity shown him: the Lord thinks me worthy to minister to Him, as a Levite, in His house, and there is not one of the people of the Lord who thinks me worthy to receive his hospitality."

his house, mixed fodder for his asses (יָבוֹל from בָּלַל, a *denom.* verb from בְּלִיל, to make a mixture, to give fodder to the beasts), and waited upon his guest with washing of feet, food, and drink (see Gen. xviii. 4 sqq., xix. 2).—Ver. 22. Whilst they were enjoying themselves, some worthless men of the city surrounded the house, knocking continuously at the door (הִתְדַּפֵּק, a form indicative of gradual increase), and demanding of the master of the house that he would bring out the man who had entered his house, that they might know him,—the very same demand that the Sodomites had made of Lot (Gen. xix. 6 sqq.). The construct state אַנְשֵׁי בְנֵי־בְלִיַּעַל is used instead of אֲנָשִׁים בְּנֵי־בל׳ (Deut. xiii. 14, etc.), because בְנֵי בְלִיַּעַל is regarded as *one* idea : people of worthless fellows. Other cases of the same kind are given by *Ewald*, Lehrb. § 289, *c.*—Vers. 23 sqq. The old man sought, as Lot had done, to defend his guests from such a shameful crime by appealing to the sacred rights of hospitality, and by giving up his own virgin daughter and the concubine of his guest (see the remarks on Gen. xix. 7, 8). נְבָלָה, *folly*, used to denote shameful licentiousness and whoredom, as in Gen. xxxiv. 7 and Deut. xxii. 21. עַנּוּ אוֹתָם, "humble them." The masculine is used in אוֹתָם and לָהֶם as the more general gender, instead of the more definite feminine, as in Gen. xxxix. 9, Ex. i. 21, etc.—Vers. 25 sqq. But as the people would not listen to this proposal, the man (no doubt the master of the house, according to ver. 24) took his (the guest's) concubine (of course with the consent of his guest) and led her out to them, and they abused her the whole night. It is not stated how it was that they were satisfied with this ; probably because they felt too weak to enforce their demand. הִתְעַלֵּל בְּ, to exercise his power or wantonness upon a person (see Ex. x. 2).—Ver. 26. When the morning drew on (*i.e.* at the first dawn of day), the woman fell down before the door of the house in which אֲדוֹנֶיהָ, "her lord," *i.e.* her husband, was, and lay there till it was light, *i.e.* till sunrise.—Ver. 27. There her husband found her, when he opened the house-door to go his way (having given up all thought of receiving her back again from the barbarous crowd), "*lying before the house-door, and her hands upon the threshold*" (*i.e.* with outstretched arms), and giving no answer to his word, having died, that is to say, in consequence of the ill-treatment of the night. He then took the corpse upon his ass to carry it to his place, *i.e.* to his home.—Ver. 29. As soon as he arrived there, he cut up the body, according to its bones (as they cut slaughtered animals in pieces : see at Lev. i. 6), into twelve pieces, and sent

them (the corpse in its pieces) into the whole of the territory of
Israel, *i.e.* to all the twelve tribes, in the hope that every one who
saw it would say : No such thing has happened or been seen since
the coming up of Israel out of Egypt until this day. Give ye heed
to it (שִׂימוּ for שִׂימוּ לֵב) ; make up your minds and say on, *i.e.* decide
how this unparalleled wickedness is to be punished. Sending the
dissected pieces of the corpse to the tribes was a symbolical act, by
which the crime committed upon the murdered woman was placed
before the eyes of the whole nation, to summon it to punish the
crime, and was naturally associated with a verbal explanation of
the matter by the bearer of the pieces. See the analogous proceeding on the part of Saul (1 Sam. xi. 7), and the Scythian custom
related by *Lucian* in Toxaris, c. 48, that whoever was unable to
procure satisfaction for an injury that he had received, cut an ox
in pieces and sent it round, whereupon all who were willing to help
him to obtain redress took a piece, and swore that they would stand
by him to the utmost of their strength. The perfects וְהָיָה — וְאָמַר
(ver. 30) are not used for the imperfects *c. vav consec.* וַיְהִי — וַיֹּאמֶר,
as *Hitzig* supposes, but as simple perfects (*perfecta conseq.*), expressing the result which the Levite expected from his conduct ;
and we have simply to supply לֵאמֹר before וְהָיָה, which is often
omitted in lively narrative or animated conversation (compare, for
example, Ex. viii. 5 with Judg. vii. 2). The perfects are used by the
historian instead of imperfects with a simple *vav*, which are commonly employed in clauses indicating intention, "because what he
foresaw would certainly take place, floated before his mind as a
thing already done " (*Rosenmüller*). The moral indignation, which
the Levite expected on the part of all the tribes at such a crime
as this, and their resolution to avenge it, are thereby exhibited not
merely as an uncertain conjecture, but a fact that was sure to
occur, and concerning which, as chap. xx. clearly shows, he had not
deceived himself.

Chap. xx. WAR WITH BENJAMIN ON THE PART OF ALL THE
OTHER TRIBES.—The expectation of the Levite was fulfilled. The
congregation of Israel assembled at Mizpeh to pass sentence upon
Gibeah, and formed the resolution that they would not rest till the
crime was punished as it deserved (vers. 1–10). But when the
Benjaminites refused to deliver up the offenders in Gibeah, and
prepared to offer resistance, the other tribes began to make war
upon Gibeah and Benjamin (vers. 11–19), but were twice defeated

by the Benjaminites with very great loss (vers. 20–28). At length, however, they succeeded by an act of stratagem in taking Gibeah and burning it to the ground, and completely routing the Benjaminites, and also in putting to death all the men and cattle that they found in the other towns of this tribe, and laying the towns in ashes, whereby the whole of the tribe of Benjamin was annihilated, with the exception of a very small remnant (vers. 29–48).

Vers. 1–11. *Decree of the Congregation concerning Gibeah.*— Vers. 1, 2. All the Israelites went out (rose up from their dwelling-places) to assemble together as a congregation like one man; all the tribes from Dan, the northern boundary of the land (*i.e.* Dan-laish, chap. xviii. 29), to Beersheba, the most southerly town of Canaan (see at Gen. xxi. 31), and the land of Gilead, *i.e.* the inhabitants of the land to the east of the Jordan, "*to Jehovah at Mizpeh*" in Benjamin, *i.e.* the present *Nebi-samwil,* in the neighbourhood of Kirjath-jearim, on the western border of the tribe of Benjamin (see at Josh. xviii. 26). It by no means follows with certainty from the expression "*to Jehovah,*" that there was a sanctuary at Mizpeh, or that the ark of the covenant was taken thither, but simply that the meeting took place in the sight of Jehovah, or that the congregation assembled together to hold a judicial court, which they held in the name of Jehovah, analogous to the expression *el-Elohim* in Ex. xxi. 6, xxii. 7. It was not essential to a judicial proceeding that the ark should be present. At this assembly the *pinnoth* (the corner-pillars) *of the whole nation presented themselves, i.e.* the heads and fathers as the supports of the congregation or of the state organism (*vid.* 1 Sam. xiv. 38, Isa. xix. 13), even of all the tribes of Israel, four hundred thousand men on foot, drawing the sword, *i.e.* armed foot soldiers ready for battle.—Ver. 3. "*The Benjaminites heard that the children of Israel* (the rest of the Israelites, the eleven tribes) *had come up to Mizpeh ;*" but they themselves were not found there. This follows from the fact that nothing is said about the Benjaminites coming, and still more clearly from ver. 13, where it is stated that the assembled tribes sent men to the Benjaminites, after holding their deliberations and forming their resolutions, to call them to account for the crime that had been committed in the midst of them. Consequently the question with which the whole affair was opened, "*Say, how did this wicked deed take place?*" is not to be regarded as addressed to the two parties, the inhabitants of Gibeah or the Benjaminites *and* the Levite (*Bertheau*), but as a summons to all who were assembled to relate

what any one knew respecting the occurrence.—Vers. 4–7. Then
the Levite, the husband of the murdered woman, described the
whole affair. בַּעֲלֵי הַגִּבְעָה, the owners or citizens of Gibeah (see at
chap. ix. 2). *"Me they intended to kill:"* the Levite draws this
conclusion from what had happened to his wife ; the men of Gibeah
had not expressed any such intention in chap. xix. 22. *"All the
country (lit. field) of the inheritance of Israel,"* i.e. all the land of
the Israelites. זִמָּה is applied to the vice of lewdness, as in Lev.
xviii. 17, which was to be punished with death. הָבוּ לָכֶם וגו׳, *"give
yourselves* (לָכֶם is *dat. comm.*) *word and counsel here,"* i.e. make up
your minds and pass sentence (*vid.* 2 Sam. xvi. 20). הֲלֹם, here,
where you are all assembled together.—Ver. 8. Then all the people
rose up as one man, saying, *"We will not any of us go into his tent,
neither will we any of us return to his house,"* sc. till this crime is
punished. The sentence follows in ver. 9 : *"This is the thing that
we will do,"* i.e. this is the way in which we will treat Gibeah :
"against it by lot" (*sc.* we will act). The *Syriac* gives the sense
correctly—We will cast lots upon it ; but the LXX. quite erro
neously supply ἀναβησόμεθα (we will go up) ; and in accordance
with this, many expositors connect the words with ver. 10 in the
following sense : "We will choose one man out of every ten by lot,
to supply the army with the necessary provision during the expedition." This is quite a mistake, because in this way a subordinate
point, which only comes into consideration in connection with the
execution of the sentence, would be made the chief point, and the
sentence itself would not be given at all. The words *"against it
by lot"* contain the resolution that was formed concerning the sinful
town, and have all the enigmatical brevity of judicial sentences,
and are to be explained from the course laid down in the Mosaic
law with regard to the Canaanites, who were to be exterminated,
and their land divided by lot among the Israelites. Consequently
the meaning is simply this : "Let us proceed with the lot against
Gibeah," i.e. let us deal with it as with the towns of the Canaanites,
conquer it, lay it in ashes, and distribute its territory by lot. In
ver. 10 a subordinate circumstance is mentioned, which was necessary to enable them to carry out the resolution that had been made.
As the assembled congregation had determined to keep together
for the purpose of carrying on war (ver. 8), it was absolutely
necessary that resources should be provided for those who were
actively engaged in the war. For this purpose they chose one man
in every ten *"to fetch provision for the people,"* לַעֲשׂוֹת לְבוֹאָם, *"that*

*they might do on their coming to Gibeah of Benjamin according to all
the folly which had been done in Israel,"* i.e. might punish the
wickedness in Gibeah as it deserved.—Ver. 11. Thus the men of
Israel assembled together against Gibeah, united as one man.
חֲבֵרִים, *lit.* as comrades, simply serves to strengthen the expression
"as one man." With this remark, which indicates briefly the
carrying out of the resolution that was adopted, the account of the
meeting of the congregation is brought to a close; but the actual
progress of the affair is really anticipated, inasmuch as what is
related in vers. 12–21 preceded the expedition in order of time.

Vers. 12–19. Before the tribes of Israel entered upon the war,
they sent men to all the tribes of Benjamin, who were to demand
that the culprits in Gibeah should be given up to be punished, that
the evil might thus be exterminated from Israel, according to the
law in Deut. xxii. 22 as compared with chap. xiii. 6 and xvii. 12.
"*The tribes of Benjamin*" are the same as "the families of Benjamin:" the historian pictured to himself the different divisions of
the tribe of Benjamin as warlike powers about to carry on a war
with the other tribes of Israel. The word *shebet* (tribe) is used in
a different way in Num. iv. 18. But the Benjaminites would not
hearken to the voice of their brethren, the other tribes of Israel.
The *Keri* (sons of Benjamin) is a needless alteration, since *Benjamin* may be construed with the plural as a collective term. By
refusing this just demand on the part of the other tribes, the
Benjaminites took the side of the culprits in Gibeah, and compelled
the congregation to make war upon the whole tribe.—Vers. 14
sqq. Both sides now made their preparations. The Benjaminites
assembled together at Gibeah out of their different towns, and
"*were mustered 26,000 men drawing the sword, beside the inhabitants
of Gibeah they were mustered, 700 picked men*" (הִתְפָּקְדוּ, with the
reduplication dropped, like the *Hothpael* in Num. i. 47). "*Out of
all this people there were 700 picked men, lamed in the right hand,
all these* (were) *slinging with a stone* (hitting) *at a hair's breadth
without fail.*" These statements are not quite clear. Since, according to the distinct words of ver. 16, the 700 slingers with their
left hands were "out of the whole people," i.e. out of the whole
number of fighting men mentioned in ver. 16, they cannot be the
same as the 700 chosen men referred to in ver. 15, notwithstanding
the similarity in the numbers and the expression "chosen men."
The obscurity arises chiefly from the word הִתְפָּקְדוּ in ver. 15, which
is separated by the Masoretic accents from מ' שֶׁבַע, and connected

with the previous words : " *Beside the inhabitants of Gibeah they* (the men of the towns of Benjamin) *were mustered.*" On the other hand, the earlier translators took the clause as a relative one : " Beside the inhabitants of Gibeah, who were mustered 700 men." And this seems absolutely necessary, because otherwise the following words, " 700 picked men," would stand without any connection ; whilst we should certainly expect at least to find the *cop. vav*, if these 700 men were not inhabitants of Gibeah. But even if התפקדו should be taken as a simple repetition of ויתפקדו, according to the analogy of Deut. iii. 5 and 1 Kings v. 30, the statement which follows could not be understood in any other way than as referring to the number of the fighting men of Gibeah. There is something striking too in the fact that only Benjaminites " out of the cities" are mentioned, and that emphasis is laid upon this by the repetition of the expression " out of the cities" (vers. 14, 15). Some have inferred from this, that the Benjaminites as the rulers had settled in the towns, whilst the Canaanites who had been subdued settled as dependants in the villages (*Bertheau*) ; or that the Benjaminites had formed military brotherhoods, the members of which lived unmarried in the towns, and that this may possibly account for the abominable crime to which the inhabitants of Gibeah were addicted, and in relation to which the whole tribe took their part (*O. v. Gerlach*). But such inferences as these are extremely uncertain, as the cities may be mentioned *a potiori* for all the places inhabited by this tribe. There is another difficulty in the numbers. According to vers. 14, 15, the total number of the fighting men of Benjamin amounted to 26,000 and 700, without reckoning Gibeah. But, according to the account of the battle, 25,100 were slain (ver. 35), viz. 18,000 in the principal engagement, 5000 as a gleaning, and 2000 in the pursuit, *i.e.* 25,000 men in all (vers. 44–46), and only 600 were left, who fled into the desert to the rock Rimmon (ver. 47). According to these accounts, the whole tribe would have contained only 25,100 + 600 = 25,700 fighting men, or 25,000 + 600 = 25,600. Accordingly, in ver. 15, the LXX. (*Cod. Al.* etc.) and *Vulgate* give only 25,000 men ; whilst the rest of the ancient versions have 26,000, in agreement with the Masoretic text. *Josephus* (Ant. v. 2, 10) also gives the number of fighting men in Benjamin as 25,600, of whom 600 were splendid slingers ; but he has merely taken the numbers from vers. 44–47. Now, although mistakes do frequently occur in the numbers given, it is a most improbable supposition that we have a mistake of this kind (26,000 for 25,000) in the instance before us, since even the latter number would not agree with vers. 44 sqq. ; and the assumption, that in vers. 35 and 44 sqq. we have an account of *all* the Benjaminites who fell, finds no support whatever in the history itself. In the verses referred to we have simply a statement of the number of Benjaminites who fell in the defeat which they sustained on the third day, whereas the victories which they gained on the first and second days could hardly have been obtained without some loss on their part; on the contrary, we may confidently assume that they would not lose less than a thousand men, though these are not mentioned in the brief account before us. The other difference between ver. 35 and vers. 44–46, viz. that 25,100 are given in the one and 25,000 in the other, may be explained on the simple assumption that we have only the full thousands mentioned in the latter, whilst the exact number is given in the former. " *Left-handed :*" see at chap. iii. 15.—Vers. 17, 18. The forces of the other tribes amounted when numbered to 400,000 men. These numbers (26,000 Benjaminites and 400,000 Israelites) will not appear too great if we consider that the whole of the congregation of Israel took part in the war, with the simple exception of Jabesh in Gilead (chap. xxi. 8), and that in the time of Moses the twelve tribes numbered more than 600,000 men of twenty years old and upwards (Num. xxvi.), so that not much more than two-thirds of the whole of the fighting men went out to the war.—Ver. 18. Before opening the campaign the Israelites went to Bethel, to inquire of God which tribe should commence the war, *i.e.* should fight at the head of the other tribes (on the fact itself, see chap. i. 1); and God appointed the tribe of Judah, as in chap. i. 2. They went to Bethel,[1] not to Shiloh, where the tabernacle was standing, because that place was too far from the seat of war. The ark of the covenant was therefore brought to Bethel, and Phinehas the high priest inquired of the Lord before it through the Urim and Thummim (vers. 27, 28). Bethel was on the northern boundary of the tribe of Benjamin, and was consecrated to this purpose before any other place by the revelations of God which had been made to the patriarch Jacob there (Gen. xxviii. and xxxv.).—Ver. 19. Thus equipped, the Israelites proceeded against Gibeah.

Vers. 20–28. As soon as the Israelites had posted themselves at Gibeah in battle array (עֲרֹךְ מִלְחָמָה, to put in a row, or arrange the war or conflict, *i.e.* to put themselves in battle array, 1 Sam. iv. 2,

---

[1] Rendered " the house of God" in the English version.—Tr

xvii 2, etc.), the Benjaminites came out and destroyed 22,000 men of Israel upon that day. הִשְׁחִית אָרְצָה, to destroy to the earth, *i.e.* to lay dead upon the ground.—Ver. 22. Notwithstanding this terrible overthrow, the people strengthened themselves, and prepared again for battle, " at the same place" where they had made ready on the first day, " seeking out of pure vainglory to wipe out the stains and the disgrace which their previous defeat had brought upon them" (Berleb. Bible).—Ver. 23. But before renewing the conflict they went up to Bethel, wept there before Jehovah, *i.e.* before the sanctuary of the ark, where Jehovah was present in the midst of His people, enthroned between the cherubim, until the evening, and then inquired of the Lord (again through the high priest), " *Shall I again draw near to war with the children of Benjamin my brother*" (*i.e.* renew the war with him)? The answer ran thus: " *Advance against him.*"—Vers. 24, 25. But on the second day also the Benjaminites brought 18,000 of them to the ground. " The second day" is not the day following the first engagement, as if the battles had been fought upon two successive days, but the second day of actual fighting, which took place some days after the first, for the inquiry was made at Bethel as to the will of God between the two engagements.—Vers. 26 sqq. After this second terrible overthrow, " *the children of Israel*" (*i.e.* those who were engaged in the war), and " *all the people*," *i.e.* the rest of the people, those members of the congregation who were not capable of bearing arms, old men and women, came to Bethel, to complain to the Lord of their misfortune, and secure His favour by fasting and sacrifices. The congregation now discovered, from this repeated defeat, that the Lord had withdrawn His grace, and was punishing them. Their sin, however, did not consist in the fact that they had begun the war itself,—for the law in Deut. xxii. 22, to which they themselves had referred in ver. 13, really required this,—but rather in the state of mind with which they had entered upon the war, their strong self-consciousness, and great confidence in their own might and power. They had indeed inquired of God (*Elohim*) who should open the conflict; but they had neglected to humble themselves before Jehovah the covenant God, in the consciousness not only of their own weakness and sinfulness, but also of grief at the moral corruption of their brother-tribe. It is certainly not without significance, that in ver. 18 it is stated that " *they asked God*" (יִשְׁאֲלוּ בֵאלֹהִים), *i.e.* they simply desired a supreme or divine decision as to the question who should lead the van in the war; whereas, after the first defeat, they wept before *Jehovah*, and inquired of *Jehovah* (ver. 23), the covenant God, for whose law and right they were about to contend. But even then there were still wanting the humility and penitence, without which the congregation of the Lord could not successfully carry on the conflict against the ungodly. The remark in ver. 22, " *The people felt* (showed) *themselves strong, and added* (continued) *to set in array the war*," is thoroughly expressive of the feeling of the congregation. They resolved upon the continuance of the war, in the full consciousness of their superior power and numerical strength ; and it was not till afterwards that they complained to the Lord of their misfortune, and inquired whether they should renew the conflict. The question was followed by a corresponding answer on the part of God, " *Go up against him*," which certainly sanctioned the continuance of the war, but gave no promise as to the result, because the people, thinking that they might be certain of success, had not inquired about that at all. It was not till after the second severe defeat, when 22,000 and 18,000, the tenth part of the whole army, had fallen, that they humbled themselves before the Lord. They not only wept because of the calamity which had befallen them, but fasted the same day before the Lord, — the fasting being the manifest expression of the bending of the heart before God, — and offered burnt-offerings and peace-offerings. The *shelamim* here are not thank-offerings, but supplicatory offerings, presented to implore the gracious assistance of God, and to commemorate the enjoyment of fellowship with the Lord, through the sacrificial meal associated with this sacrifice (as in chap. xxi. 4, 1 Sam. xiii. 9, 2 Sam. xxiv. 25).—Vers. 27, 28. Having made these preparations, they inquired of the Lord whether they should continue the war, and received this reply : " *Go up* (against Benjamin) ; *for to-morrow I will give it unto thy hand*" (דְֽיָ, the hand of the congregation carrying on the war). To this the supplementary remark is appended, that the ark of the covenant was at Bethel in those days, and the high priest served before it. The expression " in those days" implies that the ark of the covenant was only temporarily at Bethel, and therefore had been brought thither from the tabernacle at Shiloh during this war.

Vers. 29–48. *The Victory on the Third Day's Engagement.*—Ver. 29. The account of this commences with the most important point, so far as their success was concerned : Israel set liers in wait (troops in ambush) round about Gibeah.—Ver. 30. They then advanced as on the former occasions.—Vers. 31, 32. The Benjaminites came out again to meet the people (of Israel), and were drawn away from the town (the perfect הָנְתְּקוּ without וְ is subordinate to the preceding verb, and defines more precisely the advance itself, whilst the mode in which they were drawn away from the town is not described more fully till vers. 32, 33), and began to smite the beaten of the people (who pretended to fly) as formerly upon the roads (where two roads part), of which one led up to Bethel and the other to Gibeah, into the field (Gibeah is the town at which the battle took place, that is to say, somewhere in the neighbourhood, so that a road might easily run from the field of battle towards the town into the field), "about (sc. putting to death) thirty men of Israel." This statement introduces the more precise definition of the חֲלָלִים.—Ver. 32. Then the Benjaminites supposed that Israel was beaten by them as before ; but the Israelites said : We will flee, and draw it (the tribe of Benjamin) away from the town to the roads (the highroads mentioned in ver. 31). On the Dagesh dirimens in נְתַקְנוּהוּ, see Ewald, § 92, c.—Ver. 33. Carrying out this plan, " all the men of Israel rose up from their place," i.e. left the place they had occupied, drew back, " and set themselves in battle array" in Baalthamar, i.e. palm-place, which still existed, according to the Onom., in the time of Eusebius, as a small place in the neighbourhood of Gibeah, bearing the name of Bethamar. While this was going on, the ambush of Israel broke forth from its position " from the plains of Geba." The ἀπ. λεγ. מַעֲרֵה, from עָרָה to strip, denotes a naked region destitute of wood. גֶּבַע is the masculine form for גִּבְעָה, and מִמַּעֲרֵה־גָבַע a more precise definition of מִמְּקוֹמוֹ. This rendering, which is the one given in the Targum, certainly appears the simplest explanation of a word that has been rendered in very different ways, and which the LXX. left untranslated as a proper name, Μαρααγαβέ. The objection raised to this, viz. that a naked level country was not a place for an ambush, has no force, as there is no necessity to understand the words as signifying that the treeless country formed the actual hiding-place of the ambush ; but the simple meaning is, that when the men broke from their hiding-place, they came from the treeless land towards the town. The rendering given by Rashi, Trem., and others, " on account of the stripping of Gibeah," is much less suitable, since, apart from the difficulty of taking מִן in different senses so close together, we should at least expect to find הָעִיר (the city) instead of גֶּבַע.—Ver. 34. Through the advance of the ambush there came 10,000 picked men of all

Israel " from opposite to Gibeah" (who now attacked in the rear
the Benjaminites who were pursuing the flying army of Israel);
" *and the contest became severe, since they* (the Benjaminites) *did not
know that the calamity was coming upon them.*"—Ver. 35. And
Jehovah smote Benjamin before Israel (according to His promise
in ver. 28), so that the Israelites destroyed of Benjamin on that
day twenty and five thousand and an hundred men (*i.e.* twenty-five
thousand and upwards).

This was the result of the battle, which the historian gives at
once, before entering more minutely into the actual account of the
battle itself. He does this in vers. 36–46 in a series of explanations,
of which one is attached to the other, for the most part in the form
of circumstantial clauses, so that it is not till ver. 46 that he again
comes to the result already announced in ver. 35.[1]—Ver. 36. The
Benjaminites, for instance, saw (this is the proper rendering of
וַיִּרְאוּ with *vav consec.*, which merely indicates the order of thought,
not that of time) that they were beaten, and the men of Israel
vacated the field before Benjamin (נָתַן מָקוֹם, to give place by falling
back and flying), because they relied upon the ambush which they
had placed against Gibeah. The Benjaminites did not perceive
this till the ambush fell upon their rear. But the ambush itself, as
is added in ver. 37 by way of further explanation, hastened and
fell (fell as quickly as possible) into Gibeah, and went thither and
smote the whole town with the edge of the sword. To this there is
added the further explanation in ver. 38 : " *And the arrangement
of the Israelites with the ambush was this : multiply, to cause smoke-
rising to ascend* (*i.e.* cause a great cloud of smoke to ascend) *out of
the city.*" The only objection that can be raised to this view of
הֶרֶב, as the imperative *Hiphil* of רָבָה, is the suffix ־ם attached to
לְהַעֲלוֹתָם, since this is unsuitable to a direct address. This suffix can
only be explained by supposing that there is an admixture of two
constructions, the direct appeal, and the indirect explanation, that
they were to cause to ascend. If this be not admitted, however, we
can only follow *Studer*, and erase the suffix as an error of the pen
occasioned by the following word מַשְׂאַת ; for the other course sug-

---

[1] The opinions expressed by *De Wette*, etc., that ver. 35 is spurious, and by
Bertheau, that vers. 36–46 contain a different account of the battle, simply
prove that they have overlooked this peculiarity in the Hebrew mode of writing
history, viz. that the general result of any occurrence is given as early as
possible, and then the details follow afterwards; whilst these critics have not
succeeded in adducing even apparent differences in support of their opinions.

gested by *Bertheau,* namely that הֶרֶב should be struck out as a gloss, is precluded by the circumstance that there is no possible way of explaining the interpolation of so appar̨ently unsuitable a word into the text. It certainly stood in the text used by the LXX., though they have most foolishly confounded הֶרֶב with חֶרֶב, and rendered it μάχαιρα.—Ver. 39. "*And the men of Israel turned in the battle:*" that is to say, as is afterwards more fully explained in vers. 39, 40, in the form of a long new circumstantial clause, whilst Benjamin had begun to smite, etc. (repeated from vers. 31, 32), and the cloud (הַמַּשְׂאֵת = מַשְׂאַת הֶעָשָׁן, ver. 38) had begun to ascend out of the city as a pillar of smoke, and Benjamin turned back, and behold the whole city ascended towards heaven (in smoke), Israel turned (fighting) and Benjamin was terrified, for it saw that misfortune had come upon it (see ver. 34). In ver. 41*a,* the thread of the narrative, which was interrupted by the long circumstantial clause, is again resumed by the repetition of "*and the men of Israel turned.*"— Ver. 42. The Benjaminites "*now turned* (flying) *before the Israelites to the way of the desert,*" *i.e.* no doubt the desert which rises from Jericho to the mountains of Bethel (Josh. xvi. 1). They fled therefore towards the north-east; but the battle had overtaken (reached or seized) them, and those out of the towns (had perished). The difficult expression וַאֲשֶׁר מֵהֶעָרִים, of which very different, and for the most part arbitrary, explanations have been given, can only be in apposition to the suffix attached to the verb: "Benjamin, and in fact those who had come to the help of Gibeah out of the towns of Benjamin" (see vers. 14, 15), *i.e.* all the Benjaminites. The following words, מַשְׁחִיתִים וגו', are a circumstantial clause explanatory of the previous clause, וְהַמִּלְחָמָה הדב': "*since they* (the men of Israel) *destroyed him* (Benjamin) *in the midst of it.*" The singular suffix בְּתוֹכוֹ does not refer to Benjamin, as this would yield no sense at all, but to the preceding words, "the way of the desert" (see ver. 45).— In ver. 43 the account is continued by three perfects attached to one another without a copula: "*they enclosed* (hedged round) *Benjamin, pursued him; at the place of rest they trod him down to before Gibeah eastwards.*" מְנוּחָה is not used adverbially in the sense of "quietly," which would not give any fitting meaning, but is an *accus. loci,* and signifies place of rest, as in Num. x. 33. The notice "to before Gibeah" refers to all three verbs.—Ver. 44. In this battle there fell of Benjamin 18,000 men, all brave men. The אֵת before כָּל־אֵלֶּה is not a preposition, "*with*" (as the LXX., *Cod. Al.,* and *Bertheau* render it), but a sign of the accusative. It serves to show that the thought which follows is governed by the principal clause, " *so far as all these were concerned, they were brave men.*"—Ver. 45. The remainder fled to the desert, to the rock (of the place) *Rimmon*, which is described in the *Onom.* (*s. v. Remmon*) as a *vicus* fifteen Roman miles to the north of Jerusalem. It has been preserved in the village of *Rummôn*, which stands upon and around the summit of a conical limestone mountain, and is visible in all directions (*Rob.* Pal. ii. p. 113). " *And they* (the Israelites) *smote as a gleaning upon the roads* 5000 *men.*" עוֹלֵל, to have a gleaning of the battle, *i.e.* to smite or slay, as it were, as a gleaning of the principal battle (*vid.* Jer. vi. 9). *Mesilloth* are the high-roads mentioned in ver. 31. " *And pursued them to Gideom, and smote of them* 2000 *more.*" The situation of Gideom, which is only met with here, is not precisely known ; but it must have been somewhere between Gibeah and Rimmon, as the rock Rimmon, according to ver. 47, afforded a safe place of refuge to the fugitives.—Ver. 46. On the total number of the slain, see the remarks on ver. 15.—In ver. 47 the statement already made in ver. 45 with regard to the flight is resumed ; and it is still further related, that 500 men reached the rock Rimmon, and dwelt there four months, *i.e.* till the occurrence described in chap. xxi. 13 sqq.—Ver. 48. The Israelites turned (from any further pursuit of the fugitive warriors of Benjamin) to the children of Benjamin, *i.e.* to such of the people of the tribe of Benjamin as were unarmed and defenceless, and smote them with the edge of the sword, " *from the town* (or towns) *onwards, men to cattle* (*i.e.* men, women, children, and cattle), *to every one who was found ;*" *i.e.* they cut down men and cattle without quarter, from the towns onwards even to those who were found elsewhere. עַד כָּל־הַנִּמְצָא (to all that was found) corresponds to מֵעִיר (from the city), and מְתֹם עַד־בְּהֵמָה (men to beast) serves as a more precise definition of the עִיר (city) : everything that was in the city, man and beast. מְתֹם is pointed wrongly for מְתִם, *men*, the reading in several MSS. and most of the early editions (see Deut. ii. 34, iii. 6). They also set fire to all the towns that were met with, *i.e.* all without exception. Thus they did the same to the Benjaminites as to the Canaanites who were put under the ban, carrying out the ban with the strictest severity.

PRESERVATION OF THE TRIBE OF BENJAMIN—THE REMNANT
PROVIDED WITH WIVES.—CHAP. XXI.

Through the extraordinary severity with which the tribes of
Israel had carried on the war against Benjamin, this tribe had been
reduced to 600 men, and thus brought very near to extermination.
Such a conclusion to the sanguinary conflict went to the heart of
the congregation. For although, when forming the resolution to
punish the unparalleled wickedness of the inhabitants of Gibeah
with all the severity of the law, they had been urged on by nothing
else than the sacred duty that was binding upon them to root out
the evil from their midst, and although the war against the whole
tribe of Benjamin was justified by the fact that they had taken the
side of the culprits, and had even received the approval of the
Lord ; there is no doubt that in the performance of this resolution,
and the war that was actually carried on, feelings of personal
revenge had disturbed the righteous cause in consequence of the
defeat which they had twice sustained at the hands of the Benjaminites, and had carried away the warriors into a war of extermination which was neither commanded by the law nor justified by
the circumstances, and had brought about the destruction of a whole
tribe from the twelve tribes of the covenant nation with the exception of a small vanishing remnant.   When the rash deed was done,
the congregation began most bitterly to repent.   And with repentance there was awakened the feeling of brotherly love, and also a
sense of duty to provide for the continuance of the tribe, which
had been brought so near to destruction, by finding wives for those
who remained, in order that the small remnant might grow into a
vigorous tribe again.

Vers. 1–14. The proposal to find wives for the six hundred
Benjaminites who remained was exposed to this difficulty, that the
congregation had sworn at Mizpeh (as is supplemented in ver. 1 to
the account in chap. xx. 1–9) that no one should give his daughter
to a Benjaminite as a wife.—Vers. 2, 3. After the termination of
the war, the people, *i.e.* the people who had assembled together for
the war (see ver. 9), went again to Bethel (see at chap. xx. 18, 26),
to weep there for a day before God at the serious loss which the
war had brought upon the congregation.   Then they uttered this
lamentation : " *Why, O Lord God of Israel, is this come to pass in
Israel, that a tribe is missing to-day from Israel ?*"   This lamentation
involved the wish that God might show them the way to avert the

threatened destruction of the missing tribe, and build up the six hundred who remained. To give a practical expression to this wish, they built an altar the next morning, and offered burnt-offerings and supplicatory offerings upon it (see at chap. xx. 26), knowing as they did that their proposal would not succeed without reconciliation to the Lord, and a return to the fellowship of His grace. There is something apparently strange in the erection of an altar at Bethel, since sacrifices had already been offered there during the war itself (chap. xx. 26), and this could not have taken place without an altar. Why it was erected again, or another one built, is a question which cannot be answered with any certainty. It is possible, however, that the first was not large enough for the number of sacrifices that had to be offered now. Ver. 5. The congregation then resolved upon a plan, through the execution of which a number of virgins were secured for the Benjaminites. They determined that they would carry out the great oath, which had been uttered when the national assembly was called against such as did not appear, upon that one of the tribes of Israel which had not come to the meeting of the congregation at Mizpeh. The deliberations upon this point were opened (ver. 5) with the question, " *Who is he who did not come up to the meeting of all the tribes of Israel, to Jehovah ?*" In explanation of this question, it is observed at ver. 5, " *For the great oath was uttered upon him that came not up to Jehovah to Mizpeh : he shall be put to death.*" We learn from this supplementary remark, that when important meetings of the congregation were called, all the members were bound by an oath to appear. The meeting at Mizpeh is the one mentioned in chap. xx. 1 sqq. The " great oath" consisted in the threat of death in the case of any that were disobedient. To this explanation of the question in ver. 5*a*, the further explanation is added in vers. 6, 7, that the Israelites felt compassion for Benjamin, and wished to avert its entire destruction by procuring wives for such as remained. The word וַיִּנָּחֲמוּ in ver. 6 is attached to the explanatory clause in ver. 5*b*, and is to be rendered as a pluperfect: " *And the children of Israel had shown themselves compassionate towards their brother Benjamin, and said, A tribe is cut off from Israel to-day ; what shall we do to them, to those that remain with regard to wives, as we have sworn?*" etc. (compare ver. 1). The two thoughts—(1) the oath that those who had not come to Mizpeh should be punished with death (ver. 5*b*), and (2) anxiety for the preservation of this tribe which sprang from compassion towards Benjamin, and was shown in their endeavour to provide such as remained with wives, without violating the oath that none of them would give them their own daughters as wives—formed the two factors which determined the course to be adopted by the congregation. After the statement of these two circumstances, the question of ver. 5a, " *Who is the one* (only one) *of the tribes of Israel which,*" etc., is resumed and answered : " *Behold, there came no one into the camp from Jabesh in Gilead, into the assembly.*" שֵׁבֶט is used in vers. 8, 5, in a more general sense, as denoting not merely the tribes as such, but the several subdivisions of the tribes.—Ver. 9. In order, however, to confirm the correctness of this answer, which might possibly have been founded upon a superficial and erroneous observation, the whole of the (assembled) people were mustered, and not one of the inhabitants of Jabesh was found there (in the national assembly at Bethel). The situation of *Jabesh* in Gilead has not yet been ascertained. This town was closely be-sieged by the Ammonite *Nahash*, and was relieved by Saul (1 Sam. xi. 1 sqq.), on which account the inhabitants afterwards showed themselves grateful to Saul (1 Sam. xxxi. 8 sqq.). *Josephus* calls *Jabesh* the metropolis of Gilead (Ant. vi. 5, 1). According to the *Onom.* (*s. v. Jabis*), it was six Roman miles from Pella, upon the top of a mountain towards Gerasa. *Robinson* (Bibl. Res. p. 320) supposes it to be the ruins of *ed Deir* in the Wady *Jabes*.—Vers. 10 sqq. To punish this unlawful conduct, the congregation sent 12,000 brave fighting men against Jabesh, with orders to smite the inhabitants of the town with the edge of the sword, together with their wives and children, but also with the more precise instructions (ver. 11), "to ban all the men, and women who had known the lying with man" (*i.e.* to slay them as exposed to death, which implied, on the other hand, that virgins who had not lain with any man should be spared). The fighting men found 400 such virgins in Jabesh, and brought them to the camp at Shiloh in the land of Canaan. אֹתָם (ver. 12) refers to the virgins, the masculine being used as the more common genus in the place of the feminine. *Shiloh*, with the additional clause " in the land of Canaan," which was occasioned by the antithesis Jabesh in *Gilead*, as in Josh. xxi. 2, xxii. 9, was the usual meeting-place of the con-gregation, on account of its being the seat of the tabernacle. The representatives of the congregation had moved thither, after the deliberations concerning Jabesh, which were still connected with the war against Benjamin, were concluded.—Ver. 13. The con-gregation then sent to call the Benjaminites, who had taken refuge upon the rock Rimmon, and gave them as wives, when they returned (*sc.* into their own possessions), the 400 virgins of Jabesh who had been preserved alive. "*But so they sufficed them not*" (כֵּן, so, *i.e.*, in their existing number, 400 : *Bertheau*). In this remark there is an allusion to what follows.

Vers. 15–25. Of the six hundred Benjaminites who had escaped, there still remained two hundred to be provided with wives. To these the congregation gave permission to take wives by force at a festival at Shiloh. The account of this is once more introduced, with a description of the anxiety felt by the congregation for the continuance of the tribe of Benjamin. Vers. 15, 16, and 18 are only a repetition of vers. 6 and 7, with a slight change of expression. The "*breach (perez) in the tribes of Israel*" had arisen from the almost complete extermination of Benjamin. "*For out of Benjamin is* (every) *woman destroyed,*" viz. by the ruthless slaughter of the whole of the people of that tribe (chap. xx. 48). Consequently the Benjaminites who were still unmarried could not find any wives in their own tribe. The fact that four hundred of the Benjaminites who remained were already provided with wives is not noticed here, because it has been stated just before, and of course none of them could give up their own wives to others.— Ver. 17. Still Benjamin must be preserved as a tribe. The elders therefore said, "*Possession of the saved shall be for Benjamin,*" *i.e.* the tribe-land of Benjamin shall remain an independent possession for the Benjaminites who have escaped the massacre, so that a tribe may not be destroyed out of Israel. It was necessary, therefore, that they should take steps to help the remaining Benjaminites to wives. The other tribes could not give them their daughters, on account of the oath which has already been mentioned in vers. 1 and 7b and is repeated here (ver. 18). Consequently there was hardly any other course open, than to let the Benjaminites seize upon wives for themselves. And the elders lent them a helping hand by offering them this advice, that at the next yearly festival at Shiloh, at which the daughters of Shiloh carried on dances in the open air (outside the town), they should seize upon wives for themselves from among these daughters, and promising them that when the thing was accomplished they would adjust it peaceably (vers. 19–22). The "*feast of Jehovah,*" which the Israelites kept from year to year, was one of the three great annual festivals, probably one which lasted seven days, either the passover or the feast of tabernacles,—most likely the former, as the dances of the daughters of Shiloh were apparently an imitation of the dances of the Israelitish women at the Red Sea under the superintendence of Miriam (Ex. xv. 20). The minute description of the situation of Shiloh (ver. 19), viz. " to the north of Bethel, on the east of the road which rises from Bethel to Shechem, and on the south of *Lebonah*" (the present village of *Lubban*, on the north-west of Seilun : see *Rob.* Pal. iii. p. 89), serves to throw light upon the scene which follows, *i.e.* to show how the situation of Shiloh was peculiarly fitted for the carrying out of the advice given to the Benjaminites; since, as soon as they had issued from their hiding-places in the vineyards at Shiloh, and seized upon the dancing virgins, they could easily escape into their own land by the neighbouring high-road which led from Bethel to Shechem, without being arrested by the citizens of Shiloh.—Ver. 20. The *Kethibh* וַיְצַו in the singular may be explained on the ground that one of the elders spoke and gave the advice in the name of the others. חָטַף in ver. 21 and Ps. x. 9, to seize hold of, or carry off as prey = חָתַף.—Ver. 22. "*And when the fathers or brethren of the virgins carried off, come to us to chide with us, we* (the elders) *will say to them* (in your name), *Present them to us* (אוֹתָם as in ver. 12); *for we did not receive every one his wife through the war* (with Jabesh) ; *for ye have not given them to them; now would ye be guilty.*" The words " Present them to us," etc., are to be understood as spoken in the name of the Benjaminites, who were accused of the raid, to the relatives of the virgins who brought the complaint. This explains the use of the pronoun in the first person in חַנּוּנוּ and לְקַחְנוּ, which must not be altered therefore into the third person.[1] The two clauses commencing with כִּי are co-ordinate, and contain two points serving to enforce the request, " Present them," etc. The first is pleaded in the name of the Benjaminites ; the second is adduced, as a general ground on the part of the elders of the congregation, to pacify the fathers and brothers making the complaint, on account of the oath which the Israelites had taken, that none of them would give their daughters as wives to the Benjaminites. The meaning

[1] One circumstance which is decisive against this alteration of the text is, that the Seventy had the Masoretic text before them, and founded their translation upon it (ἐλεήσατε ἡμῖν αὐτάς, ὅτι οὐκ ἐλάβομεν ἀνὴρ γυναῖκα αὐτοῦ ἐν τῷ πολέμῳ). The different rendering of *Jerome* given in the *Vulgate*—*miseremini eorum! non enim rapuerunt eas jure bellantium atque victorum*—is nothing but an unfortunate and unsuccessful attempt to get rid of the difficulties connected with the readings in the text.

is the following: Ye may have your daughters with the Benjaminites who have taken them by force, for ye have not given them voluntarily, so as to have broken your oath by so doing. In the last clause בָּעֵת has an unusual meaning: " at the time" (or *now*), *i.e. in that case*, ye would have been guilty, viz. if ye had given them voluntarily. — Ver. 23. The Benjaminites adopted this advice. They took to themselves wives according to their number, *i.e.* two hundred (according to ver. 12, compared with chap. xx. 47), whom they caught from the dancing daughters of Shiloh, and returned with them into their inheritance, where they rebuilt the towns that had been reduced to ashes, and dwelt therein.

In vers. 24 and 25, the account of this event is brought to a close with a twofold remark: (1) that the children of Israel, *i.e.* the representatives of the congregation who were assembled at Shiloh, separated and returned every man into his inheritance to his tribe and family ; (2) that at that time there was no king in Israel, and every man was accustomed to do what was right in his own eyes. Whether the fathers or brothers of the virgins who had been carried off brought any complaint before the congregation concerning the raid that had been committed, the writer does not state, simply because this was of no moment so far as the history was concerned, inasmuch as, according to ver. 22, the complaint made no difference in the facts themselves.[1] With the closing remark in ver. 25, however, with which the account returns to its commencement in chap. xix. 1, the prophetic historian sums up his judgment upon the history in the words, "At that time every man did what was right in his own eyes, because there was no king in Israel," in which the idea is implied, that under the government of a king, who administered right and justice in the kingdom, such things could not possibly have happened. This not only refers to the conduct of the Israelites towards Benjamin in the war, the severity of which was not to be justified (see p. 458), but also to their con duct towards the inhabitants of Jabesh, as described in chap. xxi. 5 sqq. The congregation had no doubt a perfect right, when all the people were summoned to deliberate upon important matters affecting

---

[1] "No doubt the fathers and brothers of the virgins demanded them both from the Benjaminites themselves, and also from the elders of Israel, or at any rate petitioned that the Benjaminites might be punished : but the elders replied as they had said that they should ; and the persons concerned were satisfied with the answer, and so the affair was brought to a peaceable termination."— *Seb. Schmidt.*

the welfare of the whole nation, to utter the "great oath" against
such as failed to appear, *i.e.* to threaten them with death and carry
out this threat upon such as were obstinate; but such a punishment
as this could only be justly inflicted upon persons who were really
guilty, and had rebelled against the congregation as the supreme
power, and could not be extended to women and children unless
they had also committed a crime deserving of death.   But even if
there were peculiar circumstances in the case before us, which have
been passed over by our author, who restricts himself simply to
points bearing upon the main purpose of the history, but which
rendered it necessary that the ban should be inflicted upon all the
inhabitants of Jabesh, it was at any rate an arbitrary exemption to
spare all the marriageable virgins, and one which could not be
justified by the object contemplated, however laudable that object
might be.   This also applies to the oath taken by the people, that
they would not give any of their daughters as wives to the Benjaminites, as well as to the advice given by the elders to the remaining two hundred, to carry off virgins from the festival at
Shiloh.   However just and laudable the moral indignation may
have been, which was expressed in that oath by the nation generally
at the scandalous crime of the Gibeites, a crime unparalleled in
Israel, and at the favour shown to the culprits by the tribe of
Benjamin, the oath itself was an act of rashness, in which there
was not only an utter denial of brotherly love, but the bounds of
justice were broken through.   When the elders of the nation came
to a better state of mind, they ought to have acknowledged their
rashness openly, and freed themselves and the nation from an oath
that had been taken in such sinful haste.   "Wherefore they would
have acted far more uprightly, if they had seriously confessed
their fault and asked forgiveness of God, and given permission to
the Benjaminites to marry freely.   In this way there would have
been no necessity to cut off the inhabitants of Jabesh from their
midst by cruelty of another kind" (*Buddeus*).   But if they felt
themselves bound in their consciences to keep the oath inviolably,
they ought to have commended the matter to the Lord in prayer,
and left it to His decision; whereas, by the advice given to the
Benjaminites, they had indeed kept the oath in the letter, but had
treated it in deed and truth as having no validity whatever.

THE BOOK OF RUTH.[1]

—◆—

INTRODUCTION.

CONTENTS, CHARACTER, AND ORIGIN OF THE BOOK OF RUTH.

THE book of *Ruth* ('Ρούθ) introduces us to the family life of the ancestors of king David, and informs us, in a simple and attractive form of historical narrative, and one in harmony with the tender and affectionate contents, how *Ruth* the Moabitess, a daughter-in-law of the Beth-lehemite Elimelech, of the family of Judah, who had emigrated with his wife and his two sons into the land of Moab on account of a famine, left father and mother, fatherland and kindred, after the death of her husband, and out of childlike affection to her Israelitish mother-in-law Naomi, whose husband had also died in the land of Moab, and went with her to Judah, to take refuge under the wings of the God of Israel (chap. i.); and how, when there, as she was going in her poverty to glean some ears of corn in the field of a wealthy man, she came apparently by accident to the field of Boaz, a near relation of Elimelech, and became acquainted with this honourable and benevolent man (chap. ii.); how she then sought marriage with him by the wish of her mother-in-law (chap. iii.), and was taken by him as a wife, according to the custom of Levirate marriage, in all the ordinary legal forms, and bare a son in this marriage, named Obed. This Obed was the grandfather of David (chap. iv. 1–17), with whose genealogy the book closes (chap. iv. 18–22).

---

[1] The book of *Ruth* does not indeed belong to the prophetical books of history so far as its historical character is concerned, and even in the Hebrew canon it is placed among the hagiographa; but as its contents directly follow upon those of the book of Judges, it seemed advisable to place the exposition immediately after that of Judges.

In this conclusion the meaning and tendency of the whole narrative is brought clearly to light. The genealogical proof of the descent of David from Perez through Boaz and the Moabitess Ruth (chap. iv. 18–22) forms not only the end, but the starting-point, of the history contained in the book. For even if we should not attach so much importance to this genealogy as to say with *Auberlen* that "the book of Ruth contains, as it were, the inner side, the spiritually moral background of the genealogies which play so significant a part even in the Israelitish antiquity;" so much is unquestionably true, that the book contains a historical picture from the family life of the ancestors of David, intended to show how the ancestors of this great king walked uprightly before God and man in piety and singleness of heart, and in modesty and purity of life. "Ruth, the Moabitish great-great-grandmother of David, longed for the God and people of Israel with all the deepest earnestness of her nature, and joined herself to them with all the power of love; and Boaz was an upright Israelite, without guile, full of holy reverence for every ordinance of God and man, and full of benevolent love and friendliness towards the poor heathen woman. From such ancestors was the man descended in whom all the nature of Israel was to find its royal concentration and fullest expression" (*Auberlen*). But there is also a Messianic trait in the fact that Ruth, a heathen woman, of a nation so hostile to the Israelites as that of Moab was, should have been thought worthy to be made the tribe-mother of the great and pious king David, on account of her faithful love to the people of Israel, and her entire confidence in Jehovah, the God of Israel. As Judah begat Perez from Tamar the Canaanitish woman (Gen. xxxviii.), and as Rahab was adopted into the congregation of Israel (Josh. vi. 25), and according to ancient tradition was married to Salmon (Matt. i. 5), so the Moabitess Ruth was taken by Boaz as his wife, and incorporated in the family of Judah, from which Christ was to spring according to the flesh (see Matt. i. 3, 5, where these three women are distinctly mentioned by name in the genealogy of Jesus).

The incidents described in the book fall within the times of the judges (chap. i. 1), and most probably in the time of Gideon (see at chap. i. 1); and the book itself forms both a supplement to the book of Judges and an introduction to the books of Samuel, which give no account of the ancestors of David. So far as its contents are concerned it has its proper place, in the Septuagint, the Vulgate, the Lutheran and other versions, between the book of Judges and those of Samuel. In the Hebrew Codex, on the contrary, it is placed among the *hagiographa*, and in the Talmud (*baba bathr. f.* 14*b*) it is even placed at the head of them before the Psalms; whilst in the Hebrew MSS. it stands among the five *megilloth : Canticles, Ruth, Lamentations, Ecclesiastes, Esther.* The latter position is connected with the liturgical use of the book in the synagogue, where it was read at the feast of weeks; whilst its place among the hagiographa is to be explained from the principle upon which the general arrangement of the Old Testament canon was founded,— namely, that the different books were divided into three classes according to the relation in which their authors stood to God and to the theocracy, and the books themselves in their contents and spirit to the divine revelation (see *Keil*, Lehrbuch der Einleitung, § 155). The latter is therefore to be regarded as the original classification, and not the one in the Septuagint rendering, where the original arrangement has unquestionably been altered in the case of this and other books, just because this principle has been overlooked.[1]

---

[1] Many critics of the present day, indeed, appeal to the testimony of Josephus and the earlier fathers as favouring the opposite view, viz. that the book of Ruth was originally placed at the close of the book of Judges, to which it formed an appendix. *Josephus* (c. Ap. i. 8) reckons, as is well known, only twenty-two books of the Old Testament; and the only way by which this number can be obtained is by joining together the books of Judges and Ruth, so as to form one book. Again, *Melito* of *Sardes*, who lived in the second century, and took a journey into Palestine for the purpose of obtaining correct information concerning the sacred writings of the Jews (πόσα τὸν ἀριθμὸν καὶ ὁποῖα τὴν τάξιν εἶεν), places Ruth after Judges in the list which has been preserved by *Eusebius* (h. e. iv. 26), but does not give the number of the books, as *Bertheau* erroneously maintains, nor observes that "Judges and Ruth form one book under the name of *Shofetim.*" This is first done by *Origen* in his list as given by *Eusebius* (h. e. vi. 25), where he states that the Hebrews had twenty-two ἐνδιαθήκους βίβλους, and then adds in the case of Ruth, παρ' αὐτοῖς ἐν ἑνὶ Σωφετίμ. Ruth occupies the same place in the lists of the later Greek fathers, as in *Rufinus* (Expos. in Symb. Apost.) and *Jerome* (in Prolog. Gal.), the latter of whom makes this remark on the book of Judges, *Et in eundem compingunt Ruth, quia in diebus Judicum facta ejus narratur historia;* and after enumerating the twenty-two books of the Old Testament, adds, *Quanquam nonnulli Ruth et Kinoth inter Hagiographa scriptitent et hos libros in suo putent numero supputandos,* etc. But all these testimonies prove nothing more than that the Hellenistic Jews, who made use of the Old Testament in the Greek rendering of the LXX., regarded the book of Ruth as an appendix of the book of Judges, and not that the book of Ruth ever followed the book of Judges in the Hebrew canon, so as to form one book. The reduction of the sacred writings of the Old Testament to twenty-two is nothing more than the product of the cabbalistic and mystical numbers wrought out by the Hellenistic or Alexandrian Jews. If this numbering had been the original

The book of Ruth is not a mere (say a third) appendix to the book of Judges, but a small independent work, which does indeed resemble the two appendices of the book of Judges, so far as the incidents recorded in it fall within the period of the Judges, and are not depicted in the spirit of the prophetic view of history; but, on the other hand, it has a thoroughly distinctive character both in form and contents, and has nothing in common with the book of Judges either in style or language: on the contrary, it differs essentially both in substance and design from the substance and design of this book and of its two appendices, for the simple reason that at the close of the history (chap. iv. 17), where Obed, the son

one, the Hebrew Jews would never have increased the number to twenty-four, since the Hebrew alphabet never contained twenty-four letters. *Josephus*, however, is not a witness with regard to the orthodox opinions of the Hebrew Jews, but was an eclectic and a Hellenist, who used the Old Testament in the Septuagint version and not in the original text, and who arranged the books of the Old Testament in the most singular manner. The fathers, too, with the exception of *Jerome*, whenever they give any account of their inquiries among the Jews with regard to the number and order of the books accepted by them as canonical, never give them in either the order or number found in the Hebrew canon, but simply according to the Septuagint version, which was the only one that the Christians understood. This is obvious in the case of *Melito*, from the fact that he reckons Βασιλειῶν τέσσαρα and Παραλειπομένων δύο, and places *Daniel* between the twelve minor prophets and Ezekiel. We find the same in *Origen*, although he gives the Hebrew names to the different books, and states in connection with the four books of Kings and the two books of *Paralipomena*, that the Hebrews named and numbered them differently. Lastly, it is true that *Jerome* arranges the writings of the Old Testament in his Prol. Gal. according to the three classes of the Hebrew canon; but he endeavours to bring the Hebrew mode of division and enumeration as much as possible into harmony with the Septuagint numbering and order as generally adopted in the Christian Church, and to conceal all existing differences. You may see this very clearly from his remarks as to the number of these books, and especially from the words, *Porro quinque litteræ duplices apud Hebræos sunt, Caph, Mem, Nun, Pe, Sade* . . . . *Unde et quinque a plerisque libri duplices existimantur, Samuel, Melachim, Dibre Hajamim, Esdras, Jeremias cum Kinoth, i.e. Lamentationibus suis.* For the *plerique* who adopt two books of Samuel, Kings, and Chronicles, are not Hebrew but Hellenistic Jews, as the Hebrew Jews did not divide these writings in their canon into two books each, but this mode of dividing them was first introduced into the Hebrew Bibles by *Dan. Bomberg* from the *Septuagint* or *Vulgate*. The further remark of this father, *quanquam nonnulli Ruth et Kinoth inter hagiographa scriptitent*, etc., is also to be estimated in the same way, and the word *nonnulli* to be attributed to the conciliatory efforts of Jerome. And lastly, his remark concerning the connection between the book of Ruth and that of Judges is not to be regarded as any evidence of the position which this book occupied in the Hebrew canon, but simply as a proof of the place assigned it by the Hellenistic Jews.

of Boaz and Ruth, is described as the grandfather of David, and still more clearly in the genealogy of Perez, which is brought down to David (chap. iv. 18–22), the book passes beyond the times of the Judges. In this simple fact the author very plainly shows that his intention was not to give a picture of the family life of pious Israelites in the time of the judges from a civil and a religious point of view, but rather to give a biographical sketch of the pious ancestors of David the king.

The *origin* of the book of Ruth is involved in obscurity. From its contents, and more especially from the object so apparent in the close of the book, it may be inferred with certainty that it was not written earlier than the time of David's rule over Israel, and indeed not before the culminating point of the reign of this great king. There would therefore be an interval of 150 to 180 years between the events themselves and the writing of the book, during which time the custom mentioned in chap. iv. 7, of taking off the shoe in acts of trade and barter, which formerly existed in Israel, may have fallen entirely into disuse, so that the author might think it necessary to explain the custom for the information of his contemporaries. We have not sufficient ground for fixing a later date, say the time of the captivity; and there is no force in the arguments that have been adduced in support of this (see my Lehrb. der Einl. § 137). The discovery that words and phrases such as מַרְגְּלוֹת (chap. iii. 7, 8, 14), פָּרַשׂ כְּנָפִים (chap. iii. 9), מִקְרֶה, chance (chap. ii. 3), either do not occur at all or only very rarely in the earlier writings, simply because the thing itself to which they refer is not mentioned, does not in the least degree prove that these words were not formed till a later age. The supposed Chaldaisms, however,—namely the forms תַּעֲבוּרִי and תִּדְבָּקִין (chap. ii. 8, 21), יִקְצֹרוּן (chap. ii. 9), שָׁכַבְתִּי, יָרַדְתִּי, שָׂמְתִּי (chap. iii. 3, 4), מָרָא for מָרָה (chap. i. 20), or the use of לָהֶן, and of the ἅπ. λεγ. עָנַן (chap. i. 13), etc.,— we only meet with in the speeches of the persons acting, and never where the author himself is narrating; and consequently they furnish no proofs of the later origin of the book, but may be simply and fully explained from the fact, that the author received these forms and words from the language used in common conversation in the time of the judges, and has faithfully recorded them. We are rather warranted in drawing the conclusion from this, that he did not derive the contents of his work from oral tradition, but made use of written documents, with regard to the origin and nature of which, however, nothing certain can be determined.

EXPOSITION.

RUTH GOES WITH NAOMI TO BETHLEHEM.—CHAP. I.

In the time of the judges Elimelech emigrated from Bethlehem in Judah into the land of Moab, along with his wife Naomi, and his two sons Mahlon and Chilion, because of a famine in the land (vers. 1, 2). There Elimelech died; and his two sons married Moabitish women, named Orpah and Ruth. But in the course of ten years they also died, so that Naomi and her two daughters-in-law were left by themselves (vers. 3–5). When Naomi heard that the Lord had once more blessed the land of Israel with bread, she set out with Orpah and Ruth to return home. But on the way she entreated them to turn back and remain with their relations in their own land; and Orpah did so (vers. 6–14). But Ruth declared that she would not leave her mother-in-law, and went with her to Bethlehem (vers. 15–22).

Vers. 1–5. *Elimelech's Emigration* (vers. 1, 2).—By the word וַיְהִי the following account is attached to other well-known events (see at Josh. i. 1); and by the definite statement, " *in the days when judges judged,*" it is assigned to the period of the judges generally. " *A famine in the land,*" i.e. in the land of Israel, and not merely in the neighbourhood of Bethlehem. The time of this famine cannot be determined with certainty, although it seems very natural to connect it, as *Seb. Schmidt* and others do, with the devastation of the land by the Midianites (Judg. vi.); and there are several things which favour this. For example, the famine must have been a very serious one, and not only have extended over the whole of the land of Israel, but have lasted several years, since it compelled Elimelech to emigrate into the land of the Moabites; and it was not till ten years had elapsed, that his wife Naomi, who survived him, heard that Jehovah had given His people bread again, and returned to her native land (vers. 4, 5). Now the Midianites oppressed Israel for seven years, and their invasions were generally attended by a destruction of the produce of the soil (Judg. vi. 3, 4), from which famine must necessarily have ensued. Moreover, they extended their devastations as far as Gaza (Judg. vi. 4). And although it by no means follows with certainty from this, that they also came into the neighbourhood of Bethlehem, it is still less possible to draw the opposite conclusion, as *Bertheau* does, from the fact they encamped in the valley of Jezreel (Judg. vi. 33), and were defeated there by Gideon, namely, that they did not devastate the mountains of Judah, because the road from the plain of Jezreel to Gaza did not lie across those mountains. There is just as little force in the other objection raised by *Bertheau*, namely, that the genealogical list in chap. iv. 18 sqq. would not place Boaz in the time of Gideon, but about the time of the Philistian supremacy over Israel, since this objection is founded partly upon an assumption that cannot be established, and partly upon an erroneous chronological calculation. For example, the assumption that every member is included in this chronological series cannot be established, inasmuch as unimportant members are often omitted from the genealogies, so that Obed the son of Boaz might very well have been the grandfather of Jesse. And according to the true chronological reckoning, the birth of David, who died in the year 1015 B.C. at the age of seventy, fell in the year 1085, *i.e.* nine or ten years after the victory gained by Samuel over the Philistines, or after the termination of their forty years' rule over Israel, and only ninety-seven years after the death of Gideon (see the chronological table, p. 289). Now David was the youngest of the eight sons of Jesse. If therefore we place his birth in the fiftieth year of his father's life, Jesse would have been born in the first year of the Philistian oppression, or forty-eight years after the death of Gideon. Now it is quite possible that Jesse may also have been a younger son of Obed, and born in the fiftieth year of his father's life; and if so, the birth of Obed would fall in the last years of Gideon. From this at any rate so much may be concluded with certainty, that Boaz was a contemporary of Gideon, and the emigration of Elimelech into the land of Moab may have taken place in the time of the Midianitish oppression. " *To sojourn in the fields of Moab*," *i.e.* to live as a stranger there. The form שְׂדֵי (vers. 1, 2, 22, and chap. ii. 6) is not the construct state singular, or only another form for שָׂדֶה, as *Bertheau* maintains, but the construct state plural of the absolute שָׂדִים, which does not occur anywhere, it is true, but would be a perfectly regular formation (comp. Isa. xxxii. 12, 2 Sam. i. 21, etc.), as the construct state singular is written שְׂדֵה even in this book (ver. 6 and chap. iv. 3). The use of the singular in these passages for the land of the Moabites by no means proves that שְׂדֵי must also be a singular, but may be explained from the fact that the expression " the field (= the territory) of Moab" alternates with the plural, " the fields of Moab."—Vers. 2, 3. אֶפְרָתִים, the plural of אֶפְרָתִי, an adjective

formation, not from אֶפְרַיִם, as in Judg. xii. 5, but from אֶפְרָת (Gen.
xlviii. 7) or אֶפְרָתָה (chap. iv. 11, Gen. xxxv. 19), the old name for
Bethlehem, *Ephrathite, i.e.* sprung from Bethlehem, as in 1 Sam.
xvii. 12. The names—*Elimelech, i.e.* to whom God is King; *Naomi*
(נָעֳמִי, a contraction of נָעֳמִית, LXX. Νοομμείν, *Vulg. Noēmi*), *i.e.*
the gracious; *Machlon, i.e.* the weakly; and *Chilion,* pining—are
genuine Hebrew names; whereas the names of the Moabitish
women, *Orpah* and *Ruth,* who were married to Elimelech's sons,
cannot be satisfactorily explained from the Hebrew, as the meaning
given to *Orpah,* " turning the back," is very arbitrary, and the
derivation of *Ruth* from רֵעוּת, a friend, is quite uncertain. According to chap. iv. 10, Ruth was the wife of the elder son Mahlon.
Marriage with daughters of the Moabites was not forbidden in the
law, like marriages with Canaanitish women (Deut. vii. 3); it was
only the reception of Moabites into the congregation of the Lord
that was forbidden (Deut. xxiii. 4).—Ver. 5. " *Thus the woman*
(Naomi) *remained left* (alone) *of her two sons and her husband.*"

Vers. 6–14. After the loss of her husband and her two sons, Naomi
rose up out of the fields of Moab to return into the land of Judah, as
she had heard that Jehovah had visited His people, *i.e.* had turned
His favour towards them again to give them bread. From the place
where she had lived Naomi went forth, along with her two daughters-
in-law. These three went on the way to return to the land of Judah.
The expression " to return," if taken strictly, only applies to Naomi,
who really *returned* to Judah, whilst her daughters-in-law simply
wished to accompany her thither.—Vers. 8 sqq. " *On the way,*" *i.e.*
when they had gone a part of the way, Naomi said to her two daughters-in-law, " *Go, return each one to her mother's house,*"—not her
father's, though, according to chap. ii. 11, Ruth's father at any rate
was still living, but her mother's, because maternal love knows best
how to comfort a daughter in her affliction. " *Jehovah grant you that
ye may find a resting-place, each one in the house of her husband,*" *i.e.*
that ye may both be happily married again. She then kissed them,
to take leave of them (*vid.* Gen. xxxi. 28). The daughters-in-law,
however, began to weep aloud, and said, " *We will return with thee
to thy people.*" כִּי before a direct statement serves to strengthen it,
and is almost equivalent to a positive assurance.—Ver. 11. Naomi
endeavoured to dissuade them from this resolution, by setting before
them the fact, that if they went with her, there would be no hope
of their being married again, and enjoying the pleasures of life once
more. " *Have I yet sons in my womb, that they may be your hus-*

bands?" Her meaning is : 1 am not pregnant with sons, upon whom, as the younger brothers of Mahlon and Chilion, there would rest the obligation of marrying you, according to the Levirate law (Deut. xxv. 5 ; Gen. xxxviii. 8). And not only have I no such hope as this, but, continues Naomi, in vers. 12, 13, I have no prospect of having a husband and being blessed with children : "*for I am too old to have a husband;*" yea, even if I could think of this altogether improbable thing as taking place, and assume the impossible as possible ; "*if I should say, I have hope* (of having a husband), *yea, if I should have a husband to-night, and should even bear sons, would ye then wait till they were grown, would ye then abstain from having husbands?*" The כִּי (*if*) before אָמַרְתִּי refers to both the perfects which follow. לָהֵן is the third pers. plur. neuter suffix הֵן with the prefix לְ, as in Job xxx. 24, where הֵן is pointed with seghol, on account of the toned syllable which follows, as here in pause in ver. 9 : *lit.* in these things, in that case, and hence in the sense of *therefore* = לָכֵן, as in Chaldee (*e.g.* Dan. ii. 6, 9, 24, etc.). תֵּעָגֵנָה (*vid.* Isa. lx. 4, and *Ewald*, § 195, *a.*), from עָגַן ἁπ. λεγ. in Hebrew, which signifies in Aramæan to hold back, shut in ; hence in the Talmud עֲגוּנָה, a woman who lived retired in her own house without a husband. Naomi supposes three cases in ver. 12, of which each is more improbable, or rather more impossible, than the one before ; and even if the impossible circumstance should be possible, that she should bear sons that very night, she could not in that case expect or advise her daughters-in-law to wait till these sons were grown up and could marry them, according to the Levirate law. In this there was involved the strongest persuasion to her daughters-in-law to give up their intention of going with her into the land of Judah, and a most urgent appeal to return to their mothers' houses, where, as young widows without children, they would not be altogether without the prospect of marrying again. One possible case Naomi left without notice, namely, that her daughters-in-law might be able to obtain other husbands in Judah itself. She did not hint at this, in the first place, and perhaps chiefly, from delicacy on account of the Moabitish descent of her daughters-in-law, in which she saw that there would be an obstacle to their being married in the land of Judah ; and secondly, because Naomi could not do anything herself to bring about such a connection, and wished to confine herself therefore to the one point, of making it clear to her daughters that in her present state it was altogether out of her power to provide connubial and domestic happiness for them in the land of Judah.

She therefore merely fixed her mind upon the different possibilities of a Levirate marriage.[1] אַל בְּנֹתַי, "*not my daughters*," *i.e.* do not go with me; "*for it has gone much more bitterly with me than with you.*" מָרַר relates to her mournful lot. מִכֶּם is comparative, "before you;" not "it grieveth me much on your account," for which עֲלֵיכֶם would be used, as in 2 Sam. i. 26. Moreover, this thought would not be in harmony with the following clause: "for the hand of the Lord has gone out against me," *i.e.* the Lord has sorely smitten me, namely by taking away not only my husband, but also my two sons.—Ver. 14. At these dissuasive words the daughters-in-law broke out into loud weeping again (תִּשֶּׂנָה with the א dropped for תִּשֶּׂאנָה, ver. 9), and Orpah kissed her mother-in-law, and took leave of her to return to her mother's house; but Ruth clung to her (דָּבַק as in Gen. ii. 24), forsaking her father and mother to go with Naomi into the land of Judah (*vid.* chap. ii. 11).

Vers. 15–22. To the repeated entreaty of Naomi that she would follow her sister-in-law and return to her people and her God, Ruth replied: "*Entreat me not to leave thee, and to return away behind thee: for whither thou goest, I will go; and where thou stayest, I will stay; thy people is my people, and thy God my God! where thou diest, I will die, and there will I be buried. Jehovah do so to me, and*

---

[1] The objections raised by *J. B. Carpzov* against explaining vers. 12 and 13 as referring to a Levirate marriage,—namely, that this is not to be thought of, because a Levirate marriage was simply binding upon brothers of the deceased by the same father and mother, and upon brothers who were living when he died, and not upon those born afterwards,—have been overthrown by *Bertheau* as being partly without foundation, and partly beside the mark. In the first place, the law relating to the Levirate marriage speaks only of brothers of the deceased, by which, according to the design of this institution, we must certainly think of sons by one father, but not necessarily of sons by the same mother. Secondly, the law does indeed expressly require marriage with the sister-in-law only of a brother who should be in existence when her husband died, but it does not distinctly exclude a brother born afterwards; and this is the more evident from the fact that, according to the account in Gen. xxxviii. 11, this duty was binding upon brothers who were not grown up at the time, as soon as they should be old enough to marry. Lastly, Naomi merely says, in ver. 12*a*, that she was not with child by her deceased husband; and when she does take into consideration, in vers. 12*b* and 13, the possibility of a future pregnancy, she might even then be simply thinking of an alliance with some brother of her deceased husband, and therefore of sons who would legally be regarded as sons of Elimelech. When *Carpzov* therefore defines the meaning of her words in this manner, "I have indeed no more children to hope for, to whom I could marry you in time, and I have no command over others," the first thought does not exhaust the meaning of the words, and the last is altogether foreign to the text.

more also (*lit.* and so may He add to do)! *Death alone shall divide between me and thee.*" The words כֹּה יַעֲשֶׂה י׳ . . . יֹסִיף are a frequently recurring formula in connection with an oath (cf. 1 Sam. iii. 17, xiv. 44, xx. 13, etc.), by which the person swearing called down upon himself a severe punishment in case he should not keep his word or carry out his resolution. The following כִּי is not a particle used in swearing instead of אִם in the sense of "if," equivalent to "surely not," as in 1 Sam. xx. 12, in the oath which precedes the formula, but answers to ὅτι in the sense of *quod* introducing the declaration, as in Gen. xxii. 16, 1 Sam. xx. 13, 1 Kings ii. 23, 2 Kings iii. 14, etc., signifying, I swear that death, and nothing else than death, shall separate us. Naomi was certainly serious in her intentions, and sincere in the advice which she gave to Ruth, and did not speak in this way merely to try her and put the state of her heart to the proof, "that it might be made manifest whether she would adhere stedfastly to the God of Israel and to herself, despising temporal things and the hope of temporal possessions" (*Seb. Schmidt*). She had simply the earthly prosperity of her daughter-in-law in her mind, as she herself had been shaken in her faith in the wonderful ways and gracious guidance of the faithful covenant God by the bitter experience of her own life.[1] With Ruth, however, it was evidently not merely strong affection and attachment by which she felt herself so drawn to her mother-in-law that she wished to live and die with her, but a leaning of her heart towards the God of Israel and His laws, of which she herself was probably not yet fully conscious, but which she had acquired so strongly in her conjugal relation and her intercourse with her Israelitish connections, that it was her earnest wish never to be separated from this people and its God (cf. chap. ii. 11).—Ver. 18. As she insisted strongly upon going with her (הִתְאַמֵּץ, to stiffen one's self firmly upon a thing), Naomi gave up persuading her any more to return.—Ver. 19. So they two went until they came to Bethlehem. When they arrived, the whole town was in commotion on their account (תֵּהֹם, imperf. *Niph.* of הוּם, as in 1 Sam. iv. 5, 1 Kings i. 45). They said, "*Is this Naomi?*" The subject to תֹּאמַרְנָה is the inhabitants of the town, but chiefly the female portion

---

[1] "She thought of earthly things alone; and as at that time the Jews almost universally were growing lax in the worship of God, so she, having spent ten years among the Moabites, thought it of little consequence whether they adhered to the religion of their fathers, to which they had been accustomed from their infancy or went over to the Jewish religion."—*Carpzov.*

of the inhabitants, who were the most excited at Naomi's return. This is the simplest way of explaining the use of the feminine in the verbs תֹּאמַרְנָה and תִּקְרֶאנָה. In these words there was an expression of amazement, not so much at the fact that Naomi was still alive, and had come back again, as at her returning in so mournful a condition, as a solitary widow, without either husband or sons; for she replied (ver. 20), " *Call me not Naomi (i.e. gracious), but Marah*" (the bitter one), *i.e.* one who has experienced bitterness, "*for the Almighty has made it very bitter to me. I, I went away full, and Jehovah has made me come back again empty. Why do ye call me Naomi, since Jehovah testifies against me, and the Almighty has afflicted me?*" "*Full,*" *i.e.* rich, not in money and property, but in the possession of a husband and two sons; a rich mother, but now deprived of all that makes a mother's heart rich, bereft of both husband and sons. "*Testified against me,*" by word and deed (as in Ex. xx. 16, 2 Sam. i. 16). The rendering "*He hath humbled me*" (LXX., *Vulg., Bertheau,* etc.) is incorrect, as עָנָה with בְ and the construct state simply means to trouble one's self with anything (Eccl. i. 13), which is altogether unsuitable here.—With ver. 22 the account of the return of Naomi and her daughter-in-law is brought to a close, and the statement that "*they came to Bethlehem in the time of the barley harvest*" opens at the same time the way for the further course of the history. הַשָּׁבָה is pointed as a third pers. perf. with the article in a relative sense, as in chap. ii. 6 and iv. 3. Here and at chap. ii. 6 it applies to Ruth; but in chap. iv. 3 to Naomi. הֵמָּה, the masculine, is used here, as it frequently is, for the feminine הֵנָּה, as being the more common gender. The harvest, as a whole, commenced with the barley harvest (see at Lev. xxiii. 10, 11).

RUTH GLEANS IN THE FIELD OF BOAZ.—CHAP. II.

Ruth went to the field to glean ears of corn, for the purpose of procuring support for herself and her mother-in-law, and came by chance to the field of Boaz, a relative of Naomi, who, when he heard that she had come with Naomi from Moabitis, spoke kindly to her, and gave her permission not only to glean ears in his field and even among the sheaves, but to appease her hunger and thirst with the food and drink of his reapers (vers. 1–16), so that in the evening she returned to her mother-in-law with a plentiful gleaning, and told her of the gracious reception she had met with from this man, and then learned from her that Boaz was a relation of her own (vers. 17–23).

Vers. 1–7. The account of this occurrence commences with a statement which was necessary in order to make it perfectly intelligible, namely that Boaz, to whose field Ruth went to glean, was a relative of Naomi through her deceased husband Elimelech. The *Kethibh* מירע is to be read מְיֻדָּע, an acquaintance (cf. Ps. xxxi. 12, lv. 14). The *Keri* מוֹדַע is the construct state of מוֹדָע, *lit.* acquaintanceship, then an acquaintance or friend (Prov. vii. 4), for which מוֹדַעַת occurs afterwards in chap. iii. 2 with the same meaning. That the acquaintance or friend of Naomi through her husband was also a relation, is evident from the fact that he was " of the family of Elimelech." According to the rabbinical tradition, which is not well established however, Boaz was a nephew of Elimelech. The לְ before אִישָׁה is used instead of the simple construct state, because the reference is not to *the* relation, but to *a* relation of her husband; at the same time, the word מוֹדָע has taken the form of the construct state notwithstanding this לְ (compare *Ewald*, § 292, *a.*, with § 289, *b.*). גִּבּוֹר חַיִל generally means the brave man of war (Judg. vi. 12, xi. 1, etc.); but here it signifies a man of property. The name *Boaz* is not formed from בּוֹ עָ, in whom is strength, but from a root, בָּעַז, which does not occur in Hebrew, and signifies *alacrity.*— Vers. 2, 3. Ruth wished to go to the field and glean at (among) the ears, *i.e.* whatever ears were left lying upon the harvest field (cf. ver. 7), אַחַר אֲשֶׁר, behind him in whose eyes she should find favour. The Mosaic law (Lev. xix. 9, xxiii. 22, compared with Deut. xxiv. 19) did indeed expressly secure to the poor the right to glean in the harvest fields, and prohibited the owners from gleaning themselves; but hard-hearted farmers and reapers threw obstacles in the way of the poor, and even forbade their gleaning altogether. Hence Ruth proposed to glean after him who should generously allow it. She carried out this intention with the consent of Naomi, and chance led her to the portion of the field belonging to Boaz, a relation of Elimelech, without her knowing the owner of the field, or being at all aware of his connection with Elimelech. וַיִּקֶר מִקְרֶהָ, *lit.* " her chance chanced to hit upon the field." —Vers. 4 sqq. When Boaz came from the town to the field, and had greeted his reapers with the blessing of a genuine Israelite, " *Jehovah be with you,*" and had received from them a corresponding greeting in return, he said to the overseer of the reapers, " *Whose damsel is this ?*" to which he replied, " *It is the Moabitish damsel who came back with Naomi from the fields of Moab, and she has said* (asked), *Pray, I will glean* (*i.e.* pray allow me to glean) *and gather among the sheaves after the reapers, and has come and stays* (here) *from morning till now; her sitting in the house that is little.*" מֵאָז, *lit.* a conjunction, here used as a preposition, is stronger than מִן, "*from then*," from the time of the morning onwards (see *Ewald*, § 222, *c.*). It is evident from this answer of the servant who was placed over the reapers, (1) that Boaz did not prohibit any poor person from gleaning in his field; (2) that Ruth asked permission of the over-seer of the reapers, and availed herself of this permission with untiring zeal from the first thing in the morning, that she might get the necessary support for her mother-in-law and herself; and (3) that her history was well known to the overseer, and also to Boaz, although Boaz saw her now for the first time.

Vers. 8–16. The good report which the overlooker gave of the modesty and diligence of Ruth could only strengthen Boaz in his purpose, which he had probably already formed from his affection as a relation towards Naomi, to make the acquaintance of her daughter-in-law, and speak kindly to her. With fatherly kind-ness, therefore, he said to her (vers. 8, 9), "*Dost thou hear, my daughter?* (*i.e.* 'thou hearest, dost thou not?' *interrogatio blande affirmat;*) *go not to reap in another field, and go not away from here, and keep so to my maidens* (*i.e.* remaining near them in the field). *Thine eyes* (directed) *upon the field which they reap, go behind them* (*i.e.* behind the maidens, who probably tied up the sheaves, whilst the men-servants cut the corn). *I have commanded the young men not to touch thee* (to do thee no harm); *and if thou art thirsty* (צָמֵא, from צָמָה = צָמֵא: see *Ewald*, § 195, *b.*), *go to the vessels, and drink of what the servants draw.*"—Ver. 10. Deeply affected by this generosity, Ruth fell upon her face, bowing down to the ground (as in 1 Sam. xxv. 23, 2 Sam. i. 2; cf. Gen. xxiii. 7), to thank him reverentially, and said to Boaz, "*Why have I found favour in thine eyes, that thou regardest me, who am only a stranger?*" הִכִּיר, to look at with sympathy or care, to receive a person kindly (cf. ver. 19).—Vers. 11, 12. Boaz replied, "*Everything has been told me that thou hast done to* (אֵת, prep. as in Zech. vii. 9, 2 Sam. xvi. 17) *thy mother-in-law since the death of thy husband, that thou hast left thy father and thy mother, and thy kindred, and hast come to a people that thou knewest not heretofore*" (hast therefore done what God commanded Abraham to do, Gen. xii. 1). "*The Lord recompense thy work, and let thy reward be perfect* (recalling Gen. xv. 1) *from the Lord the God of Israel, to whom thou hast come to seek refuge under His wings !"* For this figurative expression, which is derived from Deut. xxxii. 11, compare Ps. xci. 4, xxxvi. 8, lvii. 2. In these words of Boaz we see the genuine piety of a true Israelite. —Ver. 13. Ruth replied with true humility, *" May I find favour in thine eyes ; for thou hast comforted me, and spoken to the heart of thy maiden* (see Judg. xix. 3), *though I am not like one of thy maidens," i.e.* though I stand in no such near relation to thee, as to have been able to earn thy favour. In this last clause she restricts the expression "thy maiden." *Carpzov* has rightly pointed this out : "But what am I saying when I call myself thy maiden ? since I am not worthy to be compared to the least of thy maidens." The word אֶמְצָא is to be taken in an optative sense, as expressive of the wish that Boaz might continue towards her the kindness he had already expressed. To take it as a present, "I find favour" (*Clericus* and *Bertheau*), does not tally with the modesty and humility shown by Ruth in the following words.—Ver. 14. This unassuming humility on the part of Ruth made Boaz all the more favourably disposed towards her, so that at meal-time he called her to eat along with his people (לָה without *Mappik*, as in Num. xxxii. 42, Zech. v. 11 ; cf. *Ewald*, § 94, *b.* 3). *" Dip thy morsel in the vinegar."* *Chomez*, a sour beverage composed of vinegar (wine vinegar or sour wine) mixed with oil; a very refreshing drink, which is still a favourite beverage in the East (see *Rosenmüller*, A. and N. Morgenland, iv. p. 68, and my Bibl. Archäologie, ii. p. 16). *"And he reached her parched corn."* The subject is Boaz, who, judging from the expression "come hither," either joined in the meal, or at any rate was present at it. קָלִי are roasted grains of wheat (see at Lev. ii. 14, and my Bibl. Arch. ii. p. 14), which are still eaten by the reapers upon the harvest field, and also handed to strangers.[1] Boaz gave her an abundant supply of it, so that she was not only satisfied, but left some, and was able to take it home to her mother (ver. 18).—Vers. 15, 16. When she rose up to glean again after eating, Boaz commanded his people, saying, *" She may*

---

[1] Thus *Robinson* (Pal. ii. p. 394) gives the following description of a harvest scene in the neighbourhood of Kubeibeh : " In one field nearly two hundred reapers and gleaners were at work, the latter being nearly as numerous as the former. A few were taking their refreshment, and offered us some of their ' parched corn.' In the season of harvest, the grains of wheat not yet fully dry and hard, are roasted in a pan or on an iron plate, and constitute a very palatable article of food ; this is eaten along with bread, or instead of it."

also glean between the sheaves (which was not generally allowed), *and ye shall not shame her* (do her any injury, Judg. xviii. 7); *and ye shall also draw out of the bundles for her, and let them lie* (the ears drawn out), *that she may glean them, and shall not scold her,"* sc. for picking up the ears that have been drawn out. These directions of Boaz went far beyond the bounds of generosity and compassion for the poor; and show that he felt a peculiar interest in Ruth, with whose circumstances he was well acquainted, and who had won his heart by her humility, her faithful attachment to her mother-in-law, and her love to the God of Israel,—a fact important to notice in connection with the further course of the history.

Vers. 17-23. Thus Ruth gleaned till the evening in the field; and when she knocked out the ears, she had about an ephah (about 20-25 lbs.) of barley.—Ver. 18. This she brought to her mother-in-law in the city, and *"drew out* (sc. from her pocket, as the Chaldee has correctly supplied) *what she had left from her sufficiency,"* i.e. of the parched corn which Boaz had reached her (ver. 14).—Ver. 19. The mother inquired, *"Where hast thou gleaned to-day, and where wroughtest thou?"* and praised the benefactor, who, as she conjectured from the quantity of barley collected and the food brought home, had taken notice of Ruth: *"blessed be he that did take knowledge of thee!"* When she heard the name of the man, Boaz, she saw that this relative of her husband had been chosen by God to be a benefactor of herself and Ruth, and exclaimed, *"Blessed be he of the Lord, that he has not left off* (withdrawn) *his favour towards the living and the dead!"* On עֲזֹב חַסְדּוֹ see Gen. xxiv. 27. This verb is construed with a double accusative here; for אֵת cannot be a preposition, as in that case מֵאֵת would be used like מֵעִם in Gen. *l.c.* *"The living,"* etc., forms a second object: as regards (with regard to) the living and the dead, in which Naomi thought of herself and Ruth, and of her husband and sons, to whom God still showed himself gracious, even after their death, through His care for their widows. In order to enlighten Ruth still further upon the matter, she added, *"The man* (Boaz) *is our relative, and one of our redeemers."* He *"stands near to us,"* sc. by relationship. גֹּאֲלֵנוּ, a defective form for גֹּאֲלֵינוּ, which is found in several MSS. and editions. On the significance of the *goël*, or redeemer, see at Lev. xxv. 26, 48, 49, and the introduction to chap. iii.—Ver. 21. Ruth proceeded to inform her of his kindness: גַּם כִּי, *"also* (know) *that he said to me, Keep with my people, till the harvest is all ended."* The masculine הַנְּעָרִים, for which we should rather expect the feminine נְעָרוֹת in accordance with vers. 8, 22, 23, is quite in place as the more comprehensive gender, as a designation of the reapers generally, both male and female; and the expression אֲשֶׁר לִי in this connection in the sense of *my* is more exact than the possessive pronoun: the people who belong to my house, as distinguished from the people of other masters.—Ver. 22. Naomi declared herself fully satisfied with this, because Ruth would be thereby secured from insults, which she might receive when gleaning in strange fields. "*That they meet thee not,*" *lit.* "that they do not fall upon thee." פָּגַע בְּ signifies to fall upon a person, to smite and ill-treat him.—Ver. 23. After this Ruth kept with the maidens of Boaz during the whole of the barley and wheat harvests gleaning ears of corn, and lived with her mother-in-law, *sc.* when she returned in the evening from the field. In this last remark there is a tacit allusion to the fact that a change took place for Ruth when the harvest was over.

RUTH SEEKS FOR MARRIAGE WITH BOAZ.—CHAP. III.

After the harvest Naomi advised Ruth to visit Boaz on a certain night, and ask him to marry her as redeemer (vers. 1–5). Ruth followed this advice, and Boaz promised to fulfil her request, provided the nearer redeemer who was still living would not perform this duty (vers. 6–13), and sent her away in the morning with a present of wheat, that she might not return empty to her mother-in-law (vers. 14–18). To understand the advice which Naomi gave to Ruth, and which Ruth carried out, and in fact to form a correct idea of the further course of the history generally, we must bear in mind the legal relations which came into consideration here. According to the theocratical rights, Jehovah was the actual owner of the land which He had given to His people for an inheritance; and the Israelites themselves had merely the usufruct of the land which they received by lot for their inheritance, so that the existing possessor could not part with the family portion or sell it at his will, but it was to remain for ever in his family. When any one therefore was obliged to sell his inheritance on account of poverty, and actually did sell it, it was the duty of the nearest relation to redeem it as *goël*. But if it should not be redeemed, it came back, in the next year of jubilee, to its original owner or his heirs without compensation. Consequently no actual sale took place in our sense of the word, but simply a sale of the yearly produce till the year of jubilee (see Lev. xxv. 10, 13–16, 24–28). There was also an old customary right, which had received the sanction of God, with certain limitations, through the Mosaic law,—namely, the custom of Levirate marriage, or the marriage of a brother-in-law, which we meet with as early as Gen. xxxviii., viz. that if an Israelite who had been married died without children, it was the duty of his brother to marry the widow, that is to say, his sister-in-law, that he might establish his brother's name in Israel, by begetting a son through his sister-in-law, who should take the name of the deceased brother, that his name might not become extinct in Israel. This son was then the legal heir of the landed property of the deceased uncle (cf. Deut. xxv. 5 sqq.). These two institutions are not connected together in the Mosaic law; nevertheless it was a very natural thing to place the Levirate duty in connection with the right of redemption. And this had become the traditional custom. Whereas the law merely imposed the obligation of marrying the childless widow upon the brother, and even allowed him to renounce the obligation if he would take upon himself the disgrace connected with such a refusal (see Deut. xxv. 7–10); according to chap. iv. 5 of this book it had become a traditional custom to require the Levirate marriage of the redeemer of the portion of the deceased relative, not only that the landed possession might be permanently retained in the family, but also that the family itself might not be suffered to die out.

In the case before us Elimelech had possessed a portion at Bethlehem, which Naomi had sold from poverty (chap. iv. 3); and Boaz, a relation of Elimelech, was the redeemer of whom Naomi hoped that he would fulfil the duty of a redeemer,—namely, that he would not only ransom the purchased field, but marry her daughter-in-law Ruth, the widow of the rightful heir of the landed possession of Elimelech, and thus through this marriage establish the name of her deceased husband or son (Elimelech or Mahlon) upon his inheritance. Led on by this hope, she advised Ruth to visit Boaz, who had shown himself so kind and well-disposed towards her, during the night, and by a species of bold artifice, which she assumed that he would not resist, to induce him as redeemer to grant to Ruth this Levirate marriage. The reason why she adopted this plan for the accomplishment of her wishes, and did not appeal to Boaz directly, or ask him to perform this duty of affection to her deceased husband, was probably that she was afraid lest she should fail to attain her end in this way, partly because the duty of a Levirate marriage was not legally binding upon the redeemer, and partly because Boaz was not so closely related to her husband that she could justly require this of him, whilst there was actually a nearer redeemer than he (chap. iii. 12). According to our customs, indeed, this act of Naomi and Ruth appears a very objectionable one from a moral point of view, but it was not so when judged by the customs of the people of Israel at that time. ·Boaz, who was an honourable man, and, according to chap. iii. 10, no doubt somewhat advanced in years, praised Ruth for having taken refuge with him, and promised to fulfil her wishes when he had satisfied himself that the nearer redeemer would renounce his right and duty (chap. iii. 10, 11). As he acknowledged by this very declaration, that under certain circumstances it would be his duty as redeemer to marry Ruth, he took no offence at the manner in which she had approached him and proposed to become his wife. On the contrary, he regarded it as a proof of feminine virtue and modesty, that she had not gone after young men, but offered herself as a wife to an old man like him. This conduct on the part of Boaz is a sufficient proof that women might have confidence in him that he would do nothing unseemly. And he justified such confidence. "The modest man," as *Bertheau* observes, "even in the middle of the night did not hesitate for a moment what it was his duty to do with regard to the young maiden (or rather woman) towards whom he felt already so strongly attached; he made his own personal inclinations subordinate to the traditional custom, and only when this permitted him to marry Ruth was he ready to do so. And not knowing whether she might not have to become the wife of the nearer *goël*, he was careful for her and her reputation, in order that he might hand her over unblemished to the man who had the undoubted right to claim her as his wife."

Vers. 1-5. As Naomi conjectured, from the favour which Boaz had shown to Ruth, that he might not be disinclined to marry her as *goël*, she said to her daughter-in-law, " *My daughter, I must seek rest for thee, that it may be well with thee.*" In the question הֲלֹא אֲבַקֶּשׁ, the word הֲלֹא is here, as usual, an expression of general admission or of undoubted certainty, in the sense of " Is it not true, I seek for thee? it is my duty to seek for thee." מְנוּחָה = מָנוֹחַ (chap. i. 9) signifies the condition of a peaceful life, a peaceful and well-secured condition, " a secure life under the guardian care of a husband" (*Rosenmüller*). " *And now is not Boaz our relation, with whose maidens thou wast ? Behold, he is winnowing the barley floor* (barley on the threshing-floor) *to-night*," *i.e.* till late in the night, to avail himself of the cool wind, which rises towards evening (Gen. iii. 8), for the purpose of cleansing the corn. The threshing-floors of the Israelites were, and are still in Palestine, made under the open heaven, and were nothing more than level places in the field stamped quite hard.[1]—Vers. 3, 4. " *Wash and anoint thyself* (סָכְתְּ, from סוּךְ = נָסַךְ), *and put on thy clothes* (thy best clothes), *and go down* (from Bethlehem, which stood upon the ridge of a hill) *to the threshing-floor; let not thyself be noticed by the man* (Boaz) *till he has finished eating and drinking. And when he lies down, mark the place where he will sleep, and go* (when he has fallen asleep) *and uncover the place of his feet, and lay thyself down; and he will tell thee what thou shalt do.*"—Ver. 5. Ruth promised to do this. The אֵלַי, which the Masorites have added to the text as *Keri non scriptum*, is quite unnecessary. From the account which follows of the carrying out of the advice given to her, we learn that Naomi had instructed Ruth to ask Boaz to marry her as her redeemer (cf. ver. 9).

Vers. 6–13. Ruth went accordingly to the threshing-floor and did as her mother-in-law had commanded; *i.e.* she noticed where Boaz went to lie down to sleep, and then, when he had eaten and drunken, and lay down cheerfully, at the end of the heap of sheaves or corn, and, as we may supply from the context, had fallen asleep, came to him quietly, uncovered the place of his feet, *i.e.* lifted up the covering over his feet, and lay down.—Ver. 8. About midnight the man was startled, namely, because on awaking he observed that there was some one lying at his feet; and he " bent himself" forward, or on one side, to feel who was lying there, " *and behold a woman was lying at his feet.*" מַרְגְּלֹתָיו is *accus. loci.*—Ver. 9. In answer to his inquiry, " *Who art thou?*" she said, " *I am Ruth, thine handmaid; spread thy wing over thine handmaid, for thou art a redeemer.*" כְּנָפֶךָ is a dual according to the Masoretic pointing, as we cannot look upon it as a pausal form on account of the position of the word, but it is most probably to be regarded as a singular; and the figurative expression is not taken from birds, which spread their wings over their young, *i.e.* to protect them, but refers, according to Deut. xxiii. 1, xxvii. 20, and Ezek. xvi. 8, to the wing, *i.e.* the corner of the counterpane, referring to the fact that a man

---

[1] " A level spot is selected for the threshing-floors, which are then constructed near each other, of a circular form, perhaps fifty feet in diameter, merely by beating down the earth hard."—*Robinson*, Pal. ii. p. 277.

spreads this over his wife as well as himself. Thus Ruth entreated Boaz to marry her because he was a redeemer. On this reason for the request, see the remarks in the introduction to the chapter.— Ver. 10. Boaz praised her conduct : " *Blessed be thou of the Lord, my daughter* (see chap. ii. 20) ; *thou hast made thy later love better than the earlier, that thou hast not gone after young men, whether poor or rich.*" Ruth's earlier or first love was the love she had shown to her deceased husband and her mother-in-law (comp. chap. ii. 11, where Boaz praises this love) ; the later love she had shown in the fact, that as a young widow she had not sought to win the affections of young men, as young women generally do, that she might have a youthful husband, but had turned trustfully to the older man, that he might find a successor to her deceased husband, through a marriage with him, in accordance with family custom (*vid.* chap. iv. 10). " *And now,*" added Boaz (ver. 11), " *my daughter, fear not ; for all that thou sayest I will do to thee : for the whole gate of my people* (*i.e.* all my city, the whole population of Bethlehem, who go in and out at the gate : see Gen. xxxiv. 24, Deut. xvii. 2) *knoweth that thou art a virtuous woman.*" Consequently Boaz saw nothing wrong in the fact that Ruth had come to him, but regarded her request that he would marry her as redeemer as perfectly natural and right, and was ready to carry out her wish as soon as the circumstances would legally allow it. He promised her this (vers. 12, 13), saying, " *And now truly I am a redeemer ; but there is a nearer redeemer than I. Stay here this night* (or as it reads at the end of ver. 13, ' lie till the morning'), *and in the morning, if he will redeem thee, well, let him redeem ; but if it does not please him to redeem thee, I will redeem thee, as truly as Jehovah liveth.*" כִּי אִם (*Kethibh,* ver. 12), after a strong assurance, as after the formula used in an oath, " *God do so to me,*" etc., 2 Sam. iii. 35, xv. 21 (*Kethibh*), and 2 Kings v. 20, is to be explained from the use of this particle in the sense of *nisi,* except that, = only : " only I am redeemer," equivalent to, assuredly I am redeemer (cf. *Ewald,* § 356, *b.*). Consequently there is no reason whatever for removing the אִם from the text, as the Masorites have done (in the *Keri*).[1] Ruth was to lie till morning, because she could not easily return to

---

[1] What the ל *majusc.* in לִינִי signifies, is uncertain. According to the smaller Masora, it was only found among the eastern (*i.e.* Palestinian) Jews. Consequently *Hiller* (in his Arcanum Keri et Ctibh, p. 163) conjectures that they used it to point out a various reading, viz. that לִנִי should be the reading here. But this is hardly correct.

the city in the dark at midnight; but, as is shown in ver. 14, she did not stay till actual daybreak, but " *before one could know another, she rose up, and he said* (*i.e.* as Boaz had said), *It must not be known that the woman came to the threshing-floor.*" For this would have injured the reputation not only of Ruth, but also of Boaz himself.—Ver. 15. He then said, "Bring the cloak that thou hast on, and lay hold of it" (to hold it open), and measured for her six measures of barley into it as a present, that she might not go back empty to her mother-in-law (ver. 17). מִטְפַּחַת, here and Isa. iii. 22, is a broad upper garment, *pallium*, possibly only a large shawl. "As the cloaks worn by the ancients were so full, that one part was thrown upon the shoulder, and another gathered up under the arm, Ruth, by holding a certain part, could receive into her bosom the corn which Boaz gave her" (*Schröder*, De vestit. mul. p. 264). *Six* (measures of) *barley :* the measure is not given. According to the Targum and the Rabbins, it was six seahs = two ephahs. This is certainly incorrect; for Ruth would not have been able to carry that quantity of barley home. When Boaz had given her the barley he measured out, and had sent her away, he also went into the city. This is the correct rendering, as given by the *Chaldee*, to the words וַיָּבֹא הָעִיר; though Jerome referred the words to Ruth, but certainly without any reason, as יָבֹא cannot stand for תָּבֹא. This reading is no doubt found in some of the MSS., but it merely owes its origin to a mistaken interpretation of the words.—Vers. 16-18. When Ruth returned home, her mother-in-law asked her, "*Who art thou?*" *i.e.* as what person, in what circumstances dost thou come? The real meaning is, What hast thou accomplished? Whereupon she related all that the man had done (cf. vers. 10-14), and that he had given her six measures of barley for her mother. The Masorites have supplied אֵלַי after אָמַר, as at ver. 5, but without any necessity. The mother-in-law drew from this the hope that Boaz would now certainly carry out the matter to the desired end. "*Sit still,*" *i.e.* remain quietly at home (see Gen. xxxviii. 11), "*till thou hearest how the affair turn out,*" namely, whether the nearer redeemer mentioned by Boaz, or Boaz himself, would grant her the Levirate marriage. The expression "fall," in this sense, is founded upon the idea of the falling of the lot to the ground; it is different in Ezra vii. 20. "*For the man will not rest unless he has carried the affair to an end this day.*" כִּי־אִם, except that, as in Lev. xxii. 6, etc. (see *Ewald*, § 356, *b.*).

BOAZ MARRIES RUTH.—CHAP. IV.

To redeem the promise he had given to Ruth, Boaz went the next morning to the .gate of the city, and calling to the nearer redeemer as he passed by, asked him, before the elders of the city, to redeem the piece of land which belonged to Elimelech and had been sold by Naomi; and if he did this, at the same time to marry Ruth, to establish the name of the deceased upon his inheritance (vers. 1-5). But as he renounced the right of redemption on account of the condition attached to the redemption of the field, Boaz undertook the redemption before the assembled people, together with the obligation to marry Ruth (vers. 6-12). The marriage was blessed with a son, who became the father of Jesse, the father of David (vers. 13-17). The book closes with a genealogical proof of the descent of David from Perez (vers. 18-22).

Vers. 1-5. "*Boaz had gone up to the gate, and had sat down there.*" This circumstantial clause introduces the account of the further development of the affair. The gate, *i.e.* the open space before the city gate, was the forum of the city, the place where the public affairs of the city were discussed. The expression "went up" is not to be understood as signifying that Boaz went up from the threshing-floor where he had slept to the city, which was situated upon higher ground, for, according to chap. iii. 15, he had already gone to the city before he went up to the gate; but it is to be explained as referring to the place of justice as an ideal eminence to which a man went up (*vid.* Deut. xvii. 8). The redeemer, of whom Boaz had spoken—that is to say, the nearer relation of Elimelech—then went past, and Boaz requested him to come near and sit down. סוּר as in Gen. xix. 2, etc. : "*Sit down here, such a one.*" פְּלֹנִי אַלְמֹנִי, any one, a certain person, whose name is either unknown or not thought worth mentioning (cf. 1 Sam. xxi. 3, 2 Kings vi. 8). Boaz would certainly call him by his name; but the historian had either not heard the name, or did not think it necessary to give it.—Ver. 2. Boaz then called ten of the elders of the city as witnesses of the business to be taken in hand, and said to the redeemer in their presence, "*The piece of field which belonged to our brother* (*i.e.* our relative) *Elimelech* (as an hereditary family possession), *Naomi has sold, and I have thought* (lit. ' I said,' *sc.* to myself; cf. Gen. xvii. 17, xxvii. 41), *I will open thine ear* (*i.e.* make it known, disclose it) : *get it before those who sit here, and* (indeed) *before the elders of my people.*" As the field had been sold to another, getting it (קָנָה) could only be accomplished by virtue of the right of redemption. Boaz therefore proceeded to say, " *If thou wilt redeem, redeem; but if thou wilt not redeem, tell me, that I may know it: for there is not beside thee* (any one more nearly entitled) *to redeem, and I am* (the next) *after thee*." הַיֹּשְׁבִים is rendered by many, those dwelling, and supposed to refer to the inhabitants of Bethlehem. But we could hardly think of the inhabitants generally as present, as the word "before" would require, even if, according to ver. 9, there were a number of persons present besides the elders. Moreover they would not have been mentioned first, but, like " *all the people*" in ver. 9, would have been placed after the elders as the principal witnesses. On these grounds, the word must be taken in the sense of sitting, and, like the verb in ver. 2, be understood as referring to the elders present; and the words " before the elders of my people" must be regarded as explanatory. The expression יִגְאַל (third pers.) is striking, as we should expect the second person, which is not only found in the Septuagint, but also in several codices, and is apparently required by the context. It is true that the third person may be defended, as it has been by *Seb. Schmidt* and others, on the assumption that Boaz turned towards the elders and uttered the words as addressed to them, and therefore spoke of the redeemer as a third person: " *But if he, the redeemer there, will not redeem*." But as the direct appeal to the redeemer himself is resumed immediately afterwards, the supposition, to our mind at least, is a very harsh one. The person addressed said, " *I will redeem*." Boaz then gave him this further explanation (ver. 5): " *On the day that thou buyest the field of the hand of Naomi, thou buyest it of the hand of Ruth the Moabitess, of the wife of the deceased* (Mahlon, the rightful heir of the field), *to set up* (that thou mayest set up) *the name of the deceased upon his inheritance*." From the meaning and context, the form קָנִיתִי must be the second pers. masc.; the *yod* at the end no doubt crept in through an error of the pen, or else from a וֹ, so that the word is either to be read קָנִיתָ (according to the *Keri*) or קָנִיתוֹ, " *thou buyest it*." So far as the fact itself was concerned, the field, which Naomi had sold from want, was the hereditary property of her deceased husband, and ought therefore to descend to her sons according to the standing rule of right; and in this respect, therefore, it was Ruth's property quite as much as Naomi's. From the negotiation between Boaz and the nearer redeemer, it is very evident that Naomi had sold the field which was the hereditary property of her husband, and was

lawfully entitled to sell it. But as landed property did not descend
to wives according to the Israelitish law, but only to children, and
when there were no children, to the nearest relatives of the husband (Num. xxvii. 8–11), when Elimelech died his field properly
descended to his sons; and when they died without children, it
ought to have passed to his nearest relations. Hence the question
arises, what right had Naomi to sell her husband's field as her own
property? The Rabbins suppose that the field had been presented
to Naomi and Ruth by their husbands (vid. Selden, de success. in
bona def. c. 15). But Elimelech could not lawfully give his hereditary property to his wife, as he left sons behind him when he died,
and they were the lawful heirs; and Mahlon also had no more right
than his father to make such a gift. There is still less foundation
for the opinion that Naomi was an heiress, since even if this were
the case, it would be altogether inapplicable to the present affair,
where the property in question was not a field which Naomi had
inherited from her father, but the field of Elimelech and his sons.
The true explanation is no doubt the following: The law relating
to the inheritance of the landed property of Israelites who died
childless did not determine the time when such a possession should
pass to the relatives of the deceased, whether immediately after the
death of the owner, or not till after the death of the widow who
was left behind (vid. Num. xxvii. 9 sqq.). No doubt the latter
was the rule established by custom, so that the widow remained in
possession of the property as long as she lived; and for that length
of time she had the right to sell the property in case of need, since
the sale of a field was not an actual sale of the field itself, but
simply of the yearly produce until the year of jubilee. Consequently
the field of the deceased Elimelech would, strictly speaking, have
belonged to his sons, and after their death to Mahlon's widow,
since Chilion's widow had remained behind in her own country
Moab. But as Elimelech had not only emigrated with his wife
and children and died abroad, but his sons had also been with him
in the foreign land, and had married and died there, the landed
property of their father had not descended to them, but had
remained the property of Naomi, Elimelech's widow, in which
Ruth, as the widow of the deceased Mahlon, also had a share.
Now, in case a widow sold the field of her deceased husband for
the time that it was in her possession, on account of poverty, and a
relation of her husband redeemed it, it was evidently his duty not
only to care for the maintenance of the impoverished widow, but if

she were still young, to marry her, and to let the first son born of such a marriage enter into the family of the deceased husband of his wife, so as to inherit the redeemed property, and perpetuate the name and possession of the deceased in Israel. Upon this right, which was founded upon traditional custom, Boaz based this condition, which he set before the nearer redeemer, that if he redeemed the field of Naomi he must also take Ruth, with the obligation to marry her, and through this marriage to set up the name of the deceased upon his inheritance.

Vers. 6–13. The redeemer admitted the justice of this demand, from which we may see that the thing passed as an existing right in the nation. But as he was not disposed to marry Ruth, he gave up the redemption of the field.—Ver. 6. "*I cannot redeem it for myself, lest I mar mine own inheritance.*" The redemption would cost money, since the yearly produce of the field would have to be paid for up to the year of jubilee. Now, if he acquired the field by redemption as his own permanent property, he would have increased by so much his own possessions in land. But if he should marry Ruth, the field so redeemed would belong to the son whom he would beget through her, and he would therefore have parted with the money that he had paid for the redemption merely for the son of Ruth, so that he would have withdrawn a certain amount of capital from his own possession, and to that extent have detracted from its worth. "*Redeem thou for thyself my redemption,*" i.e. the field which I have the first right to redeem.—Vers. 7, 8. This declaration he confirmed by what was a usual custom at that time in renouncing a right. This early custom is described in ver. 7, and there its application to the case before us is mentioned afterwards. "*Now this was* (took place) *formerly in Israel in redeeming and exchanging, to confirm every transaction: A man took off his shoe and gave it to another, and this was a testimony in Israel.*" From the expression "*formerly,*" and also from the description given of the custom in question, it follows that it had gone out of use at the time when our book was composed. The custom itself, which existed among the Indians and the ancient Germans, arose from the fact that fixed property was taken possession of by treading upon the soil, and hence taking off the shoe and handing it to another was a symbol of the transfer of a possession or right of ownership (see the remarks on Deut. xxv. 9 and my Bibl. Archäol. ii. p. 66). The *Piel* קִיֵּם is rarely met with in Hebrew; in the present instance it was probably taken from the old legal phraseology.

The only other places in which it occurs are Ezek. xiii. 6, Ps. cxix 28, 106, and the book of Esther, where it is used more frequently as a Chaldaism.—Vers. 9, 10. After the nearest redeemer had thus renounced the right of redemption with all legal formality, Boaz said to the elders and all the (rest of the) people, *" Ye are witnesses this day, that I have acquired this day all that belonged to Elimelech, and to Mahlon and Chilion* (*i.e.* the field of Elimelech, which was the rightful inheritance of his sons Mahlon and Chilion), *at the hand of Naomi; and also Ruth the Moabitess, the wife of Mahlon, I have acquired as my wife, to raise up the name of the deceased upon his inheritance, that the name of the deceased may not be cut off among his brethren and from the gate of his people"* (*i.e.* from his native town Bethlehem; cf. chap. iii. 11). On the fact itself, see the introduction to chap. iii.; also the remarks on the Levirate marriages at Deut. xxv. 5 sqq.—Ver. 11. The people and the elders said, *" We are witnesses,"* and desired for Boaz the blessing of the Lord upon this marriage. For Boaz had acted as unselfishly as he had acted honourably in upholding a laudable family custom in Israel. The blessing desired is the greatest blessing of marriage: *" The Lord make the woman that shall come into thine house* (the participle בָּאָה refers to what is immediately about to happen) *like Rachel and like Leah, which two did build the house of Israel* ("build" as in Gen. xvi. 2, xxx. 3); *and do thou get power in Ephratah, and make to thyself a name in Bethlehem."* עֲשֵׂה חַיִל does not mean "get property or wealth," as in Deut. viii. 17, but get *power*, as in Ps. lx. 14 (cf. Prov. xxxi. 29), *sc.* by begetting and training worthy sons and daughters. *" Make thee a name,"* literally "call out a name." The meaning of this phrase, which is only used here in this peculiar manner, must be the following: "Make to thyself a well-established name through thy marriage with Ruth, by a host of worthy sons who shall make thy name renowned."— Ver. 12. *" May thy house become like the house of Perez, whom Tamar bore to Judah"* (Gen. xxxviii.). It was from *Perez* that the ancestors of Boaz, enumerated in vers. 18 sqq. and 1 Chron. ii. 5 sqq., were descended. As from Perez, so also from the seed which Jehovah would give to Boaz through Ruth, there should grow up a numerous posterity.

Vers. 13–17. This blessing began very speedily to be fulfilled. When Boaz had married Ruth, Jehovah gave her conception, and she bare a son.—Ver. 14. At his birth the women said to Naomi, *" Blessed be the Lord, who hath not let a redeemer be wanting to thee to-day.*" This redeemer was not Boaz, but the son just born. They called him a redeemer of Naomi, not because he would one day redeem the whole of Naomi's possessions (*Carpzov, Rosenmüller,* etc.), but because as the son of Ruth he was also the son of Naomi (ver. 17), and as such would take away the reproach of childlessness from her, would comfort her, and tend her in her old age, and thereby become her true *goël, i.e.* her deliverer (*Bertheau*). "*And let his name be named in Israel,*" *i.e.* let the boy acquire a celebrated name, one often mentioned in Israel.—Ver. 15. "*And may the boy come to thee a refresher of the soul, and a nourisher of thine old age; for thy daughter-in-law, who loveth thee* (who hath left her family, her home, and her gods, out of love to thee), *hath born him; she is better to thee than seven sons.*" *Seven,* as the number of the works of God, is used to denote a large number of sons of a mother whom God has richly blessed with children (*vid.* 1 Sam. ii. 5). A mother of so many sons was to be congratulated, inasmuch as she not only possessed in these sons a powerful support to her old age, but had the prospect of the permanent continuance of her family. Naomi, however, had a still more valuable treasure in her mother-in-law, inasmuch as through her the loss of her own sons had been supplied in her old age, and the prospect was now presented to her of becoming in her childless old age the tribe-mother of a numerous and flourishing family.—Ver. 16. Naomi therefore adopted this grandson as her own child; she took the boy into her bosom, and became his nurse.—Ver. 17. And the neighbours said, "*A son is born to Naomi,*" and gave him the name of *Obed.* This name was given to the boy (the context suggests this) evidently with reference to what he was to become to his grandmother. *Obed,* therefore, does not mean "servant of Jehovah" (*Targum*), but "*the serving one,*" as one who lived entirely for his grandmother, and would take care of her, and rejoice her heart (*O. v. Gerlach,* after *Josephus,* Ant. v. 9, 4). The last words of ver. 17, "*he is the father of Jesse, the father of David,*" show the object which the author kept in view in writing down these events, or composing the book itself. This conjecture is raised into a certainty by the genealogy which follows, and with which the book closes.

Vers. 18–20. "*These are the generations of Perez,*" *i.e.* the families descended from Perez in their genealogical order (*toledoth :* see at Gen. ii. 4). The genealogy only goes back as far as *Perez,* because he was the founder of the family of Judah which was named after him (Num. xxvi. 20), and to which Elimelech and Boaz belonged.

Perez, a son of Judah by Tamar (Gen. xxxviii. 29), begat *Hezrom*, who is mentioned in Gen. xlvi. 12 among the sons of Judah who emigrated with Jacob into Egypt, although (as we have shown in our comm. on the passage) he was really born in Egypt. Of this son *Ram* (called *Aram* in the *Sept. Cod. Al.*, and from that in Matt. i. 3) nothing further is known, as he is only mentioned again in 1 Chron. ii. 9. His son *Amminadab* was the father-in-law of Aaron, who had married his daughter (Ex. vi. 23), and the father of *Nahesson* (*Nahshon*), the tribe-prince of the house of Judah in the time of Moses (Num. i. 7, ii. 3, vii. 12). According to this there are only four or five generations to the 430 years spent by the Israelites in Egypt, if we include both Perez and Nahesson; evidently not enough for so long a time, so that some of the intermediate links must have been left out even here. But the omission of unimportant members becomes still more apparent in the statement which follows, viz. that Nahshon begat *Salmah*, and Salmah *Boaz*, in which only two generations are given for a space of more than 250 years, which intervened between the death of Moses and the time of Gideon. *Salmah* (שַׂלְמָה or שַׂלְמָא, 1 Chron. ii. 11) is called *Salmon* in ver. 21; a double form of the name, which is to be explained from the fact that *Salmah* grew out of *Salmon* through the elision of the *n*, and that the terminations *an* and *on* are used promiscuously, as we may see from the form שִׂרְיָה in Job xli. 18 when compared with שִׂרְין in 1 Kings xxii. 34, and שִׂרְיוֹן in 1 Sam. xvii. 5, 38 (see *Ewald*, § 163–4). According to the genealogy of Christ in Matt. i. 5, Salmon married Rahab; consequently he was a son, or at any rate a grandson, of Nahshon, and therefore all the members between Salmon and Boaz have been passed over. Again, the generations from Boaz to David (vers. 21, 22) may possibly be complete, although in all probability one generation has been passed over even here between Obed and Jesse (see p. 471). It is also worthy of notice that the whole chain from *Perez* to *David* consists of ten links, five of which (from Perez to Nahshon) belong to the 430 years of the sojourn in Egypt, and five (from Salmon to David) to the 476 years between the exodus from Egypt and the death of David. This symmetrical division is apparently as intentional as the limitation of the whole genealogy to ten members, for the purpose of stamping upon it through the number ten as the seal of completeness the character of a perfect, concluded, and symmetrical whole.

The genealogy closes with David, an evident proof that the

book was intended to give a family picture from the life of the
pious ancestors of this great and godly king of Israel. But for us
the history which points to David acquires a still higher signification, from the fact that all the members of the genealogy of David
whose names occur here are also found in the genealogy of Jesus
Christ. " The passage is given by Matthew word for word in the
genealogy of Christ, that we may see that this history looks not so
much to David as to Jesus Christ, who was proclaimed by all as
the Saviour and Redeemer of the human race, and that we may
learn with what wonderful compassion the Lord raises up the lowly
and despised to the greatest glory and majesty" (Brentius).

COMMENTARY ON THE OLD TESTAMENT

C. F. KEIL and F. DELITZSCH

1 AND 2 SAMUEL

TRANSLATED BY

JAMES MARTIN

TABLE OF CONTENTS

THE BOOKS OF SAMUEL.

INTRODUCTION.

EXPOSITION.

THE SECOND BOOK OF SAMUEL.

THE BOOKS OF SAMUEL

---◆---

INTRODUCTION.

TITLE, CONTENTS, CHARACTER, AND ORIGIN OF THE BOOKS OF SAMUEL.

THE books of Samuel originally formed one undivided work, and in the Hebrew MSS. they do so still. The division into two books originated with the Alexandrian translators (LXX.), and was not only adopted in the Vulgate and other versions, but in the sixteenth century it was introduced by Daniel Bomberg into our editions of the Hebrew Bible itself. In the Septuagint and Vulgate, these books are reckoned as belonging to the books of the Kings, and have the heading, Βασιλειῶν πρώτη, δευτέρα (*Regum*, i. *et* ii.). In the Septuagint they are called "books of the kingdoms," evidently with reference to the fact that each of these works contains an account of the history of a double kingdom, viz.: the books of Samuel, the history of the kingdoms of Saul and David; and the books of Kings, that of the kingdoms of Judah and Israel. This title does not appear unsuitable, so far as the books before us really contain an account of the rise of the monarchy in Israel. Nevertheless, we cannot regard it as the original title, or even as a more appropriate heading than the one given in the Hebrew canon, viz. "*the book of Samuel*," since this title not only originated in the fact that the first half (*i.e.* our first book) contains an account of the acts of the prophet Samuel, but was also intended to indicate that the spirit of Samuel formed the soul of the true kingdom in Israel, or that the earthly throne of the Israelitish kingdom of God derived its strength and perpetuity from the Spirit of the Lord which lived in the prophet. The division into two books answers to the contents, since the death of Saul, with which the first book closes, formed a turning-point in the development of the kingdom.

The books of Samuel contain the history of the kingdom of God in Israel, from the termination of the age of the judges to the close of the reign of king David, and embrace a period of about 125 years, viz. from about 1140 to 1015 B.C. The *first* book treats of the judgeship of the prophet Samuel and the reign of king Saul, and is divided into three sections, answering to the three epochs formed by the judicial office of Samuel (ch. i.-vii.), the reign of Saul from his election till his rejection (ch. viii.-xv.), and the decline of his kingdom during his conflict with David, whom the Lord had chosen to be the leader of His people in the place of Saul (ch. xvi.-xxxi.). The renewal of the kingdom of God, which was now thoroughly disorganized both within and without, commenced with Samuel. When the pious Hannah asked for a son from the Lord, and Samuel was given to her, the sanctuary of God at Shiloh was thoroughly desecrated under the decrepit high priest Eli by the base conduct of his worthless sons, and the nation of Israel was given up to the power of the Philistines. If Israel, therefore, was to be delivered from the bondage of the heathen, it was necessary that it should be first of all redeemed from the bondage of sin and idolatry, that its false confidence in the visible pledges of the gracious presence of God should be shaken by heavy judgments, and the way prepared for its conversion to the Lord its God by deep humiliation. At the very same time, therefore, at which Samuel was called to be the prophet of God, the judgment of God was announced upon the degraded priesthood and the desecrated sanctuary. The *first* section of our book, which describes the history of the renewal of the theocracy by Samuel, does not commence with the call of Samuel as prophet, but with an account on the one hand of the character of the national religion in the time of Eli, and on the other hand of the piety of the parents of Samuel, especially of his mother, and with an announcement of the judgment that was to fall upon Eli's house (ch. i. ii.). Then follow first of all the call of Samuel as prophet (ch. iii.), and the fulfilment of the judgment upon the house of

Eli and the house of God (ch. iv.); secondly, the manifestation of the omnipotence of God upon the enemies of His people,
by the chastisement of the Philistines for carrying off the ark of
the covenant, and the victory which the Israelites gained over
their oppressors through Samuel's prayer (ch. v.–vii. 14); and
lastly, a summary of the judicial life of Samuel (ch. vii. 15–17).
The *second* section contains, first, the negotiations of the people
with Samuel concerning the appointment of a king, the anointing
of Saul by the prophet, and his election as king, together with
the establishment of his kingdom (ch. viii.–xii.); and secondly,
a brief survey of the history of his reign, in connection with
which the only events that are at all fully described are his first
successful conflicts with the Philistines, and the war against the
Amalekites which occasioned his ultimate rejection (ch. xiii.–
xv.). In the *third* section (ch. xvi.–xxxi.) there is a much more
elaborate account of the history of Saul from his rejection till
his death, since it not only describes the anointing of David and
his victory over Goliath, but contains a circumstantial account
of his attitude towards Saul, and the manifold complications
arising from his long-continued persecution on the part of Saul,
for the purpose of setting forth the gradual accomplishment of
the counsels of God, both in the rejection of Saul and the election of David as king of Israel, to warn the ungodly against hardness of heart, and to strengthen the godly in their trust in the
Lord, who guides His servants through tribulation and suffering
to glory and honour. The *second* book contains the history of
the reign of David, arranged in four sections: (1) his reign over
Judah in Hebron, and his conflict with Ishbosheth the son of
Saul, whom Abner had set up as king over the other tribes of
Israel (ch. i.–iv.) : (2) the anointing of David as king over all
Israel, and the firm establishment of his kingdom through the
conquest of the citadel of Zion, and the elevation of Jerusalem
into the capital of the kingdom ; the removal of the ark of the
covenant to Jerusalem ; the determination to build a temple to
the Lord ; the promise given him by the Lord of the everlasting duration of his dominion ; and lastly, the subjugation of
all the enemies of Israel (ch. v.–viii. 14), to which there is
appended a list of the principal officers of state (ch. viii. 15–18),
and an account of the favour shown to the house of Saul in the
person of Mephibosheth (ch. ix.) : (3) the disturbance of his

reign through his adultery with Bathsheba during the Ammonitish and Syrian war, and the judgments which came upon
his house in consequence of this sin through the wickedness of
his sons, viz. the incest of Amnon and rebellion of Absalom,
and the insurrection of Sheba (ch. x.–xx.) : (4) the close of
his reign, his song of thanksgiving for deliverance out of the
hand of all his foes (ch. xxii.), and his last prophetic words
concerning the just ruler in the fear of God (ch. xxiii. 1–7).
The way is prepared for these, however, by an account of the
expiation of Saul's massacre of the Gibeonites, and of various
heroic acts performed by his generals during the wars with the
Philistines (ch. xxi.) ; whilst a list of his several heroes is afterwards appended in ch. xxiii. 8–39, together with an account of
the numbering of the people and consequent pestilence (ch.
xxiv.), which is placed at the close of the work, simply because
the punishment of this sin of David furnished the occasion
for the erection of an altar of burnt-offering upon the site of
the future temple. His death is not mentioned here, because
he transferred the kingdom to his son Solomon before he died ;
and the account of this transfer forms the introduction to the
history of Solomon in the first book of Kings, so that the close
of David's life was most appropriately recorded there.

So far as the *character* of the historical writing in the books
of Samuel is concerned, there is something striking in the
contrast which presents itself between the fulness with which
the writer has described many events of apparently trifling
importance, in connection with the lives of persons through
whom the Lord secured the deliverance of His people and kingdom from their foes, and the summary brevity with which he
disposes of the greatest enterprises of Saul and David, and the
fierce and for the most part tedious wars with the surrounding
nations ; so that, as Thenius says, " particular portions of the
work differ in the most striking manner from all the rest, the
one part being very brief, and written almost in the form of a
chronicle, the other elaborate, and in one part composed with
really biographical fulness." This peculiarity is not to be
accounted for from the nature of the sources which the author
had at his command ; for even if we cannot define with precision the nature and extent of these sources, yet when we
compare the accounts contained in these books of the wars

between David and the Ammonites and Syrians with those in the books of Chronicles (2 Sam. viii. and x. with 1 Chron. xviii. xix.), we see clearly enough that the sources from which those accounts were derived embraced more than our books have given, since there are several places in which the chronicler gives fuller details of historical facts, the truth of which is universally allowed. The preparations for the building of the temple and the organization of the army, as well as the arrangement of the official duties of the Levites which David undertook, according to 1 Chron. xxii.–xxviii., in the closing years of his life, cannot possibly have been unknown to the author of our books. Moreover, there are frequent allusions in the books before us to events which are assumed as known, though there is no record of them in the writings which have been handed down to us, such as the removal of the tabernacle from Shiloh, where it stood in the time of Eli (1 Sam. i. 3, 9, etc.), to Nob, where David received the shewbread from the priests on his flight from Saul (ch. xxi. 1 sqq.); the massacre of the Gibeonites by Saul, which had to be expiated under David (2 Sam. xxi.); the banishment of the necromancers out of the land in the time of Saul (1 Sam. xxviii. 3); and the flight of the Beerothites to Gittaim (2 Sam. iv. 3). From this also we must conclude, that the author of our books knew more than he thought it necessary to mention in his work. But we certainly cannot infer from these peculiarities, as has often been done, that our books are to be regarded as a compilation. Such an inference as this simply arises from an utter disregard of the plan and object, which run through both books and regulate the selection and arrangement of the materials they contain. That the work has been composed upon a definite plan, is evident from the grouping of the historical facts, in favour of which the chronological order generally observed in both the books has now and then been sacrificed. Thus, in the history of Saul and the account of his wars (1 Sam. xiv. 47, 48), the fact is also mentioned, that he smote the Amalekites; whereas the war itself, in which he smote them, is first described in detail in ch. xv., because it was in that war that he forfeited his kingdom through his transgression of the divine command, and brought about his own rejection on the part of God. The sacrifice of the chronological order to the material grouping of kindred events, is still more evident in the history of David. In 2 Sam. viii. all his wars with foreign nations are collected together, and even the wars with the Syrians and Ammonites are included, together with an account of the booty taken in these wars; and then after this, viz. in ch. x.-xii., the war with the Ammonites and Syrians is more fully described, including the circumstances which occasioned it, the course which it took, and David's adultery which occurred during this war. Moreover, the history of Saul, as well as that of David, is divided into two self-contained periods, answering indeed to the historical course of the reigns of these two kings, but yet so distinctly marked off by the historian, that not only is the turning-point distinctly given in both instances, viz. the rejection of Saul and the grievous fall of David, but each of these periods is rounded off with a comprehensive account of the wars, the family, and the state officials of the two kings (1 Sam. xiv. 47-52, and 2 Sam. viii.). So likewise in the history of Samuel, after the victory which the Israelites obtained over the Philistines through his prayer, everything that had to be related concerning his life as judge is grouped together in ch. vii. 15-17, before the introduction of the monarchy is described; although Samuel himself lived till nearly the close of the reign of Saul, and not only instituted Saul as king, but afterwards announced his rejection, and anointed David as his successor. These comprehensive accounts are anything but proofs of compilations from sources of different kinds, which ignorance of the peculiarities of the Semitic style of writing history has led some to regard them as being; they simply serve to round off the different periods into which the history has been divided, and form resting-places for the historical review, which neither destroy the material connection of the several groups, nor throw any doubt upon the unity of the authorship of the books themselves. And even where separate incidents appear to be grouped together, without external connection or any regard to chronological order, on a closer inspection it is easy to discover the relation in which they stand to the leading purpose of the whole book, and the reason why they occupy this position and no other (see the introductory remarks to 2 Sam. ix. xxi.-xxiv.).

If we look more closely, however, at the contents of these books, in order to determine their character more precisely, we

find at the very outset, in Hannah's song of praise, a prophetic
glance at the anointed of the Lord (ch. ii. 10), which foretells
the establishment of the monarchy that was afterwards accomplished under Saul and David.   And with this there is associated the rise of the new name, *Jehovah Sabaoth*, which is
never met with in the Pentateuch or in the books of Joshua
and Judges; whereas it occurs in the books before us from the
commencement (ch. i. 3, 11, etc.) to the close. (For further
remarks on the origin and signification of this divine name, see
at ch. i. 3.)   When Israel received a visible representative of
its invisible God-king in the person of an earthly monarch;
Jehovah, the God of Israel, became the God of the heavenly
hosts.   Through the establishment of the monarchy, the people
of Jehovah's possession became a "world-power;" the kingdom
of God was elevated into a kingdom of the world, as distinguished from the other ungodly kingdoms of the world, which
it was eventually to overcome in the power of its God.   In this
conflict Jehovah manifested himself as the Lord of hosts, to
whom all the nations and kingdoms of this world were to become
subject.   Even in the times of Saul and David, the heathen
nations were to experience a foretaste of this subjection.   When
Saul had ascended the throne of Israel, he fought against all
his enemies round about, and extended his power in every
direction in which he turned (ch. i. 14, 47, 48).   But David
made all the nations who bordered upon the kingdom of God
tributary to the people of the Lord, as the Lord gave him
victory wherever he went (ch. ii. 8, 14, 15); so that his son
Solomon reigned over all the kingdoms, from the stream (the
Euphrates) to the boundary of Egypt, and they all brought him
presents, and were subject to him (1 Kings v. 1).   But the Israelitish monarchy could never thus acquire the power to secure
for the kingdom of God a victory over all its foes, except as the
king himself was diligent in his endeavours to be at all times
simply the instrument of the God-king, and exercise his authority
solely in the name and according to the will of Jehovah.   And
as the natural selfishness and pride of man easily made this
concentration of the supreme earthly power in a single person
merely an occasion for self-aggrandisement, and therefore the
Israelitish kings were exposed to the temptation to use the
plenary authority entrusted to them even in opposition to the

will of God ; the Lord raised up for Himself organs of His own
Spirit, in the persons of the prophets, to stand by the side of
the kings, and make known to them the will and counsel of
God.   The introduction of the monarchy was therefore preceded by the development of the prophetic office into a spiritual
power in Israel, in which the kingdom was to receive not only
a firm support to its own authority, but a strong bulwark against
royal caprice and tyranny.   Samuel was called by the Lord to
be His prophet, to convert the nation that was sunk in idolatry
to the Lord its God, and to revive the religious life by the
establishment of associations of prophets, since the priests had
failed to resist the growing apostasy of the nation, and had
become unfaithful to their calling to instruct and establish the
congregation in the knowledge and fear of the Lord.   Even
before the call of Samuel as a prophet, there was foretold to
the high priest Eli by a man of God, not only the judgment that
would fall upon the degenerate priesthood, but the appointment
of a faithful priest, for whom the Lord would build a permanent
house, that he might ever walk before His anointed (1 Sam.
ii. 27–36).   And the first revelation which Samuel received
from God had reference to the fulfilment of all that the Lord
had spoken against the house of Eli (ch. iii. 11 sqq.).   The
announcement of a faithful priest, who would walk before the
anointed of the Lord, also contained a prediction of the establishment of the monarchy, which foreshadowed its worth and
great significance in relation to the further development of the
kingdom of God.   And whilst these predictions of the anointed
of the Lord, before and in connection with the call of Samuel,
show the deep spiritual connection which existed between the
prophetic order and the regal office in Israel ; the insertion of
them in these books is a proof that from the very outset the
author had this new organization of the Israelitish kingdom of
God before his mind, and that it was his intention not simply
to hand down biographies of Samuel, Saul, and David, but to
relate the history of the Old Testament kingdom of God at the
time of its elevation out of a deep inward and outward decline
into the full authority and power of a kingdom of the Lord,
before which all its enemies were to be compelled to bow.

   Israel was to become a kingship of priests, i.e. a kingdom
whose citizens were priests and kings.   The Lord had announced

this to the sons of Israel before the covenant was concluded at Sinai, as the ultimate object of their adoption as the people of His possession (Ex. xix. 5, 6). Now although this promise reached far beyond the times of the Old Covenant, and will only receive its perfect fulfilment in the completion of the kingdom of God under the New Covenant, yet it was to be realized even in the people of Israel so far as the economy of the Old Testament allowed. Israel was not only to become a priestly nation, but a royal nation also; not only to be sanctified as a congregation of the Lord, but also to be exalted into a kingdom of God. The establishment of the earthly monarchy, therefore, was not only an eventful turning-point, but also an " epoch-making" advance in the development of Israel towards the goal set before it in its divine calling. And this advance became the pledge of the ultimate attainment of the goal, through the promise which David received from God (2 Sam. vii. 12–16), that the Lord would establish the throne of his kingdom for ever. With this promise God established for His anointed the eternal covenant, to which David reverted at the close of his reign, and upon which he rested his divine announcement of the just ruler over men, the ruler in the fear of God (2 Sam. xxiii. 1–7). Thus the close of these books points back to their commencement. The prophecy of the pious mother of Samuel, that the Lord would give strength unto His king, and exalt the horn of His anointed (1 Sam. ii. 10), found a fulfilment in the kingdom of David, which was at the same time a pledge of the ultimate completion of the kingdom of God under the sceptre of the Son of David, the promised Messiah.

This is one, and in fact the most conspicuous, arrangement of the facts connected with the history of salvation, which determined the plan and composition of the work before us. By the side of this there is another, which does not stand out so prominently indeed, but yet must not be overlooked. At the very beginning, viz. in ch. i., the inward decay of the house of God under the high priest Eli is exhibited; and in the announcement of the judgment upon the house of Eli, a long-continued oppression of the dwelling-place (of God) is foretold (ch. ii. 32). Then, in the further course of the narrative, not only is the fulfilment of these threats pointed out, in the events described in 1 Sam. iv., vi. 19–vii. 2, and xxii. 11–19 ; but it is also shown how David first of all brought the ark of the covenant, about which no one had troubled himself in the time of Saul, out of its concealment, had a tent erected for it in the capital of his kingdom upon Mount Zion, and made it once more the central point of the worship of the congregation ; and how after that, when God had given him rest from his enemies, he wished to build a temple for the Lord to be the dwelling-place of His name ; and lastly, when God would not permit him to carry out this resolution, but promised that his son would build the house of the Lord, how, towards the close of his reign, he consecrated the site for the future temple by build-ing an altar upon Mount Moriah (2 Sam. xxiv. 25). Even in this series of facts the end of the work points back to the be-ginning, so that the arrangement and composition of it accord-ing to a definite plan, which has been consistently carried out, are very apparent. If, in addition to this, we take into account the deep-seated connection between the building of the temple as designed by David, and the confirmation of his monarchy on the part of God as exhibited in 2 Sam. vii., we cannot fail to observe that the historical development of the true kingdom, in accordance with the nature and constitution of the Old Tes-tament kingdom of God, forms the leading thought and purpose of the work to which the name of Samuel has been attached, and that it was by this thought and aim that the writer was influenced throughout in his selection of the historical materials which lay before him in the sources that he employed.

The full accounts which are given of the birth and youth of Samuel, and the life of David, are in the most perfect har-mony with this design. The lives and deeds of these two men of God were of significance as laying the foundation for the development and organization of the monarchical kingdom in Israel. Samuel was the model and type of the prophets; and embodied in his own person the spirit and nature of the pro-phetic office, whilst his attitude towards Saul foreshadowed the position which the prophet was to assume in relation to the king. In the life of David, the Lord himself educated the king of His kingdom, the prince over His people, to whom He could continue His favour and grace even when he had fallen so deeply that it was necessary that he should be chastised for his sins. Thus all the separate parts and sections are fused together as an organic whole in the fundamental thought of the work before us. And this unity is not rendered at all questionable by differences such as we find in the accounts of the mode of Saul's death as described in 1 Sam. xxxi. 4 and 2 Sam. i. 9, 10, or by such repetitions as the double account of the death of Samuel, and other phenomena of a similar kind, which can be explained without difficulty; whereas the assertion sometimes made, that there are some events of which we have two different accounts that contradict each other, has never yet been proved, and, as we shall see when we come to the exposition of the passages in question, has arisen partly from unscriptural assumptions, partly from ignorance of the formal peculiarities of the Hebrew mode of writing history, and partly from a mistaken interpretation of the passages themselves.

With regard to the *origin* of the books of Samuel, all that can be maintained with certainty is, that they were not written till after the division of the kingdom under Solomon's successor. This is evident from the remark in 1 Sam. xxvii. 6, that "*Ziklag pertaineth unto the kings of Judah unto this day.*" For although David was king over the tribe of Judah alone for seven years, it was not till after the falling away of the ten tribes from the house of David that there were really "kings of Judah." On the other hand, nothing can be inferred with certainty respecting the date of composition, either from the distinction drawn between Israel and Judah in 1 Sam. xi. 8, xvii. 52, xviii. 16, and 2 Sam. iii. 10, xxiv. 1, which evidently existed as early as the time of David, as we may see from 2 Sam. ii. 9, 10, v. 1–5, xix. 41, xx. 2; or from the formula "*to this day,*" which we find in 1 Sam. v. 5, vi. 18, xxx. 25, 2 Sam. iv. 3, vi. 18, xviii. 18, since the duration of the facts to which it is applied is altogether unknown; or lastly, from such passages as 1 Sam. ix. 9, 2 Sam. xiii. 18, where explanations are given of expressions and customs belonging to the times of Saul and David, as it is quite possible that they may have been altogether changed by the time of Solomon. In general, the contents and style of the books point to the earliest times after the division of the kingdom; since we find no allusions whatever to the decay of the kingdoms which afterwards took place, and still less to the captivity; whilst the style and language are classical throughout, and altogether free from Chaldaisms and later forms, such as we meet with in the writings of the Chaldean period, and even in those of the time of the captivity. The author himself is quite unknown; but, judging from the spirit of his writings, he was a prophet of the kingdom of Judah. It is unanimously admitted, however, that he made use of written documents, particularly of prophetic records made by persons who were contemporaries of the events described, not only for the history of the reigns of Saul and David, but also for the life and labours of Samuel, although no written sources are quoted, with the exception of the " book of Jasher," which contained the elegy of David upon Saul and Jonathan (2 Sam. i. 18); so that the sources employed by him cannot be distinctly pointed out. The different attempts which have been made to determine them minutely, from the time of Eichhorn down to G. Em. Karo (*de fontibus librorum qui feruntur Samuelis Dissert. Berol.* 1862), are lacking in the necessary proofs which hypotheses must bring before they can meet with adoption and support. If we confine ourselves to the historical evidence, according to 1 Chron. xxix. 29, the first and last acts of king David, *i.e.* the events of his entire reign, were recorded in the "*dibre* of Samuel the seer, of Nathan the prophet, and of Gad the seer." These prophetic writings formed no doubt the leading sources from which our books of Samuel were also drawn, since, on the one hand, apart from sundry deviations arising from differences in the plan and object of the two authors, the two accounts of the reign of David in 2 Sam. viii.–xxiv. and 1 Chron. xi.–xxi. agree for the most part so thoroughly word for word, that they are generally regarded as extracts from one common source; whilst, on the other hand, the prophets named not only lived in the time of David but throughout the whole of the period referred to in the books before us, and took a very active part in the progressive development of the history of those times (see not only 1 Sam. i.–iii. vii.–x. xii. xv. xvi., but also 1 Sam. xix. 18–24, xxii. 5, 2 Sam. vii. 12, xxiv. 11–18). Moreover, in 1 Chron. xxvii. 24, there are " chronicles (diaries or annals) of king David" mentioned, accompanied with the remark that the result of the census appointed by David was not inserted in them, from

which we may infer that all the principal events of his reign
were included in these chronicles.   And they may also have
formed one of the sources for our books, although nothing certain can be determined concerning the relation in which they
stood to the writings of the three prophets that have been mentioned.   Lastly, it is very evident from the character of the
work before us, that the author had sources composed by eye-
witnesses of the events at his command, and that these were
employed with an intimate knowledge of the facts and with
historical fidelity, inasmuch as the history is distinguished by
great perspicuity and vividness of description, by a careful
delineation of the characters of the persons engaged, and by
great accuracy in the accounts of localities, and of subordinate
circumstances connected with the historical events.

EXPOSITION.

I. HISTORY OF THE PEOPLE OF ISRAEL UNDER THE PROPHET SAMUEL.

1 SAM. I.–VII.

THE call of Samuel to be the prophet and judge of Israel
formed a turning-point in the history of the Old Testament
kingdom of God.   As the prophet of Jehovah, Samuel was to
lead the people of Israel out of the times of the judges into
those of the kings, and lay the foundation for a prosperous
development of the monarchy.   Consecrated like Samson as a
Nazarite from his mother's womb, Samuel accomplished the
deliverance of Israel out of the power of the Philistines, which
had been only commenced by Samson ; and that not by the
physical might of his arm, but by the spiritual power of his word
and prayer, with which he led Israel back from the worship
of dead idols to the Lord its God.   And whilst as one of the
judges, among whom he classes himself in 1 Sam. xii. 11, he
brought the office of judge to a close, and introduced the
monarchy ; as a prophet, he laid the foundation of the prophetic office, inasmuch as he was the first to naturalize it, so

to speak, in Israel, and develope it into a power that continued henceforth to exert the strongest influence, side by side with the priesthood and monarchy, upon the development of the covenant nation and kingdom of God. For even if there were prophets before the time of Samuel, who revealed the will of the Lord at times to the nation, they only appeared sporadically, without exerting any lasting influence upon the national life; whereas, from the time of Samuel onwards, the prophets sustained and fostered the spiritual life of the congregation, and were the instruments through whom the Lord made known His purposes to the nation and its rulers. To exhibit in its origin and growth the new order of things which Samuel introduced, or rather the deliverance which the Lord sent to His people through this servant of His, the prophetic historian goes back to the time of Samuel's birth, and makes us acquainted not only with the religious condition of the nation, but also with the political oppression under which it was suffering at the close of the period of the judges, and during the high-priesthood of Eli. At the time when the pious parents of Samuel were going year by year to the house of God at Shiloh to worship and offer sacrifice before the Lord, the house of God was being profaned by the abominable conduct of Eli's sons (ch. i. ii.). When Samuel was called to be the prophet of Jehovah, Israel lost the ark of the covenant, the soul of its sanctuary, in the war with the Philistines (ch. iii. iv.). And it was not till after the nation had been rendered willing to put away its strange gods and worship Jehovah alone, through the influence of Samuel's exertions as prophet, that the faithful covenant God gave it, in answer to Samuel's intercession, a complete victory over the Philistines (ch. vii.). In accordance with these three prominent features, the history of the judicial life of Samuel may be divided into three sections, viz.: ch. i. ii.; iii.–vi.; and vii.

SAMUEL'S BIRTH AND DEDICATION TO THE LORD. HANNAH'S SONG OF PRAISE.—CHAP. I.–II. 10.

While Eli the high priest was judging Israel, and at the time when Samson was beginning to fight against the Philistines, a pious Israelitish woman prayed to the Lord for a son (vers.

1–18). Her prayer was heard. She bore a son, to whom she gave the name of Samuel, because he had been asked for from the Lord. As soon as he was weaned, she dedicated him to the Lord for a lifelong service (vers. 19–28), and praised the Lord in a song of prophetic character for the favour which He had shown to His people through hearkening to her prayer (ch. ii. 1–10).

Vers. 1–8. *Samuel's pedigree.*—Ver. 1. His father was a man of Ramathaim-Zophim, on the mountains of Ephraim, and named Elkanah. *Ramathaim-Zophim*, which is only mentioned here, is the same place, according to ver. 3 (comp. with ver. 19 and ch. ii. 11), which is afterwards called briefly *ha-Ramah*, *i.e.* the height. For since Elkanah of Ramathaim-Zophim went year by year out of his city to Shiloh, to worship and sacrifice there, and after he had done this, returned to his house to Ramah (ver. 19, ch. ii. 11), there can be no doubt that he was not only a native of Ramathaim-Zophim, but still had his home there; so that Ramah, where his house was situated, is only an abbreviated name for Ramathaim-Zophim.[1] This Ramah (which is invariably written with the article, ha-Ramah), where Samuel was not only born (vers. 19 sqq.), but lived, laboured, died (ch. vii. 17, xv. 34, xvi. 13, xix. 18, 19, 22, 23), and was buried (ch. xxv. 1, xxviii. 3), is not a different place, as has been frequently assumed,[2] from the Ramah in Benjamin (Josh. xviii. 25), and is not to be sought for in Ramleh near Joppa (v. Schubert, etc.), nor in Soba on the north-west of Jerusalem (Robinson, *Pal.* ii. p. 329), nor three-quarters of an hour to the north of Hebron (Wolcott, v. de Velde), nor anywhere else in the tribe of Ephraim, but is identical with Ramah of Benjamin,

---

[1] The argument lately adduced by Valentiner in favour of the difference between these two names, viz. that " examples are not wanting of a person being described according to his original descent, although his dwelling-place had been already changed," and the instance which he cites, viz. Judg. xix. 16, show that he has overlooked the fact, that in the very passage which he quotes the temporary dwelling-place is actually mentioned along with the native town. In the case before us, on the contrary, Ramathaim-Zophim is designated, by the use of the expression " from his city," in ver. 3, as the place where Elkanah lived, and where " his house" (ver. 19) was still standing.

[2] For the different views which have been held upon this point, see the article " Ramah," by Pressel, in Herzog's *Cyclopædia.*

and was situated upon the site of the present village of er-Râm, two hours to the north-west of Jerusalem, upon a conical mountain to the east of the Nablus road (see at Josh. xviii. 25). This supposition is neither at variance with the account in ch. ix. x. (see the commentary upon these chapters), nor with the statement that Ramathaim-Zophim was upon the mountains of Ephraim, since the mountains of Ephraim extended into the tribe-territory of Benjamin, as is indisputably evident from Judg. iv. 5, where Deborah the prophetess is said to have dwelt between Ramah and Bethel in the mountains of Ephraim. The name Ramathaim-Zophim, *i.e.* " the two heights (of the) Zophites," appears to have been given to the town to distinguish it from other Ramahs, and to have been derived from the Levitical family of Zuph or Zophai (see 1 Chron. vi. 26, 35), which emigrated thither from the tribe of Ephraim, and from which Elkanah was descended. The full name, therefore, is given here, in the account of the descent of Samuel's father ; whereas in the further history of Samuel, where there was no longer the same reason for giving it, the simple name Ramah is invariably used.[1] The connection between Zophim and Zuph is confirmed by the fact that Elkanah's ancestor, Zuph, is called Zophai in 1 Chron. vi. 26, and Zuph or Ziph in 1 Chron. vi. 35. Zophim therefore signifies the descendants of Zuph or Zophai, from which the name " land of Zuph," in ch. ix. 5, was also derived (see the commentary on this passage). The tracing back of Elkanah's family through four generations to Zuph agrees with the family registers in 1 Chron. vi., where the ancestors of Elkanah are mentioned twice,—first of all in the genealogy of the Kohathites (ver. 26), and then in that of Heman, the leader of the singers, a grandson of Samuel (ver.

---

[1] The fuller and more exact name, however, appears to have been still retained, and the use of it to have been revived after the captivity, in the ʹΡαμαθέμ of 1 Macc. xi. 34, for which the Codd. have ʹΡαθαμείν and ʹΡαμαθαΐμ, and Josephus ʹΡαμαθά, and in the Arimathæa of the gospel history (Matt. xxvii. 57). " For the opinion that this Ramathaim is a different place from the city of Samuel, and is to be sought for in the neighbourhood of Lydda, which Robinson advocates (*Pal.* iii. pp. 41 sqq.), is a hasty conclusion, drawn from the association of Ramathaim with Lydda in 1 Macc. xi. 34,—the very same conclusion which led the author of the *Onomasticon* to transfer the city of Samuel to the neighbourhood of Lydda" (Grimm on 1 Macc. xi. 34).

33),—except that the names Elihu, Tohu, and Zuph, are given as Eliab, Nahath, and Zophai in the first instance, and Eliel, Toah, and Ziph (according to the *Chethibh*) in the second,—various readings, such as often occur in the different genealogies, and are to be explained partly from the use of different forms for the same name, and partly from their synonymous meanings. *Tohu* and *Toah,* which occur in Arabic, with the meaning to press or sink in, are related in meaning to *nachath* or *nuach,* to sink or settle down. From these genealogies in the Chronicles, we learn that Samuel was descended from Kohath, the son of Levi, and therefore was a Levite. It is no valid objection to the correctness of this view, that his Levitical descent is never mentioned, or that Elkanah is called an Ephrathite. The former of these can very easily be explained from the fact, that Samuel's work as a reformer, which is described in this book, did not rest upon his Levitical descent, but simply upon the call which he had received from God, as the prophetic office was not confined to any particular class, like that of priest, but was founded exclusively upon the divine calling and endowment with the Spirit of God. And the difficulty which Nägelsbach expresses in Herzog's *Cycl.,* viz. that " as it was stated of those two Levites (Judg. xvii. 7, xix. 1), that they lived in Bethlehem and Ephraim, but only after they had been expressly described as Levites, we should have expected to find the same in the case of Samuel's father," is removed by the simple fact, that in the case of both those Levites it was of great importance, so far as the accounts which are given of them are concerned, that their Levitical standing should be distinctly mentioned, as is clearly shown by Judg. xvii. 10, 13, and xix. 18 ; whereas in the case of Samuel, as we have already observed, his Levitical descent had no bearing upon the call which he received from the Lord. The word *Ephrathite* does not belong, so far as the grammatical construction is concerned, either to *Zuph* or *Elkanah,* but to " *a certain man,*" the subject of the principal clause, and signifies an Ephraimite, as in Judg. xii. 5 and 1 Kings xi. 26, and not an inhabitant of Ephratah, *i.e.* a Bethlehemite, as in ch. xvii. 12 and Ruth i. 2 ; for in both these passages the word is more precisely defined by the addition of the expression " of Bethlehem-Judah," whereas in this verse the explanation is to be found in the expression " of

Mount Ephraim." Elkanah the Levite is called an Ephraimite, because, so far as his civil standing was concerned, he belonged to the tribe of Ephraim, just as the Levite in Judg. xvii. 7 is described as belonging to the family of Judah. The Levites were reckoned as belonging to those tribes in the midst of which they lived, so that there were Judæan Levites, Ephraimitish Levites, and so on (see Hengstenberg, *Diss.* vol. ii. p. 50). It by no means follows, however, from the application of this term to Elkanah, that Ramathaim-Zophim formed part of the tribe-territory of Ephraim, but simply that Elkanah's family was incorporated in this tribe, and did not remove till afterwards to Ramah in the tribe of Benjamin. On the division of the land, dwelling-places were allotted to the Levites of the family of Kohath, in the tribes of Ephraim, Dan, and Manasseh (Josh. xxi. 5, 21 sqq.). Still less is there anything at variance with the Levitical descent of Samuel, as Thenius maintains, in the fact that he was dedicated to the Lord by his mother's vow for he was not dedicated to the service of Jehovah generally through this vow, but was set apart to a lifelong service at the house of God as a Nazarite (vers. 11, 22); whereas other Levites were not required to serve till their twenty-fifth year, and even then had not to perform an uninterrupted service at the sanc-tuary. On the other hand, the Levitical descent of Samuel receives a very strong confirmation from his father's name. All the Elkanahs that we meet with in the Old Testament, with the exception of the one mentioned in 2 Chron. xxviii. 7, whose genealogy is unknown, can be proved to have been Levites; and most of them belong to the family of Korah, from which Samuel was also descended (see Simonis, *Onomast.* p. 493). This is no doubt connected in some way with the meaning of the name *Elkanah,* the man whom God has bought or acquired; since such a name was peculiarly suitable to the Levites, whom the Lord had set apart for service at the sanctuary, in the place of the first-born of Israel, whom He had sanctified to himself when He smote the first-born of Egypt (Num. iii. 13 sqq., 44 sqq.; see Hengstenberg, *ut sup.*).—Vers. 2, 3. Elkanah had two wives, Hannah (grace or gracefulness) and Peninnah (coral), the latter of whom was blessed with children, whereas the first was childless. He went with his wives year by year (מִיָּמִים יָמִימָה, as in Ex. xiii. 10, Judg. xi. 40), according to the instructions of the law (Ex. xxxiv. 23, Deut. xvi. 16), to the tabernacle at Shiloh (Josh. xviii. 1), to worship and sacrifice to the Lord of hosts. "*Jehovah Zebaoth*" is an abbreviation of "*Jehovah Elohe Zebaoth*," or יְהוָֹה אֱלֹהֵי הַצְּבָאוֹת ; and the connection of *Zebaoth* with *Jehovah* is not to be regarded as the construct state, nor is *Zebaoth* to be taken as a genitive dependent upon *Jehovah*. This is not only confirmed by the occurrence of such expressions as "*Elohim Zebaoth*" (Ps. lix. 6, lxxx. 5, 8, 15, 20, lxxxiv. 9) and "*Adonai Zebaoth*" (Isa. x. 16), but also by the circumstance that *Jehovah*, as a proper name, cannot be construed with a genitive. The combination "Jehovah Zebaoth" is rather to be taken as an ellipsis, where the general term Elohe (God of), which is implied in the word *Jehovah*, is to be supplied in thought (see Hengstenberg, *Christol.* i. p. 375, English translation) ; for frequently as this expression occurs, especially in the case of the prophets, *Zebaoth* is never used alone in the Old Testament as one of the names of God. It is in the Septuagint that the word is first met with occasionally as a proper name (Σαβαώθ), viz. throughout the whole of the first book of Samuel, very frequently in Isaiah, and also in Zech. xiii. 2. In other passages, the word is translated either κύριος, or θεὸς τῶν δυνάμεων, or παντοκράτωρ ; whilst the other Greek versions use the more definite phrase κύριος στρατιῶν instead.

This expression, which was not used as a divine name until the age of Samuel, had its roots in Gen. ii. 1, although the title itself was unknown in the Mosaic period, and during the times of the judges (see p. 7). It represented Jehovah as ruler over the heavenly hosts (*i.e.* the angels, according to Gen. xxxii. 2, and the stars, according to Isa. xl. 26), who are called the " armies" of Jehovah in Ps. ciii. 21, cxlviii. 2 ; but we are not to understand it as implying that the stars were supposed to be inhabited by angels, as Gesenius (*Thes. s. v.*) maintains, since there is not the slightest trace of any such notion in the whole of the Old Testament. It is simply applied to Jehovah as the God of the universe, who governs all the powers of heaven, both visible and invisible, as He rules in heaven and on earth. It cannot even be proved that the epithet Lord, or God of Zebaoth, refers chiefly and generally to the sun, moon, and stars, on account of their being so peculiarly adapted, through their visible splendour, to keep alive the consciousness of the

omnipotence and glory of God (Hengstenberg on Ps. xxiv. 10).
For even though the expression צְבָאָם (their host), in Gen. ii. 1,
refers to the heavens only, since it is only to the heavens (vid.
Isa. xl. 26), and never to the earth, that a "host" is ascribed, and
in this particular passage it is probably only the stars that are
to be thought of, the creation of which had already been mentioned in Gen. i. 14 sqq.; yet we find the idea of an army of
angels introduced in the history of Jacob (Gen. xxxii. 2, 3),
where Jacob calls the angels of God who appeared to him the
" camp of God," and also in the blessing of Moses (Deut.
xxxiii. 2), where the " ten thousands of saints" (*Kodesh*) are
not stars, but angels, or heavenly spirits; whereas the fighting
of the stars against Sisera in the song of Deborah probably
refers to a natural phenomenon, by which God had thrown the
enemy into confusion, and smitten them before the Israelites
(see at Judg. v. 20). We must also bear in mind, that whilst
on the one hand the tribes of Israel, as they came out of Egypt,
are called Zebaoth Jehovah, " the hosts of Jehovah" (Ex. vii. 4,
xii. 41), on the other hand the angel of the Lord, when appearing in front of Jericho in the form of a warrior, made himself
known to Joshua as " the prince of the army of Jehovah,"
i.e. of the angelic hosts. And it is in this appearance of the
heavenly leader of the people of God to the earthly leader of
the hosts of Israel, as the prince of the angelic hosts, not only
promising him the conquest of Jericho, but through the miraculous overthrow of the walls of this strong bulwark of the
Canaanitish power, actually giving him at the same time a practical proof that the prince of the angelic hosts was fighting for
Israel, that we have the material basis upon which the divine
epithet " Jehovah God of hosts" was founded, even though it
was not introduced immediately, but only at a later period,
when the Lord began to form His people Israel into a kingdom,
by which all the kingdoms of the heathen were to be overcome.
It is certainly not without significance that this title is given
to God for the first time in these books, which contain an
account of the founding of the kingdom, and (as Auberlen has
observed) that it was by Samuel's mother, the pious Hannah,
when dedicating her son to the Lord, and prophesying of the
king and anointed of the Lord in her song of praise (ch. ii. 10),
that this name was employed for the first time, and that God

was addressed in prayer as "Jehovah of hosts" (ver. 11). Consequently, if this name of God goes hand in hand with the prophetic announcement and the actual establishment of the monarchy in Israel, its origin cannot be attributed to any antagonism to Sabæism, or to the hostility of pious Israelites to the worship of the stars, which was gaining increasing ground in the age of David, as Hengstenberg (on Ps. xxiv. 10) and Strauss (on Zeph. ii. 9) maintain ; to say nothing of the fact, that there is no historical foundation for such an assumption at all. It is a much more natural supposition, that when the invisible sovereignty of Jehovah received a visible manifestation in the establishment of the earthly monarchy, the sovereignty of Jehovah, if it did possess and was to possess any reality at all, necessarily claimed to be recognised in its all-embracing power and glory, and that in the title "God of (the heavenly) hosts" the fitting expression was formed for the universal government of the God-king of Israel,—a title which not only served as a bulwark against any eclipsing of the invisible sovereignty of God by the earthly monarchy in Israel, but overthrew the vain delusion of the heathen, that the God of Israel was simply the national deity of that particular nation.[1]

The remark introduced in ver. 3*b*, "*and there were the two sons of Eli, Hophni and Phinehas, priests of the Lord*," *i.e.* performing the duties of the priesthood, serves as a preparation for what follows. This reason for the remark sufficiently explains why the sons of Eli only are mentioned here, and not Eli himself, since, although the latter still presided over the sanctuary as high priest, he was too old to perform the duties connected with the offering of sacrifice. The addition made by the LXX., Ἠλὶ καὶ, is an arbitrary interpolation, occasioned by a misapprehension of the reason for mentioning the sons of Eli.—Vers. 4, 5. "*And it came to pass, the day, and he*

---

[1] This name of God was therefore held up before the people of the Lord even in their war-songs and pæans of victory, but still more by the prophets, as a banner under which Israel was to fight and to conquer the world. Ezekiel is the only prophet who does not use it, simply because he follows the Pentateuch so strictly in his style. And it is not met with in the book of Job, just because the theocratic constitution of the Israelitish nation is never referred to in the problem of that book.

offered sacrifice" (for, " on which he offered sacrifice "), that
he gave to Peninnah and her children portions of the flesh of
the sacrifice at the sacrificial meal ; but to Hannah he gave
מָנָה אַחַת אַפָּיִם, " *one portion for two persons,*" *i.e.* a double
portion, because he loved her, but Jehovah had shut up her
womb : *i.e.* he gave it as an expression of his love to her, to
indicate by a sign, " thou art as dear to me as if thou hadst
born me a child " (O. v. Gerlach). This explanation of the
difficult word אַפָּיִם, of which very different interpretations
have been given, is the one adopted by Tanchum Hieros., and
is the only one which can be grammatically sustained, or yields
an appropriate sense. The meaning *face* (*facies*) is placed
beyond all doubt by Gen. iii. 19 and other passages ; and
the use of לְאַפֵּי as a synonym for לִפְנֵי in ch. xxv. 23, also
establishes the meaning " person," since פָּנִים is used in this
sense in 2 Sam. xvii. 11. It is true that there are no other
passages that can be adduced to prove that the singular אַף was
also used in this sense ; but as the word was employed promiscuously in both singular and plural in the derivative sense of
anger, there is no reason for denying that the singular may also
have been employed in the sense of *face* (πρόσωπον). The
combination of אַפָּיִם with מָנָה אַחַת in the absolute state is supported by many other examples of the same kind (see Ewald,
§ 287, *h*). The meaning *double* has been correctly adopted in
the Syriac, whereas Luther follows the *tristis* of the Vulgate,
and renders the word *traurig*, or sad. But this meaning, which
Fr. Böttcher has lately taken under his protection, cannot be
philologically sustained either by the expression נָפְלוּ פָנֶיךָ (Gen.
iv. 6), or by Dan. xi. 20, or in any other way. אַף and אַפָּיִם
do indeed signify anger, but anger and sadness are two very
different ideas. But when Böttcher substitutes " angrily or
unwillingly " for sadly, the incongruity strikes you at once :
" he gave her a portion unwillingly, because he loved her !"
For the custom of singling out a person by giving double or
even large portions, see the remarks on Gen. xliii. 34.—Ver. 6.
" *And her adversary* (Peninnah) *also provoked her with provocation, to irritate her.*" The גַּם is placed before the noun
belonging to the verb, to add force to the meaning. רָעַם
(*Hiphil*), to excite, put into (inward) commotion, not exactly to
make angry.—Ver. 7. " *So did he* (Elkanah) *from year to year*

(namely give to Hannah a double portion at the sacrificial meal), *as often as she went up to the house of the Lord.* *So did she* (Peninnah) *provoke her* (Hannah), *so that she wept, and did not eat.*" The two כֵּן correspond to one another. Just as Elkanah showed his love to Hannah at every sacrificial festival, so did Peninnah repeat her provocation, the effect of which was that Hannah gave vent to her grief in tears, and did not eat.—Ver. 8. Elkanah sought to comfort her in her grief by the affectionate appeal: "*Am I not better to thee* (טוֹב, *i.e.* dearer) *than ten children?*" *Ten* is a round number for a large number.

Vers. 9–18. *Hannah's prayer for a son.*—Vers. 9–11. "*After the eating at Shiloh, and after the drinking,*" *i.e.* after the sacrificial meal was over, Hannah rose up with a troubled heart, to pour out her grief in prayer before God, whilst Eli was sitting before the door-posts of the palace of Jehovah, and vowed this vow: "*Lord of Zebaoth, if Thou regardest the distress of Thy maiden, and givest men's seed to Thy maiden, I will give him to the Lord all his life long, and no razor shall come upon his head.*" The choice of the infinitive absolute שָׁתֹה instead of the infinitive construct is analogous to the combination of two nouns, the first of which is defined by a suffix, and the second written absolutely (see *e.g.* עָזִּי וְזִמְרָת, Ex. xv. 2; cf. 2 Sam. xxiii. 5, and Ewald, § 339, *b*). The words from וְעֵלִי onwards to מָרַת נֶפֶשׁ form two circumstantial clauses inserted in the main sentence, to throw light upon the situation and the further progress of the affair. The tabernacle is called "*the palace of Jehovah*" (cf. ch. ii. 22), not on account of the magnificence and splendour of the building, but as the dwelling-place of Jehovah of hosts, the God-king of Israel, as in Ps. v. 8, etc. מְזוּזָה is probably a porch, which had been placed before the curtain that formed the entrance into the holy place, when the tabernacle was erected permanently at Shiloh. מָרַת נֶפֶשׁ, troubled in soul (cf. 2 Kings iv. 27). וּבָכֹה תִבְכֶּה is really subordinate to תִּתְפַּלֵּל, in the sense of "weeping much during her prayer." The depth of her trouble was also manifest in the crowding together of the words in which she poured out the desire of her heart before God: "*If Thou wilt look upon the distress of Thine handmaid, and remember and not forget,*" etc. "*Men's seed*" (*semen virorum*), *i.e.* a male child. אֲנָשִׁים

is the plural of אִישׁ, a man (see Ewald, § 186–7), from the root
אֵשׁ, which combines the two ideas of fire, regarded as life,
and giving life and firmness. The vow contained two points :
(1) she would give the son she had prayed for to be the Lord's
all the days of his life, *i.e.* would dedicate him to the Lord for
a lifelong service, which, as we have already observed at p. 18,
the Levites as such were not bound to perform ; and (2) no
razor should come upon his head, by which he was set apart as
a Nazarite for his whole life (see at Num. vi. 2 sqq., and Judg.
xiii. 5). The Nazarite, again, was neither bound to perform a
lifelong service nor to remain constantly at the sanctuary, but
was simply consecrated for a certain time, whilst the sacrifice
offered at his release from the vow shadowed forth a complete
surrender to the Lord. The second point, therefore, added a
new condition to the first, and one which was not necessarily
connected with it, but which first gave the true consecration to
the service of the Lord at the sanctuary. At the same time,
the qualification of Samuel for priestly functions, such as the
offering of sacrifice, can neither be deduced from the first point
in the vow, nor yet from the second. If, therefore, at a later
period, when the Lord had called him to be a prophet, and had
thereby placed him at the head of the nation, Samuel officiated
at the presentation of sacrifice, he was not qualified to perform
this service either as a Levite or as a lifelong Nazarite, but
performed it solely by virtue of his prophetic calling.—Vers.
12–14. But when Hannah prayed much (*i.e.* a long time)
before the Lord, and Eli noticed her mouth, and, as she was
praying inwardly, only saw her lips move, but did not hear her
voice, he thought she was drunken, and called out to her :
" *How long dost thou show thyself drunken ? put away thy wine
from thee,*" *i.e.* go away and sleep off thine intoxication (cf. ch.
xxv. 37). מְדַבֶּרֶת עַל לִבָּהּ, *lit.* speaking to her heart. עַל is not
to be confounded with אֶל (Gen. xxiv. 45), but has the subordinate idea of a comforting address, as in Gen. xxxiv. 3, etc.—
Vers. 15, 16. Hannah answered : " *No, my lord, I am a woman
of an oppressed spirit. I have not drunk wine and strong drink,
but have poured out my soul before the Lord* (see Ps. xlii. 5).
*Do not count thine handmaid for a worthless woman, for I have
spoken hitherto out of great sighing and grief.*" נָתַן לִפְנֵי, to set
or lay before a person, *i.e.* generally to give a person up to

another ; here to place him in thought in the position of another, *i.e.* to take him for another. שִׂיחַ, meditation, inward movement of the heart, sighing.—Ver. 17. Eli then replied : *" Go in peace, and the God of Israel give* (grant) *thy request* (שְׁלָתֵךְ for שְׁאֵלָתֵךְ), *which thou hast asked of Him."* This word of the high priest was not a prediction, but a pious wish, which God in His grace most gloriously fulfilled.—Ver. 18. Hannah then went her way, saying, *" Let thine handmaid find grace in thine eyes,"* *i.e.* let me be honoured with thy favour and thine intercession, and was strengthened and comforted by the word of the high priest, which assured her that her prayer would be heard by God ; and she did eat, *" and her countenance was no more,"* sc. troubled and sad, as it had been before. This may be readily supplied from the context, through which the word countenance (פָּנִים) acquires the sense of a troubled countenance, as in Job ix. 27.

Vers. 19–28. *Samuel's birth, and dedication to the Lord.*— Vers. 19, 20. The next morning Elkanah returned home to Ramah (see at ver. 1) with his two wives, having first of all worshipped before the Lord ; after which he knew his wife Hannah, and Jehovah remembered her, *i.e.* heard her prayer. *" In the revolution of the days,"* *i.e.* of the period of her conception and pregnancy, Hannah conceived and bare a son, whom she called Samuel ; *" for* (she said) *I have asked him of the Lord."* The name שְׁמוּאֵל (Σαμουήλ, LXX.) is not formed from שֵׁם=שְׁמוֹ and אֵל, name of God (Ges. *Thes.* p. 1434), but from שְׁמוּעַ אֵל, *heard of God, a Deo exauditus,* with an elision of the ע (see Ewald, § 275, *a*, Not. 3) ; and the words *" because I have asked him of the Lord"* are not an etymological explanation of the name, but an exposition founded upon the facts. Because Hannah had asked him of Jehovah, she gave him the name, *" the God-he d,"* as a memorial of the hearing of her prayer.— Vers. 21, 22. When Elkanah went up again with his family to Shiloh, to present his yearly sacrifice and his vow to the Lord, Hannah said to her husband that she would not go up till she had weaned the boy, and could present him to the Lord, that he might remain there for ever. זֶבַח הַיָּמִים, the sacrifice of the days, *i.e.* which he was accustomed to offer on the days when he went up to the sanctuary ; really, therefore, the annual sacrifice. It follows from the expression *" and his vow,"* that Elkanah had also vowed a vow to the Lord, in case the beloved Hannah should have a son. The vow referred to the presentation of a sacrifice. And this explains the combination of אֶת־נִדְרוֹ with לִזְבֹּחַ.[1] Weaning took place very late among the Israelites. According to 2 Macc. vii. 28, the Hebrew mothers were in the habit of suckling their children for three years. When the weaning had taken place, Hannah would bring her son up to the sanctuary, to appear before the face of the Lord, and remain there for ever, i.e. his whole life long. The Levites generally were only required to perform service at the sanctuary from their twenty-fifth to their fiftieth year (Num. viii. 24, 25); but Samuel was to be presented to the Lord immediately after his weaning had taken place, and to remain at the sanctuary for ever, i.e. to belong entirely to the Lord. To this end he was to receive his training at the sanctuary, that at the very earliest waking up of his spiritual susceptibilities he might receive the impressions of the sacred presence of God. There is no necessity, therefore, to understand the word נָּמַל (wean) as including what followed the weaning, namely, the training of the child up to

[1] The LXX. add to τὰς εὐχὰς αὐτοῦ the clause καὶ πάσας τὰς δεκάτας τῆς γῆς αὐτοῦ ("and all the tithes of his land"). This addition is just as arbitrary as the alteration of the singular נִדְרוֹ into the plural τὰς εὐχὰς αὐτοῦ. The translator overlooked the special reference of the word נִדְרוֹ to the child desired by Elkanah, and imagined—probably with Deut. xii. 26, 27 in his mind, where vows are ordered to be paid at the sanctuary in connection with slain offerings and sacrificial meals—that when Elkanah made his annual journey to the tabernacle he would discharge all his obligations to God, and consequently would pay his tithes. The genuineness of this additional clause cannot be sustained by an appeal to Josephus (Ant. v. 10, 3), who also has δεκάτας τε ἔφερον, for Josephus wrote his work upon the basis of the Alexandrian version. This statement of Josephus is only worthy of notice, inasmuch as it proves the incorrectness of the conjecture of Thenius, that the allusion to the tithes was intentionally dropped out of the Hebrew text by copyists, who regarded Samuel's Levitical descent as clearly established by 1 Chron. vi. 7–13 and 19–21. For Josephus (l. c. § 2) expressly describes Elkanah as a Levite, and takes no offence at the offering of tithes attributed to him in the Septuagint, simply because he was well acquainted with the law, and knew that the Levites had to pay to the priests a tenth of the tithes that they received from the other tribes, as a heave-offering of Jehovah (Num. xviii. 26 sqq. ; cf. Neh. x. 38). Consequently the presentation of tithe on the part of Elkanah, if it were really well founded in the biblical text, would not furnish any argument against his Levitical descent.

his thirteenth year (Seb. Schmidt), on the ground that a child of three years old could only have been a burden to Eli : for the word never has this meaning, not even in 1 Kings xi. 20 ; and, as O. v. Gerlach has observed, his earliest training might have been superintended by one of the women who worshipped at the door of the tabernacle (ch. ii. 22).—Ver. 23. Elkanah expressed his approval of Hannah's decision, and added, " *only the Lord establish His word*," *i.e,* fulfil it. By "His word" we are not to understand some direct revelation from God respecting the birth and destination of Samuel, as the Rabbins suppose, but in all probability the word of Eli the high priest to Hannah, " The God of Israel grant thy petition " (ver. 17), which might be regarded by the parents of Samuel after his birth as a promise from Jehovah himself, and therefore might naturally excite the wish and suggest the prayer that the Lord would graciously fulfil the further hopes, which the parents cherished in relation to the son whom they had dedicated to the Lord by a vow. The paraphrase of דְּבָרוֹ in the rendering given by the LXX., τὸ ἐξελθὸν ἐκ τοῦ στόματός σου, is the subjective view of the translator himself, and does not warrant an emendation of the original text.—Vers. 24, 25. As soon as the boy was weaned, Hannah brought him, although still a נַעַר, *i.e.* a tender boy, to Shiloh, with a sacrifice of three oxen, an ephah of meal, and a pitcher of wine, and gave him up to Eli when the ox (bullock) had been slain, *i.e.* offered in sacrifice as a burnt-offering. The striking circumstance that, according to ver. 24, Samuel's parents brought three oxen with them to Shiloh, and yet in ver. 25 the ox (הַפָּר) alone is spoken of as being slain (or sacrificed), may be explained very simply on the supposition that in ver. 25 that particular sacrifice is referred to, which was associated with the presentation of the boy, that is to say, the burnt-offering by virtue of which the boy was consecrated to the Lord as a spiritual sacrifice for a lifelong service at His sanctuary, whereas the other two oxen served as the yearly festal offering, *i.e.* the burnt-offerings and thank-offerings which Elkanah presented year by year, and the presentation of which the writer did not think it needful to mention, simply because it followed partly from ver. 3 and partly from the Mosaic law.[1]—Vers.

[1] The interpretation of בְּפָרִים שְׁלֹשָׁה by ἐν μόσχῳ τριετίζοντι (LXX.), upon which Thenius would found an alteration of the text, is proved to be

26–28. When the boy was presented, his mother made herself known to the high priest as the woman who had previously prayed to the Lord at that place (see vers. 11 sqq.), and said, " *For this child I prayed; and the Lord hath granted me my request which I asked of Him : therefore I also make him one asked of the Lord all the days that he liveth; he is asked of the Lord.*" וְגַם אָנֹכִי : *I also; et ego vicissim* (Cler.). הִשְׁאִיל, to let a person ask, to grant his request, to give him what he asks (Ex. xii. 36), signifies here to make a person " asked " (שָׁאוּל). The meaning to lend, which the lexicons give to the word both here and Ex. xii. 36, has no other support than the false rendering of the LXX., and is altogether unsuitable both in the one and the other. Jehovah had not *lent* the son to Hannah, but had *given* him (see ver. 11); still less could a man *lend* his son to the Lord. The last clause of ver. 28, " *and he worshipped the Lord there,*" refers to Elkanah, *qui in votum Hannæ consenserat*, and not to Samuel. On a superficial glance, the plural יִשְׁתַּחֲווּ, which is found in some Codd., and in the Vulgate, Syriac, and Arabic, appears the more suitable; but when we look more closely at the connection in which the clause stands, we see at once that it does not wind up the foregoing account, but simply introduces the closing act of the transference of Samuel. Consequently the singular is perfectly appropriate; and notwithstanding the fact that the subject is not mentioned, the allusion to Samuel is placed beyond all doubt. When Hannah had given up her son to the high priest, his father Elkanah first of all worshipped before the Lord in the sanctuary, and then Hannah worshipped in the song of praise, which follows in ch. ii. 1–10.

both arbitrary and wrong by the fact that the translators themselves afterwards mention the θυσία, which Elkanah brought year by year, and the μόσχος, and consequently represent him as offering at least two animals, in direct opposition to the μόσχῳ τριετίζοντι. This discrepancy cannot be removed by the assertion that in ver. 24 the sacrificial animal intended for the dedication of the boy is the only one mentioned; and the presentation of the regular festal sacrifice is taken for granted, for an ephah of meal would not be the proper quantity to be offered in connection with a single ox, since, according to the law in Num. xv. 8, 9, only three-tenths of an ephah of meal were required when an ox was presented as a burnt-offering or slain offering. The presentation of an ephah of meal presupposes the offering of three oxen, and therefore shows that in ver. 24 the materials are mentioned for all the sacrifices that Elkanah was about to offer.

Chap. ii. 1–10. *Hannah's song of praise.*—The prayer in which Hannah poured out the feelings of her heart, after the dedication of her son to the Lord, is a song of praise of a prophetic and Messianic character. After giving utterance in the introduction to the rejoicing and exulting of her soul at the salvation that had reached her (ver. 1), she praises the Lord as the only holy One, the only rock of the righteous, who rules on earth with omniscience and righteousness, brings down the proud and lofty, kills and makes alive, maketh poor and maketh rich (vers. 2–8). She then closes with the confident assurance that He will keep His saints, and cast down the rebellious, and will judge the ends of the earth, and exalt the power of His king (vers. 9, 10).

This psalm is the mature fruit of the Spirit of God. The pious woman, who had gone with all the earnest longings of a mother's heart to pray to the Lord God of Israel for a son, that she might consecrate him to the lifelong service of the Lord, " discerned in her own individual experience the general laws of the divine economy, and its signification in relation to the whole history of the kingdom of God" (Auberlen, p. 564). The experience which she, bowed down and oppressed as she was, had had of the gracious government of the omniscient and holy covenant God, was a pledge to her of the gracious way in which the nation itself was led by God, and a sign by which she discerned how God not only delivered at all times the poor and wretched who trusted in Him out of their poverty and distress, and set them up, but would also lift up and glorify His whole nation, which was at that time so deeply bowed down and oppressed by its foes. Acquainted as she was with the destination of Israel to be a *kingdom*, from the promises which God had given to the patriarchs, and filled as she was with the longing that had been awakened in the nation for the realization of these promises, she could see in spirit, and through the inspiration of God, the *king* whom the Lord was about to give to His people, and through whom He would raise it up to might and dominion.

The refusal of modern critics to admit the genuineness of this song is founded upon an *a priori* and utter denial of the supernatural saving revelations of God, and upon a consequent inability to discern the prophetic illumination of the pious

Hannah, and a complete misinterpretation of the contents of her song of praise. The "proud and lofty," whom God humbles and casts down, are not the heathen or the national foes of Israel, and the " poor and wretched" whom He exalts and makes rich are not the Israelites as such; but the former are the *ungodly*, and the latter the *pious*, in Israel itself. And the description is so well sustained throughout, that it is only by the most arbitrary criticism that it can be interpreted as referring to definite historical events, such as the victory of David over Goliath (Thenius), or a victory of the Israelites over heathen nations (Ewald and others). Still less can any argument be drawn from the words of the song in support of its later origin, or its composition by David or one of the earliest of the kings of Israel. On the contrary, not only is its genuineness supported by the general consideration that the author of these books would never have ascribed a song to Hannah, if he had not found it in the sources he employed; but still more decisively by the circumstance that the songs of praise of Mary and Zechariah, in Luke i. 46 sqq. and 68 sqq., show, through the manner in which they rest upon this ode, in what way it was understood by the pious Israelites of every age, and how, like the pious Hannah, they recognised and praised in their own individual experience the government of the holy God in the midst of His kingdom.

The first verse forms the introduction to the song. Holy joy in the Lord at the blessing which she had received impelled the favoured mother to the praise of God :

> Ver. 1. My heart is joyful in the Lord,
> My horn is exalted in the Lord,
> My mouth is opened wide over mine enemies :
> For I rejoice in Thy salvation.

Of the four members of this verse, the first answers to the third, and the second to the fourth. The heart rejoices at the lifting up of her horn, the mouth opens wide to proclaim the salvation before which the enemies would be dumb. "*My horn is high*" does not mean 'I am proud' (Ewald), but "my power is great in the Lord." The horn is the symbol of strength, and is taken from oxen whose strength is in their horns (*vid.* Deut. xxxiii. 17; Ps. lxxv. 5, etc.). The power was high or exalted by the salvation which the Lord had manifested to her. To Him all the glory was due, because He had proved himself to be the holy One, and a rock upon which a man could rest his confidence.

Ver. 2. None is holy as the Lord; for there is none beside Thee;
And no rock is as our God.

3. Speak ye not much lofty, lofty;
Let (not) insolence go out of thy mouth!
For the Lord is an omniscient God,
And with Him deeds are weighed.

God manifests himself as holy in the government of the kingdom of His grace by His guidance of the righteous to salvation (see at Ex. xix. 6). But holiness is simply the moral reflection of the glory of the one absolute God. This explains the reason given for His holiness, viz. "there is not one (a God) beside thee" (cf. 2 Sam. xxii. 32). As the holy and only One, God is the rock (vid. Deut. xxxii. 4, 15; Ps. xviii. 3) in which the righteous can always trust. The wicked therefore should tremble before His holiness, and not talk in their pride of the *lofty* things which they have accomplished or intend to perform. גְּבֹהָה is defined more precisely in the following clause, which is also dependent upon אַל by the word עָתָק, as insolent words spoken by the wicked against the righteous (see Ps. xxxi. 19). For Jehovah hears such words; He is "*a God of knowledge*" (*Deus scientiarum*), a God who sees and knows every single thing. The plural דֵּעוֹת has an intensive signification. לֹא נִתְכְּנוּ עֲלִלוֹת might be rendered "deeds are not weighed, or equal" (cf. Ezek. xviii. 25, 26, xxxiii. 17). But this would only apply to the actions of men; for the acts of God are always just, or weighed. But an assertion respecting the actions of men does not suit the context. Hence this clause is reckoned in the Masora as one of the passages in which לֹא stands for לוֹ (see at Ex. xxi. 8). "*To Him* (with Him) *deeds are weighed*:" that is to say, the acts of God are weighed, *i.e.* equal or just. This is the real meaning according to the passages in Ezekiel, and not "the actions of men are weighed by Him" (De Wette, Maurer, Ewald, etc.): for God weighs the minds and hearts of men (Prov. xvi. 2, xxi. 2, xxiv. 12), not their actions. This expression never occurs. The weighed or righteous acts of God are described in vers. 4–8 in great and general traits, as displayed in the government of His kingdom through the marvellous changes which occur in the circumstances connected with the lives of the righteous and the wicked.

> Ver. 4. Bow-heroes are confounded,
> And stumbling ones gird themselves with strength ;
>
> 5. Full ones hire themselves out for bread,
> And hungry ones cease to be.
> Yea, the barren beareth seven (children),
> And she that is rich in children pines away.
>
> 6. The Lord kills and makes alive ;
> Leads down into hell, and leads up.
>
> 7. The Lord makes poor and makes rich,
> Humbles and also exalts.
>
> 8. He raises mean ones out of the dust,
> He lifts up poor ones out of the dunghill,
> To set them beside the noble ;
> And He apportions to them the seat of glory :
> For the pillars of the earth are the Lord's,
> And He sets the earth upon them.

In ver. 4, the predicate חַתִּים is construed with the *nomen rectum* גִּבֹּרִים, not with the *nomen regens* קֶשֶׁת, because the former is the leading term (*vid.* Ges. § 148, 1, and Ewald, § 317, *d*). The thought to be expressed is, not that the bow itself is to be broken, but that the heroes who carry the bow are to be confounded or broken inwardly. " *Bows of the heroes*" stands for heroes carrying bows. For this reason the verb is to be taken in the sense of confounded, not broken, especially as, apart from Isa. li. 56, חָתַת is not used to denote the breaking of outward things, but the breaking of men.—Ver. 5. שְׂבֵעִים are the rich and well to do ; these would become so poor as to be obliged to hire themselves out for bread. חָדֵל, to cease to be what they were before. The use of עַד as a conjunction, in the sense of " yea" or " in fact," may be explained as an elliptical expression, signifying " it comes to this, that." " *Seven children*" are mentioned as the full number of the divine blessing in children (see Ruth iv. 15). " The mother of many children" pines away, because she has lost all her sons, and with them her support in her old age (see Jer. xv. 9). This comes from the Lord, who kills, etc. (cf. Deut. xxxii. 39). The words of ver. 6 are figurative. God hurls down into death and the danger of death, and also rescues therefrom (see Ps. xxx. 3, 4).

The first three clauses of ver. 8 are repeated *verbatim* in Ps. cxiii. 7, 8. *Dust* and the *dunghill* are figures used to denote the deepest degradation and ignominy. The antithesis to this is, sitting upon the chair or throne of glory, the seat occupied by noble princes. The Lord does all this, for He is the creator and upholder of the world. *The pillars* (מְצֻקֵי, from צוּק = יָצַק) *of the earth are the Lord's;* i.e. they were created or set up by Him, and by Him they are sustained. Now as Jehovah, the God of Israel, the Holy One, governs the world with His almighty power, the righteous have nothing to fear. With this thought the last strophe of the song begins :

> Ver. 9. The feet of His saints He will keep,
> And the wicked perish in darkness ;
> For by power no one becomes strong.
>
> 10. The Lord—those who contend against Him are confounded.
> He thunders above him in the heavens ;
> The Lord will judge the ends of the earth,
> That He may lend might to His king,
> And exalt the horn of His anointed.

The Lord keeps the feet of the righteous, so that they do not tremble and stumble, *i.e.* so that the righteous do not fall into adversity and perish therein (*vid.* Ps. lvi. 14, cxvi. 8, cxxi. 3). But the wicked, who oppress and persecute the righteous, will perish in darkness, *i.e.* in adversity, when God withdraws the light of His grace, so that they fall into distress and calamity. For no man can be strong through his own power, so as to meet the storms of life. All who fight against the Lord are destroyed. To bring out the antithesis between man and God, " Jehovah" is written absolutely at the commencement of the sentence in ver. 10 : "*As for Jehovah, those who contend against Him are broken,*" both inwardly and outwardly (חָתַת, as in ver. 4). The word עָלָו, which follows, is not to be changed into עֲלֵיהֶם. There is simply a rapid alternation of the numbers, such as we frequently meet with in excited language. " *Above him,*" i.e. above every one who contends against God, He thunders. Thunder is a premonitory sign of the approach of the Lord to judgment. In the thunder, man is made to feel in an alarming way the presence of the omnipotent God. In the words, " *The Lord will judge the ends of the earth,*" *i.e.* the earth to its utmost extremities, or the whole world, Hannah's prayer rises up to a prophetic glance at the consummation of the kingdom of God. As certainly as the Lord God keeps the righteous at all times, and casts down the wicked, so certainly will He judge the whole world, to hurl down all His foes, and perfect His kingdom which He has founded in Israel. And as every kingdom culminates in its throne, or in the full might and government of a king, so the kingdom of God can only attain its full perfection in the king whom the Lord will give to His people, and endow with His might. *The king*, or the *anointed of the Lord*, of whom Hannah prophesies in the spirit, is not one single king of Israel, either David or Christ, but an ideal king, though not a mere personification of the throne about to be established, but the actual king whom Israel received in David and his race, which culminated in the Messiah. The exaltation of the horn of the anointed of Jehovah commenced with the victorious and splendid expansion of the power of David, was repeated with every victory over the enemies of God and His kingdom gained by the successive kings of David's house, goes on in the advancing spread of the kingdom of Christ, and will eventually attain to its eternal consummation in the judgment of the last day, through which all the enemies of Christ will be made His footstool.

SAMUEL'S SERVICE BEFORE ELI. UNGODLINESS OF ELI'S SONS. DENUNCIATION OF JUDGMENT UPON ELI AND HIS HOUSE. —CHAP. II. 11–36.

Vers. 11–17. *Samuel the servant of the Lord under Eli. Ungodliness of the sons of Eli.*—Ver. 11 forms the transition to what follows. After Hannah's psalm of thanksgiving, Elkanah went back with his family to his home at Ramah, and the boy (Samuel) was serving, *i.e.* ministered to the Lord, in the presence of Eli the priest. The fact that nothing is said about Elkanah's wives going with him, does not warrant the interpretation given by Thenius, that Elkanah went home alone. It was taken for granted that his wives went with him, according to ch. i. 21 (" all his house"). שֵׁרֵת אֶת־יְהוָֹה, which signifies literally, both here and in ch. iii. 1, to serve the Lord, and which is used interchangeably with שֵׁרֵת אֶת־פְּנֵי יי (ver. 18), to serve in the presence of the Lord, is used to denote the duties performed both by priests and Levites in connection with the worship of God, in which Samuel took part, as he grew up, under the superintendence of Eli and according to his instructions.—Ver. 12. But Eli's sons, Hophni and Phinehas (ver. 34), were בְּנֵי בְלִיַּעַל, worthless fellows, and knew not the Lord, *sc.* as He should be known, *i.e.* did not fear Him, or trouble themselves about Him (*vid.* Job xviii. 21; Hos. viii. 2, xiii. 4).— Vers. 13, 14. "*And the right of the priests towards the people was* (the following)." *Mishpat* signifies the right which they had usurped to themselves in relation to the people. "*If any one brought a sacrifice* (כָּל־אִישׁ זֹבֵחַ זֶבַח is placed first, and construed absolutely : ' as for every one who brought a slain-offering'), *the priest's servant* (*lit.* young man) *came while the flesh was boiling, with a three-pronged fork in his hand, and thrust into the kettle, or pot, or bowl, or saucepan. All that the fork brought up the priest took. This they did to all the Israelites who came thither to Shiloh.*"—Vers. 15, 16. They did still worse. "*Even before the fat was consumed,*" *i.e.* before the fat portions of the sacrifice had been placed in the altar-fire for the Lord (Lev. iii. 3–5), the priest's servant came and demanded flesh of the person sacrificing, to be roasted for the priest; "*for he will not take boiled flesh of thee, but only* חַי, raw, *i.e.* fresh meat." And if the person sacrificing replied, "*They will burn the fat directly* (*lit.* ' at this time,' as in Gen. xxv. 31, 1 Kings xxii. 5), *then take for thyself, as thy soul desireth,*" he said, "*No* (לֹא for לֹו), *but thou shalt give now ; if not, I take by force.*" These abuses were practised by the priests in connection with the thank-offerings, with which a sacrificial meal was associated. Of these offerings, the portion which legally fell to the priest as his share was the heave-leg and wave-breast. And this he was to receive after the fat portions of the sacrifice had been burned upon the altar (see Lev. vii. 30–34). To take the flesh of the sacrificial animal and roast it before this offering had been made, was a crime which was equivalent to a robbery of God, and is therefore referred to here with the emphatic particle גַּם, as being the worst crime that the sons of Eli committed. Moreover, the priests could not claim any of the flesh which the offerer of the sacrifice boiled for the sacrificial meal, after burning the fat portions upon the altar and giving up the portions which belonged to them, to say nothing of their taking it forcibly out of the pots while it was being boiled.—Ver. 17. Such conduct as this on the part of the young men (the priests' servants), was a great sin in the sight of the Lord, as they thereby brought the sacrifice of the Lord into contempt. נִאֵץ, causative, to bring into contempt, furnish occasion for blaspheming (as in 2 Sam. xii. 14). " The robbery which they committed was a small sin in comparison with the contempt of the sacrifices themselves, which they were the means of spreading among the people" (O. v. Gerlach). *Minchah* does not refer here to the meat-offering as the accompaniment to the slain-offerings, but to the sacrificial offering generally, as a gift presented for the Lord.

Vers. 18–21. *Samuel's service before the Lord.*—Ver. 18. Samuel served as a boy before the Lord by the side of the worthless sons of Eli, girt with an ephod of white material (בַּד, see at Ex. xxviii. 42). The ephod was a shoulder-dress, no doubt resembling the high priest's in shape (see Ex. xxviii. 6 sqq.), but altogether different in the material of which it was made, viz. simple white cloth, like the other articles of clothing that were worn by the priests. At that time, according to ch. xxii. 18, all the priests wore clothing of this kind ; and, according to 2 Sam. vi. 14, David did the same on the occasion of a religious festival. Samuel received a dress of this kind even when a boy, because he was set apart to a lifelong service before the Lord. חָגוּר is the technical expression for putting on the ephod, because the two pieces of which it was composed were girt round the body with a girdle.—Ver. 19. The small מְעִיל also (*Angl.* "coat"), which Samuel's mother made and brought him every year, when she came with her husband to Shiloh to the yearly sacrifice, was probably a coat resembling the *meïl* of the high priest (Ex. xxviii. 31 sqq.), but was made of course of some simpler material, and without the symbolical ornaments attached to the lower hem, by which that official dress was distinguished.—Ver. 20. The priestly clothing of the youthful Samuel was in harmony with the spiritual relation in which he stood to the high priest and to Jehovah. Eli blessed his parents for having given up the boy to the Lord, and expressed this wish to the father : " *The Lord lend thee seed of this woman in the place of the one asked for* (הַשְּׁאֵלָה)*, whom they* (one) *asked for from the Lord.*" The striking use of the third pers. masc. שָׁאַל instead of the second singular or plural may be

accounted for on the supposition that it is an indefinite form of
speech, which the writer chose because, although it was Hannah
who prayed to the Lord for Samuel in the sight of Eli, yet Eli
might assume that the father, Elkanah, had shared the wishes
of his pious wife. The apparent harshness disappears at once
if we substitute the passive; whereas in Hebrew active constructions were always preferred to passive, wherever it was
possible to employ them (Ewald, § 294, *h*). The singular
suffix attached to לִמְקוֹמוֹ after the plural הָלְכוּ may be explained
on the simple ground, that a dwelling-place is determined by
the husband, or master of the house.—Ver. 21. The particle כִּי,
"*for*" (Jehovah visited), does not mean *if, as,* or *when,* nor is
it to be regarded as a copyist's error. It is only necessary to
supply the thought contained in the words, "*Eli blessed Elkanah,*" viz. that Eli's blessing was not an empty fruitless
wish; and to understand the passage in some such way as this:
Eli's word was fulfilled, or still more simply, *they went to their
home blessed;* for *Jehovah visited Hannah,* blessed her with
"*three sons and two daughters; but the boy Samuel grew up
with the Lord,*" *i.e.* near to Him (at the sanctuary), and under
His protection and blessing.

Vers. 22–26. *Eli's treatment of the sins of his sons.*—Ver.
22. The aged Eli reproved his sons with solemn warnings on
account of their sins; but without his warnings being listened
to. From the reproof itself we learn, that beside the sin noticed
in vers. 12–17, they also committed the crime of lying with
the women who served at the tabernacle (see at Ex. xxxviii. 8),
and thus profaned the sanctuary with whoredom. But Eli,
with the infirmities of his old age, did nothing further to prevent these abominations than to say to his sons, "*Why do ye
according to the sayings which I hear, sayings about you which
are evil, of this whole people.*" אֶת־דִּבְרֵיכֶם רָעִים is inserted to
make the meaning clearer, and מֵאֵת כָּל־ה' is dependent upon
שֹׁמֵעַ. "*This whole people*" signifies all the people that came
to Shiloh, and heard and saw the wicked doings there.—Ver.
24. אַל בָּנַי, "*not, my sons,*" *i.e.* do not such things, "*for the
report which I hear is not good; they make the people of Jehovah
to transgress.*" מַעֲבִרִים is written without the pronoun אַתֶּם in
an indefinite construction, like מִשַׁלְּחִים in ch. vi. 3 (Maurer).
Ewald's rendering as given by Thenius, "The report which I

hear the people of God bring," is just as inadmissible as the
one proposed by Böttcher, "The report which, as I hear, the
people of God are spreading." The assertion made by Thenius,
that הֶעֱבִיר, without any further definition, cannot mean to cause
to sin or transgress, is correct enough no doubt; but it does not
prove that this meaning is inadmissible in the passage before
us, since the further definition is actually to be found in the
context.—Ver. 25. "*If man sins against man, God judges him;
but if a man sins against Jehovah, who can interpose with entreaty
for him?*" In the use of פִּלְלוֹ and יִתְפַּלֶּל־לֹו there is a parono-
masia which cannot be reproduced in our language. פָּלַל signifies to decide or pass sentence (Gen. xlviii. 11), then to arbitrate,
to settle a dispute as arbitrator (Ezek. xvi. 52, Ps. cvi. 30), and
in the *Hithpael* to act as mediator, hence to entreat. And
these meanings are applicable here. In the case of one man's
sin against another, God settles the dispute as arbitrator through
the proper authorities; whereas, when a man sins against God,
no one can interpose as arbitrator. Such a sin cannot be disposed of by intercession. But Eli's sons did not listen to this
admonition, which was designed to reform daring sinners with
mild words and representations; "*for*," adds the historian,
"*Jehovah was resolved to slay them.*" The father's reproof
made no impression upon them, because they were already
given up to the judgment of hardening. (On hardening as a
divine sentence, see the discussions at Ex. iv. 21.)—Ver. 26.
The youthful Samuel, on the other hand, continued to grow in
stature, and in favour with God and man (see Lev. ii. 52).

Vers. 27–36. *Announcement of the judgment upon Eli and
his house.*—Ver. 27. Before the Lord interposed in judgment,
He sent a prophet (a "*man of God,*" as in Judg. xiii. 6) to the
aged Eli, to announce as a warning for all ages the judgment
which was about to fall upon the worthless priests of his house.
In order to arouse Eli's own conscience, he had pointed out to
him, on the one hand, the grace manifested in the choice of
his father's house, *i.e.* the house of Aaron, to keep His sanctuary (vers. 27*b* and 28), and, on the other hand, the desecra-
tion of the sanctuary by the wickedness of his sons (ver. 29).
Then follows the sentence: The choice of the family of Aaron
still stood fast, but the deepest disgrace would come upon the
despisers of the Lord (ver. 30): the strength of his house

would be broken; all the members of his house were to die early deaths. They were not, however, to be removed entirely from service at the altar, but to their sorrow were to survive the fall of the sanctuary (vers. 31–34). But the Lord would raise up a faithful priest, and cause him to walk before His anointed, and from him all that were left of the house of Eli would be obliged to beg their bread (vers. 35, 36). To arrive at the true interpretation of this announcement of punishment, we must picture to ourselves the historical circumstances that come into consideration here. Eli the high priest was a descendant of Ithamar, the younger son of Aaron, as we may see from the fact that his great-grandson Ahimelech was "of the sons of Ithamar" (1 Chron. xxiv. 3). In perfect agreement with this, Josephus (*Ant.* v. 11, 5) relates, that after the high priest Ozi of the family of Eleazar, Eli of the family of Ithamar received the high-priesthood. The circumstances which led to the transfer of this honour from the line of Eleazar to that of Ithamar are unknown. We cannot imagine it to have been occasioned by an extinction of the line of Eleazar, for the simple reason that, in the time of David, Zadok the descendant of Eleazar is spoken of as high priest along with Abiathar and Ahimelech, the descendants of Eli (2 Sam. viii. 17, xx. 25). After the deposition of Abiathar he was reinstated by Solomon as sole high priest (1 Kings ii. 27), and the dignity was transmitted to his descendants. This fact also overthrows the conjecture of Clericus, that the transfer of the high-priesthood to Eli took place by the command of God on account of the grievous sins of the high priests of the line of Eleazar; for in that case Zadok would not have received this office again in connection with Abiathar. We have, no doubt, to search for the true reason in the circumstances of the times of the later judges, namely in the fact that at the death of the last high priest of the family of Eleazar before the time of Eli, the remaining son was not equal to the occasion, either because he was still an infant, or at any rate because he was too young and inexperienced, so that he could not enter upon the office, and Eli, who was probably related by marriage to the high priest's family, and was no doubt a vigorous man, was compelled to take the oversight of the congregation; and, together with the supreme administration of the affairs of the nation as

judge, received the post of high priest as well, and filled it till
the time of his death, simply because in those troublous times
there was not one of the descendants of Eleazar who was able
to fill the supreme office of judge, which was combined with
that of high priest. For we cannot possibly think of an unjust
usurpation of the office of high priest on the part of Eli, since
the very judgment denounced against him and his house presupposes that he had entered upon the office in a just and
upright way, and that the wickedness of his sons was all that
was brought against him. For a considerable time after the
death of Eli the high-priesthood lost almost all its significance.
All Israel turned to Samuel, whom the Lord established as His
prophet by means of revelations, and whom He also chose as
the deliverer of His people. The tabernacle at Shiloh, which
ceased to be the scene of the gracious presence of God after
the loss of the ark, was probably presided over first of all after
Eli's death by his grandson Ahitub, the son of Phinehas, as his
successor in the high-priesthood. He was followed in the time
of Saul by his son Ahijah or Ahimelech, who gave David the
shew-bread to eat at Nob, to which the tabernacle had been
removed in the meantime, and was put to death by Saul in
consequence, along with all the priests who were found there.
His son Abiathar, however, escaped the massacre, and fled to
David (ch. xxii. 9–20, xxiii. 6). In the reign of David he is
mentioned as high priest along with Zadok; but he was afterwards deposed by Solomon (2 Sam. xv. 24, xvii. 15, xix. 12,
xx. 25; 1 Kings ii. 27).

Different interpretations have been given of these verses.
The majority of commentators understand them as signifying
that the loss of the high-priesthood is here foretold to Eli, and
also the institution of Zadok in the office. But such a view is
too contracted, and does not exhaust the meaning of the words.
The very introduction to the prophet's words points to something greater than this: " *Thus saith the Lord, Did I reveal
myself to thy father's house, when they were in Egypt at the
house of Pharaoh?*" The ה interrogative is not used for הֲלֹא
(*nonne*), but is emphatic, as in Jer. xxxi. 20. The question is
an appeal to Eli's conscience, which he cannot deny, but is
obliged to confirm. By Eli's father's house we are not to
understand Ithamar and his family, but Aaron, from whom Eli

was descended through Ithamar. God revealed himself to the tribe-father of Eli by appointing Aaron to be the spokesman of Moses before Pharaoh (Ex. iv. 14 sqq. and 27), and still more by calling Aaron to the priesthood, for which the way was prepared by the fact that, from the very beginning, God made use of Aaron, in company with Moses, to carry out His purpose of delivering Israel out of Egypt, and entrusted Moses and Aaron with the arrangements for the celebration of the passover (Ex. xii. 1, 43). This occurred when they, the fathers of Eli, Aaron and his sons, were still in Egypt at the house of Pharaoh, *i.e.* still under Pharaoh's rule.—Ver. 28. " *And did I choose him out of all the tribes for a priest to myself.*" The interrogative particle is not to be repeated before וּבָחוֹר, but the construction becomes affirmative with the inf. abs. instead of the perfect. " *Him*" refers back to " *thy father*" in ver. 27, and signifies Aaron. The expression " *for a priest*" is still further defined by the clauses which follow: לַעֲלוֹת עַל מ׳, " *to ascend upon mine altar,*" *i.e.* to approach my altar of burnt-offering and perform the sacrificial worship; " *to kindle incense,*" *i.e.* to perform the service in the holy place, the principal feature in which was the daily kindling of the incense, which is mentioned *instar omnium;* " *to wear the ephod before me,*" *i.e.* to perform the service in the holy of holies, which the high priest could only enter when wearing the ephod to represent Israel before the Lord (Ex. xxviii. 12). " *And have given to thy father's house all the firings of the children of Israel*" (see at Lev. i. 9). These words are to be understood, according to Deut. xviii. 1, as signifying that the Lord had given to the house of Aaron, *i.e.* to the priesthood, the sacrifices of Jehovah to eat in the place of any inheritance in the land, according to the portions appointed in the sacrificial law in Lev. vi. vii., and Num. xviii.—Ver. 29. With such distinction conferred upon the priesthood, and such careful provision made for it, the conduct of the priests under Eli was an inexcusable crime. " *Why do ye tread with your feet my slain-offerings and meat-offerings, which I have commanded in the dwelling-place?*" Slain-offering and meat-offering are general expressions embracing all the altar-sacrifices. מָעוֹן is an accusative (" *in the dwelling*"), like בַּיִת, in the house. " *The dwelling*" is the tabernacle. This reproof applied to the priests generally, including

Eli, who had not vigorously resisted these abuses. The words which follow, " *and thou honourest thy sons more than me,*" relate to Eli himself, and any other high priest who like Eli should tolerate the abuses of the priests. " *To fatten yourselves with the first of every sacrificial gift of Israel, of my people.*" לְעַמִּי serves as a periphrasis for the genitive, and is chosen for the purpose of giving greater prominence to the idea of עַמִּי (my people). רֵאשִׁית, the first of every sacrificial gift (*minchah,* as in ver. 17), which Israel offered as the nation of Jehovah, ought to have been given up to its God in the altar-fire because it was the best; whereas, according to vers. 15, 16, the sons of Eli took away the best for themselves.—Ver. 30. For this reason, the saying of the Lord, " *Thy house* (*i.e.* the family of Eli) *and thy father's house* (Eli's relations in the other lines, *i.e.* the whole priesthood) *shall walk before me for ever*" (Num. xxv. 13), should henceforth run thus : " *This be far from me ; but them that honour me I will honour, and they that despise me shall be despised.*" The first declaration of the Lord is not to be referred to Eli particularly, as it is by C. a Lapide and others, and understood as signifying that the high-priesthood was thereby transferred from the family of Eleazar to that of Ithamar, and promised to Eli for his descendants for all time. This is decidedly at variance with the fact, that although "walking before the Lord" is not a general expression denoting a pious walk with God, as in Gen. xvii. 1, but refers to the service of the priests at the sanctuary as walking before the face of God, yet it cannot possibly be specially and exclusively restricted to the right of entering the most holy place, which was the prerogative of the high priest alone. These words of the Lord, therefore, applied to the whole priesthood, or the whole house of Aaron, to which the priesthood had been pro- mised, " *for a perpetual statute*" (Ex. xxix. 9). This promise was afterwards renewed to Phinehas especially, on account of the zeal which he displayed for the honour of Jehovah in connection with the idolatry of the people at Shittim (Num. xxv. 13). But even this renewed promise only secured to him an eternal *priesthood* as a covenant of peace with the Lord, and not specially the high-priesthood, although that was included as the culminating point of the priesthood. Consequently it was not abrogated by the temporary transfer of the high-priest-

hood from the descendants of Phinehas to the priestly line of
Ithamar, because even then they still retained the priesthood.
By the expression " *be it far from me*," *sc.* to permit this to
take place, God does not revoke His previous promise, but
simply denounces a false trust therein as irreconcilable with
His holiness. That promise would only be fulfilled so far as
the priests themselves honoured the Lord in their office, whilst
despisers of God, who dishonoured Him by sin and presumptuous wickedness, would be themselves despised.

This contempt would speedily come upon the house of Eli.
—Ver. 31. " *Behold, days come*,"—a formula with which prophets were accustomed to announce future events (see 2 Kings
xx. 17 ; Isa. xxxix. 6 ; Amos iv. 2, viii. 11, ix. 13 ; Jer. vii.
32, etc.),—"*then will I cut off thine arm, and the arm of thy
father's house, that there shall be no old man in thine house.*" To
cut off the arm means to destroy the strength either of a man
or of a family (see Job xxii. 9 ; Ps. xxxvii. 17). The strength
of a family, however, consists in the vital energy of its members, and shows itself in the fact that they reach a good old
age, and do not pine away early and die. This strength was to
vanish in Eli's house ; no one would ever again preserve his
life to old age.—Ver. 32. " *And thou wilt see oppression of the
dwelling in all that He has shown of good to Israel.*" The
meaning of these words, which have been explained in very
different ways, appears to be the following : In all the benefits
which the Lord would confer upon His people, Eli would see
only distress for the dwelling of God, inasmuch as the tabernacle would fall more and more into decay. In the person of
Eli, the high priest at that time, the high priest generally is
addressed as the custodian of the sanctuary ; so that what is
said is not to be limited to him personally, but applies to all the
high priests of his house. מָעוֹן is not Eli's dwelling-place, but
the dwelling-place of God, *i.e.* the tabernacle, as in ver. 29, and
is a genitive dependent upon צַר. הֵיטִיב, in the sense of benefit-
ing a person, doing him good, is construed with the accusative
of the person, as in Deut. xxviii. 63, viii. 16, xxx. 5. The
subject to the verb יֵיטִיב is *Jehovah*, and is not expressly mentioned, simply because it is so clearly implied in the words
themselves. This threat began to be fulfilled even in Eli's own
days. The distress or tribulation for the tabernacle began with

the capture of the ark by the Philistines (ch. iv. 11), and continued during the time that the Lord was sending help and deliverance to His people through the medium of Samuel, in their spiritual and physical oppression. The ark of the covenant—the heart of the sanctuary—was not restored to the tabernacle in the time of Samuel; and the tabernacle itself was removed from Shiloh to Nob, probably in the time of war; and when Saul had had all the priests put to death (ch. xxi. 2, xxii. 11 sqq.), it was removed to Gibeon, which necessarily caused it to fall more and more into neglect. Among the different explanations, the rendering given by Aquila (καὶ ἐπιβλέψει (? ἐπιβλέψῃς) ἀντίζηλον κατοικητηρίου) has met with the greatest approval, and has been followed by Jerome (et videbis æmulum tuum), Luther, and many others, including De Wette. According to this rendering, the words are either supposed to refer to the attitude of Samuel towards Eli, or to the deposition of Abiathar, and the institution of Zadok by Solomon in his place (1 Kings ii. 27). But צָר does not mean the antagonist or rival, but simply the oppressor or enemy; and Samuel was not an enemy of Eli any more than Zadok was of Abiathar. Moreover, if this be adopted as the rendering of צָר, it is impossible to find any suitable meaning for the following clause. In the second half of the verse the threat of ver. 31 is repeated with still greater emphasis. כָּל־הַיָּמִים, all the time, i.e. so long as thine house shall exist.—Ver. 33. "And I will not cut off every one to thee from mine altar, that thine eyes may languish, and thy soul consume away; and all the increase of thine house shall die as men." The two leading clauses of this verse correspond to the two principal thoughts of the previous verse, which are hereby more precisely defined and explained. Eli was to see the distress of the sanctuary; for to him, i.e. of his family, there would always be some one serving at the altar of God, that he might look upon the decay with his eyes, and pine away with grief in consequence. אִישׁ signifies every one, or any one, and is not to be restricted, as Thenius supposes, to Ahitub, the son of Phinehas, the brother of Ichabod; for it cannot be shown from ch. xiv. 3 and xxii. 20, that he was the only one that was left of the house of Eli. And secondly, there was to be no old man, no one advanced in life, in his house; but all the increase of the house was to die in the full bloom of manhood. אֲנָשִׁים, in contrast with זְקֵן, is used to denote men in the prime of life.

Ver. 34. "*And let this be the sign to thee, what shall happen to* (come upon) *thy two sons, Hophni and Phinehas ; in one day they shall both die.*" For the fulfilment of this, see ch. iv. 11. This occurrence, which Eli lived to see, but did not long survive (ch. iv. 17 sqq.), was to be the sign to him that the predicted punishment would be carried out in its fullest extent.—Ver. 35. But the priesthood itself was not to fall with the fall of Eli's house and priesthood ; on the contrary, the Lord would raise up for himself a tried priest, who would act according to His heart. "*And I will build for him a lasting house, and he will walk before mine anointed for ever.*"—Ver. 36. Whoever, on the other hand, should still remain of Eli's house, would come "*bowing before him* (to get) *a silver penny and a slice of bread,*" and would say, "*Put me, I pray, in one of the priests' offices, that I may get a piece of bread to eat.*" אֲגוֹרָה, *that which is collected,* signifies some small coin, of which a collection was made by begging single coins. Commentators are divided in their opinions as to the historical allusions contained in this prophecy. By the "tried priest," Ephraem Syrus understood both the prophet Samuel and the priest Zadok. "As for the facts themselves," he says, "it is evident that, when Eli died, Samuel succeeded him in the government, and that Zadok received the high-priesthood when it was taken from his family." Since his time, most of the commentators, including Theodoret and the Rabbins, have decided in favour of Zadok. Augustine, however, and in modern times Thenius and O. v. Gerlach, give the preference to Samuel. The fathers and earlier theologians also regarded Samuel and Zadok as the type of Christ, and supposed the passage to contain a prediction of the abrogation of the Aaronic priesthood by Jesus Christ.[1] This higher

---

[1] Theodoret, *qu.* vii. in 1 Reg. Οὐκοῦν ἡ πρόῤῥησις κυρίως μὲν ἁρμόττει τῷ σωτῆρι Χριστῷ. κατὰ δὲ ἱστορίαν τῷ Σαδούκ, ὅς ἐκ τοῦ Ἐλεάζαρ κατάγων τὸ γένος, τὴν ἀρχιερωσύνην διὰ τοῦ Σολομῶνος ἐδέξατο. Augustine says (*De civit. Dei* xvii. 5, 2) : "Although Samuel was not of a different tribe from the one which had been appointed by the Lord to serve at the altar, he was not of the sons of Aaron, whose descendants had been set apart as priests ; and thus the change is shadowed forth, which was afterwards to be introduced through Jesus Christ." And again, § 3 : "What follows (ver. 35) refers to

reference of the words is in any case to be retained; for the rabbinical interpretation, by which Grotius, Clericus, and others abide,—namely, that the transfer of the high-priesthood from the descendants of Eli to Zadok, the descendant of Eleazar, is all that is predicted, and that the prophecy was entirely fulfilled when Abiathar was deposed by Solomon (1 Kings ii. 27),—is not in accordance with the words of the text. On the other hand, Theodoret and Augustine both clearly saw that the words of Jehovah, "I revealed myself to thy father's house in Egypt," and, "Thy house shall walk before me for ever," do not apply to Ithamar, but to Aaron. "Which of his fathers," says Augustine, "was in that Egyptian bondage, from which they were liberated when he was chosen to the priesthood, excepting Aaron? It is with reference to his posterity, therefore, that it is here affirmed that they would not be priests for ever; and this we see already fulfilled." The only thing that appears untenable is the manner in which the fathers combine this historical reference to Eli and Samuel, or Zadok, with the Messianic interpretation, viz. either by referring vers. 31–34 to Eli and his house, and then regarding the sentence pronounced upon Eli as simply a type of the Messianic fulfilment, or by admitting the Messianic allusion simply as an allegory. The true interpretation may be obtained from a correct insight into the relation in which the prophecy itself stands to its fulfilment. Just as, in the person of Eli and his sons, the threat announces deep degradation and even destruction to all the priests of the house of Aaron who should walk in the footsteps of the sons of Eli, and the death of the two sons of Eli in one day was to be merely a sign that the threatened punishment would be completely fulfilled upon the ungodly priests; so, on the other hand, the promise of the raising up of the tried priest, for whom God would build a lasting house, also refers to all the priests whom

that priest, whose figure was borne by Samuel when succeeding to Eli." So again in the Berleburger Bible, to the words, "I will raise me up a faithful priest," this note is added: "Zadok, of the family of Phinehas and Eleazar, whom king Solomon, as the anointed of God, appointed high priest by his ordinance, setting aside the house of Eli (1 Kings ii. 35; 1 Chron. xxix. 22). At the same time, just as in the person of Solomon the Spirit of prophecy pointed to the true Solomon and Anointed One, so in this priest did He also point to Jesus Christ the great High Priest."

the Lord would raise up as faithful servants of His altar, and only receives its complete and final fulfilment in Christ, the true and eternal High Priest. But if we endeavour to determine more precisely from the history itself, which of the Old Testament priests are included, we must not exclude either Samuel or Zadok, but must certainly affirm that the prophecy was partially fulfilled in both. Samuel, as the prophet of the Lord, was placed at the head of the nation after the death of Eli ; so that he not only stepped into Eli's place as judge, but stood forth as priest before the Lord and the nation, and "had the important and sacred duty to perform of going before the anointed, the king, whom Israel was to receive through him ; whereas for a long time the Aaronic priesthood fell into such contempt, that, during the general decline of the worship of God, it was obliged to go begging for honour and support, and became dependent upon the new order of things that was introduced by Samuel" (O. v. Gerlach). Moreover, Samuel acquired a strong house in the numerous posterity that was given to him by God. The grandson of Samuel was Heman, "the king's seer in the words of God," who was placed by David over the choir at the house of God, and had fourteen sons and three daughters (1 Chron. vi. 33, xxv. 4, 5). But the very fact that these descendants of Samuel did not follow their father in the priesthood, shows very clearly that a lasting house was not built to Samuel as a tried priest through them, and therefore that we have to seek for the further historical fulfilment of this promise in the priesthood of Zadok. As the word of the Lord concerning the house of Eli, even if it did not find its only fulfilment in the deposition of Abiathar (1 Kings ii. 27), was at any rate partially fulfilled in that deposition ; so the promise concerning the tried priest to be raised up received a new fulfilment in the fact that Zadok thereby became the sole high priest, and transmitted the office to his descendants, though this was neither its last nor its highest fulfilment. This final fulfilment is hinted at in the vision of the new temple, as seen by the prophet Ezekiel, in connection with which the sons of Zadok are named as the priests, who, because they had not fallen away with the children of Israel, were to draw near to the Lord, and perform His service in the new organization of the kingdom of God as set forth in that vision

(Ezek. xl. 46, xliii. 19, xliv. 15, xlviii. 11). This fulfilment is effected in connection with Christ and His kingdom. Consequently, the anointed of the Lord, before whom the tried priest would walk for ever, is not Solomon, but rather David, and the Son of David, whose kingdom is an everlasting kingdom.

SAMUEL CALLED TO BE A PROPHET.—CHAP. III.

Vers. 1–9. At the time when Samuel served the Lord before Eli, both as a boy and as a young man (ch. ii. 11, 21, 26), the word of the Lord had become *dear*, *i.e.* rare, in Israel, and "*prophecy was not spread.*" נִפְרָץ, from פָּרַץ, to spread out strongly, to break through copiously (cf. Prov. iii. 10). The "*word of the Lord*" is the word of God announced by prophets : the "*vision*," "*visio prophetica.*" It is true that Jehovah had promised His people, that He would send prophets, who should make known His will and purpose at all times (Deut. xviii. 15 sqq. ; cf. Num. xxiii. 23) ; but as a revelation from God presupposed susceptibility on the part of men, the unbelief and disobedience of the people might restrain the fulfilment of this and all similar promises, and God might even withdraw His word to punish the idolatrous nation. Such a time as this, when revelations from God were universally rare, had now arisen under Eli, in whose days, as the conduct of his sons sufficiently proves, the priesthood had fallen into very deep corruption.—Vers. 2–4. The word of the Lord was then issued for the first time to Samuel. Vers. 2–4 form one period. The clause, "*it came to pass at that time*" (ver. 2*a*), is continued in ver. 4*a*, "*that the Lord called*," etc. The intervening clauses from וְעֵלִי to אֲרוֹן אֱלֹהִים are circumstantial clauses, intended to throw light upon the situation. The clause, "*Eli was laid down in his place*," etc., may be connected logically with "*at that time*" by the insertion of "*when*" (as in the English version : Tr.). The dimness of Eli's eyes is mentioned, to explain Samuel's behaviour, as afterwards described. Under these circumstances, for example, when Samuel heard his own name called out in sleep, he might easily suppose that Eli was calling him to render some assistance. The "*lamp of God*" is the light of the candlestick in the tabernacle, the seven lamps of which were put up and lighted every evening, and burned through the night till all the oil was consumed (see Ex. xxx. 8, Lev. xxiv. 2, 2 Chron. xiii. 11, and the explanation given at Ex. xxvii. 21). The statement that this light was not yet extinguished, is equivalent to " before the morning dawn." " *And Samuel was lying* (sleeping) *in the temple of Jehovah, where the ark of God was.*" הֵיכָל does not mean the holy place, as distinguished from the " most holy," as in 1 Kings vi. 5, vii. 50,[1] but the whole tabernacle, the tent with its court, as the palace of the God-king, as in ch. i. 9, Ps. xi. 4. Samuel neither slept in the holy place by the side of the candlestick and table of shew-bread, nor in the most holy place in front of the ark of the covenant, but in the court, where cells were built for the priests and Levites to live in when serving at the sanctuary (see at ver. 15). *The ark of God, i.e.* the ark of the covenant, is mentioned as the throne of the divine presence, from which the call to Samuel proceeded.—Vers. 5–9. As soon as Samuel heard his name called out, he hastened to Eli to receive his commands. But Eli bade him lie down again, as he had not called him. At first, no doubt, he thought the call which Samuel had heard was nothing more than a false impression of the youth, who had been fast asleep. But the same thing was repeated a second and a third time ; for, as the historian explains in ver. 6, " *Samuel had not yet known Jehovah, and* (for) *the word of Jehovah was not yet revealed to him.*" (The perfect יָדַע after טֶרֶם, though very rare, is fully supported by Ps. xc. 2 and Prov. viii. 25, and therefore is not to be altered into יֵדַע, as Dietrich and Böttcher propose.) He therefore imagined again that Eli had called him. But when he came to Eli after the third call, Eli perceived that the Lord was calling, and directed Samuel, if the call were repeated, to answer, " *Speak, Lord ; for Thy servant heareth.*"

Vers. 10–18. When Samuel had lain down again, " *Jehovah came and stood,*" *sc.* before Samuel. These words show that the revelation of God was an objectively real affair, and not a mere dream of Samuel's. " *And he called to him as at*

---

[1] The Masoretes have taken הֵיכָל in this sense, and therefore have placed the *Athnach* under שֹׁכֵב, to separate שֹׁכֵב וּשְׁמוּאֵל from בְּהֵיכַל יְיָ, and thus to guard against the conclusion, which might be drawn from this view of הֵיכָל, that Samuel slept in the holy place.

other times" (see Num. xxiv. 1; Judg. xvi. 20, etc.). When Samuel replied in accordance with Eli's instructions, the Lord announced to him that He would carry out the judgment that had been threatened against the house of Eli (vers. 11–14). "*Behold, I do a thing in Israel, at which both the ears of every one that heareth it shall tingle,*" *sc.* with horror (see 2 Kings xxi. 12; Jer. xix. 3; Hab. i. 5).—Ver. 12. "*On that day I will perform against Eli all that I have spoken concerning his house* (see ch. ii. 30 sqq.), *beginning and finishing it,*" *i.e.* completely. הָקִים אֶת־אֲשֶׁר דִּבֶּר, to set up the word spoken, *i.e.* to carry it out, or accomplish it. In ver. 13 this word is communicated to Samuel, so far as its essential contents are concerned. God would judge "*the house of Eli for ever because of the iniquity, that he knew his sons were preparing a curse for themselves and did not prevent them.*" To judge on account of a crime, is the same as to punish it. עַד־עוֹלָם, *i.e.* without the punishment being ever stopped or removed. מְקַלְלִים לָהֶם, cursing themselves, *i.e.* bringing a curse upon themselves. "*Therefore I have sworn to the house of Eli, that the iniquity of the house of Eli shall not* (אִם, a particle used in an oath, equivalent to assuredly not) *be expiated by slain-offerings and meat-offerings* (through any kind of sacrifice) *for ever.*" The oath makes the sentence irrevocable. (On the facts themselves, see the commentary on ch. ii. 27–36.) —Ver. 15. Samuel then slept till the morning; and when he opened the doors of the house of Jehovah, he was afraid to tell Eli of the revelation which he had received. Opening the doors of the house of God appears to have been part of Samuel's duty. We have not to think of doors opening into the holy place, however, but of doors leading into the court. Originally, when the tabernacle was simply a tent, travelling with the people from place to place, it had only curtains at the entrance to the holy place and court. But when Israel had become possessed of fixed houses in the land of Canaan, and the dwelling-place of God was permanently erected at Shiloh, instead of the tents that were pitched for the priests and Levites, who encamped round about during the journey through the desert, there were erected fixed houses, which were built against or inside the court, and not only served as dwelling-places for the priests and Levites who were officiating, but were also used for the reception and custody of the gifts that were brought as offerings to the sanctuary. These buildings in all probability supplanted entirely the original tent-like enclosure around the court; so that instead of the curtains at the entrance, there were folding doors, which were shut in the evening and opened again in the morning. It is true that nothing is said about the erection of these buildings in our historical books, but the fact itself is not to be denied on that account. In the case of Solomon's temple, notwithstanding the elaborate description that has been given of it, there is nothing said about the arrangement or erection of the buildings in the court; and yet here and there, principally in Jeremiah, the existence of such buildings is evidently assumed. מַרְאָה, *visio*, a sight or vision. This expression is applied to the word of God which came to Samuel, because it was revealed to him through the medium of an inward sight or intuition.—Vers. 16–18. When Samuel was called by Eli and asked concerning the divine revelation that he had received, he told him all the words, without concealing anything; whereupon Eli bowed in quiet resignation to the purpose of God: " *It is the Lord; let Him do what seemeth Him good.*" Samuel's communication, however, simply confirmed to the aged Eli what God had already made known to him through a prophet. But his reply proves that, with all his weakness and criminal indulgence towards his wicked sons, Eli was thoroughly devoted to the Lord in his heart. And Samuel, on the other hand, through his unreserved and candid communication of the terribly solemn word of God with regard to the man, whom he certainly venerated with filial affection, not only as high priest, but also as his own parental guardian, proved himself to be a man possessing the courage and the power to proclaim the word of the Lord without fear to the people of Israel.

Vers. 19–21. Thus Samuel grew, and Jehovah was with him, and let none of his words fall to the ground, *i.e.* left no word unfulfilled which He spoke through Samuel. (On הִפִּיל, see Josh. xxi. 45, xxiii. 14, 1 Kings viii. 56.) By this all Israel from Dan to Beersheba (see at Judg. xx. 1) perceived that Samuel was found trustworthy, or approved (see Num xii. 7) as a prophet of Jehovah. And the Lord continued to appear at Shiloh; for He revealed himself there to Samuel " *in the word of Jehovah,*" *i.e.* through a prophetic announcement of

His word. These three verses form the transition from the call of Samuel to the following account of his prophetic labours in Israel. At the close of ver. 21, the LXX. have appended a general remark concerning Eli and his sons, which, regarded as a deduction from the context, answers no doubt to the paraphrastic treatment of our book in that version, but in a critical aspect is utterly worthless.

WAR WITH THE PHILISTINES. LOSS OF THE ARK. DEATH OF ELI AND HIS SONS.—CHAP. IV.

At Samuel's word, the Israelites attacked the Philistines, and were beaten (vers. 1, 2). They then fetched the ark of the covenant into the camp according to the advice of the elders, that they might thereby make sure of the help of the almighty covenant God ; but in the engagement which followed they suffered a still greater defeat, in which Eli's sons fell and the ark was taken by the Philistines (vers. 3–11). The aged Eli, terrified at such a loss, fell from his seat and broke his neck (vers. 12–18); and his daughter-in-law was taken in labour, and died after giving birth to a son (vers. 19–22). With these occurrences the judgment began to burst upon the house of Eli. But the disastrous result of the war was also to be a source of deep humiliation to all the Israelites. Not only were the people to learn that the Lord had departed from them, but Samuel also was to make the discovery that the deliverance of Israel from the oppression and dominion of its foes was absolutely impossible without its inward conversion to its God.

Vers. 1, 2. The two clauses, " *The word of Samuel came to all Israel,*" and " *Israel went out,*" etc., are to be logically connected together in the following sense: "At the word or instigation of Samuel, Israel went out against the Philistines to battle." The Philistines were ruling over Israel at that time. This is evident, apart from our previous remarks concerning the connection between the commencement of this book and the close of the book of Judges (see vol. iv. pp. 280 sqq.), from the simple fact that the land of Israel was the scene of the war, and that nothing is said about an invasion on the part of the Philistines. The Israelites encamped at Ebenezer, and the Philistines were encamped at Aphek. The name *Ebenezer*

("the stone of help") was not given to the place so designated
till a later period, when Samuel set up a memorial stone there
to commemorate a victory that was gained over the Philistines
upon the same chosen battle-field after the lapse of twenty
years (ch. vii. 12). According to this passage, the stone was
set up between *Mizpeh* and *Shen*. The former was not the
Mizpeh in the lowlands of Judah (Josh. xv. 38), but the *Mizpeh*
of Benjamin (Josh. xviii. 26), *i.e.*, according to Robinson, the
present *Neby Samwil,* two hours to the north-west of Jerusalem,
and half an hour to the south of Gibeon (see at Josh. xviii. 26).
The situation of *Aphek* has not been discovered. It cannot
have been far from Mizpeh and Ebenezer, however, and was
probably the same place as the Canaanitish capital mentioned
in Josh. xii. 18, and is certainly different from the *Aphekah*
upon the mountains of Judah (Josh. xv. 53) ; for this was on
the south or south-west of Jerusalem, since, according to the
book of Joshua, it belonged to the towns that were situated in
the district of Gibeon.—Ver. 2. When the battle was fought,
the Israelites were defeated by the Philistines, and in battle-
array four thousand men were smitten upon the field. עֲרֹךְ, *sc.*
מִלְחָמָה, as in Judg. xx. 20, 22, etc. בַּמַּעֲרָכָה, in battle-array, *i.e.*
upon the field of battle, not in flight. "*In the field*," *i.e.* the
open field where the battle was fought.

Vers. 3–11. On the return of the people to the camp, the
elders held a council of war as to the cause of the defeat they
had suffered. "*Why hath Jehovah smitten us to-day before the
Philistines?*" As they had entered upon the war by the word
and advice of Samuel, they were convinced that Jehovah had
smitten them. The question presupposes at the same time that
the Israelites felt strong enough to enter upon the war with
their enemies, and that the reason for their defeat could only
be that the Lord, their covenant God, had withdrawn His help.
This was no doubt a correct conclusion ; but the means which
they adopted to secure the help of their God in continuing the
war were altogether wrong. Instead of feeling remorse and
seeking the help of the Lord their God by a sincere repentance
and confession of their apostasy from Him, they resolved to
fetch the ark of the covenant out of the tabernacle at Shiloh
into the camp, with the delusive idea that God had so inseparably bound up His gracious presence in the midst of His people

with this holy ark, which He had selected as the throne of His gracious appearance, that He would of necessity come with it into the camp and smite the foe. In ver. 4, the ark is called "*the ark of the covenant of Jehovah of hosts, who is enthroned above the cherubim,*" partly to show the reason why the people had the ark fetched, and partly to indicate the hope which they founded upon the presence of this sacred object. (See the commentary on Ex. xxv. 20–22.) The remark introduced here, "*and the two sons of Eli were there with the ark of the covenant of God,*" is not merely intended to show who the guardians of the ark were, viz. priests who had hitherto disgraced the sanctuary, but also to point forward at the very outset to the result of the measures adopted.—Ver. 5. On the arrival of the ark in the camp, the people raised so great a shout of joy that the earth rang again. This was probably the first time since the settlement of Israel in Canaan, that the ark had been brought into the camp, and therefore the people no doubt anticipated from its presence a renewal of the marvellous victories gained by Israel under Moses and Joshua, and for that reason raised such a shout when it arrived.—Vers. 6–8. When the Philistines heard the noise, and learned on inquiry that the ark of Jehovah had come into the camp, they were thrown into alarm, for "*they thought* (lit. said), *God* (Elohim) *is come into the camp, and said,* "*Woe unto us! For such a thing has not happened yesterday and the day before* (i.e. never till now). *Woe to us! Who will deliver us from the hand of these mighty gods? These are the very gods that smote Egypt with all kinds of plagues in the wilderness.*" The Philistines spoke of the God of Israel in the plural, הָאֱלֹהִים הָאַדִּירִים, as heathen who only knew of *gods*, and not of one Almighty God. Just as all the heathen feared the might of the gods of other nations in a certain degree, so the Philistines also were alarmed at the might of the God of the Israelites, and that all the more because the report of His deeds in the olden time had reached their ears (see Ex. xv. 14, 15). The expression "*in the wilderness*" does not compel us to refer the words "smote with all the plagues" exclusively to the destruction of Pharaoh and his army in the Red Sea (Ex. xiv. 23 sqq.). "*All the plagues*" include the rest of the plagues which God inflicted upon Egypt, without there being any necessity to supply the copula וֹ before בַּמִּדְבָּר, as in the LXX. and Syriac.

By this addition an antithesis is introduced into the words, which, if it really were intended, would require to be indicated by a previous בָּאָרֶץ or בְּאַרְצָם. According to the notions of the Philistines, all the wonders of God for the deliverance of Israel out of Egypt took place in the desert, because even when Israel was in Goshen they dwelt on the border of the desert, and were conducted thence to Canaan.—Ver. 9. But instead of despairing, they encouraged one another, saying, " *Show your-selves strong, and be men, O Philistines, that we may not be obliged to serve the Hebrews, as they have served you; be men, and fight!*"—Vers. 10, 11. Stimulated in this way, they fought and smote Israel, so that every one fled home ("to his tent," see at Josh. xxii. 8), and 30,000 men of Israel fell. The ark also was taken, and the two sons of Eli died, *i.e.* were slain when the ark was taken,—a practical proof to the degenerate nation, that Jehovah, who was enthroned above the cherubim, had departed from them, *i.e.* had withdrawn His gracious presence.[1]

Vers. 12–22. The tidings of this calamity were brought by a Benjaminite, who came as a messenger of evil tidings, with his clothes rent, and earth upon his head—a sign of the deepest mourning (see Josh. vii. 6)—to Shiloh, where the aged Eli was sitting upon a seat by the side (יַד is a copyist's error for יַד) of the way watching; for his heart trembled for the ark of God, which had been taken from the sanctuary into the camp without the command of God. At these tidings the whole city cried out with terror, so that Eli heard the sound of the cry, and asked the reason of this loud noise (or tumult), whilst the messenger was hurrying towards him with the news.—Ver. 15. Eli was ninety-eight years old, and " *his eyes stood,*" *i.e.* were

---

[1] "It is just the same now, when we take merely a historical Christ outside us for our Redeemer. He must prove His help chiefly internally by His Holy Spirit, to redeem us out of the hand of the Philistines; though externally He must not be thrown into the shade, as accomplishing our justification. If we had not Christ, we could never stand. For there is no help in heaven and on earth beside Him. But if we have Him in no other way than merely without us and under us, if we only preach about Him, teach, hear, read, talk, discuss, and dispute about Him, take His name into our mouth, but will not let Him work and show His power in us, He will no more help us than the ark helped the Israelites."—*Berleburger Bible.*

stiff, so that he could no more see (*vid.* 1 Kings xiv. 4). This
is a description of the so-called black cataract (*amaurosis*),
which generally occurs at a very great age from paralysis of the
optic nerves.—Vers. 16 sqq. When the messenger informed him
of the defeat of the Israelites, the death of his sons, and the
capture of the ark, at the last news Eli fell back from his seat
by the side of the gate, and broke his neck, and died. The loss
of the ark was to him the most dreadful of all—more dreadful
than the death of his two sons. Eli had judged Israel forty
years. The reading *twenty* in the Septuagint does not deserve
the slightest notice, if only because it is perfectly incredible
that Eli should have been appointed judge of the nation in
his seventy-eighth year.—Vers. 19–22. The judgment which
fell upon Eli through this stroke extended still further. His
daughter-in-law, the wife of Phinehas, was with child (near) to
be delivered. לָלַת, contracted from לָלֶדֶת (from יָלַד : see Ges.
§ 69, 3, note 1; Ewald, § 238, *c*). When she heard the
tidings of the capture (אֶל־הִלָּקַח, " *with regard to the being taken
away*") of the ark of God, and the death of her father-in-law
and husband, she fell upon her knees and was delivered, for
her pains had fallen upon her (*lit.* had turned against her), and
died in consequence. Her death, however, was but a subordinate matter to the historian. He simply refers to it casually in
the words, " *and about the time of her death*," for the purpose
of giving her last words, in which she gave utterance to her
grief at the loss of the ark, as a matter of greater importance
in relation to his object. As she lay dying, the women who
stood round sought to comfort her, by telling her that she had
brought forth a son; but " *she did not answer, and took no
notice* (שִׁית לֵב = שׂוֹם לֵב, *animum advertere ;* cf. Ps. lxii. 11),
but called to the boy (*i.e.* named him), *Ichabod* (אִי כָבוֹד, no glory),
saying, The glory of Israel is departed*," referring to the capture
of the ark of God, and also to her father-in-law and husband.
She then said again, " *Gone* (גָּלָה, wandered away, carried off)
is the glory of Israel, for the ark of God is taken.*" The repetition of these words shows how deeply the wife of the godless
Phinehas had taken to heart the carrying off of the ark, and
how in her estimation the glory of Israel had departed with it.
Israel could not be brought lower. With the surrender of the
earthly throne of His glory, the Lord appeared to have abolished

His covenant of grace with Israel ; for the ark, with the tables of the law and the capporeth, was the visible pledge of the covenant of grace which Jehovah had made with Israel.

HUMILIATION OF THE PHILISTINES BY MEANS OF THE ARK OF THE COVENANT.—CHAP. V.-VII. 1.

Whilst the Israelites were mourning over the loss of the ark of God, the Philistines were also to derive no pleasure from their booty, but rather to learn that the God of Israel, who had given up to them His greatest sanctuary to humble His own degenerate nation, was the only true God, beside Whom there were no other gods. Not only was the principal deity of the Philistines thrown down into the dust and dashed to pieces by the glory of Jehovah; but the Philistines themselves were so smitten, that their princes were compelled to send back the ark into the land of Israel, together with a trespass-offering, to appease the wrath of God, which pressed so heavily upon them.

Chap. v. THE ARK IN THE LAND OF THE PHILISTINES.—Vers. 1–6. The Philistines carried the ark from Ebenezer, where they had captured it, into their capital, *Ashdod* (*Esdud ;* see at Josh. xiii. 3), and placed it there in the temple of Dagon, by the side of the idol Dagon, evidently as a dedicatory offering to this god of theirs, by whose help they imagined that they had obtained the victory over both the Israelites and their God. With regard to the image of *Dagon,* compounded of man and fish, *i.e.* of a human body, with head and hands, and a fish's tail, see, in addition to Judg. xvi. 23, Stark's *Gaza,* pp. 248 sqq., 308 sqq., and Layard's *Nineveh and its Remains,* pp. 466–7, where there is a bas-relief from Khorsabad, in which " a figure is seen swimming in the sea, with the upper part of the body resembling a bearded man, wearing the ordinary conical tiara of royalty, adorned with elephants' tusks, and the lower part resembling the body of a fish. It has the hand lifted up, as if in astonishment or fear, and is surrounded by fishes, crabs, and other marine animals" (Stark, p. 308). As this bas-relief represents, according to Layard, the war of an Assyrian king with the inhabitants of the coast of Syria, most probably of Sargon, who had to carry on a long conflict with the Philistian towns, more especially with Ashdod, there can hardly be any doubt that we have a representation of the Philistian Dagon here. This deity was a personification of the generative and vivifying principle of nature, for which the fish with its innumerable multiplication was specially adapted, and set forth the idea of the giver of all earthly good.—Ver. 3. The next morning the Ashdodites found Dagon lying on his face upon the ground before the ark of Jehovah, and restored him to his place again, evidently supposing that the idol had fallen or been thrown down by some accident.—Ver. 4. But they were obliged to give up this notion when they found the god lying on his face upon the ground again the next morning in front of the ark of Jehovah, and in fact broken to pieces, so that Dagon's head and the two hollow hands of his arms lay severed upon the threshold, and nothing was left but the trunk of the fish (דָּגוֹן). The word *Dagon*, in this last clause, is used in an appellative sense, viz. the fishy part, or fish's shape, from דָּג, a fish. הַמִּפְתָּן is no doubt the threshold of the door of the recess in which the image was set up. We cannot infer from this, however, as Thenius has done, that with the small dimensions of the recesses in the ancient temples, if the image fell forward, the pieces named might easily fall upon the threshold. This naturalistic interpretation of the miracle is not only proved to be untenable by the word כְּרֻתוֹת, since כָּרוּת means *cut off*, and not broken off, but is also precluded by the improbability, not to say impossibility, of the thing itself. For if the image of Dagon, which was standing by the side of the ark, was thrown down towards the ark, so as to lie upon its face in front of it, the pieces that were broken off, viz. the head and hands, could not have fallen sideways, so as to lie upon the threshold. Even the first fall of the image of Dagon was a miracle. From the fact that their god Dagon lay upon its face before the ark of Jehovah, *i.e.* lay prostrate upon the earth, as though worshipping before the God of Israel, the Philistines were to learn, that even their supreme deity had been obliged to fall down before the majesty of Jehovah, the God of the Israelites. But as they did not discern the meaning of this miraculous sign, the second miracle was to show them the annihilation of their idol through the God of Israel, in such a way as to preclude every thought of accident. The disgrace attending the annihilation of their idol was probably to be heightened by the fact, that the pieces of Dagon that were smitten off were lying upon the threshold, inasmuch as what lay upon the threshold was easily trodden upon by any one who entered the house. This is intimated in the custom referred to in ver. 5, that in consequence of this occurrence, the priests of Dagon, and all who entered the temple of Dagon at Ashdod, down to the time of the historian himself, would not step upon the threshold of Dagon, *i.e.* the threshold where Dagon's head and hands had lain, but stepped over the threshold (not " leaped over," as many commentators assume on the ground of Zeph. i. 5, which has nothing to do with the matter), that they might not touch with their feet, and so defile, the place where the pieces of their god had lain.—Ver. 6. The visitation of God was not restricted to the demolition of the statue of Dagon, but affected the people of Ashdod as well. " *The hand of Jehovah was heavy upon the Ashdodites, and laid them waste.*" הֵשַׁם, from שָׁמֵם, when applied to men, as in Micah vi. 13, signifies to make desolate not only by diseases, but also by the withdrawal or diminution of the means of subsistence, the devastation of the fields, and such like. That the latter is included here, is evident from the dedicatory offerings with which the Philistines sought to mitigate the wrath of the God of the Israelites (ch. vi. 4, 5, 11, 18), although the verse before us simply mentions the diseases with which God visited them.[1] " *And He smote them with* עֳפָלִים, *i.e. boils :*" according to the Rabbins, swellings on the anus, *mariscæ* (see at Deut. xxviii. 27). For עפלים the Masoretes have invariably substituted מְחֹרִים,

---

[1] At the close of vers. 3 and 6 the Septuagint contains some comprehensive additions ; viz. at the close of ver. 3 : Καὶ ἐβαρύνθη χεὶρ Κυρίου ἐπὶ τοὺς Ἀζωτίους καὶ ἐβασάνιζεν αὐτούς, καὶ ἐπάταξεν αὐτοὺς εἰς τὰς ἕδρας αὐτῶν, τὴν Ἄζωτον καὶ τὰ ὅρια αὐτῆς ; and at the end of ver. 4 : Καὶ μέσον τῆς χώρας αὐτῆς ἀνεφύησαν μύες καὶ ἐγένετο σύγχυσις θανάτου μεγάλη ἐν τῇ πόλει. This last clause we also find in the Vulgate, expressed as follows : *Et eballiverunt villæ et agri in medio regionis illius, et nati sunt mures, et facta est confusio mortis magnæ in civitate.* Ewald's decision with regard to these clauses (*Gesch.* ii. p. 541) is, that they are not wanted at ch. v. 3, 6, but that they are all the more necessary at ch. vi. 1 ; whereas at ch. v. 3, 6, they would rather injure the sense. Thenius admits that the clause appended to ver. 3 is nothing more than a second translation of our sixth verse, which has been interpolated by a copyist of the Greek in the wrong place ; whereas that of ver. 6 contains the original though somewhat

which is used in ch. vi. 11, 17, and was probably regarded as more decorous. *Ashdod* is a more precise definition of the word *them*, viz. Ashdod, *i.e.* the inhabitants of Ashdod and its territory.

Vers. 7–12. " *When the Ashdodites saw that it was so,*" they were unwilling to keep the ark of the God of Israel any longer, because the hand of Jehovah lay heavy upon them and their god Dagon ; whereupon the princes of the Philistines (סַרְנֵי, as in Josh. xiii. 3, etc.) assembled together, and came to the resolution to " *let the ark of the God of Israel turn* (*i.e.* be taken) *to Gath*" (ver. 8). The princes of the Philistines probably imagined that the calamity which the Ashdodites attributed to the ark of God, either did not proceed from the ark, *i.e.* from the God of Israel, or if actually connected with the presence of the ark, simply arose from the fact that the city itself was hateful to the God of the Israelites, or that the Dagon of Ashdod was weaker than the Jehovah of Israel : they therefore resolved to let the ark be taken to Gath in order to pacify the Ashdodites. According to our account, the city of *Gath* seems to have stood between Ashdod and Ekron (see at Josh. xiii. 3). —Ver. 9. But when the ark was brought to Gath, the hand of Jehovah came upon that city also with very great alarm. מְהוּמָה גְּדוֹלָה is subordinated to the main sentence either adverbially or in the accusative. Jehovah smote the people of the city, small and great, so that boils broke out upon their hinder parts.—Vers. 10–12. They therefore sent the ark of God to *Ekron, i.e. Akir,* the north-western city of the Philistines (see

corrupt text, according to which the Hebrew text should be emended. But an impartial examination would show very clearly, that all these additions are nothing more than paraphrases founded upon the context. The last part of the addition to ver. 6 is taken *verbatim* from ver. 11, whilst the first part is a conjecture based upon ch. vi. 4, 5. Jerome, if indeed the addition in our text of the Vulgate really originated with him, and was not transferred into his version from the Itala, did not venture to suppress the clause interpolated in the Alexandrian version. This is very evident from the words *confusio mortis magnæ*, which are a literal rendering of σύγχυσις θανάτου μεγάλη ; whereas in ver. 11, Jerome has given to מְהוּמַת מָוֶת, which the LXX. rendered σύγχυσις θανάτου, the much more accurate rendering *pavor mortis*. Moreover, neither the Syriac nor *Targum Jonath.* has this clause ; so that long before the time of Jerome, the Hebrew text existed in the form in which the Masoretes have handed it down to us.

at Josh. xiii. 3). But the Ekronites, who had been informed of what had taken place in Ashdod and Gath, cried out, when the ark came into their city, " *They have brought the ark of the God of Israel to me, to slay me and my people*" (these words are to be regarded as spoken by the whole town) ; and they said to all the princes of the Philistines whom they had called together, " *Send away the ark of the God of Israel, that it may return to its place, and not slay me and my people. For deadly alarm* (מְהוּמַת מָוֶת, *confusion of death, i.e. alarm* produced by many sudden deaths) *ruled in the whole city ; very heavy was the hand of God there. The people who did not die were smitten with boils, and the cry of the city ascended to heaven.*" From this description, which simply indicates briefly the particulars of the plagues that God inflicted upon Ekron, we may see very clearly that Ekron was visited even more severely than Ashdod and Gath. This was naturally the case. The longer the Philistines resisted and refused to recognise the chastening hand of the living God in the plagues inflicted upon them, the more severely would they necessarily be punished, that they might be brought at last to see that the God of Israel, whose sanctuary they still wanted to keep as a trophy of their victory over that nation, was the omnipotent God, who was able to destroy His foes.

Chap. vi.–vii. 1. THE ARK OF GOD SENT BACK.—Vers. 1–3. The ark of Jehovah was in the land (*lit.* the fields, as in Ruth i. 2) of the Philistines for seven months, and had brought destruction to all the towns to which it had been taken. At length the Philistines resolved to send it back to the Israelites, and therefore called their priests and diviners (see at Num. xxiii. 23) to ask them, " *What shall we do with regard to the ark of God ; tell us, with what shall we send it to its place ?*" " *Its place*" is the land of Israel, and בַּמֶּה does not mean " in what manner" (*quomodo:* Vulgate, Thenius), but *with what, wherewith* (as in Micah vi. 6). There is no force in the objection brought by Thenius, that if the question had implied with what presents, the priests would not have answered, " *Do not send it without a present ;*" for the priests did not confine themselves to this answer, in which they gave a general assent, but proceeded at once to define the present more minutely. They replied, " *If they send away the ark of the God of Israel* (מְשַׁלְּחִים is to be

taken as the third person in an indefinite address, as in ch. ii.
24, and not to be construed with אַתֶּם supplied), *do not send it
away empty* (*i.e.* without an expiatory offering), *but return Him*
(*i.e.* the God of Israel) *a trespass-offering.*" אָשָׁם, *lit.* guilt, then
the gift presented as compensation for a fault, the trespass-
offering (see at Lev. v. 14–26). The gifts appointed by the
Philistines as an *asham* were to serve as a compensation and
satisfaction to be rendered to the God of Israel for the robbery
committed upon Him by the removal of the ark of the covenant, and were therefore called *asham,* although in their nature
they were only expiatory offerings. For the same reason the
verb הֵשִׁיב, to return or repay, is used to denote the presentation
of these gifts, being the technical expression for the payment of
compensation for a fault in Num. v. 7, and in Lev. v. 23 for
compensation for anything belonging to another, that had been
unjustly appropriated. " *Are ye healed then, it will show you why
His hand is not removed from you,*" *sc.* so long as ye keep back the
ark. The words אָז תֵּרָפְאוּ are to be understood as conditional,
even without אִם, which the rules of the language allow (see
Ewald, § 357, *b*) ; this is required by the context. For, according to ver. 9, the Philistine priests still thought it a possible
thing that any misfortune which had befallen the Philistines
might be only an accidental circumstance. With this view,
they could not look upon a cure as certain to result from the
sending back of the ark, but only as possible ; consequently
they could only speak conditionally, and with this the words
" *we shall know* " agree.

Vers. 4–6. The trespass-offering was to correspond to the
number of the princes of the Philistines. מִסְפַּר is an accusative
employed to determine either measure or number (see Ewald,
§ 204, *a*), lit. " *the number of their princes :* " the compensations
were to be the same in number as the princes. " *Five golden
boils, and five golden mice,*" *i.e.*, according to ver. 5, images
resembling their boils, and the field-mice which overran the
land ; the same gifts, therefore, for them all, " *for one plague is
to all and to your princes,*" *i.e.* the same plague has fallen upon
all the people and their princes. The change of person in the
two words, לְכֻלָּם, " *all of them,*" *i.e.* the whole nation of the
Philistines, and לְסַרְנֵיכֶם, " *your princes,*" appears very strange to
us with our modes of thought and speech, but it is by no means

unusual in Hebrew. The selection of this peculiar kind of expiatory present was quite in accordance with a custom, which was not only widely spread among the heathen but was even adopted in the Christian church, viz. that after recovery from an illness, or rescue from any danger or calamity, a representation of the member healed or the danger passed through was placed as an offering in the temple of the deity, to whom the person had prayed for deliverance; [1] and it also perfectly agrees with a custom which has prevailed in India, according to Tavernier (Ros. *A. u. N. Morgenland* iii. p. 77), from time immemorial down to the present day, viz. that when a pilgrim takes a journey to a pagoda to be cured of a disease, he offers to the idol a present either in gold, silver, or copper, according to his ability, of the shape of the diseased or injured member, and then sings a hymn. Such a present passed as a practical acknowledgment that the god had inflicted the suffering or evil. If offered after recovery or deliverance, it was a public expression of thanksgiving. In the case before us, however, in which it was offered before deliverance, the presentation of the images of the things with which they had been chastised was probably a kind of fine or compensation for the fault that had been committed against the Deity, to mitigate His wrath and obtain a deliverance from the evils with which they had been smitten. This is contained in the words, "Give glory unto the God of Israel! peradventure He will lighten His (punishing) hand from off you, and from off your

---

[1] Thus, after a shipwreck, any who escaped presented a tablet to Isis, or Neptune, with the representation of a shipwreck upon it ; gladiators offered their weapons, and emancipated slaves their fetters. In some of the nations of antiquity even representations of the private parts, in which a cure had been obtained from the deity, were hung up in the temples in honour of the gods (see Schol. ad Aristoph. *Acharn.* 243, and other proofs in Winer's *Real-wörterbuch,* ii. p. 255). Theodoret says, concerning the Christians of the fourth century (*Therapeutik. Disp.* viii.) : Ὅτι δὲ τυγχάνουσιν ὧνπερ αἰτοῦσιν οἱ πιστῶς ἐπαγγέλλοντες, ἀναφανδὸν μαρτυρεῖ τὰ τούτων ἀναθήματα, τὴν ἰατρείαν δηλοῦντα, οἱ μὲν γὰρ ὀφθαλμῶν, οἱ δὲ ποδῶν, ἄλλοι δὲ χειρῶν προσφέρουσιν ἐκτυπώματα· καὶ οἱ μὲν ἐκ χρυσοῦ, οἱ δὲ ἐξ ὕλης ἀργύρου πεποιημένα. δέχεται γὰρ ὁ τούτων Δεσπότης καὶ τὰ σμικρά τε καὶ εὔωνα, τῇ τοῦ προσφέροντος δυνάμει τὸ δῶρον μετρῶν. δηλοῖ δὲ ταῦτα προχείμενα τῶν παθημάτων τὴν λύσιν, ἧς ἀνετέθη μνημεῖα παρὰ τῶν ἀρτίων γεγενημένων. And at Rome they still hang up a picture of the danger, from which deliverance had been obtained after a vow, in the church of the saint invoked in the danger.

gods, and from off your land." The expression is a pregnant one for " make His heavy hand light and withdraw it," *i.e.* take away the punishment. In the allusion to the representations of the field-mice, the words " that devastate the land " are added, because in the description given of the plagues in ch. v. the devastation of the land by mice is not expressly mentioned. The introduction of this clause after עַכְבְּרֵיכֶם, when contrasted with the omission of any such explanation after עָפְלֵיכֶם, is a proof that the plague of mice had not been described before, and therefore that the references made to these in the Septuagint at ch. v. 3, 6, and ch. vi. 1, are nothing more than explanatory glosses. It is a well-known fact that field-mice, with their enormous rate of increase and their great voracity, do extraordinary damage to the fields. In southern lands they sometimes destroy entire harvests in a very short space of time (Aristot. *Animal.* vi. 37 ; Plin. *h. n.* x. c. 65 ; Strabo, iii. p. 165 ; Ælian, etc., in Bochart, *Hieroz.* ii. p. 429, ed. Ros.).—Ver. 6. " *Wherefore,*" continued the priests, " *will ye harden your heart, as the Egyptians and Pharaoh hardened their hearts?* (Ex. vii. 13 sqq.) *Was it not the case, that when He* (Jehovah) *had let out His power upon them* (הִתְעַלֵּל בְּ, as in Ex. x. 2), *they* (the Egyptians) *let them* (the Israelites) *go, and they departed?* " There is nothing strange in this reference, on the part of the Philistian priests, to the hardening of the Egyptians, and its results, since the report of those occurrences had spread among all the neighbouring nations (see at ch. iv. 8). And the warning is not at variance with the fact that, according to ver. 9, the priests still entertained some doubt whether the plagues really did come from Jehovah at all : for their doubts did not preclude the possibility of its being so ; and even the possibility might be sufficient to make it seem advisable to do everything that could be done to mitigate the wrath of the God of the Israelites, of whom, under existing circumstances, the heathen stood not only no less, but even more, in dread, than of the wrath of their own gods.

Vers. 7–12. Accordingly they arranged the sending back in such a manner as to manifest the reverence which ought to be shown to the God of Israel as a powerful deity (vers. 7–9). The Philistines were to take a new cart and make it ready (עָשָׂה), and to yoke two milch cows to the cart upon which no yoke had ever come, and to take away their young ones (calves) from them into the house, *i.e.* into the stall, and then to put the ark upon the cart, along with the golden things to be presented as a trespass-offering, which were to be in a small chest by the side of the ark, and to send it (*i.e.* the ark) away, that it might go, viz. without the cows being either driven or guided. From the result of these arrangements, they were to learn whether the plague had been sent by the God of Israel, or had arisen accidentally. " *If it* (the ark) *goeth up by the way to its border towards Bethshemesh, He* (Jehovah) *hath done us this great evil; but if not, we perceive that His hand hath not touched us. It came to us by chance,*" *i.e.* the evil came upon us merely by accident. In עֲלֵיהֶם, בְּנֵיהֶם, and מֵאַחֲרֵיהֶם (ver. 7), the masculine is used in the place of the more definite feminine, as being the more general form. This is frequently the case, and occurs again in vers. 10 and 12. אַרְגַּז, which only occurs again in vers. 8, 11, and 15, signifies, according to the context and the ancient versions, a chest or little case. The suffix to אֹתוֹ refers to the ark, which is also the subject to יַעֲלֶה (ver. 9). גְּבוּלוֹ, the territory of the ark, is the land of Israel, where it had its home. מִקְרֶה is used adverbially : by chance, or accidentally. The new cart and the young cows, which had never worn a yoke, corresponded to the holiness of the ark of God. To place it upon an old cart, which had already been used for all kinds of earthly purposes, would have been an offence against the holy thing; and it would have been just the same to yoke to the cart animals that had already been used for drawing, and had had their strength impaired by the yoke (see Deut. xxi. 3). The reason for selecting cows, however, instead of male oxen, was no doubt to be found in the further object which they hoped to attain. It was certainly to be expected, that if suckling cows, whose calves had been kept back from them, followed their own instincts, without any drivers, they would not go away, but would come back to their young ones in the stall. And if the very opposite should take place, this would be a sure sign that they were driven and guided by a divine power, and in fact by the God whose ark they were to draw into His own land. From this they would be able to draw the conclusion, that the plagues which had fallen upon the Philistines were also sent by this God. There was no special sagacity in this advice of the priests ; it was nothing more than a cleverly devised attempt to put the power of the God of the Israelites to the test, though they thereby unconsciously and against their will furnished the occasion for the living God to display His divine glory before those who did not know Him.—Vers. 10–12. The God of Israel actually did what the idolatrous priests hardly considered possible. When the Philistines, in accordance with the advice given them by their priests, had placed the ark of the covenant and the expiatory gifts upon the cart to which the two cows were harnessed, " *the cows went straight forward on the way to Bethshemesh; they went along a road going and lowing* (*i.e.* lowing the whole time), *and turned not to the right or to the left; and the princes of the Philistines went behind them to the territory of Bethshemesh.*" יִשַּׁרְנָה בַדֶּרֶךְ, *lit.* " *they were straight in the way,*" *i.e.* they went straight along the road. The form יִשַּׁרְנָה for יִישַׁרְנָה is the imperf. *Kal*, third pers. plur. fem., with the preformative י instead of ת, as in Gen. xxx. 38 (see Ges. § 47, Anm. 3; Ewald, § 191, *b*). *Bethshemesh*, the present *Ain-shems*, was a priests' city on the border of Judah and Dan (see at Josh. xv. 10).

Vers. 13–18. The inhabitants of Bethshemesh were busy with the wheat-harvest in the valley (in front of the town), when they unexpectedly saw the ark of the covenant coming, and rejoiced to see it. The cart had arrived at the field of Joshua, a Bethshemeshite, and there it stood still before a large stone. And they (the inhabitants of Bethshemesh) chopped up the wood of the cart, and offered the cows to the Lord as a burnt-offering. In the meantime the Levites had taken off the ark, with the chest of golden presents, and placed it upon the large stone; and the people of Bethshemesh offered burnt-offerings and slain-offerings that day to the Lord. The princes of the Philistines stood looking at this, and then returned the same day to Ekron. That the Bethshemeshites, and not the Philistines, are the subject to וַיִּבְקְעוּ, is evident from the correct interpretation of the clauses; viz. from the fact that in ver. 14*a* the words from וְהָעֲנָלָה to אֶבֶן גְּדוֹלָה are circumstantial clauses introduced into the main clause, and that וַיִּבְקְעוּ is attached to וַיִּשְׂמְחוּ לִרְאוֹת, and carries on the principal clause.—Ver. 15*a* contains a supplementary remark, therefore הוֹרִידוּ is to be translated as a pluperfect. After sacrificing the cart, with the cows, as a burnt-offering to the Lord, the inhabitants of Bethshemesh

gave a further practical expression to their joy at the return of
the ark, by offering burnt-offerings and slain-offerings in praise
of God. In the burnt-offerings they consecrated themselves
afresh, with all their members, to the service of the Lord; and
in the slain-offerings, which culminated in the sacrificial meals,
they sealed anew their living fellowship with the Lord. The
offering of these sacrifices at Bethshemesh was no offence
against the commandment, to sacrifice to the Lord at the place
of His sanctuary alone. The ark of the covenant was the
throne of the gracious presence of God, before which the
sacrifices were really offered at the tabernacle. The Lord had
sanctified the ark afresh as the throne of His presence, by the
miracle which He had wrought in bringing it back again.—In
vers. 17 and 18 the different atoning presents, which the Philistines sent to Jehovah as compensation, are enumerated once
more : viz. five golden boils, one for each of their five principal
towns (see at Josh. xiii. 3), and "*golden mice, according to the
number of all the Philistian towns of the five princes, from the
fortified city to the village of the inhabitants of the level land*"
(*perazi;* see at Deut. iii. 5). The priests had only proposed that
five golden mice should be sent as compensation, as well as five
boils (ver. 4). But the Philistines offered as many images of
mice as there were towns and villages in their five states, no
doubt because the plague of mice had spread over the whole
land, whereas the plague of boils had only fallen upon the
inhabitants of those towns to which the ark of the covenant
had come. In this way the apparent discrepancy between ver.
4 and ver. 18 is very simply removed. The words which follow,
viz. אֲשֶׁר הִנִּיחוּ עָלֶיהָ וגו, "*upon which they had set down the ark,*"
show unmistakeably, when compared with vers. 14 and 15, that
we are to understand by אָבֵל הַגְּדוֹלָה the great stone upon which
the ark was placed when it was taken off the cart. The conjecture of Kimchi, that this stone was called *Abel* (*luctus*), on
account of the mourning which took place there (see ver. 19),
is extremely unnatural. Consequently there is no other course
left than to regard אבל as an error in writing for אֶבֶן, according
to the reading, or at all events the rendering, adopted by the
LXX. and *Targum*. But וְעַד (even unto) is quite unsuitable
here, as no further local definition is required after the foregoing וְעַד כֹּפֶר הַפְּרָזִי, and it is impossible to suppose that the

Philistines offered a golden mouse as a trespass-offering for the great stone upon which the ark was placed. We must therefore alter וְעַד into וְעֵד : " *And the great stone is witness* (for וְעֵד in this sense, see Gen. xxxi. 52) *to this day in the field of Joshua the Bethshemeshite,*" *sc.* of the fact just described.

Ver. 19–ch. vii. 1. DISPOSAL OF THE ARK OF GOD.—
Ver. 19. As the ark had brought evil upon the Philistines, so the inhabitants of Bethshemesh were also to be taught that they could not stand in their unholiness before the holy God : "*And He* (God) *smote among the men of Bethshemesh, because they had looked at the ark of Jehovah, and smote among the people seventy men, fifty thousand men.*" In this statement of numbers we are not only struck by the fact that the 70 stands before the 50,000, which is very unusual, but even more by the omission of the copula וּ before the second number, which is altogether unparalleled. When, in addition to this, we notice that 50,000 men could not possibly live either in or round Bethshemesh, and that we cannot conceive of any extraordinary gathering having taken place out of the whole land, or even from the immediate neighbourhood ; and also that the words חֲמִשִּׁים אֶלֶף אִישׁ are wanting in several Hebrew MSS., and that Josephus, in his account of the occurrence, only speaks of *seventy* as having been killed (*Ant.* vi. 1, 4) ; we cannot come to any other conclusion than that the number 50,000 is neither correct nor genuine, but a gloss which has crept into the text through some oversight, though it is of great antiquity, since the numbers stood in the text employed by the Septuagint and Chaldee translators, who attempted to explain them in two different ways, but both extremely forced. Apart from this number, however, the verse does not contain anything either in form or substance that could furnish occasion for well-founded objections to its integrity. The repetition of וַיַּךְ simply resumes the thought that had been broken off by the parenthetical clause כִּי רָאוּ בַאֲרוֹן יְיָ ; and בָּעָם is only a general expression for בְּאַנְשֵׁי ב' שׁ'. The stroke which fell upon the people of Bethshemesh is sufficiently accounted for in the words, " *because they had looked,*" etc. There is no necessity to understand these words, however, as many Rabbins do, as signifying " they looked *into* the ark," *i.e.* opened it and looked in ; for if this had been the meaning, the

opening would certainly not have been passed over without notice. רָאָה with בְּ means to look *upon* or *at* a thing with lust or malicious pleasure ; and here it no doubt signifies a foolish staring, which was incompatible with the holiness of the ark of God, and was punished with death, according to the warning expressed in Num. iv. 20. This severe judgment so alarmed the people of Bethshemesh, that they exclaimed, " *Who is able to stand before Jehovah, this holy God!* " Consequently the Bethshemeshites discerned correctly enough that the cause of the fatal stroke, which had fallen upon them, was the unholiness of their own nature, and not any special crime which had been committed by the persons slain. They felt that they were none of them any better than those who had fallen, and that sinners could not approach the holy God. Inspired with this feeling, they added, " *and to whom shall He go away from us ?* " The subject to יַעֲלֶה is not the ark, but Jehovah who had chosen the ark as the dwelling-place of His name. In order to avert still further judgments, they sought to remove the ark from their town. They therefore sent messengers to Kirjath-jearim to announce to the inhabitants the fact that the ark had been sent back by the Philistines, and to entreat them to fetch it away.

Ch. vii. 1. The inhabitants of Kirjath-jearim complied with this request, and brought the ark into the house of Abinadab upon the height, and sanctified Abinadab's son Eleazar to be the keeper of the ark. *Kirjath-jearim*, the present *Kuryet el Enab* (see at Josh. ix. 17), was neither a priestly nor a Levitical city. The reason why the ark was taken there, is to be sought for, therefore, in the situation of the town, *i.e.* in the fact that Kirjath-jearim was the nearest large town on the road from Bethshemesh to Shiloh. We have no definite information, however, as to the reason why it was not taken on to Shiloh, to be placed in the tabernacle, but was allowed to remain in the house of Abinadab at Kirjath-jearim, where a keeper was expressly appointed to take charge of it ; so that we can only confine ourselves to conjectures. Ewald's opinion (*Gesch.* ii. 540), that the Philistines had conquered Shiloh after the victory described in ch. iv., and had destroyed the ancient sanctuary there, *i.e.* the tabernacle, is at variance with the accounts given in ch. xxi. 6, 1 Kings iii. 4, 2 Chron. i. 3, respecting the continuance of worship in the tabernacle at Nob and Gibeon. There

is much more to be said in support of the conjecture, that the
carrying away of the ark by the Philistines was regarded as a
judgment upon the sanctuary, which had been desecrated by the
reckless conduct of the sons of Eli, and consequently, that even
when the ark itself was recovered, they would not take it back
without an express declaration of the will of God, but were
satisfied, as a temporary arrangement, to leave the ark in Kirjath-jearim, which was farther removed from the cities of the
Philistines. And there it remained, because no declaration of
the divine will followed respecting its removal into the tabernacle, and the tabernacle itself had to be removed from Shiloh
to Nob, and eventually to Gibeon, until David had effected the
conquest of the citadel of Zion, and chosen Jerusalem as his
capital, when it was removed from Kirjath-jearim to Jerusalem (2 Sam. vi.). It is not stated that Abinadab was a
Levite; but this is very probable, because otherwise they would
hardly have consecrated his son to be the keeper of the ark, but
would have chosen a Levite for the office.

CONVERSION OF ISRAEL TO THE LORD BY SAMUEL.   VICTORY
  OVER THE PHILISTINES.   SAMUEL AS JUDGE OF ISRAEL.—
  CHAP. VII. 2–17.

Vers. 2–4. *Purification of Israel from idolatry.*—Twenty
years passed away from that time forward, while the ark remained at Kirjath-jearim, and all Israel mourned after Jehovah.
Then Samuel said to them, " *If ye turn to the Lord with all
your heart, put away the strange gods from the midst of you, and the
Astartes, and direct your heart firmly upon the Lord, and serve
Him only, that He may save you out of the hand of the Philistines.*" And the Israelites listened to this appeal. The single
clauses of vers. 2 and 3 are connected together by *vav consec.*,
and are not to be separated from one another. There is no
gap between these verses; but they contain the same closely
and logically connected thought,[1] which may be arranged in

---

[1] There is no force at all in the proofs which Thenius has adduced of a
gap between vers. 2 and 3. It by no means follows, that because the
Philistines had brought back the ark, their rule over the Israelites had
ceased, so as to make the words " he will deliver you," etc., incomprehen-
sible. Moreover, the appearance of Samuel as *judge* does not presuppose

one period in the following manner : " And it came to pass, when the days multiplied from the time that the ark remained at Kirjath-jearim, and grew to twenty years, and the whole house of Israel mourned after Jehovah, that Samuel said," etc. The verbs וַיִּרְבּוּ, וַיִּהְיוּ, and וַיִּנָּהוּ, are merely continuations of the infinitive שֶׁבֶת, and the main sentence is resumed in the words וַיֹּאמֶר שְׁמוּאֵל. The contents of the verses require that the clauses should be combined in this manner. The statement that twenty years had passed can only be understood on the supposition that some kind of turning-point ensued at the close of that time. The complaining of the people after Jehovah was no such turning-point, but became one simply from the fact that this complaining was followed by some result. This result is described in ver. 3. It consisted in the fact that Samuel exhorted the people to put away the strange gods (ver. 3); and that when the people listened to his exhortation (ver. 4), he helped them to gain a victory over the Philistines (vers. 5 sqq.). יִנָּהוּ, from נָהָה, to lament or complain (Micah ii. 4; Ezek. xxxii. 18). "The phrase, *to lament after God*, is taken from human affairs, when one person follows another with earnest solicitations and complaints, until he at length assents. We have an example of this in the Syrophenician woman in Matt. xv." (Seb. Schmidt). The meaning "to assemble together," which is the one adopted by Gesenius, is forced upon the word from the Chaldee אִתְנְהִי, and it cannot be shown that the word was ever used in this sense in Hebrew. Samuel's appeal in ver. 3 recalls to mind Josh. xxiv. 14, and Gen. xxxv. 2; but the words, " *If ye do return unto the Lord with all your hearts*," assume that the turning of the people to the Lord their God had already inwardly commenced, and indeed,

that his assumption of this office must necessarily have been mentioned before. As a general rule, there was no such formal assumption of the office, and this would be least of all the case with Samuel, who had been recognised as an accredited prophet of Jehovah (ch. iii. 19 sqq.). And lastly, the reference to idols, and to their being put away in consequence of Samuel's appeal, is intelligible enough, without any express account of their falling into idolatry, if we bear in mind, on the one hand, the constant inclination of the people to serve other gods, and if we observe, on the other hand, that Samuel called upon the people to turn to the Lord with all their heart and serve Him alone, which not only does not preclude, but actually implies, the outward continuance of the worship of Jehovah.

as the participle שָׁבִים expresses duration, had commenced as a
permanent thing, and simply demand that the inward turning
of the heart to God should be manifested outwardly as well,
by the putting away of all their idols, and should thus be
carried out to completion. The "strange gods" (see Gen.
xxxv. 2) are described in ver. 4 as "*Baalim.*" On *Baalim* and
Ashtaroth, see at Judg. ii. 11, 13. הָכִין לֵב, to direct the heart
firmly: see Ps. lxxviii. 8 ; 2 Chron. xxx. 19.

Vers. 5-14. *Victory obtained over the Philistines through
Samuel's prayer.*—Vers. 5, 6. When Israel had turned to the
Lord with all its heart, and had put away all its idols, Samuel
gathered together all the people at Mizpeh, to prepare them
for fighting against the Philistines by a solemn day for penitence and prayer. For it is very evident that the object of
calling all the people to Mizpeh was that the religious act
performed there might serve as a consecration for battle, not
only from the circumstance that, according to ver. 7, when the
Philistines heard of the meeting, they drew near to make war
upon Israel, but also from the contents of ver. 5 : "*Samuel
said* (sc. to the heads or representatives of the nation), *Gather
all Israel to Mizpeh, and I will pray for you unto the Lord.*"
His intention could not possibly have been any other than to
put the people into the right relation to their God, and thus to
prepare the way for their deliverance out of the bondage of the
Philistines. Samuel appointed *Mizpeh, i.e. Nebi Samwil*, on
the western boundary of the tribe of Benjamin (see at Josh.
xviii. 26), as the place of meeting, partly no doubt on historical
grounds, viz. because it was there that the tribes had formerly
held their consultations respecting the wickedness of the inhabitants of Gibeah, and had resolved to make war upon Benjamin
(Judg. xx. 1 sqq.), but still more, no doubt, because Mizpeh,
on the western border of the mountains, was the most suitable
place for commencing the conflict with the Philistines.—
Ver. 6. When they had assembled together here, "*they drew
water and poured it out before Jehovah, and fasted on that day,
and said there, We have sinned against the Lord.*" Drawing
water and pouring it out before Jehovah was a symbolical act,
which has been thus correctly explained by the Chaldee, on the
whole : "They poured out their heart like water in penitence
before the Lord." This is evident from the figurative expres-

sions, " poured out like water," in Ps. xxii. 15, and " pour out
thy heart like water," in Lam. ii. 19, which are used to denote
inward dissolution through pain, misery, and distress (see 2
Sam. xiv. 14). Hence the pouring out of water before God
was a symbolical representation of the temporal and spiritual
distress in which they were at the time,—a practical confession
before God, " Behold, we are before Thee like water that has
been poured out ;" and as it was their own sin and rebellion
against God that had brought this distress upon them, it was
at the same time a confession of their misery, and an act of the
deepest humiliation before the Lord. They gave a still further
practical expression to this humiliation by fasting (צוּם), as a
sign of their inward distress of mind on account of their sin,
and an oral confession of their sin against the Lord. By the
word שָׁם, which is added to וַיֹּאמְרוּ, " they said *there*," *i.e.* at
Mizpeh, the oral confession of their sin is formally separated
from the two symbolical acts of humiliation before God, though
by this very separation it is practically placed on a par with
them. What they did symbolically by the pouring out of water
and fasting, they explained and confirmed by their verbal confession. שָׁם is never an adverb of time signifying "*then ;*"
neither in Ps. xiv. 5, cxxxii. 17, nor Judg. v. 11. " *And thus
Samuel judged the children of Israel at Mizpeh.*" וַיִּשְׁפֹּט does not
mean " he became judge" (Mich. and others), any more than
" he punished every one according to his iniquity" (Thenius,
after David Kimchi). Judging the people neither consisted in
a censure pronounced by Samuel afterwards, nor in absolution
granted to the penitent after they had made a confession of
their sin, but in the fact that Samuel summoned the nation to
Mizpeh to humble itself before Jehovah, and there secured for
it, through his intercession, the forgiveness of its sin, and a
renewal of the favour of its God, and thus restored the proper
relation between Israel and its God, so that the Lord could
proceed to vindicate His people's rights against their foes.

When the Philistines heard of the gathering of the Israelites at Mizpeh (vers. 7, 8), their princes went up against Israel
to make war upon it ; and the Israelites, in their fear of the
Philistines, entreated Samuel, " *Do not cease to cry for us to the
Lord our God, that He may save us out of the hand of the Philistines.*"—Ver. 9. " *And Samuel took a milk-lamb* (a lamb that

was still sucking, probably, according to Lev. xxii. 27, a lamb
seven days old), *and offered it whole as a burnt-offering to the
Lord.*" כָּלִיל is used adverbially, according to its original meaning as an adverb, "*whole.*" The Chaldee has not given the
word at all, probably because the translators regarded it as
pleonastic, since every burnt-offering was consumed upon the
altar whole, and consequently the word כָּלִיל was sometimes
used in a substantive sense, as synonymous with עוֹלָה (Deut.
xxxiii. 10; Ps. li. 21). But in the passage before us, כָּלִיל is
not synonymous with עוֹלָה, but simply affirms that the lamb was
offered upon the altar without being cut up or divided. Samuel
selected a young lamb for the burnt-offering, not "as being the
purest and most innocent kind of sacrificial animal,"—for it
cannot possibly be shown that very young animals were regarded as purer than those that were full-grown,—but as being
the most suitable to represent the nation that had wakened up
to new life through its conversion to the Lord, and was, as it
were, new-born. For the burnt-offering represented the man,
who consecrated therein his life and labour to the Lord. The
sacrifice was the substratum for prayer. When Samuel offered
it, he cried to the Lord for the children of Israel; and the
Lord "*answered,*" *i.e.* granted, his prayer.—Ver. 10. When the
Philistines advanced during the offering of the sacrifice to fight
against Israel, "*Jehovah thundered with a great noise,*" *i.e.* with
loud peals, against the Philistines, and threw them into confusion, so that they were smitten before Israel. The thunder,
which alarmed the Philistines and threw them into confusion
(יְהֻמֵּם, as in Josh. x. 10), was the answer of God to Samuel's
crying to the Lord.—Ver. 11. As soon as they took to flight,
the Israelites advanced from Mizpeh, and pursued and smote
them to below *Beth-car.* The situation of this town or locality,
which is only mentioned here, has not yet been discovered.
Josephus (*Ant.* vi. 2, 2) has μέχρι Κορραίων.—Ver. 12. As a
memorial of this victory, Samuel placed a stone between Mizpeh
and Shen, to which he gave the name of *Eben-ha-ezer, i.e.* stone
of help, as a standing memorial that the Lord had thus far
helped His people. The situation of *Shen* is also not known.
The name *Shen* (*i.e.* tooth) seems to indicate a projecting point
of rock (see ch. xiv. 4), but may also signify a place situated
upon such a point.—Ver. 13. Through this victory which was

obtained by the miraculous help of God, the Philistines were
so humbled, that they no more invaded the territory of Israel,
i.e. with lasting success, as they had done before. This limitation of the words "*they came no more*" (*lit.* "they did not
add again to come into the border of Israel"), is implied in
the context; for the words which immediately follow, "*and
the hand of Jehovah was against the Philistines all the days of
Samuel*," show that they made attempts to recover their lost
supremacy, but that so long as Samuel lived they were unable
to effect anything against Israel. This is also manifest from
the successful battles fought by Saul (ch. xiii. and xiv.), when
the Philistines had made fresh attempts to subjugate Israel
during his reign. The defeats inflicted upon them by Saul also
belong to the days of Samuel, who died but a very few years
before Saul himself. Because of these battles which Saul
fought with the Philistines, Lyra and Brentius understand the
expression "all the days of Samuel" as referring not to the
lifetime of Samuel, but simply to the duration of his official
life as judge, viz. till the commencement of Saul's reign. But
this is at variance with ver. 15, where Samuel is said to have
judged Israel all the days of his life. Seb. Schmidt has given,
on the whole, the correct explanation of ver. 13 : "They came
no more so as to obtain a victory and subdue the Israelites
as before; yet they did return, so that the hand of the Lord
was against them, *i.e.* so that they were repulsed with great
slaughter, although they were not actually expelled, or the
Israelites delivered from tribute and the presence of military
garrisons, and that all the days that the judicial life of Samuel
lasted, in fact all his life, since they were also smitten by Saul."
—Ver. 14. In consequence of the defeat at Ebenezer, the Philistines were obliged to restore to the Israelites the cities which
they had taken from them, "*from Ekron to Gath*." This definition of the limits is probably to be understood as *exclusive, i.e.*
as signifying that the Israelites received back their cities up to
the very borders of the Philistines, measuring these borders
from Ekron to Gath, and not that the Israelites received Ekron
and Gath also. For although these chief cities of the Philistines had been allotted to the tribes of Judah and Dan in the
time of Joshua (Josh. xiii. 3, 4, xv. 45, 46), yet, notwithstanding the fact that Judah and Simeon conquered Ekron,

together with Gaza and Askelon, after the death of Joshua (Judg. i. 18), the Israelites did not obtain any permanent possession. " *And their territory*" (coasts), *i.e.* the territory of the towns that were given back to Israel, not that of Ekron and Gath, " *did Israel deliver out of the hands of the Philistines. And there was peace between Israel and the Amorites;*" *i.e.* the Canaanitish tribes also kept peace with Israel after this victory of the Israelites over the Philistines, and during the time of Samuel. The Amorites are mentioned, as in Josh. x. 6, as being the most powerful of the Canaanitish tribes, who had forced the Danites out of the plain into the mountains (Judg. i. 34, 35).

Vers. 15–17. *Samuel's judicial labours.*—With the calling of the people to Mizpeh, and the victory at Ebenezer that had been obtained through his prayer, Samuel had assumed the government of the whole nation; so that his office as judge dates from this period, although he had laboured as prophet among the people from the death of Eli, and had thereby prepared the way for the conversion of Israel to the Lord. As his prophetic labours were described in general terms in ch. iii. 19–21, so are his labours as judge in the verses before us: viz. in ver. 15 their duration,—" *all the days of his life,*" as his activity during Saul's reign and the anointing of David (ch. xv. xvi.) sufficiently prove; and then in vers. 16, 17 their general character,—" *he went round from year to year*" (וְסָבַב serves as a more precise definition of וְהָלַךְ, he went and travelled round) *to Bethel, i.e.* Beitin (see at Josh. vii. 2), *Gilgal, and Mizpeh* (see at ver. 5), and judged Israel at all these places. Which Gilgal is meant, whether the one situated in the valley of the Jordan (Josh. iv. 19), or the *Jiljilia* on the higher ground to the south-west of Shiloh (see at Josh. viii. 35), cannot be determined with perfect certainty. The latter is favoured partly by the order in which the three places visited by Samuel on his circuits occur, since according to this he probably went first of all from Ramah to Bethel, which was to the north-east, then farther north or north-west to Jiljilia, and then turning back went towards the south-east to Mizpeh, and returning thence to Ramah performed a complete circuit; whereas, if the Gilgal in the valley of the Jordan had been the place referred to, we should expect him to go there first of all from Ramah, and then towards the north-east to Bethel, and from that to the south-west to Mizpeh ; and partly also by the circumstance that, according to 2 Kings ii. 1 and iv. 38, there was a school of the prophets at Jiljilia in the time of Elijah and Elisha, the founding of which probably dated as far back as the days of Samuel. If this conjecture were really a well-founded one, it would furnish a strong proof that it was in this place, and not in the Gilgal in the valley of the Jordan, that Samuel judged the people. But as this conjecture cannot be raised into a certainty, the evidence in favour of Jiljilia is not so conclusive as I myself formerly supposed (see also the remarks on ch. ix. 14). אֵת כָּל־הַמְּקוֹמוֹת is grammatically considered an accusative, and is in apposition to אֶת־יִשְׂרָאֵל, *lit. Israel,* viz. all the places named, *i.e.* Israel which inhabited all these places, and was to be found there. "*And his return was to Ramah ;*" *i.e.* after finishing the annual circuit he returned to Ramah, where he had his house. There he judged Israel, and also built an altar to conduct the religious affairs of the nation. Up to the death of Eli, Samuel lived and laboured at Shiloh (ch. iii. 21). But when the ark was carried away by the Philistines, and consequently the tabernacle at Shiloh lost what was most essential to it as a sanctuary, and ceased at once to be the scene of the gracious presence of God, Samuel went to his native town Ramah, and there built an altar as the place of sacrifice for Jehovah, who had manifested himself to him. The building of the altar at Ramah would naturally be suggested to the prophet by these extraordinary circumstances, even if it had not been expressly commanded by Jehovah.

II. THE MONARCHY OF SAUL FROM HIS ELECTION TILL HIS ULTIMATE REJECTION.

CHAP. VIII.-XV.

The earthly monarchy in Israel was established in the time of Samuel, and through his mediation. At the pressing desire of the people, Samuel installed the Benjaminite Saul as king, according to the command of God. The reign of Saul may be divided into two essentially different periods: viz. (1) the establishment and vigorous development of his regal supremacy (ch. viii.-xv.); (2) the decline and gradual overthrow of his monarchy (ch. xvi.-xxxi.). The establishment of the monarchy is introduced by the negotiations of the elders of Israel with Samuel concerning the appointment of a king (ch. viii.). This is followed by (1) the account of the anointing of Saul as king (ch. ix. 1-x. 16), of his election by lot, and of his victory over the Ammonites and the confirmation of his monarchy at Gilgal (ch. x. 17-xi. 15), together with Samuel's final address to the nation (ch. xii.); (2) the history of Saul's reign, of which only his earliest victories over the Philistines are given at all elaborately (ch. xiii. 1-xiv. 46), his other wars and family history being disposed of very summarily (ch. xiv. 47-52); (3) the account of his disobedience to the command of God in the war against the Amalekites, and the rejection on the part of God with which Samuel threatened him in consequence (ch. xv.). The brevity with which the history of his actual reign is treated, in contrast with the elaborate account of his election and confirmation as king, may be accounted for from the significance and importance of Saul's monarchy in relation to the kingdom of God in Israel.

The people of Israel traced the cause of the oppression and distress, from which they had suffered more and more in the time of the judges, to the defects of their own political constitution. They wished to have a king, like all the heathen nations, to conduct their wars and conquer their enemies. Now, although the desire to be ruled by a king, which had existed in the nation even from the time of Gideon, was not in itself at variance with the appointment of Israel as a kingdom of God, yet the motive which led the people to desire it was both wrong and hostile to God, since the source of all the evils and misfortunes from which Israel suffered was to be found in the apostasy of the nation from its God, and its coquetting with the gods of the heathen. Consequently their self-willed obstinacy in demanding a king, notwithstanding the warnings of Samuel, was an actual rejection of the sovereignty of Jehovah, since He had always manifested himself to His people as their king by delivering them out of the power of their foes, as soon as they returned to Him with simple penitence of heart. Samuel

pointed this out to the elders of Israel, when they laid their petition before him that he would choose them a king. But Jehovah
fulfilled their desires. He directed Samuel to appoint them a
king, who possessed all the qualifications that were necessary to
secure for the nation what it looked for from a king, and who
therefore might have established the monarchy in Israel as
foreseen and foretold by Jehovah, if he had not presumed upon
his own power, but had submitted humbly to the will of God
as made known to him by the prophet. Saul, who was chosen
from Benjamin, the smallest but yet the most warlike of all
the tribes, a man in the full vigour of youth, and surpassing
all the rest of the people in beauty of form as well as bodily
strength, not only possessed "warlike bravery and talent, unbroken courage that could overcome opposition of every kind,
a stedfast desire for the well-being of the nation in the face of
its many and mighty foes, and zeal and pertinacity in the execution of his plans" (Ewald), but also a pious heart, and an
earnest zeal for the maintenance of the provisions of the law,
and the promotion of the religious life of the nation. He would
not commence the conflict with the Philistines until sacrifice
had been offered (ch. xiii. 9 sqq.); in the midst of the hot pursuit of the foe he opposed the sin committed by the people in
eating flesh with the blood (ch. xiv. 32, 33); he banished the
wizards and necromancers out of the land (ch. xxviii. 3, 9); and
in general he appears to have kept a strict watch over the observance of the Mosaic law in his kingdom. But the consciousness of his own power, coupled with the energy of his character,
led him astray into an incautious disregard of the commands of
God; his zeal in the prosecution of his plans hurried him on
to reckless and violent measures; and success in his undertakings heightened his ambition into a haughty rebellion against
the Lord, the God-king of Israel. These errors come out very
conspicuously in the three great events of his reign which are
the most circumstantially described. When Saul was preparing
for war against the Philistines, and Samuel did not appear at
once on the day appointed, he presumptuously disregarded the
prohibition of the prophet, and offered the sacrifice himself
without waiting for Samuel to arrive (ch. xiii. 7 sqq.). In the
engagement with the Philistines, he attempted to force on the
annihilation of the foe by pronouncing the ban upon any one

in his army who should eat bread before the evening, or till he had avenged himself upon his foes. Consequently, he not only diminished the strength of the people, so that the overthrow of the enemy was not great, but he also prepared humiliation for himself, inasmuch as he was not able to carry out his vow (ch. xiv. 24 sqq.). But he sinned still more grievously in the war with the Amalekites, when he violated the express command of the Lord by only executing the ban upon that nation as far as he himself thought well, and thus by such utterly unpardonable conduct altogether renounced the obedience which he owed to the Lord his God (ch. xv.). All these acts of transgression manifest an attempt to secure the unconditional gratification of his own self-will, and a growing disregard of the government of Jehovah in Israel; and the consequence of the whole was simply this, that Saul not only failed to accomplish that deliverance of the nation out of the power of its foes which the Israelites had anticipated from their king, and was unable to inflict any lasting humiliation upon the Philistines, but that he undermined the stability of his monarchy, and brought about his own rejection on the part of God.

From all this we may see very clearly, that the reason why the occurrences connected with the election of Saul as king are fully described on the one hand, and on the other only such incidents connected with his enterprises after he began to reign as served to bring out the faults and crimes of his monarchy, was, that Israel might learn from this, that royalty itself could never secure the salvation it expected, unless the occupant of the throne submitted altogether to the will of the Lord. Of the other acts of Saul, the wars with the different nations round about are only briefly mentioned, but with this remark, that he displayed his strength and gained the victory in whatever direction he turned (ch. xiv. 47), simply because this statement was sufficient to bring out the brighter side of his reign, inasmuch as this clearly showed that it might have been a source of blessing to the people of God, if the king had only studied how to govern his people in the power and according to the will of Jehovah. If we examine the history of Saul's reign from this point of view, all the different points connected with it exhibit the greatest harmony. Modern critics, however, have discovered irreconcilable contradictions in the history, simply because, instead of studying it for the purpose of fathoming the plan and purpose which lie at the foundation, they have entered upon the inquiry with a twofold assumption : viz. (1) that the government of Jehovah over Israel was only a subjective idea of the Israelitish nation, without any objective reality ; and (2) that the human monarchy was irreconcilably opposed to the government of God. Governed by these axioms, which are derived not from the Scriptures, but from the philosophical views of modern times, the critics have found it impossible to explain the different accounts in any other way than by the purely external hypothesis, that the history contained in this book has been compiled from two different sources, in one of which the establishment of the earthly monarchy was treated as a violation of the supremacy of God, whilst the other took a more favourable view. From the first source, ch. viii., x. 17–27, xi., xii., and xv. are said to have been derived ; and ch. ix.–x. 17, xiii., and xiv. from the second.

ISRAEL'S PRAYER FOR A KING.—CHAP. VIII.

As Samuel had appointed his sons as judges in his old age, and they had perverted justice, the elders of Israel entreated him to appoint them a king after the manner of all the nations (vers. 1–5). This desire not only displeased Samuel, but Jehovah also saw in it a rejection of His government ; nevertheless He commanded the prophet to fulfil the desire of the people, but at the same time to set before them as a warning the prerogatives of a king (vers. 6–9). This answer from God, Samuel made known to the people, describing to them the prerogatives which the king would assume to himself above the rest of the people (vers. 10–18). As the people, however, persisted in their wish, Samuel promised them, according to the direction of God, that their wishes should be gratified (vers. 19–22).

Vers. 1–5. The reason assigned for the appointment of Samuel's sons as judges is his own advanced age. The inference which we might draw from this alone, namely, that they were simply to support their father in the administration of justice, and that Samuel had no intention of laying down his office, and still less of making the supreme office of judge hereditary in his family, is still more apparent from the fact that

they were stationed as judges of the nation in Beersheba, which
was on the southern border of Canaan (Judg. xx. 1, etc. ; see at
Gen. xxi. 31). The sons are also mentioned again in 1 Chron.
vi. 13, though the name of the elder has either been dropped
out of the Masoretic text or has become corrupt.—Ver. 3. The
sons, however, did not walk in the ways of their father, but set
their hearts upon gain, took bribes, and perverted justice, in
opposition to the command of God (see Ex. xxiii. 6, 8 ; Deut.
xvi. 19).—Vers. 4, 5. These circumstances (viz. Samuel's age
and the degeneracy of his sons) furnished the elders of Israel
with the opportunity to apply to Samuel with this request:
"*Appoint us a king to judge us, as all the nations*" (the heathen),
sc. have kings. This request resembles so completely the law
of the king in Deut. xvii. 14 (observe, for example, the expression כְּכָל־הַגּוֹיִם), that the distinct allusion to it is unmistakeable.
The custom of expressly quoting the book of the law is met with
for the first time in the writings of the period of the captivity.
The elders simply desired what Jehovah had foretold through
His servant Moses, as a thing that would take place in the
future and for which He had even made provision.

Vers. 6–9. Nevertheless "*the thing displeased Samuel when
they said*," etc. This serves to explain הַדָּבָר, and precludes the
supposition that Samuel's displeasure had reference to what
they had said concerning his own age and the conduct of his
sons. At the same time, the reason why the petition for a king
displeased the prophet, was not that he regarded the earthly
monarchy as irreconcilable with the sovereignty of God, or
even as untimely ; for in both these cases he would not have
entered into the question at all, but would simply have refused
the request as ungodly or unseasonable. But " *Samuel prayed
to the Lord*," *i.e.* he laid the matter before the Lord in prayer,
and the Lord said (ver. 7) : "*Hearken unto the voice of the people
in all that they say unto thee.*" This clearly implies, that not only
in Samuel's opinion, but also according to the counsel of God,
the time had really come for the establishment of the earthly
sovereignty in Israel. In this respect the request of the elders
for a king to reign over them was perfectly justifiable; and
there is no reason to say, with Calvin, "they ought to have
had regard to the times and conditions prescribed by God, and
it would no doubt have come to pass that the regal power would

have grown up in the nation. Although, therefore, it had not yet been established, they ought to have waited patiently for the time appointed by God, and not to have given way to their own reasons and counsels apart from the will of God." For God had not only appointed no particular time for the establishment of the monarchy; but in the introduction to the law for the king, " When thou shalt say, I will set a king over me," He had ceded the right to the representatives of the nation to deliberate upon the matter. Nor did they err in this respect, that while Samuel was still living, it was not the proper time to make use of the permission that they had received; for they assigned as the reason for their application, that Samuel had grown old : consequently they did not petition for a king instead of the prophet who had been appointed and so gloriously accredited by God, but simply that Samuel himself would give them a king in consideration of his own age, in order that when he should become feeble or die, they might have a judge and leader of the nation. Nevertheless the Lord declared, "*They have not rejected thee, but they have rejected me, that I should not reign over them. As they have always done from the day that I brought them up out of Egypt unto this day, that they have forsaken me and served other gods, so do they also unto thee.*" This verdict on the part of God refers not so much to the desire expressed, as to the feelings from which it had sprung. Externally regarded, the elders of Israel had a perfect right to present the request; the wrong was in their hearts.[1] They not only declared to the prophet their confidence in his administration of his office, but they implicitly declared him incapable of any further superintendence of their civil and political affairs. This mistrust was founded upon mistrust in the Lord and His

---

[1] Calvin has correctly pointed out how much would have been warrantable under the circumstances : "They might, indeed, have reminded Samuel of his old age, which rendered him less able to attend to the duties of his office, and also of the avarice of his sons and the corruptness of the judges; or they might have complained that his sons did not walk in his footsteps, and have asked that God would choose suitable men to govern them, and thus have left the whole thing to His will. And if they had done this, there can be no doubt that they would have received a gracious and suitable answer. But they did not think of calling upon God; they demanded that a king should be given them, and brought forward the customs and institutions of other nations."

guidance. In the person of Samuel they rejected the Lord and His rule. They wanted a king, because they imagined that Jehovah their God-king was not able to secure their constant prosperity. Instead of seeking for the cause of the misfortunes which had hitherto befallen them in their own sin and want of fidelity towards Jehovah, they searched for it in the faulty constitution of the nation itself. In such a state of mind as this, their desire for a king was a contempt and rejection of the kingly government of Jehovah, and was nothing more than forsaking Jehovah to serve other gods. (See ch. x. 18, 19, and ch. xii. 7 sqq., where Samuel points out to the people still more fully the wrong that they have committed.)—Ver. 9. In order to show them wherein they were wrong, Samuel was instructed to bear witness against them, by proclaiming the right of the king who would rule over them. הָעֵד תָּעִיד בָּהֶם neither means "warn them earnestly" (De Wette), nor "explain and solemnly expound to them" (Thenius). הֵעִיד בּ means *to bear witness*, or give testimony against a person, *i.e.* to point out to him his wrong. The following words, וְהִגַּדְתָּ וגו, are to be understood as explanatory, in the sense of "*by proclaiming to them.*" "*The manner (mishpat) of the king*" is the *right* or *prerogative* which the king would claim, namely, such a king as was possessed by all the other nations, and such an one as Israel desired in the place of its own God-king, *i.e.* a king who would rule over his people with arbitrary and absolute power.

Vers. 10–18. In accordance with the instructions of God, Samuel told the people all the words of Jehovah, *i.e.* all that God had said to him, as related in vers. 7–9, and then proclaimed to them the right of the king.—Ver. 11. "*He will take your sons, and set them for himself upon his chariots, and upon his saddle-horses, and they will run before his chariot;*" *i.e.* he will make the sons of the people his retainers at court, his charioteers, riders, and runners. The singular suffix attached to בְּמֶרְכַּבְתּוֹ is not to be altered, as Thenius suggests, into the plural form, according to the LXX., Chald., and Syr., since the word refers, not to war-chariots, but to the king's state-carriage; and פָּרָשׁ does not mean a rider, but a saddle-horse, as in 2 Sam. i. 6, 1 Kings v. 6, etc.—Ver. 12. "*And to make himself chiefs over thousands and over fifties;*"—the greatest and smallest military officers are mentioned, instead of all the soldiers and officers (comp. Num. xxxi. 14, 2 Kings i. 9 sqq., with Ex. xviii. 21, 25). וְלָשׂוּם is also dependent upon יִקַּח (ver. 11),—"*and to plough his field* (חָרִישׁ, lit. the ploughed), *and reap his harvest, and make his instruments of war and instruments of his chariots.*"—Ver. 13. "*Your daughters he will take as preparers of ointments, cooks, and bakers,*" sc. for his court.—Vers. 14 sqq. All their possessions he would also take to himself : the good (*i.e.* the best) fields, vineyards, and olive-gardens, he would take away, and give to his servants ; he would tithe the sowings and vineyards (*i.e.* the produce which they yielded), and give them to his courtiers and servants. סָרִים, lit. the eunuch ; here it is used in a wider sense for the *royal chamberlains.* Even their *slaves* (men-servants and maid-servants) and their *beasts of draught and burden* he would take and use for his own work, and *raise the tithe of the flock.* The word בַּחוּרֵיכֶם, between the slaves (men-servants and maid-servants) and the asses, is very striking and altogether unsuitable ; and in all probability it is only an ancient copyist's error for בְּקַרֵיכֶם, your oxen, as we may see from the LXX. rendering, τὰ βουκόλια. The servants and maids, oxen and asses, answer in that case to one another ; whilst the young men are included among the sons in vers. 11, 12. In this way the king would make all the people into his servants or slaves. This is the meaning of the second clause of ver. 17 ; for the whole are evidently summed up in conclusion in the expression, "*and ye shall be his servants.*"—Ver. 18. Israel would then cry out to God because of its king, but the Lord would not hear it then. This description, which contains a fearful picture of the tyranny of the king, is drawn from the despotic conduct of the heathen kings, and does not presuppose, as many have maintained, the times of the later kings, which were so full of painful experiences.

Vers. 19—22. With such a description of the "*right of the king*" as this, Samuel had pointed out to the elders the dangers connected with a monarchy in so alarming a manner, that they ought to have been brought to reflection, and to have desisted from their demand. "*But the people refused to hearken to the voice of Samuel.*" They repeated their demand, "*We will have a king over us, that we also may be like all the nations, and that our king may judge us, and go out before us, and conduct our battles.*"—Vers. 21, 22. These words of the people were laid by Samuel before the Lord, and the Lord commanded him to give the people a king. With this answer Samuel sent the men of Israel, *i.e.* the elders, away. This is implied in the words, "*Go ye every man unto his city*," since we may easily supply from the context, "till I shall call you again, to appoint you the king you desire."

ANOINTING OF SAUL AS KING.—CHAP. IX.–X. 16.

When the Lord had instructed Samuel to appoint a king over the nation, in accordance with its own desire, He very speedily proceeded to show him the man whom He had chosen. Saul the Benjaminite came to Samuel, to consult him as a seer about his father's she-asses, which had been lost, and for which he had been seeking in all directions in vain (ch. ix. 1–14). And the Lord had already revealed to the prophet the day before, that He would send him the man who had been set apart by Him as the king of Israel; and when Samuel met with Saul, He pointed him out as the man to whom He had referred (vers. 15–17). Accordingly, Samuel invited Saul to be his guest at a sacrificial meal, which he was about to celebrate (vers. 18–24). After the meal he made known to him the purpose of God, anointed him as king (vers. 25–27, ch. x. 1), and sent him away, with an announcement of three signs, which would serve to confirm his election on the part of God (ch. x. 2–16). This occurrence is related very circumstantially, to bring out distinctly the miraculous interposition of God, and to show that Saul did not aspire to the throne; and also that Samuel did not appoint of his own accord the man whom he was afterwards obliged to reject, but that Saul was elected by God to be king over His people, without any interference on the part of either Samuel or himself.[1]

Ch. ix. 1–10. *Saul searches for his father's asses.*—Vers. 1, 2. The elaborate genealogy of the Benjaminite Kish, and the minute description of the figure of his son Saul, are in-

---

[1] There is no tenable ground for the assumption of Thenius and others, that this account was derived from a different source from ch. viii., x. 17–27, and xi. sqq.; for the assertion that ch. x. 17–27 connects itself in the most natural way with ch. viii. is neither well-founded nor correct. In the first place, it was certainly more natural that Samuel, who was to place a king over the nation according to the appointment of God, should be

tended to indicate at the very outset the importance to which Saul attained in relation to the people of Israel. *Kish* was the son of *Abiel :* this is in harmony with ch. xiv. 51. But when, on the other hand, it is stated in 1 Chron. viii. 33, ix. 39, that *Ner* begat *Kish*, the difference may be reconciled in the simplest manner, on the assumption that the *Ner* mentioned there is not the father, but the grandfather, or a still more remote ancestor of *Kish*, as the intervening members are frequently passed over in the genealogies. The other ancestors of *Kish* are never mentioned again. גִּבּוֹר חַיִל refers to *Kish*, and signifies not a brave man, but a man of property, as in Ruth ii. 1. This son *Saul* (*i.e.* " *prayed for :*" for this meaning of the word, comp. ch. i. 17, 27) was " *young and beautiful.*" It is true that even at that time Saul had a son grown up (viz. Jonathan), according to ch. xiii. 2 ; but still, in contrast with his father, he was " a young man," *i.e.* in the full vigour of youth, probably about forty or forty-five years old. There is no necessity, therefore, to follow the Vulgate rendering *electus*. No one equalled him in beauty. " *From his shoulder upwards he was higher than any of the people.*" Such a figure as this was well adapted to commend him to the people as their king (cf. ch. x. 24), since size and beauty were highly valued in rulers, as signs of manly strength (see Herod. iii. 20, vii. 187 ; Aristot. *Polit.* iv. c. 24).—Vers. 3–5. Having been sent out by his father to search for his she-asses which had strayed, Saul went with his servant through the mountains of Ephraim, which ran south-wards into the tribe-territory of Benjamin (see at ch. i. 1), then through the land of Shalishah and the land of Shaalim, and after that through the land of Benjamin, without finding the asses ; and at length, when he had reached the land of Zuph, he deter-mined to return, because he was afraid that his father might turn his mind from the asses, and trouble himself about them (the son and servant). חָדַל מִן, to desist from a thing, to give it up or renounce it.

made acquainted with the man whom God had appointed, before the people elected him by lot. And secondly, Saul's behaviour in hiding himself when the lots were cast (ch. x. 21 sqq.), can only be explained on the supposition that Samuel had already informed him that he was the appointed king ; whereas, if this had not been the case, it would be altogether incompre-hensible.

As Saul started in any case from Gibeah of Benjamin, his own home (ch. x. 10 sqq., 26, xi. 4, xv. 34, xxiii. 19, xxvi. 1), *i.e.* the present *Tuleil el Phul,* which was an hour or an hour and a half to the north of Jerusalem (see at Josh. xviii. 28), and went thence into the mountains of Ephraim, he no doubt took a north-westerly direction, so that he crossed the boundary of Benjamin somewhere between Bireh and Atarah, and passing through the crest of the mountains of Ephraim, on the west of Gophnah (Jifna), came out into the land of Shalishah. *Sha-lishah* is unquestionably the country round (or of) *Baal-shalishah* (2 Kings iv. 42), which was situated, according to Eusebius (*Onom. s.v.* Βαιθσαρισάθ : *Beth-sarisa* or *Beth-salisa*), *in regione Thamnitica,* fifteen Roman miles to the north of Diospolis (Lydda), and was therefore probably the country to the west of Jiljilia, where three different wadys run into one large wady, called Kurawa ; and according to the probable conjecture of Thenius, it was from this fact that the district received the name of *Shalishah,* or *Three-land.* They proceeded thence in their search to the land of *Shaalim :* according to the *Onom.* (*s.v.*), " a village seven miles off, *in finibus Eleutheropoleos contra occidentem.*" But this is hardly correct, and is most likely connected with the mistake made in transposing the town of Samuel to the neighbourhood of Diospolis (see at ch. i. 1). For since they went on from Shaalim into the land of Benjamin, and then still further into the land of Zuph, on the south-west of Benjamin, they probably turned eastwards from Shalishah, into the country where we find *Beni Mussah* and *Beni Salem* marked upon Robinson's and v. de Velde's maps, and where we must therefore look for the land of *Shaalim,* that they might proceed thence to explore the land of Benjamin from the north-east to the south-west. If, on the contrary, they had gone from Shaalim in a southerly or south-westerly direction, to the district of Eleutheropolis, they would only have entered the land of Benjamin at the south-west corner, and would have had to go all the way back again in order to go thence to the land of Zuph. For we may infer with certainty that the land of Zuph was on the south-west of the tribe-territory of Benjamin, from the fact that, according to ch. x. 2, Saul and his companion passed Rachel's tomb on their return thence to their own home, and then came to the border of

Benjamin. On the name *Zuph*, see at ch. i. 1.—Ver. 6. When
Saul proposed to return home from the land of Zuph, his
servant said to him, " *Behold, in this city* ('*this*,' referring to
the town which stood in front of them upon a hill) *is a man of
God, much honoured; all that he saith cometh surely to pass :
now we will go thither; perhaps he will tell us our way that we
have to go*" (*lit.* have gone, and still go, *sc.* to attain the object
of our journey, viz. to find the asses). The name of this town
is not mentioned either here or in the further course of this
history. Nearly all the commentators suppose it to have been
Ramah, Samuel's home. But this assumption has no foundation at all in the text, and is irreconcilable with the statements
respecting the return in ch. x. 2–5. The servant did not say
there *dwells* in this city, but there is in this city (ver. 6 ; comp.
with this ver. 10, " They went into the city where the man of
God was," not " dwelt"). It is still more evident, from the
answer given by the drawers of water, when Saul asked them,
" *Is the seer here?*" (ver. 11),—viz. " *He came to-day to the
city, for the people have a great sacrifice upon the high place*"
(ver. 12),—that the seer (Samuel) did not live in the town, but
had only come thither to a sacrificial festival. Moreover, " every
impartial man will admit, that the fact of Samuel's having
honoured Saul as his guest at the sacrificial meal of those who
participated in the sacrifice, and of their having slept under the
same roof, cannot possibly weaken the impression that Samuel
was only there in his peculiar and official capacity. It could not
be otherwise than that the presidency should be assigned to him
at the feast itself as priest and prophet, and therefore that the
appointments mentioned should proceed from him. And it is
but natural to assume that he had a house at his command for
any repetition of such sacrifices, which we find from 2 Kings
iv. to have been the case in the history of Elisha" (Valentiner).
And lastly, the sacrificial festival itself does not point to Ramah;
for although Samuel had built an altar to the Lord at Ramah
(ch. vii. 17), this was by no means the only place of sacrifice in
the nation. If Samuel offered sacrifice at Mizpeh and Gilgal
(ch. vii. 9, x. 8, xiii. 8 sqq.), he could also do the same at other
places. What the town really was in which Saul met with him,
cannot indeed be determined, since all that we can gather from
ch. x. 2 is, that it was situated on the south-west of Bethlehem.

—Vers. 7–10. Saul's objection, that they had no present to bring to the man of God, as the bread was gone from their vessels, was met by the servant with the remark, that he had a quarter of a shekel which he would give.—Ver. 9. Before proceeding with the further progress of the affair, the historian introduces a notice, which was required to throw light upon what follows; namely, that beforetime, if any one wished to inquire of God, *i.e.* to apply to a prophet for counsel from God upon any matter, it was customary in Israel to say, We will go to the seer, because "*he that is now called a prophet was beforetime called a seer.*" After this parenthetical remark, the account is continued in ver. 10. Saul declared himself satisfied with the answer of the servant; and they both went into the town, to ask the man of God about the asses that were lost.

Vers. 11–17. As they were going up to the high place of the town, they met maidens coming out of the town to draw water; and on asking them whether the seer was there, they received this answer: "*Yes; behold, he is before thee: make haste now, for he has come into the town to-day; for the people have a sacrifice to-day upon the high place.*" Bamah (in the singular) does not mean the height or hill generally; but throughout it signifies *the high place*, as a place of sacrifice or prayer.— Ver. 13. "*When ye come into the city, ye will find him directly, before he goes up to the high place to eat.*" כֵּן not only introduces the apodosis, but corresponds to כְּ, *as, so* : here, however, it is used with reference to time, in the sense of our " immediately." "*For the people are not accustomed to eat till he comes, for he blesses the sacrifice,*" etc. בֵּרֵךְ, like εὐλογεῖν, refers to the thanksgiving prayer offered before the sacrificial meal. "*Go now for him; ye will meet him even to-day.*" The first אֹתוֹ is placed at the beginning for the sake of emphasis, and then repeated at the close. כְּהַיּוֹם, "*Even to-day.*"—Ver. 14. When they went into the town, Samuel met them on his way out to go to the high place of sacrifice. Before the meeting itself is described, the statement is introduced in vers. 15–17, that the day before Jehovah had foretold to Samuel that the man was coming to him whom he was to anoint as captain over his people. גָּלָה אֹזֶן, to *open any one's ear*, equivalent to *reveal* something to him (ch. xx. 12 ; 2 Sam. vii. 27, etc.). אֶשְׁלַח, *I will send thee, i.e.* "I will so direct his way in my overruling providence, that he shall come to thee" (J. H. Mich.). The words, "*that he may save my people out of the hand of the Philistines; for I have looked upon my people, for their cry is come unto me*," are not at all at variance with ch. vii. 13. In that passage there is simply the assertion, that there was no more any permanent oppression on the part of the Philistines in the days of Samuel, such as had taken place before; but an attempt to recover their supremacy over Israel is not only not precluded, but is even indirectly affirmed (see the comm. on ch. vii. 13). The words before us simply show that the Philistines had then begun to make a fresh attempt to contend for dominion over the Israelites. "*I have looked upon my people;*" this is to be explained like the similar passage in Ex. ii. 25, "God looked upon the children of Israel," and Ex. iii. 7, "I have looked upon the misery of my people." God's looking was not a quiet, inactive looking on, but an energetic look, which brought help in trouble. "*Their cry is come unto me:*" this is word for word the same as in Ex. iii. 9. As the Philistines wanted to tread in the footsteps of the Egyptians, it was necessary that Jehovah should also send His people a deliverer from these new oppressors, by giving them a king. The reason here assigned for the establishment of a monarchy is by no means at variance with the displeasure which God had expressed to Samuel at the desire of the people for a king (ch. viii. 7 sqq.); since this displeasure had reference to the state of heart from which the desire had sprung. Ver. 17. When Samuel saw Saul, the Lord answered him, *sc.* in reply to the tacit inquiry, ' *Is this he?*' "*Behold, this is the man of whom I spake to thee.*" עָצַר, *coercere imperio.*

Vers. 18–24. The thread of the narrative, which was broken off in ver. 15, is resumed in ver. 18. Saul drew near to Samuel in the gate, and asked him for the seer's house. The expression בְּתוֹךְ הַשָּׁעַר is used to define more precisely the general phrase in ver. 14, בָּאִים בְּתוֹךְ הָעִיר; and there is no necessity to alter הָעִיר in ver. 14 into הַשָּׁעַר, as Thenius proposes, for בּוֹא בְּתוֹךְ הָעִיר does not mean to go (or be) in the middle of the town, as he imagines, but to *go into*, or enter, *the town;* and the entrance to the town was through the gate.—Ver. 19. Samuel replied, "*I am the seer: go up before me to the high place, and eat with me to-day; and to-morrow I will send thee away, and make known to thee all that is in thy heart.*" Letting a person go in front was a sign of great esteem. The change from the singular עֲלֵה to the plural אֲכַלְתֶּם may be explained on the ground that, whilst Samuel only spoke to Saul, he intended expressly to invite his servant to the meal as well as himself. "*All that is in thine heart*" does not mean "all that thou hast upon thy heart," *i.e.* all that troubles thee, for Samuel relieved him of all anxiety about the asses at once by telling him that they were found ; but simply the thoughts of thy heart generally. Samuel would make these known to him, to prove to him that he was a prophet. He then first of all satisfied him respecting the asses (ver. 20) : "*As for the asses that were lost to thee to-day three days* (three days ago), *do not set thy heart upon them* (*i.e.* do not trouble thyself about them), *for they are found.*" After this quieting announcement, by which he had convinced Saul of his seer's gift, Samuel directed Saul's thoughts to that higher thing which Jehovah had appointed for him : "*And to whom does all that is worth desiring of Israel belong? is it not to thee, and to all thy father's house?*" "The desire of Israel" (*optima quæque Israel*, Vulg. ; "the best in Israel," Luther) is not all that Israel desires, but all that Israel possesses of what is precious or *worth desiring* (see Hag. ii. 7). "The antithesis here is between the asses and every desirable thing" (Seb. Schmidt). Notwithstanding the indefinite character of the words, they held up such glorious things as in prospect for Saul, that he replied in amazement (ver. 21), "*Am not I a Benjaminite, of the smallest of the tribes of Israel? and my family is the least of all the families of the tribe of Benjamin* (שִׁבְטֵי בנ is unquestionably a copyist's error for שֵׁבֶט בנ') ; *and how speakest thou such a word to me?*" Samuel made no reply to this, as he simply wanted first of all to awaken the expectation in Saul's mind of things that he had never dreamt of before.—Ver. 22. When they arrived at the high place, he conducted Saul and his servant into the cell (the apartment prepared for the sacrificial meal), and gave them (the servant as well as Saul, according to the simple customs of antiquity, as being also his guest) a place at the upper end among those who had been invited. There were about thirty persons present, no doubt the most distinguished men of the city, whilst the rest of the people probably encamped in the open air.—Vers. 23, 24. He then ordered the cook to bring the piece which he had directed him to set aside, and to

place it before Saul, namely the leg and הֶעָלֶיהָ (the article in
the place of the relative; see Ewald, § 331, *b*); *i.e.* not what
was over it, viz. the broth poured upon it (Dathe and Maurer),
but what was attached to it (Luther). The reference, however,
is not to the kidney as the choicest portion (Thenius), for the
kidneys were burned upon the altar in the case of all the slain
sacrifices (Lev. iii. 4), and only the flesh of the animals offered
in sacrifice was applied to the sacrificial meal. What was at
tached to the leg, therefore, can only have been such of the fat
upon the flesh as was not intended for the altar. Whether the
right or left leg, is not stated: the earlier commentators decide
in favour of the left, because the right leg fell to the share of
the priests (Lev. vii. 32 sqq.). But as Samuel conducted the
whole of the sacrificial ceremony, he may also have offered the
sacrifice itself by virtue of his prophetic calling, so that the
right leg would fall to his share, and he might have it reserved
for his guest. In any case, however, the leg, as the largest and
best portion, was to be a piece of honour for Saul (see Gen.
xliii. 34). There is no reason to seek for any further symbolical meaning in it. The fact that it was Samuel's intention
to distinguish and honour Saul above all his other guests, is
evident enough from what he said to Saul when the cook had
brought the leg: "*Behold, that which is reserved is set before
thee* (שִׂים is the passive participle, as in Num. xxiv. 21); *for
unto this time hath it been kept for thee, as I said I have invited
the people*" לַמּוֹעֵד is either "*to the appointed time of thy
coming*," or possibly, "*for the* (this) *meeting together*." Samuel
mentions this to give Saul his guest to understand that he
had foreseen his coming in a supernatural way. לֵאמֹר, *saying*,
i.e. as I said (to the cook).

Vers. 25—27. When the sacrificial meal was over, Samuel
and Saul went down from the high place into the town, and he
(Samuel) talked with him upon the roof (of the house into
which Samuel had entered). The flat roofs of the East were
used as places of retirement for private conversation (see at
Deut. xxii. 8). This conversation did not refer of course to
the call of Samuel to the royal dignity, for that was not made
known to him as a word of Jehovah till the following day (ver.
27); but it was intended to prepare him for that announcement: so that O. v. Gerlach's conjecture is probably the correct

one, viz. that Samuel " talked with Saul concerning the deep
religious and political degradation of the people of God, the
oppression of the heathen, the causes of the inability of the
Israelites to stand against these foes, the necessity for a conversion of the people, and the want of a leader who was entirely
devoted to the Lord." [1]—Ver. 26. *" And they rose up early in*

[1] For עַל הַגָּג וַיְדַבֵּר עִם־שָׁאוּל the LXX. have καὶ διέστρωσαν τῷ Σαοὺλ
ἐπὶ τῷ δώματι καὶ ἐκοιμήθη, " they prepared Saul a bed upon the, house,
and he slept," from which Clericus conjectured that these translators had
read וירבדו לשאול (וַיִּרְבְּדוּ) or וַיִּרְבְּדוּ ; and Ewald and Thenius propose to
alter the Hebrew text in this way. But although וַיַּשְׁכִּמוּ וְגוּ' (ver. 26) no
doubt presupposes that Saul had slept in Samuel's house, and in fact upon
the roof, the remark of Thenius, " that the private conversation upon the
roof (ver. 25) comes too early, as Saul did not yet know, and was not to
learn till the following day, what was about to take place," does not
supply any valid objection to the correctness of the Masoretic text, or any
argument in favour of the Septuagint rendering or interpretation, since it
rests upon an altogether unfounded and erroneous assumption, viz. that
Samuel had talked with Saul about his call to the throne. Moreover, " the
strangeness" of the statement in ver. 26, " they rose up early," and then
" when the morning dawned, Samuel called," etc., cannot possibly throw
any suspicion upon the integrity of the Hebrew text, as this " strangeness " vanishes when we take וַיְהִי כַּעֲלוֹת וְגוּ' as a more precise definition of
וַיַּשְׁכִּמוּ. The Septuagint translators evidently held the same opinion as
their modern defenders. They took offence at Samuel's private conversation with Saul, because he did not make known to him the word of God
concerning his call to the throne till the next morning ; and, on the other
hand, as their rising the next morning is mentioned in ver. 26, they felt
the absence of any allusion to their sleeping, and consequently not only
interpreted ידבר by a conjectural emendation as standing for ירבד, because
רְבַד מַרְבַדִּים is used in Prov. vii. 16 to signify the spreading of mats or
carpets for a bed, but also identified וַיִּשְׁכְּמוּ with יִשְׁכְּבוּ, and rendered it
ἐκοιμήθη. At the same time, they did not reflect that the preparation of
the bed and their sleeping during the night were both of them matters of
course, and there was consequently no necessity to mention them; whereas
Samuel's talking with Saul upon the roof was a matter of importance in
relation to the whole affair, and one which could not be passed over in
silence. Moreover, the correctness of the Hebrew text is confirmed by all
the other ancient versions. Not only do the Chaldee, Syriac, and Arabic
follow the Masoretic text, but Jerome does the same in the rendering
adopted by him, *"Et locutus est cum Saule in solario.   Cumque mane
surrexissent ;"* though the words *" stravitque Saul in solario et dormivit "*
have been interpolated probably from the Itala into the text of the Vulgate which has come down to us.

the morning: namely, when the morning dawn arose, Samuel called to Saul upon the roof (*i.e.* he called from below within the house up to the roof, where Saul was probably sleeping upon the balcony; cf. 2 Kings iv. 10), *Get up, I will conduct thee.*" As soon as Saul had risen, "*they both (both Samuel and Saul) went out* (into the street)." And when they had gone down to the extremity of the town, *Samuel said to Saul,* "*Let the servant pass on before us (and he did so), and do thou remain here for the present; I will show thee a word of God.*"

Ch. x. 1. Samuel then took the oil-flask, poured it upon his (Saul's) head, kissed him, and said, "*Hath not Jehovah* (equivalent to 'Jehovah assuredly hath') *anointed thee to be captain over His inheritance?*" הֲלוֹא, as an expression of lively assurance, receives the force of an independent clause through the following כִּי, "*is it not so?*" *i.e.* "yea, it is so, that," etc., just as it does before אִם in Gen. iv. 7. נַחֲלָתוֹ, His (Jehovah's) possession, was the nation of Israel, which Jehovah had acquired as the people of His own possession through their deliverance out of Egypt (Deut. iv. 20, ix. 26, etc.). Anointing with oil was a symbol of endowment with the Spirit of God; as the oil itself, by virtue of the strength which it gives to the vital spirits, was a symbol of the Spirit of God as the principle of divine and spiritual power (see at Lev. viii. 12). Hitherto there had been no other anointing among the people of God than that of the priests and sanctuary (Ex. xxx. 23 sqq.; Lev. viii. 10 sqq.). When Saul, therefore, was consecrated as king by anointing, the monarchy was inaugurated as a divine institution, standing on a par with the priesthood; through which henceforth the Lord would also bestow upon His people the gifts of His Spirit for the building up of His kingdom. As the priests were consecrated by anointing to be the media of the ethical blessings of divine grace for Israel, so the king was consecrated by anointing to be the vehicle and medium of all the blessings of grace which the Lord, as the God-king, would confer upon His people through the institution of a civil government. Through this anointing, which was performed by Samuel under the direction of God, the king was set apart from the rest of the nation as "anointed of the Lord" (cf. ch. xii. 3, 5, etc.), and sanctified as the נָגִיד, *i.e.* its captain, its leader and commander. *Kissing* was probably not a sign of homage or reverence towards the anointed of the Lord, so much as "a kiss of affection, with which the grace of God itself was sealed" (Seb. Schmidt).[1]

Vers. 2–7. To confirm the consecration of Saul as king over Israel, which had been effected through the anointing, Samuel gave him three more signs which would occur on his journey home, and would be a pledge to him that Jehovah would accompany his undertakings with His divine help, and practically accredit him as His anointed. These signs, therefore, stand in the closest relation to the calling conveyed to Saul through his anointing.—Ver. 2. *The first sign: "When thou goest away from me to-day (i.e. now), thou wilt meet two men at Rachel's sepulchre, on the border of Benjamin at Zelzah; and they will say unto thee, The asses of thy father, which thou wentest to seek, are found. Behold, thy father hath given up* אֶת־דִּבְרֵי הָאֲתֹנוֹת, *the words (i.e. talking) about the asses, and troubleth himself about you, saying, What shall I do about my son?"* According to Gen. xxxv. 16 sqq., Rachel's sepulchre was on the way from Bethel

---

[1] The LXX. and Vulgate have expanded the second half of this verse by a considerable addition, which reads as follows in the LXX. : οὐχὶ κέχρικέ σε κύριος εἰς ἄρχοντα ἐπὶ τὸν λαὸν αὐτοῦ ἐπὶ Ἰσραήλ; καὶ σὺ ἄρξεις ἐν λαῷ κυρίου, καὶ σὺ σώσεις αὐτὸν ἐκ χειρὸς ἐχθρῶν αὐτοῦ κυκλόθεν, καὶ τοῦτό σοι τὸ σημεῖον ὅτι ἔχρισέ σε κύριος ἐπὶ κληρονομίαν αὐτοῦ εἰς ἄρχοντα. And in the Vulgate : *Ecce, unxit te Dominus super hæreditatem suam in principem, et liberabis populum suum de manibus inimicorum ejus, qui in circuitu ejus sunt. Et hoc tibi signum, quia unxit te Deus in principem.* A comparison of these two texts will show that the LXX. interpolated their addition between הֲלוֹא and כִּי, as the last clause, ὅτι ἔχρισέ σε κύριος ἐπὶ κληρονομίαν αὐτοῦ εἰς ἄρχοντα, is a verbal translation of כִּי מְשָׁחֲךָ יְהוָה עַל־נַחֲלָתוֹ לְנָגִיד. In the Vulgate, on the other hand, the first clause, *ecce unxit—in principem,* corresponds word for word with the Hebrew text, from which we may see that Jerome translated our present Hebrew text; and the addition, *et liberabis,* etc., was interpolated into the Vulgate from the Itala. The text of the Septuagint is nothing more than a gloss formed from ch. ix. 16, 17, which the translator thought necessary, partly because he could not clearly see the force of הֲלוֹא כִּי, but more especially because he could not explain the fact that Samuel speaks to Saul of signs, without having announced them to him as such. But the author of the gloss has overlooked the fact that Samuel does not give Saul a σημεῖον, but three σημεῖα, and describes the object of them in ver. 7 as being the following, namely, that Saul would learn when they took place what he had to do, for Jehovah was with him, and not that they would prove that the Lord had anointed him to be captain.

to Bethlehem, only a short distance from the latter place, and therefore undoubtedly on the spot which tradition has assigned to it since the time of Jerome, viz. on the site of the *Kubbet Rahil*, half an hour to the north-west of Bethlehem, on the left of the road to Jerusalem, about an hour and a half from the city (see at Gen. xxxv. 20). This suits the passage before us very well, if we give up the groundless assumption that Saul came to Samuel at Ramah and was anointed by him there, and assume that the place of meeting, which is not more fully defined in ch. ix., was situated to the south-west of Bethlehem.[1] The expression " in the border of Benjamin" is not at variance with this. It is true that *Kubbet Rahil* is about an hour and a quarter from the southern boundary of Benjamin, which ran past the *Rogel* spring, through the valley of Ben-Hinnom (Josh. xviii. 16) ; but the expression עִם קְבוּרָה must not be so pressed as to be restricted to the actual site of the grave, since otherwise the further definition " *at Zelzah*" would be superfluous, as Rachel's tomb was unquestionably a well-known locality at that time. If we suppose the place called Zelzah, the situation of which has not yet been discovered,[2] to have been about midway between Rachel's tomb and the *Rogel* spring, Samuel could very well describe the spot where Saul would meet the

[1] As the account of Saul's meeting with Samuel, in ch. ix., when properly understood, is not at variance with the tradition concerning the situation of Rachel's tomb, and the passage before us neither requires us on the one hand to understand the Ephratah of Gen. xxxv. 19 and xlviii. 7 as a different place from Bethlehem, and erase " *that is Bethlehem*" from both passages as a gloss that has crept into the text, and then invent an *Ephratah* in the neighbourhood of Bethel between Benjamin and Ephraim, as Thenius does, nor warrants us on the other hand in transferring Rachel's tomb to the neighbourhood of Bethel, in opposition to the ordinary tradition, as Kurtz proposes ; so the words of Jer. xxxi. 15, " A voice was heard in Ramah, lamentation and bitter weeping, Rachel weeping for her children," etc., furnish no evidence that Rachel's tomb was at Ramah (*i.e. er Râm*). " For here (in the cycle of prophecy concerning the restoration of all Israel, Jer. xxx.–xxxiii.) Rachel's weeping is occasioned by the fact of the exiles of Benjamin having assembled together in Ramah (Jer. xl. 1), without there being any reason why Rachel's tomb should be sought for in the neighbourhood of this Ramah" (Delitzsch on Gen. xxxv. 20).

[2] Ewald (*Gesch.* iii. p. 29) supposes Zelzah to be unsuitable to the context, if taken as the name of a place, and therefore follows the ἀλλομένους μεγάλα of the LXX., and renders the word " in great haste ;" but he has neither given any reason why the name of a place is unsuitable here, nor

two men in the way that he has done. This sign, by confirming
the information which Samuel had given to Saul with reference
to the asses, was to furnish him with a practical proof that what
Samuel had said to him with regard to the monarchy would
quite as certainly come to pass, and therefore not only to deliver
him from all anxiety as to the lost animals of his father, but
also to direct his thoughts to the higher destiny to which God
had called him through Samuel's anointing.

The second sign (vers. 3, 4): " *Then thou shalt go on forward from thence, and thou shalt come to the terebinth of Tabor;
and there shall meet thee there three men going up to God to
Bethel, carrying one three kids, one three loaves of bread, and
one a bottle of wine. They will ask thee after thy welfare, and
give thee two loaves; receive them at their hands.*" The terebinth of *Tabor* is not mentioned anywhere else, and nothing
further can be determined concerning it, than that it stood by
the road leading from Rachel's tomb to Gibeah.[1] The fact
that the three men were going up to God at Bethel, shows that
there was still a place of sacrifice consecrated to the Lord at
Bethel, where Abraham and Jacob had erected altars to the
Lord who had appeared to them there (Gen. xii. 8, xiii. 3, 4,
xxviii. 18, 19, xxxv. 7); for the kids and loaves and wine
were sacrificial gifts which they were about to offer. שָׁאַל לְשָׁלוֹם,
to ask after one's welfare, *i.e.* to greet in a friendly manner
(cf. Judg. xviii. 15; Gen. xliii. 27). The meaning of this
double sign consisted in the fact that these men gave Saul
two loaves from their sacrificial offerings. In this he was to

considered that the Septuagint rendering is merely conjectural, and has
nothing further to support it than the fact that the translators rendered
צָלַח ἐφήλατο, " he sprang upon him," in ver. 6 and ch. xi. 6, and took צלצח
to be an emphatic form of צלח.

[1] The opinion expressed by Ewald and Thenius, that Deborah's mourning oak (Gen. xxxv. 8) is intended, and that *Tabor* is either a different
form of *Deborah*, or that *Tabor* should be altered into Deborah, has no
foundation to rest upon; for the fact that the oak referred to stood below
(*i.e.* to the south of) Bethel, and the three men whom Saul was to meet at
the terebinth of *Tabor* were going to Bethel, by no means establishes the
identity of the two, as their going up to Bethel does not prove that they
were already in the neighbourhood of Bethel. Moreover, the Deborah oak
was on the north of Gibeah, whereas Saul met the three men between
Rachel's tomb and Gibeah, *i.e.* to the south of Gibeah.

discern a homage paid to the anointed of the Lord; and he was therefore to accept the gift in this sense at their hand.

The third sign (vers. 5, 6) Saul was to receive at Gibeah of God, where posts of the Philistines were stationed. *Gibeath ha-Elohim* is not an appellative, signifying a high place of God, *i.e.* a high place dedicated to God, but a proper name referring to *Gibeah* of Benjamin, the native place of Saul, which was called *Gibeah of Saul* from the time when Saul resided there as king (ver. 16 : cf. ch. xi. 4, xv. 34; 2 Sam. xxi. 6; Isa. x. 29). This is very apparent from the fact that, according to vers. 10 sqq., all the people of Gibeah had known Saul of old, and therefore could not comprehend how he had all at once come to be among the prophets. The name *Gibeah of God* is here given to the town on account of a *bamah* or sacrificial height which rose within or near the town (ver. 13), and which may possibly have been renowned above other such heights, as the seat of a society of prophets. נְצִבֵי פְלִשְׁתִּים are not bailiffs of the Philistines, still less columns erected as signs of their supremacy (Thenius), but military posts of the Philistines, as ch. xiii. 3, 4, and 2 Sam. viii. 6, 14, clearly show. The allusion here to the posts of the Philistines at Gibeah is connected with what was about to happen to Saul there. At the place where the Philistines, those severe oppressors of Israel, had set up military posts, the Spirit of God was to come upon Saul, and endow him with the divine power that was required for his regal office. *"And it shall come to pass, when thou comest to the town there, thou wilt light upon a company of prophets coming down from the high place (bamah, the sacrificial height), before them lyre and tambourin, and flute, and harp, and they prophesying."* חֶבֶל signifies a rope or cord, then a *band* or *company* of men. It does not follow that because this band of prophets was coming down from the high place, the high place at Gibeah must have been the seat of a school of the prophets. They might have been upon a pilgrimage to Gibeah. The fact that they were preceded by musicians playing, seems to indicate a festal procession. *Nebel* and *kinnor* are stringed instruments which were used after David's time in connection with the psalmody of divine worship (1 Chron. xiii. 8, xv. 20, 21; Ps. xxxiii. 2, xliii. 4, etc.). The *nebel* was an instrument resembling a *lyre*, the *kinnor* was more like a *guitar* than a harp. *Toph :* the *tambourin,* which was played by Miriam at the Red Sea (Ex. xv. 20). *Chalil:* the *flute ;* see my *Bibl. Archæology,* ii. § 137. By the prophesying of these prophets we are to understand an ecstatic utterance of religious feelings to the praise of God, as in the case of the seventy elders in the time of Moses (Num. xi. 25). Whether it took the form of a song or of an enthusiastic discourse, cannot be determined ; in any case it was connected with a very energetic action indicative of the highest state of mental excitement. (For further remarks on these societies of prophets, see at ch. xix. 18 sqq.)—Ver. 6. "*And the Spirit of Jehovah will come upon thee, and thou wilt prophesy with them, and be changed into another man.*" " Ecstatic states," says Tholuck (*die Propheten,* p. 53), "have something infectious about them. The excitement spreads involuntarily, as in the American revivals and the preaching mania in Sweden, even to persons in whose state of mind there is no affinity with anything of the kind." But in the instance before us there was something more than psychical infection. The Spirit of Jehovah, which manifested itself in the prophesying of the prophets, was to pass over to Saul, so that he would prophesy along with them (הִתְנַבִּיתָ formed like a verb ל״ה for הִתְנַבֵּאת ; so again in ver. 13), and was entirely to transform him. This transformation is not to be regarded indeed as regeneration in the Christian sense, but as a change resembling regeneration, which affected the entire disposition of mind, and by which Saul was lifted out of his former modes of thought and feeling, which were confined within a narrow earthly sphere, into the far higher sphere of his new royal calling, was filled with kingly thoughts in relation to the service of God, and received "*another heart*" (ver. 9). *Heart* is used in the ordinary scriptural sense, as the centre of the whole mental and psychical life of will, desire, thought, perception, and feeling (see Delitzsch, *Bibl. Psychol.* pp. 248 sqq., ed. 2). Through this sign his anointing as king was to be inwardly sealed. — Ver. 7. " *When these signs are come unto thee* (the *Kethibh* תבאינה is to be read תְּבֹאֶינָה, as in Ps. xlv. 16 and Esther iv. 4 ; and the *Keri* תְּבֹאֶנָה is a needless emendation), *do to thee what thy hand findeth, i.e.* act according to the circumstances (for this formula, see Judg. ix. 33) ; *for God will be with thee.*" The occurrence of the signs mentioned was to assure him of the certainty that

God would assist him in all that he undertook as king. The first opportunity for action was afforded him by the Ammonite Nahash, who besieged Jabesh-gilead (ch. xi.).

Ver. 8. In conclusion, Samuel gave him an important hint with regard to his future attitude : " *And goest thou before me down to Gilgal ; and, behold, I am coming down to thee, to offer burnt-offerings, and to sacrifice peace-offerings : thou shalt wait seven days, till I come to thee, that I may show thee what thou art to do.*" The infinitive clause וגו' לְהַעֲלוֹת is undoubtedly dependent upon the main clause וְיָרַדְתָּ, and not upon the circumstantial clause which is introduced as a parenthesis. The thought therefore is the following : If Saul went down to Gilgal to offer sacrifice there, he was to wait till Samuel arrived. The construction of the main clause itself, however, is doubtful, since, grammatically considered, יָרַדְתָּ can either be a continuation of the imperative עֲשֵׂה (ver. 7), or can be regarded as independent, and in fact conditional. The latter view, according to which יָרַדְתָּ supposes his going down as a possible thing that may take place at a future time, is the one required by the circumstantial clause which follows, and which is introduced by וְהִנֵּה ; for if וְיָרַדְתָּ were intended to be a continuation of the imperative which precedes it, so that Samuel commanded Saul to go down to Gilgal before him, he would have simply announced his coming, that is to say, he would either have said וְיָרַדְתִּי or וַאֲנִי אֵרֵד. The circumstantial clause " *and behold I am coming down to thee*" evidently presupposes Saul's going down as a possible occurrence, in the event of which Samuel prescribes the course he is to pursue. But the conditional interpretation of וְיָרַדְתָּ is still more decidedly required by the context. For instance, when Samuel said to Saul that after the occurrence of the three signs he was to do what came to his hand, he could hardly command him immediately afterwards to go to Gilgal, since the performance of what came to his hand might prevent him from going to Gilgal. If, however, Samuel meant that after Saul had finished what came to his hand he was to go down to Gilgal, he would have said, " And after thou hast done this, go down to Gilgal," etc. But as he does not express himself in this manner, he can only have referred to Saul's going to Gilgal as an occurrence which, as he foresaw, would take place at some time or other. And to Saul himself this must not only have presented itself as a possible occurrence, but under the existing circumstances as one that was sure to take place; so that the whole thing was not so obscure to him as it is to us, who are only able to form our conclusions from the brief account which lies before us. If we suppose that in the conversation which Samuel had with Saul upon the roof (ch. ix. 25), he also spoke about the manner in which the Philistines, who had pushed their outposts as far as Gibeah, could be successfully attacked, he might also have mentioned that Gilgal was the most suitable place for gathering an army together, and for making the necessary preparations for a successful engagement with their foes. If we just glance at the events narrated in the following chapters, for the purpose of getting a clear idea of the thing which Samuel had in view; we find that the three signs announced by Samuel took place on Saul's return to Gibeah (vers. 9–16). Samuel then summoned the people to Mizpeh, where Saul was elected king by lot (vers. 17–27); but Saul returned to Gibeah to his own house even after this solemn election, and was engaged in ploughing the field, when messengers came from Jabesh with the account of the siege of that town by the Ammonites. On receiving this intelligence the Spirit of Jehovah came upon him, so that he summoned the whole nation with energy and without delay to come to battle, and proceeded to Jabesh with the assembled army, and smote the Ammonites (ch. xi. 1–11). Thereupon Samuel summoned the people to come to Gilgal and renew the monarchy there (ch. xi. 12–15); and at the same time he renewed his office of supreme judge (ch. xii.), so that now for the first time Saul actually commenced his reign, and began the war against the Philistines (ch. xiii. 1), in which, as soon as the latter advanced to Michmash with a powerful army after Jonathan's victorious engagement, he summoned the people to Gilgal to battle, and after waiting there seven days for Samuel in vain, had the sacrifices offered, on which account as soon as Samuel arrived he announced to him that his rule would not last (ch. xiii. 13 sqq.). Now, it cannot have been the first of these two gatherings at Gilgal that Samuel had in his mind, but must have been the second. The first is precluded by the simple fact that Samuel summoned the people to go to Gilgal for the purpose of renewing the monarchy; and therefore, as

the words "come and let us go to Gilgal" (ch. xi. 14) unquestionably imply, he must have gone thither himself along with
the people and the king, so that Saul was never in a position to
have to wait for Samuel's arrival. The second occurrence at
Gilgal, on the other hand, is clearly indicated in the words of
ch. xiii. 8, "*Saul tarried seven days, according to the set time
that Samuel had appointed*," in which there is almost an express
allusion to the instructions given to Saul in the verse before us.
But whilst we cannot but regard this as the only true explanation, we cannot agree with Seb. Schmidt, who looks upon the
instructions given to Saul in this verse as "a rule to be observed
throughout the whole of Samuel's life," that is to say, who
interprets יֵרַדְתָּ in the sense of "as often as thou goest down to
Gilgal."   For this view cannot be grammatically sustained,
although it is founded upon the correct idea, that Samuel's
instructions cannot have been intended as a solitary and arbitrary command, by which Saul was to be kept in a condition
of dependence.   According to our explanation, however, this is
not the case ; but there was an inward necessity for them,
so far as the government of Saul was concerned.   Placed as
he was by Jehovah as king over His people, for the purpose
of rescuing them out of the power of those who were at that
time its most dangerous foes, Saul was not at liberty to enter
upon the war against these foes simply by his own will, but was
directed to wait till Samuel, the accredited prophet of Jehovah,
had completed the consecration through the offering of a solemn
sacrifice, and had communicated to him the requisite instructions from God, even though he should have to wait for seven
days.[1]

Vers. 9–16. When Saul went away from Samuel, to return
to Gibeah, "*God changed to him another heart*,"—a pregnant
expression for "God changed him, and gave him another heart"

[1] The difficulty in question has been solved on the whole quite correctly by Brentius.   "It is not to be supposed," he says, "that Samuel
was directing Saul to go at once to Gilgal as soon as he should go away
from him, and wait there for seven days ; but that he was to do this after
he had been chosen king by public lot, and having conquered the Ammonites and been confirmed in the kingdom, was about to prepare to make
war upon the Philistines, on whose account chiefly it was that he had been
called to the kingdom.   For the Lord had already spoken thus to Samuel
concerning Saul : ' He will save my people from the hands of the Phili-

(see at ver. 6) ; and all these signs (the signs mentioned by Samuel) happened on that very day. As he left Samuel early in the morning, Saul could easily reach Gibeah in one day, even if the town where he had met with Samuel was situated to the south-west of Rachel's tomb, as the distance from that tomb to Gibeah was not more than three and a half or four hours.— Ver. 10. The third sign is the only one which is minutely described, because this caused a great sensation at Gibeah, Saul's home. " *And they* (Saul and his attendant) *came thither to Gibeah.*" " *Thither*" points back to " thither to the city" in ver. 5, and is defined by the further expression " to Gibeah" (Eng. version, " to the hill :" Tr.).   The rendering ἐκεῖθεν (LXX.) does not warrant us in changing שָׁם into מִשָּׁם ; for the latter would be quite superfluous, as it was self-evident that they came to Gibeah from the place where they had been in the company of Samuel.—Ver. 11. When those who had known Saul of old saw that he prophesied with the prophets, the people said one to another, " *What has happened to the son of Kish? Is Saul also among the prophets?*" This expression presupposes that Saul's previous life was altogether different from that of the disciples of the prophets.—Ver. 12. And one from thence (*i.e.* from Gibeah, or from the crowd that was gathered round the prophets) answered, " *And who is their father?*" *i.e.* not " who is their president?" which would be a very gratuitous question ; but, " is *their* father a prophet then ?" *i.e.*, according to the explanation given by Oehler (Herzog's *Real. Enc.* xii. p. 216), " have they the prophetic spirit by virtue of their birth?" Understood in this way, the retort forms a very appropriate " answer" to the expression of surprise and the inquiry, how it came to pass that Saul was among the prophets. If those prophets had not obtained the gift of prophecy by inheritance, but as a free gift of the Lord, it was equally possible for the Lord to communi-

stines, because I have looked upon my people.' This is the meaning therefore of Samuel's command : Thou hast been called to the kingdom chiefly for this purpose, that thou mayest deliver Israel from the tyranny of the Philistines. When therefore thou shalt enter upon this work, go down into Gilgal and wait there seven days, until I shall come to thee : for thou shalt then offer a holocaust, though not before I come to thee, and I will show thee what must be done in order that our enemies the Philistines may be conquered. The account of this is given below in ch. xiii., where we learn that Saul violated this command."

cate the same gift to Saul. On the other hand, the alteration of the text from אֲבִיהֶם (their father) into אָבִיהוּ (his father), according to the LXX., Vulg., Syr., and Arab., which is favoured by Ewald, Thenius, and others, must be rejected, for the simple reason that the question, Who is his father? in the mouth of one of the inhabitants of Gibeah, to whom Saul's father was so well known that they called Saul the son of Kish at once, would have no sense whatever. From this the proverb arose, "Is Saul also among the prophets?"—a proverb which was used to express astonishment at the appearance of any man in a sphere of life which had hitherto been altogether strange to him.—Vers. 13 sqq. When Saul had left off prophesying, and came to Bamah, his uncle asked him and his attendant where they had been; and Saul told him, that as they had not found the asses anywhere, they had gone to Samuel, and had learned from him that the asses were found. But he did not relate the words which had been spoken by Samuel concerning the monarchy, from unambitious humility (cf. vers. 22, 23) and not because he was afraid of unbelief and envy, as Thenius follows Josephus in supposing. From the expression " he came to Bamah" (Eng. ver. " to the high place"), we must conclude, that not only Saul's uncle, but his father also, lived in Bamah, as we find Saul immediately afterwards in his own family circle (see vers. 14 sqq.).

SAUL ELECTED KING. HIS ELECTION CONFIRMED.
CHAP. X. 17—XI. 15.

Vers. 17–27. Saul's Election by Lot.—After Samuel had secretly anointed Saul king by the command of God, it was his duty to make provision for a recognition of the man whom God had chosen on the part of the people also. To this end he summoned the people to Mizpeh, and there instructed the tribes to choose a king by lot. As the result of the lot was regarded as a divine decision, not only was Saul to be accredited by this act in the sight of the whole nation as the king appointed by the Lord, but he himself was also to be more fully assured of the certainty of his own election on the part of God.[1]—Ver. 17.

[1] Thenius follows De Wette, and adduces the incompatibility of ch. viii. and ch. x. 17–27 with ch. ix. 1–10, 16, as a proof that in vers. 17–27 we

הָעָם is the nation in its heads and representatives. *Samuel*
selected *Mizpeh* for this purpose, because it was there that he
had once before obtained for the people, by prayer, a great
victory over the Philistines (ch. vii. 5 sqq.).—Vers. 18, 19.
" But before proceeding to the election itself, Samuel once more
charged the people with their sin in rejecting God, who had
brought them out of Egypt, and delivered them out of the hand
of all their oppressors, by their demand for a king, that he might
show them how dangerous was the way which they were taking
now, and how bitterly they would perhaps repent of what they
had now desired" (O. v. Gerlach ; see the commentary on
ch. viii.). The masculine הַלְּחָצִים is construed *ad sensum* with
הַפַּמְלָכוֹת. In וַתֹּאמְרוּ לוֹ the early translators have taken לוֹ for
לֹא, which is the actual reading in some of the Codices. But
although this reading is decidedly favoured by the parallel passages, ch. viii. 19, xii. 12, it is not necessary ; since כִּי is used to
introduce a direct statement, even in a declaration of the opposite, in the sense of our " *no but*" (*e.g.* in Ruth i. 10, where
לֹה precedes). There is, therefore, no reason for exchanging
לוֹ for לֹא.—Vers. 20, 21. After this warning, Samuel directed
the assembled Israelites to come before Jehovah (*i.e.* before the
altar of Jehovah which stood at Mizpeh, according to ch. vii. 9)
according to their tribes and families (*alaphim :* see at Num.
i. 16) ; " *and there was taken* (by lot) *the tribe of Benjamin.*"

have a different account of the manner in which Saul became king from
that given in ch. ix. 1-10, 16, and one which continues the account in
ch. viii. 22. " It is thoroughly inconceivable," he says, " that Samuel
should have first of all anointed Saul king by the instigation of God, and
then have caused the lot to be cast, as it were, for the sake of further confirmation ; for in that case either the prophet would have tempted God, or
he would have made Him chargeable before the nation with an unworthy
act of jugglery." Such an argument as this could only be used by critics
who deny not only the inspiration of the prophets, but all influence on the
part of the living God upon the free action of men, and cannot therefore
render the truth of the biblical history at all doubtful. Even Ewald sees
no discrepancy here, and observes in his history (*Gesch.* iii. p. 32) : " If we
bear in mind the ordinary use made of the sacred lot at that time, we shall
find that there is nothing but the simple truth in the whole course of the
narrative. The secret meeting of the seer with Saul was not sufficient to
secure a complete and satisfactory recognition of him as king ; it was also
necessary that the Spirit of Jehovah should single him out publicly in a
solemn assembly of the nation, and point him out as the man of Jehovah."

הִלָּכֵד, *lit.* to be snatched out by Jehovah, namely, through the lot (see Josh. vii. 14, 16). He then directed the tribe of Benjamin to draw near according to its families, *i.e.* he directed the heads of the families of this tribe to come before the altar of the Lord and draw lots; and *the family of Matri was taken.* Lastly, when the heads of the households in this family came, and after that the different individuals in the household which had been taken, the lot fell upon *Saul the son of Kish.* In the words, *"Saul the son of Kish was taken,"* the historian proceeds at once to the final result of the casting of the lots, without describing the intermediate steps any further.[1] When the lot fell upon Saul, they sought him, and he could not be found.— Ver. 22. Then they inquired of Jehovah, *" Is any one else come hither?"* and Jehovah replied, *"Behold, he* (whom ye are seeking) *is hidden among the things."* The inquiry was made through the high priest, by means of the Urim and Thummim, for which שָׁאַל בַּיהוָֹה was the technical expression, according to Num. xxvii. 21 (see Judg. xx. 27, 28, i. 1, etc.). There can be no doubt, that in a gathering of the people for so important a purpose as the election of a king, the high priest would also be present, even though this is not expressly stated. Samuel presided over the meeting as the prophet of the Lord. The answer given by God, *" Behold, he is hidden,"* etc., appears to have no relation to the question, *" Is any one else come?"* The Sept. and Vulg. have therefore altered the question into εἰ ἔτι ἔρχεται ὁ ἀνήρ, *utrumnam venturus esset;* and Thenius would adopt this

---

[1] It is true the Septuagint introduces the words καὶ προσάγουσι τὴν φυλὴν Ματταρὶ εἰς ἄνδρας before וַיִּלָּכֵד, and this clause is also found in a very recent Hebrew MS. (viz. 451 in Kennicott's *dissert. gener.* p. 491). But it is very evident that these words did not form an integral part of the original text, as Thenius supposes, but were nothing more than an interpolation of the Sept. translators, from the simple fact that they do not fill up the supposed gap at all completely, but only in a very partial, and in fact a very mistaken manner; for the *family of Matri* could not come to the lot εἰς ἄνδρας (man by man), but only κατ᾽ οἴκους (by households: Josh. vii. 14). Before the household (*beth-aboth*, father's house) of Saul could be taken, it was necessary that the נְּבָרִים (ἄνδρες), *i.e.* the different heads of households, should be brought; and it was not till then that Kish, or his son Saul, could be singled out as the appointed of the Lord. Neither the author of the gloss in the LXX., nor the modern defender of the gloss, has thought of this.

as an emendation. But he is wrong in doing so; for there was no necessity to ask whether Saul would still come : they might at once have sent to fetch him. What they asked was rather, whether any one else had come besides those who were present, as Saul was not to be found among them, that they might know where they were to look for Saul, whether at home or anywhere else. And to this question God gave the answer, " He is present, only hidden among the things." By כֵּלִים (the *things* or *vessels*, Eng. ver. the stuff) we are to understand the *travelling baggage* of the people who had assembled at Mizpeh. Saul could neither have wished to avoid accepting the monarchy, nor have imagined that the lot would not fall upon him if he hid himself. For he knew that God had chosen him; and Samuel had anointed him already. He did it therefore simply from humility and modesty. " In order that he might not appear to have either the hope or desire for anything of the kind, he preferred to be absent when the lots were cast" (Seb. Schmidt).— Vers. 23, 24. He was speedily fetched, and brought into the midst of the (assembled) people ; and when he came, he was a head taller than all the people (see ch. ix. 2). And Samuel said to all the people, " *Behold ye whom the Lord hath chosen ! for there is none like him in all the nation.*" Then all the people shouted aloud, and cried, " *Let the king live !*" Saul's bodily stature won the favour of the people (see the remarks on ch. ix. 2).

Samuel then communicated to the people the right of the monarchy, and laid it down before Jehovah. " *The right of the monarchy*" (*meluchah*) is not to be identified with the right of the king (*melech*), which is described in ch. viii. 11 and sets forth the right or prerogative which a despotic king would assume over the people ; but it is the right which regulated the attitude of the earthly monarchy in the theocracy, and determined the duties and rights of the human king in relation to Jehovah the divine King on the one hand, and to the nation on the other. This right could only be laid down by a prophet like Samuel, to raise a wholesome barrier at the very outset against all excesses on the part of the king. Samuel therefore wrote it in a document which was laid down before Jehovah, *i.e.* in the sanctuary of Jehovah ; though certainly not in the sanctuary at Bamah in Gibeah, as Thenius supposes, for nothing is known respecting any such sanctuary. It was no doubt placed in the tabernacle, where the law of Moses was also deposited, by the side of the fundamental law of the divine state in Israel. When the business was all completed, Samuel sent the people away to their own home.—Ver. 26. Saul also returned to his house at Gibeah, and there went with him the crowd of the men whose hearts God had touched, *sc.* to give him a royal escort, and show their readiness to serve him. הַחַיִל is not to be altered into בְּנֵי הַחַיִל, according to the free rendering of the LXX., but is used as in Ex. xiv. 28; with this difference, however, that here it does not signify a large military force, but a crowd of brave men, who formed Saul's escort of honour. —Ver. 27. But as it generally happens that, where a person is suddenly lifted up to exalted honours or office, there are sure to be envious people found, so was it here : there were בְּנֵי בְלִיַּעַל, *worthless people,* even among the assembled Israelites, who spoke disparagingly of Saul, saying, " *How will this man help us ?*" and who brought him no present. *Minchah:* the present which from time immemorial every one has been expected to bring when entering the presence of the king; so that the refusal to bring a present was almost equivalent to rebellion. But Saul was " *as being deaf,"* *i.e.* he acted as if he had not heard. The objection which Thenius brings against this view, viz. that in that case it would read וְהוּא הָיָה כְּמ׳, exhibits a want of acquaintance with the Hebrew construction of a sentence. There is no more reason for touching וַיְהִי than וַיֵּלְכוּ in ver. 26. In both cases the apodosis is attached to the protasis, which precedes it in the form of a circumstantial clause, by the *imperfect,* with *vav consec.* According to the genius of our language, these protases would be expressed by the conjunction *when,* viz.: "*when Saul also went home, . . . there went with him,*" etc.; and " *when loose* (or idle) *people said, etc., he was as deaf.*"

Ch. xi. SAUL's VICTORY OVER THE AMMONITES.—Even after the election by lot at Mizpeh, Saul did not seize upon the reins of government at once, but returned to his father's house in Gibeah, and to his former agricultural occupation ; not, however, merely from personal humility and want of ambition, but rather from a correct estimate of the circumstances. The monarchy was something so new in Israel, that the king could not expect a general and voluntary recognition of his regal dignity and authority, especially after the conduct of the worthless people mentioned in ch. x. 27, until he had answered their expectations from a king (ch. viii. 6, 20), and proved himself a deliverer of Israel from its foes by a victorious campaign. But as Jehovah had chosen him ruler over his people without any seeking on his part, he would wait for higher instructions to act, before he entered upon the government. The opportunity was soon given him.

Vers. 1–5. Nahash, the king of the Ammonites (cf. ch. xii. 12 ; 2 Sam. x. 2), attacked the tribes on the east of the Jordan, no doubt with the intention of enforcing the claim to a part of Gilead asserted by his ancestor in the time of Jephthah (Judg. xi. 13), and besieged *Jabesh* in Gilead,[1]—according to Josephus the metropolis of Gilead, and probably situated by the Wady Jabes (see at Judg. xxi. 8) ; from which we may

---

[1] The time of this campaign is not mentioned in the Hebrew text. But it is very evident from ch. xii. 12, where the Israelites are said to have desired a king, when they saw that Nahash had come against them, that Nahash had invaded Gilead before the election of Saul as king. The Septuagint, however, renders the words וַיְהִי כְּמַחֲרִישׁ (ch. x. 27) by καὶ ἐγενήθη ὡς μετὰ μῆνα, and therefore the translators must have read כְּמֵחֹדֶשׁ, which Ewald and Thenius would adopt as an emendation of the Hebrew text. But all the other ancient versions give the Masoretic text, viz. not only the Chaldee, Syriac, and Arabic, but even Jerome, who renders it *ille vero dissimulabat se audire*. It is true that in our present Vulgate text these words are followed by *et factum est quasi post mensem;* but this addition has no doubt crept in from the Itala. With the general character of the Septuagint, the rendering of כְּמַחֲרִישׁ by ὡς μετὰ μῆνα is no conclusive proof that the word in their Hebrew Codex was כְּמֵחֹדֶשׁ ; it simply shows that this was the interpretation which they gave to כמחריש. And Josephus (vi. 5, 1), who is also appealed to, simply establishes the fact that ὡς μετὰ μῆνα stood in the Sept. version of his day, since he made use of this version and not of the original text. Moreover, we cannot say with Ewald, that this was the last place in which the time could be overlooked ; for it is perfectly evident that Nahash commenced the siege of Jabesh shortly after the election of Saul at Mizpeh, as we may infer from the verb וַיַּעַל, when taken in connection with the fact implied in ch. xii. 12, that he had commenced the war with the Israelites before this. And lastly, it is much more probable that the LXX. changed כמחריש into כמחדש, than that the Hebrew readers of the Old Testament should have altered כמחדש into כמחריש, without defining the time more precisely by אֶחָד, or some other number.

see that he must have penetrated very far into the territory of the Israelites. The inhabitants of Jabesh petitioned the Ammonites in their distress, "*Make a covenant with us, and we will serve thee;*" i.e. grant us favourable terms, and we will submit.—Ver. 2. But Nahash replied, "*On this condition* (בְּזֹאת, *lit.* at this price, בְּ *pretii*) *will I make a covenant with you, that I may put out all your right eyes, and so bring a reproach upon all Israel.*" From the fact that the infinitive נְקוֹר is continued with וְשַׂמְתִּיו, it is evident that the subject to נְקוֹר is Nahash, and not the Israelites, as the Syriac, Arabic, and others have rendered it. The suffix to שַׂמְתִּיהָ is neuter, and refers to the previous clause: "*it*," i.e. the putting out of the right eye. This answer on the part of Nahash shows unmistakeably that he sought to avenge upon the people of Israel the shame of the defeat which Jephthah had inflicted upon the Ammonites.—Ver. 3. The elders of Jabesh replied: "*Leave us seven days, that we may send messengers into all the territory of Israel; and if there is no one who saves us, we will come out to thee,*" i.e. will surrender to thee. This request was granted by Nahash, because he was not in a condition to take the town at once by storm, and also probably because, in the state of internal dissolution into which Israel had fallen at that time, he had no expectation that any vigorous help would come to the inhabitants of Jabesh. From the fact that the messengers were to be sent into all the territory of Israel, we may conclude that the Israelites had no central government at that time, and that neither Nahash nor the Jabeshites had heard anything of the election that had taken place; and this is still more apparent from the fact that, according to ver. 4, their messengers came to Gibeah of Saul, and laid their business before the people generally, without applying at once to Saul. —Ver. 5. Saul indeed did not hear of the matter till he came (returned home) from the field behind the oxen, and found the people weeping and lamenting at these mournful tidings. "*Behind the oxen,*" i.e., judging from the expression "yoke of oxen" in ver. 7, the pair of oxen with which he had been ploughing.

Vers. 6–11. When the report of the messengers had been communicated to him, "*the Spirit of Jehovah came upon him, and his anger was kindled greatly,*" sc. at the shame which the

Ammonites had resolved to bring upon all Israel.—Ver. 7. He took a yoke of oxen, cut them in pieces, and sent (the pieces) into every possession of Israel by messengers, and said, " *Who-ever cometh not forth after Saul and Samuel, so shall it be done unto his oxen.*" The introduction of Samuel's name after that of Saul, is a proof that Saul even as king still recognised the authority which Samuel possessed in Israel as the prophet of Jehovah. This symbolical act, like the cutting up of the woman in Judg. xix. 29, made a deep impression. " *The fear of Jehovah fell upon the people, so that they went out as one man.*" By "the fear of Jehovah " we are not to understand δεῖμα πανικόν (Thenius and Böttcher), for *Jehovah* is not equi-valent to *Elohim*, nor the fear of Jehovah in the sense of fear of His punishment, but a fear inspired by Jehovah. In Saul's energetic appeal the people discerned the power of Jehovah, which inspired them with fear, and impelled them to immediate obedience.—Ver. 8. Saul held a muster of the people of war, who had gathered together at (or near) *Bezek*, a place which was situated, according to the *Onom.* (*s. v. Bezek*), about seven hours to the north of Nabulus towards Beisan (see at Judg. i. 4). The number assembled were 300,000 men of Israel, and 30,000 of Judah. These numbers will not appear too large, if we bear in mind that the allusion is not to a regular army, but that Saul had summoned all the people to a general levy. In the distinction drawn between the children of Judah and the children of Israel we may already discern a trace of that separation of Judah from the rest of the tribes, which even-tually led to a formal secession on the part of the latter.— Ver. 9. The messengers from Jabesh, who had been waiting to see the result of Saul's appeal, were now despatched with this message to their fellow-citizens : " *To-morrow you will have help, when the sun shines hot,*" *i.e.* about noon.—Ver. 10. After receiving these joyful news, the Jabeshites announced to the Ammonites : " *To-morrow we will come out to you, and ye may do to us what seemeth good to you,*"—an untruth by which they hoped to assure the besiegers, so that they might be fallen upon unexpectedly by the advancing army of Saul, and thoroughly beaten.—Ver. 11. The next day Saul arranged the people in three divisions (רָאשִׁים, as in Judg. vii. 16), who forced their way into the camp of the foe from three different sides, in the morning watch (between three and six o'clock in the morning), smote the Ammonites "*till the heat of the day*," and routed them so completely, that those who remained were all scattered, and there were not two men left together.

Vers. 12—15. RENEWAL OF THE MONARCHY.—Saul had so thoroughly acted the part of a king in gaining this victory, and the people were so enthusiastic in his favour, that they said to Samuel, viz. after their return from the battle, "*Who is he that said, Saul should reign over us!*" The clause שָׁאוּל יִמְלֹךְ עָלֵינוּ contains a question, though it is indicated simply by the tone, and there is no necessity to alter שָׁאוּל into הֲשָׁאוּל. These words refer to the exclamation of the worthless people in ch. x. 27. "*Bring the men* (who spoke in this manner), *that we may put them to death.*" But Saul said, "*There shall not a man be put to death this day; for to-day Jehovah hath wrought salvation in Israel;*" and proved thereby not only his magnanimity, but also his genuine piety.[1]—Ver. 14. Samuel turned this victory to account, by calling upon the people to go with him to Gilgal, and there renew the monarchy. In what the renewal consisted is not clearly stated; but it is simply recorded in ver. 15 that "*they* (the whole people) *made Saul king there before the Lord in Gilgal.*" Many commentators have supposed that he was anointed afresh, and appeal to David's second anointing (2 Sam. ii. 4 and v. 3). But David's example merely proves, as Seb. Schmidt has correctly observed, that the anointing could be repeated under certain circumstances; but it does not prove that it was repeated, or must have been repeated, in the case of Saul. If the ceremony of anointing had been performed, it would no doubt have been mentioned, just as it is in 2 Sam. ii. 4 and v. 3. But יַמְלִכוּ does not mean "they anointed," although the LXX. have rendered it ἔχρισε Σαμουήλ, according to their own subjective interpretation. The renewal of the monarchy may very well have consisted in nothing more than

---

[1] "Not only signifying that the public rejoicing should not be interrupted, but reminding them of the clemency of God, and urging that since Jehovah had shown such clemency upon that day, that He had overlooked their sins, and given them a glorious victory, it was only right that they should follow His example, and forgive their neighbours' sins without bloodshed."—*Seb. Schmidt.*

a solemn confirmation of the election that had taken place at Mizpeh, in which Samuel once more laid before both king and people the right of the monarchy, receiving from both parties in the presence of the Lord the promise to observe this right, and sealing the vow by a solemn sacrifice. The only sacrifices mentioned are *zebachim shelamim*, *i.e.* peace-offerings. These were thank-offerings, which were always connected with a sacrificial meal, and when presented on joyous occasions, formed a feast of rejoicing for those who took part, since the sacrificial meal shadowed forth a living and peaceful fellowship with the Lord. *Gilgal* is in all probability the place where Samuel judged the people every year (ch. vii. 16). But whether it was the Gilgal in the plain of the Jordan, or Jiljilia on higher ground to the south-west of Shiloh, it is by no means easy to determine. The latter is favoured, apart from the fact that Samuel did not say "Let us go down," but simply "Let us go" (cf. ch. x. 8), by the circumstance that the solemn ceremony took place after the return from the war at Jabesh ; since it is hardly likely that the people would have gone down into the valley of the Jordan to Gilgal, whereas Jiljilia was close by the road from Jabesh to Gibeah and Ramah.

SAMUEL'S ADDRESS AT THE RENEWAL OF THE MONARCHY.— CHAP. XII.

Samuel closed this solemn confirmation of Saul as king with an address to all Israel, in which he handed over the office of judge, which he had hitherto filled, to the king, who had been appointed by God and joyfully recognised by the people. The good, however, which Israel expected from the king depended entirely upon both the people and their king maintaining that proper attitude towards the Lord with which the prosperity of Israel was ever connected. This truth the prophet felt impelled to impress most earnestly upon the hearts of all the people on this occasion. To this end he reminded them, that neither he himself, in the administration of his office, nor the Lord in His guidance of Israel thus far, had given the people any reason for asking a king when the Ammonites invaded the land (vers. 1–12). Nevertheless the Lord had given them a king, and would not withdraw His hand from them, if they would only fear Him and confess their sin (vers. 13--15). This address was then confirmed by the Lord at Samuel's desire, through a miraculous sign (vers. 16-18); whereupon Samuel gave to the people, who were terrified by the miracle and acknowledged their sin, the comforting promise that the Lord would not forsake His people for His great name's sake, and then closed his address with the assurance of his continued intercession, and a renewed appeal to them to serve the Lord with faithfulness (vers. 19-25). With this address Samuel laid down his office as judge, but without therefore ceasing as prophet to represent the people before God, and to maintain the rights of God in relation to the king. In this capacity he continued to support the king with his advice, until he was compelled to announce his rejection on account of his repeated rebellion against the commands of the Lord, and to anoint David as his successor.

Vers. 1-6. The time and place of the following address are not given. But it is evident from the connection with the preceding chapter implied in the expression וַיֹּאמֶר, and still more from the introduction (vers. 1, 2) and the entire contents of the address, that it was delivered on the renewal of the monarchy at Gilgal.—Vers. 1, 2. Samuel starts with the fact, that he had given the people a king in accordance with their own desire, who would now walk before them. הִנֵּה with the participle expresses what is happening, and will happen still. הִתְהַלֵּךְ לִפְנֵי must not be restricted to going at the head in war, but signifies the general direction and government of the nation, which had been in the hands of Samuel as judge before the election of Saul as king. "And I have grown old and grey (שַׂבְתִּי from שִׂיב); and my sons, behold, they are with you." With this allusion to his sons, Samuel simply intended to confirm what he had said about his own age. By the further remark, "and I have walked before you from my childhood unto this day," he prepares the way for the following appeal to the people to bear witness concerning his conduct in office.—Ver. 3. "Bear witness against me before the Lord," i.e. looking up to the Lord, the omnipotent and righteous God-king, "and before His anointed," the visible administrator of His divine government, whether I have committed any injustice in my office of judge, by appropriating another's property, or by oppression and violence (רָצַץ, to pound or crush in pieces, when used to denote an act of violence, is stronger than עָשַׁק, with which it is connected here and in many other passages, *e.g.* Deut. xxviii. 33; Amos iv. 1), or by taking atonement money (כֹּפֶר, redemption or atonement money, is used, as in Ex. xxi. 30 and Num. xxxv. 31, to denote a payment made by a man to redeem himself from capital punishment), "*so that I had covered my eyes with it*," viz. to exempt from punishment a man who was worthy of death. The בּוֹ, which is construed with הֶעְלִים, is the ב *instrumenti*, and refers to כֹּפֶר; consequently it is not to be confounded with מִן, "to hide from," which would be quite unsuitable here. The thought is not that the judge covers his eyes from the *copher*, that he may not see the bribe, but that he covers his eyes with the money offered him as a bribe, so as not to see and not to punish the crime committed. —Ver. 4. The people answered Samuel, that he had not done them any kind of injustice.—Ver. 5. To confirm this declaration on the part of the people, he then called Jehovah and His anointed as witnesses against the people, and they accepted these witnesses. כָּל־יִשְׂרָאֵל is the subject to וַיֹּאמֶר; and the *Keri* וַיֹּאמְרוּ, though more simple, is by no means necessary. Samuel said, "*Jehovah be witness against you*," because with the declaration which the people had made concerning Samuel's judicial labours they had condemned themselves, inasmuch as they had thereby acknowledged on oath that there was no ground for their dissatisfaction with Samuel's administration, and consequently no well-founded reason for their request for a king.— Ver. 6. But in order to bring the people to a still more thorough acknowledgment of their sin, Samuel strengthened still more their assent to his solemn appeal to God, as expressed in the words "*He is witness*," by saying, "*Jehovah* (*i.e.* yea, the witness is Jehovah), *who made Moses and Aaron, and brought your fathers out of the land of Egypt*." The context itself is sufficient to show that the expression "is witness" is understood; and there is no reason, therefore, to assume that the word has dropped out of the text through a copyist's error. עָשָׂה, to make, in a moral and historical sense, *i.e.* to make a person what he is to be; it has no connection, therefore, with his physical birth, but simply relates to his introduction upon the stage of history, like ποιεῖν, Heb. iii. 2. But if Jehovah, who redeemed Israel out of Egypt by the hands of Moses and Aaron, and exalted it into His own nation, was witness of the unselfishness and impartiality of Samuel's conduct in his office of judge, then Israel had grievously sinned by demanding a king. In the person of Samuel they had rejected Jehovah their God, who had given them their rulers (see ch. viii. 7). Samuel proves this still further to the people from the following history.

Vers. 7–12. "*And now come hither, and I will reason with you before the Lord with regard to all the righteous acts which He has shown to you and your fathers.*" צְדָקוֹת, righteous acts, is the expression used to denote the benefits which Jehovah had conferred upon His people, as being the results of His covenant fidelity, or as acts which attested the righteousness of the Lord in the fulfilment of the covenant grace which He had promised to His people. –Ver. 8. The first proof of this was furnished by the deliverance of the children of Israel out of Egypt, and their safe guidance into Canaan ("*this place*" is the land of Canaan). The second was to be found in the deliverance of the people out of the power of their foes, to whom the Lord had been obliged to give them up on account of their apostasy from Him, through the judges whom He had raised up for them, as often as they turned to Him with penitence and cried to Him for help. Of the hostile oppressions which overtook the Israelites during this period of the judges, the following are singled out in ver. 9: (1) that by Sisera, the commander-in-chief of Hazor, *i.e.* that of the Canaanitish king Jabin of Hazor (Judg. iv. 2 sqq.) ; (2) that of the Philistines, by which we are to understand not so much the hostilities of that nation described in Judg. iii. 31, as the forty years' oppression mentioned in Judg. x. 2 and xiii. 1 ; and (3) the Moabitish oppression under Eglon (Judg. iii. 12 sqq.). The first half of ver. 10 agrees almost word for word with Judg. x. 10, except that, according to Judg. x. 6, the Ashtaroth are added to the Baalim (see at ch. vii. 4 and Judg. ii. 13). Of the judges whom God sent to the people as deliverers, the following are named, viz. Jerubbaal (see at Judg. vi. 32), *i.e.* Gideon (Judg. vi.), and Bedan, and Jephthah (see Judg. xi.), and Samuel. There is no judge named *Bedan* mentioned either in the book of Judges or anywhere else. The name *Bedan* only occurs again in 1 Chron. vii. 17, among the descendants of Machir the Manassite : consequently some of the commentators suppose *Jair* of Gilead to be the judge intended. But such a supposition is perfectly arbitrary, as it is not rendered probable by any identity in the two names, and Jair is not described as having delivered Israel from any hostile oppression.   Moreover, it is extremely improbable that Samuel should have mentioned a judge here, who had been passed over in the book of Judges on account of his comparative insignificance.   There is also just as little ground for rendering *Bedan* as an appellative, *e.g.* the Danite (*ben-Dan*), as Kimchi suggests, or *corpulentus* as Böttcher maintains, and so connecting the name with Samson.   There is no other course left, therefore, than to regard *Bedan* as an old copyist's error for *Barak* (Judg. iv.), as the LXX., Syriac, and Arabic have done,—a conclusion which is favoured by the circumstance that Barak was one of the most celebrated of the judges, and is placed by the side of Gideon and Jephthah in Heb. xi. 32. The Syriac, Arabic, and one Greek MS. (see Kennicott in the *Addenda* to his *Dissert. Gener.*), have the name of *Samson* instead of *Samuel*.   But as the LXX., Chald., and Vulg. all agree with the Hebrew text, there is no critical ground for rejecting Samuel, the more especially as the objection raised to it, viz. that Samuel would not have mentioned himself, is far too trivial to overthrow the reading supported by the most ancient versions ; and the assertion made by Thenius, that Samuel does not come down to his own times until the following verse, is altogether unfounded.   Samuel could very well class himself with the deliverers of Israel, for the simple reason that it was by him that the people were delivered from the forty years' tyranny of the Philistines, whilst Samson merely commenced their deliverance and did not bring it to completion. Samuel appears to have deliberately mentioned his own name along with those of the other judges who were sent by God, that he might show the people in the most striking manner (ver. 12) that they had no reason whatever for saying to him, "*Nay, but a king shall reign over us*," as soon as the Ammonites invaded Gilead.   "*As Jehovah your God is your King*," *i.e.* has ever proved himself to be your King by sending judges to deliver you.

Vers. 13–18*a*. After the prophet had thus held up before the people their sin against the Lord, he bade them still further consider, that the king would only procure for them the anticipated deliverance if they would fear the Lord, and give up

their rebellion against God.—Ver. 13. " *But now behold the
king whom ye have chosen, whom ye have asked for! behold,
Jehovah hath set a king over you.*" By the second וְהִנֵּה, the
thought is brought out still more strongly, that Jehovah had
fulfilled the desire of the people. Although the request of the
people had been an act of hostility to God, yet Jehovah had fulfilled it. The word בְּחַרְתֶּם, relating to the choice by lot (ch. x.
17 sqq.), is placed before אֲשֶׁר שְׁאֶלְתֶּם, to show that the demand
was the strongest act that the people could perform. They had
not only chosen the king with the consent or by the direction
of Samuel; they had even demanded a king of their own self-
will.—Ver. 14. Still, since the Lord had given them a king,
the further welfare of the nation would depend upon whether
they would follow the Lord from that time forward, or whether
they would rebel against Him again. " *If ye will only fear the
Lord, and serve Him, . . . and ye as well as the king who rules
over you will be after Jehovah your God.*" אִם, in the sense of
modo, if only, does not require any apodosis, as it is virtually
equivalent to the wish, " *O that ye would only !*" for which
אִם with the imperfect is commonly used (*vid.* 2 Kings xx.
19; Prov. xxiv. 11, etc.; and Ewald, § 329, *b*). There is also
nothing to be supplied to וִהְיִתֶם . . . אַחַר יְהֹוָה, since הָיָה אַחַר, to
be after or behind a person, is good Hebrew, and is frequently
met with, particularly in the sense of attaching one's self to the
king, or holding to him (*vid.* 2 Sam. ii. 10; 1 Kings xii. 20,
xvi. 21, 22). This meaning is also at the foundation of the
present passage, as Jehovah was the God-king of Israel.—
Ver. 15. " *But if ye do not hearken to the voice of Jehovah, and
strive against His commandment, the hand of Jehovah will be
heavy upon you, as upon your fathers.*" וְ in the sense of *as*,
i.e. used in a comparative sense, is most frequently placed
before whole sentences (see Ewald, § 340, *b*); and the use of
it here may be explained, on the ground that בַּאֲבֹתֵיכֶם contains
the force of an entire sentence: " *as it was upon your fathers.*"
The allusion to the fathers is very suitable here, because the
people were looking to the king for the removal of all the calamities, which had fallen upon them from time immemorial. The
paraphrase of this word, which is adopted in the Septuagint,
ἐπὶ τὸν βασιλέα ὑμῶν, is a very unhappy conjecture, although
Thenius proposes to alter the text to suit it.—Ver. 16. In order

to give still greater emphasis to his words, and to secure their
lasting, salutary effect upon the people, Samuel added still
further : Even now ye may see that ye have acted very
wickedly in the sight of Jehovah, in demanding a king. This
chain of thought is very clearly indicated by the words גַּם־עַתָּה,
" yea, even now." " Even now come hither, and see this great
thing which Jehovah does before your eyes." The words גַּם־עַתָּה,
which are placed first, belong, so far as the sense is concerned,
to רְאוּ אֶת־הד׳ ; and הִתְיַצְּבוּ (" place yourselves," i.e. make yourselves ready) is merely inserted between, to fix the attention of
the people more closely upon the following miracle, as an event
of great importance, and one which they ought to lay to heart.
" Is it not now wheat harvest? I will call to Jehovah, that He
may give thunder (קֹלוֹת, as in Ex. ix. 23, etc.) and rain. Then
perceive and see, that the evil is great which ye have done in the
eyes of Jehovah, to demand a king." The wheat harvest occurs
in Palestine between the middle of May and the middle of June
(see my Bibl. Arch. i. § 118). And during this time it scarcely
ever rains. Thus Jerome affirms (ad Am. c. 4) : " Nunquam
in fine mensis Junii aut in Julio in his provinciis maximeque in
Judæa pluvias vidimus." And Robinson also says in his Palestine (ii. p. 98) : " In ordinary seasons, from the cessation of the
showers in spring until their commencement in October and
November, rain never falls, and the sky is usually serene" (see
my Arch. i. § 10). So that when God sent thunder and rain
on that day in answer to Samuel's appeal to him, this was a
miracle of divine omnipotence, intended to show to the people
that the judgments of God might fall upon the sinners at any
time. Thunderings, as " the voices of God" (Ex. ix. 28), are
harbingers of judgment.

Vers. 18b–25. This miracle therefore inspired the people
with a salutary terror. " All the people greatly feared the Lord
and Samuel," and entreated the prophet, " Pray for thy servants
to the Lord thy God, that we die not, because we have added to
all our sins the evil thing, to ask us a king."—Vers. 20, 21.
Samuel thereupon announced to them first of all, that the Lord
would not forsake His people for His great name's sake, if they
would only serve Him with uprightness. In order, however,
to give no encouragement to any false trust in the covenant
faithfulness of the Lord, after the comforting words, " Fear

not," he told them again very decidedly that they had done wrong, but that now they were not to turn away from the Lord, but to serve Him with all their heart, and not go after vain idols. To strengthen this admonition, he repeats the לֹא תָסוּרוּ in ver. 21, with the explanation, that in turning from the Lord they would fall away to idols, which could not bring them either help or deliverance. To the כִּי after תָסוּרוּ the same verb must be supplied from the context : "*Do not turn aside* (from the Lord), *for* (ye turn aside) *after that which is vain.*" הַתֹּהוּ, the vain, worthless thing, signifies the *false gods.* This will explain the construction with a plural : "*which do not profit and do not save, because they are emptiness*" (*tohu*), *i.e.* worthless beings (*elilim,* Lev. xix. 4 ; cf. Isa. xliv. 9 and Jer. xvi. 19).—Ver. 22. " *For* (כִּי gives the reason for the main thought of the previous verse, ' Fear not, but serve the Lord,' etc.) *the Lord will not forsake His people for His great name's sake ; for it hath pleased the Lord* (for הוֹאִיל, see at Deut. i. 5) *to make you His people.*" The emphasis lies upon *His.* This the Israelites could only be, when they proved themselves to be the people of God, by serving Jehovah with all their heart. " *For His great name's sake,*" *i.e.* for the great name which He had acquired in the sight of all the nations, by the marvellous guidance of Israel thus far, to preserve it against misapprehension and blasphemy (see at Josh. vii. 9).—Ver. 23. Samuel then promised the people his constant intercession : " *Far be it from me to sin against the Lord, that I should cease to pray for you, and to instruct you in the good and right way,*" *i.e.* to work as prophet for your good. " In this he sets a glorious example to all rulers, showing them that they should not be led astray by the ingratitude of their subordinates or subjects, and give up on that account all interest in their welfare, but should rather persevere all the more in their anxiety for them" (*Berleb. Bible*).—Vers. 24, 25. Lastly, he repeats once more his admonition, that they would continue stedfast in the fear of God, threatening at the same time the destruction of both king and people if they should do wrong (on ver. 24*a*, see ch. vii. 3 and Josh. xxiv. 14, where the form יְראוּ is also found). " *For see what great things He has done for you*" (shown to you), not by causing it to thunder and rain at Samuel's prayer, but by giving them a king. הִגְדִּיל עִם, as in Gen. xix. 19.

SAUL'S REIGN, AND HIS UNSEASONABLE SACRIFICE IN THE WAR AGAINST THE PHILISTINES.—CHAP. XIII.

The history of the reign of Saul commences with this chapter ;[1] and according to the standing custom in the history of the kings, it opens with a statement of the age of the king when he began to reign, and the number of years that his reign lasted. If, for example, we compare the form and contents of this verse with 2 Sam. ii. 10, v. 4, 1 Kings xiv. 21,

[1] The connection of vers. 8–11 of this chapter with ch. x. 8 is adduced in support of the hypothesis that ch. xiii. forms a direct continuation of the account that was broken off in ch. x. 16. This connection must be admitted ; but it by no means follows that in the source from which the books before us were derived, ch. xiii. was directly attached to ch. viii. 16, and that Samuel intended to introduce Saul publicly as king here in Gilgal immediately before the attack upon the Philistines, to consecrate him by the solemn presentation of sacrifices, and to connect with this the religious consecration of the approaching campaign. For there is not a word about any such intention in the chapter before us or in ch. x. 8, nor even the slightest hint at it. Thenius has founded this view of his upon his erroneous interpretation of יָרַדְתָּ in ch. x. 8 as an imperative, as if Samuel intended to command Saul to go to Gilgal immediately after the occurrence of the signs mentioned in ch. x. 2 sqq. : a view which is at variance with the instructions given to him, to do what his hand should find after the occurrence of those signs (see p. 101). To this we may also add the following objections : How is it conceivable that Saul, who concealed his anointing even from his own family after his return from Samuel to Gibeah (ch. x. 16), should have immediately after chosen 3000 men of Israel to begin the war against the Philistines? How did Saul attain to any such distinction, that at his summons all Israel gathered round him as their king, even before he had been publicly proclaimed king in the presence of the people, and before he had secured the confidence of the people by any kingly heroic deed ? The fact of his having met with a band of prophets, and even prophesied in his native town of Gibeah after his departure from Samuel, and that this had become a proverb, is by no means enough to explain the enterprises described in ch. xiii. 1–7, which so absolutely demand the incidents that occurred in the meantime as recorded in ch. x. 17–xii. 25 even to make them intelligible, that any writing in which ch. xiii. 2 sqq. followed directly upon ch. x. 16 would necessarily be regarded as utterly faulty. This fact, which I have already adduced in my examination of the hypothesis defended by Thenius in my *Introduction to the Old Testament* (p. 168), retains its force undiminished, even though, after a renewed investigation of the question, I have given up the supposed connection between ch. x. 8 and the proclamation mentioned in ch. xi. 14 sqq., which I defended there.

xxii. 42, 2 Kings viii. 26, and other passages, where the age
is given at which Ishbosheth, David, and many of the kings of
Judah began to reign, and also the number of years that their
reign lasted, there can be no doubt that our verse was also
intended to give the same account concerning Saul, and therefore that every attempt to connect this verse with the one
which follows is opposed to the uniform historical usage. Moreover, even if, as a matter of necessity, the second clause of
ver. 1 could be combined with ver. 2 in the following manner:
He was two years king over Israel, then Saul chose 3000 men,
etc.; the first half of the verse would give no reasonable sense,
according to the Masoretic text that has come down to us.
בֶּן־שָׁנָה שָׁאוּל בְּמָלְכוֹ cannot possibly be rendered "*jam per annum
regnaverat Saul*," "Saul had been king for a year," or "Saul
reigned one year," but can only mean "*Saul was a year old
when he became king.*" This is the way in which the words have
been correctly rendered by the Sept. and Jerome; and so also
in the Chaldee paraphrase ("Saul was an innocent child when
he began to reign") this is the way in which the text has been
understood. It is true that this statement as to his age is
obviously false; but all that follows from that is, that there is
an error in the text, namely, that between בֶּן and שָׁנָה the age
has fallen out,—a thing which could easily take place, as there
are many traces to show that originally the numbers were not
written in words, but only in letters that were used as numerals.
This gap in the text is older than the Septuagint version, as
our present text is given there. There is, it is true, an *anony-
mus* in the *hexapla*, in which we find the reading υἱὸς τριάκοντα
ἐτῶν Σαούλ; but this is certainly not according to ancient
MSS., but simply according to a private conjecture, and that an
incorrect one. For since Saul already had a son, Jonathan,
who commanded a division of the army in the very first years
of his reign, and therefore must have been at least twenty
years of age, if not older, Saul himself cannot have been
less than forty years old when he began to reign. Moreover,
in the second half of the verse also, the number given is evidently a wrong one, and the text therefore equally corrupt;
for the rendering "*when he had reigned two years over Israel*" is
opposed both by the parallel passages already quoted, and also
by the introduction of the name Saul as the subject in ver. 2*a*,

which shows very clearly that ver. 2 commences a fresh sentence, and is not merely the apodosis to ver. 1*b*. But Saul's reign must have lasted longer than two years, even if, in opposition to all analogies to be found elsewhere, we should understand the two years as merely denoting the length of his reign up to the time of his rejection (ch. xv.), and not till the time of his death. Even then he reigned longer than that; for he could not possibly have carried on all the wars mentioned in ch. xiv. 47, with Moab, Ammon, Edom, the kings of Zobah and the Philistines, in the space of two years. Consequently a numeral, say כ, twenty, must also have dropped out before שְׁתֵּי שָׁנִים (two years); since there are cogent reasons for assuming that his reign lasted as long as twenty or twenty-two years, reckoning to the time of his death. We have given the reasons themselves in connection with the chronology of the period of the judges (vol. iv. pp. 283-4).[1]

Vers. 2-7. *The war with the Philistines* (ch. xiii. xiv.) certainly falls, at least so far as the commencement is concerned, in the very earliest part of Saul's reign. This we must infer partly from the fact, that at the very time when Saul was seeking for his father's asses, there was a military post of the Philistines at Gibeah (ch. x. 5), and therefore the Philistines had already occupied certain places in the land; and partly also from the fact, that according to this chapter Saul selected an army of 3000 men out of the whole nation, took up his post at Michmash with 2000 of them, placing the other thousand at Gibeah under his son Jonathan, and sent the rest of the people home (ver. 2), because his first intention was simply to check the further advance of the Philistines. The dismission of the rest of the people to their own homes presupposes that the whole of the fighting men of the nation were assembled together. But as no other summoning together of the people has been

---

[1] The traditional account that Saul reigned forty years (Acts xiii. 24, and Josephus, *Ant.* vi. 14, 9) is supposed to have arisen, according to the conjecture of Thenius (on 2 Sam. ii. 10), from the fact that his son Ishbosheth was forty years old when he began to reign, and the notion that as he is not mentioned among the sons of Saul in 1 Sam. xiv. 49, he must have been born after the commencement of Saul's own reign. This conjecture is certainly a probable one; but it is much more natural to assume that as David and Solomon reigned forty years, it arose from the desire to make Saul's reign equal to theirs.

mentioned before, except to the war upon the Ammonites at Jabesh (ch. xi. 6, 7), where all Israel gathered together, and at the close of which Samuel had called the people and their king to Gilgal (ch. xi. 14), the assumption is a very probable one, that it was there at Gilgal, after the renewal of the monarchy, that Saul formed the resolution at once to make war upon the Philistines, and selected 3000 fighting men for the purpose out of the whole number that were collected together, and then dismissed the remainder to their homes. In all probability Saul did not consider that either he or the Israelites were sufficiently prepared as yet to undertake a war upon the Philistines generally, and therefore resolved, in the first place, only to attack the outpost of the Philistines, which was advanced as far as Gibeah, with a small number of picked soldiers. According to this simple view of affairs, the war here described took place at the very commencement of Saul's reign ; and the chapter before us is closely connected with the preceding one.—Ver. 2. Saul posted himself at Michmash and on the mount of Bethel with his two thousand men. *Michmash*, the present *Mukhmas*, a village in ruins upon the northern ridge of the Wady *Suweinit*, according to the *Onom.* (*s. v. Machmas*), was only nine Roman miles to the north of Jerusalem, whereas it took Robinson three hours and a half to go from one to the other (*Pal.* ii. p. 117). *Bethel* (*Beitin ;* see at Josh. vii. 2) is to the north-west of this, at a distance of two hours' journey, if you take the road past Deir-Diwan. The mountain (הַר) of Bethel cannot be precisely determined. Bethel itself was situated upon very high ground ; and the ruins of Beitin are completely surrounded by heights (Rob. ii. p. 126; and v. Raumer, *Pal.* pp. 178–9). Jonathan stationed himself with his thousand men at (by) Gibeah of Benjamin, the native place and capital of Saul, which was situated upon *Tell el Phul* (see at Josh. xviii. 28), about an hour and a half from Michmas.—Ver. 3. "*And Jonathan smote the garrison of the Philistines that was at Geba,*" probably the military post mentioned in ch. x. 5, which had been advanced in the meantime as far as Geba. For *Geba* is not to be confounded with *Gibeah*, from which it is clearly distinguished in ver. 16 as compared with ver. 15, but is the modern *Jeba*, between the Wady *Suweinit* and Wady *Fara*, to the north-west of Ramah (er-Râm ; see at Josh. xviii. 24). " *The Philistines heard this. And Saul had the trumpet blown throughout the whole land, and proclamation made: let the Hebrews hear it."* לֵאמֹר after תָּקַע בַּשּׁוֹפָר points out the proclamation that was made after the alarm given by the *shophar* (see 2 Sam. xx. 1; 1 Kings i. 34, 39, etc.). The object to " let them hear" may be easily supplied from the context, viz. Jonathan's feat of arms. Saul had this trumpeted in the whole land, not only as a joyful message for the Hebrews, but also as an indirect summons to the whole nation to rise and make war upon the Philistines. In the word שָׁמַע (hear), there is often involved the idea of observing, laying to heart that which is heard. If we understand יִשְׁמְעוּ in this sense here, and the next verse decidedly hints at it, there is no ground whatever for the objection which Thenius, who follows the LXX., has raised to יִשְׁמְעוּ הָעִבְרִים. He proposes this emendation, יִפְשְׁעוּ הָעִבְרִים, " let the Hebrews fall away," according to the Alex. text ἠθετήκασιν οἱ δοῦλοι, without reflecting that the very expression οἱ δοῦλοι is sufficient to render the Alex. reading suspicious, and that Saul could not have summoned the people in *all* the land to fall away from the Philistines, since they had not yet conquered and taken possession of the whole. Moreover, the correctness of יִשְׁמְעוּ is confirmed by וְכָל־יִשְׂרָאֵל שָׁמְעוּ in ver. 4. *" All Israel heard,"* not the call to fall away, but the news, *" Saul has smitten a garrison of the Philistines, and Israel has also made itself stinking with the Philistines,"* *i.e.* hated in consequence of the bold and successful attack made by Jonathan, which proved that the Israelites would no longer allow themselves to be oppressed by the Philistines. *" And the people let themselves be called together after Saul to Gilgal."* הִצָּעֵק, to permit to summon to war (as in Judg. vii. 23, 24). The words are incorrectly rendered by the Vulgate, *" clamavit ergo populus post Saul,"* and by Luther, " Then the people cried after Saul to Gilgal." Saul drew back to Gilgal, when the Philistines advanced with a large army, to make preparations for the further conflict (see at ver. 13).—Ver. 5. The Philistines also did not delay to avenge the defeat at Geba. They collected an innumerable army: 30,000 chariots, 6000 horsemen, and people, *i.e.* foot-soldiers, without number (as the sand by the sea-shore; cf. Judg. vii. 12, Josh. xi. 4, etc.). רֶכֶב by the side of פָּרָשִׁים can only mean war chariots. 30,000 war chariots, however, bear no proportion

whatever to 6000 horsemen, not only because the number of
war chariots is invariably smaller than that of the horsemen
(cf. 2 Sam. x. 18 ; 1 Kings x. 26 ; 2 Chron. xii. 3), but also, as
Bochart observes in his *Hieroz.* p. i. lib. ii. c. 9, because such a
number of war chariots is never met with either in sacred or
profane history, not even in the case of nations that were much
more powerful than the Philistines. The number is therefore
certainly corrupt, and we must either read 3000 (שְׁלֹשֶׁת אֲל
instead of שְׁלֹשִׁים אֶל), according to the Syriac and Arabic, or
else simply 1000 ; and in the latter case the origin of the number
thirty must be attributed to the fact, that through the oversight
of a copyist the ל of the word יִשְׂרָאֵל was written twice, and
consequently the second ל was taken for the numeral thirty.
This army was encamped " *at Michmash, before* (*i.e.* in the
front, or on the western side of) *Bethaven:*" for, according to
Josh. vii. 2, Bethaven was to the east of Michmash ; and קִדְמַת,
when it occurs in geographical accounts, does not " always
mean to the east," as Thenius erroneously maintains, but invariably means simply " in front" (see at Gen. ii. 14).[1]—Vers.
6, 7. When the Israelites saw that they had come into a strait
(צַר לֹו), for the people were oppressed (by the Philistines), they
hid themselves in the caves, thorn-bushes, rocks (*i.e.* clefts
of the rocks), fortresses (צְרִחִים ; see at Judg. ix. 46), and pits
(which were to be found in the land) ; and Hebrews also went
over the Jordan into the land of Gad and Gilead, whilst Saul
was still at Gilgal ; and all the people (the people of war who
had been called together, ver. 4) trembled behind him, *i.e.* were
gathered together in his train, or assembled round him as leader,
trembling or in despair.

The *Gilgal* mentioned here cannot be Jiljilia, which is
situated upon the high ground, as assumed in the *Comm. on
Joshua,* p. 94, but must be the Gilgal in the valley of the
Jordan. This is not only favoured by the expression יֵרְדוּ (the
Philistines will come *down* from Michmash to Gilgal, ver. 12),

---

[1] Consequently there is no ground whatever for altering the text
according to the confused rendering of the LXX., ἐν Μαχμὰς ἐξ ἐναντίας
Βαιθωρὼν κατὰ νότου, for the purpose of substituting for the correct statement in the text a description which would be geographically wrong, viz.
to the south-east of Beth-horon, since Michmash was neither to the south
nor to the south-east, but to the east of Beth-horon.

but also by וַיַּעַל (Samuel went *up* from Gilgal to Gibeah, ver.
15), and by the general attitude of Saul and his army towards
the Philistines. As the Philistines advanced with a powerful
army, after Jonathan's victory over their garrison at Geba (to
the south of Michmash), and encamped at Michmash (ver.
5); and Saul, after withdrawing from Gilgal, where he had
gathered the Israelites together (vers. 4, 8, 12), with Jonathan
and the six hundred men who were with him when the muster
took place, took up his position at Geba (vers. 15, 16), from
which point Jonathan attacked the Philistine post in the pass of
Michmash (ver. 23, and ch. xiv. 1 sqq.): Saul must have drawn
back from the advancing army of the Philistines to the Gilgal
in the Jordan valley, to make ready for the battle by collecting soldiers and presenting sacrifices, and then, after this had
been done, must have advanced once more to Gibeah and Geba
to commence the war with the army of the Philistines that was
encamped at Michmash. If, on the other hand, he had gone
northwards to Jiljilia from Michmash, where he was first
stationed, to escape the advancing army of the Philistines; he
would have had to attack the Philistines from the north when
they were encamped at Michmash, and could not possibly have
returned to Geba without coming into conflict with the Philistines, since Michmash was situated between Jiljilia and Geba.

Vers. 8–15. *Saul's untimely sacrifice.*—Vers. 8, 9. Saul
waited seven days for Samuel's coming, according to the time
appointed by Samuel (see at ch. x. 8), before proceeding to
offer the sacrifices through which the help of the Lord was to
be secured for the approaching campaign (see ver. 12); and as
Samuel did not come, the people began to disperse and leave
him. The *Kethib* וייחל is either the *Niphal* וַיִּיָחֶל, as in Gen. viii.
12, or *Piel* וַיְיַחֵל; and the *Keri* וַיּוֹחֶל (*Hiphil*) is unnecessary. The
verb יָעַד may very easily be supplied to אֲשֶׁר שְׁמוּאֵל from the word
לְמוֹעֵד (see *Ges. Lehrgeb.* p. 851).—Ver. 9. Saul then resolved,
in his anxiety lest the people should lose all heart and forsake
him altogether if there were any further delay, that he would
offer the sacrifice without Samuel. וַיַּעַל הָעֹלָה does not imply
that Saul offered the sacrifice with his own hand, *i.e.* that he
performed the priestly function upon this occasion. The co-
operation of the priests in performing the duties belonging to
them on such an occasion is taken for granted, just as in the

case of the sacrifices offered by David and Solomon (2 Sam. xxiv. 25; 1 Kings iii. 4, viii. 63).—Vers. 10 sqq. The offering of the sacrifice was hardly finished when Samuel came and said to Saul, as he came to meet him and salute him, " *What hast thou done?* " Saul replied, "*When I saw that the people were scattered away from me, and thou camest not at the time appointed, and the Philistines were assembled at Michmash, I thought the Philistines will come down to me to Gilgal now* (to attack me), *before I have entreated the face of Jehovah; and I overcame myself, and offered the burnt-offering.*" חִלָּה פְנֵי יי': see Ex. xxxii. 11.—Ver. 13. Samuel replied, " *Thou hast acted foolishly,* (and) *not kept the commandment of Jehovah thy God, which He commanded thee: for now* (sc. if thou hadst obeyed His commandment) *Jehovah would have established thy sovereignty over Israel for ever; but now* (sc. since thou hast acted thus) *thy sovereignty shall not continue.*" The antithesis of עַתָּה הֵכִין and וְעַתָּה לֹא תָקוּם requires that we should understand these two clauses conditionally. The conditional clauses are omitted, simply because they are at once suggested by the tenor of the address (see Ewald, § 358, a). The כִּי (for) assigns the reason, and refers to נִסְכַּלְתָּ ("thou hast done foolishly"), the לֹא שָׁמַרְתָּ וגו' being merely added as explanatory. The non-continuance of the sovereignty is not to be regarded as a rejection, or as signifying that Saul had actually lost the throne so far as he himself was concerned; but לֹא תָקוּם (shall not continue) forms the antithesis to הֵכִין עַד־עוֹלָם (established for ever), and refers to the fact that it was not established in perpetuity by being transmitted to his descendants. It was not till his second transgression that Saul was rejected, or declared unworthy of being king over the people of God (ch. xv.). We are not compelled to assume an immediate rejection of Saul even by the further announcement made by Samuel, "*Jehovah hath sought him a man after his own heart; him hath Jehovah appointed prince over His people;*" for these words merely announce the purpose of God, without defining the time of its actual realization. Whether it would take place during Saul's reign, or not till after his death, was known only to God, and was made contingent upon Saul's further behaviour. But if Saul's sin did not consist, as we have observed above, in his having interfered with the prerogatives of the priests by offering the sacrifice himself, but simply in the fact that he had transgressed the commandment of God as revealed to him by Samuel, to postpone the sacrifice until Samuel arrived, the punishment which the prophet announced that God would inflict upon him in consequence appears a very severe one, since Saul had not come to the resolution either frivolously or presumptuously, but had been impelled and almost forced to act as he did by the difficulties in which he was placed in consequence of the prophet delaying his coming. But wherever, as in the present instance, there is a definite command given by the Lord, a man has no right to allow himself to be induced to transgress it, by fixing his attention upon the earthly circumstances in which he is placed. As Samuel had instructed Saul, as a direct command from Jehovah, to wait for his arrival before offering sacrifice, Saul might have trusted in the Lord that he would send His prophet at the right time and cause His command to be fulfilled, and ought not to have allowed his confidence to be shaken by the pressing danger of delay. The interval of seven days and the delay in Samuel's arrival were intended as a test of his faith, which he ought not to have lightly disregarded. Moreover, the matter in hand was the commencement of the war against the principal enemies of Israel, and Samuel was to tell him what he was to do (ch. x. 8). So that when Saul proceeded with the consecrating sacrifice for that very conflict, without the presence of Samuel, he showed clearly enough that he thought he could make war upon the enemies of his kingdom without the counsel and assistance of God. This was an act of rebellion against the sovereignty of Jehovah, for which the punishment announced was by no means too severe.—Ver. 15. After this occurrence Samuel went up to Gibeah, and Saul mustered the people who were with him, about six hundred men. Consequently Saul had not even accomplished the object of his unseasonable sacrifice, namely, to prevent the dispersion of the people. With this remark the account of the occurrence that decided the fate of Saul's monarchy is brought to a close.

Vers. 16-23. *Disarming of Israel by the Philistines.*—The following account is no doubt connected with the foregoing, so far as the facts are concerned, inasmuch as Jonathan's brave heroic deed, which brought the Israelites a splendid victory over the Philistines, terminated the war for which Saul had entreated the help of God by his sacrifice at Gilgal; but it is not formally connected with it, so as to form a compact and complete account of the successive stages of the war. On the contrary, the 16th verse, where we have an account of the Israelitish warriors and their enemies, commences a new section of the history, in which the devastating march of the Philistines through the land, and the disarming of the Israelites by these their enemies, are first of all depicted (vers. 17–23); and then the victory of the Israelites through Jonathan's daring and heroic courage, notwithstanding their utter prostration, is recorded (ch. xiv. 1–46), for the purpose of showing how the Lord had miraculously helped His people.[1]

Ver. 16. The two clauses of this verse are circumstantial clauses: "*But Saul, and Jonathan his son, and the people that were with him, were sitting,* i.e. tarrying, *in Geba of Benjamin* (the present Jeba; see at ver. 3); *and the Philistines had encamped at Michmash.*" Just as in vers. 2–4 it is not stated when or why Saul went from Michmash or Geba to Gilgal,

---

[1] From this arrangement of the history, according to which the only two points that are minutely described in connection with the war with the Philistines are those which bring out the attitude of the king, whom the nation had desired to deliver it from its foes, towards Jehovah, and the way in which Jehovah acted towards His people, whilst all the rest is passed over, we may explain the absence of any closer connection between ver. 15 and ver. 16, and not from a gap in the text. The LXX., however, adopted the latter supposition, and according to the usual fashion filled up the gap by expanding ver. 15 in the following thoughtless manner: καὶ ἀνέστη Σαμουὴλ καὶ ἀπῆλθεν ἐκ Γαλγάλων· καὶ τὸ κατάλειμμα τοῦ λαοῦ ἀνέβη ὀπίσω Σαοὺλ εἰς ἀπάντησιν ὀπίσω τοῦ λαοῦ τοῦ πολεμιστοῦ· αὐτῶν παραγενομένων ἐκ Γαλγάλων εἰς Γαβαὰ Βενιαμὶν καὶ ἐπεσκέψατο Σαοὺλ, κ.τ.λ. For there is no sense in εἰς ἀπάντησιν ὀπίσω, and the whole thought, that the people who were left went up after Saul to meet the people of war, is unintelligible, since it is not stated whence the people of war had come, who are said to have met with those who had remained behind with Saul, and to have gone up with him from Gilgal to Gibeah. If, however, we overlook this, and assume that when Saul returned from Gilgal to Gibeah a further number of fighting men came to him from different parts of the land, how does this assumption agree with the account which follows, viz. that when Saul mustered the people he found only six hundred men,—a statement which is repeated again in ch. xiv. 2? The discrepancy remains even if we adopt Ewald's conjecture (*Gesch.* iii. 43), that εἰς ἀπάντησιν is a false rendering of לְקְרָב, "to the conflict." Moreover, even with the Alexandrian filling up, no natural connection is secured between vers. 15 and 16, unless we identify *Geba* of Ben-

but this change in his position is merely hinted at indirectly at
the close of ver. 4; so here Saul's return from Gilgal to Geba
with the fighting men who remained with him is not distinctly
mentioned, but simply taken for granted as having already
occurred.—Vers. 17, 18. Then the spoiler went out of the
camp of the Philistines in three companies. שְׁלֹשָׁה רָאשִׁים is
made subject to the verb to define the mode of action (see
Ewald, § 279, c); and *rashim* is used here, as in ch. xi. 11.
הַמַּשְׁחִית, according to the context, is a hostile band that went
out to devastate the land. The definite article points it out as
well known. One company took the road to *Ophrah* into the
land of *Shual, i.e.* went in a north-easterly direction, as, according to the *Onom., Ophrah* of Benjamin was five Roman miles
to the east of Bethel (see at Josh. xviii. 23). Robinson supposes it to have been on the site of *Tayibeh.* The land of
Shual (fox-land) is unknown; it may possibly have been identical with the land of *Saalim* (ch. ix. 5). The other company
turned on the road to Beth-horon (Beit-ur : see at Josh. x. 11),
that is to say, towards the west; the third, "the way to the
territory that rises above the valley of *Zeboim* towards the

---

jamin with *Gibeah,* as the Septuagint and its latest defenders have done,
and not only change the participle יֹשְׁבִים (ver. 16) into the aorist ἐκάθισαν,
but interpolate καὶ ἔκλαιον after " at *Geba* of Benjamin ;" whereas the
statement of the text "at *Geba* in Benjamin" is proved to be correct by
the simple fact that Jonathan could only attempt or carry out the heroic
deed recorded in ch. xiv. from *Geba* and not from *Gibeah;* and the alteration of the participle into the aorist is just as arbitrary as the interpolation
of καὶ ἔκλαιον. From all this it follows that the Septuagint version has not
preserved the original reading, as Ewald and Thenius suppose, but contains
nothing more than a mistaken attempt to restore the missing link. It is
true the Vulgate contains the same filling up as the Septuagint, but with
one alteration, which upsets the assertion made by Thenius, that the repetition of the expression מִן הַגִּלְגָּל, ἐκ Γαλγάλων, caused the reading contained
in the Septuagint to be dropped out of the Hebrew text. For the text of
the Vulgate runs as follows : *Surrexit autem Samuël et ascendit de Galgalis
in Gabaa Benjamin. Et reliqui populi ascenderunt post Saul obviam populo,
qui expugnabant eos venientes de Galgala in Gabaa in colle Benjamin. Et
recensuit Saul, etc.* Jerome has therefore rendered the first two clauses of
ver. 15 in perfect accordance with the Hebrew text ; and the addition
which follows is nothing more than a gloss that has found its way into his
translation from the Itala, and in which *de Galgala in colle Benjamin* is
still retained, whereas Jerome himself rendered מִן הַגִּלְגָּל *de Galgalis.*

desert." These descriptions are obscure ; and the valley of
Zeboim altogether unknown. There is a town of this name
(צְבֹעִים, different from צְבֹיִים, Deut. xxix. 22, Gen. xiv. 2, 8 ;
or צְבֹאִים, Hos. xi. 8, in the vale of Siddim) mentioned in Neh.
xi. 34, which was inhabited by Benjaminites, and was apparently situated in the south-eastern portion of the land of Benjamin, to the north-east of Jerusalem, from which it follows that
the third company pursued its devastating course in a south-
easterly direction from Michmash towards Jericho. " *The
wilderness*" is probably the desert of Judah. The intention of
the Philistines in carrying out these devastating expeditions,
was no doubt to entice the men who were gathered round Saul
and Jonathan out of their secure positions at Gibeah and Geba,
and force them to fight.—Vers. 19 sqq. The Israelites could not
offer a successful resistance to these devastating raids, as there
was no smith to be found in the whole land : " *For the Philistines thought the Hebrews might make themselves sword or spear*"
(אָמַר followed by פֶּן, " to say, or think, that not," equivalent to
being unwilling that it should be done). Consequently (as
the words clearly imply) when they proceeded to occupy the
land of Israel as described in ver. 5, they disarmed the people
throughout, *i.e.* as far as they penetrated, and carried off the
smiths, who might have been able to forge weapons ; so that, as
is still further related in ver. 20, all Israel was obliged to go to
the Philistines, every one to sharpen his edge-tool, and his
ploughshare, and his axe, and his chopper. According to Isa.
ii. 4, Micah iv. 3, and Joel iv. 10, אֵת is an iron instrument
used in agriculture ; the majority of the ancient versions render
it *ploughshare*. The word מַחֲרֵשָׁתוֹ is striking after the previous
מַחֲרַשְׁתּוֹ (from מַחֲרֶשֶׁת) ; and the meaning of both words is uncertain. According to the etymology, מַחֲרֶשֶׁת might denote any
kind of edge-tool, even the ploughshare. The second מַחֲרֵשָׁתוֹ
is rendered τὸ δρέπανον αὐτοῦ (his sickle) by the LXX., and
sarculum by Jerome, a small garden hoe for loosening and
weeding the soil. The fact that the word is connected with
קַרְדֹּם, the axe or hatchet, favours the idea that it signifies a *hoe*
or *spade* rather than a sickle. Some of the words in ver. 21
are still more obscure. וְהָיְתָה, which is the reading adopted by
all the earlier translators, indicates that the result is about to
be given of the facts mentioned before : " *And there came to*

pass," *i.e.* so that there came to pass (or arose), הִפָּצִירָה פִּים, "*a blunting of the edges*." פְּצִירָה, bluntness, from פָּצַר, to tear, hence to make blunt, is confirmed by the Arabic فطار, *gladius fissuras habens, obtusus ensis*, whereas the meaning to hammer, *i.e.* to sharpen by hammering, cannot be established. The insertion of the article before פְּצִירָה is as striking as the omission of it before פִּים; also the *stat. abs.* instead of the construct פְּצִירַת. These anomalies render it a very probable conjecture that the reading may have been הַפְצִיר הַפִּים (*inf. Hiph. nomin.*). Accordingly the rendering would be, "*so that bluntness of the edges occurred in the edge-tools, and the plough-shares, and the trident, and the axes, and the setting of the goad*." שְׁלֹשׁ קִלְּשׁוֹן is to be regarded as a *nom. comp.* like our trident, denoting an instrument with three prongs, according to the Chaldee and the Rabbins (see Ges. *Thes.* p. 1219). דָּרְבָן, *stimulus*, is probably a pointed instrument generally, since the meaning goad is fully established in the case of דָּרְבֹן by Eccl. xii. 11.[1]—Ver. 22. On the day of battle, therefore, the people with Saul and Jonathan were without either sword or spear; Saul and Jonathan were the only persons provided with them. The account of the expedition of the Israelites, and their victory over the Ammonites, given in ver. 11, is apparently at variance with this description of the situation of the Israelites, since the

[1] Ver. 21 runs very differently in the LXX., namely, καὶ ἦν ὁ τρυγητὸς ἕτοιμος τοῦ θερίζειν, τὰ δὲ σκεύη ἦν τρεῖς σίκλοι εἰς τὸν ὀδόντα, καὶ τῇ ἀξίνῃ καὶ τῷ δρεπάνῳ ὑπόστασις ἦν ἡ αὐτή; and Thenius and Böttcher propose an emendation of the Hebrew text accordingly, so as to obtain the following meaning: "And the sharpening of the edges in the case of the spades and ploughshares was done at three shekels a tooth (*i.e.* three shekels each), and for the axe and sickle it was the same" (Thenius); or, "and the same for the sickles, and for the axes, and for setting the prong" (Böttcher). But here also it is easy enough to discover that the LXX. had not another text before them that was different from the Masoretic text, but merely confounded הפציר with הבציר, τρυγητός, and took שְׁלֹשׁ קִלְּשׁוֹן, which was unintelligible to them, *e conjectura* for שְׁלֹשׁ שֶׁק' שֵׁן הַשֵּׁן, altogether regardless of the sense or nonsense of their own translation. The latest supporters of this senseless rendering, however, have neither undertaken to prove the possibility of translating ὀδόντα (ὀδούς), "each single piece" (*i.e.* each), or inquired into the value of money at that time, so as to see whether three shekels would be an unexampled charge for the sharpening of an axe or sickle.

war in question not only presupposes the possession of weapons by the Israelites, but must also have resulted in their capturing a considerable quantity. The discrepancy is very easily removed, however, when we look carefully at all the circumstances. For instance, we can hardly picture the Israelites to ourselves as amply provided with ordinary weapons in this expedition against the Ammonites. Moreover, the disarming of the Israelites by the Philistines took place for the most part if not entirely after this expedition, viz. at the time when the Philistines swept over the land with an innumerable army after Jonathan had smitten their garrison at Geba (vers. 3, 5), so that the fighting men who gathered round Saul and Jonathan after that could hardly bring many arms with them. Lastly, the words "there was neither sword nor spear found in the hands of all the people with Saul and Jonathan" must not be too closely pressed, but simply affirm that the 600 fighting men of Saul and Jonathan were not provided with the necessary arms, because the Philistines had prevented the possibility of their arming themselves in the ordinary way by depriving the people of all their smiths.

Ver. 23 forms the transition to the heroic act of Jonathan described in ch. xiv.: "*An outpost of the Philistines went out to the pass of Michmash;*" i.e. the Philistines pushed forward a company of soldiers to the pass (מַעֲבַר, the crossing place) of Michmash, to prevent an attack being made by the Israelites upon their camp. Between *Geba* and *Michmash* there runs the great deep Wady *es Suweinit,* which goes down from Beitin and Bireh (Bethel and Beeroth) to the valley of the Jordan, and intersects the ridge upon which the two places are situated, so that the sides of the wady form very precipitous walls. When Robinson was travelling from Jeba to Mukhmas he had to go down a very steep and rugged path into this deep wady (*Pal.* ii. p. 116). "The way," he says in his *Biblical Researches,* p. 289, "was so steep, and the rocky steps so high, that we were compelled to dismount; while the baggage mules got along with great difficulty. Here, where we crossed, several short side wadys came in from the south-west and north-west. The ridges between these terminate in elevating points projecting into the great wady; and the most easterly of these bluffs on each side were probably the outposts of the two gar-

risons of Israel and the Philistines. The road passes around
the eastern side of the southern hill, the post of Israel, and
then strikes up over the western part of the northern one, the
post of the Philistines, and the scene of Jonathan's adventure."

JONATHAN'S HEROIC ACT, AND ISRAEL'S VICTORY OVER THE
PHILISTINES.   SAUL'S WARS AND FAMILY.—CHAP XIV.

Vers. 1–15. *Jonathan's heroic act.*—With strong faith and
confidence in the might of the Lord, that He could give the
victory even through the hands of very few, Jonathan resolved
to attack the outpost of the Philistines at the pass of Mukhmas,
accompanied by his armour-bearer alone, and the Lord crowned
his enterprise with a marvellous victory.—Ver. 1. Jonathan
said to his armour-bearer, " *We will go over to the post of the
Philistines, that is over there.*" To these words, which introduce
the occurrences that followed, there are attached from וּלְאָבִיו to
ver. 5 a series of sentences introduced to explain the situation,
and the thread of the narrative is resumed in ver. 6 by a repetition of Jonathan's words. It is first of all observed that
Jonathan did not disclose his intentions to his father, who
would hardly have approved of so daring an enterprise. Then
follows a description of the place where Saul was stationed
with the six hundred men, viz. " *at the end of Gibeah* (*i.e.* the
extreme northern end), *under the pomegranate-tree* (*Rimmon*)
which is by Migron." *Rimmon* is not the rock Rimmon (Judg.
xx. 45), which was on the north-east of Michmash, but is an
appellative noun, signifying *a pomegranate-tree*. *Migron* is a
locality with which we are not acquainted, upon the north side
of Gibeah, and a different place from the Migron which was
on the north or north-west of Michmash (Isa. x. 28). *Gibeah*
(*Tuleil el Phul*) was an hour and a quarter from *Geba*, and
from the pass which led across to Michmash. Consequently,
when Saul was encamped with his six hundred men on the
north of Gibeah, he may have been hardly an hour's journey
from Geba.—Ver. 3. Along with Saul and his six hundred
men, there was also *Ahiah*, the son of Ahitub, the (elder)
brother of Ichabod, the son of Phinehas, the son of Eli, the
priest at Shilóh, and therefore a great-grandson of Eli, wearing
the ephod, *i.e.* in the high priest's robes. *Ahiah* is generally

supposed to be the same person as *Ahimelech*, the son of Ahitub (ch. xxii. 9 sqq.), in which case *Ahiah* (אֲחִיָּה, brother, *i.e.* friend of Jehovah) would be only another form of the name Ahimelech (*i.e.* brother or friend of the King, viz. Jehovah). This is very probable, although Ahimelech might have been Ahiah's brother, who succeeded him in the office of high priest on account of his having died without sons, since there is an interval of at least ten years between the events related in this chapter and those referred to in ch. xxii. Ahimelech was afterwards slain by Saul along with the priests of Nob (ch. xxii. 9 sqq.); the only one who escaped being his son Abiathar, who fled to David and, according to ch. xxx. 7, was invested with the ephod. It follows, therefore, that Ahiah (or Ahimelech) must have had a son at least ten years old at the time of the war referred to here, viz. the Abiathar mentioned in ch. xxx. 7, and must have been thirty or thirty-five years old himself, since Saul had reigned at least twenty-two years, and Abiathar had become high priest a few years before the death of Saul. These assumptions may be very easily reconciled with the passage before us. As Eli was ninety-eight years old when he died, his son Phinehas, who had been killed in battle a short time before, might have been sixty or sixty-five years old, and have left a son of forty years of age, namely Ahitub. Forty years later, therefore, *i.e.* at the beginning of Saul's reign, Ahitub's son Ahiah (Ahimelech) might have been about fifty years old; and at the death of Ahimelech, which took place ten or twelve years after that, his son Abiathar might have been as much as thirty years of age, and have succeeded his father in the office of high priest. But Abiathar cannot have been older than this when his father died, since he was high priest during the whole of David's forty years' reign, until Solomon deposed him soon after he ascended the throne (1 Kings ii. 26 sqq.). Compare with this the remarks on 2 Sam. viii. 17. Jonathan had also refrained from telling the people anything about his intentions, so that they did not know that he had gone.

In vers. 4, 5, the locality is more minutely described. Between the passes, through which Jonathan endeavoured to cross over to go up to the post of the Philistines, there was a sharp rock on this side, and also one upon the other. One of these was called *Bozez*, the other *Seneh ;* one (formed) a pillar (מָצוּק), *i.e.* a steep height towards the north opposite to Michmash, the other towards the south opposite to Geba. The expression "*between the passes*" may be explained from the remark of Robinson quoted above, viz. that at the point where he passed the Wady Suweinit, side wadys enter it from the south-west and north-west. These side wadys supply so many different crossings. Between them, however, on the north and south walls of the deep valley, were the jagged rocks *Bozez* and *Seneh*, which rose up like pillars to a great height. These were probably the "hills" which Robinson saw to the left of the pass by which he crossed: "Two hills of a conical or rather spherical form, having steep rocky sides, with small wadys running up behind so as almost to isolate them. One is on the side towards Jeba, and the other towards Mukhmas" (*Pal.* ii. p. 116).—Ver. 6. And Jonathan said to his armour-bearer, "*Come, we will go over to the post of these uncircumcised; it may be that Jehovah will work for us; for* (there is) *no hindrance for Jehovah to work salvation by many or few.*" Jonathan's resolution arose from the strong conviction that Israel was the nation of God, and possessed in Jehovah an omnipotent God, who would not refuse His help to His people in their conflict with the foes of His kingdom, if they would only put their whole trust in Him.—Ver. 7. As the armour-bearer approved of Jonathan's resolution (נְטֵה לָךְ, *turn thither*), and was ready to follow him, Jonathan fixed upon a sign by which he would ascertain whether the Lord would prosper his undertaking.— Vers. 8 sqq. "*Behold, we go over to the people and show our-selves to them. If they say to us, Wait* (דֹּמּוּ, *keep quiet*) *till we come to you, we will stand still in our place, and not go up to them; but if they say thus, Come up unto us, then we will go up, for Jehovah hath* (in that case) *delivered them into our hand.*" The sign was well chosen. If the Philistines said, "Wait till we come," they would show some courage; but if they said, "Come up to us," it would be a sign that they were cowardly, and had not courage enough to leave their position and attack the Hebrews. It was not tempting God for Jonathan to fix upon such a sign by which to determine the success of his enterprise; for he did it in the exercise of his calling, when fighting not for personal objects, but for the kingdom of God, which the uncircumcised were threatening to annihilate, and in

the most confident belief that the Lord would deliver and preserve His people. Such faith as this God would not put to
shame.—Vers. 11 sqq. When the two showed themselves to
the garrison of the Philistines, they said, "*Behold, Hebrews come
forth out of the holes in which they have hidden themselves.*" And
the men of the garrison cried out to Jonathan and his armour-
bearer, "*Come up to us, and we will tell you a word,*" *i.e.* we will
communicate something to you. This was ridicule at the daring
of the two men, whilst for all that they had not courage enough
to meet them bravely and drive them back. In this Jonathan
received the desired sign that the Lord had given the Philistines into the hand of the Israelites : he therefore clambered
up the rock on his hands and feet, and his armour-bearer after
him; and "*they* (the Philistines) *fell before Jonathan,*" *i.e.* were
smitten down by him, "*and his armour-bearer was slaying behind him.*"—Ver. 14. The first stroke that Jonathan and his
armour-bearer struck was (amounted to) about twenty men "*on
about half a furrow of an acre of field.*" מַעֲנָה, *a furrow,* as
in Ps. cxxix. 3, is in the absolute state instead of the construct,
because several nouns follow in the construct state (cf. Ewald,
§ 291, *a*). צֶמֶד, *lit.* things bound together, then a pair ; here it
signifies a pair or *yoke of oxen,* but in the transferred sense
of a piece of land that could be ploughed in one morning with
a yoke of oxen, like the Latin *jugum, jugerum.* It is called the
furrow of an acre of land, because the *length* only of half an
acre of land was to be given, and not the breadth or the entire
circumference. The Philistines, that is to say, took to flight in
alarm as soon as the brave heroes really ascended, so that the
twenty men were smitten one after another in the distance of
half a rood of land. Their terror and flight are perfectly conceivable, if we consider that the outpost of the Philistines was
so stationed upon the top of the ridge of the steep mountain
wall, that they could not see how many were following, and
the Philistines could not imagine it possible that two Hebrews
would have ventured to climb the rock alone and make an
attack upon them. Sallust relates a similar occurrence in connection with the scaling of a castle in the Numidian war (*Bell.
Jugurth.* c. 89, 90).—Ver. 15. And there arose a *terror in the
camp upon the field* (*i.e.* in the principal camp) *as well as among
all the people* (of the advanced outpost of the Philistines) ; *the*

garrison (*i.e.* the army that was encamped at Michmash), *and the spoilers, they also trembled, and the earth quaked, sc.* with the noise and tumult of the frightened foe; " *and it grew into a trembling of God," i.e.* a supernatural terror miraculously infused by God into the Philistines. The subject to the last וַתְּהִי is either חֲרָדָה, the alarm in the camp, or all that has been mentioned before, *i.e.* the alarm with the noise and tumult that sprang out of it.

Vers. 16–23. *Flight and defeat of the Philistines.*—Ver. 16. The spies of Saul at Gibeah saw how the multitude (in the camp of the Philistines) melted away and was beaten more and more. The words וַיֵּלֶךְ וַהֲלֹם are obscure. The Rabbins are unanimous in adopting the explanation *magis magisque frangebatur,* and have therefore probably taken הֲלֹם as an inf. absol. הָלוֹם, and interpreted הָלַם according to Judg. v. 26. This was also the case with the Chaldee; and Gesenius (*Thes.* p. 383) has adopted the same rendering, except that he has taken הָלַם in the sense of *dissolutus, dissipatus est.* Others take הֲלֹם as adverbial (" *and thither*"), and supply the correlate הֲלֹם (hither), so as to bring out the meaning " *hither and thither."* Thus the LXX. render it ἔνθεν καὶ ἔνθεν, but they have not translated וַיֵּלֶךְ at all.—Ver. 17. Saul conjectured at once that the excitement in the camp of the Philistines was occasioned by an attack made by Israelitish warriors, and therefore commanded the people: פְּקָדוּ־נָא, " *Muster* (number) *now, and see who has gone away from us;"* and " *Jonathan and his armour-bearer were not there," i.e.* they were missing.—Vers. 18 sqq. Saul therefore resolved to ask God, through the priest Ahiah, what he should do; whether he should go out with his army against the Philistines or no. But whilst he was talking with the priest, the tumult in the camp of the Philistines became greater and greater, so that he saw from that what ought to be done under the circumstances, and stopped the priest's inquiring of God, and set out with his people without delay. We are struck, however, with the expression in ver. 18, " *Bring hither the ark of God,"* and the explanation which follows, " *for the ark of God was at that time with the children of Israel,"* inasmuch as the ark was then deposited at Kirjath-jearim, and it is a very improbable thing that it should have been in the little camp of Saul. Moreover, in other cases where the high priest is spoken of as inquiring

the will of God, there is no mention made of the ark, but only
of the ephod, the high priest's shoulder-dress, upon which there
were fastened the Urim and Thummim, through which inquiry
was made of God. And in addition to this, the verb הַגִּישָׁה is
not really applicable to the ark, which was not an object that
could be carried about at will; whereas this verb is the current
expression used to signify the fetching of the ephod (*vid.* ch.
xxiii. 9, xxx. 7). All these circumstances render the correctness of the Masoretic text extremely doubtful, notwithstanding
the fact that the Chaldee, the Syriac, the Arabic, and the
Vulgate support it, and recommend rather the reading adopted
by the LXX., προσάγαγε τὸ Ἐφούδ· ὅτι αὐτὸς ἦρεν τὸ Ἐφοὺδ
ἐν τῇ ἡμέρᾳ ἐκείνῃ ἐνώπιον Ἰσραήλ, which would give as the
Hebrew text, הַגִּישָׁה הָאֵפוֹד כִּי הוּא נָשָׂא הָאֵפוֹד בַּיּוֹם הַהוּא לִפְנֵי יִשְׂרָאֵל.
In any case, וּבְנֵי יִשְׂרָאֵל at the end of the verse should be read
לִפְנֵי or לִפְנֵי יִשׂ', since ו gives no sense at all.—Ver. 19. "*It
increased more and more ;*" *lit.* increasing and becoming
greater. The subject וְהֶהָמוֹן וגו' is placed absolutely at the
head, so that the verb וַיֵּלֶךְ is appended in the form of an apodosis. אֱסֹף יָדֶךָ, "*draw thy hand in*" (back); *i.e.* leave off now.
—Ver. 20. "*And* (*i.e.* in consequence of the increasing tumult
in the enemy's camp) *Saul had himself, and all the people with
him, called,*" *i.e.* called together for battle; and when they came
to the war, *i.e.* to the place of conflict, "*behold, there was the
sword of the one against the other, a very great confusion,*" in
consequence partly of terror, and partly of the circumstance
alluded to in ver. 21.—Ver. 21. "*And the Hebrews were with
the Philistines as before* (yesterday and the day before yesterday), *who had come along with them in the camp round about;
they also came over to Israel, which was with Saul and Jonathan.*"
סָבִיב means distributed round about among the Philistines.
Those Israelites whom the Philistines had incorporated into
their army are called *Hebrews*, according to the name which
was current among foreigners, whilst those who were with Saul
are called *Israel*, according to the sacred name of the nation.
The difficulty which many expositors have found in the word
לִהְיוֹת has been very correctly solved, so far as the sense is concerned, by the earlier translators, by the interpolation of "*they
returned :*" תָּבוּ (Chald.), ἐπεστράφησαν (LXX.), *reversi sunt*
(Vulg.), and similarly the Syriac and Arabic. We are not at

liberty, however, to amend the Hebrew text in this manner, as nothing more is omitted than the finite verb הָיוּ before the infinitive לִהְיוֹת (for this construction, see Gesenius, *Gramm.* § 132, 3, Anm. 1), and this might easily be left out here, since it stands at the beginning of the verse in the main clause. The literal rendering would be, they were to be with Israel, *i.e.* they came over to Israel. The fact that the Hebrews who were serving in the army of the Philistines came over to Saul and his host, and turned their weapons against their oppressors, naturally heightened the confusion in the camp of the Philistines, and accelerated their defeat; and this was still further increased by the fact that the Israelites who had concealed themselves on the mountains of Ephraim also joined the Israelitish army, as soon as they heard of the flight of the Philistines (ver. 22).—Ver. 23. " *Thus the Lord helped Israel that day, and the conflict went out beyond Bethaven.*" Bethaven was on the east of Michmash, and, according to ver. 31, the Philistines fled westwards from Michmash to Ajalon. But if we bear in mind that the camp of the Philistines was on the eastern side of Michmash before Bethaven, according to ch. xiii. 5, and that the Israelites forced their way into it from the south, we shall see that the battle might easily have spread out beyond Bethaven, and that eventually the main body of the enemy might have fled as far as Ajalon, and have been pursued to that point by the victorious Israelites.

Vers. 24–31. *Saul's precipitate haste.*—Ver. 24. The men of Israel *were pressed* (*i.e.* fatigued) *on that day*, *sc.* through the military service and fighting. Then Saul adjured the people, saying, " *Cursed be the man that eateth bread until the evening, and* (till) *I have avenged myself upon mine enemies.*" וַיֹּאֶל, *fut. apoc.* of וַיַּאֲלֶה for וַיַּאֲלֶה, from אָלָה, to swear, *Hiphil* to adjure or require an oath of a person. The people took the oath by saying " *amen*" to what Saul had uttered. This command of Saul did not proceed from a proper attitude towards the Lord, but was an act of false zeal, in which Saul had more regard to himself and his own kingly power than to the cause of the kingdom of Jehovah, as we may see at once from the expression נִקַּמְתִּי וגו׳, " till *I* have avenged *myself* upon mine enemies." It was a despotic measure which not only failed to accomplish its object (see vers. 30, 31), but brought Saul into the unfortunate position of being unable to carry out the oath (see ver. 45). All the people kept the command. "*They tasted no bread.*" וְלֹא־טָעַם is not to be connected with וַיְנַקְמֵהוּ as an apodosis.—Ver. 25. "*And all the land* (*i.e.* all the people of the land who had gathered round Saul : *vid.* ver. 29) *came into the woody country; there was honey upon the field.*" יַעַר signifies here a woody district, in which forests alternated with tracts of arable land and meadows.—Ver. 26. When the people came into the wood and saw *a stream of honey* (of wild or wood bees), "*no one put his hand to his mouth* (*sc.* to eat of the honey), *because they feared the oath.*"—Ver. 27. But Jonathan, who had not heard his father's oath, dipped (in the heat of pursuit, that he might not have to stop) the point of his staff in the new honey, and put it to his mouth, "*and his eyes became bright ;*" his lost strength, which is reflected in the eye, having been brought back by this invigorating taste. The *Chethibh* תראנה is probably to be read תֵּרְאֶנָה, the eyes became seeing, received their power of vision again. The Masoretes have substituted as the *Keri* תָּאֹרְנָה, from אוֹר, to become bright, according to ver. 29; and this is probably the correct reading, as the letters might easily be transposed. —Vers. 28 sqq. When one of the people told him thereupon of his father's oath, in consequence of which the people were exhausted (וַיָּעַף הָעָם belongs to the man's words ; and וַיָּעַף is the same as in Judg. iv. 21), Jonathan condemned the prohibition. "*My father has brought the land* (*i.e.* the people of the land, as in ver. 25) *into trouble* (עָכַר, see at Gen. xxxiv. 30) : *see how bright mine eyes have become because I tasted a little of this honey. How much more if the people had eaten to-day of the booty of its enemies, would not the overthrow among the Philistines truly have then become great ?*" אַף כִּי, *lit.* to this (there comes) also that = not to mention how much more ; and כִּי עַתָּה is an emphatic introduction of the apodosis, as in Gen. xxxi. 42, xliii. 10, and other passages, and the apodosis itself is to be taken as a question.

Vers. 31–46. *Result of the battle, and consequences of Saul's rashness.*—Ver. 31. "*On that day they smote the Philistines from Michmash to Ajalon,*" which has been preserved in the village of *Yâlo* (see at Josh. xix. 42), and was about three geographical miles to the south-west of Michmash ; "*and the people were very faint,*" because Saul had forbidden them to

eat before the evening (ver. 24).—Ver. 32. They therefore
"*fell voraciously upon the booty*"—(the *Chethibh* וַיַּעַשׂ is no doubt
merely an error in writing for וַיַּעַט, *imperf. Kal* of עִיט with
Dagesh forte implic. instead of וַיָּעַט, as we may see from ch. xv.
19, since the meaning required by the context, viz. to fall upon
a thing, cannot be established in the case of עָשָׂה with אֶל.   On
the other hand, there does not appear to be any necessity to
supply the article before שָׁלָל, and this *Keri* seems only to have
been taken from the parallel passage in ch. xv. 19),—"*and took
sheep, and oxen, and calves, and slew them on the ground* (אַרְצָה,
lit. to the earth, so that when they were slaughtered the animal
fell upon the ground, and remained lying in its blood, and was
cut in pieces), *and ate upon the blood*" (עַל הַדָּם, with which אֶל הַדָּם,
"*lying to the blood*," is interchanged in ver. 34), *i.e.* the flesh
along with the blood which adhered to it, by doing which they
sinned against the law in Lev. xix. 26.   This sin had been
occasioned by Saul himself through the prohibition which he
issued.—Vers. 33, 34. When this was told to Saul, he said,
"*Ye act faithlessly towards Jehovah*" by transgressing the laws
of the covenant; "*roll me now* (*lit.* this day) *a large stone.
Scatter yourselves among the people, and say to them, Let every
one bring his ox and his sheep to me, and slay here*" (upon the
stone that has been rolled up), viz. so that the blood could run
off properly upon the ground, and the flesh be separated from
the blood.   This the people also did.—Ver. 35. As a thanksgiving for this victory, Saul built an altar to the Lord.   אֹתוֹ
הֵחֵל לִבְנוֹת, "*he began to build it*," *i.e.* he built this altar at the
beginning, or as the first altar.   This altar was probably not
intended to serve as a place of sacrifice, but simply to be a
memorial of the presence of God, or the revelation of God
which Saul had received in the marvellous victory.—Ver. 36.
After the people had strengthened themselves in the evening
with food, Saul wanted to pursue the Philistines still farther
during the night, and to plunder among them until the light
(*i.e.* till break of day), and utterly destroy them.   The people
assented to this proposal, but the priest (Ahiah) wished first of
all to obtain the decision of God upon the matter.   "*We will
draw near to God here*" (before the altar which has just been
built).—Ver. 37. But when Saul inquired of God (through
the Urim and Thummim of the high priest), "*Shall I go down*

after the Philistines? wilt Thou deliver them into the hand of Israel?" God did not answer him. Saul was to perceive from this, that the guilt of some sin was resting upon the people, on account of which the Lord had turned away His countenance, and was withdrawing His help.—Vers. 38, 39. When Saul perceived this, he directed all the heads of the people (*pinnoth,* as in Judg. xx. 2) to draw near to learn whereby (wherein) the sin had occurred that day, and declared, *" As truly as Jehovah liveth, who has brought salvation to Israel, even if it were upon Jonathan my son, he shall die."* The first כִּי in ver. 39 is explanatory; the second and third serve to introduce the words, like ὅτι, *quod;* and the repetition serves to give emphasis, *lit.* *" that even if it were upon my son, that he shall die."* *" And of all the people no one answered him,"* from terror at the king's word.—Ver. 40. In order to find out the guilt, or rather the culprit, Saul proceeded to the lot; and for this purpose he made all the people stand on one side, whilst he and his son Jonathan went to the other, and then solemnly addressed Jehovah thus: *" God of Israel, give innocence* (of mind, *i.e.* truth). *And the lot fell upon Saul and Jonathan* (יִלָּכֵד, as in ch. x. 20, 21); *and the people went out,"* *sc.* without the lot falling upon them, *i.e.* they went out free.—Ver. 42. When they proceeded still further to cast lots between Saul and his son (הַפִּילוּ, *sc.* גּוֹרָל ; cf. 1 Chron. xxvi. 14, Neh. xi. 11, etc.), *Jonathan was taken.*[1]—Vers. 43,

---

[1] In the Alex. version, vers. 41 and 42 are lengthened out with long paraphrases upon the course pursued in casting the lots: καὶ εἶπε Σαούλ, Κύριε ὁ θεὸς Ἰσραὴλ τί ὅτι οὐκ ἀπεκρίθης τῷ δούλῳ σου σήμερον; εἰ ἐν ἐμοὶ ἢ ἐν Ἰωνάθαν τῷ υἱῷ μου ἡ ἀδικία ; κύριε ὁ θεὸς Ἰσραὴλ δὸς δήλους· καὶ ἐὰν τάδε εἴπῃ, δὸς δὴ τῷ λαῷ σου Ἰσραήλ, δὸς δὴ ὁσιότητα, καὶ κληροῦται Ἰωνάθαν καὶ Σαούλ, καὶ ὁ λαὸς ἐξῆλθε. Ver. 42 : Καὶ εἶπε Σαούλ, Βάλλετε ἀνὰ μέσον ἐμοῦ καὶ ἀνὰ μέσον Ἰωνάθαν τοῦ υἱοῦ μου· ὃν ἂν κατακληρώσηται Κύριος ἀποθανέτω. Καὶ εἶπεν ὁ λαὸς πρὸς Σαούλ, Οὐκ ἔστι τὸ ῥῆμα τοῦτο. Καὶ κατεκράτησε Σαοὺλ τοῦ λαοῦ, καὶ βάλλουσιν ἀνὰ μέσον αὐτοῦ καὶ ἀνὰ μέσον Ἰωνάθαν τοῦ υἱοῦ αὐτοῦ, καὶ κατακληροῦται Ἰωνάθαν. One portion of these additions is also found in the text of our present Vulgate, and reads as follows : *Et dixit Saul ad Dominum Deum Israel: Domine Deus Israel, da indicium! quid est quod non responderis servo tuo hodie? Si in me aut in Jonatha filio meo est iniquitas, da ostensionem; aut si hæc iniquitas est in populo tuo, da sanctitatem. Et deprehensus est Jonathas et Saul, populus autem exivit.* The beginning and end of this verse, as well as ver. 42, agree here most accurately with the Hebrew text. But the words from *quid est quod* to *da sanctitatem* are interpolated, so that הָבָה תָמִים are translated twice;

44. When Saul asked him what he had done, Jonathan confessed that he had tasted a little honey (see ver. 27), and resigned himself to the punishment suspended over him, saying, "*Behold, I shall die ;*" and Saul pronounced sentence of death upon him, accompanying it with an oath ("*God do so,*" etc.: *vid.* Ruth i. 17).—Ver. 45. But the people interposed, "*Shall Jonathan die, who has achieved this great salvation* (victory) *in Israel? God forbid! As truly as Jehovah liveth, not a hair shall fall from his head upon the ground; for he hath wrought* (the victory) *with God to-day.*" Thus the people delivered Jonathan from death. The objection raised by the people was so conclusive, that Saul was obliged to yield.

What Jonathan had done was not wrong in itself, but became so simply on account of the oath with which Saul had

first in the words *da indicium*, and then in the interpolation *da ostensionem.* This repetition of the same words, and that in different renderings, when taken in connection with the agreement of the Vulgate with the Hebrew text at the beginning and end of the verse, shows clearly enough, that the interpolated clauses did not originate with Jerome, but are simply inserted in his translation from the Itala. The additions of the LXX., in which τάδε εἴπη is evidently only a distortion of ἡ ἀδικία, are regarded by Ewald (*Gesch.* iii. p. 48) and Thenius as an original portion of the text which has dropped out from the Masoretic text. They therefore infer, that instead of תָּמִים we ought to read תֻּמִּים (*Thummim*), and that we have here the full formula used in connection with the use of the Urim and Thummim, from which it may be seen, that this mode of divine revelation consisted simply in a sacred lot, or in the use of two dice, the one of which was fixed upon at the outset as meaning *no*, and the other as meaning *yes.* So much at any rate is indisputable, that the Septuagint translator took תמים in the sense of *thummim*, and so assumed that Saul had the guilty person discovered by resorting to the Urim and Thummim. But this assumption is also decidedly erroneous, together with all the inferences based upon it. For, in the first place, the verbs הִפִּיל and יִלָּכֵד can be proved to be never used throughout the whole of the Old Testament to signify the use of the Urim and Thummim, and to be nothing more than technical expressions used to denote the casting of a simple lot (see the passages cited above in the text). Moreover, such passages as ch. x. 22, and ii. 5, 23, show most unmistakeably that the divine oracle of the Urim and Thummim did not consist merely in a sacred lot with yes and no, but that God gave such answers through it as could never have been given through the lots. The Septuagint expansions of the text are nothing more, therefore, than a subjective and really erroneous interpretation on the part of the translators, which arose simply from the mistaken idea that תמים was *thummim*, and which is therefore utterly worthless.

forbidden it. But Jonathan did not hear the oath, and therefore had not even consciously transgressed. Nevertheless a
curse lay upon Israel, which was to be brought to light as a
warning for the culprit. Therefore Jehovah had given no
reply to Saul. But when the lot, which had the force of a
divine verdict, fell upon Jonathan, sentence of death was not
thereby pronounced upon him by God; but it was simply made
manifest, that through his transgression of his father's oath,
with which he was not acquainted, guilt had been brought upon
Israel. The breach of a command issued with a solemn oath,
even when it took place unconsciously, excited the wrath of
God, as being a profanation of the divine name. But such a
sin could only rest as guilt upon the man who had committed,
or the man who occasioned it. Now where the command in
question was one of God himself, there could be no question,
that even in the case of unconscious transgression the sin fell
upon the transgressor, and it was necessary that it should either
be expiated by him or forgiven him. But where the command
of a man had been unconsciously transgressed, the guilt might
also fall upon the man who issued the command, that is to say,
if he did it without being authorized or empowered by God.
In the present instance, Saul had issued the prohibition without divine authority, and had made it obligatory upon the people
by a solemn oath. The people had conscientiously obeyed the
command, but Jonathan had transgressed it without being
aware of it. For this Saul was about to punish him with death,
in order to keep his oath. But the people opposed it. They
not only pronounced Jonathan innocent, because he had broken
the king's command unconsciously, but they also exclaimed that
he had gained the victory for Israel " *with God*." In this
fact (Jonathan's victory) there was a divine verdict. And
Saul could not fail to recognise now, that it was not Jonathan,
but he himself, who had sinned, and through his arbitrary and
despotic command had brought guilt upon Israel, on account
of which God had given him no reply.—Ver. 46. With the
feeling of this guilt, Saul gave up any further pursuit of the
Philistines : he " *went up*" (*sc.* to Gibeah) " *from behind the
Philistines*," *i.e.* desisting from any further pursuit. But the
Philistines went to their place, *i.e.* back into their own
land.

Vers. 47–52. GENERAL SUMMARY OF SAUL'S OTHER WARS, AND ACCOUNT OF HIS FAMILY.—Ver. 47. *" But Saul had taken the sovereignty."* As Saul had first of all secured a recognition of himself as king on the part of all the·tribes of Israel, through his victory over the Ammonites at Jabesh (ch. xi. 12 sqq.), so it was through the victory which he had gained over the Philistines, and by which these obstinate foes of Israel were driven back into their own land, that he first acquired the kingship over Israel, *i.e.* first really secured the regal authority over the Israelites. This is the meaning of לָכַד הַמְּלוּכָה; and this statement is not at variance either with the election of Saul by lot (ch. x. 17 sqq.), or with his confirmation at Gilgal (ch. xi. 14, 15). But as Saul had to fight for the sovereignty, and could only secure it by successful warfare, his other wars are placed in the foreground in the summary account of his reign which follows (vers. 47, 48), whilst the notices concerning his family, which stand at the very beginning in the case of the other kings, are not mentioned till afterwards (vers. 49–51). Saul fought successfully against all the enemies of Israel round about; against Moab, the Ammonites, Edom, the kings of Zobah, a district of Syria on this side the Euphrates (see at 2 Sam. viii. 3), and against the Philistines. The war against the Ammonites is described in ch. xi.; but with the Philistines Saul had to wage repeated war all the days of his life (ver. 52). The other wars are none of them more fully described, simply because they were of no importance to the history of the kingdom of God, having neither furnished occasion for any miraculous displays of divine omnipotence, nor brought about the subjection of hostile nations to the power of Israel. *" Whithersoever he turned, he inflicted punishment."* This is the rendering which Luther has very aptly given to יַרְשִׁיעַ; for הִרְשִׁיעַ signifies to declare wrong, hence to condemn, more especially as applied to judges: here it denotes sentence or condemnation *by deeds.* Saul chastised these nations for their attacks upon Israel.— Ver. 48. *" And he acquired power;"* עָשָׂה חַיִל (as in Num. xxiv. 18) does not merely signify he proved himself brave, or he formed an army, but denotes the development and unfolding of power in various respects. Here it relates more particularly to the development of strength in the war against Amalek, by virtue of which Saul smote this arch-enemy of Israel, and put an end to their depredations. This war is described more fully in ch. xv., on account of its consequences in relation to Saul's own sovereignty.—Vers. 49–51. *Saul's family.*—Ver. 49. Only three of his sons are mentioned, namely those who fell with him, according to ch. xxxi. 2, in the war with the Philistines. *Jisvi* is only another name for Abinadab (ch. xxxi. 2; 1 Chron. viii. 33, ix. 39). In these passages in the Chronicles there is a fourth mentioned, *Esh-baal*, *i.e.* the one who is called *Ish-bosheth* in 2 Sam. ii. 8, etc., and who was set up by Abner as the antagonist of David. The reason why he is not mentioned here it is impossible to determine. It may be that the name has fallen out simply through some mistake in copying: the daughters *Michal* and *Merab* are mentioned, with special reference to the occurrence described in ch. xviii. 17 sqq.—Vers. 50, 51. *Abner* the general was also Saul's cousin. For " *son of Abiel*" (*ben Abiel*) we must read "*sons of Abiel*" (*bne Abiel:* see ch. ix. 1). —Ver. 52. The statement, " *and the war was hard* (severe) *against the Philistines as long as Saul lived*," merely serves to explain the notice which follows, namely, that Saul took or drew to himself every strong man and every brave man that he saw. If we observe this, which is the true relation between the two clauses in this verse, the appearance of abruptness which we find in the first notice completely vanishes, and the verse follows very suitably upon the allusion to the general. The meaning might be expressed in this manner : And as Saul had to carry on a severe war against the Philistines his whole life long, he drew to himself every powerful man and every brave man that he met with.

WAR WITH AMALEK. SAUL'S DISOBEDIENCE AND REJECTION.—CHAP. XV.

As Saul had transgressed the commandment of God which was given to him through Samuel, by the sacrifice which he offered at Gilgal in the war with the Philistines at the very commencement of his reign, and had thereby drawn upon himself the threat that his monarchy should not be continued in perpetuity (ch. xiii. 13, 14) ; so his disobedience in the war against the Amalekites was followed by his rejection on the part of God. The Amalekites were the first heathen nation to attack the Israelites after their deliverance out of Egypt, which they did in the most treacherous manner on their journey from Egypt to Sinai; and they had been threatened by God with extermination in consequence. This Moses enjoined upon Joshua, and also committed to writing, for the Israelites to observe in all future generations (Ex. xvii. 8–16). As the Amalekites afterwards manifested the same hostility to the people of God which they had displayed in this first attack, on every occasion which appeared favourable to their ravages, the Lord instructed Samuel to issue the command to Saul, to wage war against Amalek, and to smite man and beast with the ban, *i.e.* to put all to death (vers. 1–3). But when Saul had smitten them, he not only left Agag the king alive, but spared the best of the cattle that he had taken as booty, and merely executed the ban upon such animals as were worthless (vers. 4–9). He was rejected by the Lord for this disobedience, so that he was to be no longer king over Israel. His rejection was announced to him by Samuel (vers. 10–23), and was not retracted in spite of his prayer for the forgiveness of his sin (vers. 24–35). In fact, Saul had no excuse for this breach of the divine command; it was nothing but open rebellion against the sovereignty of God in Israel; and if Jehovah would continue King of Israel, He must punish it by the rejection of the rebel. For Saul no longer desired to be the medium of the sovereignty of Jehovah, or the executor of the commands of the God-king, but simply wanted to reign according to his own arbitrary will. Nevertheless this rejection was not followed by his outward deposition. The Lord merely took away His Spirit, had David anointed king by Samuel, and thenceforward so directed the steps of Saul and David, that as time advanced the hearts of the people were turned away more and more from Saul to David; and on the death of Saul, the attempt of the ambitious Abner to raise his son Ishbosheth to the throne could not possibly have any lasting success.

Vers. 1–3. The account of the war against the Amalekites is a very condensed one, and is restricted to a description of the conduct of Saul on that occasion. Without mentioning either the time or the immediate occasion of the war, the narrative commences with the command of God which Samuel solemnly communicated to Saul, to go and exterminate that people.

Samuel commenced with the words, " *Jehovah sent me to anoint thee to be king over His people, over Israel,*" in order to show to Saul the obligation which rested upon him to receive his commission as coming from God, and to proceed at once to fulfil it. The allusion to the anointing points back not to ch. xi. 15, but to ch. x. 1.—Ver. 2. " *Thus saith the Lord of Zebaoth, I have looked upon what Amalek did to Israel, that it placed itself in his way when he came up out of Egypt*" (Ex. xvii. 8). Samuel merely mentions this first outbreak of hostility on the part of Amalek towards the people of Israel, because in this the same disposition was already manifested which now made the people ripe for the judgment of extermination (*vid.* Ex. xvii. 14). The hostility which they had now displayed, according to ver. 33, there was no necessity for the prophet to mention particularly, since it was well known to Saul and all Israel. When God looks upon a sin, directs His glance towards it, He must punish it according to His own holiness. This פָּקַדְתִּי points at the very outset to the punishment about to be proclaimed.—Ver. 3. Saul is to smite and ban everything belonging to it without reserve, *i.e.* to put to death both man and beast. The last clause וְהֵמַתָּה וגו' is only an explanation and exemplification of וְהַחֲרַמְתֶּם וגו'. " *From man to woman,*" etc., *i.e.* men and women, children and sucklings, etc.

Vers. 4-9. Saul summoned the people to war, and mustered them (those who were summoned) at *Telaim* (this was probably the same place as the *Telem* mentioned in Josh. xv. 24, and is to be looked for in the eastern portion of the Negeb). " *Two hundred thousand foot, and ten thousand of the men of Judah :*" this implies that the two hundred thousand were from the other tribes. These numbers are not too large ; for a powerful Bedouin nation, such as the Amalekites were, could not possibly be successfully attacked with a small army, but only by raising the whole of the military force of Israel.—Ver. 5. He then advanced as far as the city of the Amalekites, the situation of which is altogether unknown, and placed an ambush in the valley. וַיָּרֶב does not come from רִיב, to fight, *i.e.* to quarrel, not to give battle, but was understood even by the early translators as a contracted form of וַיָּאָרֶב, the *Hiphil* of אָרַב. And modern commentators have generally understood it in the same way ; but Olshausen (*Hebr. Gramm.* p. 572) questions the correctness

of the reading, and Thenius proposes to alter וַיָּרֶב בַּנַּחַל into
וַיַּעֲרֹךְ מִלְחָמָה. נַחַל refers to a valley in the neighbourhood of the
city of the Amalekites.—Ver. 6. Saul directed the Kenites to
come out from among the Amalekites, that they might not
perish with them (אֹסְפְּךָ, *imp. Kal* of אָסַף), as they had shown
affection to the Israelites on their journey out of Egypt (compare Num. x. 29 with Judg. i. 16). He then smote the Amalekites from Havilah in the direction towards Shur, which lay
before (to the east of) Egypt (cf. Gen. xxv. 18). *Shur* is the
desert of Jifar, *i.e.* that portion of the desert of Arabia which
borders upon Egypt (see at Gen. xvi. 7). *Havilah*, the country
of the *Chaulotæans*, on the border of Arabia Petræa towards
Yemen (see at Gen. x. 29).—Vers. 8, 9. Their king, *Agag*, he
took alive (on the name, see at Num. xxiv. 7), but all the people
he banned with the edge of the sword, *i.e.* he had them put to
death without quarter. "*All,*" *i.e.* all that fell into the hands
of the Israelites. For it follows from the very nature of the
case that many escaped, and consequently there is nothing
striking in the fact that Amalekites are mentioned again at a
later period (ch. xxvii. 8, xxx. 1 ; 2 Sam. viii. 12). The last
remnant was destroyed by the Simeonites upon the mountains
of Seir in the reign of Hezekiah (1 Chron. iv. 43). Only, king
Agag did Saul and the people (of Israel) spare, also "*the best
of the sheep and oxen, and the animals of the second birth, and the
lambs and everything good; these they would not ban.*" מִשְׁנִים,
according to D. Kimchi and R. Tanch., are שְׁנַיִם לֶבֶטֶן, *i.e.
animalia secundo partu edita*, which were considered superior to
the others (*vid.* Roediger in *Ges. Thes.* p. 1451); and כָּרִים,
pasture lambs, *i.e.* fat lambs. There is no necessity, therefore,
for the conjecture of Ewald and Thenius, מַשְׁמַנִּים, fattened, and
כְּרָמִים, vineyards; nor for the far-fetched explanation given by
Bochart, viz. camels with two humps and camel-saddles, to say
nothing of the fact that camel-saddles and vineyards are altogether out of place here. In "*all that was good*" the things
already mentioned singly are all included. הַמְּלָאכָה, the property;
here it is applied to cattle, as in Gen. xxxiii. 14. נִבְזֶה = נְמִבְזֶה,
despised, undervalued. The form of the word is not contracted from a noun מִבְזֶה and the participle נִבְזֶה (*Ges. Lehrgeb.*
p. 463), but seems to be a *participle Niph.* formed from a noun
מִבְזֶה. But as such a form is contrary to all analogy, Ewald

and Olshausen regard the reading as corrupt. נָמֵס (from מָסַס) : flowing away; used with reference to diseased cattle, or such as have perished. The reason for sparing the best cattle is very apparent, namely selfishness. But it is not so easy to determine why Agag should have been spared by Saul. It is by no means probable that he wished thereby to do honour to the royal dignity. O. v. Gerlach's supposition, that vanity or the desire to make a display with a royal slave was the actual reason, is a much more probable one.

Vers. 10-23. The word of the Lord came to Samuel: "*It repenteth me that I have made Saul king, for he hath turned away from me, and not set up* (carried out) *my word.*" (On the repentance of God, see the remarks on Gen. vi. 6.) That this does not express any changeableness in the divine nature, but simply the sorrow of the divine love at the rebellion of sinners, is evident enough from ver. 29. שׁוּב מֵאַחֲרֵי יְיָ, to turn round from following God, in order to go his own ways. This was Saul's real sin. He would no longer be the follower and servant of the Lord, but would be absolute ruler in Israel. Pride arising from the consciousness of his own strength, led him astray to break the command of God. What more God said to Samuel is not communicated here, because it could easily be gathered and supplied from what Samuel himself proceeded to do (see more particularly vers. 16 sqq.). In order to avoid repetitions, only the principal feature in the divine revelation is mentioned here, and the details are given fully afterwards in the account of the fulfilment of the instructions. Samuel was deeply agitated by this word of the Lord. "*It burned* (in) *him,*" sc. wrath (אַף, compare Gen. xxxi. 36 with xxx. 2), not on account of the repentance to which God had given utterance at having raised up Saul as king, nor merely at Saul's disobedience, but at the frustration of the purpose of God in calling him to be king in consequence of his disobedience, from which he might justly dread the worst results in relation to the glory of Jehovah and his own prophetic labours.[1] The opinion

---

[1] "Many grave thoughts seem to have presented themselves at once to Samuel and disturbed his mind, when he reflected upon the dishonour which might be heaped upon the name of God, and the occasion which the rejection and deposition of Saul would furnish to wicked men for blaspheming God. For Saul had been anointed by the ministry of Samuel, and he

that יָחַר לְ is also used to signify deep distress cannot be established from 2 Sam. iv. 8. " *And he cried to Jehovah the whole night*," *sc.* praying for Saul to be forgiven. But it was in vain. This is evident from what follows, where Samuel maintains the cause of his God with strength and decision, after having wrestled with God in prayer.—Ver. 12. The next morning, after receiving the revelation from God (ver. 11), Samuel rose up early, to go and meet Saul as he was returning from the war. On the way it was told him, " *Saul has come to Carmel*"— *i.e. Kurmul*, upon the mountains of Judah to the south-east of Hebron (see at Josh. xv. 55)—" *setting himself a memorial*" (יָד, a hand, then a memorial or monument, inasmuch as the hand calls attention to anything: see 2 Sam. xviii. 18), " *and has turned and proceeded farther, and gone down to Gilgal*" (in the valley of the Jordan, as in ch. xiii. 4).—Ver. 13. When Samuel met him there, Saul attempted to hide his consciousness of guilt by a feigned friendly welcome. " *Blessed be thou of the Lord*" (*vid.* Ruth ii. 20, Gen. xiv. 19, etc.) was his greeting to the prophet; " *I have set up the word of Jehovah.*"—Vers. 14, 15. But the prophet stripped his hypocrisy at once with the question, " *What then is this bleating of sheep in my ears, and a lowing of oxen that I hear?*" Saul replied (ver. 15), " *They have brought them from the Amalekites, because the people spared the best sheep and oxen, to sacrifice them to the Lord thy God; and the rest we have banned.*" So that it was not Saul, but the people, who had transgressed the command of the Lord, and that with the most laudable intention, viz. to offer the best of the cattle that had been taken, as a thank-offering to the Lord. The falsehood and hypocrisy of these words lay upon the very surface; for even if the cattle spared were really intended as sacrifices to the Lord, not only the people, but Saul also, would have had their own interests in view (*vid.* ver. 9), since the flesh of thank-offerings was appropriated to sacrificial meals.—Vers. 16 sqq.

had been chosen by God himself from all the people, and called by Him to the throne. If, therefore, he was nevertheless deposed, it seemed likely that so much would be detracted from the authority of Samuel and the confidence of the people in his teaching, and, moreover, that the worship of God would be overturned, and the greatest disturbance ensue; in fact, that universal confusion would burst upon the nation. These were probably the grounds upon which Samuel's great indignation rested."—*Calvin.*

Samuel therefore bade him be silent. הֶרֶף, " leave off," excusing
thyself any further. " I will tell thee what Jehovah hath said to
me this night." (The Chethibh וַיֹּאמְרוּ is evidently a copyist's
error for וַיֹּאמֶר.) " Is it not true, when thou wast little in thine
eyes (a reference to Saul's own words, ch. ix. 21), thou didst
become head of the tribes of Israel? and Jehovah anointed thee
king over Israel, and Jehovah sent thee on the way, and said,
Go and ban the sinners, the Amalekites, and make war against
them, until thou exterminatest them. And wherefore hast thou
not hearkened to the voice of Jehovah, and hast fallen upon the
booty," etc.? (תַּעַט, see at ch. xiv. 32.)

Even after this Saul wanted to justify himself, and to
throw the blame of sparing the cattle upon the people.—Ver.
20. " Yea, I have hearkened to the voice of Jehovah (אֲשֶׁר serving,
like כִּי, to introduce the reply: here it is used in the sense of
asseveration, utique, yea), and have brought Agag the king of the
Amalekites, and banned Amalek." Bringing Agag he mentioned
probably as a practical proof that he had carried out the war
of extermination against the Amalekites.—Ver. 21. Even the
sparing of the cattle he endeavoured to defend as the fulfilment
of a religious duty. The people had taken sheep and oxen from
the booty, " as firstlings of the ban," to sacrifice to Jehovah.
Sacrificing the best of the booty taken in war as an offering of
first-fruits to the Lord, was not indeed prescribed in the law,
but was a praiseworthy sign of piety, by which all honour was
rendered to the Lord as the giver of the victory (see Num.
xxxi. 48 sqq.). This, Saul meant to say, was what the people
had done on the present occasion; only he overlooked the fact,
that what was banned to the Lord could not be offered to Him
as a burnt-offering, because, being most holy, it belonged to
Him already (Lev. xxvii. 29), and according to Deut. xiii. 16,
was to be put to death, as Samuel had expressly said to Saul
(ver. 3).—Vers. 22, 23. Without entering, therefore, into any
discussion of the meaning of the ban, as Saul only wanted to
cover over his own wrong-doings by giving this turn to the
affair, Samuel put a stop to any further excuses, by saying,
" Hath Jehovah delight in burnt-offerings and slain-offerings as
in hearkening to the voice of Jehovah? (i.e. in obedience to His
word.) Behold, hearing (obeying) is better than slain-offerings,
attending better than fat of rams." By saying this, Samuel did

not reject sacrifices as worthless ; he did not say that God took no pleasure in burnt-offerings and slain-offerings, but simply compared sacrifice with obedience to the command of God, and pronounced the latter of greater worth than the former. " It was as much as to say that the sum and substance of divine worship consisted in obedience, with which it should always begin, and that sacrifices were, so to speak, simple appendices, the force and worth of which were not so great as of obedience to the precepts of God" (Calvin). But it necessarily follows that sacrifices without obedience to the commandments of God are utterly worthless; in fact, are displeasing to God, as Ps. l. 8 sqq., Isa. i. 11 sqq., lxvi. 3, Jer. vi. 20, and all the prophets, distinctly affirm. There was no necessity, however, to carry out this truth any further. To tear off the cloak of hypocrisy, with which Saul hoped to cover his disobedience, it was quite enough to affirm that God's first demand was obedience, and that observing His word was better than sacrifice ; because, as the *Berleb. Bible* puts it, "in sacrifices a man offers only the strange flesh of irrational animals, whereas in obedience he offers his own will, which is rational or spiritual worship" (Rom. xii. 8). This spiritual worship was shadowed forth in the sacrificial worship of the Old Testament. In the sacrificial animal the Israelite was to give up and sanctify his own person and life to the Lord. (For an examination of the meaning of the different sacrifices, see *Pent.* vol. ii. pp. 274 sqq., and Keil's *Bibl. Archäol.* i. § 41 sqq.) But if this were the design of the sacrifices, it was clear enough that God did not desire the animal sacrifice in itself, but first and chiefly obedience to His own word. In ver. 22, טוֹב is not to be connected as an adjective with זֶבַח, "more than good sacrifice," as the Sept. and Thenius render it ; it is rather to be taken as a predicate, "*better than slain-offerings,*" and מִזֶּבַח is placed first simply for the sake of emphasis. Any contrast between good and bad sacrifices, such as the former construction would introduce into the words, is not only foreign to the context, but also opposed to the parallelism. For חֵלֶב אֵילִים does not mean fat rams, but the fat of rams ; the fat portions taken from the ram, which were placed upon the altar in the case of the slain-offerings, and for which חֵלֶב is the technical expression (compare Lev. iii. 9, 16, with vers. 4, 11, etc.). " *For,*" continued Samuel (ver. 23), "*rebellion is the sin of soothsaying, and opposition is heathenism and idolatry.*" מְרִי and הַפְצַר are the subjects, and synonymous in their meaning. חַטַּאת קֶסֶם, the sin of soothsaying, *i.e.* of divination in connection with the worship of idolatrous and demoniacal powers. In the second clause idols are mentioned instead of idolatry, and compared to resistance, but without any particle of comparison. Opposition is keeping idols and teraphim, *i.e.* it is like worshipping idols and teraphim. אָוֶן, nothingness, then an idol or image (*vid.* Isa. lxvi. 3; Hos. iv. 15, x. 5, 8). On the *teraphim* as domestic and oracular deities, see at Gen. xxxi. 19. Opposition to God is compared by Samuel to soothsaying and oracles, because idolatry was manifested in both of them. All conscious disobedience is actually idolatry, because it makes self-will, the human I, into a god. So that all manifest opposition to the word and commandment of God is, like idolatry, a rejection of the true God. "*Because thou hast rejected the word of Jehovah, He hath rejected thee, that thou mayst be no longer king.*" מְהִיוֹת מֶלֶךְ = מִמֶּלֶךְ (ver. 26), away from being king.

Vers. 24—35. This sentence made so powerful an impression upon Saul, that he confessed, "*I have sinned : for I have transgressed the command of the Lord and thy words, because I feared the people, and hearkened to their voice.*" But these last words, with which he endeavoured to make his sin appear as small as possible, show that the consciousness of his guilt did not go very deep. Even if the people had really desired that the best of the cattle should be spared, he ought not as king to have given his consent to their wish, since God had commanded that they should all be banned (*i.e.* destroyed); and even though he had yielded from weakness, this weakness could not lessen his guilt before God. This repentance, therefore, was rather the effect of alarm at the rejection which had been announced to him, than the fruit of any genuine consciousness of sin. "It was not true and serious repentance, or the result of genuine sorrow of heart because he had offended God, but was merely repentance of the lips arising from fear of losing the kingdom, and of incurring public disgrace" (C. v. Lapide). This is apparent even from ver. 25, but still more from ver. 30. In ver. 25 he not only entreats Samuel for the forgiveness of his sin, but says, "*Return with me, that I may pray to the Lord.*"

The שׁוּב presupposes that Samuel was about to go away after executing his commission. Saul entreated him to remain that he might pray, *i.e.* not only in order to obtain for him the forgiveness of his sin through his intercession, but, according to ver. 30, to show him honour before the elders of the people and before Israel, that his rejection might not be known.—Vers. 26, 27. This request Samuel refused, repeating at the same time the sentence of rejection, and turned to depart. "*Then Saul laid hold of the lappet of his mantle* (*i.e.* his upper garment), *and it tore*" (*lit.* was torn off). That the *Niphal* וַיִּקָּרַע is correct, and is not to be altered into וַיִּקְרַע אֹתָהּ, "Saul tore off the lappet," according to the rendering of the LXX., as Thenius supposes, is evident from the explanation which Samuel gave of the occurrence (ver. 28): "*Jehovah hath torn the sovereignty of Israel from thee to-day, and given it to thy neighbour, who is better than thou.*" As Saul was about to hold back the prophet by force, that he might obtain from him a revocation of the divine sentence, the tearing of the mantle, which took place accidentally, and evidently without any such intention on the part of Saul, was to serve as a sign of the rending away of the sovereignty from him. Samuel did not yet know to whom Jehovah would give it; he therefore used the expression לְרֵעֶךָ, as רֵעַ is applied to any one with whom a person associates. To confirm his own words, he adds in ver. 29: "*And also the Trust of Israel doth not lie and doth not repent, for He is not a man to repent.*" נֵצַח signifies constancy, endurance, then confidence, trust, because a man can trust in what is constant. This meaning is to be retained here, where the word is used as a name for God, and not the meaning *gloria*, which is taken in 1 Chron. xxix. 11 from the Aramæan usage of speech, and would be altogether unsuitable here, where the context suggests the idea of unchangeableness. For a man's repentance or regret arises from his changeableness, from the fluctuations in his desires and actions. This is never the case with God; consequently He is נֵצַח יִשְׂרָאֵל, *the unchangeable One, in whom Israel can trust, since He does not lie or deceive, or repent of His purposes.* These words are spoken θεοπρεπῶς (theomorphically), whereas in ver. 11 and other passages, which speak of God as repenting, the words are to be understood ἀνθρωποπαθῶς (anthropomorphically; cf. Num. xxiii. 19).—Vers. 30,

31. After this declaration as to the irrevocable character of the determination of God to reject Saul, Samuel yielded to the renewed entreaty of Saul, that he would honour him by his presence before the elders and the people, and remained whilst Saul worshipped, not merely "for the purpose of preserving the outward order until a new king should take his place" (O. v. Gerlach), but also to carry out the ban upon Agag, whom Saul had spared.—Ver. 32. After Saul had prayed, Samuel directed him to bring Agag the king of the Amalekites. Agag came מַעֲדַנֹּת, *i.e.* in a contented and joyous state of mind, and said (in his heart), "*Surely the bitterness of death is vanished,*" not from any special pleasure at the thought of death, or from a heroic contempt of death, but because he thought that his life was to be granted him, as he had not been put to death at once, and was now about to be presented to the prophet (Clericus).—Ver. 33. But Samuel pronounced the sentence of death upon him : "*As thy sword hath made women childless, so be thy mother childless before women!*" מִנָּשִׁים is to be understood as a comparative : more childless than (other) women, *i.e.* the most childless of women, namely, because her son was the king. From these words of Samuel, it is very evident that Agag had carried on his wars with great cruelty, and had therefore forfeited his life according to the *lex talionis.* Samuel then hewed him in pieces "*before the Lord at Gilgal,*" *i.e.* before the altar of Jehovah there ; for the slaying of Agag being the execution of the ban, was an act performed for the glory of God.—Vers. 34, 35. After the prophet had thus maintained the rights of Jehovah in the presence of Saul, and carried out the ban upon Agag, he returned to his own home at Ramah ; and Saul went to his house at Gibeah. From that time forward Samuel broke off all intercourse with the king whom Jehovah had rejected. "*For Samuel was grieved for Saul, and it repented the Lord that he had made Saul king,*" *i.e.* because Samuel had loved Saul on account of his previous election ; and yet, as Jehovah had rejected him unconditionally, he felt that he was precluded from doing anything to effect a change of heart in Saul, and his reinstatement as king.

III. SAUL'S FALL AND DAVID'S ELECTION.

Chap. XVI.-XXXI.

Although the rejection of Saul on the part of God, which was announced to him by Samuel, was not followed by immediate deposition, but Saul remained king until his death, the consequences of his rejection were very speedily brought to light. Whilst Samuel, by the command of God, was secretly anointing David, the youngest son of Jesse, at Bethlehem, as king (ch. xvi. 1–13), the Spirit of Jehovah departed from Saul, and an evil spirit began to terrify him, so that he fell into melancholy; and his servants fetched David to the court, as a man who could play on stringed instruments, that he might charm away the king's melancholy by his playing (ch. xvi. 14–23). Another war with the Philistines soon furnished David with the opportunity for displaying his heroic courage, by the defeat of the giant Goliath, before whom the whole army of the Israelites trembled; and to attract the eyes of the whole nation to himself, as the deliverer of Israel from its foes (ch. xvii. 1–54), in consequence of which Saul placed him above the men of war, whilst Saul's brave son Jonathan formed a bond of friendship with him (ch. xvii. 55–xviii. 5). But this victory, in commemorating which the women sang, " Saul hath slain a thousand, David ten thousand" (ch. xviii. 7), excited the jealousy of the melancholy king, so that the next day, in an attack of madness, he threw his spear at David, who was playing before him, and after that not only removed him from his presence, but by elevating him to the rank of chief captain, and by the promise to give him his daughter in marriage for the performance of brave deeds, endeavoured to entangle him in such conflicts with the Philistines as should cost him his life. And when this failed, and David prospered in all his undertakings, he began to be afraid of him, and cherished a lifelong hatred towards him (ch. xviii. 6–30). Jonathan did indeed try to intercede and allay his father's suspicions, and effect a reconciliation between Saul and David; but the evil spirit soon drove the jealous king to a fresh attack upon David's life, so that he was obliged to flee not only from the presence of Saul, but from his own house also, and went to Ramah, to the prophet Samuel, whither, however, Saul soon followed him, though he was so overpowered by the Spirit of the prophets, that he could not do anything to David (ch. xix.). Another attempt on the part of Jonathan to change his father's mind entirely failed, and so excited the wrath of Saul, that he actually threw the spear at his own son; so that no other course now remained for David, than to separate himself from his noble friend Jonathan, and seek safety in flight (ch. xx.). He therefore fled with his attendant first of all to Nob, where Ahimelech the high priest gave him some of the holy loaves and the sword of Goliath, on his representing to him that he was travelling hastily in the affairs of the king. He then proceeded to Achish, the king of the Philistines, at Gath; but having been recognised as the conqueror of Goliath, he was obliged to feign madness in order to save his life; and being driven away by Achish as a madman, he went to the cave of Adullam, and thence into the land of Moab. But he was summoned by the prophet to return to his own land, and went into the wood Hareth, in the land of Judah; whilst Saul, who had been informed by the Edomite Doeg of the occurrence at Nob, ordered all the priests who were there to be put to death, and the town itself to be ruthlessly destroyed, with all the men and beasts that it contained. Only one of Ahimelech's sons escaped the massacre, viz. Abiathar; and he took refuge with David (ch. xxi. xxii.). Saul now commenced a regular pursuit of David, who had gradually collected around him a company of 600 men. On receiving intelligence that David had smitten a marauding company of Philistines at Keilah, Saul followed him, with the hope of catching him in this fortified town; and when this plan failed, on account of the flight of David into the wilderness of Ziph, because the high priest had informed him of the intention of the inhabitants to deliver him up, Saul pursued him thither, and had actually surrounded David with his warriors, when a messenger arrived with the intelligence of an invasion of the land by the Philistines, and he was suddenly called away to make war upon these foes (ch. xxiii.). But he had no sooner returned from the attack upon the Philistines, than he pursued David still farther into the wilderness of Engedi, where he entered into a large cave,

behind which David and his men were concealed, so that he
actually fell into David's hands, who might have put him to
death.   But from reverence for the anointed of the Lord,
instead of doing him any harm, David merely cut off a corner
of his coat, to show his pursuer, when he had left the cave, in
what manner he had acted towards him, and to convince him
of the injustice of his hostility.   Saul was indeed moved to
tears ; but he was not disposed for all that to give up any
further pursuit (ch. xxiv.).   David was still obliged to wander
about from place to place in the wilderness of Judah ; and at
length he was actually in want of the necessaries of life, so that
on one occasion, when the rich Nabal had churlishly turned
away the messengers who had been sent to him to ask for a
present, he formed the resolution to take bloody revenge upon
this hard-hearted fool, and was only restrained from carrying
the resolution out by the timely and friendly intervention of the
wise Abigail (ch. xxv.).   Soon after this Saul came a second
time into such a situation, that David could have killed him ;
but during the night, whilst Saul and all his people were
sleeping, he slipped with Abishai into the camp of his enemy,
and carried off as booty the spear that was at the king's head,
that he might show him a second time how very far he was
from seeking to take his life (ch. xxvi.).   But all this only
made David's situation an increasingly desperate one ; so that
eventually, in order to save his life, he resolved to fly into the
country of the Philistines, and take refuge with Achish, the
king of Gath, by whom he was now received in the most
friendly manner, as a fugitive who had been proscribed by the
king of Israel.   At his request Achish assigned him the town
of Ziklag as a dwelling-place for himself and his men, whence
he made sundry excursions against different Bedouin tribes of
the desert.   In consequence of this, however, he was brought into
a state of dependence upon this Philistian prince (ch. xxvii.) ;
and shortly afterwards, when the Philistines made an attack
upon the Israelites, he would have been perfectly unable to
escape the necessity of fighting in their ranks against his own
people and fatherland, if the other princes of the Philistines
had not felt some mistrust of " these Hebrews," and compelled
Achish to send David and his fighting men back to Ziklag (ch.
xxix.).   But this was also to put an end to his prolonged flight.

Saul's fear of the power of the Philistines, and the fact that he could not obtain any revelation from God, induced him to have recourse to a necromantist woman, and he was obliged to hear from the mouth of Samuel, whom she had invoked, not only the confirmation of his own rejection on the part of God, but also the announcement of his death (ch. xxviii.). In the battle which followed on the mountains of Gilboa, after his three sons had been put to death by his side, he fell upon his own sword, that he-might not fall alive into the hands of the archers of the enemy, who were hotly pursuing him (ch. xxxi.), whilst David in the meantime chastised the Amalekites for their attack upon Ziklag (ch. xxx.).

It is not stated anywhere how long the pursuit of David by Saul continued ; the only notice given is that David dwelt a year and four months in the land of the Philistines (ch. xxvii. 7). If we compare with this the statement in 2 Sam. v. 4, that David was thirty years old when he became king (over Judah), the supposition that he was about twenty years old when Samuel anointed him, and therefore that the interval between Saul's rejection and his death was about ten years, will not be very far from the truth. The events which occurred during this interval are described in the most elaborate way, on the one hand because they show how Saul sank deeper and deeper, after the Spirit of God had left him on account of his rebellion against Jehovah, and not only was unable to procure any longer for the people that deliverance which they had expected from the king, but so weakened the power of the throne through the conflict which he carried on against David, whom the Lord had chosen ruler of the nation in his stead, that when he died the Philistines were able to inflict a total defeat upon the Israelites, and occupy a large portion of the land of Israel ; and, on the other hand, because they teach how, after the Lord had anointed David ruler over His people, and had opened the way to the throne through the victory which he gained over Goliath, He humbled him by trouble and want, and trained him up as king after His own heart. On a closer examination of these occurrences, which we have only briefly hinted at, giving their main features merely, we see clearly how, from the very day when Samuel announced to Saul his rejection by God, he hardened himself more and more against

the leadings of divine grace, and continued steadily ripening
for the judgment of death.   Immediately after this announcement an evil spirit took possession of his soul, so that he fell
into trouble and melancholy ; and when jealousy towards David
was stirred up in his heart, he was seized with fits of raving
madness, in which he tried to pierce David with a spear, and
thus destroy the man whom he had come to love on account of
his musical talent, which had exerted so beneficial an influence
upon his mind (ch. xvi. 23, xviii. 10, 11, xix. 9, 10).   These
attacks of madness gradually gave place to hatred, which developed itself with full consciousness, and to a most deliberately
planned hostility, which he concealed at first not only from
David but also from all his own attendants, with the hope that
he should be able to put an end to David's life through his
stratagems, but which he afterwards proclaimed most openly as
soon as these plans had failed.   When his hostility was first
openly declared, his eagerness to seize upon his enemy carried
him to such a length that he got into the company of prophets
at Ramah, and was so completely overpowered by the Spirit of
God dwelling there, that he lay before Samuel for a whole day
in a state of prophetic ecstasy (ch. xix. 22 sqq.).   But this
irresistible power of the Spirit of God over him produced no
change of heart.   For immediately afterwards, when Jonathan
began to intercede for David, Saul threw the spear at his own
son (ch. xx. 33), and this time not in an attack of madness or
insanity, but in full consciousness; for we do not read in this
instance, as in ch. xviii. xix., that the evil spirit came upon
him.   He now proceeded to a consistent carrying out of his
purpose of murder.   He accused his courtiers of having conspired against him like Jonathan, and formed an alliance with
David (ch. xxii. 6 sqq.), and caused the priests at Nob to be
murdered in cold blood, and the whole town smitten with the
edge of the sword, because Ahimelech had supplied David
with bread; and this he did without paying any attention to
the conclusive evidence of his innocence (ch. xxii. 11 sqq.).
He then went with 3000 men in pursuit of David ; and even
after he had fallen twice into David's hands, and on both occasions had been magnanimously spared by him, he did not desist
from plotting for his life until he had driven him out of the
land ; so that we may clearly see how each fresh proof of the

righteousness of David's cause only increased his hatred, until at length, in the war against the Philistines, he rashly resorted to the godless arts of a necromancer which he himself had formerly prohibited, and eventually put an end to his own life by falling upon his sword.

Just as clearly may we discern in the guidance of David, from his anointing by Samuel to the death of Saul, how the Lord, as King of His people, trained him in the school of affliction to be His servant, and led him miraculously on to the goal of his divine calling. Having been lifted up as a young man by his anointing, and by the favour which he had acquired with Saul through his playing upon the harp, and still more by his victory over Goliath, far above the limited circumstances of his previous life, he might very easily have been puffed up in the consciousness of the spiritual gifts and powers conferred upon him, if God had not humbled his heart by want and tribulation. The first outbursts of jealousy on the part of Saul, and his first attempts to get rid of the favourite of the people, only furnished him with the opportunity to distinguish himself still more by brave deeds, and to make his name still dearer to the people (ch. xviii. 30). When, therefore, Saul's hostility was openly displayed, and neither Jonathan's friendship nor Samuel's prophetic authority could protect him any longer, he fled to the high priest Ahimelech, and from him to king Achish at Gath, and endeavoured to help himself through by resorting to falsehood. He did save himself in this way no doubt, but he brought destruction upon the priests at Nob. And he was very soon to learn how all that he did for his people was rewarded with ingratitude. The inhabitants of Keilah, whom he had rescued from their plunderers, wanted to deliver him up to Saul (ch. xxiii. 5, 12); and even the men of his own tribe, the Ziphites, betrayed him twice, so that he was no longer sure of his life even in his own land. But the more this necessarily shook his confidence in his own strength and wisdom, the more clearly did the Lord manifest himself as his faithful Shepherd. After Ahimelech had been put to death, his son Abiathar fled to David with the light and right of the high priest, so that he was now in a position to inquire the will and counsel of God in any difficulty into which he might be brought (ch. xxiii. 6). On two occasions God brought his mortal foe Saul into his hand, and David's conduct in both these cases shows how the deliverance of God which he had hitherto experienced had strengthened his confidence in the Lord, and in the fulfilment of His promises (compare ch. xxiv. with ch. xxvi.). And his gracious preservation from carrying out his purposes of vengeance against Nabal (ch. xxv.) could not fail to strengthen him still more. Nevertheless, when his troubles threatened to continue without intermission, his courage began to sink and his faith to waver, so that he took refuge in the land of the Philistines, where, however, his wisdom and cunning brought him into a situation of such difficulty that nothing but the grace and fidelity of his God could possibly extricate him, and out of which he was delivered without any act of his own.

In this manner was the divine sentence of rejection fulfilled upon Saul, and the prospect which the anointing of David had set before him, of ascending the throne of Israel, carried out to completion. The account before us of the events which led to this result of the various complications, bears in all respects so thoroughly the stamp of internal truth and trustworthiness, that even modern critics are unanimous in acknowledging the genuine historical character of the biblical narrative upon the whole. At the same time, there are some things, such as the supposed irreconcilable discrepancy between ch. xvi. 14–23 and ch. xvii. 55–58, and certain repetitions, such as Saul's throwing the spear at David (ch. xviii. 10 and xix. 9, 10), the treachery of the Ziphites (ch. xxiii. 19 sqq. and xxvi. 1 sqq.), David's sparing Saul (ch. xxiv. 4 sqq. and xxvi. 5 sqq.), which they cannot explain in any other way than by the favourite hypothesis that we have here divergent accounts, or legendary traditions derived from two different sources that are here woven together; whereas, as we shall see when we come to the exposition of the chapters in question, not only do the discrepancies vanish on a more thorough and minute examination of the matter, but the repetitions are very clearly founded on facts.

ANOINTING OF DAVID. HIS PLAYING BEFORE SAUL.—
CHAP. XVI.

After the rejection of Saul, the Lord commanded Samuel the prophet to go to Bethlehem and anoint one of Jesse's sons as king; and when he went to carry out this commission, He pointed out David, the youngest of eight sons, as the chosen one, whereupon the prophet anointed him (vers 1–13). Through the overruling providence of God, it came to pass after this, that David was brought to the court of Saul, to play upon the harp, and so cheer up the king, who was troubled with an evil spirit (vers. 14–23).

Vers. 1–13. ANOINTING OF DAVID.—Ver. 1. The words in which God summoned Samuel to proceed to the anointing of another king, " *How long wilt thou mourn for Saul, whom I have rejected, that he may not be king over Israel?*" show that the prophet had not yet been able to reconcile himself to the hidden ways of the Lord; that he was still afraid that the people and kingdom of God would suffer from the rejection of Saul; and that he continued to mourn for Saul, not merely from his own personal attachment to the fallen king, but also, or perhaps still more, from anxiety for the welfare of Israel. He was now to put an end to this mourning, and to fill his horn with oil and go to Jesse the Bethlehemite, for the Lord had chosen a king from among his sons.—Ver. 2. But Samuel replied, " *How shall I go? If Saul hear it, he will kill me.*" This fear on the part of the prophet, who did not generally show himself either hesitating or timid, can only be explained, as we may see from ver. 14, on the supposition that Saul was already given up to the power of the evil spirit, so that the very worst might be dreaded from his madness, if he discovered that Samuel had anointed another king. That there was some foundation for Samuel's anxiety, we may infer from the fact that the Lord did not blame him for his fear, but pointed out the way by which he might anoint David without attracting attention (vers. 2, 3). " *Take a young heifer with thee, and say* (*sc.* if any one ask the reason for your going to Bethlehem), *I am come to sacrifice to the Lord.*" There was no untruth in this, for Samuel was really about to conduct a sacrificial festival and was to invite Jesse's

family to it, and then anoint the one whom Jehovah should
point out to him as the chosen one. It was simply a concealment of the principal object of his mission from any who might
make inquiry about it, because they themselves had not been
invited. "There was no dissimulation or falsehood in this,
since God really wished His prophet to find safety under the
pretext of the sacrifice. A sacrifice was therefore really offered,
and the prophet was protected thereby, so that he was not
exposed to any danger until the time of full revelation arrived"
(Calvin).—Ver. 4. When Samuel arrived at Bethlehem, the
elders of the city came to meet him in a state of the greatest
anxiety, and asked him whether his coming was peace, or
promised good. The singular וַיֹּאמֶר may be explained on the
ground that one of the elders spoke for the rest. The anxious
inquiry of the elders presupposes that even in the time of Saul
the prophet Samuel was frequently in the habit of coming unexpectedly to one place and another, for the purpose of reproving
and punishing wrong-doing and sin.—Ver. 5. Samuel quieted
them with the reply that he was come to offer sacrifice to the
Lord, and called upon them to sanctify themselves and take
part in the sacrifice. It is evident from this that the prophet
was accustomed to turn his visits to account by offering sacrifice, and so building up the people in fellowship with the Lord.
The reason why sacrifices were offered at different places was,
that since the removal of the ark from the tabernacle, this
sanctuary had ceased to be the only place of the nation's
worship. הִתְקַדֵּשׁ, to sanctify one's self by washings and legal
purifications, which probably preceded every sacrificial festival
(vid. Ex. xix. 10, 22). The expression, "Come with me to the
sacrifice," is constructio prægnans for "Come and take part in
the sacrifice." "Call to the sacrifice" (ver. 3) is to be understood in the same way. זֶבַח is the slain-offering, which was
connected with every sacrificial meal. It is evident from the
following words, "and he sanctified Jesse and his sons," that
Samuel addressed the general summons to sanctify themselves
more especially to Jesse and his sons. For it was with them
that he was about to celebrate the sacrificial meal.—Vers. 6 sqq.
When they came, sc. to the sacrificial meal, which was no doubt
held in Jesse's house, after the sacrifice had been presented upon
an altar, and when Samuel saw the eldest son Eliab, who was

tall and handsome according to ver. 7, " *he thought (lit.* he said, *sc.* in his heart), *Surely His anointed is before Jehovah,*" *i.e.* surely the man is now standing before Jehovah whom He hath chosen to be His anointed.   But Jehovah said to him in the spirit, " *Look not at his form and the height of his stature, for I have rejected him : for not as man seeth (sc.* do I see) ; *for man looketh at the eyes, and Jehovah looketh at the heart.*"   The eyes, as contrasted with the heart, are figuratively employed to denote the outward form.—Vers. 8 sqq. When Jesse thereupon brought up his other sons, one after another, before Samuel, the prophet said in the case of each, " *This also Jehovah hath not chosen.*" As Samuel must be the subject to the verb וַיֹּאמֶר in vers. 8–10, we may assume that he had communicated the object of his coming to Jesse.—Ver. 11. After the seventh had been presented, and the Lord had not pointed any one of them out as the chosen one, " *Samuel said to Jesse, Are these all the boys?*" When Jesse replied that there was still *the smallest, i.e.* the youngest, left, and he was keeping the sheep, he directed him to fetch him; " *for,*" said he, " *we will not sit down till he has come hither.*"   סָבַב, to surround, *sc.* the table, upon which the meal was arranged.   This is implied in the context.—Vers. 12, 13. When David arrived,—and he was *ruddy,* also *of beautiful eyes and good looks* (אַדְמוֹנִי, used to denote the reddish colour of the hair, which was regarded as a mark of beauty in southern lands, where the hair is generally black.   עַם is an adverb here = therewith), and therefore, so far as his looks and figure were concerned, well fitted, notwithstanding his youth, for the office to which the Lord had chosen him, since corporeal beauty was one of the outward distinctions of a king,—the Lord pointed him out to the prophet as the chosen one; whereupon he anointed him in the midst of his brethren. Along with the anointing the Spirit of Jehovah came upon David from that day forward.   But Samuel returned to Ramah when the sacrificial meal was over. There is nothing recorded concerning any words of Samuel to David at the time of the anointing and in explanation of its meaning, as in the case of Saul (ch. x. 1). In all probability Samuel said nothing at the time, since, according to ver. 2, he had good reason for keeping the matter secret, not only on his own account, but still more for David's sake; so that even the brethren of David who were present knew nothing about the meaning and object of the anointing, but may have imagined that Samuel merely intended to consecrate David as a pupil of the prophets. At the same time, we can hardly suppose that Samuel left Jesse, and even David, in uncertainty as to the object of his mission, and of the anointing which he had performed. He may have communicated all this to both of them, without letting the other sons know. It by no means follows, that because David remained with his father and kept the sheep as before, therefore his calling to be king must have been unknown to him; but only that in the anointing which he had received he did not discern either the necessity or obligation to appear openly as the anointed of the Lord, and that after receiving the Spirit of the Lord in consequence of the anointing, he left the further development of the matter to the Lord in childlike submission, assured that He would prepare and show him the way to the throne in His own good time.

Vers. 14–23. DAVID's INTRODUCTION TO THE COURT OF SAUL.—Ver. 14. With the rejection of Saul on the part of God, the Spirit of Jehovah had departed from him, and an evil spirit from Jehovah had come upon him, who filled him with fear and anguish. The "*evil spirit from Jehovah*" which came into Saul in the place of the Spirit of Jehovah, was not merely an inward feeling of depression at the rejection announced to him, which grew into melancholy, and occasionally broke out in passing fits of insanity, but a higher evil power, which took possession of him, and not only deprived him of his peace of mind, but stirred up the feelings, ideas, imagination, and thoughts of his soul to such an extent that at times it drove him even into madness. This demon is called "*an evil spirit*" (coming) *from Jehovah,*" because Jehovah had sent it as a punishment, or "*an evil spirit of God*" (*Elohim :* ver. 15), or briefly "*a spirit of God*" (*Elohim*), or "*the evil spirit*" (ver. 23, compare ch. xviii. 10), as being a supernatural, spiritual, evil power; but never "the Spirit of Jehovah," because this is the Spirit proceeding from the holy God, which works upon men as the spirit of strength, wisdom, and knowledge, and generates and fosters the spiritual or divine life. The expression רוּחַ יְהוָֹה רָעָה (ch. xix. 9) is an abbreviated form for רוּחַ רָעָה מֵאֵת יְהֹוָה, and is to be interpreted accordingly.—Ver.

15. When Saul's attendants, *i.e.* his officers at court, perceived the mental ailment of the king, they advised him to let the evil spirit which troubled him be charmed away by instrumental music. *"Let our lord speak* (command) ; *thy servants are before thee* (*i.e.* ready to serve thee) : *they will seek a man skilled in playing upon the harp; so will it be well with thee when an evil spirit of God comes upon thee, and he* (the man referred to) *plays with his hand."* The powerful influence exerted by music upon the state of the mind was well known even in the earliest times; so that the wise men of ancient Greece recommended music to soothe the passions, to heal mental diseases, and even to check tumults among the people. From the many examples collected by Grotius, Clericus, and more especially Bochart in the *Hieroz.* P. i. l. 2, c. 44, we will merely cite the words of Censorinus (*de die natali*, c. 12) : *"Pythagoras ut animum sua semper divinitate imbueret, priusquam se somno daret et cum esset expergitus, cithara ut ferunt cantare consueverat, et Asclepiades medicus phreneticorum mentes morbo turbatas sæpe per symphoniam suæ naturæ reddidit."*—Vers. 17, 18. When Saul commanded them to seek out a good player upon a stringed instrument in accordance with this advice, one of the youths (נְעָרִים, a lower class of court servants) said, *" I have seen a son of Jesse the Bethlehemite, skilled in playing, and a brave man, and a man of war, eloquent, and a handsome man, and Jehovah is with him."* The description of David as *" a mighty man"* and *"a man of war"* does not presuppose that David had already fought bravely in war, but may be perfectly explained from what David himself afterwards affirmed respecting his conflicts with lions and bears (ch. xvii. 34, 35). The courage and strength which he had then displayed furnished sufficient proofs of heroism for any one to discern in him the future warrior.—Vers. 19, 20. Saul thereupon sent to ask Jesse for his son David; and Jesse sent him with a present of an ass's burden of bread, a bottle of wine, and a buck-kid. Instead of the singular expression חֲמוֹר לֶחֶם, an ass with bread, *i.e.* laden with bread, the LXX. read חֹמֶר לֶחֶם, and rendered it γόμορ ἄρτων; but this is certainly wrong, as they were not accustomed to measure bread in bushels. These presents show how simple were the customs of Israel and in the court of Saul at that time.—Ver. 21. When David came to Saul and stood before him, *i.e.* served him by playing upon his harp, Saul took a great liking to him, and nominated him his armour-bearer, *i.e.* his adjutant, as a proof of his satisfaction with him, and sent to Jesse to say, "*Let David stand before me,*" *i.e.* remain in my service, "*for he has found favour in my sight.*" The historian then adds (ver. 23) : "*When the* (evil) *spirit of God came to Saul* (אֶל, as in ch. xix. 9, is really equivalent to עַל), *and David took the harp and played, there came refreshing to Saul, and he became well, and the evil spirit departed from him.*" Thus David came to Saul's court, and that as his benefactor, without Saul having any suspicion of David's divine election to be king of Israel. This guidance on the part of God was a school of preparation to David for his future calling. In the first place, he was thereby lifted out of his quiet and homely calling in the country into the higher sphere of court-life; and thus an opportunity was afforded him not only for intercourse with men of high rank, and to become acquainted with the affairs of the kingdom, but also to display those superior gifts of his intellect and heart with which God had endowed him, and thereby to gain the love and confidence of the people. But at the same time he was also brought into a severe school of affliction, in which his inner man was to be trained by conflicts from without and within, so that he might become a man after God's heart, who should be well fitted to found the true monarchy in Israel.

DAVID'S VICTORY OVER GOLIATH.—CHAP. XVII. 1–54.

A war between the Philistines and the Israelites furnished David with the opportunity of displaying before Saul and all Israel, and greatly to the terror of the enemies of his people, that heroic power which was firmly based upon his bold and pious trust in the omnipotence of the faithful covenant God (vers. 1–3). A powerful giant, named Goliath, came forward from the ranks of the Philistines, and scornfully challenged the Israelites to produce a man who would decide the war by a single combat with him (vers. 4–11). David, who had returned home for a time from the court of Saul, and had just been sent into the camp by his father with provisions for his elder brothers who were serving in the army, as soon as he heard the challenge and the scornful words of the Philistine, offered to fight with him (vers. 15–37), and killed the giant with a stone from a sling; whereupon the Philistines took to flight, and were pursued by the Israelites to Gath and Ekron (vers. 38–54).

Vers. 1–11. Some time after David first came to Saul for the purpose of playing, and when he had gone back to his father to Bethlehem, probably because Saul's condition had improved, the Philistines made a fresh attempt to subjugate the Israelites. They collected their army together (*machaneh*, as in Ex. xiv. 24, Judg. iv. 16) to war at *Shochoh*, the present *Shuweikeh*, in the Wady *Sumt*, three hours and a half to the south-west of Jerusalem, in the hilly region between the mountains of Judah and the plain of Philistia (see at Josh. xv. 35), and encamped between *Shochoh* and *Azekah*, at *Ephes-dammim*, which has been preserved in the ruins of *Damûm*, about an hour and a half east by north of Shuweikeh; so that *Azekah*, which has not yet been certainly traced, must be sought for to the east or north-east of Damûm (see at Josh. x. 10).— Vers. 2, 3. Saul and the Israelites encamped opposite to them in the *terebinth* valley (*Emek ha-Elah*), *i.e.* a plain by the Wady *Musur*, and stood in battle array opposite to the Philistines, in such order that the latter stood *on that side against the mountain* (on the slope of the mountain), and the Israelites *on this side against the mountain; and the valley* (הַגַּיְא, the deeper cutting made by the brook in the plain) *was between them.*—Vers. 4 sqq. And *the* (well-known) *champion* came out of the camps of the Philistines (אִישׁ הַבֵּנַיִם, the middle-man, who decides a war between two armies by a single combat; Luther, "*the giant*," according to the ἀνὴρ δυνατός of the LXX., although in ver. 23 the Septuagint translators have rendered the word correctly ἀνὴρ ὁ ἀμεσσαῖος, which is probably only another form of ὁ μεσαῖος), named *Goliath* of Gath, one of the chief cities of the Philistines, where there were Anakim still left, according to Josh. xi. 22. His height was *six cubits and a span* (6¼ cubits), *i.e.*, according to the calculation made by Thenius, about nine feet two inches Parisian measure,—a great height no doubt, though not altogether unparalleled, and hardly greater than that of the great uncle of Iren, who came to Berlin in the year 1857 (see Pentateuch, vol. iii. p. 303, note).[1] The armour

---

[1] According to Pliny (*h. n.* vii. 16), the giant *Pusio* and the giantess *Secundilla*, who lived in the time of Augustus, were ten feet three inches

of Goliath corresponded to his gigantic stature : *" a helmet of brass upon his head, and clothed in scale armour, the weight of which was five thousand shekels of brass."* The meaning *scales* is sustained by the words קַשְׂקֶשֶׂת in Lev. xi. 9, 10, and Deut. xiv. 9, 10, and קַשְׂקְשׂוֹת in Ezek. xxix. 4. שִׁרְיוֹן קַשְׂקַשִׂים, therefore, is not θώραξ ἁλυσιδωτός (LXX.), a coat of mail made of rings worked together like chains, such as were used in the army of the Seleucidæ (1 Macc. vi. 35), but according to Aquila's φολιδωτόν (scaled), a coat made of plates of brass lying one upon another like scales, such as we find upon the old Assyrian sculptures, where the warriors fighting in chariots, and in attendance upon the king, wear coats of scale armour, descending either to the knees or ankles, and consisting of scales of iron or brass, which were probably fastened to a shirt of felt or coarse linen (see Layard, *Nineveh and its Remains*, vol. ii. p. 335). The account of the weight, 5000 shekels, *i.e.* according to Thenius, 148 Dresden pounds, is hardly founded upon the actual weighing of the coat of mail, but probably rested upon a general estimate, which may have been somewhat too high, although we must bear in mind that the coat of mail not only covered the chest and back, but, as in the case of the Assyrian warriors, the lower part of the body also, and therefore must have been very large and very heavy.[1]—Ver. 6. And *" greaves of brass upon his feet, and a brazen lance* (hung) *between his shoulders,"* *i.e.* upon his back. כִּידוֹן signifies a lance, or small spear. The LXX. and Vulgate, however, adopt the rendering ἀσπὶς χαλκῆ, *clypeus æneus ;* and Luther has followed them, and translates

---

(Roman) in height ; and a Jew is mentioned by Josephus (*Ant.* xviii. 4, 5), who was seven cubits in height, *i.e.* ten Parisian feet, or if the cubits are Roman, nine and a half.

[1] According to Thenius, the cuirass of *Augustus* the Strong, which has been preserved in the historical museum at Dresden, weighed fifty-five pounds; and from that he infers, that the weight given as that of Goliath's coat of mail is by no means too great. Ewald, on the other hand, seems to have no idea of the nature of the Hebrew weights, or of the bodily strength of a man, since he gives 5000 lbs. of brass as the weight of Goliath's coat of mail (*Gesch.* iii. p. 90), and merely observes that the pounds were of course much smaller than ours. But the shekel did not even weigh so much as our full ounce. With such statements as these you may easily turn the historical character of the scriptural narrative into incredible myths ; but they cannot lay any claim to the name of science.

it a brazen shield. Thenius therefore proposes to alter כִּידוֹן into מָגֵן, because the expression " between his shoulders" does not appear applicable to a spear or javelin, which Goliath must have suspended by a strap, but only to a small shield slung over his back, whilst his armour-bearer carried the larger צִנָּה in front of him. But the difficulty founded upon the expression " *between his shoulders*" has been fully met by Bochart (*Hieroz.* i. 2, c. 8), in the examples which he cites from Homer, Virgil, etc., to prove that the ancients carried their own swords slung over their shoulders (ἀμφὶ δ' ὤμοισιν : *Il.* ii. 45, etc.). And Josephus understood the expression in this way (*Ant.* vi. 9, 1). Goliath had no need of any shield to cover his back, as this was suffi- ciently protected by the coat of mail. Moreover, the allusion to the כִּידוֹן in ver. 45 points to an offensive weapon, and not to a shield.—Ver. 7. " *And the shaft of his spear was like a weaver's beam, and the point of it six hundred shekels of iron*" (about seventeen pounds). For חֵץ, according to the *Keri* and the parallel passages, 2 Sam. xxi. 19, 1 Chron. xx. 5, we should read עֵץ, wood, *i.e.* a shaft. Before him went the bearer of the *zinnah, i.e.* the great shield.—Ver. 8. This giant stood and cried to the ranks of the Israelites, " *Why come ye out to place yourselves in battle array? Am I not the Philistine, and ye the servants of Saul? Choose ye out a man who may come down to me*" (into the valley where Goliath was standing). The meaning is : " Why would you engage in battle with us ? I am the man who represents the strength of the Philistines, and ye are only servants of Saul. If ye have heroes, choose one out, that we may decide the matter in a single combat."—Ver. 9. " *If he can fight with me, and kill me, we will be your servants ; if I overcome him, and slay him, ye shall be our servants, and serve us.*" He then said still further (ver. 10), " *I have mocked the ranks of Israel this day* (the mockery consisted in his desig- nating the Israelites as servants of Saul, and generally in the triumphant tone in which he issued the challenge to single combat) ; *give me a man, that we may fight together !*"—Ver. 11. At these words Saul and all Israel were dismayed and greatly afraid, because not one of them dared to accept the challenge to fight with such a giant.

Vers. 12–31. *David's arrival in the camp, and wish to fight with Goliath.*—David had been dismissed by Saul at that time, and having returned home, he was feeding his father's sheep once more (vers. 12–15). Now, when the Israelites were standing opposite to the Philistines, and Goliath was repeating his challenge every day, David was sent by his father into the camp to bring provisions to his three eldest brothers, who were serving in Saul's army, and to inquire as to their welfare (vers. 16–19). He arrived when the Israelites had placed themselves in battle array; and running to his brethren in the ranks, he saw Goliath come out from the ranks of the Philistines, and heard his words, and also learned from the mouth of an Israelite what reward Saul would give to any one who would defeat this Philistine (vers. 20–25). He then inquired more minutely into the matter; and having thereby betrayed his own intention of trying to fight with him (vers. 26, 27), he was sharply reproved by his eldest brother in consequence (vers. 28, 29). He did not allow this to deter him, however, but turned to another with the same question, and received a similar reply (ver. 30); whereupon his words were told to the king, who ordered David to come before him (ver. 31). This is, in a condensed form, the substance of the section, which introduces the conquest of Goliath by David in the character of an episode. This first heroic deed was of the greatest importance to David and all Israel, for it was David's first step on the way to the throne, to which Jehovah had resolved to raise him. This explains the fulness and circumstantiality of the narrative, in which the intention is very apparent to set forth most distinctly the marvellous overruling of all the circumstances by God himself. And this circumstantiality of the account is closely connected with the form of the narrative, which abounds in repetitions, that appear to us tautological in many instances, but which belong to the characteristic peculiarities of the early Hebrew style of historical composition.[1]

[1] On account of these repetitions and certain apparent differences, the LXX. (*Cod. Vat.*) have omitted the section from ver. 12 to ver. 31, and also that from ver. 55 to ch. xviii. 5 ; and on the ground of this omission, Houbigant, Kennicott, Michaelis, Eichhorn, Dathe, Bertheau, and many others, have pronounced both these sections later interpolations; whereas the more recent critics, such as De Wette, Thenius, Ewald, Bleek, Stähelin, and others, reject the hypothesis that they are interpolations, and infer from the supposed discrepancies that ch. xvii. and xviii. were written by some one who was ignorant of the facts mentioned in ch. xvi., and was

Vers. 12–15 are closely connected with the preceding words, "*All Israel was alarmed at the challenge of the Philistine; but David the son of that Ephratite (Ephratite*, as in Ruth i. 1, 2) *of Bethlehem in Judah, whose name was Jesse*," etc. The verb and predicate do not follow till ver. 15 ; so that the words occur here in the form of an anacolouthon. The traditional introduction of the verb הָיָה between וְדָוִד and בֶּן־אִישׁ (David *was* the son of that Ephratite) is both erroneous and misleading. If the words were to be understood in this way, הָיָה could no more be omitted here than הָיְתָה in 2 Chron. xxii. 3, 11. The true explanation is rather, that vers. 12–15 form one period expanded by parentheses, and that the historian lost sight of

altogether a different person from the author of this chapter. According to ch. xvi. 21 sqq., they say, David was Saul's armour-bearer already, and his family connections were well known to the king, whereas, according to ch. xvii. 15, David was absent just at the time when he ought as armour-bearer to have been in attendance upon Saul ; whilst in ch. xvii. 33 he is represented as a shepherd boy who was unaccustomed to handle weapons, and as being an unauthorized spectator of the war, and, what is still more striking, even his lineage is represented in vers. 55 sqq. as unknown both to Abner and the king. Moreover, in ver. 12 the writer introduces a notice concerning David with which the reader must be already well acquainted from ch. xvi. 5 sqq., and which is therefore, to say the least, superfluous ; and in ver. 54 Jerusalem is mentioned in a manner which does not quite harmonize with the history, whilst the account of the manner in which he disposed of Goliath's armour is apparently at variance with ch. xxi. 9. But the notion, that the sections in question are interpolations that have crept into the text, cannot be sustained on the mere authority of the Septuagint version ; since the arbitrary manner in which the translators of this version made omissions or additions at pleasure is obvious to any one. Again, the assertion that these sections cannot well be reconciled with ch. xvi., and emanated from an author who was unacquainted with the history in ch. xvi., is overthrown by the unquestionable reference to ch. xvi. which we find in ver. 12, "David the son of *that* Ephratite,"—where Jerome has correctly paraphrased הַזֶּה, *de quo supra dictum est*,—and also by the remark in ver. 15, that David went backwards and forwards from Saul to feed his father's sheep in Bethlehem. Neither of these can be pronounced interpolations of the compiler, unless the fact can be established that the supposed discrepancies are really well founded. But it by no means follows, that because Saul loved David on account of the beneficial effect which his playing upon the harp produced upon his mind, and appointed him his armour-bearer, therefore David had really to carry the king's armour in time of war. The appointment of armour-bearer was nothing more than conferring upon him the title of aide-de-camp, from which it cannot be the construction with which he commenced in the intermediate clauses; so that he started afresh with the subject וְדָוִד in ver. 15, and proceeded with what he had to say concerning David, doing this at the same time in such a form that what he writes is attached, so far as the sense is concerned, to the parenthetical remarks concerning Jesse's eldest sons. To bring out distinctly the remarkable chain of circumstances by which David was led to undertake the conflict with Goliath, he links on to the reference to his father certain further notices respecting David's family and his position at that time. Jesse had eight sons and was an old man in the time of Saul. בָּא בַאֲנָשִׁים, "*come among the weak.*" אֲנָשִׁים generally means, no doubt,

inferred that David had already become well known to the king through the performance of warlike deeds. If Joab, the commander-in-chief, had *ten* armour-bearers (2 Sam. xviii. 15, compare ch. xxiii. 37), king Saul would certainly have other armour-bearers besides David, and such as were well used to war. Moreover, it is not stated anywhere in ch. xvi. that Saul took David at the very outset into his regular and permanent service, but, according to ver. 22, he merely asked his father Jesse that David might stand before him, *i.e.* might serve him; and there is no contradiction in the supposition, that when his melancholy left him for a time, he sent David back to his father to Bethlehem, so that on the breaking out of the war with the Philistines he was living at home and keeping sheep, whilst his three eldest brothers had gone to the war. The circumstance, however, that when David went to fight with Goliath, Saul asked Abner his captain, "Whose son is this youth?" and Abner could give no explanation to the king, so that after the defeat of Goliath, Saul himself asked David, "Whose son art thou?" (vers. 55-58), can hardly be comprehended, if all that Saul wanted to ascertain was the name of David's father. For even if Abner had not troubled himself about the lineage of Saul's harpist, Saul himself could not well have forgotten that David was a son of the Bethlehemite Jesse. But there was much more implied in Saul's question. It was not the name of David's father alone that he wanted to discover, but what kind of man the father of a youth who possessed the courage to accomplish so marvellous a heroic deed really was; and the question was put not merely in order that he might grant him an exemption of his house from taxes as the reward promised for the conquest of Goliath (ver. 25), but also in all probability that he might attach such a man to his court, since he inferred from the courage and bravery of the son the existence of similar qualities in the father. It is true that David merely replied, "The son of thy servant Jesse of Bethlehem;" but it is very evident from the expression in ch. xviii. 1, "when he had made an end of speaking unto Saul," that Saul conversed with him still further about his family affairs, since the very words imply a lengthened conversation. The other difficulties are very trivial, and will be answered in connection with the exposition of the passages in question.

people or men. But this meaning does not give any appropriate sense here ; and the supposition that the word has crept
in through a slip of the pen for בַּשָּׁנִים, is opposed not only by
the authority of the early translators, all of whom read אֲנָשִׁים,
but also by the circumstance that the expression בּוֹא בַשָּׁנִים does
not occur in the whole of the Old Testament, and that בּוֹא בַיָּמִים
alone is used with this signification.—Ver. 13. " *The three great
(i.e.* eldest) *sons of Jesse had gone behind Saul into the war.*"
הָלְכוּ, which appears superfluous after the foregoing וַיֵּלְכוּ, has
been defended by Böttcher, as necessary to express the pluperfect, which the thought requires, since the *imperfect consec.*
וַיֵּלְכוּ, when attached to a substantive and participial clause,
merely expresses the force of the aorist. Properly, therefore,
it reads thus : " *And then* (in Jesse's old age) *the three eldest
sons followed, had followed, Saul ;*" a very ponderous construction indeed, but quite correct, and even necessary, with the
great deficiency of forms, to express the pluperfect. The names
of these three sons agree with ch. xvi. 6–9, whilst the third,
Shammah, is called *Shimeah* (שִׁמְעָה) in 2 Sam. xiii. 3, 32, שִׁמְעִי
in 2 Sam. xxi. 21, and שִׁמְעָא in 1 Chron. ii. 13, xx. 7.—Ver. 15.
" *But David was going and returning away from Saul :*" *i.e.* he
went backwards and forwards from Saul to feed his father's
sheep in Bethlehem ; so that he was not in the permanent
service of Saul, but at that very time was with his father.
The latter is to be supplied from the context.—Ver. 16. The
Philistine drew near (to the Israelitish ranks) morning and
evening, and stationed himself for forty days (in front of them).
This remark continues the description of Goliath's appearance,
and introduces the account which follows. Whilst the Philistine was coming out every day for forty days long with his
challenge to single combat, Jesse sent his son David into the
camp. " *Take now for thy brethren this ephah of parched grains*
(see Lev. xxiii. 14), *and these ten loaves, and bring them quickly
into the camp to thy brethren.*"—Ver. 18. " *And these ten slices
of soft cheese* (so the ancient versions render it) *bring to the
chief captain over thousand, and visit thy brethren to inquire after
their welfare, and bring with you a pledge from them*"—a pledge
that they are alive and well. This seems the simplest explanation of the word עֲרֻבָּתָם, of which very different renderings were
given by the early translators.—Ver. 19. " *But Saul and they*

(the brothers), *and the whole of the men of Israel, are in the terebinth valley,"* etc. This statement forms part of Jesse's words.—Vers. 20, 21. In pursuance of this commission, David went in the morning *to the waggon-rampart,* when the army, which was going out (of the camp) into battle array, raised the war-cry, and Israel and the Philistines placed themselves *battle-array against battle-array.* וְהַחַיִל וגו' is a circumstantial clause, and the predicate is introduced with וְהֵרֵעוּ, as וְהַחַיִל וגו' is placed at the head absolutely : " *and as for the army which,* etc., *it raised a shout.*" הֵרֵעַ בַּמִּלְחָמָה, *lit.* to make a noise in war, *i.e.* to raise a war-cry.—Ver. 22. David left the vessels with the provisions in the charge of the keeper of the vessels, and ran into the ranks to inquire as to the health of his brethren.—Ver. 23. Whilst he was talking with them, the champion (middle-man) Goliath drew near, and spoke according to those words (the words contained in vers. 8 sqq.), and David heard it. מִפַּעֲרוֹת פל' is probably an error for מִמַּעַרְכוֹת פל' (*Keri*, LXX., Vulg.; cf. ver. 26). If the *Chethibh* were the proper reading, it would suggest an Arabic word signifying a crowd of men (Dietrich on *Ges. Lex.*).—Vers. 24, 25. All the Israelites fled from Goliath, and were sore afraid. They said (אִישׁ יִשְׂרָאֵל is a collective noun), " *Have ye seen this man who is coming?* (הַרְּאִיתֶם, with *Dagesh dirim.* as in ch. x. 24.) *Surely to defy Israel is he coming; and whoever shall slay him, the king will enrich him with great wealth, and give him his daughter, and make his father's house (i.e. his family) free in Israel,*" viz. from taxes and public burdens. There is nothing said afterwards about the fulfilment of these promises. But it by no means follows from this, that the statement is to be regarded as nothing more than an exaggeration, that had grown up among the people, of what Saul had really said. There is all the less probability in this, from the fact that, according to ver. 27, the people assured him again of the same thing. In all probability Saul had actually made some such promises as these, but did not feel himself bound to fulfil them afterwards, because he had not made them expressly to David himself.—Ver. 26. When David heard these words, he made more minute inquiries from the bystanders about the whole matter, and dropped some words which gave rise to the supposition that he wanted to go and fight with this Philistine himself. This is implied in the words, "*For who is the Philistine, this uncircumcised one* (*i.e.* standing as he does outside the covenant with Jehovah), *that he insults the ranks of the living God!*" whom he has defied in His army. "He must know," says the *Berleburger Bible*, "that he has not to do with men, but with God. With a living God he will have to do, and not with an idol."—Ver. 28. David's eldest brother was greatly enraged at his talking thus with the men, and reproved David: "*Why hast thou come down* (from Beth-lehem, which stood upon high ground, to the scene of the war), *and with whom hast thou left those few sheep in the desert?*" "*Those few sheep,*" the loss of only one of which would be a very great loss to our family. "*I know thy presumption, and the wickedness of thy heart; for thou hast come down to look at the war;*" *i.e.* thou art not contented with thy lowly calling, but aspirest to lofty things; it gives thee pleasure to look upon bloodshed. Eliab sought for the splinter in his brother's eye, and was not aware of the beam in his own. The very things with which he charged his brother—presumption and wicked-ness of heart—were most apparent in his scornful reproof.— Vers. 29, 30. David answered very modestly, and so as to put the scorn of his reprover to shame: "*What have I done, then? It was only a word*"—a very allowable inquiry certainly. He then turned from him (Eliab) to another who was standing by; and having repeated his previous words, he received the same answer from the people.—Ver. 31. David's words were told to Saul, who had him sent for immediately.

Vers. 32—40. *David's resolution to fight with Goliath; and his equipment for the conflict.*—Ver. 32. When in the presence of Saul, David said, "*Let no man's heart* (*i.e.* courage) *fail on his account* (on account of the Philistine, about whom they had been speaking): *thy servant will go and fight with this Phili-stine.*"—Vers. 33 sqq. To Saul's objection that he, a mere youth, could not fight with this Philistine, a man of war from his youth up, David replied, that as a shepherd he had taken a sheep out of the jaws of a lion and a bear, and had also slain them both. The article before אֲרִי and דּוֹב points out these animals as the *well-known* beasts of prey. By the expression וְאֶת־הַדּוֹב the bear is subordinated to the lion, or rather placed afterwards, as something which came in addition to it; so that אֵת is to be taken as a *nota accus.* (*vid.* Ewald, § 277, *a*), though it is not to be understood as implying that the lion and the bear went together in search of prey. The subordination or addition is merely a logical one : not only the lion, but also the bear, which seized the sheep, did David slay. זֶה, which we find in most of the editions since the time of Jac. Chayim, 1525, is an error in writing, or more correctly in hearing, for שֶׂה, a sheep. *" And I went out after it ; and when it rose up against me, I seized it by its beard, and smote it, and killed it."* זָקָן, beard and chin, signifies *the bearded chin.* Thenius proposes, though without any necessity, to alter בִּזְקָנוֹ into בִּגְרוֹנוֹ, for the simple but weak reason, that neither lions nor bears have any actual beard. We have only to think, for example, of the λῖς ἠϋγένειος in Homer (*Il.* xv. 275, xvii. 109), or the *barbam vellere mortuo leoni* of Martial (x. 9). Even in modern times we read of lions having been killed by Arabs with a stick (see Rosenmüller, *Bibl. Althk.* iv. 2, pp. 132–3). The constant use of the *singular* suffix is sufficient to show, that when David speaks of the lion and the bear, he connects together two different events, which took place at different times, and then proceeds to state how he smote both the one and the other of the two beasts of prey.—Ver. 36. *" Thy servant slew both the lion and the bear ; and the Philistine, this uncircumcised one, shall become like one of them (i.e.* the same thing shall happen to him as to the lion and the bear), *because he has defied the ranks of the living God."* *" And,"* he continued (ver. 37), *" the Lord who delivered me out of the hand* (the power) *of the lion and the bear, he will deliver me out of the hand of this Philistine."* David's courage rested, therefore, upon his confident belief that the living God would not let His people be defied by the heathen with impunity. Saul then desired for him the help of the Lord in carrying out his resolution, and bade him put on his own armour-clothes, and gird on his armour. מַדָּיו (his clothes) signifies probably a peculiar kind of clothes which were worn under the armour, a kind of armour-coat to which the sword was fastened.—Vers. 39, 40. When he was thus equipped with brazen helmet, coat of mail, and sword, David began to walk, but soon found that he could do nothing with these. He therefore said to Saul, *" I cannot go in these things, for I have not tried them ; "* and having taken them off, he took his shepherd's staff in his hand, sought out five smooth stones from the brook-valley, and put them in the shepherd's thing that he had, namely his shepherd's bag. He then took the sling in his hand, and went up to the Philistine. In the exercise of his shepherd's calling he may have become so skilled in the use of the sling, that, like the Benjaminites mentioned in Judg. xx. 16, he could sling at a hair's-breadth, and not miss.

Vers. 41-54. *David and Goliath: fall of Goliath, and flight of the Philistines.*—Ver. 41. The Philistine came closer and closer to David.—Vers. 42 sqq. When he saw David, "*he looked at him, and despised him,*" *i.e.* he looked at him contemptuously, because he was a youth (as in ch. xvi. 12) ; "*and then said to him, Am I a dog, that thou comest to me with sticks ?* " (the plural מַקְלוֹת is used in contemptuous exaggeration of the armour of David, which appeared so thoroughly unfit for the occasion) ; "*and cursed David by his God* (*i.e.* making use of the name of Jehovah in his cursing, and thus defying not David only, but the God of Israel also), *and finished with the challenge, Come to me, and I will give thy flesh to the birds of heaven and the beasts of the field*" (to eat). It was with such threats as these that Homer's heroes used to defy one another (*vid.* Hector's threat, for example, in *Il.* xiii. 831-2).—Vers. 45 sqq. David answered this defiance with bold, believing courage : " *Thou comest to me with sword, and javelin, and lance; but I come to thee in the name of the Lord of Sabaoth, the God of the ranks of Israel, whom thou hast defied. This day will Jehovah deliver thee into my hand; and I shall smite thee, and cut off thine head, and give the corpse of the army of the Philistines to the birds this day. . . . And all the world shall learn that Israel hath a God; and this whole assembly shall discover that Jehovah bringeth deliverance* (victory) *not by sword and spear: for war belongeth to Jehovah, and He will give you into our hand.*" Whilst Goliath boasted of his strength, David founded his own assurance of victory upon the Almighty God of Israel, whom the Philistine had defied. פֶּגֶר is to be taken collectively. יֵשׁ אֱלֹהִים לְיִשְׂרָאֵל does not mean " God is for Israel," but "Israel hath a God," so that *Elohim* is of course used here in a pregnant sense. This *God* is Jehovah; war is his, *i.e.* He is the Lord of war, who has both war and its results in His power.—Vers. 48, 49. When the Philistine rose up, drawing near towards David (קָם and יֵלֶךְ simply serve to set forth the occurrence in a more pictorial manner), *David hastened and ran to the battle array to meet him,* took a stone out of his pocket, hurled it, and hit the Philistine on his temples, so that the stone entered them, and Goliath fell upon his face to the ground.—Ver. 50 contains a remark by the historian with reference to the result of the conflict : *"Thus was David stronger than the Philistine, with sling and stone, and smote the Philistine, and slew him without a sword in his hand."* And then in ver. 51 the details are given, namely, that David cut off the head of the fallen giant with his own sword. Upon the downfall of their hero the Philistines were terrified and fled ; whereupon the Israelites rose up with a cry to pursue the flying foe, and pursued them *"to a valley, and to the gates of Ekron."* The first place mentioned is a very striking one. The *"valley"* cannot mean the one which divided the two armies, according to ver. 3, not only because the article is wanting, but still more from the facts themselves. For it is neither stated, nor really probable, that the Philistines had crossed that valley, so as to make it possible to pursue them into it again. But if the word refers to some other valley, it seems very strange that nothing further should be said about it. Both these circumstances render the reading itself, גיא, suspicious, and give great probability to the conjecture that גיא is only a copyist's error for *Gath,* which is the rendering given by the LXX., especially when taken in connection with the following clause, *" to Gath and to Ekron"* (ver. 52).—Ver. 52. *" And wounded of the Philistines fell on the way to Shaaraim, and to Gath and to Ekron."* Shaaraim is the town of *Saarayim,* in the lowland of Judah, and has probably been preserved in the Tell *Kefr Zakariya* (see at Josh. xv. 36). On *Gath* and *Ekron,* see at Josh. xiii. 3.—Ver. 53. After returning from the pursuit of the flying foe, the Israelites plundered the camp of the Philistines. דָּלַק אַחֲרֵי, to pursue hotly, as in Gen. xxxi. 36.—Ver. 54. But David took the head of Goliath and brought it to Jerusalem, and put his armour in his tent. אֹהֶל is an antiquated term for a dwelling-place, as in ch. iv. 10, xiii. 2, etc. The reference is to David's house at Bethlehem, to which he returned with the booty after the defeat of Goliath, and that by the road which ran past Jerusalem, where he left the head of Goliath. There is no anachronism in these statements ; for the assertion made by some, that Jerusalem was not yet in the possession of the Israelites, rests upon a confusion between the citadel of Jebus upon Zion, which

was still in the hands of the Jebusites, and the city of Jerusalem, in which Israelites had dwelt for a long time (see at
Josh. xv. 63, and Judg. i. 8).   Nor is there any contradiction
between this statement and ch. xxi. 9, where Goliath's sword
is said to have been preserved in the tabernacle at Nob : for it
is not affirmed that David *kept* Goliath's armour in his own
home, but only that he took it thither ; and the supposition that
Goliath's sword was afterwards deposited by him in the sanctuary
in honour of the Lord, is easily reconcilable with this.   Again, the
statement in ch. xviii. 2, to the effect that, after David's victory
over Goliath, Saul did not allow him to return to his father's
house any more, is by no means at variance with this explanation of the verse before us.   For the statement in question must
be understood in accordance with ch. xvii. 15, viz. as signifying
that from that time forward Saul did not allow David to return
to his father's house to keep the sheep as he had done before,
and by no means precludes his paying brief visits to Bethlehem.

JONATHAN'S FRIENDSHIP.   SAUL'S JEALOUSY AND PLOTS
AGAINST DAVID.—CHAP. XVII. 55—XVIII. 30.

David's victory over Goliath was a turning-point in his life,
which opened the way to the throne.   But whilst this heroic
deed brought him out of his rural shepherd life to the scene of
Israel's conflict with its foes, and in these conflicts Jehovah
crowned all his undertakings with such evident success, that
the Israelites could not fail to discern more and more clearly
in him the man whom God had chosen as their future king;
it brought him, on the other hand, into such a relation to the
royal house, which had been rejected by God, though it still
continued to reign, as produced lasting and beneficial results in
connection with his future calling.   In the king himself, from
whom the Spirit of God had departed, there was soon stirred
up such jealousy of David as his rival to whom the kingdom
would one day come, that he attempted at first to get rid of
him by stratagem; and when this failed, and David's renown
steadily increased, he proceeded to open hostility and persecution.   On the other hand, the heart of Jonathan clung more
and more firmly to David with self-denying love and sacrifice.
This friendship on the part of the brave and noble son of the

king, not only helped David to bear the more easily all the
enmity and persecution of the king when plagued by his evil
spirit, but awakened and strengthened in his soul that pure
feeling of unswerving fidelity towards the king himself, which
amounted even to love of his enemy, and, according to the
marvellous counsel of the Lord, contributed greatly to the
training of David for his calling to be a king after God's own
heart. In the account of the results which followed David's
victory over Goliath, not only for himself but also for all Israel,
the friendship of Jonathan is mentioned first (ver. 55–ch. xviii.
5); and this is followed by an account of the growing jealousy
of Saul in its earliest stages (vers. 6–30).

Ch. xvii. 55–xviii. 5. *Jonathan's friendship.*—Vers. 55–58.
The account of the relation into which David was brought to
Saul through the defeat of Goliath is introduced by a supplementary remark, in vers. 55, 56, as to a conversation which
took place between Saul and his commander-in-chief Abner
concerning David, whilst he was fighting with the giant. So
far, therefore, as the actual meaning is concerned, the verbs
in vers. 55 and 56 should be rendered as pluperfects. When
Saul saw the youth walk boldly up to meet the Philistine, he
asked Abner whose son he was; whereupon Abner assured him
with an oath that he did not know. In our remarks concerning
the integrity of this section (p. 177) we have already observed,
with regard to the meaning of the question put by Saul, that
it does not presuppose an actual want of acquaintance with the
person of David and the name of his father, but only ignorance of the social condition of David's family, with which
both Abner and Saul may hitherto have failed to make themselves more fully acquainted.[1]—Vers. 57, 58. When David
returned "*from the slaughter of the Philistine,*" *i.e.* after the
defeat of Goliath, and when Abner, who probably went as commander to meet the brave hero and congratulate him upon his
victory, had brought him to Saul, the king addressed the same
question to David, who immediately gave him the information
he desired. For it is evident that David said more than is

[1] The common solutions of this apparent discrepancy, such as that Saul
pretended not to know David, or that his question is to be explained on
the supposition that his disease affected his memory, have but little probability in them, although Karkar still adheres to them.

here communicated, viz. "*the son of thy servant Jesse the Beth-lehemite,*" as we have already observed, from the words of ch. xviii. 1, which presuppose a protracted conversation between Saul and David. The only reason, in all probability, why this conversation has not been recorded, is that it was not followed by any lasting results either for Jesse or David.

Ch. xviii. 1–5. The bond of friendship which Jonathan formed with David was so evidently the main point, that in ver. 1 the writer commences with the love of Jonathan to David, and then after that proceeds in ver. 2 to observe that Saul took David to himself from that day forward; whereas it is very evident that Saul told David, either at the time of his conversation with him or immediately afterwards, that he was henceforth to remain with him, *i.e.* in his service. "*The soul of Jonathan bound itself* (*lit.* chained itself; cf. Gen. xliv. 30) *to David's soul, and Jonathan loved him as his soul.*" The *Chethibh* וַיֶּאֱהָבוּ with the suffix וֹ attached to the imperfect is very rare, and hence the *Keri* וַיֶּאֱהָבֵהוּ (*vid.* Ewald, § 249, *b*, and Olshausen, *Gramm.* p. 469). לָשׁוּב, to return to his house, viz. to engage in his former occupation as shepherd.—Ver. 3. Jonathan *made a covenant* (*i.e.* a covenant of friendship) *and* (*i.e.* with) *David*, because he loved him as his soul.—Ver. 4. As a sign and pledge of his friendship, Jonathan gave David *his clothes and his armour. Meil*, the upper coat or cloak. *Maddim* is probably the *armour coat* (*vid.* ch. xvii. 39). This is implied in the word וְעַד, which is repeated three times, and by which the different arms were attached more closely to מַדָּיו. For the act itself, compare the exchange of armour made by Glaucus and Diomedes (Hom. *Il.* vi. 230). This seems to have been a common custom in very ancient times, as we meet with it also among the early Celts (see Macpherson's *Ossian*).—Ver. 5. And David *went out, sc.* to battle; *whithersoever Saul sent him, he acted wisely and prosperously* (יַשְׂכִּיל, as in Josh. i. 8: see at Deut. xxix. 8). Saul placed him above the men of war in consequence, made him one of their commanders; and he pleased all the people, and the servants of Saul also, *i.e.* the courtiers of the king, who are envious as a general rule.

Vers. 6–16. *Saul's jealousy towards David.*[1]—Saul had no

---

[1] The section vers. 6–14 is supposed by Thenius and others to have been taken by the compiler from a different source from the previous one, and

sooner attached the conqueror of Goliath to his court, than he
began to be jealous of him.   The occasion for his jealousy was
the celebration of victory at the close of the war with the
Philistines.—Vers. 6, 7. "*When they came,*" *i.e.* when the warriors
returned with Saul from the war, "*when* (as is added to explain
what follows) *David returned from the slaughter,*" *i.e.* from the
war in which he had slain Goliath, the women came out of all
the towns of Israel, "*to singing and dancing,*" *i.e.* to celebrate
the victory with singing and choral dancing (see the remarks
on Ex. xv. 20), "*to meet king Saul with tambourines, with joy,
and with triangles.*" שִׂמְחָה is used here to signify expressions
of joy, a *fête*, as in Judg. xvi. 23, etc.   The striking position
in which the word stands, viz. between two musical instruments,
shows that the word is to be understood here as referring
specially to songs of rejoicing, since according to ver. 7 their
playing was accompanied with singing.   The women who
"*sported*" (מְשַׂחֲקוֹת), *i.e.* performed mimic dances, sang in alternate choruses ("*answered,*" as in Ex. xv. 21), "*Saul hath slain

not to have been written by the same author : (1) because the same thing
is mentioned in vers. 13, 14, as in ver. 5, though in a somewhat altered
form, and vers. 10, 11 occur again in ch. xix. 9, 10, with a few different
words, and in a more appropriate connection ; (2) because the contents of
ver. 9, and the word מִמָּחֳרָת in ver. 10, are most directly opposed to vers.
2 and 5.   On these grounds, no doubt, the LXX. have not only omitted
the beginning of ver. 6 from their version, but also vers. 9–11.   But the
supposed discrepancy between vers. 9 and 10 and vers. 2 and 5,—viz. that
Saul could not have kept David by his side from attachment to him, or
have placed him over his men of war after several prosperous expeditions,
as is stated in vers. 2 and 5, if he had looked upon him with jealous eyes
from the very first day, or if his jealousy had broken out on the second
day in the way described in vers. 10, 11,—is founded upon two erroneous
assumptions ; viz. (1) that the facts contained in vers. 1–5 were contemporaneous with those in vers. 6–14 ; and (2) that everything contained in
these two sections is to be regarded as strictly chronological.   But the fact
recorded in ver. 2, namely, that Saul took David to himself, and did not
allow him to go back to his father's house any more, occurred unquestionably some time earlier than those mentioned in vers. 6 sqq. with their
consequences.   Saul took David to himself immediately after the defeat of
Goliath, and before the war had been brought to an end.   But the celebration of the victory, in which the pæan of the women excited jealousy in
Saul's mind, did not take place till the return of the people and of the
king at the close of the war.   How long the war lasted we do not know ;
but from the fact that the Israelites pursued the flying Philistines to Gath

his thousands, and David his ten thousands."—Ver. 8. Saul was enraged at this. The words displeased him, so that he said, " *They have given David ten thousands, and to me thousands, and there is only the kingdom more for him*" (*i.e.* left for him to obtain). " In this foreboding utterance of Saul there was involved not only a conjecture which the result confirmed, but a deep inward truth : if the king of Israel stood powerless before the subjugators of his kingdom at so decisive a period as this, and a shepherd boy came and decided the victory, this was an additional mark of his rejection" (O. v. Gerlach).— Ver. 9. From that day forward Saul *was looking askance* at David. עָוַן, a denom. verb, from עַיִן, an eye, looking askance, is used for עֹיֵן (*Keri*).—Vers. 10, 11. The next day the evil spirit fell upon Saul (" *the evil spirit of God;*" see at ch. xvi. 14), so that he raved *in his house,* and threw his javelin at David, who played before him "*as day by day,*" but did not hit him, because David *turned away before him twice.* הִתְנַבֵּא does not

and Ekron, and then plundered the camp of the Philistines after that (ch. xvii. 52, 53), it certainly follows that some days, if not weeks, must have elapsed between David's victory over Goliath and the celebration of the triumph, after the expulsion of the Philistines from the land. Thus far the events described in the two sections are arranged in their chronological order ; but for all the rest the facts are arranged antithetically, according to their peculiar character, whilst the consequences, which reached further than the facts that gave rise to them, and were to some extent contemporaneous, are appended immediately to the facts themselves. Thus David's going out whithersoever Saul sent him (ver. 5) may indeed have commenced during the pursuit of the flying Philistines ; but it reached far beyond this war, and continued even while Saul was looking upon him with jealous eyes. Ver. 5 contains a general remark, with which the historian brings to a close one side of the relation between David and Saul, which grew out of David's victory. He then proceeds in ver. 6 to give the other side, and rounds off this paragraph also (vers. 14–16) with a general remark, the substance of which resembles, in the main, the substance of ver. 5. At the same time it implies some progress, inasmuch as the delight of the people at the acts performed by David (ver. 5) grew into love to David itself. This same progress is also apparent in ver. 13 (" *Saul made him captain over a thousand*"), as compared with ver. 5 (" *Saul set him over the men of war* "). Whether the elevation of David into a captain over a thousand was a higher promotion than his appointment over the men of war, or the latter expression is to be taken as simply a more general or indefinite term, denoting his promotion to the rank of commander-in-chief, is a point which can hardly be determined with certainty.

mean to prophesy in this instance, but " *to rave*." This use of
the word is founded upon the ecstatic utterances, in which the
supernatural influence of the Spirit of God manifested itself in
the prophets (see at ch. x. 5). וַיָּטֶל, from טוּל, he hurled the
javelin, and said (to himself), " *I will pierce David and the
wall.*" With such force did he hurl his spear ; but David
turned away from him, *i.e.* eluded it, twice. His doing so a
second time presupposes that Saul hurled the javelin twice ;
that is to say, he probably swung it twice without letting it go
out of his hand,—a supposition which is raised into certainty
by the fact that it is not stated here that the javelin entered
the wall, as in ch. xix. 10. But even with this view יָטֶל is not
to be changed into יִפֹּל, as Thenius proposes, since the verb נָטַל
cannot be proved to have ever the meaning to swing. Saul
seems to have held the javelin in his hand as a sceptre, according to ancient custom.—Vers. 12, 13. " *And Saul was afraid
of David, because the Spirit of Jehovah was with him, and had
departed from Saul ;*" he " *removed him therefore from him,*"
i.e. from his immediate presence, by appointing him chief
captain over thousand. In this fear of David on the part of
Saul, the true reason for his hostile behaviour is pointed out
with deep psychological truth. The fear arose from the consciousness that the Lord had departed from him,—a consciousness which forced itself involuntarily upon him, and drove him
to make the attempt, in a fit of madness, to put David to death.
The fact that David did not leave Saul immediately after this
attempt upon his life, may be explained not merely on the
supposition that he looked upon this attack as being simply an
outburst of momentary madness, which would pass away, but
still more from his firm believing confidence, which kept him
from forsaking the post in which the Lord had placed him
without any act of his own, until he saw that Saul was plotting
to take his life, not merely in these fits of insanity, but also at
other times, in calm deliberation (*vid.* ch. xix. 1 sqq.).—Vers. 14
sqq. As chief commander over thousand, he went out and in
before the people, *i.e.* he carried out military enterprises, and
that so wisely and prosperously, that the blessing of the Lord
rested upon all he did. But these successes on David's part
increased Saul's fear of him, whereas all Israel and Judah came
to love him as their leader. David's success in all that he took

in hand compelled Saul to promote him; and his standing with
the people increased with his promotion. But as the Spirit of
God had departed from Saul, this only filled him more and
more with dread of David as his rival. As the hand of the
Lord was visibly displayed in David's success, so, on the other
hand, Saul's rejection by God was manifested in his increasing
fear of David.

Vers. 17–30. *Craftiness of Saul in the betrothal of his
daughters to David.*—Vers. 17 sqq. As Saul had promised to
give his daughter for a wife to the conqueror of Goliath (ch.
xvii. 25), he felt obliged, by the growing love and attachment
of the people to David, to fulfil this promise, and told him that
he was ready to do so, with the hope of finding in this some
means of destroying David. He therefore offered him his elder
daughter *Merab* with words that sounded friendly and kind:
" *Only be a brave man to me, and wage the wars of the Lord.*"
He called the wars with the Philistines " *wars of Jehovah,*" *i.e.*
wars for the maintenance and defence of the kingdom of God,
to conceal his own cunning design, and make David feel all the
more sure that the king's heart was only set upon the welfare
of the kingdom of God. Whoever waged the wars of the
Lord might also hope for the help of the Lord. But Saul had
intentions of a very different kind. He thought ("said," *sc.* to
himself), " *My hand shall not be upon him, but let the hand of
the Philistines be upon him;*" *i.e.* I will not put him to death;
the Philistines may do that. When Saul's reason had returned,
he shrank from laying hands upon David again, as he had done
before in a fit of madness. He therefore hoped to destroy him
through the medium of the Philistines.—Ver. 18. But David
replied with true humility, without suspecting the craftiness of
Saul: " *Who am I, and what is my condition in life, my father's
family in Israel, that I should become son-in-law to the king?*"
מִי חַיַּי is a difficult expression, and has been translated in
different ways, as the meaning which suggests itself first (viz.
" *what is my life*") is neither reconcilable with the מִי (the
interrogative personal pronoun), nor suitable to the context.
Gesenius (*Thes.* p. 471) and Böttcher give the meaning " *people*"
for חַיִּים, and Ewald (*Gramm.* § 179, *b*) the meaning " *family.*"
But neither of these meanings can be established. חַיִּים seems
evidently to signify the condition in life, the relation in which

a person stands to others, and מִי is to be explained on the ground that David referred to the persons who formed the class to which he belonged. "*My father's family*" includes all his relations. David's meaning was, that neither on personal grounds, nor on account of his social standing, nor because of his lineage, could he make the slightest pretension to the honour of becoming the son-in-law of the king.—Ver. 19. But Saul did not keep his promise. When the time arrived for its fulfilment, *he gave his daughter to Adriel the Meholathite*, a man of whom nothing further is known.[1]—Vers. 20-24. *Michal is married to David.*—The pretext under which Saul broke his promise is not given, but it appears to have been, at any rate in part, that Merab had no love to David. This may be inferred from vers. 17, 18, compared with ver. 20. *Michal, the younger daughter of Saul, loved David.* When Saul was told this, the thing was quite right in his eyes. He said, "*I will give her to him, that she may become a snare to him, and the hand of the Philistines may come upon him*" (*sc.* if he tries to get the price which I shall require as dowry; cf. ver. 25). He therefore said to David, "*In a second way* (בִּשְׁתַּיִם, as in Job xxxiii. 14) *shalt thou become my son-in-law.*" Saul said this casually to David; but he made no reply, because he had found out the fickleness of Saul, and therefore put no further trust in his words.—Ver. 22. Saul therefore employed his courtiers to persuade David to accept his offer. In this way we may reconcile in a very simple manner the apparent discrepancy, that Saul is said to have offered his daughter to David himself, and yet he commissioned his servants to talk to David privately of the king's willingness to give him his daughter. The omission of ver. 21*b* in the Septuagint is to be explained partly from the fact that בִּשְׁתַּיִם points back to vers. 17-19, which are wanting in this version, and partly also in all probability from the idea entertained by the translators that the statement itself is at variance with vers. 22 sqq. The courtiers were to talk to David בַּלָּט, "*in private,*" *i.e.* as though they were doing it behind the king's back.—Ver. 23. David replied to the courtiers, "*Does it seem to you a little thing to become son-in-law to the king, seeing that I*

---

[1] Vers. 17-19 are omitted from the Septuagint version; but they are so, no doubt, only because Saul's first promise was without result so far as David was concerned.

am a poor and humble man?" "*Poor,*" *i.e.* utterly unable to
offer anything like a suitable dowry to the king. This reply
was given by David in perfect sincerity, since he could not
possibly suppose that the king would give him his daughter
without a considerable marriage portion.—Vers. 24 sqq. When
this answer was reported to the king, he sent word through his
courtiers what the price was for which he would give him his
daughter. He required no dowry (see at Gen. xxxiv. 12), but
only a hundred foreskins of the Philistines, *i.e.* the slaughter of
a hundred Philistines, and the proof that this had been done, to
avenge himself upon the enemies of the king ; whereas, as the
writer observes, Saul supposed that he should thus cause David
to fall, *i.e.* bring about his death by the hand of the Philistines.
—Vers. 26, 27. But David was satisfied with Saul's demand,
since he had no suspicion of his craftiness, and loved Michal.
Even before the days were full, *i.e.* before the time appointed
for the delivery of the dowry and for the marriage had arrived,
he rose up with his men, smote two hundred Philistines, and
brought their foreskins, which were placed in their full number
before the king; whereupon Saul was obliged to give him
Michal his daughter to wife. The words "*and the days were
not full*" (ver. 26) form a circumstantial clause, which is to be
connected with the following sentence, "*David arose,*" etc.
David delivered twice the price demanded. "*They made them
full to the king,*" *i.e.* they placed them in their full number
before him.—Vers. 28, 29. The knowledge of the fact that
David had carried out all his enterprises with success had
already filled the melancholy king with fear. But when the
failure of this new plan for devoting David to certain death
had forced the conviction upon him that Jehovah was with
David, and that he was miraculously protected by Him ; and
when, in addition to this, there was the love of his daughter
Michal to David; his fear of David grew into a lifelong enmity.
Thus his evil spirit urged him ever forward to greater and
greater hardness of heart.—Ver. 30. The occasion for the
practical manifestation of this enmity was the success of David
in all his engagements with the Philistines. As often as the
princes of the Philistines went out (*sc.* to war with Israel),
David acted more wisely and prosperously than all the servants
of Saul, so that his name was held in great honour. With this

general remark the way is prepared for the further history of Saul's conduct towards David.

JONATHAN'S INTERCESSION FOR DAVID. SAUL'S RENEWED ATTEMPTS TO MURDER HIM. DAVID'S FLIGHT TO SAMUEL. —CHAP. XIX.

Vers. 1-7. Jonathan warded off the first outbreak of deadly enmity on the part of Saul towards David. When Saul spoke to his son Jonathan and all his servants about his intention to kill David (לְהָמִית אֶת־דָּוִד, *i.e.* not that they should kill David, but "*that he intended to kill him*"), Jonathan reported this to David, because he was greatly attached to him, and gave him this advice : "*Take heed to thyself in the morning ; keep thyself in a secret place, and hide thyself. I will go out and stand beside my father in the field where thou art, and I will talk to my father about thee* (דִּבֶּר בְּ, as in Deut. vi. 7, Ps. lxxxvii. 3, etc., to talk of or about a person), *and see what* (*sc.* he will say), *and show it to thee.*" David was to conceal himself in the field near to where Jonathan would converse with his father about him ; not that he might hear the conversation in his hiding-place, but that Jonathan might immediately report to him the result of his conversation, without there being any necessity for going far away from his father, so as to excite suspicion that he was in league with David.—Vers. 4, 5. Jonathan then endeavoured with all the modesty of a son to point out most earnestly to his father the grievous wickedness involved in his conduct towards David. "*Let not the king sin against his servant, against David ; for he hath not sinned against thee, and his works are very good* (*i.e.* very useful) *to thee. He hath risked his life* (see at Judg. xii. 3), *and smitten the Philistines, and Jehovah hath wrought a great salvation of all Israel. Thou hast seen it, and rejoiced ; and wherefore wilt thou sin against innocent blood, to slay David without a cause?*"—Vers. 6, 7. These words made an impression upon Saul. He swore, "*As Jehovah liveth, he* (David) *shall not be put to death ;*" whereupon Jonathan reported these words to David, and brought him to Saul, so that he was with him again as before. But this reconciliation, unfortunately, did not last long.

Vers. 8-17. Another great defeat which David had inflicted

upon the Philistines excited Saul to such an extent, that in a fit of insanity he endeavoured to pierce David with his javelin as he was playing before him. The words *Ruach Jehovah* describe the attack of madness in which Saul threw the javelin at David according to its higher cause, and that, as implied in the words *Ruach Jehovah* in contrast with *Ruach Elohim* (ch. xviii. 10, xvi. 15), as inflicted upon him by Jehovah. The thought expressed is, that the growth of Saul's melancholy was a sign of the hardness of heart to which Jehovah had given him up on account of his impenitence. David happily escaped this javelin also. He slipped away from Saul, so that he hurled the javelin into the wall; whereupon David fled and escaped the same night, *i.e.* the night after this occurrence. This remark somewhat anticipates the course of the events, as the author, according to the custom of Hebrew historians, gives the result at once, and then proceeds to describe in detail the more exact order of the events.—Ver. 11. " *Saul sent messengers to David's house,*" to which David had first fled, " *to watch him* (that he might not get away again), *and to put him to death in the* (next) *morning.*" Michal made him acquainted with this danger, and then let him down through the window, so that he escaped. The danger in which David was at that time is described by him in Ps. lix., from which we may see how Saul was surrounded by a number of cowardly courtiers, who stirred up his hatred against David, and were busily engaged in getting the dreaded rival out of the way.—Vers. 13, 14. Michal then took the *teraphim,*—*i.e.* in all probability an image of the household gods of the size of life, and, judging from what follows, in human form,—laid it in the bed, and put a piece of woven goats' hair *at his head, i.e.* either round or over the head of the image, and *covered it with the garment* (*beged*, the upper garment, which was generally only a square piece of cloth for wrapping round), and told the messengers whom Saul had sent to fetch him that he was ill. Michal probably kept *teraphim* in secret, like Rachel, because of her barrenness (see at Gen. xxxi. 19). The meaning of כְּבִיר הָעִזִּים is doubtful. The earlier translators took it to mean goat-skin, with the exception of the Seventy, who confounded כְּבִיר with כָּבֵד, *liver*, upon which Josephus founds his account of Michal having placed a still moving goat's liver in the bed, to make the messengers believe that there was a breathing invalid beneath. כְּבִיר, from כָּבַר, signifies something woven, and עִזִּים goats' hair, as in Ex. xxv. 4. But it is impossible to decide with certainty what purpose the cloth of goats' hair was to serve; whether it was merely to cover the head of the teraphim with hair, and so make it like a human head, or to cover the head and face as if of a person sleeping. The definite article not only before תְּרָפִים and בֶּגֶד, but also with כְּבִיר הָעִזִּים, suggests the idea that all these things belonged to Michal's house furniture, and that כְּבִיר עִזִּים was probably a counterpane made of goats' hair, with which persons in the East are in the habit of covering the head and face when sleeping.—Vers. 15 sqq. But when Saul sent the messengers again to see David, and that with the command, " *Bring him up to me in the bed,*" and when they only found the teraphim in the bed, and Saul charged Michal with this act of deceit, she replied, " *He* (David) *said to me, Let me go; why should I kill thee?*"—"*Behold, teraphim were* (laid) *in the bed.*" The verb can be naturally supplied from ver. 13. In the words " *Why should I kill thee?*" Michal intimates that she did not mean to let David escape, but was obliged to yield to his threat that he would kill her if she continued to refuse. This prevarication she seems to have considered perfectly justifiable.

Vers. 18–24. David fled to Samuel at Ramah, and reported to him all that Saul had done, partly to seek for further advice from the prophet who had anointed him, as to his further course, and partly to strengthen himself, by intercourse with him, for the troubles that still awaited him. He therefore went along with Samuel, and dwelt with him in *Naioth.* נוית (to be read נְוִית according to the *Chethibh,* for which the Masoretes have substituted the form נָיוֹת, vers. 19, 23, and xx. 1), from נָוֶה or נָוֶה, signifies dwellings; but here it is in a certain sense a proper name, applied to the *coenobium* of the pupils of the prophets, who had assembled round Samuel in the neighbourhood of Ramah. The plural נְוִית points to the fact, that this coenobium consisted of a considerable number of dwelling-places or houses, connected together by a hedge or wall.— Vers. 19, 20. When Saul was told where this place was, he sent messengers to fetch David. But as soon as the messengers saw the company of prophets prophesying, and Samuel standing there as their leader, the Spirit of God came upon them, so that they also prophesied. The singular וַיַּרְא is certainly very striking here; but it is hardly to be regarded as merely a copyist's error for the plural וַיִּרְאוּ, because it is extremely improbable that such an error as this should have found universal admission into the MSS. ; so that it is in all probability to be taken as the original and correct reading, and understood either as relating to the leader of the messengers, or as used because the whole company of messengers were regarded as one body. The ἀπ. λεγ. לַהֲקָה signifies, according to the ancient versions, an assembly, equivalent to קְהִלָּה, from which it arose according to Kimchi and other Rabbins by simple inversion.—Ver. 21. The same thing happened to a second and third company of messengers, whom Saul sent one after another when the thing was reported to him.—Vers. 22 sqq. Saul then set out to Ramah himself, and inquired, as soon as he had arrived at the great pit at *Sechu* (a place near Ramah with which we are not acquainted), where Samuel and David were, and went, according to the answer he received, to the Naioth at Ramah. There the Spirit of God came upon him also, so that he went along prophesying, until he came to the Naioth at Ramah ; and there he even took off his clothes, and prophesied before Samuel, and lay there naked all that day, and the whole night as well. עָרוֹם, γυμνός, does not always signify complete nudity, but is also applied to a person with his upper garment off (cf. Isa. xx. 2 ; Micah i. 8 ; John xxi. 7). From the repeated expression " *he also,*" in vers. 23, 24, it is not only evident that Saul came into an ecstatic condition of prophesying as well as his servants, but that the prophets themselves, and not merely the servants, took off their clothes like Saul when they prophesied. It is only in the case of וַיִּפֹּל עָרֹם that the expression " he also" is not repeated ; from which we must infer, that Saul alone lay there the whole day and night with his clothes off, and in an ecstatic state of external unconsciousness ; whereas the ecstasy of his servants and the prophets lasted only a short time, and the clear self-consciousness returned earlier than with Saul. This difference is not without significance in relation to the true explanation of the whole affair. Saul had experienced a similar influence of the Spirit of God before, namely, immediately after his anointing by Samuel, when he met a company of prophets who were prophesying at Gibeah, and he had been thereby changed into another man (ch. x. 6 sqq.). This miraculous seizure by the Spirit of God was repeated again here, when he came near to the seat of the prophets; and it also affected the servants whom he had sent to apprehend David, so that Saul was obliged to relinquish the attempt to seize him. This result, however, we cannot regard as the principal object of the whole occurrence, as Vatablus does when he says, " The spirit of prophecy came into Saul, that David might the more easily escape from his power." Calvin's remarks go much deeper into the meaning : " God," he says, " changed their (the messengers') thoughts and purpose, not only so that they failed to apprehend David according to the royal command, but so that they actually became the companions of the prophets. And God effected this, that the fact itself might show how He holds the hearts of men in His hand and power, and turns and moves them according to His will." Even this, however, does not bring out the full meaning of the miracle, and more especially fails to explain why the same thing should have happened to Saul in an intensified degree. Upon this point Calvin simply observes, that " Saul ought indeed to have been strongly moved by these things, and to have discerned the impossibility of his accomplishing anything by fighting against the Lord; but he was so hardened that he did not perceive the hand of God : for he hastened to Naioth himself, when he found that his servants mocked him;" and in this proceeding on Saul's part he discovers a sign of his increasing hardness of heart. Saul and his messengers, the zealous performers of his will, ought no doubt to have learned, from what happened to them in the presence of the prophets, that God had the hearts of men in His power, and guided them at His will; but they were also to be seized by the might of the Spirit of God, which worked in the prophets, and thus brought to the consciousness, that Saul's raging against David was fighting against Jehovah and His Spirit, and so to be led to give up the evil thoughts of their heart. Saul was seized by this mighty influence of the Spirit of God in a more powerful manner than his servants were, both because he had most obstinately resisted the leadings of divine grace, and also in order that, if it were possible, his hard heart might be broken and subdued by the power of grace. If, however, he should nevertheless continue obstinately in his rebellion against God, he

would then fall under the judgment of hardening, which would
be speedily followed by his destruction. This new occurrence in
Saul's life occasioned a renewal of the proverb : " *Is Saul also
among the prophets ?*" The words " *wherefore they say*" do not
imply that the proverb was first used at this time, but only that
it received a new exemplification and basis in the new event in
Saul's experience. The origin of it has been already mentioned
in ch. x. 12, and the meaning of it was there explained.

This account is also worthy of note, as having an important
bearing upon the so-called *Schools of the Prophets* in the time
of Samuel, to which, however, we have only casual allusions.
From the passage before us we learn that there was a company
of prophets at Ramah, under the superintendence of Samuel,
whose members lived in a common building (נוית), and that
Samuel had his own house at Ramah (ch. vii. 17), though he
sometimes lived in the *Naioth* (cf. vers. 18 sqq.). The origin
and history of these schools are involved in obscurity. If we
bear in mind, that, according to ch. iii. 1, before the call of
Samuel as prophet, the prophetic word was very rare in Israel,
and prophecy was not widely spread, there can be no doubt
that these unions of prophets arose in the time of Samuel, and
were called into existence by him. The only uncertainty is
whether there were other such unions in different parts of the
land beside the one at Ramah. In ch. x. 5, 10, we find a band
of prophesying prophets at Gibeah, coming down from the
sacrificial height there, and going to meet Saul ; but it is not
stated there that this company had its seat at Gibeah, although
it may be inferred as probable, from the name " *Gibeah of God*"
(see the commentary on ch. x. 5, 6). No further mention is
made of these in the time of Samuel ; nor do we meet with
them again till the times of Elijah and Elisha, when we find
them, under the name of *sons of the prophets* (1 Kings xx. 35),
living in considerable numbers at Gilgal, Bethel, and Jericho
(*vid.* 2 Kings iv. 38, ii. 3, 5, 7, 15, iv. 1, vi. 1, ix. 1). According to ch. iv. 38, 42, 43, about a hundred sons of the prophets
sat before Elisha at Gilgal, and took their meals together. The
number at Jericho may have been quite as great ; for fifty men
of the sons of the prophets went with Elijah and Elisha to the
Jordan (comp. ch. ii. 7 with vers. 16, 17). These passages
render it very probable that the sons of the prophets also lived

in a common house. And this conjecture is raised into a certainty by ch. vi. 1 sqq. In this passage, for example, they are represented as saying to Elisha : " The place where we sit before thee is too strait for us; let us go to the Jordan, and let each one fetch thence a beam, and build ourselves a place to dwell in there." It is true that we might, if necessary, supply לְפָנֶיךָ from ver. 1, after לָשֶׁבֶת שָׁם, " to sit before thee," and so understand the words as merely referring to the erection of a more commodious place of meeting. But if they built it by the Jordan, we can hardly imagine that it was merely to serve as a place of meeting, to which they would have to make pilgrimages from a distance, but can only assume that they intended to live there, and assemble together under the superintendence of a prophet. In all probability, however, only such as were unmarried lived in a common building. Many of them were married, and therefore most likely lived in houses of their own (2 Kings iv. 1 sqq.). We may also certainly assume the same with reference to the unions of prophets in the time of Samuel, even if it is impossible to prove that these unions continued uninterruptedly from the time of Samuel down to the times of Elijah and Elisha. Oehler argues in support of this, " that the historical connection, which can be traced in the influence of prophecy from the time of Samuel forwards, may be most easily explained from the uninterrupted continuance of these supports ; and also that the large number of prophets, who must have been already there according to 1 Kings xviii. 13 when Elijah first appeared, points to the existence of such unions as these." But the historical connection in the influence of prophecy, or, in other words, the uninterrupted succession of prophets, was also to be found in the kingdom of Judah both before and after the times of Elijah and Elisha, and down to the Babylonian captivity, without our discovering the slightest trace of any schools of the prophets in that kingdom. All that can be inferred from 1 Kings xviii. is, that the large number of prophets mentioned there (vers. 4 and 13) were living in the time of Elijah, but not that they were there when he first appeared. The first mission of Elijah to king Ahab (ch. xvii.) took place about three years before the events described in 1 Kings xviii., and even this first appearance of the prophet in the presence of the king is not to be regarded as the commencement of his prophetic labours.

How long Elijah had laboured before he announced to Ahab the judgment of three years' drought, cannot indeed be decided; but if we consider that he received instructions to call Elisha to be his assistant and successor not very long after this period of judgment had expired (1 Kings xix. 16 sqq.), we may certainly assume that he had laboured in Israel for many years, and may therefore have founded unions of the prophets. In addition, however, to the absence of any allusion to the continuance of these schools of the prophets, there is another thing which seems to preclude the idea that they were perpetuated from the time of Samuel to that of Elijah, viz. the fact that the schools which existed under Elijah and Elisha were only to be found in the kingdom of the ten tribes, and never in that of Judah, where we should certainly expect to find them if they had been handed down from Samuel's time. Moreover, Oehler also acknowledges that "the design of the schools of the prophets, and apparently their constitution, were not the same under Samuel as in the time of Elijah." This is confirmed by the fact, that the members of the prophets' unions which arose under Samuel are never called "sons of the prophets," as those who were under the superintendence of Elijah and Elisha invariably are (see the passages quoted above). Does not this peculiar epithet seem to indicate, that the "sons of the prophets" stood in a much more intimate relation to Elijah and Elisha, as their spiritual fathers, than the חֶבֶל הַנְּבִיאִים or לַהֲקַת הַנְּבִיאִים did to Samuel as their president? (1 Sam. xix. 20.) בְּנֵי הַנְּבִיאִים does not mean *filii prophetæ*, i.e. sons who are prophets, as some maintain, though without being able to show that בְּנֵי is ever used in this sense, but *filii prophetarum*, disciples or scholars of the prophets, from which it is very evident that these sons of the prophets stood in a relation of dependence to the prophets (Elijah and Elisha), i.e. of subordination to them, and followed their instructions and admonitions. They received commissions from them, and carried them out (*vid.* 2 Kings ix. 1). On the other hand, the expressions חֶבֶל and לַהֲקָה simply point to combinations for common working under the presidency of Samuel, although the words נִצָּב עֲלֵיהֶם certainly show that the direction of these unions, and probably the first impulse to form them, proceeded from Samuel, so that we might also call these societies schools of the prophets.

The opinions entertained with regard to the nature of these unions, and their importance in relation to the development of the kingdom of God in Israel, differ very widely from one another. Whilst some of the fathers (Jerome for example) looked upon them as an Old Testament order of monks ; others, such as Tennemann, Meiners, and Winer, compare them to the Pythagorean societies. Kranichfeld supposes that they were free associations, and chose a distinguished prophet like Samuel as their president, in order that they might be able to cement their union the more firmly through his influence, and carry out their vocation with the greater success.[1] The truth lies between these two extremes. The latter view, which precludes almost every relation of dependence and community, is not reconcilable with the name "sons of the prophets," or with ch. xix. 20, where Samuel is said to have stood at the head of the prophesying prophets as נִצָּב עֲלֵיהֶם, and has no support whatever in the Scriptures, but is simply founded upon the views of modern times and our ideas of liberty and equality. The prophets' unions had indeed so far a certain resemblance to the monastic orders of the early church, that the members lived together in the same buildings, and performed certain sacred duties in common ; but if we look into the aim and purpose of monasticism, they were the very opposite of those of the prophetic life. The prophets did not wish to withdraw from the tumult of the world into solitude, for the purpose of carrying on a contemplative life of holiness in this retirement from the earthly life and its affairs ; but their unions were associations formed for the purpose of mental and spiritual training, that they might exert a more powerful influence upon their contemporaries. They were called into existence by chosen instruments of the Lord, such as Samuel, Elijah, and Elisha, whom the Lord had called to be His prophets, and endowed with a peculiar measure of His Spirit for this particular calling, that they might check the decline of religious life in the nation, and bring back the rebellious "to the law and the testimony."

---

[1] Compare Jerome (*Epist.* iv. *ad Rustic. Monach.* c. 7) : "The sons of the prophets, whom we call the monks of the Old Testament, built themselves cells near the streams of the Jordan, and, forsaking the crowded cities, lived on meal and wild herbs." Compare with this his *Epist.* xiii. *ad Paulin*, c. 5.

Societies which follow this as their purpose in life, so long as they do not lose sight of it, will only separate and cut themselves off from the external world, so far as the world itself opposes them, and pursues them with hostility and persecution. The name "schools of the prophets" is the one which expresses most fully the character of these associations; only we must not think of them as merely educational institutions, in which the pupils of the prophets received instruction in prophesying or in theological studies.[1] We are not in possession indeed of any minute information concerning their constitution. Prophesying could neither be taught nor communicated by instruction, but was a gift of God which He communicated according to His free will to whomsoever He would. But the communication of this divine gift was by no means an arbitrary thing, but presupposed such a mental and spiritual disposition on the part of the recipient as fitted him to receive it; whilst the exercise of the gift required a thorough acquaintance with the law and the earlier revelations of God, which the schools of the prophets were well adapted to promote. It is therefore justly and generally assumed, that the study of the law and of the history of the divine guidance of Israel formed a leading feature in the occupations of the pupils of the prophets, which also included the cultivation of sacred poetry and music, and united exercises for the promotion of the prophetic inspiration. That the study of the earlier revelations of God was carried on, may be very safely inferred from the fact that from the time of Samuel downwards the writing of sacred history formed an essential part of the prophet's labours, as has been already observed at vol. iv. pp. 9, 10 (translation). The cultivation of sacred music and poetry may be inferred partly from the fact that, according to ch. x. 5, musicians walked in front of the

---

[1] Thus the Rabbins regarded them as בָּתֵּי מִדְרָשׁ; and the earlier theologians as colleges, in which, as Vitringa expresses it, "philosophers, or if you please theologians, and candidates or students of theology, assembled for the purpose of devoting themselves assiduously to the study of divinity under the guidance of some one who was well skilled as a teacher;" whilst others regarded them as schools for the training of teachers for the people, and leaders in the worship of God. The English Deists—Morgan for example—regarded them as seats of scientific learning, in which the study of history, rhetoric, poetry, natural science, and moral philosophy was carried on.

prophesying prophets, playing as they went along, and partly also from the fact that sacred music not only received a fresh impulse from David, who stood in a close relation to the association of prophets at Ramah, but was also raised by him into an integral part of public worship. At the same time, music was by no means cultivated merely that the sons of the prophets might employ it in connection with their discourses, but also as means of awakening holy susceptibilities and emotions in the soul, and of lifting up the spirit to God, and so preparing it for the reception of divine revelations (see at 2 Kings iii. 15). And lastly, we must include among the spiritual exercises prophesying in companies, as at Gibeah (ch. x. 5) and Ramah (ch. xix. 20).

The outward occasion for the formation of these communities we have to seek for partly in the creative spirit of the prophets Samuel and Elijah, and partly in the circumstances of the times in which they lived. The time of Samuel forms a turning-point in the development of the Old Testament kingdom of God. Shortly after the call of Samuel the judgment fell upon the sanctuary, which had been profaned by the shameful conduct of the priests : the tabernacle lost the ark of the covenant, and ceased in consequence to be the scene of the gracious presence of God in Israel. Thus the task fell upon Samuel, as prophet of the Lord, to found a new house for that religious life which he had kindled, by collecting together into closer communities, those who had been awakened by his word, not only for the promotion of their own faith under his direction, but also for joining with him in the spread of the fear of God and obedience to the law of the Lord among their contemporaries. But just as, in the time of Samuel, it was the fall of the legal sanctuary and priesthood which created the necessity for the founding of schools of the prophets ; so in the times of Elijah and Elisha, and in the kingdom of the ten tribes, it was the utter absence of any sanctuary of Jehovah which led these prophets to found societies of prophets, and so furnish the worshippers of Jehovah, who would not bend their knees to Baal, with places and means of edification, as a substitute for what the righteous in the kingdom of Judah possessed in the temple and the Levitical priesthood. But the reasons for the establishment of prophets' schools were not to be found merely in the circumstances of the times. There was a higher reason still, which must not be overlooked in our examination of these unions, and their importance in relation to the theocracy. We may learn from the fact that the disciples of the prophets who were associated together under Samuel are found prophesying (ch. x. 10, xix. 20), that they were also seized by the Spirit of God, and that the Divine Spirit which moved them exerted a powerful influence upon all who came into contact with them. Consequently the founding of associations of prophets is to be regarded as an operation of divine grace, which is generally manifested with all the greater might where sin most mightily abounds. As the Lord raised up prophets for His people at the times when apostasy had become great and strong, that they might resist idolatry with almighty power; so did He also create for himself organs of His Spirit in the schools of the prophets, who united with their spiritual fathers in fighting for His honour. It was by no means an accidental circumstance, therefore, that these unions are only met with in the times of Samuel and of the prophets Elijah and Elisha. These times resembled one another in the fact, that in both of them idolatry had gained the upper hand; though, at the same time, there were some respects in which they differed essentially from one another. In the time of Samuel the people did not manifest the same hostility to the prophets as in the time of Elijah. Samuel stood at the head of the nation as judge even during the reign of Saul; and after the rejection of the latter, he still stood so high in authority and esteem, that Saul never ventured to attack the prophets even in his madness. Elijah and Elisha, on the other hand, stood opposed to a royal house which was bent upon making the worship of Baal the leading religion of the kingdom; and they had to contend against priests of calves and prophets of Baal, who could only be compelled by hard strokes to acknowledge the Lord of Sabaoth and His prophets. In the case of the former, what had to be done was to bring the nation to a recognition of its apostasy, to foster the new life which was just awakening, and to remove whatever hindrances might be placed in its way by the monarchy. In the time of the latter, on the contrary, what was needed was " a compact phalanx to stand against the corruption which had penetrated so deeply into the nation." These differences in the times would certainly not be

without their influence upon the constitution and operations of
the schools of the prophets.

JONATHAN'S LAST ATTEMPT TO RECONCILE HIS FATHER TO DAVID.—CHAP. XX.–XXI. 1.

Vers. 1-11. After the occurrence which had taken place at
Naioth, David fled thence and met with Jonathan, to whom he
poured out his heart.[1] Though he had been delivered for the
moment from the death which threatened him, through the marvellous influence of the divine inspiration of the prophets upon
Saul and his messengers, he could not find in this any lasting
protection from the plots of his mortal enemy. He therefore
sought for his friend Jonathan, and complained to him, "What
have I done? what is my crime, my sin before thy father, that
he seeks my life?"—Ver. 2. Jonathan endeavoured to pacify
him: "*Far be it! thou shalt not die: behold, my father does nothing great or small* (*i.e.* not the smallest thing; cf. ch. xxv. 36
and Num. xxii. 18) *that he does not reveal to me; why should my
father hide this thing from me? It is not so.*" The לֹו after הִנֵּה
stands for לֹא: the *Chethibh* עָשָׂה is probably to be preferred to
the *Keri* יַעֲשֶׂה, and to be understood in this sense: " My father
has (hitherto) done nothing at all, which he has not told to me."
This answer of Jonathan does not presuppose that he knew
nothing of the occurrences described in ch. xix. 9–24, although
it is possible enough that he might not have been with his father
just at that time; but it is easily explained from the fact that
Saul had made the fresh attack upon David's life in a state of
madness, in which he was no longer master of himself; so that
it could not be inferred with certainty from this that he would

---

[1] According to Ewald and Thenius, this chapter was not written by the
author of the previous one, but was borrowed from an earlier source, and
ver. 1 was inserted by the compiler to connect the two together. But the
principal reason for this conjecture—namely, that David could never have
thought of sitting at the royal table again after what had taken place, and
that Saul would still less have expected him to come—is overthrown by the
simple suggestion, that all that Saul had hitherto attempted against David,
according to ch. xix. 8 sqq., had been done in fits of insanity (cf. ch. xix.
9 sqq.), which had passed away again; so that it formed no criterion by
which to judge of Saul's actual feelings towards David when he was in a
state of mental sanity.

still plot against David's life in a state of clear consciousness.
Hitherto Saul had no doubt talked over all his plans and undertakings with Jonathan, but he had not uttered a single word to
him about his deadly hatred, or his intention of killing David;
so that Jonathan might really have regarded his previous
attacks upon David's life as nothing more than symptoms of
temporary aberration of mind.—Ver. 3. But David had looked
deeper into Saul's heart. He replied with an oath (" he sware
again," *i.e.* a second time), " *Thy father knoweth that I have
found favour in thine eyes* (*i.e.* that thou art attached to me) ;
*and thinketh Jonathan shall not know this, lest he be grieved.
But truly, as surely as Jehovah liveth, and thy soul liveth, there is
hardly a step* (*lit.* about a step) *between me and death.*" כִּי introduces the substance of the oath, as in ch. xiv. 44, etc.—Ver.
4. When Jonathan answered, "*What thy soul saith, will I do to
thee,*" *i.e.* fulfil every wish, David made this request, " *Behold,
to-morrow is new moon, and I ought to sit and eat with the king :
let me go, that I may conceal myself in the field* (*i.e.* in the open
air) *till the third evening.*" This request implies that Saul gave
a feast at the new moon, and therefore that the new moon was
not merely a religious festival, according to the law in Num.
x. 10, xxviii. 11–15, but that it was kept as a civil festival also,
and in the latter character for two days; as we may infer both
from the fact that David reckoned to the third evening, *i.e.*
the evening of the third day from the day then present, and
therefore proposed to hide himself on the new moon's day and
the day following, and also still more clearly from vers. 12, 27,
and 34, where Saul is said to have expected David at table on
the day after the new moon. We cannot, indeed, conclude
from this that there was a religious festival of two days' duration; nor does it follow, that because Saul supposed that David
might have absented himself on the first day on account of
Levitical uncleanness (ver. 26), therefore the royal feast was a
sacrificial meal. It was evidently contrary to social propriety
to take part in a public feast in a state of Levitical uncleanness,
even though it is not expressly forbidden in the law.—Ver. 6.
" *If thy father should miss me, then say, David hath asked permission of me to hasten to Bethlehem, his native town; for there is
a yearly sacrifice for the whole family there.*" This ground of
excuse shows that families and households were accustomed to

keep united sacrificial feasts once a year. According to the law
in Deut. xii. 5 sqq., they ought to have been kept at the tabernacle; but at this time, when the central sanctuary had fallen
into disuse, they were held in different places, wherever there
were altars of Jehovah—as, for example, at Bethlehem (cf. ch.
xvi. 2 sqq.). We see from these words that David did not look
upon prevarication as a sin.—Ver. 7. *"If thy father says, It is
well, there is peace to thy servant (i.e.* he cherishes no murderous
thoughts against me); *but if he be very wroth, know that evil is
determined by him."* כָּלָה, to be completed; hence to be firmly
and unalterably determined (cf. ch. xxv. 17; Esther vii. 7). Seb.
Schmidt infers from the closing words that the fact was certain
enough to David, but not to Jonathan. Thenius, on the other
hand, observes much more correctly, that "it is perfectly obvious
from this that David was not quite clear as to Saul's intentions,"
though he upsets his own previous assertion, that after what
David had gone through, he could never think of sitting again
at the king's table as he had done before.—Ver. 8. David made
sure that Jonathan would grant this request on account of his
friendship, as he had *brought him into a covenant of Jehovah
with himself.* David calls the covenant of friendship with
Jonathan (ch. xviii. 3) a *covenant of Jehovah,* because he had
made it with a solemn invocation of Jehovah. But in order to
make quite sure of the fulfilment of his request on the part of
Jonathan, David added, *" But if there is a fault in me, do thou
kill me* (אַתָּה used to strengthen the suffix); *for why wilt thou
bring me to thy father?"* sc. that he may put me to death.—
Ver. 9. Jonathan replied, *" This be far from thee!"* sc. that I
should kill thee, or deliver thee up to my father. חָלִילָה points
back to what precedes, as in ver. 2. *" But* (כִּי after a previous
negative assertion) *if I certainly discover that evil is determined
by my father to come upon thee, and I do not tell it thee,"* sc.
" may God do so to me," etc. The words are to be understood
as an asseveration on oath, in which the formula of an oath is
to be supplied in thought. This view is apparently a more
correct one, on account of the cop. ו before לֹא, than to take
the last clause as a question, " Shall I not tell it thee?"—Ver.
10. To this friendly assurance David replied, *" Who will tell
me?"* sc. how thy father expresses himself concerning me; *" or
what will thy father answer thee roughly?"* sc. if thou shouldst

attempt to do it thyself. This is the correct explanation given by De Wette and Maurer. Gesenius and Thenius, on the contrary, take אִם in the sense of "*if perchance.*" But this is evidently incorrect; for even though there are certain passages in which אִם may be so rendered, it is only where some other case is supposed, and therefore the meaning *or* still lies at the foundation. These questions of David were suggested by a correct estimate of the circumstances, namely, that Saul's suspicions would leave him to the conclusion that there was some understanding between Jonathan and David, and that he would take steps in consequence to prevent Jonathan from making David acquainted with the result of his conversation with Saul.—Ver. 11. Before replying to these questions, Jonathan asked David to go with him to the field, that they might there fix upon the sign by which he would let him know, in a way in which no one could suspect, what was the state of his father's mind.

Vers. 12–23. In the field, where they were both entirely free from observation, Jonathan first of all renewed his covenant with David, by vowing to him on oath that he would give him information of his father's feelings towards him (vers. 12, 13); and then entreated him, with a certain presentiment that David would one day be king, even then to maintain his love towards him and his family for ever (vers. 14–16); and lastly, he made David swear again concerning his love (ver. 17), and then gave him the sign by which he would communicate the promised information (vers. 18–23).—Vers. 12 and 13*a* are connected. Jonathan commences with a solemn invocation of God: "*Jehovah, God of Israel!*" and thus introduces his oath. We have neither to supply "Jehovah is *witness*," nor "as truly as Jehovah *liveth*," as some have suggested. "*When I inquire of my father about this time to-morrow, the day after to-morrow* (a concise mode of saying 'to-morrow or the day after'), *and behold it is* (stands) *well for David, and then I do not send to thee and make it known to thee, Jehovah shall do so to Jonathan,*" etc. ("The Lord do so," etc., the ordinary formula used in an oath: see ch. xiv. 44). The other case is then added without an adversative particle: "*If it should please my father evil against thee* (*lit.* as regards evil), *I will make it known to thee, and let thee go, that thou mayest go in peace; and Jehovah be with thee, as He has been with my father.*" In this wish there is

expressed the presentiment that David would one day occupy
that place in Israel which Saul occupied then, *i.e.* the throne.
—In vers. 14 and 15 the Masoretic text gives no appropriate
meaning. Luther's rendering, in which he follows the Rabbins
and takes the first וְלֹא (ver. 14) by itself, and then completes
the sentence from the context ("but if I do it not, show me no
mercy, because I live, not even if I die"), contains indeed a
certain permissible sense when considered in itself; but it is
hardly reconcilable with what follows, "*and do not tear away
thy compassion for ever from my house.*" The request that he
would show no compassion to him (Jonathan) even if he died,
and yet would not withdraw his compassion from his house for
ever, contains an antithesis which would have been expressed
most clearly and unambiguously in the words themselves, if this
had been really what Jonathan intended to say. De Wette's
rendering gives a still more striking contradiction : "*But let not*
(Jehovah be with thee) *if I still live, and thou showest not the
love of Jehovah to me, that I die not, and thou withdrawest not
thy love from my house for ever.*" There is really no other
course open than to follow the Syriac and Arabic, as Maurer,
Thenius, and Ewald have done, and change the וְלֹא in the first
two clauses of ver. 14 into וְלוּ or וְלֻא, according to the analogy
of the form לוּא (ch. xiv. 30), and to render the passage thus :
"And mayest thou, if I still live, mayest thou show to me the
favour of the Lord, and not if I die, not withdraw thy favour
from my house for ever, not even (וְלֹא) when Jehovah shall cut
off the enemies of David, every one from the face of the earth!"
"*The favour of Jehovah*" is favour such as Jehovah shows to
His people. The expression "when Jehovah shall cut off,"
etc., shows very clearly Jonathan's conviction that Jehovah
would give to David a victory over all his enemies.—Ver.
16. Thus Jonathan concluded a covenant with the house of
David, namely, by bringing David to promise kindness to his
family for ever. The word בְּרִית must be supplied in thought
to יִכְרֹת, as in ch. xxii. 8 and 2 Chron. vii. 18. "*And Jehovah
required it* (what Jonathan had predicted) *at the hand of
David's enemies.*" Understood in this manner, the second
clause contains a remark of the historian himself, namely, that
Jonathan's words were really fulfilled in due time. The
traditional rendering of וּבִקֵּשׁ as a relative preterite, with אָמַר

understood, " *and said, Let Jehovah take vengeance*," is not only
precluded by the harshness of the introduction of the word
"saying," but still more by the fact, that if אָמַר (saying) is
introduced between the copula *vav* and the verb בִּקֵּשׁ, the
perfect cannot stand for the optative בְּקֵּשׁ, as in Josh. xxii. 23.
—Ver. 17. " *And Jonathan adjured David again by his love to
him, because he loved him as his own soul*" (cf. ch. xviii. 1, 3);
i.e. he once more implored David most earnestly with an oath
to show favour to him and his house.—Vers. 18 sqq. He then
discussed the sign with him for letting him know about his
father's state of mind : " *To-morrow is new moon, and thou wilt
be missed, for thy seat will be empty*," *sc.* at Saul's table (see
at ver. 5). " *And on the third day come down quickly* (from
thy sojourning place), *and go to the spot where thou didst hide
thyself on the day of the deed, and place thyself by the side of
the stone Ezel.*" The first words in this (19th) verse are not
without difficulty. The meaning " on the third day" for the
verb שָׁלֵשׁ cannot be sustained by parallel passages, but is fully
established, partly by הַשְּׁלִשִׁית, the third day, and partly by the
Arabic usage (*vid.* Ges. *Thes. s. v.*). מָאֹד after תֵּרֵד, *lit.* " *go
violently down*," is more striking still. Nevertheless the correctness of the text is not to be called in question, since שִׁלַּשְׁתָּ
is sustained by τρισσεύσει in the Septuagint, and תֵּרֵד מָאֹד by
descende ergo festinus in the Vulgate, and also by the rendering
in the Chaldee, Arabic, and Syriac versions, " and on the third
day thou wilt be missed still more," which is evidently merely
a conjecture founded upon the context. The meaning of
בְּיוֹם הַמַּעֲשֶׂה is doubtful. Gesenius, De Wette, and Maurer
render it " on the day of the deed," and understand it as referring to Saul's deed mentioned in ch. xix. 2, viz. his design of
killing David ; others render it " on the day of business," *i.e.*
the working day (Luther, after the LXX. and Vulgate), but
this is not so good a rendering. The best is probably that of
Thenius, " on the day of the business" (which is known to thee).
Nothing further can be said concerning the stone Ezel than
that Ezel is a proper name.—Ver. 20. " *And I will shoot off
three arrows to the side of it* (the stone Ezel), *to shoot for me at
the mark*," *i.e.* as if shooting at the mark. The article attached
to הַחִצִּים is either to be explained as denoting that the historian
assumed the thing as already well known, or on the supposition

that Jonathan went to the field armed, and when giving the sign pointed to the arrows in his quiver. In the word צִדָּה the *Raphe* indicates that the suffix of הָ— is not a mere toneless ה, although it has no mappik, having given up its strong breathing on account of the harsh צ sound.—Ver. 21. "*And, behold* (הִנֵּה, directing attention to what follows as the main point), *I will send the boy* (saying), *Go, get the arrows. If I shall say to the boy, Behold, the arrows are from thee hitherwards, fetch them; then come, for peace is to thee, and it is nothing, as truly as Jehovah liveth.*"—Ver. 22. "*But if I say to the youth, Behold, the arrows are from thee farther off; then go, for Jehovah sendeth thee away,*" *i.e.* bids thee flee. The appointment of this sign was just as simple as it was suitable to the purpose.—Ver. 23. This arrangement was to remain an eternal secret between them. "*And* (as for) *the word that we have spoken, I and thou, behold, the Lord is between me and thee for ever,*" namely, a witness and judge in case one of us two should break the covenant (*vid.* Gen. xxxi. 48, 49). This is implied in the words, without there being any necessity to assume that עֵד had dropped out of the text. "*The word*" refers not merely to the sign agreed upon, but to the whole matter, including the renewal of the bond of friendship.

Vers. 24–34. David thereupon concealed himself in the field, whilst Jonathan, as agreed upon, endeavoured to apologize for his absence from the king's table.—Vers. 24, 25. On the new moon's day Saul sat at table, and as always, *at his seat by the wall*, *i.e.* at the top, just as, in eastern lands at the present day, the place of honour is the seat in the corner (see *Harmar Beobachtungen* ii. pp. 66 sqq.). "*And Jonathan rose up, and Abner seated himself by the side of Saul, and David's place remained empty.*" The difficult passage, "*And Jonathan rose up,*" etc., can hardly be understood in any other way than as signifying that, when Abner entered, Jonathan rose from his seat by the side of Saul, and gave up the place to Abner, in which case all that is wanting is an account of the place to which Jonathan moved. Every other attempted explanation is exposed to much graver difficulties. The suggestion made by Gesenius, that the cop. וְ should be supplied before אַבְנֵר, and וַיֵּשֶׁב referred to Jonathan ("and Jonathan rose up and sat down, and Abner (sat down) by the side of Saul"), as in the Syriac, is open to this objection, that in addition to the necessity of supplying ו, it is impossible to see why Jonathan should have risen up for the purpose of sitting down again. The rendering " and Jonathan came," which is the one adopted by Maurer and De Wette, cannot be philologically sustained; inasmuch as, although קוּם is used to signify rise up, in the sense of the occurrence of important events, or the appearance of celebrated persons, it never means simply "to come." And lastly, the conjecture of Thenius, that וַיָּקָם should be altered into וַיְקַדֵּם, according to the senseless rendering of the LXX., προέφθασε τὸν Ἰονάθαν, is overthrown by the fact, that whilst קִדֵּם does indeed mean to anticipate or come to meet, it never means to sit in front of, i.e. opposite to a person.—Ver. 26. On this (first) day Saul said nothing, sc. about David's absenting himself, "for he thought there has (something) happened to him, that he is not clean; surely (כִּי) he is not clean" (vid. Lev. xv. 16 sqq.; Deut. xxiii. 11).—Vers. 27 sqq. But on the second day, the day after the new moon (lit. the morrow after the new moon, the second day: הַשֵּׁנִי is a nominative, and to be joined to וַיְהִי, and not a genitive belonging to הַחֹדֶשׁ), when David was absent from table again, Saul said to Jonathan, " Why is the son of Jesse not come to meat, neither yesterday nor to-day?" Whereupon Jonathan answered, as arranged with David (compare vers. 28 and 29 with ver. 6). " And my brother, he hath commanded me," i.e. ordered me to come. צִוָּה as in Ex. vi. 13, and אָחִי, the elder brother, who was then at the head of the family, and arranged the sacrificial meal.—Vers. 30, 31. Saul was greatly enraged at this, and said to Jonathan, " Son of a perverse woman (נַעֲוַת is a participle, Niph. fem. from עָוָה) of rebellion,"—i.e. son of a perverse and rebellious woman (an insult offered to the mother, and therefore so much the greater to the son), hence the meaning really is, "Thou perverse, rebellious fellow,"—"do I not know that thou hast chosen the son of Jesse to thine own shame, and to the shame of thy mother's nakedness?" בָּחַר, to choose a person out of love, to take pleasure in a person; generally construed with בְּ pers., here with לְ, although many Codd. have בְּ here also. "For as long as the son of Jesse liveth upon the earth, thou and thy kingdom (kingship, throne) will not stand." Thus Saul evidently suspected David as his rival, who would either wrest the

government from him, or at any rate after his death from his
son. " *Now send and fetch him to me, for he is a child of death,*"
i.e. he has deserved to die, and shall be put to death.—Vers.
32 sqq. When Jonathan replied, " *My father, why shall he die?
what has he done?*" Saul was so enraged that he hurled his
javelin at Jonathan (cf. ch. xviii. 11). Thus Jonathan saw
that his father had firmly resolved to put David to death, and
rose up from the table in fierce anger, and did not eat that day ;
for he was grieved concerning David, because his father had
done him shame. כָּלָה is a substantive in the sense of unalter-
able resolution, like the verb in ver. 9. בְּיוֹם־הַחֹדֶשׁ הַשֵּׁנִי, on the
second day of the new moon or month.

Vers. 35–42. The next morning Jonathan made David
acquainted with what had occurred, by means of the sign agreed
upon with David. The account of this, and of the meeting
between Jonathan and David which followed, is given very
concisely, only the main points being touched upon. In the
morning (after what had occurred) Jonathan went to the field,
לְמוֹעֵד דָּוִד, either " *at the time agreed upon with David,*" or " *to
the meeting with David,*" or perhaps better still, " *according to
the appointment* (agreement) *with David,*" and a small boy with
him.—Ver. 36. To the latter he said, namely as soon as they
had come to the field, Run, get the arrows which I shoot. The
boy ran, and he shot off the arrows, " *to go out beyond him,*" *i.e.*
so that the arrows flew farther than the boy had run. The form
חֵצִי for חֵץ only occurs in connection with disjunctive accents ;
beside the present chapter (vers. 36, 37, 38, *Chethibh*) we find
it again in 2 Kings ix. 24. The singular is used here with
indefinite generality, as the historian did not consider it necessary to mention expressly, after what he had previously written,
that Jonathan shot off three arrows one after another.—Ver. 37.
When the boy came to the place of the shot arrow (*i.e.* to the
place to which the arrow had flown), Jonathan called after him,
" *See, the arrow is* (lies) *away from thee, farther off ;*" and again,
" *Quickly, haste, do not stand still,*" that he might not see David,
who was somewhere near ; and the boy picked up the arrow and
came to his lord. The *Chethibh* הַחֵצִי is evidently the original
reading, and the singular is to be understood as in ver. 37 ;
the *Keri* הַחִצִּים is an emendation, according to the meaning of
the words. The writer here introduces the remark in ver. 39,

that the boy knew nothing of what had been arranged between Jonathan and David.—Ver. 40. Jonathan then gave the boy his things (bow, arrows, and quiver), and sent him with them to the town, that he might be able to converse with David for a few seconds after his departure, and take leave of him unobserved.—Ver. 41. When the boy had gone, *David rose* (from his hiding-place) *from the south side, fell down upon his face to the ground, and bowed three times* (before Jonathan); they then kissed each other, and wept for one another, "*till David wept strongly,*" *i.e.* to such a degree that David wept very loud. מֵאֵצֶל הַנֶּגֶב, "*from the side of the south,*" which is the expression used to describe David's hiding-place, according to its direction in relation to the place where Jonathan was standing, has not been correctly rendered by any of the early translators except Aquila and Jerome. In the Septuagint, the Chaldee, the Syriac, and the Arabic, the statement in ver. 19 is repeated, simply because the translators could not see the force of מֵאֵצֶל הַנֶּגֶב, although it is intelligible enough in relation to what follows, according to which David fled from thence *southwards to Nob.*—Ver. 42. All that is given of the conversation between the two friends is the parting word spoken by Jonathan to David: "*Go in peace. What we two have sworn in the name of the Lord, saying, The Lord be between me and thee, and between my seed and thy seed for ever:*" *sc.* let it stand, or let us abide by it. The clause contains an aposiopesis, which may be accounted for from Jonathan's deep emotion, and in which the apodosis may be gathered from the sense. For it is evident, from a comparison of ver. 23, that the expression "for ever" must be understood as forming part of the oath.—Ch. xxi. 1. David then set out upon his journey, and Jonathan returned to the town. This verse ought, strictly speaking, to form the conclusion of ch. xx.[1] The subject to "*arose*" is David; not because Jonathan was the last one spoken of (Thenius), but because the following words, "and Jonathan came," etc., are in evident antithesis to "he arose and went."

[1] In our English version it does; but in the Hebrew, which is followed here, it forms the opening verse of ch. xxi. In the exposition of the following chapter it has been thought better to follow the numbering of the verses in our version rather than that of the original, although the latter is conformed to the Hebrew.—TR.

DAVID'S FLIGHT TO NOB, AND THENCE TO GATH.
CHAP. XXI. 2-16.

After the information which David had received from Jonathan, nothing remained for him in order to save his life but immediate flight. He could not return to the prophets at Ramah, where he had been miraculously preserved from the first outbreak of Saul's wrath, because they could not ensure him permanent protection against the death with which he was threatened. He therefore fled first of all to Nob, to Ahimelech the high priest, to inquire the will of God through him concerning his future course (ch. xxii. 10, 15), and induced him to give him bread and the sword of Goliath also, under the pretext of having to perform a secret commission from the king with the greatest speed ; for which Saul afterwards took fearful vengeance upon the priests at Nob when he was made acquainted with the affair through the treachery of Doeg (vers. 1–9). David then fled to Gath to the Philistian king Achish ; but here he was quickly recognised as the conqueror of Goliath, and obliged to feign insanity in order to save his life, and then to flee still farther (vers. 10–15). The state of his mind at this time he poured out before God in the words of Ps. lvi., lii., and xxxiv.

Vers. 1–9. *David at Nob.*—The town of *Nob* or *Nobeh* (unless indeed the form נֹבֶה stands for נֹבָה here and in ch. xxii. 9, and the ה attached is merely ה local, as the name is always written נֹב in other places : *vid.* ch. xxii. 11, 32 ; 2 Sam. xxi. 16 ; Isa. x. 32 ; Neh. xi. 32) was at that time a priests' city (ch. xxii. 19), in which, according to the following account, the tabernacle was then standing, and the legal worship carried on. According to Isa. x. 30, 32, it was between Anathoth (*Anata*) and Jerusalem, and in all probability it has been preserved in the village of *el-Isawiyeh, i.e.* probably the village of Esau or Edom, which is midway between Anata and Jerusalem, an hour from the latter, and the same distance to the south-east of Gibeah of Saul (Tell el Phul), and which bears all the marks of an ancient place, partly in its dwellings, the stones of which date from a great antiquity, and partly in many marble columns which are found there (*vid.* Tobler, *Topogr. v. Jerusalem* ii. p. 720). Hence v. Raumer (*Pal.* p. 215, ed. 4) follows Kiepert in the map which he has appended to Robinson's *Biblical Re-searches*, and set down this place as the ancient *Nob*, for which Robinson indeed searched in vain (see *Pal.* ii. p. 150). Ahime-lech, the son of Ahitub, most probably the same person as Ahiah (ch. xiv. 3), was "*the priest*," *i.e.* the high priest (see at ch. xiv. 3). When David came to him, the priest "*went trem-bling to meet him*" (יֶחֱרַד לִקְרַאת) with the inquiry, " *Why art thou alone, and no one is with thee ?*" The unexpected appearance of David, the son-in-law of the king, without any attendants, alarmed Ahimelech, who probably imagined that he had come with a commission from the king which might involve him in danger. David had left the few servants who accompanied him in his flight somewhere in the neighbourhood, as we may gather from ver. 2, because he wished to converse with the high priest alone. Ahimelech's anxious inquiry led David to resort to the fabrication described in ver. 2 : " *The king hath commanded me a business, and said to me, No one is to know anything of this matter, in which* (*lit.* in relation to the matter with regard to which) *I send thee, and which I have entrusted to thee* (*i.e.* no one is to know either the occasion or the nature of the commission): *and the servants I have directed to such and such a place.*" יוֹדַע, *Poel*, to cause to know, point, show. Ahimelech had re-ceived no information as yet concerning the most recent occur-rences between Saul and David ; and David would not confess to him that he was fleeing from Saul, because he was evidently afraid that the high priest would not give him any assistance, lest he should draw down the wrath of the king. This false-hood brought the greatest calamities upon Ahimelech and the priests at Nob (ch. xxii. 9–19), and David was afterwards obliged to confess that he had occasioned it all (ch. xxii. 22).— Ver. 3. "*And now what is under thy hand ? give into my hand* (*i.e.* hand me) *five loaves, or whatever* (else) *is to be found.*" David asked for five loaves, because he had spoken of several attendants, and probably wanted to make provision for two or three days (Thenius).—Ver. 4. The priest answered that he had no common bread, but only holy bread, viz., according to ver. 6, shew-bread that had been removed, which none but priests were allowed to eat, and that in a sacred place ; but that he was willing to give him some of these loaves, as David had said that he was travelling upon an important mission from the king, provided only that " *the young men had kept themselves at least from women*," *i.e.* had not been defiled by sexual inter-course (Lev. xv. 18). If they were clean at any rate in this respect, he would in such a case of necessity depart from the Levitical law concerning the eating of the shew-bread, for the sake of observing the higher commandment of love to a neigh-bour (Lev. xix. 18 ; cf. Matt. xii. 5, 6, Mark ii. 25, 26).[1]—Ver. 5. David quieted him concerning this scruple, and said, " *Nay, but women have been kept from us since yesterday and the day before.*" The use of כִּי אִם may be explained from the fact, that in David's reply he paid more attention to the sense than to the form of the priest's scruple, and expressed himself as concisely as possible. The words, " if the young men have only kept themselves from women," simply meant, if only they are not unclean ; and David replied, That is certainly not the case, *but* women have been kept from us ; so that כִּי אִם has the meaning *but* in this passage also, as it frequently has after a previous negative, which is implied in the thought here as in 2 Sam. xiii. 33. " *When I came out, the young men's things were holy* (Levitically clean) ; *and if it is an unholy way, it becomes even holy through the instrument.*" David does not say that the young men were clean when he came out (for the rendering given to כְּלִי הַנְּעָרִים in the Septuagint, πάντα τὰ παιδάρια, is without any critical value, and is only a mistaken attempt to explain the word כְּלִי, which was unintelligible to the translator), but simply affirms that כְּלִי הַנְּעָרִים קֹדֶשׁ, *i.e.*, according to Luther's rendering (*der Knaben Zeug war heilig*), the young men's things (clothes, etc.) were holy. כֵּלִים does not mean merely vessels, arms, or tools, but also the dress (Deut. xxii. 5), or rather the clothes as well as such things as were most necessary to meet the wants of life. By the *coitus*, or strictly speaking, by the *emissio seminis* in connection with the *coitus*, not only were the persons themselves defiled, but also every article of clothing or leather upon which any of the *semen* fell (Lev. xv. 18) ; so that it was necessary for the purpose of purification that the things which a man had on should all be washed. David ex-plains, with evident allusion to this provision, that the young

---

[1] When Mark (ii. 26) assigns this action to the days of Abiathar the high priest, the statement rests upon an error of memory, in which Ahime-lech is confounded with Abiathar.

men's things were holy, *i.e.* perfectly clean, for the purpose of assuring the priest that there was not the smallest Levitical uncleanness attaching to them. The clause which follows is to be taken as conditional, and as supposing a possible case : " *and if it is an unholy way.*" דֶּרֶךְ, the way that David was going with his young men, *i.e.* his purpose or enterprise, by which, however, we are not to understand his request of holy bread from Ahimelech, but the performance of the king's commission of which he had spoken. וְאַף כִּי, *lit.* besides (there is) also that, = moreover there is also the fact, that it becomes holy through the instrument; *i.e.*, as O. v. Gerlach has correctly explained it, " on the supposition of the important royal mission, upon which David pretended to be sent, *through me* as an ambassador of the anointed of the Lord," in which, at any rate, David's meaning really was, "the way was sanctified before God, when he, as His chosen servant, the preserver of the true kingdom of God in Israel, went to him in his extremity." That כְּלִי in the sense of instrument is also applied to *men*, is evident from Isa. xiii. 5 and Jer. l. 25.—Ver. 6. The priest then gave him (what was) holy, namely the shew-loaves "*that were taken from before Jehovah,*" *i.e.* from the holy table, upon which they had lain before Jehovah for seven days (*vid.* Lev. xxiv. 6–9).—In ver. 7 there is a parenthetical remark introduced, which was of great importance in relation to the consequences of this occurrence. There at the sanctuary there was a man of Saul's servants, נֶעְצָר, *i.e.* " *kept back* (shut off) *before Jehovah :*" *i.e.* at the sanctuary of the tabernacle, either for the sake of purification or as a proselyte, who wished to be received into the religious communion of Israel, or because of supposed leprosy, according to Lev. xiii. 4. His name was Doeg the Edomite, אַבִּיר הָרֹעִים, " *the strong one (i.e.* the overseer) *of the herdsmen of Saul.*"[1]—Ver. 8.

---

[1] The Septuagint translators have rendered these words νέμων τὰς ἡμιόνους, " feeding the mules of Saul ;" and accordingly in ch. xxii. 9 also they have changed Saul's servants into mules, in accordance with which Thenius makes Doeg the upper herdsman of Saul. But it is very evident that the text of the LXX. is nothing more than a subjective interpretation of the expression before us, and does not presuppose any other text, from the simple fact that all the other ancient versions are founded upon the Hebrew text both here and in ch. xxii. 9, including even the Vulgate (*potentissimus pastorum*) ; and the clause contained in some of the MSS. of the Vulgate (*hic pascebat mulas Saul*) is nothing more than a gloss that has

David also asked Ahimelech whether he had not a sword or a javelin at hand ; "*for I have neither brought my sword nor my* (other) *weapons with me, because the affair of the king was pressing*," *i.e.* very urgent, נָחוּץ, ἀπ. λεγ., literally, compressed.—Ver. 9. The priest replied, that there was only the sword of Goliath, whom David slew in the terebinth valley (ch. xvii. 2), wrapped up in a cloth hanging behind the ephod (the high priest's shoulder-dress),—a sign of the great worth attached to this dedicatory offering. He could take that. David accepted it, as a weapon of greater value to him than any other, because he had not only taken this sword as booty from the Philistine, but had cut off the head of Goliath with it (see ch. xvii. 51). When and how this sword had come into the tabernacle is not known (see the remarks on ch. xvii. 54). The form בְּזֶה for בָּזֶה is only met with here. On the *Piska*, see at Josh. iv. 1.

Vers. 10–15. *David with Achish at Gath.*—David fled from Nob to Achish of Gath. This Philistian king is called *Abimelech* in the heading of Ps. xxxiv., according to the standing title of the Philistian princes at Gath. The fact that David fled at once out of the land, and that to the Philistines at Gath, may be accounted for from the great agitation into which he had been thrown by the information he had received from Jonathan concerning Saul's implacable hatred. As some years had passed since the defeat of Goliath, and the conqueror of Goliath was probably not personally known to many of the Philistines, he might hope that he should not be recognised in Gath, and that he might receive a welcome there with his few attendants, as a fugitive who had been driven away by Saul, the leading foe of the Philistines.[1] But in this he

crept in from the Itala ; and this is still more obvious in ch. xxii. 9, where וְהוּא נִצָּב is applicable enough to עַבְדֵי, but is altogether unsuitable in connection with פַּרְדֵי, since נָצַב is no more applied in Hebrew to herdsmen or keepers of animals, than we should think of speaking of presidents of asses, horses, etc. Moreover, it is not till the reign of David that we read of mules being used as riding animals by royal princes (2 Sam. xiii. 29, xviii. 9) ; and they are mentioned for the first time as beasts of burden, along with asses, camels, and oxen, in 1 Chron. xii. 40, where they are said to have been employed by the northern tribes to carry provisions to Hebron to the festival held at the recognition of David as king. Before David's time the sons of princes rode upon asses (*vid.* Judg. x. 4, xii. 14).

[1] This removes the objection raised by modern critics to the historical

was mistaken. He was recognised at once by the courtiers of Achish. They said to their prince, " *Is not this David the king of the land? Have they not sung in circles, Saul hath slain his thousands, and David his ten thousands?*" (cf. ch. xviii. 6, 7.) "*King of the land*" they call David, not because his anointing and divine election were known to them, but on account of his victorious deeds, which had thrown Saul entirely into the shade. Whether they intended by these words to celebrate David as a hero, or to point him out to their prince as a dangerous man, cannot be gathered from the words themselves, nor can the question be decided with certainty at all (cf. ch. xxix. 5).—Ver. 12. But David took these words to heart, and was in great fear of Achish, lest he should treat him as an enemy, and kill him. In order to escape this danger, "*he disguised his understanding (i.e.* pretended to be out of his mind) *in their eyes (i.e.* before the courtiers of Achish), *behaved insanely under their hands* (when they tried to hold him as a madman), *scribbled upon the door-wings, and let his spittle run down into his beard.*" The suffix to וַיְשַׁנּוֹ is apparently superfluous, as the object, אֶת־טַעְמוֹ, follows immediately afterwards. But it may be accounted for from the circumstantiality of the conversation of every-day life, as in 2 Sam. xiv. 6, and (though these cases are not perfectly parallel) Ex. ii. 6, Prov. v. 22, Ezek. x. 3 (cf. Gesenius' *Gramm.* § 121, 6, Anm. 3). וַיְתָו, from תָּוָה, to make signs, *i.e.* to scribble. The Sept.

credibility of the narrative before us, namely, that David would certainly not have taken refuge at once with the Philistines, but would only have gone to them in the utmost extremity (Thenius). It is impossible to see how the words "he fled *that day for fear of Saul*" (ver. 11) are to prove that this section originally stood in a different connection, and are only arbitrarily inserted here (Thenius). Unless we tear away the words in the most arbitrary manner from the foregoing word וַיִּבְרַח, they not only appear quite suitable, but even necessary, since David's journey to Abimelech was not a flight, or at all events it is not described as a flight in the text; and David's flight from Saul really began with his departure from Nob. Still less can the legendary origin of this account be inferred from the fact that some years afterwards David really did take refuge with Achish in the Philistian country (ch. xxvii. and xxix.), or the conjecture sustained that this is only a distorted legend of that occurrence. For if the later sojourn of David with Achish be a historical fact, the popular legend could not possibly have assumed a form so utterly different as the account before us, to say nothing of the fact that this occurrence has a firm historical support in Ps. xxxiv. 1.

and Vulgate render it ἐτυμπάνιζειν, impingebat, he drummed, smote with his fists upon the wings of the door, which would make it appear as if they had read וַיֵּתָו (from תָּפַף), which seems more suitable to the condition of a madman whose saliva ran out of his mouth.—Vers. 14, 15. By this dissimulation David escaped the danger which threatened him; for Achish thought him mad, and would have nothing to do with him. "Wherefore do ye bring him to me? Have I need of madmen, that ye have brought this man hither to rave against me? Shall this man come into my house?" Thus Achish refused to receive him into his house. But whether he had David taken over the border, or at any rate out of the town; or whether David went away of his own accord; or whether he was taken away by his servants, and then hurried as quickly as possible out of the land of the Philistines, is not expressly mentioned, as being of no importance in relation to the principal object of the narrative. All that is stated is, that he departed thence, and escaped to the cave Adullam.

DAVID'S WANDERINGS IN JUDAH AND MOAB.   MASSACRE OF
PRIESTS BY SAUL.—CHAP. XXII.

Vers. 1–5. Having been driven away by Achish, the Philistian king at Gath, David took refuge in the cave Adullam, where his family joined him. The cave Adullam is not to be sought for in the neighbourhood of Bethlehem, as some have inferred from 2 Sam. xxiii. 13, 14, but near the town Adullam, which is classed in Josh. xv. 35 among the towns in the lowlands of Judah, and at the foot of the mountains; though it has not yet been traced with any certainty, as the caves of Deir Dubban, of which Van de Velde speaks, are not the only large caves on the western slope of the mountains of Judah. When his brethren and his father's house, i.e. the rest of his family, heard of his being there, they came down to him, evidently because they no longer felt themselves safe in Bethlehem from Saul's revenge. The cave Adullam cannot have been more than three hours from Bethlehem, as Socoh and Jarmuth, which were near to Adullam, were only three hours and a half from Jerusalem (see at Josh. xii. 15).—Ver. 2. There a large number of malcontents gathered together round David, viz. all who

were in distress, and all who had creditors, and all who were embittered in spirit (bitter of soul), *i.e.* people who were dissatisfied with the general state of affairs or with the government of
Saul,—about four hundred men, whose leader he became. David
must in all probability have stayed there a considerable time.
The number of those who went over to him soon amounted to
six hundred men (xxiii. 13), who were for the most part brave
and reckless, and who ripened into heroic men under the command of David during his long flight. A list of the bravest of
them is given in 1 Chron. xii., with which compare 2 Sam.
xxiii. 13 sqq. and 1 Chron. xi. 15 sqq. — Vers. 3–5. David
proceeded thence to *Mizpeh* in Moab, and placed his parents
in safety with the king of the Moabites. His ancestress Ruth
was a Moabitess. *Mizpeh :* literally a watch-tower or mountain
height commanding a very extensive prospect. Here it is
probably a proper name, belonging to a mountain fastness on
the high land, which bounded the Arboth Moab on the eastern
side of the Dead Sea, most likely on the mountains of Abarim
or Pisgah (Deut. xxxiv. 1), and which could easily be reached
from the country round Bethlehem, by crossing the Jordan near
the point where it entered the Dead Sea. As David came to
the king of Moab, the Moabites had probably taken possession
of the most southerly portion of the eastern lands of the Israelites; we may also infer this from the fact that, according to ch.
xiv. 47, Saul had also made war upon Moab, for *Mizpeh Moab*
is hardly to be sought for in the actual land of the Moabites, on
the south side of the Arnon (Mojeb). אֶתְכֶם . . . יֵצֵא־נָא, " *May
my father and my mother go out with you.*" The construction
of יֵצֵא with אֵת is a pregnant one : to go out of their home and
stay with you (Moabites). " *Till I know what God will do to
me.*" Being well assured of the justice of his cause, as contrasted with the insane persecutions of Saul, David confidently
hoped that God would bring his flight to an end. His parents
remained with the king of Moab as long as David was בַּמְּצוּדָה,
i.e. upon the mountain height, or citadel. This can only refer
to the place of refuge which David had found at Mizpeh Moab.
For it is perfectly clear from ver. 5, where the prophet Gad
calls upon David not to remain any longer בַּמְּצוּדָה, but to return
to the land of Judah, that the expression cannot refer either
to the cave Adullam, or to any other place of refuge in the

neighbourhood of Bethlehem. The prophet *Gad* had probably come to David from Samuel's school of prophets; but whether he remained with David from that time forward to assist him with his counsel in his several undertakings, cannot be determined, on account of our want of information. In 1 Chron. xxi. 9 he is called David's seer. In the last year of David's reign he announced to him the punishment which would fall upon him from God on account of his sin in numbering the people (2 Sam. xxiv. 11 sqq.); and according to 1 Chron. xxix. 29 he also wrote the acts of David. In consequence of this admonition, David returned to Judah, and went into the wood *Hareth,* a woody region on the mountains of Judah, which is never mentioned again, and the situation of which is unknown. According to the counsels of God, David was not to seek for refuge outside the land; not only that he might not be estranged from his fatherland and the people of Israel, which would have been opposed to his calling to be the king of Israel, but also that he might learn to trust entirely in the Lord as his only refuge and fortress.

Vers. 6–23. Murder of the Priests by Saul.—Vers. 6 sqq. When Saul heard that David and the men with him *were known, i.e.* that information had been received as to their abode or hiding-place, he said to his servants when they were gathered round him, "*Hear,*" etc. The words, "*and Saul was sitting at Gibeah under the tamarisk upon the height,*" etc., show that what follows took place in a solemn conclave of all the servants of Saul, who were gathered round their king to deliberate upon the more important affairs of the kingdom. This sitting took place at Gibeah, the residence of Saul, and in the open air "*under the tamarisk.*" בָּרָמָה, *upon the height,* not "under a grove at Ramah" (*Luther*); for *Ramah* is an appellative, and בָּרָמָה, which belongs to תַּחַת הָאֶשֶׁל, is a more minute definition of the locality, which is indicated by the definite article (*the* tamarisk upon *the* height) as the well-known place where Saul's deliberative assemblies were held. From the king's address ("*hear, ye Benjaminites; will the son of Jesse also give you all fields and vineyards?*") we perceive that Saul had chosen his immediate attendants from the members of his own tribe, and had rewarded their services right royally.

נֵּם־לְכֻלְּכֶם is placed first for the sake of emphasis, " *You Ben-jaminites also,*" and not rather to Judahites, the members of his own tribe. The second לְכֻלְּכֶם (before יִשִּׂים) is not a dative; but ל merely serves to give greater prominence to the object which is placed at the head of the clause: *As for all of you, will he make* (you: see Ewald, § 310, *a*).—Ver. 8. " *That you have all of you conspired against me, and no one informs me of it, since my son makes a covenant with the son of Jesse.*" בִּכְרֹת, *lit.* at the making of a covenant. Saul may possibly have heard something of the facts related in ch. xx. 12–17; at the same time, his words may merely refer to Jonathan's friendship with David, which was well known to him. וְאֵין־חֹלֶה, " *and no one of you is grieved on my account . . . that my son has set my servant* (David) *as a lier in wait against me,*" *i.e.* to plot against my life, and wrest the throne to himself. We may see from this, that Saul was carried by his suspicions very far beyond the actual facts. " *As at this day :*" cf. Deut. viii. 18, etc.—Vers. 9, 10. The Edomite Doeg could not refrain from yielding to this appeal, and telling Saul what he had seen when staying at Nob ; namely, that Ahimelech had inquired of God for David, and given him food as well as Goliath's sword. For the fact itself, see ch. xxi. 1–10, where there is no reference indeed to his inquiring of God; though it certainly took place, as Ahimelech (ver. 15) does not disclaim it. Doeg is here designated נִצָּב, " *the superintendent of Saul's servants,*" so that apparently he had been invested with the office of marshal of the court.—Vers. 11 sqq. On receiving this information, Saul immediately summoned the priest Ahimelech and " *all his father's house,*" *i.e.* the whole priesthood, to Nob, to answer for what they had done. To Saul's appeal, " *Why have ye conspired against me, thou and the son of Jesse, by giving him bread?*" Ahimelech, who was not conscious of any such crime, since David had come to him with a false pretext, and the priest had probably but very little knowledge of what took place at court, replied both calmly and worthily (ver. 14): " *And who of all thy servants is so faithful* (proved, attested, as, in Num. xii. 7) *as David, and son-in-law of the king, and having access to thy private audience, and honoured in thy house?*" The true explanation of סָר אֶל־מִשְׁמַעְתֶּךָ may be gathered from a comparison of 2 Sam. xxiii. 23 and 1 Chron. xi. 25, where מִשְׁמַעַת occurs

again, as the context clearly shows, in the sense of a privy councillor of the king, who hears his personal revelations and converses
with him about them, so that it corresponds to our " *audience*."
סוּר, *lit.* to turn aside from the way, to go in to any one, or to
look after anything (Ex. iii. 3; Ruth iv. 1, etc.); hence in the
passage before us " *to have access*," to be attached to a person.
This is the explanation given by Gesenius and most of the
modern expositors, whereas the early translators entirely misunderstood the passage, though they have given the meaning
correctly enough at 2 Sam. xxiii. 23. But if this was the
relation in which David stood to Saul,—and he had really done
so for a long time,—there was nothing wrong in what the high
priest had done for him; but he had acted according to the
best of his knowledge, and quite conscientiously as a faithful
subject of the king. Ahimelech then added still further (ver.
15): " *Did I then begin to inquire of God for him this day?*"
i.e. was it the first time that I had obtained the decision of God
for David concerning important enterprises, which he had to
carry out in the service of the king? " *Far be from me*," sc.
any conspiracy against the king, like that of which I am accused. " *Let not the king lay it as a burden upon thy servant,
my whole father's house* (the omission of the *cop.* ו before
בְּכָל-בֵּית may be accounted for from the excitement of the
speaker); *for thy servant knows not the least of all this.*"
בְּכָל-זֹאת, of all that Saul had charged him with.—Vers. 16, 17.
Notwithstanding this truthful assertion of his innocence, Saul
pronounced sentence of death, not only upon the high priest,
but upon all the priests at Nob, and commanded his רָצִים,
" *runners*," *i.e.* halberdiers, to put the priests to death, because,
as he declared in his wrath, " *their hand is with David* (*i.e.*
because they side with David), *and because they knew that he
fled and did not tell me.*" Instead of the *Chethibh* אָזְנוֹ, it is
probably more correct to read אָזְנִי, according to the *Keri*,
although the *Chethibh* may be accounted for if necessary from
a sudden transition from a direct to an indirect form of address: " *and* (as he said) *had not told him.*" This sentence
was so cruel, and so nearly bordering upon madness, that the
halberdiers would not carry it out, but refused to lay hands
upon " *the priests of Jehovah.*"—Ver. 18. Saul then commanded Doeg to cut down the priests, and he at once per-

formed the bloody deed. On the expression "*wearing the linen ephod*," compare the remarks at ch. ii. 18. The allusion to the priestly clothing, like the repetition of the expression "*priests of Jehovah*," serves to bring out into its true light the crime of the bloodthirsty Saul and his executioner Doeg. The very dress which the priests wore, as the consecrated servants of Jehovah, ought to have made them shrink from the commission of such a murder.—Ver. 19. But not content with even this revenge, Saul had the whole city of Nob destroyed, like a city that was laid under the ban (*vid.* Deut. xiii. 13 sqq.). So completely did Saul identify his private revenge with the cause of Jehovah, that he avenged a supposed conspiracy against his own person as treason against Jehovah the God-king.—Vers. 20–23. The only one of the whole body of priests who escaped this bloody death was a son of Ahimelech, named Abiathar, who "*fled after David*," *i.e.* to David the fugitive, and informed him of the barbarous vengeance which Saul had taken upon the priests of the Lord. Then David recognised and confessed his guilt. "*I knew that day that the Edomite Doeg was there, that he* (*i.e.* that as the Edomite Doeg was there, he) *would tell Saul: I am the cause of all the souls of thy father's house*," *i.e.* of their death. סָבַב is used here in the sense of being the cause of a thing, which is one of the meanings of the verb in the Arabic and Talmudic (*vid.* Ges. *Lex. s.v.*). "*Stay with me, fear not; for he who seeks my life seeks thy life: for thou art safe with me.*" The abstract *mishmereth*, protection, keeping (Ex. xii. 6, xvi. 33, 34), is used for the concrete, in the sense of protected, well kept. The thought is the following: As no other is seeking thy life than Saul, who also wants to kill me, thou mayest stay with me without fear, as I am sure of divine protection. David spoke thus in the firm belief that the Lord would deliver him from his foe, and give him the kingdom. The action of Saul, which had just been reported to him, could only strengthen him in this belief, as it was a sign of the growing hardness of Saul, which must accelerate his destruction.

DAVID DELIVERS KEILAH. HE IS BETRAYED BY THE ZIPHITES, AND MARVELLOUSLY SAVED FROM SAUL IN THE DESERT OF MAON.—CHAP. XXIII

The following events show how, on the one hand, the Lord gave pledges to His servant David that he would eventually become king, but yet on the other hand plunged him into deeper and deeper trouble, that He might refine him and train him to be a king after His own heart. Saul's rage against the priests at Nob not only drove the high priest into David's camp, but procured for David the help of the "light and right" of the high priest in all his undertakings. Moreover, after the prophet Gad had called David back to Judah, an attack of the Philistines upon Keilah furnished him with the opportunity to show himself to the people as their deliverer. And although this enterprise of his exposed him to fresh persecutions on the part of Saul, who was thirsting for revenge, he experienced in connection therewith not only the renewal of Jonathan's friendship on this occasion, but a marvellous interposition on the part of the faithful covenant God.

Vers. 1–14. RESCUE OF KEILAH.—After his return to the mountains of Judah, David received intelligence that Philistines, *i.e.* a marauding company of these enemies of Israel, were fighting against Keilah, and plundering the threshing-floors, upon which the corn that had been reaped was lying ready for threshing. *Keilah* belonged to the towns of the lowlands of Judah (Josh. xv. 44); and although it has not yet been discovered, was certainly very close to the Philistian frontier.— Ver. 2. After receiving this information, David inquired of the Lord (through the Urim and Thummim of the high priest) whether he should go and smite these Philistines, and received an affirmative answer.—Vers. 3–5. But his men said to him, " *Behold, here in Judah we are in fear* (*i.e.* are not safe from Saul's pursuit); *how shall we go to Keilah against the ranks of the Philistines?*" In order, therefore, to infuse courage into them, he inquired of the Lord again, and received the assurance from God, " *I will give the Philistines into thy hand.*" He then proceeded with his men, fought against the Philistines, drove off their cattle, inflicted a severe defeat upon them, and thus delivered the inhabitants of Keilah. In ver. 6 a supplementary remark is added in explanation of the expression " *inquired of the Lord*," to the effect that, when Abiathar fled to David to Keilah, the ephod had come to him. The words " *to David to Keilah*" are not to be understood as signifying that Abiathar did not come to David till he was in Keilah, but that when he fled after David (ch. xxii. 20), he met with him as he was already preparing for the march to Keilah, and immediately proceeded with him thither. For whilst it is not stated in ch. xxii. 20 that Abiathar came to David in the wood of Hareth, but the place of meeting is left indefinite, the fact that David had already inquired of Jehovah (*i.e.* through the oracle of the high priest) with reference to the march to Keilah, compels us to assume that Abiathar had come to him before he left the mountains for Keilah. So that the brief expression " to David to Keilah," which is left indefinite because of its brevity, must be interpreted in accordance with this fact.—Vers. 7–9. As soon as Saul received intelligence of David's march to Keilah, he said, " *God has rejected him* (and delivered him) *into my hand.*" נִכַּר does not mean simply to look at, but also to find strange, and treat as strange, and then absolutely *to reject* (Jer. xix. 4, as in the Arabic in the fourth conjugation). This is the meaning here, where the construction with בְּיָדִי is to be understood as a pregnant expression : " *rejected and delivered into my hand*" (*vid.* Ges. *Lex. s.v.*). The early translators have rendered it quite correctly according to the sense מָכַר, πέπρακεν, *tradidit*, without there being any reason to suppose that they read מָכַר instead of נִכַּר. " *For he hath shut himself in, to come* (= coming, or by coming) *into a city with gates and bolts.*"— Ver. 8. He therefore called all the people (*i.e.* men of war) together to war, to go down to Keilah, and to besiege David and his men.—Vers. 9 sqq. But David heard that Saul was *preparing mischief against him* (*lit.* forging, הַחֲרִישׁ, from חָרַשׁ : Prov. iii. 29, vi. 14, etc.), and he inquired through the oracle of the high priest whether the inhabitants of Keilah would deliver him up to Saul, and whether Saul would come down ; and as both questions were answered in the affirmative, he departed from the city with his six hundred men, before Saul carried out his plan. It is evident from vers. 9–12, that when the will of God was sought through the Urim and Thummim, the person making the inquiry placed the matter before God in prayer, and received an answer; but always to *one* particular question. For when David had asked the two questions given in ver. 11, he received the answer to the second question only, and had to ask the first again (ver. 12).—Ver. 13. " *They went whithersoever they could go* " (*lit.* " they wandered about where they wandered about"), *i.e.* wherever they could go without danger. —Ver. 14. David retreated into the desert (of Judah), to the mountain heights (that were to be found there), and remained on the mountains in the desert of Ziph. The "*desert of Judah*" is the desert tract between the mountains of Judah and the Dead Sea, in its whole extent, from the northern boundary of the tribe of Judah to the Wady Fikreh in the south (see at Josh. xv. 61). Certain portions of this desert, however, received different names of their own, according to the names of different towns on the border of the mountains and desert. The desert of *Ziph* was that portion of the desert of Judah which was near to and surrounded the town of *Ziph*, the name of which has been retained in the ruins of *Tell Zif*, an hour and three-quarters to the south-east of Hebron (see at Josh. xv. 55). —Ver. 14b. " *And Saul sought him all the days, but God delivered him not into his hand.*" This is a general remark, intended to introduce the accounts which follow, of the various attempts made by Saul to get David into his power. " *All the days,*" *i.e.* as long as Saul lived.

Vers. 15–28. DAVID IN THE DESERTS OF ZIPH AND MAON. —The history of David's persecution by Saul is introduced in vers. 15–18, with the account of an attempt made by the noble-minded prince Jonathan, in a private interview with his friend David, to renew his bond of friendship with him, and strengthen David by his friendly words for the sufferings that yet awaited him. Vers. 15, 16 are to be connected together so as to form one period : " *When David saw that Saul was come out . . . and David was in the desert of Ziph, Jonathan rose up and went to David into the wood.*" חֹרְשָׁה, from חֹרֶשׁ, with ה paragogic, signifies a wood or thicket ; here, however, it is probably a proper name for a district in the desert of Ziph that was overgrown with wood or bushes, and where David was stopping at that time. " There is no trace of this wood now. The land lost its ornament of trees centuries ago through the desolating hand of man" (v. de Velde). "*And strengthened his hand in God,*" *i.e.* strengthened his heart, not by supplies, or by money, or any subsidy of that kind, but by consolation drawn from his innocence, and the promises of God (*vid.* Judg. ix. 24 ; Jer. xxiii. 14). "*Fear not,*" said Jonathan to him, "*for the hand of Saul my father will not reach thee ; and thou wilt become king over Israel, and I will be the second to thee ; and Saul my father also knows that it is so.*" Even though Jonathan had heard nothing from David about his anointing, he could learn from David's course thus far, and from his own father's conduct, that David would not be overcome, but would possess the sovereignty after the death of Saul. Jonathan expresses here, as his firm conviction, what he has intimated once before, in ch. xx. 13 sqq. ; and with the most loving self-denial entreats David, when he shall be king, to let him occupy the second place in the kingdom. It by no means follows from the last words ("*Saul my father knoweth*"), that Saul had received distinct information concerning the anointing of David, and his divine calling to be king. The words merely contain the thought, he also sees that it will come. The assurance of this must have forced itself involuntarily upon the mind of Saul, both from his own rejection, as foretold by Samuel, and also from the marvellous success of David in all his undertakings.—Ver. 18. After these encouraging words, they two made a covenant before Jehovah : *i.e.* they renewed the covenant which they had already made by another solemn oath ; after which Jonathan returned home, but David remained in the wood.

The *treachery of the Ziphites* forms a striking contrast to Jonathan's treatment of David. They went up to Gibeah to betray to Saul the fact that David was concealed in the wood upon their mountain heights, and indeed "*upon the hill Hachilah, which lies to the south of the waste.*" The hill of *Ziph* is a flattened hill standing by itself, of about a hundred feet in height. "There is no spot from which you can obtain a better view of David's wanderings backwards and forwards in the desert than from the hill of *Ziph,* which affords a true panorama. The Ziphites could see David and his men moving to and fro in the mountains of the desert of *Ziph,* and could also perceive how he showed himself in the distance upon the hill *Hachilah* on the south side of *Ziph* (which lies to the right by the desert); whereupon they sent as quickly as possible to Saul, and betrayed to him the hiding-place of his enemy" (v. de Velde, ii. pp. 104–5). *Jeshimon* does not refer here to the waste land on the north-eastern coast of the Dead Sea, as in Num. xxi. 20, xxiii. 28, but to the western side of that sea, which is also desert.—Ver. 20 reads literally thus: " *And now, according to all the desire of thy soul, O king, to come down* (from Gibeah, which stood upon higher ground), *come down, and it is in us to deliver him* (David) *into the hand of the king.*" —Ver. 21. For this treachery Saul blessed them: " *Be blessed of the Lord, that ye have compassion upon me.*" In his evil conscience he suspected David of seeking to become his murderer, and therefore thanked God in his delusion that the Ziphites had had compassion upon him, and shown him David's hiding-place.—Ver. 22. In his anxiety, however, lest David should escape him after all, he charged them, " *Go, and give still further heed* (הָכִין without לֵב, as in Judg. xii. 6), *and reconnoitre and look at his place where his foot cometh* (this simply serves as a more precise definition of the pronominal suffix in מְקוֹמוֹ, his place), *who hath seen him there* (sc. let them inquire into this, that they may not be deceived by uncertain or false reports): *for it is told me that he dealeth very subtilly.*"—Ver. 23. They were to search him out in every corner (the object to וּדְעוּ must be supplied from the context). " *And come ye again to me with the certainty* (*i.e.* when you have got some certain intelligence concerning his hiding-place), *that I may go with you; and if he is in the land, I will search him out among all the thousands* (*i.e.* families) *of Judah.*"—Ver. 24. With this answer the Ziphites arose and " *went to Ziph before Saul*" (who would speedily follow with his warriors): but David had gone farther in the meantime, and was with his men " *in the desert of Maon, in the steppe to the south of the wilderness.*" Maon, now *Maïn*, is about three hours and three-quarters s.s.e. of Hebron (see at Josh. xv. 55), and therefore only two hours from Ziph, from which it is visible. " The table-land appears to terminate here; nevertheless the principal ridge of the southern mountains runs for a considerable distance towards the south-west, whereas towards the south-east the land falls off more and more into a lower table-land." This is the *Arabah* or steppe on the right of the wilderness (v. de Velde, ii. pp. 107–8).—Ver. 25. Having been informed of the arrival of Saul and his men (warriors), David went down the rock, and remained in the desert of Maon. *"The rock"* is probably the conical mountain of *Main* (*Maon*), the top of which is now surrounded with ruins, probably remains of a tower (Robinson, *Pal.* ii. p. 194), as the rock from which David came down can only have been the mountain (ver. 26), along one side of which David went with his men whilst Saul and his warriors went on the other, namely when Saul pursued him into the desert of Maon.—Vers. 26, 27. *"And David was anxiously concerned to escape from Saul, and Saul and his men were encircling David and his men to seize them; but a messenger came to Saul. . . . Then Saul turned from pursuing David."* The two clauses, "for Saul and his men" (ver. 26b), and "there came a messenger" (ver. 27), are the circumstantial clauses by which the situation is more clearly defined: the apodosis to וַיְהִי דָוִד does not follow till וַיָּשָׁב in ver. 28. The apodosis cannot begin with וּמַלְאָךְ, because the verb does not stand at the head. David had thus almost inextricably fallen into the hands of Saul; but God saved him by the fact that at that very moment a messenger arrived with the intelligence, "Hasten and go (come), for Philistines have fallen into the land," and thus called Saul away from any further pursuit of David.—Ver. 28. From this occurrence the place received the name of *Sela-hammahlekoth*, *"rock of smoothnesses,"* i.e. of slipping away or escaping, from חָלַק, in the sense of being smooth. This explanation is at any rate better supported than "rock of divisions, *i.e.* the rock at which Saul and David were separated" (Clericus), since חָלַק does not mean to separate.

DAVID SPARES SAUL IN THE CAVE.—CHAP. XXIV.

Vers. 1–8. Whilst Saul had gone against the Philistines, David left this dangerous place, and went to the mountain heights of *Engedi*, i.e. the present *Ain-jidy* (goat-fountain), in the middle of the western coast of the Dead Sea (see at Josh. xv. 62), which he could reach from Maon in six or seven hours. The soil of the neighbourhood consists entirely of limestone; but the rocks contain a considerable admixture of chalk and flint. Round about there rise bare conical mountains, and even ridges of from two to four hundred feet in height, which mostly run down to the sea. The steep mountains are intersected by wadys running down in deep ravines to the sea. "On all sides the country is full of caverns, which might then serve as lurking-places for David and his men, as they do for outlaws at the present day" (Rob. *Pal.* p. 203).—Vers. 1, 2. When Saul had returned from his march against the Philistines, and was informed of this, he set out thither with three thousand picked men to search for David and his men in the wild-goat rocks. The expression "*rocks of the wild goats*" is probably not a proper name for some particular rocks, but a general term applied to the rocks of that locality on account of the number of wild goats and chamois that were to be found in all that region, as mountain goats are still (Rob. *Pal.* ii. p. 204). —Ver. 3. When Saul came to the sheep-folds by the way, where there was a cave, he entered it to cover his feet, whilst David and his men sat behind in the cave. V. de Velde (*R.* ii. p. 74) supposes the place, where the sheep-folds by the roadside were, to have been the Wady *Chareitun*, on the south-west of the Frank mountain, and to the north-east of Tekoah, a very desolate and inaccessible valley. "Rocky, precipitous walls, which rise up one above another for many hundred feet, form the sides of this defile. Stone upon stone, and cliff above cliff, without any sign of being habitable, or of being capable of affording even a halting-place to anything but wild goats." Near the ruins of the village of *Chareitun*, hardly five minutes' walk to the east, there is a large cave or chamber in the rock, with a very narrow entrance entirely concealed by stones, and with many side vaults in which the deepest darkness reigns, at least to any one who has just entered the limestone vaults from the dazzling light of day. It may be argued in favour of the conjecture that this is the cave which Saul entered, and at the back of which David and his men were concealed, that this cave is on the road from Bethlehem to Ain-jidy, and one of the largest caves in that district, if not the largest of all, and that, according to Pococke (*Beschr. des Morgenl.* ii. p. 61), the Franks call it a labyrinth, the Arabs *Elmaama, i.e.* hiding-place, whilst the latter relate how at one time thirty thousand people hid themselves in it "to escape an evil wind," in all probability the simoom. The only difficulty connected with this supposition is the distance from Ain-jidy, namely about four or five German miles (fifteen or twenty English), and the nearness of Tekoah, according to which it belongs to the desert of Tekoah rather than to that of Engedi. *" To cover his feet"* is a euphemism according to most of the ancient versions, as in Judg. iii. 24, for performing the necessities of nature, as it is a custom in the East to cover the feet. It does not mean " to sleep," as it is rendered in this passage in the *Peschito,* and also by Michaelis and others; for although what follows may seem to favour this, there is apparently no reason why any such euphemistic expression should have been chosen for sleep. *" The sides of the cave :"* *i.e.* the outermost or farthest sides. —Ver. 4. Then David's men said to him, *" See, this is the day of which Jehovah hath said to thee, Behold, I give thine enemy into thy hand, and do to him what seemeth good to thee."* Although these words might refer to some divine oracle which David had received through a prophet, Gad for example, what follows clearly shows that David had received no such oracle ; and the meaning of his men was simply this, " Behold, to-day is the day when God is saying to thee :" that is to say, the speakers regarded the leadings of providence by which Saul had been brought into David's power as a divine intimation to David himself to take this opportunity of slaying his deadly enemy, and called this intimation a word of Jehovah. *David then rose up, and cut off the edge of Saul's cloak privily.* Saul had probably laid the *meil* on one side, which rendered it possible for David to cut off a piece of it unobserved.—Ver. 5. But *his heart smote him* after he had done it ; *i.e.* his conscience reproached him, because he regarded this as an injury done to the king himself.—Ver. 6. With all the greater firmness, therefore, did he repel the suggestions of his men : *" Far be it to me from Jehovah* (on Jehovah's account : see at Josh. xxii. 29), *that* (אִם, a particle denoting an oath) *I should do such a thing to my lord, the anointed of Jehovah, to stretch out my hand against him."* These words of David show clearly enough that no word of Jehovah had come to him to do as he liked with Saul.—Ver. 7. Thus he kept back his people with words (שִׁסַּע, *verbis dilacere*), and did not allow them to rise up against Saul, *sc.* to slay him.

Vers. 8–16. But when Saul had gone out of the cave, David

went out, and called, "*My lord king*," that when the king looked round he might expostulate with him, with the deepest reverence, but yet with earnest words, that should sharpen his conscience as to the unfounded nature of his suspicion and the injustice of his persecution. "*Why dost thou hearken to words of men, who say, Behold, David seeketh thy hurt? Behold, this day thine eyes have seen that Jehovah hath given thee to-day into my hand in the cave, and they said* (אָמַר, thought) *to kill thee, and I spared thee:*" lit. it (mine eye) spared thee (cf. Gen. xlv. 20, Deut. vii. 16, etc., which show that עֵינִי is to be supplied).— Ver. 11. To confirm what he said, he then showed him the lappet of his coat which he had cut off, and said, "*My father, see.*" In these words there is an expression of the childlike reverence and affection which David cherished towards the anointed of the Lord. "*For that I cut off the lappet and did not kill thee, learn and see* (from this) *that* (there is) *not evil in my hand* (i.e. that I do not go about for the purpose of injury and crime), *and that I have not sinned against thee, as thou nevertheless layest wait for my soul to destroy it.*"—Vers. 12, 13. After he had proved to the king in this conclusive manner that he had no reason whatever for seeking his life, he invoked the Lord as judge between him and his adversary: "*Jehovah will avenge me upon thee, but my hand will not be against thee. As the proverb of the ancients* (הַקַּדְמֹנִי *is used* collectively) *says, Evil proceedeth from the evil, but my hand shall not be upon thee.*" The meaning is this: Only a wicked man could wish to avenge himself; I do not.—Ver. 14. And even if he should wish to attack the king, he did not possess the power. This thought introduces ver. 14: "*After whom is the king of Israel gone out? After whom dost thou pursue? A dead dog, a single flea.*" By these similes David meant to describe himself as a perfectly harmless and insignificant man, of whom Saul had no occasion to be afraid, and whom the king of Israel ought to think it beneath his dignity to pursue. A dead dog cannot bite or hurt, and is an object about which a king ought not to trouble himself (cf. 2 Sam. ix. 8 and xvi. 9, where the idea of something contemptible is included). The point of comparison with a flea is the insignificance of such an animal (cf. ch. xxvi. 20).—Ver. 15. As Saul had therefore no good ground for persecuting David, the latter could very calmly commit his cause to the Lord God, that He might decide it as judge, and deliver him out of the hand of Saul : " *Let Him look at it, and conduct my cause,*" etc.

Vers. 16–22 These words made an impression upon Saul. David's conduct went to his heart, so that he wept aloud, and confessed to him : " *Thou art more righteous than I, for thou hast shown me good, and I* (have shown) *thee evil;* and thou hast given me a proof of this to-day."—Ver. 19. "*If a man meet with his enemy, will he send him* (let him go) *in peace?*" This sentence is to be regarded as a question, which requires a negative reply, and expresses the thought : When a man meets with an enemy, he does not generally let him escape without injury. But thou hast acted very differently towards me. This thought is easily supplied from the context, and what follows attaches itself to this : " *The Lord repay thee good for what thou hast done to me this day.*"—Vers. 20, 21. This wish was expressed in perfect sincerity. David's behaviour towards him had conquered for the moment the evil demon of his heart, and completely altered his feelings. In this better state of mind he felt impelled even to give utterance to these words, " *I know that thou wilt be king, and the sovereignty will have perpetuity in thy hand.*" Saul could not prevent this conviction from forcing itself upon him, after his own rejection and the failure of all that he attempted against David ; and it was this which drove him to persecute David whenever the evil spirit had the upper hand in his soul. But now that better feelings had arisen in his mind, he uttered it without envy, and merely asked David to promise on oath that he would not cut off his descendants after his death, and seek to exterminate his name from his father's house. A name is exterminated when the whole of the descendants are destroyed,—a thing of frequent occurrence in the East in connection with a change of dynasties, and one which occurred again and again even in the kingdom of the ten tribes (*vid.* 1 Kings xv. 28 sqq., xvi. 11 sqq. ; 2 Kings x.). —Ver. 22. When David had sworn this, Saul returned home. But David remained upon the mountain heights, because he did not regard the passing change in Saul's feelings as likely to continue. הַמְּצוּדָה (translated " *the hold*") is used here to denote the mountainous part of the desert of Judah. It is different in ch. xxii. 5.

DEATH OF SAMUEL. NABAL AND ABIGAIL.—CHAP. XXV.

Ver. 1. The *death of Samuel* is inserted here, because it occurred at that time. The fact that all Israel assembled together to his burial, and lamented him, *i.e.* mourned for him, was a sign that his labours as a prophet were recognised by the whole nation as a blessing for Israel. Since the days of Moses and Joshua, no man had arisen to whom the covenant nation owed so much as to Samuel, who has been justly called the reformer and restorer of the theocracy. They buried him "*in his house at Ramah.*" The expression "his house" does not mean his burial-place or family tomb, nor his native place, but the house in which he lived, with the court belonging to it, where Samuel was placed in a tomb erected especially for him. After the death of Samuel, David went down into the desert of *Paran, i.e.* into the northern portion of the desert of Arabia, which stretches up to the mountains of Judah (see at Num. x. 12); most likely for no other reason than because he could no longer find sufficient means of subsistence for himself and his six hundred men in the desert of Judah.

Vers. 2–44. The following history of *Nabal's* folly, and of the wise and generous behaviour of his pious and intelligent wife Abigail towards David, shows how Jehovah watched over His servant David, and not only preserved him from an act of passionate excitement, which might have endangered his calling to be king of Israel, but turned the trouble into which he had been brought into a source of prosperity and salvation.

Vers. 2–13. At *Maon, i.e.* Main or the mountains of Judah (see at Josh. xv. 55), there lived a rich man (גָּדוֹל, *great* through property and riches), who had his establishment at *Carmel.* מַעֲשֶׂה, work, occupation, then establishment, possessions (*vid.* Ex. xxiii. 16). *Carmel* is not the promontory of that name (Thenius), but the present *Kurmul* on the mountains of Judah, scarcely half an hour's journey to the north-west of Maon (see at Josh. xv. 55). This man possessed three thousand sheep and a thousand goats, and was at the sheep-shearing at Carmel. His name was *Nabal* (*i.e.* fool): this was hardly his proper name, but was a surname by which he was popularly designated on account of his folly. His wife *Abigail* was "*of good understanding,*" *i.e.* intelligent, "*and of beautiful figure;*"

but the husband was "*harsh and evil in his doings.*" He
sprang from the family of *Caleb.* This is the rendering
adopted by the Chaldee and Vulgate, according to the *Keri*
כְּלִבִּי. The *Chethibh* is to be read כְּלִבּוֹ, "according to his
heart;" though the LXX. (ἄνθρωπος κυνικός) and Josephus, as
well as the Arabic and Syriac, derive it from כְּלֶב, and understand it as referring to the dog-like, or shameless, character
of the man.—Vers. 4, 5. When David heard in the desert (cf.
ver. 1) that Nabal was shearing his sheep, which was generally
accompanied with a festal meal (see at Gen. xxxviii. 12), he
sent ten young men up to Carmel to him, and bade them wish
him peace and prosperity in his name, and having reminded
him of the friendly services rendered to his shepherds, solicit
a present for himself and his people. שְׁאַל לוֹ לְשָׁלוֹם, ask him
after his welfare, *i.e.* greet him in a friendly manner (cf. Ex.
xviii. 7). The word לֶחָי is obscure, and was interpreted by the
early translators merely according to uncertain conjectures.
The simplest explanation is apparently *in vitam,* long *life,*
understood as a wish in the sense of "good fortune to you"
(Luther, Maurer, etc.); although the word חַי in the singular
can only be shown to have the meaning *life* in connection with
the formula used in oaths, חֵי נַפְשְׁךָ, etc. But even if חַי must
be taken as an adjective, it is impossible to explain לֶחָי in any
other way than as an elliptical exclamation meaning "good
fortune to the living man." For the idea that the word is to
be connected with אֲמַרְתֶּם, "say to the living man," *i.e.* to the
man if still alive, is overthrown by the fact that David had no
doubt that Nabal was still living. The words which follow
are also to be understood as a wish, "*May thou and thy house,
and all that is thine, be well!*" After this salutation they were
to proceed with the object of their visit: "*And now I have
heard that thou hast sheep-shearers. Now thy shepherds have been
with us; we have done them no harm* (הִכְלַמְנוּם, as in Judg. xviii.
7: on the form, see Ges. § 53, 3, Anm. 6), *and nothing was
missed by them so long as they were in Carmel.*" When living
in the desert, David's men had associated with the shepherds of
Nabal, rendered them various services, and protected them and
their flocks against the southern inhabitants of the desert (the
Bedouin Arabs); in return for which they may have given
them food and information. Thus David proved himself a

protector of his people even in his banishment. וַיִּמְצְאוּ, "so
may the young men (those sent by David) find favour in thine
eyes! for we have come to a good (i.e. a festive) day. Give, I
pray, what thy hand findeth (i.e. as much as thou canst) to thy
servant, and to thy son David." With the expression "thy son"
David claims Nabal's fatherly goodwill. So far as the fact
itself is concerned, "on such a festive occasion near a town or
village even in our own time, an Arab sheikh of the neighbouring desert would hardly fail to put in a word either in person
or by message; and his message both in form and substance
would be only the transcript of that of David" (Robinson,
Palestine, p. 201).—Ver. 9. David's messengers delivered their
message to Nabal, וַיָּנוּחוּ, "and sat down," sc. awaiting the fulfilment of their request. The rendering given by the Chaldee
(פְּסָקוּ, cessaverunt loqui) and the Vulgate (siluerunt) is less
suitable, and cannot be philologically sustained. The Septuagint, on the other hand, has καὶ ἀνεπήδησε, "and he (Nabal)
sprang up," as if the translators had read וַיָּקָם (vid. LXX. at
ch. xx. 34). This rendering, according to which the word
belongs to the following clause, gives a very appropriate sense,
if only, supposing that וַיָּקָם really did stand in the text, the
origin and general adoption of וַיָּנוּחוּ could in any way be explained.—Ver. 10. Nabal refused the petitioners in the most
churlish manner: "Who is David? who the son of Jesse?" i.e.
what have I to do with David? "There be many servants now-
a-days who tear away every one from his master." Thus, in
order to justify his own covetousness, he set down David as a
vagrant who had run away from his master.—Ver. 11. "And
I should take my bread and my water (i.e. my food and drink),
and my cattle, . . . and give them to men whom I do not know
whence they are?" וְלָקַחְתִּי is a perfect with vav consec., and the
whole sentence is to be taken as a question.—Vers. 12, 13.
The messengers returned to David with this answer. The
churlish reply could not fail to excite his anger. He therefore
commanded his people to gird on the sword, and started with
400 men to take vengeance upon Nabal, whilst 200 remained
behind with the things.

Vers. 14–31. However intelligible David's wrath may
appear in the situation in which he was placed, it was not right
before God, but a sudden burst of sinful passion, which was

unseemly in a servant of God. By carrying out his intention, he would have sinned against the Lord and against His people. But the Lord preserved him from this sin by the fact that, just at the right time, Abigail, the intelligent and pious wife of Nabal, heard of the affair, and was able to appease the wrath of David by her immediate and kindly interposition.—Vers. 14, 15. Abigail heard from one of (Nabal's) servants what had taken place (בָּרַךְ, to wish any one prosperity and health, i.e. to salute, as in ch. xiii. 10; and יָעַט, from עִיט, to speak wrathfully: on the form, see at ch. xv. 19 and xiv. 32), and also what had been praiseworthy in the behaviour of David's men towards Nabal's shepherds; how they had not only done them no injury, had not robbed them of anything, but had defended them all the while. "They were a wall (i.e. a firm protection) round us by night and by day, as long as we were with them feeding the sheep," i.e. a wall of defence against attacks from the Bedouins living in the desert.—Ver. 17. "And now," continued the servant, "know and see what thou doest; for evil is determined (cf. ch. xx. 9) against our master and all his house: and he (Nabal) is a wicked man, that one cannot address him."—Vers. 18, 19. Then Abigail took as quickly as possible a bountiful present of provisions,—two hundred loaves, two bottles of wine, five prepared (i.e. slaughtered) sheep (עֲשׂוּוֹת, a rare form for עֲשׂוּיֹת : see Ewald, § 189, a), five seahs (an ephah and two-thirds) of roasted grains (Kali: see ch. xvii. 17), a hundred צִמֻּקִים (dried grapes, i.e. raisin-cakes: Ital. simmuki), and two hundred fig-cakes (consisting of pressed figs joined together),—and sent these gifts laden upon asses on before her to meet David, whilst she herself followed behind to appease his anger by coming to meet him in a friendly manner, but without saying a word to her husband about what she intended to do.—Ver. 20. When she came down riding upon the ass by a hidden part of the mountain, David and his men came to meet her, so that she lighted upon them. סֵתֶר הָהָר, a hidden part of the mountain, was probably a hollow between two peaks of a mountain. This would explain the use of the word יָרַד, to come down, with reference both to Abigail, who approached on the one side, and David, who came on the other. —Vers. 21 and 22 contain a circumstantial clause introduced parenthetically to explain what follows: but David had said,

Only for deception (*i.e.* for no other purpose than to be deceived in my expectation) *have I defended all that belongs to this man* (Nabal) *in the desert, so that nothing of his was missed, and* (for) *he hath repaid me evil for good. God do so to the enemies of David, if I leave,* etc.; *i.e.* " as truly as God will punish the enemies of David, so certainly will I not leave till the morning light, of all that belongeth to him, one that pisseth against the wall." This oath, in which the punishment of God is not called down upon the swearer himself (God do so *to me*), as it generally is, but upon the enemies of David, is analogous to that in ch. iii. 17, where punishment is threatened upon the person addressed, who is there made to swear; except that here, as the oath could not be uttered in the ears of the person addressed, upon whom it was to fall, the enemies generally are mentioned instead of " *to thee.*" There is no doubt, therefore, as to the correctness of the text. The substance of this imprecation may be explained from the fact that David is so full of the consciousness of fighting and suffering for the cause of the kingdom of God, that he discerns in the insult heaped upon him by Nabal an act of hostility to the Lord and the cause of His kingdom. The phrase מַשְׁתִּין בְּקִיר, *mingens in parietem,* is only met with in passages which speak of the destruction of a family or household to the very last man (viz., besides this passage, 1 Kings xiv. 10, xvi. 11, xxi. 21 ; 2 Kings ix. 8), and neither refers primarily to dogs, as Ephraem Syrus, Juda ben Karish, and others maintain; nor to the lowest class of men, as Winer, Maurer, and others imagine; nor to little boys, as L. de Dieu, Gesenius, etc., suppose; but, as we may see from the explanatory clause appended to 1 Kings xiv. 10, xxi. 21, 2 Kings ix. 8, to every male (*quemcumque masculi generis hominem : vid.* Bochart, *Hieroz.* i. pp. 776 sqq., and Rödiger on Ges. *Thes.* pp. 1397–8).—Ver. 23 is connected with ver. 20.

When Abigail saw David, she descended hastily from the ass, fell upon her face before him, bowed to the ground, and fell at his feet, saying, " *Upon me, me, my lord, be the guilt; allow thy handmaid to reveal the thing to thee.*" She takes the guilt upon herself, because she hopes that David will not avenge it upon her.—Ver. 25. She prayed that David would take no notice of Nabal, for he was what his name declared—*a fool, and folly in him;* but she (Abigail) had not seen the messengers of David. "The prudent woman uses a good argument; for a wise man should pardon a fool" (Seb. Schmidt). She then endeavours to bring David to a friendly state of mind by three arguments, introduced with וְעַתָּה (vers. 26, 27), before asking for forgiveness (ver. 28). She first of all pointed to the leadings of God, by which David had been kept from committing murder through her coming to meet him.[1] *"As truly as Jehovah liveth, and by the life of thy soul! yea, the Lord hath kept thee, that thou camest not into blood-guiltiness, and thy hand helped thee"* (*i.e.* and with thy hand thou didst procure thyself help). אֲשֶׁר, introducing her words, as in ch. xv. 20, *lit.* " as truly as thou livest, (so true is it) that," etc. In the second place, she points to the fact that God is the avenger of the wicked, by expressing the wish that all the enemies of David may become fools like Nabal; in connection with which it must be observed, in order to understand her words fully, that, according to the Old Testament representation, folly is a correlate of ungodliness, which inevitably brings down punishment.[2] The predicate to the sentence *" and they that seek evil to my lord"* must be supplied from the preceding words, viz. *" may they become just such fools."*— Ver. 27. It is only in the third line that she finally mentions the present, but in such a manner that she does not offer it directly to David, but describes it as a gift for the men in his train. *"And now this blessing* (בְּרָכָה here and ch. xxx. 26, as in Gen. xxxiii. 11: cf. ἡ εὐλογία, 2 Cor. ix. 5, 6), *which thine handmaid hath brought, let it be given to the young men in my lord's train"* (*lit.* " at the feet of :" cf. Ex. xi. 8; Judg. iv. 10, etc.).— Ver. 28. The shrewd and pious woman supports her prayer for

---

[1] " She founds her argument upon their meeting, which was so marvellously seasonable, that it might be easily and truly gathered from this fact that it had taken place through the providence of God; *i.e.* And now, because I meet thee so seasonably, do thou piously acknowledge with me the providence of God, which has so arranged all this, that innocent blood might not by chance be shed by thee."—*Seb. Schmidt.*

[2] Seb. Schmidt has justly observed, that " she reminds David of the promise of God. Not that she prophesies, but that she has gathered it from the general promises of the word of God. The promise referred to is, that whoever does good to his enemies, and takes no vengeance upon them, God himself will avenge him upon his enemies; according to the saying, *Vengeance is mine, I will repay.* And this is what Abigail says: And now thine enemies shall be as Nabal."

forgiveness of the wrong, which she takes upon herself, by promises of the rich blessing with which the Lord would recompense David. She thereby gives such clear and distinct expression to her firm belief in the divine election of David as king of Israel, that her words almost amount to prophecy: "*For Jehovah will make my lord a lasting house* (cf. ch. ii. 35; and for the fact itself, 2 Sam. vii. 8 sqq., where the Lord confirms this pious wish by His own promises to David himself); *for my lord fighteth the wars of Jehovah* (vid. ch. xviii. 17), *and evil is not discovered in thee thy whole life long.*" רָעָה, evil, *i.e.* misfortune, mischief; for the thought that he might also be preserved from wrong-doing is not expressed till ver. 31. "*All thy days*," lit. " from thy days," *i.e.* from the beginning of thy life.—Ver. 29. "*And should any one rise up to pursue thee, ... the soul of my lord will be bound up in the bundle of the living with the Lord thy God.*" The metaphor is taken from the custom of binding up valuable things in a bundle, to prevent their being injured. The words do not refer primarily to eternal life with God in heaven, but only to the safe preservation of the righteous on this earth in the grace and fellowship of the Lord. But whoever is so hidden in the gracious fellowship of the Lord in this life, that no enemy can harm him or injure his life, the Lord will not allow to perish, even though temporal death should come, but will then receive him into eternal life. "*But the soul of thine enemies, He will hurl away in the cup of the sling.*" " *The cup* (caph: cf. Gen. xxxii. 26) *of the sling*" was the cavity in which the stone was placed for the purpose of hurling.—Vers. 30, 31. Abigail concluded her intercession with the assurance that the forgiveness of Nabal's act would be no occasion of anguish of heart to David when he should have become prince over Israel, on account of his having shed innocent blood and helped himself, and also with the hope that he would remember her. From the words, "*When Jehovah shall do to my lord according to all the good that He hath spoken concerning him, and shall make thee prince over Israel,*" it appears to follow that Abigail had received certain information of the anointing of David, and his designation to be the future king, probably through Samuel, or one of the pupils of the prophets. There is nothing to preclude this assumption, even if it cannot be historically sustained. Abigail manifests such an advance and maturity in the life of faith, as could only have been derived from intercourse with prophets. It is expressly stated with regard to Elijah and Elisha, that at certain times the pious assembled together around the prophets. What prevents us from assuming the same with regard to Samuel? The absence of any distinct testimony to that effect is amply compensated for by the brief, and for the most part casual, notices that are given of the influence which Samuel exerted upon all Israel.— Ver. 31 introduces the apodosis to ver. 30 : *So will this* (*i.e.* the forgiveness of Nabal's folly, for which she had prayed in ver. 28) *not be a stumbling-block* (*pukah :* anything in the road which causes a person to stagger) *and anguish of heart* (*i.e.* conscientious scruple) *to thee, and shedding innocent blood, and that my lord helps himself.* וְלִשְׁפֹּךְ וגו׳ is perfectly parallel to לִפְוּקָה וגו׳, and cannot be taken as subordinate, as it is in the Vulgate, etc., in the sense of " that thou hast not shed blood innocently," etc. In this rendering not only is the *vav cop.* overlooked, but " not" is arbitrarily interpolated, to obtain a suitable sense, which the Vulgate rendering, *quod effuderis sanguinem innoxiam*, does not give. וְהֵיטִב is to be taken conditionally : " *and if Jehovah shall deal well with my lord, then,*" etc.

Vers. 32-38. These words could not fail to appease David's wrath. In his reply he praised the Lord for having sent Abigail to meet him (ver. 32), and then congratulated Abigail upon her understanding and her actions, that she had kept him from bloodshed (ver. 33) ; otherwise he would certainly have carried out the revenge which he had resolved to take upon Nabal (ver. 34). וְאוּלָם is strongly adversative : *nevertheless.* מֵהָרַע, inf. *constr. Hiph.* of רָעַע. כִּי, ὅτι, introduces the substance of the affirmation, and is repeated before the oath : כִּי לוּלֵי . . . כִּי אִם, (that) *if thou hadst not,* etc., (that) *truly there would not have been left* (cf. 2 Sam. ii. 27). The very unusual form תְּבָאתִי, an imperfect with the termination of the perfect, might indeed possibly be a copyist's error for תָּבֹאִי (Olsh. *Gr.* pp. 452, 525), but in all probability it is only an intensified form of the second pers. fem. imperf., like תְּבוֹאתָה (Deut. xxxiii. 16 ; cf. Ewald, § 191, *c*).—Ver. 35. David then received the gifts brought for him, and bade Abigail return to her house, with the assurance that he had granted her request for pardon. נָשָׂא פָנִים, as in Gen.

xix. 21, etc.—Ver. 36. When Abigail returned home, she found her husband *at a great feast, like a king's feast, very merry* (עָלָיו, " therewith," refers to מִשְׁתֶּה : cf. Prov. xxiii. 30), *and drunken above measure*, so that she told him nothing of what had occurred until the break of day.—Ver. 37. Then, " *when the wine had gone from Nabal*," *i.e.* when he had become sober, she related the matter to him ; whereat he was so terrified, that he was smitten with a stroke. This is the meaning of the words, " *his heart died within him, and it became as stone.*" The cause of it was not his anger at the loss he had sustained, or merely his alarm at the danger to which he had been exposed, and which he did not believe to be over yet, but also his vexation that his wife should have made him humble himself in such a manner ; for he is described as a hard, *i.e.* an unbending, self-willed man.—Ver. 38. About ten days later *the Lord smote him so that he died*, *i.e.* the Lord put an end to his life by a second stroke.

Vers. 39-44. When David heard of Nabal's death, he praised Jehovah that He had avenged his shame upon Nabal, and held him back from self-revenge. אֲשֶׁר רָב וגו׳, " *who hath pleaded the cause of my reproach* (the disgrace inflicted upon me) *against Nabal.*" " *Against Nabal*" does not belong to " *my reproach*," but to " *pleaded the cause.*" The construction of רִיב with מִן is a pregnant one, to fight (and deliver) out of the power of a person (*vid.* Ps. xliii. 1) ; whereas here the fundamental idea is that of taking vengeance upon a person.— Ver. 40. He then sent messengers to Abigail, and conveyed to her his wish to marry her, to which she consented without hesitation. With deep reverence she said to the messengers (ver. 41), " *Behold, thy handmaid as servant* (*i.e.* is ready to become thy servant) *to wash the feet of the servants of my lord ;*" *i.e.*, in the obsequious style of the East, "I am ready to perform the humblest possible services for thee."—Ver. 42. She then rose up hastily, and went after the messengers to David with five damsels in her train, and became his wife.— Ver. 43. The historian appends a few notices here concerning David's wives : " *And David had taken Ahinoam from Jezreel ; thus they also both became his wives.*" The expression " *also*" points to David's marriage with Michal, the daughter of Saul (ch. xviii. 28). *Jezreel* is not the city of that name in the tribe of Issachar (Josh. xix. 18), but the one in the mountains of Judah (Josh. xv. 56).—Ver. 44. But Saul had taken his daughter Michal away from David, and given her to *Palti* of Gallim. *Palti* is called *Paltiel* in 2 Sam. iii. 15. According to Isa. x. 30, *Gallim* was a place between Gibeah of Saul and Jerusalem. Valentiner supposes it to be the hill to the south of *Tuleil el Phul* (Gibeah of Saul) called *Khirbet el Jisr*. After the death of Saul, however, David persuaded Ishbosheth to give him Michal back again (see 2 Sam. iii. 14 sqq.).

DAVID IS BETRAYED AGAIN BY THE ZIPHITES, AND SPARES SAUL A SECOND TIME.—CHAP. XXVI.

The repetition not only of the treachery of the Ziphites, but also of the sparing of Saul by David, furnishes no proof in itself that the account contained in this chapter is only another legend of the occurrences already related in ch. xxiii. 19–xxiv. 23. As the pursuit of David by Saul lasted for several years, in so small a district as the desert of Judah, there is nothing strange in the repetition of the same scenes. And the assertion made by Thenius, that " Saul would have been a moral monster, which he evidently was not, if he had pursued David with quiet deliberation, and through the medium of the same persons, and had sought his life again, after his own life had been so magnanimously spared by him," not only betrays a superficial acquaintance with the human heart, but is also founded upon the mere assertion, for which there is no proof, that Saul was *evidently* not so ; and it is proved to be worthless by the fact, that after the first occasion on which his life was so magnanimously spared by David, he did not leave off seeking him up and down in the land, and that David was obliged to seek refuge with the Philistines in consequence, as may be seen from ch. xxvii., which Thenius himself assigns to the same source as ch. xxiv. The agreement between the two accounts reduces it entirely to outward and unessential things. It consists chiefly in the fact that the Ziphites came twice to Saul at Gibeah, and informed him that David was stopping in their neighbourhood, in the hill *Hachilah*, and also that Saul went out twice in pursuit of David with 3000 men. But the three thousand were the standing body of men that Saul had raised from the very beginning of his reign out of the whole number of those who were capable of bearing arms, for the purpose of carrying on his smaller wars (ch. xiii. 2); and the hill of *Hachilah* appears to have been a place in the desert of Judah peculiarly well adapted for the site of an encampment. On the other hand, all the details, as well as the final results of the two occurrences, differ entirely from one another. When David was betrayed the first time, he drew back into the desert of Maon before the advance of Saul; and being completely surrounded by Saul upon one of the mountains there, was only saved from being taken prisoner by the circumstance that Saul was compelled suddenly to relinquish the pursuit of David on account of the report that the Philistines had invaded the land (ch. xxiii. 25-28). But on the second occasion Saul encamped upon the hill of Hachilah, whilst David had drawn back into the adjoining desert, from which he crept secretly into Saul's encampment, and might, if he had chosen, have put his enemy to death (ch. xxvi. 3 sqq.). There is quite as much difference in the minuter details connected with the sparing of Saul. On the first occasion, Saul entered a cave in the desert of Engedi, whilst David and his men were concealed in the interior of the cave, without having the smallest suspicion that they were anywhere near (ch. xxiv. 2-4). The second time David went with Abishai into the encampment of Saul upon the hill of Hachilah, while the king and all his men were sleeping (ch. xxvi. 3, 5). It is true that on both occasions David's men told him that God had given his enemy into his hand; but the first time they added, Do to him what seemeth good in thy sight; and David cut off the lappet of Saul's coat, whereupon his conscience smote him, and he said, "Far be it from me to lay my hand upon the Lord's anointed" (ch. xxiv. 5-8). In the second instance, on the contrary, when David saw Saul in the distance lying by the carriage rampart and the army sleeping round him, he called to two of his heroes, Ahimelech and Abishai, to go with him into the camp of the sleeping foe, and then went thither with Abishai, who thereupon said to him, "God hath delivered thine enemy into thy hand : let me alone, that I may pierce him with the spear." But David rejected this proposal, and merely took away the spear and water-bowl that were at Saul's head (ch. xxvi. 6-12). And lastly, notwithstanding the fact that the words of David and replies of Saul agree in certain general thoughts, yet they differ entirely in the main. On the first occasion David showed the king that his life had been in his power, and yet he had spared him, to dispel the delusion that he was seeking his life (ch. xxiv. 10-16). On the second occasion he asked the king why he was pursuing him, and called to him to desist from his pursuit (ch. xxvi. 18 sqq.). But Saul was so affected the first time that he wept aloud, and openly declared that David would obtain the kingdom; and asked him to promise on oath, that when he did, he would not destroy his family (ch. xxiv. 17-23). The second time, on the contrary, he only declared that he had sinned and acted foolishly, and would do David no more harm, and that David would undertake and prevail; but he neither shed tears, nor brought himself to speak of David's ascending the throne, so that he was evidently much more hardened than before (ch. xxvi. 21-25). These decided differences prove clearly enough that the incident described in this chapter is not the same as the similar one mentioned in ch. xxiii. and xxiv., but belongs to a later date, when Saul's enmity and hardness had increased.

Vers. 1-12. The second betrayal of David by the Ziphites occurred after David had married Abigail at Carmel, and when he had already returned to the desert of Judah. On vers. 1 and 2 compare the explanations of ch. xxiii. 19 and xxiv. 3. Instead of " *before* (in the face of) *Jeshimon*" (*i.e.* the wilderness), we find the situation defined more precisely in ch. xxiii. 19, as " *to the right* (*i.e.* on the south) *of the wilderness*" (Jeshimon).— Vers. 3, 4. When David saw (*i.e.* perceived) in the desert that Saul was coming behind him, he sent out spies, and learned from them *that he certainly had come* (אֶל־נָכוֹן, for a certainty, as in ch. xxiii. 23).—Vers. 5 sqq. Upon the receipt of this information, David rose up with two attendants (mentioned in ver. 6) to reconnoitre the camp of Saul. When he saw the place where Saul and his general Abner were lying—Saul was lying *by the waggon rampart*, and the fighting men were encamped round about him—he said to Ahimelech and Abishai, " *Who will go down with me into the camp to Saul?*" Whereupon Abishai declared himself ready to do so ; and they both went by night, and found Saul sleeping with all the people. *Ahimelech* the Hittite is never mentioned again ; but *Abishai* the son of

Zeruiah, David's sister (1 Chron. ii. 16), and a brother of Joab, was afterwards a celebrated general of David, as was also his brother Joab (2 Sam. xvi. 9, xviii. 2, xxi. 17). Saul's spear was *pressed* (stuck) *into the ground at his head,* as a sign that the king was sleeping there, for the spear served Saul as a sceptre (cf. ch. xviii. 10).—Ver. 8. When Abishai exclaimed, " *God hath delivered thine enemy into thy hand: now will I pierce him with the spear into the ground with a stroke, and will give no second*" (*sc.* stroke: the Vulgate rendering gives the sense exactly: *et secundo non opus erit,* there will be no necessity for a second), David replied, " *Destroy him not; for who hath stretched out his hand against the anointed of the Lord, and remained unhurt?*" נִקָּה, as in Ex. xxi. 19, Num. v. 31. He then continued (in vers. 10, 11): " *As truly as Jehovah liveth, unless Jehovah smite him* (*i.e.* carry him off with a stroke; cf. ch. xxv. 38), *or his day cometh that he dies* (*i.e.* or he dies a natural death; ʻ his day' denoting the day of death, as in Job xiv. 6, xv. 32), *or he goes into battle and is carried off, far be it from me with Jehovah* (מֵיהוָה, as in ch. xxiv. 7) *to stretch forth my hand against Jehovah's anointed.*" The apodosis to ver. 10 commences with חָלִילָה, " far be it," or " the Lord forbid," in ver. 11. " *Take now the spear which is at his head, and the pitcher, and let us go.*" —Ver. 12. They departed with these trophies, without any one waking up and seeing them, because they were all asleep, as a deep sleep from the Lord had fallen upon them. מְרַאֲשֹׁתֵי שָׁאוּל stands for מִמְּרַאֲשֹׁתֵי שׁ', " from the head of Saul," with מ dropped. The expression " *a deep sleep of Jehovah,*" *i.e.* a deep sleep sent or inflicted by Jehovah, points to the fact that the Lord favoured David's enterprise.

Vers. 13–20. " *And David went over to the other side, and placed himself upon the top of the mountain afar off (the space between them was great), and cried to the people,*" etc. Saul had probably encamped with his fighting men on the slope of the hill Hachilah, so that a valley separated him from the opposite hill, from which David had no doubt reconnoitred the camp and then *gone down* to it (ver. 6), and to which he returned after the deed was accomplished. The statement that this mountain was far off, so that there was a great space between David and Saul, not only favours the accuracy of the historical tradition, but shows that David reckoned far less now upon any change in the state of Saul's mind than he had done before, when he followed Saul without hesitation from the cave and called after him (ch. xxiv. 9), and that in fact he rather feared lest Saul should endeavour to get him into his power as soon as he woke from his sleep.—Ver. 14. David called out to Abner, whose duty it was as general to defend the life of his king. And Abner replied, " *Who art thou, who criest out to the king?*" *i.e.* offendest the king by thy shouting, and disturbest his rest.—Vers. 15, 16. David in return taunted Abner with having watched the king carelessly, and made himself chargeable with his death. " *For one of the people came to destroy thy lord the king.*" As a proof of this, he then showed him the spear and pitcher that he had taken away with him. רְאֵה is to be repeated in thought before אֶת־צַפַּחַת : " *look where the king's spear is; and* (look) *at the pitcher at his head,*" sc. where it is. These reproaches that were cast at Abner were intended to show to Saul, who might at any rate possibly hear, and in fact did hear, that David was the most faithful defender of his life, more faithful than his closest and most zealous servants.—Vers. 17, 18. When Saul heard David's voice (for he could hardly have seen David, as the occurrence took place before daybreak, at the latest when the day began to dawn), and David had made himself known to the king in reply to his inquiry, David said, " *Why doth my lord pursue his servant? for what have I done, and what evil is in my hand?*" He then gave him the well-meant advice, to seek reconciliation for his wrath against him, and not to bring upon himself the guilt of allowing David to find his death in a foreign land. The words, " *and now let my lord the king hear the saying of his servant,*" serve to indicate that what follows is important, and worthy of laying to heart. In his words, David supposes two cases as conceivable causes of Saul's hostility : (1) if Jehovah hath stirred thee up against me ; (2) if men have done so. In the first case, he proposes as the best means of overcoming this instigation, that He (Jehovah) should smell an offering. The *Hiphil* יָרַח only means to smell, not to cause to smell. The subject is Jehovah. Smelling a sacrifice is an anthropomorphic term, used to denote the divine satisfaction (cf. Gen. viii. 21). The meaning of the words, " *let Jehovah smell sacrifice,*" is therefore, " let Saul appease the wrath of God by the presentation of acceptable sacrifices." What

sacrifices they are which please God, is shown in Ps. li. 18, 19;
and it is certainly not by accident merely that David uses the
word *minchah*, the technical expression in the law for the blood-
less sacrifice, which sets forth the sanctification of life in good
works. The thought to which David gives utterance here,
namely, that God instigates a man to evil actions, is met with in
other passages of the Old Testament. It not only lies at the
foundation of the words of David in Ps. li. 6 (cf. Hengstenberg
on *Psalms*), but is also clearly expressed in 2 Sam. xxiv. 1,
where Jehovah instigates David to number the people, and
where this instigation is described as a manifestation of the anger
of God against Israel; and in 2 Sam. xvi. 10 sqq., where David
says, with regard to Shimei, that God had bade him curse him.
These passages also show that God only instigates those who have
sinned against Him to evil deeds; and therefore that the instigation consists in the fact that God impels sinners to manifest
the wickedness of their hearts in deeds, or furnishes the opportunity and occasion for the unfolding and practical manifestation
of the evil desires of the heart, that the sinner may either be
brought to the knowledge of his more evil ways and also to
repentance, through the evil deed and its consequences, or, if
the heart should be hardened still more by the evil deed, that
it may become ripe for the judgment of death. The instigation of a sinner to evil is simply one peculiar way in which God,
as a general rule, punishes sins through sinners; for God only
instigates to evil actions such as have drawn down the wrath of
God upon themselves in consequence of their sin. When David
supposes the fact that Jehovah has instigated Saul against him,
he acknowledges, implicitly at least, that he himself is a sinner,
whom the Lord may be intending to punish, though without
lessening Saul's wrong by this indirect confession.

The second supposition is: "*if, however, children of men*"
(*sc.* have instigated thee against me); in which case "*let them
be cursed before the Lord; for they drive me now* (this day) *that
I dare not attach myself to the inheritance of Jehovah* (*i.e.* the
people of God), *saying, Go, serve other gods.*" The meaning is
this: They have carried it so far now, that I am obliged to separate from the people of God, to fly from the land of the Lord,
and, because far away from His sanctuary, to serve other gods.
The idea implied in the closing words was, that Jehovah could

only be worshipped in Canaan, at the sanctuary consecrated to Him, because it was only there that He manifested himself to His people, and revealed His face or gracious presence (*vid.* Ps. xlii. 2, 3, lxxxiv. 11, cxliii. 6 sqq.). " We are not to understand that the enemies of David were actually accustomed to use these very words, but David was thinking of deeds rather than words" (Calvin).—Ver. 20. " *And now let not my blood fall to the earth far away from the face of the Lord,*" *i.e.* do not carry it so far as to compel me to perish in a foreign land. " *For the king of Israel has gone out to seek a single flea* (*vid.* ch. xxiv. 15), *as one hunts a partridge upon the mountains.*" This last comparison does not of course refer to the first, so that " the object of comparison is compared again with something else," as Thenius supposes, but it refers rather to the whole of the previous clause. The king of Israel is pursuing something very trivial, and altogether unworthy of his pursuit, just as if one were hunting a partridge upon the mountains. " No one would think it worth his while to hunt a single partridge that had flown to the mountains, when they may be found in coveys in the fields" (Winer, *Bibl. R. W.* ii. p. 307). This comparison, therefore, does not presuppose that קֹרֵא must be a bird living upon the mountains, as Thenius maintains, so as to justify his altering the text according to the Septuagint. These words of David were perfectly well adapted to sharpen Saul's conscience, and induce him to desist from his enmity, if he still had an ear for the voice of truth.

Vers. 21-25. Moreover, Saul could not help confessing, " *I have sinned: return, my son David; I will do thee harm no more, because my life was precious in thine eyes that day.*" A good intention, which he never carried out. " He declared that he would never do any more what he had already so often promised not to do again ; and yet he did not fail to do it again and again. He ought rather to have taken refuge with God, and appealed to Him for grace, that he might not fall into such sins again ; yea, he should have entreated David himself to pray for him" (*Berleb. Bible*). He adds still further, " *Behold, I have acted foolishly, and have gone sore astray ;*" but yet he persists in this folly. " There is no sinner so hardened, but that God gives him now and then some rays of light, which show him all his error. But, alas ! when they are awakened by such divine movings, it is only for a few moments; and such impulses are no sooner past, than they fall back again immediately into their former life, and forget all that they have promised."—Vers. 22, 23. David then bade the king send a servant to fetch back the spear and pitcher, and reminded him again of the recompense of God : "*Jehovah will recompense His righteousness and His faithfulness to the man into whose hand Jehovah hath given thee to-day; and (for) I would not stretch out my hand against the anointed of the Lord.*"—Ver. 24. "*Behold, as thy soul has been greatly esteemed in my eyes to-day, so will my soul be greatly esteemed in the eyes of Jehovah, that He will save me out of all tribulation.*" These words do not contain any " sounding of his own praises" (Thenius), but are merely the testimony of a good conscience before God in the presence of an enemy, who is indeed obliged to confess his wrong-doing, but who no longer feels or acknowledges his need of forgiveness. For even Saul's reply to these words in ver. 25 ("*Blessed art thou, my son David: thou wilt undertake, and also prevail :*" יָכֹל תּוּכָל, *lit.* to vanquish, *i.e.* to carry out what one undertakes) does not express any genuine goodwill towards David, but only an acknowledgment, forced upon him by this fresh experience of David's magnanimity, that God was blessing all his undertakings, so that he would prevail. Saul had no more thoughts of any real reconciliation with David. "*David went his way, and Saul turned to his place*" (cf. Num. xxiv. 25). Thus they parted, and never saw each other again. There is nothing said about Saul returning to his house, as there was when his life was first spared (ch. xxiv. 23). On the contrary, he does not seem to have given up pursuing David; for, according to ch. xxvii., David was obliged to take refuge in a foreign land, and carry out what he had described in ver. 19 as his greatest calamity.

DAVID AT ZIKLAG IN THE LAND OF THE PHILISTINES.— CHAP. XXVII.

In his despair of being able permanently to escape the plots of Saul in the land of Israel, David betook himself, with his attendants, to the neighbouring land of the Philistines, to king Achish of Gath, and received from him the town of Ziklag, which was assigned him at his own request as a dwelling-place (vers. 1-7). From this point he made attacks upon certain tribes on the southern frontier of Canaan which were hostile to Israel, but described them to Achish as attacks upon Judah and its dependencies, that he might still retain the protection of the Philistian chief (vers. 8-12). David had fled to Achish at Gath once before ; but on that occasion he had been obliged to feign insanity in order to preserve his life, because he was recognised as the conqueror of Goliath. This act of David was not forgotten by the Philistines even now. But as David had been pursued by Saul for many years, Achish did not hesitate to give a place of refuge in his land to the fugitive who had been outlawed by the king of Israel, the arch-enemy of the Philistines, possibly with the hope that if a fresh war with Saul should break out, he should be able to reap some advantage from David's friendship.

Vers. 1-7. The result of the last affair with Saul, after his life had again been spared, could not fail to confirm David in his conviction that Saul would not desist from pursuing him, and that if he stayed any longer in the land, he would fall eventually into the hands of his enemy. With this conviction, he formed the following resolution : *" Now shall I be consumed one day by the hand of Saul: there is no good to me* (*i.e.* it will not be well with me if I remain in the land), *but* (כִּי after a negative) *I will flee into the land of the Philistines; so will Saul desist from me to seek me further* (*i.e.* give up seeking me) *in the whole of the territory of Israel, and I shall escape his hand."—* Ver. 2. Accordingly he went over with the 600 men who were with him to Achish, the king of Gath. *Achish*, the son of *Maoch*, is in all probability the same person not only as the king *Achish* mentioned in ch. xxi. 11, but also as *Achish* the son of *Maachah* (1 Kings ii. 39), since *Maoch* and *Maachah* are certainly only different forms of the same name ; and a fifty years' reign, which we should have in that case to ascribe to Achish, is not impossible.—Vers. 3, 4. Achish allotted dwelling-places in his capital, Gath, for David and his wives, and for all his retinue ; and Saul desisted from any further pursuit of David when he was informed of his flight to Gath. The *Chethibh* יוסף is apparently only a copyist's error for יָסַף.— Vers. 5 sqq. In the capital of the kingdom, however, David

felt cramped, and therefore entreated Achish to assign him one
of the land (or provincial) towns to dwell in; whereupon he
gave him *Ziklag* for that purpose. This town was given to
the Simeonites in the time of Joshua (Josh. xix. 5), but was
afterwards taken by the Philistines, probably not long before
the time of David, and appears to have been left without inhabitants in consequence of this conquest. The exact situation,
in the western part of the Negeb, has not been clearly ascertained (see at Josh. xv. 31). Achish appears to have given it
to David. This is implied in the remark, " *Therefore Ziklag
came to the kings of Judah (i.e.* became their property) *unto this
day.*"—Ver. 7. The statement that David remained a year and
four months in the land of the Philistines, is a proof of the
historical character of the whole narrative. The יָמִים before
the " four months" signifies *a year;* strictly speaking, a term of
days which amounted to a full year (as in Lev. xxv. 29 : see
also 1 Sam. i. 3, 20, ii. 19).

Vers. 8–12. From Ziklag David made an attack upon the
Geshurites, Gerzites, and Amalekites, smote them without
leaving a man alive, and returned with much booty. The
occasion of this attack is not mentioned, as being a matter of
indifference in relation to the chief object of the history; but it
is no doubt to be sought for in plundering incursions made by
these tribes into the land of Israel. For David would hardly
have entered upon such a war in the situation in which he was
placed at that time without some such occasion, seeing that it
would be almost sure to bring him into suspicion with Achish,
and endanger his safety. וַיַּעַל, " *he advanced,*" the verb being
used, as it frequently is, to denote the advance of an army
against a people or town (see at Josh. viii. 1). At the same
time, the tribes which he attacked may have had their seat
upon the mountain plateau in the northern portion of the desert
of Paran, so that David was obliged to march *up* to reach them.
פָּשַׁט, *to invade* for the purpose of devastation and plunder.
Geshuri is a tribe mentioned in Josh. xiii. 2 as living in the
south of the territory of the Philistines, and is a different tribe
from the Geshurites in the north-east of Gilead (Josh. xii. 5,
xiii. 11, 13; Deut. iii. 14). These are the only passages in
which they are mentioned. The *Gerzites*, or *Gizrites* according
to the *Keri*, are entirely unknown. Bonfrere and Clericus

suppose them to be the *Gerreni* spoken of in 2 Macc. xiii. 24, who inhabited the town of *Gerra*, between Rhinocolura and Pelusium (Strabo, xvi. 760), or *Gerron* (Ptol. iv. 5). This conjecture is a possible one, but is very uncertain nevertheless, as the Gerzites certainly dwelt somewhere in the desert of Arabia. At any rate Grotius and Ewald cannot be correct in their opinion that they were the inhabitants of *Gezer* (Josh. x. 33). The *Amalekites* were the remnant of this old hereditary foe of the Israelites, who had taken to flight on Saul's war of extermination, and had now assembled again (see at ch. xv. 8, 9). "*For they inhabit the land, where you go from of old to Shur, even to the land of Egypt.*" The אֲשֶׁר before מֵעוֹלָם may be explained from the fact that בּוֹאֲךָ is not adverbial here, but is construed according to its form as an infinitive : literally, "*where from of old thy coming is to Shur.*" אֲשֶׁר cannot have crept into the text through a copyist's mistake, as such a mistake would not have found its way into all the MSS. The fact that the early translators did not render the word proves nothing against its genuineness, but merely shows that the translators regarded it as superfluous. Moreover, the Alexandrian text is decidedly faulty here, and עוֹלָם is confounded with עֵלָם, ἀπὸ Γελάμ. *Shur* is the desert of *Jifar*, which is situated in front of Egypt (as in ch. xv. 7). These tribes were nomads, and had large flocks, which David took with him as booty when he had smitten the tribes themselves. After his return, David betook himself to Achish, to report to the Philistian king concerning his enterprise, and deceive him as to its true character.—Ver. 10. Achish said, "*Ye have not made an invasion to-day, have ye ?*" אַל, like μή, in an interrogative sense ; the הֲ has dropped out : vid. Ewald, § 324, b. David replied, "*Against the south of Judah, and the south of the Jerahmeelites, and into the south of the Kenites,*" sc. we have made an incursion. This reply shows that the Geshurites, Gerzites, and Amalekites dwelt close to the southern boundary of Judah, so that David was able to represent the march against these tribes to Achish as a march against the south of Judah, to make him believe that he had been making an attack upon the southern territory of Judah and its dependencies. The *Negeb* of Judah is the land between the mountains of Judah and the desert of Arabia (see at Josh. xv. 21). The *Jerahmeelites* are the descendants of

Jerahmeel, the first-born of Hezron (1 Chron. ii. 9, 25, 26), and therefore one of the three large families of Judah who sprang from Hezron. They probably dwelt on the southern frontier of the tribe of Judah (*vid.* ch. xxx. 29). The *Kenites* were *protégés* of Judah (see at ch. xv. 6, and Judg. i. 16). In ver. 11 the writer introduces the remark, that in his raid David left neither man nor woman of his enemies alive, to take them to Gath, because he thought " *they might report against us, and say, Thus hath David done.*" There ought to be a major point under עָשָׂה דָוִד, as the following clause does not contain the words of the slaughtered enemies, but is a clause appended by the historian himself, to the effect that David continued to act in that manner as long as he dwelt in the land of the Philistines. מִשְׁפָּט, the mode of procedure ; *lit.* the right which he exercised (see ch. viii. 9).—Ver. 12 is connected with ver. 10 ; Achish believed David's words, and said (to himself), " *He hath made himself stinking (i.e.* hated) *among his own people, among Israel, and will be my servant (i.e.* subject to me) *for ever.*"

DAVID IN THE ARMY OF THE PHILISTINES. ATTACK UPON ISRAEL. SAUL AND THE WITCH OF ENDOR.—CHAP. XXVIII.

Vers. 1, 2. The danger into which David had plunged through his flight into the land of the Philistines, and still more through the artifice with which he had deceived king Achish as to his real feelings, was to be very soon made apparent to him. For example, when the Philistines went to war again with Israel, Achish summoned him to go with his men in the army of the Philistines to the war against his own people and land, and David could not disregard the summons. But even if he had not brought himself into this danger without some fault of his own, he had at any rate only taken refuge with the Philistines in the greatest extremity; and what further he had done, was only done to save his own life. The faithful covenant God helped him therefore out of this trouble, and very soon afterwards put an end to his persecution by the fact that Saul lost his life in the war.—Ver. 1. "*In those days,*" *i.e.* whilst David was living in the land of the Philistines, it came to pass that the Philistines gathered their armies together for a campaign against Israel. And Achish sent word to David that he was to go with him in his army along with his men; and David answered (ver. 2), " *Thereby* (on this occasion) *thou shalt learn what thy servant will do.*" This reply was ambiguous. The words " what thy servant will do" contained no distinct promise of faithful assistance in the war with the Israelites, as the expression " *thy servant* " is only the ordinary periphrasis for "*I*" in conversation with a superior. And there is just as little ground for inferring from ch. xxix. 8 that David was disposed to help the Philistines against Saul and the Israelites; for, as Calovius has observed, even there he gives no such promise, but " merely asks for information, that he may discover the king's intentions and feelings concerning him: he simply protests that he has done nothing to prevent his placing confidence in him, or to cause him to shut him out of the battle." Judging from his previous acts, it would necessarily have been against his conscience to fight against his own people. Nevertheless, in the situation in which he was placed he did not venture to give a distinct refusal to the summons of the king. He therefore gave an ambiguous answer, in the hope that God would show him a way out of this conflict between his inmost conviction and his duty to obey the Philistian king. He had no doubt prayed earnestly for this in his heart. And the faithful God helped His servant: first of all by the fact that Achish accepted his indefinite declaration as a promise of unconditional fidelity, as his answer " *so* (לָכֵן, *itaque*, *i.e.* that being the case, if thy conduct answers to thy promise) *I will make thee the keeper of my head*" (*i.e.* of my person) implies; and still more fully by the fact that the princes of the Philistines overturned the decision of their king (ch. xxix. 3 sqq.).

Vers. 3–25. *Saul with the witch at Endor.*—The invasion of Israel by the Philistines, which brought David into so difficult a situation, drove king Saul to despair, so that in utter helplessness he had recourse to ungodly means of inquiring into the future, which he himself had formerly prohibited, and to his horror had to hear the sentence of his own death. This account is introduced with the remark in ver. 3 that Samuel was dead and had been buried at Ramah (cf. ch. xxv. 1; וּבְעִירוֹ, with an explanatory *vav*, and indeed in his own city), and that Saul had expelled "*those that had familiar spirits and the wizards out of the land*" (on the terms employed, *oboth* and *yiddonim*,

see at Lev. xix. 31).   He had done this in accordance with the
law in Lev. xix. 31, xx. 27, and Deut. xviii. 10 sqq.—Vers.
4, 5. When the Philistines advanced and encamped at *Shunem*,
Saul brought all Israel together and encamped at *Gilboa*, *i.e.*
upon the mountain of that name on the north-eastern edge of
the plain of Jezreel, which slopes off from a height of about
1250 feet into the valley of the Jordan, and is not far from
Beisan.   On the north of the western extremity of this mountain was *Shunem*, the present *Sulem* or *Solam* (see at Josh. xix.
18); it was hardly two hours distant, so that the camp of the
Philistines might be seen from Gilboa.   When Saul saw this,
he was thrown into such alarm that his heart greatly trembled.
As Saul had been more than once victorious in his conflicts with
the Philistines, his great fear at the sight of the Philistian army
can hardly be attributed to any other cause than the feeling
that God had forsaken him, by which he was suddenly overwhelmed.—Ver. 6. In his anxiety he inquired of the Lord;
but the Lord neither answered him by dreams, nor by Urim,
nor by prophets, that is to say, not by any of the three media
by which He was accustomed to make known His will to Israel.
שָׁאַל בַּיהוָה is the term usually employed to signify inquiring the
will and counsel of God through the Urim and Thummim of
the high priest (see at Judg. i. 1); and this is the case here,
with the simple difference that here the other means of inquiring
the counsel of God are also included.   On dreams, see at Num.
xii. 6.   According to Num. xxvii. 21, *Urim* denotes divine revelation through the high priest *by means of the ephod*.   But the
high priest Abiathar had been with the ephod in David's camp
ever since the murder of the priests at Nob (ch. xxii. 20 sqq.,
xxiii. 6, xxx. 7).   How then could Saul inquire of God through
the Urim?   This question, which was very copiously discussed
by the earlier commentators, and handled in different ways, may
be decided very simply on the supposition, that after the death
of Ahimelech and the flight of his son, another high priest had
been appointed at the tabernacle, and another ephod made for
him, with the *choshen* or breastplate, and the Urim and Thummim.   It is no proof to the contrary that there is nothing said
about this.   We have no continuous history of the worship at
the tabernacle, but only occasional notices.   And from these it
is perfectly clear that the public worship at the tabernacle was

not suspended on the murder of the priests, but was continued still. For in the first years of David's reign we find the tabernacle at Gibeon, and Zadok the son of Ahitub, of the line of Eleazar, officiating there as high priest (1 Chron. xvi. 39, compared with ch. v. 38 and vi. 38) ; from which it follows with certainty, that after the destruction of Nob by Saul the tabernacle was removed to Gibeon, and the worship of the congregation continued there. From this we may also explain in a very simple manner the repeated allusions to two high priests in David's time (2 Sam. viii. 17, xv. 24, 29, 35 ; 1 Chron. xv. 11, xviii. 16). The reason why the Lord did not answer Saul is to be sought for in the wickedness of Saul, which rendered him utterly unworthy to find favour with God.

Vers. 7–14. Instead of recognising this, however, and searching his own heart, Saul attempted to obtain a revelation of the future in ungodly ways. He commanded his servants (ver. 7) to seek for a woman that had a familiar spirit. *Baalath-ob:* the mistress (or possessor) of a conjuring spirit, *i.e.* of a spirit with which the dead were conjured up, for the purpose of making inquiry concerning the future (see at Lev. xix. 31). There was a woman of this kind at *Endor*, which still exists as a village under the old name upon the northern shoulder of the *Duhy* or Little Hermon (see at Josh. xvii. 11), and therefore only two German (ten English) miles from the Israelitish camp at Gilboa.—Ver. 8. Saul went to this person by night and in disguise, that he might not be recognised, accompanied by two men ; and said to her, " *Divine to me through necromancy, and bring me up whomsoever I tell thee.*" The words "bring me up," etc., are an explanation or more precise definition of "divine unto me," etc. Prophesying by the *Ob* was probably performed by calling up a departed spirit from Sheol, and obtaining prophecies, *i.e.* disclosures concerning one's own fate, through the medium of such a spirit. On the form קְסוֹמִי (*Chethibh*), see at Judg. ix. 8.—Ver. 9. Such a demand placed the woman in difficulty. As Saul had driven the necromantists out of the land, she was afraid that the unknown visitor (for it is evident from ver. 12 that she did not recognise Saul at first) might be laying a snare for her soul with his request, to put her to death, *i.e.* might have come to her merely for the purpose of spying her out as a conjurer of the dead, and then inflicting

capital punishment upon her according to the law (Lev. xx. 27).
—Vers. 10, 11. But when Saul swore to her that no punishment should fall upon her on that account (אִם יִקְּרֵךְ, "*shall
assuredly not fall upon thee*"), an oath which showed how
utterly hardened Saul was, she asked him, "*Whom shall I
bring up to thee?*" and Saul replied, "*Bring me up Samuel,*"
sc. from the region of the dead, or *Sheol*, which was thought to
be under the ground. This idea arose from the fact that the
dead were buried in the earth, and was connected with the
thought of heaven as being above the earth. Just as heaven,
regarded as the abode of God and the holy angels and blessed
spirits, is above the earth; so, on the other hand, the region
of death and the dead is beneath the ground. And with our
modes of thought, which are so bound up with time and space,
it is impossible to represent to ourselves in any other way the
difference and contrast between blessedness with God and the
shade-life in death.—Ver. 12. The woman then commenced
her conjuring arts. This must be supplied from the context,
as ver. 12 merely states what immediately ensued. "*When
the woman saw Samuel, she cried aloud,*" *sc.* at the form which
appeared to her so unexpectedly. These words imply most
unquestionably that the woman saw an apparition which she
did not anticipate, and therefore that she was not really able to
conjure up departed spirits or persons who had died, but that
she either merely pretended to do so, or if her witchcraft was
not mere trickery and delusion, but had a certain demoniacal
background, that the appearance of Samuel differed essentially
from everything she had experienced and effected before, and
therefore filled her with alarm and horror. The very fact,
however, that she recognised Saul as soon as Samuel appeared,
precludes us from declaring her art to have been nothing more
than jugglery and deception; for she said to him, "*Why hast
thou cheated me, as thou art certainly Saul?*" *i.e.* why hast thou
deceived me as to thy person? why didst thou not tell me that
thou wast king Saul? Her recognition of Saul when Samuel
appeared may be easily explained, if we assume that the woman
had fallen into a state of *clairvoyance*, in which she recognised
persons who, like Saul in his disguise, were unknown to her by
face.—Ver. 13. The king quieted her fear, and then asked her
what she had seen; whereupon she gave him a fuller descrip-

tion of the apparition : "*I saw a celestial being come up from the earth*." *Elohim* does not signify gods here, nor yet God ; still less an angel or a ghost, or even a person of superior rank, but a celestial (super-terrestrial), heavenly, or spiritual being.— Ver. 14. Upon Saul's further inquiry as to his form, she replied, "*An old man is ascending, and he is wrapped in a mantle*." *Meïl* is the prophet's mantle, such as Samuel was accustomed to wear when he was alive (see ch. xv. 27). Saul recognised from this that the person who had been called up was Samuel, and he fell upon his face to the ground, to give expression to his reverence. Saul does not appear to have seen the apparition itself. But it does not follow from this that there was no such apparition at all, and the whole was an invention on the part of the witch. It needs an opened eye, such as all do not possess, to see a departed spirit or celestial being. The eyes of the body are not enough for this.

Vers. 15–22. Then Samuel said, " *Why hast thou disturbed me* (*sc.* from my rest in Hades; cf. Isa. xiv. 9), *to bring me up ?*" It follows, no doubt, from this that Samuel had been disturbed from his rest by Saul; but whether this had been effected by the conjuring arts of the witch, or by a miracle of God himself, is left undecided. Saul replied, "*I am sore oppressed, for the Philistines fight against me, and God has departed from me, and answers me no more, either by prophets or by dreams ; then I had thee called* (on the intensified form וָאֶקְרָאֶה, *vid.* Ewald, § 228, *c*), *to make known to me what I am to do*." The omission of any reference to the Urim is probably to be interpreted very simply from the brevity of the account, and not from the fact that Saul shrank from speaking about the oracle of the high priest, on account of the massacre of the priests which had taken place by his command. There is a contradiction, however, in Saul's reply : for if God had forsaken him, he could not expect any answer from Him ; and if God did not reply to his inquiry through the regularly appointed media of His revelation, how could he hope to obtain any divine revelation through the help of a witch ? " When living prophets gave no answer, he thought that a dead one might be called up, as if a dead one were less dependent upon God than the living, or that, even in opposition to the will of God, he might reply through the arts of a conjuring woman. Truly, if he perceived that God was hostile to

him, he ought to have been all the more afraid, lest His enmity
should be increased by his breach of His laws. But fear and
superstition never reason" (Clericus). Samuel points out this
contradiction (ver. 16): "*Why dost thou ask me, since Jehovah
hath departed from thee, and is become thine enemy?*" The
meaning is: How canst thou expect an answer under these
circumstances from me, the prophet of Jehovah? עָרֶךְ, from עָר,
signifies an enemy here (from עִיר, *fervour*); and this meaning is
confirmed by Ps. cxxxix. 20 and Dan. iv. 16 (Chald.). There
is all the less ground for any critical objection to the reading,
as the Chaldee and Vulgate give a periphrastic rendering of
"enemy," whilst the Sept., Syr., and Arab. have merely paraphrased according to conjectures. Samuel then announced his
fate (vers. 17–19): "*Jehovah hath performed for himself, as He
spake by me* (לֹו, for himself, which the LXX. and Vulg. have
arbitrarily altered into לְךָ, σοί, *tibi* (to thee), is correctly explained by Seb. Schmidt, 'according to His grace, or to fulfil
and prove His truth'); *and Jehovah hath rent the kingdom out of
thy hand, and given it to thy neighbour David.*" The perfects
express the purpose of God, which had already been formed,
and was now about to be fulfilled.—Ver. 18. The reason for
Saul's rejection is then given, as in ch. xv. 23: "*Because* (כַּאֲשֶׁר,
according as) *thou . . . hast not executed the fierceness of His
anger upon Amalek, therefore hath Jehovah done this thing to thee
this day.*" "*This thing*" is the distress of which Saul had complained, with its consequences. וַיִּתֵּן, *that Jehovah may give* (= for
He will give) *Israel also with thee into the hand of the Philistines.*
"*To-morrow wilt thou and thy sons be with me* (*i.e.* in Sheol,
with the dead); *also the camp of Israel will Jehovah give into
the hand of the Philistines,*" *i.e.* give up to them to plunder.
The overthrow of the people was to heighten Saul's misery,
when he saw the people plunged with him into ruin through his
sin (O. v. Gerlach). Thus was the last hope taken from Saul.
His day of grace was gone, and judgment was now to burst
upon him without delay.—Ver. 20. These words so alarmed
him, that he fell his whole length upon the ground; for he had
been kneeling hitherto (ver. 14). He "*fell straightway* (*lit.* he
hastened and fell) *upon the ground. For he was greatly terrified
at the words of Samuel: there was also no strength in him, because
he had eaten no food the whole day and the whole night,*" *sc.* from

mental perturbation or inward excitement. Terror and bodily exhaustion caused him to fall powerless to the ground.—Vers. 21, 22. The woman then came to him and persuaded him to strengthen himself with food for the journey which he had to take. It by no means follows from the expression "*came unto Saul*," that the woman was in an adjoining room during the presence of the apparition, and whilst Samuel was speaking, but only that she was standing at some distance off, and came up to him to speak to him when he had fallen fainting to the ground. As she had fulfilled his wish at the risk of her own life, she entreated him now to gratify her wish, and let her set a morsel of bread before him and eat. "*That strength may be in thee when thou goest thy way*" (*i.e.* when thou returnest).

This narrative, when read without prejudice, makes at once and throughout the impression conveyed by the Septuagint at 1 Chron. x. 13: ἐπηρώτησε Σαοὺλ ἐν τῷ ἐγγαστριμύθῳ τοῦ ζητῆσαι, καὶ ἀπεκρίνατο αὐτῷ Σαμουὴλ ὁ προφήτης; and still more clearly at Ecclus. xlvi. 20, where it is said of Samuel: "And after his death he prophesied, and showed the king his end, and lifted up his voice from the earth in prophecy, to blot out the wickedness of the people." Nevertheless the fathers, reformers, and earlier Christian theologians, with very few exceptions, assumed that there was not a real appearance of Samuel, but only an imaginary one. According to the explanation given by Ephraem Syrus, an apparent image of Samuel was presented to the eye of Saul through demoniacal arts. Luther and Calvin adopted the same view, and the earlier Protestant theologians followed them in regarding the apparition as nothing but a diabolical spectre, a phantasm, or diabolical spectre in the form of Samuel, and Samuel's announcement as nothing but a diabolical revelation made by divine permission, in which truth is mixed with falsehood.[1] It was not till the

---

[1] Thus Luther says (in his work upon the abuses of the Mass, 1522): "The raising of Samuel by a soothsayer or witch, in 1 Sam. xxviii. 11, 12, was certainly merely a spectre of the devil; not only because the Scriptures state that it was effected by a woman who was full of devils (for who could believe that the souls of believers, who are in the hand of God, Ecclus. iii. 1, and in the bosom of Abraham, Luke xvi. 32, were under the power of the devil, and of simple men ?), but also because it was evidently in opposition to the command of God that Saul and the woman inquired of the dead. The Holy Ghost cannot do anything against this himself, nor can He help

seventeenth century that the opinion was expressed, that the apparition of Samuel was merely a delusion produced by the witch, without any real background at all. After Reginald Scotus and Balth. Becker had given expression to this opinion, it was more fully elaborated by Ant. van Dale, in his *dissert. de divinationibus idololatricis sub V. T.*; and in the so-called age of enlightenment this was the prevailing opinion, so that Thenius still regards it as an established fact, not only that the woman was an impostor, but that the historian himself regarded the whole thing as an imposture. There is no necessity to refute this opinion at the present day. Even Fr. Boettcher (*de inferis*, pp. 111 sqq.), who looks upon the thing as an imposture, admits that the first recorder of the occurrence " believed that Samuel appeared and prophesied, *contrary to the expectation* of the witch;" and that the author of the books of Samuel was convinced that the prophet was raised up and prophesied, so that after his death he was proved to be the true prophet of Jehovah, although through the intervention of ungodly arts (cf. Ezek. xiv. 7, 9). But the view held by the early church does not do justice to the scriptural narrative; and hence the more modern orthodox commentators are unanimous in the opinion that the departed prophet did really appear and announce the destruction of Saul, not, however, in consequence of the magical arts of the witch, but through a miracle wrought by the omnipotence of God. This is most decidedly favoured by the fact, that the prophetic historian speaks throughout of the appearance, not of

---

those who act in opposition to it." Calvin also regards the apparition as only a spectre (Hom. 100 in 1 Sam.): " It is certain," he says, " that it was not really Samuel, for God would never have allowed His prophets to be subjected to such diabolical conjuring. For here is a sorceress calling up the dead from the grave. Does any one imagine that God wished His prophet to be exposed to such ignominy; as if the devil had power over the bodies and souls of the saints which are in His keeping? The souls of the saints are said to rest and live in God, waiting for their happy resurrection. Besides, are we to believe that Samuel took his cloak with him into the grave? For all these reasons, it appears evident that the apparition was nothing more than a spectre, and that the senses of the woman herself were so deceived, that she thought she saw Samuel, whereas it really was not he." The earlier orthodox theologians also disputed the reality of the appearance of the departed Samuel on just the same grounds; *e.g.* Seb. Schmidt (*Comm.*); Aug. Pfeiffer; Sal. Deyling; and Buddeus, *Hist. Eccl. V. T.* ii. p. 243, and many more.

a ghost, but of Samuel himself. He does this not only in ver. 12, "When the woman saw Samel she cried aloud," but also in vers. 14, 15, 16, and 20. It is also sustained by the circumstance, that not only do the words of Samuel to Saul, in vers. 16–19, create the impression that it is Samuel himself who is speaking; but his announcement contains so distinct a prophecy of the death of Saul and his sons, that it is impossible to imagine that it can have proceeded from the mouth of an impostor, or have been an inspiration of Satan. On the other hand, the remark of Calvin, to the effect that " God sometimes gives to devils the power of revealing secrets to us, which they have learned from the Lord," could only be regarded as a valid objection, provided that the narrative gave us some intimation that the apparition and the speaking were nothing but a diabolical delusion. But it does nothing of the kind. It is true, the opinion that the witch conjured up the prophet Samuel was very properly disputed by the early theologians, and rejected by Theodoret as " unholy, and even impious ;" and the text of Scripture indicates clearly enough that the very opposite was the case, by the remark that the witch herself was terrified at the appearance of Samuel (ver. 12). Shöbel is therefore quite correct in saying: " It was not at the call of the idolatrous king, nor at the command of the witch,—neither of whom had the power to bring him up, or even to make him hear their voice in his rest in the grave,—that Samuel came ; nor was it merely by divine 'permission,' which is much too little to say. No, rather it was by the special command of God that he left his grave (?), like a faithful servant whom his master arouses at midnight, to let in an inmate of the house who has wilfully stopped out late, and has been knocking at the door. 'Why do you disturb me out of my sleep ?' would always be the question put to the unwelcome comer, although it was not by his noise, but really by his master's command, that he had been aroused. Samuel asked the same question." The prohibition of witchcraft and necromancy (Deut. xviii. 11 ; Isa. viii. 19), which the earlier writers quote against this, does not preclude the possibility of God having, for His own special reasons, caused Samuel to appear. On the contrary, the appearance itself was of such a character, that it could not fail to show to the witch and the king, that God does not allow His prohibitions to be infringed with impunity. The very same thing occurred here, which God threatened to idolaters through the medium of Ezekiel (ch. xiv. 4, 7, 8): "If they come to the prophet, I will answer them in my own way." Still less is there any force in the appeal to Luke xvi. 27 sqq., where Abraham refuses the request of the rich man in Hades, that he would send Lazarus to his father's house to preach repentance to his brethren who were still living, saying, "They have Moses and the prophets, let them hear them. If they hear not Moses and the prophets, neither will they be persuaded though one rose from the dead." For this does not affirm that the appearance of a dead man is a thing impossible in itself, but only describes it as useless and ineffectual, so far as the conversion of the ungodly is concerned.

The reality of the appearance of Samuel from the kingdom of the dead cannot therefore be called in question, especially as it has an analogon in the appearance of Moses and Elijah at the transfiguration of Christ (Matt. xvii. 3; Luke ix. 30, 31); except that this difference must not be overlooked, namely, that Moses and Elijah appeared "in glory," i.e. in a glorified form, whereas Samuel appeared in earthly corporeality with the prophet's mantle which he had worn on earth. Just as the transfiguration of Christ was a phenomenal anticipation of His future heavenly glory, into which He was to enter after His resurrection and ascension, so may we think of the appearance of Moses and Elijah "in glory" upon the mount of transfiguration as an anticipation of their heavenly transfiguration in eternal life with God. It was different with Samuel, whom God brought up from Hades through an act of His omnipotence. This appearance is not to be regarded as the appearance of one who had risen in a glorified body; but though somewhat spirit-like in its external manifestation, so that it was only to the witch that it was visible, and not to Saul, it was merely an appearance of the soul of Samuel, that had been at rest in Hades, in the clothing of the earthly corporeality and dress of the prophet, which were assumed for the purpose of rendering it visible. In this respect the appearance of Samuel rather resembled the appearances of incorporeal angels in human form and dress, such as the three angels who came to Abraham in the grove at Mamre (Gen. xviii.), and the angel who appeared to Manoah (Judg. xiii.); with this exception, however, that these angels manifested themselves in a human form, which was visible to the ordinary bodily eye, whereas Samuel appeared in the spirit-like form of the inhabitants of Hades. In all these cases the bodily form and clothing were only a dress assumed for the soul or spirit, and intended to facilitate perception, so that such appearances furnish no proof that the souls of departed men possess an immaterial corporeality.[1]

Vers. 23–25. On Saul's refusing to take food, his servants (*i.e.* his two attendants) also pressed him, so that he yielded, rose up from the ground, and sat down upon the bed (*mittah*: *i.e.* a bench by the wall of the room provided with pillows); whereupon the woman quickly sacrificed (served up) a stalled calf, baked unleavened cakes, and set the food she had prepared before the king and his servants. The woman did all this from natural sympathy for the unhappy king, and not, as Thenius supposes, to remove all suspicion of deception from Saul's mind; for she had not deceived the king at all.—Ver. 25. When Saul and his servants had eaten, they started upon their way, and went back that night to Gilboa, which was about ten miles distant, where the battle occurred the next day, and Saul and his sons fell. " Saul was too hardened in his sin to express any grief or pain, either on his own account or because of the

---

[1] Delitzsch (*bibl. Psychol.* pp. 427 sqq.) has very properly rejected, not only the opinion that Samuel and Moses were raised up from the dead for the purpose of a transient appearance, and then died again, but also the idea that they appeared in their material bodies, a notion upon which Calvin rests his argument against the reality of the appearance of Samuel. But when he gives it as his opinion, that the angels who appeared in human form assumed this form by virtue of their own power, inasmuch as they can make themselves visible to whomsoever they please, and infers still further from this, " that the outward form in which Samuel and Moses appeared (which corresponded to their form when on this side the grave) was the immaterial production of their spiritual and psychical nature," he overlooks the fact, that not only Samuel, but the angels also, in the cases referred to, appeared in men's clothing, which cannot possibly be regarded as a production of their spiritual and psychical nature. The earthly dress is not indispensable to a man's existence. Adam and Eve had no clothing before the Fall, and there will be no material clothing in the kingdom of glory; for the " fine linen, pure and white," with which the bride adorns herself for the marriage supper of the Lamb, is " the righteousness of saints" (Rev. xix. 8).

fate of his sons and his people. In stolid desperation he went to meet his fate. This was the terrible end of a man whom the Spirit of God had once taken possession of and turned into another man, and whom he had endowed with gifts to be the leader of the people of God" (O. v. Gerlach).

REMOVAL OF DAVID FROM THE ARMY OF THE PHILISTINES.— CHAP. XXIX.

Vers. 1–5. Whilst Saul derived no comfort from his visit to the witch at Endor, but simply heard from the mouth of Samuel the confirmation of his rejection on the part of God, and an announcement of his approaching fate, David was delivered, through the interposition of God, from the danger of having to fight against his own people.—Ver. 1. The account of this is introduced by a fuller description of the position of the hostile army. *" The Philistines gathered all their armies together towards Aphek, but Israel encamped at the fountain in* (at) *Jezreel."* This fountain is the present *Ain Jalûd* (or *Ain Jalût, i.e.* Goliath's fountain, probably so called because it was regarded as the scene of the defeat of Goliath), a very large fountain, which issues from a cleft in the rock at the foot of the mountain on the north-eastern border of Gilboa, forming a beautifully limpid pool of about forty or fifty feet in diameter, and then flowing in a brook through the valley (Rob. *Pal.* iii. p. 168). Consequently *Aphek*, which must be carefully distinguished from the towns of the same name in Asher (Josh. xix. 30; Judg. i. 31) and upon the mountains of Judah (Josh. xv. 53) and also at Ebenezer (1 Sam. iv. 1), is to be sought for not very far from *Shunem*, in the plain of Jezreel ; according to Van de Velde's *Mem.*, by the side of the present *el Afûleh*, though the situation has not been exactly determined. The statement in the *Onom.*, " near Endor of Jezreel where Saul fought," is merely founded upon the Septuagint, in which בְּעַיִן is erroneously rendered ἐν ᾿Ενδώρ.—Vers. 2, 3. When the princes of the Philistines (*sarne*, as in Josh. xiii. 3) advanced by hundreds and thousands (*i.e.* arranged in companies of hundreds and thousands), and David and his men came behind with Achish (*i.e.* forming the rear-guard), the (other) princes pronounced against their allowing David and his men to go with them.

This did not occur at the time of their setting out, but on the road, when they had already gone some distance (compare ver. 11 with ch. xxx. 1), probably when the five princes (Josh. xiii. 3) of the Philistines had effected a junction. To the inquiry, *" What are these Hebrews doing?"* Achish replied, *" Is not this David, the servant of Saul the king of Israel, who has been with me days already, or years already? and I have found nothing in him since his coming over unto this day."* מְאוּמָה, anything at all that could render him suspicious, or his fidelity doubtful. נָפַל, to fall away and go over to a person; generally construed with אֶל (Jer. xxxvii. 13, xxxviii. 19, etc.) or עַל (Jer. xxi. 9, xxxvii. 14; 1 Chron. xii. 19, 20), but here absolutely, as the more precise meaning can be gathered from the context.—Ver. 4. But the princes, *i.e.* the four other princes of the Philistines, not the courtiers of Achish himself, were angry with Achish, and demanded, *" Send the man back, that he may return to his place, which thou hast assigned him; that he may not go down with us into the war, and may not become an adversary (satan) to us in the war; for wherewith could he show himself acceptable to his lord (viz. Saul), if not with the heads of these men?"* הֲלוֹא, *nonne*, strictly speaking, introduces a new question to confirm the previous question. *" Go down to the battle:"* this expression is used as in ch. xxvi. 10, xxx. 24, because battles were generally fought in the plains, into which the Hebrews were obliged to come down from their mountainous land. *" These men,"* i.e. the soldiers of the Philistines, to whom the princes were pointing.— Ver. 5. To justify their suspicion, the princes reminded him of their song with which the women in Israel had celebrated David's victory over Goliath (ch. xviii. 7).

Vers. 6–11. After this declaration on the part of the princes, Achish was obliged to send David back.—Vers. 6, 7. With a solemn assertion,—swearing by Jehovah to convince David all the more thoroughly of the sincerity of his declaration,—Achish said to him, *" Thou art honourable, and good in my eyes (i.e.* quite right in my estimation) *are thy going out and coming in (i.e.* all thy conduct) *with me in the camp, for I have not found anything bad in thee; but in the eyes of the princes thou art not good (i.e.* the princes do not think thee honourable, do not trust thee). *Turn now, and go in peace, that thou mayest do nothing displeasing to the princes of the Philistines."*—Ver. 8. Partly for the sake of vindicating himself against this suspicion, and partly to put the sincerity of Achish's words to the test, David replied, " *What have I done, and what hast thou found in thy servant, since I was with thee till this day, that I am not to come and fight against the enemies of my lord the king ?*" These last words are also ambiguous, since the king whom David calls his lord might be understood as meaning either Achish or Saul. Achish, in his goodness of heart, applies them without suspicion to himself ; for he assures David still more earnestly (ver. 9), that he is firmly convinced of his uprightness. " *I know that thou art good in my eyes as an angel of God,*" *i.e.* I have the strongest conviction that thou hast behaved as well towards me as an angel could ; but the princes have desired thy removal.—Ver. 10. " *And now get up early in the morning with the servants of thy lord* (*i.e.* Saul, whose subjects David's men all were), *who have come with thee ; get ye up in the morning when it gets light for you* (so that ye can see), *and go.*"—Ver. 11. In accordance with this admonition, David returned the next morning into the land of the Philistines, *i.e.* to Ziklag ; no doubt very light of heart, and praising God for having so graciously rescued him out of the disastrous situation into which he had been brought and not altogether without some fault of his own, rejoicing that " he had not committed either sin, *i.e.* had neither violated the fidelity which he owed to Achish, nor had to fight against the Israelites" (Seb. Schmidt).

DAVID AVENGES UPON THE AMALEKITES THE PLUNDERING AND BURNING OF ZIKLAG.—CHAP. XXX.

Vers. 1–10. During David's absence the Amalekites had invaded the south country, smitten Ziklag and burnt it down, and carried off the women and children whom they found there ; whereat not only were David and his men plunged into great grief on their return upon the third day, but David especially was involved in very great trouble, inasmuch as the people wanted to stone him. But he strengthened himself in the Lord his God (vers. 1–6).—Vers. 1–4 form one period, which is expanded by the introduction of several circumstantial clauses. The apodosis to " It came to pass, when," etc. (ver. 1), does not follow till ver. 4, " Then David and the people," etc. But this is formally attached to ver. 3, "so David and his men came," with which the protasis commenced in ver. 1 is resumed in an altered form. "*It came to pass, when David and his men came to Ziklag . . . the Amalekites had invaded . . . and had carried off the wives . . . and had gone their way, and David and his men came into the town* (for 'when David and his men came,' etc.), *and behold it was burned. . . . Then David and the people with him lifted up their voice.*" "*On the third day ;*" after David's dismission by Achish, not after David's departure from Ziklag. David had at any rate gone with Achish beyond Gath, and had not been sent back till the whole of the princes of the Philistines had united their armies (ch. xxix. 2 sqq.), so that he must have been absent from Ziklag more than two days, or two days and a half. This is placed beyond all doubt by vers. 11 sqq., since the Amalekites are there described as having gone off with their booty three days before David followed them, and therefore they had taken Ziklag and burned it three days before David's return. These foes had therefore taken advantage of the absence of David and his warriors, to avenge themselves for David's invasions and plunderings (ch. xxvii. 8). Of those who were carried off, "*the women*" alone are expressly mentioned in ver. 2, although the female population and all the children had been removed, as we may see from the expression "*small and great*" (vers. 3, 6). The LXX. were therefore correct, so far as the sense is concerned, in introducing the words καὶ πάντα before אֲשֶׁר בָּהּ. "*They had killed no one, but* (only) *carried away.*" נָהַג, to carry away captive, as in Isa. xx. 4. Among those who had been carried off were David's two wives, Ahinoam and Abigail (*vid.* ch. xxv. 42, 43, xxvii. 3).—Ver. 6. David was greatly distressed in consequence ; "*for the people thought* ('said,' *sc.* in their hearts) *to stone him,*" because they sought the occasion of their calamity in his connection with Achish, with which many of his adherents may very probably have been dissatisfied. "*For the soul of the whole people was embittered* (*i.e.* all the people were embittered in their souls) *because of their sons and daughters,*" who had been carried away into slavery. "*But David strengthened himself in the Lord his God,*" *i.e.* sought consolation and strength in prayer and believing confidence in the Lord (vers. 7 sqq.). This strength he manifested in the resolution to follow the foes and rescue their

booty from them. To this end he had the ephod brought by
the high priest Abiathar (cf. ch. xxiii. 9), and inquired by means
of the Urim of the Lord, "*Shall I pursue this troop? Shall I
overtake it?*" These questions were answered in the affirmative;
and the promise was added, "*and thou wilt rescue.*" So David
pursued the enemy with his six hundred men as far as the
brook *Besor,* where the rest, *i.e.* two hundred, remained standing
(stayed behind). The words וְהַנּוֹתָרִים עָמָדוּ, which are appended
in the form of a circumstantial clause, are to be connected, so
far as the facts are concerned, with what follows: whilst the
others remained behind, David pursued the enemy still farther
with four hundred men. By the word הַנּוֹתָרִים the historian
has somewhat anticipated the matter, and therefore regards it
as necessary to define the expression still further in ver. 10*b*.
We are precluded from changing the text, as Thenius suggests,
by the circumstance that all the early translators read it in this
manner, and have endeavoured to make the expression intelligible by paraphrasing it. These two hundred men were too
tired to cross the brook and go any farther. (פָּגַר, which only
occurs here and in ver. 21, signifies, in Syriac, to be weary or
exhausted.) As Ziklag was burnt down, of course they found
no provisions there, and were consequently obliged to set out in
pursuit of the foe without being able to provide themselves with
the necessary supplies. The brook *Besor* is supposed to be the
Wady *Sheriah,* which enters the sea below Ashkelon (see v.
Raumer, *Pal.* p. 52).

Vers. 11–20. On their further march they found an
Egyptian lying exhausted upon the field; and having brought
him to David, they gave him food and drink, namely "*a slice of
fig-cake* (cf. ch. xxv. 18), *and raisin-cakes to eat; whereupon his
spirit of life returned* (*i.e.* he came to himself again), *as he had
neither eaten bread nor drunk water for three days.*"—Ver. 13.
When David asked him whence he had come (*to whom, i.e.* to
what people or tribe, *dost thou belong?*), the young man said
that he was an Egyptian, and servant of an Amalekite, and
that he had been left behind by his master when he fell sick
three days before ("*to-day three,*" *sc.* days): he also said,
"*We invaded the south of the Crethites, and what belongs to
Judah, and the south of Caleb, and burned Ziklag with fire.*"
הַכְּרֵתִי, identical with כְּרֵתִים (Ezek. xxv. 16, Zeph. ii. 5), denotes

those tribes of the Philistines who dwelt in the south-west of Canaan, and is used by Ezekiel and Zephaniah as synonymous with Philistim. The origin of the name is involved in obscurity, as the explanation which prevailed for a time, viz. that it was derived from *Creta*, is without sufficient foundation (*vid.* Stark, *Gaza*, pp. 66 and 99 sqq.). The Negeb "belonging to Judah" is the eastern portion of the Negeb. One part of it belonged to the family of Caleb, and was called Caleb's Negeb (*vid.* ch. xxv. 3).—Vers. 15, 16. This Egyptian then conducted David, at his request, when he had sworn that he would neither kill him nor deliver him up to his master, down to the hostile troops, who were spread over the whole land, eating, drinking, and making merry, on account of all the great booty which they had brought out of the land of the Philistines and Judah. —Ver. 17. David surprised them in the midst of their security, and smote them from the evening twilight till the evening of the next day, so that no one escaped, with the exception of four hundred young men, who fled upon camels. *Nesheph* signifies the evening twilight here, not the dawn,—a meaning which is not even sustained by Job vii. 4. The form מָחֳרָתָם appears to be an adverbial formation, like יוֹמָם.—Vers. 18, 19. Through this victory David rescued all that the Amalekites had taken, his two wives, and all the children great and small ; also the booty that they had taken with them, so that nothing was missing.—Ver. 20 is obscure : " *And David took all the sheep and the oxen : they drove them before those cattle, and said, This is David's booty.*" In order to obtain any meaning whatever from this literal rendering of the words, we must understand by the sheep and oxen those which belonged to the Amalekites, and the flocks taken from them as booty ; and by " *those cattle,*" the cattle belonging to David and his men, which the Amalekites had driven away, and the Israelites had now recovered from them : so that David had the sheep and oxen which he had taken from the Amalekites as booty driven in front of the rest of the cattle which the Israelites had recovered ; whereupon the drovers exclaimed, " *This* (the sheep and oxen) *is David's booty.*" It is true that there is nothing said in what goes before about any booty that David had taken from the Amalekites, in addition to what they had taken from the Israelites ; but the fact that David had really taken such booty is perfectly obvious from vers. 26–31, where he is said to have sent portions of the booty of the enemies of Jehovah to different places in the land. If this explanation be not accepted, there is no other course open than to follow the Vulgate, alter לִפְנֵי into לְפָנָיו, and render the middle clause thus: " *they drove those cattle* (viz. the sheep and oxen already mentioned) *before him*," as Luther has done. But even in that case we could hardly understand anything else by the sheep and oxen than the cattle belonging to the Amalekites, and taken from them as booty.

Vers. 21–31. When David came back to the two hundred men whom he had left by the brook Besor (יֹשִׁיבֵם, they made them sit, remain), they went to meet him and his warriors, and were heartily greeted by David.—Ver. 22. Then all kinds of evil and worthless men of those who had gone with David to the battle replied: " *Because they have not gone with us* (lit. with me, the person speaking), *we will not give them any of the booty that we have seized, except to every one his wife and his children : they may lead them away, and go.*"—Vers. 23, 24. David opposed this selfish and envious proposal, saying, " *Do not so, my brethren, with that* (אֵת, the sign of the accusative, not the preposition ; see Ewald, § 329, *a: lit.* with regard to that) *which Jehovah hath done to us, and He hath guarded us* (since He hath guarded us), *and given this troop which came upon us into our hand.* And who will hearken to you in this matter? *But* (כִּי, according to the negation involved in the question) *as the portion of him that went into the battle, so be the portion of him that stayed by the things ; they shall share together.*" הורד is a copyist's error for הַיֹּרֵד.—Ver. 25. So was it from that day and forward ; and he (David) made it (this regulation as to the booty) " *the law and right for Israel unto this day.*"—Vers. 26–31. When David returned to Ziklag, he sent portions of the booty to the elders of Judah, to his friends, with this message : " *Behold, here ye have a blessing of the booty of the enemies of Jehovah*" (which we took from the enemies of Jehovah) ; and this he did, according to ver. 31, to all the places in which he had wandered with his men, *i.e.* where he had wandered about during his flight from Saul, and in which he had no doubt received assistance. Sending these gifts could not fail to make the elders of these cities well disposed towards him, and so to facilitate his recognition as king after the death of Saul, which occurred immediately afterwards. Some of these places may have been plundered by the Amalekites, since they had invaded the *Negeb* of Judah (ver. 14). The cities referred to were *Bethel*,—not the Bethel so often mentioned, the present *Beitin*, in the tribe of Benjamin, but *Bethuel* (1 Chron. iv. 30) or *Bethul*, in the tribe of Simeon (Josh. xix. 4), which Knobel supposes to be *Elusa* or *el Khalasa* (see at Josh. xv. 30). The reading Βαιθσούρ in the Septuagint is a worthless conjecture. *Ramah* of the south, which was allotted to the tribe of Simeon, has not yet been discovered (see at Josh. xix. 8). *Jattir* has been preserved in the ruins of *Attir*, on the southern portion of the mountains of Judah (see at Josh. xv. 48). *Aroër* is still to be seen in ruins, viz. in the foundations of walls built of enormous stones in Wady Arara, where there are many cavities for holding water, about three hours E.S.E. of Bersaba, and twenty miles to the south of Hebron (*vid.* Rob. *Pal.* ii. p. 620, and v. de Velde, *Mem.* p. 288). *Siphmoth* (or *Shiphmoth*, according to several MSS.) is altogether unknown. It may probably be referred to again in 1 Chron. xxvii. 27, where Zabdi is called the *Shiphmite;* but it is certainly not to be identified with *Sepham*, on the north-east of the sea of Galilee (Num. xxxiv. 10, 11), as Thenius supposes. *Eshtemoa* has been preserved in the village of *Semua*, with ancient ruins, on the south-western portion of the mountains of Judah (see at Josh. xv. 50). *Racal* is never mentioned again, and is entirely unknown. The LXX. have five different names instead of this, the last being *Carmel*, into which Thenius proposes to alter *Racal*. But this can hardly be done with propriety, as the LXX. also introduced the Philistian *Gath*, which certainly does not belong here; whilst in ver. 30 they have totally different names, some of which are decidedly wrong. The cities of the *Jerahmeelites* and *Kenites* were situated in the Negeb of Judah (ch. xxvii. 10), but their names cannot be traced.— Ver. 30. *Hormah* in the Negeb (Josh. xv. 30) is *Zephath*, the present *Zepáta*, on the western slope of the *Rakhma* plateau (see at Josh. xii. 14). *Cor-ashan*, probably the same place as *Ashan* in the *Shephelah*, upon the border of the Negeb, has not yet been discovered (see at Josh. xv. 42). *Athach* is only mentioned here, and quite unknown. According to Thenius, it is probably a mistaken spelling for *Ether* in the tribe of Simeon

(Josh. xix. 7, xv. 43). *Hebron,* the present *el Khulil,* Abraham's city (see at Josh. x. 3 ; Gen. xxiii. 17).

DEATH AND BURIAL OF SAUL AND HIS SONS.—CHAP. XXXI.

The end of the unhappy king corresponded to his life ever since the day of his rejection as king. When he had lost the battle, and saw his three sons fallen at his side, and the archers of the enemy pressing hard upon him, without either repentance or remorse he put an end to his life by suicide, to escape the disgrace of being wounded and abused by the foe (vers. 1–7). But he did not attain his object ; for the next day the enemy found his corpse and those of his sons, and proceeded to plunder, mutilate, and abuse them (vers. 8–10). However, the king of Israel was not to be left to perish in utter disgrace. The citizens of Jabesh remembered the deliverance which Saul had brought to their city after his election as king, and showed their gratitude by giving an honourable burial to Saul and his sons (vers. 11–13). There is a parallel to this chapter in 1 Chron. x., which agrees exactly with the account before us, with very few deviations indeed, and those mostly verbal, and merely introduces a hortatory clause at the end (vers. 13, 14).

Vers. 1–7. The account of the war between the Philistines and Israel, the commencement of which has already been mentioned in ch. xxviii. 1, 4 sqq., and xxix. 1, is resumed in ver. 1 in a circumstantial clause ; and to this there is attached a description of the progress and result of the battle, more especially with reference to Saul. Consequently, in 1 Chron. x. 1, where there had been no previous allusion to the war, the participle נִלְחָמִים is changed into the perfect. The following is the way in which we should express the circumstantial clause : " Now when the Philistines were fighting against Israel, the men of Israel fled before the Philistines, and slain men fell in the mountains of Gilboa" (*vid.* ch. xxviii. 4). The principal engagement took place in the plain of Jezreel. But when the Israelites were obliged to yield, they fled up the mountains of Gilboa, and were pursued and slain there.—Vers. 2–4. The Philistines followed Saul, smote (*i.e.* put to death) his three sons (see at ch. xiv. 49), and fought fiercely against Saul himself. *When the archers* (אֲנָשִׁים בַּקֶּשֶׁת is an explanatory apposition to הַמּוֹרִים) *hit him,* i.e. overtook him, *he was greatly alarmed at them* (יָּחֶל, from חִיל or חוּל),[1] and called upon his armour-bearer to pierce him with the sword, "*lest these uncircumcised come and thrust me through, and play with me,*" i.e. cool their courage upon me by maltreating me. But as the armour-bearer would not do this, because he was very much afraid, since he was supposed to be answerable for the king's life, Saul inflicted death upon himself with his sword; whereupon the armour-bearer also fell upon his sword and died with his king, so that on that day Saul and his three sons and his armour-bearer all died; also "*all his men*" (for which we have "all his house" in the Chronicles), i.e. not all the warriors who went out with him to battle, but all the king's servants, or all the members of his house, sc. who had taken part in the battle. Neither Abner nor his son Ishbosheth was included, for the latter was not in the battle; and although the former was Saul's cousin and commander-in-chief (see ch. xiv. 50, 51), he did not belong to his house or servants.—Ver. 7. When the men of Israel upon the sides that were opposite to the valley (Jezreel) and the Jordan saw that the Israelites (the Israelitish troop) fled, and Saul and his sons were dead, they took to flight out of the cities, whereupon the Philistines took possession of them. עֵבֶר is used here to signify the side opposite to the place of conflict in the valley of Jezreel, which the writer assumed as his stand-

---

[1] The LXX. have adopted the rendering καὶ ἐτραυμάτισαν εἰς τὰ ὑποχόνδρια, they wounded him in the abdomen, whilst the Vulgate rendering is *vulneratus est vehementer a sagittariis.* In 1 Chron. x. 3 the Sept. rendering is καὶ ἐπόνεσεν ἀπὸ τῶν τόξων, and that of the Vulgate *et vulneraverunt jaculis.* The translators have therefore derived יָחֶל from חָלָה = חָלָה, and then given a free rendering to the other words. But this rendering is overthrown by the word מְאֹד, very, vehemently, to say nothing of the fact that the verb חָלַל or חָלָה cannot be proved to be ever used in the sense of wounding. If Saul had been so severely wounded that he could not kill himself, and therefore asked his armour-bearer to slay him, as Thenius supposes, he would not have had the strength to pierce himself with his sword when the armour-bearer refused. The further conjecture of Thenius, that the Hebrew text should be read thus, in accordance with the LXX., וַיָּחֶל אֶל הַמְּרֵרִים, "he was wounded in the region of the gall," is opposed by the circumstance that ὑποχόνδρια is not the gall or region of the gall, but what is under the χόνδρος, or breast cartilage, viz. the abdomen and bowels.

point (cf. ch. xiv. 40); so that עֵבֶר הָעֵמֶק is the country to the
west of the valley of Jezreel, and עֵבֶר הַיַּרְדֵּן the country to the
west of the Jordan, *i.e.* between Gilboa and the Jordan. These
districts, *i.e.* the whole of the country round about the valley
of Jezreel, the Philistines took possession of, so that the whole
of the northern part of the land of Israel, in other words the
whole land with the exception of Peræa and the tribe-land of
Judah, came into their hands when Saul was slain.

Vers. 8–10. On the day following the battle, when the
Philistines stripped the slain, they found Saul and his three sons
lying upon Gilboa; and having cut off their heads and plundered their weapons, they sent them (the heads and weapons)
as trophies into the land of the Philistines, *i.e.* round about to
the different towns and hamlets of their land, to announce the
joyful news in their idol-temples (the writer of the Chronicles
mentions the idols themselves) and to the people, and then
deposited their weapons (the weapons of Saul and his sons) in
the Astarte-houses. But the corpses they fastened to the town-
wall of Beth-shean, *i.e.* Beisan, in the valley of the Jordan (see
at Josh. xvii. 11). *Beth-azabbim* and *Beth-ashtaroth* are composite words; the first part is indeclinable, and the plural form
is expressed by the second word: *idol-houses* and *Astarte-houses*,
like *beth-aboth* (father's-houses: see at Ex. vi. 14). On the
Astartes, see at Judg. ii. 13. It is not expressly stated indeed
in vers. 9, 10, that the Philistines plundered the bodies of Saul's
sons as well, and mutilated them by cutting off their heads; but
רֹאשׁוֹ and כֵּלָיו, *his* (*i.e.* Saul's) *head* and *his weapons*, alone are
mentioned. At the same time, it is very evident from ver. 12,
where the Jabeshites are said to have taken down from the wall
of Beth-shean not Saul's body only, but the bodies of his sons
also, that the Philistines had treated the corpses of Saul's sons
in just the same manner as that of Saul himself. The writer
speaks distinctly of the abuse of Saul's body only, because it
was his death that he had chiefly in mind at the time. To the
word וַיְּשַׁלְּחוּ we must supply in thought the object רֹאשׁוֹ and כֵּלָיו
from the preceding clause. גְּוִיַּת and גְּוִיֹּת (vers. 10 and 12) are
the corpses without the heads. The fact that the Philistines
nailed them to the town-wall of Beth-shean presupposes the
capture of that city, from which it is evident that they had
occupied the land as far as the Jordan. The definite word

Beth-ashtaroth is changed by the writer of the Chronicles into *Beth-elohim*, temples of the gods; or rather he has interpreted it in this manner without altering the sense, as the Astartes are merely mentioned as the principal deities for the idols generally. The writer of the Chronicles has also omitted to mention the nailing of the corpses to the wall of Beth-shean, but he states instead that " they fastened his skull in the temple of Dagon," a fact which is passed over in the account before us. From this we may see how both writers have restricted themselves to the principal points, or those which appeared to them of the greatest importance (*vid.* Bertheau on 1 Chron. x. 10).

Vers. 11–13. When the inhabitants of Jabesh in Gilead heard this, all the brave men of the town set out to Beth-shean, took down the bodies of Saul and his sons from the wall, brought them to Jabesh, and burned them there. *" But their bones they buried under the tamarisk at Jabesh, and fasted seven days,"* to mourn for the king their former deliverer (see ch. xi.). These statements are given in a very condensed form in the Chronicles (vers. 11, 12). Not only is the fact that " they went the whole night " omitted, as being of no essential importance to the general history; but the removal of the bodies from the town-wall is also passed over, because their being fastened there had not been mentioned, and also the burning of the bodies. The reason for the last omission is not to be sought for in the fact that the author of the Chronicles regarded burning as ignominious, according to Lev. xx. 14, xxi. 9, but because he did not see how to reconcile the burning of the bodies with the burial of the bones. It was not the custom in Israel to burn the corpse, but to bury it in the ground. The former was restricted to the worst criminals (see at Lev. xx. 14). Consequently the Chaldee interpreted the word " burnt" as relating to the burning of spices, a custom which we meet with afterwards as a special honour shown to certain of the kings of Judah on the occasion of their burial (2 Chron. xvi. 14, xxi. 19 ; Jer. xxxiv. 5). But this is expressed by שָׂרַף לוֹ שְׂרֵפָה, " to make a burning for him," whereas here it is stated distinctly that " they burnt them." The reason for the burning of the bodies in the case of Saul and his sons is to be sought for in the peculiarity of the circumstances ; viz. partly in the fact that the bodies were mutilated by the removal of the heads, and therefore a regular burial of the dead was impossible, and partly in their anxiety lest, if the Philistines followed up their victory and came to Jabesh, they should desecrate the bodies still further. But even this was not a complete burning to ashes, but merely a burning of the skin and flesh; so that the bones still remained, and they were buried in the ground under a shady tree. Instead of " under the (well-known) tamarisk" (*eshel*), we have תַּחַת הָאֵלָה (under the strong tree) in 1 Chron. x. 11. David afterwards had them fetched away and buried in Saul's family grave at Zela, in the land of Benjamin (2 Sam. xxi. 11 sqq.). The seven days' fast kept by the Jabeshites was a sign of public and general mourning on the part of the inhabitants of that town at the death of the king, who had once rescued them from the most abominable slavery.

In this ignominious fate of Saul there was manifested the righteous judgment of God in consequence of the hardening of his heart. But the love which the citizens of Jabesh displayed in their treatment of the corpses of Saul and his sons, had reference not to the king as rejected by God, but to the king as anointed with the Spirit of Jehovah, and was a practical condemnation, not of the divine judgment which had fallen upon Saul, but of the cruelty of the enemies of Israel and its anointed. For although Saul had waged war almost incessantly against the Philistines, it is not known that in any one of his victories he had ever been guilty of such cruelties towards the conquered and slaughtered foe as could justify this barbarous revenge on the part of the uncircumcised upon his lifeless corpse.

THE SECOND BOOK OF SAMUEL

THIS book contains the history of *David's* reign, arranged according to its leading features: viz. (1) the commencement of his reign as king of *Judah* at Hebron, whereas the other tribes of Israel adhered to the house of Saul (ch. i.–iv.); (2) his promotion to be king over all Israel, and the victorious extension of his sway (ch. v.–ix.); (3) the decline of his power in consequence of his adultery (ch. x.–xx.); (4) the close of his reign (ch. xxi.–xxiv.). Parallels and supplements to this history, in which the reign of David is described chiefly in its connection with the development of the kingdom of God under the Old Testament, are given in ch. xi.–xxviii. of the first book of Chronicles, where we have an elaborate description of the things done by David, both for the elevation and organization of the public worship of God, and also for the consolidation and establishment of the whole kingdom, and the general administration of government.

I. DAVID KING OVER JUDAH; AND ISHBOSHETH KING OVER ISRAEL.

When David received the tidings at Ziklag of the defeat of Israel and the death of Saul, he mourned deeply and sincerely for the fallen king and his noble son Jonathan (ch. i.). He then returned by the permission of God into the land of Judah, namely to Hebron, and was anointed king of Judah by the elders of that tribe; whereas Abner, the cousin and chief general of Saul, took Ishbosheth, the only remaining son of the fallen monarch, and made him king over the other tribes

of Israel at Mahanaim (ch. ii. 1–11).   This occasioned a civil
war.   Abner marched to Gibeon against David with the forces
of Ishbosheth, but was defeated by Joab, David's commander-
in-chief, and pursued to Mahanaim, in which pursuit Abner
slew Asahel the brother of Joab, who was eagerly following
him (ch. ii. 12–32).   Nevertheless, the conflict between the
house of David and the house of Saul continued for some time
longer, but with the former steadily advancing and the latter
declining, until at length Abner quarrelled with Ishbosheth,
and persuaded the tribes that had hitherto adhered to him to
acknowledge David as king over all Israel.   After the negotiations with David for effecting this, he was assassinated by Joab
on his return from Hebron,—an act at which David not only
expressed his abhorrence by a solemn mourning for Abner, but
declared it still more openly by cursing Joab's crime (ch. iii.).
Shortly afterwards, Ishbosheth was assassinated in his own
house by two Benjaminites; but this murder was also avenged
by David, who ordered the murderers to be put to death, and
the head of Ishbosheth, that had been delivered up to him, to
be buried in Abner's tomb (ch. iv.).   Thus the civil war and
the threatened split in the kingdom were brought to an end,
though without any complicity on the part of David, but rather
against his will, viz. through the death of Abner, the author of
the split, and of Ishbosheth, whom he had placed upon the
throne, both of whom fell by treacherous hands, and received
the reward of their rebellion against the ordinance of God.
David himself, in his long school of affliction under Saul, had
learned to put all his hope in the Lord his God ; and therefore,
when Saul was dead, he took no steps to grasp by force the
kingdom which God had promised him, or to remove his rival
out of the way by crime.

DAVID'S CONDUCT ON HEARING OF SAUL'S DEATH.   HIS
ELEGY UPON SAUL AND JONATHAN.—CHAP. I.

David received the intelligence of the defeat of Israel and
the death of Saul in the war with the Philistines from an
Amalekite, who boasted of having slain Saul and handed over
to David the crown and armlet of the fallen king, but whom
David punished with death for the supposed murder of the

anointed of God (vers. 1–16). David mourned for the death of Saul and Jonathan, and poured out his grief in an elegiac ode (vers. 17–27). This account is closely connected with the concluding chapters of the first book of Samuel.

Vers. 1–16. *David receives the news of Saul's death.*—Vers. 1–4. After the death of Saul, and David's return to Ziklag from his campaign against the Amalekites, there came a man to David on the third day, with his clothes torn and earth strewed upon his head (as a sign of deep mourning: see at 1 Sam. iv. 12), who informed him of the flight and overthrow of the Israelitish army, and the death of Saul and Jonathan.—Ver. 1 may be regarded as the protasis to ver. 2, so far as the contents are concerned, although formally it is rounded off, and וַיֵּשֶׁב forms the apodosis to וַיְהִי : "*It came to pass after the death of Saul, David had returned from the slaughter of the Amalekites* (1 Sam. xxx. 1–26), *that David remained at Ziklag two days. And it came to pass on the third day*," etc. Both of these notices of the time refer to the day, on which David returned to Ziklag from the pursuit and defeat of the Amalekites. Whether the battle at Gilboa, in which Saul fell, occurred before or after the return of David, it is impossible to determine. All that follows from the juxtaposition of the two events in ver. 1, is that they were nearly contemporaneous. The man "*came from the army from with Saul*," and therefore appears to have kept near to Saul during the battle.—Ver. 4. David's inquiry, "*How did the thing happen?*" refers to the statement made by the messenger, that he had escaped from the army of Israel. In the answer, אֲשֶׁר serves, like כִּי in other passages, merely to introduce the words that follow, like our *namely* (*vid.* Ewald, § 338, *b*). "*The people fled from the fight ; and not only have many of the people fallen, but Saul and Jonathan his son are also dead.*" וְגַם . . . וְגַם : *not only . . . but also.*—Vers. 5 sqq. To David's further inquiry how he knew this, the young man replied (vers. 6–10), "*I happened to come* (נִקְרֹה = נִקְרָא) *up to the mountains of Gilboa, and saw Saul leaning upon his spear ; then the chariots* (the war-chariots for the charioteers) *and riders were pressing upon him, and he turned round and saw me, . . . and asked me, Who art thou? and I said, An Amalekite ; and he said to me, Come hither to me, and slay me, for the cramp* (שָׁבָץ according to the Rabbins) *hath seized me* (*sc.* so that I cannot defend myself, and must fall into the hands of the Philistines) ; *for my soul* (my life) *is still whole in me. Then I went to him, and slew him, because I knew that after his fall he would not live ; and took the crown upon his head, and the bracelet upon his arm, and brought them to my lord"* (David). " After his fall " does not mean " after he had fallen upon his sword or spear" (Clericus), for this is neither implied in נָפַל‎ nor in נִשְׁעָן עַל־חֲנִיתוֹ‎ (" supported, *i.e.* leaning upon his spear")', nor are we at liberty to transfer it from 1 Sam. xxxi. 4 into this passage ; but " *after his defeat*," *i.e.* so that he would not survive this calamity. This statement is at variance with the account of the death of Saul in 1 Sam. xxxi. 3 sqq. ; and even apart from this it has an air of improba- bility, or rather of untruth in it, particularly in the assertion that Saul was leaning upon his spear when the chariots and horsemen of the enemy came upon him, without having either an armour-bearer or any other Israelitish soldier by his side, so that he had to turn to an Amalekite who accidentally came by, and to ask him to inflict the fatal wound. The Amalekite invented this, in the hope of thereby obtaining the better recompense from David. The only part of his statement which is certainly true, is that he found the king lying dead upon the field of battle, and took off the crown and armlet ; since he brought these to David. But it is by no means cer- tain whether he was present when Saul expired, or merely found him after he was dead.—Vers. 11, 12. This information, the substance of which was placed beyond all doubt by the king's jewels that were brought, filled David with the deepest sorrow. As a sign of his pain he rent his clothes ; and all the men with him did the same, and mourned with weeping and fasting until the evening "*for Saul and for Jonathan his son, for the people of Jehovah, and for the house of Israel, because they had fallen by the sword*" (*i.e.* in battle). " *The people of Jehovah*" and the " *house or people of Israel*" are distinguished from one another, according to the twofold attitude of Israel, which furnished a double ground for mourning. Those who had fallen were first of all members of the people of Jehovah, and secondly, fellow-countrymen. " They were therefore asso- ciated with them, both according to the flesh and according to the spirit, and for that reason they mourned the more" (Seb. Schmidt). " The only deep mourning for Saul, with the

exception of that of the Jabeshites (1 Sam. xxxi. 11), proceeded from the man whom he had hated and persecuted for
so many years even to the time of his death; just as David's
successor wept over the fall of Jerusalem, even when it was
about to destroy Himself" (O. v. Gerlach).—Ver. 13. David
then asked the bringer of the news for further information
concerning his own descent, and received the reply that he was
the son of an Amalekite stranger, *i.e.* of an Amalekite who had
emigrated to Israel.—Ver. 14. David then reproached him for
what he had done : " *How wast thou not afraid to stretch forth
thine hand to destroy the Lord's anointed ?*" and commanded one
of his attendants to slay him (vers. 15 sqq.), passing sentence
of death in these words : " *Thy blood come upon thy head* (cf.
Lev. xx. 9, Josh. ii. 19) ; *for thy mouth hath testified against
thee, saying, I have slain the Lord's anointed.*" [1] David regarded
the statement of the Amalekite as a sufficient ground for condemnation, without investigating the truth any further ; though
it was most probably untrue, as he could see through his design
of securing a great reward as due to him for performing such a
deed (*vid.* ch. iv. 10), and looked upon a man who could attribute such an act to himself from mere avarice as perfectly
capable of committing it. Moreover, the king's jewels, which
he had brought, furnished a practical proof that Saul had
really been put to death. This punishment was by no means
so severe as to render it necessary to "estimate its morality
according to the times," or to defend it merely from the stand-
point of political prudence, on the ground that as David was
the successor of Saul, and had been pursued by him as his
rival with constant suspicion and hatred, he ought not to leave
the murder of the king unpunished, if only because the people,
or at any rate his own opponents among the people, would
accuse him of complicity in the murder of the king, if not of

---

[1] " *Thy mouth hath testified against thee,* and out of it thou art judged
(Luke xix. 22), whether thou hast done it or not. If thou hast done it,
thou receivest the just reward of thy deeds. If thou hast not done it, then
throw the blame upon thine own lying testimony, and be content with the
wages of a wicked flatterer ; for, according to thine own confession, thou
art the murderer of a king, and that is quite enough to betray thine evil
heart. David could see plainly enough that the man was no murderer : he
would show by his example that flatterers who boast of such sins as these
should get no hearing from their superiors."—*Berleb. Bible.*

actually instigating the murderer. David would never have allowed such considerations as these to lead him into unjust severity. And his conduct requires no such half vindication. Even on the supposition that Saul had asked the Amalekite to give him his death-thrust, as he said he had, it was a crime deserving of punishment to fulfil this request, the more especially as nothing is said about any such mortal wounding of Saul as rendered his escape or recovery impossible, so that it could be said that it would have been cruel under such circumstances to refuse his request to be put to death. If Saul's life was still "full in him," as the Amalekite stated, his position was not so desperate as to render it inevitable that he should fall into the hands of the Philistines. Moreover, the supposition was a very natural one, that he had slain the king for the sake of a reward. But slaying the king, the anointed of the Lord, was in itself a crime that deserved to be punished with death. What David might more than once have done, but had refrained from doing from holy reverence for the sanctified person of the king, this foreigner, a man belonging to the nation of the Amalekites, Israel's greatest foes, had actually done for the sake of gain, or at any rate pretended to have done. Such a crime must be punished with death, and that by David who had been chosen by God and anointed as Saul's successor, and whom the Amalekite himself acknowledged in that capacity, since otherwise he would not have brought him the news together with the royal diadem.

Vers. 17-27. *David's elegy upon Saul and Jonathan.*—An eloquent testimony to the depth and sincerity of David's grief for the death of Saul is handed down to us in the elegy which he composed upon Saul and his noble son Jonathan, and which he had taught to the children of Israel. It is one of the finest odes of the Old Testament; full of lofty sentiment, and springing from deep and sanctified emotion, in which, without the slightest allusion to his own relation to the fallen king, David celebrates without envy the bravery and virtues of Saul and his son Jonathan, and bitterly laments their loss. "*He said to teach,*" *i.e.* he commanded the children of Judah to practise or learn it. קֶשֶׁת, *bow; i.e.* a song to which the title *Kesheth* or bow was given, not only because the bow is referred to (ver. 22), but because it is a martial ode, and the bow was one of the principal weapons used by the warriors of that age, and one in the use of which the Benjaminites, the tribe-mates of Saul, were particularly skilful: cf. 1 Chron. viii. 40, xii. 2 ; 2 Chron. xiv. 7, xvii. 17. Other explanations are by no means so natural; such, for example, as that it related to the melody to which the ode was sung; whilst some are founded upon false renderings, or arbitrary alterations of the text, *e.g.* that of Ewald (*Gesch.* i. p. 41), Thenius, etc. This elegy was inserted in "*the book of the righteous*" (see at Josh. x. 13), from which the author of the books of Samuel has taken it.

The ode is arranged in three strophes, which gradually diminish in force and sweep (viz. vers. 19–24, 25–26, 27), and in which the vehemence of the sorrow is gradually modified, and finally dies away. Each strophe opens with the exclamation, "*How are the mighty fallen!*" The *first* contains all that had to be said in praise of the fallen heroes; the deepest mourning for their death; and praise of their bravery, of their inseparable love, and of the virtues of Saul as king. The *second* commemorates the friendship between David and Jonathan. The *third* simply utters the last sigh, with which the elegy becomes silent. The *first* strophe runs thus :

Ver. 19. The ornament, O Israel, is slain upon thy heights !
      Oh how are the mighty fallen !
   20. Tell it not in Gath, publish it not in the streets of Askelon;
      Lest the daughters of the Philistines rejoice,
      Lest the daughters of the uncircumcised triumph !
   21. Ye mountains of Gilboa, let not dew or rain be upon you, or fields
      of first-fruit offerings :
      For there is the shield of the mighty defiled,
      The shield of Saul, not anointed with oil.
   22. From the blood of the slain, from the fat of the mighty,
      The bow of Jonathan turned not back,
      And the sword of Saul returned not empty.
   23. Saul and Jonathan, beloved and kind, in life
      And in death they are not divided.
      Lighter than eagles were they ; stronger than lions.
   24. Ye daughters of Israel, weep over Saul,
      Who clothed you in purple with delight ;
      Who put a golden ornament upon your apparel !

The first clause of ver. 19 contains the theme of the entire ode. הַצְּבִי does not mean the gazelle here (as the Syriac and Clericus and others render it), the only plausible support of

which is the expression "upon thy heights," whereas the parallel
נְבוֹרִים shows that by הַצְּבִי we are to understand the two heroes
Saul and Jonathan, and that the word is used in the appellative sense of *ornament*. The king and his noble son were the
ornament of Israel. They were slain upon the heights of Israel.
Luther has given a correct rendering, so far as the sense is
concerned (*die Edelsten*, the noblest), after the *inclyti* of the
Vulgate. The pronoun "*thy* high places" refers to Israel. The
reference is to the heights of the mountains of Gilboa (see ver.
21). This event threw Israel into deep mourning, which commences in the second clause.—Ver. 20. The tidings of this
mourning were not to be carried out among the enemies of
Israel, lest they should rejoice thereat. Such rejoicing would
only increase the pain of Israel at the loss it had sustained. Only
two of the cities of Philistia are mentioned by name, viz. Gath,
which was near, and Askelon, which was farther off by the
sea. The rejoicing of the daughters of the Philistines refers to
the custom of employing women to celebrate the victories of
their nation by singing and dancing (cf. 1 Sam. xviii. 6).—Ver.
21. Even nature is to join in the mourning. May God withdraw His blessing from the mountains upon which the heroes
have fallen, that they may not be moistened by the dew and rain
of heaven, but, remaining in eternal barrenness, be memorials
of the horrible occurrence that has taken place upon them.
הָרֵי בַגִּלְבֹּעַ is an address to them; and the preposition בְּ with the
construct state is poetical: "*mountains in Gilboa*" (*vid.* Ewald,
§ 289, *b*). In עֲלֵיכֶם . . . . אַל the verb יְהִי is wanting. The following words, וּשְׂדֵי תְרוּמֹת, are in apposition to the foregoing:
"*and let not fields of first-fruit offerings be upon you*," *i.e.* fields
producing fruit, from which offerings of first-fruits were presented. This is the simplest and most appropriate explanation of
the words, which have been very differently, and in some respects
very marvellously rendered. The reason for this cursing of the
mountains of Gilboa was, that there the shield of the heroes,
particularly of Saul, had been defiled with blood, namely the
blood of those whom the shield ought to defend. נִגְעַל does not
mean to throw away (Dietrich.), but to soil or defile (as in the
Chaldee), then to abhor. "*Not anointed with oil*," *i.e.* not
cleansed and polished with oil, so that the marks of Saul's
blood still adhered to it. בְּלִי poetical for לֹא. The interpolation

of the words "*as though*" (*quasi non esset unctus oleo*, Vulgate) cannot be sustained.—Ver. 22. Such was the ignominy experienced upon Gilboa by those who had always fought so bravely, that their bow and sword did not turn back until it was satisfied with the blood and fat of the slain. The figure upon which the passage is founded is, that arrows drink the blood of the enemy, and a sword devours their flesh (*vid*. Deut. xxxii. 42; Isa. xxxiv. 5, 6; Jer. xlvi. 10). The two principal weapons are divided between Saul and Jonathan, so that the bow is assigned to the latter and the sword to the former.—Ver. 23. In death as in life, the two heroes were not divided, for they were alike in bravery and courage. Notwithstanding their difference of character, and the very opposite attitude which they assumed towards David, the noble Jonathan did not forsake his father, although his fierce hatred towards the friend whom Jonathan loved as his own soul might have undermined his attachment to his father. The two predicates, נֶאֱהָב, loved and amiable, and נְעִים, affectionate or kind, apply chiefly to Jonathan; but they were also suitable to Saul in the earliest years of his reign, when he manifested the virtues of an able ruler, which secured for him the lasting affection and attachment of the people. In his mourning over the death of the fallen hero, David forgets all the injury that Saul has inflicted upon him, so that he only brings out and celebrates the more amiable aspects of his character. The light motion or swiftness of an eagle (cf. Hab. i. 8), and the strength of a lion (*vid*. ch. xvii. 10), were the leading characteristics of the great heroes of antiquity.—Lastly, in ver. 24, David commemorates the rich booty which Saul had brought to the nation, for the purpose of celebrating his heroic greatness in this respect as well. שָׁנִי was the scarlet purple (see at Ex. xxv. 4). " With delights," or with lovelinesses, *i.e.* in a lovely manner.

The *second* strophe (vers. 25 and 26) only applies to the friendship of Jonathan :

> Ver. 25. Oh how are the mighty fallen in the midst of the battle !
> Jonathan (is) slain upon thy heights !
> 26. I am distressed for thee, my brother Jonathan :
> Thou wast very kind to me :
> Stranger than the love of woman was thy love to me !

Ver. 25 is almost a verbal repetition of ver. 19. צַר (ver.

26) denotes the pinching or pressure of the heart consequent upon pain and mourning. נִפְלְאַתָה, *third pers. fem.*, like a verb ל"ה with the termination lengthened (*vid.* Ewald, § 194, *b*), to be wonderful or distinguished. אַהֲבָתְךָ, thy love to me. Comparison to the love of woman is expressive of the deepest earnestness of devoted love.

The *third* strophe (ver. 27) contains simply a brief aftertone of sorrow, in which the ode dies away :

> Oh how are the mighty fallen,
> The instruments of war perished !

" *The instruments of war*" are not the weapons ; but the expression is a figurative one, referring to the heroes by whom war was carried on (*vid.* Isa. xiii. 5). Luther has adopted this rendering (*die Streitbaren*).

DAVID KING OVER JUDAH, AND ISHBOSHETH KING OVER ISRAEL. BATTLE AT GIBEON.—CHAP. II.

After David had mourned for the fallen king, he went, in accordance with the will of the Lord as sought through the Urim, to Hebron, and was there anointed king by the tribe of Judah. He then sent his thanks to the inhabitants of Jabesh, for the love which they had shown to Saul in burying his bones (vers. 1–7), and reigned seven years and a half at Hebron over Judah alone (vers. 10 and 11). Abner, on the other hand, put forward Ishbosheth the son of Saul, who still remained alive, as king over Israel (vers. 8 and 9) ; so that a war broke out between the adherents of Ishbosheth and those of David, in which Abner and his army were beaten, but the brave Asahel, the son-in-law of David, was slain by Abner (vers. 12–32). The promotion of Ishbosheth as king was not only a continuation of the hostility of Saul towards David, but also an open act of rebellion against Jehovah, who had rejected Saul and chosen David prince over Israel, and who had given such distinct proofs of this election in the eyes of the whole nation, that even Saul had been convinced of the appointment of David to be his successor upon the throne. But David attested his unqualified submission to the guidance of God, in contrast with this rebellion against His clearly revealed will, not only by not returning to Judah till he had received permission from the Lord, but also by the fact that after the tribe of Judah had acknowledged him as king, he did not go to war with Ishbosheth, but contented himself with resisting the attack made upon him by the supporters of the house of Saul, because he was fully confident that the Lord would secure to him in due time the whole of the kingdom of Israel.

Vers. 1–4a. *David's return to Hebron, and anointing as king over Judah.*—Ver. 1. "*After this,*" *i.e.* after the facts related in ch. i., David inquired of the Lord, namely through the Urim, whether he should go up to one of the towns of Judah, and if so, to which. He received the reply, "*to Hebron,*" a place peculiarly well adapted for a capital, not only from its situation upon the mountains, and in the centre of the tribe, but also from the sacred reminiscences connected with it from the olden time. David could have no doubt that, now that Saul was dead, he would have to give up his existing connection with the Philistines and return to his own land. But as the Philistines had taken the greater part of the Israelitish territory through their victory at Gilboa, and there was good reason to fear that the adherents of Saul, more especially the army with Abner, Saul's cousin, at its head, would refuse to acknowledge David as king, and consequently a civil war might break out, David would not return to his own land without the express permission of the Lord. Vers. 2–4a. When he went with his wives and all his retinue (*vid.* 1 Sam. xxvii. 2) to Hebron and the "*cities of Hebron,*" *i.e.* the places belonging to the territory of Hebron, the men of Judah came (in the persons of their elders) and anointed him king *over the house, i.e.* the tribe, *of Judah.* Just as Saul was made king by the tribes after his anointing by Samuel (1 Sam. xi. 15), so David was first of all anointed by Judah here, and afterwards by the rest of the tribes (ch. v. 3).

Vers. 4b–7. A new section commences with וַיִּגְּדוּ. The first act of David as king was to send messengers to Jabesh, to thank the inhabitants of this city for burying Saul, and to announce to them his own anointing as king. As this expression of thanks involved a solemn recognition of the departed king, by which David divested himself of even the appearance of a rebellion, the announcement of the anointing he had received contained an indirect summons to the Jabeshites to recognise him as their king now.—Ver. 6. *" And now,"* sc. that ye have shown this love to Saul your lord, *" may Jehovah show you grace and truth."* *" Grace and truth"* are connected together, as in Ex. xxxiv. 6, as the two sides by which the goodness of God is manifested to men, namely in His forgiving grace, and in His trustworthiness, or the fulfilment of His promises (*vid.* Ps. xxv. 10). *" And I also show you this good,"* namely the prayer for the blessing of God (ver. 5), because ye have done this (to Saul). In ver. 7 there is attached to this the demand, that now that Saul their lord was dead, and the Judæans had anointed him (David) king, they would show themselves valiant, namely valiant in their reverence and fidelity towards David, who had become their king since the death of Saul. תֶּחֱזַקְנָה יְדֵיכֶם, *i.e.* be comforted, spirited (cf. Judg. vii. 11). It needed some resolution and courage to recognise David as king, because Saul's army had fled to Gilead, and there was good ground for apprehending opposition to David on the part of Abner. Ishbosheth, however, does not appear to have been proclaimed king yet; or at any rate the fact was not yet known to David. וְגַם does not belong to אֹתִי, but to the whole clause, as אֹתִי is placed first merely for the sake of emphasis.

Vers. 8–11. *Promotion of Ishbosheth to be king over Israel.* —The account of this is attached to the foregoing in the form of an antithesis : *" But Abner, the chief captain of Saul* (see at 1 Sam. xiv. 50), *had taken Ishbosheth the son of Saul, and led him over to Mahanaim."* Ishbosheth had probably been in the battle at Gilboa, and fled with Abner across the Jordan after the battle had been lost. *Ishbosheth* (*i.e.* man of shame) was the fourth son of Saul (according to 1 Chron. viii. 33, ix. 39) : his proper name was *Esh-baal* (*i.e.* fire of Baal, probably equivalent to destroyer of Baal). This name was afterwards changed into Ishbosheth, just as the name of the god Baal was also translated into *Bosheth* (" shame," Hos. ix 10, Jer. iii. 24, etc.), and Jerubbaal changed into Jerubbosheth (see at Judg. viii. 35). Ewald's supposition, that *bosheth* was originally employed in a good sense as well, like αἰδώς and פַּחַד (Gen. xxxi. 53), cannot be sustained. *Mahanaim* was on the eastern side of the Jordan, not far from the ford of Jabbok, and was an important place for the execution of Abner's plans, partly from its historical associations (Gen. xxxii. 2, 3), and partly also from its situation. There he made Ishbosheth king *"for Gilead,"* *i.e.* the whole of the land to the east of the Jordan (as in Num. xxxii. 29, Josh. xxii. 9, etc.). *" For the Ashurites:"* this reading is decidedly faulty, since we can no more suppose it to refer to Assyria (Asshur) than to the Arabian tribe of the Assurim (Gen. xxv. 3); but the true name cannot be discovered.[1] *"And for Jezreel,"* *i.e.* not merely the city of that name, but the plain that was named after it (as in 1 Sam. xxix. 1) *" And for Ephraim, and Benjamin, and all* (the rest of) *Israel,"* of course not including Judah, where David had already been acknowledged as king.—Vers. 10, 11. *Length of the reigns of Ishbosheth over Israel, and David at Hebron.* The age of Ishbosheth is given, as is generally the case at the commencement of a reign. He was forty years old when he began to reign, and reigned *two years;* whereas David was king at Hebron over the house of Judah *seven years and a half.* We are struck with this difference in the length of the two reigns; and it cannot be explained, as Seb. Schmidt, Clericus, and others suppose, on the simple assumption that David reigned two years at Hebron over *Judah,* namely up to the time of the murder of Ishbosheth, and then five years and a half over *Israel,* namely up to the time of the conquest

---

[1] In the Septuagint we find Θασιρὶ or Θασούρ, an equally mistaken form. The Chaldee has "over the tribe of Asher," which is also unsuitable, unless we include the whole of the northern portion of Canaan, including the territory of Zebulun and Naphtali. But there is no proof that the name *Asher* was ever extended to the territory of the three northern tribes. We should be rather disposed to agree with Bachienne, who supposes it to refer to the city of Asher (Josh. xvii. 7) and its territory, as this city was in the southeast of Jezreel, and Abner may possibly have conquered this district for Ishbosheth with Gilead as a base, before he ventured to dispute the government of Israel with the Philistines, if only we could discover any reason why the inhabitants (" *the Ashurites* ") should be mentioned instead of the city *Asher,* or if it were at all likely that one city should be introduced in the midst of a number of large districts. The Syriac and Vulgate have *Geshuri,* and therefore seem to have read or conjectured הַגְּשׁוּרִי; and Thenius decides in favour of this, understanding the name *Geshur* to refer to the most northerly portion of the land on both sides of the Jordan, from Mount Hermon to the Lake of Gennesareth (as in Deut. iii. 14, Josh. xii. 5, xiii. 13, 1 Chron. ii. 23). But no such usage of speech can be deduced from any of these passages, as *Geshuri* is used there to denote the land of the Geshurites, on the north-east of Bashan, which had a king of its own in the time of David (see at ch. iii. 3), and which Abner would certainly never have thought of conquering.

of Jerusalem: for this is at variance with the plain statement in the text, that "David was king in Hebron over the house of Judah seven years and a half." The opinion that the two years of Ishbosheth's reign are to be reckoned up to the time of the war with David, because Abner played the principal part during the other five years and a half that David continued to reign at Hebron, is equally untenable. We may see very clearly from ch. iii.-v. not only that Ishbosheth was king to the time of his death, which took place after that of Abner, but also that after both these events David was anointed king over Israel in Hebron by all the tribes, and that he then went directly to attack Jerusalem, and after conquering the citadel of Zion, chose that city as his own capital. The short duration of Ishbosheth's reign can only be explained, therefore, on the supposition that he was not made king, as David was, immediately after the death of Saul, but after the recovery by Abner of the land which the Philistines had taken on this side the Jordan, which may have occupied five years.[1]

Vers. 12-32. *War between the supporters of Ishbosheth and those of David.*—Vers. 12, 13. When Abner had brought all Israel under the dominion of Ishbosheth, he also sought to make Judah subject to him, and went with this intention from Mahanaim to *Gibeon*, the present Jib, in the western portion of the tribe of Benjamin, two good hours to the north of Jerusalem (see at Josh. ix. 3), taking with him the servants, *i.e.* the fighting men, of Ishbosheth. There Joab, a son of Zeruiah, David's sister (1 Chron. ii. 16), advanced to meet him with the servants, *i.e.* the warriors of David; and the two armies met at

---

[1] From the fact that in vers. 10, 11, Ishbosheth's ascending the throne is mentioned before that of David, and is also accompanied with a statement of his age, whereas the age of David is not given till ch. v. 4, 5, when he became king over all Israel, Ewald draws the erroneous conclusion that the earlier (?) historian regarded Ishbosheth as the true king, and David as a pretender. But the very opposite of this is stated as distinctly as possible in vers. 4 sqq. (compared with ver. 8). The fact that Ishbosheth is mentioned before David in ver. 10 may be explained simply enough from the custom so constantly observed in the book of Genesis, of mentioning subordinate lines or subordinate persons first, and stating whatever seemed worth recording with regard to them, in order that the ground might be perfectly clear for relating the history of the principal characters without any interruption.

the pool of Gibeon, *i.e.* probably one of the large reservoirs that are still to be found there (see Rob. *Pal.* ii. pp. 135–6; Tobler, *Topogr. v. Jerusalem*, ii. pp. 515–6), the one encamping upon the one side of the pool and the other upon the other.—Vers. 14 sqq. Abner then proposed to Joab that the contest should be decided by single combat, probably for the purpose of avoiding an actual civil war. "*Let the young men arise and wrestle before us.*" שָׂחַק, to joke or play, is used here to denote the war-play of single combat. As Joab accepted this proposal, twelve young warriors for Benjamin and Ishbosheth, and twelve from David's men, went over, *i.e.* went out of the two camps to the appointed scene of conflict; "*and one seized the other's head, and his sword was* (immediately) *in the side of the other* (his antagonist), *so that they fell together.*" The clause וְחַרְבּוֹ בְּצַד רֵעֵהוּ is a circumstantial clause: and his sword (every one's sword) was in the side of the other, *i.e.* thrust into it. Sending the sword into the opponent's side is thus described as simultaneous with the seizure of his head. The ancient translators expressed the meaning by supplying a verb (ἐνέπηξαν, *defixit:* LXX., Vulg.). This was a sign that the young men on both sides fought with great ferocity, and also with great courage. The place itself received the name of *Helkath-hazzurim,* "*field of the sharp edges,*" in consequence (for this use of *zur,* see Ps. lxxxix. 44). Ver. 17. As this single combat decided nothing, there followed a general and very sore or fierce battle, in which Abner and his troops were put to flight by the soldiers of David. The only thing connected with this, of which we have any further account, is the slaughter of Asahel by Abner, which is mentioned here (vers. 18–23) on account of the important results which followed. Of the three sons of Zeruiah, viz. Joab, Abishai, and Asahel, Asahel was peculiarly light of foot, like one of the gazelles; and he pursued Abner most eagerly, without turning aside to the right or to the left.—Vers. 20, 21. Then Abner turned round, asked him whether he was Asahel, and said to him, "*Turn to thy right hand or to thy left, and seize one of the young men and take his armour for thyself,*" *i.e.* slay one of the common soldiers, and take his accoutrements as booty, if thou art seeking for that kind of fame. But Asahel would not turn back from Abner. Then he repeated his command that he would depart, and added, "*Why should I smite thee to the ground, and how could I then lift*

up my face to Joab thy brother?" from which we may see that
Abner did not want to put the young hero to death, out of
regard for Joab and their former friendship.—Ver. 23. But
when he still refused to depart in spite of this warning, Abner
wounded him in the abdomen with the hinder part, *i.e.* the lower
end of the spear, so that the spear came out behind, and Asahel
fell dead upon the spot. The lower end of the spear appears to
have been pointed, that it might be stuck into the ground (*vid.*
1 Sam. xxvi. 7); and this will explain the fact that the spear
passed through the body. The fate of the young hero excited
such sympathy, that all who came to the place where he had
fallen stood still to mourn his loss (cf. ch. xx. 12).—Ver. 24.
But Joab and Abishai pursued Abner till the sun set, and until
they had arrived at the hill *Ammah*, in front of *Giah*, on the
way to the desert of *Gibeon*. Nothing further is known of the
places mentioned here.—Vers. 25, 26. The Benjaminites then
gathered in a crowd behind Abner, and halted upon the top of
a hill to beat back their pursuers; and Abner cried out to Joab,
" *Shall the sword then devour for ever* (shall there be no end to
the slaughter)? *dost thou not know that bitterness arises at last?
and how long wilt thou not say to the people, to return from pursuing their brethren?"* Thus Abner warns Joab of the consequences of a desperate struggle, and calls upon him to put an
end to all further bloodshed by suspending the pursuit.—Ver.
27. Joab replied, " *If thou hadst not spoken* (*i.e.* challenged to
single combat, ver. 14), *the people would have gone away in the
morning, every one from his brother,"* *i.e.* there would have been
no such fratricidal conflict at all. The first כִּי introduces the
substance of the oath, as in 1 Sam. xxv. 34; the second gives
greater force to it (*vid.* Ewald, § 330, *b*). Thus Joab threw all
the blame of the fight upon Abner, because he had been the
instigator of the single combat; and as that was not decisive, and
was so bloody in its character, the two armies had felt obliged to
fight it out. But he then commanded the trumpet to be blown for
a halt, and the pursuit to be closed—Ver. 29. Abner proceeded
with his troops through the *Arabah*, *i.e.* the valley of the Jordan,
marching the whole night; and then crossing the river, went
through the whole of *Bithron* back to Mahanaim. *Bithron* is a
district upon the eastern side of the Jordan, which is only mentioned here. Aquila and the Vulgate identify it with *Bethhoron ;*

but there is no more foundation for this than for the suggestion of Thenius, that it is the same place as *Bethharam*, the later *Libias*, at the mouth of the Nahr Hesbân (see at Num. xxxii. 36). It is very evident that *Bithron* is not the name of a city, but of a district, from the fact that it is preceded by the word *all*, which would be perfectly unmeaning in the case of a city. The meaning of the word is a cutting; and it was no doubt the name given to some ravine in the neighbourhood of the Jabbok, between the Jordan and Mahanaim, which was on the north side of the Jabbok.—Vers. 30, 31. Joab also assembled his men for a retreat. Nineteen of his soldiers were missing besides Asahel, all of whom had fallen in the battle. But they had slain as many as three hundred and sixty of Benjamin and of Abner's men. This striking disproportion in the numbers may be accounted for from the fact that in Joab's army there were none but brave and well-tried men, who had gathered round David a long time before; whereas in Abner's army there were only the remnants of the Israelites who had been beaten upon Gilboa, and who had been still further weakened and depressed by their attempts to recover the land which was occupied by the Philistines.—Ver. 32. On the way back, David's men took up the body of Asahel, and buried it in his father's grave at Bethlehem. They proceeded thence towards Hebron, marching the whole night, so that they reached Hebron itself at daybreak. "*It got light to them* (*i.e.* the day dawned) *at Hebron.*"

DAVID ADVANCES AND ISHBOSHETH DECLINES. ABNER GOES
OVER TO DAVID, AND IS MURDERED BY JOAB.—CHAP. III.

Ver. 1. "*And the war became long* (was protracted) *between the house of Saul and the house of David; but David became stronger and stronger, and the house of Saul weaker and weaker.*" הלך, when connected with another verb or with an adjective, expresses the idea of the gradual progress of an affair (*vid.* Ges. § 131, 3, Anm. 3). The historian sums up in these words the historical course of the two royal houses, as they stood opposed to one another. "*The war*" does not mean continual fighting, but the state of hostility or war in which they continued to stand towards one another. They concluded no peace, so that David was not recognised by Ishbosheth as king, any more than Ishbosheth by David. Not only is there nothing said about any continuance of actual warfare by Abner or Ishbosheth after the loss of the battle at Gibeon, but such a thing was very improbable in itself, as Ishbosheth was too weak to be able to carry on the war, whilst David waited with firm reliance upon the promise of the Lord, until all Israel should come over to him.

Vers. 2–5. GROWTH OF THE HOUSE OF DAVID.—Proof of the advance of the house of David is furnished by the multiplication of his family at Hebron. The account of *the sons who were born to David at Hebron* does not break the thread, as Clericus, Thenius, and others suppose, but is very appropriately introduced here, as a practical proof of the strengthening of the house of David, in harmony with the custom of beginning the history of the reign of every king with certain notices concerning his family (*vid.* ch. v. 13 sqq.; 1 Kings iii. 1, xiv. 21, xv. 2, 9, etc.). We have a similar list of the sons of David in 1 Chron. iii. 1–4. The first two sons were born to him from the two wives whom he had brought with him to Hebron (1 Sam. xxv. 42, 43). The *Chethibh* ילדו is probably only a copyist's error for וַיִּוָּלְדוּ, which is the reading in many Codices. From *Ahinoam*—the first-born, *Amnon* (called Aminon in ch. xiii. 20); from *Abigail*—the second, *Chileab*. The latter is also called *Daniel* in 1 Chron. iii. 1, and therefore had probably two names. The *lamed* before Ahinoam and the following names serves as a periphrasis for the genitive, like the German *von*, in consequence of the word *son* being omitted (*vid.* Ewald, § 292, *a*). The other four were by wives whom he had married in Hebron: *Absalom* by *Maachah*, the daughter of Talmai king of Geshur, a small kingdom in the north-east of Bashan (see at Deut. iii. 14); *Adonijah* by *Haggith*; *Shephatiah* by *Abital*; and *Ithream* by *Eglah*. The origin of the last three wives is unknown. The clause appended to Eglah's name, viz. " *David's wife*," merely serves as a fitting conclusion to the whole list (Bertheau on 1 Chron. iii. 3), and is not added to show that Eglah was David's principal wife, which would necessitate the conclusion drawn by the Rabbins, that Michal was the wife intended.

Vers. 6–39. DECLINE OF THE HOUSE OF SAUL.—Vers. 6–11. *Abner's quarrel with Ishbosheth.*—During the war between the house of Saul and the house of David, Abner adhered firmly to the house of Saul, but he appropriated one of Saul's concubines to himself. When Ishbosheth charged him with this, he fell into so violent a rage, that he at once announced to Ishbosheth his intention to hand over the kingdom to David. Abner had certainly perceived the utter incapacity of Ishbosheth for a very long time, if not from the very outset, and had probably made him king after the death of Saul, merely that he might save himself from the necessity of submitting to David, and might be able to rule in Ishbosheth's name, and possibly succeed in paving his own way to the throne. His appropriation of the concubine of the deceased monarch was at any rate a proof, according to Israelitish notions, and in fact those generally prevalent in the East, that he was aiming at the throne (*vid.* ch. xvi. 21; 1 Kings ii. 21). But it may gradually have become obvious to him, that the house of Saul could not possibly retain the government in opposition to David; and this may have led to his determination to persuade all the Israelites to acknowledge David, and thereby to secure for himself an influential post under his government. This will explain in a very simple manner Abner's falling away from Ishbosheth and going over to David.—Vers. 6 and 7 constitute one period, expanded by the introduction of circumstantial clauses, the וַיְהִי (it came to pass) of the protasis being continued in the וַיֹּאמֶר (he said) of ver. 7*b*. "*It came to pass, when there was war between the house of Saul and the house of David, and Abner showed himself strong for the house of Saul, and Saul had a concubine named Rizpah, the daughter of Aiah, that he* (Ishbosheth) *said to Abner, Why hast thou gone to my father's concubine?*" The subject to "*said*" is omitted in the apodosis; but it is evident from ver. 8, and the expression "*my father,*" that *Ishbosheth* is to be supplied. Even in the second circumstantial clause, "*and Saul had a concubine,*" the reason why this is mentioned is only to be gathered from Ishbosheth's words. הִתְחַזֵּק בְּ: to prove one's self strong for, or with, a person, *i.e.* to render him powerful help. בּוֹא אֶל means "*to cohabit with.*" It was the exclusive right of the successor to the throne to cohabit with the concubines of the deceased king,

who came down to him as part of the property which he inherited.—Ver. 8. Abner was so enraged at Ishbosheth's complaint, that he replied, " *Am I a dog's head, holding with
Judah?   To-day* (*i.e.* at present) *I show affection to the house
of Saul thy father, towards his brethren and his friends, and did
not let thee fall into the hand of David, and thou reproachest me
to-day with the fault with the woman?*"   "*Dog's head*" is something thoroughly contemptible.   אֲשֶׁר לִיהוּדָה, *lit.* which (belongs)
to Judah; *i.e.* holds with Judah.—Ver. 9. " *God do so to Abner,
. . . as Jehovah hath sworn to David, so will I do to him.*"   The
repetition of כִּי serves to introduce the oath, as in ch. ii. 27.
" *To take away the kingdom from the house of Saul, and set up
the throne of David over Israel and over Judah, from Dan to
Beersheba.*"   We do not know of any oath with which God
had promised the kingdom to David ; but the promise of God
in itself is equivalent to an oath, as God is the true God, who
can neither lie nor deceive (1 Sam. xv. 29 ; Num. xxiii. 19).
This promise was generally known in Israel.   " *From Dan to
Beersheba*" (as in Judg. xx. 1).—Ver. 11. Ishbosheth could
make no reply to these words of Abner, " *because he was afraid
of him.*"

Vers. 12–21. *Abner goes over to David.*—Ver. 12. Abner
soon carried out his threat to Ishbosheth.   He sent messengers
to David *in his stead* (not " on the spot," or immediately, a rendering adopted by the Chaldee and Symmachus, but for which
no support can be found) with this message : " *Whose is the
land?*" *i.e.* to whom does it belong except to thee ? and, " *Make
a covenant with me ; behold, so is my hand with thee* (*i.e.* so will
I stand by thee), *to turn all Israel to thee.*"—Ver. 13. David
assented to the proposal on this condition : " *Only one thing
do I require of thee, namely, Thou shalt not see my face, unless
thou first of all bringest me Michal, the daughter of Saul, when
thou comest to see my face.*"   כִּי אִם־לִפְנֵי הֱבִיאֲךָ, " *except before thy
bringing,*" *i.e.* unless when thou hast first of all brought or delivered "Michal to me."   This condition was imposed by David,
not only because Michal had been unjustly taken away from
him by Saul, after he had rightfully acquired her for his wife
by paying the dowry demanded, and in spite of her love to him
(1 Sam. xviii. 27, xix. 11, 12), and given to another man (1 Sam.
xxv. 44), so that he could demand her back again with perfect

justice, and Ishbosheth could not refuse to give her up to him, but probably on political grounds also, namely, because the renewal of his marriage to the king's daughter would show to all Israel that he cherished no hatred in his heart towards the fallen king.—Ver. 14. Thereupon, namely when Abner had assented to this condition, David sent messengers to Ishbosheth with this demand: *" Give* (me) *my wife Michal, whom I espoused to me for a hundred foreskins of the Philistines"* (see 1 Sam. xviii. 25, 27). David sent to Ishbosheth to demand the restoration of Michal, that her return might take place in a duly legal form, " that it might be apparent that he had dealt justly with Paltiel in the presence of his king, and that he had received his wife back again, and had not taken her by force from her husband" (Seb. Schmidt).—Ver. 15. Ishbosheth probably sent Abner to Gallim (1 Sam. xxv. 44) to fetch Michal from her husband Paltiel (see at 1 Sam. xxv. 44), and take her back to David. The husband was obliged to consent to this separation.—Ver. 16. When he went with his wife, weeping behind her, to Bahurim, Abner commanded him to turn back; *" and he re-turned."* *Bahurim,* Shimei's home (ch. xix. 17; 1 Kings ii. 8), was situated, according to ch. xvi. 1, 5, and xvii. 18, upon the road from Jerusalem to Gilgal, in the valley of the Jordan, not far from the Mount of Olives, and is supposed by v. Schubert (*R.* iii. p. 70) to have stood upon the site of the present *Abu Dis,* though in all probability it is to be sought for farther north (see Rob. *Pal.* ii. p. 103). Paltiel had therefore followed his wife to the border of the tribe of Judah, or of the kingdom of David.—Vers. 17, 18. But before Abner set out to go to David, he had spoken to the elders of Israel (the tribes generally, with the exception of Benjamin (see ver. 19) and Judah): *" Both yester-day and the day before yesterday (i.e.* a long time ago), *ye desired to have David as king over you. Now carry out your wish: for Jehovah hath spoken concerning David, Through my servant David will I save my people Israel out of the power of the Philistines and all their enemies."* הוֹשִׁיעַ is an evident mistake in writing for אוֹשִׁיעַ, which is found in many MSS., and rendered in all the ancient versions.—Ver. 19. Abner had spoken in the same way in the ears of Benjamin. He spoke to the Benjaminites more especially, because the existing royal family belonged to that tribe, and they had reaped many advantages in consequence (*vid.* 1 Sam. xxii. 7). The verb הָיָה in the circumstantial clause (ver. 17), and the verb וַיְדַבֵּר in ver. 19, which serves as a continuation of the circumstantial clause, must be translated as pluperfects, since Abner's interview with the elders of Israel and with Benjamin preceded his interview with David at Hebron. We may see from Abner's address to the elders, that even among the northern tribes the popular voice had long since decided for David. In 1 Chron. xii. we have historical proofs of this. The word of Jehovah concerning David, which is mentioned in ver. 18, is not met with anywhere in this precise form in the history of David as it has come down to us. Abner therefore had either some expression used by one of the prophets (Samuel or Gad) in his mind, which he described as the word of Jehovah, or else he regarded the anointing of David by Samuel in accordance with the command of the Lord, and the marvellous success of all that David attempted against the enemies of Israel, as a practical declaration on the part of God, that David, as the appointed successor of Saul, would perform what the Lord had spoken to Samuel concerning Saul (1 Sam. ix. 16), but what Saul had not fulfilled on account of his rebellion against the commandments of the Lord.—Ver. 19*b*. When Abner had gained over the elders of Israel and Benjamin to recognise David as king, he went to Hebron to speak in the ears of David " *all that had pleased Israel and the whole house of Benjamin,*" *i.e.* to make known to him their determination to acknowledge him as king. There went with him twenty men as representatives of all Israel, to confirm Abner's statements by their presence; and David prepared a meal for them all.—Ver. 21. After the meal, Abner said to David, " *I will rise and go and gather together all Israel to my lord the king, that they may make a covenant with thee* (*i.e.* do homage to thee before God as king), *and thou mayest become king over all that thy soul desireth,*" *i.e.* over all the nation of God; whereupon David took leave of him, and Abner went away in peace. The expression "*in peace*" serves to prepare the way for what follows. It is not stated, however, that David sent him away in peace (without avenging himself upon him), but that " David sent him away, and he went in peace." Apart altogether from the mildness of David's own character, he had no reason whatever for treating Abner as an enemy, now that he had given up all opposition to his reigning, and had brought all the Israelites over to him. What Abner had done for Ishbosheth, including his fighting against David, was indeed a sinful act of resistance to the will of Jehovah, which was not unknown to him, and according to which Samuel had both called and anointed David king over the nation; but for all that, it was not an ordinary act of rebellion against the person of David and his rightful claim to the throne, because Jehovah had not yet caused David to be set before the nation as its king by Samuel or any other prophet, and David had not yet asserted the right to reign over all Israel, which had been secured to him by the Lord and guaranteed by his anointing, as one which the nation was bound to recognise; but, like a true servant of God, he waited patiently till the Lord should give him the dominion over all His people.

Vers. 22–30. *Abner assassinated by Joab.*—Ver. 22. After Abner's departure, the servants of David returned with much booty from a marauding expedition, and Joab at their head. The singular בָּא may be explained from the fact that Joab was the principal person in the estimation of the writer. מֵהַגְּדוּד, *lit.* from the marauding host, *i.e.* from the work of a marauding host, or from a raid, which they had been making upon one of the tribes bordering upon Judah.—Ver. 23. When Joab learned (*lit. they told him*) that Abner had been with David, and he had sent him away again, he went to David to reproach him for having done so. "*What hast thou done? Behold, Abner came to thee; why then hast thou sent him away, and he is gone quite away?*" *i.e.* so that he could go away again without being detained (for this meaning of the *inf. abs.*, see Ewald, § 280, *b*). "*Thou knowest* (or more correctly as a question, Dost thou know?) *Abner, the-son of Ner, that he came to persuade thee* (*i.e.* to make thee certain of his intentions), *and to learn thy going out and in* (*i.e.* all thine undertakings), *and to learn all that thou wilt do*" (*i.e.* all thy plans). Joab hoped in this way to prejudice David against Abner, to make him suspected as a traitor, that he might then be able to gratify his own private revenge with perfect impunity.—Ver. 26. For Abner had only just gone away from David, when Joab sent messengers after him, no doubt in David's name, though without his knowledge, and had him fetched back "from *Bor-hasirah,* *i.e.* the cistern of *Sirah.*" *Sirah* is a place which is quite unknown to us. According to

Josephus (*Ant.* vii. 1, 5), it was twenty stadia from Hebron, and called Βησιρά.—Ver. 27. When he came back, Joab *"took him aside into the middle of the gate, to talk with him in the stillness,"* *i e.* in private, and there thrust him through the body, so that he died *" for the blood of Asahel his brother,"* *i.e.* for having put Asahel to death (ch. ii. 23).—Vers. 28, 29. When David heard this, he said, *" I and my kingdom are innocent before Jehovah for ever of the blood of Abner. Let it turn* (חג, to twist one's self, to turn or fall, *irruit*) *upon the head of Joab and all his father's house* (or so-called family)! *Never shall there be wanting* (אַל יִכָּרֵת, let there not be cut off, so that there shall not be, as in Josh. ix. 23) *in the house of Joab one that hath an issue* (*vid.* Lev. xv. 2), *and a leper, and one who leans upon a stick* (*i.e.* a lame person or cripple; פֶּלֶךְ, according to the LXX. σκυτάλη, a thick round staff), *and who falls by the sword, and who is in want of bread."* The meaning is: May God avenge the murder of Abner upon Joab and his family, by punishing them continually with terrible diseases, violent death, and poverty. To make the reason for this fearful curse perfectly clear, the historian observes in ver. 30, that Joab and his brother Abishai had murdered Abner, *" because he had slain their brother Asahel at Gibeon* in the battle" (ch. ii. 23). This act of Joab, in which Abishai must have been in some way concerned, was a treacherous act of assassination, which could not even be defended as blood-revenge, since Abner had slain Asahel in battle after repeated warnings, and only for the purpose of saving his own life. The principal motive for Joab's act was the most contemptible jealousy, or the fear lest Abner's reconciliation to David should diminish his own influence with the king, as was the case again at a later period with the murder of Amasa (ch. xx. 10).

Vers. 31–39. *David's mourning for Abner's death.*—Vers. 31, 32. To give a public proof of his grief at this murder, and his displeasure at the crime in the sight of all the nation, David commanded Joab, and all the people with him (David), *i.e.* all his courtiers, and the warriors who returned with Joab, to institute a public mourning for the deceased, by tearing their clothes, putting on sackcloth, *i.e.* coarse hairy mourning and penitential clothes, and by a funeral dirge for Abner; *i.e.* he commanded them to walk in front of Abner's bier mourning and in funeral costume, and to accompany the deceased to his resting-place, whilst David as king followed the bier.—Ver. 32. Thus they buried Abner at Hebron ; and David wept aloud at his grave, and all the people with him.—Vers. 33, 34. Although the appointment of such a funeral by David, and his tears at Abner's grave, could not fail to divest the minds of his opponents of all suspicion that Joab had committed the murder with his cognizance (see at ver. 37), he gave a still stronger proof of his innocence, and of the sincerity of his grief, by the ode which he composed for Abner's death :

Ver. 33. Like an ungodly man must Abner die !

34. Thy hands were not bound, and thy feet were not placed in fetters.

As one falls before sinners, so hast thou fallen !

The first strophe (ver. 33) is an expression of painful lamentation at the fact that Abner had died a death which he did not deserve. " *The fool*" (*nabal*) is " the ungodly," according to Israelitish ideas (*vid.* Ps. xiv. 1). The meaning of ver. 34 is : Thou hadst not made thyself guilty of any crime, so as to have to die like a malefactor, in chains and bonds ; but thou hast been treacherously murdered. This dirge made such an impression upon all the people (present), that they wept still more for the dead.—Ver. 35. But David mourned so bitterly, that when all the people called upon him to take some food during the day, he declared with an oath that he would not taste bread or anything else before the setting of the sun. הַבְרוֹת לֶחֶם does not mean, as in ch. xiii. 5, to give to eat, on account of the expression " *all the people*," as it can hardly be imagined that all the people, *i.e.* all who were present, could have come to bring David food, but it signifies to make him eat, *i.e.* call upon him to eat ; whilst it is left uncertain whether David was to eat with the people (cf. ch. xii. 17), *i.e.* to take part in the funeral meal that was held after the burial, or whether the people simply urged him to take some food, for the purpose of soothing his own sorrow. כִּי אִם are to be taken separately ; כִּי, ὅτι, introducing the oath, and אִם being the particle used in an oath : " *if*," *i.e.* assuredly not.—Ver. 36. " *And all the people perceived it* (*i.e.* his trouble), *and it pleased them, as everything that the king did pleased all the people.*"— Ver. 37. All the people (*sc.* who were with the king) and all

Israel discerned on that day (from David's deep and heartfelt trouble), that the death of Abner had not happened (proceeded) from the king, as many may probably at first have supposed, since Joab had no doubt fetched Abner back in David's name. —Vers. 38, 39. Finally, David said to his (confidential) servants : " *Know ye not* (*i.e.* ye surely perceive) *that a prince and great man has this day fallen in Israel ?*" This sentence shows how thoroughly David could recognise the virtues possessed by his opponents, and how very far he was from looking upon Abner as a traitor, because of his falling away from Ishbosheth and coming over to him, that on the contrary he hoped to find in him an able general and a faithful servant. He would at once have punished the murderer of such a man, if he had only possessed the power. " *But*," he adds, " *I am this day* (still) *weak, and only anointed king ; and these men, the sons of Zeruiah, are too strong for me. The Lord reward the doer of evil according to his wickedness.*" The expression " to-day" not only applies to the word " *weak*," or tender, but also to " *anointed*" (*to-day, i.e.* only just *anointed*). As David was still but a young sovereign, and felt himself unable to punish a man like Joab according to his deserts, he was obliged to restrict himself at first to the utterance of a curse upon the deed (ver. 29), and to leave the retribution to God. He could not and durst not forgive ; and consequently, before he died, he charged Solomon, his son and successor, to punish Joab for the murder of Abner and Amasa (1 Kings ii. 5).

MURDER OF ISHBOSHETH, AND PUNISHMENT OF THE
MURDERERS.—CHAP. IV.

Vers. 1-6. *Murder of Ishbosheth.*—Ver. 1. When the son of Saul heard of the death of Abner, " *his hands slackened,*" *i.e.* he lost the power and courage to act as king, since Abner had been the only support of his throne. " *And all Israel was confounded ;*" *i.e.* not merely alarmed on account of Abner's death, but utterly at a loss what to do to escape the vengeance of David, to which Abner had apparently fallen a victim.— Vers. 2, 3. Saul's son had two leaders of military companies (for שָׁאוּל בֶן הָיוּ we must read שׁ לְבֶן הָיוּ׳) : the one was named *Baanah*, the other *Rechab*, sons of *Rimmon* the Beerothite, " *of the sons of Benjamin,"* *i.e.* belonging to them ; *" for Beeroth is also reckoned to Benjamin"* (עַל, over, above, added to). *Beeroth,* the present *Bireh* (see at Josh. ix. 17), was close to the western frontier of the tribe of Benjamin, to which it is also reckoned as belonging in Josh. xviii. 25. This remark concerning Beeroth in the verse before us, serves to confirm the statement that the Beerothites mentioned were Benjaminites ; but that statement also shows the horrible character of the crime attributed to them in the following verses. Two men of the tribe of Benjamin murdered the son of Saul, the king belonging to their own tribe.—Ver. 3. *" The Beerothites fled to Gittaim, and were strangers there unto this day."* *Gittaim* is mentioned again in Neh. xi. 33, among the places in which Benjaminites were dwelling after the captivity, though it by no means follows from this that the place belonged to the tribe of Benjamin before the captivity. It may have been situated outside the territory of that tribe. It is never mentioned again, and has not yet been discovered. The reason why the Beerothites fled to Gittaim, and remained there as strangers until the time when this history was written, is also unknown ; it may perhaps have been that the Philistines had conquered Gittaim.—Ver. 4. Before the historian proceeds to describe what the two Beerothites did, he inserts a remark concerning Saul's family, to show at the outset, that with the death of Ishbosheth the government of this family necessarily became extinct, as the only remaining descendant was a perfectly helpless cripple. He was a son of Jonathan, *smitten* (*i.e.* lamed) *in his feet.* He was five years old when the tidings came from Jezreel of Saul and Jonathan, *i.e.* of their death. His nurse immediately took him and fled, and on their hasty flight he fell and became lame. His name was *Mephibosheth* (according to Simonis, for מִפְאָה בֹשֶׁת, destroying the idol) ; but in 1 Chron. viii. 34 and ix. 40 he is called *Meribbaal* (Baal's fighter), just as Ishbosheth is also called *Eshbaal* (see at ch. ii. 8). On his future history, see ch. ix., xvi. 1 sqq., and xix. 25 sqq.—Ver. 5. The two sons of Rimmon went to Mahanaim, where Ishbosheth resided (ch. ii. 8, 12), and came in the heat of the day (at noon) into Ishbosheth's house, when he was taking his mid-day rest.—Ver. 6. *" And here they had come into the midst of the house, fetching wheat (i.e.* under the pretext of fetching wheat, probably for the soldiers in their companies), *and smote him in the abdomen; and Rechab and his brother escaped.*" The first clause in this verse is a circumstantial clause, which furnishes the explanation of the way in which it was possible for the murderers to find their way to the king. The second clause continues the narrative, and וַיַּכֻּהוּ is attached to וַיָּבֹא (ver. 5).[1]

Vers. 7–12. *Punishment of the murderers by David.*—Ver. 7. As the thread of the narrative was broken by the explanatory remarks in ver. 6, it is resumed here by the repetition of the words וַיָּבֹאוּ וגו' : "*They came into the house, as he lay upon his bed in his bed-chamber, and smote him, and slew him,*" for the purpose of attaching the account of the further progress of the affair, viz. that they cut off his head, took it and went by the way of the Arabah (the valley of the Jordan: see ch. ii. 29) the whole night, and brought the head of Ishbosheth unto David to Hebron with these words : " Behold (= there thou hast) the head of Ishbosheth, the son of Saul thine enemy,

[1] The LXX. thought it desirable to explain the possibility of Rechab and Baanah getting into the king's house, and therefore paraphrased the sixth verse as follows : καὶ ἰδοὺ ἡ θυρωρὸς τοῦ οἴκου ἐκάθαιρε πυροὺς καὶ ἐνύσταξε καὶ ἐκάθευδε, καὶ Ῥηχὰβ καὶ Βαανὰ οἱ ἀδελφοὶ διέλαθον (" and behold the doorkeeper of the house was cleaning wheat, and nodded and slept. And Rahab and Baana the brothers escaped, or went in secretly "). The first part of this paraphrase has been retained in the Vulgate, in the interpolation between vers. 5 and 6 : *et ostiaria domus purgans triticum obdormivit;* whether it was copied by Jerome from the Itala, or was afterwards introduced as a gloss into his translation. It is very evident that this clause in the Vulgate is only a gloss, from the fact that, in all the rest of ver. 6, Jerome has closely followed the Masoretic text, and that none of the other ancient translators found anything about a doorkeeper in his text. When Thenius, therefore, attempts to prove the " evident corruption of the Masoretic text," by appealing to the " nonsense (*Unsinn*) of relating the murder of Ishbosheth and the flight of the murderers twice over, and in two successive verses (see ver. 7)," he is altogether wrong in speaking of the repetition as " nonsense " whereas it is simply tautology, and has measured the peculiarities of Hebrew historians by the standard adopted by our own. J. P. F. Königsfeldt has given the true explanation when he says : " The Hebrews often repeat in this way, for the purpose of adding something fresh, as for example, in this instance, their carrying off the head." Comp. with this ch. iii. 22, 23, where the arrival of Joab is mentioned twice, viz. in two successive verses ; or ch. v. 1–3, where the assembling of the tribes of Israel at Hebron is also referred to a second time,—a repetition at which Thenius himself has taken no offence,—and many other passages of the same kind.

who sought thy life; and thus hath Jehovah avenged my lord
the king this day upon Saul and his seed." No motive is
assigned for this action. But there can be little doubt that it
was no other than the hope of obtaining a great reward from
David. Thus they presumed " to spread the name of God and
His providence as a cloak and covering over their villany, as
the wicked are accustomed to do" (*Berleb. Bible*).—Vers. 9 sqq.
But David rewarded them very differently from what they had
expected. He replied, " *As Jehovah liveth, who hath redeemed
my soul out of all adversity, the man who told me, Behold, Saul
is dead, and thought he was a messenger of good to me, I seized
and slew at Ziklag* (*vid.* i. 14, 15), *to give him a reward for his
news : how much more when wicked men have murdered a righteous man in his house upon his bed, should I not require his blood
at your hand, and destroy you from the earth?*" The several
parts of this reply are not closely linked together so as to form
one period, but answer to the excited manner in which they
were spoken. There is first of all the oath, "*As truly as Jehovah
liveth,*" and the clause appended, " *who redeemed my soul,*" in
which the thought is implied that David did not feel it necessary to get rid of his enemies by the commission of crimes.
After this (ver. 10) we have an allusion to his treatment of the
messenger who announced Saul's death to him, and pretended
to have slain him in order that he might obtain a good reward
for his tidings. כִּי, like ὅτι, simply introduces the address.
הַמַּגִּיד . . . בְּעֵינָיו is placed at the head absolutely, and made subordinate to the verb by בו after וָאֹחֲזָה. לְתִתִּי־לֹו, " *namely, to give
him.*" אֲשֶׁר is employed to introduce the explanation, like our
" *namely*" (*vid.* Ewald, § 338, *b*). בְּשֹׂרָה, good news, here "*the
reward of news.*" The main point follows in ver. 11, beginning
with אַף כִּי, " *how much more*" (*vid.* Ewald, § 354, *c*), and is
introduced in the form of a climax. The words אֲנָשִׁים . . . מִשְׁכָּבֹו
are also written absolutely, and placed at the head: " men have
slain," for " how much more in this instance, when wicked men
have slain." " *Righteous*" (*zaddik*), *i.e.* not guilty of any wicked
deed or crime. The assumption of the regal power, which Abner
had forced upon Ishbosheth, was not a capital crime in the
existing state of things, and after the death of Saul; and even
if it had been, the sons of Rimmon had no right to assassinate
him. David's sentence then follows: " *And now that this is*

the fact, that ye have murdered a righteous man, should I not," etc. בָּעֵר, to destroy by capital punishment, as in Deut. xiii. 6, etc. בִּקֵּשׁ דָּם (= דָּרַשׁ דָּם, Gen. ix. 5), to require the blood of a person, *i.e.* to take blood-revenge.—Ver. 12. David then commanded his servant to slay the murderers, and also to make the punishment more severe than usual. *" They cut off their hands and feet,"*—the hands with which they had committed the murder, and the feet which had run for the reward,—*" and hanged the bodies by the pool at Hebron"* for a spectacle and warning, that others might be deterred from committing similar crimes (cf. Deut. xxi. 22 ; J. H. Michaelis). In illustration of the fact itself, we may compare the similar course pursued by Alexander towards the murderer of king Darius, as described in Justin's history (xii. 6) and Curtius (vii. 5). They buried Ishbosheth's head in Abner's grave at Hebron. Thus David acted with strict justice in this case also, not only to prove to the people that he had neither commanded nor approved of the murder, but from heartfelt abhorrence of such crimes, and to keep his conscience void of offence towards God and towards man.

II. THE GOVERNMENT OF DAVID OVER ALL ISRAEL IN THE TIME OF ITS STRENGTH AND GLORY.

CHAP. V.–IX.

After the death of Ishbosheth, David was anointed in Hebron by all the tribes as king over the whole of Israel (ch. v. 1–5). He then proceeded to attack the Jebusites in Jerusalem, conquered their fortress Zion, and made Jerusalem the capital of his kingdom ; fortifying it still further, and building a palace in it (ch. v. 6–16), after he had twice inflicted a defeat upon the Philistines (ch. v. 17–25). But in order that the chief city of his kingdom and the seat of his own palace might also be made the religious centre of the whole nation as a congregation of Jehovah, he first of all brought the ark of the covenant out of its place of concealment, and had it conveyed in a festal procession to Zion, and deposited there in a tent which had been specially prepared for it, as a place of worship for the whole congregation (ch. vi.). He then resolved to erect for the Lord in Jerusalem a temple fitted for His name; and the Lord gave him in return the promise of the eternal perpetuity of his throne (ch. vii.). To this there is appended a cursory account of David's wars with the neighbouring nations, by which not only his own sovereignty, but the Israelitish kingdom of God, was raised into a commanding power among the nations and kingdoms of the world. In connection with all this, David still maintained his affection and fidelity towards the fallen royal family of Saul, and showed compassion towards the last remaining descendant of that family (ch. ix.).

This account of the unfolding of the power and glory of the kingdom of Israel, through the instrumentality of David and during his reign, is so far arranged chronologically, that all the events and all the enterprises of David mentioned in this section occurred in the first half of his reign over the whole of the covenant nation. The chronological arrangement, however, is not strictly adhered to, so far as the details are concerned; but the standpoint of material resemblance is so far connected with it, that all the greater wars of David are grouped together in ch. viii. (see the introduction to ch. viii.). It is obvious from this, that the plan which the historian adopted was first of all to describe the internal improvement of the Israelitish kingdom of God by David, and then to proceed to the external development of his power in conflict with the opposing nations of the world.

DAVID ANOINTED KING OVER ALL ISRAEL. JERUSALEM TAKEN, AND MADE THE CAPITAL OF THE KINGDOM. VICTORIES OVER THE PHILISTINES.—CHAP. V.

Vers. 1-5. DAVID ANOINTED KING OVER ALL ISRAEL.— Vers. 1-3 (compare with this the parallel passages in 1 Chron. xi. 1-3). After the death of Ishbosheth, all the tribes of Israel (except Judah) came to Hebron in the persons of their representatives the elders (*vid.* ver. 3), in response to the summons of Abner (ch. iii. 17-19), to do homage to David as their king. They assigned three reasons for their coming: (1.) " *Behold, we are thy bone and thy flesh,*" *i.e.* thy blood-relations, inasmuch as all the tribes of Israel were lineal descendants of Jacob (*vid.*

Gen. xxix. 14 ; Judg. ix. 2). (2.) " *In time past, when Saul was king over us, thou wast the leader of Israel* (*thou leddest out and broughtest in Israel*)," *i.e.* thou didst superintend the affairs of Israel (see at Num. xxvii. 17 ; and for the fact itself, 1 Sam. xviii. 5). הָיִיתָה מוֹצִיא is an error in writing for הָיִיתָ הַמּוֹצִיא, and מְבִי for מֵבִיא, with the א dropped, as in 1 Kings xxi. 21, etc. (*vid.* Olshausen, *Gr.* p. 69). (3.) They ended by asserting that Jehovah had called him to be the shepherd and prince over His people. The remarks which we have already made at ch. iii. 18 respecting Abner's appeal to a similar utterance on the part of Jehovah, are equally applicable to the words of Jehovah to David which are quoted here : " Thou shalt feed my people Israel," etc. On the *Piska*, see the note to Josh. iv. 1.—Ver. 3. " *All the elders of Israel came*" is a repetition of ver. 1*a*, except that the expression " all the tribes of Israel " is more distinctly defined as meaning " all the elders of Israel." " *So all the elders came ; . . . and king David made a covenant with them in Hebron before the Lord* (see at ch. iii. 21) : *and they anointed David king over* (all) *Israel.*" The writer of the Chronicles adds, " according to the word of the Lord through Samuel," *i.e.* so that the command of the Lord to Samuel, to anoint David king over Israel (1 Sam. xvi. 1, 12), found its complete fulfilment in this.—Vers. 4, 5. The age of David when he began to reign is given here, viz. thirty years old ; also the length of his reign, viz. seven years and a half at Hebron over Judah, and thirty-three years at Jerusalem over Israel and Judah. In the books of Chronicles these statements occur at the close of David's reign (1 Chron. xxix. 27).

Vers. 6–10. CONQUEST OF THE STRONGHOLD OF ZION, AND CHOICE OF JERUSALEM AS THE CAPITAL OF THE KINGDOM (cf. 1 Chron. xi. 4, 9).—These parallel accounts agree in all the main points; but they are both of them merely brief extracts from a more elaborate history, so that certain things, which appeared of comparatively less importance, are passed over either in the one or the other, and the full account is obtained by combining the two. The conquest of the citadel Zion took place immediately after the anointing of David as king over all the tribes of Israel. This is apparent, not only from the fact that the account follows directly afterwards, but also from the circumstance that, according to ver. 5, David reigned in Jerusalem just as many years as he was king over all Israel.—Ver. 6. The king went with his men (*i.e.* his fighting men : the Chronicles have " all Israel," *i.e.* the fighting men of Israel) to Jerusalem to the Jebusites, the inhabitants of the land, *i.e.* the natives or Canaanites ; "*and they said* (the singular וַיֹּאמֶר is used because הַיְבוּסִי is a singular form) *to David, Thou wilt not come hither* (*i.e.* come in), *but the blind and lame will drive thee away : to say* (*i.e.* by which they meant to say), *David will not come in.*" הֱסִירְךָ is not used for the infinitive, but has been rightly understood by the LXX., Aben Ezra, and others, as a perfect. The perfect expresses a thing accomplished, and open to no dispute; and the use of the singular in the place of the plural, as in Isa. xiv. 32, is to be explained from the fact that the verb precedes, and is only defined precisely by the subject which follows (*vid.* Ewald, § 319, *a*). The Jebusites relied upon the unusual natural advantages of their citadel, which stood upon Mount Zion, a mountain shut in by deep valleys on three different sides ; so that in their haughty self-security they imagined that they did not even need to employ healthy and powerful warriors to resist the attack made by David, but that the blind and lame would suffice.—Ver. 7. However, David took the citadel Zion, *i.e.* " the city of David." This explanatory remark anticipates the course of events, as David did not give this name to the conquered citadel, until he had chosen it as his residence and capital (*vid.* ver. 9). צִיּוֹן (*Sion*), from צִיָּה, to be dry : the dry or arid mountain or hill. This was the name of the southern and loftiest mountain of Jerusalem. Upon this stood the fortress or citadel of the town, which had hitherto remained in the possession of the Jebusites ; whereas the northern portion of the city of Jerusalem, which was upon lower ground, had been conquered by the Judæans and Benjaminites very shortly after the death of Joshua (see at Judg. i. 8).—In ver. 8 we have one circumstance mentioned which occurred in connection with this conquest. On that day, *i.e.* when he had advanced to the attack of the citadel Zion, David said, " Every one who smites the Jebusites, let him hurl into the waterfall (*i.e.* down the precipice) both the lame and blind, who are hateful to David's soul." This is most probably the proper interpretation

of these obscure words of David, which have been very differently explained. Taking up the words of the Jebusites, David
called all the defenders of the citadel of Zion " lame and
blind," and ordered them to be cast down the precipice without
quarter. צִנּוֹר signifies a waterfall (cataracta) in Ps. xlii. 8, the
only other passage in which it occurs, probably from צָנַר, to
roar. This meaning may also be preserved here, if we assume
that at the foot of the steep precipice of Zion there was a
waterfall probably connected with the water of Siloah. It is
true we cannot determine anything with certainty concerning
it, as, notwithstanding the many recent researches in Jerusalem,
the situation of the Jebusite fortress and the character of the
mountain of Zion in ancient times are quite unknown to us.
This explanation of the word *zinnor* is simpler than Ewald's
assumption that the word signifies the steep side of a rock,
which merely rests upon the fact that the Greek word καταρ-
ράκτης originally signified a plunge.[1] וַיִּגַּע should be pointed
as a *Hiphil* וַיַּגַּע. The Masoretic pointing וַיִּגַּע arises from their
mistaken interpretation of the whole sentence. The *Chethibh*
שְׂנֻאוֹ might be the *third pers. perf.*, " who hate David's soul;"
only in that case the omission of אֲשֶׁר would be surprising, and
consequently the *Keri* שְׂנֻאֵי is to be preferred. " From this,"
adds the writer, " the proverb arose, ' The blind and lame shall
not enter the house;'" in which proverb the epithet "blind and
lame," which David applied to the Jebusites who were hated
by him, has the general signification of " repulsive persons,"
with whom one does not wish to have anything to do. In the
Chronicles not only is the whole of ver. 7 omitted, with the
proverb to which the occurrence gave rise, but also the allusion

---

[1] The earliest translators have only resorted to guesses. The Seventy,
with their ἁπτέσθω ἐν παραξιφίδι, have combined צִנּוֹר with צִנָּה, which
they render now and then μάχαιρα or ῥομφαία. This is also done by
the Syriac and Arabic. The Chaldee paraphrases in this manner : " who
begins to subjugate the citadel." Jerome, who probably followed the
Rabbins, has *et tetigisset domatum fistulas* (and touched the *water-pipes*) ;
and Luther, "*und erlanget die Dachrinnen*" (like the English version,
" whosoever getteth up to the gutter : " Tr.). Hitzig's notion, that *zinnor*
signifies ear (" whosoever boxes the ears of the blind and lame ") needs
no refutation ; nor does that of Fr. Böttcher, who proposes to follow
the Alexandrian rendering, and refer *zinnor* to a " sword of honour or
marshal's staff," which David promised to the victor.

to the blind and lame in the words spoken by the Jebusites (ver. 6) ; and another word of David's is substituted instead, namely, that David would make the man who first smote the Jebusites, *i.e.* who stormed their citadel, *head and chief;* [1] and also the statement that Joab obtained the prize. The historical credibility of the statement cannot be disputed, as Thenius assumes, on the ground that Joab had already been chief (*sar*) for a long time, according to ch. ii. 13 : for the passage re ferred to says nothing of the kind ; and there is a very great difference between the commander of an army in the time of war, and a "head and chief," *i.e.* a commander-in-chief. The statement in ver. 8 with regard to Joab's part, the fortification of Jerusalem, shows very clearly that the author of the Chronicles had other and more elaborate sources in his possession, which contained fuller accounts than the author of our books has communicated.—Ver. 9. "*David dwelt in the fort,*" *i.e.* he selected the fort or citadel as his palace, "*and called it David's city.*" David may have been induced to select the citadel of Zion as his palace, and by so doing to make Jerusalem the capital of the whole kingdom, partly by the natural strength of Zion, and partly by the situation of Jerusalem, viz. on the border of the tribes of Benjamin and Judah, and tolerably near to the centre of the land. "*And David built, i.e.* fortified (the city of Zion), *round about from Millo and inwards.*" In the Chronicles we have וְעַד־הַסָּבִיב, "and to the environs or surroundings," *i.e.* to the encircling wall which was opposite to the Millo. The fortification "inwards" must have consisted in the enclosure of Mount Zion with a strong wall upon the north side, where Jerusalem joined it as a lower town, so as to defend the palace against hostile attacks on the north or town side, which had hitherto been left without fortifications. The "Millo" was at any rate some kind of fortification, probably a large tower or castle at one particular part of the surrounding wall (comp. Judg. ix. 6 with vers. 46 and 49, where *Millo* is used interchangeably with *Migdal*). The name ("the filling") probably originated in the fact that through this tower or castle the fortification of the city, or the surrounding wall, was *filled* or *completed.* The definite article before *Millo* indicates that

---

[1] This is also inserted in the passage before us by the translators of the English version : " he shall be chief and captain."—Tr.

it was a well-known fortress, probably one that had been
erected by the Jebusites. With regard to the situation of *Millo*,
we may infer from this passage, and 1 Chron. xi. 8, that the
tower in question stood at one corner of the wall, either on
the north-east or north-west, " where the hill of Zion has the
least elevation and therefore needed the greatest strengthening
from without" (Thenius on 1 Kings ix. 15). This is fully sustained both by 1 Kings xi. 27, where Solomon is said to have
closed the breach of the city of David by building (fortifying)
Millo, and by 2 Chron. xxxii. 5, where Hezekiah is said to
have built up all the wall of Jerusalem, and made *Millo* strong,
i.e. to have fortified it still further (*vid.* 1 Kings ix. 15 and 24).
—Ver. 10. And David increased in greatness, *i.e.* in power
and fame, for Jehovah the God of hosts was with him.

Vers. 11–16.—DAVID'S PALACE, WIVES AND CHILDREN
(comp. 1 Chron. xiv. 1–7).—King Hiram of Tyre sent messengers to David, and afterwards, by the express desire of, the
latter, cedar-wood and builders, carpenters and stone-masons,
who built him a house, *i.e.* a palace. *Hiram* (*Hirom* in 1 Kings
v. 32 ; *Huram* in the Chronicles ; LXX. Χειράμ ; *Josephus*,
Εἴραμος and Εἴρωμος), king of Tyre, was not only an ally
of David, but of his son Solomon also. He sent to the latter
cedar-wood and builders for the erection of the temple and of
his own palace (1 Kings v. 21 sqq. ; 2 Chron. ii. 2 sqq.), and
fitted out a mercantile fleet in conjunction with him (1 Kings
ix. 27, 28 ; 2 Chron. ix. 10) ; in return for which, Solomon not
only sent him an annual supply of corn, oil, and wine (1 Kings
v. 24 ; 2 Chron. ii. 9), but when all the buildings were finished,
twenty years after the erection of the temple, he made over to
him twenty of the towns of Galilee (1 Kings ix. 10 sqq.). It
is evident from these facts that Hiram was still reigning in the
twenty-fourth, or at any rate the twentieth, year of Solomon's
reign, and consequently, as he had assisted David with contri-
butions of wood for the erection of his palace, that he must
have reigned at least forty-five or fifty years ; and therefore that,
even in the latter case, he cannot have begun to reign earlier
than the eighth year of David's reign over all Israel, or from
six to ten years after the conquest of the Jebusite citadel upon
Mount Zion. This is quite in harmony with the account given

here ; for it by no means follows, that because the arrival of an
embassy from Hiram, and the erection of David's palace, are
mentioned immediately after the conquest of the citadel of Zion,
they must have occurred directly afterwards. The arrangement of the different events in the chapter before us is topical
rather than strictly chronological. Of the two battles fought
by David with the Philistines (vers. 17–25), the first at any
rate took place before the erection of David's palace, as it is
distinctly stated in ver. 17 that the Philistines made war upon
David when they heard that he had been anointed king over
Israel, and therefore in all probability even before the conquest
of the fortress of the Jebusites, or at any rate immediately afterwards, and before David had commenced the fortification of
Jerusalem and the erection of a palace. The historian, on the
contrary, has not only followed up the account of the capture of
the fortress of Zion, and the selection of it as David's palace,
by a description of what David gradually did to fortify and
adorn the new capital, but has also added a notice as to David's
wives and the children that were born to him in Jerusalem.
Now, if this be correct, the object of Hiram's embassy cannot
have been "to congratulate David upon his ascent of the throne,"
as Thenius maintains ; but after he had ascended the throne,
Hiram sent ambassadors to form an alliance with this powerful
monarch ; and David availed himself of the opportunity to
establish an intimate friendship with Hiram, and ask him for
cedar-wood and builders for his palace.[1]—Ver. 12. "And David

---

[1] The statements of Menander of Ephesus in Josephus (*c. Ap.* i. 18),
that after the death of *Abibal* his son *Hirom* (Εἴρωμος) succeeded him in
the government, and reigned thirty-four years, and died at the age of fifty-
three, are at variance with the biblical history. For, according to these
statements, as Hiram was still reigning " at the end of twenty years "
(according to 1 Kings ix. 10, 11), when Solomon had built his palaces and
the house of the Lord, *i.e.* twenty-four years after Solomon began to reign,
he cannot have ascended the throne before the sixty-first year of David's
life, and the thirty-first of his reign. But in that case the erection of
David's palace would fall somewhere within the last eight years of his life.
And to this we have to add the repeated statements made by Josephus (*l.c.*
and *Ant.* viii. 3, 1), to the effect that Solomon commenced the building of
the temple in Hiram's twelfth year, or after he had reigned eleven years ; so
that Hiram could only have begun to reign seven years before the death of
David (in the sixty-third year of his life), and the erection of the palace
by David must have fallen later still, and his determination to build the

perceived (*sc.* from the success of his enterprises) that Jehovah had firmly established him king over Israel, and that He had exalted his kingdom for His people Israel's sake," *i.e.* because

temple, which he did not form till he had taken possession of his house of cedar, *i.e.* the newly erected palace (ch. vii. 2), would fall in the very last years of his life, but a very short time before his death. As this seems hardly credible, it has been assumed by some that Hiram's father, Abibal, also bore the name of Hiram, or that Hiram is confounded with Abibal in the account before us (Thenius), or that Abibal's father was named Hiram, and it was he who formed the alliance with David (Ewald, *Gesch.* iv. 287). But all these assumptions are overthrown by the fact that the identity of the Hiram who was Solomon's friend with the contemporary and friend of David is expressly affirmed not only in 2 Chron. ii. 2 (as Ewald supposes), but also in 1 Kings v. 15. For whilst Solomon writes to Hiram in 2 Chron. ii. 3, " as thou didst deal with David my father, and didst send him cedars to build him an house to dwell therein," it is also stated 1 Kings v. 1 that " Hiram king of Tyre sent his servants unto Solomon ; for he had heard that they had anointed him king in the room of his father : for *Hiram was a lover of David all days* (all his life)." Movers (*Phönizier* ii. 1, p. 147 sqq.) has therefore attempted to remove the discrepancy between the statements made in Josephus and the biblical account of Hiram's friendship with David and Solomon, by assuming that in the narrative contained in the books of Samuel we have a topical and not a chronological arrangement, and that according to this arrangement the conquest of Jerusalem by David is followed immediately by the building of the city and palace, and this again by the removal of the holy ark to Jerusalem, and lastly by David's resolution to build a temple, which really belonged to the close of his reign, and indeed, according to 2 Sam. vii. 2, to the period directly following the completion of the cedar palace. There is a certain amount of truth at the foundation of this, but it does not remove the discrepancy ; for even if David's resolution to build a temple did not fall within the earlier years of his reign at Jerusalem, as some have inferred from the position in which it stands in the account given in this book, it cannot be pushed forward to the very last years of his life and reign. This is decidedly precluded by the fact, that in the promise given to David by God, his son and successor upon the throne is spoken of in such terms as to necessitate the conclusion that he was not yet born. This difficulty cannot be removed by the solution suggested by Movers (p. 149), "that the historian necessarily adhered to the topical arrangement which he had adopted for this section, because he had not said anything yet about Solomon and his mother Bathsheba :" for the expression "which shall proceed out of thy bowels" (ch. vii. 12) is not the only one of the kind ; but in 1 Chron. xxii. 9, David says to his son Solomon, "The word of the Lord came to me, saying, A son *shall be* born to thee—Solomon—he shall build an house for my name;" from which it is very obvious, that Solomon was not born at the time when David determined to build the temple and received this promise from God in conse-

He had chosen Israel as His people, and had promised to make it great and glorious.

To the building of David's palace, there is appended in

quence of his intention. To this we have also to add 2 Sam. xi. 2, where David sees Bathsheba, who gave birth to Solomon a few years later, from the roof of his palace. Now, even though the palace is simply called "the king's house" in this passage, and not the "house of cedar," as in ch. vii. 2, and therefore the house intended might possibly be the house in which David lived before the house of cedar was built, this is a very improbable supposition, and there cannot be much doubt that the "king's house" is the palace (ch. v. 11, vii. 1) which he had erected for himself. Lastly, not only is there not the slightest intimation in the whole of the account given in ch. vii. that David was an old man when he resolved to build the temple, but, on the contrary, the impression which it makes throughout is, that it was the culminating point of his reign, and that he was at an age when he might hope not only to commence this magnificent building, but in all human probability to live to complete it. The only other solution left, is the assumption that there are errors in the chronological date of Josephus, and that Hiram lived longer than Menander affirms. The assertion that Solomon commenced the erection of the temple in the eleventh or twelfth year of Hiram's reign was not derived by Josephus from Phœnician sources; for the fragments which he gives from the works of Menander and Dius in the *Antiquities* (viii. 5, 3) and *c. Apion* (i. 17, 18), contain nothing at all about the building of the temple (*vid.* Movers, p. 141), but he has made it as the result of certain chronological combinations of his own, just as in *Ant.* viii. 3, 1, he calculates the year of the building of the temple in relation both to the exodus and also to the departure of Abraham out of Haran, but miscalculates, inasmuch as he places it in the 592d year after the exodus instead of the 480th, and the 1020th year from Abraham's emigration to Canaan instead of the 1125th. And in the present instance his calculation of the exact position of the same event in relation to Hiram's reign may be just as erroneous. His statement concerning the length of Hiram's reign was no doubt taken from Menander; but even in this the numbers may be faulty, since the statements respecting *Balezorus* and *Myttonus* in the very same extract from Menander, as to the length of the reigns of the succeeding kings of Tyre, can be proved to be erroneous, and have been corrected by Movers from Eusebius and Syncellus; and, moreover, the seven years of Hiram's successor, *Baleazar*, do not tally with Eusebius and Syncellus, who both give seventeen years. Thus the proof which Movers adduces from the synchronism of the Tyrian chronology with the biblical, the Egyptian, and the Assyrian, to establish the correctness of Menander's statements concerning Hiram's reign, is rendered very uncertain, to say nothing of the fact that Movers has only succeeded in bringing out the synchronism with the biblical chronology by a very arbitrary and demonstrably false calculation of the years that the kings of Judah and Israel reigned.

vers. 13–15 the account of the increase of his house by the multiplication of his wives and concubines, and of the sons who were born to him at Jerusalem (as in 1 Chron. xiv. 3 sqq.). Taking many wives was indeed prohibited in the law of the king in Deut. xvii. 17 ; but as a large harem was considered from time immemorial as part of the court of an oriental monarch, David suffered himself to be seduced by that custom to disregard this prohibition, and suffered many a heartburn afterwards in consequence, not to mention his fearful fall in consequence of his passion for Bathsheba. The concubines are mentioned before the wives, probably because David had taken many of them to Jerusalem, and earlier than the wives. In the Chronicles the concubines are omitted, though not " intentionally," as they are mentioned in 1 Chron. iii. 9; but as being of no essential importance in relation to the list of sons which follows, because no difference was made between those born of concubines and those born of wives. " Out of Jerusalem," *i.e.* away from Jerusalem : not that the wives were all born in Jerusalem, as the words which follow, " after he was come from Hebron," clearly show. In the Chronicles, therefore, it is explained as meaning " in Jerusalem." The sons are mentioned again both in 1 Chron. xiv. 5–7 and in the genealogy in 1 Chron. iii. 5–8. *Shammua* is called *Shimea* in 1 Chron. iii. 5, according to a different pronunciation. *Shammua, Shobab, Nathan*, and *Solomon* were sons of Bathsheba according to 1 Chron. iii. 5.—Ver. 15. *Elishua* is written incorrectly in 1 Chron. iii. 6 as *Elishama*, because *Elishama* follows afterwards. There are two names after *Elishua* in 1 Chron. iii. 6, 7, and xiv. 6, 7, viz. *Eliphalet* and *Nogah*, which have not crept into the text from oversight or from a wrong spelling of other names, because the number of the names is given as nine in 1 Chron. iii. 8, and the two names must be included in order to bring out that number. And, on the other hand, it is not by the mistake of a copyist that they have been omitted from the text before us, but it has evidently been done deliberately on account of their having died in infancy, or at a very early age. This also furnishes a very simple explanation of the fact, that the name *Eliphalet* occurs again at the end of the list, namely, because a son who was born later received the name of his brother who had died young. *Eliada*, the last but one, is

called *Beeliada* in 1 Chron. xiv. 7, another form of the name,
compounded with *Baal* instead of *El.* David had therefore
nineteen sons, six of whom were born in Hebron (ch. iii. 2
sqq.), and thirteen at Jerusalem. Daughters are not mentioned
in the genealogical accounts, because as a rule only heiresses
or women who acquired renown from special causes were included in them. There is a daughter named *Thamar* mentioned afterwards in ch. xiii. 1.

Vers. 17–25. DAVID GAINS TWO VICTORIES OVER THE
PHILISTINES (compare 1 Chron. xiv. 8–17). — Both these
victories belong in all probability to the interval between the
anointing of David at Hebron over all Israel and the conquest
of the citadel of Zion. This is very evident, so far as the first
is concerned, from the words, " When the Philistines heard
that they had anointed David king over Israel " (ver. 17), not
when David had conquered the citadel of Zion. Moreover,
when the Philistines approached, David "went down to the
hold," or mountain fortress, by which we cannot possibly
understand the citadel upon Zion, on account of the expression
"went down." If David had been living upon Zion at the
time, he would hardly have left this fortification when the
Philistines encamped in the valley of Rephaim on the west of
Jerusalem, but would rather have attacked and routed the
enemy from the citadel itself. The second victory followed
very soon after the first, and must therefore be assigned to the
same period. The Philistines evidently resolved, as soon as the
tidings reached them of the union of all the tribes under the
sovereignty of David, that they would at once resist the growing power of Israel, and smite David before he had consolidated
his government.—Ver. 17. " *The Philistines went up to seek
David,*" *i.e.* to seek him out and smite him. The expression
לְבַקֵּשׁ presupposes that David had not yet taken up his abode
upon Zion. He had probably already left Hebron to make
preparations for his attack upon the Jebusites. When he
heard of the approach of the Philistines, he went down into
the mountain fortress. " The hold" cannot be the citadel of
Zion (as in vers. 7 and 9), because this was so high that they
had to go *up* to it on every side; and it is impossible to sustain
the opinion advanced by Bertheau, that the verb יָרַד (to go

down) is used for falling back into a fortification. הַמְּצוּדָה (*the* hold), with the definite article, is probably the mountain stronghold in the desert of Judah, into which David withdrew for a long time to defend himself from Saul (*vid.* ch. xxiii. 14 and 1 Chron. xii. 8). In ver. 18 the position of the Philistines is more minutely defined. The verse contains a circumstantial clause : " *The Philistines had come and spread themselves out in the valley of Rephaim,*" a valley on the west of Jerusalem, and only separated from the valley of Ben-hinnom by a narrow ridge of land (see at Josh. xv. 8). Instead of יִנָּטְשׁ the Chronicles have יִפְשְׁטוּ, they had invaded, which is perfectly equivalent so far as the sense is concerned.—Vers. 19, 20. David inquired of the Lord by the Urim whether he should go out against the foe, and whether God would give them into his hand ; [1] and when he had received an answer in the affirmative to both these questions, he went to *Baal-perazim* (*lit.* into Baalperazim), and smote them there, and said (ver. 20), " Jehovah hath broken mine enemies before me like a water-breach," *i.e.* has smitten them before me, and broken their power as a flood breaks through and carries away whatever opposes it. From these words of David, the place where the battle was fought received the name of *Baal-perazim*, *i.e.* " possessor of breaches" (equivalent to *Bruch-hausen* or *Brechendorf*, *Breach-ham* or *Break-thorpe*). The only other passage in which the place is mentioned is Isa. xxviii. 21, where this event is alluded to, but it cannot have been far from the valley of Rephaim.—Ver. 21. The Philistines left their idols behind them there. They had probably brought them to the war, as the Israelites once did their ark, as an auxiliary force. " *And David took them away.*" The Chronicles have " their gods" instead of " their idols," and " they were burned with fire " instead of יִשָּׂאֵם, " he took them

---

[1] Through the express statement that David inquired of Jehovah (viz. by the Urim) in both these conflicts with the Philistines (vers. 19 and 23), Diestel's assertion, that after the death of Saul we do not read any more about the use of the holy lot, is completely overthrown, as well as the conclusion which he draws from it, namely, that " David probably employed it for the purpose of giving a certain definiteness to his command over his followers, over whom he had naturally but little authority (1 Sam. xxii. 2 ?), rather than because he looked upon it himself with any peculiar reverence."

away,"[1] took them as booty. The reading in the Chronicles gives the true explanation of the fact, as David would certainly dispose of the idols in the manner prescribed in the law (Deut. vii. 5, 25). The same reading was also most probably to be found in the sources employed by our author, who omitted it merely as being self-evident. In this way David fully avenged the disgrace brought upon Israel by the Philistines, when they carried away the ark in the time of Eli. Vers. 22 25. Al though thoroughly beaten, the Philistines soon appeared again to repair the defeat which they had suffered. As David had not followed up the victory, possibly because he was not sufficiently prepared, the Philistines assembled again in the valley of Rephaim.—Ver. 23. David inquired once more of the Lord what he was to do, and received this answer : " *Thou shalt not go up* (*i.e.* advance to meet the foe, and attack them in front); *turn round behind them, and come upon them* (attack them) *opposite to the Baca-shrubs.*" בְּכָאִים, a word which only occurs here and in the parallel passage in 1 Chron. xiv. 14, is rendered ἀπίους, pear-trees, by the LXX., and *mulberry-trees* by the Rabbins. But these are both of them uncertain conjectures. *Baca*, according to Abulfadl, is the name given in Arabic to a shrub which grows at Mecca and resembles the balsam, except that it has longer leaves and larger and rounder fruit, and from which, if a leaf be broken off, there flows a white pungent sap, like a white tear, which in all probability gave rise to the name בְּכָא = בְּכָה, to weep (*vid.* Celsii, *Hierob.* i. pp. 338 sqq., and Gesenius, *Thes.* p. 205).—Ver. 24. " *And when thou hearest the rush of a going in the tops of the baca-shrubs, then bestir thyself,*" or hasten ; " *for Jehovah has gone out before thee, to smite the army of the Philistines.*" "The sound of a going," *i.e.* of the advance of an army, was a significant sign of the approach of an army of God, which would smite the enemies of Jehovah and of His servant David ; like the visions of Jacob (Gen. xxxii. 2, 3) and Elisha (2 Kings vi. 17). " Then thou shalt bestir thyself," *lit.* be sharp, *i.e.* active, quick : this is paraphrased in the Chronicles by " then thou shalt go out to battle."—Ver. 25. David did this, and smote the Philistines from *Geba* to the neighbourhood of *Gezer*. In the Chronicles

---

[1] This is the marginal reading in the English version, though the text has " he burned them."—TR.

we find "from *Gibeon*" instead of from *Geba*. The former is unquestionably the true reading, and *Geba* an error of the pen: for *Geba*, the present *Jeba*, was to the north of Jerusalem, and on the east of *Ramah* (see at Josh. xviii. 24) ; so that it is quite unsuitable here. But that is not the case with *Gibeon*, the present *el Jib*, on the north-west of Jerusalem (see at Josh. ix. 3); for this was on the way to *Gezer*, which was four Roman miles to the north of *Amws*, and is probably to be sought for on the site of the present *el Kubab* (see at Josh. x. 33).[1]

REMOVAL OF THE ARK TO JERUSALEM.—CHAP. VI.

After David had selected the citadel of Zion, or rather Jerusalem, as the capital of the kingdom, he directed his attention to the organization and improvement of the legally established worship of the congregation, which had fallen grievously into decay since the death of Eli, in consequence of the separation of the ark from the tabernacle. He therefore resolved first of all to fetch out the ark of the covenant, as the true centre of the Mosaic sanctuary, from its obscurity and bring it up to Zion ; and having deposited it in a tent previously prepared to receive it, to make this a place of worship where the regular worship of God might be carried on in accordance with the instructions of the law. That he should make the capital of his kingdom the central point of the worship of the whole congregation of Israel, followed so naturally from the nature of the kingdom of God, and the relation in which David stood, as the earthly

---

[1] There is no force in the objection brought by Bertheau against this view, viz. that "it is *a priori* improbable that the Philistines who were fighting against David and his forces, whose base of operations was Jerusalem, should have taken possession of the whole line from Gibeon to Gezer," as the improbability is by no means apparent, and has not been pointed out by Bertheau, whilst the assumption that Jerusalem was David's base of operations has no foundation whatever. Moreover, Bertheau's opinion, that *Geba* was the same as *Gibeah* in the tribe of Judah (Josh. xv. 57), is decidedly erroneous: for this *Gibeah* is not to be identified with the present village of *Jeba* on the south side of the Wady *Musurr*, half-way between Shocoh and Jerusalem, but was situated towards the desert of Judah (see at Josh. xv. 57) ; and besides, it is impossible to see how the Philistines, who had invaded the plain of Rephaim, could have been beaten from this Gibeah as far as to Gezer.

monarch of that kingdom, towards Jehovah the God-king, that
there is no necessity whatever to seek for even a partial explanation in the fact that David felt it desirable to have the high
priest with the Urim and Thummim always close at hand. But
why did not David remove the Mosaic tabernacle to Mount
Zion at Jerusalem at the same time as the ark of the covenant,
and so restore the divinely established sanctuary in its integrity?
This question can only be answered by conjectures. One
of the principal motives for allowing the existing separation
of the ark from the tabernacle to continue, may have been
that, during the time the two sanctuaries had been separated,
two high priests had arisen, one of whom officiated at the
tabernacle at Gibeon, whilst the other, namely Abiathar, who
escaped the massacre of the priests at Nob and fled at once to
David, had been the channel of all divine communications to
David during the time of his persecution by Saul, and had also
officiated as high priest in his camp; so that he could no more
think of deposing him from the office which he had hitherto
filled, in consequence of the reorganization of the legal worship,
than he could of deposing Zadok, of the line of Eleazar, the
officiating high priest at Gibeon. Moreover, David may from
the very first have regarded the service which he instituted in
connection with the ark upon Zion as merely a provisional
arrangement, which was to continue till his kingdom was more
thoroughly consolidated, and the way had been thereby prepared for erecting a fixed house of God, and so establishing the
worship of the nation of Jehovah upon a more durable foundation. David may also have cherished the firm belief that in the
meantime the Lord would put an end to the double priesthood
which had grown out of the necessities of the times, or at any
rate give him some direct revelation as to the arrangements
which he ought to make.

We have a parallel account of the removal of the ark of the
covenant to Zion in 1 Chron. xiii. 15 and 16, which agrees for
the most part *verbatim*, at all events in all essential points, with
the account before us; but the liturgical side of this solemn
act is very elaborately described, especially the part taken by
the Levites, whereas the account given here is very condensed,
and is restricted in fact to an account of the work of removing
the ark from Kirjath-jearim to Jerusalem as carried out by

David. David composed the 24th Psalm for the religious ceremonies connected with the removal of the ark to Mount Zion.

Vers. 1-10. *The ark fetched from Kirjath-jearim.*—Ver. 1. *" David assembled together again all the chosen men in Israel, thirty thousand."* יֹסֶף for יֹאסֶף is the *Kal* of אָסַף, as in 1 Sam. xv. 6, Ps. civ. 29. עוֹד, *again, once more,* points back to ch. v. 1 and 3, where all Israel is said to have assembled for the first time in Hebron to anoint David king. It is true that that assembly was not convened directly by David himself ; but this was not the point in question, but merely their assembling a second time (see Bertheau on 1 Chron. xiii. 5). בָּחוּר does not mean " the young men " here (*νεάνια*, LXX.), or " the fighting men," but, according to the etymology of the word, " the picked men." Instead of thirty thousand, the LXX. have seventy chiliads, probably with an intentional exaggeration, because the number of men in Israel who were capable of bearing arms amounted to more than thirty thousand. The whole nation, through a very considerable body of representatives, was to take part in the removal of the ark. The writer of the Chronicles gives a more elaborate account of the preparations for these festivities (1 Chron. xiii. 1-5); namely, that David took counsel with the heads of thousands and hundreds, and all the leaders, *i.e.* all the heads of families and households, and then with their consent collected together the whole nation from the brook of Egypt to Hamath, of course not every individual, but a large number of heads of households as representatives of the whole. This account in the Chronicles is not an expansion of the brief notice given here; but the account before us is a condensation of the fuller description given in the sources that were employed by both authors.—Ver. 2. *" David went with all the people that were with him to Baale-Jehuda, to fetch up the ark of God from thence."* The words מִבַּעֲלֵי יְהוּדָה cause some difficulty on account of the מִן, which is used instead of the accusative with ה *loc.,* like בַּעֲלָתָה in the Chronicles ; yet the translators of the Septuagint, Chaldee, Vulgate, and other versions, all had the reading מִן in their text, and בַּעֲלֵי has therefore been taken as an appellative and rendered *ἀπὸ τῶν ἀρχόντων Ἰουδά* (" from the rulers of Judah "), or as Luther renders it, " from the citizens of Judah." This is decidedly incorrect, as the word " thence " which follows is perfectly unintelligible on any other supposition than that *Baale-Jehudah* is the name of a place. *Baale-Jehudah* is another name of the city of *Kirjath-jearim* (Josh. xv. 60, xviii. 14), which is called *Baalah* in Josh. xv. 9 and 1 Chron. xiii. 6, according to its Canaanitish name, instead of which the name *Kirjath-jearim* (city of the woods) was adopted by the Israelites, though without entirely supplanting the old name. The epithet " of Judah " is a contraction of the fuller expression " city of the children of Judah " in Josh. xviii. 14, and is added to distinguish this Baal city, which was situated upon the border of the tribe of Judah, from other cities that were also named after Baal, such as *Baal* or *Baalath-beer* in the tribe of Simeon (1 Chron. iv. 33, Josh. xix. 8), *Baalath* in the tribe of Dan (Josh. xix. 44), the present *Kuryet el Enab* (see at Josh. ix. 17). The מִן (from) is either a very ancient error of the pen that crept by accident into the text, or, if genuine and original, it is to be explained on the supposition that the historian dropped the construction with which he started, and instead of mentioning *Baale-Jehudah* as the place to which David went, gave it at once as the place from which he fetched the ark ; so that the passage is to be understood in this way : " And David went, and all the people who were with him, out of Baale-Jehudah, to which they had gone up to fetch the ark of God " (Kimchi). In the sentence which follows, a difficulty is also occasioned by the repetition of the word שֵׁם in the clause עָלָיו . . . אֲשֶׁר נִקְרָא, " *upon which the name is called, the name of Jehovah of hosts, who is enthroned above the cherubim.*" The difficulty cannot be solved by altering the first שֵׁם into שָׁם, as Clericus, Thenius, and Bertheau suggest : for if this alteration were adopted, we should have to render the passage " where the name of Jehovah of hosts is invoked, who is enthroned above the cherubim (which are) upon it (*i.e.* upon the ark) ; " and this would not only introduce an unscriptural thought into the passage, but it would be impossible to find any suitable meaning for the word עָלָיו, except by making very arbitrary interpolations. Throughout the whole of the Old Testament we never meet with the idea that the name of Jehovah was invoked at the ark of the covenant, because no one was allowed to approach the ark for the purpose of invoking the name of the Lord there ; and upon the great day of atonement the high priest was only allowed to enter the most holy place with the cloud of incense, to sprinkle the blood of the atoning sacrifice upon the ark. Moreover, the standing expression for "call upon the name of the Lord" is קְרָא בְשֵׁם יי׳; whereas נִקְרָא שֵׁם יי׳ עַל פ׳ signifies "the name of Jehovah is called above a person or thing." Lastly, even if עָלָיו belonged to יֹשֵׁב הַכְּרֻבִים, it would not only be a superfluous addition, occurring nowhere else in connection with יֹשֵׁב הכ׳, not even in 1 Chron. xiii. 6 (vid. 1 Sam. iv. 4; 2 Kings xix. 15; Isa. xxxvii. 16; Ps. xcix. 1), but such an addition if made at all would necessarily require אֲשֶׁר עָלָיו (vid. Ex. xxv. 22). The only way in which we can obtain a biblical thought and grammatical sense is by connecting עָלָיו with the אֲשֶׁר before נִקְרָא: "above which (ark) the name of Jehovah-Zebaoth is named," i.e. above which Jehovah reveals His glory or His divine nature to His people, or manifests His gracious presence in Israel. "The name of God denotes all the operations of God through which He attests His personal presence in that relation into which He has entered to man, i.e. the whole of the divine self-manifestation, or of that side of the divine nature which is turned towards men" (Oehler, Herzog's Real-Encycl. x. p. 197). From this deeper meaning of "the name of God" we may probably explain the repetition of the word שֵׁם, which is first of all written absolutely (as at the close of Lev. xxiv. 16), and then more fully defined as "the name of the Lord of hosts."—Vers. 3, 4. "They set the ark of God upon a new cart, and took it away from the house of Abinadab." הִרְכִּיב means here "to put (load) upon a cart," and נָשָׂא to take away, i.e. drive off: for there are grammatical (or syntactical) reasons which make it impossible to render וַיִּשָּׂאֻהוּ as a pluperfect ("they had taken"), on account of the previous וירכבו.

The ark of the covenant had been standing in the house of Abinadab from the time when the Philistines had sent it back into the land of Israel, i.e. about seventy years (viz. twenty years to the victory at Ebenezer mentioned in 1 Sam. vii. 1 sqq., forty years under Samuel and Saul, and about ten years under David: see the chronological table in vol. iv. p. 289). The further statement, that "Uzzah and Ahio, sons of Abinadab, drove the cart," may easily be reconciled with this. These two sons were either born about the time when the ark was first taken to Abinadab's house, or at a subsequent period; or else the term *sons* is used, as is frequently the case, in the sense of grandsons. The words from חֲדָשָׁה (the last word in ver. 3) to *Gibeah* in ver. 4 are wanting in the Septuagint, and can only have been introduced through the error of a copyist, whose eye wandered back to the first עֲגָלָה in ver. 3, so that he copied a whole line twice over; for they not only contain a pure tautology, a merely verbal and altogether superfluous and purposeless repetition, but they are altogether unsuitable to the connection in which they stand. Not only is there something very strange in the repetition of the חֲדָשָׁה without an article after הָעֲגָלָה; but the words which follow, עִם אֲרוֹן ה' (with the ark of God), cannot be made to fit on to the repeated clause, for there is no sense whatever in such a sentence as this : " They brought it (the ark) out of the house of Abinadab, which is upon the hill, *with the* ark of God." The only way in which the words " with the ark " can be made to acquire any meaning at all, is by omitting the repetition referred to, and connecting them with the new cart in ver. 3 : " Uzzah and Ahio . . . drove the cart with the ark of God, and Ahio went before the ark." נָהַג, to drive (a carriage), is construed here with an accusative, in 1 Chron. xiii. 7 with בְּ, as in Isa. xi. 6.—Ver. 5. And David and all the house (people) of Israel were מְשַׂחֲקִים, sporting, *i.e.* they danced and played, before Jehovah. בְּכֹל עֲצֵי בְרוֹשִׁים, " with all kinds of woods of cypresses." This could only mean, with all kinds of instruments made of cypress wood; but this mode of expression would be a very strange one even if the reading were correct. In the Chronicles, however (ver. 8), instead of this strange expression, we find בְּכָל־עֹז וּבְשִׁירִים, " with all their might and with songs." This is evidently the correct reading, from which our text has sprung, although the latter is found in all the old versions, and even in the Septuagint, which really combines the two readings thus : ἐν ὀργάνοις ἡρμοσμένοις ἐν ἰσχύϊ καὶ ἐν ᾠδαῖς, where ἐν ὀργάνοις ἡρμοσμένοις is evidently the interpretation of בְּכֹל עֲצֵי בְרוֹשִׁים; for the text of the Chronicles cannot be regarded as an explanation of Samuel. Moreover, songs would not be omitted on such a festive occasion; and two of the instruments mentioned, viz. the *kinnor* and *nebel* (see at 1 Sam. x. 5), were generally played as accompaniments to singing. The *vav* before בְּשִׁירִים, and before the different instruments, corresponds to the Latin *et . . . et*, both . . . and. תֹּף, the timbrel. בִּמְנַעַנְעִים וּבְצֶלְצְלִים, *sistris et cymbalis*

(Vulg., Syr.), "with bells and cymbals" (Luther). מְנַעַנְעִים,
from נוּעַ, are instruments that are shaken, the σεῖστρα, *sistra*, of
the ancients, which consisted of two iron rods fastened together
at one end, either in a semicircle or at right angles, upon which
rings were hung loosely, so as to make a tinkling sound when
they were shaken.   מְצִלְתַּיִם = צֶלְצְלִים are cymbals or castanets.
Instead of מְנַעַנְעִים, we find חֲצֹצְרוֹת, trumpets, mentioned in the
Chronicles in the last rank after the cymbals. It is possible
that *sistra* were played and trumpets blown, so that the two
accounts complete each other.—Vers. 6, 7. When the procession
had reached the threshing-floor of *Nachon*, Uzzah stretched out
his hand to lay hold of the ark, *i.e.* to keep it from falling
over with the cart, because the oxen slipped. And the wrath
of the Lord was kindled, and God slew Uzzah upon the spot.
Goren nachon means "the threshing-floor of the stroke" (*nachon*
from נָכָה, not from כּוּן); in the Chronicles we have *goren chidon*,
i.e. the threshing-floor of destruction or disaster (בִּיד = כִּידֹן,
Job xxi. 20). *Chidon* is probably only an explanation of *nachon*,
so that the name may have been given to the threshing-floor,
not from its owner, but from the incident connected with the
ark which took place there. Eventually, however, this name
was supplanted by the name *Perez-uzzah* (ver. 8). The situation
of the threshing-floor cannot be determined, as all that we can
gather from this account is that the house of Obed-edom the
Gathite was somewhere near it; but no village, hamlet, or
town is mentioned.[1] Jerome paraphrases כִּי שָׁמְטוּ הַבָּקָר thus :
"Because the oxen kicked and turned it (the ark) over." But
שָׁמַט does not mean to kick; its true meaning is to let go, or
let lie (Ex. xxiii. 11; Deut. xv. 2, 3), hence to slip or stumble.
The stumbling of the animals might easily have turned the cart
over, and this was what Uzzah tried to prevent by laying hold
of the ark. God smote him there " on account of the offence "
(שַׁל, ἀπ. λεγ. from שָׁלָה, in the sense of erring, or committing a
fault). The writer of the Chronicles gives it thus : " Because

---

[1] If it were possible to discover the situation of Gath-rimmon, the home
of Obed-edom (see at ver. 10), we might probably decide the question
whether Obed-edom was still living in the town where he was born or not.
But according to the *Onom.*, Kirjath-jearim was ten miles from Jerusalem,
and Gath-rimmon twelve, that is to say, farther off. Now, if these statements are correct, Obed-edom's house cannot have been in Gath-rimmon.

he had stretched out his hand to the ark," though of course the text before us is not to be altered to this, as Thenius and Bertheau suggest.—Ver. 8. "And David was angry, because Jehovah had made a rent on Uzzah, and called the place *Perez-uzzah*" (rent of Uzzah). פָּרַץ פֶּרֶץ, to tear a rent, is here applied to a sudden tearing away from life. יִחַר לְ is understood by many in the sense of "he troubled himself;" but this meaning cannot be grammatically sustained, whilst it is quite possible to become angry, or fall into a state of violent excitement, at an unexpected calamity. The burning of David's anger was not directed against God, but referred to the calamity which had befallen Uzzah, or speaking more correctly, to the cause of this calamity, which David attributed to himself or to his undertaking. As he had not only resolved upon the removal of the ark, but had also planned the way in which it should be taken to Jerusalem, he could not trace the occasion of Uzzah's death to any other cause than his own plans. He was therefore angry that such misfortune had attended his undertaking. In his first excitement and dismay, David may not have perceived the real and deeper ground of this divine judgment. Uzzah's offence consisted in the fact that he had touched the ark with profane feelings, although with good intentions, namely to prevent its rolling over and falling from the cart. Touching the ark, the throne of the divine glory and visible pledge of the invisible presence of the Lord, was a violation of the majesty of the holy God. "Uzzah was therefore a type of all who with good intentions, humanly speaking, yet with unsanctified minds, interfere in the affairs of the kingdom of God, from the notion that they are in danger, and with the hope of saving them" (O. v. Gerlach). On further reflection, David could not fail to discover where the cause of Uzzah's offence, which he had atoned for with his life, really had lain, and that it had actually arisen from the fact that he (David) and those about him had decided to disregard the distinct instructions of the law with regard to the handling of the ark. According to Num. iv. the ark was not only to be moved by none but Levites, but it was to be carried on the shoulders, not in a carriage; and in ver. 15, even the Levites were expressly forbidden to touch it on pain of death. But instead of taking these instructions as their rule, they had followed the example of the Philistines when they sent back the ark (1 Sam. vi. 7 sqq.), and had placed it upon a new cart, and directed Uzzah to drive it, whilst, as his conduct on the occasion clearly shows, he had no idea of the unapproachable holiness of the ark of God, and had to expiate his offence with his life, as a warning to all the Israelites.— Vers. 9, 10. David's excitement at what had occurred was soon changed into fear of the Lord, so that he said, " How shall the ark of Jehovah come to me?" If merely touching the ark of God is punished in this way, how can I have it brought near me, up to the citadel of Zion? He therefore relinquished his intention of bringing it into the city of David, and placed it in the house of Obed-edom the Gathite. *Obed-edom* was a Levite of the family of the Korahites, who sprang from Kohath (compare Ex. vi. 21, xviii. 16, with 1 Chron. xxvi. 4), and belonged to the class of Levitical doorkeepers, whose duty it was, in connection with other Levites, to watch over the ark in the sacred tent (1 Chron. xv. 18, 24). He is called the *Gittite* or *Gathite* from his birthplace, the Levitical city of *Gath-rimmon* in the tribe of Dan (Josh. xxi. 24, xix. 45).

Vers. 11-19. *Removal of the ark of God to the city of David* (cf. 1 Chron. xv.).—Vers. 11, 12. When the ark had been in the house of Obed-edom for three months, and David heard that the Lord had blessed his house for the sake of the ark of God, he went thither and brought it up to the city of David with gladness, *i.e.* with festal rejoicing, or a solemn procession. (For שִׂמְחָה, in the sense of festal rejoicing, or a joyous fête, see Gen. xxxi. 27, Neh. xii. 43, etc.) On this occasion, however, David adhered strictly to the instructions of the law, as the more elaborate account given in the Chronicles clearly shows. He not only gathered together all Israel at Jerusalem to join in this solemn act, but summoned the priests and Levites, and commanded them to sanctify themselves, and carry the ark " according to the right," *i.e.* as the Lord had commanded in the law of Moses, and to offer sacrifices during the procession, and sing songs, *i.e.* psalms, with musical accompaniment. In the very condensed account before us, all that is mentioned is the carrying of the ark, the sacrificing during the march, and the festivities of the king and people. But even from these few facts we see that David had discovered his former mistake, and had given up the idea of removing the ark upon a carriage as a transgression of the law.—Ver. 13. The bearers of the ark are not particularly mentioned in this account; but it is very evident that they were Levites, as the Chronicles affirm, from the fact that the ark was carried this time, and not driven, as before. "*And it came to pass, when the bearers of the ark of Jehovah had gone six paces, he sacrificed an ox and a fatted calf*" (*i.e.* had them sacrificed). These words are generally understood as meaning, that sacrifices of this kind were offered along the whole way, at the distance of six paces apart. This would certainly have been a possible thing, and there would be no necessity to assume that the procession halted every six paces, until the sacrificial ceremony was completed, but the ark might have continued in progress, whilst sacrifices were being offered at the distances mentioned. And even the immense number of sacrificial animals that would have been required is no valid objection to such an assumption. We do not know what the distance really was: all that we know is, that it was not so much as ten miles, as Kirjath-jearim was only about twelve miles from Jerusalem, so that a few thousand oxen, and the same number of fatted calves, would have been quite sufficient. But the words of the text do not distinctly affirm that sacrifices were offered whenever the bearers advanced six paces, but only that this was done as soon as the bearers had taken the first six steps. So that, strictly speaking, all that is stated is, that when the procession had started and gone six paces, the sacrifice was offered, namely, for the purpose of inaugurating or consecrating the solemn procession. In 1 Chron. xv. this fact is omitted; and it is stated instead (ver. 26), that " when God helped the Levites that bare the ark of the covenant of the Lord, they offered seven bullocks and seven rams," *i.e.* at the close of the procession, when the journey was ended, to praise God for the fact that the Levites had been enabled to carry the ark of God to the place appointed for it, without suffering the slightest harm.[1]—Ver. 14. "*And David danced with all his might before*

[1] There is no discrepancy, therefore, between the two different accounts; but the one supplements the other in a manner perfectly in harmony with the whole affair,—at the outset, a sacrifice consisting of one ox and one fatted calf; and at the close, one of seven oxen and seven rams. Consequently there is no reason for altering the text of the verse before us, as Thenius proposes, according to the senseless rendering of the LXX., καὶ

the Lord (*i.e.* before the ark), *and was girded with a white ephod* (shoulder-dress)." Dancing, as an expression of holy enthu-siasm, was a customary thing from time immemorial : we meet with it as early as at the festival of thanksgiving at the Red Sea (Ex. xv. 20) ; but there, and also at subsequent celebra-tions of the different victories gained by the Israelites, none but women are described as taking part in it (Judg. xi. 34, xxi. 19 ; 1 Sam. xviii. 6). The white ephod was, strictly speaking, a priestly costume, although in the law it is not pre-scribed as the dress to be worn by them when performing their official duties, but rather as the dress which denoted the priestly character of the wearer (see at 1 Sam. xxii. 18) ; and for this reason it was worn by David in connection with these festivities in honour of the Lord, as the head of the priestly nation of Israel (see at 1 Sam. ii. 18). In ver. 15 it is still further related, that David and all the house (nation) of Israel brought up the ark of the Lord with jubilee and trumpet-blast. תְּרוּעָה is used here to signify the song of jubilee and the joyous shouting of the people. In the Chronicles (ver. 28) the musical instru-ments played on the occasion are also severally mentioned. —Ver. 16. When the ark came (*i.e.* was carried) into the city of David, Michal the daughter of Saul looked out of the window, and there she saw king David leaping and dancing before Jehovah, and despised him in her heart. וְהָיָה, " and it came to pass," for וַיְהִי, because there is no progress made, but only another element introduced. בָּא is a perfect : " the ark had come, . . . and Michal looked through the window, . . . there she saw," etc. Michal is intentionally designated the daughter of Saul here, instead of the wife of David, because on this occasion she manifested her father's disposition rather than her husband's. In Saul's time people did not trouble themselves about the ark of the covenant (1 Chron. xiii. 3) ; public worship was neglected, and the soul for vital religion had died out in the family of the king. Michal possessed teraphim, and in

ἦσαν μετ᾽ αὐτοῦ αἴροντες τὴν κιβωτὸν ἑπτὰ χοροί, καὶ θῦμα μόσχος καὶ ἄρνες (" with David there were bearers of the ark, seven choirs, and sacrifices of a calf and lambs"), which has also found its way into the Vulgate, though Jerome has rendered our Hebrew text faithfully afterwards (*i.e.* after the gloss, which was probably taken from the Itala, and inserted in his translation).

David she only loved the brave hero and exalted king : she therefore took offence at the humility with which the king, in his pious enthusiasm, placed himself on an equality with all the rest of the nation before the Lord.—Ver. 17. When the ark was brought to the place appointed for it upon Mount Zion, and was deposited in the tent which David had prepared for it, he offered burnt-offerings and thank-offerings before the Lord. " In its place" is still further defined as " in the midst of the tent which David," etc., *i.e.* in the Most Holy Place ; for the tent would certainly be constructed according to the type of the Mosaic tabernacle. The burnt-offerings and peace-offerings were offered to consecrate the newly erected house of God.— Vers. 18, 19. When the offering of sacrifice was over, David blessed the people in the name of the Lord, as Solomon did afterwards at the dedication of the temple (1 Kings viii. 55), and gave to all the (assembled) people, both men and women, to every one a slice of bread, a measure (of wine), and a cake for a festal meal, *i.e.* for the sacrificial meal, which was celebrated with the *shelamim* after the offering of the sacrifices, and after the king had concluded the liturgical festival with a benediction. חַלַּת לֶחֶם is a round cake of bread, baked for sacrificial meals, and synonymous with כִּכַּר־לֶחֶם (1 Chron. xvi. 3), as we may see from a comparison of Ex. xxix. 23 with Lev. viii. 26 (see the commentary on Lev. viii. 2). But the meaning of the ἀπ λεγ. אֶשְׁפָּר is uncertain, and has been much disputed. Most of the Rabbins understand it as signifying a piece of flesh or roast meat, deriving the word from אֵשׁ and פַּר ; but this is certainly false. There is more to be said in favour of the derivation proposed by L. de Dieu, viz. from the Ethiopic שִׁפֹר, *netiri*, from which Gesenius and Roediger (Ges. *Thes.* p. 1470) have drawn their explanation of the word as signifying a measure of wine or other beverage. For אֲשִׁישָׁה, the meaning grape-cake or raisin-cake is established by Song of Sol. ii. 5 and Hos. iii. 1 (*vid.* Hengstenberg, *Christol.* on Hos. iii. 1). The people returned home after the festal meal.

Vers. 20–23. When David returned home to bless his house, as he had previously blessed the people, Michal came to meet him with scornful words, saying, " *How has the king of Israel glorified himself to-day, when he stripped himself before the eyes of the maids of his servants, as only one of the loose people strips him-*

self!" The unusual combination כְּהִגָּלוֹת נִגְלוֹת is explained by
Ewald (§ 240, *e,* p. 607) in this manner, that whilst, so far as
the sense of the clause is concerned, the second verb ought to
be in the infinitive absolute, they were both written with a very
slight change of form in the infinitive construct; whereas others
regard נִגְלוֹת as an unusual form of the infinitive absolute (Ges.
Lehrgeb. p. 430), or a copyist's error for נִגְלֹה (Thenius, Olsh.
Gr. p. 600). The proud daughter of Saul was offended at the
fact, that the king had let himself down on this occasion to
the level of the people. She availed herself of the shortness
of the priests' shoulder-dress, to make a contemptuous remark
concerning David's dancing, as an impropriety that was unbe-
coming in a king. " Who knows whether the proud woman
did not intend to sneer at the rank of the Levites, as one that
was contemptible in her eyes, since their humble service may
have looked very trivial to her?" (*Berleb. Bible.*)—Vers. 21, 22.
David replied, " Before Jehovah, who chose me before thy
father and all his house, to appoint me prince over the people
of Jehovah, over Israel, before Jehovah have I played (*lit.*
joked, given utterance to my joy). And I will be still more
despised, and become base in my eyes : and with the maidens of
whom thou hast spoken, with them will I be honoured." The
copula *vav* before שִׂחַקְתִּי serves to introduce the apodosis, and
may be explained in this way, that the relative clause appended
to " before Jehovah" acquired the power of a protasis on
account of its length; so that, strictly speaking, there is an
anakolouthon, as if the protasis read thus : " Before Jehovah,
as He hath chosen me over Israel, I have humbled myself
before Jehovah" (for " before him"). With the words " who
chose me before *thy father and all his house,*" David humbles
the pride of the king's daughter. His playing and dancing
referred to the Lord, who had chosen him, and had rejected
Saul on account of his pride. He would therefore let himself
be still further despised before the Lord, *i.e.* would bear still
greater contempt from men than that which he had just
received, and be humbled in his own eyes (*vid.* Ps. cxxxi. 1) :
then would he also with the maidens attain to honour before
the Lord. For whoso humbleth himself, him will God exalt
(Matt. xxiii. 12). בְּעֵינַי is not to be altered into בְּעֵינַיִךְ, as in the
Septuagint. This alteration has arisen from a total miscon-

ception of the nature of true humility, which is of no worth in its own eyes. The rendering given by De Wette is at variance with both the grammar and the sense (" with the maidens, . . . with them will I magnify myself"); and so also is that of Thenius (" with them will I be honoured, *i.e.* indemnify myself for thy foolish contempt!").—Ver. 23. Michal was humbled by God for her pride, and remained childless to the time of her death.

DAVID'S RESOLUTION TO BUILD A TEMPLE. THE PROMISED PERPETUITY OF HIS THRONE.—CHAP. VII.

To the erection of a sanctuary for the ark upon Mount Zion there is appended an account of David's desire to build a temple for the Lord. We find this not only in the text before us, but also in the parallel history in 1 Chron. xvii. When David had acquired rest from his enemies round about, he formed the resolution to build a house for the Lord, and this resolution was sanctioned by the prophet Nathan (vers. 1–3). But the Lord revealed to the prophet, and through him to David, that He had not required the building of a temple from any of the tribes of Israel, and that He would first of all build a house himself for His servant David, and confirm the throne to his seed for ever, and then he should build Him a temple (vers. 4–17). David then gave utterance to his thanksgiving for this glorious promise in a prayer, in which he praised the unmeasurable grace of God, and prayed for the fulfilment of this renewed promise of divine grace (vers. 18–29).[1]

[1] With regard to the historical authenticity of this promise, Tholuck observes, in his *Prophets and their Prophecies* (pp. 165-6), that "it can be proved, with all the evidence which is ever to be obtained in support of historical testimony, that David actually received a prophetic promise that his family should sit upon the throne for ever, and consequently an intimation of a royal descendant whose government should be eternal. Anything like a merely subjective promise arising from human combinations is precluded here by the fact that Nathan, acting according to the best of his knowledge, gave his consent to David's plan of building a temple; and that it was not till afterwards, when he had been instructed by a divine vision, that he did the very opposite, and assured him on the contrary that God would build *him* a house." Thenius also affirms that "there is no reason for assuming, as De Wette has done, that Nathan's prophecies were not composed till after the time of Solomon;" that "their historical credibility

Vers. 1-3. When David was dwelling in his house, *i.e.* the palace of cedar (ch. v. 11), and Jehovah had given him rest from all his enemies round about, he said to Nathan the prophet : "See now, I dwell in a house of cedar, and the ark of God dwelleth within the curtains." הַיְרִיעָה in the singular is used, in Ex. xxvi. 2 sqq., to denote the inner covering, com-

is attested by Ps. lxxxix. (vers. 4, 5, 20-38, and especially ver. 20), Ps. cxxxii. 11, 12, and Isa. lv. 3 ; and that, properly interpreted, they are also Messianic." The principal evidence of this is to be found in the prophetic utterance of David in ch. xxiii., where, as is generally admitted, he takes a retrospective glance at the promise, and thereby attests the historical credibility of Nathan's prophecy (Thenius, p. 245). Nevertheless, Gust. Baur maintains that "a closer comparison of this more elaborate and simple description (ch. vii.) with the brief and altogether unexampled *last words of David*, more especially with 2 Sam. xxiii. 5, can hardly leave the slightest doubt, that the relation in which the chapter before us stands to these words, is that of a later expansion to an authentic prophetic utterance of the king himself." For example, the distinct allusion to the birth of Solomon, and the building of the temple, which was to be completed by him, is said to have evidently sprung from a later development of the original promise after the time of Solomon, on account of the incongruity apparent in Nathan's prediction between the ideal picture of the Israelitish monarchy and the definite allusion to Solomon's building of the temple. But there is no such "incongruity" in Nathan's prediction ; it is only to be found in the naturalistic assumptions of Baur himself, that the utterances of the prophets contained nothing more than subjective and *ideal* hopes of the future, and not supernatural predictions. This also applies to Diestel's opinion, that the section vers. 4-16 does not harmonize with the substance of David's glorious prayer in vers. 18-29, nor the latter again with itself, because the advice given him to relinquish the idea of building the temple is not supported by any reasons that answer either to the character of David or to his peculiar circumstances, with which the allusion to his son would have been in perfect keeping ; but the prophet's dissuasion merely alludes to the fact that Jehovah did not stand in need of a stately house at all, and had never given utterance to any such desire. On account of this "obvious" fact, Diestel regards it as credible that the original dissuasion came from God, because it was founded upon an earlier view, but that the promise of the son of David which followed proceeded from Nathan, who no doubt looked with more favourable eyes upon the building of the temple. This discrepancy is also arbitrarily foisted upon the text. There is not a syllable about any "original dissuasion" in all that Nathan says ; for he simply tells the king that Jehovah had hitherto dwelt in a tent, and had not asked any of the tribes of Israel to build a stately temple, but not that Jehovah did not need a stately house at all.

Of the different exegetical treatises upon this passage, see *Christ. Aug. Crusii Hypomnemata*, ii. 190-219, and Hengstenberg's *Christol.* i. 123 sqq.

posed of a number of lengths of tapestry sewn together, which was spread over the planks of the tabernacle, and made it into a dwelling, whereas the separate pieces of tapestry are called יְרִיעֹת in the plural ; and hence, in the later writers, יְרִיעֹות alternates sometimes with אֹהֶל (Isa. liv. 2), and at other times with אֹהָלִים (Song of Sol. i. 5 ; Jer. iv. 20, xlix. 29). Consequently הַיְרִיעָה refers here to the tent-cloth or tent formed of pieces of tapestry. "*Within* (*i.e.* surrounded by) *the tent-cloth :*" in the Chronicles we find "under curtains." From the words "when the Lord had given him rest from all his enemies round about," it is evident that David did not form the resolution to build the temple in the first years of his reign upon Zion, nor immediately after the completion of his palace, but at a later period (see the remarks on ch. v. 11, note). It is true that the giving of rest from all his enemies round about does not definitely presuppose the termination of *all* the greater wars of David, since it is not affirmed that this rest was a definitive one ; but the words cannot possibly be restricted to the two victories over the Philistines (ch. v. 17–25), as Hengstenberg supposes, inasmuch as, however important the second may have been, their foes were not even permanently quieted by them, to say nothing of their being entirely subdued. Moreover, in the promise mentioned in ver. 9, God distinctly says, " I was with thee whithersoever thou wentest, and have cut off *all* thine enemies before thee." These words also show that at that time David had already fought against all the enemies round about, and humbled them. Now, as all David's principal wars are grouped together for the first time in ch. viii. and x., there can be no doubt that the history is not arranged in a strictly chronological order. And the expression "after this" in ch. viii. 1 is by no means at variance with this, since this formula does not at all express a strictly chronological sequence. From the words of the prophet, " Go, do all that is in thy heart, for the Lord is with thee," it is very evident that David had expressed the intention to build a splendid palatial temple. The word לֵךְ, *go* (equivalent to "quite right"), is omitted in the Chronicles as superfluous. Nathan sanctioned the king's resolution " from his own feelings, and not by divine revelation" (J. H. Michaelis) ; but he did not " afterwards perceive that the time for carrying out this intention had not yet come," as Thenius and Bertheau maintain ; on the contrary, the Lord God revealed to the prophet that David was not to carry out his intention at all.

Vers. 4–17. *The revelation and promise of God.*—Ver. 4. *" That night,"* i.e. the night succeeding the day on which Nathan had talked with the king concerning the building of the temple, the Lord made known His decree to the prophet, with instructions to communicate it to the king. הַאַתָּה וגו׳, " Shouldest thou build me a house for me to dwell in ?" The question involves a negative reply, and consequently in the Chronicles we find " thou shalt not."—Vers. 6, 7. The reason assigned for this answer : " I have not dwelt in a house from the day of the bringing up of Israel out of Egypt even to this day, but I was wandering about in a tent and in a dwelling." *" And in a dwelling"* (*mishcan*) is to be taken as explanatory, viz. in a tent which was my dwelling. As a tent is a traveller's dwelling, so, as long as God's dwelling was a tent, He himself appeared as if travelling or going from place to place. " In the whole of the time that I walked among all the children of Israel, . . . have I spoken a word to one of the tribes of Israel, whom I commanded to feed my people, saying, Where- fore have ye not built me a cedar house ?" A " cedar house" is equivalent to a palace built of costly materials. The expres- sion אַחַד שִׁבְטֵי יִשְׂרָאֵל (" one of the tribes of Israel") is a striking one, as the feeding of the nation does not appear to be a duty belonging to the " tribes," and in the Chronicles we have שֹׁפְטֵי (judges) instead of שִׁבְטֵי (tribes). But if שֹׁפְטֵי had been the original expression used in the text, it would be impossible to explain the origin and general acceptance of the word שִׁבְטֵי. For this very reason, therefore, we must regard שִׁבְטֵי as the original word, and understand it as referring to the *tribes*, which had supplied the nation with judges and leaders before the time of David, since the feeding, *i.e.* the government of Israel, which was in the hands of the judges, was transferred to the tribes to which the judges belonged. This view is confirmed by Ps. lxxviii. 67, 68, where the election of David as prince, and of Zion as the site of the sanctuary, is described as the election of the *tribe* of Judah and the rejection of the tribe of Ephraim. On the other hand, the assumption of Thenius, that שִׁבְטֵי, " shepherd-staffs," is used poetically for shepherds, cannot be established on the ground of Lev. xxvii. 32 and Micah vii. 14.

Jehovah gave two reasons why David's proposal to build Him
a temple should not be carried out : (1) He had hitherto lived
in a tent in the midst of His people; (2) He had not commanded any former prince or tribe to build a temple. This
did not involve any blame, as though there had been something
presumptuous in David's proposal, or in the fact that he had
thought of undertaking such a work without an express command from God, but simply showed that it was not because of
any negligence on the part of the former leaders of the people
that they had not thought of erecting a temple, and that even
now the time for carrying out such a work as that had not yet
come.—Ver. 8. After thus declining his proposal, the Lord
made known His gracious purpose to David : "Thus saith
Jehovah of hosts" (not only *Jehovah*, as in ver. 5, but *Jehovah
Sebaoth*, because He manifests himself in the following revelation as the God of the universe) : "I have taken thee from the
pasturage (grass-plat), behind the flock, to be prince over my
people Israel ; and was with thee whithersoever thou wentest,
and exterminated all thine enemies before thee, and so made
thee, וְעָשִׂתִי (perfect with *vav* consec.), a great name, . . . and
created a place for my people Israel, and planted them, so that
they dwell in their place, and do not tremble any more (before
their oppressors) ; and the sons of wickedness do not oppress
them any further, as at the beginning, and from the day when I
appointed judges over my people Israel : and I create thee rest
from all thine enemies.   And Jehovah proclaims to thee, that
Jehovah will make thee a house."   The words עַמִּי יִשְׂ׳ . . . לְמִן הַיּוֹם
are to be joined to בָּרִאשׁוֹנָה, " as in the beginning," *i.e.* in Egypt,
and from the time of the judges ; that is to say, during the
rule of the judges, when the surrounding nations constantly
oppressed and subjugated Israel.   The plan usually adopted,
of connecting the words with וַהֲנִיחֹתִי, does not yield any suitable
thought at all, as God had not given David rest from the very
beginning of the times of the judges ; but the period of the
judges was long antecedent to the time of David, and was not
a period of rest for the Israelites.   Again, וַהֲנִיחֹתִי does not
resume what is stated in ver. 9, and is not to be rendered as a
preterite in the sense of " I have procured thee rest," but as a
perfect with *vav consec.,* " and I procure thee rest" from what
is now about to come to pass.   And וְהִגִּיד is to be taken in the

same way : the Lord shows thee, first of all through His promise (which follows), and then through the fact itself, the
realization of His word. וַהֲנִיחֹתִי refers to the future, as well as
the building of David's house, and therefore not to the rest
from all his enemies, which God had already secured for David,
but to that which He would still further secure for him, that
is to say, to the maintenance and establishment of that rest.
The commentary upon this is to be found in Ps. lxxxix. 22–24.
In the Chronicles (ver. 10) there is a somewhat different turn
given to the last clauses : "and I bend down all thine enemies,
and make it (the bending-down) known to thee (by the fact),
and a house will Jehovah build for thee." The thought is not
essentially changed by this ; consequently there is no ground
for any emendation of the text, which is not even apparently
necessary, unless, like Bertheau, we misinterpret the words,
and connect וְהִכְנַעְתִּי erroneously with the previous clause.

The connection between vers. 5–7 and 8–16 has been correctly indicated by Thenius as follows : Thou shalt not build
a house for ME; but I, who have from the very beginning
glorified myself in thee and my people (vers. 8–11), will build
a house for thee ; and thy son shall erect a house for me
(ver. 13). This thought is not merely "a play upon words
entirely in the spirit of prophecy," but contains the deep
general truth that God must first of all build a man's house,
before the man can build God's house, and applies it especially to the kingdom of God in Israel. As long as the quiet
and full possession of the land of Canaan, which had been
promised by the Lord to the people of God for their inheritance,
was disputed by their enemies round about, even the dwelling-
place of their God could not assume any other form than that
of a wanderer's tent. The kingdom of God in Israel first
acquired its rest and consolation through the efforts of David,
when God had made all his foes subject to him and established his throne firmly, *i.e.* had assured to his descendants the
possession of the kingdom for all future time. And it was this
which ushered in the time for the building of a stationary house
as a dwelling for the name of the Lord, *i.e.* for the visible
manifestation of the presence of God in the midst of His
people. The conquest of the citadel of Zion and the elevation
of this fortress into the palace of the king, whom the Lord had

given to His people, formed the commencement of the establishment of the kingdom of God. But this commencement
received its first pledge of perpetuity from the divine assurance
that the throne of David should be established for all future
time. And this the Lord was about to accomplish : He would
build David a house, and then his seed should build the house
of the Lord. No definite reason is assigned why David himself
was not to build the temple. We learn this first of all from
David's last words (1 Chron. xxviii. 3), in which he says to the
assembled heads of the nation, " God said to me, Thou shalt
not build a house for my name, because thou art a man of
wars, and hast shed blood." Compare with this the similar
words of David to Solomon in 1 Chron. xxii. 8, and Solomon's
statement in his message to Hiram, that David had been prevented from building the temple in consequence of his many
wars. It was probably not till afterwards that David was
informed by Nathan what the true reason was. As Hengstenberg has correctly observed, the fact that David was not permitted to build the temple on account of his own personal
unworthiness, did not involve any blame for what he had done ;
for David stood in a closer relation to the Lord than Solomon
did, and the wars which he waged were wars of the Lord
(1 Sam. xxv. 28) for the maintenance and defence of the
kingdom of God. But inasmuch as these wars were necessary
and inevitable, they were practical proofs that David's kingdom
and government were not yet established, and therefore that
the time for the building of the temple had not yet come, and
the rest of peace was not yet secured. The temple, as the
symbolical representation of the kingdom of God, was also to
correspond to the nature of that kingdom, and shadow forth
the peace of the kingdom of God. For this reason, David, the
man of war, was not to build the temple ; but that was to be
reserved for Solomon, the man of peace, the type of the Prince
of Peace (Isa. ix. 5).

In vers. 12–16 there follows a more precise definition of the
way in which the Lord would build a house for His servant
David : " When thy days shall become full, and thou shalt lie
with thy fathers, I will set up thy seed after thee, who shall
come from thy body, and establish his kingdom. He will build
a house for my name, and I shall establish the throne of his

kingdom for ever." הֵקִים, to set up, *i.e.* to promote to royal dignity. אֲשֶׁר יֵצֵא is not to be altered into אֲשֶׁר יָצָא, as Thenius and .others maintain. The assumption that Solomon had already been born, is an unfounded one (see the note to ch. v. 11, p. 319) ; and it by no means follows from the statement in ver. 1, to the effect that God had given David rest from all his enemies, that his resolution to build a temple was not formed till the closing years of his reign.—Vers. 14 sqq. *"I will be a father to him, and he will be a son to me ; so that if he go astray, I shall chastise him with rods of men, and with strokes of the children of men (i.e.* not 'with moderate punishment, such as parents are accustomed to inflict,' as Clericus explains it, but with such punishments as are inflicted upon all men who go astray, and from which even the seed of David is not to be excepted). *But my mercy shall not depart from him, as I caused it to depart from Saul, whom I put away before thee. And thy house and thy kingdom shall be established for ever before thee ; thy throne shall be established for ever."* It is very obvious, from all the separate details of this promise, that it related primarily to Solomon, and had a certain fulfilment in him and his reign. On the death of David, his son Solomon ascended the throne, and God defended his kingdom against the machinations of Adonijah (1 Kings ii. 12) ; so that Solomon was able to say, "The Lord hath fulfilled His word that He spoke ; for I have risen up in the stead of my father David," etc. (1 Kings viii. 20). Solomon built the temple, as the Lord said to David (1 Kings v. 19, viii. 15 sqq.). But in his old age Solomon sinned against the Lord by falling into idolatry ; and as a punishment for this, after his death his kingdom was rent from his son, not indeed entirely, as one portion was still preserved to the family for David's sake (1 Kings xi. 9 sqq.). Thus the Lord punished him with rods of men, but did not withdraw from him His grace. At the same time, however unmistakeable the allusions to Solomon are, the substance of the promise is not fully exhausted in him. The threefold repetition of the expression "for ever," the establishment of the kingdom and throne of David *for ever*, points incontrovertibly beyond the time of Solomon, and to the eternal continuance of the seed of David. The word *seed* denotes the posterity of a person, which may consist either in one son or in several children, or in a long line of successive generations. The idea of a number of persons living at the same time, is here precluded by the context of the promise, as only one of David's successors could sit upon the throne at a time. On the other hand, the idea of a number of descendants following one another, is evidently contained in the promise, that God would not withdraw His favour from the seed, even if it went astray, as He had done from Saul, since this implies that even in that case the throne should be transmitted from father to son. There is still more, however, involved in the expression "for ever." When the promise was given that the throne of the kingdom of David should continue "to eternity," an eternal duration was also promised to the seed that should occupy this throne, just as in ver. 16 the house and kingdom of David are spoken of as existing for ever, side by side. We must not reduce the idea of eternity to the popular notion of a long incalculable period, but must take it in an absolute sense, as the promise is evidently understood in Ps. lxxxix. 30 : " I set his seed for ever, and his throne as the days of heaven." No earthly kingdom, and no posterity of any single man, has eternal duration like the heaven and the earth ; but the different families of men become extinct, as the different earthly kingdoms perish, and other families and kingdoms take their place. The posterity of David, therefore, could only last for ever by running out in a person who lives for ever, *i.e.* by culminating in the Messiah, who lives for ever, and of whose kingdom there is no end. The promise consequently refers to the posterity of David, commencing with Solomon and closing with Christ : so that by the " seed" we are not to understand Solomon alone, with the kings who succeeded him, nor Christ alone, to the exclusion of Solomon and the earthly kings of the family of David ; nor is the allusion to Solomon and Christ to be regarded as a double allusion to two different objects.

But if this is established,—namely, that the promise given to the seed of David that his kingdom should endure for ever only attained its ultimate fulfilment in Christ,—we must not restrict the building of the house of God to the erection of Solomon's temple. " The building of the house of the Lord goes hand in hand with the eternity of the kingdom" (Hengstenberg). As the kingdom endures for ever, so the house built for the dwelling-place of the Lord must also endure for ever, as Solomon said at the dedication of the temple (1 Kings viii. 13) : " I have surely built Thee an house to dwell in, a settled place for Thee to abide in for ever." The everlasting continuance of Solomon's temple must not be reduced, however, to the simple fact, that even if the temple of Solomon should be destroyed, a new building would be erected in its place by the earthly descendants of Solomon, although this is also implied in the words, and the temple of Zerubbabel is included as the restoration of that of Solomon. For it is not merely in its earthly form, as a building of wood and stone, that the temple is referred to, but also and chiefly in its essential characteristic, as the place for the manifestation and presence of God in the midst of His people. The earthly form is perishable, the essence eternal. This essence was the dwelling of God in the midst of His people, which did not cease with the destruction of the temple at Jerusalem, but culminated in the appearance of Jesus Christ, in whom Jehovah came to His people, and, as God the Word, made human nature His dwelling-place (ἐσκήνωσεν ἐν ἡμῖν, John i. 14) in the glory of the only-begotten Son of the Father ; so that Christ could say to the Jews, " Destroy this temple (*i.e.* the temple of His body), and in three days I will build it up again" (John ii. 19). It is with this building up of the temple destroyed by the Jews, through the resurrection of Jesus Christ from the dead, that the complete and essential fulfilment of our promise begins. It is perpetuated within the Christian church in the indwelling of the Father and Son through the Holy Ghost in the hearts of believers (John xiv. 23; 1 Cor. vi. 19), by which the church of Jesus Christ is built up a spiritual house of God, composed of living stones (1 Tim. iii. 15, 1 Pet. ii. 5; compare 2 Cor. vi. 16, Heb. iii. 6) ; and it will be perfected in the completion of the kingdom of God at the end of time in the new Jerusalem, which shall come down upon the new earth out of heaven from God, as the true tabernacle of God with men (Rev. xxi. 1-3).

As the building of the house of God receives its fulfilment first of all through Christ, so the promise, " I will be to him a father, and he shall be to me a son," is first fully realized in Jesus Christ, the only-begotten Son of the heavenly Father (*vid.* Heb. i. 5). In the Old Testament the relation between father and son denotes the deepest intimacy of love ; and love is perfected in unity of nature, in the communication to the son of all that the father hath. The Father loveth the Son, and hath given all things into His hand (John iii. 35). Sonship therefore includes the government of the world. This not only applied to Christ, the only-begotten Son of God, but also to the seed of David generally, so far as they truly attained to the relation of children of God. So long as Solomon walked in the ways of the Lord, he ruled over all the kingdoms from the river (Euphrates) to the border of Egypt (1 Kings v. 1); but when his heart turned away from the Lord in his old age, adversaries rose up against him (1 Kings xi. 14 sqq., 23 sqq.), and after his death the greater part of the kingdom was rent from his son. The seed of David was chastised for its sins; and as its apostasy continued, it was humbled yet more and more, until the earthly throne of David became extinct. Nevertheless the Lord did not cause His mercy to depart from him. When the house of David had fallen into decay, Jesus Christ was born of the seed of David according to the flesh, to raise up the throne of His father David again, and to reign for ever as King over the house of Jacob (Luke i. 32, 33), and to establish the house and kingdom of David for ever.—In ver. 16, where the promise returns to David again with the words, " thy house and thy kingdom shall be established for ever," the expression לְפָנֶיךָ (before thee), which the LXX. and Syriac have arbitrarily changed into לְפָנַי (before me), should be particularly observed. David, as the tribe-father and founder of the line of kings, is regarded either " as seeing all his descendants pass before him in a vision," as O. v. Gerlach supposes, or as continuing to exist in his descendants.—Ver. 17. " According to all these words . . . did Nathan speak unto David," i.e. he related the whole to David, just as God had addressed it to him in the night. The clause in apposition, " according to all this vision," merely introduces a more minute definition of the peculiar form of the revelation. God spoke to Nathan in a vision which he had in the night, i.e. not in a dream, but in a waking condition, and during the night; for חִזָּיוֹן=חָזוֹן is constantly distinguished from חֲלוֹם, a revelation in a dream.

Vers. 18–29. David's prayer and thanksgiving.—Ver. 18. King David came, i.e. went into the sanctuary erected upon Zion, and remained before Jehovah. יֵּשֶׁב, remained, tarried (as in Gen. xxiv. 55, xxix. 19, etc.), not "*sat;*" for the custom of sitting before the Lord in the sanctuary, as the posture assumed in prayer, cannot be deduced from Ex. xvii. 12, where Moses is compelled to sit from simple exhaustion. David's prayer consists of two parts,—thanksgiving for the promise (vers. 18*b*–24), and supplication for its fulfilment (vers. 25–29). The thanksgiving consists of a confession of unworthiness of all the great things that the Lord had hitherto done for him, and which He had still further increased by this glorious promise (vers. 18–21), and praise to the Lord that all this had been done in proof of His true Deity, and to glorify His name upon His chosen people Israel.—Ver. 18*b*. "*Who am I, O Lord Jehovah? and who my house* (*i.e.* my family), *that Thou hast brought me hitherto?*" These words recal Jacob's prayer in Gen. xxxii. 10, "I am not worthy of the least of all the mercies," etc. David acknowledged himself to be unworthy of the great mercy which the Lord had displayed towards him, that he might give the glory to God alone (*vid.* Ps. viii. 5 and cxliv. 3).—Ver. 19. "*And this is still too little in Thine eyes, O Lord Jehovah, and Thou still speakest with regard to the house of Thy servant for a great while to come.*" לְמֵרָחוֹק, *lit.* that which points to a remote period, *i.e.* that of the eternal establishment of my house and throne. "*And this is the law of man, O Lord Jehovah.*" "The law of man" is the law which determines or regulates the conduct of man. Hence the meaning of these words, which have been very differently interpreted, cannot, with the context immediately preceding it, be any other than the following: This—namely, the love and condescension manifested in Thy treatment of Thy servant—is the law which applies to man, or is conformed to the law which men are to observe towards men, *i.e.* to the law, Thou shalt love thy neighbour as thyself (Lev. xix. 18, compare Micah vi. 8). With this interpretation, which is confirmed by the parallel text of the Chronicles (in ver. 17), "Thou sawest (*i.e.* visitedst me, or didst deal with me) according to the manner of man," the words are expressive of praise of the condescending grace of the Lord. "When God the Lord, in His treatment of poor mortals, follows the rule which He has laid down for the conduct of men one towards another, when He shows himself kind and affectionate, this must fill with adoring amazement those who know themselves and God" (Hengstenberg). Luther is wrong in the rendering which he has adopted: "This is the manner of a man, who is God the Lord;" for "Lord Jehovah" is not an explanatory apposition to "man," but an address to God, as in the preceding and following clause.—Ver. 20. "*And what more shall David speak to Thee? Thou knowest Thy servant, Lord Jehovah.*" Instead of expressing his gratitude still further in many words, David appeals to the omniscience of God, before whom his thankful heart lies open, just as in Ps. xl. 10 (compare also Ps. xvii. 3).—Ver. 21. "*For Thy word's sake, and according to Thy heart* (and therefore not because I am worthy of such grace), *hast Thou done all this greatness, to make it known to Thy servant.*" The word, for the sake of which God had done such great things for David, must be some former promise on the part of God. Hengstenberg supposes it to refer to the word of the Lord to Samuel, "Rise up and anoint him" (1 Sam. xvi. 12), which is apparently favoured indeed by the parallel in the corresponding text of 1 Chron. xvii. 19, "for Thy servant's sake," *i.e.* because Thou hast chosen Thy servant. But even this variation must contain some special allusion which does not exclude a *general* interpretation of the expression "for Thy word's sake," viz. an allusion to the earlier promises of God, or the Messianic prophecies generally, particularly the one concerning Judah in Jacob's blessing (Gen. xlix. 10), and the one relating to the ruler out of Jacob in Balaam's sayings (Num. xxiv. 17 sqq.), which contain the germs of the promise of the everlasting continuance of David's government. For the fact that David recognised the connection between the promise of God communicated to him by Nathan and Jacob's prophecy in Gen. xlix. 10, is evident from 1 Chron. xxviii. 4, where he refers to his election as king as being the consequence of the election of Judah as ruler. "According to Thine own heart" is equivalent to "according to Thy love and grace; for God is gracious, merciful, and of great kindness and truth" (Ex. xxxiv. 6, compare Ps. ciii. 8). גְּדוּלָה does not mean great things, but greatness.

The praise of God commences in ver. 22: "*Wherefore Thou art great, Jehovah God; and there is not* (one) *like Thee, and no God beside Thee, according to all that we have heard with our ears.*" By the word "wherefore," *i.e.* because Thou hast done this, the praise of the singleness of God is set forth as the result of David's own experience. God is great when He manifests the greatness of His grace to men, and brings them to acknowledge it. And in these great deeds He proves the incomparable nature of His Deity, or that He alone is the true God. (For the fact itself, compare Ex. xv. 11 ; Deut. iii. 24, iv. 35.)—Ver. 23. "*And where is* (any) *like Thy people, like Israel, a nation upon earth, which God went to redeem as a people for himself, that He might make Him a name, and do great things for you, and terrible things for Thy land before Thy people, which Thou hast redeemed for Thee out of Egypt,* (out of the) *nations and their gods?*" מִי does not really mean *where*, but *who*, and is to be connected with the words imme- diately following, viz. גּוֹי אֶחָד (one nation) ; but the only way in which the words can be rendered into good English (*German in the original* : TR.) is, "where is there any people," etc. The relative אֲשֶׁר does not belong to הָלְכוּ, which follows immediately afterwards; but, so far as the sense is concerned, it is to be taken as the object to לִפְדּוֹת, "which Elohim went to redeem." The construing of *Elohim* with a plural arises from the fact, that in this clause it not only refers to the true God, but also includes the idea of the gods of other nations. The idea, therefore, is not, "Is there any nation upon earth to which the only true God went?" but, "Is there any nation to which the deity wor- shipped by it went, as the true God went to Israel to redeem it for His own people?" The rendering given in the Septuagint to הָלְכוּ, viz. ὡδήγησεν, merely arose from a misapprehension of the true sense of the words ; and the emendation הוֹלִיךְ, which some propose in consequence, would only distort the sense. The stress laid upon the incomparable character of the things which God had done for Israel, is merely introduced to praise and celebrate the God who did this as the only true God. (For the thought itself, compare the original passage in Deut. iv. 7, 34.) In the clause וְלַעֲשׂוֹת לָכֶם, "and to do for you," David addresses the people of Israel with oratorical vivacity. Instead of saying "to do great things to (for) Israel," he says "to do great things to (for) *you.*" *For you* forms an antithesis to *him*, "to make Him a name, and to do great things for you (Israel)." The suggestion made by some, that לָכֶם is to be taken as a *dativ. comm.*, and referred to *Elohim*, no more needs a serious refutation than the alteration into לָהֶם. There have been different opinions, however, as to the object referred to in the suffix attached to לְאַרְצֶךָ, and it is difficult to decide between them; for whilst the fact that נִרְאוֹת לְאַרְצֶךָ (terrible things to Thy land) is governed by לַעֲשׂוֹת (to do) favours the allusion to Israel, and the sudden transition from the plural to the singular might be accounted for from the deep emotion of the person speaking, the words which follow ("before Thy people") rather favour the allusion to God, as it does not seem natural to take the suffix in two different senses in the two objects which follow so closely the one upon the other, viz. "*for Thy land*," and "*before Thy people;*" whilst the way is prepared for a transition from speaking of God to speaking to God by the word לָכֶם (to you). The words of Deut. x. 21 floated before the mind of David at the time, although he has given them a different turn. (On the "terrible things," see the commentary on Deut. x. 21 and Ex. xv. 11.) The connection of נִרְאוֹת (terrible things) with לְאַרְצֶךָ (to Thy land) shows that David had in mind, when speaking of the acts of divine omnipotence which had inspired fear and dread of the majesty of God, not only the miracles of God in Egypt, but also the marvellous extermination of the Canaanites, whereby Israel had been established in the possession of the promised land, and the people of God placed in a condition to found a kingdom. These acts were performed *before* Israel, before the nation, whom the Lord redeemed to himself out of Egypt. This view is confirmed by the last words, "nations and their gods," which are in apposition to "from Egypt," so that the preposition מִן should be repeated before גּוֹיִם (nations). The suffix to וֵאלֹהָיו (literally "and *its* gods") is to be regarded as distributive: "the gods of each of these heathen nations." In the Chronicles (ver. 21) the expression is simplified, and explained more clearly by the omission of "to Thy land," and the insertion of לְגָרֵשׁ, "to drive out nations from before Thy people." It has been erroneously inferred from this, that the text of our book is corrupt, and ought to be emended, or at any rate interpreted according to the Chronicles. But whilst לְאַרְצֶךָ is certainly not to be altered into לְגָרֵשׁ, it is just as wrong to do as Hengstenberg proposes,—namely, to take the thought expressed in לְגָרֵשׁ

from the preceding לַעֲשׂוֹת by assuming a *zeugma* ; for עָשָׂה, to do or make, has nothing in common with driving or clearing away.—Ver. 24. " *And Thou hast established to thyself Thy people Israel to be a people unto Thee for ever: and Thou, Jehovah, hast become a God to them.*" The first clause does not refer merely to the liberation of Israel out of Egypt, or to the conquest of Canaan alone, but to all that the Lord had done for the establishment of Israel as the people of His possession, from the time of Moses till His promise of the eternal continuance of the throne of David. Jehovah had thereby become God to the nation of Israel, *i.e.* had thereby attested and proved himself to be its God.

To this praise of the acts of the Lord there is attached in vers. 25 sqq. the prayer for the fulfilment of His glorious promise. Would Jehovah set up (*i.e.* carry out) the word which He had spoken to His servant that His name might be great, *i.e.* be glorified, through its being said, " The Lord of Sabaoth is God over Israel," and "the house of Thy servant will be firm before Thee." The prayer is expressed in the form of confident assurance.—Ver. 27. David felt himself encouraged to offer this prayer through the revelation which he had received. Because God had promised to build him a house, "therefore Thy servant hath found in his heart to pray this prayer," *i.e.* hath found joy in doing so.—Vers. 28, 29. David then briefly sums up the two parts of his prayer of thanksgiving in the two clauses commencing with עַתָּה, " and now."— In ver. 28 he sums up the contents of vers. 18*b*–24 by celebrating the greatness of the Lord and His promise; and in ver. 29 the substance of the prayer in vers. 25–27. הוֹאֵל וּבָרֵךְ, may it please Thee to bless (הוֹאִיל ; see at Deut. i. 5). " And from (out of) Thy blessing may the house of Thy servant be blessed for ever."

DAVID'S WARS, VICTORIES, AND MINISTERS OF STATE.— CHAP. VIII.

To the promise of the establishment of his throne there is appended a general enumeration of the wars by which David secured the supremacy of Israel over all his enemies round about. In this survey all the nations are included with which

war had ever been waged by David, and which he had conquered and rendered tributary : the Philistines and Moabites, the
Syrians of Zobah and Damascus, Toi of Hamath, the Ammonites,
Amalekites, and Edomites.   It is very evident from this, that
the chapter before us not only treats of the wars which David
carried on after receiving the divine promise mentioned in ch.
vii., but of all the wars of his entire reign.   The only one of
which we have afterwards a fuller account is the war with the
Ammonites and their allies the Syrians (ch. x. and xi.), and
this is given on account of its connection with David's adultery.
In the survey before us, the war with the Ammonites is only
mentioned quite cursorily in ver. 12, in the account of the booty
taken from the different nations, which David dedicated to the
Lord.   With regard to the other wars, so far as the principal
purpose was concerned,—namely, to record the history of the
kingdom of God,—it was quite sufficient to give a general statement of the fact that these nations were smitten by David and
subjected to his sceptre.   But if this chapter contains a survey
of all the wars of David with the nations that were hostile to
Israel, there can be no doubt that the arrangement of the
several events is not strictly regulated by their chronological
order, but that homogeneous events are grouped together
according to a material point of view.   There is a parallel to
this chapter in 1 Chron. xviii.

Ver. 1. SUBJUGATION OF THE PHILISTINES.—In the introductory formula, " *And it came to pass afterwards,*" the expression " *afterwards* " cannot refer specially to the contents of
ch. vii., for reasons also given, but simply serves as a general
formula of transition to attach what follows to the account just
completed, as a thing that happened afterwards.   This is incon-
testably evident from a comparison of ch. x. 1, where the war
with the Ammonites and Syrians, the termination and result of
which are given in the present chapter, is attached to what precedes by the same formula, " *It came to pass afterwards* " (cf.
ch. xiii. 1).   " *David smote the Philistines and subdued them, and
took the bridle of the mother out of the hand of the Philistines,*"
i.e. wrested the government from them and made them tributary.   The figurative expression *Metheg-ammah,* "bridle of the
mother," *i.e.* the capital, has been explained by Alb. Schultens

(on Job xxx. 11) from an Arabic idiom, in which giving up one's bridle to another is equivalent to submitting to him. Gesenius also gives several proofs of this (*Thes.* p. 113). Others, for example Ewald, render it arm-bridle; but there is not a single passage to support the rendering "arm" for *ammah*. The word is a feminine form of אֵם, mother, and only used in a tropical sense. "*Mother*" is a term applied to the chief city or capital, both in Arabic and Phœnician (*vid.* Ges. *Thes.* p. 112). The same figure is also adopted in Hebrew, where the towns dependent upon the capital are called its daughters (*vid.* Josh. xv. 45, 47). In 1 Chron. xviii. 1 the figurative expression is dropped for the more literal one: "David took Gath and its daughters out of the hand of the Philistines," *i.e.* he wrested Gath and the other towns from the Philistines. The Philistines had really five cities, every one with a prince of its own (Josh. xiii. 3). This was the case even in the time of Samuel (1 Sam. vi. 16, 17). But in the closing years of Samuel, Gath had a *king* who stood at the head of all the princes of the Philistines (1 Sam. xxix. 2 sqq., cf. xxvii. 2). Thus Gath became the capital of the land of the Philistines, which held the bridle (or reins) of Philistia in its own hand. The author of the Chronicles has therefore given the correct explanation of the figure. The one suggested by Ewald, Bertheau, and others, cannot be correct,—namely, that David wrested from the Philistines the power which they had hitherto exercised over the Israelites. The simple meaning of the passage is, that David wrested from the Philistines the power which the capital had possessed over the towns dependent upon it, *i.e.* over the whole of the land of Philistia; in other words, he brought the capital (Gath) and the other towns of Philistia into his own power. The reference afterwards made to a king of Gath in the time of Solomon in 1 Kings ii. 39 is by no means at variance with this; for the king alluded to was one of the tributary sovereigns, as we may infer from the fact that Solomon ruled over all the kings on this side of the Euphrates as far as to Gaza (1 Kings v. 1, 4).

Ver. 2. SUBJUGATION OF MOAB.—"*He smote Moab* (*i.e.* the Moabites), *and measured them with the line, making them lie down upon the ground, and measured two lines* (*i.e.* two parts)

to put to death, and one line full to keep alive." Nothing
further is known about either the occasion or the history of
this war, with the exception of the cursory notice in 1 Chron.
xi. 22, that Benaiah, one of David's heroes, smote two sons of
the king of Moab, which no doubt took place in the same war.
In the earliest period of his flight from Saul, David had met
with a hospitable reception from the king of Moab, and had
even taken his parents to him for safety (1 Sam. xxii. 3, 4).
But the Moabites must have very grievously oppressed the
Israelites afterwards, that David should have inflicted a severer
punishment upon them after their defeat, than upon any other
of the nations that he conquered, with the exception of the
Ammonites (ch. xii. 31), upon whom he took vengeance for
having most shamefully insulted his ambassadors (ch. x. 2
sqq.). The punishment inflicted, however, was of course restricted to the fighting men who had been taken prisoners by
the Israelites. They were ordered to lie down in a row upon
the earth; and then the row was measured for the purpose of
putting two-thirds to death, and leaving one-third alive. The
Moabites were then made *"servants"* to David (*i.e.* they
became his subjects), *"bringing gifts"* (*i.e.* paying tribute).

Vers. 3–8. CONQUEST AND SUBJUGATION OF THE KING
OF ZOBAH, AND OF THE DAMASCENE SYRIANS.—Ver. 3. The
situation of *Zobah* cannot be determined. The view held by
the Syrian church historians, and defended by Michaelis, viz.
that *Zobah* was the ancient *Nisibis* in northern Mesopotamia,
has no more foundation to rest upon than that of certain
Jewish writers who suppose it to have been *Aleppo*, the present
Haleb. *Aleppo* is too far north for *Zobah*, and *Nisibis* is quite
out of the range of the towns and tribes in connection with
which the name of Zobah occurs. In 1 Sam. xiv. 47, compared with ver. 12 of this chapter, Zobah, or *Aram Zobah* as
it is called in ch. x. 6 and Ps. lx. 2, is mentioned along with
Ammon, Moab, and Edom, as a neighbouring tribe and kingdom to the Israelites; and, according to vers. 3, 5, and 9 of
the present chapter, it is to be sought for in the vicinity of
Damascus and Hamath towards the Euphrates. These data
point to a situation to the north-east of Damascus and south
of Hamath, between the Orontes and Euphrates, and in fact

extending as far as the latter according to ver. 3, whilst, according to ch. x. 16, it even reached beyond it with its vassal-chiefs into Mesopotamia itself. Ewald (*Gesch.* iii. p. 195) has therefore combined *Zobah*, which was no doubt the capital, and gave its name to the kingdom, with the *Sabe* mentioned in Ptol. v. 19,—a town in the same latitude as Damascus, and farther east towards the Euphrates. The king of Zobah at the time referred to is called *Hadadezer* in the text (*i.e.* whose help is *Hadad*); but in ch. x. 16–19 and throughout the Chronicles he is called *Hadarezer*. The first is the original form; for *Hadad*, the name of the sun-god of the Syrians, is met with in several other instances in Syrian names (*vid.* Movers, *Phönizier*). David smote this king "*as he was going to restore his strength at the river* (Euphrates)." הָשִׁיב יָדוֹ does not mean to turn his hand, but signifies to return his hand, to stretch it out again over or against any one, in all the passages in which the expression occurs. It is therefore to be taken in a derivative sense in the passage before us, as signifying to restore or re-establish his sway. The expression used in the Chronicles (ver. 3), הַצִּיב יָדוֹ, has just the same meaning, since establishing or making fast presupposes a previous weakening or dissolution. Hence the subject of the sentence "as he went," etc., must be Hadadezer and not David; for David could not have extended his power to the Euphrates before the defeat of Hadadezer. The Masoretes have interpolated *P'rath* (Euphrates) after "*the river*," as in the text of the Chronicles. This is correct enough so far as the sense is concerned, but it is by no means necessary, as the *nahar* (the river κ. ἐξ.) is quite sufficient of itself to indicate the Euphrates.

There is also a war between David and Hadadezer and other kings of Syria mentioned in ch. x.; and the commentators all admit that that war, in which David defeated these kings when they came to the help of the Ammonites, is connected with the war mentioned in the present chapter. But the connection is generally supposed to be this, that the first of David's Aramæan wars is given in ch. viii., the second in ch. x.; for no other reason, however, than because ch. x. stands after ch. viii. This view is decidedly an erroneous one. According to the chapter before us, the war mentioned there terminated in the complete subjugation of the Aramæan kings and kingdoms. Aram became subject to David, paying tribute (ver. 6). Now, though the revolt of subjugated nations from their conquerors is by no means a rare thing in history, and therefore it is perfectly conceivable in itself that the Aramæans should have fallen away from David when he was involved in the war with the Ammonites, and should have gone to the help of the Ammonites, such an assumption is precluded by the fact that there is nothing in ch. x. about any falling away or revolt of the Aramæans from David; but, on the contrary, these tribes appear to be still entirely independent of David, and to be hired by the Ammonites to fight against him. But what is absolutely decisive against this assumption, is the fact that the number of Aramæans killed in the two wars is precisely the same (compare ver. 4 with ch. x. 18) : so that it may safely be inferred, not only that the war mentioned in ch. x., in which the Aramæans who had come to the help of the Ammonites were smitten by David, was the very same as the Aramæan war mentioned in ch. viii., but of which the result only is given; but also that all the wars which David waged with the Aramæans, like his war with Edom (vers. 13 sqq.), arose out of the Ammonitish war (ch. x.), and the fact that the Ammonites enlisted the help of the kings of Aram against David (ch. x. 6). We also obtain from ch. x. an explanation of the expression "as he went to restore his power (Eng. Ver. ' recover his border') at the river," since it is stated there that Hadadezer was defeated by Joab the first time, and that, after sustaining this defeat, he called the Aramæans on the other side of the Euphrates to his assistance, that he might continue the war against Israel with renewed vigour (ch. x. 13, 15 sqq.). The power of Hadadezer had no doubt been crippled by his first defeat; and in order to restore it, he procured auxiliary troops from Mesopotamia with which to attack David, but he was defeated a second time, and obliged to submit to him (ch. x. 17, 18). In this second engagement "*David took from him (i.e.* captured) *seventeen hundred horse-soldiers and twenty thousand foot*" (ver. 4, compare ch. x. 18). This decisive battle took place, according to 1 Chron. xviii. 3, in the neighbourhood of *Hamath, i.e.* Epiphania on the Orontes (see at Num. xiii. 21, and Gen. x. 18), or, according to ch. x. 18 of this book, at *Helam*,—a difference which may easily be reconciled by the simple assumption that the unknown Helam was somewhere near to Hamath. Instead of 1700 horse-soldiers, we find in the Chronicles (1, xviii. 4) 1000 chariots and 7000 horsemen. Consequently the word *receb* has no doubt dropped out after אֶלֶף in the text before us, and the numeral denoting a thousand has been confounded with the one used to denote a hundred ; for in the plains of Syria seven thousand horsemen would be a much juster proportion to twenty thousand foot than seventeen hundred. (For further remarks, see at ch. x. 18.) "*And David lamed all the cavalry*," *i.e.* he made the war-chariots and cavalry perfectly useless by laming the horses (see at Josh. xi. 6, 9),—"*and only left a hundred horses.*" The word *receb* in these clauses signifies the war-horses generally,—not merely the carriage-horses, but the riding-horses as well,—as the meaning cavalry is placed beyond all doubt by Isa. xxi. 7, and it can hardly be imagined that David would have spared the riding-horses.—Vers. 5, 6. After destroying the main force of Hadad-ezer, David turned against his ally, against *Aram-Damascus*, *i.e.* the Aramæans, whose capital was Damascus. *Dammesek* (for which we have *Darmesek* in the Chronicles according to its Aramæan form), *Damascus*, a very ancient and still a very important city of Syria, standing upon the *Chrysorrhoas* (*Phar-par*), which flows through the centre of it. It is situated in the midst of paradisaical scenery, on the eastern side of the Anti-libanus, on the road which unites Western Asia with the interior. David smote 22,000 Syrians of Damascus, placed garrisons in the kingdom, and made it subject and tributary. נְצִיבִים are not governors or officers, but military posts, garrisons, as in 1 Sam. x. 5, xiii. 3.—Ver. 7. Of the booty taken in these wars, David carried the golden shields which he took from the servants, *i.e.* the governors and vassal princes, of Hadadezer, to Jerusalem.[1] *Shelet* signifies "a shield," according to the Targums

[1] The Septuagint has this additional clause: "And Shishak the king of Egypt took them away, when he went up against Jerusalem in the days of Rehoboam the son of Solomon," which is neither to be found in the Chronicles nor in any other ancient version, and is merely an inference drawn by the Greek translator, or by some copyist of the LXX., from 1 Kings xiv. 25–28, taken in connection with the fact that the application of the brass is given in 1 Chron. xviii. 8. But, in the first place, the author of this gloss has overlooked the fact that the golden shields of Rehoboam which Shishak carried away, were not those captured by David, but those

and Rabbins, and this meaning is applicable to all the passages
in which the word occurs; whilst the meaning "equivalent"
cannot be sustained either by the rendering πανοπλία adopted
by Aquila and Symmachus in 2 Kings xi. 10, or by the renderings of the Vulgate, viz. *arma* in loc. and *armatura* in Song of
Sol. iv. 4, or by an appeal to the etymology (*vid.* Gesenius'
Thes. and Dietrich's *Lexicon*).—Ver. 8. And from the cities of
Betach and *Berothai* David took very much brass, with which,
according to 1 Chron. xviii. 8, Solomon made the brazen sea,
and the brazen columns and vessels of the temple. The LXX.
have also interpolated this notice into the text. The name
Betach is given as *Tibhath* in the Chronicles; and for *Berothai*
we have *Chun*. As the towns themselves are unknown, it cannot be decided with certainty which of the forms and names
are the correct and original ones. מִבֶּטַח appears to have been
written by mistake for מִטֶּבַח. This supposition is favoured by
the rendering of the LXX., ἐκ τῆς Μετεβάκ; and by that of
the Syriac also (viz. *Tebach*). On the other hand, the occurrence of the name *Tebah* among the sons of *Nahor the Aramæan*
in Gen. xxii. 24 proves little or nothing, as it is not known that
he founded a family which perpetuated his name; nor can anything be inferred from the fact that, according to the more
modern maps, there is a town of *Tayibeh* to the north of Damascus in 35° north lat., as there is very little in common between
the names *Tayibeh* and *Tebah*. Ewald connects *Berothai* with the
Barathena of Ptol. v. 19 in the neighbourhood of Saba. The
connection is a possible one, but it is not sufficiently certain to
warrant us in founding any conclusions upon it with regard to
the name *Chun* which occurs in the Chronicles; so that there is

which Solomon had had made, according to 1 Kings x. 16, for the retainers
of his palace; and in the second place, he has not observed that, according
to ver. 11 of this chapter, and also of the Chronicles, David dedicated to
the Lord all the gold and silver that he had taken, *i.e.* put it in the treasury of the sanctuary to be reserved for the future temple, and that at the
end of his reign he handed over to his son and successor Solomon all the
gold, silver, iron, and brass that he had collected for the purpose, to be
applied to the building of the temple (1 Chron. xxii. 14 sqq., xxix. 2 sqq.).
Consequently the clause in question, which Thenius would adopt from the
Septuagint into our own text, is nothing more than the production of a
presumptuous Alexandrian, whose error lies upon the very surface, so that
the question of its genuineness cannot for a moment be entertained.

no ground whatever for the opinion that it is a corruption of *Berothai.*

Vers. 9–12. After the defeat of the king of Zobah and his allies, Toɪ king of Hamath sought for David's friendship, sending his son to salute him, and conveying to him at the same time a considerable present of vessels of silver, gold, and brass. The name *Toi* is written *Tou* in the Chronicles, according to a different mode of interpretation; and the name of the son is given as *Hadoram* in the Chronicles, instead of *Joram* as in the text before us. The former is evidently the true reading, and *Joram* an error of the pen, as the Israelitish name *Joram* is not one that we should expect to find among Aramæans; whilst *Hadoram* occurs in 1 Chron. i. 21 in the midst of Arabic names, and it cannot be shown that the *Hadoram* or *Adoram* mentioned in 2 Chron. x. 18 and 1 Kings xii. 18 was a man of Israelitish descent. The primary object of the mission was to salute David ("to ask him of peace;" cf. Gen. xliii. 27, etc.), and to congratulate him upon his victory ("to bless him because he had fought," etc.); for Toi had had wars with Hadadezer. "*A man of wars*" signifies a man who wages wars (cf. 1 Chron. xxviii. 3; Isa. xlii. 13). According to 1 Chron. xviii. 3, the territory of the king of Hamath bordered upon that of Hadadezer, and the latter had probably tried to make king Toi submit to him. The secret object of the salutation, however, was no doubt to secure the friendship of this new and powerful neighbour.—Vers. 11, 12. David also sanctified Toi's presents to the Lord (handed them over to the treasury of the sanctuary), together with the silver and gold which he had sanctified from all the conquered nations, from Aram, Moab, etc. Instead of אֲשֶׁר הִקְדִּישׁ the text of the Chronicles has אֲשֶׁר נָשָׂא, which he took, *i.e.* took as booty. Both are equally correct; there is simply a somewhat different turn given to the thought.[1] In the enumeration of the conquered nations in ver. 12, the text of the Chronicles differs from that of the book before us. In the

---

[1] Bertheau erroneously maintains that אֲשֶׁר נָשָׂא, which he took, is at variance with 2 Sam. viii. 7, as, according to this passage, the golden shields of Hadadezer did not become the property of the Lord. But there is not a word to that effect in 2 Sam. viii. 7. On the contrary, his taking the shields to Jerusalem implies, rather than precludes, the intention to devote them to the purposes of the sanctuary.

first place, we find "*from Edom*" instead of "*from Aram*;" and secondly, the clause "*and of the spoil of Hadadezer, son of Rehob king of Zobah*," is altogether wanting there. The text of the Chronicles is certainly faulty here, as the name of *Aram* (Syria) could not possibly be omitted. *Edom* could much better be left out, not "because the conquest of Edom belonged to a later period," as Movers maintains, but because the conquest of Edom is mentioned for the first time in the subsequent verses. But if we bear in mind that in ver. 12 of both texts not only are those tribes enumerated the conquest of which had been already noticed, but all the tribes that David ever defeated and subjugated, even the Ammonites and Amalekites, to the war with whom no allusion whatever is made in the present chapter, we shall see that *Edom* could not be omitted. Consequently "*from Syria*" must have dropped out of the text of the Chronicles, and "*from Edom*" out of the one before us; so that the text in both instances ran originally thus, "from Syria, and from Edom, and from Moab." For even in the text before us, "from Aram" (Syria) could not well be omitted, notwithstanding the fact that the booty of Hadadezer is specially mentioned at the close of the verse, for the simple reason that David not only made war upon Syria-Zobah (the kingdom of Hadadezer) and subdued it, but also upon Syria-Damascus, which was quite independent of Zobah.

Vers. 13, 14. "*And David made* (himself) *a name, when he returned from smiting (i.e.* from the defeat of) *Aram,* (and smote Edom) *in the valley of Salt, eighteen thousand men.*" The words enclosed in brackets are wanting in the Masoretic text as it has come down to us, and must have fallen out from a mistake of the copyist, whose eye strayed from אֶת־אֲרָם to אֶת־אֱדוֹם; for though the text is not "utterly unintelligible" without these words, since the passage might be rendered "after he had smitten Aram in the valley of Salt eighteen thousand men," yet this would be decidedly incorrect, as the Aramæans were not smitten in the *valley of Salt,* but partly at *Medeba* (1 Chron. xix. 7) and *Helam* (ch. x. 17), and partly in their own land, which was very far away from the Salt valley. Moreover, the difficulty presented by the text cannot be removed, as Movers supposes, by changing אֶת־אֲרָם (Syria) into אֶת־אֱדוֹם (Edom), as the expression בְּשֻׁבוֹ ("when he returned") would still be unexplained. The facts were probably these : Whilst David, or rather Israel, was entangled in the war with the Ammonites and Aramæans, the Edomites seized upon the opportunity, which appeared to them a very favourable one, to invade the land of Israel, and advanced as far as the southern extremity of the Dead Sea. As soon, therefore, as the Aramæans were defeated and subjugated, and the Israelitish army had returned from this war, David ordered it to march against the Edomites, and defeated them in the valley of Salt. This valley cannot have been any other than the Ghor adjoining the Salt mountain on the south of the Dead Sea, which really separates the ancient territories of Judah and Edom (Robinson, *Pal.* ii. 483). There Amaziah also smote the Edomites at a later period (2 Kings xiv. 7). We gather more concerning this war of David from the text of the Chronicles (ver. 12) taken in connection with 1 Kings xi. 15, 16, and Ps. lx. 2. According to the Chronicles, it was Abishai the son of Zeruiah who smote the Edomites. This agrees very well not only with the account in ch. x. 10 sqq., to the effect that Abishai commanded a company in the war with the Syrians and Ammonites under the generalship of his brother Joab, but also with the heading to Ps. lx., in which it is stated that Joab returned after the defeat of Aram, and smote the Edomites in the valley of Salt, twelve thousand men ; and with 1 Kings xi. 15, 16, in which we read that when David was in Edom, Joab, the captain of the host, came up to bury the slain, and smote every male in Edom, and remained six months in Edom with all Israel, till he had cut off every male in Edom. From this casual but yet elaborate notice, we learn that the war with the Edomites was a very obstinate one, and was not terminated all at once. The difference as to the number slain, which is stated to have been 18,000 in the text before us and in the Chronicles, and 12,000 in the heading to Ps. lx., may be explained in a very simple manner, on the supposition that the reckonings made were only approximative, and yielded different results ;[1] and the fact that *David* is named

---

[1] Michaelis adduces a case in point from the Seven Years' War. After the battle of *Lissa*, eight or twelve thousand men were reported to have been taken prisoners ; but when they were all counted, including those who fell into the hands of the conquerors on the second, third, and fourth days of the flight, the number amounted to 22,000.

as the victor in the verse before us, *Joab* in Ps. lx., and *Abishai*
in the Chronicles, admits of a very easy explanation after what
has just been observed. The Chronicles contain the most literal
account. Abishai smote the Edomites as commander of the
men engaged, Joab as commander-in-chief of the whole army,
and David as king and supreme governor, of whom the writer
of the Chronicles affirms, " The Lord helped David in all
his undertakings." After the defeat of the Edomites, David
placed garrisons in the land, and made all Edom subject to
himself.

Vers. 15–18. DAVID'S MINISTERS.—To the account of
David's wars and victories there is appended a list of his official
attendants, which is introduced with a general remark as to
the spirit of his government. As king over all Israel, David
continued to execute right and justice.—Ver. 16. The chief
ministers were the following :—*Joab* (see at ch. ii. 18) was
" *over the army*," *i.e.* commander-in-chief. *Jehoshaphat* the
son of Ahilud, of whom nothing further is known, was *mazcir*,
chancellor ; not merely the national annalist, according to the
Septuagint and Vulgate (ἐπὶ τῶν ὑπομνημάτων, ὑπομνηματό-
γραφος ; *a commentariis*), *i.e.* the recorder of the most important
incidents and affairs of the nation, but an officer resembling
the *magister memoriæ* of the later Romans, or the *waka nuvis*
of the Persian court, who keeps a record of everything that
takes place around the king, furnishes him with an account of
all that occurs in the kingdom, places his *visé* upon all the
king's commands, and keeps a special protocol of all these
things (*vid.* Chardin, *Voyages* v. p. 258, and Paulsen, *Regierung
der Morgenländer*, pp. 279–80).—Ver. 17. *Zadok* the son of
Ahitub, of the line of Eleazar (1 Chron. v. 34, vi. 37, 38), and
Ahimelech the son of Abiathar, were *cohanim*, *i.e.* officiating
high priests ; the former at the tabernacle at Gibeon (1 Chron.
xvi. 39), the latter probably at the ark of the covenant upon
Mount Zion. Instead of *Ahimelech*, the Chronicles have
Abimelech, evidently through a copyist's error, as the name is
written *Ahimelech* in 1 Chron. xxiv. 3, 6. But the expression
" *Ahimelech the son of Abiathar*" is apparently a very strange
one, as Abiathar was a son of Ahimelech according to 1 Sam.
xxii. 20, and in other passages *Zadok* and *Abiathar* are men-

tioned as the two high priests in the time of David (ch. xv. 24, 35, xvii. 15, xix. 12, xx. 25). This difference cannot be set aside, as Movers, Thenius, Ewald, and others suppose, by transposing the names, so as to read Abiathar the son of Ahimelech ; for such a solution is precluded by the fact that, in 1 Chron. xxiv. 3, 6, 31, *Ahimelech* is mentioned along with Zadok as head of the priests of the line of Ithamar, and according to ver. 6 he was the son of Abiathar. It would therefore be necessary to change the name Ahimelech into Abiathar in this instance also, both in ver. 3 and ver. 6, and in the latter to transpose the two names. But there is not the slightest probability in the supposition that the names have been changed in so many passages. We are therefore disposed to adopt the view held by Bertheau and Oehler, viz. that Abiathar the high priest, the son of Ahimelech, had also a son named Ahimelech, as it is by no means a rare occurrence for grandfather and grandson to have the same names (*vid.* 1 Chron. v. 30–41), and also that this (the younger) Ahimelech performed the duties of high priest in connection with his father, who was still living at the commencement of Solomon's reign (1 Kings ii. 27), and is mentioned in this capacity, along with Zadok, both here and in the book of Chronicles, possibly because Abiathar was ill, or for some other reason that we cannot discover. As Abiathar was thirty or thirty-five years old at the time when his father was put to death by Saul, according to what has already been observed at 1 Sam. xiv. 3, and forty years old at the death of Saul, he was at least forty-eight years old at the time when David removed his residence to Mount Zion, and might have had a son of twenty-five years of age, namely the Ahimelech mentioned here, who could have taken his father's place in the performance of the functions of high priest when he was prevented by illness or other causes. The appearance of a son of Abiathar named Jonathan in ch. xv. 27, xvii. 17, 20, is no valid argument against this solution of the apparent discrepancy ; for, according to these passages, he was still very young, and may therefore have been a younger brother of Ahimelech. The omission of any allusion to Ahimelech in connection with Abiathar's conspiracy with Adonijah against Solomon (1 Kings i. 42, 43), and the reference to his son Jonathan alone, might be explained on the supposition that

Ahimelech had already died. But as there is no reference to Jonathan at the time when his father was deposed, no stress is to be laid upon the omission of any reference to Ahimelech. Moreover, when Abiathar was deposed after Solomon had ascended the throne, he must have been about eighty years of age. *Seraiah* was a scribe. Instead of *Seraiah*, we have *Shavsha* in the corresponding text of the Chronicles, and *Sheva* in the parallel passage ch. xx. 25. Whether the last name is merely a mistake for Shavsha, occasioned by the dropping of שׁ, or an abbreviated form of Shisha and Shavsha, cannot be decided. *Shavsha* is not a copyist's error, for in 1 Kings iv. 3 the same man is unquestionably mentioned again under the name of Shisha, who is called Shavsha in the Chronicles, *Sheva* (שְׁיָא) in the text of ch. xx. 25, and here Seraiah. *Seraiah* also is hardly a copyist's error, but another form for Shavsha or Shisha. The *scribe* was a secretary of state; not a military officer, whose duty it was to raise and muster the troops, for the technical expression for mustering the people was not סָפַר, but פָּקַד (cf. ch. xxiv. 2, 4, 9; 1 Chron. xxi. 5, 6, etc.).

Ver. 18. *Benaiah* the son of Jehoiada, a very brave hero of Kabzeel (see at ch. xxiii. 20 sqq.), was over the *Crethi* and *Plethi*. Instead of וְהַכְּרֵתִי, which gives no sense, and must be connected in some way with 1 Kings i. 38, 44, we must read עַל הַכְּרֵתִי according to the parallel passage ch. xx. 23, and the corresponding text of the Chronicles. The *Crethi* and *Plethi* were the king's body-guard, σωματοφύλακες (Josephus, *Ant.* vii. 5, 4). The words are adjectives in form, but with a substantive meaning, and were used to indicate a certain rank, *lit.* the executioners and runners, like הַשָּׁלִישִׁי (ch. xxiii. 8). כְּרֵתִי, from כָּרַת, to cut down or exterminate, signifies *confessor*, because among the Israelites (see at 1 Kings ii. 25), as in fact throughout the East generally, the royal halberdiers had to execute the sentence of death upon criminals. פְּלֵתִי, from פָּלַת (to fly, or be swift), is related to פָּלַט, and signifies *runners*. It is equivalent to רָץ, a courier, as one portion of the halberdiers, like the ἄγγαροι of the Persians, had to convey the king's orders to distant places (*vid.* 2 Chron. xxx. 6). This explanation is confirmed by the fact that the epithet הַכָּרִי וְהָרָצִים was afterwards applied to the king's body-guard (2 Kings xi. 4, 19), and that הַכָּרִי for הַכְּרֵתִי occurs as early as ch. xx. 23. כָּרִי, from כּוּר,

fodit, perfodit, is used in the same sense.[1]　And David's sons were כֹּהֲנִים (" confidants ") ; not priests, domestic priests, court chaplains, or spiritual advisers, as Gesenius, De Wette, and others maintain, but, as the title is explained in the corresponding text of the Chronicles, when the title had become obsolete, " the first at the hand (or side) of the king."　The correctness

---

[1] Gesenius (*Thes. s. vv.*) and Thenius (on 1 Kings i. 38) both adopt this explanation ; but the majority of the modern theologians decide in favour of Lakemacher's opinion, to which Ewald has given currency, viz. that the *Crethi* or *Cari* are Cretes or Carians, and the *Pelethi* Philistines (*vid.* Ewald, *Krit. Gramm.* p. 297, and *Gesch. des Volkes Israel,* pp. 330 sqq.; Bertheau, *zur Geschichte Israel,* p. 197 ; Movers, *Phönizier* i. p. 19). This view is chiefly founded upon the fact that the Philistines are called *C'rethi* in 1 Sam. xxx. 14, and *C'rethim* in Zeph. ii. 5 and Ezek. xxv. 16. But in both the passages from the prophets the name is used with special reference to the meaning of the word הִכְרִית, viz. to exterminate, cut off, as Jerome has shown in the case of Ezekiel by adopting the rendering *interficiam interfectores* (I will slay the slayers) for הִכְרַתִּי אֶת־כְּרֵתִים.　The same play upon the words takes place in Zephaniah, upon which Strauss has correctly observed : " Zephaniah shows that this violence of theirs had not been forgotten, calling the Philistines *Crethim* for that very reason, *ut sit nomen et omen.*"　Besides, in both these passages the true name *Philistines* stands by the side as well, so that the prophets might have used the name *Crethim* (slayers, exterminators) without thinking at all of 1 Sam. xxx. 14. In this passage it is true the name *Crethi* is applied to a branch of the Philistine people that had settled on the south-west of Philistia, and not to the Philistines generally.　The idea that the name of a portion of the royal body-guard was derived from the Cretans is precluded, *first* of all, by the fact of its combination with הַפְּלֵתִי (the Pelethites) ; for it is a totally groundless assumption that this name signifies the *Philistines,* and is a corruption of פְּלִשְׁתִּים.　There are no such contractions as these to be found in the Semitic languages, as Gesenius observes in his *Thesaurus* (*l.c.*), " Quis hujusmodi contractionem in linguis Semiticis ferat ? "　*Secondly,* it is also precluded by the strangeness of such a combination of two synonymous names to denote the royal body-guard.　" Who could believe it possible that two synonymous epithets should be joined together in this manner, which would be equivalent to saying Englishmen and Britons ? " (Ges. *Thes.* p. 1107.)　*Thirdly,* it is opposed to the title afterwards given to the body-guard, הַכָּרִי וְהָרָצִים (2 Kings xi. 4, 19), in which the *Cari* correspond to the *Crethi,* as in ch. xx. 23, and *ha-razim* to the *Pelethi ;* so that the term *pelethi* can no more signify a particular tribe than the term *razim* can.　Moreover, there are other grave objections to this interpretation.　In the first place, the hypothesis that the Philistines were emigrants from Crete is merely founded upon the very indefinite statements

of this explanation is placed beyond the reach of doubt by 1 Kings iv. 5, where the *cohen* is called, by way of explanation, "the king's friend." The title *cohen* may be explained from the primary signification of the verb כָּהַן, as shown in the corresponding verb and noun in Arabic ("*res alicujus gerere*," and "*administrator alieni negotii*"). These *cohanim*, therefore, were the king's confidential advisers.

of Tacitus (*Hist.* v. 3, 2), "*Judæos Creta insula profugos novissima Libyæ insedisse memorant*," and that of Steph. Byz. (*s. v.* Γαζα), to the effect that the city of Gaza was once called *Minoa*, from *Minos* a king of Crete,—statements which, according to the correct estimate of Strauss (*l.c.*), "have all so evidently the marks of fables that they hardly merit discussion," at all events when opposed to the historical testimony of the Old Testament (Deut. ii. 23 ; Amos ix. 7), to the effect that the Philistines sprang from *Caphtor*. And secondly, "it is *a priori* altogether improbable, that a man with so patriotic a heart, and so devoted to the worship of the one God, should have surrounded himself with a *foreign* and *heathen* body-guard" (Thenius). This argument cannot be invalidated by the remark "that it is well known that at all times kings and princes have preferred to commit the protection of their persons to foreign mercenaries, having, as they thought, all the surer pledge of their devotedness in the fact that they did not spring from the nation, and were dependent upon the ruler alone" (Hitzig). For, in the first place, the expression "at all times" is one that must be very greatly modified ; and secondly, this was only done by kings who did not feel safe in the presence of their own people, which was not the case with David. And the Philistines, those arch-foes of Israel, would have been the last nation that David would have gone to for the purpose of selecting his own body-guard. It is true that he himself had met with a hospitable reception in the land of the Philistines ; but it must be borne in mind that it was not as king of Israel that he found refuge there, but as an outlaw flying from Saul the king of Israel, and even then the chiefs of the Philistines would not trust him (1 Sam. xxix. 3 sqq.). And when Hitzig appeals still further to the fact, that according to ch. xviii. 2, David handed over the command of a third of his army to a foreigner who had recently entered his service, having emigrated from Gath with a company of his fellow-countrymen (ch. xv. 19, 20, 22), and who had displayed the greatest attachment to the person of David (ver. 21), it is hardly necessary to observe that the fact of David's welcoming a brave soldier into his army, when he had come over to Israel, and placing him over a division of the army, after he had proved his fidelity so decidedly as Ittai had at the time of Absalom's rebellion, is no proof that he chose his body-guard from the Philistines. Nor can ch. xv. 18 be adduced in support of this, as the notion that, according to that passage, David had 600 Gathites in his service as body-guard, is simply founded upon a misinterpretation of the passage mentioned.

DAVID'S KINDNESS TOWARDS MEPHIBOSHETH.—CHAP. IX.

When David was exalted to be king over all Israel, he sought to show compassion to the house of the fallen king, and to repay the love which his noble-minded friend Jonathan had once sworn to him before the Lord (1 Sam. xx. 13 sqq.; comp. xxiii. 17, 18). The account of this forms the conclusion of, or rather an appendix to, the first section of the history of his reign, and was intended to show how David was mindful of the duty of gratitude and loving fidelity, even when he reached the highest point of his regal authority and glory. The date when this occurred was about the middle of David's reign, as we may see from the fact, that Mephibosheth, who was five years old when Saul died (ch. iv. 4), had a young son at the time (ver. 12).

Vers. 1–8. When David inquired whether there was any one left of the house of Saul to whom he could show favour for Jonathan's sake (הֲכִי יֶשׁ־עוֹד: *is it so that there is any one?* = there is certainly some one left), a servant of Saul named *Ziba* was summoned, who told the king that there was a son of Jonathan living in the house of Machir at Lodebar, and that he was lame in his feet. הַאֶפֶס עוֹד אִישׁ, "*is there no one at all besides?*" The לְ before בֵּית is a roundabout way of expressing the genitive, as in 1 Sam. xvi. 18, etc., and is obviously not to be altered into מִבֵּית, as Thenius proposes. "*The kindness of God*" is love and kindness shown in God, and for God's sake (Luke vi. 36). *Machir* the son of Ammiel was a rich man, judging from ch. xvii. 27, who, after the death of Saul and Jonathan, had received the lame son of the latter into his house. *Lodebar* (לוֹדְבָר, written לֹאדְבָר in ch. xvii. 27, but erroneously divided by the Masoretes into two words in both passages) was a town on the east of Mahanaim, towards Rabbath Amman, probably the same place as Lidbir (Josh. xiii. 26); but it is not further known.—Vers. 5 sqq. David sent for this son of Jonathan (*Mephibosheth*: cf. ch. iv. 4), and not only restored his father's possessions in land, but took him to his own royal table for the rest of his life. "*Fear not,*" said David to Mephibosheth, when he came before him with the deepest obeisance, to take away any anxiety lest the king should intend to slay the descendants of the fallen king, according to the custom of eastern usurpers. It is evident from the words, " *I will restore thee all the land of Saul thy father*," that the landed property belonging to Saul had either fallen to David as crown lands, or had been taken possession of by distant relations after the death of Saul. " *Thou shalt eat bread at my table continually*," *i.e.* eat at my table all thy life long, or receive thy food from my table.—Ver. 8. Mephibosheth expressed his thanks for this manifestation of favour with the deepest obeisance, and a confession of his unworthiness of any such favour. On his comparison of himself to a " *dead dog*," see at 1 Sam. xxiv. 15.

Vers. 9–13. David then summoned Ziba the servant of Saul, told him of the restoration of Saul's possessions to his son Mephibosheth, and ordered him, with his sons and servants, to cultivate the land for the son of his lord. The words, " *that thy master's son may have food to eat*," are not at variance with the next clause, " *Mephibosheth shall eat bread alway at my table*," as bread is a general expression, including all the necessaries of life. Although Mephibosheth himself ate daily as a guest at the king's table, he had to make provision as a royal prince for the maintenance of his own family and servants, as he had children according to ver. 12 and 1 Chron. viii. 34 sqq. Ziba had fifteen sons and twenty servants (ver. 10), with whom he had probably been living in Gibeah, Saul's native place, and may perhaps have hitherto farmed Saul's land.—Ver. 11. Ziba promised to obey the king's command. The last clause of this verse is a circumstantial clause in form, with which the writer passes over to the conclusion of his account. But the words עַל שֻׁלְחָנִי, " *at my table*," do not tally with this, as they require that the words should be taken as David's own. This is precluded, however, not only by the omission of any intimation that David spoke again after Ziba, and repeated what he had said once already, and that without any occasion whatever, but also by the form of the sentence, more especially the participle אֹכֵל. There is no other course left, therefore, than to regard שֻׁלְחָנִי (my table) as written by mistake for שֻׁלְחַן דָּוִד: " *but Mephibosheth ate at David's table as one of the king's sons.*" The further notices in vers. 12 and 13 follow this in a very simple manner. כֹּל מוֹשַׁב בֵּית, " *all the dwelling*," *i.e.* all the inhabitants of Ziba's house, namely his sons and servants, were servants of Mephibosheth, *i.e.* worked for him and cultivated his land, whilst he himself took up his abode at Jerusalem, to eat daily at the king's table, although he was lamed in both his feet.

III. DAVID'S REIGN IN ITS DECLINE.

CHAP. X.–XX.

In the first half of David's reign he had strengthened and fortified the kingdom of Israel, both within and without, and exalted the covenant nation into a kingdom of God, before which all its enemies were obliged to bow ; but in the second half a series of heavy judgments fell upon him and his house, which cast a deep shadow upon the glory of his reign.   David had brought these judgments upon himself by his grievous sin with Bathsheba.   The success of all his undertakings, and the strength of his government, which increased year by year, had made him feel so secure, that in the excitement of undisturbed prosperity, he allowed himself to be carried away by evil lusts, so as to stain his soul not only with adultery, but also with murder, and fell all the deeper because of the height to which his God had exalted him.   This took place during the war with the Ammonites and Syrians, when Joab was besieging the capital of the Ammonites, after the defeat and subjugation of the Syrians (ch. x.), and when David had remained behind in Jerusalem (ch. xi. 1).   For this double sin, the adultery with Bathsheba and the murder of her husband Uriah, the Lord announced as a punishment, that the sword should not depart from David's house, and that his wives should be openly violated ; and notwithstanding the sincere sorrow and repentance of the king, when brought to see his sin, He not only caused the fruit of his sin, the child that was born of Bathsheba, to die (ch. xii.), but very soon afterwards allowed the threatened judgments to fall upon his house, inasmuch as Amnon, his first-born son, violated his half-sister Thamar, and was murdered in consequence by her own brother Absalom (ch. xiii.), whereupon Absalom fled to his father-in-law at Geshur ; and when at length the king restored him to favour (ch. xiv.), he set on foot a rebellion, which nearly cost David his life and throne (ch. xv.–xvii. 23). And even after Absalom himself was dead (ch. xvii. 24–xix. 1), and David had been reinstated in his kingdom (ch. xix. 2–40), there arose the conspiracy set on foot by the Benjaminite Sheba, which was only stopped by the death of the chief conspirator, in the fortified city of Abel-Beth-Maachah (ch. xix. 11 xx. 26).

The period and duration of these divine visitations are not stated; and all that we are able to determine from the different data as to time, given in ch. xiii. 23, 38, xiv. 28, xv. 7, when taken in connection with the supposed ages of the sons of David, is that Amnon's sin in the case of Thamar did not take place earlier than the twentieth year of David's reign, and that Absalom's rebellion broke out seven or eight years later. Consequently the assumption cannot be far from the truth, that the events described in this section occupied the whole time between the twentieth and thirtieth years of David's reign. We are prevented from placing it earlier, by the fact that Amnon was not born till after David became king over Judah, and therefore was probably about twenty years old when he violated his half-sister Thamar. At the same time it cannot be placed later than this, because Solomon was not born till about two years after David's adultery; and he must have been eighteen or twenty years old when he ascended the throne on the death of his father, after a reign of forty years and a half, since, according to 1 Kings xiv. 21, compared with vers. 11 and 42, 43, he had a son a year old, named Rehoboam, at the time when he began to reign.

WAR WITH THE AMMONITES AND SYRIANS.—CHAP. X.

This war, the occasion and early success of which are described in the present chapter and the parallel passage in 1 Chron. xix., was the fiercest struggle, and, so far as the Israelitish kingdom of God was concerned, the most dangerous, that it ever had to sustain during the reign of David. The amount of distress which fell upon Israel in consequence of this war, and still more because the first successful battles with the Syrians of the south were no sooner over than the Edomites invaded the land, and went about plundering and devastating, in the hope of destroying the people of God, is shown very clearly in the two psalms which date from this period (the 44th and 60th), in which a pious Korahite and David himself pour out their lamentations before the Lord on account of the distress of their nation, and pray for His assistance; and not less clearly in Ps. lxviii., in which David foretels the victory of the God of Israel over all the hostile powers of the world.

Vers. 1–5. *Occasion of the war with the Ammonites.*—Ver. 1. On the expression "*it came to pass after this,*" see the remarks on ch. viii. 1. When *Nahash*, the king of the Ammonites, died, and *Hanun* his son reigned in his stead, David thought that he would show him the same kindness that Nahash had formerly shown to him. We are not told in what the love shown to David by Nahash consisted. He had most likely rendered him some assistance during the time of his flight from Saul. *Nahash* was no doubt the king of the Ammonites mentioned in 1 Sam. xi. 1, whom Saul had smitten at Jabesh. David therefore sent an embassy to Hanun, "*to comfort him for his father,*" *i.e.* to show his sympathy with him on the occasion of his father's death, and at the same time to congratulate him upon his ascent of the throne.—Ver. 3. On the arrival of David's ambassadors, however, the chiefs of the Ammonites said to Hanun their lord, "*Doth David indeed honour thy father in thine eyes* (*i.e.* dost thou really suppose that David intends to do honour to thy father), *because he has sent comforters to thee? Has David not sent his servants to thee with the intention of exploring and spying out the town, and* (then) *destroying it?*" The first question is introduced with הֲ, because a negative answer is expected; the second with הֲלוֹא, because it requires an affirmative reply. הָעִיר is the capital *Rabbah*, a strongly fortified city (see at ch. xi. 1). The suspicion expressed by the chiefs was founded upon national hatred and enmity, which had probably been increased by David's treatment of Moab, as the subjugation and severe punishment of the Moabites (ch. viii. 2) had certainly taken place a short time before. King Hanun therefore gave credence to the suspicions expressed as to David's honourable intentions, and had his ambassadors treated in the most insulting manner.— Ver. 4. He had the half of their beard shaved off, and their clothes cut off up to the seat, and in this state he sent them

away. "*The half of the beard*," *i.e.* the beard on one side.
With the value universally set upon the beard by the Hebrews
and other oriental nations, as being a man's greatest ornament,[1]
the cutting off of one-half of it was the greatest insult that
could have been offered to the ambassadors, and through them
to David their king. The insult was still further increased by
cutting off the long dress which covered the body ; so that as
the ancient Israelites wore no trousers, the lower half of the
body was quite exposed. מַדְוֵיהֶם, from מָדוּ or מַדְוֶה, the long robe
reaching down to the feet, from the root מָדַד=מָדָה, to stretch,
spread out, or measure.—Ver. 5. When David received information of the insults that had been heaped upon his ambassadors,
he sent messengers to meet them, and direct them to remain in
Jericho until their beard had grown again, that he might not
have to set his eyes upon the insult they had received.

Ver. 6. When the Ammonites saw that they had made
themselves stinking before David, and therefore that David
would avenge the insult offered to the people of Israel in the
persons of their ambassadors, they looked round for help among
the powerful kings of Syria. They hired as auxiliaries (with a
thousand talents of silver, *i.e.* nearly half a million of pounds
sterling, according to 1 Chron. xix. 6) twenty thousand foot
from *Aram-Beth-Rehob* and *Aram-Zoba*, and one thousand men
from the king of *Maacah*, and twelve thousand troops from the
men of *Tob*. *Aram-Beth-Rehob* was the Aramæan kingdom,
the capital of which was *Beth-Rehob*. This Beth-Rehob, which
is simply called *Rehob* in ver. 8, is in all probability the city of
this name mentioned in Num. xiii. 21 and Judg. xviii. 28, which
lay to the south of Hamath, but the exact position of which has
not yet been discovered : for the castle of *Hunin*, in the ruins
of which Robinson imagines that he has found Beth-Rehob

---

[1] "Cutting off a person's beard is regarded by the Arabs as an indignity
quite equal to flogging and branding among ourselves. Many would rather
die than have their beard shaved off" (Arvieux, *Sitten der Beduinen-araber*).
Niebuhr relates a similar occurrence as having taken place in modern times.
In the year 1764, a pretender to the Persian throne, named *Kerim Khan*,
sent ambassadors to *Mir Mahenna*, the prince of Bendervigk, on the Persian
Gulf, to demand tribute from him ; but he in return cut off the ambassadors' beards. *Kerim Khan* was so enraged at this, that he went the next
year with a large army to make war upon this prince, and took the city,
and almost the whole of his territory, to avenge the insult.

(*Bibl. Researches*, p. 370), is to the south-west of Tell el Kadi, the ancient Laish-Dan, the northern boundary of the Israelitish territory; so that the capital of this Aramæan kingdom would have been within the limits of the land of Israel,—a thing which is inconceivable. *Aram-Naharaim* is also mentioned in the corresponding text of the Chronicles, and for that reason many have identified Beth-Rehob with Rehoboth, on "the river" (Euphrates), mentioned in Gen. xxxvi. 37. But this association is precluded by the fact, that in all probability the latter place is to be found in *Rachabe*, which is upon the Euphrates and not more than half a mile from the river (see Ritter, *Erdk.* xv. p. 128), so that from its situation it can hardly have been the capital of a separate Aramæan kingdom, as the government of the king of Zoba extended, according to ver. 16, beyond the Euphrates into Mesopotamia. On *Aram-Zoba*, see at ch. viii. 3; and for *Maacah* at Deut. iii. 14. אִישׁ־טוֹב is not to be taken as one word and rendered as a proper name, *Ish-Tob*, as it has been by most of the earlier translators; but אִישׁ is a common noun used in a collective sense (as it frequently is in the expression אִישׁ יִשְׂרָאֵל), "*the men of Tob.*" *Tob* was the district between Syria and Ammonitis, where Jephthah had formerly taken refuge (Judg. xi. 5). The corresponding text of the Chronicles (1 Chron. xix. 6, 7) is fuller, and differs in several respects from the text before us. According to the Chronicles, Hanun sent a thousand talents of silver to hire chariots and horsemen from Aram-Naharaim, Aram-Maacah, and Zobah. With this the Ammonites hired thirty-two thousand *receb* (*i.e.* chariots and horsemen: see at ch. viii. 4), and the king of Maacah and his people. They came and encamped before *Medeba*, the present ruin of *Medaba*, two hours to the south-east of Heshbon, in the tribe of Reuben (see at Num. xxi. 30, compared with Josh. xiii. 16), and the Ammonites gathered together out of their cities, and went to the war. The Chronicles therefore mention Aram-Naharaim (*i.e.* Mesopotamia) as hired by the Ammonites instead of Aram-Beth-Rehob, and leave out the men of Tob. The first of these differences is not to be explained, as Bertheau suggests, on the supposition that the author of the Chronicles took *Beth-Rehob* to be the same city as *Rehoboth of the river* in Gen. xxxvi. 37, and therefore substituted the well-known "*Aram* of the two rivers" as an interpretation of the rarer name *Beth-Rehob*, though hardly on good ground. For this conjecture does not help to explain the omission of "the men of Tob." It is a much simpler explanation, that the writer of the Chronicles omitted *Beth-Rehob* and *Tob* as being names that were less known, this being the only place in the Old Testament in which they occur as separate kingdoms, and simply mentioned the kingdoms of *Maacah* and *Zoba*, which frequently occur; and that he included "Aram of the two rivers," and placed it at the head, because the Syrians obtained succour from Mesopotamia after their first defeat. The account in the Chronicles agrees with the one before us, so far as the number of auxiliary troops is concerned. For twenty thousand men of Zoba and twelve thousand of Tob amount to thirty-two thousand, besides the people of the king of Maacah, who sent a thousand men according to the text of Samuel. But according to that of the Chronicles, the auxiliary troops consisted of chariots and horsemen, whereas only foot-soldiers are mentioned in our text, which appears all the more remarkable, because according to ch. viii. 4, and 1 Chron. xviii. 4, the king of Zoba fought against David with a considerable force of chariots and horsemen. It is very evident, therefore, that there are copyists' errors in both texts; for the troops of the Syrians did not consist of infantry only, nor of chariots and horsemen alone, but of foot-soldiers, cavalry, and war-chariots, as we may see very clearly not only from the passages already quoted in ch. viii. 4 and 1 Chron. xviii. 4, but also from the conclusion to the account before us. According to ver. 18 of this chapter, when Hadarezer had reinforced his army with auxiliaries from Mesopotamia, after losing the first battle, David smote seven hundred *receb* and forty thousand *parashim* of Aram, whilst according to the parallel text (1 Chron. xix. 18) he smote seven thousand *receb* and forty thousand foot. Now, apart from the difference between seven thousand and seven hundred in the case of the *receb*, which is to be interpreted in the same way as a similar difference in ch. viii. 4, the Chronicles do not mention any *parashim* at all in ver. 18, but foot-soldiers only, whereas in ver. 7 they mention only *receb* and *parashim*; and, on the other hand, there are no foot-soldiers given in ver. 18 of the text before us, but riders only, whereas in ver. 6 there are none but foot-soldiers mentioned, without any riders at all. It is evident that in both engagements the Syrians fought with all three (infantry, cavalry, and chariots), so that in both of them David smote chariots, horsemen, and foot.

Vers. 7–14. When David heard of these preparations and the advance of the Syrians into the land, he sent Joab and his brave army against the foe. הַגִּבּוֹרִים (*the mighty men*) is in apposition to כָּל־הַצָּבָא (*all the host*) : the whole army, namely the heroes or mighty men, *i.e.* the brave troops that were well used to war. It is quite arbitrary on the part of Thenius to supply *vav* before הַגִּבּוֹרִים ; for, as Bertheau has observed, we never find a distinction drawn between the *gibborim* and the whole army.—Ver. 8. On the other hand, the Ammonites came out (from the capital, where they had assembled), and put themselves in battle array before the gate. The Syrians were alone on the field, *i.e.* they had taken up a separate position on the broad treeless table-land (cf. Josh. xiii. 16) by Medeba. *Medeba* lay about four geographical miles in a straight line to the south-west of *Rabbath-Ammon.*—Ver. 9. When Joab saw that " the front of the war was (directed) against him both before and behind," he selected a picked body out of the Israel-itish army, and posted them (the picked men) against the children of Aram (*i.e.* the Syrians). The rest of the men he gave to his brother Abishai, and stationed them against the Ammonites. " *The front of the battle :*" *i.e.* the face or front of the hostile army, when placed in battle array. Joab had this in front and behind, as the Ammonites had taken their stand before Rabbah at the back of the Israelitish army, and the Syrians by *Medeba* in their front, so that Joab was attacked both before and behind. This compelled him to divide his army. *He chose out,* *i.e.* made a selection. Instead of בְּחוּרֵי בְיִשְׂרָאֵל (the picked men in Israel) the Chronicles have בָּחוּר בְּיִשְׂרָאֵל (the men in Israel), the singular בָּחוּר being more commonly employed than the plural to denote the men of war. The בְּ before יִשְׂרָאֵל is not to be regarded as suspicious, although the early translators have not expressed it, and the Masoretes wanted to expunge it. " The choice of Israel" signifies those who were selected in Israel for the war, *i.e.* the Israelitish soldiers. Joab himself took up his station opposite to the Syrians with a picked body of men, because they were the stronger force of the two. He then made this arrangement with Abishai (ver. 11): "*If Aram becomes stronger than I* (*i.e.* overpowers me), *come to my help; and if the Ammonites should overpower thee, I will go to help thee.*" Consequently the attack was not to be made upon both the armies of the enemy simultaneously; but Joab proposed to attack the Aramæans (Syrians) first (cf. ver. 13), and Abishai was merely to keep the Ammonites in check, though there was still a possibility that the two bodies of the enemy might make their attack simultaneously.— Ver. 12. "*Be firm, and let us be firm* (strong) *for our people, and for the towns of our God: and Jehovah will do what seemeth Him good.*" Joab calls the towns of Israel the towns of our God, inasmuch as the God of Israel had given the land to the people of Israel, as being His own property. Joab and Abishai were about to fight, in order that Jehovah's possessions might not fall into the hands of the heathen, and become subject to their gods.—Ver. 13. Joab then advanced with his army to battle against Aram, and "*they fled before him.*"—Ver. 14. When the Ammonites perceived this, they also fled before Abishai, and drew back into the city (Rabbah); whereupon Joab returned to Jerusalem, probably because, as we may infer from ch. xi. 1, it was too late in the year for the siege and capture of Rabbah.

Vers. 15–19. The Aramæans, however, gathered together again after the first defeat, to continue the war; and Hadarezer, the most powerful of the Aramæan kings, sent messengers to Mesopotamia, and summoned it to war. It is very evident, not only from the words "he sent and brought out Aram, which was beyond the river," but also from the fact that Shobach, Hadarezer's general (*Shophach* according to the Chronicles), was at the head of the Mesopotamian troops, that the Mesopotamian troops who were summoned to help were under the supreme rule of Hadarezer. This is placed beyond all possible doubt by ver. 19, where the kings who had fought with Hadarezer against the Israelites are called his "servants," or vassals. וַיָּבֹא חֵילָם (ver. 16) might be translated "and their army came;" but when we compare with this the וַיָּבֹא חֶלְאָמָה of ver. 17, we are compelled to render it as a proper name (as in the Septuagint, Chaldee, Syriac, and Arabic)—"*and they* (the men from beyond the Euphrates) *came* (marched) *to Helam*"—and to take

חֵילָם as a contracted form of חֶלְאָם. The situation of this place has not yet been discovered. Ewald supposes it to be connected with the Syrian town *Alamatha* upon the Euphrates (Ptol. *Geogr.* v. 15) ; but this is not to be thought of for a moment, if only because it cannot be supposed that the Aramæans would fall back to the Euphrates, and wait for the Israelites to follow them thither before they gave them battle ; and also on account of ch. viii. 4 and 1 Chron. xviii. 3, from which it is evident that *Helam* is to be sought for somewhere in the neighbourhood of Hamath (see p. 360). For וַיָּבֹא חֶלְאָמָה we find וַיָּבֹא אֲלֵיהֶם, " David came to them" (the Aramæans), in the Chronicles : so that the author of the Chronicles has omitted the unknown place, unless indeed אֲלֵיהֶם has been written by mistake for חֶלְאָם.—Vers. 17 sqq. David went with all Israel (all the Israelitish forces) against the foe, and smote the Aramæans at *Helam,* where they had placed themselves in battle array, slaying seven hundred charioteers and forty thousand horsemen, and so smiting (or wounding) the general *Shobach* that he died there, *i.e.* that he did not survive the battle (Thenius). With regard to the different account given in the corresponding text of the Chronicles as to the number of the slain, see the remarks on ver. 6 (pp. 376–7). It is a fact worthy of notice, that the number of men who fell in the battle (seven hundred *receb* and forty thousand *parashim*, according to the text before us ; seven thousand *receb* and forty thousand *ragli*, according to the Chronicles) agrees quite as well with the number of Aramæans reported to be taken prisoners or slain, according to ch. viii. 4 and 1 Chron. xviii. 4, 5 (viz. seventeen hundred *parashim* or a thousand *receb*, and seven thousand *parashim* and twenty thousand *ragli* of Aram-Zoba, and twenty-two thousand of Aram-Damascus), as could possibly be expected considering the notorious corruption in the numbers as we possess them ; so that there is scarcely any doubt that the number of Aramæans who fell was the same in both accounts (ch. viii. and x.), and that in the chapter before us we have simply a more circumstantial account of the very same war of which the result is given in ch. viii. and 1 Chron. xviii.—Ver. 19. " *And when all the kings, the vassals of Hadarezer, saw that they were smitten before Israel, they made peace with Israel, and became subject to them ; and Aram was afraid to render any further help to the Ammonites.*" It might appear from the first half of this verse, that it was only the vassals of Hadarezer who made peace with Israel, and became subject to it, and that Hadarezer himself did not. But the last clause, " and the Aramæans were afraid," etc., shows very clearly that Hadarezer also made peace with the Israelites, and submitted to their rule ; so that the expression in the first half of the verse is not a very exact one.

SIEGE OF RABBAH. DAVID'S ADULTERY.—CHAP. XI.

Ver. 1 (cf. 1 Chron. xx. 1). SIEGE OF RABBAH.—" *And it came to pass at the return of the year, at the time when the kings marched out, that David sent Joab, and his servants with him, and all Israel; and they destroyed the Ammonites and besieged Rabbah: but David remained in Jerusalem.*" This verse is connected with ch. x. 14, where it was stated that after Joab had put to flight the Aramæans who came to the help of the Ammonites, and when the Ammonites also had fallen back before Abishai in consequence of this victory, and retreated into their fortified capital, Joab himself returned to Jerusalem. He remained there during the winter or rainy season, in which it was impossible that war should be carried on. At the return of the year, *i.e.* at the commencement of spring, with which the new year began in the month Abib (Nisan), the time when kings who were engaged in war were accustomed to open their campaign, David sent Joab his commander-in-chief with the whole of the Israelitish forces to attack the Ammonites once more, for the purpose of chastising them and conquering their capital. The *Chethibh* הַמְּלָאכִים should be changed into הַמְּלָכִים, according to the *Keri* and the text of the Chronicles. The א interpolated is a perfectly superfluous *mater lectionis*, and probably crept into the text from a simple oversight. The " *servants* " of David with Joab were not the men performing military service, or soldiers, (in which case " all Israel " could only signify the people called out to war in extraordinary circumstances,) but the king's military officers, the military commanders ; and " *all Israel,*" the whole of the military forces of Israel. Instead of " the children of Ammon " we find " the country of the children of Ammon," which explains the meaning more fully. But there was no necessity to insert אֶרֶץ (the land

or country), as הִשְׁחִית is applied to men in other passages in the
sense of "cast to the ground," or destroy (e.g. 1 Sam. xxvi. 15).
Rabbah was the capital of Ammonitis (as in Josh. xiii. 25): the
fuller name was *Rabbath* of the children of Ammon. It has
been preserved in the ruins which still exist under the ancient
name of *Rabbat-Ammân*, on the Nahr Ammân, *i.e.* the upper
Jabbok (see at Deut. iii. 11). The last clause, " *but David
sat* (remained) *in Jerusalem,*" leads on to the account which
follows of David's adultery with Bathsheba (vers. 2–27 and ch.
xii. 1–25), which took place at that time, and is therefore inserted here, so that the conquest of Rabbah is not related till
afterwards (ch. xii. 26–31).

Vers. 2–27. DAVID'S ADULTERY.—David's deep fall forms
a turning-point not only in the inner life of the great king, but
also in the history of his reign. Hitherto David had kept free
from the grosser sins, and had only exhibited such infirmities
and failings as simulation, prevarication, etc., which clung to
all the saints of the Old Covenant, and were hardly regarded
as sins in the existing stage of religious culture at that time,
although God never left them unpunished, but invariably
visited them upon His servants with humiliations and chastisements of various kinds. Among the unacknowledged sins
which God tolerated because of the hardness of Israel's heart
was polygamy, which encouraged licentiousness and the tendency to sensual excesses, and to which but a weak barrier had
been presented by the warning that had been given for the
Israelitish kings against taking many wives (Deut. xvii. 17),
opposed as such a warning was to the notion so prevalent in
the East both in ancient and modern times, that a well-filled
harem is essential to the splendour of a princely court. The
custom to which this notion gave rise opened a dangerous precipice in David's way, and led to a most grievous fall, that can
only be explained, as O. v. Gerlach has said, from the intoxication consequent upon undisturbed prosperity and power, which
grew with every year of his reign, and occasioned a long series
of most severe humiliations and divine chastisements that marred
the splendour of his reign, notwithstanding the fact that the
great sin was followed by deep and sincere repentance.

Vers. 2–5. Towards evening David walked upon the roof

of his palace, after rising from his couch, *i.e.* after taking his mid-day rest, and saw from the roof a woman bathing, namely in the uncovered court of a neighbouring house, where there was a spring with a pool of water, such as you still frequently meet with in the East. " *The woman was beautiful to look upon.*" Her outward charms excited sensual desires.—Ver. 3. David ordered inquiry to be made about her, and found (וַיֹּאמֶר, " *ho, i.e.* the messenger, *said;*" or indefinitely, " they said ") that she was Bathsheba, the wife of Uriah the Hethite. הֲלֹא, *nonne,* is used, as it frequently is, in the sense of an affirmation, " it is indeed so." Instead of *Bathsheba* the daughter of Eliam, we find the name given in the Chronicles (1 Chron. iii. 5) as *Bathshua* the daughter of Ammiel. The form בַּת־שׁוּעַ may be derived from בַּת־שֶׁוַע, in which ב is softened into ו; for Bathsheba (with *beth*) is the correct and original form, as we may see from 1 Kings i. 11, 15, 28. *Eliam* and *Ammiel* have the same signification; the difference simply consists in the transposition of the component parts of the name. It is impossible to determine, however, which of the two forms was the original one.—Ver. 4. The information brought to him, that the beautiful woman was married, was not enough to stifle the sensual desires which arose in David's soul. " When lust hath conceived, it bringeth forth sin" (Jas. i. 15). David sent for the woman, and lay with her. In the expression " he took her, and she came to him," there is no intimation whatever that David brought Bathsheba into his palace through craft or violence, but rather that she came at his request without any hesitation, and offered no resistance to his desires. Consequently Bathsheba is not to be regarded as free from blame. The very act of bathing in the uncovered court of a house in the heart of the city, into which it was possible for any one to look down from the roofs of the houses on higher ground, does not say much for her feminine modesty, even if it was not done with an ulterior purpose, as some commentators suppose. Nevertheless in any case the greatest guilt rests upon David, that he, a man upon whom the Lord had bestowed such grace, did not resist the temptation to the lust of the flesh, but sent to fetch the woman. " *When she had sanctified herself from her uncleanness, she returned to her house.*" Defilement from sexual intercourse rendered unclean till the evening (Lev. xv. 18). Bathsheba thought it her duty to observe this statute most scrupulously, though she did not shrink from committing the sin of adultery. —Ver. 5. When she discovered that she was with child, she sent word to David. This involved an appeal to him to take the necessary steps to avert the evil consequences of the sin, inasmuch as the law required that both adulterer and adulteress should be put to death (Lev. xx. 10).

Vers. 6–13. David had Uriah the husband of Bathsheba sent to him by Joab, under whom he was serving in the army before Rabbah, upon some pretext or other, and asked him as soon as he arrived how it fared with Joab and the people (*i.e.* the army) and the war. This was probably the pretext under which David had had him sent to him. According to ch. xxiii. 39, Uriah was one of the *gibborim* (" mighty men ") of David, and therefore held some post of command in the army, although there is no historical foundation for the statement made by Josephus, viz. that he was Joab's armour-bearer or aide-de-camp. The king then said to him, " *Go down to thy house* (from the palace upon Mount Zion down to the lower city, where Uriah's house was situated), *and wash thy feet;* " and when he had gone out of the palace, he sent a royal present after him. The Israelites were accustomed to wash their feet when they returned home from work or from a journey, to take refreshment and rest themselves. Consequently these words contained an intimation that he was to go and refresh himself in his own home. David's wish was that Uriah should spend a night at home with his wife, that he might afterwards be regarded as the father of the child that had been begotten in adultery. מַשְׂאֵת, a present, as in Amos v. 11, Jer. xl. 5, Esther ii. 18.—Ver. 9. But Uriah had his suspicions aroused. The connection between his wife and David may not have remained altogether a secret, so that it may have reached his ears as soon as he arrived in Jerusalem. " *He lay down to sleep before the king's house with all the servants of his lord* (*i.e.* the retainers of the court), *and went not down to his house.*" " Before, or at, the door of the king's house," *i.e.* in the court of the palace, or in a building adjoining the king's palace, where the court servants lived.—Ver. 10. When this was told to David (the next morning), he said to Uriah, " *Didst thou not come from the way* (*i.e.* from a journey)? *why didst thou not go down* (as men generally do when they return from a journey)?" Uriah replied (ver. 11), "*The ark* (ark of the covenant), *and Israel, and Judah, dwell in the huts, and my lord Joab and the servants of my lord encamp in the field; and should I go to my house to eat and to drink, and to lie with my wife? By thy life, and by the life of thy soul, I do no such thing!*" יָשַׁב בַּסֻּכּוֹת, to sit or sojourn in huts, is the same practically as being encamped in the field. Uriah meant to say; Whereas the ark, *i.e.* Jehovah with the ark, and all Israel, were engaged in conflict with the enemies of God and of His kingdom, and therefore encamped in the open country, it did not become a warrior to seek rest and pleasure in his own home. This answer expressed the feelings and the consciousness of duty which ought to animate one who was fighting for the cause of God, in such plain and unmistakeable terms, that it was well adapted to prick the king to the heart. But David's soul was so beclouded by the wish to keep clear of the consequences of his sin in the eyes of the world, that he did not feel the sting, but simply made a still further attempt to attain his purpose with Uriah. He commanded him to stop in Jerusalem all that day, as he did not intend to send him away till the morrow.—Ver. 13. The next day he invited him to his table and made him drunken, with the hope that when in this state he would give up his intention of not going home to his wife. But Uriah lay down again the next night to sleep with the king's servants, without going down to his house; for, according to the counsel and providence of God, David's sin was to be brought to light to his deep humiliation.

Vers. 14–27. When the king saw that his plan was frustrated through Uriah's obstinacy, he resolved upon a fresh and still greater crime. He wrote a letter to Joab, with which he sent Uriah back to the army, and the contents of which were these: "Set ye Uriah opposite to the strongest contest, and then turn away behind him, that he may be slain, and die."[1] David was so sure that his orders would be executed, that he

---

[1] " We may see from this how deep a soul may fall when it turns away from God, and from the guidance of His grace. This David, who in the days of his persecution would not even resort to means that were really plausible in order to defend himself, was now not ashamed to resort to the greatest crimes in order to cover his sin. O God! how great is our strength

did not think it necessary to specify any particular crime of which Uriah had been guilty.—Ver. 16. The king's wishes were fully carried out by Joab. "*When Joab watched* (*i.e.* blockaded) *the city, he stationed Uriah just where he knew that there were brave men*" (in the city).—Ver. 17. "*And the men of the city came out* (*i.e.* made a sally) *and fought with Joab, and some of the people of the servants of David fell, and Uriah the Hethite died also.*" The literal fulfilment of the king's command does not warrant us in assuming that Joab suspected how the matter stood, or had heard a rumour concerning it. As a general, who was not accustomed to spare human life, he would be a faithful servant of his lord in this point, in order that his own interests might be served another time.—Vers. 18–21. Joab immediately despatched a messenger to the king, to give him a report of the events of the war, and with these instructions: "When thou hast told all the things of the war to the king to the end, in case the anger of the king should be excited (תַּעֲלֶה, ascend), and he should say to thee, Why did ye advance so near to the city to fight? knew ye not that they would shoot from the wall? Who smote Abimelech the son of Jerubbosheth (*i.e.* Gideon, see at Judg. vi. 32)? did not a woman throw down a millstone from the wall, that he died in Thebez (Judg. ix. 53)? why went ye so nigh to the wall? then only say, Thy servant Uriah the Hethite has perished." Joab assumed that David might possibly be angry at what had occurred, or at any rate that he might express his displeasure at the fact that Joab had sacrificed a number of warriors by imprudently approaching close to the wall: he therefore instructed the messenger, if such should be the case, to announce Uriah's death to the king, for the purpose of mitigating his wrath. The messenger seems to have known that Uriah was in disgrace with the king. At the same time, the words "thy servant Uriah is dead also" might be understood or interpreted as meaning that it was without, or even in opposition to, Joab's command, that Uriah went so far with his men,

when we lay firm hold of Thee! And how weak we become as soon as we turn away from Thee! The greatest saints would be ready for the worst of deeds, if Thou shouldst but leave them for a single moment without Thy protection. Whoever reflects upon this, will give up all thought of self-security and spiritual pride."—*Berleburg Bible.*

and that he was therefore chargeable with his own death and that of the other warriors who had fallen.—Vers. 22 sqq. The messenger brought to David all the information with which Joab had charged him (שָׁלַח with a double accusative, to send or charge a person with anything), but he so far condensed it as to mention Uriah's death at the same time. " When the men (of Rabbah) became strong against us, and came out to us into the field, and we prevailed against them even to the gate, the archers shot at thy servants down from the wall, so that some of the servants of the king died, and thy servant Uriah the Hethite is dead also." The א in the forms וַיִּרְאוּ הַמּוֹרְאִים instead of וַיֹּרוּ הַמּוֹרִים is an Aramaic mode of writing the words.—Ver. 25. David received with apparent composure the intelligence which he was naturally so anxious to hear, and sent this message back to Joab : " *Let not this thing depress thee, for the sword devours thus and thus, Keep on with the battle against the city, and destroy it.*" The construction of אַל־יֵרַע with אֵת *obj.* is analogous to the combination of a passive verb with אֵת : " Do not look upon this affair as evil" (disastrous). David then sent the messenger away, saying, " Encourage thou him" (*lit.* strengthen him, put courage into him), to show his entire confidence in the bravery and stedfastness of Joab and the army, and their ultimate success in the capture of Rabbah.—In ver. 26 the account goes back to its starting-point. When Uriah's wife heard of her husband's death, she mourned for her husband. When her mourning was over, David took her home as his wife, after which she bore him a son (the one begotten in adultery). The ordinary mourning of the Israelites lasted seven days (Gen. l. 10 ; 1 Sam. xxxi. 13). Whether widows mourned any longer we do not know. In the case before us Bathsheba would hardly prolong her mourning beyond the ordinary period, and David would certainly not delay taking her as his wife, in order that she might be married to the king as long as possible before the time of childbirth. The account of these two grievous sins on the part of David is then closed with the assurance that " the thing that David had done displeased the Lord," which prepares the way for the following chapter.

NATHAN'S REPROOF AND DAVID'S REPENTANCE.   CONQUEST
OF RABBAH.—CHAP. XII.

The Lord left David almost a whole year in his sin, before
sending a prophet to charge the haughty sinner with his mis-
deeds, and to announce the punishment that would follow.   He
did this at length through Nathan, but not till after the birth
of Bathsheba's child, that had been begotten in adultery (compare vers. 14, 15 with ch. xi. 27).   Not only was the fruit
of the sin to be first of all brought to light, and the hardened
sinner to be deprived of the possibility of either denying or
concealing his crimes, but God would first of all break his
unbroken heart by the torture of his own conscience, and
prepare it to feel the reproaches of His prophet.   The reason
for this delay on the part of God in the threatening of judgment
is set forth very clearly in Ps. xxxii., where David describes
most vividly the state of his heart during this period, and the
sufferings that he endured as long as he was trying to conceal
his crime.   And whilst in this Psalm he extols the blessedness
of a pardoned sinner, and admonishes all who fear God, on the
ground of his own inmost experience after his soul had tasted
once more the joy and confidence arising from the full forgiveness of his iniquities; in the fifty-first Psalm, which was
composed after Nathan had been to him, he shows clearly
enough that the promise of divine forgiveness, which the prophet
had given him in consequence of his confession of his guilt, did
not take immediate possession of his soul, but simply kept him
from despair at first, and gave him strength to attain to a
thorough knowledge of the depth of his guilt through prayer
and supplication, and to pray for its entire removal, that his
heart might be renewed and fortified through the Holy Ghost.
But Nathan's reproof could not possibly have borne this saving
fruit, if David had still been living in utter blindness as to the
character of his sin at the time when the prophet went to him.

Vers. 1–14. NATHAN'S REPROOF.—Vers. 1 sqq. To ensure
the success of his mission, viz. to charge the king with his
crimes, Nathan resorted to a parable by which he led on the
king to pronounce sentence of death upon himself.   The
parable is a very simple one, and drawn from life.   Two men

were living in a certain city: the one was rich, and had many
sheep and oxen; the other was poor, and possessed nothing at
all but one small lamb which he had bought and nourished
(יְחַיֶּה, *lit.* kept alive), so that it grew up in his house along
with his son, and was treated most tenderly and loved like a
daughter. The custom of keeping pet-sheep in the house, as
we keep lap-dogs, is still met with among the Arabs (*vid.*
Bochart, *Hieroz* i p 594). There came a traveller (הֵלֶךְ, a
journey, for a traveller) to the rich man (לְאִישׁ without an
article, the express definition being introduced afterwards in
connection with the adjective הֶעָשִׁיר; *vid.* Ewald, § 293*a*, p.
741), and he grudged to take of his own sheep and oxen to
prepare (*sc.* a meal) for the traveller who had come to his
house; "and he took the poor man's lamb, and dressed it for
the man that had come to him."—Vers. 5, 6. David was so
enraged at this act of violence on the part of the rich man,
that in the heat of his anger he pronounced this sentence at
once: "*As the Lord liveth, the man who did this deserves to die;
and the lamb he shall restore fourfold.*" The fourfold restoration corresponds to the law in Ex. xxi. 37. The culprit himself
was also to be put to death, because the forcible robbery of a
poor man's pet-lamb was almost as bad as man-stealing.—Vers.
7 sqq. The parable was so selected that David could not suspect that it had reference to him and to his sin. With all the
greater shock therefore did the words of the prophet, "*Thou art
the man,*" come upon the king. Just as in the parable the sin
is traced to its root—namely, insatiable covetousness—so now, in
the words of Jehovah which follow, and in which the prophet
charges the king directly with his crime, he brings out again in
the most unsparing manner this hidden background of all sins,
for the purpose of bringing thoroughly home to his heart the
greatness of his iniquity, and the condemnation it deserved.
"*Jehovah the God of Israel hath said, I anointed thee king over
Israel, and I delivered thee out of the hand of Saul, and I gave
thee thy master's house and thy master's wives into thy bosom.*"
These words refer to the fact that, according to the general
custom in the East, when a king died, his successor upon the
throne also succeeded to his harem, so that David was at liberty
to take his predecessor's wives; though we cannot infer from
this that he actually did so: in fact this is by no means probable,

since, according to 1 Sam. xiv. 50, Saul had but one wife, and
according to 2 Sam. iii. 7 only one concubine, whom Abner
appropriated to himself. " *And gave thee the house of Israel
and Judah ;*" *i.e.* I handed over the whole nation to thee as
king, so that thou couldst have chosen young virgins as wives
from all the daughters of Judah and Israel. וְאִם מְעָט, " *and if*
(all this was) *too little, I would have added to thee this and that.*"
—Ver. 9. " *Why hast thou despised the word of Jehovah, to do
evil in His eyes?   Thou hast slain Uriah the Hethite with the
sword, and taken his wife to be thy wife, and slain him with the
sword of the Ammonites.*" The last clause does not contain
any tautology, but serves to strengthen the thought by defining
more sharply the manner in which David destroyed Uriah. הָרַג,
to murder, is stronger than הִכָּה; and the fact that it was by the
sword of *the Ammonites,* the enemies of the people of God, that
the deed was done, added to the wickedness.—Vers. 10–12. The
punishment answers to the sin.   There is first of all (ver. 10)
the punishment for the murder of Uriah : " *The sword shall not
depart from thy house for ever, because thou hast despised me,
and hast taken the wife,*" etc.   " *For ever* " must not be toned
down to the indefinite idea of a long period, but must be held
firmly in its literal signification.   The expression " thy house,"
however, does not refer to the house of David as continued in
his descendants, but simply as existing under David himself
until it was broken up by his death.   The fulfilment of this
threat commenced with the murder of Amnon by Absalom
(ch. xiii. 29); it was continued in the death of Absalom the
rebel (ch. xviii. 14), and was consummated in the execution
of Adonijah (1 Kings ii. 24, 25).—Vers. 11, 12. But David
had also sinned in committing adultery.   It was therefore announced to him by Jehovah, " *Behold, I raise up mischief over
thee out of thine own house, and will take thy wives before thine
eyes, and give them to thy neighbour, that he may lie with thy
wives before the eyes of this sun* (for the fulfilment of this by
Absalom, see ch. xvi. 21, 22).   *For thou hast done it in secret ;
but I will do this thing before all Israel, and before* (in the face
of) *the sun.*"   David's twofold sin was to be followed by a twofold punishment.   For his murder he would have to witness
the commission of murder in his own family, and for his
adultery the violation of his wives, and both of them in an

intensified form. As his sin began with adultery, and was consummated in murder, so the law of just retribution was also carried out in the punishment, in the fact that the judgments which fell upon his house commenced with Amnon's incest, whilst Absalom's rebellion culminated in the open violation of his father's concubines, and even Adonijah lost his life, simply because he asked for Abishag the Shunammite, who had lain in David's bosom to warm and cherish him in his old age (1 Kings ii. 23, 24).—Ver. 13. These words went to David's heart, and removed the ban of hardening which pressed upon it. He confessed to the prophet, "*I have sinned against the Lord.*" "The words are very few, just as in the case of the publican in the Gospel of Luke (xviii. 13). But that is a good sign of a thoroughly broken spirit. . . . There is no excuse, no cloaking, no palliation of the sin. There is no searching for a loophole, . . . no pretext put forward, no human weakness pleaded. He acknowledges his guilt openly, candidly, and without prevarication" (*Berleb. Bible*). In response to this candid confession of his sin, Nathan announced to him, "*The Lord also hath let thy sin pass by* (*i.e.* forgiven it). *Thou wilt not die. Only because by this deed thou hast given the enemies of the Lord occasion to blaspheme, the son that is born unto thee shall die.*" נֵאֵץ, *inf. abs. Piel*, with chirek, because of its similarity in sound to the following perfect (see Ewald, § 240, *c*). גַּם, with which the apodosis commences, belongs to the הַבֵּן which follows, and serves to give emphasis to the expression: "Nevertheless the son" (*vid.* Ges. § 155, 2, *a*). David himself had deserved to die as an adulterer and murderer. The Lord remitted the punishment of death, not so much because of his heartfelt repentance, as from His own fatherly grace and compassion, and because of the promise that He had given to David (ch. vii. 11, 12),—a promise which rested upon the assumption that David would not altogether fall away from a state of grace, or commit a mortal sin, but that even in the worst cases he would turn to the Lord again and seek forgiveness. The Lord therefore punished him for this sin with the judgments announced in vers. 10–12, as about to break upon him and his house. But as his sin had given occasion to the enemies of the Lord—*i.e.* not only to the heathen, but also to the unbelieving among the Israelites themselves—to blaspheme or ridicule his religion and that of all other believers also, the child that was begotten in adultery and had just been born should die; in order, on the one hand, that the father should atone for his adultery in the death of the son, and, on the other hand, that the visible occasion for any further blasphemy should be taken away: so that David was not only to feel the pain of punishment in the death of his son, but was also to discern in it a distinct token of the grace of God.

Vers. 15–25. David's penitential Grief, and the Birth of Solomon.—Ver. 15. The last-mentioned punishment was inflicted without delay. When Nathan had gone home, the Lord smote the child, so that it became very ill.— Vers. 16, 17. Then David sought God (in prayer) for the boy, and fasted, and went and lay all night upon the earth. רָבֹא, "he came," not into the sanctuary of the Lord (ver. 20 is proof to the contrary), but into his house, or into his chamber, to pour out his heart before God, and bend beneath His chastising hand, and refused the appeal of his most confidential servants, who tried to raise him up, and strengthen him with food. "The elders of his house," judging from Gen. xxiv. 2, were the oldest and most confidential servants, "the most highly honoured of his servants, and those who had the greatest influence with him" (Clericus).—Ver. 18. On the seventh day, when the child died, the servants of David were afraid to tell him of its death; for they said (to one another), "Behold, while the child was still living, we spoke to him, and he did not hearken to our voice; how should we say to him, now the child is dead, that he should do harm?" (i.e. do himself an injury in the depth of his anguish.)—Vers. 19, 20. David saw at once what had happened from their whispering conversation, and asked whether the child was dead. When they answered in the affirmative, he rose up from the ground, washed and anointed himself, and changed his clothes; that is to say, he laid aside all the signs of penitential grief and mourning, went into the house of the Lord (the holy tent upon Mount Zion) and worshipped, and then returned to his house, and had food set before him.—Vers. 21 sqq. When his servants expressed their astonishment at all this, David replied, "As long as the boy lived, I fasted and wept: for

I thought (said), *Perhaps* (who knows) *the Lord may be gracious to me, that the child may remain alive. But now he is dead, why should I fast? can I bring him back again? I shall go to him, but he will not return to me.*" On this O. v. Gerlach has the following admirable remarks: " In the case of a man whose penitence was so earnest and so deep, the prayer for the pre-servation of his child must have sprung from some other source than excessive love of any created object. His great desire was to avert the stroke, as a sign of the wrath of God, in the hope that he might be able to discern, in the preservation of the child, a proof of divine favour consequent upon the restora-tion of his fellowship with God. But when the child was dead, he humbled himself under the mighty hand of God, and rested satisfied with His grace, without giving himself up to fruitless pain." This state of mind is fully explained in Ps. li., though his servants could not comprehend it. The form יְחָנַּנִי is the imperfect *Kal*, יְחָנֵּנִי according to the *Chethibh*, though the Masoretes have substituted as the *Keri* וְחַנַּנִי, the perfect with *vav consec.*—Ver. 23*b* is paraphrased very correctly by Cleri-cus: " I shall go to the dead, the dead will not come to me."— Ver. 24. David then comforted his wife Bathsheba, and lived with her again ; and she bare a son, whom he called *Solomon*, the man of peace (cf. 1 Chron. xxii. 9). David gave the child this name, because he regarded his birth as a pledge that he should now become a partaker again of peace with God, and not from any reference to the fact that the war with the Ammonites was over, and peace prevailed when he was born ; although in all probability Solomon was not born till after the capture of Rabbah and the termination of the Ammonitish war. His birth is mentioned here simply because of its connection with what immediately precedes. The writer adds (in vers. 24, 25), "*And Jehovah loved him, and sent by the hand* (through the medium) *of Nathan the prophet; and he called his son Jedidiah* (*i.e.* beloved of Jehovah), *for Jehovah's sake.*" The subject to וַיִּשְׁלַח (he sent) cannot be David, because this would not yield any appropriate sense, but must be *Jehovah*, the subject of the clause immediately preceding. " To send by the hand," *i.e.* to make a mission by a person (*vid.* Ex. iv. 13, etc.), is equiva-lent to having a commission performed by a person, or entrust-ing a person with a commission to another. We learn from what follows, in what the commission with which Jehovah entrusted Nathan consisted : " *And he* (Nathan, not Jehovah) *called his* (the boy's) *name Jedidiah.*" And if Nathan is the subject to " called," there is nothing to astonish in the expression " because of the Lord." The idea is this : Nathan came to David according to Jehovah's instructions, and gave Solomon the name *Jedidiah* for Jehovah's sake, *i.e.* because Jehovah loved him. The giving of such a name was a practical declaration on the part of Jehovah that He loved Solomon, from which David could and was intended to discern that the Lord had blessed his marriage with Bathsheba. *Jedidiah*, therefore, was not actually adopted as Solomon's name.

Vers. 26–31. Conquest of Rabbah, and Punishment of the Ammonites (comp. 1 Chron. xx. 1–3).—"*Joab fought against Rabbah of the children of Ammon, and took the king's city.*" עִיר הַמְּלוּכָה, the capital of the kingdom, is the city with the exception of the acropolis, as ver. 27 clearly shows, where the captured city is called " the water-city." *Rabbah* was situated, as the ruins of *Ammân* show, on both banks of the river (*Moiet*) *Ammân* (the upper Jabbok), in a valley which is shut in upon the north and south by two bare ranges of hills of moderate height, and is not more than 200 paces in breadth. " The northern height is crowned by the castle, the ancient acropolis, which stands on the north-western side of the city, and commands the whole city" (see Burckhardt, *Syria* ii. pp. 612 sqq., and Ritter, *Erdkunde* xv. pp. 1145 sqq.). After taking the water-city, Joab sent messengers to David, to inform him of the result of the siege, and say to him, " *Gather the rest of the people together, and besiege the city* (*i.e.* the acropolis, which may have been peculiarly strong), *and take it, that I may not take the city* (also), *and my name be named upon it*," *i.e.* the glory of the conquest be ascribed to me. Luther adopts this explanation in his free rendering, " and I have a name from it." —Ver. 29. Accordingly David " *gathered together all the people*," —*i.e.* all the men of war who had remained behind in the land ; from which we may see that Joab's besieging army had been considerably weakened during the long siege, and at the capture of the water-city,—" *and fought against the acropolis, and took it.*"—Ver. 30. He then took their king's crown (" *their king*," viz. the king of the Ammonites) from off his (the king's) head; so that he had either been taken prisoner or slain at the capture of the city. The weight of the crown was "*a talent of gold, and precious stones*" (*sc.* were upon it): as the writer of the Chronicles has correctly explained it by supplying בָּהּ. The Hebrew talent (equal to 3000 shekels) was 83½ Dresden pounds. But the strongest man could hardly have borne a crown of this weight upon his head for however short a time; and David could scarcely have placed it upon his own head. We must therefore assume that the account of the weight is not founded upon actual weighing, but simply upon an approximative estimate, which is somewhat too high. David also took a great quantity of booty out of the city.—Ver. 31. He also had the inhabitants executed, and that with cruel tortures. "*He sawed them in pieces with the saw and with iron harrows.*" וַיָּשֶׂם בַּמְּגֵרָה, "he put them into the saw," does not give any appropriate sense; and there can be no doubt, that instead of וַיָּשֶׂם we should read וַיָּשַׂר (from שׂוּר) : "he cut (sawed) them in pieces." וּבְמַגְזְרוֹת הַבַּרְזֶל, "*and with iron cutting tools.*" The meaning of the ἀπ. λεγ. מַגְזֵרוֹת cannot be more precisely determined. The current rendering, "axes or hatchets," is simply founded upon the circumstance that גָּזַר, to cut, is applied in 2 Kings vi. 4 to the felling of trees. The reading in the Chronicles, וּבַמְּגֵרוֹת, is evidently a copyist's error, as we have already had בַּמְּגֵרָה, "with the saw." The meaning of the next clause is a disputed point, as the reading itself varies, and the Masoretes read בַּמַּלְבֵּן instead of the *Chethibh* במלכן, "he made them go through brick-kilns," *i.e.* burnt them in brick-kilns, as the LXX. and Vulgate render it. On the other hand, Thenius takes the *Chethibh* under his protection, and adopts Kimchi's explanation: "he led them through *Malchan, i.e.* through the place where the Ammonites burned their children in honour of their idol." Thenius would therefore alter בְּמַלְכָּן into בְּמַלְכָּם or בַּמִּלְבֹּם : "he offered them as sacrifices in their image of Moloch." But this explanation cannot be even grammatically sustained, to say nothing of the arbitrary character of the alteration proposed; for the technical expression הֶעֱבִיר בָּאֵשׁ לַמֹּלֶךְ, "to cause to go through the fire for Moloch" (Lev. xviii. 21), is essentially different from הֶעֱבִיר בַּמֹּלֶךְ, to cause to pass through Moloch, an expression that we never meet with. Moreover, it is impossible to see how burning the Ammonites in the image of Moloch could possibly be " an obvious mode of punishing idolatry," since the idolatry itself consisted in the fact that the Ammonites burned their children to Moloch. So far as the circumstances themselves are concerned, the cruelties inflicted upon the prisoners are not to be softened down, as Daaz and others propose, by an arbitrary perversion of the words into a mere sentence to hard labour, such as sawing wood, burning bricks, etc. At the same time, the words of the text do not affirm that *all* the inhabitants of Rabbah were put to death in this cruel manner. הָעָם אֲשֶׁר בָּהּ (without כֹּל) refers no doubt simply to the fighting men that were taken prisoners, or at the most to the male population of the acropolis of Rabbah, who probably consisted of fighting men only. In doing this, David merely retaliated upon the Ammonites the cruelties with which they had treated their foes; since according to Amos i. 13 they ripped up women who were with child, and according to 1 Sam. xi. 2 their king Nahash would only make peace with the inhabitants of Jabesh upon the condition that the right eye of every one of them should be put out. It is sufficiently evident from this, that the Ammonites had aimed at the most shameful extermination of the Israelites. " *Thus did he unto all the cities of the Ammonites*," *i.e.* to all the fortified cities that resisted the Israelites. After the close of this war, David returned to Jerusalem with all the men of war. The war with the Syrians and Ammonites, including as it did the Edomitish war as well, was the fiercest in which David was ever engaged, and was also the last great war of his life.

AMNON'S INCEST, AND ABSALOM'S FRATRICIDE.—CHAP. XIII.

The judgments threatened to king David in consequence of his sin with Bathsheba soon began to fall upon him and upon his house, and were brought about by sins and crimes on the part of his own sons, for which David was himself to blame, partly because of his own indulgence and want of discipline, and partly because of the bad example that he had set them. Having grown up without strict paternal discipline, simply under the care of their different mothers, who were jealous of one another, his sons fancied that they might gratify their own fleshly lusts, and carry out their own ambitious plans; and from this there arose a series of crimes, which nearly cost the king his life and throne. Amnon, David's eldest son, led the way with his forcible violation of his step-sister Tamar (vers. 1–22). The crime was avenged by her own brother Absalom, who treacherously assassinated Amnon, in consequence of which he was obliged to flee to Geshur and take refuge with his father in law (vers. 23–39).

Vers. 1–22. AMNON'S INCEST.—Vers. 1–14. The following occurrences are assigned in a general manner to the times succeeding the Ammonitish war, by the words "*And it came to pass after this;*" and as David did not marry Maacah the mother of Absalom and Tamar till after he had been made king at Hebron (see ch. iii. 3), they cannot well have taken place before the twentieth year of his reign. *Amnon*, the eldest son of David by *Ahinoam* the Jezreelite (ch. iii. 2), loved Tamar, the beautiful sister of his step-brother Absalom, so passionately that he became ill in consequence, because he could not get near to her as she was a virgin. Vers. 1 and 2 form one period. וַיֵּצֶר is a continuation of וַיְהִי אַחֲרֵי־כֵן; and the words from וּלְאַבְשָׁלוֹם to בֶּן־דָּוִד are a circumstantial clause. וַיֵּצֶר: literally "it became narrow (anxious) to Amnon, even to making himself ill," *i.e.* he quite pined away, not "he pretended to be ill" (Luther), for it was not till afterwards that he did this according to Jonadab's advice (ver. 5). הִתְחַלּוֹת: to make one's self ill, here to become ill, in ver. 5 to pretend to be ill. The clause כִּי בְתוּלָה הִיא is to be joined to the one which follows: "*because she was a virgin, and it seemed impossible to him to do anything to her.*" The maidenly modesty of Tamar evidently raised an insuperable barrier to the gratification of his lusts.—Vers. 3–5. Amnon's miserable appearance was observed by his cousin Jonadab, a very crafty man, who asked him what was the reason, and then gave him advice as to the way in which he might succeed in gratifying his desires. *Shimeah* is called *Shammah* in 1 Sam. xvi. 9.— Ver. 4. "*Why art thou so wasting away* (דַּל, thin, spare, here equivalent to wasting away, looking miserable), *king's son, from morning to morning?*" *i.e.* day by day. "The morning" is mentioned because sick persons look worst in the morning. The advice given in ver. 5,—viz. "Lay thee down upon thy bed, and

pretend to be ill; and when thy father comes to visit thee, say
to him, May my sister Tamar come to me, and give me to eat?"
etc.,—was very craftily devised, as Amnon's wretched appearance
would favour his pretence that he was ill, and it might be hoped
that an affectionate father would gratify him, since even if the
wish seemed a strange one, it might easily be accounted for from
the marvellous desires of persons who are ill, particularly with
regard to food,—desires which it is often very difficult to gratify.
—Vers. 6 sqq. Amnon acted upon the advice, and begged his
father, when he came to ask him how he was, to allow his sister
Tamar to come and bake two heart-cakes for him before his
eyes, which she very speedily did. לָבֵב is a *denom.* from לְבִבוֹת,
to make or bake heart-cakes. לְבִבוֹת is a heart-strengthening
kind of pastry, a kind of pancake, which could be very quickly
made. It is evident from these verses that the king's children
lived in different houses. Probably each of the king's wives
lived with her children in one particular compartment of the
palace.—Vers. 9 sqq. "And she took the pan and shook out
(what she had prepared) before him. The ἀπ. λεγ. מַשְׂרֵת signifies a frying-pan or sauce-pan, according to the ancient versions.
The etymology is uncertain. But Amnon refused to eat, and,
like a whimsical patient, he then ordered all the men that were
with him to go out; and when this had been done, he told
Tamar to bring the food into the chamber, that he might eat it
from her hand; and when she handed him the food, he laid
hold of her, and said, "Come, lie with me, my sister!"—Vers.
12, 13. Tamar attempted to escape by pointing to the wickedness of such a desire: "Pray, do not, my brother, do not humble
me; for they do not such things in Israel: do not this folly."
The words recal Gen. xxxiv. 7, where the expression "folly"
(*nebalah*) is first used to denote a want of chastity. Such a
sin was altogether out of keeping with the calling and holiness
of Israel (*vid.* Lev. xx. 8 sqq.). "*And I, whither should I
carry my shame?*" *i.e.* shame and contempt would meet me
everywhere. "*And thou wouldst be as one of the fools in
Israel.*" We should both of us reap nothing but shame from
it. What Tamar still further said, "*Now therefore, I pray
thee, speak to the king, for he will not refuse me to thee,*" is no
doubt at variance with the law which prohibits marriage between step-brothers and sisters (Lev. xviii. 9, 11, xx. 17); but

it by no means proves that the laws of Leviticus were not in existence at the time, nor does it even presuppose that Tamar was ignorant of any such law. She simply said this, as Clericus observes, " that she might escape from his hands by any means in her power, and to avoid inflaming him still more and driving him to sin by precluding all hope of marriage."[1] We cannot therefore even infer from these words of hers, that she really thought the king could grant a dispensation from the existing hindrances to their marriage.—Ver. 14. Amnon would not listen to her, however, but overpowered her, forced her, and lay with her.

Vers. 15-22. Amnon had no sooner gratified his animal passion, than his love to the humbled sister turned into hatred, which was even greater than his (previous) love, so that he commanded her to get up and go. This sudden change, which may be fully explained from a psychological point of view, and is frequently exemplified still in actual life, furnishes a striking proof that lust is not love, but simply the gratification of the animal passions.—Ver. 16. Tamar replied, " *Do not become the cause of this great evil*, (which is) *greater than another that thou hast done to me, to thrust me away*," *i.e.* do not add to the great wrong which thou hast done me the still greater one of thrusting me away. This is apparently the only admissible explanation of the difficult expression אַל־אֹדוֹת, as nothing more is needed than to supply תְּהִי. Tamar calls his sending her away a greater evil than the one already done to her, because it would inevitably be supposed that she had been guilty of some shameful conduct herself, that the seduction had come from her; whereas she was perfectly innocent, and had done nothing but what affection towards a sick brother dictated, whilst it was impossible for her to call for help (as prescribed in Deut. xxii. 27), because Amnon had sent the servants away, and Tamar could not in any case expect assistance from them.—Ver. 17. Amnon then called the boy who waited upon him, and ordered him to put out this person (the sister he had humbled), and to bolt the door behind her, so that it had the appearance of her having made a shameful proposal to him.—Ver. 18. Before stating that this command was obeyed, the writer inserts this

---

[1] Josephus adopts this explanation : " This she said, as desirous to avoid her brother's violent passion at present " (*Ant.* viii. 8, 1).

remark: " *She* (Tamar) *wore a long dress with sleeves* (see Gen.
xxxvii. 3); *for in this manner did the virgin daughters of the
king dress themselves with mantles.*" מְעִילִים is an accusative
belonging to תִּלְבַּשְׁנָה, and the meaning is that the king's daughters, who were virgins, wore long dresses with sleeves as cloaks.
The *cetoneth passim* was not an ordinary under-garment, but
was worn over the plain *cetoneth* or tunic, and took the place of
the ordinary *meïl* without sleeves.   Notwithstanding this dress,
by which a king's daughter could at once be recognised, Amnon's
servant treated Tamar like a common woman, and turned her out
of the house.—Ver. 19. And Tamar took ashes upon her head,
rent her sleeve-dress (as a sign of grief and pain at the disgrace
inflicted upon her), laid her hand upon her head (as a sign that
a grievous trouble had come upon her, that the hand of God
was resting as it were upon her: *vid.* Jer. ii. 37), and "*went
going and cried,*" *i.e.* crying aloud as she went along.—Ver. 20.
Then Absalom said to her, namely when she came home mourning in this manner, "*Has Amnon thy brother been with thee?*"
This was a euphemism for what had taken place (cf. Gen. xxxix.
10), as Absalom immediately conjectured.   "*And now, my
sister, be silent; it is thy brother, do not take this thing to heart.*"
Absalom quieted the sister, because he was determined to take
revenge, but wished to conceal his plan of vengeance for the
time.   So Tamar remained in her brother's house, "*and indeed
desolate,*" *i.e.* as one laid waste, with the joy of her life hopelessly destroyed.   It cannot be proved that שֹׁמֵם ever means
single or solitary.—Vers. 21, 22. When David heard "all these
things," he became very wrathful; but Absalom did not speak
to Amnon "*from good to evil*" (*i.e.* either good or evil, not a
single word: Gen. xxiv. 50), because he hated him for having
humbled his sister.   The LXX. add to the words "he (David)
was very wroth," the following clause: " He did not trouble
the spirit of Amnon his son, because he loved him, for he was
his first-born." This probably gives the true reason why David
let such a crime as Amnon's go unpunished, when the law enjoined that incest should be punished with death (Lev. xx. 17);
at the same time it is nothing but a subjective conjecture of
the translators, and does not warrant us in altering the text.
The fact that David was contented to be simply angry is probably to be accounted for partly from his own consciousness of

guilt, since he himself had been guilty of adultery; but it arose chiefly from his indulgent affection towards his sons, and his consequent want of discipline. This weakness in his character bore very bitter fruit.

Vers. 23–39. ABSALOM'S REVENGE AND FLIGHT.—Vers. 23, 24. Absalom postponed his revenge for two full years. He then *"kept sheep shearing,"* which was celebrated as a joyous festival (see 1 Sam. xxv. 2, 8), *"at Baal-Hazor, near Ephraim,"* where he must therefore have had some property. The situation of *Baal-Hazor* cannot be precisely determined. The clause *"which* (was) *beside Ephraim"* points to a situation on the border of the tribe-territory of Ephraim (*juxta Ephraim*, according to the *Onom. s.v. Baalasor*); for the Old Testament never mentions any city of that name. This definition does not exactly tally with v. Raumer's conjecture (*Pal.* p. 149), that *Baal-Hazor* may have been preserved in *Tell Asûr* (Rob. *Pal.* ii. p. 151, iii. p. 79); for this Tell is about five Roman miles to the north-east of Bethel, *i.e.* within the limits of the tribe of Ephraim. There is greater probability in the suggestion made by Ewald and others, that Baal-Hazor is connected with the *Hazor* of Benjamin (Neh. xi. 33), though the situation of Hazor has not yet been thoroughly decided; and it is merely a conjecture of Robinson's that it is to be found in *Tell Asûr.* The following statement, that *"Absalom invited all the king's sons"* (*sc.* to the feast), somewhat anticipates the course of events: for, according to ver. 24, Absalom invited the king himself, together with his courtiers; and it was not till the king declined the invitation for himself, that Absalom restricted his invitation to the royal princes.—Ver. 25. The king declined the invitation, that he might not be burdensome to Absalom. Absalom pressed him indeed, but he would not go, and blessed him, *i.e.* wished him a pleasant and successful feast (see 1 Sam. xxv. 14). —Ver. 26. Then Absalom said, *"And not (i.e.* if thou dost not go), *may my brother Amnon go with me?"* The king would not give his consent to this; whether from suspicion cannot be determined with certainty, as he eventually yielded to Absalom's entreaties and let Amnon and all the other king's sons go. From the length of time that had elapsed since Amnon's crime was committed, without Absalom showing any wish for revenge,

David might have felt quite sure that he had nothing more to fear. But this long postponement of revenge, for the purpose of carrying it out with all the more certainty, is quite in the spirit of the East.—Ver. 28. Absalom then commanded his servants to put Amnon to death without fear, as he had commanded, as soon as his heart should become merry with wine and he (Absalom) should tell them to smite him. The arrangement of the meal is passed over as being quite subordinate to the main purpose of the narrative; and the clause added by the LXX. at the close of ver. 27, καὶ ἐποίησεν Ἀβεσσαλὼν πότον κατὰ τὸν πότον τοῦ βασιλέως, is nothing more than an explanatory gloss, formed according to 1 Sam. xxv. 36. The words "Have not I commanded you?" implied that Absalom would take the responsibility upon himself.—Ver. 29. The servants did as he commanded, whereupon the other king's sons all fled upon their mules.—Ver. 30. But whilst they were on the road, the report of what Absalom had done reached the ears of the king, and, as generally happens in such cases, with very great exaggeration: "*Absalom hath slain all the king's sons, and there is not one of them left.*"—Ver. 31. The king rent his clothes with horror at such a deed, and sat down upon the ground, and all his servants (courtiers) stood motionless by, with their clothes rent as well. This is the rendering adopted by Böttcher, as נצב has frequently the idea of standing perfectly motionless (*e.g.* Num. xxii. 23, 24; Ex. v. 20, etc.).—Ver. 32. Then Jonadab, the same person who had helped Amnon to commit his crime, said, "*Let not my lord say* (or think) *that they have slain all the young men the king's sons, but Amnon alone is dead; for it was laid upon the mouth of Absalom from the day that he forced his sister Tamar.*" The meaning is either "they might see it (the murder of Amnon) by his mouth," or "they might gather it from what he said." הָיְתָה שׂוּמָה: it was a thing laid down, *i.e.* determined (*vid.* Ex. xxi. 13). The subject, viz. the thing itself, or the intended murder of Amnon, may easily be supplied from the context. כִּי אִם is undoubtedly used in the sense of "*no but.*" The negation is implied in the thought: Let the king not lay it to heart, that they say all the king's sons are dead; it is not so, but only Amnon is dead. Jonadab does not seem to speak from mere conjecture; he is much too sure of what he says. He might possibly have heard expressions from Absalom's lips which made him certain as to how the matter stood.—Ver. 34. "And Absalom fled." This statement follows upon ver. 29. When the king's sons fled upon their mules, Absalom also took to flight.—Vers. 30-33 are a parenthesis, in which the writer describes at once the impression made upon the king and his court by the report of what Absalom had done. The apparently unsuitable position in which this statement is placed may be fully explained from the fact, that the flight of Absalom preceded the arrival of the rest of the sons at the king's palace. The alteration which Böttcher proposes to make in the text, so as to remove this statement altogether on account of its unsuitable position, is proved to be inadmissible by the fact that the account of Absalom's flight cannot possibly be left out, as reference is made to it again afterwards (vers. 37, 38, "Absalom had fled"). The other alterations proposed by Thenius in the text of vers. 34, 37, 38, are just as arbitrary and out of place, and simply show that this critic was ignorant of the plan adopted by the historian. His plan is the following : To the account of the murder of Amnon, and the consequent flight of the rest of the king's sons whom Absalom had invited to the feast (ver. 29), there is first of all appended a notice of the report which preceded the fugitives and reached the king's ears in an exaggerated form, together with the impression which it made upon the king, and the rectification of that report by Jonadab (vers. 30-33). Then follows the statement that Absalom fled, also the account of the arrival of the king's sons (vers. 34-36). After this we have a statement as to the direction in which Absalom fled, the king's continued mourning, and the length of time that Absalom's banishment lasted (vers. 37, 38), and finally a remark as to David's feelings towards Absalom (ver. 39).

Jonadab's assertion, that Amnon only had been slain, was very speedily confirmed (ver. 34). The young man, the spy, *i.e.* the young man who was looking out for the return of those who had been invited to the feast, "lifted up his eyes and saw," *i.e.* saw as he looked out into the distance, "much people (a crowd of men) coming from the way behind him along the side of the mountain." מִדֶּרֶךְ אַחֲרָיו, ἐν τῇ ὁδῷ ὄπισθεν αὐτοῦ (LXX.), *per iter devium* (Vulg.), is obscure; and אַחַר, "behind," is probably to be understood as meaning "to the west :" from the way at the back of the spy, *i.e.* to the west of his station. The following words, מִצַּד הָהָר, also remain obscure, as the position of the spy is not given, so that the allusion may be to a mountain in the north-west of Jerusalem quite as well as to one on the west.[1] When the spy observed the crowd of men approaching, Jonadab said to the king (ver. 35), "Behold, the king's sons are coming: as thy servant said, so has it come to pass."—Ver. 36. Jonadab had hardly said this when the king's sons arrived and wept aloud, *sc.* as they related what had occurred; whereupon the king and all his retainers broke out in loud weeping.—Ver. 37. "Only Absalom had fled and gone to Talmai the son of Ammihud, the king of Geshur." These words form a circumstantial clause, which the writer has inserted as a parenthesis, to define the expression "the king's sons" more particularly. If we take these words as a parenthesis, there will be no difficulty in explaining the following word "mourned," as the subject (David) may very easily be supplied from the preceding words "the king," etc. (ver. 36). To the remark that David mourned all his life for his son (Amnon), there is attached, just as simply and quite in accordance with the facts, the more precise information concerning Absalom's flight, that he remained in Geshur three years. The repetition of the words "Absalom had fled and gone to Geshur" may be accounted for from the general diffuseness of the Hebrew style. *Talmai* the king of *Geshur* was the father of *Maacah*, Absalom's mother (ch. iii. 3). The LXX. thought it necessary expressly to indicate this by inserting εἰς γῆν Χαμαχάαδ (*al.* γῆν Μαχάδ). —Ver. 39. "*And it* (this) *held king David back from going out*

---

[1] The LXX. have very comprehensive additions here: first of all, after ἐκ πλευρᾶς τοῦ ὄρους, they have the more precise definition ἐν τῇ καταβάσει, and then the further clause, "and the spy came and announced to the king," Ἄνδρας ἑώρακα ἐκ τῆς ὁδοῦ τῆς ὠρωνὴν (?) ἐκ μέρους τοῦ ὄρους, partly to indicate more particularly the way by which the king's sons came, and partly to fill up a supposed gap in the account. But they did not consider that the statement in ver. 35, "and Jonadab said to the king, Behold, the king's sons are coming," does not square with these additions; for if the spy had already informed the king that his sons were coming, there was no necessity for Jonadab to do it again. This alone is sufficient to show that the additions made by the LXX. are nothing but worthless glosses, introduced according to subjective conjectures and giving no foundation for alterations of the text.

to Absalom, for he comforted himself concerning Amnon, because he was dead." In adopting this translation of the difficult clause with which the verse commences, we take וַתְּכַל in the sense of כָּלָא, as the verbs כלה and כלא frequently exchange their forms; we also take the third pers. fem. as the neuter impersonal, so that the subject is left indefinite, and is to be gathered from the context. Absalom's flight to Geshur, and his stay there, were what chiefly prevented David from going out to Absalom. Moreover, David's grief on account of Amnon's death gradually diminished as time rolled on. צֵאת אֶל־אַבשׁ׳ is used in a hostile sense, as in Deut. xxviii. 7, to go out and punish him for his wickedness. The כִּי before נָחַם might also be rendered "*but*," as after a negative clause, as the principal sentence implies a negation: "*He did not go out against Absalom, but comforted himself.*" There is not only no grammatical difficulty in the way of this explanation of the verse, but it also suits the context, both before and after. All the other explanations proposed are either at variance with the rules of the language, or contain an unsuitable thought. The old Jewish interpretation (adopted in the Chaldee version, and also by the Rabbins), viz. David longed (his soul pined) to go out to Absalom (*i.e.* to see or visit him), is opposed, as Gusset has shown (in his *Lex*. pp. 731–2), to the conduct of David towards Absalom as described in ch. xiv.,—namely, that after Joab had succeeded by craft in bringing him back to Jerusalem, David would not allow him to come into his presence for two whole years (ch. xiv. 24, 28). Luther's rendering, "and king David left off going out against Absalom," is not only precluded by the feminine תְּכַל, but also by the fact that nothing has been said about any pursuit of Absalom on the part of David. Other attempts at emendations there is no need whatever to refute.

ABSALOM'S RETURN, AND RECONCILIATION TO THE KING.— CHAP. XIV.

As David did not repeal the banishment of Absalom, even after he had comforted himself for Amnon's death, Joab endeavoured to bring him back to Jerusalem by stratagem (vers. 1–20); and when this succeeded, he proceeded to effect his reconciliation to the king (vers. 21–33). He may have

been induced to take these steps partly by his personal attachment to Absalom, but the principal reason no doubt was that
Absalom had the best prospect of succeeding to the throne, and
Joab thought this the best way to secure himself from punishment for the murder which he had committed. But the issue
of events frustrated all such hopes. Absalom did not succeed
to the throne, Joab did not escape punishment, and David was
severely chastised for his weakness and injustice.

Vers. 1–20. When Joab perceived that the king's heart was
against Absalom, he sent for a cunning woman from Tekoah,
to work upon the king and change his mind, so that he might
grant forgiveness to Absalom. Ver. 1 is understood by the
majority of commentators, in accordance with the Syriac and
Vulgate, as signifying that Joab learned that the king's heart
was inclined towards Absalom, was well disposed towards him
again. But this explanation is neither philologically sustained,
nor in accordance with the context. לֵב, written with עַל and
without any verb, so that הָיָה has to be supplied, only occurs
again in Dan. xi. 28, where the preposition has the meaning
"*against.*" It is no argument against this meaning here, that
if David had been ill disposed towards Absalom, there would
have been no necessity to state that Joab perceived it; for we
cannot see why Joab should only have perceived or noticed
David's friendly feelings, and not his unfriendly feelings as
well. If, however, Joab had noticed the re-awakening of
David's good feelings towards Absalom, there would have been
no necessity for him to bring the cunning woman from Tekoah
to induce him to consent to Absalom's return. Moreover, David
would not in that case have refused to allow Absalom to see
his face for two whole years after his return to Jerusalem
(ver. 24). *Tekoah,* the home of the prophet Amos, the present
Tekua, two hours to the south of Bethlehem (see at Josh. xv.
59, LXX.). The " wise woman" was to put on mourning, as
a woman who had been mourning for a long while for some
one that was dead (הִתְאַבֵּל, to set or show herself mourning),
and to go to the king in this attire, and say what Joab had put
into her mouth.—Ver. 4. The woman did this. All the old
translators have given as the rendering of וַתֹּאמֶר הָאִשָּׁה " the
woman came (went) to the king," as if they had read וַתָּבֹא.
This reading is actually found in some thirty *Codd.* of De Rossi,

and is therefore regarded by Thenius and the majority of critics as the original one. But Böttcher has very justly urged, in opposition to this, that וַתֹּאמֶר cannot possibly be an accidental corruption of וַתָּבֹא, and that it is still less likely that such an alteration should have been intentionally made. But this remark, which is correct enough in itself, cannot sustain the conjecture which Böttcher has founded upon it, namely that two whole lines have dropt out of the Hebrew text, containing the answer which the woman of Tekoah gave to Joab before she went to the king, since there is not one of the ancient versions which contains a single word more than the Masoretic text. Consequently we must regard וַתֹּאמֶר as the original reading, and interpret it as a *hysteron-proteron*, which arose from the fact that the historian was about to relate at once what the woman said to the king, but thought it desirable to mention her falling down at the feet of the king before giving her actual words, " *Help, O king*," which he introduces by repeating the word וַתֹּאמֶר.—Vers. 5 sqq. When the king asked her, " What aileth thee ?" the woman described the pretended calamity which had befallen her, saying that she was a widow, and her two sons had quarrelled in the field; and as no one interposed, one of them had killed the other. The whole family had then risen up and demanded that the survivor should be given up, that they might carry out the avenging of blood upon him. Thus they sought to destroy the heir also, and extinguish the only spark that remained to her, so as to leave her husband neither name nor posterity upon the earth. The suffix attached to וַיַּכּוֹ, with the object following (" he smote him, the other," ver. 6), may be explained from the diffuseness of the style of ordinary conversation (see at 1 Sam. xxi. 14). There is no reason whatever for changing the reading into יַכּוּ, as the suffix וֹ, though unusual with verbs ל״ה, is not without parallel; not to mention the fact that the plural יַכּוּ is quite unsuitable. There is also quite as little reason for changing וְנַשְׁמִידָה into וְיַשְׁמִידוּ, in accordance with the Syriac and Arabic, as Michaelis and Thenius propose, on the ground that " the woman would have described her relatives as diabolically malicious men, if she had put into their mouths such words as these, ' We will destroy the heir also.' " It was the woman's intention to describe the conduct of the relations and their pursuit of blood-revenge in the harshest terms possible, in order that she might obtain help from the king. She begins to speak in her own name at the word וְכִבּוּ ‎("and so they shall quench and"), where she resorts to a figure, for the purpose of appealing to the heart of the king to defend her from the threatened destruction of her family, saying, "And so they shall quench the burning coal which is left." גַּחֶלֶת is used figuratively, like τὸ ζώπυρον, the burning coal with which one kindles a fresh fire, to denote the last remnant. לְבִלְתִּי שׂוּם : "so as not to set," i.e. to preserve or leave name and remnant (i.e. posterity) to my husband.

This account differed, no doubt, from the case of Absalom, inasmuch as in his case no murder had taken place in the heat of a quarrel, and no avenger of blood demanded his death; so that the only resemblance was in the fact that there existed an intention to punish a murderer. But it was necessary to disguise the affair in this manner, in order that David might not detect her purpose, but might pronounce a decision out of pity for the poor widow which could be applied to his own conduct towards Absalom.—Ver. 8. The plan succeeded. The king replied to the woman, "*Go home, I will give charge concerning thee,*" i.e. I will give the necessary commands that thy son may not be slain by the avenger of blood. This declaration on the part of the king was perfectly just. If the brothers had quarrelled, and one had killed the other in the heat of the quarrel, it was right that he should be defended from the avenger of blood, because it could not be assumed that there was any previous intention to murder. This declaration therefore could not be applied as yet to David's conduct towards Absalom. But the woman consequently proceeded to say (ver. 9), "My lord, O king, let the guilt be upon me and upon my father's house, and let the king and his throne be guiltless." כִּסֵּא, the throne, for the government or reign. The meaning of the words is this : but if there should be anything wrong in the fact that this bloodshed is not punished, let the guilt fall upon me and my family. The king replied (ver. 10), "*Whosoever speaketh to thee, bring him to me; he shall not touch thee any more.*" אֵלַיִךְ does not stand for עָלַיִךְ, "against thee;" but the meaning is, whoever speaks to thee any more about this, i.e. demands thy son of thee again.—Ver. 11. The crafty woman was not yet satisfied with this, and sought by repeating her petition to induce the king to confirm his promise on oath, that she might bind him the more firmly. She therefore said still further: "*I pray thee, let the king remember Jehovah thy God, that the avenger of blood may no more prepare destruction, and that they may not destroy my son.*" The *Chethib* הַרְבִּית is probably a copyist's error for הַרְבּוֹת, for which the Masoretes would write הַרְבַּת, the construct state of הַרְבָּה,—a form of the inf. abs. which is not commonly used, and which may possibly have been chosen because הַרְבֵּה had become altogether an adverb (*vid.* Ewald, § 240, *e*). The context requires the inf. constr. הַרְבּוֹת: that the avenger of blood may not multiply (make much) to destroy, *i.e.* may not add to the destruction; and הַרְבִּית is probably only a verbal noun used instead of the infinitive. The king immediately promised on oath that her son should not suffer the least harm.—Vers. 12, 13. When the woman had accomplished so much, she asked permission to speak one word more; and having obtained it, proceeded to the point she wanted to reach: "*And wherefore thinkest thou such things against people of God? And because the king speaketh this word, he is as one inculpating himself, since the king does not let his own rejected one return.*" כְּאָשֵׁם, "like one who has laden himself with guilt," is the predicate to the clause וּמִדַּבֵּר וגו׳. These words of the woman were intentionally kept indefinite, rather hinting at what she wished to place before the king, than expressing it distinctly. This is more particularly applicable to the first clause, which needs the words that follow to render it intelligible, as חָשַׁבְתָּה כָּזֹאת is ambiguous; so that Dathe and Thenius are wrong in rendering it, "Why dost thou propose such things towards the people of God?" and understanding it as relating to the protection which the king was willing to extend to her and to her son. חָשַׁב with עַל does not mean to think or reflect "with regard to," but "*against*" a person. Ewald is quite correct in referring the word כָּזֹאת to what follows: such things, *i.e.* such thoughts as thou hast towards thy son, whose blood-guiltiness thou wilt not forgive. עַל־עַם אֱלֹהִים, without the article, is intentionally indefinite, "against people of God," *i.e.* against members of the congregation of God. "*This word*" refers to the decision which the king had pronounced in favour of the widow. לְבִלְתִּי הָשִׁיב, literally, in not letting him return.

In order to persuade the king to forgive, the crafty woman reminded him (ver. 14) of the brevity of human life and of the mercy of God : "*For we must die, and* (are) *as water spilt upon the ground, which is not* (cannot be) *gathered up, and God does not take a soul away, but thinks thoughts, that He may not thrust from Him one expelled.*" Although these thoughts are intentionally expressed quite generally, their special allusion to the case in hand can easily be detected. We must all die, and when dead our life is irrevocably gone. Thou mightest soon experience this in the case of Absalom, if thou shouldst suffer him to continue in exile. God does not act thus; He does not deprive the sinner of life, but is merciful, and does not cast off for ever.—Ver. 15. After these allusions to David's treatment of Absalom, the woman returned again to her own affairs, to make the king believe that nothing but her own distress had led her to speak thus : "*And now that I have come to speak this word to the king my lord, was* (took place) *because the people have put me in fear* (*sc.* by their demand that I should give up my son to the avenger of blood) ; *thy handmaid said* (*i.e.* thought), *I will indeed go to the king, perhaps the king will do his handmaid's word,*" *i.e.* grant her request.—Ver. 16. "*Yea, the king will hear, to save his handmaid out of the hand of the man that would destroy me and my son from the inheritance of God.*" אֲשֶׁר must be supplied before לְהַשְׁמִיד : who is to destroy, *i.e.* who is seeking to destroy (*vid.* Gesenius, § 132, 3). "The inheritance of God" was the nation of Israel (as in 1 Sam. xxvi. 19 ; cf. Deut. xxxii. 9).—Ver. 17. "*Then thine handmaid thought, may the word of my lord the king be for rest* (*i.e.* tend to give me rest) ; *for as the angel of God* (the angel of the covenant, the mediator of the blessings of divine grace to the covenant-nation), *so is my lord the king to hear good and evil* (*i.e.* listening to every just complaint on the part of his subjects, and granting help to the oppressed), *and Jehovah thy God be with thee!*"—Vers. 18 sqq. These words of the woman were so well considered and so crafty, that the king could not fail to see both what she really meant, and also that she had not come with her petition of her own accord. He therefore told her to answer the question without disguise : whether the hand of Joab was with her in all this. She replied, "*Truly there is not* (אִם) *anything to the right hand or to the left of all that my lord the king saith,"* *i.e.* the king always hits the right point in everything that he says. " *Yea, thy servant Joab, he hath commanded me, and he hath put all these words into thy servant's mouth.*" אִשׁ is not a copyist's error, but a softer form of יֵשׁ, as in Micah vi. 10 (*vid.* Ewald, § 53c, and Olshausen, *Gramm.* p. 425).—Ver. 20. " *To turn the appearance of the king (i.e.* to disguise the affair in the finest way) *Joab hath done this; my lord (i.e.* the king), *however, is wise, like the wisdom of the angel of God, to know all that is* (happens) *upon earth.*" She hoped by these flattering words to gain the king completely over.

Vers. 21-33. David then promised Joab, that the request which he had presented through the medium of the woman of Tekoah should be fulfilled, and commanded him to fetch Absalom back. The *Chethib* עָשִׂיתִי (ver. 21) is the correct reading, and the *Keri* עָשִׂיתָ has arisen from a misunderstanding. —Ver. 22. Joab thanked the king for this, and blessed him: " *To-day thy servant knoweth that I have found grace in thy sight, my lord, O king, in that the king hath fulfilled the request of his servant.*" It is pretty evident from this, that Joab had frequently applied to David for Absalom's return, without any attention being paid to his application. David therefore suspected that Joab had instructed the woman of Tekoah. The *Chethib* עַבְדּוֹ is not to be exchanged for the *Keri* עַבְדֶּךָ.— Ver. 23. Joab then went to *Geshur* (see ch. xiii. 37), and fetched Absalom back to Jerusalem. —Ver. 24. But David could not forgive Absalom altogether. He said to Joab, " *Let him turn to his own house, and my face he shall not see.*" This half forgiveness was an imprudent measure, and bore very bitter fruit. The further account of Absalom is introduced in vers. 25-27 with a description of his personal appearance and family affairs.—Ver. 25. There was no man in all Israel so handsome as Absalom. לְהַלֵּל מְאֹד, " to much praising," *i.e.* so that he was greatly praised. From the sole of the foot even to the crown of his head, there was no fault (מוּם, bodily blemish) in him.— Ver. 26. " *When he polled his head, and it took place from year to year that he polled it; for it became heavy upon him* (too heavy for him), *and so he polled it: they weighed the hair of his head, two hundred shekels by the king's weight.*" A strong growth of hair was a sign of great manly power, and so far a proof of

Absalom's beauty. The statement as to the weight of the hair cut off, viz. two hundred shekels, is in any case a round number, and much too high, although we do not know what the difference between the royal and the sacred shekel really was. According to the sacred reckoning, two hundred shekels would be about six pounds; so that if we were to assume that the royal shekel was about half the other, the number would be still much too high. It is evident, therefore, that there is an error in the text, such as we frequently meet with in the case of numbers, though we have no means of rectifying it, as all the ancient versions contain the same number.—Ver. 27. Unto Absalom there were born three sons, and one daughter named Tamar, who was beautiful in figure. Contrary to general usage, the names of the sons are not given, in all probability for no other reason than because they died in infancy. Consequently, as Absalom had no sons, he afterwards erected a pillar to preserve his name (ch. xviii. 18). The daughter's name is probably given as a proof of Absalom's great affection for his sister Tamar, whom Amnon had violated.[1]—Vers. 28–30. After Absalom had sat for two whole years in his house at Jerusalem without seeing the king's face, he sent to Joab that he might obtain for him the king's full forgiveness. But as Joab would not come to him, even after he had sent for him twice, Absalom commanded his servants to set fire to one of Joab's fields which adjoined his own and was then full of barley, for the purpose of compelling him to come, as he foresaw that Joab would not take this destruction of his property quietly, but would come to him to complain. אֶל יָדִי, literally " at my hand," *i.e.* by the side of my field or property. The *Chethib* וְהוֹצִיתִיהָ (" come, I will set it on fire") is a *Hiphil* formation, according to verbs פ"ו, for which the *Keri* has וְהַצִּיתוּהָ, the ordinary *Hiphil* form of יָצַת in the second person plural, " go and set it on fire."— —Vers. 31, 32. When Joab came to Absalom's house in conse-

---

[1] The LXX. have this additional clause, καὶ γίνεται γυνὴ Ῥοβοὰμ υἱῷ Σαλωμὼν καὶ τίκτει αὐτῷ τὸν Ἀβιά (and she became the wife of Rehoboam the son of Solomon, and bore him a son named Abia). Although this is quite at variance with 1 Kings xv. 2, where it is stated that the wife of Rehoboam and mother of Abia (Abijam) was named *Maacah*, the clause has been adopted by Thenius, who regards it as original, though for reasons which Böttcher has shown to be worthless.

quence of this, and complained of it, Absalom said to him, " See, I have sent to thee, to say to thee, Come hither, and I will send thee to the king, to say to him, Wherefore have I come from Geshur? it were better for me that I were there still : and now I will see the king's face ; and if there is any iniquity in me, let him put me to death." This half forgiving was really worse than no forgiveness at all. Absalom might indeed very properly desire to be punished according to the law, if the king could not or might not forgive him ; although the manner in which he sought to obtain forgiveness by force manifested an evident spirit of defiance, by which, with the well-known mildness of David's temper, he hoped to attain his object, and in fact did attain it. For (ver. 33) when Joab went to the king, and announced this to him, the king sent for Absalom, and kissed him, as a sign of his restoration to favour. Nothing was said by Absalom about forgiveness ; for his falling down before the king when he came into his presence, was nothing more than the ordinary manifestation of reverence with which a subject in the East approaches his king.

ABSALOM'S REBELLION AND DAVID'S FLIGHT.— CHAP. XV.–XVI. 14.

After his restoration to favour, Absalom soon began to aspire to the throne, setting up a princely court, and endeavouring to turn the hearts of the people towards himself, by addressing in a friendly manner any who came to seek redress from the king in matters in dispute, and by saying things adapted to throw suspicion upon his father's rule (vers. 1–6). When he had succeeded in this, he asked permission from the king to take a journey to Hebron, under the pretence of wanting to fulfil a vow which he had made during his banishment ; and when once there, he soon proceeded with his rebellious intentions (vers. 7–12). As soon as David heard of it, he determined to fly from Jerusalem, and crossed the Kidron with his faithful adherents. Having sent the priests with the ark of the covenant back to the city, he went up to the Mount of Olives, amidst the loud lamentations of the people. Hushai, who came to meet him, he sent to the city, to frustrate the counsel of Ahithophel, who was one of the conspirators, and to send

information to him of what was going forward (vers. 13–37).
When he reached the top, Ziba, Mephibosheth's servant, came
to meet him with provisions and succour (ch. xvi. 1–4); whilst
Shimei, a relation of the house of Saul, followed him with curses
and stones (vers. 5–14).

With this rebellion the calamities which Nathan had predicted to David on account of his sin with Bathsheba began to
burst upon him in all their fulness.   The success of the rebellion itself may be accounted for, from the fact that the consciousness of his own fault not only made David weak towards
his sons, but produced a want of firmness in his resolutions;
whilst the imperfections and defects in the internal administration of the kingdom, when the time of the brilliant victories was
past, became more and more perceptible to the people, and furnished occasion for dissatisfaction with his government, which
Absalom was skilful enough to bend to his own purposes.
During the time that this rebellion was in progress, David
poured out his lamentations to the Lord (in Ps. xli. and lv.)
as to the faithlessness of his most confidential councillors, and
prayed for the judgment of retribution upon the conduct of this
wicked band.   After it had broken out, he uttered his longings
to return to the sanctuary at Jerusalem, and his firm confidence
that he should be delivered out of his distresses and reinstated
in his kingdom, first of all in Ps. iii. and lxiii. during his flight
in the desert of Judah, and in Ps. lxi. and lxii. during his stay
in the land to the east of the Jordan.

Vers. 1–6. *Absalom seeks to secure the people's favour.*—
Ver. 1. Soon afterwards (this seems to be the meaning of
מֵאַחֲרֵי כֵן as distinguished from אַחֲרֵי כֵן; cf. ch. iii. 28) Absalom
set up a carriage (*i.e.* a state-carriage; cf. 1 Sam. viii. 11) and
horses, and fifty men as runners before him, *i.e.* to run before
him when he drove out, and attract the attention of the people
by a display of princely pomp, as Adonijah afterwards did
(1 Kings i. 5).   He then went early in the morning to the side
of the road to the gate of the palace, and called out to every
one who was about to go to the king " for judgment," *i.e.* seek
justice in connection with any matter in dispute, and asked
him, " Of what city art thou?" and also, as we may see from
the reply in ver. 3, inquired into his feelings towards the king,
and then said, " Thy matters are good and right, but there is

no hearer for thee with the king." שֹׁמֵעַ signifies the judicial officer, who heard complainants and examined into their different causes, for the purpose of laying them before the king for settlement. Of course the king himself could not give a hearing to every complainant, and make a personal investigation of his cause; nor could his judges procure justice for every complainant, however justly they might act, though it is possible that they may not always have performed their duty conscientiously.—Ver. 4. Absalom also said, " *Oh that I might be judge in the land, and every one who had a cause might come before me; I would procure him justice !"* מִי יְשִׂמֵנִי is a wish : " who might (*i.e.* oh that one might) appoint me judge," an analogous expression to מִי יִתֵּן (*vid.* Gesenius, § 136, 1, and Ewald, § 329, *c*). עָלַי placed before יבֹא for the sake of emphasis, may be explained from the fact that a judge sat, so that the person who stood before him rose above him (comp. Ex. xviii. 13 with Gen. xviii. 8). הִצְדִּיק, to speak justly, or help to justice.—Ver. 5. And when any one came near to him to prostrate himself before him, he took him by the hand and kissed him. It was by conduct of this kind that Agamemnon is said to have secured the command of the Grecian army (Euripid. *Iphig. Aul.* v. 337 sqq.).—Ver. 6. Thus Absalom stole the heart of the men of Israel. גַּנֵּב לֵב does not mean to deceive or cheat, like גָּנַב לֵב in the *Kal* in Gen. xxxi. 20, but to steal the heart, *i.e.* to bring a person over to his side secretly and by stratagem.

Vers. 7–12. *Absalom's rebellion.*—Vers. 7, 8. After the lapse of forty (?) years Absalom said to the king, " *Pray I will go (i.e.* pray allow me to go) *and perform a vow in Hebron which I vowed to the Lord during my stay at Geshur"* (ver. 8). The number forty is altogether unsuitable, as it cannot possibly be understood either as relating to the age of Absalom or to the year of David's reign : for Absalom was born at Hebron after David had begun to reign, and David only reigned forty years and a half in all, and Absalom's rebellion certainly did not take place in the last few weeks of his reign. It is quite as inappropriate to assume, as the *terminus a quo* of the forty years, either the commencement of Saul's reign, as several of the Rabbins have done, as well as the author of the marginal note in *Cod.* 380 of De Rossi (למלכות שאול), or the anointing of David

at Bethlehem, as Luther (in the marginal note) and Lightfoto
do ; for the word " after" evidently refers to some event in
the life of Absalom, to which allusion has previously been made,
namely, either to the time of his reconciliation with David (ch.
xiv. 33), or (what is not so probable) to the period of his return
from Geshur to Jerusalem (ch. xiv. 23). Consequently the
reading adopted by the Syriac, Arabic, and Vulgate, also by
Theodoret and others, viz. " *four* years," must certainly be the
correct one, and not " forty days," which we find in Codd. 70
and 96 in Kennicott, since forty days would be far too short
a time for maturing the rebellion. It is true, that with the
reading אַרְבַּע we should expect, as a rule, the plural שָׁנִים. At
the same time, the numbers from two to ten are sometimes
construed with a singular noun (*e.g.* 2 Kings xxii. 1 ; cf. Gesenius, § 120, 2). The pretended vow was, that if Jehovah
would bring him back to Jerusalem, he would serve Jehovah.
עָבַד אֶת־יְהוָֹה, " to do a service to Jehovah," can only mean to
offer a sacrifice, which is the explanation given by Josephus.
The *Chethib* יָשִׁיב is not the infinitive, but the imperfect *Hiphil :
si reduxerit, reduxerit me*, which is employed in an unusual
manner instead of the *inf. absol.*, for the sake of emphasis.
The *Keri* יָשׁוּב would have to be taken as an adverb " again ;"
but this is quite unnecessary.—Ver. 9. The king consented,
and Absalom went to Hebron. Absalom had selected this city,
probably assigning as the reason that he was born there, but
really because his father David had been made king there, and
also possibly because there may have been many persons there
who had been displeased by the removal of the court to Jerusalem.—Ver. 10. When Absalom went to Hebron, he sent spies
into all the tribes of Israel to say, " *When ye hear the sound of
the trumpet, say, Absalom has become king in Hebron.*" We must
suppose the sending of the spies to have been contemporaneous
with the removal of Absalom to Hebron, so that וַיִּשְׁלַח is used
quite regularly, and there is no reason for translating it as a
pluperfect. The messengers sent out are called "spies," because
they were first of all to ascertain the feelings of the people in
the different tribes, and were only to execute their commission
in places where they could reckon upon support. The conspiracy had hitherto been kept very secret, as we may see from
the statement in ver. 11 : " *With Absalom there had gone two*

hundred men out of Jerusalem, invited (to the sacrificial festival), *and going in their simplicity, who knew nothing at all of the affair.*" (לֹא כָל־דָּבָר: nothing at all.)—Ver. 12. Moreover, Absalom sent for Ahithophel, David's councillor, to come from his own town Giloh, when he offered the sacrifices. The unusual construction of יִשְׁלַח אֵת with מֵעִירוֹ may be explained from the pregnant character of the expression : he sent and bade come, *i.e.* he summoned Ahithophel out of his city. *Giloh,* Ahithophel's home, was upon the mountains of Judah, to the south or south-west of Hebron (see at Josh. xv. 51). Ahithophel had no doubt been previously initiated into Absalom's plans, and had probably gone to his native city, merely that he might come to him with the greater ease ; since his general place of abode, as king's councillor, must have been in Jerusalem. "*And the conspiracy became strong; for the people multiplied continually with Absalom*" (the latter is a circumstantial clause). These words give a condensed summary of the result of the enterprise.

Vers. 13–21. *David's flight from Jerusalem.*—Vers. 13, 14. When this intelligence reached David, "*The heart of the men of Israel is after Absalom*" (הָיָה אַחַר, as in ch. ii. 10, to be attached to a person as king; see at 1 Sam. xii. 14), he said to his servants that were with him in Jerusalem, "*Arise, let us flee, for there will be no escape for us from Absalom! Make speed to depart, lest he overtake us suddenly, and drive the calamity* (the judgment threatened in ch. xii. 10, 11) *over us, and smite the city with the edge of the sword.*" David was perhaps afraid that Jerusalem might fall into Absalom's power through treachery, and therefore resolved to fly as speedily as possible, not only in order to prevent a terrible massacre, but also to give his own faithful adherents time to assemble.—Vers. 15, 16. As his servants declared themselves ready to follow him, the king went out of the city with all his family in his train (*lit.* at his feet, as in Judg. iv. 10, 15, etc.), but left ten concubines behind to keep the palace.—Ver. 17. When outside the city the king and all the people in his suite (*i.e.* the royal family and their servants) halted at "the house of the distance." הַמֶּרְחָק is probably a proper name given to a house in the neighbourhood of the city and on the road to Jericho, which was called "the farthest house," viz. from the city.—

Ver. 18. And all his servants, *i.e.* his state officers and attendants, went along by his side, and the whole body-guard (the
Crethi and *Plethi*: see at ch. viii. 18); and all the Gathites,
namely the six hundred men who had come in his train from
Gath, went along in front of the king. David directed the
fugitives to fall into rank, the servants going by his side, and
the body-guard and the six hundred old companions in arms,
who probably also formed a kind of body-guard, marching in
front. The verb עָבַר (passed on) cannot be understood as
signifying to defile past on account of its connection with
עַל־יָדוֹ (beside him, or by his side). The expression *Gittim* is
strange, as we cannot possibly think of actual Gathites or
Philistines from Gath. The apposition (the six hundred men,
etc.) shows clearly enough that the six hundred old companions
in arms are intended, the men who gathered round David on
his flight from Saul and emigrated with him to Gath (1 Sam.
xxvii. 2, 3), who afterwards lived with him in Ziklag (1 Sam.
xxvii. 8, xxix. 2, xxx. 1, 9), and eventually followed him to
Hebron and Jerusalem (ch. ii. 3, v. 6). In all probability
they formed a separate company of well-tried veterans or a
kind of body-guard in Jerusalem, and were commonly known
as *Gathites*.[1]—Ver. 19. A military commander named *Ittai*,
who had emigrated from Gath and come over to David not
long before, also accompanied the king from the city. It is
evident from ch. xviii. 2, where Ittai is said to have commanded a third part of the army sent against Absalom, and to
have been placed on an equality with Joab and Abishai the
most experienced generals, that Ittai was a Philistian general
who had entered David's service. The reason for his going
over to David is not known. According to ver. 22 of this
chapter, Ittai did not come alone, but brought all his family
with him (*taph*: the little ones). The opinion expressed by

---

[1] The Septuagint also has πάντες οἱ Γεθαῖοι, and has generally rendered
the Masoretic text correctly. But כָּל־עֲבָדָיו has been translated incorrectly,
or at all events in a manner likely to mislead, viz. πάντες οἱ παῖδες αὐτοῦ.
But in the Septuagint text, as it has come down to us, another paraphrase
has been interpolated into the literal translation, which Thenius would
adopt as an emendation of the Hebrew text, notwithstanding the fact that
the critical corruptness of the Alexandrian text must be obvious to every
one.

Thenius, that he had come to Jerusalem as a hostage, is merely founded upon a false interpretation of the last two clauses of the verse before us. David said to Ittai, "*Wherefore goest thou also with us? return and stay with the king; for thou art a stranger, and also emigrating to thy place.*" There is no irony in the words "stay with the king," as Thenius and Clericus suppose (viz. "with the man who behaves as if he were king"); nor is there an acknowledgment of Absalom as king, which certainly could never have emanated from David. The words contain nothing more than the simple thought: Do you remain with whoever is or shall be king, since there is no necessity for you as a stranger to take sides at all. This is the explanation given by Seb. Schmidt: "It is not your place to decide this contest as to who ought to be king; but you may remain quiet and see whom God shall appoint as king, and whether it be I or Absalom, you can serve the one that God shall choose." This is the only way in which we can explain the reason assigned for the admonition, viz. "Thou art a stranger," and not an Israelite. There is some difficulty connected with the following words (rendered in the Eng. version "and also an exile"). In the Septuagint and Vulgate they are rendered καὶ ὅτι μετῴκησας σὺ ἐκ τοῦ τόπου σου, *et egressus es de loco tuo* (and thou hast gone out from thine own place); but in adopting this rendering the translators have not only passed over the גַּם (also), but have taken לִמְקוֹמֶךָ for מִמְּקוֹמֶךָ. Nevertheless Thenius proposes to bring the text into harmony with these versions for the purpose of bringing out the meaning, "and moreover thou art one carried away from his own home." But this is decidedly a mistake; for David would never have made a Philistine—who had just before been carried away from his own home, or, as Thenius understands it, who had been brought to Jerusalem as a hostage—the commander of a third of his army. The meaning is rather the following: "And thou hast still no fatherland," *i.e.* thou art still wandering about through the earth like an exile from his country: wherever thou findest a place, and art allowed to settle, there only canst thou dwell.—Ver. 20. "*Thy coming is yesterday* (from yesterday), *and should I disturb thee to-day to go with us, when I am going just where I go?*" *i.e.* wherever my way may lie (I go I know not whither; Chald.: cf. 1 Sam. xxiii. 13). The

Chethib אֲנִיעֵךְ is a copyist's error. The thought requires the *Hiphil* אֲנִיעֵךְ (*Keri*), as נוּע in the *Kal* has the intransitive meaning, to totter, sway about, or move hither and thither. "*Return and take thy brethren back; grace and truth be with thee.*" It is evidently more in accordance with the train of thought to separate עִמָּךְ from the previous clause and connect it with חֶסֶד וָאֱמֶת, though this is opposed to the accents, than to adopt the adverbial interpretation, "take back thy brethren with thee in grace and truth," as Maurer proposes. (For the thought itself, see Prov. iii. 3.) The reference is to the grace and truth (faithfulness) of God, which David desired that Ittai should receive upon his way. In the Septuagint and Vulgate the passage is paraphrased thus : "Jehovah show thee grace and truth," after ch. ii. 6; but it by no means follows from this that יְהוָֹה יַעֲשֶׂה עִמָּךְ has fallen out of the Hebrew text. —Ver. 21. But Ittai replied with a solemn oath, "*Assuredly at the place where my lord the king shall be* (stay), *whether for death or life, there will thy servant be.*" כִּי אִם means "*only*," as in Gen. xl. 14, Job xlii. 8; here, in a declaration on oath, it is equivalent to *assuredly* (*vid.* Ewald, § 356, *b*). The *Chethib* is therefore correct, and the erasure of אִם in the *Keri* is a bad emendation. The כִּי in the apodosis is either an emphatic declaration, *yea*, or like ὅτι merely introduces a distinct assertion.—Ver. 22. After this assurance of his devotedness, David let Ittai do as he pleased. לֵךְ וַעֲבֹר, "go and pass on." עָבַר does not mean to pass by, but to go forward. Thus Ittai and his men and all his family that was with him went forward with the king. By "the little ones" (*taph*) we are to understand a man's whole family, as in many other instances (see at Ex. xii. 37).

Vers. 22–29. *The king crosses the Kidron, and sends the priests back with the ark to Jerusalem.*—Ver. 23. All the land (as in 1 Sam. xiv. 25) wept aloud when all the people went forward; and the king went over the brook Kidron, and all the people went over in the direction of (*lit.* in the face of) the way to the desert. The brook *Kidron* is a winter torrent, *i.e.* a mountain torrent which only flows during the heavy rains of winter (χείμαρρος τοῦ Κεδρών, John xviii. 1). It is on the eastern side of Jerusalem, between the city and the Mount of Olives, and derives its name from the appearance of the water

when rendered muddy through the melting of the snow (cf.
Job vi. 16). In summer it is nothing more than a dry channel
in the valley of Jehoshaphat (see Robinson, *Pal.* i. 396, and
v. Raumer, *Pal.* p. 309, note 81). *" The wilderness"* (*midbar*)
is the northern part of the desert of Judah, through which
the road to Jericho and the Jordan lay.—Ver. 24. Zadok the
priest and all the Levites (who were in Jerusalem) left the
city with the fugitive king, bearing the ark of the covenant :
*"And they set down the ark of God, and Abiathar came up, till
all the people had come completely over from the city."* וַיַּעַל,
ἀνέβη, *ascendit* (LXX., Vulg.), may probably be accounted for
from the fact that Abiathar did not come to join the fugitives
till the procession halted at the Mount of Olives ; so that עָלָה,
like ἀναβαίνειν, merely refers to his actually going up, and
וַיַּעַל affirms that Abiathar joined them until all the people from
the city had arrived. The rendering proposed by Michaelis
and Böttcher (" he offered sacrifices") is precluded by the fact
that עָלָה never means to sacrifice when written without עוֹלָה, or
unless the context points distinctly to sacrifices, as in ch. xxiv.
22, 1 Sam. ii. 28. The ark of the covenant was put down,
because those who went out with the king made a halt, to give
the people who were still coming time to join the procession.—
Vers. 25 sqq. Then the king said to Zadok, *" Take back the ark
of God into the city ! If I find favour in the eyes of Jehovah,
He will bring me back and let me see Him* (*i.e.* himself : the
reference is to God) *and His dwelling* (*i.e.* the ark of the
covenant as the throne of the divine glory in the tent that had
been set up for it). *But if He thus say, I have not delight in thee;
behold, here am I, let Him do to me as seemeth good to Him."*
Thus David put his fate in believing confidence into the hand
of the Lord, because he felt that it was the Lord who was
chastising him for his sins through this rebellion.—Ver. 27.
He also said still further to Zadok, *" Thou seer ! return into the
city in peace."* הֲרוֹאֶה אַתָּה, with הֲ *interrog.*, does not yield any
appropriate sense, as הֲ cannot stand for הֲלוֹא here, simply
because it does not relate to a thing which the person addressed
could not deny. Consequently the word must be pointed thus,
הָרֹאֶה (with the article), and rendered as a vocative, as it has
been by Jerome and Luther. רֹאֶה, seer, is equivalent to
prophet. He applies this epithet to Zadok, as the high priest

who received divine revelations by means of the Urim. The meaning is, Thou Zadok art equal to a prophet; therefore thy proper place is in Jerusalem (O. v. Gerlach). Zadok was to stand as it were upon the watch there with Abiathar, and the sons of both to observe the events that occurred, and send him word through their sons into the plain of the Jordan. "*Behold, I will tarry by the ferries of the desert, till a word comes from you to show me*," *sc.* what has taken place, or how the things shape themselves in Jerusalem. Instead of בְּעַבְרוֹת, the earlier translators as well as the Masoretes adopted the reading בְּעַרְבוֹת, " in the steppes of the desert." The allusion in this case would be to the steppes of Jericho (2 Kings xxv. 5). But Böttcher has very properly defended the *Chethib* on the strength of ch. xvii. 16, where the *Keri* has עֲרָבוֹת again, though עֲבָרוֹת is the true reading (cf. ch. xix. 19). The "ferries of the desert" are the places where the Jordan could be crossed, the fords of the Jordan (Josh. ii. 7; Judg. iii. 28).—Ver. 29. Zadok and Abiathar then returned to the city with the ark of God.

Vers. 30–37. *Ahithophel and Hushai.*—Vers. 30, 31. When David was going by the height of the olive-trees, *i.e.* the Mount of Olives, weeping as he went, with his head covered, and barefooted, as a sign of grief and mourning (see Esther vi. 12; Ezek. xxiv. 17), and with the people who accompanied him also mourning, he received intelligence that Ahithophel (see at ver. 12) was with Absalom, and among the conspirators. וְדָוִד הִגִּיד gives no sense; for David cannot be the subject, because the next clause, " and David said," etc., contains most distinctly an expression of David's on receiving some information. Thenius would therefore alter הִגִּיד into the *Hophal* הֻגַּד, whilst Ewald (§ 131, *a*) would change it into הִגִּיד, an unusual form of the *Hophal*, " David was informed," according to the construction of the *Hiphil* with the accusative. But although this construction of the *Hiphil* is placed beyond all doubt by Job xxxi. 37, xxvi. 4, and Ezek. xliii. 10, the *Hiphil* is construed as a rule, as the *Hophal* always is, with לְ of the person who receives information. Consequently דָּוִד must be altered into לְדָוִד, and הִגִּיד taken as impersonal, "they announced to David." Upon receipt of this intelligence David prayed to the Lord, that He would " turn the counsel of Ahithophel into foolishness," make it appear as folly, *i.e.* frustrate it,—a prayer which God answered (*vid.* ch. xvii. 1 sqq.).—Vers. 32, 33. On David's arrival at the height where people were accustomed to worship, *i.e.* upon the top of the Mount of Olives, the Archite *Hushai* came to meet him with his clothes rent and earth upon his head, that is to say, in the deepest mourning (see 1 Sam. iv. 12). It is evident from the words אֲשֶׁר־יִשְׁתַּחֲוֶה וגו' that there was a place of worship upon the top of the Mount of Olives, probably a *bamah*, such as continued to exist in different places throughout the land, even after the building of the temple. According to ver. 37, ch. xvi. 16, and 1 Chron. xxvii. 33, *Hushai* was רֵעֶה, a friend of David, *i.e.* one of his privy councillors. הָאַרְכִּי (the Archite), if we may judge from Josh. xvi. 2, was the name of a family whose possessions were upon the southern boundary of the tribe of Ephraim, between Bethel and Ataroth. *Hushai* was probably a very old man, as David said to him (vers. 33, 34), "If thou goest with me, thou wilt be a burden to me. But if thou returnest to the city and offerest Absalom thy services, thou canst bring for me the counsel of Ahithophel to nought. If thou sayest to Absalom, I will be thy servant, O king ; servant of thy father (*i.e.* as regards this) I was that of old, but now I am thy servant." The ו before אֲנִי introduces the apodosis both times (*vid.* Ewald, § 348, *a*).—Vers. 35, 36. David then commissioned him to communicate to the priests Zadok and Abiathar all that he should hear of the king's house, and send word to him through their sons.—Ver. 37. So Hushai went into the city when Absalom came to Jerusalem. The ו before the second clause, followed by the imperfect יָבוֹא, indicates contemporaneous occurrence (*vid.* Ewald, § 346, *b*).

Ch. xvi. 1–4. *Ziba's faithless conduct towards Mephibosheth.* —Ver. 1. When David had gone a little over the height (of the Mount of Olives : הָרֹאשׁ points back to ch. xv. 32), Mephibosheth's servant Ziba came to meet him, with a couple of asses saddled, and laden with two hundred loaves, a hundred raisin-cakes, a hundred date or fig-cakes, and a skin of wine. The word קַיִץ corresponds to the Greek ὀπώρα, as the LXX. have rendered it in Jer. xl. 10, 12, and is used to signify summer fruits, both here and in Amos viii. 1 (Symm.). The early translators rendered it lumps of figs in the present passage (παλάθαι ; cf. Ges. *Thes.* p. 1209). The Septuagint only has ἑκατὸν φοίνικες. The latter is certainly the more correct, as the dried lumps of figs or fig-cakes were called דְּבֵלִים (1 Sam. xxv. 18) ; and even at the present day ripe dates, pressed together in lumps like cakes, are used in journeys through the desert, as a satisfying and refreshing food (vid. Winer, bibl. Realwörterbuch, i. 253).—Ver. 2. When the king asked him, " What are these for thee?" i.e. what art thou going to do with them ? Ziba replied, " The asses are for the king's family to ride upon (to ride upon in turn), the bread and summer fruits for the young men (the king's servants) to eat, and the wine for those that are faint in the desert to drink" (see at ch. xv. 23). The Chethib ולהלחם is evidently a copyist's error for וְהַלֶּחֶם.—Ver. 3. To the further question put by the king, "Where is thy lord (Mephibosheth)? Ziba replied, " Behold, he sits (is staying) in Jerusalem ; for he said, To-day will the house of Israel restore the kingship (government) of my father." The " kingship of my father," inasmuch as the throne would have passed to Jonathan if he had outlived Saul. It is obvious enough, apart altogether from ch. xix. 25 sqq., that Ziba was calumniating his master Mephibosheth, in the hope of getting possession of the lands that he was farming for him. A cripple like Mephibosheth, lame in both feet, who had never put in any claim to the throne before, could not possibly have got the idea now that the people of Israel, who had just chosen Absalom as king, would give the throne of Saul to such a cripple as he was. It is true that Ziba's calumny was very improbable ; nevertheless, in the general confusion of affairs, it was not altogether an inconceivable thing that the oppressed party of Saul might avail themselves of this opportunity to make an attempt to restore the power of that house, which many greatly preferred to that of David, under the name of Mephibosheth.—Ver. 4. And in the excited state in which David then was, he was weak enough to give credence to Ziba's words, and to commit the injustice of promising the calumniator all that belonged to Mephibosheth,—a promise for which he most politely thanked him. הִשְׁתַּחֲוֵיתִי, " I bow myself," equivalent to, I lay myself at thy feet. " May I find favour in the eyes of my lord the king!" i.e. may the king grant me his favour (vid. 1 Sam. i. 18).

Vers. 5–14. Shimei's cursing.—Vers. 5, 6. When the king had come to Bahurim, on the other side of the Mount of Olives,

but not far off (see at ch. iii. 16), there came out of that place
a man of the family of the house of Saul, *i.e.* a distant relation
of Saul, cursing him; and he pelted David and all his servants
with stones, although all the people and all the heroes (the
household troops and body-guard: ch. xv. 17, 18) were (marching) on the right and left of the king. The words "all the
people," etc., are a circumstantial clause.—Vers. 7, 8. Shimei
cursed thus: " *Out, out* (away, away), thou man of blood, and
worthless man! Jehovah hath repaid thee (now) for all the
blood of the house of Saul, in whose stead thou hast become
king, and hath given the kingdom into the hand of Absalom
thy son. Behold, now thou art in thy misfortune, for thou
art a man of blood." אִישׁ הַדָּמִים, a man of drops of blood, *i.e.*
one who has shed blood or committed murder. What Shimei
meant by "*all the blood of the house of Saul*," which David
had shed, and because of which he was a man of blood, it is
impossible to determine with certainty. He may possibly have
attributed to David the murder of Ishbosheth and Abner, notwithstanding the fact that David was innocent of the death of
both (see ch. iii. 27 sqq., and 4, 6 sqq.). By "*in whose stead
thou hast reigned*," he meant whose throne thou hast forcibly
usurped; and by הִנְּךָ בְּרָעָתֶךָ, "it is for this that punishment hath
overtaken thee now."—Vers. 9, 10. Abishai wanted to put an
end to this cursing (on the expression "dead dog," see ch. ix. 8).
"Let me go," said he to David, "and take away his head,"
i.e. chop off his head. But David replied, "What have I to
do with you, ye sons of Zeruiah?" Joab probably joined with
Abishai. The formula "what to me and you?" signifies that
a person did not wish to have anything in common with the
feelings and views of another (cf. 1 Kings xvii. 18, Josh. xxii.
24; and τί ἐμοὶ καὶ σοί, John ii. 4. For the thing itself, comp.
Luke ix. 52–56). "If he curses, and if Jehovah hath said to
him, Curse David, who shall then say, Wherefore hast thou
done so?" For כִּי יְקַלֵּל וְכִי יה' (*Chethib*), the Masoretes give us
the *Keri*, כֹּה יְקַלֵּל כִּי יה', "so let him curse, for Jehovah," etc.
This thought lies at the foundation of the rendering adopted by
the LXX., who have inserted, by way of explanation, καὶ ἄφετε
αὐτὸν καὶ: so let him go, and so may he curse. The Vulgate
is just the same: *dimittite eum ut maledicat*. This interpolation
is taken from ver. 11, and, like the *Keri*, is nothing more than

a conjecture, which was adopted simply because כִּי was taken
as a causal particle, and then offence was taken at וְכִי. But כִּי
signifies if, *quando*, in this passage, and the ו before the following וּמִי introduces the apodosis.—Vers. 11, 12. David said still
further to Abishai and all his servants : " Behold, my own son
seeketh after my life ; how much more then the Benjaminite !
(who belongs to a hostile race.) Let him curse, for Jehovah
hath bidden him. Perhaps Jehovah will look upon my guilt,
and Jehovah will requite me good for the curse which befals
me this day." בַּעֲוֹנִי (*Chethib*) has been altered by the Masoretes into בְּעֵינִי, " upon mine eye," probably in the sense of
" upon my tears ;" and קִלְלָתִי into קִלְלָתוֹ,—from pure misapprehension. בַּעֲוֹנִי does not mean "upon my misery," for עָוֹן never
has this meaning, but upon the guilt which really belongs to me,
in contrast with that with which Shimei charges me ; and קִלְלָתִי
is the curse that has come upon me. Although David had
committed no murder upon the house of Saul, and therefore
Shimei's cursing was nothing but malicious blasphemy, he felt
that it came upon him because of his sins, though not for
the sin imputed to him. He therefore forbade their putting
the blasphemer to death, and said Jehovah had commanded
him to curse ; regarding the cursing as the consequence of the
wrath of God that was bringing him low (comp. the remarks
on 1 Sam. xxvi. 19). But this consciousness of guilt also
excited the assurance that the Lord would look upon his sin.
When God looks upon the guilt of a humble sinner, He will
also, as a just and merciful God, avert the evil, and change
the suffering into a blessing. David founded upon this the
hope, that the Lord would repay him with good for the curse
with which Shimei was pursuing him now.—Ver. 13. " So
David went with his men on the way, whilst Shimei went on
the slope of the hill opposite to him, cursing continually, and
pelted with stones over against him, and with earth." לְעֻמָּתוֹ
means over against him in both instances. It is not expressly
stated that Shimei threw stones and earth at David, but this is
implied in the context.—Ver. 14. The king came with his train,
pursued in this manner, to Ayephim, and refreshed himself
there. The context requires that *Ayephim* should be taken as
the name of a place. If it were an appellative, signifying
weary, there would be no information as to the place to which

David came, and to which the word עָם (there) distinctly refers. Bahurim cannot be the place alluded to, for the simple reason that, according to ch. xvii. 18, the place where David rested was a considerable distance beyond Bahurim, towards the Jordan, as we may see from the fact that it is stated there that the priests' sons, who were sent to carry information to David of what was occurring in Jerusalem, hid themselves in a well at Bahurim from the officers who were following them, and consequently had to go still further in order to convey the news to David; so that it is out of the question to supply this name from ver. 5. It is true that we never meet with the name *Ayephim* again; but this applies to many other places whose existence is not called in question.[1]

ABSALOM'S ENTRANCE INTO JERUSALEM. ADVICE OF AHITHO-PHEL AND HUSHAI.—CHAP. XVI. 15–XVII. 23.

Vers. 15–23. When Absalom and "all the people, the men of Israel," *i.e.* the people who had joined him out of all the tribes of Israel (ch. xv. 10), came to Jerusalem, and Ahithophel with him, Hushai the Archite also came and greeted him warmly as king, by exclaiming again and again, "Long live the king!"—Vers. 17. sqq. Absalom, apparently astonished at this, said to him, "Is this thy love to thy friend (David)? why wentest thou not with thy friend?" But Hushai replied, "No; but whom Jehovah hath chosen, and this people (*i.e.* the people who had entered Jerusalem with Absalom), and all the men of Israel (*i.e.* the whole nation), to him (לֹא for לוֹ, *Keri*) will I belong, and will remain with him. And again, whom should I serve? Is it not before his son? As I have served thy father, so will I be before thee" (*i.e.* serve thee). With great craftiness, Hushai declared at the very outset that Jehovah had chosen Absalom—at least he could not come to any other conclusion, judging from the results. And under such circum-

---

[1] The meaning of the word, wearied or weariness, does not warrant any conjectures, even though they should be more felicitous than that of Böttcher, who proposes to alter *Ayephim* into *Ephraim*, and assumes that there was a place of this name near Mahanaim, though without reflecting that the place where David rested was on this side of the Jordan, and somewhere near to Gilgal or Jericho (ch. xvii. 16 sqq. and 22).

stances he could not have any doubt as to whom it was his duty to serve. As he had formerly served the father, so now he would serve his son Absalom. In this way he succeeded in completely deceiving Absalom, so that he placed unbounded confidence in him.—Ver. 20. After taking possession of the capital of the kingdom, the next thing to do was to form the resolution to take and keep the throne. Absalom therefore turned to Ahithophel, and said, "Give ye counsel what we are to do." The plural הָבוּ (give ye) may be explained on the supposition that the other persons present were addressed as well as Ahithophel, as being capable of giving advice.—Ver. 21. Ahithophel gave the following counsel : "Go to thy father's concubines, whom he hath left behind to keep the house (*i.e.* lie with them : for בּוֹא אֶל, compare ch. iii. 7, etc.) ; so will all Israel hear that thou hast made thyself stinking with thy father, and the hands of all those who are with thee will strengthen themselves." This advice was sagacious enough. Lying with the king's concubines was an appropriation of the royal harem, and, as such, a complete usurpation of the throne (see at ch. iii. 7), which would render any reconciliation between Absalom and his father utterly impossible, and therefore would of necessity instigate the followers of Absalom to maintain his cause with all the greater firmness. This was what Ahithophel hoped to attain through his advice. For unless the breach was too great to be healed, with the affection of David towards his sons, which might in reality be called weakness, it was always a possible thing that he should forgive Absalom ; and in that case Ahithophel would be the one to suffer. But under the superintendence of God this advice of Ahithophel was to effect the fulfilment, without any such intention on his part, of the threat held over David in ch. xii. 8.—Ver. 22. Absalom had a tent put up on the roof of the king's palace, that his going in to the concubines might be done publicly in the sight of all Israel. For (as the historian adds in ver. 23 by way of explanation) the counsel of Ahithophel, which he counselled in those days, was like a divine oracle both with David and with Absalom. The words from וַעֲצַת to הָהֵם are placed at the commencement absolutely : " and (as for) the counsel of Ahithophel, . . . as if one inquired the word of God, so was every counsel of Ahithophel." The Masoretes have supplied אִישׁ as the *Keri* to יִשְׁאַל. This is

correct so far as the sense is concerned, but it is quite unnecessary, as יִשְׁאַל may be taken impersonally. שָׁאַל בִּדְבַר הָאֱלֹהִים is to
be explained from the formula שָׁאַל בֵּאלֹהִים (see at Judg. i. 1).

Chap. xvii. 1-14. *Ahithophel's advice frustrated by Hushai.*
—Vers. 1-3. Ahithophel said still further to Absalom, " I will
choose out twelve thousand men, and arise, and pursue after
David this night ; and fall upon him when he is exhausted and
weak, and fill him with alarm · so shall all the people that are
with him flee ; and I will smite the king alone (when he is
alone), and will bring back all the people to thee." הַלַּיְלָה, *the*
night, is the night following the day of David's flight and
Absalom's entrance into Jerusalem, as we may see very clearly
from ver. 16. This advice was sagaciously conceived ; for if
David had been attacked that night by a powerful army, he
might possibly have been defeated. אָשִׁיבָה, *to bring back*,
may be explained on the supposition that Ahithophel regarded
Absalom as king, and those who had fled with David as rebels,
who were to be brought back under Absalom's sceptre. The
following words, כְּשׁוּב הַכֹּל וגו׳, " *as the return of the whole* (the
whole nation) *is the man*," *i.e.* the return of all is dependent
upon David, for whom thou liest in wait, are somewhat difficult,
though the meaning of Ahithophel is evident enough from what
precedes : viz. if he is beaten, they will all come over to thee ;
" the whole nation will be at peace " (שָׁלוֹם is used adverbially).[1]
—Vers. 4, 5. Although this advice pleased Absalom and all the
elders of Israel (present), Absalom sent for Hushai the Archite
to hear his opinion. נַם־הוּא serves to strengthen the suffix in
בְּפִיו (cf. Ewald, § 311, *a*).—Vers. 6, 7. In answer to Absalom's
inquiry, " Shall we do his word (*i.e.* follow Ahithophel's advice)
or not ?" Hushai said, " The advice is not good that Ahithophel
hath given this time ;" and then still further explained (ver. 8):

[1] Consequently no conjectures are needed as to the rendering of the
words in the Septuagint, viz. καθὼς (al. ὅν τρόπον) ἐπιστρέφει ἡ νύμφη πρὸς
τὸν ἄνδρα αὐτῆς· πλὴν ψυχὴν ἀνδρὸς ἑνός σὺ ζητεῖς, such as Ewald, Thenius,
and Böttcher have attempted. For 't is very obvious that ἡ νύμφη πρὸς
τὸν ἄνδρα αὐτῆς owes its origin simply to a false reading of הַכֹּל הָאִישׁ as
הַכַּלָּה אִישׁ, and that πλὴν ψυχὴν ἀνδρὸς ἑνός has been interpolated by way
of explanation from nothing but conjecture. No other of the ancient
versions contains the slightest trace of a different reading from that given
in the text.

" Thou knowest thy father and his men, that they are heroes,
and of a ferocious disposition (like Judg. xviii. 25), like a bear
in the field robbed of her young ; and thy father is a man of
war, and will not pass the night with the people," *sc.* so that it
would be possible to come upon him unawares and slay him (לִין
with אֶת, as in Job xix. 4). The idea that יָלִין is to be taken as
a *Hiphil*, in the sense of " and does not let the people lodge for
the night" (Böttcher), is quite untenable, since it does not tally
with ver. 9, " Behold, he is hid now in one of the pits, or one of
the places (פְּחָתִים are hiding-places that are strong by nature,
מְקוֹמֹת are places rendered strong by art) ; and it comes to pass
that he falls upon them at the first : so will men hear it, and
say a defeat has taken place among the people that follow
Absalom." נָפַל with בְּ, as in Josh. xi. 7, to fall upon a person.
The subject to נָפַל is David, but it is not mentioned as being
evident enough from the context ; so that there is no necessity
for the emendation נָפְלוּ, which Thenius proposes. The suffix
בָּהֶם relates to those making the attack, the hosts of Absalom.
Thenius has given the meaning correctly : " The report that
David has made an attack will be sufficient to give rise to the
belief that our men have sustained a severe defeat."—Ver. 10.
" And even if he (the hearer, ver. 9) be a brave man, who has a
lion's heart (lion-like courage), he will be thrown into despair ;
for all Israel knows that thy father is a hero, and brave men
(are those) who are with him."—Ver. 11. " Yea (כִּי, *profecto*),
I advise : let all Israel be gathered round thee from Dan to
Beersheba (see at Judg. xx. 1), numerous as the sand by the
sea ; and thou thyself go into the war." פָּנֶיךָ, thy person, *i.e.*
thou thyself be marching. The plural הֹלְכִים is used because of
פָּנֶיךָ. For הָלַךְ בְּ, to enter into anything, see 1 Kings xix. 4,
Isa. xlv. 16, xlvi. 2. קְרָב, war, the early translators have confounded with קֶרֶב.—Ver. 12. " And come we to him (if we
come upon him) in one of the places where he is found, we let
ourselves down upon him, as the dew falls upon the earth ; and
of him and all the men with him there will not be one left."
נַחְנוּ might be a contraction of אֲנַחְנוּ, as in Gen. xlii. 11, Ex.
xvi. 7, 8, etc. : " so we upon him," equivalent to " so shall we
come upon him." But if this were the meaning, we should
expect וְהָיִינוּ עָלָיו. It is more correct, therefore, to take נַחְנוּ as the
first pers. perf. of נוּחַ, as the early translators have done : so do we

let ourselves down upon him. (For נוּחַ as applied to an army encamping, see Isa. vii. 2, 19; and as denoting the swarming of flies
and grasshoppers, Isa. vii. 19 and Ex. x. 14.) In Ahithophel's
opinion, it would be possible with a very small army to crush
David and his little band, however brave his followers might
be, and in fact to annihilate them altogether.—Ver. 13. "And
if he draw back into a city, all Israel lays ropes to that city, and
we drag it to the brook, till there is not even a little stone found
there." עַד־הַנַּחַל : inasmuch as fortified cities were generally
built upon mountains. צְרוֹר signifies a little stone, according
to the ancient versions. Hushai speaks in hyperboles of the
irresistible power which the whole nation would put forth when
summoned together for battle, in order to make his advice
appear the more plausible.—Ver. 14. And he secured his end.
Absalom and all Israel thought his advice better than that of
Ahithophel; for it was intended to commend itself to Absalom
and his supporters. "The counsel appeared safe; at the same
time it was full of a certain kind of boasting, which pleased
the younger men" (Clericus). All that Hushai had said about
the bravery and heroism of David and his followers, was well
founded. The deception lay in the assumption that all the
people from Dan to Beersheba would crowd around Absalom as
one man; whereas it might easily be foreseen, that after the first
excitement of the revolution was over, and greater calmness
ensued, a large part of the nation and army would gather round
David. But such a possibility as this never entered the minds
of Absalom and his supporters. It was in this that the divine
sentence referred to in ver. 14b was seen: "The Lord had
commanded (appointed) it, to defeat the good counsel of Ahithophel, that he might bring the evil (intended) upon Absalom."

Vers. 15–23. *David is informed of what has occurred.*—
Vers. 15, 16. Hushai communicated without delay to the
priests Zadok and Abiathar the advice which had been given
to Absalom both by Ahithophel and himself, and requested
them to make it known to David as quickly as possible. "*Stay
not the night,*" he said, "*by the ferries* (עֲבְרוֹת, as in ch. xv. 28)
*of the desert; but rather go over, lest the king and all the people
with him be destroyed.*" וְגַם, "and indeed," or after a negative
clause, "but rather." יְבֻלַּע לַמֶּלֶךְ is either "there will be a
devouring," *i.e.* destruction, to the king, it will fall upon him;

or if we supply the subject from the previous clause עֲבוֹר תַּעֲבוֹר,
as Böttcher proposes, "that it (the crossing over) may not be
swallowed up or cut off from the king." There is nothing to
justify Ewald's explanation, "it (misfortune) is swallowed by
him." Hushai recommended of course an immediate crossing
of the Jordan; because he did not know whether Absalom
would really act upon his advice, although he had expressed
his approval of it, or whether he might not change his mind
and follow Ahithophel's counsel.—Ver. 17. "Jonathan and
Ahimaaz (the sons of the priests: ch. xv. 27) stood at the
Rogel spring (the present well of Job or Nehemiah, at the
south-east corner of Jerusalem: see at Job xv. 7), and the
maid-servant (of one of the high priests) went and told them
(Hushai's message), and they went and told it to king David;
for they durst not let themselves be seen to come into the city."
They had therefore been staying at the Rogel spring outside
the city. After what had taken place publicly, according to
ch. xv. 24 sqq., Absalom could not be in any doubt as to the
views of the high priests. Consequently their sons could not
come into the city, with the intention of leaving it again directly,
to inform David of the occurrences that had taken place there
as he had requested (ch. xv. 28). The clause "*and they went
and told David*" anticipates the course of the affair, according
to the general plan adopted by Hebrew historians, of communicating the result at the very outset wherever they possibly
could.—Ver. 18. "*And a lad* (servant) *saw them, and told
Absalom.*" Absalom had most likely set spies to watch the
priests and their sons. But the two sons who had noticed the
spy hurried into the house of a man at Bahurim, who had a
well (or cistern that was dry at the time) in his court, and
went down into the well.—Ver. 19. And the man's wife spread
a covering (הַמָּסָךְ, the covering which she had close at hand)
over the well (over the opening into the cistern), and scattered
groats (רִיפוֹת, peeled barley: Prov. xxvii. 22) upon it, so that
nothing was noticed. The Vulgate explanation is a very good
one: "*quasi siccans ptisanas*" (as if drying peeled barley).—
Ver. 20. When Absalom's servants came and asked for the
priest's sons, the woman said, They have gone over the little
water-brook (מִיכַל הַמָּיִם, *ἀπ. λεγ.*), and thus led them wrong, so
that they did not find them.—Vers. 21, 22. When they had

gone away, the priest's sons came up out of the well and brought David the news, saying, "Go quickly over the water, for thus hath Ahithophel counselled against you;" whereupon David and all the people with him went hastily over the Jordan. "Till the morning dawn not one was missed who had not gone over." עַד אֶחָד, *lit.* even to one there was not any one missed.—Ver. 23. It is still further stated in conclusion, that when Ahithophel saw that his advice was not carried out, he saddled his ass and returned to his home, and there set his house in order and hanged himself, because he could foresee that Absalom would lose his cause through not taking his advice, and it would then be all over with himself. Thus was David's prayer (ch. xv. 31) fulfilled.

ABSALOM'S DEFEAT AND DEATH.—CHAP. XVII. 24—XIX. 1.

The account of the civil war, which terminated with Absalom's defeat and death, is introduced in vers. 24–26 with a description of the relative position of the two hostile parties. David had come to Mahanaim, a city, probably a fortified one, on the east of the Jordan, not far from a ford of the Jabbok (see at ch. ii. 8). Absalom had also gone over the Jordan, "he and all the men with him," *i.e.* all the fighting men that he had gathered together according to Hushai's advice, and encamped in the land of Gilead.—Ver. 25. Absalom had made Amasa captain over his army instead of Joab, who had remained true to David, and had gone with his king to Mahanaim. Amasa was the son of a man named *Jithra*, הַיִּשְׂרְאֵלִי, who had gone in to (*i.e.* had seduced) Abigail, the daughter of Nahash and sister of Zeruiah, Joab's mother. He was therefore an illegitimate cousin of Joab. The description given of *Jithra* as יִשְׂרְאֵלִי is very striking, since there was no reason whatever why it should be stated that Amasa's father was an *Israelite*. The Seventy have therefore given ὁ Ἰεζραηλίτης, *i.e.* sprung from Jezreel, where David's wife Ahinoam came from (1 Sam. xxvii. 3); but they have done so apparently from mere conjecture. The true reading is evidently הַיִּשְׁמְעֵאלִי, an Ishmaelite, according to 1 Chron. ii. 17, where the name is written Jether, a contracted form of Jithra. From the description given of Abigail as a daughter of Nahash and sister of Zeruiah, not of David, some of the earlier commentators have very justly concluded that Abigail and Zeruiah were only step-sisters of David, *i.e.* daughters of his mother by Nahash and not by Jesse.—Vers. 27–29. When David came to Mahanaim, some of the wealthier citizens of the land to the east of the Jordan supplied the men who were with him with provisions. This is mentioned as the first sign that the people had not all fallen away from David, but that some of the more distinguished men were still firm in their adherence. *Shobi,* the son of Nahash of *Rabbah,* the capital of the Ammonites (see ch. xi. 1), was possibly a son of Nahash the deceased king of the Ammonites, and brother of Hanun, who was defeated by David (ch. x. 1, 2), and one of those to whom David had shown favour and kindness when Rabbah was taken. At the same time, it is also quite possible that *Shobi* may have been an Israelite, who was merely living in the capital of the Ammonites, which had been incorporated into the kingdom of David, as it is evident from ver. 25 that Nahash was not an uncommon name among the Israelites. *Machir* the son of Ammiel of *Lodebar* (see at ch. ix. 4), and *Barsillai* of *Roglim* the Gileadite. *Roglim* was a town in Gilead, which is only mentioned once again, viz. in ch. xix. 32, and of which nothing further is known. They brought " bedding, basins, earthenware, and wheat, barley, meal, and parched grains, beans, lentils and *parched.*" The position of the verb, which is not placed between the subject and the object of the sentence, but only at the close of the whole series of objects, is certainly unusual; but this does not warrant any alteration of the text. For if we were to supply a verb before מִשְׁכָּב, as having fallen out of the text, it would be necessary, since הַגִּישׁוּ follows without a copula, to divide the things enumerated into two classes, so as to connect one portion of the objects with הַגִּישׁוּ, which is obviously un-natural. The early translators who interpolate a verb before the objects have therefore also supplied the copula ו before הַגִּישׁוּ. There is still less ground for supplying the number 10, as having dropped out before מִשְׁכָּב and סַפּוֹת, as the LXX. have done, since none of the translators of the other ancient versions had any such reading. מִשְׁכָּב, couch or bed, is used here for bedding. סַפּוֹת, basins, probably field-kettles. The repetition of וְקָלִי is very striking; nevertheless the second must not be struck out without further ground as a supposed copyist's error. As they not only ate parched ears or grains of wheat (see at Lev. ii. 14), but were also in the habit of drying pulse, pease, and lentils before eating them (*vid.* Harmar, *Beobachtungen,* i. pp. 255-6), the second קָלִי may be understood as referring to parched pulse. The *ἀπ. λεγ.* שְׁפוֹת בָּקָר signifies, according to the Chaldee and the Rabbins, cheese of oxen (*i.e.* of cows), and according to the conjecture of Roediger (Ges. *Thes.* p. 1462), a peculiar kind of cheese, such as the *Aeneze* in the province of Nedjid still make,[1] and for which the term σαφὼθ βοῶν retained by the LXX. was probably the technical name. Theodotus, on the other hand, has γαλαθηνὰ μοσχάρια, milch-calves; and the Vulgate *pingues vitulos,*—both of them renderings which can certainly be sustained from the Arabic usage of speech, and would be more in accordance with the situation of the words, viz. after צָא. כִּי אָמְרוּ, " for they said (or thought) the people have become hungry and faint and thirsty in the desert," *i.e.* in their flight to Mahanaim.

Chap. xviii. 1-5. *Preparation for war.*—Vers. 1, 2. David mustered the people that were with him, and placed over them captains of thousands and hundreds, and divided them into three companies, under the generals Joab, Abishai, and Ittai the Gathite, who had given such decided proofs, according to ch. xv. 21, 22, of his fidelity to David. שִׁלַּח בְּיַד, to leave to the hand of a person, *i.e.* to his power, is used here in the sense of placing under his direction. The people opposed in the most decided manner the wish of the king to go with them to the war, saying (ver. 3), " Thou shalt not go out: for if we flee, they will take no heed of us (*i.e.* attach no importance to this) ; and if half of us die, they will take no heed of us : for thou art as ten thousand of us (we must evidently read אַתָּה for עַתָּה, and עַתָּה has merely got into the text in consequence of וְעַתָּה following) : and now it is good that thou be ready to give us help from the city" (the *Chethib* לַעְזִיר, *inf. Hiphil* for לְהַעֲזִיר, is not to be disputed). David was to stay behind in the city with a reserve,

---

[1] According to Burckhardt's account (*Die Beduinen,* p. 48), "after they have taken the butter from the butter-milk, they beat the latter again till it coagulates, and then dry it till it is quite hard. It is then rubbed to pieces, and in the spring every family stores up two or three lasts of it, which they eat mixed with butter."

that he might be able to come to their relief in case of need.—
Vers. 4, 5. The king gave his consent to these proposals, and
went to the side of the gate, whilst the people went out by
hundreds and thousands; but in the hearing of all he commanded the principal generals, " *Mildly for me* (*i.e.* deal gently
for my sake) *with the boy Absalom.*" לְאַט is not the imperative of לָאַט, to cover over, which would not suit the connection,
and could not be construed with לְ, but an adverb from אַט, as
in Isa. viii. 6, 1 Kings xxi. 27, Job xv. 11.

Vers. 6–18. *Battle in the wood of Ephraim, and death of
Absalom.*—Vers. 6, 7. When the people, *i.e.* David's army,
had advanced into the field against Israel (those who followed
Absalom), a battle was fought " in the wood of Ephraim,"
when Israel was smitten by David's warriors and sustained
a loss of 20,000 men. The question, where the " *wood of
Ephraim*" was situated, is a disputed one. But both the name
and the fact that, according to Josh. xvii. 15, 16, the tribe-
land of Ephraim abounded in forests, favour the idea that it
was a wood in the inheritance of Ephraim, on this side of the
Jordan; and this is in perfect harmony with the statement in
ver. 23, that Ahimaaz took the way of the Jordan valley to
bring the news of the victory to David, who was staying behind
in Mahanaim. Nevertheless the majority of commentators
have supposed that the place alluded to was a woody region on
the other side of the Jordan, which had received the name of
" wood Ephraim" probably after the defeat of the Ephraimites in the time of Jephthah (Judg. xii. 1–5). The reasons
assigned are, *first*, that according to ch. xvii. 26, Absalom had
encamped in Gilead, and it is not stated that he had crossed the
Jordan again; *secondly*, that ver. 3 (" that thou succour us out
of the city") presupposes that the battle took place in the
neighbourhood of Mahanaim (Thenius); and *thirdly*, that after
the victory the army returned to Mahanaim; whereas if the
battle had been fought on this side of the Jordan, it would
evidently have been much better for it to remain there and
occupy Jerusalem (Ewald, *Gesch.* iii. p. 237). But neither of
these reasons is decisive, and there is no force in the other
arguments employed by Thenius. There was no necessity for
an immediate occupation of Jerusalem by David's victorious
army, since all Israel fled to their tents after the fall of Absa-

lom and the defeat of his army (ver. 17 and ch. xix. 9) ; that
is to say, such of Absalom's followers as had not fallen in or
after the battle, broke up and returned home, and therefore the
revolution was at an end.　Consequently there was nothing
left for David's army to do but to return to its king at Mahanaim, and fetch him back to Jerusalem, and reinstate him in
his kingdom.　The other two reasons might have some force in
them, if the history before us contained a complete account of
the whole course of the war.　But even Ewald admits that it
is restricted to a notice of the principal battle, which completely
crushed the rebellion.　There can be no doubt, however, that
this was preceded, if not by other battles, yet by such military
operations as accompany every war.　This is clearly indicated
in ver. 6, where it is stated that the army advanced into the
field against Israel (ver. 6), which evidently refers to such an
advance on the part of David's army as might compel Absalom
to draw back from Gilead across the Jordan, until at length a
decisive battle was fought, which ended in the complete destruction of his army and his own death.　Ewald observes still
further, that " it seems impossible, at any rate so far as the
name is concerned, to assume that the wood of Ephraim was
on the other side of the Jordan, whilst according to ch. xviii.
23, the messenger who reported the victory went from the field
of battle towards the Jordan valley in order to get to David."
But the way in which Ewald tries to set aside this important
point, as bearing upon the conclusion that the battle took place
on this side of the Jordan,—namely, by adopting this rendering
of ver. 23, " he ran after the manner of *Kikkar*, running, and
therefore overtook *Kushi*,"—is far too unnatural to meet with
acceptance.　Under all these circumstances, therefore, we decide in favour of the assumption that the wood of Ephraim is
to be sought for in the tribe-territory of Ephraim.

　　The nature of the ground contributed a great deal to the
utter defeat of Absalom.—Ver. 8. The conflict extended over
the surface of the whole land, *i.e.* the whole of that region (the
Chethib נפצות is not the plural נְפֹצוֹת, which would be quite
unsuitable, but is most probably a noun, נְפֻצוּת, signifying bursting asunder, or wild flight; the *Keri* נָפֹצֶת is a *Niphal* participle,
fem. gen.) ; " and the wood devoured more of the people than
the sword ate on the same day."　The woody region was most

likely full of ravines, precipices, and marshes, into which the
flying foe was pursued, and where so many perished.—Ver. 9.
"And Absalom was lighted upon (יִקָּרֵא = יִקָּרֶה) by the servants
of David, riding upon the mule; and the mule had come under
the thick branches of the great terebinth, and his head fastened
itself (remained hanging) on the terebinth, so that he was held
(hung) between heaven and earth, as the mule under him went
away." The imperfects, וַיָּבֹא, וַיֶּחֱזַק, and וַיֻּתַּן, are only a combination of the circumstantial clause וְאַבְשָׁלֹם רֹכֵב. With regard to
the fact itself, it is not clearly stated in the words that Absalom hung only by his hair, but simply that his hair entangled
him in the thick branches, and his head was fastened in the
terebinth, namely, by being jammed between the strong boughs.
—Ver. 10. A man (one of David's men) saw him in this situation, and told Joab. Joab replied (ver. 11), "Behold, thou
hast seen it, and wherefore hast thou not smitten him there to
the ground? and it was for me to give thee ten silverlings and
a girdle;" *i.e.* if thou hadst slain him, it would have been my
duty to reward thee.—Ver. 12. But the man replied, "*And I
. . . not weighing a thousand shekels in my hand . . . might not
stretch out my hand to the king's son,*" *i.e.* I could not do it for
a reward of a thousand shekels. This is the meaning of the
Chethib וְלֹא; the Masoretes, on the other hand, have substituted וְלוֹ, which is the reading adopted in most of the ancient
versions, and the one preferred by the majority of expositors:
"if I weighed . . . I would not," etc. But there is no necessity
for this alteration, as the *Chethib* is quite in accordance with
the character of the words. "*For before our ears the king commanded*" (cf. ver. 5): שִׁמְרוּ מִי, "*take care whoever* (it be) *of the
boy Absalom.*" On this use of מִי, see Ewald, § 104 *d, a.* The
Keri לִי is merely a conjecture, notwithstanding the fact that all
the versions follow it, and that one of the Codices in Kennicott
has לִי. "*Or,*" continued the man (ver. 13), "*should I have
acted deceitfully towards his life* (*i.e.* have slain him secretly,
which he calls שֶׁקֶר, cheating, because it was opposed to the
king's open command): *and nothing remains hidden from the
king; . . . thou wouldst have set thyself in opposition to me,*" *i.e.*
have risen up against me before the king. The middle clause
is a circumstantial one, as the fact that וְכָל־דָּבָר is placed first
clearly shows; so that it cannot be regarded as introducing the

apodosis, which really follows in the clause commencing with וְאַתָּה.—Ver. 14. Joab replied, "*Not so will I wait before thee,*" *i.e.* I will not leave the thing to thee. He then took three staffs in his hand, and thrust them into Absalom's heart. שְׁבָטִים is rendered by the LXX. and Vulgate, βέλη, *lanceas;* and Thenius would adopt שְׁלָחִים accordingly, as an emendation of the text. But in the earlier Hebrew שֶׁלַח only occurs in poetical writings in the sense of a missile or dart (Job xxxiii. 18, xxxvi. 12; Joel ii. 8); and it is not till after the captivity that we find it used to denote a weapon generally. There is no necessity, however, for altering the text. Joab caught up in his hurry the first thing that he found, namely pointed staffs, and pierced Absalom with them to the heart. This explains the reason for his taking *three,* whereas one javelin or dart would have been sufficient, and also the fact that Absalom was not slain, notwithstanding their being thrust at his heart. The last clause of the verse belongs to what follows : " *Still living* (*i.e.* as he was still alive) *in the midst of the terebinth, ten young men, Joab's armour-bearers, surrounded him, and smote him to death.*"
—Ver. 16. Immediately afterwards Joab stopped any further pursuit, " for Joab spared the people," *i.e.* he wanted to spare them.—Ver. 17. But Absalom they cast into a great pit in the wood, and threw up over him a very large heap of stones, as an ignominious monument, like those thrown up over Achan (Josh. vii. 26) and the king of Ai (Josh. viii. 29). This was the end of Absalom and his rebellion. " All Israel (that had crowded round him) had fled, every one to his tent" (*i.e.* home: see at Deut. xvi. 7).—Ver. 18. Absalom had erected a monument to himself in the king's valley during his lifetime; " for he said, I have no son to preserve the remembrance of my name, and he called the monument by his own name ; and so it was called hand (memorial) of Absalom unto this day." The לָקַח before וַיַּצֶּב is apparently pleonastic; but it belongs to the diffuse and circumstantial character of the antiquated Hebrew diction (as in Num. xvi. 1). מַצֶּבֶת, a memorial of stone ; whether in the form of a column, or an obelisk, or a monolith, cannot be determined (*vid.* Gen. xxviii. 22, xxxi. 52). The king's valley, which received its name from the event narrated in Gen. xiv. 17, was two stadia from Jerusalem according to Josephus (*Ant.* vii. 10, 3), and therefore not " close to the

Dead Sea," or *in regione transjordanensi* (Ges. *Thes.* pp. 1045, 1377), or " in the Jordan valley in Ephraim" (Tuch and Winer). It was on the eastern side of Jerusalem, in the Kidron valley ; though Absalom's pillar, which ecclesiastical tradition has transferred thither, a monument about forty feet in height and pointed like a pyramid, is not of early Hebrew, but of Grecian origin. On the words " I have no son," see at ch. xiv. 27.

Vers. 19–32. *David is informed of the victory, and of the death of Absalom.*—Vers. 19, 20. Ahimaaz, the son of Zadok, wanted to carry the news to David, that Jehovah had " procured the king justice out of the hand of his enemies" (שָׁפַט with מִן is a pregnant expression signifying to procure justice and deliver out of) ; but Joab, knowing how David would receive the tidings of the death of Absalom, replied, " Thou art no man of good tidings to-day; thou shalt take the news on another day, not on this, even because (כִּי עַל־כֵּן, see at Gen. xviii. 5) the king's son is dead." The *Keri* כִּי עַל־כֵּן is to be preferred to the *Chethib* כִּי־עַל ; and כֵּן has no doubt been dropt out merely because of בֶּן which follows. The *Chethib* does not give any suitable sense ; for the absence of the article before מֵת is decisive against the explanation proposed by Maurer, viz. " for (tidings have to be carried) concerning the king's son dead." If מֵת were to be construed as an adverb with בֶּן־מֶלֶךְ, it would of necessity have the article.—Ver. 21. Joab therefore entrusted *the Cushite* with the duty of conveying to David the announcement of what had occurred. It cannot be decided with certainty whether הַכּוּשִׁי or *Cushi* is the proper name of an Israelite, or whether it signifies the " Cushite," *i.e.* a descendant of Cush. The form of the name rather favours the latter view, in which case it would suggest the idea of a Moorish slave in the service of Joab.— Vers. 22, 23. As Ahimaaz still expressed a wish to hasten to the king, even after Cushi had been sent, and could not be induced to relinquish his purpose by the repeated expostulations of Joab, the latter at length permitted him to run. And he ran so fast, that he got before Cushi. וִיהִי מָה : let whatever will happen. וּלְכָה is the pronoun " to thee," as in Gen. xxvii. 37, and not the imperative of הָלַךְ, " thou mayest go." The meaning is, " and there is no striking message for thee," no message that strikes the mark, or affects anything. We must supply

" he said" in thought before ver. 23. There was the less necessity to write it here (as in 1 Sam. i. 20), since it is perfectly obvious from the repetition of וַיְהִי מָה that it is Ahimaaz who is speaking. Ahimaaz then ran by the way of the plain, *i.e.* the way which lies through or across the plain of the Jordan. Now he could not possibly have taken this road, if the battle had been fought in a wood on the eastern side of the Jordan, and he had wanted to hurry from the scene of battle to Mahanaim; for in that case he would have taken a circuitous route two or three times the distance of the straight road, so that it would have been utterly impossible for him to get there before the Cushite, however quickly he might run. This notice therefore furnishes a decisive proof that the battle was fought upon the mountains of Ephraim, in the land to the west of the Jordan, since the straight road thence to Mahanaim would lie through the valley of the Jordan.—Ver. 24. David was sitting between the two gates of Mahanaim waiting for tidings of the result of the battle. The two gates are the outer and inner gate of the fortified city wall, between which there was a small court, where David was sitting. The watchman then went up to the roof of the gate by the wall, probably the outer gate in the city wall, and as he looked he saw a man running alone.— Ver. 25. When he announced this to the king, he said, " If he (is or comes) alone, there is good news in his mouth," namely, because several runners would have shown themselves if it had been a flight. As the first messenger came nearer and nearer, the watchman saw another man running, and shouted this into the gate (הַשֹּׁעֵר is wrongly pointed for הַשַּׁעַר, according to the LXX., Syr., and Vulgate); whereupon the king replied, " This is also a good messenger."—Ver. 27. When the watchman saw by the running of the first that it was Ahimaaz, recognising him probably by the swiftness of his running, and announced it to the king, he replied, " He is a good man, and cometh with good tidings," because Joab would not have selected him to bring any other than good news.—Ver. 28. Ahimaaz then called out to the king, " *Shalom*," *i.e. Hail!* and fell down before him to greet him reverentially, and said, " Blessed be Jehovah thy God, who hath given up the men that lifted up their hand against my lord the king."—Ver. 29. In answer to the king's inquiry, " Is it well with the young man Absalom?" Ahimaaz

replied, " I saw the great tumult (that arose) when Joab sent
off the king's servant, and thy servant, and know not what"
(*sc.* had occurred).   Ahimaaz spoke as if he had been sent off
before Absalom's fate had been decided or could be known.
"*The king's servant*" is the Cushite, whom Ahimaaz saw just
approaching, so that he could point to him.   *Joab* is the subject, which is sometimes written after the object in the case of
an infinitive construction (*vid.* Gesenius, § 133, 3 Anm.); and
the expression " thy servant" is a conventional one for " me"
(viz. Ahimaaz).—Ver. 30. And the king said, " Turn, and
stand here," that he might hear the further news from the
Cushite, who had just arrived.—Ver. 31. The Cushite said,
" Let my lord the king receive good tidings, for Jehovah hath
procured thee justice to-day out of the hand of all who have
risen up against thee" (cf. ver. 19).—Ver. 32. When asked
about the welfare of Absalom, the Cushite replied, " May it
happen to the enemies of my lord the king, and all who have
risen up against thee for evil (*i.e.* to do thee harm), as to the
young man."   The death of Absalom was indicated clearly
enough in these words.

Ver. 33. The king understood the meaning of the words.
He was agitated, and went up to the balcony of the gate (the
room above the entrance) and wept, and said, walking about,
" My son Absalom, my son, my son Absalom!   Oh that I
had died for thee, Absalom, my son, my son!"   To understand this passionate utterance of anguish, we must bear in
mind not only the excessive tenderness, or rather weakness, of
David's paternal affection towards his son, but also his anger
that Joab and his generals should have paid so little regard to
his command to deal gently with Absalom.   With the king's
excitable temperament, this entirely prevented him from taking
a just and correct view of the crime of his rebel son, which
merited death, and of the penal justice of God which had been
manifested in his destruction.

DAVID REINSTATED IN HIS KINGDOM.—CHAP. XIX. 1-39.

In his passionate and sinful sorrow on account of Absalom's
death, David not only forgot altogether what it was his duty to
do, in order to recover the affections of the people, so that Joab

was obliged to remind him of this duty which was binding upon him as king (vers. 1–8) ; but he even allowed himself to be carried away into the most inconsiderate measures (vers. 9–14), and into acts of imprudence and injustice (vers. 16–23, 24–30), which could not contribute to the strengthening of his throne, however much the affection with which he wished to reward the old man Barzillai for his faithful services (vers. 31–40) might show that the king was anxious to promote the welfare of his subjects.

Vers. 1–8. *David's mourning, and Joab's reproof.*—Vers. 1–6. When Joab was told that the king was mourning and weeping for Absalom, he went to him into the house to expostulate with him. Ver. 5 introduces the continuation of ver. 1 ; vers. 2–4 contain parenthetical sentences, describing the impression made upon the people by the king's mourning. Through the king's deep trouble, the salvation (the victory) upon that day became mourning for all the people who had fought for David, and they went by stealth into the city (יִתְגַּנֵּב לָבוֹא : they stole to come, came by stealth), "as people steal away who have covered themselves with shame, when they flee in battle."—Ver. 4. But the king had covered his face, and cried aloud, "My son Absalom," etc.—Ver. 5. Then Joab went into the house to the king, and said to him, "Thou hast shamed this day the faces of all thy servants who have saved thy life, and the life of thy sons and daughters, thy wives and concubines" (covered them with shame, by deceiving their hope that thou wouldest rejoice in the victory).—Ver. 6. לְאַהֲבָה, "to love" (*i.e.* in that thou lovest) " those who hate thee, and hatest those who love thee ; for thou hast given to know to-day (through thy conduct) that chiefs and servants (commanders and soldiers) are nothing (are worth nothing) ; for I have perceived to-day (or I perceive to-day) that if (לֹא for לוּ) Absalom were alive, and we had all perished, that it would be right in thine eyes."—Ver. 7. "And now rise up, go out and speak to the heart of thy servants (*i.e.* speak to them in a friendly manner : Gen. xxxiv. 3, l. 21, etc.) : for I swear by Jehovah, if thou go not out, verily not a man will stay with thee to-night ; and this will be worse to thee than all the evil that has come upon thee from thy youth until now." Joab was certainly not only justified, but bound in David's own interests, to expostulate with him upon his conduct, and to urge

him to speak in a friendly manner to the people who had exposed their lives for him, inasmuch as his present conduct would
necessarily stifle the affection of the people towards their king,
and might be followed by the most serious results with reference to his throne.   At the same time, he did this in so heart-
less and lordly a manner, that the king could not fail to be
deeply hurt by his words.—Ver. 8. Nevertheless David was
obliged to yield to his representations.   " *The king rose up, and
sat in the gate, and . . . all the people came before the king,*" *i.e.*
the troops marched before the king, who (as we may supply from
the context) manifested his good-will in both looks and words.
But Israel, *i.e.* that portion of the people which had followed
Absalom, had returned to its tents (*i.e.* gone home: cf. ch. xviii.
17).   This sentence forms the transition to the account which
follows.

Vers. 9–14. *Preliminaries to the return of David to Jerusalem.*—Vers. 9, 10. As the rebellion was entirely crushed by
Absalom's death, and the dispersion of his followers to their
respective homes, there arose a movement among all the tribes
in favour of David.   " All the people were disputing (נָדוֹן, casting reproaches at one another) in all the tribes of Israel, saying,
The king has saved us out of the hand of our enemies, . . .
and now he is fled out of the land before Absalom.   But
Absalom, whom we anointed over us, is dead in battle; and
now why do ye keep still, to bring back the king?"   This
movement arose from the consciousness of having done an injustice to the king, in rising up in support of Absalom.—Vers.
11, 12. When these words of all Israel were reported to David,
he sent to the priests Zadok and Abiathar, saying, "Speak to
the elders of Judah, why will ye be the last to bring back the
king to his palace? . . . Ye are my brethren, my bones and
flesh (*i.e.* my blood relations): why then," etc.?   The last
clause of ver. 11, " *the speech of all Israel is come to the king,
even to his house,*" is a circumstantial clause inserted in the
midst of David's words, to explain the appeal to the men of
Judah not to be the last.   In the LXX., and some Codices of
the Vulgate, this sentence occurs twice, viz. at the end of ver.
10, and also of ver. 11; and Thenius, Ewald, and Böttcher
regard the clause at the end of ver. 10 as the original one, and
the repetition of it at the close of ver. 11 as a gloss.   But this

is certainly a mistake : for if the clause, " and the speech of all Israel came to the king to his house (at Mahanaim)," ought to stand at the close of ver. 10, and assigns the reason for David's sending to Zadok and Abiathar, ver. 11 would certainly, or rather necessarily, commence with וַיִּשְׁלַח הַמֶּלֶךְ : " The word of all Israel came to the king, and then king David sent," etc. But instead of this, it commences with וְהַמֶּלֶךְ דָּוִד שָׁלַח, " But king David sent." This construction of the sentence decidedly favours the correctness of the Hebrew text; whereas the text of the Septuagint, apart altogether from the tautological repetition of the whole of the sentence in question, shows obviously enough that it is nothing more than a conjecture, by which the attempt was made to remove the difficulty occasioned by the striking position in which the circumstantial clause occurred. —Ver. 13. " And say ye to Amasa, Art thou not my bone and flesh ? so shall God do to me, and so add, if thou shalt not be prince of the army (chief captain) before me continually in the place of Joab."—Ver. 14. Thus he (David) inclined the heart of all the people as of one man, and they sent to the king, saying, " Return thou, with all thy servants." The result of David's message to the priests is given summarily here. The subject to וַיֵּט is David, not Amasa or Zadok. So far as the fact itself is concerned, it was certainly wise of David to send to the members of his own tribe, and appeal to them not to be behind the rest of the tribes in taking part in his restoration to the kingdom, lest it should appear as though the tribe of Judah, to which David himself belonged, was dissatisfied with his victory, since it was in that tribe that the rebellion itself first broke out ; and this would inevitably feed the jealousy between Judah and the rest of the tribes. But it was not only unwise, but unjust, to give to Amasa, the traitor-general of the rebels, a promise on oath that he should be commander-in-chief in the place of Joab ; for even if the promise was only given privately at first, the fact that it had been given could not remain a secret from Joab very long, and would be sure to stir up his ambition, and lead him to the commission of fresh crimes, and in all probability the enmity of this powerful general would become dangerous to the throne of David. For however Joab might have excited David's anger by slaying Absalom, and by the offensive manner in which he had reproved the king for giving way to his grief,

David ought to have suppressed his anger in his existing circumstances, and ought not to have rendered evil for evil,
especially as he was not only about to pardon Amasa's crime,
but even to reward him as one of his faithful servants.

Vers. 15–30. *Return of the king ; and occurrences at the
crossing of the Jordan.*—Vers. 15–23. *Pardon of Shimei.*—
Vers. 15, 16. When David reached the Jordan on his return,
and Judah had come to Gilgal "to meet him, to conduct the
king over the Jordan," *i.e.* to form an escort at the crossing,
Shimei the Benjaminite hastened down from Bahurim (see ch.
xvi. 5 sqq.) with the men of Judah to meet David.—Vers. 17
sqq. There also came along with Shimei a thousand men of Benjamin, and Ziba the servant of the house of Saul, with his fifteen
sons and twenty servants (see ch. ix. 10); and they went over the
Jordan before the king, viz. through a ford, and the ferry-boat
had crossed over to carry over the king's family, and to do
whatever seemed good to him, *i.e.* to be placed at the king's
sole disposal. And Shimei fell down before the king, בְּעָבְרוֹ,
i.e. "*when he* (David) *was about to cross over the Jordan,*" not
" when Shimei had crossed over the Jordan ;" for after what
has just been stated, such a remark would be superfluous :
moreover, it is very doubtful whether the infinitive with בְּ can
express the sense of the pluperfect. Shimei said, " Let not my
lord impute to me any crime, and do not remember how thy
servant hath sinned."—Ver. 20. " For thy servant knoweth
(*i.e.* I know) that I have sinned, and behold I have come to-day
the first of the whole house of Joseph, to go to meet my lord
the king." By "*the whole house of Joseph*" we are to understand the rest of the tribes with the exception of Judah, who
are called "*all Israel*" in ver. 12. There is no reason for
the objection taken by Thenius and Böttcher to the expression
בֵּית־יוֹסֵף. The rendering of the LXX. (παντὸς Ἰσραὴλ καὶ
οἴκου Ἰωσήφ) does not prove that כָּל־יִשְׂרָאֵל was the original
reading, but only that the translator thought it necessary to
explain οἴκου Ἰωσήφ by adding the gloss παντὸς Ἰσραὴλ ;
and the assertion that it was only in the oratorical style of a
later period, when the kingdom had been divided, that Joseph
became the party name of all that were not included in Judah,
is overthrown by 1 Kings xi. 28. The designation of the tribes
that opposed Judah by the name of the leading tribe (*Joseph :*

Josh. xvi. 1) was as old as the jealousy between these tribes and Judah, which did not commence with the division of the kingdom, but was simply confirmed thereby into a permanent distinction. Shimei's prayer for the forgiveness of his sin was no more a proof of sincere repentance than the reason which he adduced in support of his petition, namely that he was the first of all the house of Joseph to come and meet David. Shimei's only desire was to secure impunity for himself. Abishai therefore replied (ver. 21), " Shall not Shimei be put to death for this (תַּחַת זאֹת, for this, which he has just said and done), because he hath cursed the anointed of Jehovah ? " (*vid.* ch. xvi. 5 sqq.) But David answered (ver. 22), " What have I to do with you, ye sons of Zeruiah (cf. ch. xvi. 10), for ye become opponents to me to-day ? " שָׂטָן, *an opponent*, who places obstacles in the way (Num. xxii. 22) ; here it signifies one who would draw away to evil. " Should any one be put to death in Israel to-day ? for do I not know that I am this day king over Israel ? " The reason assigned by David here for not punishing the blasphemer as he had deserved, by taking away his life, would have been a very laudable one if the king had really forgiven him. But as David when upon his death-bed charged his successor to punish Shimei for this cursing (1 Kings ii. 8, 9), the favour shown him here was only a sign of David's weakness, which was not worthy of imitation, the more especially as the king swore unto him (ver. 24) that he should not die.

Vers. 24–30. *David's conduct towards Mephibosheth* admits still less of justification.—Ver. 24. Mephibosheth, the son, *i.e.* grandson, of Saul, had also come down (from Jerusalem to the Jordan) to meet David, and had not " *made his feet and his beard,*" *i.e.* had not washed his feet or arranged his beard (עָשָׂה, as in Deut. xxi. 12), and had not washed his clothes—all of them signs of deep mourning (cf. Ezek. xxiv. 17)—since the day that the king had gone (*i.e.* had fled from Jerusalem) until the day that he came (again) in peace.—Ver. 25. " *Now when Jerusalem* (*i.e.* the inhabitants of the capital) *came to meet the king,*" [1] David said to him (*i.e.* to Mephibosheth, who was

---

[1] Dathe and Thenius propose to alter יְרוּשָׁלַיִם into מִירוּשָׁלַיִם (*from Jerusalem*), from a simple misunderstanding of the true meaning of the words ; for, as Böttcher has observed, the latter (*from* Jerusalem) would

with the deputation from the capital which welcomed David at the Jordan), "*Why wentest thou not with me, Mephibosheth?*" David was justified in putting this question after what Ziba, had told him concerning Mephibosheth (ch. xvi. 3).—Ver. 26. Mephibosheth replied, "My lord king, my servant hath deceived me : for thy servant thought I will have the ass saddled and go to the king; for thy servant is lame." If we understand אֶחְבְּשָׁה as signifying that Mephibosheth had the ass saddled by a servant, and not that he saddled it with his own hands, the meaning is obvious, and there is no ground whatever for altering the text. חָבַשׁ is certainly used in this sense in Gen. xxii. 3, and it is very common for things to be said to be done by a person, even though not done with his own hands. The rendering adopted by the LXX. and Vulgate, "Thy servant said to him (the servant), Saddle me the ass," is not true to the words, though correct so far as the sense is concerned. —Vers. 27, 28. "And he (Ziba) slandered thy servant to my lord the king." Mephibosheth had not merely inferred this from David's words, and the tone in which they were spoken, but had certainly found it out long ago, since Ziba would not delay very long to put David's assurance, that all the possessions of Mephibosheth should belong to him, in force against his master, so that Mephibosheth would discover from that how Ziba had slandered him. "And my lord the king is as the angel of God," *i.e.* he sees all just as it really is (see at ch. xiv. 17); "and do what is good in thy sight : for all my father's house (the whole of my family) were but men of death against my lord the king (*i.e.* thou mightest have had us all put to death), and thou didst set thy servant among thy companions at table

be quite superfluous, as it is already contained in the previous יָרַד. But Böttcher's emendation of בָּא into בָּאָה, because Jerusalem or the population of Jerusalem is a feminine notion, is equally unnecessary, since towns and lands are frequently construed as masculines when the inhabitants are intended (*vid.* Ewald, § 318, *a*). On the other hand, the rendering adopted by the LXX., and by Luther, Michaelis, and Maurer, in which יְרוּשָׁלַיִם is taken as an accusative in the sense of "when Mephibosheth came to Jerusalem to meet the king," is altogether wrong, and has been very properly given up by modern expositors, inasmuch as it is at variance not only with the word יָרַד, but also with ch. xvi. 3 and ix. 13, where Mephibosheth is said to have lived in Jerusalem.

(see ch. ix. 7, 11); and what right or (what) more have I still to cry (for help) to the king?" The meaning is, "I cannot assert any claims, but will yield to anything you decide concerning me." It must have been very evident to David from these words of Mephibosheth, that he had been deceived by Ziba, and that he had formed an unfounded prejudice against Mephibosheth, and committed an act of injustice in handing over his property to Ziba. He therefore replied, in evident displeasure (ver. 29), "Why talkest thou still of thine affairs? I have said, thou and Ziba shall divide the field?" to which Mephibosheth answered (ver. 30), "He may take the whole, since my lord the king has returned in peace to his own house." This reply shows very clearly that an injustice had been done to Mephibosheth, even if it is not regarded as an expression of wounded feeling on the part of Mephibosheth because of David's words, but, according to the view taken by Seb. Schmidt and others, as a vindication of himself, as said not to blame the king for the opinion he had formed, but simply to defend himself. But this completely overthrows the opinion held by Thenius and O. v. Gerlach, that David's words in ver. 30 contain nothing more than a revocation of his hasty declaration in ch. xvi. 4, and a confirmation of his first decision in ch. ix. 7 10, and are to be understood as signifying, "Let everything be as I settled it at first; hold the property jointly," inasmuch as Ziba and his sons had of course obtained their living from the produce of the land. Moreover, the words "thou and Ziba divide the land" are directly at variance with the promise in ch. ix. 7, "I will restore thee *all* the land of Saul thy father," and the statement in ch. ix. 9, "I have given unto thy master's son all that pertained to Saul, and to all his house." By the words, "*I have said, thou and Ziba divide the land,*" David retracted the hasty decree in ch. xvi. 4, so as to modify to some extent the wrong that he had done to Mephibosheth, but he had not courage enough to retract it altogether. He did not venture to dispute the fact that Mephibosheth had really been calumniated by Ziba, which was placed beyond all doubt by his mourning during the whole period of David's flight, as described in ver. 24. There is no ground for Winer's statement, therefore, that "it is impossible now to determine whether Mephibosheth was really innocent or not."

Vers. 31–39. *Barzillai comes to greet David.*—Ver. 31. Barzillai the octogenarian " had also come down from Roglim and gone across the Jordan with the king, to escort him over the river." אֶת־בַּיַּרְדֵּן is the portion in, or over, the Jordan. אֶת is the sign of the accusative, " the piece in the Jordan," and no further. This is the correct explanation as given by Böttcher, after Gesenius and Maurer ; and the *Keri* הַיַּרְדֵּן is a bad emendation.—Vers. 32, 33. As Barzillai had supplied the king with provisions during his stay in Mahanaim (שִׂיבָה for שִׂיבָה, like צוֹאָה for יְצוֹאָה, and other words of the same kind), because he was very wealthy (*lit.* great), David would gladly have taken him with him to Jerusalem, to repay him there for his kindness ; but Barzillai replied (vers. 34 sqq.), " How many days are there of the years of my life (*i.e.* how long shall I have yet to live), that I should go up with the king to Jerusalem ? I am now eighty years old ; can I (still) distinguish good and evil, or will thy servant taste what I eat and drink, or listen again to the voice of the singing men and singing women ? and why should thy servant be yet a burden unto my lord the king ? Thy servant would go over the Jordan with the king for a short time (*i.e.* could not remain long with him), and why does the king wish to repay me this favour ?" יָשָׁב־נָא : " Let thy servant return, that I may die in my city (my home), at the grave of my parents ; and behold thy servant Chimham (*i.e.* according to the explanation given by Josephus, Barzillai's son, who had come down with his father, as we may infer from 1 Kings ii. 7) may go over with my lord the king ; and do to him what seemeth good to thee," *i.e.* show him favours at thy pleasure.—Ver. 38. David consented to this, and said, " All that thou desirest of me I will do to him." בָחַר with עַל is a pregnant construction, signifying to choose and impose, " *choose upon me*," *i.e.* the thing for me to grant thee.—Ver. 39. Thus all the people went over the Jordan ; and when the king had crossed over, he kissed Barzillai (to take leave of him : *vid.* Ruth i. 9) ; and he (Barzillai) blessed him, and turned to his place (returned home). Barzillai only escorted the king over the Jordan, and the conversation (vers. 31–38) probably took place as they were crossing.

DISCONTENT IN ISRAEL, AND SHEBA'S REBELLION.—
CHAP. XIX. 40–XX. 26.

Vers. 40–43. *Quarrel between Israel and Judah about the restoration of the king.*—Ver. 40. David went across to Gilgal (in the plain of the Jordan: Josh. iv. 19), and Chimham (*Chimhan* is a modified form for *Chimham* : ver. 37) had gone over with him, and all the people of Judah had brought the king over (the *Keri* הֶעֱבִירוּ is an easier reading than the *Chethib* וַיַּעֲבִירוּ, "and as for the people, they had," etc.), and also "half the people of Israel," namely, beside the thousand Benjaminites who came with Shimei (ver. 17), other Israelites who dwelt in the neighbourhood.—Ver. 41. *All the men of Israel, i.e.* the representatives of the other tribes of Israel, came to meet the king in Gilgal ; and being annoyed at the fact that the men of Judah had anticipated them, they exclaimed, "Why have our brethren the men of Judah stolen thee away?" *i.e.* fetched thee thus secretly without saying a word to us. "*All David's men*" were all his faithful adherents who had fled with him from Jerusalem (ch. xv. 17 sqq.).—Ver. 42. The men of Judah replied against (עַל) the men of Israel: "The king stands near to us" (inasmuch as he belonged to their tribe), "and wherefore then art thou angry at this matter? Have we eaten from the king (*i.e.* derived any advantage from our tribe-relationship to him, as the Benjaminites did from Saul, according to 1 Sam. xxii. 7), or received anything for ourselves therefrom?" נִשֵּׂאת is an infinitive *abs. Niph.* with a feminine termination, borrowed from לֵ״ה; literally, "*or has taking been taken for us.*"—Ver. 43. The Israelites were annoyed at this answer, and retorted, "I (Israel) have ten portions in the king, and also more than thou in David ; and wherefore hast thou despised me?" They considered that they had ten shares in the king, because they formed ten tribes, in opposition to the one tribe of Judah, as the Levites did not come into considera-tion in the matter. Although David was of the tribe of Judah, he was nevertheless king of the whole nation, so that the ten tribes had a larger share than one tribe. הֲקִלֹּתַנִי refers to the fact, that Judah took no notice at all of the tribes of Israel when fetching back the king. וְלֹא־הָיָה וגו׳, "*and was not my speech the first to fetch back my king?*" (On the fact itself, see ch. xix. 10, 11.) לְ is an emphatic *dat. commodi*, and is to be taken in connection with לְהָשִׁיב, notwithstanding the accents. "And the speech of the men of Judah became fiercer (more violent) than the speech of the men of Israel." With these words the historian sums up briefly the further progress of the dispute, for the purpose of appending the account of Sheba's rebellion, to which it gave rise.

Chap. xx. 1–22. SHEBA'S REBELLION.—Ver. 1. There happened to be a worthless man there, named *Sheba*, a Benjaminite. He blew the trumpet, and said, "We have no part in David, nor inheritance in the son of Jesse. Every man to his tents, O Israel!" "*To his tents*," *i.e.* to his home, as in ch. xix. 9, etc.—Ver. 2. All the men of Israel responded to this call, and went up (to the mountains) away from David and after Sheba; but the men of Judah adhered to their king from the Jordan to Jerusalem. The construction of דָּבַק with וְעַד . . . מִן is a pregnant one: they adhered to and followed him. The expression "*from Jordan*" does not prove that Sheba's rebellion broke out at the Jordan itself, and before David's arrival in Gilgal, but may be accounted for from the fact that the men of Judah had already fetched the king back across the Jordan.—Ver. 3. As soon as David returned to his palace at Jerusalem, he brought the ten concubines whom he had left behind, and with whom Absalom had lain, into a place of safety, and took care of them, without going in unto them any more. The masculine suffixes attached to יִתְּנֵם, יְכַלְכְּלֵם, and אֲלֵיהֶם are used, as they frequently are, as being the more general and indefinite, instead of the feminine, which is the more definite form. Thus were they shut up in lifelong widowhood until the day of their death. אַלְמְנוּת is an adverbial accusative, and חַיּוּת signifies "condition in life;" literally, in widowhood of life.—Ver. 4. David then ordered Amasa to call the men of Judah to pursue Sheba the rebel, and attack him within three days, and then to present himself to him again. This commission was intended as the commencement of the fulfilment of the promise which David had given to Amasa (ch. xix. 14). It was no doubt his intention to give him the command over the army that marched against Sheba, and after the defeat of the rebel to make him commander-in-chief. But this first step towards the fulfilment

ﬡ the promise was a very imprudent act, like the promise itself,
since Joab, who had been commander of the army for so many
years, was grievously offended by it; and moreover, being a
well-tried general, he had incomparably more distinction in the
tribe of Judah than Amasa, who had taken part in Absalom's
rebellion and even led the rebel army, could possibly have.—
Vers. 5, 6. But when Amasa stayed out beyond the time fixed
for the execution of the royal commission (the *Chethib* וייחר is
the *Piel* וַיְיַחֵר, whilst the *Keri* is either the *Hiphil* וַיֹּיחֶר, or the
imperfect *Kal* of יָחַר = אָחַר, cf. תֵּחַז, ver. 9, and is quite unnecessary), probably because the men of Judah distrusted him,
and were not very ready to respond to his summons, David
said to Abishai, "Now will Sheba the son of Bichri be more
injurious (more dangerous) to us than Absalom. Take thou
the servants (soldiers) of thy lord and pursue after him, lest he
reach fortified cities, and *tear out our eye*," *i.e.* do us a serious
injury. This is the correct explanation given by Böttcher, who
refers to Deut. xxxii. 10 and Zech. ii. 12, where the apple of
the eye is the figure used to signify the most valuable possession; for the general explanation, "and withdraw from our
eye," cannot be grammatically sustained.—Ver. 7. *Thus there
went after him* (Abishai) *Joab's men.* (the corps commanded by
Joab), *and the Crethi and Plethi* (see at ch. viii. 18), out of
Jerusalem, to pursue Sheba.—Ver. 8. "When they were by the
great stone at Gibeon, and Amasa came to meet them (there),
Joab was girded with his armour-coat as his clothing, and the
girdle of the sword was bound over it upon his loins in its
sheath, which came out, and it fell (*i.e.* the sheath came out
of the sword-belt in which it was fastened, and the sword fell
to the ground), Joab said to Amasa," etc. The eighth verse
contains only circumstantial clauses, the latter of which (from
וְיוֹאָב onwards) are subordinate to the earlier ones, so that וַיֹּאמֶר
(ver. 9) is attached to the first clause, which describes the
meeting between the advancing army and Amasa.

There is something striking, however, in the fact that Joab
appears among them, and indeed, as we see from what follows,
as the commander of the forces; for according to ver. 6, David
had commissioned Abishai, Joab's brother, to pursue Sheba,
and even in ver. 7 Joab's men only are mentioned. This difficulty can hardly be solved in any other manner than by the

simple assumption that David had told Abishai to go out with Joab, and that this circumstance is passed over in the brief account in ver. 6, in which the principal facts alone are given, and consequently the name of Joab does not occur there. Clericus adopts the following explanation. "Mention," he says, "has hitherto been made simply of the command given to Abishai, but this included an order to Joab to go as well; and there is nothing to preclude the supposition that Joab's name was mentioned by the king, although this is not distinctly stated in the brief account before us."[1]—Ver. 9. Joab asked Amasa how he was, and laid hold of his beard with his right hand to kiss him. And as Amasa took no heed of the sword in Joab's hand, he smote him with it in the paunch (abdomen), and shed out his bowels upon the ground, " *and repeated not* (the stroke) *to him*" (cf. 1 Sam. xxvi. 8). Laying hold of the beard to kiss is still customary among Arabs and Turks as a sign of friendly welcome (*vid.* Arvieux, *Merkwürdige Nachrichten,* iv. p. 182, and Harmar, *Beobachtungen,* ii. p. 61). The reason for this assassination was Joab's jealousy of Amasa. Joab and Abishai then followed Sheba.—Ver. 11. One of Joab's attendants remained standing by him (Amasa), no doubt at Joab's command, and said to the people who came thither, *i.e.* to the men of Judah who were collected together by Amasa (*vid.* ver. 4), " He that favoureth Joab, and he that (is) for David, let him (go) after Joab," *i.e.* follow him to battle against Sheba.— Vers. 12, 13. Amasa lay wallowing in blood in the midst of the road; and when the man (the attendant) saw that all the

---

[1] This difficulty cannot be removed by emendations of the text, inasmuch as all the early translators, with the exception of the Syriac, had our Hebrew text before them. Thenius does indeed propose to alter *Abishai* into *Joab* in ver. 6, after the example of Josephus and the Syriac; but, as Böttcher observes, if *Joab* had originally formed part of the text, it could not have been altered into Abishai either accidentally or intentionally, and the Syriac translators and Josephus have inserted *Joab* merely from conjecture, because they inferred from what follows that Joab's name ought to be found here. But whilst this is perfectly true, there is no ground for Böttcher's own conjecture, that in the original text ver. 6 read as follows: " Then David said to Joab, Behold, the three days are gone : shall we wait for Amasa ?" and through the copyist's carelessness a whole line was left out. For this conjecture has no tenable support in the senseless reading of the *Cod. Vat.,* πρὸς 'Αμεσσαΐ for 'Αβισαΐ.

people stood still (by the corpse), he turned (pushed) Amasa from the road to the field, and threw a cloth over him, whereupon they all passed by and went after Joab.—Ver. 14. But Joab "went through all the tribes of Israel to Abela, and Beth-Maacah, and all Berim." *Abela* (ver. 15), or *Abel* (ver. 18), has been preserved in the large Christian village of *Abil*, a place with ruins, and called *Abil-el-Kamh* on account of its excellent wheat (*Kamh*), which lies to the north-west of Lake Huleh, upon a Tell on the eastern side of the river *Derdâra;* not in *Ibl-el-Hawa*, a place to the north of this, upon the ridge between *Merj Ayun* and *Wady et Teim* (*vid.* Ritter, *Erdk.* xv. pp. 240, 241; Robinson, *Bibl. Researches*, pp. 372 3; and v. de Velde, *Mem.* p. 280). *Beth-Maacah* was quite close to Abela; so that the names of the two places are connected together in ver. 15, and afterwards, as *Abel-Beth-Maacah* (*vid.* 1 Kings xv. 20, and 2 Kings xv. 29), also called *Abel-Maim* in 2 Chron. xvi. 4. *Berim* is the name of a district which is unknown to us; and even the early translators did not know how to render it. There is nothing, however, either in the πάντες ἐν χαρρί of the LXX or the *omnes viri electi* of the Vulgate, to warrant an alteration of the text. The latter, in fact, rests upon a mere conjecture, which is altogether unsuitable; for the subject to וַיִּקָּהֲלוּ cannot be כָּל־הַבֵּרִים on account of the *vav consec.*, but must be obtained from בְּכָל־שִׁבְטֵי יִשְׂרָאֵל. The *Chethib* ויקלהו is evidently a slip of the pen for וַיִּקָּהֲלוּ.—Ver. 15. They besieged him (Sheba) in Abel-Beth-Maacah, and *piled up a rampart against the city*, so that *it rose up by the town-moat* (חֵל, the moat with the low wall belonging to it); and *all the people with Joab destroyed to throw down the wall.*

Vers. 16 sqq. Then a wise woman of the city desired to speak to Joab, and said (from the wall) to him (ver. 18), " They were formerly accustomed to say, ask Abel; and so they brought (a thing) to pass." These words show that Abel had formerly been celebrated for the wisdom of its inhabitants. —Ver. 19. " I am of the peaceable, faithful in Israel: thou seekest to slay a city and mother in Israel; wherefore wilt thou destroy the inheritance of Jehovah?" The construing of אָנֹכִי with a predicate in the plural may be explained on the simple ground that the woman spoke in the name of the city as well as in its favour, and therefore had the citizens in her mind at

the time, as is very evident from the figurative expression אֵם
(mother) for mother-city or capital.[1] The woman gave Joab
to understand, in the first place, that he ought to have asked
the inhabitants of Abela whether they intended to fight for
Sheba before commencing the siege and destruction of the
town, according to the law laid down in Deut. xx. 10 sqq. with
reference to the siege of foreign towns; and secondly, that he
ought to have taken into consideration the peaceableness and
fidelity of the citizens of Abela, and not to destroy peace-
loving citizens and members of the nation of God.—Ver. 20.
The woman's words made an impression upon Joab. He felt
the truthfulness of her reproaches, and replied, "Far be it, far
be it from me, to swallow up or destroy." אֵם, as in the case of
oaths: "*truly not*."—Ver. 21. "It is not so (*sc.* as thou sayest),
but a man of the mountains of Ephraim (which extended into
the tribe of Benjamin: see at 1 Sam. i. 1), Sheba the son of
Bichri, hath lifted up his hand against the king David. Only
give him up, and I will draw away from the city." The woman
promised him this: "Behold, his head shall be thrown out to
thee over the wall."—Ver. 22. She then came to all the people
(*i.e.* the citizens of the town) "*with her wisdom*," *i.e.* with the
wise counsel which she had given to Joab, and which he had
accepted; whereupon the citizens cut off Sheba's head, and
threw it out to Joab. Then Joab had a trumpet blown for a
retreat, and the men disbanded, whilst he himself returned to
Jerusalem to the king.

Vers. 23–26. DAVID'S MINISTERS OF STATE.—The second
section of the history of David's reign closes, like the first (ch.
viii. 16 sqq.), with a list of the leading ministers of state. The
author evidently found the two lists in his sources, and included

---

[1] The correctness of the text is not to be called in question, as Thenius
and Böttcher suppose, for the simple reason that all the older translators
have followed the Hebrew text, including even the LXX. with their ἐγώ
εἰμι εἰρηνικὰ τῶν στηριγμάτων ἐν Ἰσραήλ; whereas the words ἃ ἔθεντο οἱ
πιστοὶ τοῦ Ἰσραήλ, which some of the MSS. contain at the close of ver. 18
after εἰ ἐξέλιπον, and upon which Thenius and Böttcher have founded their
conjectures, are evidently a gloss or paraphrase of וְכֵן הֵתַמּוּ, and of so little
value on critical grounds, that Tischendorf did not even think the reading
worth mentioning in his edition of the Septuagint.

them both in his work, for the simple reason that they belonged
to different periods, as the difference in the names of some of
the officers clearly shows, and that they supplemented one
another. The list before us belongs to a later period of David's
reign than the one in ch. viii. 16–18. In addition to the office-
bearers mentioned in ch. viii., we find here *Adoram* over the
tribute, and *Ira* the Jairite a confidential counsellor (*cohen* :
see at ch. viii. 18), in the place of the sons of David noticed
in ch. viii. 18. The others are the same in both lists. The
Chethib הכרי is to be read הַכָּרִי (cf. 2 Kings xi. 4, 19), from
כּוּר, *perfodit*, and is synonymous with הַכְּרֵתִי (see at ch. viii. 18).
Adoram is the same person as Adoniram, who is mentioned in
1 Kings iv. 6 and v. 28 as overseer over the tributary service
in the time of Solomon ; as we may see from the fact, that the
latter is also called Adoram in 1 Kings xii. 18, and Hadoram
in 2 Chron. x. 18. Hadoram is apparently only a contracted
form of the name, and not merely a copyist's mistake for
Adoniram. But when we find that, according to the passages
cited, the same man filled this office under three kings, we must
bear in mind that he did not enter upon it till the close of
David's reign, as he is not mentioned in ch. viii. 16 sqq., and
that his name only occurs in connection with Rehoboam's ascent
of the throne ; so that there is no ground for assuming that he
filled the office for any length of time under that monarch.
הַמַּס does not mean *vectigal, i.e.* tribute or tributary service, but
tributary labourers. The derivation of the word is uncertain,
and has been disputed. The appointment of a special prefect
over the tributary labourers can hardly have taken place before
the closing years of David's reign, when the king organized
the internal administration of the kingdom more firmly than
before. On the tributary labourers, see at 1 Kings v. 27. Ira
the Jairite is never mentioned again. There is no ground for
altering *Jairi* (the Jairite) into *Jithri* (the Jithrite), as Thenius
proposes, since the rendering given in the Syriac (" from
Jathir") is merely an inference from ch. xxiii. 38 ; and the
assumption upon which this conclusion is founded, viz. that
Ira, the hero mentioned in ch. xxiii. 38, is the same person as
Ira the royal *cohen*, is altogether unfounded.

IV. CLOSE OF DAVID'S REIGN.

CHAP. XXI.–XXIV.

After the suppression of the rebellion headed by Sheba, David spent the remaining years of his reign in establishing the kingdom upon a firmer basis, partly by organizing the army, the administration of justice, and the general government of the realm, and partly by making preparations for the erection of the temple, and enacting rules for the service of the Levites; that he might be able to hand over the government in a firm and satisfactory state to his youthful son Solomon, whom the Lord had appointed as his successor. The account of these regulations and enactments fills up the whole of the last section of the history of David's reign in the first book of Chronicles. But in the book before us, several other things—(1) two divine punishments inflicted upon Israel, with the expiation of the sins that occasioned them (ch. xxi. 1–14, and ch. xxiv.); (2) David's psalm of praise for deliverance out of the hand of all his enemies (ch. xxii.), and his last prophetic words (ch. xxiii. 1–7); and (3) a few brief notices of victorious acts performed in the wars with the Philistines (ch. xxi. 15–22), and a longer list of David's heroes (ch. xxiii. 8–39)—form, as it were, a historical framework for these poetical and prophetic portions. Of the two divine visitations mentioned, the pestilence occasioned by the numbering of the people (ch. xxiv.) occurred undoubtedly in the closing years of David's reign; whereas the famine, and the expiation connected with it (ch. xxi. 1–14), happened most probably at an earlier period, and are merely introduced here because no fitting opportunity had presented itself before. The kernel and centre of this last section of the history of David is to be found unquestionably in the psalm of thanksgiving in ch. xxii., and the prophetic announcement of an exalted and blessed king. In the psalm of thanksgiving David looks back at the close of his life upon all the mercy and faithfulness which he had experienced throughout his reign, and praises the Lord his God for the whole. In his "last words" he looks forward into the time to come, and on the strength of the promise which he has received, of the eternal duration of the dominion of his house, sees in spirit the just Ruler, who will one day arise from his seed, and take the throne of his kingdom for ever. These two lyrical and prophetic productions of David, the ripest spiritual fruit of his life, form a worthy conclusion to his reign. To this there is appended the list of his heroes, in the form of a supplement (ch. xxiii. 8–39); and finally in ch. xxiv. the account of the numbering of the people, and the pestilence which fell upon Israel, as a punishment for this fault on the part of David. This account is placed at the close of the books of Samuel, merely because the altar which was built to expiate the wrath of God, together with the sacrifices offered upon it, served to consecrate the site for the temple, which was to be erected after David's death, in accordance with the divine promise (ch. vii. 13), by his son and successor Solomon.

THREE YEARS' FAMINE. HEROIC ACTS PERFORMED IN THE WARS WITH THE PHILISTINES.—CHAP. XXI.

Vers. 1–14. THREE YEARS' FAMINE. — A three years' famine in the land, the occasion of which, as Jehovah declared to the king, was Saul's crime with regard to the Gibeonites, was expiated by David's delivering up to the Gibeonites, at their own request, seven of Saul's descendants, who were then hung by them upon a mountain before Jehovah. This occurrence certainly did not take place in the closing years of David's reign; on the other hand, it is evident from the remark in ver. 7, to the effect that Mephibosheth was spared, that it happened after David had received tidings of Mephibosheth, and had taken him to his own table (ch. ix.). This is mentioned here as a practical illustration, on the one hand of the manner in which Jehovah visited upon the house of Saul, even after the death of Saul himself, a crime which had been committed by him; and, on the other hand, of the way in which, even in such a case as this, when David had been obliged to sacrifice the descendants of Saul to expiate the guilt of their father, he showed his tenderness towards him by the honourable burial of their bones.

Vers. 1–6a. A famine, which lasted for three successive years, induced David to seek the face of Jehovah, i.e. to approach God in prayer and ask the cause of this judgment which had fallen upon the land. The Lord replied, "Because of Saul, and because of the house of blood-guiltiness, because he hath slain the Gibeonites." The expression "because of the house of blood-guiltiness" is in apposition to "Saul," and determines the meaning more precisely : "because of Saul, and indeed because of the blood-guiltiness which rests upon his house." בֵּית הַדָּמִים signifies the house upon which blood that had been shed still rested as guilt, like עִיר הַדָּמִים in Ezek. xxii. 2, xxiv. 6, 9, and אִישׁ דָּמִים in Ps. v. 7, xxvi. 9, etc. Nothing further is known about the fact itself. It is simply evident from the words of the Gibeonites in ver. 5, that Saul, in his pretended zeal for the children of Israel, had smitten the Gibeonites, *i.e.* had put them to death. Probably some dissatisfaction with them had furnished Saul with a pretext for exterminating these Amoritish heathen from the midst of the people of God.—Ver. 2. In consequence of this answer from God, which merely indicated in a general manner the cause of the visitation that had come upon the land, David sent for the Gibeonites to ask them concerning the wrong that had been done them by Saul. But before the historian communicates their answer, he introduces an explanation respecting the Gibeonites, to the effect that they were not Israelites, but remnants of the Amorites, to whom Joshua had promised on oath that their lives should be preserved (*vid.* Josh. ix. 3 sqq.). They are called *Hivites* in the book of Joshua (ch. ix. 7) ; whereas here they are designated *Amorites*, according to the more general name which is frequently used as comprehending all the tribes of Canaan (see at Gen. x. 16 and xv. 16). David said to the Gibeonites, "What shall I do for you, and wherewith shall I expiate" (*sc.* the wrong done you), "that ye may bless the inheritance (*i.e.* the nation) of Jehovah?" On the use of the imperative וּבָרְכוּ to denote the certain consequences, see Ewald, § 347.—Ver. 4. The Gibeonites answered, "I have not to do with silver and gold concerning Saul and his house" (*lit.* it is not, does not stand, to me at silver and gold with Saul and his house), *i.e.* I have no money to demand of Saul, require no pecuniary payment as compensation for the blood which he shed among us (*vid.* Num. xxxv. 31). The *Chethib* לִּי is not to be touched, notwithstanding the לָנוּ which follows. The use of the singular may be explained on the simple ground that the speaker thought of the Gibeonites as a corporation. "And it does not pertain to us to put any one to death in Israel" (*sc.* of our own accord). When David inquired still further, "What do you mean, then, that I should do to you?" they replied, "(As for) the man who consumed us, and who thought against us, that we should be destroyed (נִשְׁמַדְנוּ without כִּי, subordinate to דִּמָּה, like אֲשֶׁר in the previous verse), so as not to continue in the whole of the territory of Israel, let seven men of his sons be given us, that we may crucify them to Jehovah at Gibeah of Saul, the chosen of Jehovah." אִישׁ אֲשֶׁר וגו׳ is placed at the head absolutely (cf. Gesenius, § 145, 2). On crucifixion as a capital punishment, see at Num. xxv. 4, where it has already been observed that criminals were not impaled or fastened to the cross alive, but were first of all put to death. Consequently the Gibeonites desired that the massacre, which had taken place among them by the command of Saul, should be expiated by the execution of a number of his sons—blood for blood, according to Num. xxxv. 31. They asked for the crucifixion for Jehovah, *i.e.* that the persons executed might be impaled, as a public exhibition of the punishment inflicted, before the face of the Lord (*vid.* ver. 9), as the satisfaction required to expiate His wrath. Seven was a sacred number, denoting the performance of a work of God. This was to take place in Gibeah, the home and capital of Saul, who had brought the wrath of God upon the land through his crime. There is a sacred irony in the epithet applied to Saul, "chosen of the Lord." If Saul was the chosen of Jehovah, his actions ought to have been in accordance with his divine election.

Vers. 6*b*–10. David granted the request, because, according to the law in Num. xxxv. 33, blood-guiltiness when resting upon the land could only be expiated by the blood of the criminal; but in delivering up the members of Saul's house for whom they asked, he spared Mephibosheth the son of Jonathan and grandson of Saul, for the sake of the bond of friendship which he had formed with Jonathan on oath (1 Sam. xviii. 3, xx. 8, 16), and gave up to the Gibeonites two sons of Rizpah, a concubine of Saul (*vid.* ver. 11 and ch. iii. 7), and five sons of Merab the daughter of Saul, whom she had borne to Adriel of Meholah. The name of *Michal*, which stands in the text, is founded upon an error of memory or a copyist's mistake; for it was not Michal, but *Merab*, Saul's eldest daughter, who was given to Adriel the Meholathite as his wife (1 Sam. xviii. 19). The Gibeonites crucified those who were delivered up to them upon the mountain at Gibeah before Jehovah (see the remarks on ver. 6). " *Thus fell seven at once.*" The *Chethib* שְׁבַעְתָּיִם, at which the Masoretes took such offence that they wanted to change it into שְׁבַעְתָּם, is defended by Böttcher very properly, on the ground that the dual of the numeral denotes what is uniformly repeated as if by pairing; so that here it expresses what was extraordinary in the event in a more pictorial manner than the *Keri*: "They fell sevenfold at once," *i.e.* seven in the same way. The further remark, "they were slain in the first days of harvest, at the beginning of the barley harvest," belongs to what follows, for which it prepares the way. The two *Keris*, וְהֵמָּה for וְהֵם, and בִּתְחִלַּת for תְּחִלַּת, are needless emendations. תְּחִלַּת is an adverbial accusative (*vid.* Ges. § 118, 2). The harvest began with the barley harvest, about the middle of Nisan, our April.—Ver. 10. And Rizpah took sackcloth, *i.e.* the coarse hairy cloth that was worn as mourning, and spread it out for herself by the rock—not as a tent, as Clericus supposes, still less as a covering over the corpses of those who had been executed, according to the exegetical handbook, but for a bed—"*from the beginning of the harvest till water was poured out upon them* (the crucified) *from heaven*," *i.e.* till rain came as a sign that the plague of drought that had rested upon the land was appeased; after which the corpses could be openly taken down from the stakes and buried,—a fact which is passed over in the account before us, where only the principal points are given. This is the explanation which Josephus has correctly adopted; but his assumption that the rain fell at once, and before the ordinary early rain, has no foundation in the text of the Bible. "And suffered not the birds of heaven to settle upon the corpses by day, or the wild beasts by night." Leaving corpses without burial, to be consumed by birds of prey and wild beasts, was regarded as the greatest ignominy that could befal the dead (see at 1 Sam. xvii. 44). According to Deut. xxi. 22, 23, persons executed were not to remain hanging through the night upon the stake, but to be buried before evening. This law, however, had no application whatever to the case before us, where the expiation of guilt that rested upon the whole land was concerned. In this instance the expiatory sacrifices were to remain exposed before Jehovah, till the cessation of the plague showed that His wrath had been appeased.

Vers. 11–14. When this touching care of Rizpah for the dead was told to David, he took care that the bones of the whole of the fallen royal house should be buried in the burial-place of Saul's family. He therefore sent for the bones of Saul and Jonathan, which the men of Jabesh had taken away secretly from the wall of Beisan, where the Philistines had fastened the bodies, and which had been buried in Jabesh (1 Sam. xxxi. 10 sqq.), and had the bones of the sons and grand-sons of Saul who had been crucified at Gibeah collected together, and interred all these bones at Zela in the land of Benjamin, in the family grave of Kish the father of Saul. גָּנַב, to take away secretly. מֵרְחֹב בֵּית־שָׁן, from the *market-place* of Bethshan, does not present any contradiction to the statement in 1 Sam. xxxi. 10, that the Philistines fastened the body to the *wall* of Bethshan, as the *rechob* or market-place in eastern towns is not in the middle of the town, but is an open place against or in front of the gate (cf. 2 Chron. xxxii. 6; Neh. viii. 1, 3, 16). This place, as the common meeting-place of the citizens, was the most suitable spot that the Philistines could find for fasten-ing the bodies to the wall. The *Chethib* תְּלֻם is the true Hebrew form from תָּלָה, whereas the *Keri* תְּלָאוּם is a formation resembling the Aramæan (cf. Ewald, § 252, a). The *Keri* שָׁמָּה פְלִשְׁתִּים is correct, however, as פְלִשְׁתִּים, being a proper name, does not take any article. In בְּיוֹם הַכּוֹת the literal meaning of יוֹם (day) must not be strictly pressed, but the expression is to be taken in the sense of "at the time of the smiting;" for the hanging up of the bodies did not take place till the day after the battle (1 Sam. xxxi. 8 sqq.).—In ver. 14 the account is abridged, and the bones of the crucified persons are not men-tioned again. The situation of *Zela* is unknown (see at Josh. xviii. 28). After this had been carried out in accordance with the king's command, God suffered himself to be entreated for the land, so that the famine ceased.

Vers. 15–22. HEROIC ACTS PERFORMED IN THE WARS WITH THE PHILISTINES.—The brief accounts contained in

these verses of different heroic feats were probably taken from
a history of David's wars drawn up in the form of chronicles,
and are introduced here as practical proofs of the gracious
deliverance of David out of the hand of all his foes, for which
he praises the Lord his God in the psalm of thanksgiving which
follows, so that the enumeration of these feats is to be regarded
as supplying a historical basis for the psalm.—Vers. 15–17. The
Philistines had war with Israel again. עוֹד (again) refers generally to earlier wars with the Philistines, and has probably been
taken without alteration from the chronicles employed by our
author, where the account which follows was attached to notices
of other wars. This may be gathered from the books of the
Chronicles, where three of the heroic feats mentioned here are
attached to the general survey of David's wars (vid. 1 Chron.
xx. 4). David was exhausted in this fight, and a Philistian
giant thought to slay him ; but Abishai came to his help and
slew the giant. He was called *Yishbo benob* (Keri, *Yishbi*), *i.e.*
not *Yishbo* at *Nob*, but *Yishbobenob*, a proper name, the meaning of which is probably "his dwelling is on the height," and
which may have been given to him because of his inaccessible
castle. He was one of the descendants of Raphah, *i.e.* one of
the gigantic race of Rephaim. *Raphah* was the tribe-father of
the Rephaim, an ancient tribe of gigantic stature, of whom
only a few families were left even in Moses' time (vid. Deut.
ii. 11, iii. 11, 13, and the commentary on Gen. xiv. 5). The
weight of his lance, *i.e.* of the metal point to his lance, was
three hundred shekels, or eight pounds, of brass, half as
much as the spear of Goliath (1 Sam. xvii. 7) ; "and he was
girded with new armour." Böttcher has no doubt given the
correct explanation of the word חֲדָשָׁה ; he supposes the feminine
to be used in a collective sense, so that the noun (" armour,"
כֵּלָיו) could be dispensed with. (For parallels both to the words
and facts, *vid.* Judg. xviii. 11 and Deut. i. 41.) וַיֹּאמֶר, he
said (*sc.* to himself), *i.e.* he thought.—Ver. 17. The danger
into which the king had been brought in this war, and out of
which he had been rescued solely by Abishai's timely help,
induced his attendants to make him swear that he would not
go into battle any more in person. נִשְׁבַּע לוֹ, administered an
oath to him, *i.e.* fixed him by a promise on oath. וְלֹא תְכַבֶּה,
"and shalt not extinguish the light of Israel." David had

become the light of Israel from the fact that Jehovah was his light (ch. xxii. 29), or, according to the parallel passage in Ps. xviii. 29, that Jehovah had lighted his lamp and enlightened his darkness, *i.e.* had lifted him out of a state of humiliation and obscurity into one of honour and glory. The light (or lamp) is a figure used to represent the light of life as continually burning, *i.e.* life in prosperity and honour. David's regal life and actions were the light which the grace of God had kindled for the benefit of Israel. This light he was not to extinguish, namely by going into the midst of war and so exposing his valuable life to danger.—Ver. 18 (compare 1 Chron. xx. 4). In a second war, *Sibbechai* the Hushathite slew *Saph* the Rephaite at Gob. According to 1 Chron. xxvii. 11, *Sibbechai*, one of the *gibborim* of David (1 Chron. xi. 29), was the leader of the eighth division of the army (see at ch. xxiii. 27). הַחֻשָׁתִי is a patronymic from חוּשָׁה in 1 Chron. iv. 4. The scene of conflict is called *Gob* in our text, and *Gezer* in the Chronicles. As *Gob* is entirely unknown, Thenius supposes it to be a slip of the pen for Gezer; but this is improbable, for the simple reason that *Gob* occurs again in ver. 19. It may possibly have been a small place somewhere near to *Gezer*, which some suppose to have stood on the site of *el Kubab*, on the road from *Ramleh* to *Yalo* (see at Josh. x. 33). The name *Saph* is written *Sippai* in the Chronicles.—Ver. 19 (*vid.* 1 Chron. xx. 5). In another war with the Philistines at Gob, *Elhanan* the son of *Yaare-Orgim* of Bethlehem smote *Goliath* of Gath, whose spear was like a weaver's beam. In the Chronicles, however, we find it stated that " *Elhanan* the son of *Jair* smote *Lahmi* the brother of Goliath of Gath, whose spear," etc. The words of our text are so similar to those of the Chronicles, if we only leave out the word ארגים, which probably crept in from the next line through oversight on the part of a copyist, that they presuppose the same original text, so that the difference can only have arisen from an error in copying. The majority of the expositors (*e.g.* Piscator, Clericus, Michaelis, Movers, and Thenius) regard the text of the Chronicles as the true and original one, and the text before us as simply corrupt. But Bertheau and Böttcher maintain the opposite opinion, because it is impossible to see how the reading in 2 Sam. could grow out of that in the Chronicles; whereas the reading in the

Chronicles might have arisen through conscious alteration ori-
ginating in the offence taken by some reader, who recalled the
account of thē conflict between David and Goliath, at the
statement that Elhanan smote a giant named Goliath, and who
therefore altered בית הלחמי את into את לחמי אחי.　But apart
from the question whether there were two Goliaths, one of
whom was slain by David and the other by Elhanan, the fact
that the conjecture of Bertheau and Böttcher presupposes a
deliberate alteration of the text, or rather, to speak more correctly, an intentional falsification of the historical account, is
quite sufficient to overthrow it, as not a single example of
anything of the kind can be adduced from the whole of the
Chronicles.　On the other hand, the recollection of David's
celebrated officer *Elhanan* of Bethlehem (ch. xxiii. 24; 1 Chron.
xi. 26) might easily lead to an identification of the Elhanan
mentioned here with that officer, and so occasion the alteration
of את לחמי into בית הלחמי.　This alteration was then followed
by that of אחי גלית into את גלית, and all the more easily from
the fact that the description of Lahmi's spear corresponds word
for word with that of Goliath's spear in 1 Sam. xvii. 7.　Consequently we must regard the reading in the Chronicles as the
correct one, and alter our text accordingly; since the assumption
that there were two Goliaths is a very improbable one, and
there is nothing at all strange in the reference to a brother of
Goliath, who was also a powerful giant, and carried a spear
like Goliath.　Elhanan the son of *Jairi* is of course a different
person from *Elhanan* the Bethlehemite, the son of Dodo (ch.
xxiii. 24).　The Chronicles have יָעוּר instead of *Jairi* (the
reading according to the *Chethib*), and the former is probably
the correct way of writing the name.—Vers. 20, 21 (cf. 1 Chron.
xx. 6, 7). In another war at Gath, a Philistian warrior, who
had six fingers on each hand and six toes on each foot,[1] defied
Israel, and was slain by Jonathan the son of Shimeah, the
brother of David (see at ch. xiii. 3).　The *Chethib* מדין is probably to be read מִדִּין, an archaic plural ("a man of measures,

---

[1] Men with six fingers and six toes have been met with elsewhere.
Pliny (*h. nat.* xi. 43) speaks of certain *sedigiti* (six-fingered) Romans.
This peculiarity is even hereditary in some families.　Other examples are
collected by Trusen (*Sitten, Gebräuche, und Krankheiten der alten Hebräer*,
pp. 198-9, ed. 2) and Friedreich (*zur Bibel*, i. 298-9).

or extensions:" de Dieu, etc.) ; in the Chronicles we find the singular מִדָּה instead.—Ver. 22 (cf. 1 Chron. xx. 8). This verse contains a postscript, in which the previous verses are summed up. The accusative אֶת־אַרְבַּעַת may be explained from a species of attraction, *i.e.* from the fact that the historian had יֻלְּדוּ (ver. 21) still in his mind : " As for these four, they were born to *Rapha*," *i.e.* they were descendants of the Rephaite family at Gath, where remnants of the aboriginal Canaanitish tribes of gigantic stature were still to be found, as in other towns of the Philistines (*vid.* Josh. xi. 22). "They fell by the hand of David, and by the hand of his servants." " By the hand of David " refers to the fact that David had personally fought with *Yishbobenob* (ver. 16).

DAVID'S PSALM OF THANKSGIVING FOR VICTORY OVER ALL HIS ENEMIES.—CHAP. XXII.

In the following psalm of thanksgiving, David praises the Lord as his deliverer out of all dangers during his agitated life and conflicts with his foes (vers. 2–4). In the first half he pictures his marvellous deliverance out of all the troubles which he passed through, especially in the time of Saul's persecutions, under the image of an extraordinary theophany (vers. 5–20), and unfolds the ground of this deliverance (vers. 21–28). In the second half he proclaims the mighty help of the Lord, and his consequent victories over the foreign enemies of his government (vers. 29–46), and closes with renewed praise of God for all His glorious deeds (vers. 47–51). The psalm is thus arranged in two leading divisions, with an introductory and concluding strophe. But we cannot discover any definite system of strophes in the further arrangement of the principal divisions, as the several groups of thoughts are not rounded off symmetrically.

The contents and form of this song of praise answer to the fact attested by the heading, that it was composed by David in the later years of his reign, when God had rescued him from all his foes, and helped his kingdom to victory over all the neighbouring heathen nations. The genuineness of the psalm is acknowledged to be indisputable by all the modern critics, except J. Olshausen and Hupfeld,[1] who, with hypercritical scepticism, dispute the Davidic origin of the psalm on subjective grounds of æsthetic taste. This psalm is found in the Psalter as Ps. xviii., though with many divergences in single words and clauses, which do not, however, essentially affect the meaning. Commentators are divided in opinion as to the relation in which the two different forms of the text stand to one another. The idea that the text of 2 Sam. rests upon a careless copy and tradition must decidedly be rejected : for, on the one hand, by far the larger portion of the deviations in our text from that of the Psalter are not to be attributed to carelessness on the part of copyists, but are evidently alterations made with thoughtfulness and deliberation : *e.g.* the omission of the very first passage (ver. 1), "I will love Thee, O Lord, my strength ;" the change of אֵלִי צוּרִי (my God, my strength, or rock) into אֱלֹהֵי צוּרִי (the God of my rock), as "the God of the rock" occurs again in ver. 47 of the text before us ; or the substitution of וַיֵּרָא (He was seen, ver. 11) for וַיֵּדֶא (He did fly), etc. On the other hand, the original reading has undoubtedly been retained in many passages of our text, whilst simpler and more common forms have been substituted in that of the Psalms ; *e.g.*

---

[1] Even Hitzig observes (*die Psalmen*, i. p. 95) : "There is no ground whatever for calling in question the Davidic authorship of the psalm, and therefore the statement made in the heading ; and, in fact, there is all the more reason for adhering to it, because it is attested twice. The recurrence of the psalm as one of Davidic origin in 2 Sam. xxii. is of some weight, since not the slightest suspicion attaches to any of the other songs or sayings attributed to David in the second book of Samuel (*e.g.* iii. 33, 34, v. 8, vii. 18–29, xxiii. 1–7). Moreover, the psalm is evidently ancient, and suited to the classical period of the language and its poetry. Ver. 31 is quoted as early as Prov. xxx. 5, and ver. 34 in Hab. iii. 19. The psalm was also regarded as Davidic at a very early period, as the '*diaskeuast*' of the second book of Samuel met with the heading, which attributes the psalm to David. No doubt this opinion might be founded upon ver. 51 ; and with perfect justice if it were : for if the psalm was not composed by David, it must have been composed in his name and spirit ; and who could have been this contemporaneous and equal poet?" Again, after quoting several thoroughly Davidic signs, he says at p. 96 : "It is very obvious with how little justice the words of ver. 51, relating to 2 Sam. vii. 12–16, 26, 29, have been pronounced spurious. Besides, the psalm can no more have concluded with לִמְשִׁיחוֹ (ver. 51) than with ver. 50 ; and if David refers to himself by name at the commencement in 2 Sam. xxiii. 1, and in the middle in ch. vii. 20, why should he not do the same at the close?"

in ver. 5, מֹשְׁבְּרֵי מָוֶת instead of חֶבְלֵי מָוֶת; in ver. 8, מוֹסְדוֹת הַשָּׁמַיִם
(the foundations of the heavens) for מוֹסְדֵי הָרִים (the foundations
of the hills); in ver. 12, חַשְׁרַת־מַיִם for חֶשְׁכַת־מַיִם; in ver. 16,
וְעֵינֶיךָ עַל־רָמִים תַּשְׁפִּיל for אֲפִיקֵי מַיִם; in ver. 28, for אֲפִיקֵי יָם
; וַיִּתֵּן תָּמִים דַּרְכִּי for וַיַּתֵּר תָּמִים דַּרְכּוֹ; in ver. 33, וְעֵינַיִם רָמוֹת תַּשְׁפִּיל
and in ver. 44, תִּשְׁמְרֵנִי לְרֹאשׁ for תְּשִׂימֵנִי לְרֹאשׁ, and several others.
In general, however, the text of the Psalms bears the stamp of
poetical originality more than the text before us, and the latter
indicates a desire to give greater clearness and simplicity to
the poetical style. Consequently neither of the two texts that
have come down to us contains the original text of the psalm
of David unaltered; but the two recensions have been made
quite independently of each other, one for the insertion of the
psalm in the Psalter intended for liturgical use, and the other
when it was incorporated into the history of David's reign,
which formed the groundwork of our books of Samuel. The
first revision may have been made by David himself when he
arranged his Psalms for liturgical purposes; but the second
was effected by the prophetic historian, whose object it was,
when inserting David's psalm of praise in the history of his
reign, not so much to give it with diplomatic literality, as to
introduce it in a form that should be easily intelligible and true
to the sense.

Ver. 1. The heading is formed precisely according to the
introductory formula of the song of Moses in Deut. xxxi. 30, and
was no doubt taken from the larger historical work employed
by the author of our books. It was probably also adopted
from this into the canonical collection of the Psalter, and
simply brought into conformity with the headings of the other
psalms by the alteration of וַיְדַבֵּר דָּוִד (and David said) into
לְעֶבֶד יְהֹוָה לְדָוִד אֲשֶׁר דִּבֶּר (" of David, the servant of the Lord,
who spake:" Eng. ver.), and the insertion of לַמְנַצֵּחַ (" to the
chief musician :" Eng. ver.) at the head (see Delitzsch on the
Psalms). "In the day," i.e. at the time, "when Jehovah had
delivered him." Deliverance "out of the hand of Saul" is
specially mentioned, not because this was the last, but because
it was the greatest and most glorious,—a deliverance out of
the deepest misery into regal might and glory. The psalm
is opened by וַיֹּאמַר in both texts.—Vers. 2–4 form the introduction.

Ver. 2 Jehovah is my rock, my castle, and my deliverer to me ;
    3 My Rock-God, in whom I trust :
      My shield and horn of my salvation, my fortress and my refuge,
      My Saviour ; from violence Thou redeemest me.
    4 I call upon the praised one, Jehovah,
      And I am saved from my enemies.

This introduction contains the sum and substance of the whole psalm, inasmuch as David groups the many experiences of divine deliverance in his agitated life into a long series of predicates, in all of which he extols God as his defence, refuge, and deliverer. The heaping up of these predicates is an expression both of liveliest gratitude, and also of hope for the future. The different predicates, however, are not to be taken as in apposition to *Jehovah*, or as vocatives, but are declarations concerning God, how He had proved himself faithful to the Psalmist in all the calamities of his life, and would assuredly do so still. David calls God סַלְעִי וּמְצֻדָתִי (my rock, and my castle) in Ps. xxxi. 4 as well (cf. Ps. lxxi. 4). The two epithets are borrowed from the natural character of Palestine, where steep and almost inaccessible rocks afford protection to the fugitive, as David had often found at the time when Saul was pursuing him (*vid*. 1 Sam. xxiv. 23, xxii. 5). But whilst David took refuge in rocks, he placed his hopes of safety not in their inaccessible character, but in God the Lord, the eternal spiritual rock, whom he could see in the earthly rock, so that he called Him his true castle. מְפַלְטִי לִי (my deliverer to me) gives the real explanation of the foregoing figures. The לִי (to me) is omitted in Ps. xviii. 2, and only serves to strengthen the suffix, " my, yea *my* deliverer." " *My Rock-God*," equivalent to, God who is my Rock : this is formed after Deut. xxxii. 4, where Moses calls the Lord the Rock of Israel, because of His unchangeable faithfulness ; for *zur*, a rock, is a figure used to represent immoveable firmness. In Ps. xviii. 3 we find אֵלִי צוּרִי, " my God " (strong one), " my rock," two synonyms which are joined together in our text, so as to form one single predicate of God, which is repeated in ver. 47. The predicates which follow, " *my horn and my salvation-shield*," describe God as the mighty protector and defender of the righteous. A shield covers against hostile attacks. In this respect God was Abraham's shield (Gen. xv. 1), and the helping shield of Israel

(Deut. xxxiii. 29 ; cf. Ps. iii. 4, lix. 12). He is the "horn of salvation," according to Luther, because He overcomes enemies, and rescues from foes, and gives salvation. The figure is borrowed from animals, which have their strength and defensive weapons in their horns (see at 1 Sam. ii. 1). *"My fortress:"* *misgab* is a high place, where a person is secure against hostile attacks (see at Ps. ix. 10). The predicates which follow, viz. *my refuge*, etc., are not given in Ps. xviii. 3, and are probably only added as a rhythmical completion to the strophe, which was shortened by the omission of the introductory lines, "I love thee heartily, Jehovah" (Ps. xviii. 1). The last clause, *"My Saviour, who redeemest me from violence,"* corresponds to אֶחֱסֶה־בּוֹ in the first hemistich. In ver. 4, David sums up the contents of his psalm of thanksgiving in a general sentence of experience, which may be called the theme of the psalm, for it embraces "the result of the long life which lay behind him, so full of dangers and deliverances." מְהֻלָּל, "*the praised one*," an epithet applied to God, which occurs several times in the Psalms (xlviii. 2, xcvi. 4, cxiii. 3, cxlv. 3). It is in apposition to Jehovah, and is placed first for the sake of emphasis : "I invoke Jehovah as the praised one." The imperfects אֶקְרָא and אִוָּשֵׁעַ are used to denote what continually happens. In ver. 5 we have the commencement of the account of the deliverances out of great tribulations, which David had experienced at the hand of God.

> Ver. 5 For breakers of death had compassed me,
>   Streams of wickedness terrified me.
> 6 Cords of hell had girt me about,
>   Snares of death overtook me.
> 7 In my distress I called Jehovah,
>   And to my God I called ;
>   And He heard my voice out of His temple,
>   And my crying came into His ears.

David had often been in danger of death, most frequently at the time when he was pursued by Saul, but also in Absalom's conspiracy, and even in several wars (cf. ch. xxi. 16). All these dangers, out of which the Lord delivered him, and not merely those which originated with Saul, are included in vers. 5, 6. The figure *"breakers or waves of death"* is analogous to that of the *"streams of Belial."* His distress is represented in both of them under the image of violent floods of water. In the psalm we find חֶבְלֵי מָוֶת, "snares of death," as in Ps. cxvi. 3, death being regarded as a hunter with a net and snare (cf. Ps. xci. 3) : this does not answer so well to the parallel נַחֲלֵי, and therefore is not so good, since חֶבְלֵי שְׁאוֹל follows immediately. בְּלִיַּעַל (Belial), *uselessness* in a moral sense, or *worthlessness*. The meaning " mischief," or injury in a physical sense, which many expositors give to the word in this passage on account of the parallel " death," cannot be grammatically sustained. *Belial* was afterwards adopted as a name for the devil (2 Cor. vi. 15). Streams of wickedness are calamities that proceed from wickedness, or originate with worthless men. קִדֵּם, to come to meet with a hostile intention, *i.e.* to fall upon (*vid.* Job xxx. 27). הֵיכָל, the *temple* out of which Jehovah heard him, was the heavenly abode of God, as in Ps. xi. 4 ; for, according to vers. 8 sqq., God came down from heaven to help him.

> Ver. 8 Then the earth swayed and trembled,
>   The foundations of the heavens shook
>   And swayed to and fro, because He was wroth.
>   9 Smoke ascended in His nose,
>   And fire out of His mouth devoured,
>   Red-hot coals burned out of Him.
>   10 And He bowed the heavens and came down,
>   And cloudy darkness under His feet.

Jehovah came down from heaven to save His servant, as He had formerly come down upon Sinai to conclude His covenant with Israel in the midst of terrible natural phenomena, which proclaimed the wrath of the Almighty. The theophany under which David depicts the deliverance he had experienced, had its type in the miraculous phenomenon which accompanied the descent of God upon Sinai, and which suggested, as in the song of Deborah (Judg. v. 4, 5), the idea of a terrible storm. It is true that the deliverance of David was not actually attended by any such extraordinary natural phenomena ; but the saving hand of God from heaven was so obviously manifested, that the deliverance experienced by him could be poetically described as a miraculous interposition on the part of God. When the Lord rises up from His heavenly temple to come down upon the earth to judgment, the whole world trembles at the fierceness of His wrath. Not only does the earth tremble, but the foundations of the heavens shake : the whole universe is moved. In the psalm we have " the foundations of the hills " instead of " *the foundations of the heavens*,"—a weaker expression, signifying the earth to its deepest foundations. The *Hithpael* יִתְגָּעַשׁ, *lit. to sway itself*, expresses the idea of continuous swaying to and fro. כִּי חָרָה לוֹ, "*for it* (sc. wrath) *burned to him,*" it flamed up like a fire; cf. Deut. xxxii. 22, xxix. 19. "*Smoke,*" the forerunner of fire, "*ascended in His nose.*" The figurative idea is that of snorting or violent breathing, which indicates the rising of wrath. Smoke is followed by fire, which devours out of the mouth, *i.e.* bursts forth devouring or consuming all that opposes it. The expression is strengthened still further by the parallel: "*red-hot coals come out of Him,*" *i.e.* the flame of red-hot coals pours out of Him as out of a glowing furnace (cf. Gen. xv. 17). This description is based entirely upon Ex. xix. 18, where the Lord comes down upon Sinai in smoke and fire. We are not to picture to ourselves flashes of lightning; for all these phenomena are merely the forerunners of the appearance of God in the clouds, which is described in ver. 10, "He bowed the heavens" to come down. עֲרָפֶל, which is frequently connected with עָנָן, signifies cloudy darkness, or dark clouds. The substratum of this description is the fact that in a severe storm the heavens seem to sink down upon the earth with their dark clouds. The Lord draws near riding upon black thunder-clouds, "that the wicked may not behold His serene countenance, but only the terrible signs of His fierce wrath and punishment" (J. H. Michaelis).

> Ver. 11 He rode upon a cherub and flew hither,
>   And appeared upon the wings of the wind.
> 12 He made darkness round about Him as pavilions,
>   Water-gathering, thick clouds.
> 13 Out of the splendour before Him
>   Burned red-hot coals of fire.

These three verses are a further expansion of ver. 10, and ver. 11 of ver. 10a. The *cherub* is not a personified earthly creature, for *cherubim* are angels around the throne of God (see at Gen. iii. 22). The poetical figure "riding upon the cherub" is borrowed from the fact that God was enthroned between the two cherubim upon the lid of the ark of the covenant, and above their outspread wings (Ex. xxv. 20, 21). As the idea of His "dwelling between the cherubim" (ch. vi. 2; 1 Sam. iv. 4; Ps. lxxx. 2) was founded upon this typical manifestation of the gracious presence of God in the Most Holy place, so here David depicts the descent of Jehovah from heaven as "riding upon a cherub," picturing the cherub as a throne upon which God appears in the clouds of heaven, though without therefore imagining Him as riding upon a sphinx or driving in a chariot-throne. Such notions as these are precluded by the addition of the term וַיָּעֹף, "did fly." The "*flying*" is also suggested by the wings of the cherubim. As the divine "*shechinah*" was enthroned above the ark of the covenant upon the wings of the cherubim, David in his poetical description represents the cherub and his wings as carrying the throne of God, to express the thought that Jehovah came down from heaven as the judge and saviour of His servants in the splendour of His divine glory, surrounded by cherubim who stand as His highest servants around His throne, just as Moses in his blessing (Deut. xxxiii. 2) speaks of Jehovah as coming out of myriads of His holy angels. The elementary substratum of this was the wings of the wind, upon which He appeared. In the psalm we have וַיֵּרֶא, from דָּאָה, to soar (Deut. xxviii. 49 ; Jer. xlviii. 40), which suggests the idea of flying better than וַיֵּרָא (He was seen), though the latter gives the real explanation. In vers. 12 and 13, the "cloudy darkness under His feet" (ver. 10*b*) is still further expanded, so as to prepare the way for the description of thunder and lightning in vers. 14 sqq. God in His wrath withdraws His face from man. He envelopes himself in clouds. The darkness round about him is the black thunder-cloud which forms His hut or tent. The plural *succoth* is occasioned by the plural סְבִיבֹתָיו, "His surroundings:" it is used with indefinite generality, and is more probably the original term than סֻכָּתוֹ in the psalm. The "*darkness*" is still further explained in the second clause, חַשְׁרַת מַיִם, *water-gatherings*. חַשְׁרָה (ἀπ. λεγ.) signifies, according to the Arabic, a gathering or collection. The expression used in the psalm is חֶשְׁכַת מַיִם, *water-darkness*, which, if not less appropriate, is at any rate not the original term. עָבֵי שְׁחָקִים, *clouds of clouds*, *i.e.* the thickest clouds; a kind of superlative, in which a synonym is used instead of the same noun.—Ver. 13. The splendour of the divine nature enveloped in clouds breaks through the dark covering in burning coals of fire. The coals of fire which burst forth, *i.e.* which break out in flame from the dark clouds, are the lightning which shoots forth from the dark storm-clouds in streams of fire.

Ver. 14 Jehovah thundered from the heavens,
And the Most High gave His voice.
15 He sent arrows, and scattered them ;
Lightning, and discomfited them.
16 Then the beds of the sea became visible ;
The foundations of the world were uncovered,
Through the threatening of Jehovah,
By the snorting of the breath of His nostrils.

God sent lightning as arrows upon the enemies along with violent thunder, and threw them thereby into confusion. הָמַם, to throw into confusion, and thereby to destroy, is the standing expression for the destruction of the foe accomplished by the miraculous interposition of God (*vid.* Ex. xiv. 24, xxiii. 27; Josh. x. 10; Judg. iv. 15; 1 Sam. vii. 10). To the thunder there were added stormy wind and earthquake, as an effect of the wrath of God, whereby the foundations of the sea and land were laid bare, *i.e.* whereby the depth of the abyss and of the hell in the interior of the earth, into which the person to be rescued had fallen, were disclosed.[1]

Ver. 17 He reached out of the height, He laid hold of me ;
Drew me out of great waters :
18 Saved me from my enemy strong ;
From my haters, because they were too strong for me.
19 They fell upon me in my day of calamity :
Then Jehovah became my stay,
20 And led me out into a broad place ;
Delivered me, because He had pleasure in me.

---

[1] In vers. 13–16 the text of the Psalms deviates greatly and in many instances from that before us. In ver. 13 we find עָבָיו עָבְרוּ בָּרָד וְגַחֲלֵי אֵשׁ instead of בָּעֲרוּ גַחֲלֵי אֵשׁ ; and after ver. 14 בָּרָד וְגַחֲלֵי אֵשׁ is repeated in the psalm. In ver. 15 we have וּבְרָקִים רָב for בָּרָק, and in ver. 16 אֲפִיקֵי מַיִם for אֲפִיקֵי יָם. The other deviations are inconsiderable. So far as the repetition of בָּרָד וְגַחֲלֵי אֵשׁ at the end of ver. 14 is concerned, it is not only superfluous, but unsuitable, because the lightning following the thunder is described in ver. 15, and the words repeated are probably nothing more than a gloss that has crept by an oversight into the text. The אֲפִיקֵי מַיִם in ver. 16 is an obvious softening down of the אֲפִיקֵי יָם of the text before us. In the other deviations, however, the text of the Psalms is evidently the more original of the two ; the abridgment of the second clause of ver. 13 is evidently a simplification of the figurative description in the psalm, and בְּרָקִים רָב in the 15th verse of the psalm is more poetical and a stronger expression than the mere בָּרָק of our text.

The Lord stretched His hand from the height into the deep abysses, which had been uncovered through the threatening of the wrath of God, and drew out the sinking man. יִשְׁלַח without יָד is used to denote the stretching out of the hand, and in the sense of reaching out to a thing (as in ch. vi. 6). מַיִם רַבִּים (great waters) does not refer to the enemy, but to the calamities and dangers (waves of death and streams of Belial, ver. 5) into which the enemies of the Psalmist had plunged him. יַמְשֵׁנִי, from מָשָׁה (Ex. ii. 10), from which the name of *Moses* was derived, to whom there is probably an allusion made. As Moses was taken out of the waters of the Nile, so David was taken out of great (many) waters. This deliverance is still further depicted in more literal terms in vers. 18 sqq. אֹיְבִי עָז, my enemy strong, poetical for my strong enemy, does not refer to one single enemy, namely Saul; but, as the parallel " my haters " shows, is a poetical personification of all his enemies. They were stronger than David, therefore the Lord had to deliver him with an almighty hand. The " *day of calamity* " in which the enemy fell upon him (קֵדֶם : see at ver. 6) was the time when David wandered about in the desert helpless and homeless, fleeing from the pursuit of Saul. The Lord was then his support, or a staff on which he could support himself (*vid.* Ps. xxiii. 4), and led him out of the strait into the broad, *i.e.* into a broad space where he could move freely, because God had pleasure in him, and had chosen him in His grace to be His servant. This reason for his deliverance is carried out still further in what follows.

> Ver. 21 Jehovah rendered to me according to my righteousness,
>   According to the cleanness of my hands He recompensed me.
> 22 For I have observed the ways of Jehovah,
>   And have not wickedly departed from my God.
> 23 For all His rights are before my eyes;
>   And His statutes,—I do not depart from them.
> 24 And I was innocent towards Him,
>   And kept myself from mine iniquity.

גָּמַל signifies to do to a person good or evil, like the Greek εὖ and κακῶς πράττειν τινά. The *righteousness* and *cleannness of hands*, *i.e.* the innocence, which David attributed to himself, were not perfect righteousness or holiness before God, but the righteousness of his endeavours and deeds as contrasted with the unrighteousness and wickedness of his adversaries and pursuers, and consisted in the fact that he endeavoured earnestly and sincerely to walk in the ways of God and to keep the divine commandments. רָשַׁע מִן, *to be wicked from*, is a pregnant expression, signifying to depart wickedly from God. לְנֶגְדִּי, *i.e.* as a standard before my eye. In the psalm we find תָּמִים עִמּוֹ, innocent in intercourse with the Lord, instead of תָּמִים לוֹ (see Deut. xviii. 13); and for the fact itself, David's own testimony in 1 Sam. xxvi. 23, 24, the testimony of God concerning him in 1 Kings xiv. 8, and the testimony of history in 1 Kings xv. 5. מֵעֲוֹנִי, from mine iniquity, *i.e.* from the iniquity which I might have committed.

> Ver. 25 Thus Jehovah repaid me according to my righteousness,
>   According to my cleanness before His eyes.
> 26 Towards the pious Thou showest thyself pious,
>   Towards the perfectly innocent Thou showest thyself innocent.
> 27 Towards the genuine Thou showest thyself genuine,
>   And towards the perverse Thou showest thyself crooked.
> 28 And afflicted people Thou helpest,
>   And Thine eyes are against the haughty; them Thou humblest.

The motive for deliverance, which was expounded in vers. 21–24, is summed up briefly in ver. 25; and then in vers. 26 and 27 it is carried back to the general truth, that the conduct of God towards men is regulated according to the conduct of men towards God. The *vav cons.* in וַיָּשֶׁב expresses the logical consequence. כְּבֹרִי is used instead of כְּבֹר יָדַי in ver. 21, which is repeated in the psalm simply for the sake of variation. The truth that God treats every man in accordance with his conduct towards Him, is expounded in four parallel clauses, in which the conduct of God is expressed in verbs in the *Hithpael*, formed from the adjectives used to describe the conduct of men towards God. To the חָסִיד, the pious or devoted to God, He also shows himself pious; and innocent, blameless, to the גְּבוֹר תָּמִים, the man strong in innocence, who walks in perfect innocence. נָבָר, a *Niphal* participle, from בָּרַר, he who keeps himself pure, strives after purity of walk. תִּתְבָּר, an anomalous contraction of תִּתְבָּרַר (Ps.), analogous to the formation of נָבָר for נִבְרַר. The form תִּתַּפָּל for תִּתְפַּתָּל, to show one's self perverse or crooked, is still more anomalous. God shows himself so towards the perverse, by giving him up to his perverseness (Rom. i. 28).

This general truth is applied in ver. 28 to the congregation of God, in the contrast which it presents of humble and haughty, and is expounded from the conduct of God, as displayed in the history of Israel, towards these two classes of men, into which the nation was divided. In the psalm, therefore, we find כִּי אַתָּה, for which the simple ו is substituted here, because the verse does not contain any actual reason for what goes before. עַם עָנִי, afflicted people, is used to denote the pious and depressed in the nation; רָמִים, *the high*, *i.e.* the haughty, or godless rich and mighty in the nation. תַּשְׁפִּיל is to be taken as a relative: whom Thou humblest (see Ewald, § 332, *b*; and for the thought, Isa. ii. 11). In the psalm the unusual mode of expression in the second clause is changed into the more common phrase, " Thou bringest down high, *i.e.* proud looks" (cf. Prov. vi. 17, xxi. 4, xxx. 13; Ps. cxxxi. 1, etc.).

Ver. 29 commences the description of the help which David had already received from God in his conflict with the enemies of Israel, and which he would still receive.

> Ver. 29 For Thou art my lamp, O Jehovah!
>   And Jehovah maketh my darkness bright.
>   30 For through Thee I run troops,
>   And through my God I leap walls.
>   31 God—innocent is His way.
>   The word of Jehovah is refined,
>   A shield is He to all who trust in Him.

The explanatory כִּי, with which the new description of the divine mercy commences, refers to the thought implied in ver. 28, that David belonged to the " afflicted people," whom the Lord always helps. As the Lord delivered him out of the danger of death, because He took pleasure in him, so He also gave him power over all his enemies. For He was his lamp, *i.e.* He had lifted him out of a condition of depression and contempt into one of glory and honour (see at ch. xxi. 17), and would still further enlighten his darkness, *i.e.* " would cause the light of His salvation to shine upon him and his tribe in all the darkness of their distress" (Hengstenberg). In the psalm the verse reads thus: " For Thou lightest (makest bright) my lamp (or candle), Jehovah my God enlighteneth my darkness;" the bold figure " Jehovah the lamp of David" being more literally explained. The figure is analogous to the one in Ps.

xxvii. 1, " The Lord is my light;" whilst the form נֵיר is a later mode of writing נֵר.—Ver. 30. In the strength of his God he could run hostile troops and leap walls, *i.e.* overcome every hostile power. אָרוּץ, not from רָצַץ, to smash in pieces, but from רוּץ, to run ; construed with the accusative according to the analogy of verbs of motion.—Ver. 31. He derives this confidence from the acts of God, and also from His word. הָאֵל (God) is written absolutely, like הַצּוּר in Deut. xxxii. 4. The article points back to בֵּאלֹהַי. Jehovah is *the* God (הָאֵל), whose way is perfect, without blemish; and His word is refined brass, pure silver (cf. Ps. xii. 7). He who trusts in Him is safe from all foes. The last two clauses occur again in Agur's proverbs (Prov. xxx. 5). The thought of the last clause is still further explained in vers. 32 sqq.

> Ver. 32 For who is God save Jehovah,
> And who a rock save our God ?
> 33 This God is my strong fortress,
> And leads the innocent his way.
> 34 He makes my feet like the hinds,
> And setteth me upon my high places ;
> 35 He teacheth my hands to fight,
> And my arms span brazen bows.

There is no true God who can help, except or by the side of Jehovah (cf. Deut. xxxii. 31; 1 Sam. ii. 2). צוּר, as in ver. 2. This God is " my strong fortress :" for this figure, comp. Ps. xxxi. 5 and xxvii. 1. חַיִל, strength, might, is construed with מָעוּזִי, by free subordination : " my fortress, a strong one," like מַחְסִי עֹז (Ps. lxxi. 7 ; cf. Ewald, § 291, *b*). יַתֵּר for יְתֵר, from תּוּר (*vid.* Ges. § 72 ; Olshausen, *Gram.* p. 579), in the sense of leading or taking round, as in Prov. xii. 26. God leads the innocent his way, *i.e.* He is his leader and guide therein. The *Keri* דַּרְכִּי rests upon a misunderstanding. There is an important difference in the reading of this verse in Ps. xviii., viz. " The God who girdeth me with strength, and makes my way innocent." The last clause is certainly an alteration which simplifies the meaning, and so is also the first clause, the thought of which occurs again, word for word, in ver. 40*a*, with the addition of לַמִּלְחָמָה. אַיָּלָה or אַיֶּלֶת, the hind, or female stag, is a figure of speech denoting swiftness in running. " *Like the hinds :*" a condensed simile for " like the hinds' feet," such as we frequently meet with in Hebrew (*vid.* Ges. § 144, Anm.). The reference is to swiftness in pursuit of the foe (*vid.* ch. ii. 18; 1 Chron. xii. 8). רַגְלָיו, *his* feet, for רַגְלַי (*my* feet) in the psalm, may be accounted for from the fact, that David had spoken of himself in the third person as the innocent one. "*My high places*" were not the high places of the enemy, that became his by virtue of conquest, but the high places of his own land, which he maintained triumphantly, so that he ruled the land from them. The expression is formed after Deut. xxxii. 13, and is imitated in Hab. iii. 19. לִמֵּד is generally construed with a double accusative: here it is written with an accusative and לְ, and signifies to instruct for the war. נִחַת, in the psalm נִחֲתָה, on account of the feminine זְרוֹעֹתַי, is not the *Niphal* of חָתַת, to be broken in pieces, but the *Piel* of נָחַת, to cause to go down, to press down the bow, *i.e.* to set it. The bow of brass is mentioned as being the strongest: setting such a bow would be a sign of great heroic strength. The two verses (34 and 35) are simply a particularizing description of the power and might with which the Lord had endowed David to enable him to conquer all his foes.

> Ver. 36 And Thou reachest me the shield of my salvation,
>   And Thy hearing makes me great.
>   37 Thou makest my steps broad under me,
>   And my ankles have not trembled.

The Lord bestows the true strength for victory in His salvation. The shield of salvation is the shield which consists of salvation, of the helping grace of the Lord. עֲנֹתְךָ, for which we find in the psalm עַנְוָתְךָ, thy humility, *i.e.* God's condescending grace, does not mean "thy humiliation," but "*thy hearkening*," *i.e.* that practical hearkening on the part of God, when called upon for help, which was manifested in the fact that God made his steps broad, *i.e.* provided the walker with a broad space for free motion, removing obstructions and stumbling-blocks out of the way. God had done this for David, so that his ankles had not trembled, *i.e.* he had not been wanting in the power to take firm and safe steps. In this strength of his God he could destroy all his foes.

> Ver. 38 I will pursue my enemies and destroy them,
>   I will not turn till they are consumed.

39 I will consume them and dash them in pieces, that they may
    not arise,
    And may fall under my feet.
40 And Thou girdest me with strength for war,
    Thou bowest mine adversaries under me.
41 And Thou makest mine enemies turn the back to me;
    My haters, I root them out.

The optative form אֲרִדְּפָה serves to make the future signification of אֶרְדֹּף (in the psalm) the more apparent. Consequently
it is quite out of the question to take the other verbs as preterites. We are not compelled to do this by the interchange
of imperfects *c. vav consec.* with simple imperfects, as the *vav
consec.* is not used exclusively as expressive of the past. On
the contrary, the substance of the whole of the following description shows very clearly that David refers not only to the
victories he has already won, but in general to the defeat of all
his foes in the past, the present, and the future ; for he speaks
as distinctly as possible not only of their entire destruction
(vers. 38, 39, 43), but also of the fact that God makes him the
head of the nations, and distant and foreign nations do him
homage. Consequently he refers not only to his own personal
dominion, but also, on the strength of the promise which he
had received from God, to the increase of the dominion of the
throne of his house, whilst he proclaims in the Spirit the
ultimate defeat of all the enemies of the kingdom of God.
This Messianic element in the following description comes out
in a way that cannot be mistaken, in the praise of the Lord
with which he concludes in vers. 47—51. וָאַשְׁמִידֵם, " *I destroy
them*," is stronger than וָאֲשִׂיגֵם, " I reach them " (in the psalm).
In ver. 39 the words are crowded together, to express the utter
destruction of all foes. In the psalm וַאֲכַלֵּם is omitted. וַתַּזְרֵנִי
for וַתְּאַזְּרֵנִי in the psalm is not a poetical Syriasm, and still less
a "careless solecism" (Hupfeld), but a simple contraction,
such as we meet with in many forms : *e.g.* מַלְּפֵנוּ for מְאַלְּפֵנוּ
(Job xxxv. 11 ; cf. Ewald, § 232, *b*). The form תַּתָּה for
נָתַתָּה (in the psalm) is unusual, and the aphæresis of the נ
can only be accounted for from the fact that this much-used
word constantly drops its נ as a radical sound in the imperfect (see Ewald, § 195, *c*). The phrase תַּתָּה לִּי עֹרֶף is formed
after Ex. xxiii. 27. " Giving the enemy to a person's back "

means causing them to turn the back, *i.e.* putting them to flight.

> Ver. 42 They look out, but there is no deliverer ;
> For Jehovah, but He answereth them not.
> 43 And I rub in pieces as the dust of the earth,
> Like the mire of the streets I crush them and stamp upon them.

The cry of the foe for help is not attended to ; they are annihilated without quarter. יְשַׁעוּ, to look out to God for help (with אֶל and עַל; *vid.* Isa. xvii. 7, 8), is more poetical than יְשַׁוְּעוּ, " they cry " (in the psalm) ; and כְּעַפַר־אָרֶץ is more simple than כְּעָפָר עַל־פְּנֵי־רוּחַ (in the psalm), " I crush them as dust before the wind," for the wind does not crush the dust, but carries it away. In the second clause of ver. 43, אֲדִקֵּם is used instead of אֲרִיקֵם in the psalm, and strengthened by אֶרְקָעֵם. אֲדִקֵּם, from דָּקַק, *to make thin*, to crush ; so that instead of " I pour them out like mire of the streets which is trodden to pieces," the Psalmist simply says, " I crush and stamp upon them like mire of the streets." Through the utter destruction of the foe, God establishes the universal dominion to which the throne of David is to attain.

> Ver. 44 And Thou rescuest me out of the strivings of my people,
> Preservest me to be the head of the heathen.
> People that I knew not serve me.
> 45 The sons of the stranger dissemble to me,
> Upon hearsay they obey me.
> 46 The sons of the stranger despair,
> And tremble out of their castles.

By " *the strivings of my people* " the more indefinite expression in the psalm, "strivings of the people," is explained. The words refer to the domestic conflicts of David, out of which the Lord delivered him, such as the opposition of Ishbosheth and the rebellions of Absalom and Sheba. These deliverances formed the prelude and basis of his dominion over the heathen. Consequently תִּשְׁמְרֵנִי (*Thou preservest me* to be the head of the nations) occurs quite appropriately in the second clause ; and תְּשִׂימֵנִי, " Thou settest me," which occurs in the psalm, is a far less pregnant expression. עַם before לֹא יָדַעְתִּי is used indefinitely to signify foreign nations. *Toi* king of Hamath (ch. viii. 10) was an example, and his subjugation was a prelude of the future subjection of all the heathen to the sceptre of the Son of David, as predicted in Ps. lxxii. In ver. 45 the two clauses of the psalm are very appropriately transposed. The *Hithpael* יִתְכַּחֲשׁוּ, as compared with יְכַחֲשׁוּ, is the later form. In the primary passage (Deut. xxxiii. 29) the *Niphal* is used to signify the dissembling of friendship, or of involuntary homage on the part of the vanquished towards the victor. לִשְׁמוֹעַ אֹזֶן, " *by the hearing of the ear*," *i.e.* by hearsay, is a simple explanation of לְשֵׁמַע אֹזֶן, at the rumour of the ears (*vid.* Job xlii. 5), *i.e.* at the mere rumour of David's victories. The foreign nations pine away, *i.e.* despair of ever being able to resist the victorious power of David. יַחְגְּרוּ, "*they gird themselves*," does not yield any appropriate meaning, even if we should take it in the sense of equipping themselves to go out to battle. The word is probably a misspelling of יַחְרְגוּ, which occurs in the psalm, חָרַג being a ἅπ. λεγ. in the sense of being terrified, or trembling: they tremble out of their castles, *i.e.* they come trembling out of their castles (for the thought itself, see Micah vii. 17). It is by no means probable that the word חָגַר, which is so frequently met with in Hebrew, is used in this one passage in the sense of "*to limp*," according to Syriac usage.

In conclusion, the Psalmist returns to the praise of the Lord, who had so highly favoured him.

> Ver. 47 Jehovah liveth, and blessed is my rock,
>   And the God of my refuge of salvation is exalted.
>   48 The God who giveth me vengeance,
>   And bringeth nations under me;
>   49 Who leadeth me out from mine enemies,
>   And exalteth me above mine adversaries,
>   Delivereth me from the man of violence.

The formula חַי־יְהוָה does not mean "let Jehovah live," for the word יְחִי would be used for that (*vid.* ch. xvi. 16, 1 Sam. x. 24), but is a declaration: "the Lord is living." The declaration itself is to be taken as praise of God, for "praising God is simply ascribing to Him the glorious perfections which belong to him; we have only to give Him what is His own" (Hengstenberg). The following clauses also contain simply declarations; this is evident from the word יָרוּם, since the optative יָרֹם would be used to denote a wish. The Lord is living or alive when He manifests His life in acts of omnipotence. In the last clause, the expression צוּר (rock) is intensified into אֱלֹהֵי צוּר יִשְׁעִי (the God of my refuge, or rock, of salvation), *i.e.* the God who is my saving rock (cf. ver. 3). In the predicates of God in vers. 48, 49, the saving acts depicted by David in vers. 5–20 and 29–46 are summed up briefly. Instead of מוֹרִיד, "He causes to go down under me," *i.e.* He subjects to me, we find in the psalm וַיַּדְבֵּר, "He drives nations under me," and מְפַלְּטִי instead of מוֹצִיאִי; and lastly, instead of אִישׁ חָמָס in the psalm, we have here אִישׁ חֲמָסִים, as in Ps. cxl. 2. Therefore the praise of the Lord shall be sounded among all nations.

> Ver. 50 Therefore will I praise Thee, O Jehovah, among the nations,
>   And sing praise to Thy name.
>   51 As He who magnifies the salvation of His king,
>   And showeth grace to His anointed,
>   To David, and his seed for ever.

The grace which the Lord had shown to David was so great, that the praise thereof could not be restricted to the narrow limits of Israel. With the dominion of David over the nations, there spread also the knowledge, and with this the praise, of the Lord who had given him the victory. Paul was therefore perfectly justified in quoting the verse before us (ver. 50) in Rom. xvi. 9, along with Deut. xxxii. 43 and Ps. cxvii. 1, as a proof that the salvation of God was intended for the Gentiles also. The king whose salvation the Lord had magnified, was not David as an individual, but David and his seed for ever,—that is to say, the royal family of David which culminated in Christ. David could thus sing praises upon the ground of the promise which he had received (ch. vii. 12–16), and which is repeated almost verbatim in the last clause of ver. 51. The *Chethib* מגדיל is the *Hiphil* participle מַגְדִּיל, according to Ps. xviii. 51; and the *Keri* מִגְדּוֹל, "tower of the fulness of salvation," is a singular conjecture.

DAVID'S LAST WORDS.—CHAP. XXIII. 1–7.

The psalm of thanksgiving, in which David praised the Lord for all the deliverances and benefits that he had experienced throughout the whole of his life, is followed by the prophetic will and testament of the great king, unfolding the importance of his rule in relation to the sacred history of the future. And whilst the psalm may be regarded (ch. xxii.) as a great hallelujah, with which David passed away from the stage of life, these "last words" contain the divine seal of all that he has sung and prophesied in several psalms concerning the eternal dominion of his seed, on the strength of the divine promise which he received through the prophet Nathan, that his throne should be established for ever (ch. vii.). These words are not merely a lyrical expansion of that promise, but a prophetic declaration uttered by David at the close of his life and by divine inspiration, concerning the true King of the kingdom of God. "The aged monarch, who was not generally endowed with the gift of prophecy, was moved by the Spirit of God at the close of his life, and beheld a *just Ruler in the fear of God*, under whose reign blessing and salvation sprang up for the righteous, and all the wicked were overcome. The pledge of this was the eternal covenant which God had concluded with him" (Tholuck: *die Propheten und ihre Weissagungen*, p. 166). The heading "*these are the last words of David*" serves to attach it to the preceding psalm of thanksgiving.

> Ver. 1 Divine saying of David the son of Jesse,
> Divine saying of the man, the highly exalted,
> Of the anointed of the God of Jacob,
> And of the lovely one in the songs of praise of Israel.
> 2 The Spirit of Jehovah speaks through me,
> And His word is upon my tongue.

This introduction to the prophetic announcement rests, both as to form and substance, upon the last sayings of Balaam concerning the future history of Israel (Num. xxiv. 3, 15). This not only shows to what extent David had occupied himself with the utterances of the earlier men of God concerning Israel's future; but indicates, at the same time, that his own prophetic utterance was intended to be a further expansion of Balaam's prophecy concerning the Star out of Jacob and the Sceptre out of Israel. Like Balaam, he calls his prophecy a נְאֻם, *i.e.* a *divine saying* or oracle, as a revelation which he had received directly from God (see at Num. xxiv. 3). But the recipient of this revelation was not, like Balaam the son of Beor, a man with closed eye, whose eyes had been opened by a vision of the Almighty, but "*the man who was raised up on high*" (עָל, adverbially "*above*," is, strictly speaking, a substantive, "*height*," used in an adverbial sense, as in Hos. xi. 7, and probably also ch. vii. 16), *i.e.* whom God had lifted up out of humiliation to be the ruler of His people, yea, even to be the head of the nations (ch. xxii. 44). Luther's rendering, "who is assured of the Messiah of the God of Jacob," is based upon the Vulgate, "*cui constitutum est de Christo Dei Jacob*," and cannot be grammatically sustained. David was exalted on the one hand as "*the anointed of the God of Jacob*," *i.e.* as the one whom the God of Israel had anointed king over His people, and on the other hand as "*the lovely one in Israel's songs of praise*," *i.e.* the man whom God had enabled to sing lovely songs of praise in celebration of His grace and glory. זְמִיר = זִמְרָה does not mean a song generally, but a song of praise in honour of God (see at Ex. xv. 2), like מִזְמוֹר in the headings to the psalms. As David on the one hand had firmly established the kingdom of God in an earthly and political respect as the anointed of Jehovah, *i.e.* as king, so had he on the other, as the composer of Israel's songs of praise, promoted the spiritual edification of that kingdom. The idea of נְאֻם is explained in ver. 2. The Spirit of Jehovah speaks through him; his words are the inspiration of God. The preterite דִּבֶּר relates to the divine inspiration which preceded the utterance of the divine saying. דִּבֶּר בְּ, literally to speak into a person, as in Hos. i. 2. The saying itself commences with ver. 3.

> Ver. 3 The God of Israel saith,
>   The Rock of Israel speaketh to me:
>   A Ruler over men, just,
>   A Ruler in the fear of God.
> 4 And as light of the morning, when the sun rises,
>   As morning without clouds:
>   From shining out of rain (springeth) green out of the earth.
> 5 For is not my house thus with God?
>   For He hath made me an everlasting covenant,
>   Provided with all, and attested;
>   For all my salvation and all good pleasure.
>   Should He then not cause it to grow?

As the prophets generally preface their saying with "thus saith the Lord," so David commences his prophetic saying with "*the God of Israel saith*," for the purpose of describing it most emphatically as the word of God. He designates God "*the*

God" and "*the Rock*" (as in ch. xxii. 3) of Israel, to indicate that the contents of his prophecy relate to the salvation of the people of Israel, and are guaranteed by the unchangeableness of God. The saying which follows bears the impress of a divine oracle even in its enigmatical brevity. The verbs are wanting in the different sentences of vers. 3*b* and 4. "*A ruler over men*," *sc.* "will arise," or there will be. בָּאָדָם does not mean "among men," but "*over men;*" for בְּ is to be taken as with the verb מָשַׁל, as denoting the object ruled over (cf. Gen. iii. 16, iv. 7, etc.). הָאָדָם does not mean certain men, but the human race, humanity. This ruler is "*just*" in the fullest sense of the word, as in the passages founded upon this, viz. Jer. xxiii. 5, Zech. ix. 9, and Ps. lxxii. 2. The justice of the ruler is founded in his "*fear of God.*" יִרְאַת אֱלֹהִים is governed freely by מוֹשֵׁל. (On the fact itself, see Isa. xi. 2, 3.) The meaning is, "A ruler over the human race will arise, a just ruler, and will exercise his dominion in the spirit of the fear of God."—Ver. 4 describes the blessing that will proceed from this ruler. The idea that ver. 4 should be connected with ver. 3*b* so as to form one period, in the sense of "when one rules justly over men (as I do), it is as when a morning becomes clear," must be rejected, for the simple reason that it overlooks Nathan's promise (ch. vii.) altogether, and weakens the force of the saying so solemnly introduced as the word of God. The ruler over men whom David sees in spirit, is not any one who rules righteously over men ; nor is the seed of David to be regarded as a collective expression indicating a merely ideal personality, but, according to the Chaldee rendering, the Messiah himself, the righteous Shoot whom the Lord would raise up to David (Jer. xxiii. 5), and who would execute righteousness and judgment upon earth (Jer. xxxiii. 15).—Ver. 4 is to be taken by itself as containing an independent thought, and the connection between it and ver. 3 must be gathered from the words themselves: the appearance (the rise) of this Ruler will be "*as light of the morning, when the sun rises.*" At the same time, the Messiah is not to be regarded as the subject to אוֹר בֹּקֶר (the light of the morning), as though the ruler over men were compared with the morning light; but the subject compared to the morning light is intentionally left indefinite, according to the view adopted by Luther in his exposition, "In the time of the Messiah it will be like the light of the morning." We are precluded from regarding the Messiah as the subject, by the fact that the comparison is instituted not with the sun, but with the morning dawn at the rising of the sun, whose vivifying effects upon nature are described in the second clause of the verse. The words יִזְרַח שָׁמֶשׁ are to be taken relatively, as a more distinct definition of the morning light. The clause which follows, "morning without clouds," is parallel to the foregoing, and describes more fully the nature of the morning. The light of the rising sun on a cloudless morning is an image of the coming salvation. The rising sun awakens the germs of life in the bosom of nature, which had been slumbering through the darkness of the night. "The state of things before the coming of the ruler resembles the darkness of the night" (Hengstenberg). The verb is also wanting in the second hemistich. "From the shining from rain (is, comes) fresh green out of the earth." נֹגַהּ signifies the brightness of the rising sun; but, so far as the actual meaning is concerned, it relates to the salvation which attends the coming of the righteous ruler. מִמָּטָר is either subordinate to מִנֹּגַהּ, or co-ordinate with it. In the former case, we should have to render the passage, "from the shining of the sun which proceeds out of rain," or "from the shining after rain;" and the allusion would be to a cloudless morning, when the shining of the sun after a night's rain stimulates the growth of the plants. In the latter case, we should have to render it "from the shining (and) from the rain;" and the reference would be to a cloudless morning, on which the vegetation springs up from the ground through sunshine followed by rain. Grammatically considered, the first view (? the second) is the easier of the two; nevertheless we regard the other (? the first) as the only admissible one, inasmuch as rain is not to be expected when the sun has risen with a cloudless sky. The rays of the sun, as it rises after a night of rain, strengthen the fresh green of the plants. The rain is therefore a figurative representation of blessing generally (cf. Isa. xliv. 3), and the green grass which springs up from the earth after the rain is an image of the blessings of the Messianic salvation (Isa. xliv. 4, xlv. 8).

In Ps. lxxii. 6, Solomon takes these words of David as the basis of his comparison of the effects resulting from the govern-

ment of the true Prince of peace to the coming down of the
rain upon the mown grass.

In ver. 5, the prophecy concerning the coming of the just
ruler is sustained by being traced back to the original promise
in ch. vii., in which David had received a pledge of this.   The
first and last clauses of this verse can only be made to yield a
meaning in harmony with the context, by being taken interro-
gatively : *"for is not my house so with God?"*   The question
is only indicated by the tone (כִּי לֹא = כִּי הֲלֹא : ch. xix. 23), as
is frequently the case, even before clauses commencing with לֹא
(*e.g.* Hos. xi. 5, Mal. ii. 15 : cf. Ewald, § 324, *a*).   לֹא־כֵן (not
so) is explained by the following clause, though the כִּי which
follows is not to be taken in the sense of *"that."*   Each of the
two clauses contains a distinct thought.   That of the first is,
"Does not my house stand in such a relation to God, that the
righteous ruler will spring from it?"   This is then explained
in the second : "for He hath made an everlasting covenant
with me."   David calls the promise in ch. vii. 12 sqq., that
God would establish his kingdom to his seed for ever, a covenant, because it involved a reciprocal relation,—namely, that
Jehovah would first of all found for David a permanent house,
and then that the seed of David was to build the house of the
Lord.   This covenant is עֲרוּכָה בַכֹּל, "*equipped (or provided) with
all*" that could help to establish it.   This relates more especially
to the fact that all eventualities were foreseen, even the falling
away of the bearers of the covenant of God, so that such an
event as this would not annul the covenant (ch. vii. 14, 15).
וּשְׁמֻרָה, "*and preserved*," *i.e.* established by the assurance that
even in that case the Lord would not withdraw His grace.
David could found upon this the certainty, that God would
cause all the salvation to spring forth which had been pledged
to his house in the promise referred to.   כָּל־יִשְׁעִי, "*all my salvation*," *i.e.* all the salvation promised to me and to my house.
כָּל־חֵפֶץ, not "all my desire," but "*all the good pleasure*" of
God, *i.e.* all the saving counsel of God expressed in that covenant.   The כִּי before לֹא is an energetic repetition of the כִּי
which introduces the explanatory thought, in the sense of a
firm assurance : "*for all my salvation and all good pleasure,
yea, should He not cause it to spring forth?*"

Ver. 6 But the worthless, as rejected thorns are they all ;
    For men do not take them in the hand.
  7 And the man who touches them
    Provides himself with iron and spear-shaft,
    And they are utterly burned with fire where they dwell.

The development of salvation under the ruler in righteousness and the fear of God is accompanied by judgment upon the ungodly. The abstract בְּלִיַּעַל, *worthlessness*, is stronger than אִישׁ בְּלִיַּעַל, the worthless man, and depicts the godless as personified worthlessness. מֻנַד, in the *Keri* מֻנָּד, the *Hophal* of נוד or נָדַד, literally "*scared*" or hunted away. This epithet does not apply to the thorns, so well as to the ungodly who are compared to thorns. The reference is to thorns that men root out, not to those which they avoid on account of their prickles. בְּלָהֶם, an antiquated form for כֻּלָּם (see Ewald, § 247, *d*). To root them out, or clean the ground of them, men do not lay hold of them with the bare hand; but "*whoever would touch them equips himself* (יִמָּלֵא, *sc.* יָדוֹ, to '*fill the hand*' with anything: 2 Kings ix. 24) *with iron, i.e.* with iron weapons, *and spear-shaft*" (*vid.* 1 Sam. xvii. 7). This expression also relates to the godless rather than to the thorns. They are consumed בְּשֶׁבֶת, "*at the dwelling,*" *i.e.* as Kimchi explains, at the place of their dwelling, the place where they grow. For בְּשֶׁבֶת cannot mean "on the spot" in the sense of without delay. The burning of the thorns takes place at the final judgment upon the ungodly (Matt. xiii. 30).

DAVID'S HEROES.—CHAP. XXIII. 8–39.

The following list of David's heroes we also find in 1 Chron. xi. 10–47, and expanded at the end by sixteen names (vers. 41–47), and attached in ver. 10 to the account of the conquest of the fortress of Zion by the introduction of a special heading. According to this heading, the heroes named assisted David greatly in his kingdom, along with all Israel, to make him king, from which it is evident that the chronicler intended by this heading to justify his appending the list to the account of the election of David as king over all the tribes of Israel (1 Chron. xi. 1), and of the conquest of Zion, which followed immediately afterwards. In every other respect the two lists agree with one another, except that there are a considerable number of errors of the text, more especially in the names, which are frequently corrupt in both texts, so that the true reading cannot be determined with certainty. The heroes enumerated are divided into three classes. The *first* class consists of three, viz. *Jashobeam, Eleazar,* and *Shammah,* of whom certain brave deeds are related, by which they reached the first rank among David's heroes (vers. 8–12). They were followed by *Abishai* and *Benaiah,* who were in the *second* class, and who had also distinguished themselves above the rest by their brave deeds, though they did not come up to the first three (vers. 18–23). The others all belonged to the *third* class, which consisted of thirty-two men, of whom no particular heroic deeds are mentioned (vers. 24–39). Twelve of these, viz. the five belonging to the first two classes and seven of the third, were appointed by David commanders of the twelve detachments into which he divided the army, each detachment to serve for one month in the year (1 Chron. xxvii.). These heroes, among whom we do not find Joab the commander-in-chief of the whole of the forces, were the king's aides-de-camp, and are called in this respect הַשָּׁלִשִׁי (ver. 8), though the term הַשָּׁלִשִׁים (the *thirty,* vers. 13, 23, 24) was also a very customary one, as their number amounted to thirty in a round sum. It is possible that at first they may have numbered exactly thirty; for, from the very nature of the case, we may be sure that in the many wars in which David was engaged, other heroes must have arisen at different times, who would be received into the corps already formed. This will explain the addition of sixteen names in the Chronicles, whether the chronicler made use of a different list from that employed by the author of the books before us, and one belonging to a later age, or whether the author of our books merely restricted himself to a description of the corps in its earlier condition.

Vers. 8–12. *Heroes of the first class.*—The short heading to our text, with which the list in the Chronicles also begins (1 Chron. xi. 11), simply gives the names of these heroes. But instead of "the *names* of the mighty men," we have in the Chronicles "the *number* of the mighty men." This variation is all the more striking, from the fact that in the Chronicles the total number is not given at the close of the list as it is in our

text. At the same time, it can hardly be a copyist's error for
מִבְחָר (*selection*), as Bertheau supposes, but must be attributable
to the fact that, according to vers. 13, 23, and 24, these heroes
constituted a corps which was named from the number of
which it originally consisted. The first, *Jashobeam*, is called
" the chief of the thirty" in the Chronicles. Instead of יָשָׁבְעָם
(*Jashobeam*), the reading in the Chronicles, we have here
יֹשֵׁב בַּשֶּׁבֶת (*Josheb-basshebeth*), unquestionably a spurious reading, which probably arose, according to Kennicott's conjecture,
from the circumstance that the last two letters of ישבעם were
written in one MS. under בַּשֶּׁבֶת in the line above (ver. 7), and
a copyist took בשבת from that line by mistake for עם. The
correctness of the reading *Jashobeam* is established by 1 Chron.
xxvii. 2. The word תַּחְכְּמֹנִי is also faulty, and should be
corrected, according to the Chronicles, into בֶּן־חַכְמוֹנִי (*Ben-
hachmoni*); for the statement that Jashobeam was a son (or
descendant) of the family of *Hachmon* (1 Chron. xxvii. 32)
can easily be reconciled with that in 1 Chron. xxvii. 2, to the
effect that he was a son of Zabdiel. Instead of רֹאשׁ הַשָּׁלִשִׁים
(*head of the thirty*), the reading in the Chronicles, we have here
רֹאשׁ הַשָּׁלִשִׁי (*head of the three*). Bertheau would alter our text
in accordance with the Chronicles, whilst Thenius proposes to
bring the text of the Chronicles into accordance with ours.
But although the many unquestionable corruptions in the verse
before us may appear to favour Bertheau's assumption, we
cannot regard either of the emendations as necessary, or even
warrantable. The proposed alteration of הַשָּׁלִשִׁי is decidedly
precluded by the recurrence of רֹאשׁ הַשָּׁלִשִׁי in ver. 18, and the
alteration of הַשָּׁלִשִׁים in the Chronicles by the repeated allusion
to the שָׁלִשִׁים, not only in vers. 15, 42, ch. xii. 4, and ch. xxvii. 6
of the Chronicles, but also in vers. 13, 23, and 24 of the chapter
before us. The explanation given of שָׁלִשִׁי and שָׁלִשִׁים, as signifying chariot-warriors, is decidedly erroneous;[1] for the singular
הַשָּׁלִישׁ is used in all the passages in which the word occurs to
signify the royal aide-de-camp (2 Kings vii. 2, 17, 19, ix. 25,

---

[1] This explanation, which we find in Gesenius (*Thes.* and *Lex.*) and
Bertheau, rests upon no other authority than the testimony of Origen, to
the effect that an obscure writer gives this interpretation of τριστάτης, the
rendering of שָׁלִישׁ, an authority which is completely overthrown by the
writer of the gloss in *Octateuch.* (Schleussner, *Lex. in* LXX. t. v. p. 338),

xv. 25), and the plural שָׁלִישִׁים the royal body-guard, not only in 2 Kings x. 25, but even in 1 Kings ix. 22, and Ex. xiv. 7, xv. 4, from which the meaning chariot-warriors has been derived. Consequently רֹאשׁ הַשָּׁלִישִׁי is the head of the king's aides-de-camp, and the interchange of הַשָּׁלִישִׁי with the הַשָּׁלִשִׁים of the Chronicles may be explained on the simple ground that David's thirty heroes formed his whole body of adjutants. The singular שָׁלִישִׁי is to be explained in the same manner as הָבְּרֵתִי (see at ch. viii. 18). Luther expresses the following opinion in his marginal gloss with regard to the words which follow (הוּא עֲדִינוֹ הָעֶצְנוֹ): "We believe the text to have been corrupted by a writer, probably from some book in an unknown character and bad writing, so that *orer* should be substituted for *adino*, and *ha-eznib* for *eth hanitho ;*" that is to say, the reading in the Chronicles, "he swung his spear," should be adopted (cf. ver. 18). This supposition is certainly to be preferred to the attempt made by Gesenius (*Lex.*) and v. Dietrich (*s.v.* עָדִין) to find some sense in the words by assuming the existence of a verb עָדֵן and a noun עֶצֶן, a spear, since these words do not occur anywhere else in Hebrew; and in order to obtain any appropriate sense, it is still necessary to resort to alterations of the text. "*He swung his spear over eight hundred slain at once.*" This is not to be understood as signifying that he killed eight hundred men at one blow, but that in a battle he threw his spear again and again at the foe, until eight hundred men had been slain. The Chronicles give three hundred instead of eight hundred; and as that number occurs again in ver. 18, in the case of Abishai, it probably found its way from that verse into this in the book of Chronicles.—Vers. 9, 10. "*After him* (*i.e.* next to him in rank) was *Eleazar* the son of *Dodai* the Ahohite, among the three heroes with David when they defied the Philistines, who had assembled there, and the Israelites drew near." The *Chethib* דֹדִי is to be read דּוֹדַי, *Dodai,* according to 1 Chron. xxvii. 4, and the form דּוֹדוֹ (*Dodo*) in the parallel text (1 Chron. xi. 12) is only a variation in the form of the name. Instead of בֶּן־אֲחֹחִי (*the son of Ahohi*) we find הָאֲחֹחִי (*the Ahohite*) in the

who gives this explanation of τριστάτας: τοὺς παρὰ χεῖρα τοῦ βασιλέως ἀριστερὰν τρίτης μοίρας ἄρχοντας. Suidas and Hesychius give the same explanation (*s.v.* τριστάται). Jerome also observes (ad Ezek. xxiii.): "It is the name of the second rank next to the king."

Chronicles; but the בֶּן must not be struck out on that account as spurious, for "the son of an Ahohite" is the same as "the Ahohite." For בִּשְׁלֹשָׁה נְבֹרִים we must read בִּשְׁלֹשָׁה הַגִּבֹּרִים, according to the *Keri* and the Chronicles. שְׁלֹשָׁה is not to be altered, since the numerals are sometimes attached to substantives in the absolute state (see *Ges.* § 120, 1). "*The three heroes*" are Jashobeam, Eleazar, and Shammah (ver. 11), who reached the first rank, according to ver. 19, among the heroes of David. Instead of בְּחָרְפָם בַּפְּלִשְׁתִּים (*when they defied the Philistines*), we find in the Chronicles בַּפַּס דַּמִּים וְהַפְּלִשְׁתִּים, "*at Pas-dammim*," *i.e.* most probably *Ephes-dammim* (1 Sam. xvii. 1), where the Philistines were encamped when Goliath defied the Israelites. Thenius, Bertheau, and Böttcher therefore propose to alter our text so as to make it correspond to that of the Chronicles, and adduce as the reason the fact that in other passages חֵרֵף is construed with the accusative, and that שָׁם, which follows, presupposes the previous mention of the place referred to. But the reasons are neither of them decisive. חֵרֵף is not construed with the accusative alone, but also with לְ (2 Chron. xxxii. 17), so that the construction with בְ is quite a possible one, and is not at variance with the idea of the word. שָׁם again may also be understood as referring to the place, not named, where the Philistines fought with the Israelites. The omission of אֲשֶׁר before נֶאֶסְפוּ is more difficult to explain; and וְהַפְּלִשְׁתִּים, which we find in the Chronicles, has probably dropped out after בַּפְּלִשְׁתִּים. The reading in the Chronicles בַּפַּס דַּמִּים (בְּאֶפֶס) is probably only a more exact description of the locality, which is but obscurely indicated in our text by בְּחָרְפָם בַּפְּלִשְׁתִּים; for these words affirm that the battle took place where the Israelites had once been defied by the Philistines (1 Sam. xvii. 10), and where they repaid them for this defiance in a subsequent conflict. The Philistines are at any rate to be regarded as the subject to נֶאֶסְפוּ, and these words are a circumstantial clause: the Philistines had assembled together there to battle, and the Israelites had advanced to the attack. The heroic act of Eleazar is introduced with "he arose." He arose and smote the Philistines till his hand was weary and clave to his sword, *i.e.* was so cramped as to be stiffened to the sword. Through this Jehovah wrought a great salvation for Israel on that day, "and the people (the soldiers) turned after him only to plunder," *sc.*

because he had put the enemy to flight by himself. שׁוּב אַחֲרָיו
does not mean to turn back from flight after him, but is the
opposite of שׁוּב מֵאַחֲרֵי, to turn away from a person (1 Sam. xv.
11, etc.), so that it signifies " to turn to a person and follow
behind him." Three lines have dropped out from the parallel
text of the Chronicles, in consequence of the eye of a copyist
having wandered from פְּלִשְׁתִּים נֶאֱספוּ in ver. 9 to וַיֵּאָספוּ פְלִשְׁתִּים
in ver. 11. Vers. 11, 12. The third leading hero was *Shammah*,
the son of *Age* the Hararite (הָרָרִי is probably contracted from
הַהֲרָרִי, ver. 33). He also made himself renowned by a great
victory over the Philistines. The enemy had gathered together
לַחַיָּה, " *as a troop*," or in a crowd. This meaning of חַיָּה (here
and ver. 13, and possibly also in Ps. lxviii. 11) is thoroughly
established by the Arabic (see Ges. *Thes.* p. 470). But it seems
to have fallen into disuse afterwards, and in the Chronicles it
is explained in ver. 13 by מִלְחָמָה, and in ver. 15 by מַחֲנֶה. " On
a portion of a field of lentils there," *sc.* where the Philistines
had gathered together, the people (of Israel) were smitten.
Then Shammah stationed himself in the midst of the field, and
יַּצִּילֶהָ, " *wrested it*," from the foe, and smote the Philistines.
Instead of עֲדָשִׁים, *lentils*, we find in the Chronicles שְׂעֹרִים,
barley, a very inconsiderable difference.

Vers. 13–17. To this deed there is appended a similar heroic
feat performed by three of the thirty heroes whose names are
not given. The *Chethib* שְׁלֹשִׁים is evidently a slip of the pen
for שְׁלֹשָׁה (*Keri* and Chronicles). The thirty chiefs are the
heroes named afterwards (see above at p. 491). As שְׁלֹשָׁה
has no article either in our text or the Chronicles, the three
intended are not the three already mentioned (Jashobeam,
Eleazar, and Shammah), but three others out of the number
mentioned in vers. 24 sqq. These three came to David in the
harvest time unto the cave of Adullam (see at 1 Sam. xxii. 1),
when a troop of the Philistines was encamped in the valley of
Rephaim, and David was on the mountain fortress, and a
Philistian post was then in Bethlehem. And David longed
for water, and said, " Oh that one would bring me water to
drink out of the well of Bethlehem at the gate !" The encampment of the Philistines in the valley of Rephaim, and the
position of David on the mountain fortress (בַּמְּצוּדָה), render it
probable that the feat mentioned here took place in the war

with the Philistines described in ch. v. 17 sqq. Robinson could not discover any well in Bethlehem, "especially none 'by the gate,' except one connected with the aqueduct on the south" (*Palestine*, vol. ii. p. 158). בַּשַּׁעַר need not be understood, however, as signifying that the well was *in* or *under* the gate; but the well referred to may have been at the gate outside the city. The well to which tradition has given the name of "David's well" (*cisterna David*), is about a quarter of an hour's walk to the north-east of Bethlehem, and, according to Robinson's description, is "merely a deep and wide cistern or cavern now dry, with three or four narrow openings cut in the rock." But Ritter (*Erdk.* xvi. p. 286) describes it as "deep with clear cool water, into which there are three openings from above, which Tobler speaks of as bored;" and again as a cistern "built with peculiar beauty, from seventeen to twenty-one feet deep, whilst a house close by is pointed out to pilgrims as Jesse's house."—Ver. 16. The three heroes then broke through the camp of the Philistines at Bethlehem, *i.e.* the outpost that occupied the space before the gate, fetched water out of the well, and brought it to David. He would not drink it, however, but poured it out upon the ground to the Lord, as a drink-offering for Jehovah. "He poured it out upon the earth, rendering Him thanks for the return of the three brave men" (Clericus). And he said, "Far be it from me, O Jehovah, to do this! The blood of the men who went with their lives (*i.e.* at the risk of their lives)," *sc.* should I drink it? The verb אֶשְׁתֶּה is wanting in our text, but is not to be inserted according to the Chronicles as though it had fallen out; the sentence is rather to be regarded as an *aposiopesis*. יְהוָה after חָלִילָה לִי is a vocative, and is not to be altered into מֵיהוָה, according to the מֵאֱלֹהַי of the Chronicles. The fact that the vocative does not occur in other passages after חָלִילָה לִּי proves nothing. It is equivalent to the oath חַי יְהוָה (1 Sam. xiv. 45). The chronicler has endeavoured to simplify David's exclamation by completing the sentence. בְּנַפְשׁוֹתָם, "*for the price of their souls*," *i.e.* at the risk of their lives. The water drawn and fetched at the risk of their lives is compared to the soul itself, and the soul is in the blood (Lev. xvii. 11). Drinking this water, therefore, would be nothing else than drinking their blood.

Vers. 18–23. *Heroes of the second class.*—Vers. 18, 19.

Abishai, Joab's brother (see 1 Sam. xxvi. 6), was also chief of the body-guard, like Jashobeam (ver. 8 : the *Chethib* הַשָּׁלִשִׁי is correct; see at ver. 8). He swung his spear over three hundred slain. "He had a name among the three," *i.e.* the three principal heroes, Jashobeam, Eleazar, and Shammah. The following words, מִן־הַשְּׁלֹשָׁה, make no sense. הַשְּׁלֹשָׁה is an error in writing for הַשְּׁלֹשִׁים, as ver. 23 shows in both the texts (ver. 25 of the Chronicles): an error the origin of which may easily be explained from the word שְׁלֹשָׁה, which stands immediately before. " He was certainly honoured before the thirty (heroes of David), and became their chief, but he did not come to the three," *i.e.* he was not equal to Jashobeam, Eleazar, and Shammah. הֲכִי has the force of an energetic assurance : "*is it so that,*" *i.e.* it is certainly so (as in ch. ix. 1; Gen. xxvii. 36, xxix. 15).— Vers. 20–23. *Benaiah,* the son of Jehoiada, " Jehoiada the priest" according to 1 Chron. xxvii. 5, possibly the one who was "prince for Aaron," *i.e.* of the family of Aaron, according to 1 Chron. xii. 27, was captain of the Crethi and Plethi according to ch. viii. 18 and xx. 23. He was the son of a brave man, rich in deeds (חַי is evidently an error for חַיִל in the Chronicles), of Kabzeel in the south of Judah (Josh. xv. 21). "*He smote the two Ariels of Moab.*" The Arabs and Persians call every remarkably brave man *Ariel,* or lion of God (*vid.* Bochart, *Hieroz.* ii. pp. 7, 63). They were therefore two celebrated Moabitish heroes. The supposition that they were sons of the king of the Moabites is merely founded upon the conjecture of Thenius and Bertheau, that the word בְּנֵי (sons of) has dropped out before Ariel. " He also slew the lion in the well on the day of the snow," *i.e.* a lion which had been driven into the neighbourhood of human habitations by a heavy fall of snow, and had taken refuge in a cistern. The *Chethib* הָאֲרִיָּה and בְּאֵר are the earlier forms for the *Keris* substituted by the Masoretes הָאֲרִי and הַבּוֹר, and consequently are not to be altered. He also slew an Egyptian of distinguished size. According to the *Keri* we should read אִישׁ מַרְאֶה (instead of אֲשֶׁר מַרְאֶה), " *a man of appearance,*" *i.e.* a distinguished man, or a man of great size, ἄνδρα ὁρατόν (LXX.); in the Chronicles it is simplified as אִישׁ מִדָּה, a man of measure, *i.e.* of great height. This man was armed with a spear or javelin, whereas Benaiah was only armed with a stick; nevertheless the latter smote him, took away his spear, and slew him with his own weapon. According to the Chronicles the Egyptian was five cubits high, and his spear like a weaver's beam. Through these feats Benaiah acquired a name among the three, though he did not equal them (vers. 22, 23, as in vers. 18, 19); and David made him a member of his privy council (see at 1 Sam. xxii. 14).

Vers. 24–39. *Heroes of the third class.*—Ver. 24. "*Asahel*, the brother of Joab, among the thirty," *i.e.* belonging to them. This definition also applies to the following names; we therefore find at the head of the list in the Chronicles, וּגִבּוֹרֵי הַחֲיָלִים, "and brave heroes (were)." The names which follow are for the most part not further known. *Elhanan*, the son of *Dodo* of Bethlehem, is a different man from the Bethlehemite of that name mentioned in ch. xxi. 19. *Shammah* the Harodite also must not be confounded with the Shammahs mentioned in vers. 11 and 33. In the Chronicles we find *Shammoth*, a different form of the name; whilst הַהֲרוֹרִי is an error in writing for הַחֲרֹדִי, *i.e.* sprung from *Harod* (Judg. vii. 1). This man is called *Shamhut* in 1 Chron. xxvii. 8; he was the leader of the fifth division of David's army. *Elika* of *Harod* is omitted in the Chronicles; it was probably dropped out in consequence of the *homoioteleuton* הַחֲרֹדִי.—Ver. 26. *Helez* the Paltite; *i.e.* sprung from *Beth-Pelet* in the south of Judah (Judg. xv. 27). He was chief of the seventh division of the army (compare 1 Chron. xxvii. 10 with 1 Chron. xi. 27, though in both passages הַפַּלְטִי is misspelt הַפְּלֹנִי). *Ira* the son of *Ikkesh* of Tekoah in the desert of Judah (ch. xiv. 2), chief of the sixth division of the army (1 Chron. xxvii. 9).—Ver. 27. *Abiezer* of Anathoth (Anata) in Benjamin (see at Josh. xviii. 24), chief of the ninth division of the army (1 Chron. xxvii. 12). *Mebunnai* is a mistake in spelling for *Sibbechai* the Hushathite (compare ch. xxi. 18 and 1 Chron. xi. 29). According to 1 Chron. xxvii. 11, he was chief of the eighth division of the army.—Ver. 28. *Zalmon* the Ahohite, *i.e.* sprung from the Benjaminite family of Ahoah, is not further known. Instead of *Zalmon* we find Ilai in the Chronicles (ver. 29); but which of the two names is the correct one it is impossible to decide. *Maharai* of *Netophah*: according to Ezra ii. 22 and Neh. vii. 26, Netophah was a place in the neighbourhood of Bethlehem, but it has not yet been discovered, as *Beit Nattif*, which might be thought of, is too far from Bethlehem (*vid.* Rob. *Pal.* ii. p. 344, and Tobler, *Dritte Wanderung*, pp. 117–8). According to 1 Chron. xxvii. 13, *Maharai* belonged to the Judahite family of Serah, and was chief of the tenth division of the army.—Ver. 29. *Cheleb*, more correctly *Cheled* (1 Chron. xi. 30 ; or *Cheldai*, 1 Chron. xxvii. 15), also of Netophah, was chief of the twelfth division of the army. *Ittai* (*Ithai* in the Chronicles), the son of Ribai of Gibeah of Benjamin, must be distinguished from *Ittai* the Gathite (ch. xv. 19). Like all that follow, with the exception of Uriah, he is not further known.—Ver. 30. *Benaiah* of *Phir'aton* in the tribe of Ephraim, a place which has been preserved in the village of *Fer'ata*, to the south-west of Nablus (see at Judg. xii. 13). *Hiddai* (wrongly spelt *Hudai* in the Chronicles), out of the valleys of *Gaash*, in the tribe of Ephraim by the mountain of *Gaash*, the situation of which has not yet been discovered (see at Josh. xxiv. 30).—Ver. 31. *Abi-Albon* (written incorrectly *Abiel* in the Chronicles) the Arbathite, *i.e.* from the place called *Beth-haarabah* or *Arabah* (Josh. xv. 61 and xviii. 18, 22) in the desert of Judah, on the site of the present *Kasr Hajla* (see at Josh. xv. 6). *Azmaveth* of *Bahurim :* see at ch. xvi. 5.—Vers. 32, 33. *Eliahba* of *Shaalbon* or *Shaalbin*, which may possibly have been preserved in the present *Selbit* (see at Josh. xix. 42). The next two names, שַׁמָּה הַהֲרָרִי and בְּנֵי יָשֵׁן יְהוֹנָתָן (*Bneyashen Jehonathan* and *Shammah the Hararite*), are written thus in the Chronicles (ver. 34), בְּנֵי הָשֵׁם הַגִּזוֹנִי יוֹנָתָן בֶּן־שָׁגֵא הַהֲרָרִי : " *Bnehashem the Gizonite, Jonathan the son of Sage the Hararite.*" The text of the Chronicles is evidently the more correct of the two, as *Bne Jashen Jehonathan* does not make any sense. The only question is whether the form בְּנֵי הָשֵׁם is correct, or whether בְּנֵי has not arisen merely through a misspelling. As the name does not occur again, all that can be said is that *Bne hashem* must at any rate be written as one word, and therefore should be pointed differently. The place mentioned, *Gizon*, is unknown. שַׁמָּה for בֶּן־שָׁגֵא probably arose from ver. 11. *Ahiam* the son of *Sharar* or *Sacar* (Chron.) the Ararite (in the Chronicles the Hararite).—Ver. 34. The names in 34*a*, *Eliphelet ben-Ahasbai ben-Hammaacathi*, read thus in the Chronicles (vers. 35, 36) : Eliphal ben-Ur ; *Hepher hanmecerathi.* We see from this that in *ben-Ahasbai ben* two names have been fused together ; for the text as it lies before us is rendered suspicious partly by the fact that the names of both father and grandfather are given, which does not occur in connection with any other name in the whole list, and partly by the circumstance that בֶּן cannot properly be written with הַמַּעֲכָתִי, which is a *Gentile noun*. Consequently the following is probably the correct way of restoring the text, אֱלִיפֶלֶט חֵפֶר בֶּן־אוּר הַמַּעֲכָתִי, *Eliphelet* (a name which frequently occurs) *the son of Ur; Hepher the Maachathite, i.e.* of Maacah in the north-east of Gilead (see at ch. x. 6 and Deut. iii. 14). *Eliam* the son of Ahithophel the Gilonite, the clever but treacherous counsellor of David (see at ch. xv. 12). This name is quite corrupt in the Chronicles.—Ver. 35. *Hezro* the Carmelite, *i.e.* of Carmel in the mountains of Judah (1 Sam. xxv. 2). *Paarai* the Arbite, *i.e.* of Arab, also in the mountains of Judah (Josh. xv. 52). In the Chronicles we find *Naarai ben-Ezbi*: the latter is evidently an error in writing for *ha-Arbi*; but it is impossible to decide which of the two forms, *Paarai* and *Naarai*, is the correct one.—Ver. 36. *Jigal* the son of Nathan of Zoba (see at ch. viii. 3): in the Chronicles, Joel the brother of Nathan. *Bani* the Gadite: in the Chronicles we have *Mibhar* the son of Hagri. In all probability the names in the Chronicles are corrupt in this instance also.—Ver. 37. *Zelek* the Ammonite, *Nacharai* the Beerothite (of Beeroth : see at ch. iv. 2), the armour-bearer of Joab. Instead of נִשָּׂאִי, the *Keri* and the Chronicles have נֹשֵׂא : the latter reading is favoured by the circumstance, that if more than one of the persons named had been Joab's armour-bearers, their names would most probably have been linked together by a copulative *vav*.—Ver. 38. *Ira* and *Gareb*, both of them Jithrites, *i.e.* sprung from a family in Kirjath-jearim (1 Chron. ii. 53). *Ira* is of course a different man from the *cohen* of that name (ch. xx. 26).—Ver. 39. *Uriah* the Hittite is well known from ch. xi. 3. "*Thirty and seven in all.*" This number is correct, as there were *three* in the first class (vers. 8–12), *two* in the second (vers. 18–23), and *thirty-two* in the third (vers. 24–39), since ver. 34 contains three names according to the amended text.

NUMBERING OF THE PEOPLE, AND PESTILENCE.—CHAP. XXIV.

For the purpose of ascertaining the number of the people, and their fitness for war, David ordered Joab, his commander-in-chief, to take a census of Israel and Judah. Joab dissuaded him from such a step; but inasmuch as the king paid no attention to his dissuasion, he carried out the command with the help of the military captains (vers. 1–9). David very speedily saw, however, that he had sinned; whereupon the prophet Gad went to him by the command of Jehovah to announce the coming punishment, and give him the choice of three different judgments which he placed before him (vers. 10–13). As David chose rather to fall into the hand of the Lord than into the hand of men, God sent a pestilence, which carried off seventy thousand men in one day throughout the whole land, and had reached Jerusalem, when the Lord stopped the destroying angel in consequence of the penitential prayer of David (vers. 14–17), and sent Gad to the king to direct him to build an altar to the Lord on the spot where the destroying angel had appeared to him (ver. 18). Accordingly David bought the threshing-floor of Araunah the Jebusite, built an altar upon it, and sacrificed burnt-offerings and thank-offerings, after which the plague was stayed (vers. 19–25).

This occurrence, which is introduced in the parallel history in 1 Chron. xxi. between David's wars and his arrangements for a more complete organization of the affairs of the nation, belongs undoubtedly to the closing years of David's reign. The mere taking of a census, as a measure that would facilitate the general organization of the kingdom, could not in itself be a sinful act, by which David brought guilt upon himself, or upon the nation, before God. Nevertheless it is not only represented in ver. 1 as a manifestation of the wrath of God against Israel, but in ver. 3 Joab seeks to dissuade the king from it as being a wrong thing; and in ver. 10 David himself admits that it was a grievous sin against God, and as a sin it is punished by the Lord (vers. 12 sqq.). In what, then, did David's sin consist? Certainly not in the fact that, when taking the census, "he neglected to demand the atonement money, which was to be raised, according to Ex. xxx. 12 sqq., from all who were numbered, because the numbering of the people was regarded in itself as an undertaking by which the anger of God might easily be excited," as Josephus and Bertheau maintain; for the Mosaic instructions concerning the atonement money had reference to the incorporation of the people into the army of

Jehovah (see at Ex. xxx. 13, 14), and therefore did not come into consideration at all in connection with the census appointed by David as a purely political measure. Nor can we imagine that David's sin consisted merely in the fact that he "entered upon the whole affair from pride and vain boasting," or that "he commanded the census from vanity, inasmuch as he wanted to have it distinctly set before his own eyes how strong and mighty he was" (Buddeus, Hengstenberg, and others); for although pride and vanity had something to do with it, as the words of Joab especially seem to indicate, David was far too great a man to allow us to attribute to him a childish delight in the mere number of souls in his kingdom. The census had certainly a higher purpose than this. It is very evident from 1 Chron. xxvii. 23, 24, where it is mentioned again that it was connected with the military organization of the people, and probably was to be the completion of it. David wanted to know the number of his subjects, not that he might be able to boast of their multitude, nor that he might be able to impose all kinds of taxes upon every town and village according to their houses and inhabitants, as Ewald maintains; but that he might be fully acquainted with its defensive power, though we can neither attribute to him the definite purpose " of transforming the theocratic sacred state into a conquering world-state" (Kurtz), nor assume that through this numbering the whole nation was to be enrolled for military service, and that thirst for conquest was the motive for the undertaking. The true kernel of David's sin was to be found, no doubt, in self-exaltation, inasmuch as he sought for the strength and glory of his kingdom in the number of the people and their readiness for war. This sin was punished. "Because David was about to boast proudly and to glory in the number of his people, God determined to punish him by reducing their number either by famine, war, or pestilence" (Seb. Schmidt). At the same time, the people themselves had sinned grievously against God and their king, through the two rebellions headed by Absalom and Sheba.

Vers. 1–9. "Again the anger of Jehovah was kindled against Israel; and He moved David against them, saying, Go, number Israel and Judah." וַיָּסֶף . . . לֶחֱרוֹת points back to the manifestation of the wrath of God, which Israel had experienced in the three years' famine (ch. xxi.). Just as that plague had burst upon the land on account of the guilt which rested upon the people, so the kindling of the wrath of God against Israel a second time also presupposes guilt on the part of the nation ; and as this is not expressly pointed out, we may seek for it generally in the rebellions of Absalom and Sheba against the divinely established government of David. The subject to "*moved*" is *Jehovah*, and the words "*against them*" point back to *Israel*. Jehovah instigated David against Israel to the performance of an act which brought down a severe judgment upon the nation. With regard to the idea that God instigates to sin, see the remarks on 1 Sam. xxvi. 19. In the parallel text of the Chronicles, Satan is mentioned as the tempter to evil, through whom Jehovah led David to number the people.—Ver. 2. David entrusted the task to his commander-in-chief Joab. אֲשֶׁר אִתּוֹ, "*who was with him:*" the meaning is, "when he was with him" (David). We are not warranted in attempting any emendations of the text, either by the expression אֲשֶׁר אִתּוֹ, or by the reading in the Chronicles, וְאֶל־שָׂרֵי הָעָם ("and to the rulers of the people"); for whilst the latter reading may easily be seen to be a simplification founded upon ver. 4, it is impossible to show how שַׂר־הַחַיִל אֲשֶׁר אִתּוֹ, which is supported by all the ancient versions (with the sole exception of the Arabic), could have originated in וְאֶל־שָׂרֵי הָעָם. "*Go now through all the tribes of Israel, from Dan to Beersheba* (see at Judg. xx. 1), *and muster the people.*" פָּקַד, to muster or number, as in Num. i. 44 sqq. The change from the singular שׁוּט to the plural פִּקְדוּ may be explained very simply, from the fact that, as a matter of course, Joab was not expected to take the census by himself, but with the help of several assistants.— Ver. 3. Joab discountenanced the thing: " Jehovah thy God add to the nation, as it is, a hundredfold as many, and may the eyes of my lord the king see it. But why doth my lord the king delight in this thing?" The ו before יוֹסֵף stands at the commencement, when what is said contains a sequel to something that has gone before (*vid.* Ges. § 255, 1, *a*). The thought to which Joab's words are appended as a sequel, is implied in what David said, "that I may know the number of the people;" and if expressed fully, his words would read somewhat as follows : " If thou hast delight in the greatness of the number of

the people, may Jehovah," etc. Joab evidently saw through
the king's intention, and perceived that the numbering of the
people could not be of any essential advantage to David's
government, and might produce dissatisfaction among the
people, and therefore endeavoured to dissuade the king from
his purpose. וְכָהֶם כָּהֶם, " *as they* (the Israelites) *just are*," *i.e.*
in this connection, " just as many as there are of them."
From a grammatical point of view, כָּהֶם is to be taken as the
object to יֹסֵף, as in the parallel passages, Deut. i. 11, 2 Sam.
xii. 8. Not only did he desire that God would multiply the
nation a hundredfold, but that He would do it during the lifetime of David, so that his eyes might be delighted with the
immense numbers.—Vers. 4, 5. But as the king's word prevailed against Joab and against the captains of the army, they
(Joab and the other captains) went out to number Israel. יַּחֲנוּ,
they encamped, *i.e.* they fixed their headquarters in the open
field, because great crowds assembled together. This is only
mentioned here in connection with the place where the numbering commenced; but it is to be understood as applying to
the other places as well (Thenius). In order to distinguish
Aroer from the place of the same name on the Arnon, in the
tribe of Reuben (Josh. xii. 2; Num. xxxii. 34, etc.), it is defined more precisely as "the town in the brook-valley of Gad,"
i.e. Aroer of Gad before Rabbah (Josh. xiii. 25; Judg. xi. 33),
in the Wady *Nahr Ammân*, to the north-east of Ammân (see
at Josh. xiii. 25). וְאֶל־יַעְזֵר (and to *Jazer*) : this is a second place
of encampment, and the preposition אֶל is to be explained on the
supposition that יָבֹאוּ (they came), which follows, was already in
the writer's thoughts. *Jazer* is probably to be found in the
ruins of *es Szir*, at the source of the *Nahr Szir* (see at Num.
xxi. 32).—Ver. 6. "And they came to *Gilead*," *i.e.* the mountainous district on the two sides of the Jabbok (see at Deut. iii.
10). The words which follow, viz. "into the land תַּחְתִּים חָדְשִׁי,"
are quite obscure, and were unintelligible even to the earlier
translators. The Septuagint has γῆν 'Εθαὼν 'Αδασαί, or γῆν
Θαβασών (also γῆν χεττιείμ) ἥ ἐστιν 'Αδασαί. Symmachus
has τὴν κατωτέραν ὁδόν; Jonathan לְאַרְעָא דָרוֹמָא לְחָדְשִׁי (" into
the southland *Chodshi*"); and the Vulgate *in terram inferiorem.*
The singular form תַּחְתִּים, and the fact that we never read of
a land called *Chodshi*, render the conjecture a very probable

one that the text is corrupt. But it is no longer possible to discover the correct reading. Ewald imagines that we should
read *Hermon* instead of the unintelligible *Chodshi;* but this is
not very probable. Böttcher supposes תחתים to be a mistake
in writing for תַּחַת יָם, "below the lake," namely the lake
of Gennesareth, which might have been called *Chodshi* (the
new-moon-like), since it had very much the appearance of a
crescent when seen from the northern heights. This is inge-
nious, but incredible. The order of the places named points to
the eastern side of the sea of Galilee; for they went thence
to *Dan-Jaan, i.e.* the Dan in northern Peræa, mentioned in
Gen. xiv. 14, to the south-west of Damascus, at that time probably the extreme north-eastern boundary of the kingdom of
David, in the direction towards Syria (see at Gen. xiv. 14) :
" and round to *Sidon,*" the extreme north-western boundary of
the kingdom.—Ver. 7. Thence southwards to the fortress of
Zor, i.e. Tyre (see at Josh. xix. 29), and " *into all the towns of
the Hivites and Canaanites,*" *i.e.* the towns in the tribes of
Naphtali, Zebulun, and Issachar, or the (subsequent) province
of Galilee, in which the Canaanites had not been exterminated
by the Israelites, but had only been made tributary.—Vers.
8, 9. When they had traversed the whole land, they came back
to Jerusalem, at the end of nine months and twenty days, and
handed over to the king the number of the people mustered :
viz. 800,000 men of Israel fit for military service, drawing the
sword, and 500,000 men of Judah. According to the Chronicles
(ver. 5), there were 1,100,000 Israelites and 470,000 Judæans.
The numbers are not given by thousands, and therefore are only
approximative statements in round numbers; and the difference
in the two texts arose chiefly from the fact, that the statements
were merely founded upon oral tradition, since, according to
1 Chron. xxvii. 4, the result of the census was not inserted in
the annals of the kingdom. There is no ground, however, for
regarding the numbers as exaggerated, if we only bear in mind
that the entire population of a land amounts to about four times
the number of those who are fit for military service, and therefore 1,300,000, or even a million and a half, would only represent a total population of five or six millions,—a number which
could undoubtedly have been sustained in Palestine, according
to thoroughly reliable testimony as to its unusual fertility (see

the discussion of this subject at Num. i.–iv., vol. iii. pp. 4–13).
Still less can we adduce as a proof of exaggeration the fact,
that according to 1 Chron. xxvii. 1–15, David had only an army
of 288,000 ; for it is a well-known fact, that in all lands the
army, or number of men in actual service, is, as a rule, much
smaller than the total number of those who are capable of
bearing arms. According to 1 Chron. xxi. 6, the tribes of
Levi and Benjamin were not numbered, because, as the chronicler adds, giving his own subjective view, " the word of the
king was an abomination to Joab," or, as it is affirmed in
1 Chron. xxvii. 4, according to the objective facts, " because
the numbering was not completed." It is evident from this,
that in consequence of Joab's repugnance to the numbering of
the people, he had not hurried with the fulfilment of the king's
command; so that when David saw his own error, he revoked
the command before the census was complete, and so the tribe
of Benjamin was not numbered at all, the tribe of Levi being
of course *eo ipso* exempt from a census that was taken for the
sake of ascertaining the number of men who were capable of
bearing arms.

Vers. 10–18. David's heart, *i.e.* his conscience, smote him,
after he had numbered the people, or had given orders for the
census to be taken. Having now come to a knowledge of his
sin, he prayed to the Lord for forgiveness, because he had
acted foolishly. The sin consisted chiefly in the self-exaltation
which had led to this step (see the introductory remarks).—
Vers. 11–13. When he rose up in the morning, after he had
calmly reflected upon the matter during the night upon his
bed, and had been brought to see the folly of his determination, the prophet Gad came to him by the command of God,
pointed out to him his fault, and foretold the punishment that
would come from God. " Shall seven years of famine come
upon thy land, or three months of flight before thine oppressors that they may pursue thee, or shall there be three days of
pestilence in thy land? Now mark and see what answer I
shall bring to Him that sendeth me." These three verses form
one period, in which נָר וַיָּבֹא (ver. 13) answers as the consequent
to וגו' דָּוִד וַיָּקֶם in ver. 11, and the words from יְהֹוָה וּדְבַר (ver.
11*b*) to וְאֶעֱשֶׂה־לָּךְ (ver. 12) form a circumstantial clause inserted
between. וגו' יְהֹוָה וּדְבַר : " and the word of the Lord had taken

place (gone forth) to Gad, David's seer, saying, Go . . . thus
saith Jehovah, I lay upon thee three (things or evils) ; choose
thee one of them that I may do it to thee." Instead of נֹטֵל עַל,
to lay upon, we find נֹטֶה in the Chronicles, "to turn upon
thee." The three things are mentioned first of all in connection with the execution of Gad's commission to the king.
Instead of *seven* years of famine, we find *three* years in the
Chronicles; the Septuagint has also the number three in the
passage before us, and apparently it is more in harmony with
the connection, viz. *three* evils to choose from, and each lasting
through *three* divisions of time. But this agreement favours
the *seven* rather than the *three*, which is open to the suspicion
of being intentionally made to conform to the rest. נֻסְךָ is
an infinitive : "thy fleeing," for that thou fliest before thine
enemies. In the Chronicles the last two evils are described
more fully, but the thought is not altered in consequence.—
Ver. 14. David replied, "I am in great trouble. Let us fall
into the hand of the Lord, for His mercy is great ; but let me
not fall into the hand of men." Thus David chose the third
judgment, since pestilence comes directly from God. On the
other hand, in flight from the enemy, he would have fallen
into the hands of men. It is not easy to see, however, how
far this could apply to famine ; probably inasmuch as it tends
more or less to create dependence upon those who are still in
possession of the means of life.—Ver. 15. God then gave
(sent) a pestilence into (upon) Israel, "from the morning till
the time of the assembly ;" and there died of the people in the
whole land (from Dan to Beersheba) seventy thousand men.
"*From the morning :*" on which Gad had foretold the punishment. The meaning of וְעַד־עֵת מוֹעֵד is doubtful. The rendering "*to the time appointed*," *i.e.* "till the expiration of the three
days," in support of which the Vulgate (*ad tempus constitutum*)
is wrongly appealed to, is precluded not only by the circumstance that, according to ver. 16, the plague was stayed earlier
because God repented Him of the evil, so that it did not last
so long as was at first appointed, but also by the grammatical
difficulty that עֵת מוֹעֵד has no article, and can only be rendered
"for *an* (not for *the*) appointed time." We meet with two
different explanations in the ancient versions : one in the
Septuagint, ἕως ὥρας ἀρίστου, "till the hour of breakfast," *i.e.*

till the sixth hour of the day, which is the rendering also adopted by the Syriac and Arabic as well as by Kimchi and several of the Rabbins; the other in the Chaldee (Jonathan), "from the time at which the sacrifice is commonly slain until it is consumed." Accordingly Bochart explains עֵת מוֹעֵד as signifying "the time at which the people came together for evening prayers, about the ninth hour of the day, *i.e.* the third hour in the afternoon" (*vid.* Acts iii. 1). The same view also lies at the foundation of the Vulgate rendering, according to the express statement of Jerome (*traditt. Hebr. in* 2 *libr. Regum*): "He calls that the *time appointed*, in which the evening sacrifice was offered." It is true that this meaning of מוֹעֵד cannot be established by precisely analogous passages, but it may be very easily deduced from the frequent employment of the word to denote the meetings and festivals connected with the worship of God, when it generally stands without an article, as for example in the perfectly analogous יוֹם מוֹעֵד (Hos. ix. 5; Lam. ii. 7, 22); whereas it is always written with the article when it is used in the general sense of a fixed time, and some definite period is referred to.[1] We must therefore decide in favour of the latter. But if the pestilence did not last a whole day, the number of persons carried off by it (70,000 men) exceeded very considerably the number destroyed by the most violent pestilential epidemics on record, although they have not unfrequently swept off hundreds of thousands in a very brief space of time. But the pestilence burst upon the people in this instance with supernatural strength and violence, that it might be seen at once to be a direct judgment from God.—Ver. 16. The general statement as to the divine judgment and its terrible effects is followed by a more minute

---

[1] The objections brought against this have no force in them, viz. that, according to this view, the section must have been written a long time after the captivity (Clericus and Thenius), and that " the perfectly general expression ' *the time of meeting*' could not stand for the time of the afternoon or evening meeting" (Thenius) : for the former rests upon the assumption that the daily sacrifice was introduced after the captivity,—an assumption quite at variance with historical facts; and the latter is overthrown by the simple remark, that the indefinite expression derived its more precise meaning from the legal appointment of the morning and evening sacrifice as times of meeting for the worship of God, inasmuch as the evening meeting was the only one that could be placed in contrast with the morning.

description of the judgment itself, and the arrest of the plague. "When the destroying angel ('*the angel*' is defined immediately afterwards as '*the angel that destroyed the people*') stretched out his hand towards Jerusalem to destroy it, Jehovah repented of the evil (for this expression, see Ex. xxxii. 14, Jer. xxvi. 13, 19, etc.; and for the repentance of God, the remarks on Gen. vi. 6), and He commanded the angel, Enough! stay now thine hand." This implies that the progress of the pestilence was stayed before Jerusalem, and therefore that Jerusalem itself was spared. "*And the angel of Jehovah was at the threshing-floor of Aravnah the Jebusite.*" These words affirm most distinctly that the destroying angel was visible. According to ver. 17, David saw him there. The visible appearance of the angel was to exclude every thought of a natural land plague. The appearance of the angel is described more minutely in the Chronicles: David saw him standing by the threshing-floor of Aravnah between heaven and earth with a drawn sword in his hand, stretched out over Jerusalem. The drawn sword was a symbolical representation of the purpose of his coming (see at Num. xxii. 23 and Josh. v. 13). The threshing-floor of Aravnah was situated, like all other threshing-floors, outside the city, and upon an eminence, or, according to the more precise statement which follows, to the north-east of Zion, upon Mount Moriah (see at ver. 25). According to the *Chethib* of ver. 16, the name of the owner of the floor was הָאֲוַרְנָה, of ver. 18 אֲרַנְיָה, and of ver. 20 (twice) אֲרַוְנָה. The last form also occurs in vers. 22, 23, and 24, and has been substituted by the Masoretes as the *Keri* in vers. 16 and 18. In the Chronicles, on the other hand, the name is always written אָרְנָן (*Ornan*), and hence in the Septuagint we find Ὄρνα in both texts. "The form אֲרַוְנָה (*Aravnah*) has not a Hebrew stamp, whereas *Orna* and *Ornan* are true Hebrew formations. But for this very reason *Aravnah* appears to be derived from an ancient tradition" (Bertheau).—Ver. 17. When David saw the angel, he prayed to the Lord (he and the elders being clothed in mourning costume: Chron.): "Behold, *I* have sinned, and *I* have acted perversely; but these, the flock, what have they done? Let Thy hand come upon me and my house." The meaning is: I the shepherd of Thy people have sinned and transgressed, but the nation is innocent; *i.e.* not indeed free from every kind of blame, but only from the sin which God was punishing by the pestilence. It belongs to the very nature of truly penitential prayer, that the person praying takes all the blame upon himself, acknowledges before God that he alone is deserving of punishment, and does not dwell upon the complicity of others for the sake of palliating his own sin in the sight of God. We must not infer, therefore, from this confession on the part of David, that the people, whilst innocent themselves, had had to atone only for an act of transgression on the part of their king.—Ver. 18. David's prayer was heard. The prophet Gad came and said to him by command of Jehovah, "Go up, and erect an altar to the Lord upon the floor of Aravnah the Jebusite." This is all that is communicated here of the word of Jehovah which Gad was to convey to the king; the rest is given afterwards, as is frequently the case, in the course of the subsequent account of the fulfilment of the divine command (ver. 21). David was to build the altar and offer burnt-offerings and supplicatory-offerings upon it, to appease the wrath of Jehovah. The plague would then be averted from Israel.

Vers. 19-25. David went up to Aravnah according to the command of God.—Vers. 20, 21. When Aravnah saw the king coming up to him with his servants (וַיַּשְׁקֵף, " he looked out," viz. from the enclosure of the threshing-floor), he came out, bowed low even to the earth, and asked the king what was the occasion of his coming; whereupon David replied, " To buy the floor from thee, to build an altar to the Lord, that the plague may be turned away from the people."—Ver. 22. Aravnah replied, " Let my lord the king take and offer up what seemeth good unto him : behold (i.e. there thou hast) the ox for the burnt-offering, and the threshing-machine, and the harness of the ox for wood" (i.e. for fuel). הַבָּקָר, the pair of oxen yoked together in front of the threshing-machine. כְּלֵי הַבָּקָר, the wooden yokes. " All this giveth Aravnah, O king, to the king." הַמֶּלֶךְ is a vocative, and is simply omitted by the LXX., Vulgate, Syriac, and Arabic, because the translators regarded it as a nominative, which is quite unsuitable, as Aravnah was not a king. When Thenius, on the other hand, objects to this, for the purpose of throwing suspicion upon the passage, that the sentence is thus stamped as part of Aravnah's address to the king, and that in that case the words that follow, " and Aravnah said," would be altogether superfluous; the former remark is correct enough, for the words " all this giveth Aravnah . . . to the king" must form part of what Aravnah said, inasmuch as the remark, " all this gave Aravnah to the king," if taken as the historian's own words, would be in most glaring contradiction to what follows, where the king is said to have bought the floor and the oxen from Aravnah. And the words that follow (" and Aravnah said") are not superfluous on that account, but simply indicate that Aravnah did not proceed to say the rest in the same breath, but added it after a short pause, as a word which did not directly bear upon the question put by the king. וַיֹּאמֶר (and he said) is often repeated, where the same person continues speaking (see for example ch. xv. 4, 25, 27). " Jehovah thy God accept thee graciously," i.e. fulfil the request thou presentest to Him with sacrifice and prayer.—Ver. 24. The king did not accept the offer, however, but said, " No; but I will buy it of thee at a price, and will not offer burnt-offerings to the Lord my God without paying for them." Thus David bought the threshing-floor and the oxen for fifty shekels of silver. Instead of this, the Chronicles give "shekels of gold, in weight six hundred." This difference cannot be reconciled by assuming that David paid his fifty shekels in gold coin, which would have been worth as much as six hundred shekels of silver, since gold was worth twelve times as much as silver. For there is nothing about gold shekels in our text; and the words of the Chronicles cannot be interpreted as meaning that the shekels of gold were worth six hundred shekels of silver. No other course is left, therefore, than to assume that the number must be corrupt in one of the texts. Apparently the statement in the Chronicles is the more correct of the two: for if we consider that Abraham paid four hundred shekels of silver for the site of a family burial-place, at a time when the land was very thinly populated, and therefore land must certainly have been much cheaper than it was in David's time, the small sum of fifty shekels of silver (about £6) appears much too low a price; and David would certainly pay at least fifty shekels of gold. But we are not warranted in any case in speaking of the statement in the Chronicles, as Thenius does, as " intentionally exaggerated."

This style of criticism, which carries two kinds of weights and measures in its bag, explaining the high numbers in the books of Samuel and Kings as corruptions of the text, and those in the Chronicles as intentional exaggerations on the part of the chronicler, is sufficiently dealt with by the remark of Bertheau, that " this (*i.e.* the charge of exaggeration) could only be sustained if it were perfectly certain that the chronicler had our present text of the books of Samuel before him at the time."— Ver. 25. After acquiring the threshing-floor by purchase, David built an altar to the Lord there, and offered burnt-offerings and supplicatory-offerings (*shelamim*: as in Judg. xx. 26, xxi. 4; 1 Sam. xiii. 9) upon it to the Lord. " So Jehovah was entreated, and the plague was turned away from Israel."

This remark brings to a close not only the account of this particular occurrence, but also the book itself; whereas in the Chronicles it is still further stated that Jehovah answered David with fire from heaven, which fell upon the burnt-offering; and that after his prayer had been answered thus, David not only continued to offer sacrifice upon the floor of Aravnah, but also fixed upon it as the site for the temple which was afterwards to be built (1 Chron. xxi. 27, xxii. 1); and to this there is appended, in ch. xxii. 2 sqq., an account of the preparations which David made for the building of the temple. It is not affirmed in the Chronicles, however, that David fixed upon this place as the site for the future temple in consequence of a revelation from God, but simply that he did this, because he saw that the Lord had answered him there, and because he could not go to Gibeon, where the tabernacle was standing, to seek the Lord there, on account of the sword of the angel, *i.e.* on account of the pestilence. The command of God to build an altar upon the threshing-floor of Aravnah, and offer expiatory sacrifices upon it, when connected with His answering his prayer by turning away the plague, could not fail to be taken as a distinct intimation to David, that the site of this altar was the place where the Lord would henceforth make known His gracious presence to His people; and this hint was quite sufficient to determine the site for the temple which his son Solomon was to build.